Everyman's

ENCYCLOPAEDIA

OF GARDENING

A volume in

EVERYMAN'S REFERENCE LIBRARY

By the same author

GARDENER'S EARTH

IN YOUR FLOWER GARDEN

IN YOUR KITCHEN GARDEN

THE WINTER GARDEN

GARDEN WEEDS AND THEIR CONTROL

BASIC GARDENING

Everyman's
ENCYCLOPAEDIA
OF GARDENING

by

STANLEY B. WHITEHEAD, D.Sc.

LONDON: J. M. DENT & SONS LTD

AN ENCYCLOPAEDIA OF GARDENING
W. P. Wright, *Everyman's Library*, 1911

THE WRIGHT ENCYCLOPAEDIA OF GARDENING 1933

EVERYMAN'S ENCYCLOPAEDIA OF GARDENING 1952
Revised by Stanley B. Whitehead, D.Sc., from Walter P. Wright

EVERYMAN'S ENCYCLOPAEDIA OF GARDENING
Rewritten by Stanley B. Whitehead, D.Sc.
First published 1970

© J. M. DENT & SONS LTD, 1970

Made in Great Britain
at the
Aldine Press · Letchworth · Herts
for
J. M. DENT & SONS LTD
Aldine House · Bedford Street · London

SBN: 460 03021 3

PREFACE

FIFTY-NINE years have gone by since *Everyman's Encyclopaedia of Gardening* was first published under the authorship of Walter P. Wright, and acclaimed as 'the companion of the gardener's pleasure and his ready help in all times of trouble'; a description which has been held in mind throughout its many editions and revisions, with which I have been associated since 1952.

Three years ago, however, it was recognized and decided that in view of the great social and economic changes affecting gardening and gardeners in recent years, and the momentous advances made in horticultural practice and science, the whole book should be recast and rewritten. This it has been my privilege and task to do.

For ease of reference the same basic alphabetical sequence of entries has been retained. In it the entries devoted to cultivated and garden plants, shrubs and trees are given under their botanical names to a standard pattern of description, origins, methods of cultivation and propagation, with species and varietal recommendations, straightforward to follow, while their common names are given in cross-references.

This has permitted a great increase in the number of plants described. Nevertheless to include every plant known to garden cultivation would have required more than one volume. Consequently it has been thought most practical and useful to include only those plants and their varieties readily available in commerce and offered by nurserymen and grower specialists in their lists and catalogues to the Everyman Gardener.

Articles on fruits, herbs and vegetables are, however, given under their common names, together with details of their modern culture with due attention to the influence of modern research and the breeding of newer varieties.

Scientific and technical terms used in horticulture will be found well defined, and where necessary with expanded details, while care has been taken to bring plant names up to date in accordance with the rules of botanical nomenclature. Attention has also been given to give some guidance in the pronunciation of the Latin names of plants, so often a matter of controversy.

In addition articles are included on all aspects and features of gardening covering such vital matters as landscaping and design, flower borders, garden pools, rock gardens and greenhouse gardening, and such practical matters as fertilizers, their nature and uses, manures, soils, herbicides and weed control, disease and pest control and new developments in horticultural practices.

In recent years increasing concern has been expressed about the consequences of widespread use of the newer insecticides, especially those belonging to the chlorinated hydro-carbon group: aldrin, chlordane, DDT, dieldrin, endrin and gamma-BHC.

Although remarkably effective in their control of a wide range of insect pests, their persistent nature constitutes a threat to animal, bird and human life. Apart from drifting and being carried by wind and rain from where they are applied, their residues in the soil escape in drainage waters to rivers, lakes and seas, and appear in regions remote from their area of application.

The chemicals absorbed by organisms feeding in a contaminated environment, accumulate in their fatty tissues, to become most concentrated in those predatory birds and animals, which includes ourselves, at the end of food chains. There are indications that health and reproductive powers are thereby likely to be impaired.

Since 1967, aldrin, dieldrin and endrin have been removed from the market as far as gardeners are concerned. Chlordane is only approved for limited application (to lawns) under the Pesticides Safety Precautions Scheme, sponsored by the Ministry of Agriculture. Although the use of DDT is now banned or restricted in such countries as Sweden, Canada and some states of America, it remains on the list of products approved by the Ministry of Agriculture with the proviso that 'This chemical should only be used where there is no effective and less persistent alternative'. Gamma-BHC remains approved without such qualification, possibly because it is more susceptible to break-down.

It is in the light of the above facts that the insecticidal recommendations throughout this book have been made.

To supplement the text a complete new series of line drawings has been made, and for these I am greatly indebted to my wife, Josephine, without whose help and encouragement through the many months of work on this book my task would have been much harder.

In short, my endeavour has been to make this new *Everyman's Encyclopaedia of Gardening* as practical and helpful a tool of reference to the gardeners of today as its older editions were to those of yesterday.

STANLEY B. WHITEHEAD

January 1970

Everyman's

ENCYCLOPAEDIA
OF GARDENING

A

Aaron's Beard. See *Hypericum caly-inum.*

Aaron's Rod. See *Verbascum thapsus.*

Abele (a-beel'). See *Populus alba.*

Abelia (a-be'li-a.) Fam. Caprifoliaceae). Half-hardy deciduous and evergreen shrubs with showy tubular flowers having persistent reddish calyces of autumnal beauty. Chiefly from E. Asia and China, also Mexico.

Selection. A. chinensis, D., 3–5 ft, with sweet-scented white flowers in summer; *floribunda*, E., Mexico, 3–4 ft, with pendulous clusters of rose-purple flowers in spring; and *uniflora*, E., China, 5 ft, with orange-throated, white, pink-tinged flowers in June, have long been popular for growing under glass. *A. schumannii*, D., 4–5 ft, China, with rose-pink flowers in summer, is the best of more recent introductions. *A. × grandiflora* (*chinensis × uniflora*), E., to 5 ft, is the hardiest, with white, tinged pink, flowers for late summer, by sheltered, warm sunny walls.

Cultivation. Well-drained, loam soil. Plant October or April. Prune lightly after flowering.

Propagation. By cuttings of firm young shoots in July–August, in frame. By layering low shoots in March.

Abeliophyllum (a-be-li-o-fil'lum. Fam. Oleaceae). A one-species genus of deciduous hardy shrub, *A. distichum*, 5–6 ft, from Korea, with white, orange-centred, 4-petalled flowers along bare shoots of previous year's growth in January–March. Ordinary loam soil, but should have shelter against flower damage by spring frosts. Propagate by softwood cuttings in summer in propagating case.

Abies, Silver Firs (a'bees, Fam. Pinaceae). About 40 species, hardy evergreen coniferous trees, pyramidal or cylindrical in habit, with branches usually whorled; leaves persistent, needle-like, flattened, grooved and lustrous above, cones erect.

Selection. A. alba, European Silver Fir, to 150 ft; *amabilis*, Red Silver Fir of British Columbia, to 70 ft here, needing lime-free soil; *balsamea*, Balsam Fir, Balm of Gilead, Canada, N. U.S.A., 30–50 ft; *cephalonica*, Greek Fir, 100 ft; *concolor*, Colorado or White Fir, 100–120 ft, Rocky Mts of U.S.A.; *forrestii*, China, 25–60 ft; *grandis*, Giant Fir, western N. America, 120 ft; *homolepsis*, Japanese Fir, 60–80 ft; *koreana*, 30–50 ft, Korea; *magnifica*, Red Fir, Oregon and California, 100 ft and up, for lime-free soil; *mariesii*, Japan, 60–80 ft; *nobilis* (*procera*), California, 200 ft; *nordmanniana*, Caucasian Fir, Caucasus, Asia Minor, 150–200 ft; *numidica*, Algerian Fir, N. Africa, 70 ft; *pindrow*, Western Himalaya, to 200 ft; *pinsapo*, Spanish Fir, S. Spain, to 100 ft; *sachalinensis*, Japan, Saghalien, 55–100 ft; *veitchii*, Central Japan, 60–80 ft; and *venusta*, Bristle-cone Fir, California, 100–150 ft.

Cultivation. Well-drained sandy loams. Must have pure air, though tolerate partial shade. Do not readily attain full height in this country. Plant October or April.

Propagation. By seeds, ½-in. deep in sandy loam in April.

Abobra (a-bob'ra. Fam. Cucurbitaceae). A genus of one species, *A. tenuifolia* (*viridiflora*), half-hardy S. American, tuberous-rooted climbing perennial, 10 ft or so, with pale green fragrant flowers in summer, dioecious, followed by small oval scarlet fruits on female plants when grown together. May be cultivated like Dahlias, storing the tuberous roots during winter under frost-proof conditions.

Abronia (a-bro'ne-a. Fam. Nyctaginaceae). Californian genus of trailing plants, with verbena-like heads of flowers, grown as half-hardy annual or perennial plants in the rock garden or as basket plants.

Selection A. fragrans, white, May;

latifolia (Sand Verbena), yellow, July; *mellifera*, white, July; *umbellata*, rose-pink, are perennial, to be grown as half-hardy annuals, or potted and given glass protection for the winter.

Cultivation. Well-drained, lightish soil; sunny positions in rock gardens.

Propagation. By seeds, sown shallowly, March, under glass, 15·5–18° C. (60–65° F.), bottom heat. By young stem cuttings, in summer, under glass or closed frame.

Abrus (a′brus. Fam. Leguminosae). A tropical genus of deciduous climbing plants of which *A. precatorius*, the Crab's Eye Vine, Weather Plant, or Rosary Pea, is grown as a deciduous stove plant, to 12 ft, carrying pale purplish to rose, pea flowers in spring, followed by bright scarlet and black seeds, often strung for necklaces and rosaries, but poisonous if eaten.

Cultivation. Moist, sandy loam soil compost. Temp. Winter 15·5–18° C. (60–65° F.); summer 21–27° C. (70–80° F.). Water freely in growth.

Propagation. By seeds, in sandy loam, with bottom heat of 21–27° C. (70–80° F.).

Abscission. Literally, a cutting-away, as when a plant part such as a leaf is separated from the parent plant by the

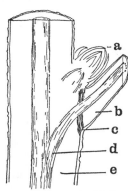

FIG.1   Abscission at leaf-fall: a. axillary bud; b. leaf stalk; c. absciss layer; d. vascular bundle; e. main stem.

formation of a layer of special (cork) cells between the base of the leaf stalk and the parent stem, shutting off its food supply.

Absorption. The process by which the plant takes in the materials needed for growth and development from its environment; soluble nutrient salts and water from the soil by the root hairs, carbon dioxide and oxygen through the leaves and their stomata.

Abutilon (a-bu′ti-lon. Fam. Malvaceae). Half-hardy evergreen shrubs of warm climes, chiefly grown to grace greenhouses or for sheltered borders, trained up pillars, walls, and rafters. With large, cordate leaves, and pendant, brightly coloured, bell-like flowers produced from August to November, they are of attractive beauty at all times.

Selection. A. megapotamicum, Brazil, 4–8 ft, red and yellow flowers, requires less heat than most; v. *variegatum* has pretty foliage; *darwinii*, Brazil, 3–4 ft, with orange, red veined flowers; *insigne*, Columbia, a delectable small shrub with white, carmine-veined flowers; *striatum*, Brazil, 3 ft, orange flowers, and striking v. *thompsonii* with richly mottled leaves; *venosum*, Brazil, to 6 ft, golden orange, red-veined flowers; *vitifolium*, Chile, to 15 ft, pale purplish-blue flowers, and its white v. *alba*; and *bedfordianum*, Brazil, to 15 ft, with handsome yellow, red-lined flowers. Hybrids available from specialist nurseries include 'Boule de Neige', white; 'Firefly', scarlet; 'Red Gauntlet', dark red; 'Golden Fleece', yellow; 'Ashford Red', glowing red; and 'Delicatum', rose.

Cultivation. In pots, compost of two parts fibrous loam, one part peat, and coarse sand to give good drainage. Pot in March. Temp. winter 7–13° C. (45–55° F.); summer 15·5–18° C. (60–65° F.). Water freely in growth, moderately in winter. Trim and cut away old wood in February–March.

Propagation. By seeds sown ⅛-in. deep, with bottom heat of 21° C. (70° F.), standard seed compost. By 5-in. cuttings of young shoots, taken in autumn or February, to be rooted with bottom heat, 15·5° C. (60° F.), under glass, and potted on to plant out in late May for bedding purposes, if desired. Pinch out growing tips once or twice to induce lateral branching.

Abyssinian Primrose. See *Primula verticillata*.

Acacallis (ak-a-kal′is. Fam. Orchidaceae). A genus of one species, *A. cyanea* epiphytic Brazilian orchid, beautiful with arching scapes of dainty pale lavender-blue and white flowers, with a frilled purplish lip and ochre-yellow crest.

Cultivation. Best grown on a raft with a thin layer of Osmunda fibre and sphagnum moss in equal quantities; moist buoyant atmosphere, minimum night temp. 18° C. (65° F.), shaded from direct sun.

Propagation. By severing branch with two pseudobulbs and roots from parent rhizome.

Acacia, Mimosa, Wattle (a-ka′sha. Fam. Leguminosae). There are over 500 species to this genus of tallish evergreen shrubs and trees, distinctive for their bipinnate leaves and adult phyllodes, and yellow or white small flowers freely borne in rounded heads or cones. Mostly native to Australia, none is reliably hardy in Britain, except in very mild gardens of the south-west. Otherwise, chiefly grown in cool greenhouse or conservatory.

Selection. A. armata, Kangaroo Thorn, 3–10 ft, yellow; *baileyana*, 3–15 ft, yellow; *decurrens* v. *dealbata (A. dealbata)*, the florist's Mimosa, or Silver Wattle; *drummondii*, 3–6 ft, pale yellow, excellent as a pot plant; *longifolia*, 10–15ft, Golden Wattle, yellow, and v. *mucronata*, much grown as greenhouse pot plants and kept to within 3–4 ft by annual pruning; *pendula*, weeping Myall, to 25 ft, yellow; *pulchella*, shrub, rich yellow; *retinoides*, 20 ft, pale yellow; *riceana*, small tree to 20 ft, pale clear yellow; all flower in late winter or early spring. *A. farnesiana*, Opoponax, to 20 ft, grown for the perfume, needs tropical conditions.

Cultivation. Soil compost of equal parts loam, leaf-mould (or peat) with coarse sand to give good drainage. Pot in spring. Temp. winter 10–13° C. (50–55° F.); summer 13–18° C. (55–65° F.). Water freely in growth, moderately in winter. Stand plants in pots outdoors May to September. Prune straggling shoots after flowering.

Propagation. By seeds sown ⅛-in. deep, March, bottom heat of 18° C. (65° F.), after soaking seeds 4 hours. By young shoot cuttings taken with a heel of older wood, July, August, inserted in sandy loam in a closed propagating frame.

Acacia, False. See *Robinia*.

Acaena (a-ke′na. Fam. Rosaceae). Hardy, evergreen, trailing perennials for rock gardens. Native to New Zealand or S. America.

Selection. A. argentea, Chile, reddish burrs of flowers without petals, summer; *buchananii*, whitish-green leaves, red burrs; *glabra*, shiny leaves, purplish-red burrs; *inermis*, glaucous leaves, mat-like, red burrs; *microphyllya*, mat-like, crimson burrs; *myriophylla*, Chile, fern-like, tufted foliage; *novae-zealandiae*, silky foliage, purple burrs; *sanguisorbae*, large leaves, rather rampant, with purplish burrs.

Cultivation. Ordinary soil, good drainage, sun or partial shade. Plant October or April.

Propagation. By seeds, shallowly, in sandy compost, in spring. By division in April. By cuttings of young shoots taken in August.

Acalypha (a-kal′i-fa, Fam. Euphorbiaceae). Tropical evergreen shrubs, grown as stove plants, chiefly for their ornamental foliage.

Selection. A. godseffiana, New Guinea, has shining green leaves with creamy-white margins; *hispida*, New Guinea, Red-hot Cat's-tail, Chenille Plant, to 10 ft, has bright green foliage and long, bright red, tassel-like spikes of flowers; *wilkesiana*, South Sea Isles, 6–10 ft, has mottled red and coppery-green foliage, of which *macafeeana*, *marginata* and *triumphans* are beautifully marked forms.

Cultivation. Equal parts sandy loam and leaf-mould (or peat). Pot in March. Water freely to September, then moderately. Temp. winter 15·5–18° C. (60–65° F.); summer 21–27° C. (70–80° F.). Prune in March–April.

Propagation. By cuttings of young shoots taken just below a node, with a little bottom heat, in early spring.

Acantholimon, Prickly Thrift (a-kantho-li′mon. Fam. Plumbaginaceae). Dwarf evergreen rock garden perennials of rather slow growth.

Selection. A. glumaceum, Armenia, 6 in., sharp-pointed, dark green leaves, spikes of bright rose flowers in summer; and *venustum*, Cilicia, with silvery-grey foliage and stiff rose flowers, are most commonly cultivated.

Cultivation. Light, sandy loam, in

warm, sunny positions of rock garden. Plant October or April.

Propagation. By seeds sown shallowly in frame in March, germination slow. By cuttings taken in August, in propagating frame or under cloche. By plant division in April.

Acanthopanax, Angelica Shrub (a-kan-tho-pa'nacks, Fam. Araliaceae). Erect-growing, prickly shrubs or trees, chiefly esteemed for their handsome palmately-leafleted deciduous foliage, tolerant of town and smoky atmospheres.

Selection. A. pentaphyllus, a Japanese shrub, 8 ft, and its v. *variegatus* with cream-edged leaves are chiefly grown; *henryi, ricinifolius* and *sessiliflorus* may be grown for subtropical bedding schemes.

Cultivation. Well-drained, humus-rich soil; sun or partial shade. May be pruned in April. Remove suckers for propagation.

Propagation. By seeds, with bottom heat, 18° C. (65° F.), under glass. By root cuttings or suckers in March; by cuttings of ripe shoots in August, in frame or under cloches.

Acanthus, Bear's Breeches, Bear's Foot (a-kan'thus. Fam. Acanthaceae). Hardy herbaceous perennials, with beautiful leaves, held to be the inspiration of the Corinthian school of architecture, and tall spikes of clustered tubular flowers; native to the Mediterranean region.

Selection. A. mollis, 3–4 ft, white or rose, summer, and v. *latifolius*, the finest form; and *spinosus*, 3–4 ft, purplish flowers, are chiefly grown.

Cultivation. Well-drained loam soil; sunny warm positions; winter protection of crowns with litter.

Propagation. By seeds, ⅛-in. deep, in spring; by plant division in autumn or spring.

Acaulis. Flowers stemless or apparently so. Ex. *Primula acaulis.*

Acclimatization. The inuring of plants to a climate different from their native one; not supported by scientific evidence.

Acephalous. Without a head. Ex. *Brassica oleracea* v. *acephala* (Kale).

Acer, Maple (a'ker. Fam. Aceraceae). A genus of some 100 species of deciduous or semi-evergreen trees, grown for their foliage.

FIG. 2 **Leaves** of Acer species (Maples). 1. *Acer griseum* (Chinese Maple). 2. *Acer palmatum* (Japanese Maple). 3. *Acer platanoides* (Norway Maple).

Selection. A. argutum, Japan, to 25 ft, yellowing in autumn; *campestre,* native Field Maple, 25–35 ft, and variegated forms; *capillipes,* Snake-barked Maple, to 30 ft; *cappadocicum,* Caucasus, to 40 ft, and vs. *aureum* and *rubrum* for leaf colour; *circinatum,* Vine Maple, western N. America, to 30 ft; *davidi,* Striated-barked Maple, China, 30–40 ft; *ginnala,* Far East, to 20 ft, fine autumn colour, fragrant flowers; *griseum,* China, to 25 ft, autumn colour; *negundo,* Box Elder, N. America, to 60 ft, esteemed for its variegated forms *aureum marginatum, aureum variegatum* and *variegatum; nikoense,* Japan, China, to 25 ft, colours and keeps leaves long in autumn; *palmatum,* the small finely cut leafed Japanese Maple, 10–20 ft, outstanding forms being *atropurpureum, dissectum, dissectum atropurpureum, flavescens, heptalobum elegans, h. lutescens, h.* 'Osakazuki', *h. rubrum; pennsylvanicum,* N. American Striated-barked Maple, to 20 ft; *platanoides,* the Norway Maple, Europe, 60 ft, and its v. *schwedlerii* for leaf colour; *pseudoplatanus,* the Syca-more, best grown in its form *brilliantis-simum,* to 30 ft; but *saccharinum,* the Silver Maple, to 100 ft, and *saccharum,* the Sugar Maple, to 130 ft, both of N. America, are forms for park-like gardens.

Cultivation. Need well-drained, humus-rich, moist loam; reasonable shelter from fretting winds, and exposure to spring frosts. Plant October–April.

Propagation. By seeds, ½-in. deep, in sandy loam, sheltered position in Octo-ber; by layering in September. Choice varieties may be budded (August) or grafted (summer) on stocks of the species. By softwood cuttings under mist propagation (q.v.).

Aceras (a'ker-as. Fam. Orchidaceae). Most interesting species is *A. anthropo-phora,* the Green Man Orchis, a native tuberous-rooted plant, which may be grown in dry, chalky loam and sun in SE. England. Plant October–April. Propagate by tuber division when dormant.

Acerose. Needle-shaped. Ex. *Coprosma acerosa.*

Achene. A hard, dry, one-seeded fruit or pericarp; such as the seeds of straw-berries.

FIG. 3 The Achenes on a Strawberry, with single achene below.

Achillea, Milfoil, Yarrow (a-kil'e-a. Fam. Compositae). Hardy perennial plants, chiefly herbaceous for borders, but some alpine for rock gardens; distinguished by rayed flowers usually borne in corymbs.

Selection. For borders: *A. filipendula,* Caucasus, 3 ft, and vs. 'Coronation Gold', 'Gold Plate'; *millefolium,* Europe, 1–3 ft, and vs. 'Cerise Queen', 'Fire King'; *ptarmica,* Europe, 2 ft, vs. 'The Pearl', 'Perry's White' and 'Snowball'; *taygetea,* Levant, 2–3 ft, golden yellow; *ageratum,* SW. Europe, 1–1½ ft, yellow, is the Sweet Maudlin. For rock gardens: *A. clavenae,* 6 in., Alps, white; and hybrids such as × 'King Edward', × *jaborneggii; ageratifolia,* N. Greece, 2–4 in.; *clypeolata,* Greece, 9 in., yellow, silver foliage; *tomentosa,* Europe, 9 in., yellow; *umbellata,* 4 in. white; all flowering during summer.

Cultivation. Ordinary well-drained soil, open position. Plant October–April.

Propagation. By seeds in spring, in cold frame or outdoor seed-bed. By plant division in autumn or spring.

Achimenes (a-ki-me'nees. Fam. Ges-neriacae). Herbaceous stoloniferous or tuberous-rooted perennials, native to the tropical zone of S. America, which make showy plants with rather oblique, brilliant tubular flowers, lasting long indoors, when grown in pots or pans, or in hanging baskets.

Selection. Notable species are *A. coccinea,* 18 in., brick red; *longiflora,* 12 in., violet-blue, with vs. *alba,* white, and *grandiflora,* large crimson; *pedunculata*

2 ft, orange and yellow; but species crosses have given many fine hybrids, best sought in nurserymen's lists.

Cultivation. Plant batches of tubercles February–April, five or six per 5-in. pot, sandy loam, temp. 15·5–18° C. (60–65° F.); in darkness until shoots are 2 in. high, and then bring to light in warm greenhouse; watering increasingly, with atmosphere kept moist, to flower in summer, when plants welcome good light but not direct sun. After flowering, reduce watering gradually, with none when dormant, keeping through winter at 10° C. (50° F.).

Propagation. Division of roots in February. By cuttings of young shoots and leaves, April to May. By seeds in March, with bottom heat of 24° C. (75° F.), minimum; 2–3 years to flowering.

Acicular. Needle-shaped. Ex. *Rosa acicularis.*

Acid. Chemically, a substance which forms hydrogen ions in solution; a substance which contains hydrogen replaceable by metals to form a salt; a substance tending to lose protons. Acids tend to turn litmus paper red, are sour to taste, and corrosive. Inorganic A.s include boracic, carbonic, chromic, hydrochloric, nitric, nitrous, phosphoric, phosphorous, sulphuric and sulphurous. Organic A.s found in plants include acetic, benzoic, citric, formic, gallic, lactic, malic, oxalic, palmitic, salicyclic, stearic, tartaric.

Acidanthera (ak-i-dan'the-ra. Fam. Iridaceae). Cormous summer-flowering plants from Ethiopia, with large tubular flowers of graceful beauty; grown as pot plants in a cool greenhouse or outdoors in mild districts.

Section. A. bicolor, 2 ft, white with purplish centre, is the hardiest, but preferred in its v. *murielae,* 3 ft, highly scented white flowers, purple basal blotch; *candida,* 1 ft, white, and *capensis,* 1 ft, white with red or yellow blotch, are for greenhouse culture.

Cultivation. Plant corms 3 in. deep, 9 in. apart, sandy loam, April–May; water freely with growth; dry off after flowering, store at 15·5° C. (60° F.), in dry warm place.

Propagation. By seeds, 18° C. (65° F.) bottom heat, April. By offsets in spring.

Acis. See *Leucojum.*

Aconite, Winter. See *Eranthis.*

Aconitum, Monk's Hood, Wolf's Bane (ak-on-i'tum. Fam. Ranunculaceae). A genus of 60 species of hardy herbaceous perennials, all of which, however, contain a poisonous alkaloid, and should not be planted where cattle may have access or where the roots may be mistaken for edible horse-radish.

Selection. A. fischeri (*carmichaelii*), Kamtschatka, 3 ft, pale blue; *napellus,* Monk's Hood, in 'Spark's variety', 5 ft, violet-blue, autumn; *variegatum,* E. Alps., 2 ft, blue and white, and v. *bicolor,* or 'Blue Sceptre'; *volubile,* twining to 12 ft, violet, late summer; *lycoctonum,* Wolf's Bane, 4 ft, yellow, late summer; *vulparia,* Alps, 3 ft, yellow, summer; and *wilsonii* 'Barker's variety', China, 6 ft, blue, September, one of the best.

Cultivation. Thrive in most moist soils, partial shade or sun, as rear border plants, among shrubs, or under trees. Plant October to March; should be well-marked in view of poisonous nature.

Propagation. By seeds, sown outdoors or in cold frame as soon as ripe. By careful division of plants in autumn or spring.

Acorn. The fruit or seed of Oaks (*Quercus* sp.).

Acorus (ak'or-us. Fam. Acaceae). Rhizomatous herbaceous perennials for the water garden and moist soils, and margins of pools or streams.

Selection. A. calamus, the Sweet Flag, native to Britain and Europe, 2–3 ft, has greenish-yellow flowers in June, and sword-like leaves, enhanced in v. *variegatus* by being striped cream and gold; *gramineus,* Japan, 8 in., has tufts of grass-like leaves, yellow flowers, and white-striped leaves in v. *variegatus.*

Cultivation. Plant in shallow water or moist soil, March. Sunny position.

Propagation. By root division, March–April.

Acris. Bitter, acrid. Ex. *Ranunculus acris.*

Acroclinium. See *Helipterum.*

Actaea, Baneberry (ak'te-a. Fam. Ranunculaceae). Hardy herbaceous perennials, best suited to the wild garden, and cool shade among shrubs and trees. The fruits or berries are poisonous.

Selection. A. spicata, 1–1½ ft, the native

Baneberry, has white flowers in summer followed by shining black berries; *alba*, with whitish fruits, and *rubra*, with red fruits, are similar but of N. American origin.

Cultivation. Ordinary soil; partial shade; plant October–March.

Propagation. By seeds sown outdoors in April; by division of roots in March.

Actinella (ak-tin-el'la. Fam. Compositae). Reasonably hardy small herbaceous perennials of western U.S.A., suitable for the rock garden or front of flower borders.

Selection. A. grandiflora, 6–9 in., with pinnate leaves, and 2-in. yellow ray flowers in summer; and *scaposa*, 9 in., with hairy linear leaves, and 1-in. yellow flowers, summer.

Cultivation. Well-drained soil, and sun. Plant in March–April.

Propagation. By seeds, April; by root division in April.

Actinidia (ak-tin-id'i-a. Fam. Actinidiaceae). Deciduous climbing shrubs, chiefly from China and Japan, hardy except in cold districts, grown for their large, long-stalked toothed leaves, and summer flowers.

Selection. A. arguta, to 50 ft, fine dark green leaves, fragrant white flowers, June; *chinensis*, Chinese Gooseberry, to 25 ft, handsome downy leaves, creamy white to yellow flowers, August, sometimes followed by hairy, gooseberry-flavoured fruits; *kolomikta*, 10–20 ft, leaves flushed red to tips, white scented flowers in June, beloved by cats; *melanandra*, more of a tall shrub, white purple-anthered white flowers, June; *polygama*, 15–18 ft, silvered foliage, white, fragrant flowers, May–June; and *purpurea*, to 25 ft, white fragrant June flowers, sometimes purple autumn fruits.

Cultivation. Well-drained loam soil, warm sheltered position; do well rambling into trees. Plant October–April.

Propagation. By cuttings of young ripening shoots in propagating case, summer. By seeds in spring, bottom heat 18° C. (65° F.)

Actinomyces (Streptomyces). A genus of ray fungi, chiefly found in the soil. *A. scabies* causes potato Scab infection.

Aculeate. Prickly. Ex. *Ruscus aculeatus.*

FIG. 4   An acuminate leaf (*Magnolia acuminata*).

Acuminate. Long and narrowly pointed. Ex. *Magnolia acuminata.*

Acute. Sharp or short-pointed. Ex. *Calceolaria acutifolia.*

Ada (a'da. Fam. Orchidacae). Genus of two epiphytic, evergreen orchids, easily grown in a cool greenhouse, minimum temp. 10° C. (50° F.).

Selection. A. aurantiaca, Columbia, with spikes of orange, spotted black, flowers; and *lehmanni*, orange, with white lip, and grey-marbled foliage, are commonly grown.

Cultivation. Compost of 2 parts of Osmunda, 1 part sphagnum moss, suits. Pot in March. Partial shade; no rest period, so water the year round, more moderately in winter.

Propagation. By division in spring.

Adam's Apple. See *Tabernaemontana.*

Adam's Needle. See *Yucca.*

Adder's Tongue. See *Ophioglossum.*

Adenandra (a-den-an'dra. Fam. Rutaceae). Half-hardy evergreen bright flowering shrubs of S. Africa, for the cool greenhouse.

Selection. A. amoena, 2 ft, white and red flowers, June; *fragrans*, 2 ft, scented rose flowers, June–July.

Cultivation. Pot in March; compost of loam and peat, with sand for drainage; winter temp. 10° C. (50° F.), moderate watering, increasing with growth.

Propagation. By cuttings of young

shoots, in spring, in propagating frame; or by seeds.

Adenocarpus (a-den-o-kar′pus. Fam. Leguminosae). Half-hardy shrubs, akin to Cytisus; of which *A. viscosus*, 2–3 ft, may be grown in a cool greenhouse, winter temp. 7° C. (45° F.), for its dense racemes of pea-like, small yellow flowers in April–May.

Propagation. By seeds, sown in March, under glass; by cuttings of young shoots taken in June, in propagating case.

Adenophora, Gland Bell-Flower (a-den-op′ora. Fam. Campanulaceae). Pretty herbaceous perennials, with drooping blue, campanulate flowers in summer for the border.

Selection. A. bulleyana, China, 4 ft, pale blue, August; *lilifolia*, Europe, 18 in. blue; *palustris*, China, 2 ft, lavender-blue; *potaninii*, China, 2 ft, blue; *berticillata*, Japan, 2–3 ft, blue, are good representatives.

Cultivation. Reasonably well drained ordinary soil. Plant October–March. Sun.

Propagation. Most readily grown by seed, sown in early spring, in cold frame.

Adiantum (ad-i-an′tum. Fam. Polypodiaceae). A genus of more than 200 semi-tropical and tropical ferns, few of which are hardy. Chiefly grown for their frond beauty in the greenhouse.

Selection. Hardiest species is *A. pedatum*, to 2 ft, with fine form ‘Klondyke’, having young fronds reddish tinged, eligible for cool sheltered places out of doors. *A. capillus-veneris*, the cosmopolitan and native Maidenhair, and its forms, require winter protection or cool greenhouse; *aethiopicum*, 6–9 in., and vs., *assimile*, 6 in.; *affine*, 6–8 in.; and *hispidulum*, of New Zealand and the antipodes, 6–15 in.; *cuneatum*, 6 to 9 in. and vs.; *excisum*, 2–3 in., and vs.; *palmatum*, to 3½ ft; *rubellum*, 4 to 6 in.; and *williamsii*, S. America, 6–8 in.; and *reniforme*, Madeira, 4–6 in., may be grown in the cool greenhouse, partial shade, winter temp. 10–13° C. (50–55° F.). The tropical *caudatum*, 2–4 in.; *concinnum*, 12 in.; *digitatum*, 1–3 ft; *fergusonii*, 2–3 ft; *fragrantissimum*, 1–1½ ft; *henslovianum*, 1–1½ ft; *lucidum*, 9–15 in.; *macrophyllum*, 9–15 in.; *moorei*, 15 in.; *peruvianum*, 9–18 in.; *princeps*, 1–2 ft; *pulverulentum*, 4–8 in.; × *rhodophyllum*, 1 ft; *tenerum*, 1–3 ft, and many vs., par-

ticularly *farleyense*, *ghiesbreghtii*, and ‘Glory of Moordrecht’; *tetraphyllum*, and vs.; *tinctum*, 6–9 in.; *trapeziforme*, 1–2 ft; and *villosum*, require stove conditions, winter temp. 15·5° C. (60° F.), and moist though buoyant atmosphere. *A. cuneatum*, Brazil, 1–1½ ft, and its vs. *dissectum*, *elegans*, *fasciculatum*, *mundulum*, *pacoti*, and *strictum*, are much grown as room plants, with the fronds cut back annually in autumn.

Cultivation. Compost of 4 parts loam, 2 parts peat, 2 parts leaf-mould, and 1 part coarse sand is suitable. Soft, diffused light, without direct sun and fairly humid atmosphere are needed, with watering regulated according to growth, more in summer, less in winter.

Propagation. By spores, evenly spread on fine sandy peat, in propagating case, 10–15·5° C. (50–60° F.). By division in spring.

Adlumia, Alleghany Vine (ad-lu′mi-a. Fam. Papaveraceae). A genus of one species, *A. fungosa*, a biennial N. American climber, to 15 ft, with pale green fern-like foliage, and pale rose or white flowers in August. Hardy only in mild districts.

Cultivation. Seeds are sown in August, in greenhouse or frame, and planted out the following spring; or sown in spring, protected over the winter, where they are to grow and flower. Plant in humus-rich loam, partial shade.

Adnate. Grown to, or joined together, usually of one organ united to a different one, as when a stamen is jointed to a pistil, or a leaf carried up and joined to the stem.

Adonis (a-do′nis. Fam. Ranunculaceae). A genus of annual and perennial flowering plants.

Selection. A. aestivalis, Pheasant's Eye, S. Europe, 12 in., crimson flowers in June; and *autumnalis*, Europe and Britain, the native Pheasant's Eye or Red Morocco, blood-red, black-eyed flowers; are annuals, to be raised from fresh seed, sown autumn or spring out of doors. *A. amurensis*, 1–1½ ft, is an early spring, golden-yellow flowering perennial from Manchuria and Japan; and *vernalis* is the brilliant native ‘Ox-eye’, with fennel-like foliage and large yellow flowers in spring.

Cultivation. Ordinary, humus-rich soil,

in borders. Plant perennials in rock garden, October, when plants may be divided.

Adpressed. Pressed against.

Aduncous. Hooked or hook-shaped. Ex. *Tropaeolum aduncum.*

Adventitious (of roots). Accidental or abnormal, as of roots arising from parts other than the radicle, such as the stem roots of lilies, aerial roots of vines.

Aechmea (ayk'me-a. Fam. Bromeliaceae). A genus of epiphytic plants of tropical America, with very handsome rosettes of sword-like leaves, and large flower spikes, for growing in the warm greenhouse or as house plants in heated rooms.

Selection. A. fasciata, Brazil, rosy-pink bracted flower spike, leaves banded white; *fulgens,* Cayenne, purple flower spike, August; and v. *discolor,* with deep green leaves, purple beneath; *mariaereginae,* Costa Rica, 2 ft, blue and salmon, June; *spectabilis,* Guatemala, 2 ft, pale pink, winter; and *weilbachii,* Brazil, bright lilac flowers, autumn, is somewhat smaller.

Cultivation. Equal parts Osmunda fibre, leaf-mould, and half a part each of coarse sand and sphagnum moss, makes a 'rooting' compost. Minimum winter temp. 7° C. (45° F.); water moderately, keeping central rosette full of water; good light without direct sun; water more freely with growth in summer.

Propagation. By suckers or offsets detached from base of plants, whenever available, to grow on in small pots, compost as above, temp. 18–24° C. (65–75° F.).

Aegle (ai'gle. Fam. Rutaceae). A genus of one species, *A. marmelos,* India, deciduous, spiny small tree, to 10 ft, with highly fragrant white flowers, April, followed by greenish-yellow orange-like hard-skinned fruits the following year. Known as the Ball Tree in India.

Cultivation. A humus-rich loam; warm greenhouse conditions, winter temp. 13° C. (55° F.), very moderate watering in winter; more in spring and summer, with overhead syringing on sunny days.

Propagation. By cuttings of freshly matured shoots; or by seeds, with bottom heat, 18° C. (65° F.).

Aeonium (ay-o'ni-um. Fam. Crassulaceae). A genus of somewhat fleshy-leaved

perennials, chiefly native to the Canary Isles and region, of which several are grown as greenhouse or window plants in the home.

Selection. A. arboreum, Morocco, 2–3 ft, bright yellow flowers, January to March; × *barbatum,* 6 in., golden-yellow, May, June, almost hardy; *canariense,* 2 ft, rosette of soft flannelly green leaves, pale yellow, April, May; *simsii,* tufted leaves, golden, April, May; *tabulaeforme,* rosette of pale green leaves, pale yellow, July, August; and *undulatum,* erect stem to 2 or 3 ft, topped with a rosette of leaves, bright yellow, summer.

Cultivation. Well-drained soil or compost; good light, ample water in summer, little in winter; minimum temp. 7° C. (45° F.).

Propagation. By division in spring, or by leaves inserted at the base in sandy loam.

Aerides (air'i-des. Fam. Orchidaceae). A large genus of epiphytic orchids, sometimes called Air Plants; native to the tropics of the Old World. Need hot or stove house conditions, minimum winter temp. 15·5° C. (60° F.).

Selection. A. crispum, India, 2½ ft, white, flushed purple, May–July; *fieldingii,* Fox-brush Aerides, Assam, 3 ft, white, mottled rose, May to July; *multiflorum,* India, 18 in., white, spotted rose-red, May to July; *odoratum,* India, etc., 3½ ft, creamy-white, tipped pink, highly fragrant, June, July; and *quinquevulnerum,* Philippines, 2½ ft, white and purple, highly fragrant.

Cultivation. Grow in sphagnum moss, with a little charcoal, in very well crocked pots; water freely in spring and summer, temp. 21–27° C. (70–80° F.), moist atmosphere.

Propagation. By division in August, when plants are repotted.

Aerosol. Method of dispersing fungicides, insecticides and herbicides in fine mist form under pressure.

Aesculus, Horse Chestnut (ais'ku-lus, Fam. Hippocastanaceae). A genus of about 25 species of deciduous trees or shrubs, several of ornamental and flowering beauty.

Selection. A. hippocastanum, the Horse Chestnut, 70–100 ft, white candle-like spikes of flowers, May, followed by prickly fruits, containing brown rounded seeds ('conkers'), is native to Greece and Albania; introduced early 17th century; double-flowering v. *flore pleno* is sterile and yields no 'conkers'—to boys' regret. Other Horse Chestnuts are *chinensis*, Chinese, to 80 ft; *indica*, Indian, 60 ft, very hardy, flowering in June; *turbinata*, Japanese, to 90 ft, with largest leaves; and hybrid × *carnea*, 30–50 ft, with deep rosy red flowers; brighter in form *briotii*. N. American species, known as Buckeye, make smaller trees, and do best in the southern half of England; *pavia*, to 20 ft, bright red, June; *parviflora*, more a tall shrub to 15 ft, white, August; *californica*, 30–40 ft, white, fragrant flowers in late summer; and *octandra*, the Sweet Buckeye, to 60 ft, yellow flowers in May–June.

Cultivation. Most soils, even clay, which incline to be loamy. Plant October–March, firming and staking well; spaced well apart.

Propagation. Preferably by seeds, sown 2–3 in. deep, outdoors, in early spring. Choice varieties by grafting or budding on seedlings, using lower dormant buds, spring.

Aestivalis. Pertaining to summer. Ex. *Adonis aestivalis.*

Aestivation. The manner in which calyx, flower parts, and petals are arranged in the flower bud.

Aethionema (ai′thi-on-e′ma. Fam. Cruciferae). Choice evergreen perennials, valued for the rock garden and walls.

Selection. A. coridifolium, 6–8 in., rosy-lilac, June; and vs. 'Warley Rose' and 'Warley ruber', are excellent glaucous-leaved perennials; *grandiflorum*, to 15 in., rose, May to August; *armenum*, 4 in., pink, June; *iberideum*, 6 in., white, April, May; *pulchellum*, 9 in., pink, spring; and *stylosum*, 3–4 in., pink, May, are perennial; while *cappadocicum*, pale red, June, and *saxatile*, 8 in., purplish, June, are annual, to raise from seeds.

Cultivation. Well-drained, lightish soil. Sunny positions. Plant October or March.

Propagation. By seeds, under glass, bottom heat 18° C. (65° F.) in March. By cuttings of young shoots, in sandy loam, in July, August.

Affinis. Related. Ex. *Nicotiana affinis.*
African Corn Lily. See *Ixia.*
African Hemp. See *Sparmannia.*
African Lily. See *Agapanthus.*

African Marigold. See *Tagetes.*
African Violet. See *Saintpaulia.*
Agapanthus, African Lily (ag-a-pan′-thus. Fam. Amaryllidaceae). Decorative perennials from S. Africa, with short rootstocks and fleshy roots, long linear leaves, and huge rounded umbels of blue or violet flowers, late summer or autumn.

Selection: A. africanus, to 2 ft, deep blue; *campanulatus*, 3 ft, sky-blue; and *orientalis*, 2–4 ft, blue, with white forms *albus* and *maximus albus*, are often wrongly named *umbellatus*, and are ever-green; not perfectly hardy, and best grown in tubs or pots, to winter under glass. *Hollandi*, 3 ft, deep blue; *inapertus*, 5 ft, blue; and *patens*, 3 ft, bright blue, are deciduous, nominally hardy, given winter top protection.

Cultivation. In tubs, grow in JI compost No. 3; place outdoors May–October; under cool glass for winter. Deciduous kinds are planted in sheltered positions, and given cover of litter for the winter.

Propagation. By seeds, sown in early spring, cool greenhouse, potted on and grown 2 to 3 years in frames to flowering size. By offsets in spring.

Agaric. One of the Agaricaceae, family of the Gill fungi, including mushroom and toadstools.

Agastache (ag-as-tak′e. Fam. Labiatae). Aromatic perennials of which *A mexicana*, 2½ ft, coarsely toothed lanceolate leaves, and rose to crimson flowers in spikes, July, may be grown in warm, sheltered gardens, in loam soil. As a Mexican, the crown may need winter protection with litter.

Propagation. By seeds, in spring. By division of plants in April.

Agathaea. See *Felicia.*

Agathis, Kauri Pine (ag′a-this. Fam. Pinaceae). A genus of evergreen coniferous gum- and timber-yielding pines native to New Zealand, Australia, Fiji and Malaya, but too tender to succeed in Britain. *A. australis*, New Zealand Kauri Pine, yields copal; *vitiensis*, Fijian Kauri Pine, yields resin; sometimes offered for growth in conservatories, while juvenile

Agave (a-ga′ve. Fam. Agavaceae) Tender evergreen plants, once commonly grown for their huge rosettes of leathery toothed and spine-tipped leaves, and occasional spikes of greenish-yellow o brownish flowers. Slow-growing, and named Century Plants, under the mistaken impression that the plants took a hundred years to flower. Actually, some flower at eight years, others may take up to forty years.

Selection. A. americana, grey-green leaves to 3 ft long, has a golden or white margined form, *marginata*, and may be grown in large tubs, but attains to 25-ft stems in time; *albicans*, 3–4 ft, *filifera*, 10–12 ft, and *parviflora*, 4–5 ft, are smaller species; all natives of Mexico.

Cultivation. Well-drained, fairly rich soil compost. Sun and open air in summer; winter shelter under glass.

Propagation. By offsets, potted in April, May, in cool greenhouse.

Ageratum, Floss Flower (aj-er-a′tum. Fam. Compositae). Pretty, half-hardy dwarf annuals, native to Mexico, used for edging and bedding.

Selection. A. houstonianum, blue, summer, is best-known species, but selected forms and hybrids such as 'Blue Mink', 'Blue Chip', 'Violet Cloud', and 'White Cushion' should be sought in seedsmen's lists.

Cultivation. Ordinary garden soil. Plant out in June. Specimen plants may also be grown in cool greenhouse as pot plants.

Propagation. By seeds, sown under glass, bottom heat 18° C. (65° F.), March, to be potted or pricked out, and hardened in cold frame. Exceptional plants can be increased by summer cuttings, grown on in cool greenhouse.

Aggregate. Broken bricks, rubble, stone or shingle, used for foundation of paths and drives, and in concrete-making.

Aggregate Fruit. A fruit formed by joining of fertilized pistils, separate in the flower. Ex. Blackberry.

Aglaonema, Poison Dart (ag-la-o-ne′ma. Fam. Araceae). Native to the monsoon areas of SE. Asia, several of the species of this genus make compact plants, with beautiful, coloured foliage and arum-like summer flowers, for indoor growth as house or cool greenhouse plants.

Selection. A. commutatum, 9-in. leaves, deep green, spotted paler green and white; *costatum*, ovate leaves, dark green, spotted and veined white; *modestum*,

slender, pointed shining green leaves; *pictum*, deep green leaves, blotched grey and white, white flower; and others.

Cultivation. Humus-rich compost; warm humid conditions, winter temp. 18° C. (65° F.); liberal watering in summer growth; little at other times.

Propagation. By root division in March.

Agrestis. Of the fields. Ex. *Veronica agrestis.*

Agrostemma. See *Lychnis* and *Silene.*

Agrostis, Bent Grass (a-gros′tis. Fam. Gramineae). A genus of over 100 species of grasses, of which annuals such as *A. nebulosa*, Cloud Grass, 15 in., and *elagans*, 12 in., are grown from spring-sown seed for their ornamental prettiness, and drying for winter decoration. Several perennial spp., notably *canina*, Velvet Bent; *stolonifera* and vs., Creeping Bent; and *tenuis*, Browntop Bent, are excellent turf grasses for lawns.

Ailanthus, Tree of Heaven (ail-an′-thus. Fam. Simarubaceae). The chief hardy sp. is *A. altissima*, a Chinese tree, growing to 60 ft, remarkable for its huge pinnate leaves, but more suitable to southern and mild districts than to the north; dioecious, female trees are to be preferred as the flowers of the male smell disagreeably. Thrives in towns, preferring deep, humus-rich soil and shelter from cold winds. May be propagated by suckers, or by root cuttings in winter. Plant October to March.

Air, Atmospheric. Composition varies very slightly according to altitude and locality, but pure dry air at sea level is composed of about 78 per cent nitrogen, 21 per cent oxygen, 0·93 per cent argon, and 0·03 per cent carbon dioxide, with traces of neon, helium, krypton, xenon. A. air usually also carries water vapour, sulphurous and hydrocarbonic compounds, hydrogen peroxide, and dust particles, all of which play some part in the life and growth of plants.

Air Plant. *See* Epiphyte.

Ajuga, Bugle (a-jug′a. Fam. Labiatae). Low-growing, creeping, hardy perennials, valued for their coloured foliage and whorled spikes of summer flowers. European.

Selection. A. genevensis, 6 in., with blue to rose or white flowers, June–July;

pyramidalis, 6 in., brilliant blue, May, June; and v. *crispa* (*metallica crispa*) with curled, metallic lustrous leaves; *reptans*, 3–4 in., blue, May–July; and its coloured-leafed forms *atropurpurea*, purple; *variegata*, white, tinged rose, and green leaves; and *multicolor*, rose, white and green leaves, make useful plants for rock gardens and ground cover in wild gardens.

Cultivation. Ordinary soil; sun or shade; easily grown; plant October–April.

Propagation. By seeds sown out of doors, in spring; or by root division, October or March.

Akebia (a-ke′bi-a. Fam. Lardizabalaceae). Charming twining, vigorous shrubs from China and Japan, with handsome foliage, and unisexual flowers, borne male and female on the same racemes, sometimes followed by sausage-shaped fruits. Hardy in mild localities.

Selection. A. lobata (*trifoliata*) is deciduous, to 30 ft, with wavy-margined, ovate leaves, and racemes of purplish small flowers in April; *quinata*, deciduous or semi-evergreen, grows 30–40 ft, with 5-leafleted leaves, and purplish flowers in April, May.

Cultivation. Well-drained, humus-rich soil; plant October or March, on sunny south wall, or to cover arbours or pergolas. Prune straggling shoots after flowering is over.

Propagation. By cuttings of young firm shoots in summer, in frame or under bell-glass. By layering or suitable low shoots in spring.

Ala (pl. **Alae**). Wing; usually used for the side petals of the pea-like flowers of the Leguminosae.

Alatus (-a, -um). Winged. Ex. *Thunbergia alata*.

Albizzia (al-biz′zi-a. Fam. Leguminosae). Deciduous tall shrubs or trees, hardy in Cornwall but requiring greenhouse shelter elsewhere, valued for fine fernlike foliage, and pinkish, many-stamened small flowers in bottle-brush-like spikes in summer.

Selection. A. julibrissin, 10–30 ft, and v. *rosea*, somewhat dwarfer; and *lophantha*, W. Australia, 10–35 ft, may be attempted.

Cultivation. Open, well-drained loam; sunny, sheltered position outdoors; or in large pots under glass. Plant in March. Winter temp. 10° C. (50° F.).

Propagation. By seeds, sown in spring, bottom heat of 24° C. (75° F.).

Albumens, Albumins. Water-soluble proteins and nutrient substances, stored and forming the food supply of seed embryos; hence 'albuminous seeds'. *See also* Exalbuminous.

Alburnum. Sapwood, or the youngest wood of a tree, just beneath the bark.

Albus (-a, -um). White. Ex. *Potentilla alba*.

Alchemilla, Lady's Mantle (al-kem-il′la. Fam. Rosaceae). Herbaceous perennials.

Selection. A. alpina. native, 6 in., with silvery divided leaves, and greenish flowers in summer, may be grown in rock gardens; *mollis* (*major*) to 12 in., with round hairy leaves and yellow corymbs of flowers, is very hardy for the front of borders; *vulgaris* is the native Lady's Mantle.

Cultivation. Ordinary, well-drained soil. Plant October or March.

Propagation. By division in October or March.

Alder. *See* Alnus.

Aldrin. Synthetic insecticide of the chlorinated hydrocarbon group, not recommended for garden use owing to its persistent toxicity and danger to bird and animal life.

Aleuron Grains. Granules of proteids and mineral compounds found chiefly in seeds.

Alexanders. Common name of *Smyrnium olusatrum*, a native plant once grown as a pot-herb or vegetable, to be earthed up and blanched like celery; strongly flavoured.

Alexandrian Laurel. See *Danae racemosa*.

Algae. A Class of simple plants found in the sea, in fresh water, in moist places and in soil; often grouped with the Fungi (q.v.) to form the Thallophyta division of the Plant Kingdom, but differing by possessing chlorophyll (q.v.). A. are grouped according to colour into Green, Brown, Red and Blue-green. Probably the first living green plants, A. are simple in structure; many being single-celled, others thread-forming or filamentous, up to the elaborate structures of sea-weeds. Without roots or flower structures, A. reproduce by the association of filaments, the cells of which send out tubes, and by cell division. In horticulture certain soil-algae play a part in increasing soil fertility. Others green paths and soil surfaces and can be a nuisance. Filamentous A., forming blanketweed or green masses, are obnoxious in pools. Larger A., seaweeds, provide valuable organic manure for soils. Some A., entering into partnership with Fungi, form lichens on trees, lawns, etc.

Algerian Iris. See *Iris unguicularis.*

Alisma, Water Plantain (a-lis'ma. Fam. Alismataceae). Aquatic perennial plants, of which the native *A. plantago-aquatica,* with long-stalked, lance-shaped leaves, and panicles of pale rose flowers, 2–3 ft., may be grown in shallow water at the edge of pools. Plant autumn or spring. Increase by seeds sown in spring, or by plant division in October or March.

Alkaloids. Basic organic nitrogenous substances formed in plants by their metabolism; many of them having physiological actions which make them valuable in medicine. Exs. Digitalis from Foxglove; Morphine from Poppy; Coniine from Hemlock, etc.

Alkanet. See *Alkanna.*

Alkanet, Evergreen. *Pentaglottis sempervirens,* a weed.

Alkanna (al-kan'na. Fam. Boraginaceae). *A. tinctoria,* hardy perennial of S. Europe, 6 in., with hairy oblong leaves, and deep blue flowers, June, may be grown in well-drained light soil, sunny position, and is the Alkanet from the roots of which a red dye was once much extracted. Propagate by division in spring.

Allamanda (al-la-man'da. Fam. Apocynaceae). Beautiful climbing evergreen plants of S. America, with large trumpet-shaped yellow flowers in summer, when grown in the hot or stove house.

Selection. A. cathartica, Guinea, 5–10 ft, golden yellow flowers, June; and vs. *hendersonii,* orange-yellow, *nobilis,* bright yellow, and *schottii,* yellow, richly striped brown, are excellent for training along rafters. The hybrid × *chelsonii* grows more stiffly with extra-large yellow flowers.

Cultivation. Rich loam, 2 parts, with 1 part leaf-mould, 1 part coarse sand and a little charcoal, or JIP 3 compost. Plant in large pots, spring. Water freely in growth, then moderately. Train shoots near to glass roof. Summer temp. 21–27° C. (70 to 80° F.); minimum in winter 13° C. (55° F.). Prune previous year's shoots in January, to just above the first node from base.

Propagation. By 3-in. cuttings of young shoots in February–April, with bottom heat of 21° C. (70° F.), and moist atmosphere.

All-heal. See *Valeriana.*

Alliaceous. Of the Onion genus, *Allium,* chiefly in reference to the odour.

Alligator Apple. See *Annona glabra.*

Alligator Pear. See *Persea gratissima.*

Allium (al'li-um. Fam. Amaryllidoceae). Large genus of bulbous plants, including valuable food plants, found under Chives, Garlic, Leek, Onion and Shallot. Ornamental species are distinctive for their linear leaves, and umbels of small, colourful flowers borne on cylindrical stems, in late spring and summer.

Selection. A. albopilosum, 12–15 in., lilac, June; *caeruleum (azureum),* 1–2 ft, deep sky-blue, June, July; *cyaneum,*

FIG. 5 *Allium neapolitanum.*

China, 6 in., blue, summer; *giganteum*, Himalaya, 3–4 ft, rose lilac, July; *karataviense*, Turkestan, 6 in., distinctive broad leaves and large lilac flowerheads, May; *moly*, Mediterranean, 12 in., yellow, June; *narcissiflorum*, 6–12 in., mauve, spring; *neapolitanum*, 1 ft, white, spring; *ostrowskianum*, Turkestan, 8–12 in., rose, June; *rosenbachianum*, Central Asia, 2½ ft, dark violet, May; *roseum*, Mediterranean, 9–12 in., rose, May; and *triquetum*, S. Europe, 6–12 in., triangular stems, white, summer.

Cultivation. Well-drained loam soil, sunny positions in rock garden or border for dwarf forms; shrubbery for tall species. Plant August–October; lift and divide every 3 or 4 years.

Propagation. By division of offset bulbs, autumn. By seeds sown in spring; 3 years to flowering.

Alloplectus (al-lo-plek'tus. Fam. Gesneriaceae). Evergreen shrubs of tropical America, decorative for the warm greenhouse, with tubular, axillary flowers in early summer.

Selection. A. hirtellus, Brazil, climber, blood-red, scarlet and yellow clubshaped flowers; *schlimii*, Colombia, cinnabar, spotted green; June.

Cultivation. 2 parts loam, 2 parts peat, 1 part coarse sand; in pots. Summer temp. 18–24° C. (65–75° F.); winter not less than 10° C. (50° F.). Water freely and syringe in summer; very moderately in winter.

Propagation. By cuttings in summer, bottom heat 21° C. (70° F.).

Allotment, Allotment Garden. As defined by the Allotments Act, 1922, an A. Garden means an allotment not exceeding 40 poles (¼ acre) in extent which is wholly or mainly cultivated by the occupier for the production of vegetable and fruit crops for consumption by himself or his family. The laws governing A.s are the Allotments Acts of 1922 and 1925, as amended by the Act of 1950. The important provisions are: The normal notice to quit is 12 months, expiring on or before 6th April or on or after 29th September, in any year. The tenant is entitled to compensation for growing crops and manures applied to the land, at whatever period of the year notice to quit expires, or re-entry is made. The tenant is entitled to compen-

sation for disturbance, usually one year's rent, except when re-entry is made for non-payment of rent, breach of regulations, etc., or when a full year's notice to quit is given. The tenant is permitted to keep hens or rabbits, properly housed, notwithstanding agreements to the contrary, on allotments, privately, and where not prejudicial to health or a nuisance. On the other hand, the landlord has the right to recover compensation for deterioration if the tenant fails to keep his plot clean and in a good state of cultivation and fertility. The landlord is entitled to deduct any rent owing from the compensation payable. Boroughs and Urban District Councils, with a population of 10,000, or upwards, are not obliged to provide individual A.s of more than 20 poles (⅛ acre); but those of smaller populations and parishes are obliged to provide A.s of ¼ acre. The rent to be paid by a tenant is 'such rent as a tenant may reasonably be expected to pay'.

Obtaining the Land. An A. can be obtained by application to the local authority (borough, parish, rural or urban council) without much difficulty. It is very useful if the land is reasonably near to one's home, but attention should be given to soil and its fertility, and its situation in relation to surrounding land. Too often A.s are laid out in low or valley situations, subject to poor drainage, and/or frost. A 10-pole (1/16 acre) plot is usually big enough to provide sufficient vegetables for the small family of 3 or 4 persons when properly cropped. Twenty poles (⅛ acre) is a good average size; while 40 poles (¼ acre) permits fruit and cut flower growing, as well as vegetable cropping. Advice on particular locations, soil needs, etc., can be obtained from local authorities or the local allotment or gardening society. Full rules governing the application for A.s and their management may be obtained from The National Allotments and Gardens Society, 22 High Street, Flitwick, Bedfordshire. The membership of the local society usually carries privileges of economical purchase of seeds, manures, fertilizers, etc., and advisory services.

Cultivation. A.s are grouped together, often in parallel strips or rectangles. This means that any neglect in cultivation by one tenant is liable quickly to affect his neighbours. Diseases and pests can spread rapidly; and weeds invade from one plot to another easily. Apart, therefore, from the need to maintain an allotment in high cultivation, with regular organic manuring, correction of lime status, and balanced fertilizing, the tenant should also be conversant with the various chemical aids to the prevention and control of noxious weeds, infectious diseases and pests, and their correct application.

Buildings on Allotment Gardens. Greenhouses, arbours, huts and storesheds used in connection with A.s and erected on the site are classed as 'agricultural buildings' and therefore exempted from rates. They should be of sound construction, properly aligned, and well maintained, if only for the good name of the tenant and the good appearance of the site.

Allspice. See *Calycanthus*.

Almond, See *Prunus communis.*

Alnus, Alder (al'nus. Fam. Betulaceae). Deciduous trees and shrubs, largely of the northern hemisphere, hardy, the most garden-worthy being:

Selection. A. cordata, Corsica, to 60 ft, handsome pyramidal growth, cordate leaves, long catkins in March; *glutinosa*, common Alder, Europe, 40–80 ft, is useful for damp places, its vs. *aurea*, with golden leaves, *imperialis*, with deeply lobed leaves, and *incisa*, the thorn-leaved alder, have much foliage beauty; *incana*, the grey alder, is best in v. *incisa*, with finely and deeply cut leaves, 40 ft; *pendula*, Japan, 25 ft, makes an attractive small weeping tree.

Cultivation. Best suited by moist, heavy soils, damp situations or waterside. Plant October to March.

Propagation. Species by seeds sown in March on outdoor beds, loam soil. Varieties by grafting on seedling species stocks, spring.

Aloe (al'o-e or a'lo. Fam. Liliaceae). Evergreen succulent plants, with fleshy leaves, usually in rosette form, chiefly native to Africa, S. Africa and offshore islands, grown in greenhouses, or planted out for summer in subtropical gardening, chiefly in the south-west.

Selection. A. aristata, S. Africa, the hardiest, slender-leaved rosettes of 6 in.,

reddish-yellow flowers, July, 12 in.; *brevifolia*, Cape Province, thick pale green leaves, red flowers, July; *ciliaris*, Cape Province, long, slender-stemmed and tall; *humilis*, Natal, stemless, toothed leaves, red on yellow flowers; with varietal forms, 4–8 in.; *mitriformis*, Cape Province, stemmed, with thick leaves, yellow-toothed, heads of red flowers; *striata*, Cape Province, stemless with pale greyish leaves, pink-margined, coral red flowers, and hybrids; and *variegata*, S. Africa, the Partridge-breasted Aloe, with stemless rosettes of white blotched, dark green leaves, spike of red flowers; much grown as a house plant.

Cultivation. Loam soil compost or JIP 2. Ample sun, liberal watering in summer, little in winter. Minimum winter temp. 7° C. (45° F.).

Propagation. By sucker offsets detached in spring, temp. 15·5° C. (60° F.).

Aloides. Aloe-like. Ex. *Kniphofia aloides.*

Alonsoa, Mask Flower (al-on-so'a. Fam. Scrophulariaceae). Half-hardy perennials of the Peruvian Alps, grown as half-hardy annuals in pots in a cool greenhouse, or for sunny beds.

Selection. A. linifolia, 1–1½ ft, bright scarlet summer flowers; and *warscewiczii*, 1½ to 2 ft, cinnabar-red, and its v. *compacta*, 1½ ft, scarlet, are good for bedding. *Incisifolia*, 1–2 ft, hooded scarlet flowers all summer, may be grown as a cool greenhouse shrub.

Cultivation. Well-drained soil, sun. Raise plants from seed to plant out in late May.

Propagation. By seeds, sown thinly, March, bottom heat 15·5° C. (60° F.), to prick out, and harden off for outdoors or to grow in pots.

Aloysia. See *Lippia*.

Alpine House. Technically, a glasshouse or greenhouse designed to give conditions of light, airiness, low humidity and protection from the inclemencies of our weather, needed by true alpine plants grown in Britain, and to enable others, especially the early flowering, to be grown more perfectly.

Design. The alpine house is usually a rectangular, span-roofed, glazed structure, on brick foundations and walls to a height of 33 in.; or on wooden walls. The walls are fitted with air-bricks or sliding ventilators, arranged staggered, not opposite, to give air circulation without draughts. The width of the house should be at least 8 ft 6 in., and as long as practicable, bearing in mind that it is more difficult to maintain equable conditions in a smaller house. The glazed structure should rise 18–30 in. to the eaves, with all side panels hinged at the top and capable of being opened. The span roof rises to a height of 7–9 ft, and is fitted with top lights to open all along on both sides. Only the ends are glazed with fixed panels. A central hard pathway of stone flags or concrete, at least 30 in. wide, gives access to staging along two sides and one end, with a half-glazed door at one end.

Although various plastic substitutes have been developed for glazing, clear 24-oz. glass is still most satisfactory for a permanent structure, for both light admission and durability, and for freedom from yellowing and readiness to scratch and collect atmospheric dust and impurities.

Staging. In a house of 8 ft 6 in. wide, the staging can be 2 ft 6 in. wide; or 4 ft in a house of 12 to 13 ft wide. The minimum height is 2 ft 9 in., though it may be carried up to 3 ft 2 in. if more convenient. The staging is best carried on brick or concrete pillars, or best of all, constructed of patent slotted angle-iron. Wooden staging is less strong and less durable. The stages should consist of strong corrugated galvanized iron, or corrugated asbestos or PVC plastic sheeting, cut so that the corrugations run sideways not lengthways. There must be adequate cross supports, and the front of the stage can be finished with a raised board, 5 in. × 1 in., preservatively treated. The stages are covered with about a 4-in. layer of gravel and coarse sand mixture; on and in which the pots and pans containing the alpine plants are put.

It is, of course, possible to buy manufactured alpine houses, but a reputable maker should be chosen, since construction is rather more exacting than that of the ordinary garden greenhouse. Western Red Cedar wood construction is very durable, though other woods last well if first treated with an organic solvent preservative. Aluminium alloy houses are most costly to buy but score in low maintenance costs.

Heating. It is possible to grow a wide range of alpine plants without heat; but the installation of heating apparatus to offset damp, fog, and air stagnancy at certain times of the winter is an insurance against losses. Electrical tubular heaters, thermostatically controlled, provide an efficient system.

Site. It is usual to site an alpine house on a north–south orientation, but deviation from the strict line is unlikely to make much difference. The half-glazed door should be at the northern end. It is important for the house to be in the open full sun, and not in a low-lying frost-pocket.

Shading. Some shading will be needed against hot direct sun, either by the use of a proprietary shading wash, applied to the inside glass; or movable screening with green plastic sheeting or netting, or muslin, during summer.

Plants in the Alpine House. Alpine plants under glass are grown in pans, deep pans, half-pots and pots, of various sizes. It is usually wise to choose the deeper containers for all but known shallow-rooting species.

Innumerable formulae for soil composts have been put forward. The essentials are, however, good fibrous medium loam, preferably sterilized, humus in the form of moist granulated peat or first-class leaf-mould, and clean coarse sand, to assure perfect drainage. A mixture of these ingredients in equal parts by volume will suit most alpine plants. For the lime-tolerant, a little ground limestone ($\frac{3}{4}$ oz. per bushel) may be added; for the lime-intolerant, a lime-free loam is necessary. Only in relatively few instances should it be necessary to depart from these simple mixtures. A top-dressing of chippings—limestone for the lime-tolerant, granite for the lime-intolerant—will provide the essential good surface drainage needed by plants in pans.

Watering should increase with growth and rising temperatures, decrease to once a week or so in winter; early morning is probably the best time to water; and take care not to wet foliage in dull, dampish weather. Ventilation must be carefully controlled but thorough, increasing as temperatures rise, but closing the house in advance of falling night temperatures. Stagnant humidity and damp, rather than cold, are to be most feared.

Choice of Plants. No more than a limited list of choice plants can be attempted here, selected for their beauty and relative ease of culture.

Acantholimon venustum; *Aethionema armenum* and vs., *A. grandiflorum, A. iberideum*; *Allium cyaneum, A. narcissiflorum*; *Alyssum montanum, A. serpyllifolium*; *Andromeda polifolia* and vs.; *Androsace carnea* and vs., *A. ciliata, A. pyrenaica, A. villosa*; *Anemone obtusiloba* v. *patula*; *Aquilegia bernardii, A. flabellata* and vs., *A. pyrenaica*; *Arabis androsacea, A. blepharophylla*; *Arenaria purpurascens*; *Armeria caespitosa*, and 'Bevan's variety'; *Artemisia lanata*; *Asperula arcadiensis, A. suberosa*; *Aster alpinus* and vs.; *Astilbe × crispa, A. glaberrima saxatilis*; *Brodiaea elegans, B. stellaris*; *Bulbocodium vernum*; *Calceolaria darwinii, C. tenella*; *Callianthemum kernerianum*; *Campanula allionii* and vs., *C. arvatica, C. cenisia, C. pilosa, C. raineri, C. tridentata*; *Cassiope lycopodioides, C. tetragona*; *Ceanothus prostratus*; *Celmisia argentea*; *Chionodoxa luciliae, C. tmoli*; *Codonopsis ovata*; *Crassula sarcocaulis*; *Crocus asturicus, C. biflorus, C. chrysanthus* and vs., *C. hyemalis, C. medius, C. speciosus, C. versicolor*; *Cyananthus microphyllus, C. sherriffii*; *Cyclamen africanum, C. balearicum, C. cilicium, C. europaeum, C. libanoticum, C. orbiculatum* and vs., *C. repandum*; *Cytisus ardoinii, C. demissus*; *Daphne petraea, D. retusa*; *Dianthus alpinus, D. freynii, D. haematocalyx, D. neglectus, D. simulans*; *Diapensia lapponica*; *Dionysia bryoides*; *Douglasia montana*; *Draba bryoides* and v. *imbricata, D. rigida*; *Dryas octopetala* v. *minor*; *Erigeron aureus, E. leiomerus*; *Erinacea anthyllis*; *Erinus alpinus* 'Dr Hanele'; *Erodium chrysanthemum, E. corsicum*; *Erythronium revolutum* and vs., *E. tuolumnense*; *Euryops evansii*; *Felicia pappei*; *Gentiana acaulis* and vs., *G. farreri, G. × 'Inverleith', G. × macauleyi, G. ornata, G. saxosa, G. verna*; *Geranium argenteum, G. dalmaticum, G. napuligerum*; *Geum reptans*; *Globularia*

incanescens; *Gypsophila aretioides* and v. *caucasica*; *Helichrysum bellidioides, H. frigidum*; *Houstonia caerulea* and vs.; *Hypericum coris, H. cuneatum, H. olympicum*; *Iberis correaefolia, I. saxatilis, I. taurica*; *Ilex crenata* v. *mariesii*; *Iris aucheri, I. bakeriana; I. histrio, I. gracilipes, I. lacustris, I. pumila, I. planifolia, I. verna*; *Jankaea heldreichii*; *Jasminum parkeri*; *Lapeirousia laxa*; *Lewisia cotyledon, L. howellii* and vs.; *Linum alpinum, L. arboreum, L. salsoloides*; *Lithospermum diffusum*; *L. oleifolium*; *Lupinus lyallii, L. ornatus*; *Meconopsis quintuplinervia*; *Mertensia maritima*; *Micromeria corsica*; *Mimulus primuloides*; *Minuartia aretioides*; *Morisia monantha*; *Myosotis alpestris, M. azorica, M. rupicola, Narcissus asturiensis, N. bulbocodium* and vs., *N. cyclamineus* and vs., *N. minor, N. rupicola, N. watieri*; *Nertera granadensis*; *Nierembergia repens*; *Nomocharis mairei* and vs.; *Omphalodes luciliae*; *Onosma albo-pilosum, O. nanum*; *Ophrys apifera*; *Orchis maculata*; *Oxalis adenophylla, O. enneaphylla*; *Penstemon davidsonii, P. menziesii, P. pinifolius, P. scouleri, P. × 'Six Hills'*; *Petrocallis pyrenaica*; *Phlox caespitosa* and vs., *P. douglasii, P. nana* v. *ensifolia (mesoleuca), Phyteuma comosum*; *Pinguicula vulgaris*; *Pleione formosana, P. pricei*; *Polygala chamaebuxus* and vs., *P. vayredae*; *Potentilla aurea, P. fruticosa* v. *beesii, P. nitida, P. verna*; *Primula allionii* and vs., *P. auricula* and vs., *P. clusiana, P. marginata* and vs., etc.; *Ptilotrichum spinosum*; *Pulsatilla alpina, P. vernalis*; *Puschkinia scilloides* and vs.; *Raffenaldia primuloides*; *Ramonda myconi* and vs.; *Ranunculus crenatus, R. glacialis*; *Raoulia australis*; *Rhododendron anthopogon; R. × 'Blue Diamond', R. ferrugineum, R. hirsutum, R. intricatum, R. leucaspis, R. russatum*, etc.; *Rhodohypoxis baurii*; *Rosa chinensis minima, R. gallica pumila*; *Salix × boydii*; *Saponaria caespitosa, S. pumila*; *Saxifraga aizoon* and vs., *S. × 'Arco Valleyi', S. × 'Bellisant', S. × boydii, S. burseriana*, and many vs., *S. callosa* and vs., *S. cotyledon* and vs., *S. dispensioides, S. grisebachii*, and v. 'Wisley', *S. × irvingii, S. longifolia, S. oppositifolia* and vs., *S. porophylla* and vs., *S. retusa, S. scardica, S. stribrnyi, S. ×* 'Tumbling Waters', and others; *Scilla adlamii, S. bifolia, S. chinensis; Sedum brevifolium, S. cauticola, S. ellacombianum, S. populifolium, S. spathulifolium* and vs., *S. stahlii; Sempervivum arachnoideum* and vs., *S. ciliosum* and vs., *S. kosaninii, S. tectorum* and vs.; *Senecio incanus; Shortia galacifolia, S. uniflora; Silene acaulis* and vs., *S. hookeri; Sisyrinchium douglasii; Soldanella alpina, S. minima, S. villosa; Spiraea bullata, S. hacquetii; Tecophilaea cyanocrocus; Teucrium chamaedrys; Thalictrum kiusianum; Thymus carnosus, T. herba-barona, T. membranaceus, T. nitidus; Tulipa aucheriana, T. batalinii, T. clusiana, T. eichleri, T. montana, T. ostrowskiana, T. stellata, T. violacea; Veronica cinerea; Viola biflora, V. calcarata, V. gracilis; Weldenia candida.*

Alpine Plants. Botanically, alpine plants are native to the regions of the world lying between the limits of the tree line and of unmelting snow and ice. Horticulturally, they may include a wider range of plants, including some from sub-alpine conditions, but which have characteristics of growth—such as low stature, diminutive parts and miniature features—of alpines, and which have come to be grown as rock garden plants. As such, garden alpines are drawn from almost all parts of the world, from near or at sea level in arctic zones, from European Alps at heights of 5,000 ft or more above sea level, and from higher altitudes in the warmer or tropical regions. According to their tolerance for our climatic conditions, they can be successfully grown in gardens where soils and situations are favourable. In the past it has been the practice to simulate the natural habitat of alpine plants as far as possible by growing them in rock gardens, where mountain landscapes are reproduced in miniature.

Where to grow Alpine Plants. A well-constructed rock garden (q.v.) is still the ideal place for alpines. Where transport costs are high, however, stone is expensive, and construction may be costly and laborious. Moreover, small gardens, especially on flat sites, may not lend themselves readily to a rock garden feature. Alpines may, however, be grown in flat beds or 'pavements', where the excellent drainage they need can be arranged; they can be grown in, and on,

dry walls (*see* Wall), terraces, stone pathways, in stone troughs or pans, and many kinds are adaptable to border planting and window boxes. They are excellent subjects for the cold alpine house (q.v.) or frame.

Alpine Plants and their Needs. Alpines owe their dwarf stature and tough growth to their adaptation and evolution under the climatic and environmental factors of their natural habitat. Ground-hugging growth enables them to escape the full force of winds, and to bear the weight of heavy snows; while their fine-bladed, waxy, hairy, leathery or tufted foliage minimizes transpiration moisture losses, at times when replacement through the roots is made difficult by the soil being frozen or dry in drought. In their native habitat alpines have good resistance to cold. Moved to lower altitudes, where more humid and damp conditions prevail, with cloud and temperature fluctuations less severe, alpines have a tendency to grow rather more soft, lush and large and more vulnerable to damp at low temperatures. Their great need is for a porous soil, with particularly good drainage at the crowns or collars of plants; moderate humus content in the nature of well-rotted leaf-mould or peat, and light of a daily duration and intensity approximately those of where the plants are found growing naturally. The great majority of alpines are hardy and perennial and adaptable to garden conditions, where soil and site are suitable. The more difficult alpines are those which have to adjust themselves in a transition from high altitude conditions to those of lowlands. It is inevitable that seed-catching crevices and levels of the rock garden invite weed invasion, and the grower of alpines must expect to devote much time and effort to preventing weeds swamping choice plants. The plants themselves are relatively free from diseases and pests; though slugs and snails are a perennial hazard.

Alpine plants are usually raised by specialist nurserymen, and sold 'ex pots', with their roots embedded in soil. This means that they may be planted at any time of the year when soil conditions and weather are suitable; though the best times to plant are September, October,

r March to May. Many alpines may be
raised quite easily from seeds. Sowing
times are critical in certain instances,
since most alpines germinate most
readily when the seeds are sown freshly
ripe. Otherwise, germination may be
delayed by weeks, sometimes months.
Propagation can usually be attempted by
means of cuttings of shoots of the current
season's growth in summer; or division
in spring. Fuller details of the alpine
plant species and their culture will be
found under the genera given throughout
his book, as follows:

Acaena	Crassula	Lysimachia	Ramonda
Acantholimon	Cyananthus	Mazus	Ranunculus
Achillea	Dianthus	Meconopsis	Raoulia
Aethionema	Dicentra	Mentha	Rhodohypoxis
Ajuga	Dodecatheon	Mertensia	Saponaria
Alyssum	Doronicum	Micromeria	Saxifraga
Andromeda	Douglasia	Mimulus	Scabiosa
Androsace	Draba	Morisia	Scutelaria
Anemone	Dryas	Myosotis	Sedum
Antennaria	Edraianthus	Nierembergia	Sempervivum
Anthemis	Erigeron	Oenothera	Shortia
Anthyllis	Erinus	Omphalodes	Silene
Aquilegia	Eriogonum	Onosma	Sisyrinchium
Arabis	Erodium	Origanum	Soldanella
Arenaria	Felicia	Oxalis	Solidago
Armeria	Frankenia	Papaver	Spiraea
Artemisia	Gentiana	Parochetus	Synthyris
Asperula	Geranium	Paronychia	Thalictrum
Aster	Geum	Penstemon	Thymus
Astilbe	Gypsophila	Petrocallis	Tiarella
Astragalus	Haberlea	Phlox	Trachelium
Aubrieta	Helichrysum	Phyteuma	Trifolium
Bellium	Hutchinsia	Pimelea	Trillium
Calamintha	Iberis	Pinguicula	Uvularia
Calceolaria	Iris	Platycodon	Vaccinium
Campanula	Jeffersonia	Polemonium	Verbascum
Celmisia	Leontopodium	Polygala	Veronica
Cheiranthus	Leucogenes	Polygonum	Viola
Chrysanthemum	Lewisia	Potentilla	Wahlenbergia
Codonopsis	Linaria	Primula	Wulfenia
Cortusa	Linum	Prunella	
Corydalis	Lithospermum	Pulsatilla	

See Alpine House, Rock Garden, Sink
Garden.

Alpine Rose. See *Rhododendron fer-
ugineum.*

Alpinus (-a, -um). Of the alps or
mountains. Ex. *Dianthus alpinus.*

Alstroemeria, Herb Lily, Peruvian Lily
al-stro-me'ri-a. Fam. Alstroemeriaceae).
Tuberous-rooted perennials of S.

America, which may be grown outdoors
or in a cool greenhouse.

Selection. A. aurantiaca, 3 ft, with
orange-flowered head of bloom, summer,
is the hardiest, but can become rampant
in agreeable conditions; *Ligtu* hybrids,
18 in., various colours, are the gems;
chilensis, 2 ft, pink, lined yellow, is hardy;
but *pelegrina,* Lily of the Incas, 1 ft, lilac,
purple spotted, is for the cool greenhouse.

Cultivation. Well-drained, loam soil,
full sun. Plant October. In pots, use JIP
1. Winter temp. 7° C. (45° F.).

Propagation. Occasionally, by division
in October or April. By seeds, cold frame,
in March, in pans.

Alternanthera (al-ter-nan'ther-a. Fam.
Amaranthaceae). Tropical herbaceous
perennials with richly coloured foliage,
chiefly grown for carpet-bedding, and
dwarfed by frequent clipping.

Selection. A. amoena, 1–2 in.; *bettzi-
chiana* and vs.; *ficoides,* creeping; and

versicolor, are all Brazilian, with highly coloured foliage.

Cultivation. Ordinary garden soil. Full sun. Plant out in late May; lift in September, to winter under glass at 15·5° C. (60° F.), with very moderate watering.

Propagation. By cuttings, taken in March, JI compost, bottom heat 21° C. (70° F.); or root cuttings taken in August, wintered under glass in boxes, at 15·5° C. (60° F.) minimum.

Alternate. Of leaves arranged singly on alternate sides of the stem; not opposite. Ex. *Buddleia alternifolia.*

Althaea, Hollyhock (al'the-a. Fam. Malvaceae). A genus containing species, biennial and perennial plants, which are ornamental and hardy.

Selection. A. cannabina, S. France, 6 ft, rose; *officinalis*, the native Marsh Mallow, 3–4 ft, blush pink; and *sulphurea*, Persia, shrubby, sulphur-yellow, are perennials. *A. rosea*, China, to 8 ft, is the biennial Hollyhock, available in single and double flowers of various colours. *A. ficifolia*, is the Fig-leaved or Antwerp Hollyhock, Siberia, to 6 ft, yellow flowering, June.

Cultivation. Deep, well-drained loam, enriched with humus in autumn; sunny position, rear of borders, or by walls. Plant October or March–April.

A. rosea (Hollyhock) and vs. should be raised from seed, sown in early summer, to plant out in flowering positions in autumn, or to winter under glass, at 7° C. (45° F.), and plant out in April; in humus-rich soil, enriched with basic slag or bone meal, and a little complete fertilizer. Annual strains: sow under glass, February–March, bottom heat 18° C. (65° F.), hardening off to plant out in May.

Propagation. Preferably by seeds, as seedling plants show greater resistance to the Rust disease. Healthy plants may be raised from cuttings taken in spring; and choice varieties are sometimes increased by grafting pieces on roots of vigorous seedlings in spring. To safeguard against Rust plants are sprayed with a copper fungicide (q.v.) in May, repeated at 3 weeks.

Altissimus (-a, -um). Highest, very tall. Ex. *Delphinium altissimum.*

Altitude. Normally, the higher the altitude, the lower the temperature, an this has marked limiting effects upo plants and their growth. Often plant from higher altitudes in subtropical o tropical regions can be grown outdoors a lower altitudes in more temperate zones Since cold air drains from higher t lower altitudes within a garden, plant on the higher ground tend to suffer les from night frosts.

Alum Root. See *Heuchera.*

Alyssum, Madwort, Gold-dust (al'i sum. Fam. Cruciferae). A genus whicl includes dwarf annual and perennia plants, and sub-shrubs, with brigh colourful flowers.

Selection. Annuals are really forms o *Lobularia maritima*, once included i *Alyssum*, and are offered as dwarf plant for edgings, rock garden and beddin under 'Little Dorrit', white; 'Rosi O'Day', rose-pink; 'Carpet of Snow' white; 'Royal Carpet', violet-purple and 'Pink Heather', pink; 3–6 in. tall *A. saxatile* is somewhat shrubby anc perennial with golden flowers, April t June, and has vs. *citrinum*, pale yellow and *compactum*, close-growing, for rocl gardens and walls; *montanum*, 3 in. bright yellow scented flowers, spring and *alpestre*, pale yellow, 3 in., ar perennial; and *argenteum*, 1–1½ ft golden-yellow, flowers in summer.

Cultivation. Any well-drained soi suits. Annuals may be sown under glass in February, March, to be planted out ir April; or sown where they are to flower thinly, March, April. Perennials may be raised similarly from seeds, or from cuttings taken in summer, inserted ir sandy loam firmly.

Propagation. By seeds, in spring, sowr ½-in. deep, in March, April; by cuttings of young shoots in summer.

Amabilis (-e). Pleasing. Ex. *Cynoglos sum amabile.*

Amaranthus (am-ar-an'thus. Fam Amaranthaceae). Half-hardy annuals grown for their beautiful foliage and spikes of bracted flowers, in July– October.

Selection. A. caudatus, Love-Lies- Bleeding, 2–3 ft, tropical, with red drooping flower spikes; *hypochondriacus*, Prince's Feather, tropical America, 4 ft, crimson, erect flower spikes, and its vs. and *A. gangeticus*, tropical, 1–3 ft, and

Propagation. By seeds sown in April outdoors in warm, sandy loam; by division in spring; by cuttings of firm shoots in summer.

Amygdalus. See *Prunus*.

Anacharis (an-a-kar'is. Fam. Hydrocharitaceae). Perennial aquatic plants, useful for underwater oxygenation of aquaria and garden pools.

Selection. A. canadensis (*Elodea c.*) N. America, is the Canada Weed or Bavingon's Curse, introduced in 1841, growing extremely rapidly for some years, and then less rampant; *crispa*, Africa, is less rampant but more tender, useful in aquaria and sheltered pools.

Cultivation. Plant in March–June in base soil of pools. Prune as necessary to contain growth.

Propagation. By cuttings inserted in spring; by winter buds sinking to the base of the pool.

Anagallis, Pimpernel (an-a-gal'is. Fam. Primulaceae). Pretty dwarf plants with soft green foliage and open-faced flowers, grown as half-hardy annuals in borders, or for cool greenhouse decoration.

Selection. A. linifolia, Mediterranean, ft, blue, reddish beneath, and its vs. *breweri,* red, *phillipsii,* deep blue, are chiefly grown; *arvensis* is the native Pimpernel, and *tenella,* the Bog Pimpernel, with pink flowers, for moist places.

Cultivation. Ordinary garden soil, planted out in May.

Propagation. By seeds, sown under glass, bottom heat 15·5° C. (65° F.), March, to be pricked out and hardened off for planting out in May.

Ananas, Pineapple (an-an'as. Fam. Bromeliaceae). Herbaceous perennials of Brazil, of which *A. comosus* in selected strains such as 'The Queen' may be suited under stove or hot house conditions; and varieties *sativus, porteanus* and *variegatus* grown for ornamental foliage in a warm greenhouse or the house.

Cultivation. In 10-in. pots, or prepared borders; 2 parts fibrous loam, 1 part peat, ½ part coarse bone meal and charcoal, 1 part sand, compost. Growing temp. 21–27° C. (70–80° F.), with free watering, and syringing to keep atmosphere moist; minimum winter temp. 18° C. (65° F.). Less heat is needed

when plants are grown for foliage and ornamental value only.

Propagation. By suckers, when available, inserted in lightish soil, bottom heat 24° C. (75° F.). close atmosphere. By crowns—the tops of fruit—treated similarly; kept close and warm for rapid growth.

Anandrous. Without stamens.

Anaphalis (an-a'pay-lis. Fam. Compositae). Reasonably hardy perennials, with white composite flowers, lending themselves to drying as Everlasting Flowers or Immortelles for winter decoration.

Selection. A. margaritacea, N. America, 1½ ft, flat-headed corymbs of pearly-white flowers, August; *triplinervis,* Himalaya, 1 ft, with white woolly foliage and white flowers, summer, are chiefly grown.

Cultivation. Well-drained open soil; full sun. Plant October or March–April.

Propagation. By seeds, sown thinly, outdoors, in April. By division in October or April.

Anastatica, Rose of Jericho (an-as-tat'i-ka. Fam. Cruciferae). Of no great garden merit, the one species, *A. hierochuntica,* 6 in., small white flowers, June, is a desert plant of Syria, sometimes known as a 'Resurrection Plant', and may be grown as a half-hardy annual, for curiosity value.

Propagation. By seeds, sown shallowly, bottom heat 21° C. (70° F.), March, pricked off and hardened to plant out in June, or grow in pots under warm greenhouse conditions.

Anatomy. The structure of the plant, as observed and studied visually.

Anbury. *See* Club-root.

Anceps. Two-edged or two-headed. Ex. *Laelia anceps.*

Anchusa (an-koo'sa. Fam. Boragainceae). A genus containing annual, biennial and perennial plants, chiefly European and hardy, esteemed for their funnel-shaped flowers, attractive to bees.

Selection. A. azurea, Caucasus, 3 to 5 ft, large panicles of bright blue flowers, summer, and its vs. 'Dropmore', deep blue; 'Loddon Royalist', gentian blue; 'Morning Glory', dark blue; 'Opal', light blue; and 'Pride of Dover', azure blue, are good border perennials; *barrelieri,* S. Europe, 1–2 ft, bushy with blue and white flowers, May, is also useful. *Angustissima* (*caespitosa*), Crete, 6 in., bright blue, June, is a choice tufted perennial for the well-drained rock garden or alpine house. The S. African *capensis* and v. 'Bluebird', are biennial, best over-wintered in a cool greenhouse, and planted out in June for July flowering; *officinalis*, 1–2 ft, purple-blue, is the native biennial.

Cultivation. Ordinary well-drained soil; sunny position. Plant October or March–April.

Propagation. By seeds, ⅛-in. deep, March, bottom heat 13–18° C. (55–65° F.) or outdoors in April, May. Perennials by division, October.

Androecium. The male organs of the flower.

Androgynous. Having male and female flowers on the same stem or spike; monoecious (q.v.).

Andromeda (an-drom'e-da. Fam. Ericaceae). Now a genus of one species of a low-growing, evergreen shrub, Britain and north temperate zone, *A. polifolia*, the Bog Rosemary, 12 in., with clusters of bell-shaped pink flowers, May; of which *nana*, with bright rose flowers, is the best form.

Cultivation. Well-drained, humus-rich, lime-free soil essential. Plant September–October, or March–April. Partial shade.

Propagation. By seeds, in sandy peat, outdoors, March; by careful division or layering in September; by cuttings of young firm shoots, August, under bell-glass or frame.

Androsace, Rock Jasmine (an-dro'-sak-e. Fam. Primulaceae). Charming tufted, dwarf perennial alpine plants, with heads of primrose-like flowers, chiefly from mountainous regions of the northern hemisphere.

Selection. A. carnea, European Alps, 2–3 in., rose, June, and v. *brigantiaca*; *chamaejasme*, 2 to 4 in., white, red and yellow throated, June; *lanuginosa*, Himalaya, trailing, silvery haired foliage, pink, summer, and v. *leichtlinii*, white; *sarmentosa*, Himalaya, 4 in., rose, May, June, and vs. *chumbyi*, more densely tufted, *watkinsii*, smaller-leafed, and *yunnanensis*, finely compact, are among the easier plants for rock gardens. High alpines of the Aretia section, such as *alpina*, Switzerland, rose-pink, June;

ciliata, Pyrenees, rose, June; *cylindrica*, Pyrenees, white, April; *helvetica*, Switzerland, white, May; *pyrenaica*, Pyrenees, white, yellow-eyed, May, are closely tufted, and need the winter protection of overhead cover or the alpine house, with perfect soil drainage.

Cultivation. Well-drained porous soil, or scree in the rock garden, with chippings. Plant ex pots, April, sunny positions. Protect with a glass cover in winter.

Propagation. By seed in early spring, under glass, 13° C. (55° F.). By cuttings or detached runners in June–July.

Anemone, Wind Flower (a-nem-o'ne Fam. Ranunculaceae). Hardy perennial herbaceous plants, with tuberous or fleshy rootstocks, distinctive for their brightly colourful flowers, composed of petaloid sepals or petals and numerous free stamens. Chiefly native to the northern hemisphere.

Selection. For garden purposes may be divided into (*a*) the tuberous-rooted, and (*b*) herbaceous fleshy-rooted perennials. Tuberous-rooted include: *A. coronaria* brown tubers, from which the varieties of florist anemones listed as 'de Caen' with single flowers in every conceivable shade; and 'St Brigid', with semi-double flowers of striking hues, have been developed, and are sometimes called the Poppy Anemones. The tubers are planted in humus-rich, well-drained soil, December–April, 2 in. deep, with winter protection, such as a cold frame, and may remain permanently so long as flowering is satisfactory. In mild, south-west gardens, planting may go on all the year round. *A.* × *fulgens*, a hybrid of *A. pavonina* × *A. hortensis*, has given rise to brilliant, short-stemmed strains of scarlet, pink and white flowering plants which may be planted to form clumps in rock gardens, in association with dwarf Narcissi or white Arabis; plant tuber 1½–2 in. deep in autumn; *A. pavonina* 8–16 in., with carmine to whitish flowers, April, requires a sheltered spot and has given rise to a selected strain known as the St Bavo anemones, which should be treated similarly to *A. coronaria*. *A. apennina*, S. Europe, 6 in, blue, March, with white, rose and double-flowered forms, may be planted in partial shade; *blanda*, E. Europe, 6 in.

deep blue, March, needs sheltered warmth, and very well-drained soil, and has vs. in various shades of blue to white; *nemorosa*, 6 in., is the white spring-flowering native wood anemone; and *ranunculoides*, a yellow-flowering woodland species, 3 to 8 in., March, of the Caucasus; all are tuberous or rhizomatous rooted for autumn planting.

Herbaceous kinds include: *A. hupehensis* (*japonica*), China, 2–3 ft, with mauve-pink flowers, late summer, and its vs. *alba*, white, *splendens*, large, pink, and hybrids such as 'Kriemhilde', semi-double, rose-pink; 'Louis Uhink', semi-double white; and 'Montrose', rose-pink; × *lesseri*, 1–1½ ft, striking with purple-carmine, flowers; *narcissiflora*, Europe, 1–2 ft, many-flowered white umbels, May; *rivularis*, India, 1–2 ft, white with purple anthers, April; *sylvestris*, the Snowdrop Windflower, ½–1½ ft, satiny white flowers, April; all adaptable to borders or the larger rock garden, though they need disciplining from time to time as they are apt to spread at the roots, especially *A. hupehensis*.

Propagation. Species by seeds, sown in spring, in cold frame, or earlier under glass in cool greenhouse. By root division in October or March–April.

See also *Pulsatilla*.

Anemonopsis (a-nem-on-op'sis. Fam. Ranunculaceae). The one species, *A. macrophylla*, Japan, 2–3 ft, with loose racemes of purple-lilac flowers, July, is a perennial suitable for the warm herbaceous border, resembling *Anemone hupehensis*, in light, well-drained soil.

Propagation. By seeds sown in March, under glass, bottom heat 15·5° C. (60° F.), to plant out in May. By root division autumn or spring.

Anemophilous. Wind-loving. Used of flowers which depend on wind for pollination; such as conifers and catkin-bearing trees.

Anemopsis (a-nem-op'sis. Fam. Saururaceae). The sole species, *A. californica*, 15–18 in., with white-bracted, anemone-like flowers in summer, is an unusual perennial of California and Mexico, which can be grown in shallow water or swampy ground, nominally hardy. The aromatic rootstock is fashioned into beads—Apache Beads—by Indians, or infused—Yerba Mansa—

as specifics against Malaria. Plant March–April.

Propagation. By division in spring.

Angelica (an-gel'i-ka. Fam. Umbelliferae). Herbaceous perennials of compound leaves, and compound umbels of whitish flowers on tall stems, of which *A. archangelica* may be grown as a herb, the stout stem, 3–5 ft, being cut and candied for use in confectionery, etc., and the seeds being used for flavouring.

Cultivation. Deep, loam soil; plant seedlings 18 in. apart, in spring; shady position. Usually grown on for at least two years before cutting stems for use. Monocarpic.

Propagation. By fresh seeds, sown in August or early September to over-winter in cold frame.

Angelica Tree. See *Aralia elata*.

Angelonia, Whispering Bells (an-gel-o'ni-a. Fam. Scrophulariaceae). Tender herbaceous perennials, native to Mexico and S. America, which make good pot plants in the warm greenhouse.

Selection. A. grandiflora, 2 ft, fragrant lilac flowers, winter, and v. *alba*, white; and *salicariifolia*, 2 ft, blue flowers, August.

Cultivation. JIP compost, 5-in. pots, in good light; winter temp. 13° C. (55° F.), water moderately in winter, freely in active growth.

Propagation. By seeds, with bottom heat of 18° C. (65° F.); in September to flower following spring and summer; in spring for winter flowering. By cutting of young shoots, in spring.

Angel's Tears. See *Narcissus triandrus*.

Angiospermae, Angiosperms. Plants with seeds enclosed in a case (pericarp). *See* Gymnospermae.

Angraecum (an-gre'kum. Fam. Orchidaceae). Epiphytic tropical orchids which may be grown under stove or hot house conditions, with beautiful and fragrant flowers.

Selection. A. articulatum, Madagascar, dwarf, creamy white flowers in racemes; *citratum*, Madagascar, compact, creamy yellow; *eburneum*, Madagascar, 18 in., white; *leonis*, Comoro Isles, long-spurred white flowers; *falcatum*, Japan, dwarf, white; *sanderianum*, Comoro Is., 1 ft, white; *sesquipedale*, Madagascar, 15 in., ivory white, and very fine. Summer-flowering.

Cultivation. Pot March, in pots half filled with crocks and half sphagnum moss with a little charcoal. A moist, warm atmosphere is needed in growth; summer temp. 18–29° C. (65–84° F.); minimum winter temp. 15·5° C. (60° F.), more moderate watering.

Propagation. By division of offsets in March–April.

Angulate. Having angles. Ex. *Pratia angulata.*

Anguloa (an-gu-lo'a. Fam. Orchidaceae). Orchids from Colombia and Peru, with large beautiful flowers in spring, to be grown in a cool greenhouse.

Selection. A. cliftonii, yellow marked reddish; *clowesii,* fragrant golden yellow; *ruckeri* v. *sanguinea,* blood red, are the pick, but there are several others in specialists' lists.

Cultivation. Compost of 1 part loam, 1 part Osmunda fibre, 1 part sphagnum moss, with a little charcoal and finely broken crocks. Summer temp. 13–18° C. (55–65° F.), increasing watering with growth to September, little thereafter, as plants rest in winter; temp. 10–15·5° C. (50–60° F.). Place pots in shade.

Propagation. By division of pseudobulbs, when new growth just begins to show in spring.

Angustifolius (-a, -um). Narrow-leaved. Ex. *Pyracantha angustifolia.*

Anhalonium. See *Ariocarpus.*

Animal Manures. *See* Manures.

Animated Oats. See *Avena.*

Anise, Aniseed. See *Pimpinella.*

Aniseed Tree. See *Illicium.*

Annona (an-no'na. Fam. Annonaceae). Small evergreen trees of tropical America, grown commercially for their edible fruits, but of ornamental value, having fragrant leaves, under stove or hot house conditions.

Selection. A. cherimola, the Cherimoya, Peru, 12 to 20 ft, has strongly scented leaves and yellowish flowers, July; *glabra,* Alligator Apple or Cork-wood, Peru, Florida, 12–20 ft, scented, cream and red, July, inedible fruits; *muricata,* Soursop, W. Indies, to 15 ft, greenish-yellow, very large fruits with edible flesh; *reticulata,* Custard Apple or Bullock's Heart, tropical America, 15 ft, yellow and purplish flowers, edible reddish fruits, is deciduous, as is *squamosa,* Sugar Apple or Sweet Sop, tropical America,

12–18 ft, having fruits of sweet taste from which sherbet is said to be made.

Cultivation. For ornamental value may be grown in large pots, JIP compost potting in March, in summer temp. 15·5–24° C. (60–75° F.); winter minimum 13° C. (55° F.); water freely, spring and summer, with syringing overhead; moderately in winter months.

Propagation. By seeds, sown 2–3 in. deep, singly in pots, bottom heat 24° C (75° F.), spring. By leaf cuttings, summer, in propagating case.

Annual Ring. The ring of woody tissue added each year between the inner side of the cambium and the outer edge of the older wood in the stems and roots of dicotyledonous shrubs and trees. The rings can be readily seen and counted in a cross section of the stem.

Annuals. Plants which complete their life-cycle, from germination to seed-ripening, within a year; but may live longer if flower-heads are removed and seeding prevented. Horticulturally, many plants, usually exotics, which are perennial in nature may be grown and treated as annuals; being winter-killed.

As such, annuals are invaluable in gardening, since they provide plants of varying stature, beauty and colour in flowers and habit, and lend themselves to ready use in beds, borders, rock gardens, shrubbery, window boxes vases, and pots under glass. They provide a quick and rich return in garden bloom and furnishings, and are particularly valuable in the new garden, which must be economically planted, and its characteristics assessed before more permanent and more expensive stock is planted.

Horticulturally, annuals may be divided into three groups: Hardy (h.) half-hardy (h-h.) and tender (t.), according to their ability to grow under our climatic conditions and the treatment they need.

Hardy annuals are those which may be sown out of doors where they are to grow and flower, usually in March, April in prepared stations. The soil should have been dug in winter, to be broken down to a friable state with the fork; moist; and warm—at least 15·5° C. (60° F.)—for ready germination. It need not be rich. Light sandy, stony or chalky soils will benefit from added leaf-mould, sifted moist peat or thoroughly rotted manure, raked in. A light dressing of superphosphate (1–$1\frac{1}{2}$ oz. per sq. yd) helps ready rooting of seedlings, or on very poor soils, a complete spring fertilizer may be given, and raked in. Seeds are sown in groups or patches, on a grid or ring system as thinly as possible. Fine seeds may be covered by sifting soil over them; larger seeds should be sown at about 2 to 3 times their shortest diameter. Seeds may be protected against parasitic soil fungi and insect grubs by dressing with a fungicidal (Thiram, Captan) and insecticidal (gamma-BHC) seed dressing, and against birds with an anthraquinone dressing, which may be shaken up together with the seed prior to sowing. (Any left-over treated seed should be stored or disposed of in a safe manner.) Damage by slugs can be prevented by scattering metaldehyde bait pellets around the sown stations.

Germination should take place in 1 to 3 weeks, and as soon as seedlings can be grasped between finger and thumb they should be thinned, 4–12 in. apart, according to eventual stature of the plants. Seedlings do not transplant readily from open ground.

The most hardy of annuals may also be sown in August–September, to provide early bloom the following spring and early summer. *Calendula officinalis*, *Iberis amara* (Candytuft), *Collinsia bicolor*, *Godetia*, *Limnanthes douglasii*, *Nemophila insignis*, *Nigella*, *Papaver rhoeas*, *Scabiosa atropurpurea* and vs., *Saponaria calabrica*, *Silene pendula compacta*, Sweet Pea.

Hardy annuals may also be raised early by seeds sown under glass, early in the year, in the same way as half-hardy annuals (*see* page 28).

Hardy Annuals, Selection (with height and colour)

Adonis aestivalis, 1 ft, crimson
Alyssum maritimum, 4–9 in., white, rose, etc.
Anchusa capensis, $1\frac{1}{2}$ ft, blue
Argemone mexicana, 2 ft, yellow
Artemisia sacroviridis, 4–5 ft, foliage
Asperula orientalis, 1 ft, blue
Bartonia aurea, $1\frac{1}{2}$ ft, golden-yellow
Blumenbachia insignis, 2 in., white
Calendula officinalis and vs., 2 ft, yellow**s**
Carthamus tinctorius, 3 ft, orange

Centaurea cyanus and vs., $2\frac{1}{2}$ ft, white, blue, pink, etc.
Centaurea moschata (Sweet Sultan), $1\frac{1}{2}$– 2 ft, white, blue, rose, yellow
Chrysanthemum carinatum vs., 2 ft, various
Chrysanthemum coronarium vs., 1–3 ft, various
Chrysanthemum inodorum 'Bridal Robe', 9 in., white
Chrysanthemum segetum vs., $1\frac{1}{2}$ ft, gold, yellow
Clarkia elegans and vs., 2 ft, various
Cnicus benedictus, 2 ft, pale yellow
Collinsia bicolor, 1 ft, lilac and white
Collomia biflora, 1 to $1\frac{1}{2}$ ft, scarlet
Convolvulus minor (tricolor), 1 ft, blue, etc.
Crepis rubra, 1 ft, white and pink
Delphinium ajacis (Larkspur), $1\frac{1}{2}$ ft, various
Delphinium consolida, $2\frac{1}{2}$–3 ft, various
Dianthus barbatus 'Wee Willie', 6 in., various
Dianthus sinensis heddewigii, 9 in., various
Dracocephalum moldavica, $1\frac{1}{2}$ ft, blue
Erysimum perofskianum, $1\frac{1}{2}$ ft, orange
Eschscholtzia californica and vs., 1 ft, various
Eucharidium concinnum 'Pink Ribbons', 1 ft, rose
Euphorbia heterophylla, 2 ft, foliage
Euphorbia marginata, 2 ft, foliage
Gilia achilleaefolia, v. major, 1 ft, blue
Gilia capitata, 2 ft, blue
Gillia × hybrida, 6 in., various
Gillia tricolor, 9 in., yellow, white, violet
Godetia grandiflora and vs., 2 ft, various
Godetia whitneyi and vs., 1 ft, various
Gypsophila elegans and vs., 1 ft, white, rose
Helianthus annuus and vs., 3–5 ft, yellow
Humulus japonicus, climber, and v. variegatus
Humulus lupulus (Hop), climber, foliage
Iberis coronaria (Rocket), $1\frac{1}{2}$ ft, white
Iberis umbellata and vs. (Candytuft), 1 ft, various
Ionopsidium acaule, 2 in., violet
Kentranthus macrosiphon, 2 ft, rose
Lathyrus hybrids, Sweet Pea, climbers, various
Lavatera trimestris and vs., 2–4 ft, white, rose
Limnanthes douglasii, 6 in., white, and yellow

Linaria maroccana and vs., 9 in., various
Linum grandiflorum and vs., 1½ ft, red, blue
Loasa vulcanica, 2 ft, white
Lonas inodora, 1 ft, yellow
Lupinus hartwegii and vs., 2–3 ft, white, blue
Lupinus, annual vs. and hybrids, 2½ ft, various
Lychnis coeli-rosa (Silene), 1½ ft, rosy-purple
Malcolmia maritima and vs., 1 ft, various
Malope grandiflora, 3 ft, rosy-purple
Matthiola bicornis, 1 ft, lilac, scented
Nemophila menziesii and vs., 4 in., blue, white
Nicandra physaloides (Shoo Fly), 3 ft, blue
Nigella damascena and vs., 1½ ft, blue, white, pink
Omphalodes linifolia, 1 ft, white
Papaver commutatum, 1½ ft, scarlet
Papaver rhoeas and vs., 1½–2 ft, various
Phacelia campanularia, 9 in., deep blue
Reseda odorata and vs., 1 ft, green, reddish
Rhodanthe maculata, 1 ft, white, rose
Salvia horminum and vs., 1½ ft, blue, pink, white
Sanvitalia procumbens, 6 in., yellow
Saponaria calabrica, 9 in., rose
Scabiosa atropurpurea (Sweet Scabious), 3 ft, various
Silene pendula and vs., 6 in., various
Silybum marianum, 4 ft, violet
Specularia speculum (Venus's Looking-glass), 9 in., blue
Tropaeolum spp. and vs. (Nasturtium), various
Viola nigra (Black Violet), 6 in., black
Viscaria cardinalis, 1 ft, crimson
Viscaria oculata and vs., 1 ft, various
Xeranthemum annuum and vs., 2 ft, white, pink, purple
Fuller details will be found under generic names.

Half-Hardy Annuals. These are annual exotic plants, including some which are naturally perennial, that need frost-free, warm conditions to grow well and complete their life cycle. To make the most of their flowering display their seeds must be sown under glass, with heat, and grown on for planting out in May–June, when the danger of frost out of doors is past. Or in some instances, late sowings

may be made in April–early May, on warm, sheltered ground.

Under glass, a minimum temp. of 15·5–18° C. (60–65° F.) is desirable; first sowings may be made in a warm greenhouse in February; in a cool greenhouse in March, April. Soil temperatures for germination should run 3° C. (5° F.) higher than the atmospheric temperature, and this may be provided by bottom heat (q.v.) engendered electrical soil heating, or underneath source of heat. Seeds are sown thinly in pans, boxes or peat-wood fibre pots, in moist standard seeds compost (*see* Compost), lightly covered with sifted sand, vermiculite, etc.; and then with a sheet of glass and opaque paper; or inserted in a polythene bag. On germination, coverings must be removed, and ample light given, with shade from hot drying sun, until seedlings are large enough to be readily handled. They are then pricked off, spaced 2 in. apart, in deeper boxes, or singly into small pots or peat-wood fibre containers, using a richer potting compost (*see* Compost), and grown on, being transferred to cold frames two to three weeks before planting-out time, to harden off growth. Planting stations should be prepared as for hardy annuals out of doors. Plants so raised are most useful for bedding, lending themselves to self- or multi-coloured groupings, on formal or informal lines; for edgings, for filling gaps in a flower border, or even for making an annual border with plants in groups or drifts. Protection against slugs by means of metaldehyde bait pellets should be given. Taller plants benefit from some early support with twiggy stakes. If spent flower-heads are regularly removed, blooming is prolonged.

Annuals in Pots. Many hardy and half-hardy annuals lend themselves to pot culture for greenhouse decoration, notably *Anchusa capensis* 'Blue Bird', Calendula, Antirrhinum, Duchess Asters, China Asters, Capsicum, *Celosia plumosa*, Cineraria, *Cobaea scandens*, Cosmea, Cuphea, *Didiscus coeruleus*, Heliotrope, *Impatiens sultani*, Clarkia, *Ipomoea rubro-coerulea*, *Kochia trichophylla*, Tagetes (African and French Marigolds), Reseda (Mignonette), Nemesia, Petunia, *Phlox drummondii*, Salpiglossis, Schizanthus, *Thunbergia alata*, Verbena, Ursinia,

Zinnia. Seedlings are pricked off in small pots, and subsequently potted on once or twice as the roots fill the smaller pots, with watering gradually increasing as growth is made.

Half-Hardy Annuals, Selection

Alonsoa warscewiczii, 1½ ft, scarlet

Ageratum houstonianum and vs., ½–1 ft, blues

Ageratum × F₁ hybrids, 6 in., blue

Amaranthus caudatus, 2 ft, dark red

Amaranthus hypochondriacus, 2 ft, crimson

Anagallis linifolia v. *phillipsii*, 6 in., blue

*Antirrhinum in variety, 9–48 in., various

Arctotis grandis and hybrids, 1½ ft, various

Aster tanacetifolius, 1½ ft, blue and yellow

Brachycome iberidifolia, 1 ft, various

Browallia elata, 1½ ft, violet-blue

Calandrinia discolor, 1¼ ft, bright purple

Calliopsis tinctoria and vs., 1–2 ft, reds, yellows

Callistephus (China Asters) in variety, ½–2 ft, various

Canna × hybrids (Indian Shot), 2½ ft, various

Capsicum annuum, 1–2 ft, coloured fruits

Celsia arcturus, 3 ft, yellow

Chrysanthemum frutescens (Marguerite), 2½ ft, white

Cineraria maritima and vs., 1–2 ft, various

Cleome spinosa and v., 3 ft, white, pink

Cobaea scandens, climber, purplish, white

Cosmos bipannatus and vs., 3 ft, various

Cucurbita (Gourds) in variety, climbers

*Dahlia in variety, 1–4 ft, various

Datura meteloides, 2½ ft, blush-violet

Dianthus × 'Sweet Wivelsfield', 1½ ft, various

Diascia barberae, 1½ ft, rose-pink

Dimorphoteca aurantiaca and vs., 1¼ ft, various

Echium × *hybrida*, 1 ft, various

Emilia flammea (Tassel Flower), 1 ft, orange-scarlet

Felicia bergeriana, 4 in., blue

Gaillardia pulchella and vs., 2 ft, orange, reds

Gamolepis tagetes, 6 in., bright yellow

Gazania × *hybrida*, 9 in., various

Gomphrena globosa and vs., 1 ft, various

Helichrysum monstrosum and vs., 2 ft, gold, etc.

Heliophila longifolia, 1½ ft, blue and cream

Heliotropum peruvianum and vs., 2 ft, blue, white

Helipterum roseum and vs., 1¼–2 ft, white, rose

Hibiscus manihot, 3–4 ft, cream-yellow

Hibiscus trionum, 2 ft, yellow and white and purple

Impatiens balsamina and vs., 1–2 ft, various

Ipomaea cardinalis and vs., climber, red

Kochia scoparia trichophylla, 3 ft, foliage

Lagenaria leucantha and v. (Gourds), climber

Layia elegans, 1½ ft, yellow, tipped white

Lobelia erinus and vs., 6 in., blues, white

Lobelia pendula and vs., trailing, blue

Luffa cylindrica (Gourd), climber, yellow

Martynia louisiana, 2 ft, yellowish

Matthiola (Mammoth, E. Lothian, Ten-week Stocks), 1½ ft, various

Maurandia barclaiana, climber, various

Mesembryanthemum criniflorum, trailer, various

Mesembryanthemum crystallinum, 6 in., foliage

Mimulus glutinosus and vs., 4 ft, various

Mirabilis jalapa, 2 ft, various

Moluccella laevis, 1½ ft, green

Nemesia strumosa and vs., 9–12 in., various

Nicotiana affinis and vs., 1¼–2½ ft, various

Perilla frutescens and vs., 1½ ft, foliage

Petunia × *hybrida*, 9–12 in., various

Phlox drummondii and vs., 8–12 in., various

Platystemon californicus, 1 ft, cream-yellow

Portulaca grandiflora and vs., 3 in., various

Ricinus communis and vs., 4 ft, foliage

Rudbeckia bicolor and vs., 2–3 ft, golden yellow

Salpiglossis sinuata and vs., 1–2 ft, various

Salvia coccinea, 2½ ft, scarlet

Salvia splendens and vs., 1 ft, various

Schizanthus hybrids, 1–2 ft, various

Sedum cepaea, 1 ft, white

Sedum coeruleum, 6 in., light blue

Senecio arenarius, 1 ft, lilac, yellow centred

Senecio elegans (Jacobea) and vs., 1½ ft, various

Statice sinuata and vs., 1–1½ ft, various

Tagetes erecta and vs., 2–3 ft, yellow shades

Tagetes patula and vs., ½–1½ ft, yellows

Tagetes sinuata and vs., 6 in., yellow shades

Thunbergia alata, climber, various

Tithonia rotundifolia hybrid, 3 ft, orange-red

Tripteris hyoseroides, 1½ ft, orange

Ursinia anethoides hybrids, 1¾ ft, orange

Ursinia pulchra and vs., 9 in., orange shades

Venidium fastuosum and hybrids, 2½ ft, various

Verbena × *hybrida*, 1 ft, various

Zea mays v. *japonica*, 4 ft, foliage

Zinnia elegans and vs., 2–2½ ft, various

Zinnia pumila and vs., 1 ft, various

Zinnia thumbelina, 6 in., various

* Plants perennial in nature, but grown as half-hardy annuals.

Tender Annuals. These are the least hardy of the annual plants, raised under glass in the same manner as half-hardy annuals, with a little extra bottom heat to aid ready germination; and normally grown in the warm or cool greenhouse throughout their life cycle, usually in pots. They may be used out of doors in warm districts, being planted out in June.

Selection

Calonyction aculeatum, climber, white

Celosia cristata and vs., 1½ ft, various

Calceolaria × *hybrida*, 1¼ ft, various

*Coleus × *hybrida*, 3 ft, foliage

**Cordyline indivisa*, 2½ ft, foliage

**Cyperus alternifolius*, 1½ ft, foliage

Didiscus coeruleus, 1½ ft, blue

Gesneria umbellata v. *texa*, 9 in., red

**Primula malacoides*, 8 in., various

*Primula obconica, 1 ft, various

**Solanum capsicastrum* and vs., 1 ft, berries

*Stevia serrata, 1½ ft, white

*Streptocarpus × *hybrida*, 1 ft, various

*Sutera burkeana, 4 ft, white, brown centre

Torenia fournieri and vs., 9–12 in., blue

* Plants which are perennial in nature but grown as tender annuals in temperate climates.

Annular. Ring-shaped.

Annuus (-a, -um). Annual. Ex. *Helianthus annuus*.

Anoda (a-no′da. Fam. Malvaceae). Perennial plants of Mexico of which *A. cristata*, 3 ft, with hastate leaves and chalice-shaped blue or white flowers, may be grown as a half-hardy, quick-growing annual.

Cultivation. Well-drained loam soil; full sun.

Propagation. By seeds, sown under glass, March, bottom heat 18° C. (65° F.), pricked off, and hardened for planting out in late May.

Anomatheca. See *Lapeyrousia cruenta*.

Anona. See *Annona*.

Anopterus (an-op′ter-us. Fam. Saxifragaceae). Evergreen shrubs of which *A. glandulosus*, the Tasmanian Laurel, 6–12 ft, with glabrous, leathery leaves, and racemes of white bell flowers in April, May, may be grown in the cool greenhouse, and placed outdoors in warm shelter in summer.

Cultivation. Compost of 2 parts loam, 1 part each of peat and sand. Pot in spring; prune after flowering. Winter temp. 13° C. (55° F.). Moderate watering in winter; ample in spring and summer.

Propagation. By cuttings of young shoots, 3 in. long, taken in summer; rooted in propagating case.

Antennaria (an-ten-na′ri-a. Fam. Compositae). Hardy perennial plants of which *A. dioica*, a low, mat-forming creeper, Europe, etc., with greyish woolly leaves and pinkish flower-heads, June, and its v. *rosea*, deep pink, may be grown in sunny places and rock gardens to clothe rather dry poorish areas.

Cultivation. Light, well-drained soil; sunny position. Plant October or early spring.

Propagation. By seeds sown in cold frame in spring; by root division in March.

Anthemis, Chamomile (an′them-is. Fam. Compositae). A genus which provides dwarf, cushion and border plants, with finely divided foliage and heads of ray flowers.

Selection. A. carpatica, S. Europe, cushion-like, large white flower-heads, summer; *cinerea*, Balkans, 1 ft, with ash-grey foliage and large white flower-heads, summer; and *montana*, Europe, dwarf cushions of foliage, pinkish-white flower-heads, late summer, are three charming ornaments for the rock garden; *tinctoria*, the native Dyer's Chamomile, 1½ ft, yellow, summer, also provides some fine border plants in vs. 'E. C. Buxton', lemon-yellow, 'Kelway's', bright yellow, and 'Perry's', golden-yellow, and has a white form *alba*; *sancti-johannis*, 1½ ft, with grey-haired stems and intense yellow summer flowers, is a hardy plant from Bulgaria for the border.

A. nobilis is the prostrate-growing native and European aromatic-leaved herb, with white flowers, of medicinal value; and also used for the making of Chamomile lawns (q.v.).

Cultivation. Well-drained open soil and sun suits all species. Plant early autumn or March–April.

Propagation. By seeds sown in nursery bed of sandy soil, April. By division in March–April.

Anther. The pollen-bearing part of the stamen.

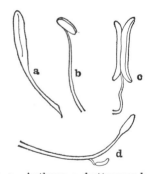

FIG. 7   Anthers: a. buttercup; b. rose; c. rye grass; d. lupin.

Anthericum (an-ther'i-kum. Fam. Liliaceae). Perennial plants with short rootstocks and fleshy tuberous roots; of which only *A. liliago*, the St Bernard's Lily, of southern European Alps, 2 ft, is grown for its beautiful summer sprays of small, white, lily-like flowers with golden anthers on a graceful stem arising from a tuft of narrow-channelled leaves.

Cultivation. Well-drained but moist humus-rich soil, and sun. Plant 4 in. deep in autumn. May also be grown in 12-in. pots in a cool greenhouse.

Propagation. By root division, September. By seeds sown thinly and shallowly, in cool greenhouse or frame, March.

Antheridium (pl. **Antheridia**). The male organ of reproduction of Ferns and their 'allies'; Horsetails and Clubmosses. It grows on the prothallus, and produces motile cells, spermatozoids, which are active agents of reproduction.

Antho-. Prefix meaning flower in compound words.

Anthocyanins. Organic compounds found in their pure state or as glycosides in plant organs and flowers which are responsible for the blue, brown, red and purple pigmentation, especially in young growth. Unrelated chemically to chlorophyll, the green colouring matter, anthocyanins, with other pigments, colour autumn foliage as chlorophyll decays.

Antholyza (an-tho-li'za. Fam. Iridaceae). A genus of one species, *A. ringens*, S. Africa, 20 in., a cormous plant with smooth linear leaves and lateral spikes of bright red flowers, with greenish tubes in summer.

Cultivation. Plant the large corms in deep boxes in cool greenhouse, March; plant out in May, 6 in. apart, in good friable loam soil, sunny position; lift in September, dry off and store corms in cool frostproof conditions until required for replanting.

Propagation. By offset corms, February, March. By seeds sown freshly ripe in October, in cool greenhouse, to germinate the following spring and plant out in early summer to grow on.

Anthracnose. A name given to certain fungus diseases characterized by darkish-coloured sunken spots or areas in affected tissues. Plants affected include Dwarf Beans, Grapes, Raspberries and Loganberries (qq.v.).

Anthriscus (an-thris'kus, Fam. Umbelliferae). The only species grown in gardens is *A. cerefolium*, the annual herb Chervil, Europe, 18 in., which is grown for its pinnately cut and curled sweetly scented and flavoured leaves which are used in salads, garnishings and seasonings. The seeds are sown successionally in spring and summer, to yield leaves for cutting in 6–8 weeks; in good friable soil, thinning plants to 4 in. apart.

Anthurium (an-thu'ri-um. Fam. Araceae). A large genus of tropical American perennial aroid plants, with handsome showy leaves, brilliant spathes and spadices of perfect flowers, of which some are grown in a stove or warm greenhouse, and one is a house plant of rising popularity.

Selection. A. andreanum, with deep green leaves, scarlet or orange-red spathe and spadix of ivory white, 1 ft h., is widely known and has been a parent of distinguished hybrids best seen at specialist nurseries; *veitchii*, 2–3 ft, long cordate leaves, markedly veined, with white spathe and rosy-white spadix, is very ornamental; *warocqueanum* is an ornamental-leafed climber, with green spathe and spadix; and *scherzerianum*, with long, oval and pointed, dark green leaves, on wiry stems, and striking flowers of a brilliant red spadix arising from a scarlet, open oval spathe, is increasingly grown as a house plant, commonly named the Flamingo or Tail Flower, and has a variety of forms.

Cultivation. Pot-grown in compost of 3 parts fibrous peat, 2 parts sphagnum moss, 1 part turfy loam, 1 part each crocks, broken charcoal, and coarse sand; or JIP, plus one-fourth sphagnum moss peat; with very thorough drainage. Need a humid atmosphere, winter temp. 15·5–21° C. (60–70° F.); water freely in growth, syringing in hot weather, moderately in winter; ample light, but shade from direct sun.

Propagation. By division of crowns in spring, each piece being furnished with roots.

Anthyllis (an-thil'lis. Fam. Leguminosae). Hardy shrubs and perennials for sun-warmed and sheltered gardens from the Mediterranean region.

Selection. A. barba-jovis, Jupiter's Beard, Spain, 6–8 ft, is evergreen with silvery-haired pinnate foliage, with roundish heads of yellow flowers at the ends of its twigs in early spring; needs a warm wall, or may be grown in a cool

greenhouse; *hermanniae*, Corsica, 2–4 ft, is a downy foliaged deciduous shrub, with heads of yellow flowers in April; *montana*, a mat-forming deciduous shrub, 4 in., with downy pinnate leaves, and heads of rosy-pink flowers in spring, may be placed in a sunny spot in the rock garden; *vulneraria* is the native Ladies' Fingers, a tufted herbaceous perennial of 6–12 in., with yellow flowers in summer, and variable forms, sometimes grown in the rock garden.

Cultivation. Lightish, porous soil; sunny positions. Plant September or March.

Propagation. Shrubs by cuttings of young shoots under bell-glass or in frame, in spring. Herbaceous perennial by seeds sown outdoors in April; or by division in autumn.

Antigonon (an-tig'o-non. Fam. Polygonaceae). Striking subtropical climbing plants, of which *A. leptopus*, Mexico, 12–15 ft, the Coral Vine, Mountain Rose, or Love's Chain, with its slender stems, handsome cordate leaves and racemes of rose-pink flowers in summer, may be grown in a warm greenhouse.

Cultivation. The tuberous rooted plant is best placed in a warm greenhouse border, training stems to near the glass, watering freely in growth; little in winter, with temperature not less than 15·5° C. (60° F.).

Propagation. By seeds in spring, bottom heat of 24° C. (75° F.).

Antirrhinum, Snapdragon (an-ti-ri'num. Fam. Scrophulariaceae). The genus is now regarded as one of some 40 species of perennial plants, originating in the Mediterranean region and California, U.S.A., greatly esteemed for their colourful abundant display of bloom in the summer months, but only hardy to winter in frost-free mild localities in this country.

Selection. A. asarina (*Asarina procumbens*), S. Europe, 6 in., procumbent, hoary leaved, and graced with single white and yellow, tinged red, flowers in summer; *glutinosa*, Spain, 4 in., prostrate sub-shrub, with pale yellow and white, streaked red, flowers, July; and *sempervirens*, Pyrenees, 8 in., prostrate evergreen, with creamy-white flowers, may be grown in warm sun on the rock garden, or in the alpine house. Interest, however, is concentrated today on *A. majus*, the Snapdragon, its varieties and hybrids, so extensively used for summer flower beds, borders and pots. With their erect, majestic spikes of tubular, broadly-lipped flowers, in an infinity of self and mingled colours, they contribute most beautifully to the summer garden scene. For convenience they may be grouped into: I. Tall-flowering forms of *A. m. grandiflorum*, growing 2–3 ft high, with tapering spikes of flowers, valuable for the rear of borders or centres of beds, and for cutting, which now include Tetraploid vs., with large ruffled petals, and a double F_1 hybrid form which is an improvement on older double flowers; and F_1 'Rocket' hybrids towering to 4 ft. II. Intermediate or semi-dwarf forms of *A. m. nanum*; growing 1½–2 ft, of somewhat bushy habit and a wide range of colours, including the Majestic and Triumph Strains, novelties such as the Penstemon-flowered, without the 'lip', and Hyacinth-flowered, with closely packed spikes of bloom, and a new race of 'Sprite' F_1 hybrids of great long-flowering vigour. III. Bedding forms of *A. m. nanum compactum*; growing 6–9 in. high, neat and compact in growth. IV. Dwarf varieties of 4–8 in. tall, listed under 'Tom Thumb' varieties, 'Little Gem' hybrids, and 'Floral Carpet' F_1 hybrids, for small beds, carpeting or in the rock garden. V. Rust Resistant varieties; growing 1½ ft, in a widening range of colour, these are invaluable where rust disease is endemic. In addition there are 'Forcing' strains offered for growing under glass, particularly for summer sowing and late winter–early spring flowering. Although many varieties have been given varietal names, the trend is for seedsmen to offer the various types of Antirrhinum by colour distinctions, and seedsmen's lists should be consulted accordingly.

Cultivation. Rock garden species need well-drained, porous soil, sunny warm positions in frost-free sites; or to be pan-grown in the cool alpine house. The garden forms of *A. majus* grow quite well in most soils, given good drainage, and humus, and appreciate the presence of lime or chalk. Plant out April–May.

Propagation. By seeds under glass, bottom heat 15·5° C. (60° F.), early March, to be pricked out and hardened off for late April–May planting. Or some plants may be potted to grow on for greenhouse decoration. For late winter, early spring, greenhouse display, sow in August, prick out, and grow in cold frame, until large enough (with 4–5 pairs of leaves) to pot in 4½-in. pots, to bring into the cool greenhouse. Water moderately in winter, minimum temp. 10° C. (50° F.). By cuttings of young shoots in summer.

Stopping. When well-grown, modern Antirrhinums should not need much restriction by stopping or pinching off the growing points of the central stem and basal side shoots, though this can be done after planting-out to induce bushiness, if desired. Tall forms may need the support of stakes in open situations. It is important to remove forming seed heads regularly to keep plants flowering. It is not wise to save seeds from garden plants. Bees will have cross-polinated many and they would not give new plants true to the parent variety.

Ants. Although not directly parasitic on plants, ants are disliked in gardens for their habit of 'farming' out colonies of aphids on plants, and visiting them for their honeydew excretions; for damage done to ripe fruits, especially wall-grown peaches, etc., and to flower buds in spring in their search for nectar; for their disfigurement of lawns, paths, etc., with their hills; and for their threat to personal comfort in the garden.

Control. If the ants can be traced to their nest, this should be opened up and dusted freely with a gamma-BHC or a trichlorphon (Tugon) insecticidal dust. If the nest cannot be found, the trails should be dusted so that the ants pick up the insecticide on their feet and carry it into the nest. Or a hole may be made in a nest with a dibber or steel bar, and a dessertspoonful of carbon bisulphide, or a teaspoonful of paradichlorbenzine inserted and the hole closed at once. Older fumigants are petrol or paraffin oil, handled with due care. A narrow band of fruit-tree grease around the base of infested plants halts ant traffic.

Anulatus (-a, -um). Ringed.

Aotus (a-o'tus. Fam. Leguminosae). Evergreen shrubs of Australia, of which

A. gracillima, 3 ft, makes an elegant plant with slender shoots, linear leaves, and axillary spikes of yellow and red pea-like flowers, May.

Cultivation. Porous soil compost, such as JIP 1, suits. Cool greenhouse conditions; prune and repot after flowering, syringing and watering freely in growth; keep just moist in winter, temp. 10° C. (50° F.).

Propagation. By cuttings of young shoots, in August, in pots, JIC compost, in shade.

Apache Beads. See *Anemopsis*.

Apetalous. Without petals. Ex. *Anemone*, *Clematis*.

Apex. The outer tip or point of a leaf, petal or part of a plant, farthest from the stem.

Aphelandra (a-pel-and'ra. Fam. Acanthaceae). Evergreen shrubs of tropical America, with handsome shining leaves, and showy spikes of flowers, requiring stove or hot house conditions.

Selection. A. aurantiaca, Mexico, 2–3 ft, orange-scarlet bracted flowers, December; *fascinator*, 1½ ft, silvery white veined leaves, scarlet flowers, autumn; *nitens*, 2–3 ft, bronzy foliage, vermilion flowers, autumn; *squarrosa*, 1–1¼ ft, white-banded leaves, yellow flowers, autumn, now best known in its v. *louisae*, with striking white-banded veins in leaves, and golden-orange flowers; *tetragona*, 3 ft, large, slender-pointed leaves, bright scarlet flowers, autumn; and others.

Cultivation. Pot in spring, equal parts loam, leaf-mould, peat and coarse sand. Grow under moist atmosphere, temp. 18–24° C. (65–75° F.), watering and syringing freely in growth, with occasional liquid feeding; keep rather drier in flower; winter at 13° C. (55° F.) minimum, keeping just moist. Prune away flower spikes when spent; prune shoots rather hard in February–March, and then repot, bearing in mind that the roots must fill pots well to promote flowering. As a house plant, *A. squarrosa* v. *louisae* needs good light, but not direct sun, winter temperature of 13° C. (55° F.), humidity with gentle watering; remove flower spike when finished, and grow on as above.

Propagation. By cuttings of young shoots, taken with a 'heel', in spring,

inserted in 3-in. pots, sandy loam, and plunged in propagating case, bottom heat 18° C. (65° F.), potting to larger pot when rooted, and growing on as for plants.

Aphis (pl. **Aphids** or **Aphides**). Green Fly, Black Fly, Plant Lice, Dolphin, Blight. The Aphididae is a huge family of hemipterous insects, important in gardening as persistent parasites of plants. The small, pear-shaped, long, slender-legged sap-sucking flies are ubiquitous and familiar, especially in summer, since they occur on a very wide range of plants, in the open, under glass

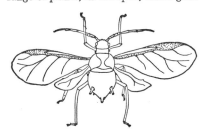

FIG. 8 Aphids, Black Fly, Green Fly: adult winged female of *Aphis rumicis*.

and indoors. They may be green, blackish-brown, yellowish or white with a waxy excretion in colour. They injure plants by piercing leaf and stem tissues to feed on the sap, reducing their vigour, often distorting growth, and admitting other disease-organisms, particularly viruses which aphids may carry from infected plants to healthy ones. Their secretion of sweet honeydew attracts ants, and may coat plant surfaces to invite Sooty Moulds which blacken leaves and interfere with photosynthesis and respiration. A few aphid species confine themselves to particular plant hosts, but many have a complicated life cycle involving two or more plant species, often with a winter and a summer host. Some aphids over-winter in egg form; others as adults. Some infest the roots of plants. Their menace lies in their powers of reproduction. Hatching from the egg-stage, adult aphids migrate to summer host plants. The females may be viviparous, producing living young parthenogenetically, or oviparous (egg-laying) at different seasons. The viviparous generations are wingless females, each of which reproduces in the same way, and in favourable weather infestations can build up at very high rates; increasing under dry, warm conditions, slowing down in dull, cold, wet periods.

Control. Ladybirds and their grubs, Hover Flies and their larvae, Lacewing Fly larvae, certain tiny wasps, and birds such as Tits, are natural predators to be regarded with a kindly eye. Under garden conditions, however, infestation can get quickly out of control, unless preventive and control measures are

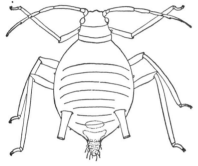

FIG. 9   Aphids: nymphal wingless viviparous female of *Aphis rumicis*, seen in summer.

taken. Broadly, aphids which overwinter in the egg-stage, chiefly on woody plants, pome fruit trees, stone fruit trees, bush currants, brambles, raspberry, roses and ornamental trees of the Prunus genus, may be vastly reduced by spraying the plants with an ovicide, tar oil, DNC or Thiol wash, while dormant in winter. In spring, the addition of an insecticide (gamma-BHC, malathion, rogor) to routine spring sprays reduces the build-up of attacks. On growing plants of all kinds the insects may be attacked directly by insecticides such as malathion, derris (safest for food crops), pyrethrum (also safe for food crops), or a gamma-BHC (Lindane) product on ornamentals. In warm weather nicotine is effective. Or protection may be given to many plants, particularly ornamental, by watering with a systemic insecticide

at least three weeks before aphid attacks are likely to occur. Under glass the above insecticides may be used in aerosol or smoke fumigating form, subject to makers' recommendations; as well as by sprays and dusts. More precise details of control are given under specific host plants and crops.

Aphyllanthes (a-pil-lan'thes. Fam. Liliaceae). The one species, *A. monspeliensis*, from the Mediterranean region, is a fibrous-rooted, dainty, dwarf perennial, for a sunny position, light well-drained soil, in the rock garden, with small basal leaves, and miniature, deep blue, lily-like flowers at the head of rush-like slender stems in June. Propagate preferably by fresh seed, sown in cool greenhouse, or careful division in late spring. Give winter protection of litter.

Aphyllus (-a, -um). Leafless. Ex. *Iris aphylla.*

Apiculate. With a small broad point at the apex (of a leaf). Ex. *Saxifraga apiculata.*

Apios (a'pi-os. Fam. Leguminosae). Hardy tuberous-rooted, twining perennial climbers, of which *A. tuberosa*, the Ground Nut or Cinnamon Vine of Pennsylvania, may be attempted in a warm, sheltered position, on light, humus-rich soil, for its graceful habit, pinnate foliage, and racemes of brownish-purple flowers which are scented in summer. The tubers are edible.

Propagation. By division of tubers, March.

Apium. *See* Celery and Celeriac.

Apocarpous. Of an ovary having the carpels free from one another in the flower.

Apogamy. The reproduction of a fern plant from the prothallus, by budding, without a sexual process.

Aponogeton (a-po-no-ge'ton. Fam. Aponogetonaceae). A genus of perennial aquatic plants with tuberous roots found in warm countries, of which *A. distachyos*, the Cape Pondweed or Water Hawthorn of S. Africa, with oblong-lanceolate floating leaves, and two-forked stems of hawthorn-scented, white flowers in spring and summer, may be grown in garden pools of more than 1 ft deep; *Kraussianus*, S. Africa, is similar with fragrant, creamy-yellow flowers, and may be grown in shallow water in sheltered conditions.

A. fenestralis (Ouvirandra fenestralis), the Lace-leaf or Lattice Leaf, of Madagascar, is entrancing with its leaves skeletonized to veins, and small white flowers, but requires to be grown in a warm greenhouse pool, with subdued light, since it is tender and a little difficult.

Cultivation. Plant rhizomes in April–May.

Propagation. By division of roots, April–May.

Appendiculatus (-a, -um). Having appendages. Ex. *Bulbophyllum appendiculatum.*

Applanatus (-a, -um). Flattened out. Ex. *Cotoneaster applanata.*

Apple. *Malus pumila* (Fam. Rosaceae), a species found wild in Europe and Western Asia, is considered the original stock from which the Apple, the most important hardy fruit now grown, has sprung, and its cultivated history goes back to ancient times. In Britain, the Apple was at first largely grown for cider-making, and the selection and development of certain varieties for culinary and eating purposes gradually followed. Being quite hardy, apples can be grown almost anywhere in Britain below the 600-ft contour line, where there is sufficient depth of soil with good sub-soil drainage to at least 3 ft. Nevertheless, several factors need to be considered before deciding whether apple-growing in a modern garden is likely to prove worth while.

Site. This should be open and well sunned, but with shelter from strong winds from the SW. and NE. quadrants. It should be as frost-free as possible, particularly in spring, and not in a valley or frost-pocket. Where there is a choice, fruit is better grown high on a slope than at the bottom, with a south to west aspect. Where spring frosts are likely it is wise to plant late-flowering varieties.

Climate. Broadly, high rainfall, over 32 in. annually, is more favourable to culinary or dual-purpose varieties than to fine dessert. It is more difficult to grow good dessert varieties in coastal areas than inland; in the west and north than in the south and east.

Soil. Although apples will grow on a wide range of soils, basically rich, heavy or clayey soils are more suitable to culinary than dessert varieties; while more open, lighter soils favour dessert kinds. To some extent, soils and their characteristics can be amended by good cultivation. The choice of the right varieties, grown on the most appropriate rootstocks, can go far in offsetting some of the less favourable environmental factors.

Rootstocks. Apple varieties are not grown from seeds (except in hybridizing work), but are propagated vegetatively in nurseries by uniting buds or shoots, termed scions, of the varieties with different rootstocks, which have growth-modifying effects on the scions. The rootstocks are usually chosen to curtail or dwarf the growth of the tree and to bring it into fruit-bearing quickly in its life. Rootstocks are chosen from what used to be called Paradise Stocks, which have fibrous and vigorous root systems. As a result of testing and classification by research stations, modern rootstocks are now known by an initial M or EM—for East Malling—plus a roman numeral, or MM—for Malling-Merton—plus an arabic numeral. Those in general use are:

M. IX. The most dwarf-growing stock, often bringing trees into bearing at 2 years old. Best for shape-trained trees for small gardens, on reasonably good soils.

M. VII. A semi-dwarfing stock, preferable to M.IX for small trees on poor soils.

MM. 106. A semi-dwarfing stock, similar to M.IX but rendering a tree immune to woolly aphis infestation.

M. I. A fairly vigorous stock, often preferred for trees to be grown on wet or heavy soils.

M. II. Also a fairly vigorous stock for trees on poorish soils.

MM. 104, and MM. 111. Alternative stocks to M. I and M. II, possessing resistance to woolly aphis infestation.

M. XVI. A vigorous stock, chiefly for half-standard and standard forms of trees.

M. XXV. An alternative vigorous stock to M. VI, but tending to bring trees into earlier bearing.

Apple Tree Forms. The use of dwarfing rootstocks makes it possible to grow apples in restricted trained forms, highly suitable for small gardens.

Cordons. Trees grown with a single straight stem to be furnished with fruiting wood or spurs along their entire length. They may be grown erectly, obliquely, or horizontally, along training wires or supports. Double and triple cordons can be grown with two or three erect stems, each stem being treated as a single cordon.

Espaliers. Trees grown with a single central main stem, with pairs of horizontally trained branches on opposite sides. It is also possible to grow trees with branches at an angle, or in the shape of a fan.

Pyramids. Trees grown with a main central stem, with branches radiating from it from low down, shortening in length higher up the tree.

Bush. grown as small trees with branches breaking from low down.

Standard and Half-Standard. Trees grown with a clean main stem or trunk, of 6 ft or 4 ft respectively before forming a branching head.

Cordons and Espaliers are ideal for growing by walls, planted 4 in. from them, and trained on wires that allow air to circulate between wall and tree. They may also be planted in line by the side of walks, or 'hedge' like. In the open, cordons are planted in line, to grow diagonally along wires strained taut between posts, rows being spaced about 6 ft apart. Pyramid and Bush trees are

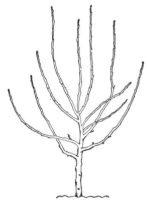

FIG. 12 A Bush Apple tree.

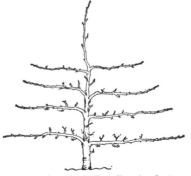

FIG. 10 An obliquely trained Cordon Apple tree.

FIG. 11 A trained Espalier Apple tree.

planted in the open to form small fruit gardens or orchards. Half-standard and standard trees are hardly suitable for small gardens, except where specimen trees are needed as much for ornamental floral beauty and shade as for their fruiting.

Yields. On dwarfing rootstocks cordons begin to bear in 2 to 3 years; pyramids in 3 to 4 years; and bushes in 4 years. On semi-dwarfing rootstocks they may take another 2 years to start fruiting. Standard and half-standard trees, on vigorous stocks, may take 7 years or more before bearing. Yields will vary much according to environmental factors and skill in management; single cordons should give 3 to 9 lb., pyramids 6 to 14 lb., bushes 25 to 40 lb. annually when established, while standards and half-standards may yield 100 to 400 lb. in full bearing. These yields should be equated with the space taken up by the plants, and ease of culture.

Planting. Apples may be planted between October and March, when weather and soil conditions are favourable. Good drainage is vital. Clay soils can be made more open by forking in gypsum, and all heavy soils are improved by incorporating sand, grit, burnt earth, and well rotted strawy manure, compost or peat. Light sandy, gravelly, or chalky soils need stiffening with clay or marl, and organic matter. Soil acidity should be corrected if below pH 6·0 (*see* pH Scale). The only fertilizers needed are sulphate of potash to potash-hungry light sands, and bone meal to all soils. In actual planting, the root system must be spread out as evenly as possible, in a large enough hole, made slightly convex at the bottom, and the point of union between stock and scion must be a few inches above ground. The soil is firmed to the roots, and a top mulch of rotted organic matter above is helpful to re-establishment. Stakes may be needed on exposed ground, preferably of oak or chestnut, treated with an organic solvent preservative, not creosote.

Cordons on M. IX stock are planted 2 ft apart; on other stocks, 2½ to 3 ft apart; in rows 6 ft apart. Pyramids on M. IX stock are planted 3 to 4 ft apart, on semi-dwarfing stocks, 4 to 5 ft apart, in rows 8 to 10 ft apart. Bushes on M. IX stock are planted 8 ft apart; on other stocks 12 to 18 ft apart, with like distances between rows. Espaliers need to be placed 12 to 15 ft apart. Half-standards and standards need 30 to 40 ft between them. Young trees transplant most satisfactorily at 2 to 4 years.

Choice of Varieties. Over 2,000 varieties of Apples have been recorded; of these the commercial fruit grower selects less than a dozen for their performance, ease in management and cropping qualities. The gardener can extend his choice to varieties of quality not considered good for commerce owing to susceptibility to injury in transport, particular cultural needs or cropping irregularities. Apart from personal preferences, the gardener's choice should be guided by the suitability of a variety for his locality and soil (and it is always wise to consult expert local experience on this), and its fertility. The trend is for the fruit nurseries to propagate fewer of the more reliable varieties, and the following represent what are considered to be good varieties for modern gardens.

Dessert—Early, to be eaten soon after gathering: Beauty of Bath, Laxton's Advance, Laxton's Epicure, Worcester Pearmain, Tydeman's Early Worcester, Merton Worcester, Laxton's Fortune, James Grieve; cropping August to early October. Mid-season: American Mother, Ellison's Orange, Charles Ross, Gravestein, Margil, Lord Lambourne, Red Ellison, Rival; for September to November. Late, for keeping; Adam's Pearmain, Blenheim Orange, Cox's Orange Pippin (not for the north), D'Arcy Spice, Golden Delicious, Granny Smith (very late), Heusgen's Golden Reinette, Merton Russet, Orleans Reinette, Ribston Pippin, Sturmer Pippin, Sunset, Laxton's Superb, Tydeman's Late Orange, Winston.

Culinary—Early: Emneth Early (Early Victoria), Arthur Turner, George Neal. Mid-season: Grenadier, Peasgood Nonesuch, Rev. W. Wilks. Late: Bramley's Seedling, Crawley Beauty, Edward VII, Howgate Wonder, Lane's Prince Albert, Newton Wonder, Ontario, Royal Jubilee, Wagener, Wellington. There are other varieties which have excellent local reputations, but a choice from the above would give a succession of fine fruit in most gardens spared extremes of climate or poor soil.

Fertilization. To mature a crop, apple blossom must be fertilized, preferably by cross-pollination. Although some varieties are termed self-fertile in that they may set or fertilize their flowers with their own pollen, others cannot, and are termed self-sterile; all varieties set more fruit when cross-pollinated by other compatible varieties. Cross-pollination is assured by interplanting compatible varieties which flower at the same time, and compatibility is a matter of the chromosome number of the variety. Most varieties have two sets of chromosomes (gene chains of hereditary material) in their cells, and are termed diploid, carrying good pollen; others have three sets and are termed triploids and form poor pollen. Diploid varieties of the same flowering period inter-pollinate very well; and two or more of such varieties should be interplanted; ideally in equal numbers, though one pollinating variety to three to six of another is usually satisfactory. Triploid varieties with three sets of chromosomes (51), need two or more diploid types flowering at the same time to ensure satisfactory inter-pollination. The flowering periods are given in the chart:

spells, and a little liquid fertilizer may be added to the water. A dressing of rotted manure or compost should be given annually in winter. On all but chalk soils, bone meal or basic slag can be given once every 3 or 4 years in autumn. The amount of nitrogen or potash given must be related to the type of tree and its performance. Broadly, dessert apples need more potash than nitrogen, and a ferti-

Early Flowering	Mid-season Flowering	Late Flowering
DIPLOID		
Adam's Pearmain	Arthur Turner	American Mother
Beauty of Bath	Charles Ross	Annie Elizabeth
Bismarck	Cox's Orange Pippin	*Court Pendu Plat
*Devonshire Quarrenden	*Duke of Devonshire	Crawley Beauty
Early Worcester	Ellison's Orange	Edward VII
*Egremont Russet	Emneth Early	Gascoyne's Scarlet
Golden Spire	Golden Noble	Heugen's Golden Reinette
Granny Smith	Grenadier	*Northern Greening
*Irish Peach	Howgate Wonder	Orleans Reinette
*Keswick Codlin	James Grieve	Royal Jubilee
Laxton's Advance	King of the Pippins	Worcester Pearmain
Laxton's Exquisite	Lane's Prince Albert	
Laxton's Fortune	Laxton's Epicure	
Lord Lambourne	Laxton's Superb	
Margil	*Lord Derby	
Rev. W. Wilks	Merton Worcester	
Sturmer Pippin	Monarch	
Sunset	Newton Wonder	
Wagener	*Norfolk Beauty	
	Ontario	
	Peasgood Nonesuch	
	Rival	
	St Everard	
	Winston	
TRIPLOID		
Gravestein	Blenheim Orange	Reinette du Canada
Ribston Pippin	Bramley's Seedling	
	Crimson Bramley	
	Warner's King	

* Varieties of local significance.

The late flowering varieties are very useful for localities prone to spring frosts. An alternative solution to the fertilization problem is to plant a family tree, consisting of two or more compatible varieties grafted on a common rootstock, especially where room is limited.

Manuring. For the first year after planting no fertilizers should be necessary. Young trees should be watered in dry

lizer of lower nitrogen and higher potash content may be given in March, proprietary, or a mixture of equal parts by weight ammonium sulphate and sulphate of potash. Culinary apples usually need more nitrogen, and a mixture of 2 parts by weight ammonium sulphate and 1 part sulphate of potash would be satisfactory, or a proprietary fruit fertilizer with a high nitrogenous content.

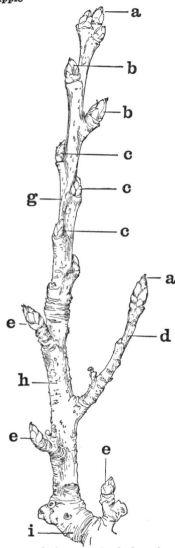

FIG. 13 A dormant Apple branch and its parts: a. terminal bud; b. fruit buds; c. leaf buds; d. lateral shoot; e. fruit spurs; g. one-year old growth shoot; h. two-year old growth shoot; i. three-year old shoot growth.

When trees are making more wood or shoot growth than is desirable, the nitrogenous dressing should be reduced. When a tree has cropped heavily, rather more nitrogen is welcome, and can be given.

Pruning. This is more of an art than a science, and needs to be approached with some appreciation of its purposes and effects on growth. The tendency is to prune too much. The purposes are (*a*) to form and maintain a shapely frame of branches or tree; (*b*) to foster the formation of flowering and fruiting spurs and regulate their performance; and (*c*) to remove dead, diseased, weakly and wrongly growing wood. At the outset it is important to differentiate between leaf or growth buds, and flower or fruit buds. The former are small and slim, lying close to the shoot, and give rise to leaves or new wood shoots. The latter are fatter at the ends of short wrinkled growths known as spurs, on two-year or older wood, and break into flower in spring. Some apple varieties, notably Bramley's and Worcesters, often form fruit buds at the ends of thinnish shoots (tip bearers) which should be left uncut.

Winter pruning may be done between leaf-fall and March; the earlier the better. It must be guided by the fact that hard or severe pruning stimulates the reaction of wood or shoot growth, and delays bearing; whereas light or no pruning encourages the formation of flower and fruit buds. The amount of pruning depends upon the age, form, vigour and variety of the tree; but broadly the weaker the growth, the more severely it may be cut. Young trees are winter-pruned to develop a good framework of branches, but once this is done, winter pruning is largely a matter of removing moribund growth and criss-crossing or in-growing shoots.

Summer pruning checks growth, and helps to maintain compact growth and fruitfulness, particularly in cordons, espaliers, pyramids and bushes. It should be used on trees making too much shoot growth, with poor fruiting.

Cordons are usually summer-pruned; in mid to late July in the south and midlands, August farther north; cutting mature lateral (side) shoots back to three leaves above the basal cluster; sub-laterals to one leaf. Secondary or later growth is cut back to one bud in autumn or winter. The leader (main shoot) is left unpruned as long as laterals are formed evenly along its length; but if stronger growth is required, it may be shortened by about one-third of the new growth in winter.

Espaliers from which another pair of horizontal branches are needed are pruned in winter, cutting the vertical central leader to within about two inches of where the new tier is to be formed; cutting above a good bud, below which are two other buds on opposite sides of the stem near together. When growth begins in spring, all other buds except the three chosen ones are rubbed off, the shoot from the top bud is trained vertically, the shoots from the side buds along canes, attached temporarily to the wire supports at 45°. The rate of growth may then be regulated by raising the weaker shoot more vertically, and lowering the stronger, so that at the end of the growing season both shoots are more or less equal and can be lowered to the horizontal. Established espaliers are pruned in summer, treating each shoot as a single cordon.

Pyramids. These are best planted as maiden or one-year-old trees. In spring the central leader is pruned fairly hard, to 1½ to 2½ ft high, and all lateral shoots to about 4 or 5 buds. The following winter the central leader is shortened by about half its new growth to a bud on the opposite side of that from which it sprang. Laterals are cut downward at outward-facing buds, 4½ to 6 in. from their base. In the following summer the leaders from these laterals, and the laterals growing from them, are shortened to five or six leaves of their base, as they mature, in July–August. This summer pruning is repeated annually. The central leader can be cut back each winter until sufficient height is secured, when it should be cut back in May.

Bushes, planted as 3-year-olds, will have several branches about the head of the main stem. The strongest and most regularly placed are shortened by one-half to two-thirds their length in winter, above a bud facing the direction in which new growth is desired, and other surplus shoots cut away at their base. In subsequent years, as long as extension

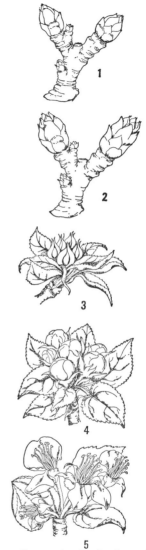

FIG. 14 Stages in Apple flower-bud development used as guidance to spring spraying: 1. Bud-break. 2. Bud Burst. 3. Green Bud or Green Cluster. 4. Pink Bud. 5. Petal Fall.

growth is needed to give a branching framework, leaders are shortened by one-third to two-thirds, according to vigour, and laterals to 3 to 5 buds of their base. A few may be left unpruned where there is room for them, and as the tree settles to a fruiting rhythm, summer pruning may be practised. Branches threatening to spoil the symmetry of the tree should be removed at base; leaders becoming overlong may be cut back to well-placed laterals which can be trained to take their place; fruit spurs may be thinned.

Half-Standards and Standards. Pruning can be managed along the lines given for bushes, but once a good framework has been built up only regulatory pruning to keep growth open and healthy should be required.

Once apple trees are fruiting, pruning should err on the light side rather than be severe. Trees that persist in vigorous shoot without fruiting may often be brought into bearing by bark-ringing or bark reversal (q.v.).

Cropping. It is unwise to allow a tree to waste its energies on carrying a crop of many fruits when it can bear fewer but larger fruits more easily. Heavy crops need to be thinned in June–July, beginning with the earliest to ripen; king or centre apples of clusters are best removed, and other clusters reduced to singles spaced six to eight inches apart, though culinary varieties may be left in pairs, well spaced.

Harvesting. Apples ripen according to the growing conditions of the season; not by the calendar; though broadly, early varieties are ready from late July to early September; mid-season with a limited keeping period, from September to October; and late keeping varieties, October and November. But the real criterion is the state of growth; apples are ready for gathering when they part easily with stalk from the tree when lifted to the horizontal or sideways. Some early varieties are subject to premature falling. This can be prevented by spraying to wet the stalk ends with a pre-harvest fruit-drop-preventing 'hormone' solution, three weeks before normal harvesting date.

Storing. In the absence of artificial cold storage, the three essentials for keeping

apples are good ventilation, steady cool, frostproof conditions (4·5–7° C. [40–45° F.]); and a moist atmosphere. Cellars are better than attics. Sound, healthy fruit is best laid out on slatted or plastic-netted trays, preferably wrapped separately in oiled paper wraps, or in boxes. Boxed and rendered mouse-proof with small-meshed netting, they can be placed against a north wall, well covered with straw and polythene sheeting.

Propagation. Chosen varieties are propagated by budding or by grafting them on chosen rootstocks. Budding is done in July and early August. The buds are taken from robust, well-developed shoots of current seasonal growth; thinly sliced, with a shield of bark, and the leaf detached. The stem of the stock is prepared by making a T-shaped incision with a sharp knife; the square-cornered pieces of bark are carefully peeled back with a blunt blade to allow the shield of the bud to be inserted with its moist slimy greenish layer of tissue in contact with that of the stock stem, and the whole swiftly secured with raffia or modern plastic budding tape. The following spring, before growth starts, the stem of the stock above the bud is

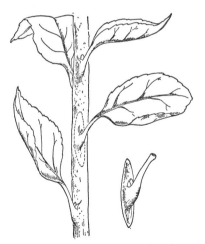

FIG. 15 Apple Budding, showing a typical shoot, and the selection and cutting out of a bud.

cut back, and the new shoot from the bud trained vertically, and at the end of the first year it is known as a maiden tree.

Grafting is done in March or April. The scion of the variety is a mature one-year-old shoot of good development, about 8 in. long, cut when dormant in winter, and kept under cool conditions, such as buried in soil or under rotted compost, in a moist position, until wanted. The scion

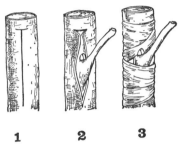

1   **2**   **3**

FIG. 16 Apple Budding: 1. The stem of the rootstock prepared with a T-shaped cut through the bark. 2. The selected shield of bark and the bud inserted. 3. The bud grafted and protected by grafting tape.

is usually prepared for tongue-grafting. It should have 3 or 4 good buds, being cut with a long slanting 2-in. cut at the lower end, on the opposite side from the lowest bud. The upper part of this cut is slit upwards to form a tongue. The stem of the stock is then prepared similarly with an upward tongue to receive the scion. This is fitted in to match the greenish cambium layers at one side (or both if possible), bound in place with raffia or tape, and sealed to exclude air with grafting wax. The strongest growth from the scion can subsequently be selected to form the maiden tree. *See* Grafting.

Apple, Custard. See *Annona*.

Apple Diseases. Unfortunately, under cultivated conditions, apples are subject to a number of diseases and parasitic pests, and prompt recognition and preventive or remedial treatment must be taken. Of diseases, chiefly caused by

infective fungi or bacteria, the following are important.

Apple Mildew (*Podosphaera leucotricha*). Occurs in spring; leaves and shoots are thin and stunted, and covered with a white mealy powder of spores. Infected shoots and fruit bud trusses should be cut out and burnt when seen. Spraying with a sulphur or karathane fungicide at green bud and pink bud stages helps to check infection. Drainage, cultural conditions, and manurial balance should be checked carefully.

Apple Scab (*Venturia inaequalis*). Causes brown or olive-green spotting on leaves, young shoots and buds; fruits with blackish spots and blotches. Often opens the way to other diseases. Helpful to destroy scabbed fallen fruit and leaves in autumn. Prevent by routine spraying in spring with lime-sulphur, captan or thiram, before and after petal-fall.

Brown Rot (*Sclerotinia fructigena*). The fungus usually infects fruits damaged by scab, insects, or hail; often developing in store. Fruit show arcs of yellowish, cushion-like pustules, tending to dry up and mummify rather than rot. The infection can spread to spurs and branches, causing canker. Infected fruit should be burnt. Scab should be controlled by spring sprays; and pests such as codling moth, caterpillars and wasps controlled if present.

Canker. May be caused by various fungi. Apple Canker (*Nectria galligena*) causes sunken areas in the bark of branches and die-back, and an eye rot of fruit; Brown Rot Cankers (*Sclerotinia fructigena, S. laxa*) may follow Brown Rot of fruit and Blossom Wilt, causing ugly swellings; Silver Leaf Canker (*Stereum purpureum*) may infect grafted trees; Papery Bark Canker may be associated with various fungi, the bark peeling in thin paper-like layers. Unchecked, cankers kill the growth above them, and if the main stem is badly cankered, the tree is best destroyed. Otherwise, cutting out the cankers for burning, protecting cuts with a fungicidal paint, and taking steps to control the fungi involved will lead to healthier growth.

Collar Rot (*Phytophthora cactorum, P. syringae*). A rotting of bark tissues at or near soil level, which, if unchecked, may lead to a failure of a tree. The infective fungi, often found in soils, gain access through wounds caused by mice or voles, or mechanical injury by machinery or tools, or by frost. Affected tissues may be cut out and burnt, and the exposed clean wood dressed with a canker paint, or creamy solution of a fungicide.

Blossom Wilt (Sclerotina laxa and form *mali).* Recognized by a wilting of the blossom trusses in spring, with leaves and flowers killed, and canker lesions forming on the branches. Lord Derby, Cox's Orange Pippin, James Grieve, and Rival are susceptible, and others may be involved. Bramley's Seedling seems relatively immune. Infected spurs and cankers must be cut out as soon as noticed and burnt. Routine spring spraying with lime-sulphur or captan is preventive.

Leaf Spots. Large, irregular dark brown areas, which cause leaves to shrivel and fall, may be caused by the fungus *Sphaeropsis malorum.* Routine spring spraying helps to hold this trouble in check, or a copper fungicide at half the normal strength can be applied in summer. Scab causes blackish brown blotches on leaves. The leaf spot, called Cox Spot, occurs in Cox's Orange Pippin, and is held to be caused by physiological disorders in dry seasons, to which adequate organic mulching may provide an answer. Tiny angular yellowish or greyish brown spots, formerly attributed to infection by *Phyllosticta angulata,* are now held to be caused by infestation by froghopper insects (*Cercopis sanguinea*).

Fly Specks (Leptothyrium pomi). Groups of small black circular dots on fruits, which are superficial, and of no infective significance. Often occur in conjunction with

Sooty Blotch (Gloeodes pomigena), which causes dark brown or greenish soot-like blotches on fruit, particularly in cold wet seasons and in shade. Routine spring spraying holds this infection in check, and pruning to admit light and air helps. Seriously blotched fruit can be cleaned by immersing for one minute in a bleaching solution ($\frac{1}{2}$ lb. chloride of lime stirred into a gallon of water, left overnight, and the clear liquid decanted for use); allow to drain for ten minutes,

wash in clear water and dry before placing in store.

Eye Rot, (Nectria galligena). Begins at the eye end of the fruit, sometimes when only half-grown, causing them to fall early or to develop with a flattened eye end. Worcester Pearmain is very susceptible. The infected areas produce white, yellowish or pinkish pustules, sporing freely. The fungus also causes cankers, and cankered growth should be cut out. Rotting fruit should be burnt. Routine spring spraying is preventive.

Storage Rots. Many fungi affecting fruit on the trees, such as Scab, Brown Rot, Eye Rot, etc., continue to develop on stored fruits. Bitter or Gloeosporium Rot (*Glomerella cingulata*) occurs chiefly on fruits in store. Other fungi: Blue Mould (*Penicillium expansum*), Grey Mould (*Botrytis cinerea*) and Pink Rot (*Trichothecium roseum*), and fusarium rots may occur in association with bad storage conditions. To reduce storage rots, the store and packages must be hygienically clean; sterilized by disinfectant if necessary; and fruit should be sound, dry, handled with care, and preferably paper-wrapped to isolate an infected fruit.

The carry-over of infection from one year to the next can be minimized if all leaves and fallen fruit are collected and burnt in the autumn.

Virus Infections. Two virus infections may be noted. An irregular yellowish mottling of leaves on the 'Lord Lambourne' variety; and a condition termed rubbery wood; and Star Cracking, which may appear on trees late to flower and leaf, and a characteristic star-shaped cracking on the fruit, especially around the eye. It has been noted on Cox's Orange Pippin, Bramley's Seedling, Charles Ross, Emneth Early, Laxton's Fortune and Monarch. Several nurseries now offer Virus Tested stock as some insurance against these as-yet incurable ills.

Physiological Disorders. On less than ideal soils and in climatically difficult seasons, apples are sensitive to physiological or nutritional disorders.

Bitter Pit. Most serious in hot dry seasons, when darkish brown spots form under the skin, scattered through the flesh, especially at the eye end, developing into sunken pits. Precise cause is not known, but it is thought to be associated with a calcium deficiency. Avoidance of excessive nitrogenous manuring, light pruning, adequate organic mulching, and foliar feeding with calcium nitrate solution (1 lb. per 10 gallons water) in summer, are suggested as corrective.

Brown Heart or Internal Breakdown. The browning and rotting of tissues around the core of an otherwise sound-looking apple are believed to be caused by very wet weather in June, early July. Brown Heart in commercially stored apples may be caused by an excess of carbon dioxide in the store atmosphere, and the tissue rot may not be confined to the core region.

Russeting and Cracking. This may be caused by some injury to the skin of developing fruits such as spring frosts, cold winds, fluctuating temperatures and rainfall, the use of the wrong spray solution or concentration, or apple mildew attacks or scab.

Water Core or Glassiness. A condition in which fruit tissues appear water-soaked or translucent, usually beginning at the core. The cause is not known, but is associated with fluctuations in rainfall and growing conditions, and faulty root action. Good culture, balanced fertilizing and adequate humus-manuring promise the best line of prevention and cure.

Insect Pests. Some one hundred or more insects resort to apple trees as food-host plants and are therefore parasitic pests to us. Only the more economically important are dealt with here.

Aphids, or *Green Fly*. The four species commonly found on apples are the Green apple aphid, *Aphis pomi*, the Apple-grass or oat apple aphid, *Rhopalosiphum insertum*, the Rosy apple aphid or blue bug, *Dysaphis mali* and the Red leaf aphid, *Dysaphis devecta*; all of which impair growth by their sap-sucking activities. Control begins by winter spraying with washes that kill over-wintering eggs on the dormant trees. In spring a malathion, dimethoate systemic or Rogor 40 insecticide may be added to routine spring sprays. Summer attacks develop from aphids migrating from other fruit trees or alternative hosts such as hawthorn in late July, and may

be fought by contact-spraying or dusting with a malathion, Rogor 40, nicotine or derris insecticide.

Apple Blossom Weevil (Anthonomus pomorum). Less common than it used to be, this long-snouted greyish weevil lays her eggs in flower buds early in their development. The grubs feed on the stamens, etc., and the petals wilt, turn brown and die, and the blossom remains unopened or capped. After petal-fall, the adult weevils emerge to feed on the leaves until July and then seek hibernation quarters in crevices in the bark, posts, hedge bottoms, etc. Good control is possible by applying gamma-BHC (dust or spray) at the breaking or bursting stage of bud development (March).

Apple Saw Fly (Hoplocampa testudinea). A tiny 4-winged, fly-like insect, active in the blossoming period, the female laying eggs just below the calyx in a hole made for the purpose. The grubs bore into the side to feed on the developing fruitlets, so that ribbon-like scars form on the fruits and a sticky mess at the point of entry. The grub is a dirty white, and brown-headed. An infested fruit smells unpleasantly. The grub leaves the fruit in June, July to pupate in brown cocoons. Compare with the behaviour of the codling moth, with which the saw fly is often confused. Effective control is possible by spraying with a gamma-BHC insecticide or nicotine seven days after petal-fall, repeating for two consecutive years.

Apple Sucker (Psylla mali). A small winged insect, related to the aphids, about the orchard from late May to November; lays yellowish eggs on shoots or spurs to over-winter and hatch into nymphs in April and May to enter into fruit trusses and suck sap. Effectively controlled by the application of a winter wash or inclusion of a gamma-BHC or dimethoate or malathion insecticide at the green bud and pink bud stages of blossom development.

Capsid Bugs (Plesiocoris rugicollis, Lygus spp.). Small yellowish nymphs or wingless bugs hatch from eggs laid in the bark in April, May, to feed on the surface of leaves, producing reddish-brown marks; after petal-fall they feed on the surface of fruitlets, provoking roughened

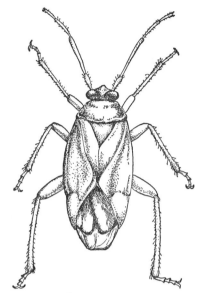

FIG. 17   A fruit tree pest: Capsid Bug,
Lygus pratensis.

corky patches that spoil appearances of the fruit without impairing their edibility. The bugs moult five times before becoming the shield-like greenish adult insects. Winter spraying kills many of the eggs, and the addition of a DDT or gamma-BHC insecticide to the spring spray at green bud and pink bud stage gives control.

Codling Moth (Cydia pomonella). Small greyish moths, marked with wavy lines and a copperish eye-like circle near the outer margin of the front wings which fly in May to July. Eggs are laid singly in surface of fruit and foliage, hatching into caterpillars which bore into fruits to feed, and cause maggoty apples. The grub is pinkish, with little odour. Entry is marked by a dark reddish irregular ring. The grubs over-winter under bark or in crevices to pupate in spring. Sometimes there is a second generation in late summer. Banding of tree stems with sacking or corrugated cardboard in June traps the caterpillars. The bands can be removed and burnt in winter. Winter

washes further reduce the caterpillars. The addition of a DDT insecticide to the petal-fall spring spray is helpful, and should be repeated 3 weeks later where infestation is serious. Fallen apples should be collected and destroyed.

Earwigs (Forficula auricularis). These insects can be troublesome where apples are grown in grass, feeding on ripening fruits from late July. A band of fruit-tree grease denies them access.

Leaf Hoppers. Many species of these lively insects are found on apples and are now regarded as possible carriers of virus diseases. Winter wash spraying considerably reduces their numbers as several species over-winter in the egg stage.

Tortrix Moths. There are several species which are found on apples. The most common is the Surface Eating Tortrix (*Archips podana* [*Cocoecia podana*]) of which the eggs are laid in June, July; the caterpillars hatch out to feed on the foliage, webbing leaves together, and later attack the fruit, before hibernating from October to March or April, and feeding on young unfolding foliage, prior to pupating in May, June, and emerging as moths in June, July. The summer Fruit Tortrix (*Adoxophyes orana*) has a similar life cycle, but the larvae hatch in July, August, and do more damage to fruit; and a second generation appears in early autumn. The above and related species of tortrix are best controlled by a late application of a DNOC/petroleum oil wash, plus DDT, at bud-breaking stage, or the addition of a DDT insecticide to a spring spray applied at bud-burst or green bud stage. The Fruitlet Mining Tortrix (*Pammene rhediella*) lays eggs in May or June, the larvae subsequently feeding on the developing fruit, often between touching fruits, sometimes leaves. The larvae hibernate in July to pupate next spring. Corrugated cardboard bands round the stems in late June will trap many larvae. In serious infestations DDT may be added to the spring spray at petal-fall.

Twig-Cutter Weevil (Rhynchites coeruleus). Small blue weevils which occur in the south, in May, laying eggs in new shoots in June, which hatch into larvae that feed on the pith; the adult weevil severs a shoot just below where an egg has been laid to fall off or hang for a time. Infested shoots should be collected and burnt. Dusting or spraying with fresh derris a fortnight after petal-fall gives good control.

Red Spider Mite (*Metatetranychus ulmi*). These sap-sucking mites over-winter in the egg stage, reddish, minute beads on spurs and shoots; to hatch as immature mites in spring and early summer, passing through several moults to become adult as small, yellowish-green to red, somewhat hairy mites; feeding on the undersides of leaves. Late winter spraying with a DNOC/petroleum oil or thiocyanate wash kills the eggs. At petal-fall, a Rogor 40 insecticide may be used. In early summer a Kelthane 20 insecticide is most effective.

Winter Moth Caterpillars. Three species, the Winter Moth (*Operophthera brumata*), the March Moth (*Alsophila aescularia*) and the Mottled Umber Moth (*Erannis defoliaria*) lay eggs on apples in autumn–winter which hatch into looper-type caterpillars which feed on buds and leaves in spring. The grease-banding of stems in late September–October traps the wingless females crawling up into the trees to lay eggs. Adding a systemic insecticide to the spring spray at green bud or pink bud stage gives good control of the caterpillars.

Woolly Aphids (*Eriosoma lanigerum*). These yellowish fly may be recognized by the waxy wool-like secretion that covers them. They often infest cankers and open a way for fungal infections. Control may be effected by adding Rogor 40, malathion or gamma-BHC insecticides to pink bud stage spring sprays. Localized colonies on established trees may be painted with a thin cream of gamma-BHC insecticide and water.

Wood-boring Moths. The Goat Moth (*Cossus cossus*) sometimes infests apples in the south, laying many eggs on stems in June, July; the caterpillars then tunnel the wood for 3 or 4 years, becoming darkish-red and yellow, and 3 to 4 in. long, and having a goat-like smell. Unfortunately, if unnoticed, their activity undermines a tree and it has to be lifted and burnt. Detected early, a squirt of gamma-BHC insecticide in the bore holes kills the caterpillars. The

Leopard Moth (*Zeuzera pyrina*) lays orange-yellow eggs on shoots and branches in June, July, to hatch into brown-headed, yellowish-white and black-spotted caterpillars which tunnel the wood to feed inside for 2 or 3 years, growing to 2 in. long, and killing the shoot. Signs of infestations are frass and sawdust on the ground and withering of the shoot. It is usually sufficient to prune the shoot away and burn it.

Other insects of lesser significance may lay eggs on apples, giving rise to leaf or fruit eating caterpillars. They include the Clouded Drab Moth (*Monima incerta*), which has bright green caterpillars seen in May to July, readily controlled by DDT or gamma-BHC in the pink bud spring spray; Eyed Hawk Moth (*Smerinthus ocellatus*) with green, white-dotted caterpillars, horned at the rear end; best destroyed by hand-picking, June, July; Brown Tail Moth (*Nygmia phaeorrhoea*), with blackish caterpillars, marked with tufted hairy brown spots in August, September, 'tenting' or nesting together, and best got rid of by cutting out the colonies for burning; the Lackey Moth (*Malacosoma neustria*) whose blue-grey with brown hairs and white and yellow-red striped caterpillars also 'tent' together, and should be collected in May–June and destroyed. Over-wintering eggs are laid in bands or bracelets on shoots, and such shoots are best pruned out when seen. The Vapourer Moth (*Orgyia antiqua*) lays over-wintering masses of eggs, attached to its empty cocoon on twigs, spurs and branches, which should be hand-picked and destroyed when seen. The caterpillars, 2 in. long, are hairy with four yellow tufts of hair on the back and long hairs at head and tail, and feed on leaves in May to August, but DDT or malathion in the petal-fall spray gives good control. The Small Ermine Moth (*Hyponomeuta malinellus*) has small spotted caterpillars which live in a silken 'tent' or nest in May, June, inviting destruction by hand collection and burning. The small round patches of eggs are laid in July, August, and the caterpillars hatch in autumn but remain under the egg case until spring. A tar oil wash in winter is useful in gaining control. Case Bearer Moth (*Coleophora nigricella*) has small caterpillars which feed on leaf surfaces in August, and then cover themselves with a small, brown, curved case for the winter hibernation, resuming feeding on newly opened leaves, eating circular holes in the leaves and forming a new straight case, fastened to the leaf, etc., in which to pupate. This pest is difficult to control, though the application of malathion in spring is promising when the caterpillars emerge to feed.

Algae, Lichens and Moss. Although not directly damaging, these greenish growths give sheltered quarters to insect pests. They are destroyed by the routine application of a winter wash.

Hares, Rabbits and Mice. These animals often damage apples by gnawing

ROUTINE DISEASE AND PEST CONTROLLING SPRAYING SCHEDULE				
Stage of Growth	*Approx. Date*	*Disease or Pest controlled*	*Material and concentration to use*	*Remarks*
Dormant*	Dec.– mid Feb.	Aphids, Apple Sucker, Scale	5–7½% tar oil wash	Also clears algae, lichen and moss
Or Breaking	Dec.–Mar.	Ditto, plus Capsid Bug, Red Spider and many moth caterpillars	5–7½% DNOC/ petroleum oil wash	Ditto
	Dec.–Mar.	Ditto	5–7½% thiocyanate oil wash	
Bud-Burst	April	Scab	Captan 2½% lime-sulphur	
	April	Tortrix moth caterpillars	DDT emulsion DDT wettable	
Green Bud* Green Cluster	Late April	Scab Tortrix and Winter Moth caterpillars	Captan 2½% lime-sulphur DDT emulsion DDT wettable	
Pink Bud*	Early May	Scab Tortrix and Winter Moth caterpillars	Captan 2% lime-sulphur Systemic DDT/BHC	
		Mildew	Karathane	Repeat at 7 to 14 days, if serious
Petal-Fall*	Late May	Scab Sawfly, Capsid Bugs, Woolly Aphids plus Red Spider	Captan BHC or gamma-BHC Emulsion Rogor 40	
Fruitlet	Mid June	Scab Mildew Codling Moth and Tortrix Red Spider	Captan Karathane Malathion Kelthane 20	As at pink bud stage

* The essential routine sprays: others as required.

the bark, and may kill a tree by girdling it. The best preventive is a collar of small-mesh wire or plastic netting, from the ground up to 2 to 3 ft, with another 6 in. bent outward at the top. A thin coating of banding grease to 3 ft high is effective for a season. Or a proprietary repellent can be applied.

Apple, Love. See *Lycopersicum* (Tomato).

Apricot (*Prunus armeniaca*. Fam. Rosaceae). This delicious stone fruit is a native of China, said to have been introduced to England by the gardener to Henry VIII. It is hardy and may be grown out of doors, but as it flowers very early, in February, it may need some cover protection when in flower, and hand pollination is helpful.

Soil. The Apricot thrives in a well-drained calcareous loam or loam soils made amenable by adding broken and ground chalk or limestone and humus-forming organic matter. Extreme light or heavy soils are less suitable.

Aspect. In SW. England and on sheltered, frost-free sites, there is no reason why the apricot should not be grown as a free-standing bush tree. It is more often grown on walls: early and mid-season varieties on west walls, late varieties on sunny south walls, though early varieties also succeed on east walls. In the north and Scotland it may be grown under glass.

Planting. Bush trees for the open orchard, fan-shaped trees for walls, are best budded on peach or apricot seedling rootstocks, rather than plum as previously used. Planting should be done in October–November, in well-dug soil, with first-class subsoil drainage, and top soil enriched with bone meal and rotted organic matter.

Pruning. The Apricot fruits on spurs on ripe older wood and on young wood. Pruning is best done in late spring and summer, consisting of disbudding, and stopping, as for peaches (*see* Peaches); and a tying-in of young shoots on a framework of mature wood in autumn. Fruits should be thinned to 5 in. apart after stones begin to form and fruits to swell.

Diseases and Pests. The Apricot is subject to a mysterious die-back in which a branch and then a whole side of a tree

may die. Poor root action, unfavourable soil conditions, and spring frosts have been indicted as causes. It has also been claimed that pruning in late May rather less severely than for peaches prevents much die-back. Other diseases and pests are similar to those suffered by Peaches (q.v.).

Varieties. All are self-fertile and may be grown singly. Early (late July–early August): Hemskirk, Royal, New Large Early. Mid-season (mid August): Breda, Kaisha, Early Orange, St Ambroise. Late (August–September): Moorpark, Shipley's, Peach. Moorpark is considered the finest, and with Hemskirk and Early Orange gives a good garden succession.

Apterous. Wingless.

Aquatic Plants. Plants which grow naturally in water, either entirely or partly submerged. *See* Water Garden.

Aquaticus (-a, -um). Living in water. Ex. *Veronica aquatica.*

Aquatilis (-e). Living under water. Ex. *Ranunculus aquatilis.*

Aquilegia, Columbine (a-qui-le'gia. Fam. Ranunculaceae). Hardy perennial plants noted for their radical, long-stalked ternate leaves, and graceful stems carrying striking colourful flowers, invaluable for spring bloom in the rock garden and herbaceous borders.

Selection. A. alpina v. 'Hensol Harebell', 1 ft, powder blue, May; *bertolonii*, *Italy*, 6 in., violet-blue, May–July; *caerulea*, Rocky Mts, 1–1½ ft, white, tinged blue, spring, and vs.; *flabellata*, Japan, 9 in., soft white, spring, and v. *pumila*, soft blue; *glandulosa*, Altai Mts, 1 ft, bright blue, May, June; and *pyrenaica*, Pyrenees, 1 ft, deep blue, spring, are delightful for the rock garden. *A. canadensis*, Canada, 1–2 ft, yellow, spring, and v. *flavescens*, pale yellow; *clematiflora hybrida*, 3–4 ft, spurless flowers, purple, pink and blue; *longissima*, Texas, 2–3 ft, pale yellow, summer; and *skinneri*, New Mexico, 2 ft, orange and red, summer, are fine species for sunny borders. *A. vulgaris*, 2 ft, is the native Columbine of which there are several forms of various colours. The border gems are, however, the long-spurred hybrids of which there are many strains, in colours of rose, blue, white, yellow, orange, pink and crimsons,

FIG. 18 *Aquilegia* × *hybrida*, long-spurred flowers of Columbine.

notably 'McKana's Giants', 2½–3 ft, exceptionally long-spurred; 'Sutton's Long-spurred Hybrids', 3 ft, which tend to supersede the 'Mrs Scott Elliott' strain.' Spring Song' is a new strain of F_1 hybrids, growing 2½ ft, and 'Dragonfly Hybrids' are shorter in stature at 18 in., with a full range of flower colours.

Cultivation. Rock garden species like well-drained, light loam soils and warm positions; border sorts succeed in most soils except the very dry or wet, appreciate lime and good light. *A. vulgaris* and its vs. do well in shade.

Propagation. By seeds sown shallowly in a cold frame in July–August; or on a nursery bed outdoors in April. Plant out

in autumn or early spring. Choice forms can be propagated by root division in October or March–April.

Arabis, Rock Cress (a′ra-bis. Fam. Cruciferae). A genus of over 100 species of annual and perennial trailing plants of which only a few are cultivated.

Selection. A. albida, the Rock Cress of SE. Europe, 6–9 in., with downy leaves, and racemes of fragrant white flowers early in the year, is a good mat-forming drape for walls, carpeter for bulbs, edging for pools, paths and borders, and ground cover for waste places, with a double-flowering v. *flore pleno*; *alpina*, 6 in., is a compact white flowering alpine for the rock garden, where a place may be found also for *aubrietioides*, a tufted dwarf with pink-purple summer flowers; and *androsacea*, 2 in., a silvery silky cushion with white flowers in summer; but *blepharophylla*, California, neat rosettes of deep green leaves and rich rose flowers, April; *bryoides*, Greece, silky white tufted rosettes, and large white flowers on 1-in. stems, April; and × *kellereri*, with silvery grey rosettes of leaves, and white flowers in May, need the shelter of the alpine house.

Cultivation. Any ordinary soil suits the hardy species. Plant in autumn. Rock garden kinds in warm sun, and well drained locations.

Propagation. By seeds outdoors in April. By cuttings of young shoots in July–August. By division of roots in October.

Araceae. The monocotyledonous Aroid or Arum Family.

Arachis, Earth Nut, Ground Nut, Monkey Nut, Pea Nut (a-ra′kis. Fam. Leguminosae). The species grown is a Brazilian annual, *A. hypogaea*, 1 ft, with yellow, pea-like flowers in May, which may be grown under stove conditions. After flowering, the flower stalks bend down, lengthen and force the pods into the soil to ripen; producing the oil-rich, edible seeds important as a food crop. Seeds may be sown in spring, 24–30° C. (75–86° F.), and grown on in large pots singly.

Arachnoid. Cobweb-like. Ex. *Sempervivum arachnoideum*.

Aralia (a-ra′li-a. Fam. Araliaceae). This genus contains herbaceous perennials, shrubs and trees, but only *A. elata*, the Angelica Tree of Japan, 10–40 ft, deciduous, with elegant double-pinnate foliage, and round umbels of small white flowers in a large panicle in August, September, is much grown, as a tall shrub or tree in sheltered gardens and deep rich loam soil. Striking forms are sometimes available in *albo-variegata*, creamy-white margined leaves; *aureo-marginata*, yellow margined leaves; and *pyramidalis* with erect habit. The herbaceous perennials, *cachemirica*, Kashmir, 5–10 ft, *cordata*, Japan, 4–6 ft, and *racemosa*, N. America, 3–4 ft, make fine foliage plants, with umbelliferous racemes of white flowers, but are not dependably hardy.

Cultivation. Deep, humus-rich loam, warm, sheltered positions. Plant in autumn or early spring.

Propagation. A. elata by suckers, April. Herbaceous plants by division in March–April or root cuttings.

Araucaria (a-raw-ka′ri-a. Fam. Pinaceae). Evergreen coniferous trees of distinctive ornamental foliage, of S. America, Australia and Pacific Islands.

Selection. A. araucana, Chile Pine, Monkey Puzzle, 50 or more feet, with its whorled branches, densely with dark green leaves, is the only hardy species, often but not always with male and female cones on separate trees; v. *aurea* has golden tinted foliage. Best grown as a specimen tree as it is difficult to place with other trees. It needs well-drained but moist soil, clean air and planting in October or March; apt to lose lower branches with age. *A. bidwillii*, the Bunya Bunya of Queensland; and *cunninghamii*, the Moreton Bay Pine, may succeed in favoured gardens in Cornwall, but are safer tub-grown in a cool greenhouse or conservatory, until too tall for retention. The Norfolk Island Pine, *excelsa*, has fine foliage, and may be pot-grown as a cool greenhouse or indoor plant, its vs. *gracilis*, compact; *leopoldii*, glaucous green foliage, and 'Silver Star', with silvery tipped shoots, being very appealing.

Cultivation. In tubs or pots, 3 parts loam, 1 part leaf-mould, and sand for drainage, or JIP compost suits well; winter temp. 7° C. (45° F.), with soil kept just moist.

Propagation. A. araucana by seeds,

1 in. deep, in March–April, in pots, temp. 18° C. (65° F.). Tender species by cuttings of the ends of upright shoots in summer, in frame or propagating case.

Arboreous, Arborescent. Tree-like, tending to tree-like form. Ex. *Lupinus arboreus*.

Arboretum. A planting of hardy trees, usually botanical.

Arbor-Vitae, See *Thuja*.

Arbour. A retreat for sitting, formed by trees, especially weeping kinds, or wood framework or trellis walled and roofed with leafy and/or flowering climbing plants.

Arbutus (ar′bu-tus. Fam. Ericaceae). Evergreen shrubs or small trees of handsome leathery foliage, and interesting habits of flowering and fruiting.

Selection. A. unedo, the Strawberry Tree, S. Europe, Eire, up to 40 ft, with panicles of white urn-shaped flowers in autumn, followed by round, pimple-surfaced red fruits with some semblance to strawberries a year later, is chiefly grown as the most hardy species; v. *rubra* has pink flowers; *Menziesii*, the Madrona, W. America, to 50 ft, has attractive smooth, flaky, light red bark, with May flowers followed by orange-red fruits, but needs mild sheltered conditions; and the hybrid × *andrachnoides* may be preferred to one of its parents *A. ardrache*, as more free-flowering, with red bark, and longer elliptical leaves, though it does not fruit well.

Cultivation. Preferably well-drained, lime-free loam, though *A. unedo* tolerates lime; sheltered warm sunny position. Plant in autumn or April.

Propagation. By seeds in pans or pots, in peaty soil, cold frame in March, rather slow. By cuttings of young shoots in August under glass.

Archegonium. Female organ of reproduction in Ferns, produced on the prothallus (q.v.) in spring and early summer, and containing the egg cells or oospheres, for release when ripe to unite with the spermatozoids of the Antheridium (q.v.).

Arches. Wooden or metal structures, bridging a path, walk or stream, or framing a view, up which ornamental climbing plants may be grown.

Arctostaphylos (ark-to-stap′il-os. Fam. Ericaceae). Rather pretty shrubs, akin to Arbutus, but only a few are satisfactorily hardy.

Selection. A. alpina is a deciduous, dwarf prostrate shrub from the colder regions of the northern hemisphere, including Scotland, growing 2 in. high, with bright green foliage, turning red in autumn, and clusters of white urn-shaped flowers in April–May, followed by purple-black berries; v. *ruber* differing in having red berries. In America the shrubs are known as Manzanita, and *A. nevadensis*, mat-forming evergreen, with compact racemes of white, tinged red, flowers in spring; and *nummularia* and its v. *myrtifolia*, California, 9 in., with white spring flowers, may be attempted in the alpine house. For the rock garden, *uva-ursi*, the Bearberry, is a useful native prostrate evergreen, spreading easily, with pinkish flowers in spring, and small brilliant red berries in autumn.

Cultivation. Lime-free, peaty soils preferred. Plant September–October or March–April.

Propagation. By cuttings of young shoots in July, under glass, bottom heat 18° C. (65° F.). By seeds in spring in cool greenhouse or frame.

Arctotis (ark-to'tis. Fam. Compositae). Pretty half-hardy flowering plants of S. Africa.

Selection. A. acaulis, 1 ft, various colours; *breviscapa*, 1 ft, orange; *grandis*, 1½ ft, white with blue disc; and large-flowering hybrids are grown as half-hardy annuals, for their summer show of large daisy-like rayed flowers.

Cultivation. Ordinary, rather porous soil; sun.

Propagation. By seeds sown under glass, temp. 18° C. (65° F.), bottom heat, March, to be pricked off and planted out in May.

Arcuate. Curved; bow-like. Ex. *Berberis arcuata.*

Arcuation. The operation of layering.

Ardisia (ar-dis'i-a. Fam. Myrsinaceae). Tropical evergreen shrubs and trees, grown in a warm greenhouse.

Selection. A. crispa (crenulata), E. Indies, 3–4 ft, is chiefly grown for its umbelliferous clusters of fragrant white flowers, June, and scarlet berries which persist in winter; *japonica*, 1–1½ ft, is somewhat hardier and similar for a cool greenhouse.

Cultivation. Pot in March, JIP or equal parts loam, peat, leaf-mould and sand; summer temp. 21–27° C. (70–80° F.); winter temp. 13° C. (55° F.). Water freely in growth; little in winter. Prune straggling growth hard in March.

Propagation. By cuttings of young shoots in March–August, bottom heat 21° C. (70° F.). By seeds in spring, under glass, bottom heat 21° C. (70° F.).

Areca (a-re'ka. Fam. Palmaceae). Tropical graceful palms of which *A. catechu*, the Betel Nut, may be grown, preferably from seed, in a warm greenhouse; JIP compost, summer temp. 24–29° C. (75–84° F.); winter not less than 15·5° C. (60° F.).

Arenaria, Sand-wort (a-ren-a'ri-a. Fam. Caryophyllaceae). Hardy annuals or herbaceous perennials, chiefly valuable for the rock garden.

Selection. A. balearica, Balearic Isles, is a creeping plant with small shining leaves, white flowers throughout summer, ideal for covering rocks in shade; *montana*, France, Spain, 4 in., is a hairy trailer, white flowers in May, June; *purpurascens*, Pyrenees, 1 in., a tufted mat with purplish flowers in spring; and *tetraquetra*, Pyrenees, with downy grey-green foliage and starry white flowers, June, are good.

Cultivation. Well-drained, porous soil. Plant March–April, in rock crevices or scree.

Propagation. By seed, April, cool frame. By division in early autumn, after flowering.

Arenose, Arenarius (-a, -um). Of sandy soils. Ex. *Arenaria.*

Areole. The organ carrying spines, bristles or hair in the leaf-axils of Cacti.

Arethusa (ar-e-thu'sa. Fam. Orchidaceae). Pretty terrestrial orchids, of which *A. bulbosum*, Carolina, 8 in., with large, scented, bright rose-purple flower, May, can be grown in a moist shady spot outdoors in mild localities; with the soil enriched with sphagnum moss and peat.

Argemone, Prickly Poppy (ar-ge-mo'ne. Fam. Papaveraceae). American herbs of which two species are grown as annuals for summer flowers.

Selection. A. grandiflora, Mexico, 2 ft, glaucous white-veined leaves, large yellow, sometimes white flowers; and *mexicana*, the Devil's Fig or Prickly

Poppy, 2 ft, handsome foliage, pale yellow or orange flowers all summer.

Cultivation. Well-drained, porous soil; full sun. Sow seeds ⅛-in. deep, where plants are to flower, in March, April. *See* Annuals.

Argenteus (-a, -um). Silvery. Ex. *Cortederia argentea.*

Argophyllus (-a, -um). Silvery-leaved. Ex. *Helianthus argophyllus.*

Argutus (-a, -um). Having sharp teeth. Ex. *Spiraea arguta.*

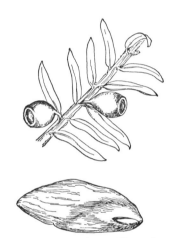

FIG. 19 Aril: *top*, of Yew (*Taxus baccata*); *bottom*, of a conifer (*Picea* sp.).

Aril. An outgrowth of the seed outside the testa; in a scarlet cup-like covering of the seed of Yew; a membraneous wing in the seeds of pine; a tuft of hairs in the seeds of Willow; a hard, small caruncle in the seeds of Euphorbia.

Ariocarpus (a-ri-o-kar'pus. Fam. Cactaceae). Spineless plants with long thick tap roots, rounded flattened stems with triangular tubercles, and short flowers from the centre.

Selection. A. fissuratus, white to purple flowers, summer; *kotschubeyanus*, carmine or purplish, summer; *retusus*, pink; and *trigonus*, yellow, with erect tubercles.

Cultivation. Well-drained, stony compost, full sun, in greenhouse or house; water very moderately.

Aristatus (-a, -um). Aristate, having awns. Ex. *Gaillardia aristata.*

Aristolochia (a-ris-to-lo'kia. Fam. Aristolochiaceae). Singular herbaceous plants, often climbing, evergreen or deciduous, mostly tender and for the greenhouse.

Selection. A. macrophylla, Dutchman's Pipe, hardy deciduous climber-twiner, eastern N. America, 15–30 ft, with curious siphon-shaped brown and yellow flowers, June, July, may be grown outdoors in warm, sheltered places, or in a tub. *A. elegans*, Calico Flower, Brazil, is graceful with yellowish flowers, August; *grandiflora* v. *sturtevantii*, Pelican Flower, W. Indies, 10 ft, with very large, striking purplish white flowers, of 20 in. long with a tail up to 3 ft, may be grown in stove conditions; summer temp. 21–24° C. (70–75° F.); winter minimum 13° C. (55° F.); water freely in growth, keep just moist in winter.

Propagation. Hardy species by ripe shoot cuttings in summer, under bell-glass. Tender species by seeds, in March, April, bottom heat 24° C. (75° F.).

Armatus (-a, -um). Armed. As with prickles or thorns. Ex. *Acacia armata.*

Armeria, Thrift (ar-me'ri-a, Fam. Plumbaginaceae). Tufted perennials, many alpine, hardy and useful for borders and the rock garden.

Selection. A. maritima, the native Thrift or Sea Pink, ½ to 1 ft, has improved forms in *alba*, white, *laucheana*, deep pink, *rubra*, red, and *splendens*, crimson pink, for June to August; *plantaginea* 'Bees' Ruby' is a taller plant with ruby red flowers on stalks up to 1½ ft. For the rock garden *A. caespitosa* 'Bevan's variety', Spain, is a beautiful dwarf, deep rose, April to May; and 'Ardendale', a bright rose; *halleri*, Pyrenees, 4 in., soft green with bright rose flowers, June; and *setacea*, S. Europe, 2 in., pink, May, are excellent.

Cultivation. Well-drained, porous soil in beds, scree or rock garden, and sun. Plant October or April–May.

Propagation. By young cuttings in June; division in autumn or spring. By seeds in spring.

Arnebia (ar-ne'bi-a. Fam. Boraginaceae). Of this genus of herbs, only the perennial, *A. echioides*, Prophet Flower, Armenia, 1 ft, is grown on dry wall or rock garden or in the border, for its yellow flowers with basal black spots, the 'marks of Mahomet' which gradually disappear, in May. It likes a well-drained, gritty porous soil, sunny position.

Propagation. By seeds, under glass, bottom heat 18° C. (65° F.), March–April; to plant out later. By cuttings taken with a 'heel' in early autumn. By root cuttings in sand, spring.

Arnica (ar'ni-ka. Fam. Compositae). Hardy herbaceous perennials, for border or rockery.

Selection. A. montana, the Mountain Tobacco of European mountains, with tufted foliage, and yellow flowers, July; and its smaller version, *nana*; *chamissonis*, 1–2 ft, yellow, summer, are chiefly grown.

Cultivation. Well-drained, loam soil. Sun. Plant in autumn or early spring.

Propagation. By seed sown shallowly in cold frame in autumn. By division of plants in spring.

Aromaticus (-a, -um). Aromatic, fragrant. Ex. *Drimys aromatica.*

Aronia, Chokeberry (a-ro'ni-a. Fam. Rosaceae). North American deciduous shrubs, attractive with corymbs of white or pinkish flowers in spring, brilliant foliage colour in autumn, and quite hardy.

Selection. A. arbutifolia, 6–8 ft, red, round fruits in autumn, bright red autumn foliage; *prunifolia* (*floribunda*) is similar but with shining purplish-black fruits, and *melanocarpa*, 1½–3 ft, has black fruits, with autumn foliage colour very attractive in v. 'Brilliant'.

Cultivation. Any ordinary soil, but useful also in moist spots; sun or partial shade. Plant October to March. Prune after flowering when necessary.

Propagation. By seeds, sown outdoors in spring after being stored in sand for the winter. By cuttings of young shoots in late summer. By division in autumn.

Arrow-head. See *Sagittaria.*

Artemisia (ar-tem-is'i-a. Fam. Compositae). A genus of aromatic herbacous perennials and shrubs, attractive for their foliage.

Selection. A. abrotanum, S. Europe, variously Southernwood, Lad's-love, Old Man, grows erectly to 3–4 ft, with downy grey finely-cut foliage, sweetly fragrant, but the flowers are only a dullish yellow; and *tridentata*, American Sage Brush, evergreen, to 6 ft, is a silvery-grey shrub with panicles of yellowish flower-heads in October. Of herbaceous perennials, *A. lactiflora*, China, 4–5 ft, has creamy-white flower spikes in autumn, splendid in the wild garden; *ludoviciana*, N. American White Sage, 3 ft; *baumgartenii*, S. Europe, 1 ft. tufted, with white downy flower-heads in August; and *stelleriana*, 2–3 ft, with yellow flowers in summer, are all finely foliaged. *A. glacialis*, Central Europe, glistening silvery foliage, yellow flowers, June; *lanata* (*pedemontana*), Central Europe, white silvery foliage; and *spicata*, Swiss Alps, silvery-white with yellow flowers, June, are dainty dwarf sub-shrubs for the rock garden or alpine house. *A. sacrorum*, Russia, to 4 ft, with fine pinnate foliage and panicles of small yellow flowers, late summer, and its v. *viride*, the Summer Fir, of pyramidal habit, deep green foliage, may be grown as annuals from seed.

Cultivation. Sound drainage and a lightish soil, with sun, suit these plants. Plant perennials October–March; rock shrubs March–April; and deciduous *abrotanum* in October–March.

Propagation. Shrubs and sub-shrubs by young cuttings in summer, inserted in sandy loam, out of doors. Perennials by division, October or March.

Arthropodium (ar-thro-po'di-um. Fam. Liliaceae). Tufted perennials with fibrous roots from New Zealand; related to Anthericum.

Selection. A. candidum, 1 ft, has grass-like tufts of leaves, with graceful racemes of white flowers in June–July, for the rock garden or alpine house; *cirrhatum*, to 3 ft, is larger with flowers in a much branched panicle, and is suitable for the cool greenhouse.

Cultivation. Sandy, humus-rich loam; warm position. Plant March–April.

Propagation. By division or suckers in spring. By seeds, under glass, bottom heat 18° C. (65° F.), spring.

Artichoke, Chinese (*Stachys affinis* [*tuberifera*]). A perennial plant, China, Japan, 1–1½ ft tall, which yields curious tuberous rhizomes in strings, often called spirals, and which are edible and said to taste like true artichokes; much grown in France as *Crosnes*; quite hardy.

Cultivation. Any ordinary well-drained soil, preferably light, previously well dug and manured; and a sunny position will suit. Plant in March–April, placing tubers 4 in. deep, 6–9 in. apart, in rows 12 in. apart; keep free from weeds, water in dry spells. Tubers may be lifted from early November onwards, as required for immediate cooking; keep frost out of the soil by a covering of straw, bracken or leaves.

Artichoke, Globe (*Cynara scolymus*). An ornamental herbaceous perennial, N. Africa, 4–5 ft tall. As a vegetable, it is grown for its unopened, bluey-green flower buds. Not truly hardy, it can be grown only in warm gardens, free of frost, and needs good, well-drained land, deeply dug, and enriched with ample rotted manure or good compost in autumn, and an open position. A complete fertilizer, at 4 oz. per sq. yd, can be forked in in March.

Planting. Rooted plants may be bought from specialist nurserymen in good strains of Green or Purple Artichokes, for planting in April. A plant should yield 12 buds at least, and have a cropping life of 3 years. Plants are spaced 4 ft apart in rows 4 ft apart, with crowns just below the surface. It is usual to plant up one third of the ground each year; by the fourth year, the first planted section can be replaced. Heads are taken in June–July, and the flowering stems then cut out. In autumn, crowns should

be given winter protection by covering with bracken or straw litter, to be removed in March. Some growers prefer weathered ashes, 6–12 in. deep, removed in March. Annual dressings of rotted manure or compost and a balanced fertilizer should be given.

Propagation. Growing plants produce suckers around the base, which should be thinned to 4 or 5, the excess being simply pulled off. Those left grow on and when 9 in. or more long may be detached with a little of the old stock and roots, and replanted to grow on for new crowns, in autumn or early spring. Plants may be raised from seeds, sown under glass, March, but seedlings are variable in character, and as it takes two to three years to measure cropping performance, vegetative propagation by suckers is safer and more rewarding. Three-year-old plants, due for discarding, will produce a crop of chards, or blanched growth, if cut to within 6 in. of the ground in July, watered freely and, when the new growth is 2 ft high, the leaves tied together, wrapped with straw or paper, and earthed up, to yield blanched chards, used like Spinach Beet, in about six weeks' time.

Artichoke, Jerusalem (*Helianthus tuberosa*). Introduced to Europe by the French from Nova Scotia, and thence to London by the Dutch under the name of Artichoke van Ter Neusen, said to have been corrupted by hawkers to Artichokes of Jerusalem, in the 17th century, this sunflower produces edible tubers freely, with little trouble; and improved modern strains are superior to older stocks.

Cultivation. The plants are hardy, and will grow in a wide range of soils, well dug and organically manured the previous autumn. Tubers are planted

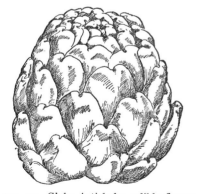

FIG. 20   Globe Artichoke, edible flower bud.

FIG. 21   Jerusalem Artichoke, edible tuber.

3 in. deep, 1½–2 ft apart, in rows about 3 ft apart in March. Plants grow 6–8 ft tall, and may be used for temporary hedging. The crop may be lifted from November onwards, and are best left in the soil until the tubers are wanted, with a top-covering of straw or litter. A proportion of tubers are retained for planting each year.

Articulatus (-a, -um). Jointed. Ex. *Celastrus articulatus.*

Artificial Manures. See Fertilizers.

Artillery Plant. See *Pilea microphylla.*

Arum (ai'rum. Fam. Araceae). Tuberous perennials, distinctive for their singular flowers, consisting of a spadix bearing male, sterile and female flowers, and a large, convolute spathe, with beautiful foliage.

Selection. A. italicum, SE. Europe, 1½ ft, greenish-white, April, followed by scarlet berries, and vs. *maculatum,* and *marmoratum* with beautifully marked leaves, and *pictum,* Spain, 1 ft, purple with green spathe, are hardy for woodland; *maculatum* is the native Cuckoo Pint or Lords and Ladies, with whitish spathe in spring and poisonous red berries in summer. In the cool greenhouse, *A. palaestinum,* Israel, with green spathe, blackish-purple inside, is the Black Calla or Solomon's Lily, and may be grown in pots, JIP compost, winter temp. 7° C. (45° F.).

Propagation. By division in spring.

Arum Lily. See *Zantedeschia aethiopica.*

Aruncus (a-run'kus. Fam. Rosaceae). Hardy herbaceous perennials of which the chief species grown is *A. sylvester* (*Spiraea aruncus*), the Goat's Beard, N. Europe, etc., 4 ft, with its ornamental foliage and long, showy panicles of creamy white flowers in June; its v. *kneiffii* has very finely cut leaves and is more dwarf.

Cultivation. A moist loam for preference; good for partial shade. Plant October–March.

Propagation. By seeds, or division in March.

Arundinaceus (-a, -um). Arundinaceous, reed-like. Ex. *Phalaris arundinacea.*

Arundinaria (a-run-din-ar'i-a. Fam. Gramineae). A genus of the woody-stemmed grasses generally called bamboos, from E. and S. Asia and S. U.S.A.

Selection. A. japonica (Bambusa metake), Japan, 10–14 ft, evergreen foliage; *fastuosa,* Japan, to 20 ft; *graminea,* Japan, to 10 ft, are the hardiest; *anceps,* Himalaya, 10–12 ft, needs warm shelter, and spreads rapidly.

Cultivation. Deep, humus-rich loam soil; with shelter from strong cold winds. Need ample moisture, especially when young. Plant April–May.

Propagation. By division, April–May. Many species have now been transferred to other genera; see *Pleioblastus, Sasa* and *Sinarundinaria.*

Arundo, Great Reed (a-run'do. Fam. Gramineae). Tall perennial reed-grasses with ornamental foliage and feathery flowering panicles, from the warm temperate zones, and therefore doubtfully hardy.

Selection. A. donax, S. Europe, to 12 ft, is the hardiest, but needs winter protection in cold localities; *conspicua,* New Zealand, 3–6 ft, does best in mild districts.

Cultivation. Plant in October or March, in moist soil or by waterside. May also be grown in large pots in cool greenhouse, winter temp. 7° C. (45° F.), minimum.

Propagation. By division in April, May.

Arvensis (-e). Of arable fields. Ex. *Ononis arvensis.*

Asarina. See Antirrhinum.

Asarum (a-sar'um. Fam. Aristolochiaceae). Perennial hardy plants with rhizomatous roots, grown for their handsome long-stalked heart- or kidney-shaped leaves and resin-scented, bell-shaped, dull brown or purplish flowers, in shady places of the rock garden or in woodland.

Selection. A. canadense, Canadian Snakeroot, bears quaint brown, long-tailed bell flowers in spring; *europaeum,* Asarabacca, with brownish flowers, has naturalized itself in Britain; *caudatum,* California, brownish-red, long-tailed flowers, are hardy enough for outdoors. Others, such as *caudigerum,* green, speckled red, flowers; *thunbergii,* Japan, purplish-green, lobed flowers; and *virginianum,* a fragrant plant, with white spotted leaves, and erect flowers, are best in a cool greenhouse, deep pans and moist leafy soil.

Propagation. By division in spring.

Ascidium (pl. **-ia**). A pitcher.

Asclepias (as-kle′pi-as. Fam. Asclepia-daceae). A genus of perennial plants and shrubs, natives of the Americas or S. Africa, attractive in flower.

Selection. A. hallii, 2–3 ft, whorled leaves, and dull pink umbels of flowers, August; *incarnata,* 2–4 ft, large leaves, red or rose, July; and *tuberosa,* Butterfly Weed, Pleurisy Root, 2 ft, showy orange flowers, autumn, are hardy N. Americans for the warm border. *A. curassavica,* tropical America, the Blood Flower, 3 ft, with showy reddish orange-scarlet flowers, summer and autumn, is best grown as an annual in the cool greenhouse, together with the fragrant Silkweed, *syriaca,* to 4 ft, pale purple flowers; while *physocarpa,* S. Africa, to 6 ft, makes a showy greenhouse shrub, with umbels of small white and cream flowers throughout summer.

Cultivation. Outdoors, well-drained, porous soil, enriched with peat; sun. Plant October or March–April. Tender species in pots, JIP compost or a sandy loam-peat mixture, and warm green-house conditions.

Propagation. All types can be raised from seeds, sown February–March, under glass, bottom heat 21° C. (70° F.). Hardy plants to be pricked off for planting in May; non-hardy to be potted on; and if retained through the winter, should be cut back after flowering, rested with very moderate watering, winter temp. 15·5° C. (60° F.), until growth begins again. Hardy perennials can be increased by division in spring.

Ascomycetes. The Sac Fungi, a large class of over 1,500 genera, many species of which are parasitic on higer plants. Their identifiable characteristic is the *ascus,* a club-shaped, cylindrical or glo-bose sac, carrying spores (ascospores), for ultimate release and propagation.

Ascospores. *See* Ascomycetes.

Ascus (pl. **Asci**). Spore cases or sacs. *See* Ascomycetes.

Asexual. Without male or female organs; applied to reproduction without the previous union of male and female cells.

Ash. *See* Fraxinus.

Ash, Mountain. *See* Sorbus.

Ashes, Coal and Coke. Ashes from coal and coke fires and furnaces find much use in the garden. When freshly drawn,

however, they may contain sulphur compounds and substances harmful to plants, and they should be weathered, exposed to the air, rain and light for some months. They may be used to provide a standing ground for pot plants, or for plunging beds. When weathered, ashes may be used to lighten heavy soils; to make aggregate beds for ring culture (q.v.); for drainage layers under lawns; for paths; and over seeds or around plants to deter mice, slugs and snails.

Ashes, Wood. Combustion reduces plants to an ash consisting of the mineral elements that entered into its composi-tion. Wood ashes are therefore inorganic, but useful sources of mineral plant nutrients. Analysis varies considerably according to kind and age of the wood or plant material burnt. Chief contents are potash (3–10 per cent), lime, as calcium oxide (30–35 per cent), magnesium (3–4 per cent); phosphorus (1–2 per cent), and traces of several other minerals. As the compounds are very soluble, it is important to keep wood ashes dry. As a potassic fertilizer, wood ashes may be used at 6 to 12 oz. per sq. yd. Vegetable waste and young wood yield richer ashes than old. Wood ashes also have a strong liming effect, and should not be used where lime-intolerant plants are grown, or where soil acidity is already negligible. In the case of soft plant material, more nutrient value is recovered by the slow combustion of the compost heap than by that of the bonfire.

Asparagus (*Asparagus officinalis*). An epicure's vegetable, one of the oldest in cultivation, Asparagus, so named by Theophrastus, has been grown in this country for over 360 years, sometimes as Spear-grass, Sperage or Sparrowgrass. The plant is native to salt steppes of E. Europe and shores of the Mediterranean and our own coasts. Perennial, with proper cultivation a planting yields for a lifetime or more.

Propagation. By seed, sown in April, ½ in. deep in drills 12 in. apart, in out-door bed of sandy loam, thinned to 9 in. apart when seedlings are large enough to handle. Plants are dioecious, and are grown on for 2 years, until they flower and the sexes can be distinguished. Then, as male plants give the better yield, the female (with pistillate flowers) are rogued out, and the male retained for planting out. Seedlings may be transplanted at one year, with wider spacing, prior to roguing and planting out. Obviously, time can be saved by buying-in two- or three-year-old selected plants from nurseries, in proven strains—Kidner's, Connover's Colossal, Martha Washington, Giant White Cap, Argenteuil.

Soil. A deep, friable, medium loam over well-drained subsoil is ideal; but other soils can be amended with gypsum, lime and organic manuring, given good drainage. Chalk needs breaking up, and given very generous manuring. On clay, beds can be raised, or plants grown in ridges. Beds are prepared in winter, double-digging the soil and incorporating manure, compost, seaweed or similar organic matter. Beds may be 4 ft wide with 2 ft wide pathways or alleys between, the top soil from the latter being added to the beds; or marked out on the flat where natural drainage is very good.

Planting. This is done in April, taking great care not to let the roots become dry at all. With two rows per bed, spacing would be 1 ft from the edges, and 1½ ft between rows. Plants are spaced 15 to 18 in. apart, and may be planted staggered in parallel rows. For each row a trench 9 in. wide and deep is taken out, and an inch of sifted rotten compost laid in the bottom. At each planting stand, a mound of good soil is made 4 in. high, and the plant placed on this with roots down the side, and promptly covered with 2 in. or so of soil. A dressing of a complete fertilizer or dried seaweed can be applied before the remainder of the soil.

Management. For the first year after planting it is only necessary to keep the beds weed-free and water to maintain good growth. In autumn, when the top growth yellows, it is cut down and removed. The bed should then be dressed with rotted manure or compost, with a little soil, and left until March, when the remains of the top-dressing is raked off, and the bed weeded. A dressing of agricultural salt (2 oz. per sq. yd) may be given to beds of other than clay soil. On heavy soils, dried seaweed manure would be better. Second year management should be as for the first, and cutting

should not begin until the third year. Then cutting may be carried out through April, May and early June, and then cease. Shoots are cut with a sharp knife or special asparagus knife about 3 to 4 in. below the surface, when they show the same amount of growth above ground. Cutting should stop in the third week of June each year, when the bed will need a dressing of a high phosphate compound fertilizer, or liquid feeding fortnightly to August. The 'Fern' is allowed to grow unhindered until it yellows, when it is removed, and the routine already outlined followed annually.

Forcing. For Christmas or early produce, asparagus may be forced by lifting strong crowns, at least 4 years old, November to February, and placing on a prepared hotbed (3 parts fresh leaves mixed with 1 part strawy stable manure, and heaped), temp. 18° C. (65° F.). This is covered with 3 in. of good soil compost, or mixture of loam and spent mushroom compost, on which the lifted crowns are placed, and covered with another 4 in. of moist soil compost, and a frame and light; syringed daily. Or crowns may be planted up in boxes of soil compost and moved into a warm greenhouse (15.5°–18° C. [60–65° F.]). The forced roots are more or less exhausted and are discarded afterwards. Crowns may be forced *in situ* by placing a frame over them, covering with 2–3 in. sifted compost in November, and then surrounding the frame with packed fresh manure, and covering with mats at night when frost threatens.

Weeds must be rigorously controlled. When time cannot be given to hand-weeding, most annual and leafy green weeds can be controlled by making an application of a paraquat herbicide in spring before any shoot buds appear, and again when cutting ceases, taking care not to wet asparagus growth. Couch grass can be controlled by a dalapon herbicide, applied to the foliage in March, April.

Diseases. The chief trouble is Rust, *Puccinia asparagi*, as a rusty-brown powdery deposit on the leaves in summer, and black streaks on the stems in autumn. It is controlled by cutting out infected shoots for burning as soon as seen. Martha Washington is a rust-resistant variety. Violet Root Rot (*Heliocobasidium purpureum*) is soil-borne but not common. The roots are covered with purple-violet web-like strands, foliage wilts and the plant dies. There is no cure, and infected plants should be carefully lifted and burnt; and the soil rested from asparagus cropping for a few years.

Pests. The most common is the Asparagus Beetle, *Crioceris asparagi*, chiefly in the south. Small, with a double black cross on reddish wing-cases, the beetles appear in May to feed on shoots. Eggs are laid in June giving rise to olive or greenish-grey humped grubs that feed on shoots and foliage for two or three weeks before pupating in the soil. Two or three broods may occur in a year. A pyrethrum insecticide is best to use in the cutting period, and repeated.

Asparagus (as-pa'ra-gus. Fam. Liliaceae). Botanically, a genus of over 100 species of the Old World, containing several evergreen and deciduous perennial climbing or trailing plants which are grown largely for their delicate fernlike branches and foliage, consisting of needle-shaped or linear phylloclades, chiefly under glass.

Selection. A. plumosus, S. Africa, the evergreen Asparagus Fern used so much for table decoration and florist's work, and *medeoloides*, S. Africa, the Smilax of florists, may be trained up strings or wires. Both have fine dwarf forms in *A. p. nanus*, which spreads horizontally; and *A. m. myrtifolius*, a finely leafed Smilax. *A. sprengeri*, Natal, 3–6 ft, and its v. *variegatus* make good room plants. *A. crispus*, S. Africa, 3–6 ft, and *scandens*, up to 6 ft, are herbaceous perennials that make good basket plants. *A. verticillatus*, Asia, is a graceful climber for pillars, 10–15 ft, with small, funnel-shaped flowers, followed by red berries, and is reputedly hardy for mild localities.

Cultivation. The tender species grows well in pots, JIP 3 compost, in a fairly warm greenhouse, shaded from hot sun, given ample ventilation; minimum winter temp. 10° C. (50° F.).

Propagation. By seeds sown under glass, March, bottom heat 18° C. (65° F.), potting off seedlings singly as soon as big enough to handle. By cuttings of ripe shoots in spring, inserted in a propagating case, with heat. By root division in March.

Aspen. See *Populus tremula*.

Asper (-ra, -rum). Asperous; rough to touch. Ex. *Asperula*—rough, of the leaves.

Asperula (as-pe'ru-la. Fam. Rubiaceae). Gardeners draw chiefly on the herbaceous perennials and one annual for their pretty flower clusters.

Selection. A. orientalis (azurea), Caucasus, is the annual, 1 ft, with freely produced clusters of scented, lavender-blue flowers in spring from an autumn sowing; in summer from a March sowing outdoors where plants are to flower. *A. odorata*, 6 in., is the native white-flowering Sweet Woodruff, smelling of new-mown hay when dry; useful in woodland or the shrubbery. Gems for the rock garden and alpine house include *A. arcadiensis*, Greece, 3 in., silvery-grey, with small long trumpets of bright pink flowers, June; *hirta*, Pyrenees, 3 in., with deep green linear leaves, small white tubular flowers, blushing pink, summer; *gussonii*, Sicily, a tufted dwarf with small pink flowers, summer; and *suberosa*, Greece, 3 in., a silvery hairy cushion, with small pink trumpet flowers on 2-in. spike, June, July.

Cultivation. Well-drained ordinary soil for the annual. Gritty porous loam for the rock garden species, and winter protection against damp. Plant in spring, in sunny positions.

Propagation. Alpines by cuttings of young shoots in June, in a propagating case with slight bottom heat. Others by seed sown outdoors.

Asphodeline (as-po-de-li'ne. Fam. Lilaceae). Hardy and easily grown herbaceous perennials from the Mediterranean region, akin to Asphodelus but with upright leafy stems.

Selection. A. lutea, Sicily, 3–4 ft, is the ancient's Asphodel or King's Spear, with narrow, furrowed leaves and a spike dense with fragrant buff and yellow flowers, June, July; *liburnica*, S. Europe, 2 ft, yellow flowers, striped green, and *taurica*, Asia Minor, 1–2 ft, white, green striped, flowers, are also grown.

Cultivation. Well-drained, humus-rich soil; plant in autumn or March, in borders or semi-wild garden, open or partial shaded positions.

Propagation. By division in early spring. *A. lutea* by seed under glass, bottom heat 21° C. (70° F.), March, to plant out in early May.

Asphodelus (as-fod'el-us. Fam. Liliaceae). Hardy herbaceous perennials, with fleshy roots, radical leaves, and six-petalled flowers.

Selection. A. cerasiferus, 4–5 ft, sword-like leaves, long upright raceme of large white, reddish-brown keeled flowers, summer, and *microcarpus,* to 3 ft, with broad, linear leathery leaves and a branching panicle of white, reddish striped flowers, summer, are both native to S. Europe, and have been previously misnamed *A. ramosus,* of old-fashioned cottage gardens; *acaulis,* Atlas Mts, is a charming alpine for the alpine house, a loose corymb of funnel-shaped, opening star-like, pale pink flowers, sweetly fragrant, opening in April–May, from a rosette of linear pointed leaves, grown in JIP 1 compost.

Cultivation. Ordinary garden soil, sun or semi-shade for the hardy perennials; planting in October or March.

Propagation. By careful division of the roots in March, April. By seeds sown outdoors in April, to transplant in autumn.

Aspidistra, Parlour Palm (as-pi-dis'tra. Fam. Liliaceae). Noted for its tolerance of shade, draughts and neglect when grown as a house plant, the best known species is *A. elatior,* introduced from Japan in 1834, and valued for its unfailing evergreen stalked leaves, with long, lanceolate and pointed blades, striped green and white in its form *variegata.* The flower is inconspicuous with mushroom-like pistil and appears close to the soil and is easily overlooked.

Cultivation. Pot in March; JIP 2 compost or one of equal parts rich loam, leaf-mould and sand. Water freely in summer, very moderately in winter; minimum temp. 10° C. (50° F.). Sponge leaves free of dust periodically; stand outdoors in warm summer showers. Variegated form needs more light than the dark-green leaved species.

Propagation. By division of the plant in spring.

Aspidium. For plants previously listed under this name, see *Dryopteris, Polystichum.*

Asplenium, Spleenwort (as-ple'ni-um.

Fam. Polypodiaceae). A very large genus of evergreen ferns of worldwide distribution, of which only the more notable can be listed here.

Selection. Tender exotics requiring stove conditions, winter temp. 15·5–21° C. (60–70° F.); summer 21–27° C. (70–80° F.), are: *A. cristatum,* tropical America, tri-pinnate fronds; *fragrans,* tropical America, scented; *longissimum,* Malacca, fronds of 2-8 ft; *lunulatum,* Tropics, simple pinnate fronds; *obtusifolium,* tropical America, broad fronds;

FIG. 22 *Asplenium nidus,* the Bird's-nest Fern.

tenerum v. *belangeri,* tropical Asia, bi-pinnate fronds; *vieillardii,* Fiji; and *viviparum,* Mascarene Isles, bearing young plants on its fronds. Half-hardy ferns for the greenhouse with minimum winter temp. 10–13° C. (50–55° F.) are: *A. bulbiferum,* Australia, New Zealand, and vs. *fabianum* and *laxum; dimorphum,* Norfolk Isle, fronds of 2–3 ft; *glandulosum,* S. Europe, dainty dwarf; *nidus,* Bird's-nest Fern, with broad, lanceolate entire fronds; *palmatum,* S. Europe; *sandersoni,* tropical Africa, narrow fronds; and *unilaterale,* Tropics. Hardy species for shady place out of doors are: *A. adiantumnigrum,* the native Black Spleenwort; *fontanum,* Rock Spleenwort; *lanceolatum* and its *crispatum* and *microdon,* Europe;

marinum, Sea Spleenwort, native and Europe; *ruta-muraria*, Wall Rue, Britain; *septentrionale*, Forked Spleenwort, Britain; *trichomanes*, Maidenhair Spleenwort, and vs.; and *viride*, Green Spleenwort, Britain, Europe.

Cultivation. Stove and greenhouse kinds usually require a humus-rich compost, of equal parts peat, leaf-mould and sandy loam; pot in March; liberal watering in summer, moderate in winter, with some shade from hot direct sun. Hardy kinds welcome well-drained but humus-rich soil, often with lime, with shade part of the day.

Propagation. Stove and greenhouse species by spores on sandy loam, when available. Hardy species by spores in cold frame, or by division in April. Some species readily produce small plantlets on their fronds which can be detached and rooted separately.

Assimilation. A term once used for the process by which the living green plant takes in carbon dioxide and water to produce sugars and starch when exposed to light, and now known as photosynthesis (q.v.).

Assurgens. Assurgent, ascending. Ex. *Spiraea assurgens.*

Aster, Michaelmas Daisy, Starwort (as'ter, Fam. Compositae). Very largely a genus of hardy herbaceous perennials, providing dwarf, spring-flowering alpines for the rock garden, and tall leafy species, usually known as Michaelmas Daisies, which are invaluable for their late summer and autumn bloom and ease of cultivation.

Selection. For the rock garden: *A. alpinus*, Europe, 6 in., bright purple flowers, June–July, is variable, with outstanding vs. such as *albus*, pure white, 'Beechwood', pale blue, *himalaicus*, no more than 4 in., reddish-purple, *ruber*, deep red, and Buxton's dwarf, purple; *bellidiastrum*, Austria, 12 in., white, June; *farreri*, Tibet, 6 in., deep violet, June; *himalaicus*, Sikkim, purplish-blue, June; *pyrenaeus*, Pyrenees, 1 ft, bright blue; *souliei limitaneus*, Tibet, purple-violet, June; *stracheyi*, Humalaya, 4 in., lilac-blue, May; and *subcaeruleus*, NW. India, 6 in., pale blue, June. Species which deserve more attention than they usually get include: *A. acris*, S. Europe, 2 ft, bright mauve, August, and its dwarf form, *nanus*; *divaricatus*, N. America, 2½ ft, white, September; × *frikartii*, a fine hybrid of 2½ ft, light blue, August, September, and its form 'Wonder of Staffa', deeper blue; *laterifolius*, N. America, to 4 ft, pale purple, August to October; *linosyris*, the native Goldilocks, 1 ft, bright yellow, August to October; and *thomsonii*, Himalaya, 1–3 ft, pale lilac, autumn. The gardener's Michaelmas Daisies are selected varieties, more rarely hybrids, of chosen species, and are grouped accordingly as they retain the main specific characteristics. The names of some well-known varieties are given here, but new kinds are added from time to time, and should be looked for at shows and show gardens, and in the annual catalogues of breeder-nurserymen.

Amellus group: erect bushy habit, branching sprays of single flowers, July–early September.

Advance, violet-blue, 2 ft.
General Pershing, lilac-pink, 2½ ft.
Jacqueline Genebrier, bright pink, 2½ ft.
King George, violet-blue, 2 ft.
Lady Hindlip, rich pink, 2 ft.
Mauve Queen, soft mauve, 1½ ft.
Mrs Ralph Woods, bright pink, 2½ ft.
Orion, ultramarine blue, 2 ft.
Preziosa, violet-purple, 2 ft.
Rudolph Von Goethe, deep lavender, 2½ ft.
Sonia, lilac-pink, 2 ft.
Ultramarine, dark violet-blue, 2 ft.
Wienholtzii, rose pink, 2½ ft.

Cordifolius group: Erect, branching habit, arching sprays of small, starry flowers, September and October.

Aldeboran, soft blue, 3½ ft.
elegans, lilac, 3 ft.
Ideal, pale blue, 3 ft.
Nancy, pale purple, 4 ft.
Profusion, lavender blue, 4 ft.
Silver Spray, white, 4 ft.
Sweet Lavender, lilac, 3 ft.

Ericoides group: Erect branching and bushy in habit, bearing small star-like flowers in elegant sprays, in September and October.

Blue Star, pale blue, 3 ft.
Chastity, white, 3½ ft.
Esther, pink, 2 ft.
Maidenhood, white, 3 ft.
Ringdove, rosy-mauve, 3 ft.
Twilight, lavender, 3 ft.

Novae-Angliae group: Tall, upright habit, bearing large flowers, single or semi-double in branching heads, September–November.

Barr's Pink, rose pink, semi-double, 5 ft.
Barr's Violet, deep violet, 5 ft.
Crimson Beauty, rose-crimson, 4 ft.
Harrington's Pink, clear pink, 4½ ft.
Hilda Morris, purple, 5 ft.
Lil Fardell, rose, 5 ft.
Mrs S. T. Wright, rosy-mauve, 4 ft.
Red Star, red, 4–5 ft.

Novi-Belgii group: Tallish, upright habit, with large single or semi-double flowers in pyramidal branching heads; late September to November.

Ada Ballard, mauve-blue, 3 ft.
Alex Wallace, mauve, semi-double, 3½ ft.
Anita Ballard, lavender, 4½ ft.
Apple Blossom, mauve-pink, semi-double, 4 ft.
Arctic, pure white, double, 3 ft.
Beechwood Beacon, rosy-crimson, 2½ ft.
Beechwood Challenger, bright red, 3½ ft.
Blandie, white, semi-double, 4 ft.
Blue Eyes, lavender blue, 3 ft.
Blue Gown, clear blue, 5 ft.
Blue Radiance, pale blue, 2½ ft.
Chequers, violet-purple, 2 ft.
Climax, light blue, 5 ft.
Crimson Brocade, red, semi-double, 3 ft.
Dick Ballard, lilac, double, 3 ft.
Ernest Ballard, carmine, semi-double, 3 ft.
Eventide, violet-blue, semi-double, 3 ft.
Fontaine, purple, semi-double, 4 ft.
Gayborder Royal, crimson, 2½ ft.
Gayborder Supreme, violet-rose, semi-double, 4 ft.
Gayborder Violet, violet-purple, 3½ ft.
Harrison's Blue, deep amethyst, 3½ ft.
Hilda Ballard, lilac-pink, semi-double, 4 ft.
Jean, rich blue-mauve, 2 ft.
Little Boy Blue, deep blue, semi-double, 2 ft.
Little Pink Lady, pink, semi-double, 2½ ft.
Margaret Ballard, rose-mauve, semi-double, 4 ft.
Marie Ballard, powder blue, double, 3 ft.

Melbourne Belle, deep rose, 2 ft.
Patricia Ballard, rich pink, double, 3 ft.
Picture, carmine red, semi-double, 4 ft.
Plenty, silvery blue, semi-double, 3½ ft.
Prosperity, rose-pink, semi-double, 4 ft.
Queen Mary, light blue, 5 ft.
Red Sunset, dark rose-red, 3 ft.
The Archbishop, purple-blue, semi-double, 3 ft.
The Cardinal, rich rose-red, 4 ft.
The Dean, warm pink, 3½ ft
The Sexton, rich blue, 3½ ft.
Twinkle, lilac-purple, semi-double, 3 ft.
Winston S. Churchill, red-purple, semi-double, 3 ft.

A. dumosus × *novi-belgii hybrids*: Of dwarf, neat, compact habit, and free-flowering, these are ideal for the front of borders, and for late colour in the rock garden; September–November.

Audrey, mauve-blue, 1 ft.
Blue Bouquet, violet-blue, 1 ft.
Lady Henry Maddocks, soft pink, 9 in.
Lilac Time, soft lilac, 1 ft.
Little Blue Baby, rich blue, semi-double, 1½ ft.
Little Red Boy, rosy red, 1½ ft.
Margaret Rose, rose-pink, 9 in.
Persian Rose, cyclamen purple, 1½ ft.
Peter Harrison, pink, 1 ft.
Rosebud, pink, semi-double, 1 ft.
Snowsprite, white, semi-double, 9 in.
Victor, pale lavender, 6 in.

A. yunnanensis 'Napsbury' is an outstanding dwarf, with large blue flowers, 1½–2 ft, that flowers in June.

Cultivation. Well-drained ordinary soil, enriched with humus-forming organic matter, suits these plants; on sunny borders or rock-garden terraces. Plant in autumn or spring. Most plants are the better for being lifted, divided and replanted every second or third year.

Propagation. By division in early spring, when growth begins; splitting into strong crowns with roots of the outer part of each plant, for replanting; the inner older parts are discarded. By cuttings of young shoots inserted in sandy loam in a frame, spring or early summer. Many species and varieties can be raised from seeds, sown under glass or in a cold frame, spring. *A. tanacetifolius,*

W. U.S.A., is an annual, bearing violet-purple flowers, and growing 1–2 ft high, which may be raised as a half-hardy annual to plant out in May.

Diseases. The worst is Wilt, caused by a fungus, *Verticillium vilmorinii*, invading and living in the rootstock from the soil. Infected plants turn brown and withered from the base upwards. Novae-angliae varieties are apparently immune, but all others are subject. Seriously infected plants are best lifted and burnt. It is possible to propagate choice plants by means of tip cuttings of new sucker growths, 1–2 in. long, in spring, before destroying the stock. Plants should be set out in fresh ground, and the old site rested from aster-growing for at least four years.

Powdery Mildew, caused by the fungus *Erysiphe cichoracearum*, coats plants greyish white, beginning near the base, in late summer. As soon as seen plants should be sprayed or dusted with a captan or sulphur fungicide, repeated at ten-day intervals. All top growth and leaves should be burnt in November.

Aster, China. The many varieties of the annual China Asters now offered by seedsmen have been developed from the Chinese *Callistephus chinensis* (Fam. Compositae), the sole species of the genus, introduced in 1731. They vary in height from 6 in. to 2½ ft, in a wide range of colour, and are adaptable for use in almost every part of a flower garden, as edgings, for bedding, to 'fill-in' herbaceous borders, and to be grown for cutting. They may be grouped according to type.

Selection. Single-flowered, 2 to 2½ ft, splendid for cutting, listed as sinensis, super sinensis, upright rainbow, mixed or by colour. *Californian Giant,* 2 ft, large, late flowering, shaggy-petalled heads like Japanese chrysanthemums; excellent for bedding and cutting, Perfection strains; *Giant Branching Comet,* 1½ ft, Crego strains, rather late flowering, branching from the base, with large double blooms, having incurved petals; *Ostrich Plume,* 1½–2 ft, large, double flowers with feathery, curling petals, good for bedding or cutting; *Giant Comet,* 1½ ft, elegant flowers, good for cutting; *Duchess,* 2 ft, with double flowers, like incurved chrysanthemums;

Princess, Super Princess, 2–2½ ft, branching, with double flowers, having centres of quilled petals; good for bedding; *Quilled,* 1½–2 ft, double flowers with quilled petals, Unicum, Radio and Amore are good strains; *Anemone-flowered,* 2 ft, double flowers with single row of flat petals around a quilled centre, Sunshine strain; *Dwarf Comet,* 9–12 in., flowers with twisted petals, for bedding; *Lilliput,* 1½ ft, small, very double flowers, for bedding, cutting and pot culture; *Paeony-flowered,* 1–1½ ft, double flowers with incurving petals; *Victoria,* 15 in., blooms to 5 in. across with petals recurving outwards; *Chrysanthemum-flowered,* 9 in., with compact habit, double flowers, outward-curving petals, for bedding or pot culture; the Colour Carpet strain belongs here; *Bouquet Powderpuff,* 1½–2 ft, very double, tightly packed heads of bloom, for bedding or cutting; *Pompone,* 1½ ft, smallish rounded flowers, for bedding or cutting. New types are added from time to time, and seedsmen's catalogues should be watched.

Cultivation. Treated as a half-hardy annual, seed is raised by sowing under glass, March, with bottom heat (18° C. [65° F.]); or outdoors on sheltered border, April. Ordinary, well-drained soils suit, enriched with rotted organic matter and bone flour.

Diseases. Sudden collapse may be caused by Black Neck, due to the Stem-rot fungus, *Phytophthora cryptogea,* turning basal stems and roots black. The soil is contaminated. Infected plants must be lifted and burnt with surrounding soil, and others watered with Cheshunt Compound. It is wise to rest the soil afterwards from aster-growing for two to three years. Rapid wilting of a plant, with stem blackening, and the appearance of a whitish or pinkish covering of spores, are caused by the Wilt fungus, *Fusarium conglutinans callistephi.* Infected plants should be destroyed, and the same procedure as for Black Neck followed, as the soil is contaminated. There are wilt-resistant strains now available.

Astilbe (as-til'be. Fam. Saxifragaceae). Pretty, hardy, herbaceous perennials with finely ternate foliage and spires or panicles of small flowers in white and all shades of pink and red. Excellent for moist soils, waterside planting and partial shade.

Selection. A. astilboides, Japan, 2–3 ft, dense, white flower spikes, June; *chinensis*, China, to 3 ft, white, tinged rose; *japonica (Spiraea japonica)*, Japan, 3 ft, white, May, which may be forced under glass; and *rivularis*, Nepal, 3 ft, yellowish white; are good for moist, sheltered situations. In the rock garden, *A. chinensis* v. *pumila*, ½–1 ft, mulberry red spikes in August; *A. simplicifolia*, Japan, 6 in., white, August, and hybrids of *A*. × *crispa* such as 'Gnome' and 'Kobold', 6 in., white or pink, are charming for late colour. Major interest, however, is in the modern hybrids, developed by Lemoine of France and Georg Arends of Ronsdorf, commonly listed under *A*. × *arendsii*, and the progeny of crossings between four species. They are valuable for moist borders and water gardens out of doors, and may be grown as pot plants under glass for earlier blooming. Fine named forms are: whites—'Betsy Cuperus', 4–5 ft, 'Avalanche', 3 ft, 'Bridal Veil', 3 ft, 'White Queen', 2½ ft; pinks—'America', 3 ft, 'Ceres', 3 ft, 'Peach Blossom', 2 ft, 'Pink Pearl', 3 ft, 'Rhineland', 3 ft, 'Venus', 2½ ft; reds—*davidii*, 4 ft, 'Fanal', 2½ ft, 'Gloria', 2½ ft, 'Granat', 3 ft, 'Koblenz', 2 ft, 'Red Sentinel', 2 ft, 'Salland', 4 ft, 'Wm Reeves', 2½ ft, flowering in July.

Cultivation. Any good soil, retentive of moisture, suits; sun or shade. Plant in October or March. Water in dry weather.

Propagation. By division in March–April.

Astragalus, Milk Vetch (as-trag′a-lus. Fam. Leguminosae). A very large genus of which few are cultivated; chiefly for their pea-like flowers.

Selection. A. alopecuroides, Europe, 2–4 ft, is an erect-growing herbaceous perennial, with long, whitish-green pinnate leaves, and short racemes of yellow flowers, June, worth trying in a warm border. Others, such as *monspessulanus*, Mediterranean, an evergreen sub-shrub, with heads of purple flowers, June; *angustifolia*, Asia Minor, 9 in., a thorny sub-shrub, white flowering, June; and *tragacantha*, the Gum Tragacanth, S. Europe, 1–2 ft, evergreen and spiny with umbels of pale reddish purple in May,

June, may be attempted in sheltered sun on the rock garden, or alpine house.

Cultivation. Well-drained, porous soil and sun. Water, if necessary, during growth. Plant in autumn or March.

Propagation. By seeds in cool frame, but slow. By short tip cuttings of young shoots in August, in propagating case or frame.

Astrantia (as-tran′ti-a. Fam. Umbelliferae). Hardy herbaceous perennials, with palmately lobed leaves and stalked umbels of flowers, chiefly valuable for shade and the wild or woodland garden.

Selection. A. carniolica, Carniola, 1 ft, white or blush pink, bracted flowers, June; and *major*, Masterwort, Europe, 1–2 ft, pinkish flowers, June, are chiefly grown; now valued for use in floral arrangements.

Cultivation. Ordinary, well-drained soil. Shade. Plant in autumn or early spring.

Propagation. By seeds, sandy loam, outdoors or in cold frame, April. By division in autumn or March.

Atamasco Lily. *See* Zephyranthes.

Ater-, Atra-, Atrum-, Atro-. Very dark, black. Ex. *Berberis thunbergii atropurpurea*.

Athrotaxis (ath-ro-tacks′is. Fam. Pinaceae). Evergreen Tasmanian conifers, which may be grown in sheltered positions, moist, humus-rich soil, in Cornwall and warm localities.

Selection. A. selaginoides, the King William Pine, to 40 ft, is the most robust; *cupressoides*, 20 ft, and *laxifolia*, 20 ft, are other possibles.

Propagation. By seeds, April, warm beds of sandy loam. By shoot cuttings, August, in a cool frame.

Athyrium (a-thi′ri-um. Fam. Polypodiaceae). A genus of ferns closely related to Asplenium, and sometimes included in it.

Selection. The most popular is *A. filixfemina*, the Lady Fern, which is native, with beautiful, finely divided fronds, 1–3 ft, long, and numerous varieties of which crested forms such as *corymbiforum, edelstenii, foliosum grandiceps*, are striking; *minutissima* is a minute form; and *victoriae* is exceptionally lovely; *crenatum*, 12-in. fronds, finely pinnate, is hardy. Others, such as *angustifolium*, Canada, 1½–2-ft fronds, simply pinnate, *drepanopterum*, Far East, and *spinulosum*, Far East, with 12-in. fronds, need cool greenhouse conditions.

Cultivation. Ordinary soils, enriched with peat; shade, even under trees. Greenhouse kinds in equal parts fibrous peat, loam and sand. Plant in autumn or spring.

Propagation. By division, March. By spores when available.

Atragene. *See* Clematis.

Atratus (-a, -um). Becoming black. Ex. *Achillea atrata*.

Atriplex (at'ri-plex. Fam. Chenopodiaceae). The annual, *A. hortensis*, may be grown as a vegetable (*see* Orache), but its form, *atrosanguinea*, with crimson stems and leaves, 4 ft, is quite ornamental in the background of the border, and the stems may be used as spinach. The shrubby species, *A. halimus*, S. Europe, 4–8 ft, silver grey, semi-evergreen, the Tree Purslane, and *portulacoides*, Europe, 1–2 ft, a native straggling shrub, are useful for seaside planting, being resistant to salt-laden winds; *canescens*, 4–6 ft, is a spreading greyishwhite evergreen shrub from N. America, for coastal areas. All like well-drained, sandy soil, and may be planted in autumn or spring.

Propagation. Shrubs by cuttings of young shoots, July, August, inserted in sandy loam.

Attenuatus (-a, -um). Attenuate, narrowing to a point.

Aubergine, Egg-plant. The fruit of *Solanum melongena* v. *esculentum*, an annual of Africa and southern Asia, also known as the Bringall, Jew's Apple and Mad Apple. Being tender, the plants are best grown in pots under glass. Seeds are sown in February, March, with bottom heat (18° C. [65° F.]); pricking off into small pots singly, and then into 6- or 7-in. pots, with JIP 3 compost; to grow in a cool greenhouse, minimum night temperature of 13° C. (55° F.), stopping at 6 in. by pinching out growing points, and supporting subsequent growth on stakes or trellis. About four fruits per plant can be expected. In warm districts plants may be planted out in June. Water freely with growth, giving liquid feeding fortnightly from setting of fruit.

Varieties are Long Purple, Dwarf Purple, Blue King.

Aubrieta, Aubrietia (aw-bree'ta, Fam. Cruciferae). Aubrietia (aw-bree'shia) is the corrupted but now accepted common name of this genus of evergreen trailers from the eastern Mediterranean and Asia Minor. The only plants offered today, however, are selected varieties and hybrids of *A. deltoidea*, which, with their long-branched trailing stems, make large cushions or hummocks of tufted greygreen foliage, covered with cruciferous flowers in early spring, though further flowering may occur in summer.

Selection. Outstanding kinds are: *aurea variegata*, golden-hued foliage; 'Barker's Double', semi-double, rosy purple; 'Bressingham's Pink', large double pink; 'Britannia', carmine pink; 'Carnival', deep violet; 'Crimson Queen', rich crimson; 'Dawn', double, light pink; 'Dr Mules', deep violet; 'Gloriosa', rosepink; 'Godstone', deep violet-purple; 'Gurgedyke', deep violet; 'Kelmscott Triumph', double, deep violet; 'Mrs Rodewall', crimson; 'Studland', lavender; 'The Queen', deep red; 'Thos T. Wood', reddish purple; 'Wirral Purple', large, purple.

Cultivation. Grow readily on any welldrained soil, limy or not, and make good wall plants, mat plants for the larger rock garden or terrace, edgings for borders and covering for banks. Plant in autumn or March. Trim hard back with shears after flowering.

Propagation. By seeds, although varieties do not come absolutely 'true'; in March or May, under glass or on outdoor nursery bed. By cuttings of young shoots, in summer. By layering or heaping soil, over long unsevered stems and leaving until autumn when roots will have formed.

Aucuba (au-ku'ba. Fam. Cornaceae). Hardy evergreen shrubs with ornamental foliage, capable of growing in almost any soil, in sun or shade, in town or country. The foliage is leathery, shining and oval, and plants are sometimes described as laurels, though of the dogwood family. Being dioecious, male and female forms are needed for a fine autumn berrying display; about one male to three or four female.

Selection. A. japonica, Japan, 6–12 ft,

of rounded form, with shining green leaves, and clusters of bright red berries; and its vs. *variegata*, a yellow-spotted leaved male; *crassifolia*, a male with thick, broad leaves; *hillieri*, female with large crimson berries; *crotonoides*, mottled golden-green leaves, male and female forms; *longifolia*, long narrow leaves in both sexes; *nana rotundifolia*, compact and free-berrying in the female form; and *salicifolia*, a female with distinctive long narrow leaves.

Cultivation. Almost any soil, well broken, will do, but humus is appreciated; sun or shade. Plant in early autumn or spring.

Propagation. By seeds in March, from berries stratified in sand, over the winter. By cuttings of shoots in porous soil in summer, rather easy, especially if covered with a handlight.

Aucuba Mosaic. Descriptive of a virus infection which causes yellow mottling of plant leaves.

Augustus (-a, -um). Majestic, noble, stately. Ex. *Crinum augustum.*

Aurantiacus (-a, -um). Orange coloured. Ex. *Dimorphotheca aurantiaca.*

Auratus (-a, -um). Golden-yellow. Ex. *Lilium auratum.*

Aureus (-a, -um). Golden. Ex. *Calochortus aureus.*

Auricula, Bear's-ear (au-rik'u-la). Botanically, what are called Auricula comprise a section of the genus *Primula*, characterized by their irregularly toothed leaves, fleshy and often farinose. Horticulturally, they may be divided into the Show or Stage Auricula, held to be derived from *Primula auricula*, and the Alpine Auricula, held to be derived from various crosses of *P. auricula* with other species, under the umbrella-name of *P.* × *pubescens*.

Show Auricula. A distinctive characteristic of these plants is the farina or meal on the flowers. As this is easily damaged by weather, Show Auriculas are usually grown under glass in rather deep frames, with staging, and given protection in frosty weather. Or they may be grown in a cool greenhouse.

Selection. Show Auriculas are classed according to flower markings as follows: (1) White-edged, such as 'Acme', 'Burley', 'Gloria', 'Heather Bell', 'Hinton Admiral' and 'White Mantle'. (2)

Grey-edged, such as 'Fancy Free,'. 'George Lightbody', 'George Rudd', 'Grey Friar', 'Love-bird', 'Nuthatch' and 'Sherfield'. (3) Green-edged, such as 'Abraham Barker', 'Antonio', 'Green Mantle', 'Linkman', 'Mystic', 'Shirley Hibberd', 'Tinklerbell' and 'Victory'. (4) Self, such as 'Blue Bird', 'Blue Fire', 'Deerleap', 'Freda', 'Harrison Weir',

FIG. 23 A Show Auricula (*Primula auricula* v.).

'King Cole', 'Loretto', 'Oakley', 'Old Gold', 'Scarlet Prince' and 'Rosebud'. Others, not falling into these classes, are termed Fancies.

Cultivation. Pot in March–June, repot after flowering. May be grown in JIP compost, or mixture of 2 parts loam, 1 part sifted leaf-mould, 1 part sifted rotted stable manure, ½ part coarse sand, plus ½ lb. bone meal per bushel. Do not like to be over-potted. Grow cool, in frames set north during summer, with free ventilation, careful but generous watering; turn frames to the south in September–April. More moderate watering in winter, minimum temp. 7° C. (45° F.), in frame or cool greenhouse. Damp and stagnant air are chief enemies in winter.

Propagation. Named varieties by offsets when repotting, severing with a razor-blade, with roots attached; dust cuts with powdered charcoal or a little fungicidal dust and root in around the rim of a pot, under handlight or in frame. By seed, though slow to germinate, and taking two years to give flowering plants, preferably when freshly ripe, in warm greenhouse.

Alpine Auriculas. Derived from crosses of *P. auricula* with other species, and grouped under *P.* × *pubescens*. There is no powder or farina on the flowers or foliage, and plants are hardier than the Show Auriculas, and may be grown out of doors or in a cold alpine house.

Selection. Good named forms are 'Basuto', crimson-maroon, gold; 'Blue Bonnet', violet-blue, white; 'Bookham Firefly', crimson, gold; 'Bookham Glory', purple, white; 'Carolina', maroon-crimson, gold; 'Gipsy', crimson, yellow; 'Gordon Douglas', violet-blue, cream; 'Kingcup', crimson, gold; 'Majestic', maroon-crimson, gold; 'Mrs L. Hearn', Cambridge blue, white; 'Spring Morning', pink, cream; and 'St Tudno', light purple, white; the second colour being that of the eye: flowering normally in May, June.

Cultivation. Out of doors, moist loam, with leaf-mould added, good drainage, partial shade, in borders or rock garden. Plant in spring. In cold greenhouse or alpine house, in pots, JIP compost; repotting after flowering.

Propagation. By division of plants, July. By seeds, sown as soon as ripe, but may be slow.

Auriculatus (-a, -um). Auriculate, having ear-like appendages, Ex. *Coreopsis auriculata.*

Australis (-e). Southern. Ex. *Cordyline australis.*

Autogamy. The term used for the process by which a flower is fertilized through its own organs without the participation of other flowers; it is said to be 'selfed'.

Autumn Crocus. *See* Colchicum.

Autumnalis (-e). Of autumn. Ex. *Colchicum autumnale.*

Auxin. A growth-regulating substance in plants associated with the elongation of cells in stems, particularly at growing points.

Avena (a-ve'na. Fam. Gramineae). Grasses with panicles of flower and seed-heads, of which *A. sativa*, or Oat, is the cereal; and *A. sterilis*, the Animated Oat, an annual of 1½–2 ft, from the Mediterranean region, may be grown for its curious ornamental value, and the habit of the seed-heads twisting and untwisting in reaction to atmospheric moisture. Seeds may be sown in autumn or spring, where the plants are to grow.

Avens. *See* Geum.

Avocado Pear. See *Persea gratissima.*

Awn. A bristle-like appendage or beard, seen especially on grasses and cereals.

FIG. 24   Axil, of leaf and stem, with axillary bud showing.

Axil. The angle formed between leaf and stem; or between two veins of leaves.

Axillaris (-e), produced in the axils of leaves. Ex. *Leucothoe axillaris.*

Axillary, growing in the axil.

Axis. The main growth of a plant, including the ascending stem and descending root.

Azalea. Although botanically Azaleas are considered a series or section of the genus Rhododendron, the earlier name persists in horticulture, and in nurseryman usage, so that for garden purposes they may well be considered apart; falling into two groups—those which are grown under glass or indoors, and those which are hardy and grown out of doors.

Indoor Azaleas. These are the so-called 'Indian' Azaleas, though in fact they are derived from *Rhododendron simsii* (*Azalea indica*), a native of China. Evergreen, they may grow to 5 ft or more, but are normally grown as pot plants under glass or indoors, and may be had in bloom from Christmas to May. Plants are usually imported each year from the Continent (Belgium, Holland), where growers specialize in raising plants with clean short stems and a head of branches, well set with flower buds.

Selection. Plants may be simply chosen for flower colour, but named varieties prepared to flower at Christmas are 'Beatrice', semi-double, orange-red; 'Kees Bier', double, red; 'Madame Gau', double, salmon pink; 'Madame Petrick', double, pink; 'Paul Schaeme', semi-double, orange; 'Perle de Noisy', double, salmon and white; 'Petrick Alba', double, white; 'Theo Findeisen', double, brick red. To flower January–March: 'Albert Elizabeth', double, white; 'Apollo', single, brick red; 'Hollandia', double, orange; 'Madame A. Haerens', double, variegated white and pink; 'Pink Pearl', double, rose-lilac; 'Vervaeneana', double, pink, edged white; and forms *rosea, rubra* and *salmonea*; and to flower March–May: 'Ernst Thiers', semi-double, red; 'Hexe', double, red; 'Madame C. van Gele', double, orange-red; 'Madame J. Haerens', double, pink; and 'Niobe', double, white.

Cultivation. Whether grown in the greenhouse or indoors, plants do not need high temperatures, unless being forced into earlier bloom; 10–18° C. (50–65° F.) is right; with regular though moderate watering. After flowering, spent flowers should be picked off, the plants kept growing, with good ventilation and watering, and may be plunged out of doors in the soil or a bed of ashes in May, watered fairly freely, syringed in hot, dry weather, and brought in again in September. Repot, if necessary, April, very firmly, in 3 parts moist peat, 1 part loam, ½ part sand, with good drainage. Prune straggling shoots or branches in April, May, but preserve short new shoots from below spent flower-heads to carry the following year's buds.

Propagation. By cuttings of young shoots, in sandy peat, spring, early summer, in propagating case, bottom heat 15·5° C. (60° F.).

Hardy Azaleas. Gloriously coloured flowering shrubs for spring, which must have lime-free soil, humus-rich with peat or leaf-mould, and reasonably good drainage. If attempted in soils containing lime, iron in an available form (see Fertilizers, *Chelated Compounds*) must be provided. They do well in sun or light shade such as open woodland, and the more dwarf kinds on rock gardens.

Selection. There are some 27 species in the Azalea Series of Rhododendron, mostly deciduous, but some evergreen. *R. (A.) albrechtii*, D., Japan, 3–5 ft, green-spotted, purple-rose, May; *arborescens*, D., E. U.S.A., 20 ft, blood red, June, July; *calendulaceum*, D., N. America, 4–9 ft, orange-scarlet, May; *luteum*, D., Asia Minor, 6–12 ft, yellow, scented, May; *molle*, D., China, 6 ft, golden yellow, May; *obtusum*, E., Japan, 3–5 ft, variable, May, and vs. *amoenum*, E., rose-purple, and *kaempferi*, D., to 8 ft, rose, May; *occidentale*, D., N. America, to 9 ft, white, June, July; *schlippenbachii*, D., Japan, 6–12 ft, pink to rose, May; and *vaseyi*, D., N. America, 8–12 ft, pale pink, May, are the pick for planting in their own right. Major garden interest, however, lies in the various hybrids, of which only a small selection can be named here. Deciduous: *Mollis (Molle)* and so-called *Mollis × sinensis* hybrids, to 4 or 5 ft, with trusses of large scentless flowers, May—'Anthony Koster', golden yellow; 'Babeuff', salmon, orange; 'Col. F. R. Durham', yellow; 'Dr M. Oosthoek', orange-red; 'Dr Reichenbach', salmon-orange; 'Hortulanus Witte', orange-yellow; 'Hugo Koster', salmon-red; 'Koster's Brilliant Red', orange-red; 'Queen Emma', deep orange. *Hardy Ghent*, 6 ft or more, with honeysuckle-like, fragrant flowers, late May, June—*coccinea speciosa*, orange-red; *davesii*, white; 'Gloria Mundi', orange; 'Pallas', red; 'Unique', orange-yellow; and double-flowering forms *narcissiflora*, sulphur yellow, 'Racine', white; 'Raphael de Smet', pale rose. *Rustica flore pleno* hybrids, with double, fragrant flowers, late May, June—'Aida', rose; 'Freya', nankeen pink; 'Phidias', cream, flushed rose; 'Phoebe', sulphur yellow.

Occidentale hybrids, very good for bedding with most sweetly scented flowers, late May, June—'Exquisita', pale rose, orange blotch; 'Graciosa', creamy-pink, orange spot; 'Irene Koster', rose-pink; 'Magnifica', creamy-white, flushed; 'Superba', creamy-pink, orange blotch. 'Exbury' hybrids, English-raised, with wide colour range, May—'Beaulieu', pink to orange; 'Cecile', salmon-orange; 'Embley Crimson'; 'Hotspur', orange-red; 'Klondyke', golden orange; etc.; 'Knap Hill' hybrids, also English raised, similar to the Exburys in range—'Fireglow', orange-vermilion; 'Harvest Moon', pale yellow; 'Persil', white; 'Pink Delight'; 'Satan', flame red; 'Tunis', orange-red.

Evergreen: Japanese Azaleas, of which the 'Kurume' hybrids were introduced from Japan fifty years ago, but which now include hybrids of various species. They may be conveniently divided into small-flowering forms, growing ultimately to 4–5 ft, of which 'Addy Wery', bright red dwarf; *amoena*, double, purple-red; 'Esmeralda', dwarf pink; 'Hinodigiri', red; 'Hinomanyo', soft pink; 'Kirin', soft pink; 'Mother's Day', salmon-red are typical; and large-flowering, such as 'Alice', salmon-red; 'Anny', orange-red; 'Jeanette', deep pink; 'Kathleen', rose-red; 'Orange Beauty'; 'Palestrina', white; 'Schubert', pink; 'Sibelius', orange-red; and 'Vuyk's Scarlet', carmine-red.

Cultivation. Lime-free soil, preferably enriched with peat or leaf-mould. Plant in October–April, somewhat shallowly. Top-dress annually with acid peat or leaves and hardwood sawdust.

Propagation. Species by seeds, sown in sandy peat, outdoor nursery bed, warm shelter. By cuttings of young shoots, taken with a 'heel', July, under hand-light or in frame, in case of hardy sorts. Indoor Azaleas by young cuttings, taken after flowering, in propagating case, with steady bottom heat, 15·5° C. (60° F.).

Azaleodendron. The name sometimes given to hybrids of species of the Azalea section and other species of Rhododendron. They require similar culture to Azaleas. The following are hardy and typical: × *azaleoides*, 6 ft or more, large trusses, white, tinged purple, fragrant flowers, June, July; × *govenianum*, light purple, June; and named forms 'Dot', rosy-crimson; 'Galloper Light', apricot-pink; and 'Nellie', white blotched yellow, flowering June.

Azara (a-za'ra. Fam. Flacourtiaceae). Evergreen shrubs from Chile, grown for their ornamental leaves with large, leaf-like stipules, and small but most pleasantly vanilla-scented flowers in early spring; but not reliably hardy.

Selection. A. microphylla, 10 ft or more, has dark shining green leaves, and tiny yellow flowers, but needs a warm, sheltered wall in other than mild areas; *variegata* is a form with creamy edged leaves; *lanceolata*, with narrowly oval leaves, soft yellow flowers in rather erect spikes, may be tried; *integrifolia*, stronger growing to 30 ft, and its vs. *brownea* and *variegata*, bear purplish flowers with bright yellow stamens, early in the year, but needs warm shelter or greenhouse conditions; *petiolaris* (*gilliesii*), to 10 ft, with creamy-yellow racemes of flowers in April, May, is best grown as a cool greenhouse shrub as a pot plant.

Cultivation. Well-drained, humus-rich soil suits, in warm, sunny positions; planting in April or October; mulching annually; and pruning, when necessary, after flowering, May.

Propagation. By cuttings, in spring, in propagating case, bottom heat of 15·5° C. (65° F.).

Azolla (a-zol'la. Fam. Salviniaceae). Floating aquatic plants of which *A. caroliniana*, America, is commonly introduced into aquaria or garden pools to give shade. With delicate, feathery foliage, it multiplies quickly by simple division, and needs watching; colours beautifully, green and red in the open.

Azureus (-a, -um). Sky blue. Ex. *Ceanothus azureus.*

B

Babiana, Baboon-root (bab-i-a′na. Fam. Iridaceae). Cormous plants of S. Africa, with lanceolate leaves and flower spikes carrying several pretty starred flowers in late spring.

Selection. B. stricta, 1 ft, with white and blue flowers, May, and its vs. *rubrocyanea,* with flowers of bright blue and crimson; *sulphurea,* pale yellow; and *villosa,* 6 in., crimson; are chiefly grown.

Cultivation. Being somewhat tender, the plants can only be grown outdoors in mild areas, planting corms in autumn or early winter, warm, sunny, sheltered position, sandy loam soil; 4–5 in. deep, 2 in. apart; lifting when foliage dies, for replanting. They are more successfully grown in pots; potted in October, porous compost, four corms to a 4-in. pot, and grown in cool greenhouse, winter temp. 5–10° C. (40–50° F.), watering regularly when shoots show through, gradually drying off when flowering is over.

Baccatus (-a, -um). Baccate, having berries. Ex. *Malus baccata.*

Baccharis (bak′kar-is. Fam. Compositae). Of nearly 300 species, two are hardy shrubs useful for seaside planting in exposed places.

Selection. B. halimifolia, the Groundel Tree, N. U.S.A., 6–12 ft, is deciduous, with glossy green leaves, dense panicles of white flowers in autumn; and *patagonica,* to 10 ft, evergreen small-leaved, nondescript yellowish-white flowers in May are grown, chiefly for cover.

Cultivation. Ordinary to poor soil. Plant October or March, April. Prune in May, June.

Propagation. By cuttings of young shoots in summer, inserted in porous soil, under handlight.

Bachelor's Buttons. *See* Ranunculus, and Lychnis.

Bacteria (Schizomycetes), or Fission Fungi. Microscopic, one-celled organisms, which increase by simple division. They may be round (cocci), rod-like (bacilli), curved (vibros), twisted (spirilla) and filamentous (clonothrix). They are present everywhere, especially in soil, and play important parts in Nature's economy. Some are parasitic, and cause disease in man, animals and plants. Many are beneficial, especially autotrophic forms such as soil types responsible for the oxidization of organic matter to humus, etc., and the fixing of nitrogen, and conversion of nitrogenous com-

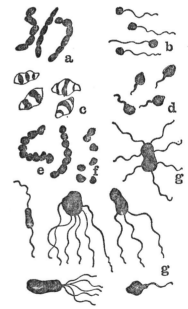

FIG. 25   Bacteria: a. rod-like *Azotobacter* sp.; b. nitrite *Nitrosomonas* sp.; c. Nodule *Radicicola*; d. tailed Nitrobacteria; e. Chain *Cocci* sp.; f. Nitrogen-fixing Azotobacter *chroococcum*; g. various forms of flagellated bacteria.

pounds into plant nutrients in the soil, and other inorganic compounds.

Bacteriosis. Plant diseases caused by bacteria.

Baeria (ba-er'i-a. Fam. Compositae). Hardy annuals of which *B. coronaria*, California, is sometimes sown in April, where it is to grow as an edging or semi-prostrate plant, with fernlike foliage, and yellow composite flowers in summer, which can be dried for winter decoration. Any ordinary soil and sun will suit.

Ball, Soil. The mass of soil, permeated by the roots of a plant, when removed from a pot, or carefully lifted from the open ground.

Balloon Flower. *See* Platycodon.

Balm (*Melissa officinalis*, Fam. Labiatae). An aromatic perennial herb of central S. Europe, growing 2 ft, in any ordinary well-drained soil. The leaves, with a pleasant lemony aroma, are used to flavour soups, stews and sauces, or for making a cooling tea, both fresh and dried. Propagated by division of rhizomes in early autumn, or may be grown from seeds sown in April, May.

Balm, Bastard. See *Melittis melissophyllum*.

Balm, Bee. See *Monarda didyma*.

Balm of Gilead. See *Populus candicans*.

Balsam. See *Impatiens balsamina*.

Balsam Poplar. *See* Populus.

Bamboo. The common name for elegant and graceful woody grasses which are now found botanically under *Arundinaria, Phyllostachys, Bambusa, Pleioblastus, Pseudosasa, Sasa* and *Sinarundinaria*.

Bambusa (bam-bu'sa. Fam. Gramineae). The genus is now one of tropical bamboos, which can be grown only in heated palm houses in Britain. *B. arundinacea*, evergreen, India, Burma and Ceylon, 30–50 ft, and *vulgaris*, Indies, Africa, S. America, evergreen to 40 ft, are found at Kew.

Banana. *See* Musa.

Baneberry. *See* Actaea.

Banks. Banks between different levels in a garden usually require some form of plant cover. Fine lawn grasses, kept well mown, are excellent, provided the slope is not too abrupt. It is best to lay turf from the bottom upward, fixing each with a wooden peg until the whole knits

and roots. Mowing is simplified by using a hover-type machine. Early spring flowering bulbs may be planted in the grass, though this inhibits cutting until the bulb foliage has withered.

Low-growing shrubs make good bank cover, such as *Hypericum calycinum, Cotoneaster dammeri, Euonymus radicans variegata, Veronica pageana, Helianthemum nummularium* vs., *Erica carnea, Erica × darleyensis, Vinca major* and *V. minor*. Taller shrubs with spreading growth such as *Cotoneaster horizontalis, C. microphylla, Forsythia suspensa, Berberis × stenophylla*, Wichuraiana ramble roses may also be used, their stems being pegged down as required. On lime-free soil, the full range of heaths and heathers may be planted, with creepers such as *Pernettya mucronata* and *Gaultheria shallon*, and possibly dwarf rhododendrons or azaleas.

Another treatment is to anchor the soil with flattish pieces of rock or paving flags, and plant evergreen perennials such as Armeria, Aubrieta, *Cerastium tomentosum*, Nepeta, *Stachys lanata, Saponaria ocymoides, Iberis sempervirens* and *Thymus serpyllum* and vs., in the interstices. A steep bank can be improved by a low retaining wall built at its base.

Banksia, Australian Honeysuckle (banks'i-a. Fam. Protaceae). Australian evergreen shrubs with beautiful foliage, and yellow flowers in dense spikes in summer. Not reliably hardy, they are best grown in a cool, airy greenhouse or conservatory.

Selection. B. dryandroides, to 5 ft, with finely divided foliage, and stems and leaves with reddish-brown hairs, very handsome; *collina*, to 8 ft, green and silvery foliage, purple flower heads; *integrifolia*, to 10 ft, large, wedge-shaped leaves, silvery beneath; *quercifolia*, 5 ft, deeply cut leaves; *marginata*, 5 ft, small, spiny leaves, white beneath; and *serrata*, to 20 ft, deeply toothed, long narrow leaves, are all delightful ornamental plants.

Cultivation. Pot in April, porous compost, water increasingly with rising temperature, and gradually decrease with winter, keeping just moist, winter temp. 10° C. (50° F.).

Propagation. By cuttings of ripe shoots, July–August, in sandy loam, in

propagating case, bottom heat 15·5° C.
(60° F.).

Baptisia (bap-tis'i-a. Fam. Leguminosae). Hardy perennials from N.
America, distinctive for their trifoliolate
leaves and racemes of pealike flowers in
early summer.

Selection. B. australis, 4 ft, with blue
flowers, is commonly grown; others are
alba, 2–4 ft, white; *leucantha*, 2 ft, white,
purple; and *tinctoria*, 2–3 ft, yellow.

Cultivation. Any good friable, porous
soil; full sun. Plant March in borders.

Propagation. By division in early
spring; by seeds sown outdoors in sandy
loam, April.

Barbados Gooseberry. See *Pereskia
aculeata*.

Barbados Lily. See *Hippeastrum
equestre*.

Barbarea (bar-ba're-a. Fam. Cruciferae). Perennial herbs, of which *B.
praecox*, Europe, is grown as a winter
salad plant (*see* Land Cress). *B. vulgaris*
v. *flore pleno*, Double *Yellow Rocket*, 15 in.
may be grown in rock or flower garden,
and propagated by spring division or by
summer cuttings.

Barbatus. Bearded. Ex. *Penstemon
barbatus*.

Barberry. *See* Berberis.

Barberton Daisy. *See* Gerbera.

Bark. Strictly, the outermost sheath of
cork cells of the stems of dicotyledons.
More generally applied to the tissues out-
lying the wood of the stem, and separated
from it by the cambium cells. *See*
Cambium.

Bark Reversal. A method of dwarfing or
checking wood growth in apple, pear and
fig trees, and promoting early bearing. A
narrow band of bark (⅜ in. wide or less) is
carefully removed from the stem or main
branches of the tree and replaced
reversed, immediately; bottom edge to
the top, top edge to the bottom of the
cut, and fastened in place with transparent adhesive tape. A razor-sharp
knife is necessary, as the operation needs
surgical precision, but it is held to be
more permanent in effect than bark-
ringing (q.v.).

Bark Slitting. A method of overcoming
a bark-bound condition, especially in
stone fruit trees, inducing fruitfulness.
A single unbroken cut is made on the
north side of the tree, from the fork of

the first branch to the ground. On bush
trees, the main branches may be slit,
running the cuts into the one in the main
stem. Carried out in early spring.

Bark-bound. A term applied to trees
when the bark fails to expand or split
naturally to allow growth. It is apt to
occur where moisture conditions are
subject to much fluctuation in ill-
drained soils.

Bark-ringing. An operation designed
to check over-vigorous growth and
induce fruiting, especially in apple and
pear trees. It consists of removing a ring
of bark tissue from the main stem or
branches in spring. The bark is cut down
to the wood. It can be removed in a
narrow (¼-in.) band in a complete band;
or two semicircles of bark, an inch or so
apart, from opposite sides of the stem,
½ in. wide, can be removed; or bark can
be removed in an interrupted ring, ½ in.
wide and 1½–2-in. long pieces. The cuts
should be covered with adhesive tape
afterwards. It takes two years to take
effect.

Barometer (*baros*, weight; *metron*, a
measure). An instrument for measuring
atmospheric weight or pressure; useful to
the gardener in helping to determine
probable changes in the weather. Various
types are available, based either on a
column of mercury (straight-tube or
siphon barometers) or a near vacuum
(aneroid barometer). A barograph is a
self-recording barometer.

Barren Wort. *See* Epimedium.

Bartonia. *See* Mentzelia.

Base. The point at which a leaf or a
shoot grows from its support plant part.

Base, Basic. Alkali, alkaline. Used of
soils, the chief base minerals being
calcium, magnesium and potassium.

Basic Slag. A by-product of steel-
making, consisting of the slag formed
when the phosphorus in iron ores unites
with lime and magnesia used for lining
the furnaces. When ground, it is used as
a slow-acting phosphatic fertilizer, also
providing lime. Quality varies, with an
analysis of 8–18·5 per cent phosphoric
acid. Solubility also varies, and is valued
according to solubility, and therefore
availability, in 2 per cent citric acid.
Effectiveness depends on the fineness of
grinding. Good quality basic slag should
be 80 per cent citric-acid-soluble,

sufficiently finely ground for 80 per cent to pass through a sieve of 10,000 meshes per square inch. Most useful for autumn or winter application at 4–8 oz. per sq. yd, for the orchard and garden generally, where lime is also helpful. On lawns, it tends to encourage clover, and is less suitable. *See* Fertilizers.

Basil, Sweet (*Ocimum basilicum*). This tropical herb may be grown as a tender annual for its foliage, which is used to flavour soups, stews, ragouts and sauces and as a salading. Seeds are sown in April under glass, to be pricked off and planted out 6–8 in. apart in a bed of porous, humus-rich soil in June, and grown on until freshly in flower, when the plants are cut and gathered for bunching and drying in airy shade. May also be pot-grown in a cool greenhouse. *O. minimum*, Bush Basil, Chile, is regarded as a dwarf form, and may be grown similarly.

Baskets, Basket Plants. Hanging baskets provide a very attractive way of growing trailing and tender plants for display in greenhouse, conservatory or porches. The baskets may be made, semi-hemispherical, in galvanized or plastic-covered wire, 10–14 in. across, or in plastic. A wired basket is first lined with fresh moss, then filled with a suitable compost such as JIP, and planted up at the same time. Good growing conditions require a temperature of 15·5–18° C. (60–65° F.), regular and liberal watering, with syringing to keep the moss fresh and green, but shade from hot scorching sun.

Plants. Baskets may be planted with one type of plants (e.g. Begonias, Achimenes, etc.) or a variety. Most suitable are *Begonia fuchsioides*, *B.* × 'Gloire de Lorraine', *Columnea banksii*, spreading Fuchsias such as 'Doctor', 'Cascade', etc., Ivy-leaved Pelargonium, Hoya, Achimenes, Lachenalia, *Saxifraga sarmentosa*, *Tradescantia* spp., *Zebrina* spp., and ferns such as *Adiantum cuneatum* and other Spleenworts, *Davallia canariense*, *Nephrolepis* spp., Selaginella. For porch or veranda baskets, 'Geraniums', *Campanula fragilis*, *C. garganica*, *C. isophylla*, and vs., and annuals such as *Lobelia gracilis*. *L. tenuior*, Nasturtiums, *Begonia lloydii* vs., and other trailers are most useful.

Bass or **Bast.** The fibres of the inner bark of Lime trees (*Tilia*), once much used for tying, but now superseded by raffia and plastic materials. Bass-mats (Archangel Mats) from Russia are useful for frame frost-protection, if available.

Bast. In botany, the growing substance of the phloem (q.v.); sieve tubes and tissue being soft bast, the fibres, hard bast.

Bastard Trenching. A method of digging in which the soil is moved to twice the depth of the spade or fork without the subsoil being brought to the top; most useful in breaking in new ground and for incorporating soil-amending materials, especially on heavier soils. *See* Digging.

Bathing-pool. When a feature of a garden, a bathing-pool should be sited in full sun, but as sheltered and secluded as possible. Permanent pools are usually of reinforced concrete or fibreglass; more temporary ones of rubber or plastic sheeting construction. Means of keeping the water hygienically clean and clear must be provided by a filtration unit or the use of chemicals. Shelter and privacy may be provided by planting evergreen hedges.

Bauera (baw'e-ra. Fam. Saxifragaceae). An Australian genus of small evergreen shrubs, of which *B. rubioides*, 15–18 in., makes a pretty shrub, with nodding pink or white flowers almost all the year round, for a cool greenhouse.

Cultivation. Pot in March–April, JIP compost, and repot annually until in 5- or 6-in. pots. May be plunged in ashes or soil out of doors, June–September. Winter temp. 5–10° C. (40–50° F.). Prune to shape in April.

Propagation. By cuttings of young half-ripe shoots in April–May, in propagating case, bottom heat of 15·5° C. (60° F.).

Bay, Bay Laurel, Bay Tree. *See* Laurus.

Bead Plant. *See* Nertera.

Beam, White. See *Sorbus aria.*

Bean Tree. *See* Ceratonia.

Beans, Broad (*Vicia faba*). This hardy annual food plant, one of the oldest in cultivation, is grown for its seeds. Does well on most soils, except the water-logged or very dry, but best on well-dug heavyish loams; organically manured for a previous crop such as potatoes or autumn cauliflower. Acid soils should be dressed with lime or basic slag in autumn. A high phosphate base fertilizer may be given prior to sowing, say 3 parts by weight superphosphate, 1 part sulphate of potash, 1 part ammonium sulphate, at 2 oz. per sq. yd.

October–November sowings may be made on well-drained soils in warm districts; 'Aquadulce Claudia' or 'Seville' v. The main crop is sown in March–April; seeds placed 3 in. deep, 9 in. apart, in double rows 10 in. apart, with 30 in. between the double rows. Dwarf vs. may be sown 6 in. apart, and are useful for early cropping under glass, sown in December–January, in deep boxes.

Varieties. White-seeded—Longpod, Giant Windsor, Aquadulce Claudia, Seville. Red-seeded—Red Emperor. Green-seeded—Green Longpod, Green Windsor. Dwarf—Sutton Dwarf, Beck's Dwarf Gem, Royal Dwarf Fan. Mazagan is a small-podded, tall variety.

Diseases. The chief is Chocolate Spot, caused by the fungus *Botrytis cinerea*; most common on autumn-sown crops and under wet conditions. Prevention lies partly in providing good drainage and an open situation, with adequate lime, phosphates and potash. A sulphur or thiram fungicide can be used to check infection. Rust, caused by the fungus *Uromyces fabae*, shows in whitish spots, turning pale brown and then dark. No special treatment can be recommended, but infected plants should be carefully burnt after cropping.

Beans, French or **Kidney** (*Phaseolus vulgaris*). A tender annual originating in subtropical America, but reaching us through France.

Cultivation. Do best in lightish, organically rich soils, with lime content, but succeed on all well-dug, properly drained soils, brought to pH 6·5–7·0 by liming, and base fertilized as for Broad Beans. Sow when soil is warm, 18° C. (65° F.), late April–July; 2 in. deep, 4–6 in. apart, in rows 18 in. apart. Mulch after rain when seedlings are well up.

Varieties. The Prince, Canadian Wonder, Masterpiece, Phoenix Claudia, etc. Mont D'or Waxpod is yellow podded. Types grown for seeds to be dried are Green Gem, Green Flageolet, and Haricots Brown Dutch and Comtesse de Chambord Improved; Tender and True is a climbing variety.

French Beans may be grown under glass, in frames or greenhouse, temp. 13–18° C. (55–65° F.), choosing vs. Fifty Days or Lightning. Sow in 8- to 10-in. pots, 1 in. deep, 3 in. apart, JIP 2 compost; stand on chippings, keep moderately watered. Sow September–March at 3- to 4-week intervals for early crops .

Beans, Scarlet Runner (*Phaseolus multiflorus*). Naturally perennial, but grown as an annual, originating from S. America, for its long pods.

Soil. May be grown in almost any soil, not waterlogged, strongly acid, shallow or dry, but does best in lightish, deep loams, rich with organic matter. Lime to bring to pH 6·5. Base fertilize as for Broad Beans. Sow in May–June, 3 in. deep, 6 in. apart, in double rows 15 in. apart; spacing double rows 6 ft apart. On heavy soils, it is worth sowing two seeds per station, removing the weaker seedling, to avoid misses. Mulch after rain when 8 in. high, and train up canes, stakes, trellis or twine to 6–10 ft.

Varieties. Prizewinner, Streamline and Sutton's Scarlet are good. Kelvedon Marvel and Princeps are less tall, 5–6 ft, and earlier cropping. Blue Coco and Scarlet Ornamental (Robin Bean) are novelties. Hammond's Dwarf Scarlet, 16–18 in., is a variety that does not need staking.

Diseases. Anthracnose is a fungus infection (*Colletotrichum lindemuthianum*) causing dark, sunken spots or blotches on French and Runner Beans, best controlled by the application of a copper or thiram fungicide, when seen. Halo Blight shows in darkish spots on leaves surrounded by light-coloured areas, and is caused by a bacterium, *Bacterium medicaginis* v. *phaseolicola*, usually in wet seasons. It seldom is very damaging, but infected plants and foliage should be burnt after cropping.

Bearberry. *See* Arctostaphylos.

Bear's Breeches. *See* Acanthus.

Bear's Foot. *See* Acanthus.

Beaufortia (bo-fort'i-a. Fam. Myrtaceae). Small, evergreen, heath-like shrubs of W. Australia, with colourful heads of flowers in early summer.

Selection. B. *decussata*, scarlet flowers, *purpurea*, purple, and *sparsa*, red, grow to about 3 ft, flowering in May–June.

Cultivation. Pot in March, equal parts loam, peat and leaf-mould, with a little coarse sand; warm greenhouse, temp. 15·5–18° C. (60–65° F.); water freely with growth, very moderately in winter, with temp. 10° C. (50° F.). Prune to shape in March.

Propagation. By cuttings of side-shoots, taken late June or July, in sandy loam, bottom heat 15·5° C. (60° F.).

Beaumontia (bo-mon′ti-a. Fam. Apocynaceae). The species chiefly grown is B. *grandiflora*, a twining climber of 15 ft or more from India, with large white trumpet-shaped flowers in summer, for the warm greenhouse; summer temp. 21–27° C. (70–80° F.); winter 15·5–18° C. (60–65° F.). May be grown in the border or a tub, compost of 2 parts each loam and peat, 1 part sand, watering freely in growth, very moderately in winter.

Propagation. By cuttings of half-ripe shoots, in spring, sandy compost, bottom heat 18° C. (65° F.).

Bed. In gardening a term descriptive of an area or piece of ground specially prepared as (*a*) a seed bed, for sowing small seeds; (*b*) a nursery bed, for raising plants from cuttings, or growing-on seedlings or small collections of young plants; (*c*) a vegetable bed (i.e. onion bed), for the growing of certain vegetables or herbs; (*d*) a flower bed, usually devoted to the growing of one or more types of flowering or ornamental plants, especially annuals and biennials, often isolated in grass, stone paving or gravel. The shape of flower beds should accord with their site and the space available. Although the outline may be as intricate as personal preference dictates, it is wise to keep it simple, especially in lawns, having regard to the time and labour which must be given to edge-trimming. Simple rectangular, circular, oval, crescent beds are easiest to maintain, bearing in mind that modern design suggests that they should be to the flanks and ends of lawns, leaving an open central space, which facilitates mowing. After all, it is the beauty and display of the plants that creates the greatest effect. In practice, the size of the bed should have some relation to the plants

chosen for it, and to the ease of maintenance in tending the plants. Broadly, the tallest plants are set in the centre of beds, and other plants graduate in size to the lowest at the outer edges of the beds, but perfect symmetry need not be too zealously pursued.

Bedding and Bedding Plants. Formerly bedding implied the planting-out of half-hardy plants, in May or June, for summer display. Today it covers the planting-out of plants for display at other seasons too, but which occupy the soil for a limited period. Hardy and non-hardy plants are used. Beds are prepared by bastard trenching, and amending to produce a fairly porous soil, provided with humus, and of a pH 6·0–6·5. Heavy clayey soils can be lightened with gypsum, coarse sand and grit. Light soils are basically improved by adding a few loads of clay or heavy loam. All soils need rotted organic matter every other year, with bone-meal; with a fertilizer high in phosphates in spring.

Spring Bedding. Plants are raised from seed in the previous year, ready to plant out when the summer show is over, in September–October. Beds can be devoted to one species in one variety or a mixture. Wallflowers, Polyanthus, Primroses, Alpine Auriculas may be used in this way. Or they may be combined with bulbs to flower at the same time, particularly tulips, such as the lily flowering, cottage and late double varieties, chosen to harmonize. Tulips, of course, are ideal bedding subjects in themselves. They may be enhanced by being accompanied by carpeting plants, such as *Alyssum saxatile compactum*, *Myosotis alpestris* (Forget-me-nots), Pansies, *Iberis sempervirens*, raised from seed. In all but cold districts, several hardy annuals can be raised from seed in summer, to bed in early autumn and flower early the following year, as ground cover for bulbs or in simple combinations. Alyssum, Calendula, Candytuft, Eschscholtzia, Linaria, Silene and annual Sweet William are usually successful. The hybrid strains of Anemone—Caen, St Bavo, St Brigid and *Anemone fulgens*—go well with the low annuals. When flowering is over, bulbs may be carefully lifted and transferred to trenches on reserve ground to finish their growth; and perennials, lifted with soil balls about their roots, can be replanted in spare ground to free the beds for summer.

Summer Bedding. For summer display beds are planted up with half-hardy and near-hardy annuals raised from seeds under glass; with non-hardy perennials which have over-wintered under frost-protection, and with certain bulbs or cormous plants. Some annuals lend themselves to populating beds on their own, in self-colours, simple harmonies or mixed. Beds of Antirrhinum, Calceolaria, Godetia, Asters, Nemesia, Penstemon, Petunia, Stocks, Sweet William, Salvia, Tropaeolum, Verbena and Zinnia are admirably long in flower. Non-hardy plants that may also be used alone are Begonias, both tuberous and multiflora types; dwarf Dahlias, Gloxinias and 'Geraniums'. Mixed plantings may be made with dwarf or carpeting annuals, drawing on such kinds as Ageratum, Alyssum, Daisies (*Bellis perennis*), Convolvulus, Clarkia, Gaillardia, Heliotrope, Marigolds, Tagetes, *Phlox drummondii*, Silene, Viola and Viscaria. Lobelia, Tagetes, white Alyssum are often used in formal bedding together with zonal 'Geraniums', especially in municipal gardens. Taller plants often employed also include Fuchsias, Abutilons, Iresines, Cannas, Solanums, Nicotiana, *Eucalyptus globosus*, etc.

Foliage contrast can be introduced by the use of *Cineraria maritima* for its silvery white leaves; *Helichrysum microphyllum*, *Eulalia japonica*, *Zea japonica gigantea quadricolor*, ornamental cabbage and kale, and grasses such as *Coix lacrima*. *Eragrostis elegans* and *Tricholaena rosea*.

Bedeguar, Moss Gall, Robin's Pin-cushion. Reddish moss-like growths or galls found on shoots of wild roses and sometimes on cultivated roses; caused by a small gall-wasp, *Rhodites rosae*, laying eggs in buds which hatch into grubs feeding on the rose and setting up the abnormal growth in reaction. It is sufficient to cut out the galls when seen.

Bee Orchis. *See* Ophrys.

Beech. *See* Fagus.

Bees, Hive or **Honey** (*Apis mellifica*). Hive or Honey Bees are very useful in gardens not only for the honey they produce but for pollination, especially valuable in cross-pollinating fruits. In orchards, the hives should be placed near together rather than scattered. A healthy colony in winter consists of 40,000 neuter or worker bees, headed by a fertile, egg-laying queen; rising to 80,000 or more in summer, when female and male bees are reared as well as workers to promote propagation, usually taking the form of swarming. In autumn males are cast out, and only colonies headed by a fertile queen can survive the winter. Bees have a foraging range of about 2 miles radius, though tending to concentrate on flower resources nearest the hive. They collect pollen and nectar from flowers for food; also need water, and a substance called propolis. A surplus of honey can only be expected when bees have access to specific flowers in abundance. Usually this depends on resources outside the average garden. Honey flows or surpluses are likely to occur from fruit blossom in spring, white clover in summer, lime in late summer, and heather in late summer and autumn. It is not possible to stock a garden with bee-flowers to keep them the year round, unless very big. Bees visit a wide range of flowers, particularly white, blue, pink, green, purple blossoms, and those heavy with pollen and/or nectar. Gardening beekeepers should concentrate on providing winter-flowering Heaths, Crocus, Snowdrops, Aconites, etc., to give early pollen for colony building; later flowering plants are Mignonette, Nepeta, Limnanthes, Lavender, Candytuft, Silene, Thymes, most herbs, and bulbs. Limes are much liked, but *Tilia × orbicularis*. *T. petiolaris* and *T. tomentosa* should be avoided as the flowers sometimes have harmful effects on bees. Extra care needs to be taken when using pesticides for the control of plant diseases and pests in all gardens, since many substances are toxic to both honey bees and wild bees. Insecticides based on BHC, DDT, Derris, Malathion, Nicotine and Pyrethrum are toxic to bees. To avoid damage (*a*) a clean water supply should be provided near hives, so that bees are less likely to drink from dew or rain contaminated with pesticide residues; (*b*) lead arsenate, which is very persistent, should not be used for spraying; (*c*) applications should be correctly timed, with a close season of no spraying or dusting when flower blossoms being visited by bees are open.

Beetroot (*Beta vulgaris*, Fam. Chenopodiaceae). This vegetable, grown for its red-fleshed swollen roots, is a biennial, but is grown as an annual, and its forms stem from a wild seashore plant of Britain, Europe, N. Africa and Asia Minor.

Soil. Well-drained sandy loam or a friable porous soil, preferably well dug and manured for a previous crop of potatoes, onions, brassicas or legumes, but not spinach or other roots; limed to bring to pH 6·5, and base-fertilized with a high phosphate dressing. Sow seeds in late April or May, 1 in. deep, in rows 1 ft apart; thinning at seedling stage to 4–6 in. apart. 'Seeds' are capsules containing several seeds, but remain viable for 10 years. For exhibition roots, make round holes, 2 ft deep, fill with JIP compost and sow one seed per hole.

Varieties. Globe, for early cropping— Detroit, Early Bunch, Show Bench. Oval or Tankard—Blood Red, Spangsbjerg Cylinder. Long—Green-top, Exhibition.

To store, lift, free from soil, twist off leaves and keep in dry, cool, frostproof place, on straw.

Spinach Beet, grown for its leaves, requires similar soil treatment; sow in April for summer use; in August for winter use, thinning seedlings to 9 in. apart.

Silver Seakale Beet (Swiss Chard). May be grown as for Spinach Beet for its fleshy leaf-stems and mid-ribs, cooked like Seakale.

Begonia (be-go'ni-a. Fam. Begoniaceae). A large genus of tender perennials found in warm climates of the world, varied in form, size and nature, but may be grouped according to type as tuberous rooted, fibrous rooted and ornamental-leaved.

Tuberous. The plants grown today are largely the race of florists' large-flowered hybrids, of which the chief parents are such species as *B. boliviensis*, *davisii*, *pearcei*, *rosaeflora* and *veitchii*, natives of S. America, and sometimes grouped as *B. tuber-hybrida*. They may be subdivided into (i) large single-flowered, deckle-edged or picot-edged petals; and (ii) large double-flowered, subdivided into rosebud or rose-flowered, camellia-

flowered (*camelliaeflora*), fimbriated or finely deckle-edged (*fimbriata*), and bicoloured (*marmorata*), according to petal formation and shape. The range of colours is great, from dark red, through copper, salmon, scarlet, pinks, orange and yellow to white. Many nurserymen simply offer them by flower colour and shape. For named forms and latest hybrids the catalogues of specialists should be consulted.

Plants are erect growing, with branching stems, 1 ft or more; with unisexual flowers, the smaller (female) usually showing below the more showy male

Cultivation. For greenhouse or indoor flowering, tubers may be planted from February onwards, singly in 5- or 6-in. pots, JIP 2 compost, or equal parts loam, leaf-mould and sand, with half a part rotted sifted farmyard manure. They need shade, regular watering and temp. of 18–21° C. (65–70° F.). For outdoor planting, tubers are started in March in shallow boxes, in a mixture of equal parts light loam and leaf-mould or moist peat; temp. 18–21° C. (65–70° F.); watered increasingly with growth, in light, airy conditions with shade from hot sun, occasional liquid feeding, and planted out in May; humus-rich, porous soil, partial shade. Lift in September, dry off tubers, and store in dryish peat, under frostproof conditions, minimum temp. 10° C. (50° F.).

Propagation. Named forms by stem cuttings of young shoots, in spring or summer, inserted in porous compost, in propagating case, bottom heat of 18° C. (65° F.). By seeds sown in February–March, with bottom heat of 21° C. (70° F.).

Small-flowered Tubers. These are offered under *B. multiflora*, and consist of compact-growing plants, of 6–10 in., bearing masses of bright, long-lasting single or double flowers, and are ideal for small beds, narrow borders, and even the rock garden, or for pots. Often offered by colour, fine named forms are Flamboyant, scarlet; Frene Eysser, salmon-copper; Jewel, orange; Le Madelon, rose-pink; Mayor Max, orange-scarlet; Helen Harms, yellow; Mrs Richard Galle, gold, crimson flushed; and Rambouillet, flame red.

Particularly suitable for hanging baskets are the pendulous forms listed under *pendula*, such as Betha, salmon pink; Dawn, yellow, flushed salmon; Golden Shower, golden yellow; Irene, pale pink; and Sunset, salmon-orange.

Fibrous-rooted. A large group of tropical or subtropical plants, consisting of many species and varieties of a shrubby habit which are chiefly grown in the warm greenhouse, and herbaceous species of which *B. semperflorens*, its varieties and hybrids, are important for summer bedding. Notable for the greenhouse, conservatory or indoor rooms are: *B. acutifolia*, Jamaica, 3–4 ft, white; *coccinea*, Brazil, 2–3 ft, red, and its hybrid 'President Carnot'; *angularis*, Brazil, to 8 ft, white; *dregei*, S. Africa, to 3 ft, white; *foliosa*, Columbia, 2 ft, white; *fuchsioides*, Mexico, 4–6 ft, scarlet; *haageana*, Brazil, 2 ft, rose-pink; *incarnata*, Mexico, 2 ft, rose; × *lucerna*, 2–4 ft, pink; *maculata*, Brazil, 2–3 ft, rose; *nitida*, Jamaica, 4–6 ft, rose; and *venosa*, Brazil, to 4 ft, white; with the exception of *B. dregei*, flowering in autumn, winter or spring. *B. albococcinea*, India, 1½ ft, rose and white, summer; *glaucophylla*, Brazil, climbing or trailing, brick-red; *heracleifolia*, Mexico, 2–4 ft, rose, winter; *hydrocotylifolia*, Mexico, 1 ft, rose, summer; and *manicata*, Mexico, 1 ft, pink, winter, are more rhizamatous-rooted. *B. socotrana*, Isle of Socotrana, 1½ ft, bright rose, winter, is interesting as the only bulbous species. Crossed with *B. dregei*, it provides some beautiful winter-flowering hybrids such as 'Gloire de Lorraine', reddish pink; 'Turnford Hall', white; 'Glory of Cincinnati', pink; 'Mrs J. A. Petersen', rose-red; 'Eve's Favourite', deep pink; and 'The Fairy', pale pink. Crossed with *B. subpeltata*, it gives 'Gloire de Sceaux', pink; and with certain tuberous species notable winter-flowering forms such as 'Altrincham Pink'; 'Clibran's Crimson', 'Clibran's Red'; 'Emita', orange-scarlet; 'Exquisite', pink; 'Fascination', orange-scarlet; 'Her Majesty', coppery orange; 'Optima', salmon; and 'Scarlet Beauty'; 1–1½ ft tall.

Cultivation. Woody or shrubby species in pots; JIP 2 compost or as for tubers. Pot in April. Water freely in active growth, moderately in winter; minimum winter temp. 15·5° C. (60° F.); give good light, but shade from hot direct sun. Winter-flowering kinds need to be rested after flowering, with little watering, temp. 10° C. (55° F.), until about early May. Give moist atmosphere in summer, by mist-spraying daily.

Propagation. By cuttings of young shoots, taken in early spring, in propagating case, bottom heat 18–21° C. (65–70° F.). By leaf cuttings in summer (*see* page 79).

Fibrous-rooted Bedding Begonias. *B. semperflorens*, Brazil, 6–12 in., white or rose flowers in summer, is the characteristic parent of an increasing range of exceptionally floriferous strains of neat plants for pots, vases, window-boxes and bedding or edging borders, in bloom all summer until the first frost. 'Coral Pink', 'Crimson Bedder', 'Loveliness' and 'Rosabella' are old favourites, but there are now improved F_1 hybrid strains commanding attention, such as 'Thousand Wonders', and up-to-date catalogues should be consulted.

Cultivation. Although perennial, the trend is to raise these plants from seed as half-hardy annuals, sowing under glass, 15·5–18° C. (60–65° F.), and growing on to plant out in late May or June. May be lifted in September and wintered in a warm greenhouse, with soil kept just moist.

Ornamental Leaved. Begonias grown for their magnificently textured, veined and coloured foliage are chiefly rhizomatous-rooted. The most valuable is probably *B. rex*, Assam, a parent of several outstanding forms such as 'King Henry', 'Hoar Frost', 'Silver Queen' and 'Isolde'. Others include *B. albopicta*, Brazil, 1½ ft, silver-spotted, glossy green; × *argenteo-guttata*, white flecked shining green, white and pink flowers; *cathayana*, China, 2–3 ft, crimson-leaved; *daedalea*, Mexico, 1 ft, green and russet; *imperialis*, Mexico, 9 in., olive and bright green; *masoniana*. Indo-China (?), 1 ft, grey-green with purple Iron Cross markings; *rajah*, Malaya, 1 ft, brown-red, green-veined; while *B. maculata* and vs., variable leaf marking, and *metallica*, Bahia, 3 ft, green and reddish, are fine foliaged fibrous-rooting kinds; and *B.* × *weltoniensis* is a tuberous hybrid, 1–3 ft, with red-veined, yellowish green leaves, tolerant of light and room conditions, and an old favourite in cottage windows.

Cultivation. On the same lines as for fibrous-rooted, greenhouse types. Many will make good house plants, given sufficient humidity, with abundant water in active growth, very moderate in winter; winter temp. 15·5–18° C. (60–65° F.).

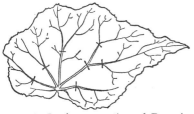

FIG. 26 Leaf propagation of Begonia; underside of leaf showing where cuts are made at vein junctions.

FIG. 27 A Begonia plantlet growing from a leaf pegged on the soil, seen in section.

Propagation. By leaf cuttings in spring and summer; taking mature leaves before drying the plants off, carefully slitting the ribs or veins on the underside, below a junction, and pegging or weighting down on the surface of soil compost, to root and form small plants which can be later pricked out and grown on in pots.

Diseases. Browning and blotching of leaves with a grey mould may occur under too damp, cold or stagnant conditions, favourable to the grey mould fungus, *Botrytis cinerea*. Detach and burn infected leaves; apply a captan fungicide. Leaf Spots are traceable to the fungi *Phyllosticta begoniae* and *Gloes-*

porium begoniae, but the use of captan or a copper fungicide give good control.

Pests. Thrips (*Euthrips parvus, Heliothrips haemorrhoidalis, Thrips flavus,* etc.), may cause irregular reddish-brown lines on leaves, rusty-brown spots underneath, and deformation. Malathion, gamma-BHC insecticides give control. Mealy Bugs (*Pseudococcus adonidum, P. citri*), White Fly (*Trialeurodes vaporariorum*) and Aphids (*Aphis gossypii, Macrosiphum begoniae*) may be troublesome, but are checked by a systemic insecticide, or one based on malathion or gamma-BHC or nicotine. Eelworms may infest plants; *Aphelenchoides fragariae* causing irregular brown leaf blotches and stunting; and *Heterodera marionii* stunting plants and forming galls on the roots, especially of tuberous Begonias. Infested plants should be burnt, and the soil in which they grew sterilized. Propagation is possible from young uninfested cuttings, however.

Belladonna Lily. See *Amaryllis*.

Bell-flower. *See* Campanula.

Bell-glass. A dome-shaped glass, with knob, now superseded by modern cloches or handlights.

Bellis, Daisy (bel′lis. Fam. Compositae). Hardy perennials of which forms of the native Daisy, *Bellis perennis*, 4–6 in., are chiefly grown, for spring bedding, as edging plants and in the rock garden; 'Dresden China', pink; and 'Pomponette' in white, pink and red, having double quilled flowers, May, June; though the latest development is F_1 hybrids of Haubner's breeding. 'Hen and Chickens' is an abnormal proliferous form, with secondary heads arising around the first larger flowers.

Cultivation. Ordinary soils, like lime; sun or shade.

Propagation. By division, after flowering. By seeds, sown in well-drained soil, April, or in boxes in frame in March; transplanting out in July.

Bellium (bel′li-um. Fam. Compositae). A small genus of free-flowering, daisy-like plants of which *B. minutum*, Mediterranean region, makes a tiny mat of fine evergreen leaves, studded with white-petalled, yellow-disked flowers in June, and may be grown in warm, sunny shelter in the rock garden, or alpine house, given well-drained light loam and peat. Propagated by division, April, or by seed in the cool greenhouse, bottom heat of 21° C. (70° F.).

Bellus (-a, -um). Beautiful. Ex. *Hoya bella.*

Beloperone, Shrimp Plant (bel-o-per-o′ne. Fam. Acanthaceae). Tropical evergreen shrubs of which *B. guttata,* Mexico, to 3 ft, with shining soft green oval leaves, and terminal arching spikes of flowers, 3–6 in. long, having brownish-pink or salmon-coloured overlapping bracts, fancifully resembling a shrimp, may be grown in a cool greenhouse, and as a house plant, as it flowers well when quite young.

Cultivation. In pots, with standard compost; in good light, spring, summer temp. 15·5–18° C. (60–65° F.), increasing watering with growth; winter temp. 10–13° C. (50–55° F.). Repot March.

Propagation. By cuttings of young shoots, spring or summer, with bottom heat, 18° C. (65° F.).

Bending. The arching or bending down of branches of fruit or ornamental trees to induce fuller and more even breaking of buds and check shoot growth.

Benedictus (-a, -um). Blessed. Ex. *Cnicus benedictus.*

Benzene Hexachloride, BHC. A powerful chlorinated hydrocarbon insecticide, of which the gamma isomer, gamma-BHC, is the most toxic to insects, and most suitable for garden use. It may be used in aerosol, dust, spray or smoke form, but not within 2 to 3 weeks of harvesting food crops. *See* Insecticides.

Berberis, Barberry (ber′ber-is. Fam. Berberidaceae). A genus of many beautiful flowering shrubs, with spiny stems, largely Asiatic or American in origin, but a few Mediterranean and European. The hardy kinds are easily grown, and provide some of the best spring-flowering and late-berrying shrubs.

Selection. The desirable garden barberries may be divided into deciduous and evergreen groups. *Deciduous:* Distinguished by their fine fruiting performance and autumn leaf colours, these are perfectly hardy, and need no regular pruning except the removal of a few older shoots to base in spring as the plants age. *B. aggregata,* China, to 6 ft, red berries in panicles, and v. 'Buccaneer', coral-red; *angulosa,* Himalaya,

FIG. 28 *Berberis* × *lologensis*, with glowing orange clusters of flowers.

3 ft, dark red edible berries; *aristata,* Himalaya, to 10 ft, red berries with blue bloom; × *carminea,* 4 ft, panicles of carmine red berries; *chitria,* to 10 ft, panicles of red, oblongish fruits; *concinna,* Sikkim, 2 ft, flowers and red fruits borne singly; *dictiophylla,* Yunnan, to 6 ft, very spiny, red berries with whitish bloom, pronounced in v. *epruinosa; francisci-ferdinandii,* China, to 8 ft, with long racemes of flowers and red fruits; *heteropoda,* Turkestan, 8 ft, blue-black berries; *jamesiana,* Yunnan, 6 ft, clusters of translucent coral berries; *koreana,* Korea, 6 ft, red berries; *lycioides,* Jaunsar, 6 ft, racemes of oval, whitish bloomed berries; *morrisonensis,* Formosa, 3 ft, clusters of bright red berries; *prattii,* China, 6 ft, clusters of bright pink, ovoid berries; × *rubrostilla,* 4 ft, small clusters of pear-shaped lustrous red berries, at their best in form *crawleyensis; thunbergii,* Japan, 4 ft, shining red berries, and its fine purple-leaved v. *atropurpurea* and *a. nana,* a dwarf of 1½ ft; *vulgaris* v. *purpurifolia,* to 8 ft, for hedging; *wilsonae,* China, 2–3 ft, round red berries in clusters, and v. *gracilis,* to 6 ft, coral red berries; and *yunnanensis,* Yunnan, 6 ft, bright red berries. All of these flower, of course, in yellow tones, between May and July.

Evergreen: Bear yellow flowers in April–May, and have blue-black, red or purple oval berries, often with a blue or whitish bloom in autumn. Outstanding hardy kinds are: *B.* × *antoniana*, 5 ft; *buxifolia*, Magellan Straits, 6 ft, and v. *nana*, 1½ ft; *calliantha*, Tibet, 3 ft, flowers in threes; *candidula*, China, 2 ft, *darwinii*, Chile, 6–8 ft, with small, shield-like leaves, many-flowered racemes; and a parent of notable hybrids, such as × *irwinii*, 2 ft, × *stenophylla*, to 10 ft, and vs. *corallina nana*, 'Crawley Gem', 2–4 ft, *gracilis*, 4–5 ft, *gracilis nana*, 1 ft, and *picturata*, coloured stems, 3 ft; *gagnepainii* v. *lanceifolia*, 4–5 ft; *hakeoides*, 4 ft; *hookeri*, Sikkim, 3 ft, and v. *viridis*; *julianae*, Tibet, to 10 ft; *lepidifolia*, Yunnan, to 6 ft; *linearifolia*, Chile, 3–4 ft; *lologensis*, Chile, 5 ft; *panlanensis*, China, 4–5 ft; *replicata*, Yunnan, to 4 ft; *taliensis*, Yunnan, 4 ft; *valdiviana*, Chile, 6 ft; *verruculosa*, China, 3–5 ft; and × *wintonensis*, 5 ft, early flowering.

Cultivation. Both deciduous and ever-green plants do best when planted young in well-drained soil, provided with humus-forming organic matter. Deci-duous species may be planted October to March; evergreen in autumn or early spring. Regular pruning is not required; but some of the older stems can be cut out to restore shapeliness, straggling shoots cut back after flowering, and hedges trimmed after flowering.

Propagation. By seeds of species, stratified in sand over the winter, sown in March–April, in pots in cold frame, or in shaded beds out of doors. Transplant seedlings the following year. By cuttings of firm young shoots, taken with a 'heel' in late summer, under cloches or in a cold frame. By layering in spring.

Bergamot. See *Monarda*.

Bergamot Mint. See *Mentha odorata*.

Bergenia, Megasea (ber-ge'ni-a. Fam. Saxifragaceae). Perennial plants with distinctive large, fleshy leaves, and large panicles of white to red bloom early in the year; excellent for wild or bog gardens, large borders and spacious rock gardens, and ground cover.

Selection. B. cordifolia, Siberia, 1 ft, sp. 2½ ft, red, March, April; and vs. *alba*, white; *purpurea*, purplish pink; and *rosea*, pink; *crassifolia*, Siberia, 1 ft, red;

× 'Ballawey', 1 ft, purple, April, May; *purpurascens*, Himalaya, 6 in.; *stracheyi*, 1 ft, pink, and v. *alba*, are all reasonably hardy.

Cultivation. Any ordinary soil, well-drained. Tolerant of shade. Plant October or March–April.

Propagation. By division after flower-ing. By seed, sown outdoors in sheltered spot, March–April.

Berry. A fleshy fruit in which seeds are embedded in pulp, e.g. Gooseberry, Blackberry, etc.

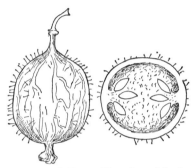

FIG. 29 A Berry (Gooseberry) fruit.

Besom. A garden broom, usually made of birch twigs and shoots bound to a wooden handle.

Bessara (bes'sa-ra. Fam. *Amaryllida-ceae*). Bulbous plants of which *B. elegans*, Mexico, 2 ft, is pretty with umbels of scarlet and white flowers in summer, in the cool greenhouse. Half-hardy, it is potted in October, standard compost, watered freely in growth, but cool and dry when foliage withers. Propagate by offsets in October.

Beta, Beet (be'ta. Fam. Chenopodia-ceae). Apart from the culinary beetroots (q.v.), interest lies chiefly in the orna-mental-leaved forms, *B. vulgaris* v. *cicla*, the Silver Beet; v. *variegata*, Chilean Beet, with leaves up to 3 ft long, hand-somely marked; and *dracaenaefolia*, 2 ft, with narrow, dark crimson leaves, for bedding. Easily raised by seeds sown ¼ in. deep, in March, under glass, bottom heat 15·5° C. (60° F.); to be planted out in May.

Bethlehem Sage. See *Pulmonaria*.

Betonica, Betony. See *Stachys.*

Betula, Birch (bet'u-la. Fam. Betulaceae). Deciduous shrubs and trees of the northern hemisphere, with unisexual flowers, the male in catkins, of graceful habit, with slender branches, and often attractive bark colouring as the trees get older.

Selection. B. pendula, Silver Birch, to 60 ft, singularly graceful with silvery white, peeling bark; is native and European, with fine vs. in *dalecarlica,* Swedish Birch, with deeply lobed leaves; *fastigiata,* columnar; and *youngii,* dome-shaped, fine weeping form; *albo-sinensis* v. *septentrionalis,* China, to 60 ft, with lovely, smooth orange-brown bark; *ermani* v. *nipponica,* Japan, to 70 ft, also has orange-brown barked branches, creamy white on the trunk; *maximowiczii,* Japan, to 60 ft, has pale orange bark, the largest leaves and the longest catkins of all birches; *papyifera,* Canoe or Paper Birch, N. America, to 70 ft, very white bark, and its v. *occidentalis,* to 130 ft, tallest of Birches; *lutea,* the Yellow Birch, N. America, to 50 ft, yellowish barked; *jacquemontii,* Himalaya, to 50 ft, creamy white bark; *lenta,* Cherry Birch, to 70 ft, black-brown bark; and *pubescens,* native White Birch, 50–60 ft, for damp places. *B. nana,* Arctic Birch, 2–3 ft, is a pretty foliage shrub for dampish places.

Cultivation. Ordinary soils, with humus, and good drainage. N. American species are not quite so good as on their native soils. Plant October–March.

Propagation. Species by seeds in pans in cold frame, in autumn, as soon as ripe.

Betulaceae. A dicotyledonous family of deciduous shrubs and trees, containing Alnus, Betulus, Carpinus, Corylus and Ostrya, dealt with in this book.

Bi- signifies two in compound words. Ex. *bicolor,* of two colours.

Biennials. Plants which produce leaves the first year, flower and seed the next, and then die, their life-cycle completed in two growing seasons or years. In gardening, plants which are naturally perennial are often grown as biennials, their first blooming being considered their best, and then uprooted.

Cultivation. Seeds are sown out of doors in June to early August, in fairly rich, well-dug, weed-free soil, out of the direct sun, pricked out into rows, and transplanted to where they are to flower in early autumn or early spring. Choice kinds can be reared in a cold frame or under cloches. Plants may be given a light mulch of sifted rotted organic matter as frost protection of the roots, and refirmed if lifted by frost in winter.

Bignonia, Trumpet Flower (big-no'-ni-a. Fam. Bignoniaceae). This genus of half-hardy, deciduous shrubs with brilliant trumpet-like flowers is botanically reduced to *B. unguis-cati,* Argentine, a useful cool greenhouse climber, with claw-like tendrils, solitary yellow flowers in summer; others, such as *B. magnifica* (correctly *Arrabidaea magnifica*), purple-crimson flowers, summer, and *chamberlaynii* (now *Anemopaegma chamberlaynii*), bright yellow, may be grown under similar conditions.

Cultivation. Standard compost or 2 parts fibrous loam, 1 part peat, 1 part coarse sand. Pot or plant February–March. Winter temp. 10° C. (50° F.). Ample sun, trained to rafters. Prune in late winter, removing weak shoots, shortening strong ones by one-third. Water increasingly with growth; ventilate freely; keep almost dry in winter.

Propagation. By cuttings of young shoots of 3–4 in. in April, in propagating frame, bottom heat 18–21° C. (65–70° F.). By layering in spring.

Bilberry. See *Vaccinium myrtillus.*

Bill Hook. Cutting tool, hooked at the tip, with short or long handle, chiefly used for hedge-trimming.

Billardiera (bill-ar-deer'a. Fam. Pittosporaceae). Australian evergreen climbers, chiefly distinctive for their autumn show of edible fruits.

Selection. B. longiflora, a slender twining climber, with yellowish-green flowers, followed by purplish-blue berries, is chiefly grown on a warm wall in mild, sunny areas, but otherwise in pots or the border of a cool greenhouse; *scandens,* cream flowers turning purplish, may also be attempted.

Cultivation. Standard compost or soil rich with peat; water freely in growth, very moderately in winter, minimum temp. 7° C. (45° F.). Intolerant of a limy or chalk soil.

Betonica, Betony. See *Stachys.*

Garden Biennials	Height	Sow	Plant out at	Colour
Adlumia cirrhosa	climber	May–July	2 ft apart	Pale rose
*Antirrhinum, various	1–3 ft	May–Aug.	6–12 in. apart	Various
*Campanula medium	2½ ft	May–July	1 ft apart	Various
Campanula patula	2 ft	June–Aug.	9 in. apart	Purple
Campanula pyramidalis	3 ft	May–July	1 ft apart	Blue
Campanula pyramidalis v. *alba*	3 ft	May–July	1 ft apart	White
Campanula rapunculus	2 ft	May–July	1 ft apart	Blue
Celsia cretica	4–6 ft	May–July	1½ ft apart	Yellow†
**Cheiranthus allionii*	1 ft	June–Aug.	9 in. apart	Orange/yellow
**Cheiranthus cheiri:* (Wallflower)	1 ft	June–Aug.	9 in. apart	Various, red/yellow
Cnicus diacantha	2½ ft	June–Aug.	1 ft apart	Purplish
Cynoglossum amabile	1–2 ft	May–July	1 ft apart	Blue/pink
**Dianthus barbatus* (Sweet William)	1½ ft	May–July	1 ft apart	Various
Digitalis purpurea (Foxglove)	2½–4 ft	May–July	1 ft apart	Various
Dipsacus sp. (Teasel)	6 ft	June–Aug.	1½ ft apart	Light purple
Gentiana crinita	6 in.	May–July	6 in. apart	Blue
Gilia rubra	3 ft	June–Aug.	1 ft apart	Red†
Lunaria annua	2½ ft	June–Aug.	1 ft apart	Purple, white
Meconopsis integrifolia	3 ft	May–July	1 ft apart	Yellow
Oenothera biennis	2½ ft	June–Aug.	1 ft apart	Yellow
Papaver nudicaule	2–3 ft	June–Aug.	9–12 in. apart	Yellow, red, white
Reseda alba	2 ft	June–Aug.	6 in. apart	White
Silene armeria	1 ft	June–Aug.	9 in. apart	Rose, white
Silene compacta	1 ft	June–Aug.	9 in. apart	Rose
Stock, Brompton	2 ft	July	1 ft apart	Various
Trachelium caeruleum	2 ft	June–Aug.	1 ft apart	Blue†
Verbascum blattaria	3 ft	June–Aug.	1 ft apart	Yellow
Verbascum bombyciferum	4 ft	June–Aug.	1½ ft apart	Soft yellow
Verbascum × hybridum	6–9 ft	June–Aug.	2 ft apart	Yellow, white
Verbascum pyramidalis	4 ft	June–Aug.	1½ ft apart	Yellow
Verbascum thapsus	3 ft	June–Aug.	1 ft apart	Yellow

* Perennials, commonly grown as biennials.
† Not reliably hardy, overwinter under glass.

Propagation. By seed in April, 18° C. (65° F.); by cuttings of young shoots in summer.

Billbergia (bill-berg′i-a. Fam. Bromeliaceae). Stemless herbaceous plants of subtropical America, with narrow, grass-like leaves, and spikes of colourful bracted flowers in late winter or spring, chiefly grown in the cool greenhouse and as house plants.

Selection. B. nutans is easy, with yellowish-green flowers, and rose-pink bracts, from Brazil; *porteana*, green, violet and red; *morelii*, blue, rose and red; *thyrsoidea*, red; *vittata*, blue and crimson; and × *windii*, greenish-yellow, rose-crimson, are other fine species.

Cultivation. Equal parts peat, leaf-mould, and loam, with half a part sharp sand, suits these epiphytes, with good drainage in pots. Pot, and repot every two years, in March; water freely in summer; only moderately in winter; minimum temp. 13–15·5° C. (60–65° F.).

Propagation. By offsets in spring, in sandy peat, bottom heat 27° C. (80° F.), reducing when rooted.

Bindweed. Common name of several native plants, apt to become troublesome weeds. Field Bindweed or Cornbine is *Convolvulus arvensis*, a perennial climber with persistent brittle rhizomatous roots, deep-penetrating in the soil. Susceptible to 2, 4-D and 2, 4, 5-T herbicides but repeated applications needed. Black Bindweed is *Polygonum convolvulus*, an annual, susceptible to a paraquat herbicide. *See* Herbicides.

Biota. See *Thuja orientalis.*

Birch. See *Betula.*

Bird Cherry. See *Prunus padus.*

Birds. On the whole, birds are more beneficial than harmful in gardens in their destruction of caterpillars, grubs, insects and small fauna. The Cuckoo, Kestrel, House Martin, Hedge-sparrow, Flycatcher, Redstart, Swallow, Swift, Barn Owl, Tawny Owl, Tits, Wagtail, Whitethroat, Woodpeckers and Wren, being largely insectivorous, do help immensely. The Blackbird, Rook, Starling and Thrush keep down many pests, such as insects, soil grubs, snails and slugs, but may damage ripening fruit, certain vegetables, and ornamental berries and fruits, in their season. Tits may raid peas. Although the Bullfinch, Chaffinch, Greenfinch, Hawfinch, House Sparrow and Jay eat many insects, they do much damage to fruit buds, spring flowers, seed beds and various crops. Stock Doves and Wood Pigeons can be wholly destructive to crops.

Complete prevention of damage is only possible by enclosing plants in nets or netted cages, chiefly valuable for the safe harvesting of fruits. Buds and flowers can be given temporary protection by the use of a bird-repellent, or a spider-like, fine-fibred, plastic webbing placed over plants. Seed-beds are protected by fine-mesh plastic netting or a criss-crossing of nylon thread on short sticks. Scares are most useful when changed often or rearranged.

Bird's-eye Primrose. See *Primula farinosa.*

Bird's-foot Trefoil. See *Lotus.*

Bird's-nest Fern. See *Asplenium nidus.*

Bird's-Tongue Flower. See *Strelitizia.*

Birthwort. See *Aristolochia.*

Bisexual. Of flowers, having stamens and pistil in the same flower.

Bishop's Weed. Also **Ground Elder.** Common name of *Aegopodium podagraria*, often a persistent weed, partially

susceptible to 2,4-D, 2,4,5-T and paraquat herbicides. *See* Herbicides.

Bitter Almond. See *Prunus communis* v. *amara.*

Bitter Vetch. See *Lathyrus vernus; Vicia orobus.*

Black Fly. *See* Aphids.

Black Hellebore. See *Helleborus.*

Black Spleenwort. See *Asplenium.*

Black Thorn. See *Prunus spinosa.*

Blackberry (*Rubus* spp.). The Blackberry, Bramble or Bumblekites are of more than one species of the native plants of Britain and Europe. Cultivated selected forms yield heavy crops of large berries, excellent for jams, jellies, canning and bottling.

Selection. Early: Bedford Giant. Mid-season: Himalaya Giant, Merton Early, Merton Thornless, Parsley-leaved. Late: John Innes. All are self-fertile and heavy-yielding. Here, too, belongs the Veitch-berry (Blackberry × November Abundance Raspberry cross), as its culture is similar.

Cultivation. Rich, deep loam preferred, but any well-drained, moist soil suits well. Plant October–March; cutting hard back to induce new shoots from the base. Usually grown on walls or wire supports; planting 12–16 ft apart, in rows 6–8 ft apart. Wires should be spaced 2, 3 and 5 ft above the ground on posts. Tie fruiting canes to top two wires; new canes to bottom wire temporarily. After fruiting, cut down old canes to base; train new canes in their place. In very vigorous kinds, such as Himalaya Berry, two to four old canes may be retained to fruit a second season. Manure liberally with organic matter in autumn, and a mixture of 2 parts steamed bone meal and 1 part sulphate of potash, 3 oz. to the sq. yd, in March.

Propagation. Peg selected tips of canes to soil to root in late summer, and transplant in winter, when rooted.

Diseases. Blackberries are susceptible to Raspberry Cane Spot (q.v.), but seldom seriously affected. Stunted, light green bushy growth is suspected of being of virus origin, known as Dwarf; affected plants should be lifted and burnt.

Pests. A Gall-mite, *Phytoptus essigi*, causes Redberry Disease; and all fruited canes should be promptly cut out and burnt; lime-sulphur at 1 part to 12 parts

water to new 4-in. long growths in spring
is also most helpful. Deformed, hard,
brown and maggoty berries suggest
infestation by the Raspberry Beetle
(*Byturus tomentosus*) (*see* Raspberry).
Aphids and Capsid Bug are sometimes
troublesome, requiring a malathion
application in spring, or derris in summer.

Blackcurrant. *See* Currants (*Ribes
nigrum*).

Bladder Fern. See *Cystopteris*.

Bladder Nut. See *Staphylea*.

Bladder Senna. See *Colutea*.

Bladderwort. See *Utricularia*.

Blade. The flat expanded part of a leaf
(Lamina).

Blaeberry. See *Vaccinium*.

Blanching. The whitening of stems and
leaves by excluding light, as with Celery,
Leeks, etc.

Blandfordia (bland-ford'i-a. Fam.
Liliaceae). Rhizomatous-rooted evergreen perennials, with pretty umbels of
flowers in summer, and linear leaves,
from Australia and Tasmania, for the
cool greenhouse.

Selection. B. flammea, 1 ft, yellow, and
v. *aurea*, golden-yellow, June; *grandiflora*, 2 ft, red and yellow; and *nobilis*,
15 in., orange, are usually grown.

Cultivation. Pot, and repot, in autumn,
standard compost, or in equal parts
sandy loam and peat. Water little in
winter, temp. 7–10° C. (45–50° F.), until
growth begins in spring; increase watering, give sun, and keep more or less dried
off till repotting time.

Propagation. By division when repotting.

Blandus (-a, -um). Pleasing. Ex.
Gladiolus blandus.

Blanket Flower. See *Gaillardia*.

Blechnum (blek'num. Fam. Polypodiaceae). Evergreen ferns, chiefly from
warm regions, though some are hardy;
with characteristic pinnate or pinnatifid
fronds.

Selection. B. brasiliense, Brazil, 2–4 ft,
a small tree fern; *fraxineum* (*longifolium*),
W. Indies, 1–2 ft; *occidentale*, tropical
America, 2 ft; need stove conditions;
winter temp. 15·5° C. (60° F.) minimum.
B. auriculatum, S. America, 18 in.;
blechnoides, Chile, 1–1½ ft; *gibbum*, New
Caledonia, 2–3 ft; and *orientale*, Australia, 3 ft; need a warm greenhouse;
winter temp. 10° C. (50° F.) minimum.

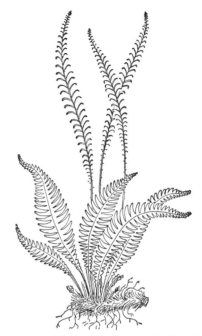

FIG. 30 *Blechnum spicant*, the Hard
Fern.

B. spicant, the Hard Fern, is found in
Britain, to 12 in., and is hardy in rather
acid soil, and shade; *durum*, Chatham
Isles, 1 ft, may also be grown out of
doors; *penna marina*, 9 in., almost hardy.

Cultivation. Greenhouse species need
potting in March, in equal parts loam,
peat, leaf-mould and sand. Water
liberally in warm months, fairly humid
atmosphere, with partial shade.

Propagation. By spores sown on sifted
sand-peat mixture, any time, bottom
heat 27° C. (80° F.), moist.

Bleeding. A term describing the
exudation of sap from a stem, caused by
injury and untimely pruning. Vines
bleed when pruned too late in winter, as
do certain trees, notably Maples, Prunus,
Limes, etc. Unlikely when plants are
pruned immediately after leaf-fall, or
when in fresh full leaf. Cuts need dressing
with a tree paint, or sealing with grafting
wax.

Bleeding Heart. See *Dicentra*.

Blessed Thistle. See *Cnicus benedictus*.

Bletilla (ble-til′la. Fam. Orchidaceae). Terrestrial orchids of which *B. striata* (*Bletia hyacinthina*), China, with handsome ribbed leaves, and racemes of amethyst-purple flowers, 12 in. long, and a white-flowered v. *alba*, are hardy enough to grow in sheltered, shady positions in a bog garden in mild localities; in a cool greenhouse elsewhere, potted in equal parts loam, peat and leaf-mould and half a part coarse sand; being kept fairly dry in winter, minimum temp. 7° C. (45° F.). Propagate by division in June.

Bletting. *See* Medlar.

Blight. A general term for a severe attack on a plant by disease (e.g. Potato Blight), or pest (e.g. American Blight), or a plant's reactions to certain weather conditions.

Blood. A quick-acting, organic, nitrogenous fertilizer; may be forked into the soil when fresh, but is messy and nauseous to use. It is usually dried as a fine powder commercially. *See* Fertilizers.

Blood Flower. See *Haemanthus*.

Blood Root, Bloodwort. See *Sanguinaria*.

Bloom. The fine, down-like, waxy covering on fruits such as grapes, plums, berries, etc.

Bloom, Blossom. A flower or group of flowers, especially of fruit trees.

Bloomeria (bloo-mer′i-a. Fam. Amaryllidaceae). Cormous perennial plants from California, for the cold greenhouse, with ribbon-like leaves, and umbels of gay long-stalked flowers on slender scapes in July.

Selection. B. aurea, 1–1½ ft, golden yellow; and *clevelandii*, similar but with smaller yellow flowers.

Cultivation. Pot in September, 2 in. deep, three or four corms to a 5-in. pot, standard compost. Keep rather dry, winter temp. 7° C. (45° F.), until growth starts, when watering is gradually increased and maintained till after flowering; dry off gradually. May be tried in warm, sheltered, sunny places, 3 in. deep, in mild areas.

Propagation. By offsets at potting time.

Blue Cedar. See *Cedrus atlantica* v. *glauca*.

Blue Cowslip. See *Pulmonaria angustifolia*.

Blue Lace Flower. See *Didiscus coeruleus*.

Blue Marguerite. See *Agathaea*.

Blue Poppy. See *Meconopsis betonicifolia*.

Blue Spruce. See *Picea pungens* and vs.

Bluebell. (Of Scotland), *Campanula rotundifolia*; (of England), *Endymion nonscriptus*.

Blueberry. See *Vaccinium*.

Bluebottle. See *Centaurea cyanus*.

Blue-gum Tree. See *Eucalyptus globulus*.

Bluets. See *Houstonia*.

Blumenbachia (blu-men-bak′i-a. Fam. Loasaceae). S. American plants, annual, biennial and perennial, but not hardy in Britain; with showy summer flowers, but leaves often covered with stinging hairs, making them unpleasant to handle.

Selection. B. insignis is a trailing plant, with white and reddish-yellow flowers, best grown as a half-hardy annual, to plant out in May. For the greenhouse, *lateritia* can be an attractive climber, with brick-red flowers, summer; *coronata*, 1½ ft, is an erect-growing cool greenhouse biennial, with glossy white flowers in June.

Cultivation. Sow in pans, standard compost, bottom heat 18° C. (65° F.), March, for summer flowering; sow biennial species in June–August, potting and wintering with soil just moist, temp. 7° C. (45° F.). Seeds are not regularly offered.

Bocconia. See *Macleaya*.

Boenninghausenia (bo-en-ing-hause′ni-a. Fam. Rutaceae.). The one species is *B. albiflora*, an Asian sub-shrubby perennial of 1½–2 ft, with blue-grey, fern-like, long-stalked leaves, and white summer flowers in large loose panicles.

Cultivation. Any well-drained soil; sheltered position, in the border. Plant in October or March–April.

Propagation. By seeds, under glass, bottom heat 18° C. (65° F.), standard compost.

Bog Arum. See *Calla*.

Bog Asphodel. *Narthecium ossifragum*, a native of bogs and moors.

Bog Bean. See *Menyanthes trifoliata*.

Bog Garden. A bog garden can be created out of naturally low-lying ground flanking a stream or pond, or made to utilize low-lying ground, much subject to waterlogging or slight flooding by its natural topography. As a rule it is desirable to add organic matter, such as peat, bark fibre or leaves, both to give a moisture-retaining sponge and avoid depressions which fill with water and invite mosquitoes to breed freely. Planting is done to create a natural rather than a formal effect, with plants tolerant of moist conditions. A short planting list can be made from: *Aconitum napellus* (Monkshood), 3–4 ft; *Aruncus sylvester*, 5–8 ft; *Asclepias incarnata*, Swamp Milkweed, 3 ft; *Astilbe* in variety, 1½–3 ft; *Astrantia major*, 2–3 ft; *Cimicifuga cordifolia*, 3–4 ft; *Eupatorium cannabinum*, Hemp Agrimony, 3–4 ft; *Filipendula* spp., 2–4 ft; *Gunnera manicata*, 8 ft; *Hemerocallis* (Day Lily) in variety, 3 ft; *Iris kaempferi* vs., 2½ ft; *Lobelia cardinalis*, 3 ft; *Lysichitum americana*, 2 ft; *Lysimachia vulgaris*, 2–3 ft; *Lythrum salicaria*, 3 ft; *Monarda didyma*, 2½ ft; *Primula* spp., *Ranunculus acris flore pleno*, 2 ft; *Rodgersia pinnata* vs., 2–3 ft; and *Senecio clivorum*. Of shorter stature are *Ajuga genevensis*, *Claytonia siberica*, *Coreopsis rosea*, *Cypripedium calceolus*, *C. reginae*, *Geum rivale*, *Hosta* spp., *Mimulus* spp., *Polygonum affine*. Ferns such as *Adiantum pedatum*, *Dryopteris thelypteris*, *Athyrium corymbiferum*, *Onoclea sensibilis* and the Royal Fern, *Osmunda regalis*, can be planted. Shrubs likely to thrive in wet ground are drawn from *Cornus* spp., *Salix* spp., *Skimmia* spp. and *Vaccinium* spp. Alders (*Alnus* spp.) and some of the bamboos (*Arundinaria*, *Pseudosasa*, *Sinarundinaria*, etc.) are useful in moist situations.

Bog Myrtle. See *Myrica*.

Bog Pimpernel. See *Anagallis tenella*.

Bog Violet. See *Pinguicula*.

Bole. The main trunk or stem of a tree.

Bolting. The running to seed prematurely of brassica vegetables, lettuce and biennials. It is sometimes caused by drought, sometimes by lack of firmness at the roots.

Boltonia (bol-to′ni-a. Fam. Compositae). Hardy herbaceous perennial plants, chiefly from N. America, resembling Michaelmas Daisies, and useful for their autumn flowering.

Selection. B. asteroides, to 6 ft, white, lilac to violet flowers and vs., and *latisquamata*, to 6 ft, bluish-violet flowers.

Cultivation. Well-dug, humus-rich soil, in borders. Plant October or March.

Propagation. By division in March.

Bone Meal, Bone Flour. See Fertilizers.

Bonfire. Although the proper place for all clean vegetable waste is the compost heap where it can be rotted down to humus-forming material, the bonfire is the best place for diseased or pest-ridden plants, cankered and dead wood, and debris that accumulates in a garden. Fire is the perfect sterilant, and the ashes of a bonfire, collected dry, provide useful amounts of mineral nutrients for plants when used as a fertilizer, chiefly calcium and potash. See Ashes, Wood. A bonfire should be lit, however, only on days when it is unlikely to be a nuisance to neighbours, and with due regard to local authority by-laws.

Bongardia (bon-gard′i-a. Fam. Bericaceae). The one species is *B. chrysogonum*, Persia, Syria, 6 in.; a tuberous-rooted perennial with radical pinnate foliage and golden-yellow, single flowers on branching stems in May. It needs well-drained light soil and a sheltered warm position in border or rock garden; protected against damp by a handlight as it easily rots. Plant April. Propagation is by division in April; by seed sown under glass, in spring, bottom heat 15·5° C. (60° F.).

Borage (*Borago officinalis*). A hardy annual aromatic herb, native to Britain and Europe, growing to 3 ft, the young leaves being used in salads, and in claret cup, for their cool, cucumber-like flavour, and the blue flowers for pot-pourri or to be candied. Sow outdoors, August–September, or March, in any well-drained soil, and sun; thinning to 15 in. apart.

Borago, Borage (bor-a′go. Fam. Boraginaceae). As well as the annual Borage (q.v.), the genus contains hardy perennial herbs of which *B. laxifolia*, Corsica, is a sprawly, decumbent, many-stemmed plant, with racemes of pale blue flowers, during summer, best suited to the wild garden; planted in autumn or spring. Propagate by division in spring. Or seeds may be sown in light soil, April–May.

Bordeaux Mixture. A copper fungicide

particularly useful in controlling fungus blights and moulds. *See* Fungicides.

Border. A gardening term usually used to describe a bed of soil, longer than wide, devoted to a particular class of plant. It may abut a wall, hedge or fence, or be isolated alongside paths or drives. It may be devoted to annual flowers, herbaceous perennials, trained fruit trees, ornamental shrubs, a mixed planting of flowering and ornamental plants, herbs or early saladings; or under glass, to greenhouse plants or crops. In all cases, the soil must be deeply dug, with provision made for good drainage, and yet adequate moisture retention by adding humus-forming organic matter. Lime should be added to bring to the pH or level of acidity most favourable to the plants to be grown. *See* Fruit, Herbaceous Border and Plants, and Shrubs.

Borealis (-e). Northern. Ex. *Linnea borealis.*

Borecole or **Kale** (*Brassica oleracea acephala*). The hardiest of all winter green vegetables, surviving and recovering from frosts well to provide vitamin-rich fresh greens in late spring and early summer, the kales are particularly valuable in the north and in cold districts, though eligible for all gardens.

Cultivation. Seeds are sown thinly, ¼ in. deep, in outdoor seed-bed, in March for early winter cropping, in April or May for late winter or spring; in June for late spring and early summer. Seedling plants are transplanted two months later to well-dug, organically manured soil, 2 ft apart, 2–3 ft between rows according to vigour. They can follow early potatoes or peas, and are often planted between rows of second-early potatoes. To induce sturdy firm growth, high nitrogenous fertilizers should be avoided at this stage. But plants may be given a liquid feed in spring (dried blood in solution, or a seaweed derivative).

Varieties. Scotch Kale is grown chiefly for its curled leaves, in tall, intermediate and dwarf strains. Asparagus Kale produces long thin shoots in late spring which may be cooked like bundles of asparagus. Thousand-headed Kale branches very freely, providing much leaf. Cottager's Kale grows 2½ ft tall, with curly margined leaves, and is very

hardy. Hungry Gap Kale is the hardiest, cropping a year hence from May–June sowings. Ormskirk Hearting Kale produces loose-hearted heads for cooking like cabbage. There are also garnishing or Ornamental Kales, prettily coloured in leaf and fringed or crested at the edges, for border decoration in autumn and winter, and subsequent eating.

Boronia (bo-ro′ni-a. Fam. Rutaceae). Australian evergreen shrubs, with pinnate leaves and four-petalled flowers, sweetly scented, for the cool greenhouse; sometimes called Australian Native Roses.

Selection. B. elatior, 4 ft, rosy carmine flowers; *heterophylla*, whorled cerise flowers, May; *megastigma*, 2 ft, racemes of maroon and yellow flowers, April; and *serrulata*, 3 ft, clusters of bright rose flowers, summer, are chiefly grown.

Cultivation. Pot, and repot, May or after flowering; standard compost, or 2 parts loam, 1 part each peat, sand and broken charcoal. Water freely March–September; moderately in winter, minimum temp. 7° C. (45° F.). May be summered out of doors in sheltered shade.

Propagation. By cuttings of young shoots in May–July, inserted in sandy compost, bottom heat 13° C. (55° F.).

Botany. The science of plant study.

Botry-. A prefix in compound words meaning bunched. Ex. *Muscari botryoides*, the Grape Hyacinth, with flowers bunched and grape-like.

Botrychium, Moon Fern, Moonwort (bo-trik′i-um. Fam. Ophioglossaceae). Small deciduous ferns, happiest in constantly moist conditions, such as a damp shaded spot in the rock garden or fernery.

Selection. B. lunaria, the native Moonwort, has pleasing fertile fronds; and *virginianum*, N. America, etc., has longer fronds; both being hardy. Although from Hudson Bay territory, *ternata* is only half-hardy and needs to be placed in a cool greenhouse fernery, in shade, winter temp. 7° C. (45° F.).

Cultivation. Plant in April. Hardy kinds do well in low grass, when kept moist.

Propagation. By root division in April.

Botrytis. A name often given to diseases caused by parasitic fungi of the genus; *B. cinerea*, the common Grey Mould; *B. allii*, Onion Neck Rot; *B. elliptica*, Lily Mould; *B. paeoniae*, Paeony Blight; and *B. tulipae*, Tulip Fire; *see under* plant hosts for details and treatment.

Bottle Brush. See *Callistemon*.

Bottle Gourd. See *Lagenaria*.

Bottom Heat. Heat supplied to the soil, usually in propagation work; by hotbed (q.v.), hot-water or steam heating-pipes in greenhouse, or by soil-heating electric wires or cable. *See* Greenhouse and Propagation.

Bougainvillea (bou-gain-vill'e-a. Fam. Nyctaginaceae). Breathtaking for their great panicles of colourful, bracted flowers, the deciduous shrubby climbers of this south American genus do well in cool greenhouses or conservatories.

Selection. B. glabra, Brazil, with bright green foliage, and bright rosy-red flowers, summer; and *B. spectabilis*, Brazil, lilac-rose, with its vs. *lateritia*, brick red, and 'Mrs Butt', bright rose; and *lindleyana* v. 'Orange King', orange-salmon, excel.

Cultivation. Best grown in the well-drained greenhouse border, but in a large pot or tub where vigour must be restrained. Plant in autumn or spring, water freely in growth; allow to dry off and rest after flowering until February. Prune by cutting away weak shoots, and reduce previous year's shoots to within a bud of the main stems in February. Minimum winter temp. 7° C. (45° F.), but increase as growth begins anew.

Propagation. By cuttings of half-ripe shoots, in a propagating case, bottom heat of 18° C. (65° F.).

Bouncing Bet. See *Saponaria*.

Bourbon Rose. *See* Roses.

Boussingaultia (boo-sin-gall'ti-a. Fam. Basellaceae). Tuberous-rooted perennial climbers of which *B. baselloides*, Ecuador, is chiefly grown in a cool greenhouse or on a warm, sunny wall in mild districts, as a twining climber to 6–12 ft, with cordate leaves, and clusters of small white scented flowers in autumn.

Cultivation. Plant tubers in February, light, humus-rich soil, water freely with growth. Dry off after flowering. Lift outdoor tubers to store in sand under frost-proof conditions.

Propagation. By brittle tubercles

detached from stems in spring, inserted in sandy loam, at 13° C. (55° F.).

Bouvardia (boo-vard'i-a, Fam. Rubiaceae). Pretty Mexican or South American evergreen shrubs with fragrant, waxy flowers to bloom early in the year in a warm greenhouse.

Selection. At one time more popular, species are *B. humboldtii corymbiflora*, 2 ft, white scented racemes; *jasminiflora*, Jasmine Plant, 2 ft, free-flowering, white; *leiantha*, 2 ft, scarlet; and *triphylla*, to 3 ft, scarlet. There are many named hybrids such as Alfred Neuner, white; Bridal Wreath, white; King of the Scarlets, red; Mrs R. Green, salmon; President Garfield, double pink; and Priory Beauty, pink.

Cultivation. Pot in March, JIP compost, or equal parts good loam, leaf-mould, peat and sand; grow on under cool greenhouse conditions, temp. 13–18° C. (55–65° F.), watering liberally; pinching back new growth to make bushy plants; ventilate freely, shade from hot sun; water moderately only in winter, minimum temp. 10° C. (50° F.). Prune flowered shoots hard back after flowering.

Propagation. By cuttings of young shoots, about 2 in. long, cut above the first joint; rooted in porous compost (JIC), bottom heat 21° C. (70° F.) or more, in propagating frame; pot on when rooted.

Bowstring Hemp. See *Sanseviera*.

Box. See *Buxus*.

Box Elder. See *Acer negundo*.

Box Thorn. See *Lycium*.

Boysenberry. American hybrid (Black-berry × Raspberry × Loganberry), with large deep red fruits. *See* Loganberry.

Brachy-. Prefix of compound words meaning short. Ex. *brachyphyllus*, short-leaved.

Brachycome (brak-i-co'me. Fam. Compositae). Of this Australian race, *B. iberidifolia*, the Swan River Daisy, 1 ft, is a graceful half-hardy annual, with blue or white rayed flowers in profusion in summer. Sow seeds in March–April, with gentle bottom heat, 13° C. (55° F.), to prick off and plant out in May, porous soil, and sun; or grow as a pot plant in a cool greenhouse.

Brachyglottis (brak-i-glot'tis. Fam. Compositae). The one species, *B. repanda*,

New Zealand, to 15 ft, is an evergreen shrub or small tree, with large, oval, handsome leaves, and large panicles of small, greenish-white mignonette-scented flowers in spring, but only eligible for a warm wall in mildest localities; planted in April, in well-drained, rich soil. Propagation by cuttings in July–August, of young firm shoots, under cloche or handlight.

Brachypodium (brak-i-pod′i-um. Fam. Gramineae). Commonly, the False Brome Grass, *B. distachyon*, Europe, 9 in., is an annual, hardy enough to be sown where it is to grow in March–April, with a distinctive inflorescence which should be cut in full flower for drying and winter decoration.

Bracken or **Brake Fern.** See *Pteridium aquilinum*.

Bracteatus (-a, -um). Bracteate, having bracts.

Bracteoles. Small secondary bracts attached to the base of flower-stalks.

Bracts. Modified or rudimentary leaves growing near the calyx of a flower or at the base of the flower stalk. They may be green and leaf-like, or coloured, as in *Clematis* and *Euphorbia pulcherrima*.

FIG. 31 Bracts. The large bracts to the small flower of *Cornus kousa*.

Brahea (bra′he-a. Fam. Palmaceae). A genus of palms with crowns of fan-shaped leaves, of which the Mexican

B. dulcis, 10 ft or more, grows slowly in a warm greenhouse; potted in February–March, in compost of equal parts loam, peat and sand; watered freely in summer, very moderately in winter, minimum temp. 10° C. (50° F.). Propagation by seeds with bottom heat of 27° C. (80° F.).

Bramble. See Blackberry.

Brandy Bottle. See *Nuphar lutea*.

Brasenia, Water Shield, Water Target (bras-en′i-a. Fam. Nymphaeaceae). The single species, *B. schreberi*, N. America, is an interesting aquatic plant, with small oval floating leaves and purple flowers in summer, to plant in pool shallows in April–May. Propagation is chiefly by offsets or root division.

Brassavola (bras-sa′vo-la. Fam. Orchidaceae). Epiphytic orchids of Brazil and W. Indies, which may be grown in a warm greenhouse (winter temp. 13–18° C. [55–65° F.]). *B. digbyana*, Honduras, is the best known, for its large, fragrant, greenish and purple, with fringed lip, flowers, and as a parent of many *Brasso-cattleya* hybrids; *glauca*, Mexico, greenish-white, with pink streaking, is also grown.

Cultivation. Pot in March, in pots or pans half-filled with crocks, and a compost of equal parts live sphagnum moss and fibrous peat, with a little crushed charcoal; water liberally in growth, give ample light, but be very sparing of water in rest period, during winter.

Propagation. By division in March.

Brassia (bras′si-a. Fam. Orchidaceae). Epiphytic orchids of the tropics which may be grown in a warm greenhouse; minimum winter temp. 13–15.5° C. (55–60° F.).

Selection. B. verrucosa, Guatemala, arching spikes of greenish, purple-brown and white flowers in spring; *brachiata*, Guatemala, yellow-green, purple-spotted, summer; *gireoudiana*, Costa Rica, greenish-yellow and reddish-brown, summer; *lanceana*, Surinam, yellow, blotched deep red, very fragrant, summer; and *lawrenceana*, Brazil, yellow, spotted brown, and green, summer.

Cultivation. Pot, and repot every three years, in pans, with very good drainage, or on blocks of wood, or baskets; compost of one part sphagnum moss and three parts Osmunda fibre; to grow in good light; water freely in summer, moderately in winter.

Propagation. By division when re-potting.

Brassica (bras'sik-a. Fam. Cruciferae). A genus largely of annual and biennial herbs with some perennials. *B. oleracea*, 2–4 ft, is the biennial wild cabbage of Europe and Britain, from which have been developed the various leafy green vegetables Borecole, Broccoli, Brussels Sprouts, Cabbage, Cauliflower, Colewort, Kale, Kohl Rabi and Savoy, often collectively described by the generic name of Brassicas. Rapes and Swede are developed from *B. napus*, and the Turnip from *B. campestris* v. *rapa*, but are also often described as Brassica vegetables; the Chinese annual, *cernua*, is parent of the Chinese Cabbage, Pet Sai; *nigra* is the Black Mustard; and *repanda*, a dwarf perennial from the European Alps, with yellow flowers in June, may be grown in the rock garden, in well-drained soil, and good sun. *See* Brassicas under crop names.

Brasso-. A prefix to various hybrid races of orchids, in which *Brassavola* species has been a parent; e.g. *Brasso-cattleya*; *Brasso-Diacrum*; *Brasso-Epi-dendrum*; *Brasso-Laelia*; and *Brasso-Laelio-cattleya*; the lists of orchid specialists may be consulted, as many of these hybrids are expensive. Treatment is on the lines given for *Cattleya* (q.v.).

Bravoa (bra-vo'a. Fam. Amaryllidaceae). A bulbous plant from Mexico, *B. geminiflora*, aptly named the Twin-flower, carries alternating pairs of rich tubular orange-red flowers on stems up to 2 ft, in summer.

Cultivation. Bulbs may be planted 4 in. deep, 9 in. apart, in warm sheltered borders, light loam soil, in September and given winter protection, or planted three bulbs to a 6-in. pot, standard compost, in the cool greenhouse.

Propagation. By offsets in September.

Breastwood. Summer shoots of fruit trees trained on walls that grow out in front of the main branches, sometimes termed foreright or forthright shoots, which are cut back or out, preserving only well-placed side-shoots for future fruiting.

Breeze. Grit-like particles of coke, sometimes used on lawns to improve surface drainage and aeration, applied after spiking in winter.

Briar or **Brier.** The common Brier or Dog Rose is *Rosa canina*, often used as a rootstock on which hybrid roses are budded or grafted. The Sweet Brier is *Rosa eglanteria*, which is one of the parents of the Penzance Briers. The Austrian Brier is *Rosa foetida*, which with its vs. *bicolor* and *persiana*, has been the source of yellow colouring in many hybrid roses. *See* Roses.

Briza, Quaking Grass (briz'a. Fam. Gramineae). Two hardy annuals, *B. maxima*, Canary Isles, 1–1½ ft, and *minor*, Mediterranean region, 1 ft, are grown for their attractive panicles of flowering spikelets and curious glumes, to cut for flower bouquets and for drying. Seeds are sown thinly in good loam soil where the plants are to grow in April. *B. media* is the native perennial Quaking Grass.

Broad Bean. *See* Beans, Broad (*Vicia faba*).

Broccoli. Botanically, there is no difference between Broccoli and Cauliflowers; both are developments of *Brassica oleracea botrytis cauliflora*. Broccoli are the hardier, providing the 'cauliflowers' harvested between November and June. The plants are somewhat coarser, with a strong tendency for the leaves to incurl and fold over the curds, and are often termed winter cauliflowers.

Selection. Varieties are numerous, but fall into four main types: (1) D'Angers, originating in Anjou, France, with greyish-blue leaves, having curled margins and long stalks, firm white heads, not too regular or deeply embedded in the leaves; reasonably hardy for cold districts, but not suitable for the more humid conditions of the south-west. (2) Roscoff, introduced from Brittany, having abundant leaves, wavy-edged, white-veined, white, firm, rounded heads when well grown, but only hardy enough for Cornwall and similar favourable places in the south-west. (3) Italian Protector, with large, thick, dark bluish-green leaves, very white heads, deeply set; only suitable for sheltered mild localities, free from severe winter frosts. (4) English Hybrids, the hardiest of all, and most suitable for the colder parts of the country. No type stands up well to long periods of snow and frost. The

Variety	Type	Sow	Season of Harvest
Roscoff Extra	Early Roscoff	March–Apr.	November
Winter Mammoth	Italian Protector	April	December
Snow's Winter White	D'Angers	April	Late December
Roscoff No. 1	Roscoff	April	December–January
Feltham Early	D'Angers	April	January–February
Roscoff No. 2	Roscoff	April	January–February
Superb Early White	D'Angers	April	February
Snow White	D'Angers	April	Late February
Penzance	English Hybrid	April	March
Roscoff No. 3	Roscoff	Late April	February–March
Mid-Feltham	D'Angers	Late April	March
Leamington	Hybrid	Late April	March–April
*Knight's Protecting	Hybrid	Late April	March–April
Roscoff No. 4	Roscoff	Early May	March–April
*St George	D'Angers	Early May	March–April
Satisfaction	D'Angers	Early May	Early April
*Royal Oak	D'Angers	May	May
Roscoff No. 5	Roscoff	May	May
Late Feltham	D'Angers	Mid May	May
*Late Queen	Hybrid	Mid May	May–early June
*May Blossom	D'Angers	Mid May	May
Markanta	Hybrid	May	May
Whitsuntide	D'Angers	May	May–early June
Extra Late Feltham	D'Angers	Late May	June
Midsummer	Hybrid	Late May	June

* Very hardy varieties.

accompanying chart gives a selected list of varieties, from which sowings can be made.

Cultivation. Seeds are sown in outdoor seed-beds $\frac{1}{4}$ in. deep, thinly, in rows 9–12 in. apart, in well-drained, friable soil, dressed with superphosphate at 1 oz. per sq. yd. Seedlings are transplanted in late May to early July to good, not too rich soil, such as one manured for a previous crop, and set out 30 in. apart in rows 30 in. apart, firmly. Lime content should give a pH of about 6·5 to 7·0. A suitable fertilizer is 4 parts hoof and horn meal, 4 parts superphosphate, 2 parts sulphate of potash at 4 oz. per sq. yd.

Diseases. The most serious is Club-root or Ambury (q.v.). Ring Spot, caused by the fungus *Mycosphaerella brassicicola*, shows as brown spots developing dark concentric rings; seldom serious except in the south and west. Prevention is more important than cure, and lies in proper crop rotation, prompt destruction of infected leaves and good culture. Downy Mildew (*Peronospora parasitica*), White Blister (*Cystopus candidus*) and Grey Mould (*Botrytis cinerea*) call for the destruction of much infected plants and remains, but are rarely serious under good culture.

Pests. Flea Beetles (*Phyllotreta* spp.) attack seedlings, but may be controlled by dressing the seeds with a gamma-BHC seed dressing, or gamma-BHC dust, applied immediately damage is seen. Cabbage Root Fly (*Delia brassicae*) flies in April, laying eggs on or near plant stems to hatch into grubs which feed on the roots; control lies in dusting plants from late April with 4 per cent Calomel dust, after planting out. Turnip Gall Weevil (*Ceuthorrhynchus pleurostigma*) causes gall-like, hollow growths, occupied by one or more larvae, on the roots; DDT dust in spring deters the pest but infested roots should be burnt where found. The caterpillars of the Cabbage White Butterflies (*Pieris brassicae, P. rapae*) and the Cabbage Moth (*Barathra brassicae*) may feed on the undersides of leaves in summer and autumn, but can be controlled with a derris insecticide. Cabbage White Fly (*Aleurodes brassicae*) and Cabbage Aphis (*Brevicoryne bras-sicae*) infestations should be promptly checked by the use of a malathion or gamma-BHC insecticide, or nicotine in hot weather.

Broccoli, Sprouting (*Brassica oleracea botrytis cymosa*). Differs from the cauli-flower broccoli in that the flower-bud heads are many and small on branching stalks, the broccoli of Italy.

Varieties. Early Purple Sprouting, sown in early April for December–February cutting; Late Purple Sprouting, sown in May for April cutting; Early White Sprouting, less hardy, and Late White Sprouting, are white-headed counterparts, grown similarly, of the Purple Sprouting varieties, but need more sheltered conditions. Calabresse or Green Sprouting, sown in March, produces a large central head which is cut in late summer; after this, the plant produces smaller heads for two or three months. Nine Star is perennial but requires about 4 sq. ft per plant.

Cultivation. More tolerant of poorer soils than cauliflower-broccoli, but responds to similar culture. Diseases and pests as for Broccoli (q.v.).

Brodiaea (bro-di-e′a. Fam. Amaryl-liaceae). Cormous perennials, native to California, with umbels of pretty flowers in early summer.

Selection. B. bridgesii, 9 in., pale lilac; *californica*, 1 ft, purple-pink; *coronaria*, ½–1½ ft, bluish-purple; are representative. Many species have been transferred to other genera. *B. uniflora* to *Ipheion*, for instance. Also see *Dichelostemma*.

Cultivation. Plant in autumn, 2–3 in. deep, in sandy, humus-rich loam, warm, sunny positions; or grow in pots, standard compost, in cool greenhouse.

Bromelia (bro-me′li-a. Fam. Bromelia-ceae). Stemless perennials with rosettes of firm, spiky, lance-shaped leaves, and panicles of rather fleshy flowers with colourful bracts, natives of tropical America, and grown as hothouse or house plants.

Selection. B. fastuosa, 2 ft, red and reddish violet, August; and *pinguin*, red and white, spring, 1–2 ft, are chiefly offered.

Cultivation. Pot in March, equal parts peat, Osmunda fibre, sand and decayed manure; water freely, summer temp. 21–

27° C. (70–80° F.); winter 15·5–18° C. (60–65° F.), slightly less water needed.

Propagation. By offsets, April, bottom heat 27° C. (80° F.).

Brompton Stocks. See Stocks, and *Matthiola*.

Bromus, Brome Grass (bro′mus. Fam. Gramineae). Grasses of which a few annual species are sometimes grown for their many-flowered spikelets in panicles, for cutting and for winter decoration when dried.

Selection. B. briziformis, Caucasus, 2 ft; *macrostachys* and v. *lanuginosus*, 1–2 ft; and *madritensis*, Europe, 1½ ft, are usually offered.

Cultivation. Ordinary soil; sow in March–April, thinly, where plants are to grow, thin 6 in. apart. Cut when freshly in flower for drying.

Broom. See *Cytisus*, *Genista* and *Spartium*.

Broom, Butcher's. See *Ruscus acu-leatus*.

Broom, Portuguese. See *Cytisus albus*.

Broom, Spanish. See *Genista* and *Spartium*.

Broom-rape. See *Orobanche*.

Broussonetia (brows-son-e′ti-a. Fam. Moraceae). Deciduous Asian shrubs and trees of which *B. papyrifera*, the Paper Mulberry of China, to 15 ft, is hardy for mild localities, with handsome cordate leaves, catkins and female red flowers in round heads, ½ in. wide, spring; reason-ably rich soil. Propagation by cuttings with a heel in summer.

Browallia (brow-al′li-a. Fam. Solana-ceae). Plants of tropical S. America, of which *B. demissa*, 1½ ft, blue, white or violet flowers, June–July, and *grandi-flora*, 1–3 ft, blue or white, July, are free-flowering, half-hardy annuals, raised from seed sown under glass in March (18° C. [65° F.]), to plant out in May, or grow in pots in a cool greenhouse. *B. speciosa major*, 2 ft, is a shrubby peren-nial of Colombia, producing deep blue, white-throated flowers freely in winter months in a cool greenhouse, from seeds sown in spring, and grown in 5- or 6-in. pots; Silver Bells is a fine white flowering form; winter temp. 10–13° C. (50–55° F.).

Bruckenthalia (bruk-en-tha′li-a. Fam. Ericaceae). The one species, *B. spiculi-folia*, SE. Europe, 6 in., is a small ever-green heath, with racemes of magenta pink flowers in June; suitable for lime-free peaty soil in mild localities, in the heath garden or border. Propagation is by division every few years at planting time in April, by young shoot cuttings in a frame in summer; by seeds, sown April.

Brugmansia. See *Datura*.

Brunfelsia (brun-fels'i-a. Fam. Solanaceae). Free-flowering evergreen shrubs of S. America for the warm greenhouse.

Selection. B. americana, W. Indies, 4–6 ft, highly fragrant yellow flowers, June; *calycina*, Brazil, 2 ft, purple, throughout summer; and vs.; and *latifolia*, tropical America, 2–3 ft, lavender to white, scented, are all elegant.

Cultivation. Pot, and repot, after flowering, 2 parts leaf-mould, 2 parts peat, 1 part loam, and 1 part sand. Water freely in active growth, moderately in winter months, minimum temp. 10° C. (50° F.); prune lightly after flowering.

Propagation. By cuttings of young firm shoots, summer, in propagating case, bottom heat 18° C. (65° F.); potting in small pots when rooted.

Brunnera (brun'ne-ra. Fam. Boraginaceae). Hardy perennials of which *B. macrophylla* (*Anchusa myostotidiflora*), Caucasus, 1½ ft, may be grown for its sky-blue sprays of forget-me-not-like flowers, May–July, in partial shade, border or woodland; any ordinary soil, moist but well drained. Propagated by seed, sown in spring out of doors.

Brussels Sprouts (*Brassica oleracea bullata gemmifera*). So called because of their development over 750 years ago near the Belgian capital, Brussels Sprouts are distinctive by reason of the stemless buds or buttons of closely enfolded leaves that form in the axils of the stem leaves, and are now grown extensively for autumn and winter food.

Varieties. Dwarf, 12–15 in., early cropping; Jade Cross F_1, Continuity, Cambridge No. 1; Medium, 1½–2 ft, early: Harrison's XXX, Wroxton, Cambridge No. 3. Mid season, maincrop: Fillbasket, Ormskirk Giant, Winter Harvest, Rous Lench. Late: Cambridge No. 5. Tall strains, 2–3 ft: early, Exhibition; mid season, Goliath, Scrymger's Giant, Irish Elegance, Cluseed Giant, Fillbasket; late, Rearguard, King of the Lates, Blue Vein. Certain strains do better in one locality than another, and

seeds should be bought from first-class seedsmen, with local advice. Red is a red-coloured novelty.

Cultivation. A long growing season, good soil and firm planting are essential. Soil should be well dug, organically manured, and limed to bring to pH 6·5 to 7·0 the preceding winter. In March a balanced fertilizer should be well raked in, or a mixture of 4 parts by weight hoof and horn meal, 4 parts superphosphate 2 parts sulphate of potash at 3 oz. per sq. yd. Liquid feeding can be done in June with dilute liquid manure or a seaweed derivative. Seeds may be sown (*a*) in autumn within a cold frame, to plant out in March–April for earliest crops; (*b*) in boxes in a cool greenhouse in February–March to plant out in April or early May; (*c*) in March out of doors on sheltered warm bed, to plant out in late May. The soil must be made very firm to the roots of the young plants. It is sensible to earth up plants where exposed to much wind, as they make growth. In late August or September sprouts can be hastened to heart up by 'cocking'—removing the small, nut-size growing point of the main stem; or later for a late variety, leaving the surrounding leaves intact. Tall plants will benefit from being staked. Sprouts are best harvested from the base at first, going over the plants at intervals, leaving the heads to the last.

Diseases and Pests. These are the same as for Broccoli (q.v.).

Bryanthus (bri-an'thus. Fam. Ericaceae). The one species, *B. gmelinii* (*musciformis*), is a rare, slow-growing prostrate shrub of N. Japan and Kamchatka, 2–3 in. high, densely crowded with tiny linear leaves, and heads of pinkish flowers in May, requiring a lime-free soil, cool shade and rather moist conditions; best provided in a cold frame or the alpine house, or a north slope of a rock garden in a mild locality.

Bryoides. Moss-like. Ex. *Saxifraga bryoides*.

Bryophyllum (bri-o-pil'lum. Fam. Crassulaceae). Somewhat shrubby perennials with succulent leaves, with heads of tubular, drooping flowers in spring; native to Madagascar, and grown in the warm greenhouse and increasingly as house plants; closely related to *Kalanchoe*.

Selection. B. crenata, 1½ ft, yellowish-brown; *proliferum*, 2 ft, yellow; *tubi-florum*, 2½ ft, red.

Cultivation. Pot, and repot, in April, standard compost; or 3 parts rich loam, 1 part leaf-mould, 1 part sand, with good drainage. Water freely in active growth; sparingly in winter, minimum temp. 10° C. (50° F.); but flower earlier in warmer conditions.

Propagation. The plants are distinctive in that small plantlets are formed along the notches of their leaves, which may be detached to root and grow when placed on damp soil.

Bryophyta. One of the Divisions of the Plant Kingdom which includes (*a*) the Liverworts or Hepaticae; and (*b*) the Mosses or *Musci*.

Buck Bean. See *Menyanthes trifoliata*.

Buckler Fern. See *Dryopteris*.

Buckthorn. See *Rhamnus*.

Buckthorn, Sea. See *Hippohae*.

Budding. A method of vegetative propagation by which a bud (or eye), called the scion, is removed from a plant and transferred to be united with a different plant, called the stock, or with another part of the same plant. The operation is carried out when the sap is circulating freely, and the bark comes away from the wood easily on the stock; usually from June to late August. Of the various ways, Shield or T-budding is most often used, particularly for propagating roses and fruit trees. Plump wood buds are selected on well-developed shoots of the current season's growth, with leaves cut off, but leaf-stalks left for handling; the bud is removed on a shield of bark, by cutting from about ½ in. below upward and behind the bud to just above it with a clean sharp knife, with no more than the thinnest sliver, if any, of wood. The stock is prepared by making a vertical cut through the bark, slightly longer than the bud shield, and a shorter horizontal cut at the top, forming a T. The bark is then eased back with a blunt blade, such as that of a budding knife, until the bud on its shield will slip in, with its greenish cambium tissue in contact with that of the stock. The bud is tied in with raffia or preferably plastic budding tape to exclude air, rain or insects, but not so tightly as to injure the bark. As soon as union is evident, the ties are examined and loosened, if necessary. The whole operation must be done quickly, without any drying out of tissues; buds can be kept moist in a damp cloth. It helps to shade budded stocks in hot dry weather. Budding is also sometimes done by removing a square, a circle or a ring of bark carrying a bud, and fitting this into a similar space on the stock, made by removing bark of the same size and shape, and then sealing with raffia or tape to exclude air, etc. This requires greater precision, as the transferred bark must fit in the bark of the stock perfectly. All budding is best done in dullish weather, morning or evening, if possible. Many ornamental trees, deciduous and evergreen, may be propagated by budding. Compatible stocks, usually of the same species or genus, sometimes within the same family, must be used.

Budding Knife. A good budding knife has a handle of ivory, ivorine or bone, shaped to a short, rounded blade at one end with which to open and lift the bark, and one or more sharp, straight cutting blades; one of which may have a rounded point, less likely to cut more than the bark in use.

Buddleia, Butterfly Bush (bud'le-a. Fam. Loganiaceae). Of the colourful flowering shrubs in this genus, the hardy kinds provide delightful summer flowers, scented and often attractive to butterflies.

Selection. B. davidii, China, to 15 ft, is deciduous, with large close spikes of lavender flowers, July–September, and has several named forms such as 'Empire Blue', 'Royal Red', 'White Bouquet' and the deep purple 'Black Knight'; all of which may be kept within bounds by pruning the previous year's growth hard back in February or March; *nanhoensis*, 4 ft, is a dwarf form with shorter flower spikes. *B. fallowiana*, 6–10 ft, with very fragrant panicles of lavender flowers in June, is even better in its white v. *alba*, and may be hard-pruned in late winter. The Orange Ball Tree, *globosa*, Chile, to 10 ft, with stalked, rounded heads of orange-yellow flowers in June, is almost evergreen in mild districts; *alternifolia*, China, to 20 ft, spreads widely with graceful weeping branches, wreathed with clusters of lilac-purple flowers,

June; and *colvilei*, Himalaya, 10–20 ft, carries crimson-maroon panicles of the largest flowers in June, but needs a mild climate and shelter. These June-flowering species may be pruned after flowering.

Cultivation. Well-drained, humus-rich soil is preferred. Plant in early autumn or April.

Propagation. By cuttings of firm shoots, inserted in a cold frame, in late summer or September. By seeds in warm light soil in spring.

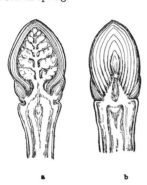

FIG. 32 Buds: a. flower bud, containing embryonic flower; b. leaf bud, to make shoot growth.

Buds. Buds are simply short, young, undeveloped shoots. On growing they may produce leaves, and with further development shoots or stems bearing leaves, or flowers. In regulating the growth of trees, particularly fruits, it is important to be able to differentiate between the thin, slim, almost conical leaf bud, and the fatter, rounded blossom bud. The development of a flower or flowers from a flower bud stops vegetative growth from it. Buds may be terminal, at the ends of stems or shoots, or axillary or lateral, in the axils of leaves and stem. Some axillary buds remain dormant, though they may grow if the stem is severed above them or injured. Buds may also form in other parts of a plant, as from the callus or healing tissue of cut stems; on leaves, and on roots, and such buds are termed adventitious.

Bugle. See *Ajuga*.
Bugloss, Viper's. See *Echium*.
Bulb. A bulb is a complete plant at a resting stage of growth, consisting of a modified shoot, formed underground, and made up of a more or less fleshy disk-like stem or plate, carrying a mass of swollen leaves or scales, containing food reserves, and enclosing or surrounding a central embryo shoot from the stem or plate, bearing the rudimentary

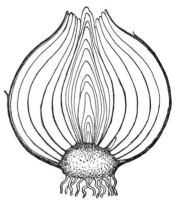

FIG. 33 A Bulb, with fleshy scales (leaves) surrounding embryo flowering shoot, from a basal plate.

leaves and inflorescence which develop into foliage and flower on growth being resumed, while from the underside of the plate adventitious roots bud and form. In the axils of the swollen leaves and from the basal stem, lateral buds form and develop into daughter bulbs, often called offsets, by which the plants propagate themselves vegetatively. In some species (e.g. Tulipa), the parent bulb dies, leaving one or more large daughter bulbs and some smaller ones developed at the base of leaves; in others the parent bulb lives on, with other bulbs developing from the basal plate at the sides (e.g. Narcissus); and others give rise to several daughter bulbs around the diminishing parent (e.g. Shallots). Bulbous plants should be allowed to grow until the foliage yellows and withers before being lifted, to ensure maximum development of the bulbs;

dried under cool conditions, not in the hot sun; and stored cool (7° C. [45° F.]). The rest period varies, and replanting should not be unduly delayed, since root development must precede top growth. The various bulbous plants are dealt with under their generic names. See *Acidanthera, Allium, Amaryllis, Babiana, Bravoa, Brodiaea, Bulbocodium, Calochortus, Camassia, Chionodoxa, Clivia, Colchicum, Crinum, Cypella, Dichelostemma, Dierama, Elisena, Endymion, Erythronium, Eucharis, Eucomis, Ferraria, Frittilaria, Galanthus, Galtonia, Gloriosa, Habranthus, Haemanthus, Hippeastrum, Hyacinthella, Hyacinthus, Hymenocallis, Ipheion, Iris, Ixia, Ixiolirion, Lachenalia, Leucojum, Lilium, Lycoris, Merendera, Muscari, Narcissus, Nerine, Nomocharis, Ornithogalum, Pancratium, Paradisea, Puschkinia, Schizostylis, Scilla, Sparaxis, Sprekelia, Sternbergia, Triteleia, Tulipa, Urceolina, Urginea, Vallota, Veltheimia, Watsonia, Zephyranthes.*

Bulbinella (bul-bin-el'la. Fam. Liliaceae). Herbaceous perennials with thick underground root stem and roots, linear leaves and erect racemes of pretty flowers in summer, from New Zealand.

Selection. B. hookeri, 2–3 ft, yellow or whitish, summer; *rossii,* 2–3 ft, orange.

Cultivation. Not reliably hardy, need well-drained loam soil, in warm, partial shade, and winter protection. Plant in April.

Propagation. By division in April.

Bulbocodium (bul-bo-ko'di-um. Fam. Liliaceae). The one species, *B. vernum,* is a hardy cormous plant of 6 in., with tubular, funnel-shaped, violet-purple flowers, resembling those of Colchicum, and strap-like leaves in early spring, from Central and Southern Europe.

Cultivation. Plant in well-drained, porous soil, autumn. Lift every other year, divide, refurbish the soil with sifted organic matter and bone meal.

Bulbophyllum (bul-bo-pil'lum. Fam. Orchidaceae). Small epiphytic orchids, requiring stove conditions.

Selection. B. barbigerum, Sierra Leone, dwarf, greenish-brown flower; *dearei,* Borneo, yellow, veined reddish; *grandiflorum,* greenish white, netted brown; *lobbii,* Siam, yellow, spotted purple; summer flowering.

Cultivation. Pot in April–May, well-drained shallow pans or baskets; in 3 parts chopped Osmunda fibre and 1 part sphagnum moss, and hang on rafters; water well in growth, shade from hot sun; minimum summer temp. 21° C. (70° F.); winter 13° C. (55° F.).

Propagation. By division of rhizomes in April.

Bullace (*Prunus insititia*). Closely related to the Plum and the Damson which are to be preferred where space is limited, the Bullace does yield small, round purplish fruits, excellent for cooking and jam, in October–November, freely on self-fertile trees, 15–20 ft tall, which might be considered as windbreak planting on the exposed sides of an orchard. There is a White Bullace with pale yellow fruits, having a whitish bloom, as well as the Black Bullace. Culture is the same as for Plums (q.v.).

Bullatus (-a, -um). Bullate, having blisters, puckers or pustules. Ex. *Cotoneaster bullata.*

Bullrush. See *Scirpus, Typha.*

Buphthalmum, Yellow Ox-eye (bup-thal'mum. Fam. Compositae). Showy, hardy herbaceous perennials with large, yellow-rayed flower-heads in summer.

Selection. B. salicifolium, Austria, 1½–2 ft, *speciosissimum,* S. Europe, 2 ft, and *speciosum,* SE. Europe, to 5 ft, are all good.

Cultivation. Any good ordinary soil suits, sunny position. *B. speciosum* does well by water.

Propagation. By division in October or March. By seeds, sown in cold frame or outdoors, April.

Bupleurum (bu-plur'um. Fam. Umbelliferae). The chief species cultivated is *B. fruticosum,* S. Europe, an evergreen shrub of 4–8 ft, with umbels of small yellow flowers in August–September; chiefly valuable for seaside planting to withstand salt-laden winds, thriving in any soil. Only hardy in southern and western mild districts.

Cultivation. Plant in early autumn or March–April; any soil, including chalk, well drained. Prune after flowering, if necessary, or in March.

Propagation. By cuttings of firm young shoots, in sandy peat soil, in cold frame, September.

Burbidgea (bur-bidj'e-a. Fam. Zingi-beraceae). Tropical rhizomatous herbaceous perennials for humid stove conditions. *B. nitida*, N. Borneo, 2–3 ft, with a head of shining orange-scarlet flowers, in summer, and *schizocheila*, Malaya, 1 ft, with orange-yellow flowers, may be grown in large pots, tubs or border, using a compost of equal parts loam, leaf-mould, peat and sand; watering freely in growth, little at other times; winter temp. 13° C. (55° F.) minimum. Propagated by division in March.

Burchellia (bur-kel'li-a. Fam. Rubiaceae). The one species, *B. capensis*, is a South African evergreen shrub, 3–5 ft, with ovate leaves, and heads of inch-long, somewhat funnel-shaped, bright scarlet flowers, April; to be grown in large pots or the border of a warm greenhouse: winter temp. 13° C. (55° F.), watering freely in active growth, moderately in winter. A standard compost, or one of equal parts loam, peat, leaf-mould and sand. Plant in March. Propagate by cuttings of young shoots, April–May, in propagating case, at 24° C. (75° F.).

Burgundy Mixture. A variant of Bordeaux Mixture, in which washing soda replaces the lime. *See* Fungicides.

Burnet Rose. See *Rosa spinosissima*.

Burning Bush. See *Dictamnus*.

Butcher's Broom. See *Ruscus*.

Butomus, Flowering Rush (bu-to'mus. Fam. Butomaceae). The one species, *B. umbellatus*, is a handsome native perennial for shallow waters or wet soil, 2–3 ft high, with slender, triquetrous leaves, and bold umbels of rose flowers in summer.

Cultivation. Plant in April, in shallow water, or rich, wet soil. Propagate by division, spring.

Butterbur. See *Petasites*.

Buttercup. See *Ranunculus*.

Butterfly Bush. See *Buddleia*.

Butterfly Flower. See *Schizanthus*.

Butterfly Orchids. Native wildings; *Platanthera bifolia, P. chlorantha*.

Butterfly Tulip. See *Calochortus*.

Butterwort. See *Pinguicula*.

Button Bush. See *Cephalanthus occidentalis*.

Buxifolius (-a, -um). Box-leaved. Ex. *Cotoneaster buxifolia*.

Buxus (buks'us. Fam. Buxaceae).

FIG. 34 The inflorescence of *Butomus umbellatus*, the Flowering Rush.

Evergreen shrubs or small trees, valued for their ornamental foliage, hardiness and willingness to stand up to trimming as formal hedges and ornamental topiary.

Selection. *B. sempervirens*, Britain, Europe, etc., grows to 20 ft naturally, but is more often used for hedges and topiary. Its vs. *argentea*, leaves edged white; *aurea pendula*, the golden weeping form, and *pendula*, elegant green weeping form; and *handsworthii*, large-leaved, make good specimens for small garden lawns. Interesting dwarfs are *elegantissima*, with narrow white-edged leaves, *myosotifolia*, tiny-leaved *myrtifolia*, with small myrtle-like leaves, *rosmarinifolia*, with narrow, rosemary-like leaves and *suffruticosa*, which is the edging box, much used for formal effect and to grow only 6–12 in. high; *pyramidalis*, erect in habit, is good for hedges; *latifolia maculata*, compact with broad leaves yellowing; and *prostrata* is a vigorous, low-spreading variety. Korea contributes *B. microphylla*, 3–4 ft, small-leaved, rounded and compact, and China *harlandii*, to 3 ft, dome-shaped with long, cuneate leaves; but not so hardy.

Cultivation. May be planted in early autumn or spring, any well-drained soil, doing well on chalk; tolerant of shade. Clipped forms may be trimmed in May and August; established hedges each August.

Propagation. By cuttings of young shoots, 3 in. long, July–September, in sandy loam, shady border; by layering in spring or late summer; by division, April.

Byzantinus (-a, -um). Of Byzantium (Turkey); Ex. *Gladiolus byzantinus.*

C

Cabbage (*Brassica oleracea capitata*). As a source of vitamins and food-minerals, the cabbage is one of the most nutritious vegetables. It may be had in season throughout the year. Like all brassicas cabbage succeeds best in well-dug soil, liberally organically manured, limed to pH 6·5, and in open, sunny positions. It may follow roots, potatoes or legumes, but not a crop of its own family. True cabbage has smooth leaves, folded inward to form a closely packed head and heart. Savoy cabbage has wrinkled leaves, though the culture is similar (*see* Savoy). Sowing times and varieties are related to the season of the year at which the vegetables are intended to mature.

Early Summer Cabbage. For cutting in June, the seeds are sown in January–February, $\frac{1}{2}$ in. deep, in a cool greenhouse or frame, to plant out in early April, about 1 ft apart. Outdoors a first sowing may be made in March, planted out 4–6 weeks later, to mature in July–August. Quick-maturing varieties such as First and Best,† Golden Acre,* Greyhound,† Primo,* Summer Triumph F_1,* Tender and True,* Harbinger,† Early Paragon Roundhead* and Velocity.* The same varieties may be sown in July to give small cabbages before the winter.

Mid-season Cabbage. For cutting in high summer and early autumn, seeds are sown $\frac{1}{2}$ in. deep, in a separate nursery bed in March to plant out in June. The soil should have been adequately prepared, winter-manured with rotted organic matter, and its lime status checked and corrected. Prior to planting a balanced brassica fertilizer should be raked in, or a mixture of 4 parts by weight hoof and horn meal, 2 parts superphosphate, 1 part sulphate of potash, at 4 oz. per sq. yd. This can be supplemented 4–6 weeks after planting with 1 oz. per sq. yd of nitro-chalk, or a liquid feeding. Firm planting is essential, setting seedlings with first true leaves at soil level.

Suitable varieties are Greyhound,† Fillgap* and Monarch F_1,* to give small to medium hearts; Enfield Market, Utility, and Webb's Emperor for large hearts.

Autumn–winter Cabbage. For cutting in late September–January, seeds are sown in April–May, and culture is similar to that for summer cabbage. Good varieties are Autumn Glory F_1,* Pride of the Market,* Winningstadt,† Autumn Pride F^1* and Winter Keeper *; and for December–January, Christmas Drumhead,* January King * and Wheeler's Imperial.†

Spring Cabbage. For cutting in April–June, seeds are sown on an outdoor seedbed of friable soil in good heart, with protection from birds by netting, if needed; and transplanted to good soil, preferably well manured for a previous crop (onions, potatoes, etc.) in September–October, preferably well-drained and lightish, and in a sheltered warm position where growth responds readily to the spring sun. Plants should be well firmed, and soil drawn to them a little before winter sets in. In February–March, a stimulatory feed of nitro-chalk or a nitrogen-high fertilizer or seaweed derivative will help hearting. Many varieties are offered, and often a tested locally recommended strain is best. Otherwise, Sutton's April,† Ellam's Dwarf Early Spring,† Durham Early,* Durham Elf,* Flower of Spring,† Harbinger, † First Early Market.†

Red Cabbage. For the largest heads for pickling, the seed is sown in autumn in a cold frame or well-sheltered conditions, to over-winter and be planted in March, for summer or autumn harvesting. Sowings can be made in March–April also. Of the drumhead type, suitable varieties are Blood Red, Red Drumhead, Stockley's Giant and Early Blood Red.

Chinese Cabbage or *Petsai* (*Brassica cernua*) is an annual, growing rapidly

---

* Round or ball headed. † Pointed headed.

with a head resembling that of a Cos
Lettuce. Seeds are sown in late May–
July, in well-drained, humus-rich soil,
where they are to grow in rows 15 in.
apart, thinning plants to 18 in. Varieties
are Chihli, light green, crisp leaves;
Petsai, white-hearted; and Wong Bok,
larger heads.

Portuguese Cabbage or *Couve Tron-
chuda (Brassica oleracea costa'a)* is grown
for the thick midribs of its great leaves,
which are flavoursome when cooked like
seakale, while the heart is used as a
cabbage. Seeds are sown in February–
March, in cool greenhouse or frame, and
seedlings planted out in May, 3 ft apart.

Diseases and Pests. These are the same
as for other brassicas; *see under* Borecole. *See* Club-root.

Cacalia. See *Emilia.*

Cactus (pl. **Cacti**). The popular common name of succulent plants of the
family *Cactaceae.* Although botanically
identifiable by floral characteristics, the
one clear readily identifiable distinction
of a cactus is the possession of a vegetative organ called the areole, a small protuberance of woolly felt or hairs from
which spines arise. Cacti are native to the
Americas. There are probably over 2,000
different species, now divided into three
tribes—Pereskieae, Opuntieae and Cere-
eae; the last being further divided into
8 subtribes. Obviously there is much
variation among cacti, and they cannot
all be treated alike. The key to their culture lies in the factors of their growth in
their native habitat. Only general broad
recommendations can be given here.

Cultivation. Cacti may be divided into
epiphytic and terrestrial kinds. Epiphytes (e.g. climbing Cereus, Epiphyllum) are native to warm, moist tropical
regions, and usually need greenhouse or
indoor conditions. Terrestrials belong to
hot dry desert regions, and require a
definite resting period, fortunately coinciding with our winters, when they
require to be kept dry, as moisture at
low temperatures can cause rotting. The
soil for all cacti must be porous and free-
draining. Although specialists put forward many pet formulae, one of equal
parts good medium to heavy loam, peat
and coarse sharp sand is sound; plus a
sprinkling of bone meal and limestone
grit for desert soils. Extra peat—leaf-

mould is less suitable—can be added for
epiphytes, though these can also be
grown in Osmunda fibre and peat, plus a
little rotted cow manure, in warm,
humid conditions. No fertilizers should
be given to cacti, except a little bone
meal. Plants are potted at the beginning
of the growing season, usually spring,
and it is important that pot size should
match plant size, neither too small nor
too large. Good crocking, and a little
charcoal, at the base is necessary for
drainage and soil sweetness. Terrestrial
cacti need no water when at rest,
between October and mid March, at
temp. 5–7° C. (40–45° F.); when growth
begins, water is best given by immersing
pots in water until the soil is evenly
soaked, and then stand to drain. Thereafter water with gradually increasing
frequency from weekly to daily in late
June to early August in hot weather;
and gradually reduce to September,
when plants must be 'ripened' or
hardened off, to no water as October
begins to elapse. Epiphytes need watering through the year, though with less in
winter, with temp. of 10° C. (50° F.)
minimum; in summer, they welcome
humidity and can be syringed in hot
weather. Cacti can be grown in cool
greenhouses, with good ventilation, and
temperatures kept just above 5° C.
(40° F.); or in indoor rooms where
they can receive good light, but not
scorching direct sun in sudden bursts.
In dry rooms, some humidity should
be provided, and it may be necessary
to give a few drops of water to
prevent undue shrinkage in winter,
but grudgingly and carefully.

Propagation. By cuttings of offsets,
pieces detached at a joint, tops of stems,
tubercles, according to type, taken at
any time of the year, though winter is
least favourable, and inserted in a
mixture of sharp sand and peat, kept
damp and close in a propagating frame
or case, at 21° C. (70° F.). By seeds,
standard compost, with bottom heat of
16–21° C. (60–70° F.), spring or early
summer. By grafting when quick propagation of slow-growing kinds is required;
scion and stock must belong to the
same family. The grafted plant, however,
is seldom so characteristic of its type as
one on its own roots.

Diseases and Pests. Cacti are rarely troubled by disease. The chief trouble is likely to be a rot started at or near the soil surface, and is usually aggravated by overwet conditions, especially when temperatures are low. A top covering of the soil with suitable stone chippings or gravel helps to prevent this.

The chief pest is Mealy Bug (*Pseudococcus* spp.) on the plants, which can be removed with tweezers, painted with white oil emulsion, carefully so as not to dissolve the waxy bloom as well as the 'wool' of the bugs, or spraying with a malathion insecticide. Root Mealy Bug (*Ripersia* spp.) attack the roots, but may be controlled by placing a few crystals of paradichlorobenzene in the drainage holes of pots. Scale Insects (*Lecanium* spp.) develop under a scaly shield on plants, and this is best picked off with tweezers when seen; in spring and summer spraying with a malathion insecticide at fortnightly intervals will usually clear an infestation. Red Spider Mites (*Tetranychus telarius*) are apt to be troublesome in dry atmospheres. In summer frequent syringing with water checks infestation, and chemical control can be achieved by fumigating the plants with Azobenzene Smoke, or spraying with a pybuthrin/derris aerosol. Aphids (Greenfly) can be defeated by using malathion in aerosol form to cover the insects, or a DDT/gamma BHC insecticide. Ants need to be discouraged not so much because of the damage they do but because of their habit of tending and transferring such pests as aphids, scale insects, etc., from plant to plant; a DDT/gamma BHC dust at the base of plants stops them, or a proprietary ant-killer may be used. Woodlice or Slaters may be controlled by dusting where they are seen with a DDT insecticide, and keeping surroundings hygienically clean, and free of decaying organic matter.

See *Cactus, Cephalocereus, Cereus, Echinocactus, Echinocereus, Echinopsis, Epiphyllum, Ferocactus, Gymnocalcycium, Lithops, Lobivia, Mamillaria, Nyctocereus, Opuntia, Pereskia, Rebutia, Rhipsalis,* and *Schlambergera* (*Zygocactus*).

Cactus (kak'tus. Fam. Cactaceae). Now a genus of few species, sometimes listed under *Melocactus*; rare, tropical and not easy to keep. The best known is *C. melocactus* (*neryi*), the Turk's Cap, Jamaica, globular, with broad ribs, forming a cephalium or woolly cap of white with reddish bristles. Others are *caesius*, Venezuela; and *intortus*, W. Indies. Water freely and syringe in summer, 21° C. (70° F.); moderately in winter, temp. 15·5° C. (60° F.).

Caeruleus (-a, -um). Blue. Ex. *Hibiscus syriacus caeruleus.*

Caesalpinia (kees-alp-in'i-a. Fam. Leguminosae). Deciduous shrubs of doubly pinnate leaves, and open flowers of much beauty; but not very hardy.

Selection. C. gilliesii, Argentine, to 10 ft, is the Bird of Paradise shrub, with 12-in. racemes of yellow, red-stamened flowers, July–August; and *japonica,* Japan, to 15 ft, canary yellow flowers, July, may be grown on sunny, warm walls in mild localities, as the hardiest.

Cultivation. Any well-drained ordinary soil. Plant autumn to March. Prune after flowering to preserve shape, or in February.

Propagation. By seeds in cold frame, April–August, porous compost, at 18–21° C. (65–70° F.).

Caladium (ka-la'di-um. Fam. Araceae). Tuberous-rhizomatous rooted tropical perennials, attractive for their huge, vari-coloured leaves, for hothouse conditions, and indoor house plants.

Selection. C. bicolor, S. America, 1 ft, and vs. *baraquinii, chantinii,* etc.; *humboldtii,* Brazil, and v. *myriostigma; picturatum* and vs.; and *schomburgkii,* Guinea, Brazil; and their hybrids.

Cultivation. Start tubers in growth in compost of equal parts loam, leaf-mould and peat, with sand for drainage, in February; temp. 21–24° C. (70–75° F.); grow on in moist atmosphere, watering freely in summer; gradually withhold water in autumn; keep almost dry in winter, temp. 13° C. (55° F.), in their pots.

Propagation. By division of tubers in February–March.

Calamintha, Calamint (kal-a-minth'a. Fam. Labiatae). Perennial herbs with thyme-like, fragrant, summer flowers, for the rock garden.

Selection. C. alpina, S. Europe, 6 in., with whorls of purplish flowers, and *grandiflora,* upright to 9 in., rose-pink flowers, are usually grown. *C. acinos,* the native annual Basil Thyme, is now *Acinos arvensis,* easily grown from seed sown in April.

Cultivation. Any well-drained soil; sunny position. Plant October–March.

Propagation. Easiest by division in March. By cuttings of young shoots in summer, under handlight.

Calandrinia (kal-an-drin′i-a. Fam. Portulacaceae). Primarily perennial, but usually grown as half-hardy annuals. *C. discolor,* Chile, 1–1½ ft, showy light purple flowers in summer; *grandiflora,* Chile, 2 ft, purple; and *umbellata,* 6 in., crimson-magenta, may be flowered in the greenhouse, or planted out in May; the latter sometimes perennating in a warm spot in the rock garden. Best grown from seed, sown under glass, bottom heat 18° C. (65° F.), March.

Calanthe (kal-anth′e Fam. Orchidaceae). Terrestrial deciduous and evergreen orchids, valuable for their tall spikes of many flowers, lasting long.

Selection. Evergreen—*C. masuca,* India, deep violet flowers, summer; *veratrifolia,* India, 2–3 ft., white flowering spikes, May–July, and vs. Deciduous— *C. vestita,* Burma, 2½ ft spikes of white flowers, winter, and many vs., and hybrids, which may be chosen from the lists of Orchid specialists.

Cultivation. Pot in March; filling pots one-third full of broken crocks, then a compost of equal parts loam, peat and sphagnum moss, with coarse sand and broken charcoal; placing bulbs well up in the pot. Water freely, syringe daily in hot weather, summer temps. 18–29° C. (65–85° F.), with good light. Keep deciduous kinds almost dry in winter, evergreens just moist temp. 15·5° C. (60° F.) minimum.

Propagation. By division of pseudobulbs, March.

Calathea (kal-a-the′a. Fam. Marantaceae). South American perennial herbs, grown for their ornamental foliage as warm greenhouse and house plants.

Selection. C. backemiana, 15 in., silvery-grey, olive green blotched leaves; *lindeniana,* to 3 ft, deep green, zoned yellow-green, and maroon beneath, leaves; *picturata,* 1 ft, green with silvery white zoned or lined leaves; and *zebrina,* 1½ ft, deep green, banded paler green,

leaves, are from Brazil; *ornata* 1½–8 ft, with leaves lined pale green and white, has several attractive vs., and *veitchinana,* Peru, to 2½ ft, has leaves of various shades of green.

Cultivation. Pot and repot, March–April, in equal parts loam, peat and leaf-mould, plus coarse sand to one-sixth; water freely in summer, temps. 21–27° C. (70–80° F.), moderately in winter, temp. 18° C. (65° F.) minimum; appreciate partial shade, some humidity.

Propagation. By division. March–April, when repotting.

Calceolaria, Slipper Flower (kal-ke-o-la′ri-a, or kal-se-o-la′ri-a. Fam. Scrophulariaceae). A genus of plants largely native to C. and S. America, distinctive for their slipper-like flowers with a pouted lower lip. Horticulturally, consider as follows.

Herbaceous species and hybrids, naturally perennial, but grown as half-hardy annuals or biennials to flower under glass. Sow the fine seeds thinly and lightly in pans, standard compost, June, in greenhouse or frame, shading from sun and keeping moist. Transplant seedlings in July–August to small 2-in. pots, potting on as required by growth, to winter in cool greenhouse (10° C. [50° F.]), finally potting to 6- or 7-in. pots in March, to flower in May–July. Or with earlier sowings and a warm greenhouse may be flowered earlier. Seeds are offered in vari-colour mixtures, and the strains *gracilis* and Glorious F_1 are good for early flowering.

Shrubby species and hybrids. These are largely grown for bedding in summer, and for cool greenhouse and conservatory as pot plants. They may be raised from seed sown in March, standard compost, bottom heat 13–15·5° C. (55–60° F.); to be potted on; hardened off for planting out in June, or finally to 6-in. pots for growing under glass. From plants, cuttings of young shoots may be taken in September in cool frame, over-wintered and potted into 4-in. pots in spring, with growing points nipped out, and grown on and hardened off for planting in early June in beds. They only need protection against hard frosts. If needed for pot growth under glass, the cuttings can be taken earlier, and grown under cool greenhouse conditions throughout, growth being pinched back to induce bushy plants. Pot on as the roots fill the pots, using standard composts. Species include: *B. amplexicaulis*, yellow; *bicolor*, Peru, white and yellow; *pavonii*, Peru, yellow and brown; *integrifolia*, Chile, to 3 ft, yellow; and hybrids such as × *burbidgei*, 2–4 ft, excellent for winter flowering; and × *profusa*, a similar large showy plant with rich yellow flowers.

Hardy species. C. mexicana, 10 in., pale yellow flowers in summer, and *scabiosifolia*, Peru, 1½ ft, yellow, may be grown as hardy annuals. *C. acutifolia*, Patagonia, 4 in., golden, June, is a low rhizomatous perennial; *arachnoidea*, Chile, 6 in., purple, June, and white v. *alba*; *biflora*, Chile, 6 in., yellow, July; *darwinii*, Patagonia, 3 in., yellow, brown-spotted, July; *polyrrhiza*, Chile, herbaceous dwarf, 6 in., yellow, purple spotted, June; and *tenella*, Chile, 4 in., yellow, June, with *uniflora*, Patagonia, 4 in., yellow, June, herbaceous, are eligible for the rock garden or alpine house, given a porous, humus soil, light shade and winter protection from wet and cold. All may be propagated by division in April, or by young shoot cuttings in July.

Calcifuge. Disliking lime. *See* Lime-tolerance in plants.

Calciole, Calciphilous. Liking lime. *See* Lime-tolerance in plants.

Calcium. An essential nutrient of plants, as a constituent of cell walls, a base for the neutralization of organic acids and for the normal development of growing points and root tips, and for nitrogen absorption. Calcium is obtained from the soil where it occurs as carbonate of lime chiefly, but is subject to loss in solution, especially under arable cultivation. *See* Lime.

Calcium Cyanamide. A nitrogenous fertilizer, 20·6 per cent nitrogen, 22 per cent lime, acting quickly with an alkaline end reaction, for application in late winter or spring, prior to sowing or planting, as an alternative to sulphate of ammonia on acid soils. It is initially caustic to plant foliage and may be used for the superficial control of weeds at 1–2 oz. per sq. yd. It is also useful as an activator or rotting agent in compost heaps.

Calcium Cyanide. A chemical which gives off toxic hydrocyanic acid gas when exposed to moisture. Once used in

greenhouses to fumigate against insect pests, but now superseded by insecticidal smokes or aerosols (*see* Greenhouse Insecticides). In proprietary form (e.g. Cyanogas), the chemical is prepared for use in controlling rabbits, rats, moles, etc., in their runs, and wasps and ants in their nests, but should be handled strictly according to the maker's recommendations, as the fumes are highly dangerous to humans, and pet animals, if inhaled.

Calendula, Pot Marigold (ka-len'dul-a. Fam. Compositae). Only *C. officinalis*, the hardy annual introduced from southern Europe nearly 400 years ago, is grown, averaging 2 ft tall, with ray-petalled flowers, single to double, in shades of orange and yellow, borne freely throughout summer. Strains of note are the double Orange King, Golden King and Lemon King; orange Radio with quilled petals; Pacific Beauties; Kelmscott Orange, and single Nova.

Cultivation. Sow under glass in February–March, 15·5° C. (60° F.), bottom heat; or outdoors in April; sow in July–August to overwinter in mild gardens, in cold frame elsewhere. Plant in any ordinary soil, remove spent flowers to prolong bloom.

Calico Bush. See *Kalmia*.

Californian Poppy. See *Eschscholtzia*.

Calla, Bog Arum (kal'la. Fam. Araceae). The one species, *C. palustris*, 6 in., is a hardy aquatic perennial with floating leaves, producing short white spathes in summer, naturalized in Britain, and suitable for pond margins or boggy soil. Plant in April, propagating by division in the same month.

Callicarpa (kal-li-kar'pa. Fam. Verbenaceae). Chiefly deciduous shrubs, attractive in flower and for their beautiful autumn berrying, but only really hardy enough for mild localities.

Selection. C. giraldiana, China, 6 ft, shining bluish-lilac berries; *dichotoma*, China, 4 ft, deep violet berries; and *japonica*, Japan, 4 ft, violet berries, are the hardiest; *rubella*, Himalaya, 3–5 ft, rose-purple, needs cool greenhouse conditions.

Cultivation. Plant in autumn or spring, good loam soil, sunny warm position; preferably more than one for good berrying. Prune in March, to shape.

Propagation. By cuttings of young

half-ripe shoots in July–August, in propagating frame or under handlight.

Calliopsis. See *Coreopsis*.

Callirhoe, Poppy Mallow (kal-ir-ho'e. Fam. Malvaceae). N. American annuals and perennials with showy single flowers in summer.

Selection. *C. involucrata*, Texas, 6 in., with large crimson flowers, and its v. *lineariloba*, lilac, white-edged, make good procumbent perennials for a sunny spot in the rock garden; *papaver*, rambles with stems to 3 ft, and has poppy-like violet-red flowers, good for dry sandy places. The annual, *pedata*, Texas, 2–3 ft, is variable with reddish to lilac flowers.

Cultivation. All may be grown from seed sown under glass, March, bottom heat 18° C. (65° F.), to plant out in April, in well-drained porous soil and sun.

Callistemon, Bottle Brush (kal-i-ste'mon. Fam. Myrtaceae). Evergreen shrubs of Australia, suitable for cool greenhouse conditions in pots, notable for their long-stamened flowers, borne in spikes.

Selection. *C. citrinus* v. *splendens*, scarlet, June; *linearis*, crimson, July; *phoeniceus*, red, July; *salignus*, yellow, June; and v. *alba*, white; and *speciosa*, deep scarlet, June–July; all 2½–5 ft when pot-grown.

Cultivation. Pot, and repot biennially, March; standard compost, or equal parts loam, peat, with sand. Prune to shape after flowering. Water freely in summer, very moderately in winter, temp. 7° C. (45° F.).

Propagation. By cuttings of firm young shoots, July–August, in cold frame, porous compost.

Callistephus (kal-i-ste'pus. Fam. Compositae). The one species, *C. chinensis*, is the parent hardy annual of the cultivated China Asters (q.v.).

Callitriche, Water Starwort (kal-lit' ri-ke. Fam. Callitrichaceae). Aquatic plants of which two native perennials, *C. autumnalis* and *verna*, are excellent oxygenators under water for garden pools and aquaria. Plant in late spring; propagate by stem cuttings inserted into the mud.

Call-me-to-you. One of the common names of the wild pansy, *Viola tricolor*, Used by Rudyard Kipling in his poem, *Our Fathers of Old*.

Calluna, Ling, Heather (kal-u'na. Fam. Ericaceae). The sole species, *C. vulgaris*, an evergreen bushy shrub, with fine linear leaves and upright racemes of small, bell-shaped flowers, July–October, is native to lime-free soils in Britain and many parts of the northern hemisphere. In its various forms it is valued in gardens for ground cover, its long-flowering period and as a bee plant. Notable vs. are *alba*, white heather; *alportii*, crimson; 'C. W. Nix', dark crimson, tall; *foxii*, purplish-pink, dwarf; *hammondii*, white, tall; 'H. E. Beale', tall, rose-pink; 'J. H. Hamilton', pink, dwarf; 'Mair's White'; *aurea*, golden leaved, pink; and *serlei*, white.

Cultivation. Plant in autumn or early spring; lime-free, peaty or humus-rich soil; trim after flowering or in February–March.

Propagation. By cuttings of young unflowered shoots in July–August, in cold frame; by division in early spring.

Callus. The new tissue produced at the base of cuttings or cut surfaces of stems, roots, etc., formed from the cambium cells, and from which buds and new roots are formed.

Calochortus, Butterfly Tulip, Mariposa Lily (kal-o-kor'tus. Fam. Liliaceae). Beautiful bulbous plants in California and Mexico, but only half-hardy and eligible for sheltered sunny positions in very mild localities, otherwise grown in pots in a cool greenhouse or frame.

Selection. *C. alba*, 1–2 ft, white, July; *amabilis*, 1 ft, golden yellow, May; *luteus*, 1 ft, yellow, lined brown, September; *pulchellus*, 1 ft, bright yellow, July; *splendens*, 1½ ft, lilac, August; and *venustus*, 1–4 ft, yellow and crimson, July, and vs.

Cultivation. Pot 8 to 10 bulbs in a 4- to 5-in. pot, November, standard compost, place in cold frame, covered with fibre or peat, bringing in to cool greenhouse, winter temp. 7–10° C. (45–50° F.), when growth shows, and watering moderately; dry off when foliage yellows. Outdoors, plant 3 in. deep.

Propagation. Chiefly by offsets in November.

Calomel. Mercurous chloride (HgCl), prepared as a dust containing 4 per cent calomel for the control of Cabbage Root Fly, Onion Fly and Club-root. *See*

Borecole, Onion and Club-root. Also used in mercurized lawn dressings to control moss. *See* Lawns.

Calonyction, Moonflower (kal-o-nik'ti-on. Fam. Convolvulaceae). Tropical twining perennials, of which *C. aculeatum*, to 10 ft, with handsome cordate leaves and large white, fragrant, trumpet-like flowers, July–August, is well worth growing from seed sown in March, bottom heat 21° C. (70° F.), potted on ultimately to a 12-in. pot, or border, in the greenhouse, kept well watered in growth, little in winter, with minimum temp. 7° C. (45° F.).

Calopogon (kal-lo-po'gon. Fam. Orchidaceae). Hardy, terrestrial, tuberous-rooted orchids from N. America, with grass-like leaves and late summer flowers. *C. pulchellus*, 1½ ft, spikes of purple, golden-bearded flowers, and *multiflorus*, amethyst-purple, may be planted in moist positions in the rock garden, bog garden or fernery in autumn, and increased by taking offsets from the roots.

Caltha (kal'tha. Fam. Ranunculaceae). Hardy, perennial herbs with buttercup-like flowers.

Selection. C. palustris, the Marsh Marigold, or King-cup, Europe, etc., 1 ft, with its spring butter-yellow flowers, and forms *plena*, doubled flowers, *pallida plena*, pale yellow, and *alba*, white, are grown in moist places, and by water; *polypetala*, Caucasus, 2 ft, has large flowers and leaves; *biflora*, 6 in., white, is a miniature. Propagated by division in spring; by seed, sown April.

Calvary Clover. See *Medicago*.

Calycanthus, Allspice (kal-i-kan'thus. Fam. Calycanthaceae). Aromatic deciduous shrubs, hardy in mild localities, but needing a sheltered, sunny wall elsewhere.

Selection. C. floridus, Carolina Allspice, 6–9 ft, reddish-purple and brown flowers, June–July, of delightful fragrance, and *occidentalis*, Californian Allspice, 8 ft, purplish-red, August.

Cultivation. Plant autumn or early spring; well-drained soil, enriched with peat, in warm sun.

Propagation. By layers in spring, or cuttings of young shoots in July–August, in a frame.

Calycinus (-a, -um). Calycinous,

having a conspicuous calyx. Ex. *Hypericum calycinum*.

Calyculatus (-a, -um). Calyculate, having calyx-like bracts. Ex. *Chamaedaphne calyculata*.

Calypso (kal-ip'so. Fam. Orchidaceae). A single species, *C. bulbosa*, a high altitude, northern hemisphere orchid, 4 in., with rose, brown and yellow crested flower, early summer, may be grown in light, peaty, moist soil and partial shade in rock garden or bog. Propagated by offsets, in March.

Calystegia (kal-is-teg'i-a. Fam. Convolvulaceae). A genus of twining perennials, apt to be invasive, and not particularly commendable here. *C. sepium*, Bellbine or Larger Bindweed, can easily become a troublesome weed.

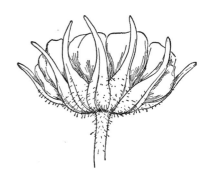

FIG. 35 A Calyx, surrounding the corolla of a flower.

Calyx. The outer whorl of leaf-like organs, usually green, occasionally coloured, below the corolla of a flower.

Camassia, Bear Grass, Quamash (ka-mas'si-a. Fam. Liliaceae). Hardy, N. American, bulbous plants, with long, linear leaves and spring-flowering spike-like racemes of starry flowers, excellent for moist soils, where they can be left undisturbed, in borders, partial shade or in water gardens.

Selection. C. cusickii, 3 ft, pale blue; *fraseri*, 1½ ft, blue; *leichtlinii*, 3–4 ft, purple-blue, with white forms; and *quamash*, 3 ft, blue or white; and v. *flore albo*, snow white.

Cultivation. Plant 4 in. deep, 6 in.

apart, moist or heavy loam, to leave undisturbed.

Propagation. By seed sown in March, out of doors; to flower in about four years. By division occasionally.

Cambium. The actively splitting layer of cells in stems and roots of dicotyledons between the phloem (bast) and xylem (wood).

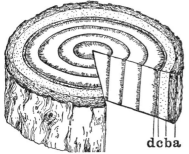

FIG. 36   Cambium in the woody stem of a plant: a. bark; b. phloem; c. cambium; d. xylem.

Camellia (ka-mel'li-a. Fam. Theaceae). Very fine evergreen shrubs with perfect, large showy flowers, from tropical and subtropical Asia, or temperate zones; some of which have proved surprisingly hardy.

Selection. C. *japonica*, Japan and Korea, and vs. are hardiest, but preferably with shelter from cold spring winds since they flower early; notable are *alba simplex*, single white; *alba plena* and *nobilissima*, double whites; 'Adolphe Audusson', 'Apollo' and 'Mercury', semi-double reds; 'Jupiter' and 'Kimberley', single red with bosses of golden stamens; 'Gloire de Nantes' and *campbelii*, semi-double, rose-pink; *elegans* and 'Preston Rose', deep pink; *mathotiana*, double crimson, and vs. *alba*, white, and *rubra*, deep pink; and *anemonaeflora*, rose-pink with a peony centre; all flowering in late March–May, and make rather slow growth to 12 ft or more over several years. Of species, *cuspidata*, China, 6 ft, small white flowers, April, is hardy, but *reticulata*, China, to 20 ft, deep rose, March; *saluenensis*, China, 12 ft, white,

rose, April; *sasanqua*, Japan, to 18 ft, white to rose, winter; *sinensis*, China, to 6 ft, the Tea Plant, dull white, May; and *tsaii*, China, to 6 ft, white, May, are only hardy for the south-west and mild localities. There are several hybrids, of which C. × 'Donation', semi-double pink; × 'J. C. Williams', single, blush pink; × 'Elizabeth Rothschild', semi-double pink; × 'Cornish Snow', single, white; and × 'Salutation', semi-double, rose pink, promise well in hardiness and beauty.

Cultivation. Plant in early autumn or spring; deep, humus-rich soil, not necessarily lime-free, but well supplied with peat or leaf-mould; sheltered from north and east winds. Prune when necessary after flowering. Camellias make excellent cool greenhouse shrubs, planted in May, large pots or tubs, compost of half peat, half loam, with provision for drainage. Roots should fill pots well. May be placed outdoors, June–September.

Propagation. By cuttings of firm young shoots in sandy peat, July–August. By layering in September. By leaf cuttings taken with stalk and axil bud intact, inserted in pots, summer.

Campanula, Bellflower (kam-pan'u-la. Fam. Campanulaceae). A large genus of perennial plants, with a few annuals and biennials, characterized by their bell-shaped or flared flowers, natives of the northern hemisphere, especially southern Europe and the Mediterranean region; providing fine plant material for outdoor beds and borders, rock garden and greenhouse.

Selection. For Borders. C. *alliariifolia*, Caucasus, 2 ft, creamy-white, tolerates shade; *carpatica*, 1–2 ft, in vs. 'China Cup', pale blue, and 'White Star', white; *glomerata*, Europe, 1–2 ft, blue; and vs. *dahurica*, violet-blue; *superba*, 2½ ft, violet; *lactiflora*, Caucasus, 5 ft, milky blue, and vs. 'Loddon Anna', 3–4 ft, lilac pink, 'Pouffe', 9 in., lavender; and 'Prichard's', 2½ ft, deep blue; *latifolia*, Europe, etc., 4–5 ft, blue, and vs. *alba*, white, 'Brantwood', violet-purple, *macrantha*, purplish blue; *latiloba*, Siberia, 1–3 ft, violet-blue, and vs. *alba*, white, and 'Percy Piper', deep blue; *longistyla*, Caucasus, 2½ ft, deep blue-purple; *persicifolia*, Europe, etc., 2–3 ft, blue, and vs. *alba*, single, *alba*

coronata, semi-double, *alba flore pleno*,
double; 'Beechwood', pale blue, 'Fleur
de Neige', white, *Moerheimii*, semi-
double white; 'Telham Beauty', rich
blue, and 'Verdun', semi-double blue;
rhomboidalis, 1½–2 ft, blue; *trachelium*,
Europe, etc., 2–3 ft, blue-purple, late
flowering, and v. *alba*, white; and × *van
houttei*, 1½ ft, deep violet.

Biennials for the border include *C.
medium*, Canterbury Bells, 1–4 ft, in
single and double and 'Cup-and-Saucer'
forms of blue, white and pink flowers;
michauxioides, 3–4 ft, 'Caria', pale blue;
pyramidalis, the Chimney Bell-flower,
4–5 ft, blue, and v. *alba*, white, for early
summer sowing to flower the following
year. Plants may also be potted up in
autumn to bring in and flower in the
cool greenhouse.

For the Rock Garden. Hardy kinds for
outdoors are *C. carpatica*, in vs. 'Ditton
Blue', 6 in. deep blue, *turbinata*, 6 in.,
purple-blue, and *t. pallida*, china-blue;
cochlearifolia, 4 in., and its vs., blues and
white; *garganica*, 4 in., blue, and vs.
'W. H. Paine' and *hirsuta*, pale blue, and
form *alba*; *portenschlagiana*, 4 in., light
purple blue; *poscharskyana*, 8 in., light
blue; *pulla*, 3 in., violet-blue, and its
hybrid × 'G. F. Wilson'; and *raineri*,
3 in., china-blue. All are alpine in origin,
and require well-drained positions in
scree or on rock terraces.

For the Alpine House. Here can be
grown some of the species that find our
winter damp too much, such as *C.
allionii*, 2 in., light purple-blue; *alpina*,
6 in., blue and white; *arvatica*, 2 in.,
violet; *caespitosa*, 6 in., clear blue;
cenisia, 3 in., bright blue; *fragilis*,
prostrate, deep blue; *rupestris*, 3 in.,
blue; and *zoysii*, 3 in., clear blue; largely
spring-flowering, southern European
alpines.

For Baskets. C. isophylla, Italy, lilac-
blue flowers on prostrate stems, and vs.
alba and *mayi*, are pretty, though not
dependably hardy.

Propagation. Border types are readily
raised from seeds sown in well-drained
soil outdoors in May–July. By division
of plants in spring. Rock garden species
may be raised from seeds sown in
spring or early summer, in boxes, in the
cool greenhouse or frame. Choice
varieties can be propagated by young

cuttings taken in spring, with gentle
bottom heat (15.5° C. [60° F.]).

There are no serious diseases of
campanulas, but slugs do much damage
unless repelled by the use of metaldehyde
bait.

Campanulatus (-a, -um). Campanulate, bell-shaped. Ex. *Enkianthus
campanulatus.*

Campestris (-e). Of the plains or fields.
Ex. *Acer campestre.*

Campion. See *Lychnis*, and *Silene.*

Campsis, Trumpet Climber (kamp'sis.
Fam. Bignoniaceae). Deciduous climbers
with pinnate leaves and clusters of large,
trumpet-shaped orange-red flowers,
autumn.

*Selection. C. chinensis (Bignonia
grandiflora)*, China, may be grown as a
pot plant in the cool greenhouse; cut
back hard each winter; *radicans
(Bignonia radicans, Tecoma radicans)*,
30 ft, may be grown out of doors in mild
localities, being from N. America; and
clings by means of aerial roots; several
forms are grown, such as *flava*, yellow,
and 'Madame Gallen', salmon.

Cultivation. A humus-rich porous soil,
and a sunny position suit *C. radicans.
C. chinensis* may be potted in equal
parts loam, peat or leaf-mould, and sand.

Propagation. By root-cutting in
spring, or young shoots taken in summer.

Canary Creeper. See *Tropaeolum
peregrinum.*

Candicans. White. Ex. *Galtonia
candicans.*

Candidissimus (-a, -um). Purest white.
Ex. *Senecio cineraria candidissima*
(White-leafed Cineraria).

Candidus (-a, -um). Shining white.
Ex. *Lilium candidum.*

Candleberry Myrtle. See *Myrica
cerifera.*

Candytuft. See *Iberis.*

Cane Spot. *See* Raspberries.

Canescens. Greyish-white, hoary. Ex.
Atriplex canescens.

Canker. Swollen bark and callus
surrounding a wound on a shrub or tree,
which may be caused by physical
injury or fungus infection. *See* Apples.

Canna, Indian Shot (kan'na. Fam.
Cannaceae). Although a genus of more
than 40 species of tropical herbaceous
perennials, those chiefly grown in
gardens are varieties or hybrids of *C.*

indica, native to tropical America and the West Indies; striking for their stately growth, unfolding oblong leaves and spikes of richly and beautifully coloured flowers in summer, 2–4 ft tall. Plants may be bought in named Dwarf or Giant forms, or by flower colour; but it is more usual to raise from seeds.

Cultivation. Seeds, which have a hard testa, are soaked for 24 hours in warm water, *or* the testa (seed-coat) is filed or chipped and sown in standard compost in boxes or pans, in February–March, with bottom heat of 18–21° C. (65–70° F.); potted singly to 3-in. pots as soon as two leaves are showing, and to larger pots as required, greenhouse temp. 15·5–18° C. (60–65° F.). Plants may be flowered in 6- or 7-in. pots in the greenhouse; or if to be used for outdoor beds, planted out in June. In autumn, when foliage dies down, the fleshy roots may be lifted to store like dahlias; those in pots dried off; and kept frostproof at 7° C. (45° F.). They may be restarted into growth the following February–March in a warm greenhouse.

Propagation. By division in early spring.

Cannabis, Indian Hemp (kan'na-bis. Fam. Moraceae). The cultivated species, *C. sativa,* central Asia, is an annual of handsome habit, to 8 ft, with large digitate leaves and female flowers in spikes, male in axillary panicles. It may be grown from seed sown in April, ⅛ in. deep, ordinary soil, sunny position, where the plants are to grow, in mild localities; otherwise seed is germinated under glass, temp. 18° C. (65° F.) in March, and planted out in May. It is the source plant of the drug hashish, however, and seedsmen are now reluctant to handle the seeds.

Canteloupe Melon. *See* Melons.

Canterbury Bell. See *Campanula medium.*

Cantua (kan'tu-a. Fam. Polemoniaceae). Attractive, S. American, evergreen shrubs with colourful tubular flowers for the cool greenhouse.

Selection. C. buxifolia, 3–4 ft, with drooping purplish-red and yellow flowers in clusters, April–May; *bicolor,* 4 ft, yellow and scarlet; and *pyrifolia,* white and yellow, grows tall.

Cultivation. Pot (and repot as necessary) in March; 2 parts good loam, 2 parts peat, 1 part sand; water freely in growth, moderately in winter, temp. 7° C. (45° F.) minimum.

Propagation. By cuttings of young shoots in sandy loam, in propagating case, with heat (13° C. [55° F.]).

Cape Gooseberry. See *Physalis.*

Cape Hyacinth. See *Galtonia.*

Cape Jasmine, or **Jessamine.** See *Gardenia.*

Cape Pondweed. See *Aponogeton.*

Cape Primrose. See *Streptocarpus.*

Capensis (-e). Of the Cape of Good Hope, or Cape Colony, S. Africa. Ex. *Crinum capense.*

Caper. See *Capparis.*

Caper Spurge. See *Euphorbia lathyrus.*

Capillary. Hair-like.

Capitatus (-a, -um). Capitate; of flowers in dense heads. Ex. *Primula capitata.*

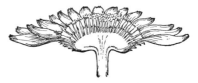

FIG. 37   A Capitulum (Daisy).

Capitulum. A close head of flowers without pedicels, as in flowers of Compositae and Scabiosa.

Capparis (kap-pa'ris. Fam. Capparidaceae). Attractive evergreen shrubs of which *C. spinosa,* S. Europe, 3 ft, the buds of which are picked and preserved as Capers, may be grown in a cool greenhouse for its white, tinged red, with purple filaments, flowers in June; winter temp. 7–10° C. (45–50° F.); *acuminata,* China, white flowers, with long stamens, and *inermis,* S. Europe, white flowering, are also sometimes grown. May succeed out of doors in warm, sunny shelter in southern counties.

Cultivation. Pot in March, standard compost, and grow in full sun, ample water in summer, very moderate in winter.

Propagation. By cuttings of firm shoots, July–August in propagating case, 18° C. (65° F.); or seeds sown in April, with bottom heat 18° C. (65° F.).

Capreolatus (-a, -um). Capreolate, twining, with tendrils. Ex. *Fumaria capreolata*.

Capsicum, Chillies, Red Pepper (kap'si-kum. Fam. Solonaceae). The plants grown for their pungent pod-like fruits, actually juiceless berries, are varieties of *C. annuum*, grown as half-hardy annuals, such as Cayenne Long Red, Long Yellow, Bull Nosed Red and Yellow, Chili and Yolo Wonder. Christmas Cheer, Rising Sun and Chameleon are dwarf varieties of $1-1\frac{1}{2}$ ft, with small ornamental fruits, often grown for their decorative effect.

Cultivation. Plants are raised from seeds in March, standard compost, with bottom heat 18° C. (65° F.); to be potted on, either for planting out in warm, sheltered, sunny borders in mild districts, in May; or grown in 6-in. pots in the cool greenhouse, with regular watering, and liquid feeding when flowers are set, syringing in hot weather. Plants for winter ornament may be placed outdoors in a deep frame until September. Fruits may be left to hang on plants until fully ripe.

Capsid Bugs. Sucking insect pests of Apples, Pears, Currants and Gooseberries, often disfiguring fruits. *See* Fig. 17 and under the fruits concerned.

Capsule. A dry dehiscent fruit or seed vessel.

Captan. Common name for N-trichloromethylthio-cyclohex-4-ene 1:2-dicarboxyimide, a modern protective fungicide against several diseases of fruits and plants. *See* Fungicides.

Caragana (kar-a-ga'na. Fam. Leguminosae). Deciduous flowering shrubs and trees, with pinnate foliage and yellow, pea-like flowers, and often spiny. Although hardy, they like to be dryish in winter, and therefore do best in full sun.

Selection. *C. arborescens*, Siberia, the Pea tree, makes a tall shrub or small tree, 15–20 ft, with clusters of slender stalked yellow flowers in May; v. *lorbergii* is remarkable for its fine, feathery foliage, and v. *nana* is a slow-growing dwarf, while v. *pendula* makes an attractive small weeping tree. *C. pygmaea*, China, 3–4 ft, with slender arching branches and single yellow flowers in May, is quite charming; others of note are *sinensis*, China, 3–4 ft, reddish-yellow flowers, June; and

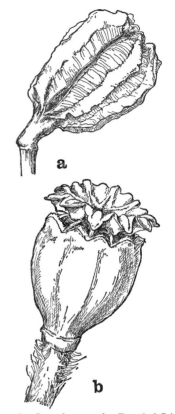

FIG. 38   Capsules: a. of a Bearded Iris; b. of an Oriental Poppy.

maximowicziana, China, Tibet, 3–4 ft, with elegant foliage and yellow flowers in May.

Cultivation. Plant in autumn to March, sunny hot positions, light, well-drained soil. Prune to shape after flowering, if necessary.

Propagation. By seeds in warm soil, April, out of doors. By cuttings or layering in summer.

Caraway (*Carum carvi*. Fam. Umbelliferae). This biennial herb, grown for its fruits or seeds, may be sown in July–August, in drills 1 ft apart, in well-drained, lightish loam, to over-winter, and bear its umbels of white flowers that ripen into seeds the following summer. Thin plants to 9 in. apart; keep free from weeds.

Carbohydrates. Organic chemical compounds of carbon, hydrogen and oxygen; the hydrogen and oxygen atoms usually in the same ratio as in water, $2:1$. They include starches, sugars, gums, insulin and cellulose, and are normally formed by plants by photosynthesis (q.v.).

Carbolic Acid. See Cresylic Acid.

Carbon. An element essential to plants as well as to all living things; charcoal, lamp-black, diamonds and graphite are forms of it. It combines readily with other elements forming carbonates, carbon dioxide, etc., and is found in mineral oils, coal, etc.

Carbon Dioxide, CO_2, carbonic acid gas. A colourless gas, forming 0.03 per cent by volume of the atmosphere normally. Vital to plants as the only source of carbon which forms a large part of their structure. It is absorbed and utilized by green plants by photosynthesis (q.v.). The supply of the gas in the atmosphere is replenished by the combustion of carbonaceous substances —coal, oil, gas, wood, etc., by animal and plant respiration and the decomposition of organic matter, and certain manufacturing processes, such as lime-burning. More recently it has been found that enriching the atmosphere artificially with CO_2 in which plants are actively growing accelerates growth and increases their produce. This has practical and commercial implications in glasshouse culture, particularly in the growing of food crops such as cucumbers and tomatoes. Metered amounts of CO_2 are released from cylinders of the compressed gas.

Carbon Disulphide, or **Carbon Bisulphide,** CS_2. A volatile, more or less colourless, extremely inflammable liquid, its vapour capable of forming an explosive mixture with air, especially in the presence of heat above $46°$ C. ($140°$ F.). It is toxic to animal and insect life, and is therefore sometimes used as a soil fumigant, against ants, wireworms, leatherjackets, chafer grubs, vine weevils, root aphids, etc., at 2 fluid oz. per 3 sq. yds; poured into holes, 6–8 in. deep, at 1-ft intervals, made with a

dibber, and promptly sealed with soil, or a special injector may be used. It should not come in touch with plants or their roots directly. See Soil and Soil Fumigation.

Carbonate of Lime (Calcium carbonate), $CaCO_3$. See Lime.

Cardamine, Cuckoo Flower, Lady's Smock (kar-dam'ine. Fam. Cruciferae). The native perennial herb, *C. pratensis*, $1-1\frac{1}{2}$ ft, deserves a place in cool damp soils, partial shade, in its v. *flore pleno*, for its seedless, double white flowers in May; *macrophylla*, Siberia, follows with pale purple flowers in June; and *trifolia*, S. Europe, 6 in., with pretty sprays of white flowers, in spring, is a useful plant for the rock garden. Plant in autumn or early spring, any soil retaining moisture. Propagate by division.

Cardinal Flower. See *Lobelia cardinalis*.

Cardinalis (-e). Scarlet. Ex. *Delphinium cardinale*.

Cardiocrinum (kar-di-o-krin'um. Fam. Liliaceae). Tall-growing monocarpic bulbous plants, formerly included in *Lilium*, for woodland and light shade.

Selection. C. *cathayanum*, China, to $4\frac{1}{2}$ ft, large, creamy-white flowers in late summer; *C. cordatum*, Japan, 4–6 ft, white, yellow streaked, funnel-shaped flowers, August; *C. giganteum*, Himalaya, 6–10 ft, white, tinged purple and green flowers, August.

Cultivation. Plant bulbs with tips just at soil level in organically enriched soil, March, in half-shade and moist conditions.

Propagation. The old bulb dies after flowering, leaving offset bulbs to grow on and flower in about four years.

Cardoon (*Cynara cardunculus*). Closely related to the Globe Artichoke, the Spanish Cardoon is grown for its succulent leaf-stalks and midribs, like celery. Seeds may be sown under glass in March, in peat-wood fibre pots, bottom heat of $15.5°$ C. ($60°$ F.), subsequently hardened off to plant out in 1-ft deep trenches in rich loam soil in May; *or* in the trenches in late April or early May, 3 or 4 seeds per station, thinned to one plant; about 2 ft apart. Enrich soil with thoroughly rotted manure or compost beforehand. Liberal watering is needed in summer. Plants grow 4–5 ft tall, and blanching can be started in September, in the same manner as for celery, by earthing up gradually, or enclosing plants in light-excluding corrugated cardboard or black sheet polythene.

Carduncellus (kar-dun-kel′lus. Fam. Compositae). Herbaceous perennials of the Mediterranean, of which *C. rhaponticoides*, 9 in., making prostrate rosettes of leaves, and bearing many tubular blue flowers in summer, is useful for the rock garden; well-drained soil in sunny position. Propagated by division in March.

Carex, Sedge (ka′rex. Fam. Cyperaceae). Hardy herbaceous perennial grasses of which a few may be used for the margins of pools and bog gardens.

Selection. C. buchanani, New Zealand, has handsome reddish foliage; *pendula*, Europe, 3–6 ft, is graceful with hanging spikes of flowers; *pseudocyperus*, cosmopolitan in temperate zones, to 3 ft, is elegant; *riparia*, Europe and native, to 5 ft, is best in ‘Bowles Golden’ form, or *variegata*, with leaves striped white. *C. arenaria*, Britain, 1 ft, may be used to bind a loose sandy seashore soil.

Cultivation. Plant in March.

Propagation. By division in March.

Carina. A keel. The basis petals of a sweet pea or similar papilionaceous flower.

Carinatus (-a, -um). Carinate, keeled. Ex. *Chrysanthemum carinatum*.

Carlina, Carline Thistle (kar-li′na. Fam. Compositae). The species usually grown are the hardy perennials *C. acanthifolia*. S. Europe, 2 ft, with spiny leaves and white flower-heads in June; and *acaulis*, Europe, 8 in., white, June, planted in ordinary soil, in early spring.

Propagation. By seeds, April, where plants are to grow.

Carmichaelia (kar-mi-ke′li-a. Fam. Leguminosae). Curiously leafless shrubs, with green flattened branches and small, yellow, pea-like flowers in clusters, early summer.

Selection. C. enysii makes a branched thicket of light green, flat branches, with fragrant violet flowers, June, for rock gardens in mild localities, or the alpine house; *flagelliformis*, 4–5 ft, erect-growing, with purplish flowers, June, may be tried at the foot of a sunny sheltered wall; *petriei*, 2–4 ft, violet-purple, and *williamsii*, 3–6 ft, creamy-

yellow, purple-stained, are tender, and need winter protection, or to be pot-grown and moved to a cool greenhouse for winter.

Cultivation. Rather light, porous soil, with humus, and sunny warmth are needed. Plant in April.

Propagation. By seeds in spring, bottom heat of 18° C. (65° F.). By cuttings, taken with a heel, July.

Carnation. The popular name for the strains of coronet-flowered plants of *Dianthus caryophyllus*, sometimes called Florist Carnations. They include:

Border Carnations. These are perennials, with stout, tall stems and large flowers, for growing out of doors in prepared borders, or in pots.

Selection. They are classed according to their colouring as follows:

Selfs—of one colour of any shade; such as ‘Afterglow’, apricot; ‘Beauty of Cambridge’, primrose; ‘Belle of Bookham’, old rose; ‘Bookham Apricot’; ‘Bookham Gleam’, scarlet; ‘Bookham Grand’, crimson; ‘Bookham Perfume’, maroon; ‘Bookham Spice’, white; ‘Crimson Model’, crimson; ‘Edenside White’, white; ‘Exquisite’, rose-pink; ‘Fiery Cross’, scarlet; ‘Grey Douglas’, heliotrope; ‘Lavender Clove’, lavender; ‘Madonna’, white; ‘Narcissus’, yellow; ‘Oakfield Clove’, crimson; ‘Rose Bradwardine’, pink; ‘Salmon Clove’, salmon pink; ‘St Joan’, old rose; ‘Sunset Glow’, buff apricot; ‘Victory’, bright scarlet; ‘White Circle’.

Bizarres—a clear ground colour, marked and flaked with two or three other colours, such as ‘Apricot Bizarre’, ‘Lilac Bizarre’, ‘Pink Bizarre’ and ‘Rose Bizarre’.

Flakes—a clear ground flaked with one colour only. Typical are ‘Cherry Flake’, cherry-red, flaked maroon; ‘Scarlet Flake’, orange-scarlet, flaked chestnut; ‘Ebor’, chocolate, flaked red; ‘Glen Glory’, white, flaked rose-pink; ‘Oriflamme’, apricot, flaked red; ‘Sunbeam’, yellow, flaked red.

Fancies—a large class of varieties not of any of the above, but having a white or yellow ground, flecked or mottled with other colours, or mottled, flaked or spotted with various colours. Typical are, with white ground, ‘Alice Forbes’, flaked dusky rose; ‘Bookham Dandy’,

striped crimson; 'Bookham Lass', barred
Tyrian rose; 'Douglas Burn', striped
garnet-lake; 'Egret', striped and edged
pink; 'Fascination', lavender grey
edged; 'Lucy Bertram', vivid pink
markings; 'Merlin Clove', edged and
marked bright purple; 'Nobility', flecked
crimson; 'Robin Thane', flaked crimson;
'Sprite', splashed rose-red; 'William
Newell', marked salmon-red. With
yellow ground, 'Bookham Favourite',
marked crimson; 'Catherine Glover',
flaked scarlet; 'Dainty', edged and
flaked soft pink; 'Douglas Fancy',
edged blood-red; 'Edenside Fairy',
edged bluey purple; 'Fascination', edged
lavender-grey; 'Happiness', edged
scarlet; 'Sunbeam', marked scarlet.
Vari-coloured, 'Afton Water', soft pink,
flush rose; 'Dawn Glory', buff, overlaid
lavender; 'Evening Glow', apricot,
barred rose, heliotrope; 'Harmony',
French grey, barred cerise; 'Leslie
Rennison', lavender, shot cerise; 'Mary
Livingstone', silvery grey, flaked rose-
pink; 'Rameses', apricot, lavender,
purple, scarlet blended; 'Spangle',
orange-buff, suffused mauve; 'Thurso',
crimson, overlaid maroon.

Picotees, with colour confined to the
margins of the petals, of plain white or
yellow ground, such as: White ground—
'E. M. Wilkinson', edged claret; 'Eva
Humphries', edged bright purple;
'Ganymede', edged crimson; 'Perfection', edged deep scarlet; 'Rose Frills',
edged rose-pink. With yellow ground—
'Crimson Frills', edged crimson; 'Firefly', heavily edged crimson claret;
'Santa Claus', edged purple; 'Togo',
heavily edged crimson.

Here, also, note may be taken of the
somewhat shorter statured race of
'Cottage' border carnations, developed
by Allwoods, with varieties in self and
various colours.

Cultivation. Out of doors, border
carnations need well-dug, free-draining
beds, enriched with rotted manure or
compost, and limed to bring to pH 6·5
to 7·0. They may be grown by themselves, or in groups in a mixed border.
Plant a chosen collection in April, and
stake with canes when flower stems arise.
Plant at 15–18 in. apart, replant every
third or fourth year. Disbud or remove
buds other than the ones chosen for

flowering when small. Liquid feeding can
be given weekly from when buds form
to their showing colour.

Propagation. By July plants produce
strong non-flowered side-shoots which
may be chosen for layering. The chosen
shoot, of good vigour, should have its
lower leaves carefully stripped off,

FIG. 39 A Carnation shoot prepared for
layering.

FIG. 40 A Carnation shoot layered from
the parent plant.

leaving about five pairs near the end. The stem is slit obliquely upwards through a node or joint, conveniently placed for bending to the soil. The tongue may be trimmed slightly, and the shoot then pinned to the soil, with the half-severed part, $\frac{1}{2}$ in. deep, to be mounded over with a mixture of sandy loam and sifted peat. Rooting takes 6 to 8 weeks, when the rooted layer can be detached and planted out separately in September. Alternately, cuttings of the end 4–6 in. of non-flowered shoots may be taken and rooted in frames or in pots, July–August. By seeds, sown in pans or pots, April–May, in cold frame or greenhouse, standard compost, with gentle heat ($15\cdot5^\circ$ C. [60° F.]) if necessary. Prick off, pot on and harden off for planting out. Seeds do not necessarily come true to variety, but reliable seeds from specialists will yield pleasing plants.

Under Glass. Border carnations may be induced to give finer flowers by judicious use of glass. They need ample light, good ventilation and airy conditions but no excess of heat. Rooted layers may be potted in 3-in. pots in early autumn, and over-wintered in a cold frame or greenhouse, with watering only just to keep the soil moist. In March, plants are potted into 5- or 6-in. pots, JIP 2 compost, and in May to 7- or 8-in. pots, JIP 3 compost, being kept close in the frame for a few days after potting, and then freely ventilated, so that by end of May they may stand outdoors on ashes or firm well-drained standing place, and watered freely with syringing in hot weather. To induce sturdy bushy growth, young plants can be pinched back at 6 in. high. Stake, disbud and liquid feed as for outdoor plants, and when buds show colour, remove to cold greenhouse to flower.

Perpetual-flowering Carnations. Sometimes called tree carnations, these plants produce flowering side-shoots from the main stem, which require training and support. They are not hardy, and are grown under glass, and with good management some may be had in flower all the year round, though flowers are fewer in winter than at other seasons. Plants need an airy greenhouse, with good ventilation and ample light, but little heat, minimum winter temps.

7–10° C. (45–50° F.), with rises of 6° C. (10° F.) in the daytime.

Selection. Varieties are numerous and growers' lists should be consulted for new introductions. A satisfactory choice can be made from: Whites—'Ashington White', 'Purity', 'White Sim'. Pinks—'Ashington Pink', 'Crowley Sim', 'Peppermint Sim', 'Peter Fisher', 'Royal Salmon'. Reds and scarlets—'Red Pimpernel', 'Robert Allwood', 'Royal Scarlet', 'William Sim'. Crimsons—'Royal Crimson', 'Topsy', 'Wivelsfield Crimson'. Yellows—'Allwood's Yellow', 'Ashington Apricot', 'Maine Sunshine', 'Miller's Yellow', 'Royal Maize'. Heliotrope and mauve—'Allwood's Market Lilac', 'Allwood's Market Joy', 'Royal Lavender', 'Ashington Purple'. Fancies —'Arthur Allwood', yellow, slashed red-bronze; 'Doris Allwood', salmon-rose, shaded grey; 'Marchioness of Headfort', salmon-red, creamy-white edged; 'Mary E. Sim', white, flaked scarlet; 'Royal Pelargonium', white and scarlet. Shorter and more compact forms, specially suited to pot culture, will be found in the 'Amateur' strain of Perpetuals.

Cultivation. Plants may be grown in pots, in special border beds, usually made of concrete troughs, 4 ft wide, 10 in. deep, filled with JIP 3 compost (or similar), or by soilless culture, using sand, gravel or vermiculite as the rooting aggregate. Plants are usually bought in 3-in. pots, in April–June. On arrival, they should be potted on to 6-in. pots, or into beds, 8 in. apart. 10 in. between the rows, and shaded until they have recovered. If they have not been 'stopped', with growth points cut off, this should be done about a week after potting, and thereafter side growth or laterals should be stopped when they have formed five or six leaves, spreading the operation by stopping one or two laterals per plant per week to July, and thus spreading the period of bloom. Support must be arranged, as plants grow 3–5 ft tall; a frame of wires on posts at 12 in. apart for plants in beds; canes for plants in pots. Water should be given when the compost begins to dry out, and plants are gently syringed on hot sunny days; in winter more moderate watering is needed and foliage should not be wetted; winter temp. 10° C. (50° F.) at night. Flowering should start in late winter or early spring. Three buds usually appear at the top of each stem, and the largest or centre one should be retained, the others rubbed off while small, and also axillary buds down the stem as far as the first strong side-shoot. After the first lot of blooms a liquid feed may be given, and repeated occasionally. Pot plants will be ready to be moved into 8- or 9-in. pots in the spring of the second year, being potted firmly, using fresh JIP 3 compost, and grown on to flower in summer or autumn. At the end of two years some or all the plants will be ready for replacement with young stock.

Propagation. By cuttings taken from healthy plants, consisting of 2–4-in. long shoots from the lower half of the plant, cut close to a node with a razor blade or sharp knife, between November and March. Bottom leaves are removed and the cuttings inserted in moist clean sand or vermiculite, bottom heat of 15·5° C. (60° F.), and when rooted, transferred to 3-in. pots, JIP 2 compost, and grown on until ready for beds or 6-in. pots.

Malmaison Carnations. These are developed from the old blush v. 'Souvenir de la Maison', noted for their big, richly scented, fully double flowers, but require more skill in growing than the Perpetuals, although treatment may be on similar lines.

Selection. 'Duchess of Westminster', salmon rose; 'Old Blush', pale pink; 'Princess of Wales', salmon pink; 'Rothschild's', deep salmon pink; 'The Queen', terra-cotta.

Cultivation. Pot young plants in August–September, in 5-in. pots, JIP 2 compost, ramming firm; grow cool in winter, very moderate watering, good ventilation, minimum temp. 7° C. (45° F.); water more often with growth, liquid feed weekly when buds form, shade from hot sun. Or may be wintered in a deep frame from which frost can be excluded. After flowering, cut out flowered stems, repot into larger pot, JIP 3 compost, ready for wintering.

Propagation. Layers root more easily than cuttings, and may be prepared from non-flowered shoots in June–July, as

for border carnations, rooting into adjacent pots.

Chabaud, Grenadin and Margaret Carnations. These are strains of *D. caryophyllus*, which are perennial, but are more often grown as half-hardy annuals; sowing seeds early in the year under glass, with heat (13–15·5° C. [55–60° F.]), potting on seedlings to plant out in May, to flower in summer. Or seeds may be sown later in early summer for plants that flower the following year. Plants grow 1–1½ ft tall, and seedsmen offer both named varieties and mixtures.

Diseases. Rust (*Uromyces caryophyllinus*), a fungus, causes chocolate-brown, powdery spotting or blotching of leaves, stems and flower buds; infected leaves, etc., should be cut away and burnt; and plants dusted or sprayed with a sulphur or thiram fungicide, and grown with good ventilation, temps. of 10–15° C. (50–58° F.), and careful watering to keep atmosphere on the dryish side. Leaf-rot or Branch-rot (*Pseudodiscosia dianthi*) attacks at or near nodes, showing in ash-grey spots which soon turn to dark brown or black. Cut out infected shoots, apply a copper fungicide, and avoid too moist conditions at low temperatures. Leaf Spot (*Septoria dianthi*) shows in roundish, light brown spots, with darker edges on leaves. Cut out and burn infected leaves, keep foliage dry, dust with a sulphur or thiram fungicide. Wilting suggests infection of the plant by soil-borne fungi (*Verticillium* sp., *Fusarium* spp.), for which there is no certain cure. Infected plants are best burnt, and propagation made from healthy plants, using new composts in which the soil fraction has been sterilized.

Pests. Aphids (*Macrosiphum solani*, *Myzus persicae*, etc.) and thrips (*Thrips tabaci*) are sap suckers and may carry the Mosaic virus, and should be promptly controlled by applying a malathion, gamma-BHC, smoke or insecticide. Red Spider Mite (*Tetranychus telarius*) can be controlled by fumigating with Azobenzene. A systemic insecticide may be used to prevent attacks of the above three insects. The Carnation Tortrix Moth (*Tortrix pronubana*) rolls leaves, spins leaves together at the tips of shoots, and larvae feed on buds, etc.;

but DDT or gamma-BHC would give control. Trouble from soil pests—wireworms, leatherjackets, chafer grubs—in borders can be prevented by use of a gamma-BHC dust at planting-out.

Carneus (-a, -um). Flesh-coloured. Ex. *Erica carnea.*

Carob Tree. See *Ceratonia.*

Carpels. The divisions of the pistil and ovary of a flower; in some cases united, in others free.

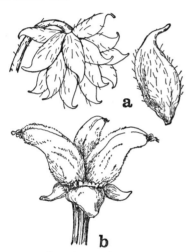

FIG. 41 Carpels: a. forming the seed head of *Geum* sp., with one shown singly; b. forming the seed head of *Paeonia* sp.

Carpenteria (kar-pen-te′ri-a. Fam. Saxifragaceae). The one species, *C. californica*, is a beautiful evergreen shrub, 6–8 ft, with clusters of white, open flowers, many-stamened and scented, in June, but being from California it is only hardy in warm, sunny, winter-mild places; otherwise a tub plant for conservatory or cool greenhouse; rich well-drained loamy soil. Propagated by cuttings of young shoots in early summer; or by layering.

Carpet Bedding. The art of planting beds with dwarf plants with coloured foliage in geometrical patterns and carpet designs is too artificial, effort, space and time wasting for modern gardeners, though still practised somewhat by local authorities in making floral clocks, coats of arms, etc. Beds are planted in May–June, using such plants as Alternanthas, Antennaria, Echeverias, Saxifrages, Sedums, Sempervivums and Mesembryanthemums, interspersed with dwarf species of Cerastium, Mentha, Sagina and similar creeping plants. Constant discipline of plants is needed to maintain the pattern. Examples of local authorities should be studied by the interested.

Carpinus, Hornbeam (kar-pi′nus. Fam. Betulaceae). Hardy, handsome deciduous trees, thriving on most soils of good drainage, except chalk.

Selection. C. betulus, native, 50–80 ft, is good for hedging, retaining its browned leaves in winter under clipping. For specimen planting, v. *asplenifolia*, with deeply cut leaves, *columnaris*, slender and spire-like, *pendula*, weeping, and *pyramidalis*, for narrow sites, are all attractive. The American Hornbeam, *caroliniana*, 30 ft, makes a graceful small tree with autumn foliage colour; the Chinese, *cordata*, 40 ft, is handsome with large cordate leaves, but too seldom offered.

Cultivation. Plant October–March, open position; ordinary soil, but not highly alkaline.

Propagation. By seeds sown ¾ in. deep in autumn, in well-drained soil, out of doors. *See* Hedges.

Carrion Flower. See *Stapelia.*

Carrot (*Daucus carota*, Fam. Umbelliferae). As a vegetable, carrots have a useful content of sugar, and a high content of carotene (vitamin A), making them health-giving and nutritive. Introduced to England in the reign of Elizabeth I, the swollen, red-rooted forms we know are developed from a hardy biennial of Europe, including Britain. The ideal soil is a sandy loam, with high water table; but they succeed in most soils which are friable and porous. Heavy soils need opening with sand, wood ashes, gypsum and rotted organic matter.

Selection. Stump-rooted or shorthorn, for early sowing (and heavy soils)—Early Nantes, Early Gem, Red-cored Early Market, Primo. Stump-rooted, intermediate — Chantenay, Autumn King. Pointed, half-long, intermediate—

Ideal, James's Scarlet, St Valery. Long-rooted for deep soils—Long Red Surrey.

Cultivation. Use ground organically manured for a previous crop. Avoid use of fresh manures. Lime to pH 6·0. Pre-fertilize with 1 part by weight sulphate of ammonia, 4 parts super-phosphate, 2 parts sulphate of potash at 3 oz. per sq. yd.

Sow from March onwards for bunching and immediate consumption, $\frac{1}{2}$ in. deep in drills 9–12 in. apart; maincrops for storing in May or early June. Thin to 4–6 in. apart as soon as practicable. Weed, especially in early stages. Lift for storing in late October; in layers in boxes, interleaved with sand, sifted ashes or fairly dry earth; store frostproof but cool (5° C. [40° F.]).

Pests. Carrot Fly (*Psila rosae*) lays eggs in May–June in soil near the plants, which hatch in 12 days into grubs that bore into and feed on the roots. A second generation occurs about 8 weeks later. The use of a DDT insecticidal dust in May or after thinning is most effective. Cover and firm soil over roots after thinning.

Carthamus, Distaff Thistle (kar-tham'us. Fam. Compositae). Hardy annuals, of which *C. tinctorius*, Egypt, 3 ft, the Saffron Thistle, is chiefly grown, from seeds sown shallowly in boxes, standard compost, in March, bottom heat 18° C. (65° F.), to be pricked off and planted out in May, for their orange-rayed, July flowers; *lanatus*, 2 ft, may be grown similarly.

Cartwheel Flower. See *Heracleum.*

Carum (kar'um. Fam. Umbelliferae). Only *C. carvi* is of garden value. *See* Caraway.

Caruncle. An outgrowth on the testa of some seeds, such as those of *Ricinus* and *Viola.*

Carya, Hickory (ka'ri-a. Fam. Juglandaceae). Handsome foliaged deciduous trees of N. America, with pinnate leaves, yellowing in autumn, and unisexual flowers; excellent for specimen planting.

Selection. C. ovata, 70 ft, fine autumn leaf colour; *C. pecan*, 100 ft, and *C. tomentosa*, 60 ft, are probably the pick.

Cultivation. As plants are seldom offered, it is best to grow from seed (nuts); winter-stored in a strong box of moist soil, stratified, placed in a shady

FIG. 42   Caruncle, on a seed of the Castor Oil Plant (*Ricinus* sp.).

place out of doors. Plant up singly in deep pots, JIP 1 compost, in March, with bottom heat of 18° C. (65° F.), in greenhouse or frame; hardening off to plant out, without injuring the tap root, in autumn, where the tree is to grow.

Caryopteris, Blue Spiraea (kari-op'ter-is. Fam. Verbenaceae). Deciduous shrubs, valuable for their late flowering, though not very hardy.

Selection. C. tangutica, China, 3–5 ft, violet-blue flowers in clusters, is the hardiest; *incana* (*mastacanthus*), China, 3 ft, violet-blue, needs warmth and shelter; but its hybrid *C. × clandonensis*, to 4 ft, bright blue, and form 'Heavenly Blue' is fairly hardy, given a congenial soil and sun.

FIG. 43   *Caryopteris × clandonensis.*

Cultivation. Best planted in March–April, good, well-drained light to medium loam, sun and shelter from winter's worst. Shoots often die back in winter; prune out and shorten growth each spring.

Propagation. By cuttings of young shoots in July; under handlight or in propagating case.

Cassandra. See *Chamaedaphne.*

Cassia (kas'si-a. Fam. Leguminosae). Of 400 species, the best known is *C. corymbosa*, 3 ft, an evergreen shrub of tropical America, with rich yellow flowers in clusters in August, and attractive pinnate leaves; and may be grown in a cool greenhouse or conservatory; winter temp. 7° C. (45° F.) minimum. *C. marylandica*, U.S.A., to 3 ft, is a more or less hardy herbaceous perennial, yellow-flowering in August.

Cultivation. Pot in March, standard compost, for the greenhouse; gradually increase watering, and syringe in hot summer weather; but water very little in winter. Prune, when necessary, in February–March. Plant *C. marylandica* in well drained loam, April.

Cassinia, Golden Bush (kas-sin'i-a. Fam. Compositae). Evergreen shrubs, heath-like in foliage and small flowers, chiefly of New Zealand, doubtfully hardy except in mild, warm localities.

Selection. C. fulvida, to 6 ft, grows dense and erect with gold-tipped leaves and white flowers, July, and is the hardiest; *retorta*, to 6 ft, more finely and silvery leafed, and *vauvilliersii*, 6 ft, dark green leaves, whitish underneath, may be tried.

Cultivation. Plant in well-drained, peat-enriched soil, autumn or early spring. Mild localities only.

Propagation. By cuttings of young shoots in summer, in a frame or under handlights.

Cassiope (kas-si'o-pe. Fam. Ericaceae). Dwarf, evergreen, heath-like, hardy shrubs, with imbricate leaves and solitary, bell-shaped, hanging flowers in spring. Of alpine or arctic origin, they need acid, lime-free soil, and are happier in the north than in the south.

Selection. C. lycopodioides, NE. Asia, almost prostrate shrublet, white flowers, April, and v. *major*, larger and more robust, are easiest to grow; *fastigiata*,

Himalaya, 9 in., white, May, and *tetragona*, 1 ft, pale green and carmine, May, are worth trying.

Cultivation. Plant in April, lime-free, well-drained soil, good light but not hot bright sun. May also be grown in the alpine house.

Propagation. By cuttings of young shoots, in August, inserted in sandy peat in propagating frame; or by seed, sown in February–March, in pan, cold frame.

Castanea (kas-ta'ne-a. Fam. Fagaceae). Deciduous trees with handsome leaves, especially on poor soils.

Selection. C. sativa, the Sweet Chestnut, S. Europe, to 100 ft, makes a fine parkland specimen, with several vs., 'Marron de Lyon' for fruit; golden- and silver-variegated forms, and a purple-leaved variety; *henryi*, China, to 60 ft, with long, slender leaves; *mollissima*, 30 ft or more, with large nuts, and *seguinii*, to 30 ft, as a small tree or tall shrub, are compatriots, and worth consideration; while *pumila*, the Chinquapin of N. America, is of shrubby habit, and with leaves white with down underneath.

Cultivation. From light to loam soils suit best; but do well on dry soils too. Plant October–March. Not quite so happy in cold districts or on wet soils.

Propagation. By seeds, sown in autumn, 3 in. deep, in sandy loam.

Castor Oil Plant. See *Ricinus.*

Catalpa (ka-tal'pa. Fam. Bignoniaceae). Handsome deciduous trees, notable for leafing out in May, and bearing panicles of flowers in July.

Selection. C. bignonioides, the Indian Bean tree, N. America, 25–40 ft, spreading, with large cordate leaves, and white, yellow and purple marked flowers in July–August; v. *aurea*, one of the finest yellow-leaved trees, make fine lawn specimens; China contributes *fargesii*, 40–60 ft, ovate leaves, hairy beneath, and rose-pink flower in June, its v. *duclouxii*, with glabrous leaves; and *bungei*, nicely pyramidal to 20 ft or more, and white, purple-spotted flowers.

Cultivation. Not unduly particular about soil, but likes a moist deep loam; does well near towns in open situations, but flowers best in the southern half of Britain. Plant October–March.

Propagation. By seeds sown 1 in. deep,

March, out of doors. By cuttings of ripe, short side-shoots in summer, inserted in frame or propagating case, with gentle bottom heat.

Catananche, Cupid's Dart (kat-an-an'ke. Fam. Compositae). The species grown is *C. caerulea*, a hardy perennial from S. Europe, growing 2–3 ft, with large blue flowers on strong wiry stems in summer, splendid for drying for winter decoration, and its vs. *alba*, white, and *bicolor*, blue and white. Seeds may be sown in March under glass, bottom heat 18° C. (65° F.), to plant out in May, in any ordinary well-drained soil, and flower the same year; or later out of doors to provide plants to flower the following year. Propagated also by division.

Catch Cropping. The practice of sowing quick-growing crops on soil prepared for other main-crop vegetables; such as lettuce, radish, spring mustard and cress on celery ridges, on ground prepared for winter greens, or between maincrop plants with a long season of growth.

Catchfly. See *Silene*.

Catchfly, German. See *Lychnis viscaria*.

Caterpillar. The larva of a butterfly or moth, though often applied to the larva of a sawfly also.

Catharticus (**-a,** **-um**). Cathartic, purgative. Ex. *Rhamnus cathartica*.

Cathcartia (kath-kart'i-a. Fam. Papaveraceae). The one species, *C. villosa*, is an alpine perennial herb of the Himalaya, with showy, yellow, poppy-like flowers on 12-in. stems in June; needs a light, humus-rich soil, and a warm, sunny sheltered position in the rock garden or border. Propagation by seed, sown under glass, bottom heat 15·5° C. (60° F.), in spring. Not reliably durable in colder parts.

Catkin. A dense, deciduous spike, usually of unisexual apetalous flowers. See *Corylus, Populus, Quercus, Salix,* etc.

Catmint. See *Nepeta*.

Cattleya (kat'le-ya. Fam. Orchidaceae). An important genus of evergreen epiphytic orchids, native to subtropical and tropical America, of some 40 species and natural hybrids, from which many other hybrids have been raised and crosses with other genera such as Laelia, Brassovola and Sophronitis. The flowers are outstanding in beauty of form and

FIG. 44   Female Catkins or Cones of *Alnus incana*.

magnificent colouring, and although the main flowering period is from early August to May, this can be extended by careful selection. Specialist lists should be consulted, for the hybrids tend to be the more rewarding in their superb and large flowers.

Selection. Note may be taken of the more outstanding species here: *C. aclandiae*, Brazil, 6 in., purple, streaked yellow, rose, July; *bicolor*, Brazil, 30 in., September, and vs., brownish green, purple; *bowringiana*, C. America, 1–2 ft, rosy purple, autumn; *citrina*, Mexico, 1 ft, lemon yellow, May–August; *dowiana*, Costa Rica, 6 in., rich purple, streaked gold, August–November; *eldorado*, C. America, 6 in., pink and purplish crimson, August–September; *gaskelliana*, Brazil, 1 ft, light rose-purple, white, August; *guttata*, Brazil, 1½–2 ft, greenish yellow, dotted crimson, October; *intermedia*, Brazil, 1½ ft, soft rose, May–July; *labiata*, Brazil, 1 ft, deep rose, September–November; *loddigesii*, Brazil, 1–2 ft, rose, marked yellow, August–September; *lueddemanniana*, Venezuela, 1 ft, purple-rose, white, September–October; *mendelii*, Brazil, 1 ft, pink, and purple, April–May; *mossiae*, La Guayra, 1 ft, rose, May–June, many vs.; *percivaliana*, Columbia, 1 ft, January–February; *rex*, Peru, 1 ft, white, yellow and crimson, July–August; *schilleriana*, Brazil, 6 in., rose-brown and purple, June–July; *skinneri*, Guatemala, 1½ ft, rosy purple, white; *trianae*, Quindiu,

1 ft, blush rose, orange and purple, January–April, many vs.; *walkeriana*, Brazil, 1 ft, rose, sweet-scented, November–December; *warneri*, Brazil, 1 ft, rose and crimson, July–August; and vs.

Cultivation. Plant up, or replant, in spring, in pots or pans, well-crocked, and in compost of 3 parts chopped Osmunda fibre to 1 part sphagnum moss; grow in ample light, but shade with roller blinds, giving dappled or broken light in sunny summer days; water freely in active growth, with syringing to maintain

good, rich soil, much space, and plants tend to be ready at the same time, in an overwhelming glut. It is not suitable for dry soils, or soils subject to waterlogging, or much summer heat.

Varieties. For early summer cropping seeds are sown under glass, with gentle bottom heat of 15·5° C. (60° F.); for later cropping they may be sown in a cold frame or out of doors in a nursery bed, and planted out. Where there is room for successional cropping, varieties may be chosen by the accompanying chart; where limited space is available,

Variety	*When sown*	*When planted out*	*To mature in*
Cambridge Earliest	January–February	April, early May	June
Super Snowball	in heat, under	April, early May	June
Forerunner	glass	April, early May	June
All the Year Round	March–April	May–June	August–September
Early Autumn Giant	April	May–June	September
Mammoth	April	May–June	September–October
Boomerang	April	May–June	September
Autumn Giant	April	May	October
Canberra	April	May–June	October–November
Sydney Market	April–May	May–June	October–November
South Pacific	April–May	May–June	Late October
Veitch's Self-protecting	April	May–June	November
Classic Forerunner Improved Snowball All the Year Round	September in cold frame to over-winter	April	June–July

buoyant atmosphere with free ventilation; summer temps. 18–29° C. (65–85° F.); water more moderately in winter, with temps. 13–15·5° C. (55–60° F.) at night. Repot every other year.

Propagation. By division of rhizomes in spring, with four bulbs per rhizome, when possible.

Caudatus (-a, -um). Caudate, having a tail. Ex. *Cypripedium caudatum*, with its tailed flowers.

Caudex. The axis of a plant, particularly of the stem of a palm or fern.

Cauliflower (*Brassica oleracea botrytis cauliflora*). The true or summer cauliflower is less hardy than its near relation, broccoli (q.v.), and is grown to crop from June to November. It is not an ideal small garden vegetable, although delectable and vitamin-rich, as it needs a

it would be better to rely on one variety such as 'All the Year Round'.

Cultivation. Cauliflowers need to be grown with as little check as possible, in soil well dug, generously manured for a previous crop or in the preceding autumn, limed to bring to about pH 6·5, and given a balanced fertilizer prior to planting out, say, 6 parts by weight fine hoof and horn meal, 3 parts superphosphate, 1 part steamed bone flour, 2 parts sulphate of potash at 3–4 oz. per sq. yd. A liquid feeding can be given 4 weeks after planting out; repeated about 2 to 3 weeks later. Plants raised under glass or in frames are set out after rain, firmly, as soon as the soil warms up, those from outdoor nursery beds as soon as true leaves are being formed, spacing small varieties 2 ft apart, large 2½–3 ft apart each way. Planting holes should be dusted with 4 per cent calomel dust where club-root or cabbage root fly has been known. Those who do not want the trouble of transplanting may sow a variety such as Sutton's Beacon in mid April, thinning to 18 in. apart, and leaving seedlings to grow on *in situ*. It helps to get blanched white heads if the leaves are tied at the tips over the curd as it begins to heart.

Diseases and Pests. See Broccoli.

Cauline. Of leaves, borne on the stem.

Cayenne Pepper. See *Capsicum*.

Ceanothus (ke-an-o'thus, often see-an-o'thus, Fam. Rhamnaceae). Evergreen and deciduous shrubs, notable for their blue flowering, chiefly Californian in origin, differing in hardiness.

Selection. Spring-flowering in May, June and evergreen are *cyaneus*, to 20 ft, intense blue; *dentatus*, 4–6 ft., fine-leaved, rich blue; × 'Delight', to 18 ft, rich blue; × *lobbianus*, 6 ft, bright blue, and v. *russellianus*, light blue; *rigidus*, to 12 ft, deep blue; *thyrsiflorus*, to 20 ft, bright blue; × *veitchianus*, to 10 ft, bright deep blue; all of which need the sheltered, warm, sunny wall in colder localities, and may be pruned after flowering when necessary. Summer–autumn flowering kinds tend to be hardier; the best being × *burkwoodii*, to 20 ft, deep blue; and × 'Autumnal Blue', soft blue, of the evergreens; and × 'Ceres', to 12 ft, lilac-pink; *azureus*, to 6 ft, deep blue; × 'Gloire de Versailles', to 12 ft, powder-blue; × 'Henri Desfosse', to 10 ft, deep violet; × 'Perle Rose', to 8 ft, lilac-rose; and × 'Topaz', to 8 ft, deep blue, all of which may be pruned fairly hardly each April, if needed.

Cultivation. Any well-drained, porous soil with humus will suit, but sun and warmth essential. Plant evergreens out of pots in early autumn or spring; deciduous kinds in mild winter weather or spring. Best as wall shrubs, though effective as shrubs in the open, given sufficient mildness.

Propagation. Evergreens from firm cuttings in summer, in propagating frame; deciduous kinds by young, 3-in. shoots, in July–August, or layering.

Cedar. See *Cedrus*.

Cedar, Incense. See *Libocedrus decurrens*.

Cedar, Red. See *Juniperus virginiana*.

Cedar, Western Red. See *Thuja plicata*.

Cedronella (ke-dron-el'la. Fam. Labiatae). Shrubby perennials of which *C. cana*, New Mexico, 2–3 ft, is hardy and neatly evergreen with hoary leaves and showy crimson flowers, July, in well-drained peaty soil and a warm spot; *triphylla*, Canary Isles, 3 ft, is the fragrant Balm of Gilead, white flowers, July, but not hardy except in the mildest of gardens.

Cultivation. Plant in April: *C. triphylla* in pots to move into the greenhouse in winter.

Propagation. By cuttings of young shoots, in propagating case, or under handlight, summer.

Cedrus, Cedar (ke'drus, see'drus, by usage. Fam. Pinaceae). Tall-growing, evergreen conifers, delightful when young, but fairly rapid in growth.

Selection. C. atlantica, Atlantic Cedar, Atlas Mts, to 120 ft, pyramidal, but finest garden form is *glauca*, with bluish-green foliage; *leodara*, Deodar or Indian Cedar, W. Himalaya, 60–150 ft, with

FIG. 45 *Cedrus libani*, cone and foliage.

pendulous branches; with coloured gold and silver-leafed versions; *libani*, Cedar of Lebanon, Lebanon Mts, Syria, 70–100 ft, makes a noble specimen, but best in the southern half of England.

Cultivation. Plant in spring, well-drained, reasonably deep soil, when young; tolerate lime.

Propagation. Species by seed, ½ in. deep, in pans in cool greenhouse, or nursery bed, in April, to transplant the following year.

Celandine, Greater. A native perennial weed, *Chelidonium majus*, with bright yellow spring flowers; a herbalist's remedy for warts.

Celandine, Lesser. A perennial weed, *Ranunculus ficaria*, with buttercup-like golden-yellow star flowers in spring. See *Ranunculus.*

Celastrus (ke-las′trus, or see-las′trus. Fam. Celastraceae). Deciduous shrubs of twining habit of which a few are grown for the rich, bright colouring of their fruits and open seed vessels in autumn. Flowers are insignificant, but sometimes unisexual, and more than one plant should be grown.

Selection. C. orbiculatus, NE. Asia, 30–40 ft, with scarlet fruits against yellow valves, autumn; *hookeri*, Himalaya, to 20 ft, red fruits and orange valves; and *scandens*, Climbing Bittersweet, N. America, to 20 ft, bright red fruits and yellow valves, are usually offered, though there are others.

Cultivation. Best raised from seeds, sown in pots, March–April, bottom heat of 18° C. (65° F.), to plant out where they are to grow on walls, trellis, pillars or posts, or an old tree; in sun or shade, well-drained soil of porous texture. Prune in March to induce branching; may be kept shrub-like by regular annual pruning.

Propagation. By layers, in spring or summer.

Celeriac. *See* Celery.

Celery (*Apium graveolens*). Developed from a biennial plant of marshy temperate places, including Britain, celery is chiefly grown for its blanched leaf stalks as a health-protecting salading, and the whole plant for cooking. It requires an abundance of moisture, and is therefore best grown in humus-rich, friable soils, easily worked, and is chiefly

grown to crop in summer–early autumn, or later autumn, and winter.

Summer Celery. This is rated from a quick-growing, self-blanching variety, Golden Self-Blanching, of American breeding. Seed is sown shallowly, mixed with a little sand as the seeds are small, in boxes, in mid to late March, under glass, bottom heat 21° C. (70° F.), otherwise germination is very slow. Seedlings are pricked off when large enough to handle, and grown on in 15·5° C. (60° F.), to harden off and plant out in mid May or June, into organically rich soil, 9–12 in. apart, which has been given a fertilizer rich in potash. The plants are grown on the soil, and later blanched with collars of kraft paper, or corrugated cardboard, for the finest produce. Or this celery may be grown in a frame, with the top off. It is ready for harvesting, as required, from late July to October.

Autumn–Winter Celery. Varieties are white-stalked such as Solid White, Wright's Grove Solid White, Sandringham Dwarf White and White Gem (dwarf); pink, Clayworth Prize Pink, Manchester Pink and Standard Bearer; and red, Solid Red, Wright's Grove Red and Incomparable. The white are held to be slightly less hardy. There are often local strains offered by seedsman.

Seeds are sown in February–March in the same way as for summer celery; or seedling plants may be bought for planting in mid May or June. These maincrops are usually grown in trenches, prepared beforehand; 12–15 in. wide for a single row, 18 in. for a double row of plants, and 8–10 in. deep. The base of the trench is enriched with rotted manure, compost or organic matter, and bone meal at 3 oz. per sq. yd; and allowed to consolidate. Lime to bring to pH 6·0 to 6·5. Plants are set 1 ft apart, singly or in pairs, watered in, and shaded at first from hot sun. Plants are blanched by earthing up in stages, beginning when they are 12–15 in. tall; carefully gathering in the stalks, and firming the soil to them only lightly, without letting soil in between the stalks, at 2–3 week intervals. Or plants can be enclosed in paper collars before actually earthing up, preferably tied loosely in position with raffia or twine.

Weeds should be kept down, and suckers at the base of plants removed.

Celeriac is a turnip-rooted form of Celery, with swollen crown and base of stem. Plants are raised from seed in the same way as for celery, and set out on similar soil on the flat, 1 ft apart, in June. Any side-shoots forming should be removed, and older leaves are removed as the plant grows and swells. At harvest the 'bulbous' part is trimmed of roots and leaves, except for the growing point, and stored in sand, cool, and used for salads or cooked like beetroot.

Cells. All plant tissues are made up of separate units known as cells. The cell is enclosed in a non-living wall termed cellulose, which is plastic and expands

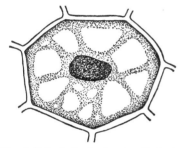

FIG. 46 Cell of plant, showing its darker nucleus in the centre, surrounded by cytoplasm, which also lines the cell, and encloses vacuoles which become one large vacuole with ageing.

as the cell grows, but becomes stiff and inflexible as soon as the cell reaches its full size. Within its walls is the living matter of the cell—protoplasm—jelly-like, almost colourless, chemically a mixture of proteins, in which other particles may be present such as starch grains (chloroplasts), and a more viscous, chemically more complex kind of proto-plasm termed the nucleus. The nucleus is held to be the centre of chemical activity, determining the size, shape and function of the cell, and controlling its living processes. The protoplasm not part of the nucleus is termed the cytoplasm, out of which the cell walls are formed. A cell also contains as it

grows fluid-full cavities, vacuoles, con-taining cell-sap, a fluid of dissolved salts, sugar or pigments in water. As the cell attains its full size the protoplasm lines the walls, and a large single vacuole occupies the centre. Cells increase by division, one into two, two into four, and so on, forming groups or tissues with specialized functions, such as a root, a stem or a leaf, and so maintaining the plant body in growth and life. In cell division, the nucleus condenses in a cell filled with protoplasm and divides first into two nuclei which move apart. A middle lamella or first layer of a new cell wall develops between the two nuclei, separating them, and the cyto-plasm then forms cellulose on each side of the lamella until two separate cells are formed, in which vacuoles develop and the cells enlarge as discrete units.

Cellular. Made up of cells.

Cellulose. The structural tissue which forms the cell walls of plants, a carbohydrate $(C_6H_{10}O_5)n$.

Celmisia (kel-mis'i-a or sel-mis'i-a. Fam. Compositae). A New Zealand genus of perennial herbs of which *C. coriacea*, $1\frac{1}{2}$–3 ft, with large, white-rayed flower heads in summer, from a rosette of long, linear woolly leaves, is hardy enough for borders in mild districts, with glass cover in winter; given well-drained soil and sunny position. Propagated by division in spring. Others, such as *gracilenta*, 3–12 in., finely tufted leaves, and small white flowers, May, and *spectabilis*, $1\frac{1}{2}$ ft, a mat-like plant, may be raised from seeds and grown as half-hardy annuals.

Celosia (kel-o'si-a or sel-o'si-a. Fam. Amaranthaceae). Tropical Asian herbs with highly coloured flowers, chiefly grown as half-hardy annuals in the cool greenhouse, as pot plants.

Selection. C. cristata, 6–9 in., the Cockscomb, is chiefly grown in selected strains for their shining, crowded, crested masses of brilliant white, gold, orange, rose and crimson flowers; and its v. *pyramidalis* (*C. plumosa*) is parent to the Feathered Cockscombs, $1\frac{1}{2}$–2 ft, with dense feathery plume-like spikes of red to yellow flowers; *argentea linearis*, 2 ft, is also offered, with creamy white flower spikes.

Cultivation. Sow seeds under glass,

standard compost, March, bottom heat 24° C. (75° F.), potting singly to 3-in. pots when large enough, and finally to 5-in. pots; grow near the glass, water regularly, temps. 15·5–18° C. (60°–65° F.). Liquid feed weekly when growing freely. May also be used for summer bedding, planted out in June.

Celsia (kel'si-a or sel'si-a. Fam. Scrophulariaceae). A Mediterranean race of plants with spikes or racemes of flowers in early summer resembling those of Verbascum, a related genus. *C. arcturus*, a half-hardy shrubby perennial, with decorative clear yellow, purple-anthered flowers, blooming from seed in six months, in a warm greenhouse, and ultimately making a shrub of 3–4 ft, sowing in March, with bottom heat of 18° C. (65° F.), and potting on by stages to 5-in. pots. Repot in April. May also be propagated by short cuttings of young shoots in June–July, in propagating frame. *C. cretica*, 4 ft, is a half-hardy biennial, best raised from seed sown in April or August, plants being over-wintered in a cool greenhouse or frame.

Centaurea (ken-tau're-a or sen-tau're-a. Fam. Compositae). A large genus of which the following are chiefly grown of its annual, biennial and perennial herbs.

Annuals. *C. cyanus*, Europe and Britain, is the Cornflower, with flowers in shades of blue, rose, pink, mauve and white, single and double, in strains growing 2–2½ ft tall; and dwarf forms such as Jubilee Gem and Polka Dot, of 1 ft. *C. moschata* (*Amberboa moschata*), Mediterranean, 2 ft, is the Sweet Sultan, with white, yellow, purple and red flowering vs., and its form *imperialis*, to 3 ft, has very large handsome flowers, eclipsing those of the species for cutting.

Cultivation. By seeds, sown thinly, in March–April, in well-drained soil, where they are to grow, thinning to 6 in. to 1 ft apart.

Perennials. *C. dealbata*, Caucasus, 1½ ft, pinnate leaves, pink flowers, August; *glastifolia*, Europe, 3–4 ft, yellow flowers, summer; *macrocephala*, Caucasus, 3 ft, yellow flowers, July; *montana*, the blue perennial cornflower of Euro e, 1½ ft, with white, pink and rose

vs., May–June; *pulcherrima*, Europe, 2½ ft, silvery foliage, rose-pink flowers, summer; and *rutifolia* (*candicissima*), Italy, chiefly grown for its silvery-white, finely divided foliage and purplish summer flowers; make good border plants. *C. simplicaulis*, Armeria, 6 in., silvery leaved, with rose-red June flowers, may be placed in gritty soil in a warm sheltered rock garden.

Cultivation. Ordinary, well-drained soil, enriched with humus, and sunny positions suit; planting in autumn or March. *C. rutifolia* and *simplicaulis* may need a cloche in winter.

Propagation. By division in autumn or spring; by seeds sown outdoors in April.

Centaurium (ken-taur'i-um. Fam. Gentianaceae). The native *C. portense* (*scilloides*), a tufted perennial of 2–3 in. high, with bright rose gentian-like flowers in summer, makes an attractive rock garden plant, for well-drained soil, planted in spring or autumn. Propagated best by seed, preferably freshly ripe, in autumn.

Centifolius (-a, -um). Very many-leaved. Ex. *Rosa centifolia*.

Centipedes. These are beneficial, carnivorous arthopods (Class *Chilopoda*), not to be confused with the plant-eating Millipedes (q.v.). They move rapidly, have flattish bodies, and only one pair of legs to each body segment. They feed on slugs, snails, insect grubs and worms. There are two common kinds; the large brown Lithobius, and the long thin yellowish Geophilus; friendly natives.

Centranthus. See *Kentranthus*.

Centropogon (ken-tro-po'gon. Fam. Campanulaceae). The chief plant grown under this name is *C.* × *lucyanus*, reputedly a French hybrid of *C. fastuosus* × *Siphocampylus betulaefolius*; highly esteemed as a winter-flowering plant for the warm greenhouse, minimum temp. 13° C. (55° F.), growing 2–2½ ft high, with rose-carmine, white-tipped, tubular flowers, grown in pots or hanging baskets, near the glass. Pot in March, equal parts peat and loam, with sand; water freely in active growth, but more moderately in winter; may be cut back and repotted each spring. Propagated by division or cuttings in April, closed propagating case, at 15·5° C. (60° F.).

Cephalanthera, Helleborine (kep-a-lan'the-ra or sep-a-lan'the-ra. Fam. Orchidaceae). *C. damasonium* (*latifolia, grandiflora*), 1–2 ft, white flowers in May–June; *longifolia* (*ensifolia*), 1–2 ft, white, May–June; and *rubra*, ½–1½ ft, rose-purple, June–July, are native Helleborines, which may be grown in a border, on chalky loam, planting in autumn.

Propagation. By division in September.

Cephalanthus (kep-a-lan'thus or sep-a-lan'thus. Fam. Rubiaceae). The hardy deciduous Button Bush, *C. occidentalis*, N. America, 4–9 ft, may be easily grown for its shining, ornamental foliage and round heads of small tubular white flowers in August, in well-drained, peat-enriched soil and sun. Propagated by spring layering, or cuttings of young firm shoots in July, under handlights.

Cephalaria (kep-a-la'ri-a or sep-a-la'ri-a. Fam. Dipsaceae). Two hardy perennials, *C. alpina*, European Alps, to 5 ft, with scabious-like, pale yellow flowers, June–July, and *tartarica*, Siberia, 5–6 ft, sulphur-yellow, July–August, may be considered for the large border or wild garden; planting in October or March, ordinary soil; sun or shade. Propagated by seed sown outdoors in spring, or by division in March.

Cephalium. The woolly cap that forms at the head of certain Cacti, increasing in size annually.

Cephalocereus (kep-al-o-ke're-us or sep-al-o-se're-us. Fam. Cactaceae). Columnar cacti, which, as they mature, form a mass of hair termed a pseudocephalium, among which almost hidden, nocturnal flowers may be produced, with age.

Selection C. senilis (*Pilocereus senilis*), the 'Old Man' cactus, with long, soft white 'hairs', is most popular; *chrysacanthus*, golden yellow spines and hair; *palmeri*, blue-green and ribbed, with long greyish hairs; *polylophus*, short yellowish wool at the aereoles, are others worth growing. All come from Mexico. Normal cactus cultivation. *See* Cacti.

Cephalotaxus (kep-al-o-tacks'us or sep-al-o-tacks'us. Fam. Taxaceae). Evergreen shrubs or small trees, closely resembling Yew, but with larger leaves, and acorn-like fruits, of China and Japan. Hardy, except in very exposed situations.

Selection. C. drupacea (*harrintoniana*). Japanese Plum-Yew or Cow's-tail Pine, 4–8 ft, makes a rugged bush; its v. *fastigiata*, grows stiffly erect; *fortunei*, Chinese Plum-Yew, is more vigorous, tree-like to 20 ft, with leaves 2–3 in. long, and olive-green seeds; v. *concolor* is a dwarf of 3–4 ft.

Cultivation. Plant in September or April–May. Almost any soil, except dry sand or gravel; sun or partial shade.

Propagation. By seeds in pots, in cold frame, in September or March to plant out at one year old. By cuttings of young shoots, in a frame or under handlight, inserted in August.

Cephalotus (kep-al-o'tus or sep-al-o'tus. Fam. Cephalotaceae). The one species, *C. follicularis*, the Australian Pitcher Plant, W. Australia, is a herbaceous, almost stemless perennial, which is insectivorous, with oval, hairy, green leaves, and other leaves which form pitchers, tinged purple, 1–3 in. long, which trap insects; the white flowers on an erect stalk are small and petalless.

Cultivation. Pot in March, compost of equal parts fibrous peat, chopped living sphagnum moss, and coarse sand; water freely, cover with bell-glass in cool shade; keep just moist in winter, minimum temp. 7° C. (45° F.).

Propagation. By division of rhizomatous roots, in March–April.

Cerasiferus (-a, -um). Cherry-bearing. Ex. *Prunus cerasifera*.

Cerastium (ker-as'ti-um or ser-as'ti-um. Fam. Caryophyllaceae). The chief species grown are the perennial *C. tomentosum*, S. Europe, or Snow-in-Summer, a mat-forming, rather rampant plant, with silvery-white foliage, and white flowers in June, which is good as a ground cover in poor soils, or for the ordinary rock garden, walls or border edge, if trimmed regularly; v. *columnae* is a more accommodating form for small gardens; *biebersteinii*, Crimea, is similar with linear foliage, flowering in May–June; *latifolium*, with bell-shaped white flowers, and *uniflorum*, with yellow-white or white flowers, are both alpines and low-growing, for July colour in a scree.

Cultivation. Plant in March–April, well-drained soil, sun or partial shade. Trim after flowering.

Propagation. By seeds sown out of doors, April; or by cuttings of young stems or division in spring.

Cerasus (Cherry). See *Prunus.*

Ceratonia, Carob-bean, Locust tree (ker-at-o′ni-a or ser-at-o′ni-a. Fam. Leguminosae). The one species, *C. siliqua,* E. Mediterranean, is an evergreen tree, 20 ft, with leathery, pinnate foliage, unisexual yellow-red flowers, giving way to long leathery pods, filled with a sweet pulp, between the seeds; interesting as the reputed food of St John the Baptist in the wilderness, while the seeds were once used as carats, measures of weight, by goldsmiths. Of no great distinction, it may be grown outdoors only in the mildest localities, otherwise it needs a cool greenhouse, winter temp. 7° C. (45° F.), well-drained soil compost, in a tub.

Ceratopteris (ker-a-top′ter-is. Fam. Ceratopteridaceae). Old World tropical aquatic ferns which may be grown in the warm greenhouse (15·5–18 C.° [60–65 ° F.]); *C. thalictroides* and *pteridoides* are grown, the spores being sown on compost of equal parts loam and leafmould in a pot submerged to the rim in water in February, or by pegging old fronds on the soil, which soon produce young plants.

Ceratostigma (ker-a-to-stig′ma or ser-a-to-stig′ma. Fam. Plumbaginaceae). Perennial or sub-shrubs, of which *C. plumbaginoides,* China, is the herbaceous Leadwort, 1–1½ ft, with bright purplish-blue flowers in late summer, and suitable for sun and porous soil in the rock garden; while *willmottianum,* W. China, is shrubby, with 2–3-ft stems, carrying clusters of bright blue flowers, August–October, and ideal for the border or shrub garden, given well-drained soil and a sunny, sheltered position; stems may die back in winter; *griffithii,* India, China, is a low, evergreen shrub, with bright blue flowers in late summer, best grown in a pot, standard JIP compost, under cold greenhouse conditions; winter temp. 5° C. (40° F.).

Propagation. By division in spring; by cuttings of young firm shoots in July–August, in a frame.

Cercidiphyllum (ker-kid-i-pil′lum or ser-sid-i-fil′lum. Fam. Cercidiphyllaceae). The only species, *C. japonicum,* Japan,

grows to a beautiful tree of 100 ft in its homeland, but makes a round-headed small tree or tall bush in Britain, with roundish or oval cordate leaves which colour magnificently in autumn; v. *sinense,* the Chinese form, is similar.

Cultivation. Plant October–March, well-drained, humus-rich loam, with shelter from strong winds.

Propagation. By seeds in pots, standard compost, in cool greenhouse, bottom heat of 15·5° C. (60° F.).

Cercis (ker′kis or ser′sis. Fam. Leguminosae). Deciduous trees or shrubs of which the only one worth attempting is *C. siliquastrum,* unfortunately dubbed the Judas Tree, of S. Europe and the Middle East. It is best grown as a small tree, in sunny, warm sheltered gardens of the south, where its cordate leaves and May flowers of clusters of bright rose purple are enchanting. It is likely to disppoint in cold districts and the north.

Cultivation. Plant while young, preferably ex pots, in March–April; well-drained soil, full sun.

Propagation. By seeds under glass, in pots, JIP compost, bottom heat of 15·5° C. (60° F.).

FIG. 47   *Cercis siliquastrum,* flowers and leaves.

Cereus (ke're-us or se're-us. Fam. Cactaceae). Now a genus of tall, columnar, ribbed cacti, chiefly native to Argentine and Brazil, with large flowers, white, opening in the late afternoon or evening, on tall plants.

Selection. C. azureus, dark bluish green with black spines; *chalybaeus*, dark blue stems; *coerulescens*, very dark green stems; *jamacaru*, deeply ribbed almost blue stems; *peruvianus*, much ribbed, deep green stems, and its v. *montrosus*, the cristate Rock Cactus.

Cultivation. Pot in spring, moving on to large pots when established, watering freely in summer; as for terrestrial cacti (*see* Cacti).

Propagation. Preferably by cuttings in spring or summer.

Cerinthe, Honeywort, Wax-flower (ker-inth'e or ser-inth'e. Fam. Boraginaceae). Pretty hardy annuals with dark green leaves and leafy racemes of vari-coloured, tubular-bell-like flowers. *C. aspera*, S. Europe, 1–2 ft, yellow, brown, purple flowers, July; and *major*, Switzerland, 1 ft, yellow, purple, July, may be sown in April, in well-drained, loamy soil and sun, where they are to flower.

Cernuus (-a, -um). Drooping. Ex. *Narcissus cernuus*.

Cestrum (kest'-rum. Fam. Solanaceae), now includes *Habrothamnus*. Striking ornamental evergreen tall-growing shrubs with clusters of tubular flowers in summer, from Mexico and S. America.

Selection. C. auranticum, Guatemala, to 8 ft, bright orange flowers; *fasciculatum*, Mexico, 5 ft, rose-carmine; *newellii*, 8 ft, crimson; *parqui*, Chile, 10 ft, yellow; *purpureum* (elegans), Mexico, 10 ft, reddish-purple; and *psittacinum*, 8 ft, bright orange.

Cultivation. May be grown on walls in warm, sheltered places, such as Cornwall; otherwise best grown in large pots or borders in a cool greenhouse, winter temps. of 10–13° C. (50–55° F.), with very moderate watering; increasing as growth becomes active through spring and summer. Prune in February.

Propagation. Cuttings of young shoots, taken in summer, in propagating frame, bottom heat of 18° C. (65° F.).

Ceterach (ke-ter'ack. Fam. Polypodiaceae). Ferns with pinnate fronds, scaly beneath, of which *C. officinarum*, the native Scale Fern, 4–6 in., loves lime and may be grown in rock garden crevices with ample summer moisture; v. *ramoso-cristatum* is a remarkable Irish crested form.

Chaenomeles (kai-no-me'les. Fam. Rosaceae). Hardy deciduous flowering shrubs of N. Asia, akin to *Cydonia* spp., and often confused with them.

Selection. C. speciosa (*Cydonia japonica, Pyrus japonica*), the Japanese Quince, 6–10 ft, with somewhat spiny branching growth, is esteemed for its clusters of apple-blossom-like scarlet to red flowers in winter and early spring; with many vs., of which 'Rowallane Seedling', 'Vermilion' and *Moerloesii* are outstanding; *C. japonica*, Japan, Maule's Quince, 3 ft, wide spreading, orange-red, April, and vs. 'Boule de Feu', 'Hever Castle' and 'Versicolor Lutescens'; × *superba*, a hybrid of the above two species, has white, pink and scarlet forms, and double-forming scarlet 'Knaphill Scarlet' and dark crimson 'Simonii'; and *cathayensis*, China, 8 ft, white, April; edible fruits for jelly-making are often borne.

Cultivation. Plant October–March, any reasonably well-drained soil; as wall shrubs, or in the open or as hedges of informal character. Prune, when necessary, after flowering, shortening the flowered shoots.

Propagation. Species by seeds, sown April, out of doors. By sucker shoots detached in autumn; by cuttings of young shoots in summer, under hand-light.

Chafers. Beetles, of which the fleshy white, brown-headed larvae, known as White Grubs, may infest the soil and do much harm by feeding on the roots of fruit bushes and trees, ornamental shrubs and young trees, trees and perennials, etc. The most destructive are the Cockchafer, *Melolontha melolontha*, the garden chafer or bracken-clock, *Phyllopertha horticola*, the summer chafer, *Amphimallus solstitialis*, and the rose chafer, *Cetonia aurata*. Soil fumigation with naphthalene (q.v.) in autumn/winter gives good control. The adult insects fly in May and June. (*See* Fig. 48, page 128.)

Chamaecyparis, Bastard or False Cypress, White Cedars (kam-ai-kip'a-ri-s.

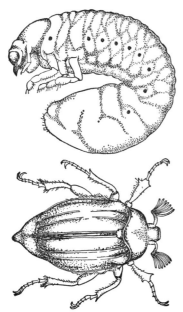

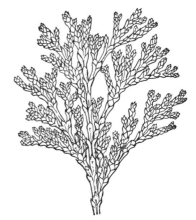

FIG. 49 A flat foliage spray of *Chamaecyparis lawsoniana*.

FIG. 48 *Melolontha melolontha*, the Cockchafer: white larva and adult beetle.

Fam. Pinaceae). A genus of evergreen coniferous trees, closely related to, and confused with Cupressus, but botanically distinct by having flattened branchlets, only two cotyledons, whereas Cupressus has two to five, and only one to five seeds per fertile scale, whereas Cupressus has six to twenty. They make very attractive trees, varying in size and stature and leaf colour, eligible for most gardens where the atmosphere is not much polluted.

Selection. C. lawsoniana, Lawson's Cypress, SW. Oregon, NW. California, U.S.A., to 100 ft, pyramidal, has over 100 varieties; good garden forms are *allumii* to 40 ft, glaucous blue; *erecta*, 20 ft, fastigiate; *fletcheri*, 12-20 ft, bushy; 'green Hedger', for hedging; *lanei*, to 45 ft, golden-leaved; *lutea*, to 50 ft, golden-yellow; 'Triomphe de Boskoop', to 50 ft, glaucous blue; and more dwarf forms such as *ellwoodii*, slowly to 12 ft, grey-green; *minima*

aurea, *m. glauca*, to 6 ft, rounded, bushy; and *pygmaea argentea*, to 3 ft, blue-green, tipped silver foliage. *C. nootkatensis*, Western N. America, to 120 ft, Yellow Cypress, smells turpentiny, does well on heavy, cold soils; vs. *argenteo-variegata*, green and creamy-white foliage; *lutea*, shaded gold; and *compacta*, a dwarf form to 12 ft, are useful. *C. obtusa*, Japanese Hinoki Cypress, 40–60 ft, attractive rich green, and vs. *crippsii*, to 25 ft, golden-leaved; *caespitosa*, very dwarf and bun-like, and *nana*, very dwarf, spreading growth, are for rock gardens. *C. pisifera*, sometimes called Retinospora, Japan, to 60 ft, has vs. *plumosa aurea*, to 25 ft, golden-leaved; *filifera*, with whip-like branchlets, and vs. *aurea*, *gracilis* and *flava*, 6–8 ft; *nana aurea*, a rock garden dwarf; *plumosa compressa* and *squarrosa compacta* are low, bun-shaped dwarfs. *C. thyoides*, the White Cypress of Eastern N. America, is not much grown, but its v. *andelyensis* makes a picturesque small tree to 10 ft, with its glaucous foliage turning plum purple in winter, for the south-west and west.

Cultivation. Plant September–November in the warmer counties, late March–May elsewhere; good light, clean air and soils that drain readily of excess moisture without drying out are suitable.

Place out of strong, cold or drying winds.

Propagation. Species from seeds sown in spring, sandy loam, to transplant two years hence. By cuttings in July–September, in cold frame.

Chamaedaphne (kam-ai-dap'ne. Fam. Ericaceae). The only species, *C. calyculata* (*Cassandra calyculata, Andromeda calyculata nana*), northern hemisphere, the Leather Leaf, is an evergreen upright shrub, 2–4 ft, with racemes of small, white, urn-shaped flowers in early spring.

Cultivation. Plant March–April, in lime-free peaty soil, with midday shade from hot sun.

Propagation. By layering in August–September. By cuttings taken in August in a cold frame. By seeds sown in peat-sand compost, in cold frame, spring.

Chamomile. See *Anthemis*.

Chamomile Lawn. The plant used for chamomile lawns is *Anthemis nobilis*, the native perennial with feathery fragrant foliage, resistant to drought, and requiring no regular cutting. Revived interest in such lawns, known since the seventeenth century, has led to leafy strains being evolved. Chamomile succeeds best in well-drained soil, such as sandy loam, with a lime content, but may suffer winter damage in cold districts and the north. It is not suitable for clay or soils subject to waterlogging. The lawn area needs good preparation, being well dug, weeded free of all perennial weed roots, levelled and firmed. It may be sown in spring, 1 oz. to 4–6 sq. yds; but seed is expensive. It is cheaper to sow seeds, ¼ in. deep, in rows 4 in. apart, on separate nursery bed, or in boxes in a cool greenhouse or frame, and plant out the seedlings, 4 in. apart, in prepared area. Or established plants can be lifted and divided, planting out the divisions 6–12 in. apart. The sward is springy, ornamental and stands up well to foot traffic, but is unsuitable for games or rough play.

Charcoal. The kind used in gardening is carbonized wood, obtained by burning with the exclusion of air. In broken or granular form it may be added to composts to aid drainage and keep the soil sweet; to orchid composts and bulb fibre. Crushed, it may be used on lawns

as a top-dressing to improve aeration and drainage and offset acidity. Pieces may be placed in the water of hyacinth glasses to help to keep the water clean.

Chards. After the main heads of Globe Artichokes have been used, selected plants may be cut to within 6 in. of the ground; new growths break and when about 2 ft high are bound round with straw and earthed up to blanch them. In about six weeks the stems are ready for gathering and cooking, as Chards.

Charieis (**Kaulfussia**) (kar'ee-is. Fam. Compositae). The one species, *C. heterophylla*, S. Africa, 1 ft, with blue or reddish rayed flowers in early summer, is grown as a hardy annual; sown in March–April, in ordinary soil, full sun, where plants are to grow; thinning to 9 in. apart.

Charlock, *Sinapis arvensis.* A persistent annual yellow-flowering weed, of cornfields and arable land.

Cheilanthes (ki-lan'thes. Fam. Polypodiaceae). Evergreen ferns of much beauty, chiefly from warm countries, and grown in the cool greenhouse.

Selection. *C. gracillima,* the Lace Fern of California, with pinnatifid fronds, 4 in.; *microphylla,* tropical America, 8-in. fronds; *myriophylla,* Mexico, 6-in. fronds, and v. *elegans*; and *tomentosa,* Mexico, 12-in. fronds, are good.

Cultivation. Pot in February–March; 2 parts peat, 1 part sandy loam and a little charcoal; water freely at the roots, but give none overhead; give good light but shade from hot sun and keep in airy atmosphere; more moderate watering in winter, minimum temp. 7° C. (45° F.). Propagated by spores.

Cheilos. A lip. See also *Platy-*.

Cheiranthus (ki-er-an'thus. Fam. Cruciferae). The important species are *C. cheiri,* the Wallflower, now available in many strains, in a range of colours containing hues and blends of red, orange, yellow, cream to white, 9–24 in. tall, and × *allionii,* the Siberian Wallflower, in golden and orange shades; naturally perennial, they are grown as hardy biennials, seeds being sown out of doors, preferably in May, seedlings being pricked out 3 in. apart, and planted out where they are to flower in September, in well-drained soil, enriched with rotted organic matter, and limed to pH 6·5. *C. semperflorens*, Morocco, 2–3 ft, cream flowers, turning purple, its v. 'Wenlock Beauty', 9 in., velvet-purple; and its hybrid × *kewensis*, 12 in., brownish-orange, are not quite so hardy, and may be grown in pots in the cool greenhouse, giving early new year flowers.

Chelidonium. *See* Celandine.

Chelone (ke-lo′ne. Fam. Scrophulariaceae). Hardy perennials from N. America which make good border plants, flowering in July–August.

Selection. C. glabra, 1–2 ft, white; *C. lyoni*, 3–4 ft, rose-purple; and *obliqua*, 2 ft, deep rose, with flowers in terminal spikes.

Cultivation. Plant in autumn or spring, any good ordinary soil, sun or partial shade.

Propagation. By division in autumn; by seeds in spring, or cuttings of young shoots in summer in a propagating frame.

Chenopodium (ken-o-po′di-um. Fam. Chenopodiaceae). Of over 100 species, several are weeds, such as the Goosefoot (*C. vulvaria, ficifolium, murale, rubrum, urbicum*) and Fat Hen (*C. album*). *C. purpurescens*, China, 3 ft, and *C. amaranticolor*, S. France, to 8 ft, red or purple flowering, summer, may be grown as half-hardy annuals (q.v.); the latter yielding leaves that may be cooked like spinach. *C. bonushenricus* is sometimes grown as a pot-herb; *see* Good King Henry.

Cherry. These delectable stone fruits fall into three groups—Sweet or Dessert Cherries, derived from *Prunus avium*, the native Bird Cherry; Sour Cherries from *P. cerasus*; and the Dukes, derived from *P. avium* × *P. cerasus* crossings, and intermediate for culinary and dessert use.

Sweet Cherries. These are more difficult to grow than sours, needing a good light to medium loam, of depth and even texture, overlying naturally well-drained subsoil such as gravel, ragstone or chalk; and succeed better in the southern half of England than in the north.

There are no dwarfing rootstocks, and varieties should be budded on the seedling wild cherry or Gean, or Malling F 12/1. Best grown in half-standard or standard form; though they may also be grown as fan-trained trees on walls

where the necessary time and skill can be given to them.

Sweet cherries are not self-fertile; cross-pollination between two or more compatible kinds is essential to cropping. Recommended varieties and pollinators are: *Early:* 1. Early Rivers (4, 9, 11). 2. Merton Bounty (1, 4). 3. Merton favourite (1, 4, 5). 4. Merton Glory (1, 2, 11). 5. Merton Heart (1, 3, 4, 11). *Mid-season:* 6. Amber Heart (8, 10, 12). 7. Bradbourne Black (5, 8, 10, 12). 8. Frogmore Early (7, 10, 12). 9. Noir de Guben (1, 4). *Late:* 10. Bigarreau Napoleon (7, 8, 12). 11. Merton Bigarreau (1, 2, 4, 5). 12. Governor Wood (1, 7, 8, 10).

Planting. This is done when trees are dormant, October–March, the earlier the better, giving ample space; half-standards and standards 25–30 ft apart; wall trees 24 ft. No fertilizers in the first year, but thereafter 2 parts by weight bone meal, 1 part sulphate of potash at 2–3 oz. per sq. yd may be given each winter, topped by an organic dressing; and basic slag (4–6 oz. per sq. yd) every third year, especially to trees in grass. A nitrogenous dressing can be given in March. Trees should not go short of water in May if premature dropping of fruit is to be avoided.

Pruning. This should be done between the last week of May and the second week of June. Standard trees only need pruning to shape and space branches when young; thereafter only dead wood and weak shoots need to be cut out, or a little thinning done. The trained tree is shaped as for peaches (q.v.), and as fruit is borne on both old and new wood, leading shoots are not shortened after shaping, but shoots growing to or from the wall are removed, and other shoots trained in to space available, or shortened to 5 or 6 leaves. Training shoots horizontally encourages new growth, and permits the removal of overlong shoots to a lateral when necessary.

Sour Cherries. The chief varieties are Morello and Kentish Red, both self-fertile, and may be grown alone. Morello does quite well on a north wall, and may be considered where sweet cherries may not succeed. Planting and manuring are as for sweet cherries. Pruning is different as fruit is borne only on the previous year's wood. Trees may be grown in standard or half-standard form or bush, or fan-trained on a wall.

Pruning should be timed as for sweet cherries, and trees shaped as for plums (q.v.). Thereafter all dead and blind wood, interlacing and inward-growing shoots should be cut away, and each year a proportion of shoots may be cut hard back to older wood to stimulate new growth.

Duke Cherries. In planting, two or more varieties should be chosen to ensure cross-pollination, on Gean or Malling F 12/1 rootstocks; and grown as the sour cherries. Varieties are May Duke, Archduke, Late Duke and Reine Hortense.

Diseases. Bacterial Canker or Die-back is the worst; caused by *Pseudomonas mors-prunorum*, with a yellowing of leaves in spring, later withering, with cracks and cankers in the bark. Infected shoots should be cut out when seen. Spraying with a copper oxychloride fungicide in mid August, mid September and mid October is the most promising control. The Silver Leaf fungus, *Stereum purpureum*, may infect cherries, giving the characteristic silvery sheen to the leaves of infected shoots or branches, which should be cut out and burnt in June, cuts painted with a fungicidal paint, and the tree reinvigorated by good culture.

Pests. The Cherry Black-fly (Aphis), *Myzus cerasi*, can curl leaves and stunt growth, but winter spraying with tar oil or DNOC petroleum oil wash is preventative, or malathion used at blossom burst to white bud stages. Cherry Fruit Moth, *Argyresthia curvella*, feeds on young fruitlets, but winter washes control, or malathion as for black-fly in early spring. Red Spider Mites, *Metatetranychus ulmi*, may trouble wall trees in hot weather, but a spray based on Rogor is effective.

Cherry, Cornelian. See *Cornus mas.*

Cherry Laurel. See *Prunus laurocerasus.*

Cherry Pie. See *Heliotropium.*

Cherry Plum. See *Prunus cerasifera.*

Chervil, Common (*Anthriscus cerefolium*). A hardy annual herb, giving sweet, aromatic leaves which may be used in salads and for seasoning.

Successional sowings may be made outdoors in good soil. March–September, cropping in 6 to 8 weeks; or in boxes, in a cool greenhouse for winter supplies.

Cheshunt Compound. A fungicide chiefly used to prevent or check soilborne diseases such as damping-off, stem rots, etc., in seedlings. Made by mixing 2 parts by weight powdered copper sulphate with 11 parts fresh ammonium carbonate in a glass or earthenware jar, corked closely for 24 hours; and then dissolving 1 oz. in a little hot water, and diluting to 2 gallons with cold water, for immediate use.

Chestnut. See *Aesculus.*

Chickling Vetch. See *Lathyrus sativus.*

Chickweed. See *Stellaria.*

Chicory (*Cichorium intybus*). A hardy perennial, grown as a biennial for its blanched heads of shoots, chicons, as winter salading, Improved Giant, Whiteloaf and Large Brussels being suitable strains. Seeds are sown, late May–early June, in light, rich soil, ½ in. deep, in rows 12 in. apart, and thinned to 9 in. apart when 1 in. high. The carrot-like roots are lifted in November, the spent top growth removed, and stored in dry soil or sand in a cool, frostproof place. To force and blanch, roots are placed in boxes or large pots, 3 in. apart, crowns 1 in. above the surface, in moist peat or soil, watered gently, and covered with a light-tight box, to be brought into a temp. of 13–18° C. (55–65° F.), in greenhouse or heated space. The blanched heads are ready in about four weeks, and with successional preparation can be had up to May.

Plants may also be grown for their ornamental value, growing 2–5 ft, with blue flowers, rose pink in v. *rosea*, in summer, but only where its rampant vigour would not be out of place.

Chilean Crocus. See *Tecophilaea.*

Chimaera, literally a fabulous monster; in gardening an abnormal composite plant, formed by the growing together of tissues of different generic constitution. See *Laburnocytisus.*

Chimney Bell-flower. See *Campanula pyramidalis.*

Chimonanthus, Winter-sweet (ki-mon-an'thus. Fam. Calycanthaceae). The species grown is *C. praecox* (*fragrans*),

FIG. 50 *Chimonanthus praecox.*

China, 8 ft or more, which bears sweetly scented, yellow and purplish, starry flowers close to its leafless shoots in winter; v. *grandiflorus* has larger, less fragrant flowers, and greater vigour; and *lutea* all-yellow flowers. Needs a porous, humus-rich loam, a warm, sheltered position, and sun, to give of its best. Flowered shoots may be shortened after flowering in March.

Propagation. By seeds, under glass, bottom heat of 15·5° C. (60° F.), March–April. By layering in early spring.

China Aster. *See* Aster and *Callistephus.*

Chionanthus, Fringe Tree (ki-o-nan'thus. Fam. Oleaceae). A deciduous shrub or small tree of 10–30 ft, *C. virginicus,* of N. America, may be grown for the beauty of its pure white, fringe-like flowers, borne in panicles in June, and yellow autumn leaf colour, in good loam soil, and full sun. The Chinese *C. retusus,* to 10 ft, is similar, but with smaller terminal panicles of flowers.

Propagation. Preferably by seed, in pots, under glass, with bottom heat of 18° C. (65° F.), spring.

Chionodoxa, Glory of the Snow (ki-on-o-docks'a. Fam. Liliaceae). Bulbous plants from the E. Mediterranean region, of which *C. luciliae,* stars of white-centred, intense blue flowers on 6-in. stalks, with white and pink-flowering forms; *sardensis,* all blue

flowers; and *gigantea,* 8 in. soft violet blue and white, flower in March–April, and may be naturalized in rock gardens, borders or shrubberies, ordinary soil. Plant bulbs in August–October, 1 in. deep, 3 in. apart; to be lifted and divided every third year.

Propagation. By freshly ripened seed in late summer, sown outdoors. By offset bulbs.

Chives (*Allium schoenoprasum*). Grown for their fine tubular leaves to flavour salads, soups, etc., with a mild onion savour, these hardy perennial, slightly bulbous plants grown in any well-drained soil from division of clumps set out in autumn or spring. May be grown from seed, sown April.

Chlamy-. A prefix signifying a covering.

Chlorophyll. The green colouring matter of plants, present in parts exposed to the light, contained in minute bodies of protoplasm, chloroplasts, in the cells. Its function is to absorb certain rays of light and utilize their energy to split water into oxygen and hydrogen and activate the reactions which result in carbohydrate foodstuffs being formed for the plant. *See* Photosynthesis.

Chlorophytum (klo-ro-pi'tum. Fam. Liliaceae). Only *C. elatum* v. *variegatum,* a S. African evergreen perennial, with long, narrow, whitish striped leaves, up to 24 in., is grown in the cool greenhouse. Pot in March, standard compost, water freely in active growth, very moderately in winter, minimum temp. 5–7° C. (40–45° F.). Propagated by division.

Chloroplasts. Minute, but the largest, bodies of protoplasm in the cytoplasm of plant cells, which contain chlorophyll, and are instrumental in the conversion of certain light rays into chemical energy.

Chlorosis. The loss of greenness in plant leaves, etc. It may accompany disease, or be caused by a mineral nutrient deficiency, such as of iron or manganese.

Choisya, Mexican Orange Blossom (koy'si-a or choy'si-a. Fam. Rutaceae). The one species, *C. ternata,* makes a rounded evergreen bush of 4–9 ft, with trifoliolate, bright green leaves, and cymes of daisy-like, scented white flowers, April–May; and despite its

Mexican origin can be grown outdoors in mild sheltered localities, or against warm walls. Needs only a porous soil and shelter from cold winds. Makes a good pot plant in cold greenhouses.

Propagation. By cuttings of young shoots in summer, in propagating case, bottom heat 18° C. (65° F.), or ripe cuttings in August, in a cold frame.

Choke Berry. See *Aronia arbutifolia*.

Chorizema (kor-i-ze'ma. Fam. Leguminosae). Highly attractive Australian evergreen shrubs of 2–3 ft, which make good pot plants for the cool greenhouse, minimum winter temp. 7° C. (45° F.), as they bear sweet-pea-like flowers over a long period. *C. cordatum*, red and yellow flowers; *dicksonii*, red; *henchmannii*, red and yellow; *illicifolium*, orange and red; and *varium*, yellow and reddish, are all good.

Cultivation. Pot, and repot every other year, in spring, 8-in. pots; standard compost; water increasingly with growth; very moderately in winter. Prune after flowering; may be stood outdoors, July–September, in sheltered spot.

Propagation. By 'heeled' cuttings under handlight or in propagating frame, July–August.

Christmas Pride. See *Ruellia*.

Christmas Rose. See *Helleborus*.

Christmas Tree. See *Picea abies*.

Christ's Thorn. See *Paliurus*.

Chromoplasts. Minute bodies which carry colouring matter or pigments other than chlorophyll, of which the chemical functions are largely unknown.

Chromosomes. Thread-like, gene-bearing bodies within the nuclei of plant cells.

Chrysalid, Chrysalis (pl. **Chrysalides**). The pupal stage of an insect, particularly of moths and butterflies.

Chrysanthemum (kri-san'the-mum. Fam. Compositae). A genus of over 100 species, annual and perennial herbs, ranging from weeds to the most gorgeous flowering hybrids. For gardening purposes they may be considered as follows:

Annual Chrysanthemums. Grown each year from seed, they include *C. carinatum*, Morocco, 2 ft, with parti-coloured, single-ray flowers, and vs. such as *burridgeanum*, white petals, crimson inner ring; 'John Bright', pure yellow; 'The Sultan', pure scarlet; 'White Queen'; *tricolor*, vari-coloured; and double-flowering hybrids; *coronarium*, S. Europe, 2–4 ft, pale yellow, and vs. *flore pleno*, double yellow and white; 'Golden Glory', 1 ft, single golden *multicaule*, Algeria, 6–12 in., golden yellow, for edging and rock gardens; *segetum*, the native Corn Marigold, with golden-yellow flowers, improved in vs. 'Evening Star', 'Golden Glow' and 'Eldorado'; × *spectabile* 'Cecilia', 2½ ft, large white, single blooms with inner golden ring; all of which bloom July–September.

Cultivation. Seeds may be sown in March–April, thinly, where plants are to grow, and thinned out; preferably in sunny positions, and well-drained soil, given a little humus and superphosphate.

Paris Daisy, Marguerite. A half-hardy shrubby perennial, *C. frutescens*, Canaries, 2–3 ft., with white or pale yellow-rayed flowers, and its vs. *brussonetii*, white; 'Etoile d'Or', lemon yellow; 'Queen Alexandra', double white; and *grandiflorum*, with larger flowers; are usually grown as pot plants in the cool greenhouse, or for window-boxes, to flower freely for most of the year.

Cultivation. Plants may be raised from seed, sown under glass, standard compost, March–April, with bottom heat of 18° C. (65° F.); to be potted on singly to 3-in., and then 5- or 6-in. pots, being pinched back at the growing points, after moves, and coming into flower in the following spring. Or plants are easily propagated by cuttings of young shoots, 3–4 in. long, inserted in sandy loam, in a cold frame, July–September; to be potted later. By regulating potting a little, a succession of plants can be brought to give bloom over a long period.

Pyrethrum. C. coccineum (*Pyrethrum roseum*), Caucasus, Persia, 1–2 ft, is the hardy perennial from which the modern border pyrethrums, so useful for early cut flowers in May–June, have been raised; single vs. such as white 'Avalanche', salmon-red 'Evenglow', scarlet, 'Kelway's Glorious', and double vs. such as crimson 'J. N. Twerdy', pale pink 'Madalene', 'White Madalene' and pink 'Queen Mary'. Here, *C. cinerarii-folium*, Dalmatia, 15 in., white, July, may be included as the source plant of the pyrethrum used in insecticides.

Cultivation. Plants may be raised from seeds sown in a cold frame, April, or out of doors, May, to grow on and plant out in early autumn. Named forms are best bought in as young plants for early autumn planting, in ordinary soil, enriched with rotted organic matter and bone meal, sheltered from wind.

Propagation. By division of plants in autumn, which should be done every third year or so.

Hardy Perennial Border Chrysanthe-mums. The native white summer-flower-ing Ox-Eye Daisy, *C. leucanthemum*, 2½ ft, deserves a place in the border, especially in its newer vs. such as 'Mount Everest' and 'Silver Prince', growing only 1½ ft tall. The Shasta Daisy, *C. maximum*, Pyrenees, 1½–2 ft, is available in several outstanding vs., 'Esther Read', 'Horace Read', 'Jennifer Read', 'Beauté Nivelloise', 'Wirral Pride', and 'Wirral Supreme', being double, white, flowering from June to August. Korean chrysanthemums, vs. of *koreanum*, make good border plants, with sprays of brightly coloured flowers late into autumn, and hardy enough for all but the most exposed gardens; new forms are constantly being introduced, but good standbys are: single-flowering —'Apollo', bronze-red and old gold; 'Astrid', soft pink; 'Carmen', rust-brown; 'Ceres', old gold and yellow; 'Daphne', pink; 'Diana', rose-pink; 'Fireflame', blood-red; 'Indian Sum-mer', coppery-orange; 'Mars', red; 'Mercury', salmon-red; 'Venus', rose-pink; 'Vulcan', clear red; and 'Wildfire', rust-red. Double-flowering are 'Bubbles', orange-red; 'Ember', madder red; 'Janté Wells', golden-yellow; and 'The Moor', wine red. There is also the 'Otley' race of Koreans of much beauty and distinction, to be looked for in the raiser's list. *C. rubellum*, 3 ft, the origins of which are not known, bears large, single pink flowers, and vs. in other colours have been developed to lend distinction to border colour in late summer and autumn. The native Fever-few, *C. parthenium*, 2–3 ft, is very appealing in its double flowering form,

while the Golden Feather, v. *aureum*, with yellow-green foliage is a good dwarf edging plant. The Hungarian, *C. uliginosum*, towers to 6 ft, with white flowers, August–October, and delights in a moist soil; but the Moroccan *mawii*, 1½ ft, white flowering, reddish beneath, is not so hardy, and may be wintered under glass, or fresh stock raised from seed each year.

FIG. 51 Chrysanthemum cutting, pre-pared for rooting.

Cultivation. The above border plants do well in most soils with reasonable drainage, enriched with organic matter and bone meal. Plants may be set out in autumn or early winter; many can be raised from seeds, sown outdoors or in a cold frame, May or June, to give plants for setting out by autumn. Established plants may be propagated by cuttings of young shoots taken in early spring, and rooted in a cool greenhouse or frame, standard JIP compost.

Rock Garden Chrysanthemums. Dwarfs suitable for the rock garden or the alpine house are *C. alpinum*, Pyrenees, 2 in., with white, shading to yellow, flowers in July; *arcticum*, Alaska, 9 in., white, tinged pink, June–July; *catananche*,

Morocco, 4 in., cream and red, May, deserving of the alpine house; *hispanicum*, Spain, 6 in., white, May, and its v. *sulphureum*, yellow; and *radicans*, Spain, 2 in., golden yellow, May.

Cultivation. A porous soil, lightish, with good sifted leaf-mould added, and bone meal, suits these plants, where they can keep dryish in winter, with a surface mulch of grit. Propagation is by seed in spring, or division in summer.

FLORIST AND SHOW CHRYSANTHEMUMS. These embrace the autumn-flowering chrysanthemums of the florist's shop, show and greenhouse, with a heritage that goes back to the Far East, where the 'Golden Flower' (*chrysos*, gold; *anthos*, flower) was cultivated in China about 500 B.C., improved by the Japanese, but only became introduced into Britain in the eighteenth century. The plants grown today are highly complex hybrids in which several species have played their parts, but it is usually accepted that the dominant parents were *C. indicum*, of China and Southern Japan, and *C. morifolium* (*sinense*), of China. Today there are many thousands of varietal forms, which are reduced to order by the Classification For Show Purposes adopted by the National Chrysanthemum Society.

LATE-FLOWERING CHRYSANTHEMUMS: Indoor Varieties
Section I. Exhibition Incurved.
  (a) Large-flowered. Ex. 'Ondine'.
  (b) Medium-flowered. Ex. 'Progress'.
Section II. Large Exhibition. Ex. 'Majestic'.
Section III. Large Exhibition Incurving. Ex. 'Candeur'.
Section IV. Medium Exhibition. Ex. 'Mona Davis'.
Section V. Reflexed Decorative. Ex. 'Loveliness'.
Section VI. Incurving Decoratives. Ex. 'Coralie'.
Section VII. Anemones.
  (a) Large-flowered, 5 in. diameter or more. Ex. 'Admiration'.
  (b) Medium-flowered, 3–5 in. diameter. Ex. 'Heloïse'.
  (c) Small-flowered, 2–3 in. diameter. Ex. 'Calliope'.
Section VIII. Pompons.
  (a) Large-flowered, 2 in. diameter or more. Ex. 'Dresden China'.

  (b) Small-flowered, less than 2 in. diameter. Ex. 'Baby'.
Section IX. Singles.
  (a) Large-flowered, 5 in. diameter or more. Ex. 'Cleone'.
  (b) Medium-flowered, 3 in., not more than 5 in. diameter. Ex. 'Golden Seal'.
  (c) Small-flowered, less than 3 in. diameter. Ex. 'Market Gem'.
Section X. Spidery, Plumed and Feathery. Ex. 'Ming of the Plumes'.
Section XI. Any other types.
OCTOBER-FLOWERING CHRYSANTHEMUMS:
Section XVI. Reflexed.
  (a) Large-flowered. Ex. 'Perfection'.
  (b) Medium-flowered. Ex. 'Yellow Gown'.
Section XVII. Incurving.
  (a) Large-flowered. Ex. 'Superlative'.
  (b) Medium-flowered. Ex. 'Estelle Normand'.
EARLY-FLOWERING CHRYSANTHEMUMS: Outdoor Varieties
Section XX. Incurved.
  (a) Large-flowered. Ex. 'Shirley Cream'.
  (b) Medium-flowered. Ex. 'Harvest Moon'.
  (c) Small-flowered. Ex. 'Moonstone'.
Section XXI. Reflexed.
  (a) Large-flowered. Ex. 'Barbara'.
  (b) Medium-flowered. Ex. 'Sweetheart'.
  (c) Small-flowered. Ex. 'Wendy'.
Section XXII. Incurving.
  (a) Large-flowered. Ex. 'Una'.
  (b) Medium-flowered. Ex. 'Migoli'.
Section XXIII. Singles.
  (a) Large-flowered. Ex. 'Daphne'.
  (b) Medium-flowered. Ex. 'Nectar'.
Section XXIV. Pompons.
  (a) Tall. Ex. 'Cream Bouquet'.
  (b) Dwarf. Ex. 'Denise'.
Section XXV. Any other types.
EARLY-FLOWERING CHRYSANTHEMUMS are defined as varieties which are normally expected to flower out of doors before 1st October, without needing protection. They are largely grown as border plants or in special beds. Good drainage is essential, and the soil should be prepared by liberal organic manuring in autumn, and a balanced chrysanthemum fertilizer, or a mixture of 2 parts by weight hoof and horn

meal, 2 parts bone flour and 1 part sulphate of potash may be given at planting-out time, 3–4 oz. per sq. yd.

Plants, whether bought-in or home-raised, usually consist of cuttings which have been rooted, and are planted out about the second and third week of May; in groups of three or four, 18 in. apart, if in the border, or 15–18 in. apart in beds, in rows 15 in. apart; using a trowel, planting firmly, but loosening the surface soil afterwards. A ring of powdered lime round each plant, or the use of a metaldehyde bait, will deter slugs. Plants must not suffer water shortage, and weeds should be controlled, at least until August. After planting, plants are *stopped* as soon as they recover by cutting out the top growth of the main stem above a leaf; and again, about the second week of June, by removing the tops of the lateral shoots then in being. The plants are then allowed to grow on without further check. For garden display, disbudding—the removal of side buds below the main or crown bud of each stem—sometimes called securing of buds, is not essential. When large blooms are wanted for cutting or exhibition, the plant is stopped when 6 in. tall; three or four lateral shoots are then allowed to grow to produce crown buds, which are secured by removing all unwanted lower buds and side-shoots from leaf-axils as they appear. By timing the stopping of shoots it is possible to regulate flowering for given dates, assuming that it takes 6 to 8 weeks, according to variety, from the securing of the chosen crown buds to open flower.

Propagation. Outdoor plants are lifted at the end of October, the roots (stools) cleaned of soil, and boxed, or placed in boxes and covered with dryish soil, to winter in a cool greenhouse at 7–10° C. (45–50° F.), or frostproof frame, kept slightly moist. Cuttings are taken of the new growths coming from the roots in February–March, consisting of short-jointed tip shoots, 2–3 in. long, which are stripped of their lower leaves, and inserted for 1 in. in 2½-in. deep boxes, pans or pots, to root. The bases of cuttings can be dressed with a root-inducing hormone. They should be kept close, and if possible given bottom heat of 15·5° C. (60° F.). When rooted, in 2 to 3 weeks, cuttings may be moved to 3-in. pots for pot growth, or to boxes, spaced 3 in. apart, for outdoors, and grown on in temperature of 10° C. (50° F.), with judicious watering and good ventilation, being moved to a cold frame to harden off before being planted out.

Selection. Varieties are now so numerous, and new introductions so frequently made, while vegetative reproduction inevitably takes its toll of many varieties, that the keen chrysanthemum grower is best advised to follow show reports and the recommendations of the National Chrysanthemum Society, and to consult the catalogues of specialists in this flower.

LATE-FLOWERING INDOOR CHRYSAN-THEMUMS.

Plants are potted from mid February onwards, when grown from rooted cuttings, in 3-in. pots, in the cool greenhouse, 10° C. (50° F.), and grown on until moved into 5- or 6-in. pots in April, with watering gradually increasing, and good aeration. They need shade from hot sun, and may be hardened off until about mid May, when they may be stood out of doors on wood boards, ashes or slates in a sheltered place, facing south or west. When the roots fill the pots, about mid June, they are potted on to 8- or 9-in. pots, with good drainage afforded by crocks, and well firmed. Standard composts such as John Innes, UC, or Levington may be used throughout. Plants must be staked adequately, usually three canes per plant, and growth tied on as necessary. Pots should be spaced to avoid foliage of plants touching, and watering may need attention two or three times a day in hot weather. If bushy plants are wanted, plants are stopped, by pinching out the growing tip of the central shoot when 6 in. high, usually in April; and the resultant shoots are stopped when they have made 5 or 6 in. growth, in early summer. For large or exhibition blooms, allow the young plant to grow until the natural break bud (the flower bud at the end of the main stem) shows in early summer; then pinch out this bud and all the shoots below except the three or four most vigorous and well-placed, each of which is allowed to grow on unstopped, and all side-shoots and side-buds are removed to concentrate growth in the first crown bud. In some varieties, however, it is recommended that the first crown buds should be removed, and second crown buds allowed to form on two shoots at the top, with all other shoots being removed. In September, or as soon as flower buds show a tinge of colour, plants should be housed under glass, with ample room and maintaining a buoyant atmosphere. Feeding may be done with a suitable proprietary liquid feed or seaweed derivative from when buds first show colour until about three-quarters open, twice weekly. Temp. 7–13° C. (45–55° F.).

Propagation. After flowering, stems and weak basal shoots are cut down, a top-dressing of soil compost added, and plants placed in a cool greenhouse or frostproof frame and watered. In four weeks or so sucker shoots grow from the roots from which sturdy, short-jointed tip cuttings of 2 to 3 in. can be taken to root in 3-in. pots, as detailed for the early-flowering chrysanthemums. Cuttings may be taken from November onwards, according to variety and purpose; though December–February is usually the most popular time. Some varieties do not yield many shoots from the roots, and it is then necessary to take stem cuttings, which do not root quite so readily, and tend to produce flower buds too early, and care must be taken to see that the selected shoots are sturdy, with good healthy growing points.

Selection. Apart from personal preferences in types of flowers, the choice of varieties is very wide, and with old favourites dropping out and new forms being introduced every year, it is wise to be guided by show reports, the recommendations of the National Chrysanthemum Society and specialists' catalogues.

The Control of Flowering. In Nature, Chrysanthemums are short-day plants, which means that they require a long dark period (or night) to bring them into flowering; consequently they normally flower in the autumn. By varying the day- or night-length artificially it is possible to quicken or retard flowering. Flowering can be delayed by exposing the plants to a period of light in the middle of the night, and hastened by subjecting them to darkness earlier in the day. Applied commercially, this photoperiodic sensitivity of chrysanthemums gives us their flowers in every month of the year.

Cascade Chrysanthemums. These are trailer strains developed in Japan, branching freely with small single flowers. Plants may be grown from seeds or from cuttings. When the young plants have made six or seven leaves, they are pinched back to the fourth or fifth leaf. This leads to the formation of three or four branches, of which the foremost is allowed to grow unchecked, while the others are stopped frequently to induce bushy growth at the base. The leading shoot is trained to a cane, pointing north at an angle of 45°; as side growths extend, they are stopped regularly until about mid September; the leading shoot is tied to the cane as it lengthens, and the cane gradually lowered to the horizontal. When flower buds have formed all over the plant, the lower part of the main stem is bound with raffia or grafting tape to prevent breakage, the cane removed, and the top growth carefully lowered to drape from a pedestal or shelf, and secured by coiling wire about the main stem and branches.

Diseases. Powdery Mildew (*Erysiphe cichoracearum*) covers leaves with a whitish powdery growth. As the spores need a moist atmosphere in which to germinate, good ventilation and careful watering help to prevent this fungus disease. Outbreaks can be checked by applying sulphur dust, Bordeaux Mixture and, on tolerant varieties, Karathane. The Grey Mould fungus, *Botrytis cinerea*, may cause a damping-off of blooms, but is best prevented by regulating heat, ventilation and watering to avoid over-moist conditions; captan dust may be used. Rust (*Puccinia chrysanthemi*) starts as blister-like swellings on leaves which burst and release masses of brown powdery spores. Good ventilation and avoidance of undue humidity reduce the risk. Affected leaves should be removed and burnt, and plants treated with a sulphur or thiram fungicide; old stems and remains of infected plants being destroyed after flowering. Petal Blight (*Itersonilia perplexans*) begins on outer petals, working inwards, turning petals brown; careful application of a zineb fungicide at 2- to 3-day intervals when disease appears checks it. Ray Blight (*Aschochyta chrysanthemi*) browns petals from the centre of blooms outwards, and spreads to stems. Zineb or captan may be used to check it; infected material must be burnt; and strict hygienic methods of culture followed. Virus Yellows is characterized by the basal yellowing of foliage and the abortion of flowers; plants should be promptly destroyed. In buying new stock it is essential to know it is healthy and virus-free, which can be ensured by treatment under what is termed 'Heat therapy'.

Pests. Aphids (Green-fly) may be controlled by use of a systemic insecticide, effective for 4 weeks; or application of malathion, gamma-BHC or nicotine insecticide; also effective against Thrips, and White-fly. Leaf-miner grubs (*Phytomyza chrysanthemi*) tunnelling leaves succumb to nicotine, but care is needed in application. Capsid or Bishop Bug (*Lygus pratensis*) may be controlled with gamma-BHC or DDT insecticide. Red Spider infestation calls for the use of a kelthane insecticide. Sciarid Fly larvae, small creamy-white, blackheaded grubs, and Symphilids, slender, active, white 'insects', may attack roots in the soil if soil sterilization is not practised. Eelworms (*Aphelenchoides ritzema-bosi*) cause yellowish-green or brown patches on the leaves, which wither and droop against the stem from the base upwards, and blight buds and flowers; although they live in the tissues, they can move on the outsides of plants when moist. The soil also becomes infested. Commercially, infestation is controlled by the use of parathion, but this toxic insecticide is not readily available to gardeners. An older, effective method is Warm Water Treatment: cut back the stems of infested stools, wash roots free of all soil, disposing of this as it will contain eelworms; immerse stools entirely in warm water at 46° C. (115° F.) for five minutes; plunge immediately into cold water, drain, and plant in clean soil. Soil in which plants have grown should be removed **or** sterilized by heat treatment.

Chrysobactron. See *Bulbinella.*

Chrysogonum (kris-og′o-num. Fam. Compositae.) The sole species, *C. virginianum*, 6 in., is a N. American hardy herbaceous perennial, with yellow-rayed flowers in May, suitable for rock gardens. Plant October–March, well drained, peaty loam. Propagated by division in March.

Chrysopsis, Golden Aster (kris-op′sis. Fam. Compositae). Hardy, herbaceous N. American perennials of which *C. villosa* v. *rutteri*, 1 ft, is grown for its yellow-rayed flowers in summer. Plant in ordinary soil, October–March; propagate by division in March, or by seeds sown in April, out of doors.

Cibotium (ki-bo′ti-um. Fam. Cyatheaceae). Tree ferns, related to Dicksonia, which may be grown in the cool greenhouse, winter temp. of 7° C. (45° F.).

Selection. C. *barometz*, Assam, tripinnate fronds; *regale*, Mexico; and *C. glaucum*, Sandwich Isles.

Cultivation. Pot in April, compost of 2 parts fibrous loam, 1 part each fibrous peat and sand; water freely to September, just keep moist in winter. Shade from hot direct sun. Propagated by spores.

Cichorium (ki-ko′ri-um. Fam. Compositae). Herbaceous plants of which *C. endivia* is the Endive (q.v.), and *C. intybus*, Chicory (q.v.).

Cilia. Fine hairs on the edges of leaves.

Ciliatus (-a, -um). Fringed with hairs. Ex. *Androsace ciliata.*

Cimicifuga, Bugwort (ki-mi-ki-fu′ga, Fam. Ranunculaceae). Handsome herbaceous perennials, with plumose racemes of flowers in summer.

Selection. C. *americana*, Eastern N. America, 2–3 ft, white; *dahurica*, Japan, 4 ft, white; *foetida intermedia*, 'White Pearl', to 5 ft; and *racemosa*, Eastern N. America, 4–8 ft, white.

Cultivation. Plant March; moisture-retentive soil, or in shade on lighter soils, in border, or water garden.

Propagation. By division in March. By seeds in a cold frame in autumn, or outdoors in April.

Cineraria. The garden or florist Cinerarias are now regarded as being derived from *Senecio cruentus*, native to the Canary Islands, naturally perennial, but grown as half-hardy biennials for their highly decorative and colourful, rayed and starry flowers, in the greenhouse.

Selection. C.s may be classified as (1) Large-flowered Singles, 15 in.; (2) Stellata strains, with star-like flowers, 2–2½ ft, and the Feltham Beauty strains, 1½ ft; (3) Intermediate vs., 15 in., free-branching with somewhat smaller flower-heads; and (4) *Multiflora*, *nana*, compact and 9–12 in., and *maxima*, 15 in. There are also double-flowering strains.

Cultivation. Sowings are made in April for winter-flowering plants; in June for spring-flowering. Seeds are sown thinly in pans, bottom heat of 15·5° C. (60° F.), shaded from hot sun; pricked off, potted into 3-in. pots, then into 5-in. for dwarf kinds, and on to 6- to 8-in. pots for larger plants. Plants need cool, moist growing conditions, shade from hot sun, regular watering, ventilation with draughts, and may be grown in frames during the summer. Minimum winter temps. 10° C. (50° F.). Use standard composts throughout.

Diseases. Young and winter plants may suffer from Black Neck, a rotting of stems at or near soil level, caused by *Phytophthora* sp. of soil fungi; prevented by use of standard composts and avoidance of over-wet conditions. Rust, *Coleosporium senecionis*, causes bright yellow spots on undersides of leaves. There is a virus disease, Spotted Wilt, which causes yellow spotting of leaves and browning veins. It is wise to destroy all diseased plants, for they are marred anyway.

Pests. Sap-sucking Aphids, Thrips, White-fly and leaf-miners may attack Cinerarias; but prevention is possible by the use of a systemic insecticide.

For other Cinerarias see *Senecio*.

Cinereus (-a, -um). Grey, ash-coloured. Ex. *Botrytis cinerea*, the Grey-mould fungus.

Cinquefoil. See *Potentilla*.

Circiniatus (-a, -um). Circiniate, curled round or inwards like a crook as with fern fronds.

Cirrhus, Cirrhatus (-a, -um). A tendril, tendril-bearing. Ex. *Arthopodium cirrhatum*.

Cissus (kis'sus. Fam. Vitaceae). A large genus of climbing plants, grown

FIG. 52 *Cissus antarctica,* Kangaroo Vine.

for the beauty of their leaves, in the greenhouse and as house plants.

Selection. C. antarctica, the Kangaroo Vine, Australia, evergreen, pretty toothed leaves, makes a good cool greenhouse climber or potted house plant; *discolor,* Java, exceptionally fine for its coloured foliage; *javalensis*, Nicaragua, 6 ft, green and velvety leaves; and *striata*, Chile, evergreen and elegant, are well worth while.

Cultivation. Pot, and repot, April; JI compost, water freely in active growth; moderately in winter, minimum temp. 10–15·5° C. (50–60° F.), though *C. discolor* likes at least 13° C. (55° F.).

Propagation. By cuttings of young shoots, taken with a heel, in summer, in propagating case, with bottom heat of 21–27° C. (70–80° F.).

Cistus (kis′tus. Fam. Cistaceae). Evergreen shrubs with rose-like flowers, of the Mediterranean region, reliably hardy only in areas escaping prolonged frosts.

Selection. C. × *corbariensis*, 2–3 ft, white flowers; × *cyprius*, 6 ft, white with central crimson blotch; *laurifolius*, 6–8 ft, white and yellow; × *loretii*, 4 ft, white and yellow; × *lusitanicus*, 1–2 ft, white, crimson-blotched; *palhinhaii*, 1–2 ft, white; × *pulverulentus*, 2–3 ft, deep purplish-pink; and × 'Silver Pink', to 2½ ft, silvery-pink, are the most promising for outdoor growing; flowers are short-lasting, fugacious, but produced freely in a long succession, June–August.

Cultivation. Dwarf shrubs can be planted in the rock garden; taller kinds in sheltered shrub borders; all need warm, sunny places, well-drained lightish soil; and to be planted April–May.

Propagation. By cuttings of young shoots, taken in July–August, rooted in propagating frame. By seeds in spring, bottom heat of 18° C. (65° F.).

Citrinus (-a, -um). Citron-coloured. Ex. *Bulbocodium citrinum.*

Citriodorus (-a, -um). Citron- or lemon-scented. Ex. *Lippia citriodora.*

Citron. See *Citrus medica.*

Citrus (kit′rus, or sit′rus. Fam. Rutaceae). Evergreen shrubs and trees, with simple leaves and fragrant white flowers, and globose juicy fruits, originating in Asia and China, but grown commercially in the warmer parts of the world. *C. aurantiifolia* is the Lime; *aurantium*, the Seville Orange; *limonia*, the Lemon; *maxima*, the Shaddock; *medica*, the Citron; *nobilis* v. *deliciosa*, the Mandarin or Tangerine; *paradisi*, the Grapefruit; and *sinensis*, the Sweet

Orange; all of which have their selected strains. Dwarf forms are sometimes offered of varieties and hybrids.

Cultivation. Pot, and repot, in March–April, standard compost, and grow under cool greenhouse conditions; water freely in active growth, moderately in winter, minimum temp. 7° C. (45° F.); prune when necessary in spring; shade from hot sun. Fruit takes two seasons to develop and ripen.

Propagation. By seeds (pips), ½ in. deep, in pots, spring–summer, bottom heat 15·5° C. (60° F.); though plants may eventually grow too big, from pips taken from bought fruits. By cuttings taken in July–August, inserted in pots, sandy loam, in frame or cool greenhouse. Selected vs. are grafted on seedling stocks in March, or budded in August.

Cladanthus (kla-dan′thus. Fam. Compositae). The sole species, *C. arabicus*, Spain, Morocco, 2–2½ ft, is a strong-growing annual, with finely cut, feathery foliage and yellow daisy-like flowers, summer. Sow in April, ordinary soil, where it is to grow.

Cladode. A flattened, leaf-like petiole or lateral shoot.

Cladrastis (kla-dras′tis. Fam. Leguminosae). Deciduous ornamental flowering trees with pinnate foliage and panicles of white, pea-like flowers.

Selection. C. lutea, N. American Yellow-wood, 15–30 ft, with drooping panicles of bloom in June, rich yellow autumnal foliage; and *sinensis*, China, to 40 ft, with white, flushed pink, erect panicles of bloom in midsummer, should be better known.

Cultivation. Plant October–March, well-drained loamy soil, full sun.

Propagation. By seeds, sown in March–April, in pots in a cold frame, after chipping the seed. By root cuttings, taken in early spring, in cold frame.

Clarkia (klark′i-a. Fam. Onagraceae). Hardy annuals of Western N. America, of which those chiefly grown are double-flowering strains of *C. elegans flore pleno*, 2 ft, with showy summer flowers in shades of crimson, purple, rose, pink, salmon, orange and white, and semi-double forms of *C. pulchella* of somewhat smaller stature.

Cultivation. Seeds may be sown in April where they are to flower out of doors, in good soil, and thinned, or in boxes in a cool greenhouse in March, for subsequent planting out; or potting up to grow as pot plants. For winter flowers, seeds are sown in a cold frame in August, thinned to 9 in. apart, pinched back to induce bushy growth, and potted in October to winter in a cool greenhouse and bloom in January–March, using standard compost. Outdoors they like a warm soil, enriched with rotted organic matter and a little superphosphate.

Clary. See *Salvia sclarea*.

Class. In Botany, one of the sub-divisions of the Plant Kingdom.

Classification. The 375,000 species of living plants that comprise the Plant Kingdom are botanically classified according to the order of their appearance in the world, as far as is known, and according to their related structural characters. Briefly, the Plant (Phyta) Kingdom is divided into two Sub-kingdoms, the thallophytes (Thallophyta) and the embryophytes (Embryophyta). These are further split into Divisions; the Divisions into Classes. The thallophytes are simple plants, dependent upon water for their reproduction, and embrace the bacteria, diatoms, algae and fungi, with which we are only incidentally concerned in this book. The embryophytes are land-dwelling plants, with roots, stems and leaves, and include the liverworts, mosses, psilophytes, club mosses, quillworts, horsetails, ferns, cycads, gymnosperms and angiosperms. The angiosperms or flowering plants are held to number about 250,000, and are the plants with which we are chiefly concerned in gardening. They are divided into two Classes, Monocotyledonae and Dicotyledonae. The Classes are divided into Orders (their names ending in *-ales*, or *-ae*), sometimes Sub-orders (ending in *-ineae*). Orders and Sub-orders are divided into Families (ending in *-aceae*, with a few exceptions such as Compositae, Gramineae, Labiatae and Leguminosae. Families (and Sub-families) are divided into Tribes and Sub-tribes if their size demands, but all divide into Genera. Each Genus is divided into Species, and Species (sp., spp.) may have varieties (v. or var.). It is common to speak also of a Race, Form or Strain of a specific

plant; while the term Clone is used of plants derived from the vegetative propagation of a selected individual. See Nomenclature.

Clavatus (-a, -um). Clavate, club-shaped, thickening from base to summit. Ex. *Calochortus clavatus*.

Clay. In soils, clay consists of the finest mineral particles, less than 0·002 mm. (1/12000 in.). Its physical properties—high water capacity, great capillarity, slow movement of water vertically, very high absorption capacity for gases, water and plant nutrients, relatively cold temperature, poor aeration, high cohesion and plasticity—impress soils containing more than 25 to 30 per cent by weight. Amendment may be sought by (a) incorporating gypsum; (b) rough-digging to leave exposed to weathering by frost; (c) liming to correct acidity to a pH 6·5; (d) organic manuring; and (e) incorporating coarse materials such as sand, grit and clay that has been burnt and sifted. By these measures the clay acquires a crumb structure more porous and exploitable by plants.

Claying. The practice of adding clay to light soils to make them more moisture retentive; the clay being strewn on the soil in autumn or early winter to weather and then worked in.

Claytonia (klay-to'ni-a. Fam. Portulacaceae). Small annual or perennial herbs for moist soils in the rock garden or wild garden. *C. alsinoides* (*sibirica*), 6 in., with rose-pink flowers in spring, seeds itself freely and has naturalized in Britain, along with *perfoliata*, which has small white flowers. N. America provides *caroliniana*, 4 in., tinged pink white flowers; and *virginica*, white, which are perennials; and *australasica* is a creeping mat of bronzy-green leaves, with pearly white flowers in spring, for the scree. All are readily grown from seed sown in spring, out of doors.

Cleistogamous. Of flowers of certain plants which may produce normal showy flowers, and later flowers with minute or no petals which do not open, but form viable seeds; such as *Oxalis acetosella* and *Viola odorata*.

Clematis (klem'a-tis. Fam. Ranunculaceae). A large genus which provides many of the most beautiful hardy climbers, a few for the greenhouse, and a few herbaceous perennials for the border.

Selection. Hardy Species. C. alpina, N. Europe and Asia, 6–8 ft, blue, April, May; *armandii*, China, 12–20 ft, evergreen, white, April–May, and vs. 'Apple Blossom' and 'Snowdrift'; *calycina*, S. Europe, evergreen, yellowish-white, winter; *chrysocoma*, China, 12 ft, white, May–June; *cirrhosa*, S. Europe, 10 ft, cream, January–March; × *durandii*, France, 10 ft, blue-violet, June; *flammula*, S. Europe, 10–15 ft, white, scented, late summer; × *jouiniana*, to 15 ft, yellowish-white to blue, autumn; *macropetala*, China, to 10 ft, violet-blue, May–June, and v. *markhamii*; *montana*, Himalaya, to 30 ft, white, May, and vs. *rubens*, rose-pink, *tetrarose*, lilac-rose, and *grandiflora*, white; *orientalis*, N. Asia, 10–15 ft, yellow, late summer; *rehderiana*, China, to 25 ft, pale yellow, autumn; *tangutica*, China, 8–12 ft, rich yellow, August–September; and *viticella* SE. Europe, 8–12 ft, blue, purple, July–September, and vs. *alba luxurians*, white, and *kermesiana*, crimson.

Large-Flowered Hybrids. With their large coloured sepals and free-flowering, the hybrids are usually grouped according to their chief parent:

Florida Group. 'Belle of Woking', lavender double flowers; 'Countess of Lovelace', deep lavender double; 'Duchess of Edinburgh', white double; and 'Proteus', mauve-pink double; flower in June from wood of previous year's growth, and later from young new shoots.

Jackmanii Group. Besides × *jackmanii*, violet-blue, vs. *rubra*, crimson red; *superba*, violet purple; 'Comtesse de Bouchard', rose; 'Gypsy Queen', dark purple; 'Hagley Hybrid', deep pink; 'Madame Ed. André', crimson; 'Perle d'Azur', deep blue; and 'Victoria', soft heliotrope, are splendid; all flowering best on shoots of the current season's growth from July onwards.

Lanuginosa Group. Some of the largest flowering kinds belong here, including 'Beauty of Worcester', deep violet-blue; 'Crimson King', best crimson; 'Blue Gem', sky-blue; 'Fairy Queen', flesh-pink; 'Henryi', white; 'King George V', deep pink; 'King Edward VII', violet, crimson-bar; 'Lady Caroline Nevill',

lavender; 'Lady Northcliffe', deep lavender blue; 'Lord Nevill', deep blue; 'Marie Boisselot', white; 'Mrs Cholmondeley', pale blue; 'Mrs Spencer Castle', pinkish heliotrope; 'W. E. Gladstone', pale blue; and 'Wm Kennett', deep lavender; flowering in July on the older wood, and later from shoots of the current season's growth.

Patens Group. 'Barbara Dibley', rose-violet; 'Barbara Jackman', violet-pink; 'Daniel Deronda', violet-blue; 'Lady Londesborough', lavender; 'Lasurstern', deep lavender blue; 'Marcel Moser', pink, striped; 'Mrs Geo. Jackman', white; 'Nelly Moser', light pink, striped carmine; and the 'President', deep violet; flower in May–June and on from the older wood, and usually

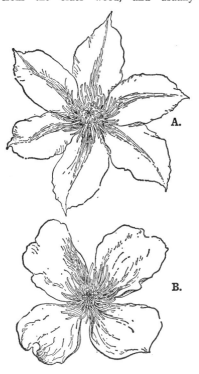

FIG. 53 Clematis flowers: A. 'Nelly Moser' hybrid. B. × *jackmanii*

again in September–October, from young shoots.

Texensis Group. 'Countess of Onslow', bright violet-purple; 'Duchess of Albany', rosy carmine; 'Grace Darling', rosy carmine; flower from July onwards from shoots of the current season's growth.

Viticella Group. 'Ascotiensis', bright blue; 'Ernest Markham', petunia red; 'Huldine', white; 'Lady Betty Balfour', violet-blue; 'M. Koster', rosy red; 'Royal Velours', deep purple; and 'Ville de Lyon'; bloom in August to autumn, on shoots of the current year's growth. New introductions are always being made, and specialists' lists should be consulted to keep abreast of new hybrids.

Cultivation. Clematis may be grown ideally to clamber through trees or hedges; on walls, trellis, pergolas they usually need support and some tying in of shoots; they may be grown in borders on pylons of weatherproofed stakes, or cylinders of plastic netting; and in some cases to ramble over banks. Plant in autumn or spring; well-drained soil, limed to pH 6·5, and liberally enriched with rotted organic matter or peat; where the roots are kept cool with partial shade, or overplanting with low growing shrubs or perennial plants. The top growth should be able to grow into the sun or good light.

Pruning. After planting, when growth is beginning in February–March, all Clematis should be cut back to strong breaking buds, 6–9 in. from the ground, to induce strong new growth, unlikely to wilt. Plants take 2 to 3 years to settle down to flowering, during which pruning should be done in late winter, to develop growth breaking from low down, cutting the year's growth back by one-third to one-half. Thereafter there is no absolute need to prune, where plants have room to spread, except to remove dead or weak growth and thin out to prevent a tangle. Where space is limited, and control is necessary, pruning should be regulated by the way in which the plant produces its flowers. Briefly, Clematis which flower in spring should be pruned after flowering; those which flower in summer or autumn from current growth are pruned in February–March, when the previous year's shoots are cut back as hard as is deemed necessary; this includes species such as *C. flammula* and hybrids of the *Jackmanii texensis* and *viticella* groups. Clematis that produce flowers from the previous year's wood and new summer shoots, chiefly those of the *florida*, *lanuginosa* and *patens* groups, may be pruned in February–March either (*a*) only lightly cutting back the shoots of the previous year's growth, after removing weak shoots, and then cutting back some of the shoots after the first flush of flowering; or (*b*) cut back all the previous year's shoots as for *jackmanii* vs., as hard as necessary; early flowers are sacrificed and flowering is concentrated into the summer and autumn.

Greenhouse Clematis. C. indivisa, New Zealand, and v. *lobata*, white, flowering in April, and evergreen, may be pot-grown in the cool greenhouse, in standard compost; winter temp. 7–10° C. (45–50° F.), moderate watering; prune after flowering. Others, too, may be grown such as *C. armandii* 'Snowdrift' and 'Apple Blossom', and *florida* v. *sieboldii*.

Propagation. By seeds, sown in spring or when ripe, in a cold frame. By cuttings, taken in July–August, cut between nodes, inserted in propagating case, bottom heat of 18–21° C. (65–70° F.). By layering in spring or summer.

Herbaceous Clematis. C. heracleifolia, China, 3 ft, makes a shrubby perennial with tubular blue flowers in July–August; 'Wyedale' is a new larger-flowering form; *recta*, S. Europe, 3–4 ft, has white flowers in June–July, and a double form, *flore pleno*. May be planted in March, or raised from seeds.

Diseases. Clematis are normally free of diseases. The worst trouble is a rather mysterious one called Wilt, the cause being unknown. It happens chiefly to young plants, which suddenly die-back in part or whole. Hard pruning after planting, and prompt cutting back of any wilted shoots, together with good culture, seem to be the best preventatives.

Pests. Slugs and snails are often attracted to Clematis. Metaldehyde bait is a good protector.

Cleome, Spider Flower (kle-o'me. Fam. Capparidaceae). *C. spinosa* (*pungens*), W. Indies, 2–3 ft, white, and its vs

'Helen Campbell', white, and 'Pink Queen', pink, are half-hardy annuals with interesting flowers having long spready stamens, reminiscent of a spider's legs. Seeds may be sown in March, standard compost, bottom heat of 18° C. (65° F.), to be pricked off and planted out in May; or grown on in pots for greenhouse decoration.

Clerodendrum, Clerodendron (kle-ro-den'drum. Fam. Verbenaceae). Only a few species of this large genus of deciduous shrubs are grown, as hardiness is doubtful.

Selection. *C. trichotomum*, Japan, 10 ft, with clusters of white flowers in summer; and *fargesii*, China, 6–10 ft, downy foliage, and equally fragrant white flowers in August, are hardy for sunny, wind-sheltered positions in mild localities, and succeed in almost any well-drained garden soil. The leaves give off an unpleasant smell if crushed. *C. bungei*, China 4 ft, with purplish-red flowers in late summer, is apt to have its top growth winter-killed, but may be tried. Propagation is by suckers removed in autumn, or cuttings of young shoots in summer in propagating case, bottom heat of 18° C. (65° F.).

C. thomsonae v. *balfourii*, W. Africa, an evergreen climber with fine panicles of crimson and white flowers in August, is a pot plant or border plant for the warm greenhouse (13° C. [55° F.]); where *speciosissimum*, Java, 3 ft, evergreen with scarlet flowers, may also be grown as a shrub. For the cool greenhouse (7° C. [45° F.] minimum) *fragrans*, China, with sweetly scented flowers in August, may be pot-grown, standard compost. Propagation is by cuttings of young shoots in July–August, in a propagating case, bottom heat of 21° C. (70° F.), or by root cuttings in early spring.

Clethra (kleth'ra. Fam. Clethraceae). Deciduous shrubs of bushy upright habit, notable for racemes or panicles of strongly perfumed small white flowers in late summer.

Selection. *C. alnifolia*, the Sweet Pepper Bush of Eastern U.S.A., 7–8 ft, is perhaps the best, with its vs. *paniculata*, larger flowers, and *rosea*, pinkish flowers; *barbinervis*, China, Japan, makes a tall shrub or small tree, flowering late,

and *fargestii*, China, to 10 ft, with downy racemes of tiny white flowers in July–August, may be considered. *C. delavayi*, W. China, to 25 ft, deciduous, with cup-shaped flowers, July–August, and the evergreen *arborea*, Madeira, to 20 ft, with nodding white flowers, August–October, are very beautiful, but only hardy enough for the mildest gardens, or cool greenhouse.

Cultivation. Plant in autumn or early spring; well-drained, lime-free, peat-enriched soil, in wind-sheltered, sunny positions.

Propagation. By cuttings of young shoots taken in July–August, in propagating case, bottom heat of 18° C. (65° F.), or by layering in early spring. By seeds sown in frame in spring.

Clianthus, Glory Pea, Parrot's Bill (kli-an'thus. Fam. Leguminosae). Only *C. puniceus*, an evergreen shrub of up to 12 ft, and clusters of rose-scarlet, pea-like flowers with long pointed keels, like a parrot's beak in summer, is worth growing. Coming from New Zealand it is only hardy enough for mild districts as a wall shrub, in well-drained soil, and south or west aspect. Elsewhere, it may be grown in a cold greenhouse in a border or large pot. It has a creamy-white flowering v. *albus*. *C. formosus*, Australia's Glory Pea, a small shrub with droopy shoots, and red with black basal boss, flowers in spring, needs a greenhouse, and is attractive in a hanging basket, but a little difficult to keep.

Propagation. By cuttings of firm young shoots taken in summer, in propagating case, bottom heat of 21° C. (70° F.). By seeds sown in pots, spring, with bottom heat.

Click Beetles. The adult insects of wireworms (q.v.).

Climbers. May be defined as plants which grow upwards to the light by using the support of other plants or objects. They may climb by means of self-adhesive suckers, aerial roots, tendrils or leaf-stalks, by hooked spines or prickles, or by twining growth. Climbers are invaluable in furnishing a garden to train up walls, fences, arches, pillars, pergolas, etc., and such features as arbours or rocks. Although many tall-growing shrubs are pressed into use on similar supporting backgrounds, they are not true climbers. The following are selections:

Hardy Woody Perennial Climbers: Deciduous—Actinidia, twining; *Akebia*, twining; *Ampelopsis*, tendrils; *Aristolochia macrophylla*, twining; *Campsis radicans*, aerial roots; *Celastrus*, twining; *Clematis*, twining; *Hydrangea petiolaris*, aerial roots; *Jasminum officinale*, twining; *Lonicera*, twining; *Polygonum baldschuanicum*, twining; *Rosa*, by hooking; *Schizophragma*, selfclinging; *Parthenocissus*, self-clinging; *Vitis*, tendrils; *Wistaria*, twining.

Evergreen: Clematis armandii, twining; *Clematis balearica*, twining; *Decumaria barbara*, self-clinging; *Hedera*, aerial roots; *Lonicera japonica*, twining; *Mutisia ilicifolia*, tendrils; *Pileostegia*, aerial roots;

Half-hardy and Tender Perennial Climbers. Suitable for sheltered, frostfree gardens or greenhouses.

Deciduous: Cobaea scandens, Jasminum beesianum, rambling; *Passiflora*, twining; *Lathyrus pubescens*, tendrils.

Evergreen: Asparagus, twining; *Bougainvillea*, rambling; *Cissus*, twining; *Clematis indivisia*, twining; *Eccremocarpus*, tendrils; *Ficus pumila*, aerial roots; *Hoya*, twining; *Ipomoea*, twining; *Lonicera implexa*, twining; *Solanum jasminoides*, twining; *Tacsonia*, tendrils.

Annual Climbers. To grow from seeds. *Calonycton*; twining; *Cuphea*, twining; *Humulus*, twining; *Ipomoea*, twining; *Lathyrus*, tendrils; *Tropaeolum*, twining.

Clintonia. See *Downingia*.

Clivia (kliv′i-a. Fam. Amaryllidaceae). Bulbous evergreen plants, with straplike leaves, and umbels of showy funnel-shaped flowers, from S. Africa, sometimes called Imantophyllums, for the cool greenhouse and indoor decoration.

Selection. C. miniata, 2 ft, with yellowscarlet flowers, and v. *aurea*, yellow, spring or summer; *nobilis*, 2 ft, reddishyellow, spring; and × *cyrtanthiflora*, 2 ft, flame red.

Cultivation. Pot in February, rich compost, such as JIP 3, 6–10-in. pots, water freely in growth, temp. 13–15·5° C. (60–65° F.); after flowering, grow on cool until October, when watering is reduced to the minimum, with temp. of 7° C. (45° F.) minimum. Topdress with fresh compost annually, repot only when essential.

Propagation. By division, or by offsets, in February–March. By seeds, in March, with bottom heat of 24° C. (75° F.).

Cloches. The term derives from the French name for large, straight-sided, round and knobbed bell-glasses, but now covers a wide range of portable glass or transparent plastic coverings for plants growing out of doors in half-round, tent, barn and high-level shapes, and handlights. They give weather protection, create an immediate environment conducive to vigorous growth, with a temperature rise of 3–5 deg. C. (5–7 deg. F.), and some protection from certain diseases and pests. They are most useful in lengthening the growing season at each end; enabling earlier sowings to be made with earlier ripening in spring, and prolonging growth and protecting late-maturing crops in autumn. They are invaluable to protect early sowings of tender plants; to help in the rooting of cuttings out of doors; and to hasten the ripening of crops such as strawberries. In use, the cover should be complete, with end stops of glass or wood in place, and the glass clean. Cloches, bell-glasses and handlights should be put in place on moist soil, preferably one to two weeks beforehand, in making sowings or plantings.

Clone. A group of individual plants, genetically uniform, derived from one individual by non-sexual vegetative propagation entirely; designated by cl. or ℅.

Cloud Grass. See *Agrostis nebulosa*.

Clove. A form of Carnation (q.v.).

Cloves. The young bulbs or segments of certain bulbs, such as Garlic and Shallots. Also the dried flower-buds of *Eugenia aromatica*, used as culinary spice. *See* Fig. 54, page 146.

Club-root, also known as Ambury, Anbury, Clubbing, Clump-foot, Fingerand-Toe, etc., characterized by the thickening, distortion and swelling of the roots of plants of the Cruciferae, growing in infected soil. The cause is a soil-borne slime fungus, *Plasmodiophora brassicae*, which thrives in wet, poorly aerated and acid soils, All leafy brassicas,

FIG. 54 Clove of Garlic, detached from the bulb.

radish, turnip, swede, candytuft, stocks, wallflowers, etc., and cruciferous weeds are suceptible. When severe, the ground must be rested from such crops and plants for at least three years, and cruciferous weeds promptly destroyed. The soil should be limed to bring to pH 6·5 to 7·0; drainage improved and better aeration developed by the use of gypsum and organic matter. Acid-reacting fertilizers, notably sulphate of ammonia and dried blood, should be avoided, also nitrate of soda. All infected plants should be lifted and burnt. On replanting, some protection can be given by dusting planting holes with 4 per cent calomel dust, or watering with mercuric bichloride (1 oz. per 10 gallons water).

Clytostoma (kli-tos-to'ma. Fam. Bignoniaceae). Very beautiful evergreen S. American climbers for the warm greenhouse, with magnificent, funnel-shaped flowers in pairs in summer; akin to Bignonia.

Selection. C. callistegioides, Brazil, pale purple and yellow, summer, and *binatum* (*purpureum*), rosy purple, with white eye, summer, are grown.

Cultivation. Pot in April, large pots, or in border, good drainage and compost of 2 parts fibrous loam, 1 peat, 1 leaf-mould and 1 of sand; water freely in growth, summer temps. 18–24° C. (65–75° F.); very moderately in winter, minimum temp. 10° C. (50° F.).

Propagation. Cuttings of good strong shoots, with three joints, in spring, in pots, in propagating case, with bottom heat of 21° C. (70° F.). By seeds, similarly.

Cnicus (kni'kus. Fam. Compositae). A large genus of herbs, of which *C. benedictus*, the Blessed Thistle, from the Mediterranean region, 2 ft, may be grown as an annual, sown under glass in March for subsequent planting out in May, for its handsome silvery-marbled foliage, with yellow summer flowers; and *diacantha*, Asia Minor, 2–3 ft, for its ornamental foliage and purplish flowers, in the same way or as a biennial, sown out of doors in July–August in a sheltered place; *spinosissimus*, 3 ft, is perennial, with clustered heads of yellow flowers in summer, and may be planted in autumn or spring.

Cobaea (ko-bai'a. Fam. Polemoniaceae). The chief species grown is *C. scandens*, a deciduous climber of tropical America, to 15 ft, with huge, bell-like, purplish flowers in summer, white in v. *alba*, and may be grown as a perennial in a cool greenhouse, trained up the rafters; though more often treated as a half-hardy annual, raised from seeds sown in March, bottom heat of 18° C. (65° F.), for subsequent hardening-off and planting out to climb by tendrils on a south sunny and warm wall, fence or trellis in May.

Cob-nut. See *Corylus* and Nut.

Coccineus (-a, -um). Scarlet. Ex. *Crataegus coccinea.*

Cochlearia (ko-klai'ri-a. Fam. Cruciferae). *C. armoracia* is the Horse-radish (q.v.); *officinalis* is the biennial Scurvy Grass, at one time valued as an anti-scorbutic herb.

Cockchafers. See Chafers.

Cockroaches. Beetle-like insects of which the black *Blatta orientalis* and the German *B. germanica* usually infest houses, while the American *Periplaneta americana*, Australian *P. australasiae*, and *Leucophaea surinamensis* may be

FIG. 55 Flowers and leaves of the climber, *Cobaea scandens*.

omnivorous pests in greenhouses, especially if heated. All feed at night, but may be readily controlled by dressings of powdered borax and pyrethrum powder, or a proprietary remedy sprinkled on staging and supports and bases of greenhouses and near heat sources.

Cockscomb. See *Celosia*.

Cocksfoot Grass. See *Dactylis glomerata*.

Cockspur Thorn. See *Crataegus crus-galli*.

Coconut Fibre. The fibre taken from between the outer skin and inner shell of the coconut is most useful for plunging potted plants and bulbs in; as storage medium for wintering Begonia tubers and cormous plants; and for mulching beds in summer. It may even be used as a medium, when wetted, for raising softwood cuttings which are to be potted up later.

Codiaeum, Croton (kod-i-ai'um. Fam. Euphorbiaceae). The one species grown, *C. variegatum* v. *pictum*, Malaya, is esteemed for its wonderfully colour-variegated, green, orange, scarlet, pink leaves, varying from plant to plant, and is pot-grown to 2 ft, in the warm greenhouse, preferably with a steady heat of 15·5° C. (60° F.), or indoor rooms, free of draughts, watering generously in summer, more moderately in winter; standard compost suits.

Codling Moth. *See* Apple, *under* Pests.

Codlins and Cream. See *Epilobium hirsutum* and *Narcissus*.

Codonopsis (ko-don-op'sis. Fam. Campanulaceae). Hardy perennial herbs, chiefly from the Himalayan region, of which *C. clematidea*, 1–2 ft, with white, blue-tinted, bell-like summer flowers, and *ovata*, 1 ft, pale blue, flowering in summer, may be grown in borders; and *C. convolvulacea*, blue flower bells, its more robust v. *forrestii*, and *tangshen*, greenish, striped purple flowers, are climbing twiners, 6–10 ft, worth trying on a sunny trellis or wall.

Cultivation. Plant in March–April, well-drained, warm soil, sunny positions.

Propagation. Easily raised from seeds, sown April, in outdoor seed-bed.

Coelestis (-e). Sky-blue. Ex. *Agathaea coelestis*.

Coelogyne (koil-og'in-e. Fam. Orchidaceae). Very charming epiphytic orchids, of which many may be grown in a cool greenhouse.

Selection. *C. cristata*, Himalaya, 6 in., snow-white flowers, with yellow lip, in late winter, and its vs. such as *lemoniana*, lemon-yellow; and *alba*, pure white; and *morreana*, Annam, 1 ft, white, golden-haired flowers, spring, are easiest to grow; others to consider are *odoratissima*, India, white, summer, and *barbata*, Assam, snow-white, spring.

Cultivation. Pot in March, in clumps, compost of equal parts live sphagnum moss and fibrous peat, well-crocked, and grow near glass but shade from hot sun. Water freely in spring and summer, very moderately in winter, minimum temp. 7–10° C. (45°–50° F.).

Propagation. By division in March.

Coeruleus (-a, -um). Blue. Ex. *Polemonium coeruleum*.

Coix, Job's Tears (ko'icks. Fam. Graminae). *C. lachryma-jobi*, tropical

Asia, is a tender ornamental grass, growing to 3 ft, with bead-like inflorescence, which becomes hard, greyish and tear-like at the ends, for use as ornament. Seeds may be sown in February–March, with bottom heat of 18° C. (65° F.), for planting out in May; or potted in large pots, and stood in saucers of water in the cool greenhouse. The v. *aurea zebrina* has yellow-striped leaf blades.

Colchicum (kol'ki-kum. Fam. Liliaceae). Cormous plants of much interest and beauty, though poisonous, which normally produce their flowers (Naked Ladies) in autumn, and their leaves with the seeds the following spring.

Selection. C. autumnale, Autumn Crocus or Meadow Saffron, 6–9 in., is native, with purplish-pink flowers, and white and double forms; *giganteum*, Turkey, rosy-purple, October; *sibthorpi*, Greece, lilac-purple, September; *kesselringii* (*crociflorum*), Turkestan, white and purple, February; *speciosum*, Persia, etc., rose-purple, September, and its vs. *rubrum, album* and *maximum*; *ancyrense* (*biebersteinii*), Russia, March; and hybrids such as 'Autumn Queen', 'Lilac

FIG. 56 Autumn flowers of *Colchicum speciosum*.

Wonder', 'Violet Queen' and 'Waterlily'. All stronger, larger and more robust in their flowering.

Cultivation. Out of doors, plant corms 4 in. deep, 1 ft apart, in drifts in light shade or in grass, where they can naturalize, and spring leaves will not be in the way. Well-drained soil, enriched with rotted organic matter, is appreciated. All kinds, especially the winter-flowering, may be grown in the cold greenhouse, potted in July–August, three corms per 6-in. pot, standard compost.

Propagation. By dividing offsets every fourth year after leaves have withered. By seeds on outdoor seed-bed, kept watered, in March, or in pans in cold frame; take 3 to 5 years to reach flowering size.

Coleus, Flame Nettle (ko'le-us. Fam. Labiatae). The plants chiefly grown are hybrid forms of the Javanese perennial *C. blumei* and its v. *verschaffeltii*, as half-hardy annuals, with their magnificent ovate, pointed leaves, vividly marked in apricot, yellow, red, copper and purple shades, on green and white. Seeds may be sown in March, under glass, bottom heat of 21° C. (70° F.), or summer (for the winter greenhouse); pricked off and potted, either for bedding out in June, or growing on as pot plants for greenhouse or indoor rooms; the young plants can be made bushy by pinching back growing tips in early growth. To winter, a temp. of 13° C. (55° F.) is needed, with moderate watering. *C. penzigii*, Abyssinia, 2 ft, whitish, hairy foliage, bright violet flowers, autumn; *shirensis*, Africa, 3 ft, blue flowers, winter, and *thyrsoideus*, Africa, 2 ft, bright blue flowers, winter, are worth growing in the warm greenhouse for their bloom, raised from seed as for the others. Choice kinds may be propagated by cuttings, when available, in small pots, shaded from sun, with bottom heat of 13–15.5° C. (55–60° F.).

Colewort, Collard. Small, rather open, hardy cabbages, maturing quickly, for sowing out of doors, in May for autumn cropping, in July for winter cropping, with plants spaced 1 ft apart, in soil organically manured for a previous crop. Rosette and Improved Hardy Green are good vs.

Collar. The junction (or neck) between stem and root in a plant.

Collinsia (kol-lins'i-a. Fam. Scrophulariaceae). An American race of annuals of which *C. bicolor*, California, 1–2 ft, is chiefly grown for its white and rose-purple lipped flowers in August; its vs. *alba*, white, *candidissima*, pure white, and 'Salmon-Beauty' extend the range; others, such as *grandiflora*, 1 ft, pale purple, and *verna*, 6 in., white and blue, are sometimes offered.

Cultivation. May be sown outdoors in April, in lightish soil, and sun, and thinned 4 in. apart.

Collinus (-a, -um). Of low hills. Ex. *Campanula collina.*

Colloidal Copper. Usually a suspension of copper oxychloride in water, for fungicidal use instead of Bordeaux Mixture, having the merit of leaving no unsightly deposit of plants.

Collomia (kol-lom'i-a. Fam. Polemoniaceae). Pretty American annuals of which *C. biflora* of Chile grows 1–1½ ft, with unusual linear leaves, deeply toothed at the ends, and dense heads of scarlet flowers in summer; *grandiflora*, Western N. America, 2 ft, has yellow, turning red, flowers, and *linearis*, 1 ft, yellow-brown. Seeds are sown in March–April, where plants are to grow, in well-drained, humus-rich soil; thinned to 4 in. apart.

Colorado Beetle (*Leptinotarsa decemlineata*). A dangerous alien pest of

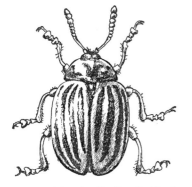

FIG. 57 Colorado Beetle, *Leptinotarsa decemlineata.*

potatoes, the presence of which must be notified at once in writing to the Ministry of Agriculture. The adult beetles are yellowish with black lines on the wing-cases and head, and may appear in July–August. The females lay masses of orange-yellow eggs on potato leaves, which hatch into brick-red, black-spotted, hump-backed grubs. These feed on the foliage for about 3 weeks, then pupate in the soil. The danger is greatest in counties near to the Continent.

Colosseus (-a, -um). Gigantic. Ex. *Nicotiana colossea.*

Coltsfoot. See *Tussilago.*

Columbine. See *Aquilegia.*

Column. The pillar-like structure formed when the sexual organs (style and stamens) are united as in orchids.

Columnea (kol-um'ne-a. Fam. Gesneriaceae). Evergreen perennial herbs of tropical America which may be grown in greenhouses or as house plants, preferably in baskets or pots where their trailing stems can drape and show off the brilliant tubular flowers.

Selection. C. gloriosa, 2 ft, fiery red, yellow-throated flowers; and purple, bronze-leaved v. *purpurea*; *microphylla*, small-leaved, orange-scarlet; *oerstediania*, with russet-orange flowers; and the hybrid × *banksii*, deep red, are all from Costa Rica, flowering freely in autumn and winter.

Cultivation. Being partly epiphytic, a compost of 2 parts peat, 1 part each of leaf-mould and sand, is suitable, with a little base fertilizer (John Innes), and plants need ample light without direct hot sun; liberal watering in summer, very moderate in winter, with minimum temps. of 13–15·5° C. (55–60° F.).

Propagation. By cuttings of young shoots in spring, in propagating case, with bottom heat of 24° C. (75° F.).

Colutea, Bladder Senna (ko-lu'te-a. Fam. Leguminosae). Deciduous shrubs with pinnate foliage, long-stalked, few-flowered racemes of pea-like flowers, followed by inflated seed pods that inspire its common name.

Selection. C. arborescens, S. Europe, to 12 ft, yellow flowers in summer, is usually grown; *orientalis*, at 6 ft, is more compact, with brownish-red flowers; and × *media*, a hybrid of the two species, to 10 ft, has orange-red flowers, and pods up to 3 in. long.

Cultivation. Plant in autumn or March, any well-drained soil, sunny position. Prune in February to shape.

Comatus (a, -um). Hairy.

Comfrey. See *Symphytum*.

Commelina (kom-me-li'na. Fam. Commelinaceae). Two species may be grown out of doors, for their fugacious flowers, lasting a day, but produced throughout the summer; *C. coelestis*, 1½ ft, blue-flowering, but with white-and-blue and white varieties; and *tuberosa*, 1½ ft, sky-blue flowers; both are from Mexico, and tuberous-rooted, and being only half-hardy the roots should be lifted in October, to store in cool, frostproof shelter, and replant in May. Any well-drained soil and warm position is suitable. Propagation by seeds, sown under glass, March, bottom heat of 18° C. (65° F.).

Comosus (-a, -um). Comose, growing in tufts. Ex. *Muscari comosum*.

Compass Plant. See *Silphium*.

Composites. Flowers of the family *Compositae*, having both ray florets and central flowers on the disk.

Compost and Compost-making. Compost consists of organic material rotted down and used as an alternative or supplement to animal manure to enrich the soil with humus, bacteria and plant nutrients. The fundamentals of compost-making are: *Materials:* almost anything of an organic nature—plant remains, grass mowings, weeds, leaves, waste vegetables, hedge clippings, prunings, kitchen waste, vacuum-cleaner dust, waste wool, peat, rags, sawdust, straw, leather clippings, hair, deep litter, etc. Tough stalks should be crushed or chopped small. Diseased or pest-infested plant material, seeding weeds, roots of perennial weeds such as couch grass, and hard wood, etc., are best burnt and the ashes added to the heap. *Site.* This should give as much shelter as possible from scorching sun, drying and cold winds, frost and weather extremes. *Size.* A free-standing heap should be not less than 5 ft wide, 5 ft long, 4 ft high, tapering from base to 3½ ft wide at the top. Smaller heaps are best made within slatted boxes, or netting enclosures, preferably in pairs so that one heap is

maturing while another is being made, minimum size of 3 ft by 3 ft by 3 ft–4 ft high. *Foundation.* Heaps should be founded on soil, not on wood, brick or concrete. It is very helpful to provide aeration by placing half round, unglazed

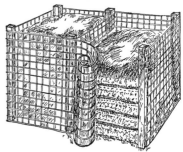

FIG. 58 A simple Compost Bin, double-bays, made with plastic mesh and posts.

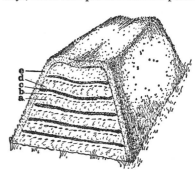

FIG. 59 A free-standing Compost Heap: a. layer of organic vegetable waste; b. decomposition activator; c. sprinkling of soil; d. dusting of lime (optional); e. jacket of soil.

earthenware tiles, bricks or logs along the base, and a first layer of coarse material—prunings, twigs, hedge-trimming, straw, etc. The heap is built in layers like a sandwich: (1) 4–8 in. of mixed organic waste, moist but not wet; (2) a half-inch covering of top soil; (3) a sprinkling of powdered lime, ground limestone or chalk; repeated until the heap is complete, and a final covering of an inch or so of soil. This will take nine to twelve months to rot, but if turned top to bottom, sides to middle, after eight to twelve weeks, it would be ready for use in about six months. Decomposition can be accelerated by the use of an activator, added to the layer of organic matter; which can consist of a 2-in. layer of animal manure, as in the Indore system; of organic fertilizers such as fish meal, guano, dried poultry manure or dried blood; of a nitrogenous fertilizer (ammonium sulphate, calcium cyanamide, nitro-chalk); of a proprietary chemical activator (Garotta, Adco), in which case the lime dressing is omitted; of a seaweed activator (Bio, Marinure, Maxicrop); or a bacterial activator (Fertosan); or of a herbal activator (QR). If the compost is intended for lime-intolerant plants, it is best prepared with a bacterial or herbal activator and lime is omitted. With activation, compost is ready in six to twelve weeks in summer, eight to sixteen weeks in winter, and should be a blackish-brown, friable, sweet-smelling, easily broken up material, with a plant nutrient value higher than that of farmyard manure, which can be used at any time to mulch or manure the soil.

Composts, Standard. These consist of standardized formulae for composts used for seed-raising and the pot growth of plants from the seedling stage onward. They have been experimentally devised and tested to give consistently good results in the propagation of a wide range of garden plants, and their use is implicit in the recommendations made for the propagation of plants in this book except where otherwise stated.

The John Innes Composts. Evolved at the John Innes Horticultural Institution, England, these have been in increasing use since 1939 without any need for modification. The chief formulae are:
John Innes Seed Compost (JIS):
  2 parts by bulk medium loam, sterilized
  1 part by bulk sedge or sphagnum moss peat
  1 part by bulk sharp, lime-free sand
    Plus per bushel (8 gallons)
  $1\frac{1}{2}$ oz. superphosphate (16–18 per cent P_2O_5)
  $\frac{3}{4}$ oz. ground chalk, limestone or whitening.

John Innes Potting Compost (JIP 1):
  7 parts by bulk medium loam, sterilized
  3 parts by bulk sedge or sphagnum moss peat
  2 parts by bulk sharp, lime-free sand
    Plus per bushel (8 gallons)
  4 oz. John Innes Base Fertilizer
  $\frac{3}{4}$ oz. ground chalk, limestone or whitening.

JIP 1 is used for the first potting-on of seedlings. For the second potting and for most plants to be over-wintered, the amounts of base fertilizer and chalk are doubled, and the compost becomes JIP 2. For the final potting and for plants grown permanently in pots, the amounts of base fertilizer and chalk are tripled, and the compost becomes JIP 3.
John Innes Base is made up of:
  2 parts by weight hoof and horn meal
  2 parts by weight superphosphate (16–18 per cent P_2O_5)
  1 part by weight sulphate of potash (48–50 per cent K_2O).
For lime-intolerant plants, a lime-free loam and the omission of the chalk are necessary.
John Innes Cuttings Compost (JIC):
  1 part by bulk medium loam, sterilized
  2 parts by bulk sedge or sphagnum moss peat
  3 parts by bulk sterilized coarse sand.
For lime-intolerant plants (Erica, Rhododendron, etc.):
  3 parts by bulk sphagnum moss peat or leaf-mould
  1 part by bulk loam (sterilized)
  2 parts by bulk coarse or sharp lime-free sand
    Plus per bushel
  4 oz. John Innes Base Fertilizer.
The UC Soilless Composts. These composts obviate the use of loam, often difficult to obtain, and have been evolved at the University of California. Five formulae have been put forward, chiefly differing in the ratio of sand to peat used. The most useful is:
UC Seed and Cuttings Compost (may be stored):
  50 per cent by bulk of *fine* clean sand
  50 per cent by bulk of sphagnum moss peat
    Plus per cubic yard (21 bushels)

4 oz potassium nitrate

4 oz. potassium sulphate

2½ lb. superphosphate (16–18 per cent P₂O₅)

7½ lb. dolomite (magnesian) ground limestone.

2½ lb. ground chalk or ordinary limestone.

UC Potting Compost (to be used within one week):

As above, but plus 2½ lb. hoof and horn meal.

UC Potting Compost No. 2 for final potting:

As for seeds, plus 5 lb. hoof and horn meal.

Various developments of soilless composts have been made and are offered under proprietary names, such as the 'Levington' composts based on peat, and now accepted as standard composts for horticultural use.

Compound. Used of leaves composed of several similar leaflets; the divisions extending to the leaf-stalks.

Comptonia, Sweet Fern (Fam. Myricaceae). The one species, *C. aspleni-*

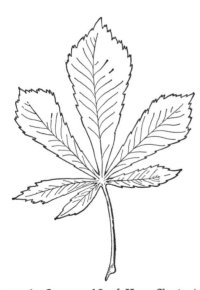

FIG. 60 Compound Leaf, Horse Chestnut (*Aesculus hippocastanum*).

folia, eastern N. America, is a deciduous, hardy shrub of 2–4 ft, chiefly grown for its pleasing pinnately lobed and fragrant foliage, though its catkin flowers in spring are intriguing. Plant October–March in lime-free peaty soil. Propagation is by layering in spring.

Conandron (ko-nan'dron. Fam. Gesneriaceae). The only species is *C. ramondioides,* a tuberous-rooted, herbaceous perennial of Japan, 6 in., with lilac-purple, orange-centred, tomato-like flowers in late spring, from a rosette of crinkled, yellow-green leaves. Only hardy enough for mild rock gardens, peaty soil, or the alpine house.

Propagation. By division in spring.

Conchi-. A prefix in compound words meaning shell-shaped. Ex. *Tigridia pavonia* v. *conchiflora.*

Concinnus (-a, -um). Neat, elegant, Ex. *Berberis concinna.*

Concolor. Of one colour or tint. Ex. *Abies concolor.*

Concrete. A mixture of Portland cement, sand and an aggregate such as shingle, broken brick or stone, gravel or clinker; plus water and often a synthetic setting agent. A standard formula is 1 part by volume cement, 2 parts sand, 4 parts aggregate, which is suitable for the making of paths, pools, etc. Large areas or where concrete is subject to much stress may be reinforced by embedding steel wire, netting, expanded metal or mesh in the concrete.

Cone. The scaly fruit of conifer (q.v.), also known as a strobilus.

Cone Flower. See *Rudbeckia.*

Congeners. Plants belonging to the same genus.

Conglomerate. Clustered or crowded.

Conidium (pl. **Conidia**). A fungus spore (spores).

Conifers, Coniferae. Comprise the major Class of Gymnosperms, largely consisting of upright-growing, evergreen trees, of garden value for their elegant form, handsome foliage beauty and colouring, and a variability that makes them adaptable to every garden, where atmospheric conditions and soil are suitable. They are native to the temperate and subtropical zones, usually on mountains. They are valuable economically as the source of various softwood timbers, and of natural oils such as turpentine, and resins. The flowers are always unisexual, the male in catkins and the female in cones with naked ovules and seeds. For garden ornamentation, conifers provide noble specimen trees, but may also be used for screens, and in some cases for hedges. Deciduous kinds, chiefly Larches and the Swamp Cypress, give autumn foliage colour. Dwarf types are effective for small gardens and rock gardens. The families of the Class are Pinaceae, Cupressaceae and Texaceae. *See* Abies, Araucaria, Cedrus, Cephalotaxus, Chamaecyparis, Cryptomeria, Cupressus, Dacrydium, Fitzroya, Juniperus, Larix, Libocedrus, Metasequoia, Picea, Pinus, Podocarpus, Pseudotsuga, Saxegothaea, Sequoia, Taxodium, Taxus, Thuja, Thujopsis, Tsuga and Wellingtonia.

Conophytum (kon-o-pi'tum. Fam. Aizoaceae). Small succulent plants, akin to Mesembryanthemum, falling into two groups; one with more or less rounded bodies, the other with more elongated round bodies and two-lobed, which are really succulent leaves. New leaves form within the old, which dry up during the rest period, to be split by the new leaves when growth is resumed; flowers appear about July, and vary in size and colouring.

Selection. C. *bilobum*, two-lobed, yellow; *elishae*, two-lobed, yellow; *minutum*, purple; *meyerae*, two-lobed, yellow; *pallidum*, purple; and *truncatellum*, pale yellow; all natives of Namaqualand, S. Africa.

Cultivation. In cool greenhouse or indoors, very well-drained compost, sun; water March–May, then no water until new growth begins in July, when watering may increase gradually; little in winter; with minimum temp. 7° C. (45° F.), atmosphere rather dry.

Propagation. By cuttings, taken with a part of the stem, in spring, rooted in moist sand.

Conservatory. Usually a lofty, airy glass structure, attached or connected to a house, with beds in which tall plants of floral or foliage merit, such as Acacias, Camellias, Palms, of a tender nature may be grown; with climbers such as Lapageria, Passiflora, Solanum, Tacsonia, Bougainvillea, etc., and tubs of

Agapanthus, Clivia, Nerine, Crinum and tender shrubs about wide spaces and paths.

Conspicuus (-a, -um). Conspicuous, easily seen. Ex. *Narcissus barii* v. *conspicuus*.

Contortus (-a, -um). Twisted. Ex. *Corylus avellana* v. *contorta*.

Convallaria, Lily of the Valley (kon-val-la'ri-a. Fam. Liliaceae). Now a genus of one species, C. *majalis*, native and common to temperate regions of the northern hemisphere, 6–8 in., well known for its twin, elliptical leaves, sheathing a raceme of nodding, sweetly scented, waxen-white bell-like flowers in spring. There are large-flowered forms in v. *major* and 'Fortin's Giant', and a rose-pink in v. *rubra*.

Cultivation. Will grow almost anywhere, but is best placed in moist soil in some shade, or as a woodland plant. Plant in October–March; top dress annually with organic matter. Earlier flowers may be obtained by potting 2- or 3-year old crowns or 'pips' in autumn or early winter, about six to a 5-in. pot, plunging in fibre or ashes for a few weeks, and then bringing into a cool greenhouse to flower. For early forcing, large crowns are potted or boxed rather closely together, the roots only loosely covered with soil or fibre, and the crowns with moss, and plunged with bottom heat of 27° C. (85° F.) and air temperature of 24° C. (75° F.), and kept well moistened. It is also possible to retard flowering by keeping the crowns at −2° C. (28° F.). Retarded crowns are often offered, and are brought into flower by potting up and placing in a cool frame for four days, and then brought into a warm greenhouse at 13–15·5° C. (55–60° F.).

Convolute. One part rolled lengthwise within another, as in some buds. *See* Aestivation and Vernation.

Convolvulus (kon-vol'vu-lus. Fam. Convolvulaceae). Although it contains the persistent and noxious weed, C. *arvensis*, or Bindweed, this genus also contains some garden-worthy flowering plants.

Selection. C. *cantabricus*, 6 in., pale red open, saucer-shaped flowers, August, and *lineatus*, 6 in., pale reddish-purple flowers, June, are deciduous perennials from S. Europe for warm corners in the rock garden or alpine house, to be propagated by division in spring, or by young cuttings in August. *C. cneorum*, a dwarf evergreen shrub, to 2 ft., with funnel-shaped, white, striped pink, flowers, June–July, comes from Spain and needs the shelter of the alpine house, with ample sun. Propagated by cuttings in summer. It is doubtful wisdom to introduce *elegantissimus* (*althaeoides*), although its summer flowers of pale red are beautiful, for it can become a rampant weed in the rock garden. The dwarf Convolvulus, *tricolor*, 1 ft, is a hardy annual, with pretty blue, yellow and white trumpet flowers, and varieties of other shades including crimson; for sowing outdoors in April, where the plants are to grow, in lightish, humus-rich soil, and sun.

Coprosma (ko-pros′ma. Fam. Rubiaceae). Evergreen shrubs, chiefly of New Zealand, of little floral beauty, but carrying colourful small fruits in season. As, however, plants are unisexual, it is necessary to plant a male with one or more females which can then produce their berry-like fruits.

Selection. *C. acerosa*, of prostrate habit, with translucent blue berries in autumn, and v. *brunnea*, and *petriei*, dwarf and prostrate, with bluish-purple fruits, are the hardiest and may be tried in mild localities, well-drained soil, and sun. *C. baueri*, to 10 ft or more, glossy foliage and orange-yellow, oval fruits, is sometimes grown in the cool greenhouse; its v. *picturata*, with variegated leaves, being colourful, but space is usually too precious except in a large greenhouse for these plants to be grown. Propagation is by cuttings in spring.

Coptis, Gold Thread (kop′tis. Fam. Ranunculaceae). The only species much grown is *C. trifolia*, 6 in., an evergreen perennial, with white spring flowers, for moist peaty ground or the bog garden; quite hardy for planting in March, and propagating by division after flowering. May also be grown from seed, sown in sandy peat, in cold frame in spring.

Coral Bells. See *Heuchera sanguinea*.

Coral Spot. A fungus, *Nectria cinnabarina*, usually recognized by the coral-red spots or pustules it produces on dead twigs and branches, as a saprophyte. It may, however, infect and parasitize red currants and various shrubs and trees, and dead wood should be collected and burnt to prevent this.

Coral Tree. See *Erythrina*.

Cordatus (-a, -um). Cordate, or heart-shaped. Ex. *Tilia cordata*.

FIG. 61 Cordate Leaf, Lime (*Tilia platyphyllos*).

Cordon. A form of tree trained to a single main stem; lateral shoots being consistently pruned back. A double cordon has two main stems. *See* Apples.

Cordyline (kor-di-li′ne. Fam. Liliaceae). Evergreen shrubs from the warmer regions of the world, chiefly grown for their handsome foliage as greenhouse and indoor plants; the leaves being long, assegai spear-shaped and channelled with a palm-like habit.

Selection. *C. australis*, tree-like in its native New Zealand, may be grown outdoors in mild Cornish gardens, but in tubs or large pots to be moved into winter shelter elsewhere, or as a cool greenhouse plant, until too big; more spectacular in its coloured-leaf forms *atropurpurea*, *aureo-striata* and *veitchii*; *indivisia* may be grown similarly, with leaves to 3 ft, with red or yellow midribs. They require a well-drained peaty soil, or standard compost (if pot-grown). *C. terminalis*, tropical Asia, is more tender and is grown in the greenhouse or as a pot plant, and has notable vs. *baptistii*, pink and yellow striped leaves;

guilfoylei, red, pink and white; *mayi*, margined red; and *norwoodiensis*, yellow-stripes, crimson edges. These require potting in spring, standard compost, liberal watering in growth, syringing in hot weather, and moderate watering in winter, with temps. of 13–15·5° C. (55–60° F.).

Propagation. By cutting back overgrown plants and using 2-in. lengths of the stem as cuttings, inserted in a propagating frame, bottom heat of 18° C. (65° F.); by suckers detached in spring; by seeds in heat in spring.

Coreopsis (kor-e-op'sis. Fam. Compositae). A genus of annual or perennial herbs with rayed flowerheads, useful for summer colour.

Selection. The annuals, often listed and grown as *Calliopsis*, are forms of Western N. American species, *C. drummondii* 'Golden Crown', 2 ft, golden-yellow and maroon, and *tinctoria*, 1–2 ft, offered in single and double-flowering vs., brightly coloured yellows to reds, and in dwarf forms of 9 in. They provide a summer of bloom, from seeds sown as half-hardy annuals under glass in March, or as hardy annuals where they are to grow in April, being thinned to 9 in. apart. The perennials make fine herbaceous plants; *grandiflora*, in strains such as 'Mayfield Giant', 2 ft., golden-yellow; 'Baby Sun', 1½ ft, yellow and red; *lanceolata*, 2 ft, bright yellow, and v. 'Sunburst'; *pubescens* (*auriculata*), 3 ft, yellow; and *verticillata*, 2 ft, golden yellow, all provide an abundance of flowers, not least for cutting, throughout the summer.

Cultivation. Any reasonably well-drained soil, and sunny position suits all kinds. Plant perennials in spring.

Propagation. By seeds, sown outdoors in April. Perennials by division in spring or by cuttings of young growths detached in summer and rooted in a frame.

Coriaceus (-a, -um). Coriaceous, leathery. Ex. *Actinidia coriacea*.

Coriander (*Coriandrum sativum*). A hardy, umbelliferous annual herb, of S. Europe, 18 in., grown chiefly for its aromatic seeds, used in flavouring confectionery, bread, curry powder, and in a mixed spice. Seeds are sown in March–April, ¼ in. deep, in drills 12 in. apart, to flower in June and ripen its seeds in September; may also be sown in autumn.

Coris (kor'is. Fam. Primulaceae). A small leafy thyme-like plant, with short racemes of lilac flowers in June. *C. monspeliensis*, from the Mediterranean region, may be grown in well-drained sandy soil, peat-enriched, and warm sun. Propagation by seed sown in a cold frame, April–May.

Cork. The outer layer of the bark of woody plants and conifers.

Cork-tree, Cork Oak. See *Quercus suber*.

Corm. The fleshy, solid and swollen underground part of a stem, in which reserve materials are stored for the nurture of a bud. It is usually annual, a new corm being formed on the old one, as in the Crocus and Gladiolus; and often has a membraneous coat. The scales are not conspicuous as with bulbs, and a bud is produced at the apex. Compare with Bulb. *See* Fig. 62, page 156.

Corn Flag. *See* Gladiolus.

Corn Marigold. See *Chrysanthemum segetum*.

Corn Salad, Lamb's Lettuce (*Valerianella locusta* (*olitoria*)). An annual salad plant which may be sown in deep rich soil, and warm shelter, in February, April or September to give leaves for picking almost all the year round. Sow in drills 1 ft apart, thinning plants to 6 in. apart. A pleasant alternative to lettuce or endive.

Cornel. See *Cornus*.

Cornelian Cherry. See *Cornus mas*.

Cornflower. See *Centaurea*.

Corniculatus (-a, -um). Having a horn or a spur. Ex. *Lotus corniculatus*.

Cornish Moneywort. See *Sibthorpia*.

Cornus, Cornel, Dogwood (kor'nus. Fam. Cornaceae). Chiefly deciduous shrubs or trees of the northern hemisphere which are hardy, and will grow in almost any ordinary soil, with reasonable drainage.

Selection. C. alba, Siberia, to 10 ft, a wide-spreading shrub, with red stems, is superior in its vs. *atrosanguinea*, brilliant red stems, more dwarf; and *spaethii* with golden-variegated foliage; N. America contributes *florida*, slow-growing to 10 ft, with beautiful white flowers, with four bracts, May; rosy-red in v. *rubra*; and a stiffly drooping form *pendula*, but

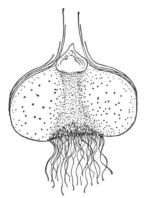

FIG. 62 Corm (*Crocus* sp.), section showing the formation of the new future corm at the top of the old flowering corm.

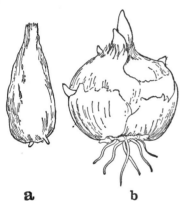

a   **b**

FIG. 63 Corms: a. *Freesia* sp.; b. *Montbretia* sp.

best planted where late spring frosts come seldom; *amomum*, to 10 ft, distinctive for clusters of blue fruits; *baileyi*, to 10 ft, with white fruits; *nuttalii*, to 15 ft, or more, the finest for its flowers with their creamy-white bracts in May; *rugosa*, to 10 ft, with woolly leaves and pale blue fruits; and *canadensis*, a dwarf of less than 1 ft, its clusters of small bracted flowers being followed by bright red fruits. The best

tree forms are *kousa* v. *chinensis*, to 20 ft, with large bracted, creamy-white June flowers; *macrophylla*, also found in China, to 30 ft or 50 ft, with attractive yellowish-white clusters of flowers in July–August; and the European Cornelian Cherry, *C. mas*, to 20 ft, with rounded umbels of yellow flowers before the leaves in February–March; with several vs. having variegated foliage. The native Dogwood, *C. sanguinea*, erect-growing, is worth while for its red winter stems, and *stolonifera* v. *flaviramea*, N. America, for its yellow-barked stems, both being cut back in late winter to ensure young stems of the brightest colour.

Cultivation. Plant October–March, in almost any soil which is decently drained and provided with humus. Many do well in damp places.

Propagation. Shrub kinds by cuttings of young firm stems in October, inserted out of doors; or all by cuttings of young shoots taken in summer, to be rooted in a frame, or by layers. Tree species by seeds, in a frame, spring.

Cornutus (-a, -um). Horn-shaped, horned. Ex. *Viola corunta*.

Corokia (kor-ok'i-a. Fam. Cornaceae). Pretty evergreen shrubs with yellow flowers in spring, natives of New Zealand.

Selection. The hardiest is *C. cotoneaster*, to 8 ft, with tortuous and much inter-laced branches, and star-shaped, bright yellow flowers to the ends of twigs in May, but apt to suffer in hard winters; *virgata*, to 10 ft, is somewhat larger-leaved, silvery-white felted beneath, with yellow flowers, sometimes followed by orange-yellow fruits, when grown on a sunny, warm, sheltered wall; but *macro-carpa*, to 20 ft, has the largest leaves, silvery beneath, yellow flowers in June, and is the most tender of the three. There are others, but not often offered.

Cultivation. Plant autumn or April, in well-drained, humus-rich soil, sheltered sunny position in the warmer counties. Prune, if required, in spring after flowering.

Propagation. By cuttings of firm shoots, with a heel, taken in August, inserted in a cold frame. By seeds, sown in March, under glass, bottom heat of 18° C. (65° F.).

Corolla. The whorl of coloured petals above the calyx, and the most conspicuous part of the flower.

FIG. 64   Corona of a Trumpet Daffodil.

Corona. A crown, such as the cup of a Narcissus or the rays of a Passiflora flower.

Coronatus (-a, -um). Crowned. Ex. *Coreopsis coronata.*

Coronilla (kor-on-il′la. Fam. Leguminosae). A mixed genus of hardy, half-hardy, evergreen or deciduous shrubs or perennials, with pinnate foliage and pea-like flowers in summer.

Selection. C. cappadocica, Asia Minor, is a prostrate trailer, with umbels of large yellow flowers, July, for the warm terrace of a rock garden; *emerus,* Europe the Scorpion Senna, to 7 ft, is a deciduous shrub, with yellow, summer flowers growing from the leaf axils; reasonably hardy for mild localities. The most popular plant is *glauca,* S. Europe, evergreen, 4–8 ft, which with its bluey foliage and clusters of rich yellow flowers in spring makes a good cool greenhouse plant, together with its variegated leaf form; while *valentina,* 4 ft, only differs in having more leaflets per leaf and larger stipules to its flowers. *C. varia,* the European Crown Vetch, white, purple or pink umbels of flowers in summer, is a useful rock garden perennial.

Cultivation. Plant outdoors in well-sheltered warm positions, peat-enriched, well-drained soil, October or March–April. Pot indoors in spring, water freely in growth, moderately in winter, minimum temp. 7° C. (45° F.).

Propagation. By layers in spring. By cuttings of young firm shoots in July–August, in a cold frame.

Correa (kor′re-a. Fam. Rutaceae). Evergreen Australian shrubs, easily cultivated, and with a long flowering season, for the cool greenhouse.

Selection. C. alba, Botany Bay Tea Tree, 2–4 ft, white or pink tubular flowers, April–June; *speciosa,* to 6 ft, crimson, and v. *pulchella,* rose-red flowers, April–June; and × *harrisii,* a shapely hybrid of 6 ft, with scarlet flowers from early spring.

Cultivation. Pot after flowering or in early autumn, standard compost; water moderately in winter, temps. 7–13° C. (45–55° F.), increasing watering as growth is made in spring. Prune after flowering; repot if necessary.

Propagation. By cuttings of young shoots, in propagating case, bottom heat of 18° C. (65° F.), spring.

Corrosive Sublimate. Mercuric chloride, $HgCl_2$. Highly poisonous white powder, sometimes used as a fungicide, to control club-root, etc.

Corsican Pine. See *Pinus nigra* v. *calabrica.*

Cortaderia, Pampas Grass (kor-ta-der′i-a. Fam. Gramineae). Large perennial grasses of which *C. selloana argentea,* temperate S. America, 6–10 ft and a spread of up to 6 ft, is grown for its magnificent plume-like inflorescences in the autumn; rising from a nest of narrow, tough, sharply edged arching leaves; there are vs. with white or yellow lined leaves, and *carminea rendatleri* has purplish plumes; but the best form for small gardens is a selected strain of v. *pumila* such as 'Sunningdale Silver', to 8 ft.

Cultivation. Plant in April, in well prepared deep soil, well-drained but moisture-retentive, and wind sheltered. Cut back or burn off old foliage in April before new growth begins.

Propagation. Plants are male or female. As the female flowers are more silky and beautiful, female plants should be cultivated and propagated by division in April. Growth may be slow for a year or two.

Cortex. The outer ring of tissue of a plant stem that becomes bark.

Cortusa (kor-tu'sa. Fam. Primulaceae). Pretty alpine woodland perennials, of which *C. matthioli*, European and Asian Mts, 6 in., bears rose-purple drooping flowers in July, its v. *pubescens* having deeply cut leaves; *semenovii*, Turkestan, is similar but with yellow flowers. Both grow well in cool shade, ordinary soil, and may be propagated by simple division in April.

Corydalis, Fumitory (ko-rid'a-lis. Fam. Papaveraceae). Mostly small herbaceous perennials, with tuberous roots, and attractive, divided foliage, and summer flowers for the rock garden.

Selection. C. cheilanthifolia, China, 8 in., yellow flowers, May; *nobilis,* Siberia, 9 in., pale yellow; *cashmeriana,* Kashmir, 6 in., bright blue, May; and *wilsonii,* China, canary-yellow, are the pick. The native *C. lutea* makes a pretty yellow flowering wall plant, sometimes rampant.

Cultivation. Plant October or March, well-drained, lightish soil, liking lime, in partial shade or sun.

Propagation. By seeds in April, outdoors. By division of roots in April.

Corylopsis (kor-il-op'sis. Fam. Hamamelidaceae). Deciduous shrubs of NE. Asia, delightful for their drooping spikes of soft yellow, fragrant flowers in early spring.

Selection. C. glabrescens, Japan, to 15 ft, is hardiest, but *pauciflora,* Japan, 4–6 ft, or *spicata,* Japan, to 6 ft, are best for small gardens, all flowering in April.

Cultivation. Plant October–March, well-drained, humus-rich soil, out of reach of spring frosts and cold winds. Prune, if necessary, after flowering.

Propagation. By cuttings of young shoots, July–August, in cold frame or under handlights.

Corylus (kor'il-us. Fam. Betulaceae). Deciduous shrubs or trees of which *C. avellana* and *maxima* are grown for their Nuts (q.v.). Ornamental are:

Selection. C. avellana v. *contorta,* Britain, a bush of intriguingly twisted and curled shoots and twigs, 6 ft; v. *aurea,* for yellow foliage; *chinensis,* the Chinese Hazel, a tall tree, to 80 ft, makes a noble specimen with large

leaves; *colurna,* the Turkish Hazel, to 70 ft, is equally distinctive; and *maxima* v. *atropurpurea,* to 15 ft, is a fine dark purple leaved Filbert.

Cultivation. Plant October–March, well-drained, loam soil, accepting lime. Little pruning needed.

Propagation. Species by seeds, sown autumn or spring. Shrubs by layering in spring.

Corymb. A raceme of flowers of which the stalks inside shorten so that the flowers make a flat head.

Corymbosus (-a, -um). Corymb-shaped. Ex. *Vaccinium corybosum.*

Coryphantha (kor-i-pan'tha. Fam. Cactaceae). Mexican cacti, closely akin to Mammillaria, with grooved tubercles and large flowers. The standard cactus treatment suits (*see* Cactus). *C. clava,* cylindrical, to 12 in, greenish-red flowers; *cornifera,* brown-yellow; *erecta,* pale yellow; and *speciosa,* golden; are all good. A watch for red spider mite infestation should be kept.

Cosmos (Cosmea) (kos'mos. Fam. Compositae). Mexican plants of which *C. bipinnatus,* 3 ft, has been developed to give profuse-flowering, graceful branching plants, in white, pink and white, rose, and crimson strains, for summer into autumn; when raised as a half-hardy annual, sown in March, under glass, bottom heat of 18° C. (65° F.), to be pricked off, and hardened off for May planting outside, 18–24 in. apart; *sulphureus,* 'Sunset', 2½ ft, carries vermilion semi-double flowers very freely, with similar treatment.

Costa, Costate. The midrib of a leaf, ribbed.

Cotoneaster (ko-to-ne-as'ter. Fam. Rosaceae). A notable genus of deciduous and evergreen shrubs, mostly hardy, and valuable for their ornamental fruits.

Selection. Deciduous. C. adpressa, China, prostrate and spreading, good for rock work, red berries; *bullata,* China, to 12 ft, brilliant red fruits, good for exposed places; *dielsiana,* China, 6–8 ft, graceful, scarlet fruits; *divaricata,* China, 6 ft, elegant, red-fruited; *frigida,* Himalaya, to 30 ft, as a small tree, bright red fruits; *horizontalis,* China, flat, herringbone branching, red fruits, excellent for walls or prostrate cover to 5 ft by 5 ft; *rotundifolia,* Himalaya,

4–6 ft, scarlet fruits, well-retained; and *simonsii*, China, to 9 ft, scarlet berries, useful for hedging and exposed positions for shelter.

Evergreen. Of the tree forms, *C. salicifolius*, China, to 18 ft, bright red fruits, is valuable, with larger leaves and fruits in v. *rugosus*; *congestus*, Himalaya, fine-leaved, red berries, is a dwarf for rock gardens; *conspicuus*, China, to 6 ft, attractive in flower and with its red berries; × *cornubia*, tree or tall shrub, to 20 ft, huge clusters of red berries; *dammeri*, China, creeps and roots, with coral-red fruits, for ground cover; *franchetii*, China, 8 ft, graceful habit, beautiful in its orange-red fruits; × *pendula*, striking for its long prostrate shoots with brilliant red berries, and when grown as a small weeping tree; *lactea*, China, to 12 ft, grey woolly leaves, red berries; *microphylla*, Himalaya, low spreading growth for banks, or to hang over rocks, fine-leaved, and scarlet berries; *serotina*, China, to 10 ft, rounded leaves, bright red persistent berries; *wardii*, Tibet, 6–9 ft, erect, with orange-red berries; and × *watereri*, fast-growing hybrid to 20 ft, as shrub or tree, weighed down with red fruits in autumn.

Cultivation. Plant deciduous kinds October–March; evergreen autumn or March–April. Well-drained soil, otherwise not difficult. Prune or trim, if thought necessary, in June–July after flowering.

Propagation. By cuttings in July–August, under handlights. By seeds, sown when ripe in autumn, or stored over winter in sand, to sow in spring on outdoor seed-bed.

Cotton Grass. See *Eriophorum*.

Cotyledon (ko-ti-le'don. Fam. Crassulaceae). Very largely a S. African genus of succulent plants, falling into two groups; one of shrubby growth with opposite leaves, the other of thick fleshy stems with alternate leaves. In both, the leaves are succulent, persistent on the shrubby plants, but being renewed each year on the others.

Selection. Of shrubby growth, *C. orbiculata*, roundish, grey-green, red-edged leaves, yellowish-red tubular flowers; and *undulata*, wavy-edged leaves, covered with white meal, pendent

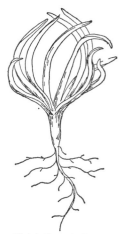

FIG. 65a   Multi-dicotyledonous seedling, typical of Fir (*Abies* spp.).

cream, red striped flowers, are beautiful growing and flowering in summer. The best of the fleshy-stemmed kinds are probably *paniculata*, to 5 ft, rosette of leaves to the top of stems, red flowers in summer; *reticulata*, short-stemmed, greenish-yellow flowers, summer; and *tuberculosa*, orange-red flowers; the plants resting in summer, forming new leaves in autumn.

FIG. 65b   Cotyledons of a Broad Bean, opened out.

Cultivation. Cool greenhouse with minimum winter temp. of 7–10° C. (45–50° F.), standard compost, sunny position. Pot and repot shrubby kinds in March–April; others September. Water moderately but regularly in growth. Fleshy-stemmed sorts need no water when leafless and resting.

Propagation. By cuttings or leaf cuttings, August.

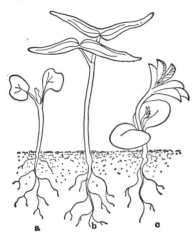

FIG. 65c Dicotyledonous seedlings: a. *Brassica* sp.; b. *Ipomoea* sp.; c. *Fabia* sp.

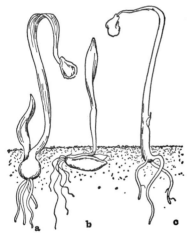

FIG. 65d Monocotyledonous seedings: a. Sweet Corn; b. Grass; c. Onion.

Cotyledons. Seed-leaves, produced singly in monocotyledons, or in pairs in dicotyledons.

Couch Grass, Quick, Scutch, Twitch (*Agropyron repens*). An agressive, persistent weed, with rhizomatous invasive underground stems, inhibitory to the growth of many garden plants; may be controlled by repeated cultivation, forking out, drying and burning the roots or composting them for 2 to 3 years; or by applying a dalapon herbicide to the foliage, which gives good control where the weed infests orchard, shrubbery or asparagus bed.

Couve Trouchuda. *See* Cabbage.

Cow-Dung. Pure cow-dung, allowed to dry, and then crumbled, is sometimes used as a fertilizer in potting composts, especially by old-time gardeners.

Cowslip. See *Primula veris*.

Cowslip, American. See *Dodecatheon*.

Crab Apple. See *Malus pumila*.

Crambe (kram'be. Fam. Cruciferae). The plant offered for its hardy ornamental foliage is *C. cordifolia*, Caucasus, 3–6 ft, with large, fleshy cordate leaves, and a huge branched panicle of white flowers in June, suitable for the wild garden; planted October–March, and propagated by division, or by seed. *C. maritima* is Seakale (q.v.).

Cranberry. The large or American Cranberry, grown for its acid, red berry-like fruits is *Vaccinium macrocarpon* (*Oxycoccus macrocarpus*), a creeping evergreen shrub, which, in selected forms, is grown on damp, acid soils, and subjected to flooding through autumn, winter and spring. The plant can be grown in a bog garden; propagated by layers, or division in spring.

Crane Flies or **Daddy-long-legs.** (*Tipula oleracea, T. paludosa, Pachyrhina maculata*). These are the familiar long-legged insects often seen skittering in May–August, the females digging their ovipositors into lawns and soil to lay the eggs that hatch into the greyish-brown to almost black cylindrical grubs which are called Leatherjackets. The grubs are often numerous and do much harm by feeding on plant roots and underground parts in autumn, winter and spring, before pupating. They may be trapped with potato slices impaled on sticks, and removed or destroyed *in situ* by spraying with a DDT or gamma-BHC insecticide.

Crane's Bill. See *Geranium*.

Crassula (kras'su-la. Fam. Crassulaceae). A large genus of succulent shrubby plants, chiefly from S. Africa, of which a selection can be grown in the cool greenhouse or as house plants.

Selection. C. arborescens, shrubby, 2-3 ft, grey-green, red-edged leaves, rarely produces its flowers; *lactea*, 2 ft, starry white flowers in a spiky raceme, autumn; and *falcata*, to 2 ft, scarlet flowers in flat corymbs, summer; make good indoor plants; *cooperi*, a low, matted cushion of a plant, with pink flowers in winter; *Justus-cordevoyi*, dwarf clump of short stems, small deep pink flowers, summer; and *C. nealeana*, a branching small shrub, with yellow flowers, summer, may be grown.

Cultivation. Pot, and repot, in spring, standard compost; grow in cool greenhouse, winter temp. 70° C. (45° F.); increasing watering with growth, very moderate in winter.

Propagation. By leaf cuttings in summer; JIC compost.

Crataego-mespilus (kra-te'go-mes'pi-lus. Fam. Rosaceae). Three interesting hybrids between the Thorn (*Crataegus oxycantha*) and the Medlar (*Mespilus germanica*), hardy and free-flowering. *C. asnieresii*, a small tree with drooping branches, white flowers and brown fruits resembling those of the thorn, and *dardari*, with slightly longer leaves, white flowers and fruits like small medlars, are graft hybrids of a Medlar grafted on a Thorn, originating in France; while × *grandiflora*, a tree up to 30 ft, has broader oval leaves, pure white flowers in spring, and yellow-brown haws. All are hardy and grow readily in any ordinary soil, planted in October–March.

Crataegus, Thorn (kra-te'gus. Fam. Rosaceae). Small deciduous trees, of which many are deserving of garden culture for their foliage, flowers and/or fruits.

Selection. C. apiifolia, S. U.S.A., 10–20 ft, the Parsley-leaved Thorn, with deeply cut leaves, white May flowers, scarlet haws; *arnoldiana*, U.S.A., to 20 ft, flowers and fruits well; but is very thorny; × *carrierei*, to 20 ft, few thorns, long, oval leaves, esteemed for persistent orange-red haws; *crus-galli*, the Cockspur Thorn, N. America, to 30 ft, white, June, rather large persistent red fruits; × *dippeliana*, to 15 ft, lobed leaves, white June flowers, dull red haws, flowers

freely; *monogyna* is the native hedgerow Thorn, to 35 ft as a tree, outstanding in its vs. *aurea*, yellow berried; *pendula rosea*, a graceful weeper; *praecox*, the Glastonbury Thorn which flowers in winter and leafs early; and *stricta*, an erect-growing form; *orientalis*, Far East, to 20 ft, thornless, with cut-lobed leaves,

FIG. 66   *Crataegus* × *carrierei* in flower.

white June flowers, and ribbed coral-red fruits; *oxycantha*, the native Hawthorn, to 20 ft, has red fruits with two stones, and its double-flowering vs. *alba plena* and *coccinea plena*, Paul's Double Scarlet, make good specimens; *maskei*, double, shell-pink flowers; *fructuluteo*, yellow-fruiting; and *pendula*, a charming, white-flowering weeping form are good; *pinnatifida* v. *major*, China, to 20 ft, white May flowers, and lobed leaves up to 6 in. long, is very effective; *tanacetifolia*, the Tansy-leaved Thorn, to

30 ft, finely cut leaves, June flowers, and bracted, yellow fruits, is very attractive.

Cultivation. Plant October–March, any ordinary soil, including chalk, but welcome humus. Prune, when necessary, in November.

Propagation. Species by seeds, extracted from ripe haws over-wintered in cool sand, in March; may be 2 to 3 years germinating, so mark seed-bed. Choice varieties are budded on common thorn seedlings in July, or grafted in March.

Crazy Paving. A path laid with irregular-shaped pieces of flat stone, the straight sides being put down first, on bed of sand or ashes, then large pieces centrally as the walking stones, and finally filling in the remaining spaces. Interstices should be grouted with cement except where spaces are left for planting carpeting plants, such as *Acaena buchananii*, *A. microphylla*, *Antenaria dioica*, *Armeria caespitosa*, *Aubrieta* sp., *Campanula garganica*, *Hutchinsia alpina*, *Mentha requienii*, *Saxifraga*, Mossy; *Sempervivum* sp., *Silene acaulis*, *Thymus serpyllum* and vs., etc.

Creeper. A plant that creeps or runs on the ground, over rock faces, etc., often rooting itself.

Creeper, Virginian. See *Parthenocissus.*

Creeping Jenny. See *Lysimachia nummularia.*

Crenatus (-a, -um). Crenate, having rounded teeth on the leaf margins. Ex. *Ilex crenata.*

FIG. 67   Crenate leaf (*Veronica* sp.).

Creosote. A product of the distillation of wood or coal-tar, often used to preserve timber from fungal and insect attacks. It is, however, caustic, its fumes are toxic to plants, and should not be used for the treatment of garden woodwork likely to be near or in touch with plants. The more refined products (Presotim, Solignum) or metallic solvents (Cuprinol) are safer.

Crepis, Hawk's-beard (kre′pis. Fam. Compositae). Annual, biennial and perennials, of which most are weeds. *C. aurea*, 6 in., is a European alpine herbaceous perennial, with orange flowerheads on single stems in autumn, and may be planted in ordinary soil, in rock garden or border; *rubra*, S. Europe, 1 ft, is a hardy annual, providing red flowers, good for cutting, in autumn, when sown where it is to grow in April, and thinned.

Propagation. Perennial species by division in April.

Cress (*Lepidium sativum*). An annual which is grown to be eaten at the seed-leaf stage with Mustard. Fresh, first-quality seed is best sown in 3-in. deep boxes, half-filled with a porous soil compost (JIS or once-used JIP), firmed and levelled, sprinkling the seed evenly and thickly, and moistening with a mist spraying of water; covered to exclude light, and grown in greenhouse or frame (in summer, outdoors under a cloche), at 10–13° C. (50–55° F.) minimum; keeping moist with mist spraying, not with watering-can; remove cover when about 1–1½ in. high, and grow on for cutting in 10–14 days. Plain or Curled varieties may be sown. Mustard (q.v.) is sown 3 to 4 days later as it germinates more quickly. May also be grown on flannel, kept moist, but rather tediously.

Cress, Land. *See* Land Cress.

Cresylic Acid. Carbolic acid; sold as a 98 per cent pure solution. It may be used instead of formaldehyde for sterilizing soil, greenhouses, frames, boxes and pots; as a 2½ per cent solution (1 part to 39 parts water); as a disinfectant. A greenhouse may be washed down inside with it at the end of the growing season; protective clothing and gloves should be worn.

Crinodendron (Tricuspidaria) (krin-o-den′dron. Fam. Elaeocarpaceae). Evergreen trees from Chile. The Lantern

Tree, *C. hookerianum* (*Tricuspidaria lanceolata*), is the best known as an evergreen with shapely elliptical leathery leaves, and crimson, urn-like flowers hanging on long stalks in May–June; it grows 10–30 ft tall, but needs mild, warm shelter, as does *C. patagua*, 30 ft, with somewhat shorter leaves and white cup-shaped flowers in August.

Cultivation. Plant October or April–May, in lime-free, humus-rich soil, preferably on a warm, frost-free wall, unless your garden is a very mild one; otherwise in a cold greenhouse. Prune to shape, if necessary, after flowering.

Propagation. By cuttings of young shoots taken with a heel, July–August, in sandy compost, placed in propagating frame, with bottom heat of 21° C. (70° F.).

Crinum (kri'num. Fam. Amaryllidaceae). Bulbous plants, with lovely flowers and bold leaves.

Selection. C. longiflorum, India, 18 in., with umbels of white, greenish tubed, trumpet flowers; *moorei*, Natal, 2 ft, white, red-flushed, funnelled flowers; and × *powellii*, 2 ft, reddish flared flowers, and its vs. *album*, pure white, and *krelagei*, pink; may prove hardy enough to be planted out of doors in warm, sheltered borders, deep, light loam, to flower in autumn. Otherwise they may be grown in a cool or warm greenhouse, together with *C. asiaticum*, tropical Asia, 2 ft, white, and its vs.; *bulbispermum*, S. Africa, 2 ft, white, red flush; and *macowanii*, Natal, 3 ft, white, tinged purple. There are also several good hybrids.

Cultivation. Pot, and repot every third year, one bulb to a 9-in. pot, in spring, standard compost; watering increasingly with growth, ample sun; more moderately in winter, temp. 10–13° C. (50–55° F.).

Propagation. By offset bulbs when repotting.

Crispus (-a, -um). Curled, wavy-edged. Ex. *Elodea crispa*.

Cristatus (-a, -um). Crested. Ex. *Pteris ensiformis cristata*.

Croceus (-a, -um). Yellow. Ex. *Lilium croceum*.

Crocks. The clean broken pieces of clay pots, used to afford drainage at the base of pots; may be replaced today by plastic mesh and crumpled plastic material.

Crocosmia (kro-kos'mi-a. Fam. Iridaceae). S. African cormous plants, allied to Tritonia, with spikes of flared, tubular flowers in July–August.

Selection. C. aurea, 2–3 ft, with golden-yellow flowers, has vs. *flore pleno*, double flowers; and *imperialis*, fiery-orange red; *pottsii*, 1½ ft, bright yellow, flushed red: and their hybrid, × *crocosmiiflora*, orange-scarlet; and *masonorum*, 3 ft, bright orange-red.

Cultivation. Plant about 4 in. deep, in well-drained, humus-rich soil, sunny position, in spring. Lift and store corms as for gladiolus for the winter, in November, except in frost-free areas. Also pot-grown in greenhouses.

Propagation. By offset corms, detached when replanting. By seeds in pans, in cold frame, April.

Crocus (kro'kus. Fam. Iridaceae). Hardy cormous perennial plants, treasured for their autumn to spring flowering.

Selection. Autumn and winter-flowering species to be planted in August–September, 2–3 in. deep, where frost or rains are least likely to mar them; *C. longiflorus*, Italy, 3 in., yellow; *medius*, Riviera, 5 in., purple; *nudiflorus*, SW. Europe, pale purple; *orchroleucus*, Israel, 3 in., buff, orange; *pulchellus*, Greece, 4 in., blue-lilac; *salzmanni*, Morocco, 4 in., lilac; *sativus*, Saffron Crocus, Asia Minor, 2 in., lilac; *speciosus*, Asia Minor, Persia, 4 in., bright lilac, feathered, and v. *aitchisoni*, pale lilac; and *kotschyanus*, Lebanon, 3 in., rosy-lilac. Spring-flowering species, February–March, to be planted October–December, 2–3 in. deep: *balansae*, Asia Minor, 2 in., orange; *biflorus*, Scotch Crocus, Italy, 4 in., lilac to white; and vs.; *chrysanthus*, Asia Minor, 3 in., orange and bronze; and improved vs. 'E. A. Bowles', 'E. P. Bowles', Canary Bird', 'Zwanenburg's Bronze' and the white 'Snow Bunting'; *etruscus*, Italy, 4 in., deep lilac; *fleischeri*, Asia Minor, 3 in., white; *imperati*, Italy, 4 in., pale purple, feathered; *minimus*, Corsica, 2 in., purple; *sieberi*, Greece, 4 in., bright lilac; *susianus*, Cloth of Gold Crocus, Caucasus, 3 in., orange, feathered brown; *tomasinianus*, Dalmatia, 3 in., pale lavender-blue; *vernus*, Europe, 3½ in., white to purple; and *versicolor*, S. European Alps, 4 in., purple to white. The large-flowering Dutch Crocus are held to be derived from *C. aureus* and *C. vernus*, and are planted in September–December, 2–3 in. deep, as much apart, and good forms are: 'Jeanne d'Arc', 'Kathleen Parlow', 'Pallas', whites; 'Early Perfection', 'Negro Boy', 'Purple Beauty', *purpureus grandiflorus* and 'The Bishop', purples; 'Little Dorrit', silvery lilac; 'Queen of the Blues', lilac-blue; 'Maximilian', china blue; 'Striped Beauty', white, striped lilac; 'Golden Yellow' and 'Yellow Giant', yellows.

Cultivation. Plant species in well-drained, humus-rich soil, with a little bone meal, in rock garden, shrubbery or borders, lift, divide and replant every third year. Plant Dutch vs., in beds or border, to naturalize in grass, allowing leaves to wither before cutting; lift and divide every fifth year or so. In pots—plant in deep pans or pots, standard compost, October–November, to place in cold frame for about six weeks, then bringing gradually into cool greenhouse, and finally indoors; plant out after flowering.

Propagation. By offset corms, on lifting and dividing. By seeds, sown out of doors, June–July; need 3 to 4 years to build up to flowering.

Crocus, Autumn. See *Colchicum*.

Crossandra (kross-an'dra. Fam. Acanthaceae). Free-flowering, beautiful, evergreen shrubs of tropical W. Africa for the warm greenhouse.

Selection. C. *flava*, 9 in., bright yellow spikes of flowers, summer; *guineensis*, 6 in., pale lilac, autumn; and *unduliflora*, E. Indies, tallest at 1–3 ft, orange flowers, summer.

Cultivation. Pot, and repot, in early spring, standard compost, water liberally in growth, summer temps. 18–24° C. (65–75° F.); more moderately in winter, 13–15·5° C. (55–60° F.).

Propagation. By cuttings, spring to autumn, with bottom heat of 21° C. (70° F.). By seeds sown in similar warmth in spring.

Cross-fertilization. The fertilizing of a flower and its ovules by pollen of another flower of the same species or another

compatible species. *See* Hybrid; Self-fertilization.

Crossing. The pollinating of the stigma of the flower of a plant with pollen from the flower of another related but different kind, to obtain a hybrid of the two, or simply to set fruit.

Croton. See *Codiaeum*.

Crowea (kro'e-a. Fam. Rutaceae). Pretty evergreen Australian shrubs, which may be grown in a cool airy greenhouse.

Selection. C. *angustifolia*, 2–3 ft, has thin, linear leaves, with star-like pale rose flowers from the axils in spring; *saligna*, 2–3 ft, has narrow, lanceolate leaves, with rich rose-red flowers in July.

Cultivation. Pot, and repot, in March, standard compost; water freely in growth; very moderately in winter, minimum temp. 7° C. (45° F.). Shorten shoots to shape.

Propagation. By seeds, if possible, sown with slight bottom heat (15·5° C. [60° F.]), spring.

Crown Imperial. See *Fritillaria*.

Cruciatus (-a, -um). Cruciate, cross-shaped. Ex. *Colletia cruciata*.

Cruciferae. A dicotyledonous family of over 200 genera; the following being included in this book: *Aethionema, Alyssum, Anastatica, Arabis, Aubrieta, Barbarea, Brassica, Cardamine, Cheiranthus, Cochlearia, Crambe, Draba, Erysimum, Heliophila, Hesperis, Hutchinisia, Iberis, Ionopsidium, Isatis, Lunaria, Malcolmia, Matthiola, Morisia, Nasturtium, Petrocallis, Raphanus, Vesicaria.*

Cruciform. Cross-shaped; the cross-like formation of the petals of the flowers of the Cruciferae.

Cruentus (-a, -um). Blood-coloured. Ex. *Senecio cruentus*.

Cryosophila (kri-o-sof'i-la. Fam. Palmaceae). *C. nana* (*Acanthorriza aculeata*) is an evergreen palm from Mexico, with much divided leaves, for the warm greenhouse. Pot in March, standard compost, watering freely in growth, moderately in winter, with temp. 10–13° C. (50–55° F.). Propagated by seeds sown in moist peat, spring, with bottom heat of 21° C. (70° F.).

Cryptanthus (krip-tan'thus. Fam. Bromeliaceae). Low-growing, stemless plants, with rosettes of leaves, reminiscent of a starfish, from Brazil, now popular as warm greenhouse and house plants.

Selection. C. bivittatus, recurved leaves, green with bands of buff, low dense head of white flowers, July; *acaulis*, 6 in., with wavy-edged, recurved green leaves; striped white in v. *zebrinus*; and *zonatus*, 9 in., with leaves banded green, white and buff, white flower head in summer.

Cultivation. Pot, and repot when necessary, in March, standard compost, watering freely in growth, moderately in winter; minimum winter temp. 15.5° C. (60° F.).

Propagation. By offsets in spring.

Cryptogamae, Cryptogams. The non-flowering members of the Plant Kingdom as defined by Linnaeus; from *kryptos*, hidden, and *gamos*, marriage; as opposed to the Phanerogamae or flowering plants. Cryptogams include ferns, horse-tails, club-mosses, mosses, liverworts and algae.

Cryptogramma (krip-to-gram'ma. Fam. Polypodioceae). Hardy deciduous ferns, of which *C. crispa*, the Mountain Parsley Fern, native and of Arctic and N. temperate zone, 10 in., is very charming, for lime-free soil in the rock garden, or as a pot-plant in the cool greenhouse in shade; *acrostichoides*, the Rock Brake of N. America, and *brunoniana* of the Himalaya, are distinguished small ferns to grow similarly.

Cultivation. Plant or pot in March; lime-free, cool, moist soil, or loam-peat compost, in cool, partially shaded positions.

Propagation. By division of roots or crowns, in March. By spores, but very slow.

Cryptomeria (krip-to-me'ri-a. Fam. Pinaceae). The one species, *C. japonica*, Japanese Cedar, is a pleasing evergreen conifer, with reddish-brown bark, to top 100 ft, in this country; but more appealing to gardeners in its vs. such as *elegans*, 20–25 ft, with green foliage turning bronzy purplish in winter; *lobbii*, of denser and more compact habit; and the dwarf forms, *albovariegata*, very dwarf, leaves touched with white; *bandai-sugi*, conical, and dwarf, to 6 ft; *elegans nana*, to 9 ft, fine foliage; *globosa nana*, bushy, to 8 ft;

pygmaea, compact dwarf; *cristata*, with curious fasciated branches; *spiralis*, with leaves curiously spiralling the branches; and the very dwarf *vilmoriniana*.

Cultivation. Plant in September–October or April; deep, loam soil, well sheltered from strong winds, with moisture always assured.

Propagation. The species by seeds, in March, out of doors or under cloches; varieties by cuttings of typical young shoots, in sandy loam, in a close frame or under handlights, August–September.

Ctenanthe, Comb-flower (ten-an'the. Fam. Marantaceae). Evergreen perennial herbs of Brazil, with tufted habit and long-stalked basal leaves and short-stalked stem leaves of appealing character, grown as house plants.

Selection. C. lubbersiana, 1½ ft, with stalked linear-ovate leaves, deep green with yellow variegation on top, pale green beneath, and *oppenheimiana*, 3 ft, with long-stalked leaves of leathery texture, purple beneath, and its v. *tricolor*, with creamy-white and pink markings, are usually offered.

Cultivation. Pot in March–April, standard compost, water freely in growth in summer, syringing foliage; very moderate watering in winter, with temp. 15.5° C. (60° F.). Propagated by division in spring, when repotting.

Cuckoo Flower. See *Cardamine*.

Cuckoo Pint. See *Arum*.

Cuckoo Spit. The frothy secretion of the nymphs of the Frog-hopper or Cuckoo-spit insects (*Cercopidae*). The froth itself does little harm, the nymphs may cause wilting of young shoots; malathion gives control.

Cucullatus (-a, -um). Cucullate; hooded. Ex. *Viola cucullata*.

Cucumber (Cucumis sativus). The origins of the tendril-climbing or trailing cucumber plant are not precisely known but are attributed to the warmer regions of Africa, Asia or East Indies. It is one of the oldest cultivated vegetables and needs warmth, humidity, moisture and a rich, friable, humus-containing soil, and is therefore most successfully grown in a heated greenhouse.

Culture under Glass. Temps. of at least 15.5° C. (60° F.) at night, 21–29° C. (70–85° F.) by day, are needed. Seeds may be sown singly in 3-in. pots, half-filled with standard compost, or in 3-in. deep boxes, $1\frac{1}{2}$ in. deep, point downwards, with bottom heat of 21–24° C. (70–75° F.); in late November for early crops, in mid December for main crops, planting out in February, or January–March, for late crops, and for plants to grow in frames or outdoors. Germination should take place in 48 to 60 hours; slow germination gives weaker plants. Plants are usually ready to plant out in 4 to 5 weeks from sowing, in prepared bed, or mound of a compost of 2 parts turfy loam, 1 part rotted stable manure, good compost, or rotted horse manure and straw, on the staging. Plants produce male and female flowers separately, but as fruits are formed parthenocarpically, male flowers (staminate) are best removed to obtain seedless fruits. Growth is trained to the glass, and fruits allowed to form on laterals only; the main stem is stopped at 4 ft. Laterals are grown to cover glass space available, but stopped at the second leaf beyond where fruit is produced; unwanted shoots are pinched out. Watering is done with water at greenhouse temperature, without wetting plants at the collar. As soon as any roots show at the surface, a covering top-dressing of soil compost should be added. Atmosphere should be kept buoyant, with syringing on hot days. Liquid feeding can be given twice weekly, when fruits are forming. The seaweed derivatives give sweet fruits.

Frame Culture. The soil should be prepared as for greenhouse culture, and the frame warm, when planted in April–June, one plant per frame. Shade from hot sun, and give protection from cool nights for first fortnight or so. Regulate ventilation according to the heat of the day; water regularly with care, syringe in hot weather. Peg out laterals to cover frame without overcrowding.

Varieties for under Glass. Smooth-skinned: Improved Telegraph, Satisfaction, Tender and True, Simex F_1, Lockie's Perfection. Spiny: Rochford's Market, Butcher's Disease Resistant, Chennell's Challenger (the last two for early sowings).

Outdoor Culture. Seeds may be sown, as above, in mid April, to plant out in late May–early June; under a handlight;

in prepared compost of rotting manure, well mixed with leaves, and topped with good loam soil. Space between plants should be 24–30 in.; nip back leading shoots at seven to nine leaves; stop laterals at two leaves beyond where fruit form. Water liberally; top dress to cover roots as necessary; liquid feed when fruits are swelling.

Varieties. Stockwood Ridge, Carter's Greenline, Baton Vert F_1, Long Green and Bedfordshire Prize Ridge. New Japanese types are Kaga, Kariha, Ochiai F_1 and Suyo. Apple and Russian Cucumbers are novelties. For pickling, Short Prickly, or Small Paris Gherkin.

Diseases. Canker or Foot Rot (*Bacterium carotovorum*), when base of stem goes brown with soft rot, is largely prevented by avoiding wet conditions at the base of plants; to combat infection dust with copper-lime dust. Anthracnose (*Colletotrichichum oligochaetum*) spreads easily when humidity is too high, paling and withering leaves and stems; infected leaves should be removed, and plants dusted with fine sulphur, repeated at 7–10-day intervals. Leaf Blotch (*Cercospora melonis*) shows in pale, turning yellow and brown, increasing spots, and affected leaves should be removed at once. Butcher's Disease Resistant variety should be grown. Gummosis (*Cladosporium cucumerinum*) causes irregular brownish spots on leaves, and sunken spots oozing an amber 'gum' on fruits, and is encouraged by over-wet conditions, low temperatures and inadequate ventilation; affected fruits should be removed, and a sulphur fungicide applied, with attention to better growing conditions. Powdery Mildew (*Erysiphe cichoracearum*) may cover leaves, but is superficial, and controlled by karathane. Virus infections may cause 'Green Mottle Mosaic', or 'Yellow Mosaic', for which there is no cure; seriously infected plants are best destroyed. Grey Mould (*Botrytis cinerea*) may show up if hygiene is neglected. In cases of severe infection, the house should be disinfected after cropping.

Pests. Aphids, Red Spider Mites, Thrips and White-fly may infest cucumbers from other plants; and care is needed in choice of insecticide. Derris, malathion, kelthane or a nicotine product may be used but not DDT or gamma-BHC.

Cultivar, Cultivar-name. A cultivated variety of a plant; the name given to it.

Cuneatus (-a, -um). Cuneate; wedge-shaped and attached by the point. Ex. *Adiantum cuneatum*.

FIG. 68 Cuneate leaves (*Adiantum cuneatum*).

Cunninghamia (kun-ning-ham'i-a. Fam. Pinaceae). Very beautiful, ever-green coniferous trees, reasonably hardy, but best planted in warm, rich soils, in mild localities and good shelter. *C. lanceolata*, the Chinese Fir, China, to 80 ft, has emerald-green foliage, turning reddish-brown in winter; *konishii*, Formosa, is more rare, and less hardy, and only suggested for the milder corners of the south-west.

Cup-and-Saucer Flower. Canterbury Bells, sometimes applied to *Cobaea scandens*.

Cuphea (ku'pe-a. Fam. Lythraceae). A genus of free-flowering, half-hardy plants from Mexico.

Selection. C. ignea, the Cigar Flower, 1 ft, of slender grace with evergreen lance-shaped leaves, and bright scarlet tubular flowers, blue-black and white to the end, in summer; and *micropetala*, 1 ft, with scarlet, yellow and white flowers, are shrubs for the cool green-house or as house plants. *C. miniata*,

to 2 ft, pale vermilion flowers, and *lanceolata*, 1½ ft, reddish violet flowers, are grown as annuals, for pot growth or summer bedding.

Cultivation. All may be raised from seeds, sown March, standard compost, bottom heat of 21° C. (70° F.); shrubby kinds to be potted on, and grown in greenhouse with winter temp. 10° C. (50° F.), freely watered in summer, very moderately in winter; annuals to be pricked out, and hardened off for plant-ing out in early June, sunny positions, well-drained soil.

Propagation. Shrubby perennials by cuttings of young shoots in spring, with bottom heat (21° C. [70° F.]).

Cupressocyparis (ku-pres-so-ki-par'is. Fam. Cupressaceae). *C.* × *leylandii*, a hybrid cypress of *Chamaecyparis noot-katensis* × *Cupressus macrocarpa*, hardy, remarkably fast-growing, may make a pyramidal tree of 80 ft or more; but is highly adaptable to forming screens or hedges, standing up to clipping and curtailment exceptionally well. Best planted September–October or March–May, ex pots, any well-drained soil of reasonable depth and moisture retention. Propagated by cuttings, July–August, under mist.

Cupressus, Cypress (ku-pres'sus. Fam. Cupressaceae). Evergreen coniferous trees, nearly related to *Chamaecyparis* (q.v.), but not quite so hardy.

Selection. The best known is *C. macrocarpa*, the Monterey Cypress, fast-growing, pyramidal, California, to 100 ft, hardy enough in the south and west, salt-resistant and good for coastal planting, but mistakenly used for hedging as it dies back under clipping; *crippsii*, stiffer habit, silvered leaves, and *lutea*, very fine golden-leaved conifer, are vs.; *lusitanica*, Mexican Cypress, or Cedar of Goa, to 100 ft, has a pendulous grace, and several vs., but is not for cold districts; *sempervirens*, Mediter-ranean Cypress, to 80 ft, may be with spreading branches as in v. *horizontalis*, or stiffly erect in v. *stricta*, the Italian form; but again only for the warmer counties.

Cultivation. Plant September–October or March–May, preferably ex pots, young, in well-drained soil, open situa-tions, where frosts and drought are not

FIG. 69 The scale-like, adpressed leaves, typical of Cypress (*Cupressus* spp.).

troublesome. Propagation by seeds, in April, sandy loam.

Cupreus (-a, -um). Copper-coloured. Ex. *Mimulus cupreus.*

Cupula, Cupule. The cupped receptacle or involucre of an acorn or a nut.

Currants, Black (*Ribes nigrum*). When established these bushes yield heavily of fruits very rich in vitamin C and health-protective nutrients. They live long, grow well in sun or partial shade, given soil that is well-drained and retentive of top-soil moisture, and may be associated with stone fruits, culinary apples or nuts in an orchard, requiring similar generous nitrogenous feeding.

Selection. Early-fruiting—Boskoop Giant, Laxton's Giant, Mendip Cross. Mid season—Wellington XXX, Seabrook's Black. Late—Baldwin, Amos Black. A succession gives June to early August cropping. Wellington XXX is first choice if only one variety is planted.

Planting. Plant October–March in soil prepared by thorough deep-digging, organic manuring and basic slag or lime to bring to pH 6·0, if needed. Plant one- or two-year-old bushes, firmly, about 6 ft apart, and then cut all shoots back to within an inch of the soil surface.

Culture. As the best fruit grows on shoots of one year or the previous year's growth, the aim is to produce a steady succession of such shoots. In the first autumn after planting, all except the strongest shoots (left for fruiting) are cut back to soil level to provoke more new shoots from the base. In the following year, after fruiting, the fruited shoots are cut back. Thereafter, pruning consists of pruning two or three of the oldest branches right out, cutting weak shoots hard back, and removing fruited wood so that new growth is made each year to maintain shape. Growers often cut off the shoots laden with the fruit, to ease harvesting and prune at the same time. Feeding must be generous—annual top-dressing with organic matter, and a dressing of Chilean potash nitrate in spring.

Propagation. By firm cuttings of shoots of current year's growth, 9 in. long, in autumn; inserted in a slit with top two buds above ground; rooted cuttings may be planted out the following autumn–winter.

Diseases. Leaf spot (*Gloeosporium ribis*) shows in tiny brown spots leading to defoliation, and calls for spraying with a copper fungicide in May. Reversion, a virus disease, causes distorted and dwarfed leaves, with fewer than five veins, lobes and teeth; and infected plants should be promptly burnt.

Pests. Aphids (Greenfly) cause leaf-curl, but may be controlled by a winter tar-oil wash, and derris insecticide,

FIG. 70 Big Bud on Currant shoots in winter.

repeated, in late spring. The worst is the gall mite (*Phytoptus ribis*) which causes a characteristic swelling of buds, known as Big Bud, apparent in winter. Spraying with lime-sulphur at the 'grape stage' of blossom development in spring stops the mites in their migrations.

Currants, Flowering. See *Ribes*.

Currants, Red and White. Hybrid in origin, these fruit bushes, with their delectable produce for pies and preserves, need different treatment from Black Currants.

Selection. Red varieties: early—Fay's Prolific, Versailles. Mid season—Earliest of Fourlands, Laxton's No. 1, Red Lake. Late—Laxton's Perfection, River's Late Red, Wilson's Long Bunch. White varieties: White Transparent, White Versailles.

Culture. Plant October–March, in well-drained soil, bastard-trenched and enriched with rotted organic matter, and, if necessary, sulphate of potash, with pH brought to 6·0–6·5 levels. Plants are grown on short single stem, if bush-shape, and should be spaced 5 ft apart; or as cordons, 15 in. apart. All shoots of bushes are cut back by one-half their length after planting, to an outward-facing bud. As these plants bear on the old better than on the new wood, pruning calls for the shortening of all lateral or side shoots to five leaves at the end of June. In winter, the laterals on bushes are cut to within an inch or so of their base, and leading shoots by one-third to one-half their new growth; as the bushes age, they can be pruned harder, with a few of the oldest branches being cut out, and new shoots will arise to take their place. Winter treatment of cordons consists of shortening the laterals to within half an inch of their base, and shortening the leader by half of its new growth. Plants should receive an annual organic top mulch, and a dressing of a high potassic fertilizer, or 1 to 1½ oz. Chilean potash nitrate per sq. yd., in March.

Propagation. By cuttings of sound shoots of the current year's growth, 12 in. long, taken in autumn; inserted with top three or four buds above soil level, retained at the top, other buds rubbed off to give a clean 5 or 6 in. of stem, and to prevent suckering from below ground. New shoots made in the first year are cut back to about four buds the following winter, for bush plants; the top shoot becomes the main leader, and others are pruned hard almost to their base.

Diseases. Similar to those of Black Currants (q.v.). Die-back may be caused by Coral Spot (*Nectria cinnabarina*) or Grey Mould (*Botrytis cinerea*) and infected growth should be cut out.

Pests. Aphids (Greenfly) cause red blistering of leaves, stunting of shoots, and are best controlled by tar-oil winter wash, and derris or malathion in late spring and summer. Currant Clearwing Moth (*Aegeria tipuliformis*) larvae may tunnel shoots from midsummer on, causing wilting; and shoots will need to be cut back to sound wood and burnt. Gooseberry Sawfly may infest foliage (*see* Gooseberry).

Cuspidatus (-a, -um). Cuspidate, sharp or spear pointed. Ex. *Camellia cuspidata*.

Cuticle. The thick outermost layer of cells of the epidermis of plants; often waxy, and serving as a protection.

Cutting back. The pruning or shortening of shoots and branches of shrubs and trees.

Cuttings. A cutting may be defined as a part of a plant separated from it and induced to form roots to become an individual plant on its own. By taking cuttings the gardener can increase his stock of a desirable plant with progeny identical in character with the parent. Theoretically, all plants can be propagated by cuttings of one kind or another In practice, many are too difficult, such as trees, others unrewarding or more easily propagated by other means.

Cuttings consist of portions of plants containing actively growing undifferentiated cells (cambiums) which can bud and form roots. They may be portions of a stem or shoot, root, or of leaves. They must be chosen of healthy, sound material, typical of the plant to be propagated. Successful propagation depends on keeping the cuttings turgid and alive until roots are formed to support new development. The essentials are air, adequate moisture, sufficient warmth and light, in a combination to stimulate growth without wilting. A porous, and therefore well-aerated, but moist rooting medium is essential, with sufficient heat to ensure rapid growth. Most cuttings can be successfully rooted in sand, vermiculite or peat, but unless moved on to richer soil as soon as rooted, they will falter and fail. It is more usual to use a compost designed for the purpose (*see* Composts).

Stem Cuttings. These consist of portions of a typical stem or shoot which may be cut at various stages of growth, usually less than one year old.

Hardwood Cuttings are taken in autumn, and consist of the leafless shoots of deciduous shrubs, trees, or woody perennials, of the current season's growth. An exception is the Willow, which roots readily from old branches (setts) as well as from young. Shoots are cut cleanly from firm, healthy lateral growth, with four to six buds; usually severed a little below a node or bud. In a few species, notably *Clematis*, the cut is made midway between nodes (internodal cuttings). These are the easiest cuttings to root. Those of hardy plants may be inserted in sandy loam at the foot of a north or sheltered wall for about one-half to two-thirds their length, and well firmed. They may be given the cover of a cloche, handlight or bell-glass, and left to grow for a year before being lifted and moved to growing quarters.

Evergreen and Conifer hardwood cuttings may also be taken in late summer and autumn. They should consist of shortish, sturdy lateral shoots, removed with a short 'heel' of older wood, by peeling them downward, carefully, from the parent branch. The heel is trimmed neatly, and to reduce loss of moisture by transpiration, lower leaves are removed. The cuttings are then inserted very firmly in a cold frame, or under cloche, handlight or even jam-jar covers, to minimize transpiration losses, and left until the following autumn before attempting transplanting. Ventilation is essential the following spring and summer when covers are lifted.

Softwood Cuttings are leafy cuttings, or half ripe, being taken from greenwood lateral shoots with a terminal bud or growing point, usually in early or mid

summer, when growth is firm enough to tend to crack at the centre when sharply bent. Such cuttings may be taken of shrubs, certain trees, and flowering plants, annual, biennial and perennial, of non-flowered shoots. The cuttings, a few inches only in length, are stripped of their lower leaves, cut cleanly below a

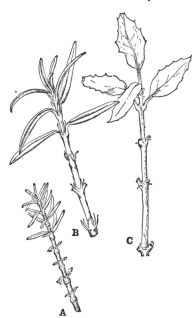

FIG. 71 Softwood or half-ripe cuttings, prepared for planting: A. *Erica carnea*; B. *Lavendula spicata*; C. *Fuchsia* hybrid. Note lower leaves have been removed.

node, and inserted in a porous rooting medium, with the warmth of bottom heat, and kept close with cover until rooted. In some cases of hardy species, it is often sufficient to firm the cuttings in light sandy loam out of doors, covered by bell-glasses or jam-jars. For consistent results, the cuttings are best inserted in a propagator (q.v.) or propagating frame, where they can be grown under controlled conditions. The cuttings must be kept moist, and shaded from hot sun. When rooted, ventilation should be given

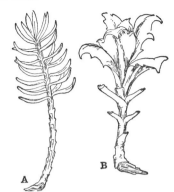

FIG. 72 Cuttings taken with a heel in early summer: A. *Iberis* sp.; B. *Aubrieta* hybrid.

increasingly, and growth hardened. After transplanting or potting on to richer compost, the rooted cuttings welcome partial shade for a few days until they regain full turgidity.

Cuttings with a Heel. These consist of half-ripened or half-mature lateral shoots of the current year's growth detached with the more fully ripened base or 'heel' of the older wood at their junction with the mature branch. They are taken in July–September. Those of hardy and easy-rooting species may be rooted out of doors in beds of porous soil, sheltered and shaded, with the cover of bell-glass, cloche or jam-jar. Slow-rooting kinds may be rooted in cold frames, or pans or pots in the cool greenhouse, or in a propagating case or frame, as with soft-wood cuttings.

Cuttings taken in the growing season vary considerably in the time they take to root or 'strike', according to the species of plant. Cuttings of many shrubs and trees are difficult to root since transpiration losses cause death before root formation can be established. Many plants, hitherto found difficult, can now be successfully rooted under controlled conditions of humidity by what is now termed Mist Propagation (q.v.). Another aid to the rooting of cuttings is to dip the cut ends into a synthetic root-inducing hormone solution or powder, which has the effect of speeding up the

FIG. 73 Woody plant cuttings, taken with a heel in late summer: A. *Veronica* hybrid; B. *Chamaecyparis* sp.; C. *Senecio greyii*.

initial stages of forming a callus from which roots are budded.

Winter and Spring Softwood Cuttings. A number of flowering plants are propagated from new shoots, offsets or suckers, appearing in late winter or spring; notably Chrysanthemums, Dahlias and some herbaceous perennials. These are dealt with under their separate headings in this book.

Root Cuttings. Many plants with rather thickish, fleshy roots may be propagated from portions of the roots, 1 in. or so long, in early spring. The portions are best cut straight across at the top, slanting at the base, as a reminder of which way up to plant them. They may be planted out of doors in a sheltered border of warm porous soil, but better still in seed boxes, 2 in. apart, or pots, with the tops just below soil surface. Species of Aralia, Ailanthus, Clerodendron, Populus, Rhus, Yucca, Robinia and Wistaria, and several herbaceous plants such as Anchusa, Echium, Phlox, Decentra, Echinops, *Papaver orientale*, Romneya, Stokesia, and others noted in this book may be propagated in this way.

Leaf Cuttings. Not many plants are propagated by leaf cuttings. Of shrubs, Camellias (q.v.) may be treated in this way, the cutting being a small section of the stem with a leaf and axillary bud on it, inserted in a propagating case with the bud just below the surface. Mist helps rooting. Most leaf cuttings, however, are of succulent plants, or cacti, and tender plants with rather prominently veined leaves. The typical case is the ornamental leaved Begonia (q.v.). Some succulents such as Bryophyllum and Crassula produce plants in the angles of leaf serrations if laid on moist sand. Others, such as *Saintpaulia*, *Ramonda*, *Haberlea*, *Gesneria* and *Streptocarpus*, may be propagated by taking leaves with a stalk, and inserting the

FIG. 74   An axillary leaf cutting (*Camellia* sp.).

stalk on the rooting medium, under close conditions, the leaf blade not coming into contact with the surface. Lilies and similar bulbs may be increased by scale, actually leaf, cuttings; the scales being detached from the bulbs, and their bases just buried in a rooting medium in a propagating case or frame. The most effective ways of taking cuttings of plants are indicated throughout this book under the generic entries.

Cutworms. The larvae or caterpillars of Owlet Moths which feed on plants at soil level.

Cyananthus (ki-an-an'thus. Fam. Campanulaceae). Hardy alpine, herbaceous perennials, with somewhat fleshy roots and bright gay blue flowers, autumn.

Selection. C. incanus, 4 in., azure blue, *lobatus*, 4 in., bright purple-blue, *microphyllus*, violet-blue, from Himalayan regions, flowers, August–September, on trailing stems, like small periwinkles.

Cultivation. Plant in spring, well-drained soil, providing adequate moisture in summer, and protection from winter dampness. May also be grown in the cold alpine house.

Propagation. By seeds, April–May, out of doors, March, under glass, slight bottom heat; or cuttings of young shoots in July.

Cyanella (ki-an-el'la. Fam. Amaryllidaceae). Small bulbous plants from S. Africa, requiring cool greenhouse or frame cultivation in Britain.

Selection. C. capensis, 1 ft, has branching stems with racemes of purple flowers, July–August; and *odoratissima*, 1 ft, rose fading to yellow flowers, scented. July–August.

Cultivation. Pot in September–October, four to a 5-in. pot, standard compost, keeping cool during winter ($7°$ C. [$45°$ F.]), giving light and air as growth appears, and grow on, watering regularly, and after flowering, until leaves die, then dry off.

Propagation. By offset bulbs when repotting.

Cyan(e)us (-a, -um). Cyaneous, clear blue. Ex. *Centaurea cyanus*.

Cyanogas. See Calcium Cyanide.

Cyclamen, Sowbread (kik'la-men or sick'la-men. Fam. Primulaceae). Cormous plants originating in the

Mediterranean region, distinguished by their beautiful reflexed flowers.

Selection. Hardy species, for rock garden or planting under shrubs, where they may be undisturbed: *C. europaeum*, 4 in., marbled cordate leaves, slightly scented carmine flowers, late summer and autumn; *coum* (*hymale, orbiculatum, hiemale, vernum, ibericum, atkinsii*) has carmine, crimson-pink, white with deep red purple-centred flowering forms in winter and early spring, against marbled dark green leaves; *graecum*, rose pink, September; *repandum* has fragrant rose flowers in April–May; *neapolitanum* may flower rose, white or rose pink, according to variety, July–November. *C. rohlfsianum*, rose pink, autumn, is tender.

FIG. 75 *Cyclamen neapolitanum.*

Cultivation. Plant as soon as corms are available, August–October, in well-drained soil, enriched with bone meal and peat, 1–2 in. below the surface (*C. neapolitanum*) with roots uppermost, 4 in. apart, in rock garden, woodland or shrubbery.

Propagation. By seeds, sown out of doors, in warm, sheltered position; spring or summer, plant out corms a year later. Protect from mice.

In the Alpine House. All the above species may be grown in the alpine house or cold greenhouse, planted in large pans, compost of equal parts loam, peat and sand, with the tubers just below the surface. Water carefully by immersion, not from overhead; top-dress with a little leaf-mould annually, and leave undisturbed. They may be joined with other not-so-hardy species, such as *C. africanum*, rose to pale pink flowers, September–October; *balearicum*, fragrant white, veined lilac, flowers, March–April; *cilicium*, light rose, and crimson markings, September–October; *creticum*, pure white, scented, April; and *libanoticum*, fragrant, white or pale rose, March. A winter temperature of 7° C. (45° F.) should be maintained.

The Florist Cyclamen. Originating in *C. persicum*, native to the Eastern Mediterranean, this large-flowering Cyclamen, grown late autumn to spring bloom, in the cool greenhouse or home, is now offered in many strains; colours of white, pink, salmon, crimson to mauve in strains such as 'Sutton's Triumph', and double flowering in Kimono F_1 hybrids. Bought-in plants need cool room conditions, 13–15·5° C. (55–60° F.), careful watering, preferably by immersion, good light but not direct sun. When growth flags in late spring, gradually dry off, place in cold frame in pots on their side. Repot in August, water moderately, increasing with growth, and grow cool. Corms give the largest flowers in first year of blooming, thereafter there may be more flowers, but smaller.

Propagation. From seeds, usually sown in August, standard compost, or equal parts leaf-mould, loam and sand, temp. 13–15·5° C. (55–60° F.); pricked off into small thumb pots when large enough to handle; over-wintered cool in even light, potted to 3-in. pots in spring; and on to 4½–5-in. pots about June; grown on in cool moist atmosphere, shaded from hot sun, in cold greenhouse or frames, to flower in November onwards.

Diseases. Unlikely with correct watering and proper drainage; no water should lodge on the corms. Soft Rot (*Bacterium carotovorum*) may attack the corms, but dusting with a copper-lime dust checks it; also Grey Mould (*Botrytis cinerea*), which may attack leaves and stalks in over-moist, stagnant conditions.

Pests. Cyclamen Mites, Aphids, Thrips and Vine Weevils may attack the plants, and a good safeguard is the use of a systemic insecticide or malathion.

Cydonia, Quince (ki-do'ni-a or si-do'ni-a. Fam. Rosaceae). Now a genus of one species, *C. oblonga,* the Quince, deciduous tree to 25 ft, grown for its pear-shaped, yellow, fragrant fruit, exquisite for jelly-making and conserves. Origin doubtful, but the Vranja Quince is considered the finest.

Cultivation. Plant October–March, reasonably well-drained soil, pH 6·5, prune to shape only, when in leaf and after flowering in May. No significant diseases or pests. Propagation by layering in spring; or more slowly by seeds in April, outdoors.

Cymbidium (kim-bid'i-um. Fam. Orchidaceae). A genus of orchids deservedly popular because they give long-lasting flowers in December–May, require less heat than most orchids and only need repotting every second or third year.

Selection. C. eburneum, Khaisia, 2½ ft, white fragrant flowers, February; *giganteum,* N. India, 2½ ft, yellow, striped reddish-brown; *grandiflorum,* Sikkim, 2½ ft, green, yellow, purple, March; *insigne,* Annam, 2½ ft, rose and white, March; *lowianum,* Burma, 2 ft, green, yellow, dark-red, March–April; and *parishii,* Burma, 2½ ft, white and orange, summer; are all good, but there are also many fine and beautiful hybrids offered, just as easy.

Cultivation. Pot, and repot biennially, March–April, compost of equal parts loam and fibrous peat, with ½ part sphagnum moss, and crocks; water freely in growth, give good light, shade from hot sun, summer temps. 15·5–21° C. (60–70° F.); water moderately in winter, with minimum temp. of 7° C. (45° F.).

Propagation. By division of large plants, April.

Cyme. An inflorescence having a terminal flower with subsidiary branches also bearing terminal flowers, as in Forget-me-not.

Cynara (ki-na'-ra. Fam. Compositae). Thistle-like perennials of the Mediter-

ranean region, of which *C. cardunculus* is the Cardoon (q.v.) and *scolymus* the Globe Artichoke (q.v.).

Cynoglossum (ki-no-glos'sum. Fam. Boraginaceae). Biennial and perennial flowering herbs, readily raised from seeds.

Selection. C. amabile, China, Tibet, 1–2 ft, with racemes of beautiful blue, pink or white flowers forming loose panicles, in July–August; *creticum,* Mediterranean region, 1–2 ft, pale violet to red, August; and *nervosum,* 2½ ft, blue, July, are hardy biennials to grow from summer sowings; *officinale,* 1–3 ft, dark purple, is the native Hound's Tongue, a common name sometimes used for the whole genus.

Cultivation. Sow seeds in June–July on prepared outdoor seed-bed, thinning seedlings, and planting out where they are to flower, in well-drained, ordinary soil, in early autumn.

Cypella (ki-pel'la. Fam. Iridaceae). Bulbous plants of tropical America, rather tender.

Selection. C. herbertii, Brazil, 12 in., pretty hued yellow flowers, July, and *peruviana,* 12 in., stalked clusters of bright yellow flowers, spotted reddish-brown, are usually offered.

Cultivation. Pot in November, 3 in. deep in 5-in. pots, standard compost,

FIG. 76   Cyme (Yellow-wort or Centaury).

four or five bulbs to a pot; plunge in ashes or fibre in a cold frame until growth begins; then bring in to cool greenhouse for early summer flowering, watering regularly; dry off when leaves wither. May be planted out of doors, 3–4 in. deep in warm, sheltered borders, mild localities, and lifted annually.

Propagation. Usually by offsets, when repotting. By seeds sown as soon as ripe, and available.

Cyperus (ki-per′us or si-per′us. Fam. Cyperaceae). A large genus of reeds or grass-like plants, chiefly native to warm climates, and therefore doubtfully hardy.

Selection. C. alternifolius, Madagascar, 1½ ft, is the Umbrella Grass, with an attractive head of foliage and pale brown spikelets of flowers; with good vs. in *gracilis,* slender growing, and *nanus compactus,* 1 ft, a dwarf form; *diffusus,* Tropics, to 3 ft, with greenish-yellow spikelets; and *papyrus,* Egypt, to 10 ft, the Paper Plant; are grown in pots, for placing in indoor pools, or outdoor ponds for the summer. *C. longus,* the native Galingale, 2–4 ft, is useful for the large pond or lake, and hardy in the south and mild districts.

Cultivation. Pot in March, standard compost, keep well watered, stand in saucer of water in hot weather (as such makes a pretty house-plant), syringe often. Water moderately in winter, temp. 7° C. (45° F.).

Propagation. By division in spring. By seeds sown in pans, spring, bottom heat of 15·5° C. (60° F.).

Cypress. See *Chamaecyparis* and *Cupressus,* and *Taxodium.*

Cypripedium, Lady's Slipper (kip-re-pe′di-um or sip-re-pe′di-um. Fam. Orchidaceae). An important and interesting genus of orchids, almost unique in possessing two fertile stamens where other orchids have only one. Sometimes referred to four separate genera. *Cypripedium, Paphiopedilum, Phragmipedilum* and *Selenipedium.* They may be considered as one here. All are characterized by the inflated pouched flower, and invite attention by their relatively easy culture, and readiness to furnish long-lasting bloom.

Selection. The true *Cypripedium* section includes hardy species, some of which can be grown outdoors under

rather cool, shady, but frostproof conditions, and well-drained peaty soil, with winter protection. *C. acaule,* N. U.S.A., greenish, rose and purple, May; *arietinum,* Canada, greenish-brown, red, May; *calceolus,* N. Asia, 1½ ft, reddish brown, yellow, summer; *candidum,* N. America, 1 ft, greenish brown and white, June–July; *guttatum,* Siberia, snow-white and rose; *japonicum,* Japan,

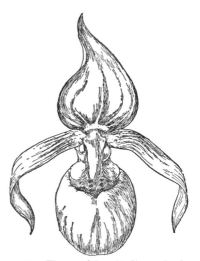

FIG. 77   Flower of *Cypripedium calceolus,* Lady's Slipper.

6 in., white and crimson, June; *macranthon,* Tibet, 1 ft, purple; *montanum,* Oregon, 1 ft, brownish-purple; *pubescens,* N. America, 1½ ft, yellowish brown and yellow, May–June; and *reginae,* American Mocassin flower, 2 ft, white and rose, June, and pure white v. *album,* are worth trying; or may be grown in pots in the cool greenhouse, together with Nepalese *insigne,* yellowish, brown and white, winter, and its vs. *chantinii,* violet-purple spotted; *sanderae,* primrose-yellow; *sanderianum,* yellow, and many others; and *villosum,* India, 1 ft, orange-red and purplish; May, and vs.; where winter temp. of at least 7° C. (45° F.) can be maintained. For the warm greenhouse, minimum winter

temp. 13° C. (55° F.), a short list in-cludes *C. barbatum*, Malacca, 1 ft, white and purple, spring and summer, and several vs.; *bellatulum*, Burma, 1 ft, white, purple-maroon, spring; and v. *album*; *boxallii*, India, 1 ft, pale green, brown, spring; *callosum*, Cochin China, 1 ft, white and chocolate, spring–summer; *charlesworthii*, Burma, 1 ft, white and rose, late summer; *druryi*, India, 6 in. greenish yellow and black; *fairieanum*, Assam, 1 ft, white and purple, autumn; *lawrenceanum*, Borneo, 1 ft, white and purple, summer; and v. *hyeanum*, white and green; *niveum*, Malaya, 6 in., white, June; and *venustum*; in most of these the foliage tends to persist, and is mottled. There are innumerable hybrids of character, which may be seen at shows, and selected from the catalogues of Orchid specialists.

Cultivation. For the greenhouse, plants are potted in April, in pots about one-third full of crocks, and a compost of 1 part fibrous loam, 2 parts peat, 1 part sphagnum moss, with coarse sand to ensure good drainage, watering liberally in active growth, syringing freely in hot weather temp. 15.5–24° C. (60–75° F.); more moderately in winter. Propagated by division in April.

Plants of the *Phragmipedilum* section belong to tropical America, and require hothouse conditions, with winter temps. of 13–15.5° C. (55–60° F.). *C. carcinum*, Peru, 1 ft, pale green and white, summer; *caudatum*, Peru, 1½ ft, creamy white, green, spring; *schlimii*, New Granada, 1 ft, white and rose, and its whiter v. *albiflorum*, winter, are well-known kinds. Few, if any, of the *Selenipedium* section appear to be in cultivation.

Cultivation. Pot in April, compost of equal parts fibrous loam, Osmunda fibre and sphagnum moss, with crushed brick and coarse sand, and pots half-crocked; water freely in growth, summer temps. of 18–27° C. (65–80° F.); sparingly in winter, temp. at night not less than 13° C. (55° F.).

Propagation. By division in April.

Cyrtomium (kir-to'mi-um. Fam. Polypodiaceae). The species chiefly grown is *C. falcatum* (*Aspidium falcatum*), native to Japan, China and S. Asia, to 1 ft, a pretty decorative fern with leathery fronds, as an indoor plant, or

for the cool greenhouse, winter temp. 7° C. (45° F.), being evergreen and durable; water freely in growth, sparingly in winter; has several vs.

Cystopteris, Bladder Fern (kis-top'ter-is. Fam. Polypodiaceae). Small, elegant hardy ferns, rather delicate and brittle, losing their fronds in autumn and being dormant to spring.

Selection. C. fragilis, 8 in., is native and charming, with vs. *dentata* and *dickieana*; and *alpina* and *montana* are rarities of Teesdale and Scottish moun-tains respectively.

Cultivation. May be grown in pots in cold frame, greenhouse or alpine house, compost of equal parts loam, fibrous peat, leaf-mould and coarse sand; or sheltered places out of doors; must have shade.

Propagation. By division in April. By spores sown in a cold frame in autumn.

Cytisus, Broom (kit'i-sus; sit'i-sus by usage. Fam. Leguminosae). Deciduous and evergreen shrubs, flowering freely in second or third year from seed, invaluable on light soils and poor soils.

Selection. C. albus, White Spanish Broom, Spain, Portugal, to 12 ft, white, pea-shaped flowers, May–June; *bat-tandieri*, NW. Africa, to 15 ft, a tree form, deciduous silvery leaves, bright yellow short racemes of flowers, June; × *dallimorei*, to 8 ft, rose and crimson, May; × *praecox*, 3–5 ft, creamy-yellow, May; *scoparius*, the Scots Broom, to 8 ft, yellow, May–June, and its vs. 'Firefly', red-brown and yellow, 'Lord Lam-bourne', crimson and yellow, 'Golden Sunlight', bright golden-yellow; and many hybrids, of which *sulphureus*, the Moonlight Broom, to 4 ft, with sulphur yellow flowers, is good. Dwarfer species for small gardens include *C. ardoinii*, 6 in., golden yellow, April–May; × *beanii*, 1½ ft, deep yellow, May; *demissus*, SE. Europe, 3 in., yellow and reddish-brown; × *kewensis*, 1½ ft, creamy yellow; *procumbens*, to 2 ft, yellow; *purpureus*, Europe, purple, May, and its v. *albus*, and *atropurpurea*, a fine purple; and × *versicolor*, 2 ft, pale yellow and purple.

The evergreens are often too tender for outdoors. *C. canariensis*, Canary Islands, to 6 ft, is the Genista of florists, with fragrant, bright yellow flowers, May–July, its v. *ramosissimus* being smaller; × *racemosus*, to 6 ft, flowers earlier; both may be grown in the cold greenhouse in pots.

Cultivation. Plant when young out of pots, in spring, well-drained, friable soil, sunny positions, as older plants do not transplant well. Prune after flowering, cutting flowered shoots back to within a bud or two of their base, but not into old wood. Plants grow very leggy in time, and it is better to replace them than to attempt regeneration.

Propagation. Most species and some hybrids are readily raised from seeds, sown in pans or boxes, standard compost, in cool greenhouse or frame; transplanted to pots as soon as large enough without root disturbance. By cuttings of young shoots in August, inserted in cold frame. Choice kinds may be grafted on Laburnum stock, particularly in making standard type brooms.

D

Daboecia, St Dabeoc's Heath (dab-oi'ki-a. Fam. Ericaceae). Sometimes described as the Irish Heath, *D. cantabrica*, of SW. Europe, the Azores and Eire, 1–3 ft, is a pretty evergreen shrub, with erect racemes of rosy-purple, pendent urn-shaped flowers, June–October; v. *alba* flowers pure white; *atropurpurea*, a darker purple; and *bicolor* has white and rosy-purple flowers on the same plant; *azorica*, Azores, 9 in., with rich crimson flowers, June–July, is more compact, but only hardy enough for warm sheltered spots in mild, frost-free localities.

Cultivation. Plant October or April–May; lime-free, peat-enriched, well-drained soil, in good light, but sheltered from hard frost. May also be grown in the alpine house, in deep pans.

Propagation. By cuttings of young shoots, in cold frame, July–August; by layering in spring; by seeds, sown in spring, in cold frame.

Dacrydium (dak-rid'i-um. Fam. Taxaceae). Ornamental evergreen conifers, resembling the Cypresses, but only hardy enough for the mildest localities, where *D. cupressinum*, the Rimu or Red Pine of New Zealand, to 30 ft, of graceful habit, and *franklinii*, the Huon Pine of Tasmania, to 30 ft, with slender drooping branches like a weeping Cypress, may be tried.

Cultivation. Plant October or March–April; well-drained, peat-enriched sandy loam, in sheltered position.

Propagation. By seeds in spring, or by cuttings, standard composts, in propagating frame, slight bottom heat of 15·5° C. (60° F.).

Dactylis (dak'til-is. Fam. Gramineae). The one species, *D. glomerata*, 1–3 ft, Cocksfoot grass, is sometimes useful for ground cover under trees, and has variegated leafed forms sometimes grown for decorative purposes. May be raised from seeds, sown in spring, ordinary soil, and propagated by division.

Daddy-long-legs. *See* Crane Flies.

Daffodil, Daffydowndilly. The common English name for *Narcissus pseudonarcissus*; and more broadly applied to Narcissi with trumpet-like flowers. See *Narcissus*.

Dahlia (dah'li-a; day'li-a by usage. Fam. Compositae). Herbaceous perennial plants with tuberous root-stocks, natives of Mexico, and grown as half-hardy perennials for the galaxy of colourful bloom furnished for the summer and autumn in flower-heads that vary from single-rayed forms with a centre disk to multi-petalled blooms, varying in size, shape and arrangement almost infinitely.

Selection. Botanically the genus is one of ten or so species, few of which, however, are in cultivation. Introduced to Madrid, Spain, in 1789, the early dahlias spread to France and England in 1802 to 1815, chiefly *D. coccinea* (parent source of single dahlias), *pinnata* (a parent of double dahlias) and *rosea* (*variabilis*) (chief parent of garden dahlias). Later *D. excelsa* and *imperialis*, species growing 6–20 ft naturally, gave stature to many garden dahlias, and *juarezii*, introduced in 1864, gave rise to the Cactus strains and intermediates. Today the garden dahlias are variations and hybrids of these species, and probably number thousands, with new additions being made every year. Horticulturally garden dahlias are now ordered according to the classifications and rules of the National Dahlia Society, as follows; Typical varieties cited.

1. *Single.* Flowers with a single outer ring of ray florets, surrounding a central disk: (*a*) Show Singles: 'Murillo'; (*b*) Singles: Coltness hybrids; (*c*) Mignon: 'G. F. Hemerick', 'Lady Aileen', 'Sneezy'.

2. *Star.* Small, single-flowered, with twisted and pointed ray florets: 'White Star'.

3. *Anemone-flowered.* Single-flowered with central disk of tubular elongated

flowers. Mixed vs.: 'Bridesmaid', 'Comet', 'Guinea', 'Honey', 'Roulette'.

4. *Collarette*. Flowers with one or more rings of flat ray florets, and an inner ring or collar of shorter florets. (*a*) Collarette Single: 'Emperor's Waltz', 'Swan Lake'. (*b*) Paeony-flowered: 'Gigolo', 'Grand Duc'. (*c*) Decorative: 'Libretto', 'Lilac Butterfly'.

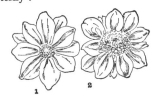

FIG. 78 Types of Dahlia flowers: 1. Single.2.Anemone-flowered.3.Decorative. 4. Cactus. 5. Show. 6. Pompon.

5. *Paeony-flowered*. Flowers with two or more rows of ray florets and a central disk. (*a*) Large, over 7 in. across; (*b*) Medium, 5–7 in. across; (*c*) Small, less than 5 in. across: 'Bishop of Landaff', 'Intensive'.

6. *Decorative*. Flowers fully double, showing no disk, with long broad ray florets, flattish or slightly twisted, usually blunt pointed, Graded: (*a*) Giant, over 10 in. across: 'Bonafide', 'Croydon Snotop', 'Epping Forest',

'Hamari Girl', 'Holland Festival', 'Lavender Perfection', 'Lavengro', 'Prime Minister', 'The Master', 'Wheezy'. (*b*) Large, 8–10 in. across: 'Alibi', 'Blarney Stone', 'Gaudy', 'Polly Bergen', 'Showman's Delight'. (*c*) Medium, 6–8 in. across: 'Arc de Triomphe', 'First Lady', 'Ballego's Glory', 'Jescot Bizan', 'Glory of Naarden', 'New Country', 'Betty Russell', 'Terpo', 'Rendevous'. (*d*) Small, 3–6 in. across: 'Amethyst', 'Angora', 'Chinese Lantern', 'Dedham', 'Gerrie Hoek', 'Glory of Heemstede', 'Honey Glow', 'Fête d'Orange', 'Horn of Plenty', 'Hamari Fiesta', 'Never Before', 'Red Emperor'. (*e*) Miniature, less than 3 in. across: 'David Howard', 'Kochelsee', 'Lark', 'Newby', 'Safe Shot', 'White Nymph'.

7. *Double Show and Fancy*. Flower-heads double, more than 4 in. across, with almost globular shape, disk florets like the outer but smaller; florets with margins incurved, tubular, short and blunt pointed: 'Bonny Blue', 'Gloire de Lyon', 'Merlin', 'Standard'.

8. *Pompon*. Flower-heads rounded, like those of Class 7 but smaller: (*a*) Large, 3–4 in. across: 'Jean Lister', 'Mary Paterson', 'Rothesay Superb'. (*b*) Medium, 2–3 in. across: 'Leo', 'Grand Willo', 'Wolf Whistle', 'Yellow Gem'. (*c*) Small, less than 2 in. across: 'Arthur Kearley', 'Crossfield Ebony', 'Golden Willo', 'Jacky Brooks', 'Kym Willo', 'Master Michael', 'Little Conn', 'Little Willo', 'Noreen', 'Rhonda', 'Sulphurea', 'Willo's Violet'.

9. *Cactus*. Flower-heads double, no disk showing; ray florets usually pointed, twisted in part, or straight or incurving. Graded: (*a*) Giant, flower-heads over 10 in. across: 'Crimson Beauty', 'Herbert Apps', 'Polar Star', 'Royal Rothesay', 'Searchlight'. (*b*) Large, 8–10 in. across: 'Arab Queen', 'Drakenburg', 'Fireglow', 'Frontispiece', 'Paul Critchley', 'Smokey', 'Surprise'. (*c*) Medium, 6–8 in. across: 'Best Seller', 'Apache', 'Fascination', 'Firerays', 'Frigid Friend', 'Raiser's Pride', 'Seranade', 'Tu Tu', 'Vuurvogel', 'Yellow Galator'. (*d*) Small, 3–6 in. across: 'Andries Orange', 'Arlett', 'Doris Day', 'Goya's Venus', 'Irena Marina', 'Klankstad Kerkrade', 'Pink Cheerio',

'Pontiac', 'Preference', 'Salmon Rays', 'Tamara'. (*e*) Miniature, less than 3 in. across.

10. *Semi-Cactus*. Flower-heads double, ray florets broad at the base, margins revolute towards tip, slightly twisted for about half their length. Graded: (*a*) Giant, flower-heads over 8 in. across: 'Amber Cocorico', 'Cocorico', 'Frontispiece', 'Respectable'. (*b*) Large, 6–8 in. across: 'Cosmopolitan', 'Glorification', 'Hoek's White', 'Margot Fonteyn', 'Nantenan'. (*c*) Medium, 3–6 in. across: 'Adare', 'Autumn Fire', 'Exotica', 'Fleur de Holland', 'Fury', 'Hamari Bride', 'Ravel', 'Rotterdam', 'Sugar Candy', 'Tracey Short'. (*d*) Small, less than 3 in. across: 'Adelaide', 'Pharos', 'Purity', 'Rose Preference', 'Vin de France'.

11. *Miscellaneous*. Any dahlias which do not fall into any one of the above classes: such as Orchid-flowered Dahlias: Wonder Dahlias.

12. *Dwarf Bedding*. Plants not exceeding 2 ft in height, which may have flower-heads characteristic of the above classes: Cactus type—'Downham', 'Janet Miner', 'Park Delight', 'Park Princess', 'Park Wonder'. Decorative type—'Arnhem', 'Elburg', 'Golden Pride', 'Rocquencourt', 'Rothesay Castle', 'Snow-white'. Single type—'Henriette', 'Red Sparks', 'Signal', 'Summer Beauty'.

Cultivation. May be planted in any soil that is of some depth, and moisture-retentive; well dug and enriched with organic matter—manure, compost, peat, etc., in autumn/winter. A sunny position is essential, but unexposed to strong winds. Plant in May or early June, when danger from spring frosts is past; at depths of 3–6 in., to accommodate roots, spacing plants at the equivalent to their average height. Stake stoutly at planting time. May be given a complete fertilizer prior to planting; and a quick-acting nitrogenous feed after establishment. Water if necessary in dry weather; top-dress with an organic mulch after rain. Remove spent flower-heads regularly. Thin branches on plants chosen to grow large or exhibition blooms to about five or six. When autumn frost blackens the foliage, cut top growth down to 4–6 in., lift the roots

carefully with a fork. The roots should be air-dried and soil removed, and then stored under temps. of 5–7° C. (42–45° F.), in an atmosphere slightly damp such as a cellar. They can be placed on slatted shelves, or placed in boxes loosely covered with peat, sand or vermiculite. It is important to see that only healthy, firm roots are stored. Dusting with a copper or sulphur fungicidal dust is a useful precaution against storage rots and tubers should be placed out of reach of mice or slugs.

Propagation. By root division. This can be done in spring. The vegetative buds from which new growth develops grow on the collar of the year-old stems. When roots are divided it is essential to see that each separated tuber is intact with a piece of stem carrying one or more buds, cutting them with a sharp knife. The tuberous divisions may be started into growth in pots under glass, or planted out where they are to grow in May.

FIG. 79   A Dahlia root, with shoots to be taken as cuttings for propagation.

By cuttings in early spring. Over-wintered roots are planted shallowly in moist peat or soil compost; watered well and started into growth in heated greenhouse (7–13° C. [45–55° F.]). When shoots reach 2–3 in. long, they are detached at the base with a piece of the collar as a 'heel', and inserted in small pots, or boxes at 3 in. apart, standard compost, kept watered and growing until it is safe to plant them out in May.

FIG. 80 A Dahlia shoot-cutting ready for rooting.

when night temps. do not fall below 7° C. (45° F.). Simple stem cuttings (without the 'heel') can also be taken but root more slowly, preferably in a propagating case with bottom heat (15·5° C. [60° F.]).

By seeds, sown in March–April, under glass, standard compost, bottom heat of 18° C. (65° F.), in pans or boxes. Most types of dahlias can be raised in this way, though specific varieties can only be propagated surely by vegetative means —division or cuttings.

Diseases. Powdery Mildew (*Erysiphe polygoni*) may appear under moist conditions in massed plants, also Smut (*Entyloma dahliae*). Infected foliage is best removed and the plants sprayed or dusted with a karathane or copper fungicide. Wilt (*Verticillium dahliae*) may attack through the roots, and calls for the resting of the soil from dahlia-growing for at least three years, and protection of subsequent replanting with a fungicidal dusting of planting holes. Stem Rot (*Sclerotinia sclerotiorum*) may cause a soft rot and wilt of a plant under wet conditions, towards the end of a season. A whitish mould shows on stems, and the fungus sclerotia develop inside the stem. Infected tissue must be carefully cut out and burnt; roots should be dusted with a fungicide before storing. Grey Mould (*Botrytis cinerea*) is sometimes troublesome in wet weather, but prompt removal of spent flower heads and the use of a copper fungicide or captan will contain it. Unfortunately, Dahlias are subject to virus infections, notably Mosaic, which shows in a yellow-mottling of leaves and stunted growth; Ring Spot shows as yellow or pale green rings or markings on leaves; Tomato Spotted Wilts as concentric rings or wavy lines; Streak as brown spots and stripes on stems and leaf stalks; and Stunt as a dwarfing of growth. Plants may not die immediately, but it is essential to rogue out virus-infected plants and burn. Good culture and proper spacing of plants are necessary to healthy stock.

Pests. Aphids (Green-fly), Leaf-hoppers, Red Spider Mites and Thrips attack dahlias, and much can be done to prevent infestations by the use of a systemic insecticide. Otherwise, malathion, gamma-BHC or a derris insecticide can be applied. The Bishop Bug (*Lygus pratensis*) may attack buds and leaves, causing distortion, in July–August; malathion may be used in control. Earwigs ascend plants to feed in blooms and cause distortion. A band of fruit-tree banding grease round the stem of a plant near the base, and its stake, stops the pests getting access, while insecticidal dusts can be applied in summer.

Daisy. See *Bellis.*

Dalapon. Common name of 2,2-dichloroproprionic acid, the active ingredient of herbicides for the control of couch and other coarse grasses. *See* Herbicides.

Damask Rose. See *Rosa damascena.*

Dame's Rocket, Dame's Violet. See *Hesperis.*

Damping Down. A watering operation carried out in the greenhouse, consisting of wetting floors, stages and walls by sprinkling. It is designed to increase humidity in warm greenhouses, to lower temperatures on hot sunny days, and maintain a good growing atmosphere for tender plants, but should be done in the earlier half of the day when temperatures are rising.

Damping Off. Describes the collapse of seedling plants at the soil surface, usually caused by a soil fungus (*Pythium* sp., etc.), and aggravated by damp conditions, low temperatures and over-crowding of seedlings. It can be prevented by use of sterilized loam composts and careful watering, or dressing seeds with a thiram fungicidal dressing. Attacks may be minimized by promptly removing infected seedlings, and watering with a fungicidal solution (such as Cheshunt Compound).

Damson and Bullace (*Prunus insititia*). The differences are arbitrary; damsons are the trees which give oval, purple, fruits; bullaces round fruits which may be black or white or intermediate in colour. As developments of the same species, both make very hardy trees of the stone fruit type, and their culture is on the same lines as for plums.

Selection. Damsons—Bradley's King, Farleigh, Merryweather, Prune and Early River's. Bullaces—Black, Langley, Shepherd's and White. Trees are usually grown as half-standards or standards, on Brompton or Common Plum root-stocks, and their culture is the same as for plums (q.v.). On account of their hardiness, however, they may be planted farther north than gages, and make good windbreaks for the exposed side of an orchard.

Danaë (da'ni. Fam. Liliaceae). The one species is *D. racemosa*, the Alexandrian Laurel, of Asia Minor and Persia, an evergreen shrub of 2–4 ft, with bright green, leaf-like cladodes on bamboo-like stems, excellent for cutting; the flowers are insignificant.

Cultivation. Plant in moist soil, in shade, October or March–April. Propagation by seeds, in spring, or by simple division, April.

Dandelion (*Taraxacum officinale*). As a weed, the common dandelion runs to over a hundred forms, and may be readily controlled by a 2,4-D selective herbicide (q.v.). Selective forms are worth growing for their leaves, used in salads when young. The seeds are sown shallowly in drills, 1 ft apart, in April, in porous loam soil, thinned to 8 in. apart, and grown on to autumn, when the roots may be lifted and stored; and subsequently forced at intervals in the dark as with Seakale (q.v.).

Danes' Blood, Danewort. See *Sambucus ebulus*.

Daphne (daf'ne. Fam. Thyme-laeaceae). Deciduous and evergreen shrubs, beautiful in spring with fragrant flowers, often of borderline hardiness.

Selection. Of the evergreens *D. arbuscula*, Hungary, 6 in., rosy-pink flowers, June; *blagayana*, Carniola and Styria, 1 ft, creamy white, April–May, needing a lime-free soil; *cneorum*, the highly fragrant Garland Flower, Central and S. Europe, ½–1 ft, deep pink, May–June; *collina*, Mediterranean, Asia Minor,

FIG. 81 *Daphne mezereum*, Mezereon.

2 ft, lilac-pink, May–June, needing warm shelter; × *neapolitana*, 2 ft, rosy lilac, March–June, tolerant of lime; *odora*, China, Japan, to 6 ft, reddish-purple, January–March, needing shelter for its early flowers; *petraea*, N. Italy, 3–6 in., spreading, rose, May–June, best in the alpine house, with its v. *grandiflora*, larger flowers; *retusa*, W. China, 1–2 ft, deep rose, May; and *sericea*, of the E. Mediterranean, 1–2 ft, rosy-pink, May–June, is best in the alpine house. Among the deciduous, *D. mezereum*, the Mezereon of Europe and Asia Minor, to 5 ft, with lilac-pink flowers, March–April, and its vs. *alba*,

white-flowering, and *grandiflora*, are the easiest to grow; × *burkwoodii* ('Somerset)', 4 ft, pale pink, May–June, is good; *genkwa*, China, lilac-blue, April–May, needs to be in lime-free soil, partial shade and on its own roots to succeed—very beautiful although the flowers are without scent; *D. laureola*, to 3 ft, is the evergreen Spurge Laurel and native, useful in woodland and shade.

Cultivation. All Daphnes appreciate good drainage, and ample humus in the soil. Plant evergreens in early autumn or March–April; deciduous October–March. Partial shade is usually appreciated. In the coldest areas, evergreens are best grown in the alpine house.

Propagation. Mostly by cuttings of firm shoots, July–August, inserted in a propagating case. By layers of prostrate forms, in spring. By seeds sown in March, standard compost, bottom heat of 15.5° C. (60° F.).

Daphniphyllum (dap-ni-pil'lum. Fam. Euphorbiaceae). The chief species grown is *D. macropodum* (*glaucescens*), China, Korea, Japan, to 8 ft, for its rather striking foliage of rich green, oblong leaves, glaucous underneath, and reasonably hardy for moist shade, and soil, in mild localities. Propagation by cuttings of firm young shoots, in propagating case, in July; *humile* is a spreading shrub from Japan, 1–2 ft, less often seen, but requiring similar culture.

Darlingtonia (dar-ling-ton'i-a. Fam. Sarraceniaceae). The sole species, *D. californica*, the Californian Pitcher Plant, is an interesting insectivorous plant, producing a rosette of hollow leaves with a hood-like top and bi-lobed appendage, mottled white and veined reddish; and inverted yellow-green and red flowers in April–May. It may be grown out of doors in mild localities, given a pocket of peat with chopped sphagnum moss and crushed charcoal, in a damp, shady spot; or in a cool greenhouse, in similar compost, in shade, and kept well watered.

Cultivation. Plant, pot and repot biennially, in early July. Stand pots in deep saucers, packed with sphagnum moss, and keep always moist.

Propagation. By division of rhizomatous roots, July. By seeds, sown on living sphagnum moss, firmed evenly, in a pan, covered by a glass, April–June.

Dasy-. Prefix of compound words, signifying hairy. Ex. *Sedum dasyphyllum* —hairy-leaved.

Date Palm. See *Phoenix dactylifera*.

Datura (da-tu'ra. Fam. Solanaceae). A genus of poisonous plants with narcotic properties, appreciated horticulturally for the beauty of their trumpet-like flowers, either annual or shrubby.

Selection. D. metel, India, 3–5 ft, has large cordate leaves, and single, white trumpet flowers, 9 in. long, 4 in. across, June; v. *fastuosa* (*D. fastuosa*), 2–3 ft, violet or red, white inside, flowers, July; *meteloides*, Texas to Mexico, 2½ ft, is naturally perennial, but grown as an annual, with bluish-violet or white, fragrant flowers, July; and *stramonium* is the native Thorn Apple, 2 ft, with white funnel-shaped flowers, July followed by prickly, apple-shaped fruits, but dangerous to cattle if allowed to get out of hand. All the above are grown as annuals, being sown under glass in March, with bottom heat of 15.5° C. (60° F.), pricked off and planted out in May, though *D. stramonium* often seeds itself out of doors. The shrubby kinds, for greenhouse culture, include *D. suaveolens*, the Angel's Trumpet of Mexico, to 10 ft, with white fragrant flowers, August, and a double form; *cornigera* (*Brugmansia knightii*), Mexico, to 10 ft, with large, creamy white trumpet flowers, summer; and *chlorantha*, 4 ft, yellow, scented flowers, August–October.

Cultivation. The shrubby types, naturally evergreen, may be treated as deciduous in a cool greenhouse, grown in the border or 12-in. pots, watered freely in growth, very little in winter, with minimum temperature of 7° C. (45° F.). Prune after flowering.

Propagation. By cuttings of firm shoots, in spring or summer, in propagating case, bottom heat of 18° C. (65° F.).

Daucus (dou'kus. Fam. Umbelliferae). Of some sixty species, the only species of interest is *D. carota*, the Carrot (q.v.).

Davallia (da-val'li-a. Fam. Polypodiaceae). Handsome ferns of tropical and warm countries for the greenhouse or as indoor plants.

Selection. D. canariensis, the Hare's-foot fern, so called from its prostrate stems covered with fine, brown hair-like scales, W. Mediterranean, is a good indoor pot plant; *bullata*, Japan, China, etc.; *denticulata* and vs., Old World Tropics; *mariesii*, pretty Japanese dwarf; *pyxidata*, New S. Wales, with large fronds; *solida*, Malaya, etc., and vs. *superba* and *fijiensis* with many forms; and *trichomanoides*, Malaya, may be grown in the cool greenhouse, as pot or basket plants, minimum winter temp. 10° C. (50° F.).

Cultivation. A compost of 3 parts fibrous peat, 1 part leaf-mould and coarse sand to give good drainage, usually suits, with sphagnum moss for basket growth. Water freely, by immersion, not overhead, in active growth; sparingly in winter; good light.

Propagation. By spores in spring; by division of rhizomatous stems, when repotting in April.

Davidia (da-vid'i-a. Fam. Cornaceae). The sole species, *D. involucrata*, W. China, is a deciduous tree, to 40 ft, with large, bright green, white felted beneath, leaves, and pendent clusters of tiny flowers, enclosed by two white bracts, one half as large as the other, in May, giving it the name of the Dove or Handkerchief tree; its v. *vilmoriniana* is more effective as the foliage is smooth on both sides and contrasts better.

Cultivation. Plant October–March, in well-drained but humus-rich, moist soil, and preferably in a sunny, warm, sheltered spot. Takes a few years to come to a flowering rhythm; and is not for cold, exposed or windy situations. Little pruning needed, but can be done after flowering.

Propagation. By cuttings in July–August, of young shoots, in cold frame. By seeds, in April.

Day Lily. See *Hemerocallis*.

DDT. Dichloro - diphenyl - trichloro-ethane; a persistent, pervasive, synthetic insecticide, harmful to wild life; to be used with great care. *See* Insecticides.

Dead Nettle. See *Lamium*.

Dealbatus (-a, -um). Mealy, powdery. Ex. *Acacia dealbata*.

Deca-. Prefix indicating ten. Ex. Decapetalous, ten-petalled.

Decaisnea (de-kais'ne-a. Fam. Lardizabalaceae). Deciduous shrubs with feathery pinnate foliage, panicles of yellow-green flowers and striking pod-like fruits. *D. fargesii*, W. China, is hardy, growing to 8 ft, with June flowers followed by metallic-blue fruits. Plant October–March, in well-drained but moisture-retentive soil, and a warm, sheltered position out of reach of late spring frost. *D. insignis*, Himalaya, is similar, with golden-yellow edible fruits, but not so hardy, and only eligible for the mildest localities.

Propagation. By cuttings, July, in a propagating case, bottom heat of 18° C. (65° F.).

Deciduous. Falling off; usually of leaves, lasting only a season.

Deciduous Cypress. See *Taxodium*.

Declinatus (-a, -um). Declinate, bent downwards. Ex. *Centaurea declinata*.

Decumaria (de-kum-a'ri-a. Fam. Saxifragaceae). Two deciduous climbing shrubs, clinging by aerial roots, for warm walls in mild localities, chiefly of the south-west.

Selection. D. barbara, SE. U.S.A., to 30 ft, has corymbs of small white flowers, June–July; and *sinensis*, Central China, to 15 ft, flowers in May with smaller corymbs of white, scented flowers.

Cultivation. Plant October–March, well-drained average soil, warm, frost-free walls. Prune after flowering, or in February to get branching.

Propagation. By cuttings of firm shoots, under handlights or in cold frame, July–August.

Decumbens. Decumbent, of prostrate stems with upturned tips. Ex. *Cytisus decumbens*.

Decurrens. Decurrent; of leaves, when the stalks and leaf tissues extend down the stem. Ex. *Libocedrus decurrens*.

Decussatus (-a, -um). Decussate, parts at right angles, to form a square, as with opposite leaves in equal rows. Ex. *Phlox decussata*.

Defoliation. The loss or shedding of leaves.

Dehiscence. The opening of fruits or pods to shed their seeds; of stamens their pollen.

Delicatus (-a, -um). Charming.

Delphinium (del-pin'i-um. Fam

Ranunculaceae). A large genus of annual, biennial and perennial flowering herbs, from which plants may be grown for the greenhouse, the herbaceous border and rock garden.

Selection. Annuals. D. adjacis, S. Europe, 1–3 ft, the Rocket Larkspur, is the parent of colourful strains of annuals, such as double Hyacinth-flowered tall kinds, and dwarf, with single spikes of closely packed flowers, in white, pinks, scarlet, mauve and blue, in early summer; *consolida*, Europe, ½–3 ft, is parent to the branching Larkspurs, long-flowering and very fine in such forms as 'Exquisite Pink', 'Los Angeles', rose-salmon; 'Rosamond', bright rose; and 'Rosy Scarlet'; and tall-growing strains such as the 'Stock-flowered', 'Giant Imperial', 'Regal' and 'Supreme', which reach to 3 or 4 ft, are well worth growing. The naturally perennial *grandiflorum* has given rise to notable dwarfer forms, 'Azure Fairy', 'Blue Butterfly', 'White Butterfly' and 'Tom Thumb', of 1–1½ ft, which are usually grown as annuals. All the above may be grown as annuals, from seeds sown under glass in March, bottom heat of 15·5° C. (60° F.), to prick off and plant out for summer flowering; or seeds may be sown in June–July, on outdoor beds, thinned and planted in flowering positions in September to flower earlier the following year.

Perennials. These are chiefly the tall, noble plants of the herbaceous border, flowering from June onwards, which underwrite the greatness of the genus. They are now classed in two groups:

1. The 'Elatum' Type, with a long central flower raceme, and hybrids of *D. cheilanthum, elatum, formosum*, etc. They are subdivided into (a) single-flowered: 'Blue Beauty', 'Wrexham Glory'; (b) semi-double-flowered: 'Agnes Brooks', gentian blue; 'Anne Page', cornflower blue; 'Betty Baseley', Reckitt's-blue; 'Blackmore's Blue', sky blue, white eye; 'Blackmore's Glorious', mauve and pale blue; 'Bridesmaid', silvery mauve; 'C. F. Langdon', blue with black eye; 'Crystal', sky blue, white eye; 'Eva Gower', gentian blue; 'Frederick Grisewood', deep blue; 'George Bishop', mauve and blue;

'Glamour Girl', cobalt blue; 'Lady Eleanor', sky blue; 'Mrs Frank Bishop', gentian blue; 'Royalist', deep blue; 'Startling', violet; 'Swanlake', white; 'Watkin Samuel', rich sky blue; and hybrids of the 'Bishop' and 'Common-wealth' strains; (c) double-flowered: 'Alice Artindale', lilac and blue; 'Lady Eleanor', sky blue; 'Purple Ruffles', purple and deep blue.

2. The 'Belladonna' Type, with branching habit of shorter racemes, and mostly single sterile flowers, such as 'Blue Bees', clear pale blue; 'Lamartine', Oxford blue; 'Isis', mauve; 'Naples', gentian blue; 'Moerheimii', white; 'Orion', clear blue; 'Pink Sensation', clear pink; and 'Wendy', deep blue. Other hybrid strains are offered under 'Giant Pacific Hybrids', raised in California, and named forms such as 'Astolat', shades of pink; 'Black Knight', dark violet, and 'Galahad', clear white; and a dwarf bushy strain as 'Connecticut Yankees' growing only to 1½ ft.

Of the species, *brunonianum*, Himalaya, 1–1½ ft, large light blue flowers, June–July; *formosum*, to 3 ft, purple-blue, August; *nudicaule*, California, 1–1½ ft, red and yellow; and *zalil*, Persia, 1–2 ft, pale yellow, are worth growing in borders or sheltered rockeries.

Cultivation. Plant in March–April, in ground well dug and organically manured in the winter; lime to bring soil to pH 6·5, if acid, and give a top-dressing of a complete fertilizer in March. It is wise to thin shoots to the strongest ones of each crown in April, and stake. Spent flower spikes may be cut, leaving the foliage; finally cutting stems to within 6 in. of the soil in autumn.

Propagation. Perennial and choice varieties are best propagated by cuttings of young shoots, 3–4 inches long, severed close to the parent crown, in spring; rooting these in standard compost in pots or boxes in the cool greenhouse or frame, to plant out in early June. Species and mixed strains may be raised from seeds, sown under glass, March, bottom heat 18°C. (65° F.), or in boxes in a cold frame; germination should take place in 2 weeks. Seedlings may be pricked off, and transplanted to

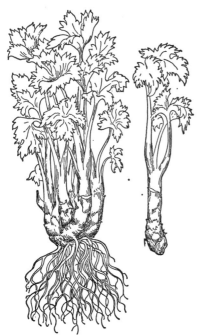

FIG. 82 A Delphinium root in spring, showing shoot detached at its base for rooting as a cutting.

outdoor positions when large enough. Seeds may also be sown in autumn, and seedlings over-wintered in a frame, with protection from slugs.

Diseases. Leaf Blotch (*Bacterium delphinii*) may cause black spotting and blotching; affected leaves may be removed and spraying with a captan fungicide carried out, though it is not easy to control the disease, and susceptible varieties could be rogued out. Powdery Mildew (*Erysiphe polygoni*) makes unsightly powdery white patches on leaves, etc., and calls for repeated applications with karathane or sulphur fungicide to bring under control. There is an incurable disorder known as 'Black Root Rot', affecting the roots of second-year plants; and stock should be lifted and burnt.

Pests. Slugs are the worst, and may be combated with metaldehyde baits, and covering crowns of plants for the winter with cinders. A dusting of a DDT, gamma-BHC insecticide when new growth begins will prevent damage by cutworm grubs, leather-jackets and wireworms.

Deltoides. Deltoid, delta- or triangular-shaped. Ex. *Dianthus deltoides*.

Dendrobium, Rock Lily (den-dro′bi-um. Fam. Orchidaceae). A huge genus of most attractive orchids, with clusters of beautiful blooms.

Selection. D. infundibulum, Burma 1–1½ ft, large, ivory-white flowers, May–June; *jamesianum*, Moulmein, 1–1½ ft, white and red lip, May–June; and *longicornu*, India, 1½ ft, white, May–June, may be grown in a cool green-house; watered freely in growth, but sparingly when dormant, winter temp. 7–13° C. (45–55° F.). *D. aureum*, India, Ceylon, 1½ ft, highly fragrant, yellow flowers, March; *chrysanthum*, Nepal, 3–6 ft, rich yellow, September, basket kind; *densiflorum*, India, 1–1½ ft, clear yellow, April–May; *fimbriatum*, India, to 4 ft, deep orange, March–April, *formosum* v. *giganteum*, Burma, to 3 ft white and gold, autumn; *monile*, China, Japan, 10 in., white; May; *nobile*, N India, etc., 2–3 ft, white and rosy pink, February–April, and several vs.; and *thyrsiflorum*, Burma, 1½–2 ft, white orange lip, spring; are for the warm greenhouse, winter temp. 13–18 C. (55–65° F.); liberal watering in growth, less in winter. Evergreen species such as *D. aggregatum*, N. India, 1 ft, orange yellow, spring; *bigibbum*, Queensland 1½ ft, magenta rose, September–October, *brymerianum*, Burma, 1–2 ft, yellow March–April; *phalaenopsis*, N. Australia 1–1½ ft, magenta and purplish red September, and vs.; need stove condi-tions, winter temps. of 15·5–21° C (60–70° F.), liberal watering March–August, then sparingly and keep cool while dormant.

Cultivation. Pot up in March–April when young growths are 2–3 in. long, in well-crocked pots, and a compost of parts Osmunda fibre, 1 part sphagnum moss and a little charcoal; well firmed and moistened.

Propagation. By division, when re-potting.

Dendromecon (den-drom'e-kon. Fam. Papaveraceae). The only species grown in gardens is *D. rigidum*, California, 2–10 ft, a half-hardy, glaucous evergreen shrub, with bright yellow, poppy-like flowers in summer; for mild localities, in well-drained, lightish loam, by a very warm and sheltered wall.

Propagation. By cuttings of well-ripened young shoots in summer, in small pots, in propagating case, with gentle bottom heat of 18° C. (65° F.).

Dens-canis. Dog's-tooth. Ex. *Erythronium dens-canis*.

Densus (-a, -um). Dense, close or crowded. Ex. *Pteris serrulata* v. *densa*.

Dentaria (den-ta'ri-a. Fam. Cruciferae). Perennial herbs, related to Cardamine, of which *D. bulbifera*, Europe, 1½–2 ft, large purple flowers, April; and *enneaphylla*, Italy, 1 ft, creamy-yellow flowers, May, may be planted in a woodland garden, in rich moist soil and shade. Propagation by careful division in spring.

Dentatus (-a, -um). Dentate, toothed, with teeth facing outward. Ex. *Ceanothus dentatus*.

FIG. 83   A dentate leaf.

Denticulatus (-a, -um). Denticulate, finely toothed. Ex. *Primula denticulata*.

Deodar. See *Cedrus deodara*.

Depressus (-a, -um). Depressed, flattened at the top. Ex. *Centaurea depressa*.

Derris. A natural insecticide prepared from the powdered tuberous root of *Derris elliptica*, a tropical climber. The most active principle is a nerve-paralysing poison, rotenone, which is toxic to most biting and sucking insects, such as Aphids, Thrips, Caterpillars, etc.; but non-toxic to humans and animals. It affects fish, however, and should not be used near fish-ponds. See Insecticides.

Desfontainea (des-fon-tain'i-a. Fam. Loganiaceae). The one species, *D. spinosa*, Chile, 4–10 ft, is a pleasing evergreen shrub, with small holly-like leaves, and attractive, funnel-shaped, shallowly lobed scarlet and yellow flowers in summer. It may be grown under warm sheltered conditions, in well-drained, humus-rich soil, in the south and west, or in a pot in the cold greenhouse. Propagation by 3-in. long tip cuttings in August, inserted in propagating frame, with slight bottom heat.

Deutzia (de-utz'i-a. Fam. Saxifragaceae). Deciduous flowering shrubs, mostly natives of China, which are hardy, and quite easy to grow.

Selection. D. discolor v. *major*, 4–6 ft, rose-tinted white flowers, June; *glomeruliflora*, to 6 ft, white flowers in clusters, May–June; *hypoglauca*, to 8 ft, blue-grey leaves, white clustered flowers, June; × *kalmiiflora*, 6 ft, pretty white and carmine, June; × *lemoinei*, to 6 ft, pure white flowers in erect panicles, May–June, and its compact form 'Boule de Neige'; *longifolia* v. *farreri* (*albida*), 12 ft, white, and v. *veitchii*, to 15 ft, the tallest of the genus, with rich rose flowers, June, and hybrids such as × 'Contraste', mauve pink, banded purple, flowers, June, and 'Magician', mauve-pink, edged white, flowers, June; × *magnifica*, 6 ft, double white, June–July; *monbeigii*, compact at 4–6 ft, white, May–June; *pulchra*, to 8 ft, drooping panicles of white, tinged pink flowers, May–June, is very fine, and has vs. *scabra*, 8–10 ft, graceful, white flowers, June–July, very fine in forms *candidissima*, double white, *macrocephala*, large panicles, 'Pride of Rochester', double white, flushed rose, and *watereri*, large flowers, white with rose outside; *setchuenensis* v. *corymbiflora*, to 6 ft, charming with white corymbs of flowers, June–July; and *vilmorinae*, 6–8 ft, white corymbs of bloom, June; these give plenty of scope for June beauty. *D. gracilis*, Japan, 3–4 ft, pure white flowers in racemes, may be forced under glass or grown outdoors, together with × *rosea*, soft rose and its forms *campanulata*, white and purple; *carminea*, purplish; and *grandiflora*, large flowering white, June; while the Chinese *grandiflora*, to 6 ft, is the earliest to flower, though its April white flowers are not too plentiful.

Cultivation. Plant October–March, any well-drained soil, with humus in it, lime-tolerant, but need sunny positions out of reach of late spring frosts. May be pruned after flowering, cutting flowered shoots hard back.

Propagation. By cuttings in propagaring case, with bottom heat of 15·5–18° C. (60–65° F.), July–August.

Devil-in-the-bush. See *Nigella*.

Dew. Condensed moisture from saturated air formed on the earth's and plant surfaces when temperatures fall rapidly during the night; if severe, the dew is converted to hoar frost.

Di-, Dis-. Prefix signifying two. Ex. *Diandrous*, with two stamens; *Disanthus*, flowers in pairs.

Dianella (di-an-el'la. Fam. Liliaceae). Herbaceous perennials, with grass-like leaves, panicles of drooping flowers and berries, but only hardy enough for outdoors in very mild localities, otherwise grown in a cool greenhouse.

Selection. D. laevis, New S. Wales, 2 ft, blue flowers in spring; *caerulea*, very similar, blue, May; *intermedia*, New Zealand's Turutu, 1½ ft, purplishwhite, and purple berries; and *tasmanica*, Tasmania, 2–3 ft, pale blue flowers, deep blue berries, are worth attempting.

Cultivation. Plant in August–September, at the foot of a south wall, well-drained, humus-rich soil. Or in pots, standard compost, in cool greenhouse, temp. 7–13° C. (45–55° F.), February–March.

Propagation. By division when dormant; by seeds sown in spring, under glass, bottom heat of 18° C. (65° F.).

Dianthus (di-an'thus. Fam. Caryophyllaceae). A large genus of perennial and annual herbs, which includes Carnations, Pinks, Sweet Williams (q.v. under separate headings) and Picotees, many species for the rock garden, and showy annuals. Plants are characterized by

stems swollen at the nodes, grass-like narrow, often grey-green foliage, and flowers borne singly or severally on strong, somewhat woody stems.

Selection. Alpine species: D. alpinus, Austrian Alps, 4 in., rose-pink, solitary flowers, May–June, with white v. *albus*; *arenarius*, N. Europe, 8 in., white, July; *freynii*, Hercegovina, dwarf cushion, pink, July; *gratianopolitanus*, the Cheddar Pink, Britain, mat-forming, 1 ft, red to pink, July, and vs.; *haematocalyx*, tufted, Greece, 6 in., purple-red, June; *cruentus*, SE. Europe, to 2 ft, purple, June; *deltoides*, the Maiden Pink, Britain, 9 in., pink, June, and vs. *albus*, 'Brilliant', red, and 'Wisley', crimson; *knappii*, Hungary, Bosnia, 15 in., yellow, June; *microleis*, Thrace, tufted, 1 in., clear pink, May; *neglectus*, SW. Europe, 6 in., rose-red, July–August; *noeanus*, Balkans, 8 in., white, June; *pindicola*, cushion, Greece, 1 in., reddish pink, July; *plumarius*, SE. Europe, the Pink, 1 ft, pink, June; *simulans*, tufted, Bulgaria, 2 in., deep pink, June; *sylvestris*, S. Alps, to 1 ft, rose, summer; and hybrid alpine pinks such as 'Ariel', 3 in., cherry red; 'Aubrey Prichard', 4 in., double, pink; × *boydii*, cushion, fringed pink; 'Bombardier', 4 in., scarlet; 'Dainty Maid', 3 in., crimson, pink, white; 'Elf', 6 in., semi-double, crimson; 'Hidcote', semi-double, deep red; 'Inchmery', 4 in., double, pale pink; 'Jupiter', 4 in., salmon-pink; 'La Bourbrille', 5 in., soft pink; 'Little Jock', 3 in., double, light pink; 'Mars', 4 in., double, red; 'Mrs. Clarke', double, blood crimson; 'Waithman's Beauty', 6 in., ruby, laced white; 'Windward Rose', 4 in., rose; all flowering July onwards.

Cultivation. Plant October or March–April, in gritty, well-drained soil, enriched with leaf-mould; sunny exposures; top-dress with chippings to keep collars from rotting. Many may be grown in a cold alpine house, standard compost, in pans or pots.

Propagation. By cuttings of unflowered shoots in July, in propagating frame or under handlights. By careful division in spring. By seeds in March, in pans, in cool greenhouse or frame.

Annual Dianthus. These are developments of the Chinese or Indian Pink,

D. chinensis and its Japanese v. *heddewigii*, offered in various strains and colours, such as 'Festival', 4–6 in. high; 'Rainbow', 12–15 in.; and dwarf 'Sensation', single and double flowering. Seeds may be sown in February under glass, bottom heat of 15·5° C. (60° F.), to give summer flowering plants; or in June, outdoors, to be planted in flowering positions in September, for flowering the following year, as biennials.

Diascia (di-as'ki-a. Fam. Scrophulariaceae). A native of S. Africa, *D. barberae*, 1½ ft, with rosy-pink, yellow-throated flowers in terminal racemes, summer, is a half-hardy annual, easily raised from seeds sown in March, under glass, standard compost, bottom heat of 18° C. (65° F.), pricked off and planted out in May, or pot-grown in the cold greenhouse.

Dibber, Dibble. A short, pointed wooden tool used in dibbling or planting out seedlings. Care is needed not to compress the soil, if heavy.

Dicentra (di-ken'tra or di-sen'tra. Fam. Papaveraceae). Handsome flowering herbaceous perennials, with tuberous rootstocks, and graceful racemes of drooping flowers.

Selection. The gem is *D. spectabilis*, Bleeding Heart or Lyre Flower, Siberia, Japan, 2 ft, with rosy-crimson to pink flowers, spring; *cucullaria*, Dutchman's Breeches, U.S.A., 5 in., white and yellow; *eximia*, U.S.A., to 1½ ft, reddish-purple, drooping flowers; *formosa*, West N. America, pink racemes, tending to branch, May–June, shade-tolerant, and *scandens*, Himalaya, slender-stemmed, semi-climber, yellow or purple flowers, summer, may be grown.

Cultivation. Plant March, well-drained, humus-rich soil, partial shade. *D. spectabilis* may be forced by potting up in March, and bringing into cool greenhouse, temp. 10–13° C. (60–65° F.).

Propagation. By division in March–April; by seeds, sown April, in cold frame or outdoor bed.

Dichelostemma (di-kel-o-stem'ma. Fam. Amaryllidaceae). Bulbous plants, formerly under *Brodiaea*, native to Western N. America, but only hardy enough for outdoors in the milder localities.

Selection. *D. congestum*, 8–12 in.,

round umbels of bright purple flowers, June; *ida-maia*, 1½–2 ft, umbels of drooping blood-red and yellow flowers, June–July; *multiflorum*, 2½ ft, violet-mauve, June; and *pulchellum*, 12 in., violet, May.

Cultivation. Plant September–November, well-drained soil, warm, sunny, sheltered places, with litter cover against frosts. Or pot up in autumn, to grow in cool greenhouse.

Dicksonia (dik-son'i-a. Fam. Cyatheaceae). Ferns with tree-like stems, and large, much-divided fronds for the moist, heated greenhouse or conservatory, winter temp. 7–10° C. (45–50° F.).

Selection. *D. antarctica*, Australia, slowly to 30 ft, and *squarrosa*, New Zealand, may be grown in large pots.

Cultivation. Pot, and repot, March–April, in 2 parts loam, 1 part leaf-mould or fibrous peat and coarse sand; water liberally in summer, moderately in winter.

Propagation. By spores, on peaty soil, spring.

Dicotyledons. The Class of flowering plants (Angiospermae) with two cotyledons or seed leaves in the embryo; growing with a branched tap-root root system, netted, branched veined leaves, and flowers with parts in fours, fives or their multiples. *See* Fig. 84, page 190.

Dictamnus (dik-tam'nus. Fam. Rutaceae). The only species, *D. albus*, Burning Bush, Dittany or Fraxinella, of E. Europe and Asia, is a hardy perennial, of 18 in., lemon or balsam scented when rubbed, with terminal racemes of white flowers in late spring, with a good v. *purpureus*, rosy-purple flowered, and a larger v. *giganteus*; of interest for its stem secretion of a volatile oil or resin, which, on a hot still summer day, may be set alight and flame briefly without harming the plant. Readily grown from seeds, sown, March–April, lightish, well-drained soil.

Didiscus (Trachymene), Blue Lace Flower (did-is'kus. Fam. Umbelliferae). The one species, *D. caeruleus*, Australia, 1–2 ft, is grown as a half-hardy annual, sowing in February–March, under glass, bottom heat 18° C. (65° F.), to prick off and plant out in May, or grow as a pot plant in the greenhouse; its umbels of

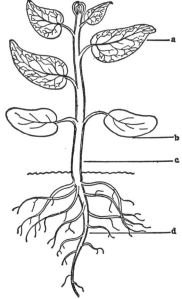

FIG. 84 Dicotyledon: main characters: a. netted veining of leaves; b. pair of seed leaves; c. stem thicker low down; d. branched tap-root system.

small blue flowers in July being lacy and pretty in effect.

Didynamous. Having four stamens, two long and two short; e.g. species of the Labiatae.

Dieback. Descriptive of shoots and branches of shrubs and trees dying. Causes may be waterlogging of the soil; severe drought; hard prolonged frost; fungal or bacterial infection, infestation by wood-boring insects or grubs. Dead growth should be cut out to clean healthy wood, and cuts treated with a suitable antiseptic paint.

Dieffenbachia (deef-en-bak'i-a. Fam. Araceae). Handsome, evergreen foliage plants of tropical America, for the warm greenhouse, or to grow as house plants. Unfortunately poisonous with an acrid sap, and no part of a plant should be sucked or touched by the lips.

Selection. D. chelsonii, dark green leaves, with grey banding, and yellowish spotting; *eburnea*, compact habit, light green; *magnifica*, white spotted and blotched dark green; *picta*, dark green with paler and white markings; *regina*, greyish, greenish and mottled; *rex*, deep green, white blotched; and *seguine'* Dumb Cane, to 6 ft, green, white spotted.

Cultivation. Pot, or repot, in spring; compost of equal parts loam, leafmould, peat and sharp sand. Water freely in active growth, syringing on hot days; moderately in winter, temp. 10–18° C. (60–65° F.); with atmosphere reasonably humid.

Propagation. By the growing tip of a stem and pieces of stem cut into 2–3-in. lengths, inserted in sandy compost, after drying off for a day or so, with bottom heat (18° C. [65° F.]), under glass.

Dielytra. *See* Dicentra, of which it is a synonym.

Dierama (di-er-a'ma. Fam. Iridaceae). Cormous perennial plants of S. Africa, of which *D. pulcherrimum*, 3–6 ft, is chiefly grown for its tall stems bearing drooping racemes of bright purple flowers in August–September; white in v. *album*, wine-red in 'Heron', pale pink in 'Kingfisher' and violet in 'Skylark'. Hardy except in very cold localities.

Cultivation. Plant in May, 4 in. deep, well-drained, but moisture-retentive soil, full sun.

Propagation. By offsets in spring. By seeds sown under glass; seedlings being planted out without root disturbance, but using peat-wood fibre pots.

Diervilla. This generic name is now reserved for a few American species, not much grown in this country. See *Weigela*.

Digging. The operation of turning over and fragmenting the soil to make it a better rooting medium for plants; a necessary preliminary when bringing fallow ground into cultivation, and periodically essential in arable cultivations. Digging admits air to the soil, temporarily improves drainage, exposes the soil to the beneficent actions of the weather, gives an opportunity to assess and expose soil-frequenting pests, facilitates weed control and fosters garden hygiene. It also provides a favourable opportunity for amending texture and structure by incorporating organic matter, and dressings of lime, gypsum and fertilizers. It results in a stimulus of biological and chemical soil activity that gives a temporary increase of fertility.

Tools. Digging may be done with the solid-bladed spade, though it is usually easier to penetrate and turn over a clay or stony soil with a flat-tined digging fork. These tools should be of first quality; of stainless steel if possible, otherwise the tool should be kept bright by cleaning and oiling after each use, to facilitate working. There is a spring-loaded type of spade which is designed to ease the labour, but it is not very successful in breaking up the soil itself. An alternative to the native handled spade or fork is the long-handled continental pointed spade, used more like a shovel. Whatever type of tool is used, it is helpful to keep the cutting edge sharp.

In digging the spade blade is thrust vertically into the soil for its full depth (a spit), the slice of soil loosened by a slight movement of the handle backward, lifted and thrown forward with a twist of the wrist, with economy of movement and effort that entails carrying the soil as little as possible. It is best to take thinnish rather than thick slices, as they will break up more readily.

When to dig. As it is desirable that the soil should reconsolidate, digging should be done well in advance of sowing or planting. Clay soils, especially, are best dug in the autumn or early winter, to allow frost to break up the clods, and weathering to take place. Light, sandy soils can be dug later and less deeply, since they reconsolidate more quickly. It is important to catch a sticky clay in the best conditions for digging, when it is neither too sticky nor too dried out. As fertility decreases with depth, it is normally unwise to invert or unduly mix the top spit and second spit (the subsoil).

Simple Digging. This means the straightforward breaking up of the soil one spit deep. It is best to divide the area to be dug into two equal parts; begin digging at one end of one half of the area by removing the first trench of soil to a width of 12 or 15 in. and placing it on the opposite end of the

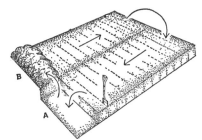

FIG. 85   The method of digging a rectangular plot; with opening trench prepared by moving soil at A to B; arrows show the direction of digging.

second half. This gives room for the turning over and forward of the soil, working up one half to the end, and then working down the second half, when, at the finish, the excavated soil of the first trench can be fitted in. Perennial weed roots should be removed, but small annual weeds can be turned in and smothered.

Bastard Trenching. Sometimes termed double-digging; the start is made in the same way as for simple digging, but making a wider trench, say to 2 ft; this exposes the subsoil, which is then forked over and broken up, before the top spit is turned on to it, and the same procedure followed in sequence. The trench should be cleaned of soil as the work proceeds. In dealing with grassland, the turf may be stripped first, 2–3 in. thick, and laid inverted on the forked-over subsoil, sprinkled with a nitrogenous fertilizer to aid decomposition, before the top spit is turned on top. This method of digging is excellent for clay and heavy soils being prepared for cultivation. It is less necessary for a naturally porous soil, or light soil with a free-draining subsoil. The opportunity of treating a subsoil with an amendment, such as gypsum to make it more friable if a sticky clay, or with organic matter if poor in texture, should be taken.

Trenching. This means working the soil to three spits deep, and is only undertaken in exceptional circumstances, such as in preparing for sweet peas, asparagus or deep-rooting permanent plants such as flower borders on stiff

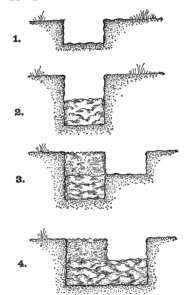

FIG. 86 Double-digging or bastard trenching: 1. Trench opened with top spit removed. 2. Second spit of subsoil broken up *in situ*. 3. Top spit of second trench turned. 4. Subsoil of second trench broken up prior to turning over third trench.

heavy soils. A first trench of top spit soil, 30 in. wide, is taken out; then the second spit for half the width of the trench. The exposed third spit is forked over, the second spit of the second half of the trench turned over on to it, and then the top spit of the next row of digging; and the sequence then repeated. It is hard work, but can be very rewarding for years to come.

Ridging. A technique in digging clay soils in which the ground is marked out in 2½-ft wide strips; at the beginning of the first strip, the top spit of soil is removed as in simple digging; the next row of soil is thrown forward in large clods, with the spadefuls from the sides being placed to the centre to form a ridge, and so expose as much soil surface to frost and wind as possible. Carried out in autumn, the soil can be easily broken

down to a good tilth in early spring. *See* No-digging Techniques.

Digitalis, Foxglove (dig-i-ta'lis. Fam. Scrophulariaceae). Biennial and perennial flowering herbs, with glove-like, finger-flower in tall racemes.

Selection. The perennials commonly cultivated are *D. grandiflora* (*ambigua*), Europe, Caucasus, Altai, 2–3 ft, with yellowish, brown-veined flowers, July–August; *lutea*, SW. Europe, NW. Africa, 2 ft, yellow, July; × *mertonensis*, 3 ft, strawberry red, summer; and *orientalis*, Anatolia, 2 ft, pale whitish flowers, July–August. They may be planted in ordinary garden soil, sun or partial shade, October or March; and propagated by division. The best known Foxglove, biennial *D. purpurea*, to 5 ft, purple to white flowers in summer, runs to many vs. such as *alba*, white; *gloxinioides*, large-flowered in various colours; and *monstrosa*, flowers more or less double; and hybrids such as the 'Excelsior', with flowers all round the stem, various colours of white, yellow, pink and purple; and 'Foxy', of 2½ ft stature. May be raised from seed, sown out of doors, April–June, and seedlings planted out 9 in. apart, when large enough to handle, in borders, or shaded places, almost any ordinary garden soil.

Digitate. Fingered.

FIG. 87 Digitate leaf (*Cannabis* sp.).

Dill (*Peucedanum graveolens*). A sweet annual herb of which the young leaves may be used to flavour soups, stews and sauces; and the seeds to flavour preserves or cakes, or to make dill vinegar

The seeds are sown in March–April, in drills 10 in. apart, ¼ in. deep, thinning to 8 in. apart and keeping weed-free; any good humus-rich, porous soil suits.

Dimorphic. Having two forms of organs on the same plant. Ex. Two different lengths of styles in Primulas.

Dimorphotheca, Cape Daisy, Cape Marigold, Star of the Veldt (di-mor-fo-the′ka. Fam. Compositae). S. African herbs or sub-shrubs, naturally perennial, but tender in this country and therefore grown as half-hardy annuals out of doors.

Selection. D. aurantiaca, 1 ft, with bright orange, rayed flowers, summer–autumn, is best in its hybrid strains, with buff, salmon and white flowers, and 'Goliath', extra large orange flowers; *calendulacea*, in mixed colours, branching freely; *ecklonis*, 2 ft, pretty white with blue disk flowers, summer; *pluvialis ringens*, 1 ft, white, blue-zoned flowers; and *sinuata* 'Orange Glory', 1¼ ft, are worth growing.

Cultivation. Sow seeds under glass, standard compost, bottom heat of 18° C. (65° F.), March, to prick off and plant out in May; or out of doors in April.

Dioecious. Having female flowers on one plant, male on another. Ex. *Taxus baccata*, *Salix* spp.

Dionaea, Venus's Fly-trap (di-o-nai′a. Fam. Droseraceae). The one species, *D. muscipula*, Carolina, 6 in., is a herbaceous perennial, interesting as an insectivorous plant, trapping flies by its leaves, which close when the bristles on the leaf lobes are touched or the lobes sharply knocked. It is grown in a pot, in a compost of peat, fine silver sand and living sphagnum moss, stood in a saucer of water, in a cool greenhouse; white flowers are borne in July–August. Propagation by seeds sown in moist sand and sphagnum moss, under bell-glass in spring; or by division in March.

Diosma (di-os′ma. Fam. Rutaceae). Evergreen, heath-like shrubs from S. Africa, with fragrant foliage, attractive flowers in spring, suitable for cool greenhouse culture.

Selection. D. ericoides, 1–2 ft, with white flowers in small clusters, spring, is chiefly grown.

Cultivation. Pot, and repot, in early summer, when new growth begins, standard compost, water freely in active growth, very moderately in winter, temp. 7° C. (45° F.) minimum. Trim shoots well back after flowering.

Propagation. By cuttings of young shoots, taken with a heel, July–August, inserted in a propagating frame, with slight bottom heat of 15·5° C. (60° F.).

Diospyros. *See* Persimmon.

Dipelta (di-pel′ta. Fam. Caprifoliaceae). Deciduous hardy shrubs from China, resembling Weigela, and easily grown.

Selection. D. floribunda, Central China, 6 ft, long-pointed ovate leaves, tubular, bell-like pink flowers, yellow-throated, May–June; *ventricosa*, W. China, to 6 ft, deep rose, orange-throated flowers, May–June; and *yunnanensis*, to 6 ft, creamy white, flushed rose, flowers, May.

Cultivation. Plant October–March, well-drained loam soil, sunny position. Prune after flowering when necessary.

Propagation. By cuttings of young shoots, July–August, in cold frame or under a handlight.

Diphylleia (di-pil-li′a. Fam. Podophyllaceae). Known as the Umbrella Leaf by reason of its peltate leaves, up to 2 ft across, *D. cymosa*, SE. U.S.A., 1–3 ft, is a rhizamatous-rooting herbaceous perennial, with loose heads of white flowers in summer, followed by blue berries, and succeeds in moist peaty soils, planted October–March, partial shade, out of reach of keen frosts and very hard winters. Propagation by division in spring.

Diphyllous. Two-leaved.

Diplacus. See *Mimulus*.

Diploid. A plant having two sets of chromosomes in its nuclei. *See* Chromosomes.

Dipsacus (dip′sa-kus. Fam. Dipsaceae). Biennial herbs with prickly stems and leaves, and fine flower-heads, which become cone-like seed-heads with hooked seeds, known as Teasels; of Europe, Asia and N. Africa.

Selection. D. fullonum, Fuller's Teasel, to 6 ft, is the species cultivated for its dried heads used in the textile industry for raising the nap of woollen cloth; also for indoor decorations, but makes a handsome garden plant; *sylvestris*, the common native Teasel, 6 ft, has pale lilac flower heads, and the dried seed heads are useful for winter decoration and may be dipped in silver or gold paint.

Cultivation. Sow seeds outdoors in April–June, transplant seedlings early to where they are to flower, any ordinary soil. Apt to seed themselves if neglected.

Diptera. An Order of Insects, containing two-winged flies.

Disa (di'sa. Fam. Orchidaceae). Terrestrial orchids, chiefly from Africa.

Selection. D. uniflora, Table Mt, 1½ ft, scarlet, veined crimson, shaded yellow flowers, June–July; and vs. *barrellii,* orange-scarlet, crimson-veined; and *superba,* bright scarlet and crimson, veined pink; and × *kewensis,* pink.

Cultivation. Pot in November–December, compost of 3 parts shredded and sifted Osmunda fibre, 2 parts sphagnum moss, 1 part oak leaf-mould, and coarse sand and crushed brick; need a moist atmosphere, airy and cool, with shade; winter temp. 7° C. (45° F.) minimum; water moderately, increasing with growth. Control thrips.

Propagation. By division, November.

Disanthus (di-san'thus. Fam. Hamamelidaceae). The sole species, *D. cercidifolia,* Japan, 8–12 ft, is a hardy deciduous shrub, with cordate bluish-green foliage, and axillary pairs of purple flowers, with narrow, ribbony petals, October. Obviously, needs autumn shelter for flowering, planting October–March, peat-enriched soil, sunny position.

Propagation. By cuttings taken in July–August, in cold frame or under handlight, sandy loam soil.

Disbudding. The pinching out and removal of unwanted buds, flowers or shoots to strengthen other growth and secure more robust shoots, finer flowers and larger fruits. *See* Figs, Peaches, Grapes, and flowers such as Chrysanthemum, Carnation and Dahlia.

Discolor. Of two or more colours. Ex. *Sorbus discolor.*

Diseases. Plants are subject to disease from two main causes: infection by parasitic organisms, such as bacteria, fungi or viruses, and functional disorders arising from adverse environmental conditions. Most parasitic diseases are

caused by fungi, only a few by bacteria, and are usually spread by spores, air- or moisture-carried, or sometimes by insects. Sooner or later they manifest in overt symptoms and signs of the parasite; often amenable to control by fungicides (q.v.). Virus diseases, however, are still not perfectly understood, being largely transmitted by insects or the transfer of infected sap from the sick plant to the healthy. Viruses involve the whole plant, and control lies largely in destroying it to remove its danger to other plants as a source of infection. Many parasitic diseases arise or are aggravated by environmental conditions which undermine the integrity and resistance of the plant, and good culture is the first and most important defence. In some instances, such as rust in antirrhinums, breeding can give resistant strains, and virus-free clones of various plants have now been raised. A healthy plant, good culture, and prompt remedial treatment at the first symptoms of disease are the essentials of parasitic disease control. Nonparasitic functional disorders may arise from adverse weather conditions, soil deficiencies, or wrong cultural treatment; while symptoms may resemble those of a disease, the evidence of a parasite is absent, though there may be secondary infection of weakened tissues by saprophytic fungi. Diseases in particular are described under the plants involved throughout this book. *See* Nutrition.

Disk, Disc. The fleshy part of the receptacle, surrounding or surmounting the ovary of a flower. More loosely

FIG. 88   Disk or Disc.

applied to the central flowers (disk florets) of the Compositae.

Dissectus (-a, -um). Dissected, cut into deeply divided lobes. Ex. *Acer palmatum* v. *dissectum*.

Disthicus (-a, -um). Distichous, in two opposite rows. Ex. *Taxodium distichum*.

Dittany. See *Dictamnus*.

Diurnal. Descriptive of flowers which open during the day but close at night. *See* Nocturnal.

Divaricatus (-a, -um). Divaricate, spreading widely. Ex. *Phlox. divaricata.*

Dizygotheca, Threadleaf (di-zi-go-the′ka. Fam. Araliaceae). Evergreen shrubs of the South Seas, sometimes offered under Aralia, for the warm greenhouse or as house plants.

Selection. D. elegantissima, New Hebrides, slow-growing with compound digitate leaves, on long, green, mottled white thready stalks; for foliage and table decoration; *kerchoveana,* South Sea Islands, graceful with digitate leaves, wavy-edged and serrate; and *veitchii* v. *gracillima,* New Caledonia, finely leafleted and ribbed white; are chiefly grown for foliage effect.

Cultivation. Pot in April, standard compost, water liberally in growth in summer, moderately in winter with minimum temp. 13° C. (55° F.), with good light, and fairly moist atmosphere.

Propagation. By cuttings of young shoots, July, in propagating case, bottom heat, 24° C. (75° F.).

Dodder (*Cascuta* spp. Fam. Calystegia). Annual parasitic plants with slender, pink, yellow or white twining stems, attached to the host plant by suckers. *C. epithymum* is the commonest in gardens, on Gorse, Heather, Heaths and related plants; *C. europaea* parasitizes Flax, Hops, Nettles, but is very rare.

Dodecatheon, American Cowslip, Shooting Stars (do-dek-ath′e-on. Fam. Primulaceae). Glabrous perennial herbs of N. America, notable for their reflexed, cyclamen-like umbels of flowers in spring.

Selection. D. integrifolium, British Columbia, 10 in., purplish pink flowers; *meadia,* Eastern N. America, to 2 ft, rose and white, and vs. *album* and *violaceum*; and *pauciflorum,* 8 in., pale lilac, are usually offered.

Cultivation. Plant September or

FIG. 89 *Dodecatheon meadia.*

March–April, in well-drained peaty soil, partial shade and sheltered positions in rock garden, shrubbery or border; or may be pot-grown in alpine house or cold greenhouse.

Propagation. By seeds, in cool frame, summer or spring, or by root division in early autumn.

Dog Rose. See *Rosa canina.*

Dog's Mercury. *Mercurialis perennis,* a common weed.

Dog's Tooth Violet. See *Erythronium.*

Dogwood. See *Cornus.*

Dolabratus (-a, -um). Dolabrate, axe-shaped. Ex. *Thuja dolabrata.*

Dolichos (dol′ikos. Fam. Leguminosae). Climbing, twining plants of which

D. lablab, the Hyacinth Bean of the Tropics, with purple, pea-like flowers in axillary racemes, July–August, and edible pods and seeds later, may be raised from seed, sown under glass, March, bottom heat 21° C. (70° F.), and grown as a greenhouse climber in pots.

Dollar Spot. A disease of lawns (q.v.).

Domesticus (-a, -um). Of the house. Ex. *Prunus domestica.*

Dondia. See *Hacquetia.*

Dormant. Resting, applied to the leafless period of deciduous shrubs and trees; also to buds, formed normally but remaining undeveloped.

Doronicum, Leopard's Bane (dor-on′i-kum. Fam. Compositae). Herbaceous, early-flowering perennials with rayed, yellow flower-heads, hardy and easy to grow.

Selection. D. austriacum, Europe, 1–1½ ft, large-flowering, spring; *caucasicum,* 1 ft, showy flowers, larger in v. *magnificum,* April; *clusii,* Austrian Alps, 1 ft, pale yellow, early summer; *cordatum* SE. Europe, 6 in., solitary flowers, spring; and *plantagineum,* Europe, 2–3 ft, and v. *excelsum* ('Harper Crewe'), May, are good for partial shade in borders; *pardalianches,* 2–3 ft, the Great Leopard's Bane, native, yellow, spring, reputedly poisonous, is for the wild garden.

Cultivation. Plant October–March, any ordinary soil, does not mind shade.

Propagation By seeds, out of doors, April. By division, October or March.

Dorsal. Growing on the back, or relating to the back of leaves, etc.

Dorycnium (dor-ik′ni-um. Fam. Leguminosae). Semi-herbaceous perennial plants, of which *D. hirsutum,* S. Europe, branching stems with trifoliolate silvery leaves, heads of white broom-like flowers, summer, is commonly grown; *rectum,* rose pink, and *suffruticosum,* 2–3 ft, pinkish white flowers, are others.

Cultivation. Plant April, well-drained lightish soil, like hot sun, in rock gardens or border.

Propagation. By seeds, April, warm bed of sandy loam.

Douglas Fir. See *Pseudotsuga taxifolia.*

Douglasia (do-glas′i-a. Fam. Primulaceae). Choice evergreen alpine plants, closely related to Androsace, with tubular, primrose-like flowers in early spring.

Selection. D. vitaliana, Spain and central Europe, of tufted, rosette habit, and solitary yellow flowers, spring, is chiefly grown; *dentata,* Cascade Mts, umbels of small violet flowers; *laevigata,* N. America, rose-pink, yellow-eyed, flowers in umbels; and *montana,* Wyoming, rose-pink flowers in ones or twos, are others.

Cultivation. Plant September or March, well-drained gritty soil, with peat or leaf-mould, in rock gardens; in pans in the alpine house, standard compost.

Propagation. By seeds, sown when ripe, or in April.

Dove Tree. See *Davidia.*

Downingia (Clintonia) (dow-nin′gi-a. Fam. Campanulaceae). Annual flowering plants from California, unusual for their two-lipped flowers, raised as half-hardy annuals, from seeds sown under glass, March, bottom heat of 18° C. (65° F.), to be pricked off and planted out in May. *D. elegans,* 6 in., blue and white flowers, and *pulchella,* to 9 in., deep blue, yellow blotch and white border, summer, are grown.

Draba, Whitlow Grass (dra′ba. Fam. Cruciferae). A rather large genus of spring-flowering plants of which only a few are cultivated in rock gardens or the alpine house.

Selection. D. acaulis, Taurus, 1 in., cushion, golden-yellow flowers, April; *aizoides,* tufted, a native, yellow flowers, spring, and the similar more vigorous *aizoon,* European Alps, sulphur-yellow flowers, spring; *bruniifolia,* Caucasus, golden-yellow, March; *bryoides,* Caucasus, 2 in., cushion, golden-yellow, April, and v. *imbricata,* smaller; *dedeana,* Pyrenees, 1 in., cushion, white, pale violet, flowers, April; and *polytricha,* Armenia, densely tufted, yellow flowers, April, are all perennial.

Cultivation. All need perfect drainage in scree or light open soil, sunny positions, planting March–April, with winter protection from rains and damp. Or may be grown in pans in the alpine house.

Propagation. By seeds, in March, in cold frame. By detachment of rosetted tufts in June, to root in a propagating case, slight bottom heat, 15·5° C. (60° F.).

Dracaena (dra-ke′na. Fam. Liliaceae). Tropical shrub- and tree-like evergreen plants, largely grown for their handsome ornamental foliage, in the greenhouse, or as house plants, being closely related to Cordyline.

Selection. *D. draco*, the Dragon-tree, Canary Islands, with a head of bluish-green, linear, pointed leaves, decorative while young, eventually too tall; *fragrans*, Guinea, broad, and glossy green leaves, striped yellow and gold in v. *lindenii*, and a central stripe of gold in *massangeana*; *godseffiana*, Congo, shrub-like with opposite or whorled oval leaves, dark green and cream-spotted; *goldieana*, West Africa, slender-stemmed with spreading leaves, ovate and broad, green with bands of silver-green, and yellow midrib; and *parrii*, tree-like with narrow, linear spiky leaves, olive green, pink splotched beneath, which with *sanderiana*, slender with thin, spreading narrowly lanceolate leaves, may be termed fairly hardy, for outdoor growth in summer.

Cultivation. Pot, February–March, well-crocked 5- or 6-in. pots, standard compost, in partial shade, warm greenhouse; water liberally in growth, moderately in winter, minimum temp. 10° C. (50° F.); likes a warm, moist atmosphere; with syringing and wiping of leaves in summer; for winter place pots inside larger ones, filling gap with moist peat, which is kept watered.

Propagation. By stem cuttings of 1–2 in., in spring or summer, placed in cuttings compost, in propagating case, bottom heat of 18° C. (65° F.).

Dracocephalum, Dragon's Head (dra-ko-kep′a-lum. Fam. Labiatae). Pretty summer-flowering annual and perennial herbaceous plants of Europe and Asia.

Selection. *D. moldavica*, the Moldavian Balm of E. Siberia, 18 in., with whorls of blue and white flowers, is a hardy annual, to sow in April, where it is to flower, or earlier under glass for transplanting. *D. austriacum*, Europe, 1½ ft, blue, July; *forrestii*, W. China, 1½ ft, spikes of deep purple-blue flowers, summer; *grandiflorum*, Siberia, to 9 in., blue; and *hemsleyanum*, Europe, purplish blue, for the rock garden; *japonicum*, Japan, 2 ft, white with blue

bordered flowers; *ruprechtii*, Turkestan, 1½ ft, rose-lilac; *ruyschianum*, Europe, 2 ft, Europe, purple, are summer-flowering perennials.

Cultivation. Plant October–May, reasonably well-drained soil, cool positions, in borders.

Propagation. By division in spring.

Dragon Tree. See *Dracaena draco*.

Dragon's Head. See *Dracocephalum*.

Drainage. With few exceptions, most garden plants and crops need good aeration at the roots, and efficient drainage is critically important and essential.

Land Drainage. A test can be made by drilling holes. 2½ ft deep in winter, covering to exclude rain, and observing the behaviour of the water table or level in them after rains. If the water rises into the top foot and is slow to subside, subsoil drainage is probably needed. If it rises and sinks relatively quickly no drainage is needed. Often improvement follows the breaking-up of a dense, clayey or panned subsoil, especially if amended by the addition of gypsum, grit and organic matter. In low-lying places it may be sufficient to raise the beds with added soil. Where the soil lies waterlogged for more than two or three weeks, a system of subsoil drainage by means of round agricultural drain tiles will be needed. This is an operation calling for some skill. The land is first opened up by trenches, 1½–3 ft deep, which are placed 20–30 ft apart in light or medium loam soils; 12–18 ft in clay, to run on a herring-bone or a grid pattern, with a fall of 1 in 200 or 300 to a main drain, which should have an outlet in a ditch, drainage system or soakaway (large pit, 6–8 ft deep, 4–6 ft square; filled with rubble or broken brick or stone). The drains are usually of 3-in. diameter pipes or tiles of porous clay or concrete or plastic, running to a main drain of 4 in. diameter. They are packed around with broken stone or rubble, which is topped with inverted sods, leaves or fibre, before the soil is replaced. A drainage system should be tested before the final filling-in.

Container Drainage. Pans, pots, boxes, vases and troughs used for plants need adequate provision for drainage. Window-boxes, for instance, should have drainage holes in the base. Holes may be kept open by a piece of nylon mesh over them, or a large crock; drainage material is then added, of broken crocks (clean broken clay pots), brick or gravel, or more recently, crunched plastic ribbon, topped with a thin layer of leaves of fibre, and then the soil compost. Orchid pots are usually crocked for half to two-thirds their depth to allow for copious watering.

Drill. A shallow trench made in the soil to take seeds, chiefly used in growing vegetable crops, raising annuals and biennials for subsequent transplanting, and in nursery beds. It may be a simple V shape, made by pushing the back of a straight rake in and along, or with a triangular hoe, guided by a line; or a shallow trench of spade-width to take large seeds such as peas, beans and tree seeds. The soil is subsequently raked over the seed and firmed.

Drimys (drim′is. Fam. Magnoliaceae). Evergreen shrubs, attractive in leaf and flower, tender, however, and only for outdoor culture in mild localities.

Selection. D. aromatica, Tasmania, to 12 ft, with light green, oblong leaves, clusters of white flowers, April–May, is aromatically pungent; and with *winteri,* Winter's Bark of S. America, to 20 ft, jasmine-scented white clusters of flowers, may be grown against a south wall in sheltered gardens.

Cultivation. Plant in April, well-drained, humus-rich soil, sunny position. Prune after flowering.

Propagation. By layers, spring; by cuttings of young shoots, July, in propagating frame, slight bottom heat.

Dropwort. See *Filipendula.*

Drosera, Sundew (dros′er-a. Fam. Droseraceae). Slender, perennial glandular herbs, interesting for their insectivorous habit and strange beauty.

Selection. D. rotundifolia, 4 in., a rosette of reddish orbicular leaves, sparkling glandular hairs, and scape bearing white flowers, July–August; *anglica,* similar but slightly larger, and *intermedia,* small and long-leaved, are native species of bogs and damp places on heaths and moors; *binnata,* Australia, 6 in., lobed leaves and large white summer flowers, *capensis,* S. Africa, with purple flowers, and *filiformis,* N.

FIG. 90 *Drosera rotundifolia,* Sundew.

America, 1 ft, divided leaves, purple flowers, summer, may also be grown.

Cultivation. Pot in pans or pots, with good drainage, in equal parts peat and sphagnum moss, kept very moist in good light, in a cool greenhouse, in spring; standing pots in saucers of water; winter temp. 7° C. (45° F.).

Propagation. By seeds on surface of peat and living sphagnum moss mixture, under handlight or bell-glass (13–18° C. [55–65° F.]), spring or summer. By division in March–April; by 1-in. root cuttings in peat-moss mixture, in propagating frame, spring.

Drupe. A fruit with a fleshy pericarp

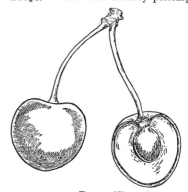

FIG. 91 Drupe (Cherry).

surrounding seed in a hardy stony kernel; a stone fruit such as a plum or sloe, or ivy berry.

Drupel. A small drupe such as the individual parts of a Blackberry which is a conglomeration or aeterio of drupels.

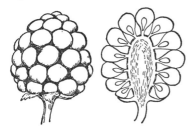

FIG. 92 Drupel. Aggregate fruit of drupels (Blackberry).

Dryas (dri'as. Fam. Rosaceae). Prostrate flowering evergreen sub-shrubs of which *D. octopetala*, Mountain Avens, a native of N. Europe and Britain, is excellent for the rock garden, with 8-petalled white flowers, June, over a mat of small, deep green ovate leaves, white beneath; vs. *integrifolia*, with smaller flowers, *lanata*, with grey downy foliage, and v. *minor*, a miniature of half the species size; *drummondii* is a N. American with yellowish flowers, and × *suendermannii*, a hybrid with *octopetala*, has droopy flowers, yellow in the bud but opening white.

Cultivation. Plant September–October or March–April, well-drained soil, with peat and lime, leave undisturbed.

Propagation. By layers, spring; by cuttings in July–August, under hand-light; by seed, sown in spring.

Dryopteris (dri-op'ter-is. Fam. Polypodiaceae). A large genus of ferns, with rhizomatous stout rootstocks and long pinnate and pinnatifid leaves forming crowns.

Selection. D. filix-mas, the Male Fern, native and cosmopolitan, and its many forms; *cristata*, Crested Buckler Fern; *aemula*, Hay-scented Buckler Fern;

spinulosa, Buckler Fern, and its vs., and *villarsii*, Rigid Buckler Fern, native and European, are hardy, and willing to grow in sun or shade, in soil affording moisture enough; though *cristata* needs rather boggy conditions, such as a peat-enriched soil near water. *D. fragrans*, Caucasus, etc.; *goldieana*, E. America; *hirtipes*, Japan, Malaya; and *nove-boracensis*, E. America, are exotics hardy enough for out of doors.

D. cana, Sikkim, finely fronded, to 12 in.; *effusa*, tropical America, pale green fronds to 4 ft.; *hispida*, New Zealand, broad fronds of 1½ ft; and *parasitica*, tropical, fronds of 1 to 2 ft, may be grown in the cool greenhouse, winter temp. 10° C. (50° F.), with shade, and liberal watering in summer, and a compost of 2 parts sandy loam, 1 part leaf-mould and peat.

Propagation. By division of mature plants, spring; by spores, April, or summer, when available.

Dubius (-a, -um). Doubtful, uncertain. Ex. *Gypsophila dubia*.

Duckweed. See *Lemna*.

Dulcis (-e). Sweet. Ex. *Dendrobium dulce*.

Dumb Cane. See *Dieffenbachia seguine*.

Dumosus (-a, -um). Busy, compact. Ex. *Aster dumosus*.

Duramen. Heartwood; the part of the wood of a tree that hardens as the plant grows and matures.

Dutchman's Breeches. See *Dicentra*.

Dutchman's Pipe. See *Aristolochia*.

Dwarf Trees. Naturally dwarf trees are usually mutations or sports of forest or woodland trees, or vegetatively propagated forms, especially among conifers. They may be trees dwarfed by growing in exposed and limiting conditions. They may be artificially dwarfed by raising tree seedlings, with roots confined by pots or containers, and the top growth contorted and restrained by training and regular pruning (*see* Trees, Dwarfing of). Fruit trees grown on stature-limiting rootstocks are also referred to as dwarf trees (*see* Apples).

Dyer's Greenwood. See *Genista tinctoria*.

E

Earthing-up. The operation of heaping soil to the stems of growing plants; practised in growing celery and leeks to blanch their stems; in potato-growing to give tubers and roots cool, dark soil conditions and facilitate spraying, etc., of top growth, and eventual harvesting; in tomato-growing to induce additional basal rooting; in Brussels sprout growing to give stability. Earthing-up should be done in stages when the soil is friable and just moist, working with a draw hoe, spade or plough.

Earthworms. Soil-inhabiting creatures of great importance to soil fertility. By tunnelling through the soil they aid drainage, aeration and root penetration. They draw leaves, etc., into their burrows, pass earth through their bodies to excrete it greatly enriched in humus and plant nutrients, sift and raise the finer mineral soil from lower to surface levels. Of the Order Oligochaeta, Fam. Lumbricidae, there are roughly twenty-five species, the commonest which throw up wormcasts at the surface being *Lumbricus terrestis,* *Allobophora longa* and *A. nocturna,* particularly in mild muggy autumnal and spring weather; but more species deposit their casts in the soil. Brandling worms (*Eisenia foetida*) occur in great numbers in compost heaps and rotting manure. Earthworms are hermaphrodite, but the eggs of one are fertilized by the sperm cells of another. Normally it is unwise to destroy them. On lawns, however, wormcasts are unsightly and often a hazard. Their numbers are best reduced by the use of expellents (Mowrah meal, potassium permanganate, lime-water), or poisons (derris, chlordane), but their absence means that regular aeration of the turf should be carried out. In other countries, notably America, earthworms are bred intensively for soil improvement. A soil can only support the population for which it provides food, however, and the simplest way to increase the earthworm population is to feed the soil with humus-forming organic matter, and keep the pH between 6·0 and 6·5 by liming.

Earwigs. Insects of the Order Dermaptera, of which there are five native species, the commonest being *Forficula auricularia.* They are copper-brown, with not often seen but large wings under their wing-cases, and a pair of forceps at the ends of their bodies, bowed in the male, more or less straight in the female. Earwigs over-winter as adults in bark crevices, leaves, rubbish, etc., and the females nest in the soil to lay their eggs and brood the nymphs. Their supposed eagerness for entering the human ear is grossly exaggerated. Earwigs are disliked in the garden since they often damage flowers and leaves of chrysanthemum, dahlias, helianthus and many annuals, and ripening fruits. A trichlorphon (Dipterex 80) or gamma-BHC insecticide, applied to the base of plants and soil surface, gives adequate control; a band of fruit-tree grease round the base of stalks and stakes stops them climbing up plants; and these measures are more effective than traps of inverted plant pots, filled with straw or hay on sticks.

Eburneus (a-, -um), Like ivory, ivory-white. Ex. *Cymbidium eburneum.*

Ecballium (ek-bal'li-um. Fam. Cucurbitaceae). The sole species, *E. elaterium,* Mediterranean region, the Squirting Cucumber, is a half-hardy annual trailing plant, without tendrils, with yellow flowers, June, followed by turgid, prickly oblong fruits, which when ripe squirt their seeds out through a hole left where it detaches from the stalk. Seeds may be sown in March, under glass, bottom heat of 21° C. (70° F.), standard compost, for hardening off and planting out in rather rich soil in May, as a plant curiosity.

Eccremocarpus (ek-kre-mo-kar'pus. Fam. Bignoniaceae). Evergreen climbers of Chile, of which *E. scaber*, 10–15 ft, is grown for its beautiful pinnate foliage and many-flowered racemes of bell-shaped orange-red flowers, with vs. *aureus*, golden flowers, and *ruber*, orangey red; to cover arbours, trellis or pergolas in summer out of doors, or as a cold greenhouse climber. May be grown from seeds as a half-hardy annual for outdoors, sowing under glass, bottom heat of 18° C. (65° F.), in March, standard compost, to plant out in May; or pot-grown perennially in the greenhouse; and may be propagated from stem cuttings in August, with gentle heat, to over-winter in cool greenhouse.

Echeveria (ek-e-ve'ri-a. Fam. Crassulaceae). Succulent plants with rosette formation of beautiful leaves, often gorgeously coloured and plush-textured with fine hairs and waxy secretion, and bell-shaped flowers, usually red or yellow.

Selection. E. carnicolor, Mexico,

orange-red flowers, March; *derenbergii*, Mexico, red-tipped leaves, orange, March; *harmsii*, Mexico, 12–18-in. stems, large red, yellow-tipped flowers, May; *secunda*, Mexico, 12 in., reddish-yellow, spring; and *setosa*, Mexico, stemless, with red, yellow-tipped flowers, spring.

Cultivation. At one time much used for carpet bedding; may be planted out for summer in beds and borders, well-drained soils, sunny position, in May. More often grown in pots in the cool greenhouse or as house plants, in standard composts, and only need temps. above freezing point in winter (7° C. [45° F.]).

Propagation. By leaves detached from basal rosette, inserted in porous compost, spring, with gentle bottom heat (15·5° C. [60° F.]); or stem cuttings.

Echinacea (ek-in-a'ke-a. Fam. Compositae). Hardy perennial native of U.S.A., *E. purpurea* (*Rudbeckia purpurea*), 3–4 ft, with rayed flower-heads of reddish-purple and orange disk, summer, and vs., may be grown in deep rich loamy soil, enriched with leaf-mould, in the border.

Cultivation. Plant in March–April, sunny position.

Propagation. By seeds sown in June, outdoors. By division in March–April.

Echinatus (-a, -um). Echinate, with hedgehog-like prickles. Ex. *Pelargonium enchinatum.*

Echinocactus (ek-in-o-kak'tus. Fam. Cactaceae). Round or cylindrical, ribbed and very spiny cacti, with woolly crowns, flowering from the top, when mature, and largely Mexican in origin; Hedgehog cacti.

Selection. Most popular is *E. grusonii*, globular, flattened top, growing very large, golden yellow spines, yellowish flowers in mature plants; *grandis*, cylindrical, dull green, large; *horizonthalonis*, short, flattened, reddish-brown spines; *ingens*, globular, dark brown spines; and *polycephalus*, forming clumps of globular heads, are usually available.

Cultivation. Pot March–April, ordinary cactus compost; to grow in cold greenhouse or as a window plant, watering in summer, very little at other times, winter temp. 7° C. (45° F.).

Propagation. By seed, sown in spring.

Echinocereus (ek-in-o-ke're-us. Fam.

Cactaceae). Cacti with globular or cylindrical stems, columnar or in clumps, with large brightly coloured flowers from the older spiny aeroles on the sides, summer.

Selection. E. blanckii, violet flowers; *pectinatus*, pink; *pentalophus*, reddish-violet; *reichenbachii*, light purple, scented; *rigidissimus*, the Rainbow Cactus, pink; *salm-dyckianus*, orange-red; and *scheerii*, pink, are all ready blooming, natives of Mexico and Texas.

Cultivation. Pot March–April, ordinary cactus compost (*see* Cactus), sunny position, cool greenhouse or windows; watering well in summer, little in winter, minimum temp. 7° C. (45° F.).

Propagation. By cuttings of stems; by seeds, spring, summer; by grafting on *Trichocereus*.

Echinofossulocactus (**Stenocactus**) (ek-in-o-fos-su-lo-kak'tus. Fam. Cactaceae). Small, terrestrial, globular cacti with thin wavy ribs, large spines, and flowers at the top, natives of Mexico.

Selection. E. albatus, white flowering; *coptonogonus*, reddish-yellow spines, purple and white flowers, summer; *hastatus*, white; and *lamellosus*, red, are worth growing.

Cultivation. Pot March–April, cactus compost, to grow in cool greenhouse or windows, watering freely in active growth, very little in winter, temp. 7° C. (45° F.).

Propagation. By seeds, or by cuttings, spring, with gentle bottom heat (18° C. [65° F.]).

Echinops, Globe Thistle (ek-in'ops. Fam. Compositae). Herbaceous perennials with handsome thistle-like foliage and roundish flower-heads of blue or white flowers in summer, for borders.

Selection. E. ritro, S. Europe, 3 ft, blue flower-heads; *humilis* v. *nivalis*, Asia, 3 ft, white flowering, and v. 'Taplow Blue'; and *sphaerocephalus*, Europe, 5 ft, silvery grey flowers, are chiefly grown.

Cultivation. Plant March–April, well-drained ordinary soil, sunny position.

Propagation. By seeds sown in April, outdoors or in cold frame; by division in spring.

Echinopsis (ek-in-op'sis. Fam. Cactaceae). Roundish, deep ribbed and spiny 'Sea Urchin' cacti, natives of S.

America, and yet surprisingly easy to grow and withstanding cold well; flower freely when mature from old aeroles.

Selection. E. eyriesii, Brazil, etc., long white flowers, summer; *huottii*, Bolivia, white; *multiplex*, S. Brazil, pale pink; *nigra*, black spines, white flowers; *oxygona*, S. Brazil, pink; *rhodotricha*, Brazil, white; and *tubiflora*, Argentina, white flowers. All flower in first half of summer.

Cultivation. Pot and repot every third year, in March–April; standard cactus compost (*see* Cactus); water freely in active growth, little in winter, minimum temp. 7° C. (45° F.), sunny greenhouse or windows.

Propagation. By seeds in pans, spring, bottom heat of 24° C. (75° F.). By offsets, spring. By cuttings, summer.

Echium (ek'i-um. Fam. Boraginaceae). Plants of the Mediterranean region and Canary Islands, of which *E. plantagineum* in its dwarf hybrid forms is grown as a hardy annual, for its open bell-like flowers, of white, pink, rose, carmine, mauve and blue, borne on 1 ft tall branching stems through the summer; from seeds sown under glass, March; or out of doors, April, where they are to flower; *creticum*, S. Europe, 6 in., reddish-violet flowers, may also be grown. *E. candicans*, Madeira, 2 ft, with conical panicles of blue flowers, and *wildprettii*, Canary Islands, 2–3 ft, pale red, are biennials for the cool greenhouse, to be sown in June in pots, to flower the following year. *E. vulgare*, the native Viper's Bugloss, 2–3 ft, with its violet-blue flowers, is a biennial for the wild garden; but its v. 'Blue Bedder', 1 ft, is a compact blue-flowering form which may be grown as a hardy annual.

Ecology. The study of the habits, lives and relationships between plants and animals and their environment (*see* Habitat).

Edelweiss. See *Leontopodium alpinum*.

Edging-iron. A half-moon or crescent-shaped, sharp, steel-bladed tool, with a straight handle; used to cut and trim the verges of lawns and turf manually.

Edgings. Beds and borders may be given edgings of dwarf annuals (Ageratum, Alyssum, Bellis, Candytuft, Linaria, Lobelia, Tagetes), of dwarf

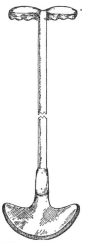

FIG. 94 Edging-iron, modern design.

perennials, or of shrubs such as dwarf Box (see *Buxus*), *Euonymus radicans* or lavender; or a strip of turf, at least 2 ft wide, kept trim and mown.

Edgings to driveways or paths can be of stone, tile or concrete kerbing, bricks or preservatively treated wood on short stakes; their sharp edging broken by suitable mat-forming plants (Aubrieta, Campanulas, Saxifrages, Nepeta, Armeria, alpine Dianthus, etc.). Lawn edges can be made easier to keep trim by means of aluminium, galvanized steel or plastic edging driven in flush with the surface of the turf.

Edraianthus (ed-ra-i-an'thus. Fam. Campanulaceae). Pretty flowering perennials, related to Campanula and Wahlenbergia, with funnel or bell-shaped early summer flowers, for rock gardens.

Selection. E. caudatus, Dalmatia, 3 in., heads of purple flowers, July; *dinaricus*, Dalmatia, 3 in., violet-blue flowers, June; *graminifolius*, Dalmatia, 3 in., heads of purple flowers, June–July, and *tenuifolius*, Dalmatia, to 6 in., violet-blue, white, summer, are all hardy for most gardens.

Cultivation. Plant March–April, well-drained, porous and deep soil, likes lime; in rock gardens; or in pans in the alpine house. Sunny positions.

Propagation. By seeds sown in March, in pans, in cold frame or greenhouse. By tufted cuttings, detached in late May–early June, inserted in propagating case.

Edulis (-e). Edible. Ex. *Physalis edulis.*

Eelworms. Belonging to the *Nemotoda*, eelworms are minute, usually microscopic, free-living, worm-like creatures, parasitic on many plants, causing galls, knots, distortion and cysts. Chrysanthemum, cucumber, melon, mushroom, narcissus, potato, currant, fern, onion, and phlox, tomato and tulip, are chiefly infested. Control may be achieved by the use of heat in hot water or soil sterilization treatment or the application of a parathion insecticide. For treatment *see under* the plants concerned.

Eggplant. See Aubergine.

Elgantine. See *Rosa eglanteria*.

Eichhornia (ak-horn'i-a. Fam. Pontederiaceae). Tropical aquatic plants with showy flowers, for a tank in the warm greenhouse.

Selection. E. azurea, Brazil, bright pale blue flowers, July; and *crasspipes* (*speciosa*), S. America, violet-blue, July, are chiefly grown; placed in the water as floating plants, shallow water, with loam soil in which the roots can root. A weed in tropical countries, it is not easy to keep under artificial conditions; winter temp. 13° C. (55° F.). Propagation by division in spring.

Elaeagnus (el-e-ag'nus. Fam. Elaeagnaceae). Deciduous and evergreen flowering shrubs, chiefly from China and Japan, and hardy except for the coldest localities.

Selection. E. angustifolia, the Oleaster, S. Europe, 15–20 ft, yellow, bell-shaped flowers, June; *argentea*, U.S.A., 6–10 ft, drooping silvery yellow flowers, small silvery fruits later; and *multiflora*, China, Japan, 6–10 ft, yellow-white flowers, April–May, and edible red fruits in autumn, are deciduous, doing best in mild localities, and lightish soils. *E. macrophylla*, Korea, Japan, to 10 ft, silvery foliage, flowers late in October; *glabra*, Japan, China, 15 ft, shining leaves with yellow and brown scales, late October, brownish white flowers; *pungens*, Japan, to 15 ft, leaves with white and brown scales, has notable vs.

in *dicksonii, maculata, simonii, tricolor* and *variegata*, grown for their lovely variegated foliage is shades of gold, yellow to white.

Cultivation. Plant deciduous spp. in October–March; evergreens September–October or March–April, in well-drained porous soil, sunny but sheltered positions. Prune, if necessary, early spring. Do not like much root disturbance.

Propagation. Deciduous kinds by seeds, sown April, under cloches or in cold frames. Evergreens by cuttings of young firm shoots, July–August, inserted in sandy loam, in cold frame or under handlights.

Elatior. Taller. Ex. *Primula elatior.*

Elatus (-a, -um). Tall. Ex. *Hypericum elatum.*

Elder. See *Sambucus.*

Elecampane. See *Inula helenium.*

Electricity in Gardening. Electricity with its great advantages of cleanliness, ease of control, reasonable capital costs and efficiency, is being increasingly used in gardening. Its chief applications are: (1) Space heating of frames and greenhouses, by fan, convector, tubular or wire heaters, thermostatically controlled. (2) Soil heating, either by insulated cable or bare wires laid in the soil. (3) Soil sterilization, preferably by heating the soil between two electrodes. (4) Provision of light to advance growth or supplement poor natural light, as in winter; or to advance or retard flowering by disrupting photoperiodism in plants sensitive to light. (5) Provision of power and/or light points in the garden for electrically driven machines such as mowers, hedge-trimmers, etc., and for floodlighting at night. *See* Greenhouse, Light, Photoperiodism, Soil Sterilization.

Elegans. Elegant, graceful. Ex. *Humea elegans.*

Elisena (el-is-e′na. Fam. Amaryllidaceae). The ornamental bulbous plant, *E. longipetala,* Lima, 3 ft, may be grown in the cool greenhouse for its magnificent umbels of white, funnel-shaped flowers in May; potted in autumn, standard compost, overwintered, and kept rather dry, at 7° C. (45° F.); with gradually increasing watering as growth is made, and till leaf growth is over in autumn.

Propagation. By offsets, when repotting.

Elk's Horn Fern. See *Platycerium.*

Ellipticus (-a, -um). Elliptical, oval, twice as long as wide, pointed at both ends. Ex. *Garrya elliptica.*

FIG. 95   Elliptic leaf.

Elm. See *Ulmus.*

Elodea (**Anacharis**) (el-o′de-a. Fam. Hydrocharidaceae). Underwater oxygenating aquatic plants for the garden pool, dioecious, and chiefly female plants grown.

Selection. E. canadensis, Canadian Pondweed, N. America, can become invasive; *crispa,* curled leaves, white flowers; and *densa,* S. America, white flowers.

Cultivation. Plant April–June, in bottom of pools; propagated by cuttings, dibbled in.

Elongatus (-a, -um). Elongate, much lengthened. Ex. *Acacia elongata.*

Elsholtzia (el-sholtz′i-a. Fam. Labiatae). The only species grown, *E. stauntonii,* N. China, to 5 ft, is an autumn-flowering shrub, with spikes of small purple-pink flowers, apt to be cut back by hard winter weather but shoots again in spring.

Cultivation. Plant early autumn or March–April; porous, humus-rich soil, sunny, sheltered position. Prune in February–March of dead and weak wood.

Propagation. By seeds, sown in spring, outdoors. By cuttings of young shoots, in summer, under handlights.

Embothrium (em-both′ri-um. Fam. Proteaceae). Evergreen shrubs or trees of S. America, of which *E. coccineum*, the Chilean Firethorn, to 40 ft, blazes with racemes of narrow, tubular, scarlet-crimson flowers, with protruding styles, in May–June, but is only eligible for mild localities, such as Cornwall, N. Wales and W. Scotland, on peaty, more or less lime-free soils, well drained and sunny; v. *longifolium*, with longer, narrower leaves, is held to be hardier. Plant in March–April; propagated by seeds, sown in spring, bottom heat of 18° C. (65° F.), in cool greenhouse.

Embryo. The rudimentary plant of an ovule after fertilization, in a seed.

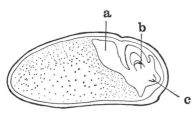

FIG. 96 Embryo. A seed in section: a. cotyledon; b. plumule; and c. radicle; constitute the embryo, in a grain of wheat.

Emilia (Cacalia), Tassel Flower (e-mil′i-a. Fam. Compositae). The chief species grown is *E. flammea* (*Cacalia coccinea*), tropical America, 1–2 ft, a half-hardy annual, with clusters of small scarlet flowers in summer; v. *lutea* has golden-yellow flowers. Seeds are sown, under glass, standard compost, bottom heat of 18° C. (65° F.), March, for planting out in May.

Eminens. Eminent, outstanding. Ex. *Cuphea eminens*.

Empetrum (em-pet′rum. Fam. Empetraceae). The one species grown is the evergreen, heath-like *E. nigrum*, or Crowberry, a native of N. Britain, and many other countries, 6–12 in., dioecious (except in v. *hermaphroditum*), pink flowers in May, brownish-black edible berries in autumn; and v. *rubrum*, brownish-purple flowers. May be planted in peaty, moist soil, autumn or spring; and propagated by cuttings of young shoots in summer, under handlights, in peaty sandy soil.

Enchytraeid Worms. Small white, or pinkish, bristled worms, often found in compost, leaf-mould, and damp soils; in pots, around aster roots and plants with an accumulation of moribund roots; also known as pot worms, not to be confused with eelworms, since the latter are not discernible to the eye.

Endemic. Belonging naturally to a region or country.

Endive (*Cichorium endivia*). A reasonably hardy annual, useful as a salading and an alternative to lettuce, especially in autumn, winter and spring, yielding leaves of good flavour, with a slight bitterness. There are two varieties: the broad-leaved Batavian which is hardier, and the Green Curled, more esteemed for salads. A warm, humus-rich soil, pH 6.5, is best. Sowings may be made in drills, ½ in. deep, 1 ft apart, in June–August, for winter–spring cropping, thinning seedlings to 12 in. apart. Earlier sowings may be made for autumn cropping, but as slow germination encourages bolting these are best made under glass, and seedlings transplanted, with as little check to growth as possible. Blanching reduces bitterness of taste, and can be done by tying outer leaves up, or by inverting flower-pots, with drainage hole covered, over plants. Plants may also be lifted with soil ball, and placed in covered frames. Steps must be taken to control slugs, which are very fond of these plants.

Endocarp. The inmost layer of a drupe; i.e. the 'stone' of a peach or plum. *See* Drupe.

Endodermis. The inner layer of the cortex of the root or stem of a dicotyledon.

Endogens. Inward growers, an old name for monocotyledons.

Endophytic. Growing inside another plant.

Endosperm. The nutritive tissue formed in the embryo sac of seeds of flowering plants. *See* Fig. 97, page 206.

Endymion (en-di′mi-on. Fam. Liliaceae). This genus now includes the bulbous plants which renew their bulbs annually formerly placed under Hyacinthus or Scilla, though some botanists hold that the correct name is Hyacinthoides.

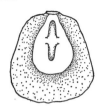

FIG. 97 Endosperm, surrounding the embryo in a seed of Corn (*Zea mays*).

Selection. E. *nonscriptus* (*Hyacintha nonscriptus*, *Scilla nutans*, *S. nonscripta*), the Bluebell or wild Hyacinth of England and W. Europe, 10–18 in., upright racemes of nodding, blue, purple, pink or white bell-like flowers, April–June; and *hispanica*, Spain, Portugal, 6–9 in., with blue, sometimes rose-purple or white, bell-shaped flowers, May; and their several varieties and hybrids.

Cultivation. Plant 3 in. deep, as much apart, in any ordinary soil; excellent for woodland and naturalizing. Propagation is easy from seeds.

Enkianthus (en-ki-an'thus. Fam. Ericaceae). Deciduous shrubs of the Far East, with whorled branches and pretty racemes of bell-like flowers in spring, needing a lime-free, well-drained soil.

Selection. E. *campanulatus*, Japan, to 12 ft, pale yellow, red-tipped flowers, May, and v. *palibinii*, with rich red flowers; *cernuus*, Japan, 5–8 ft, nodding white flowers, May, and v. *rubens*, rich red flowers; *chinensis*, China, to 20 ft, yellow-red, campanulate flowers, May; and *perulatus*, Japan, to 6 ft, white flowers, May, are the hardiest; good autumn foliage colour.

Cultivation. Plant October–April, well-drained, peaty, lime-free soil; sunny positions or light shade. Prune, if necessary, after flowering.

Propagation. By cuttings of firm shoots, in spring, in propagating frame. By seeds, sown in April.

Ensiformis (-e). Ensiform; sword-shaped as with leaves of Iris.

Entire. Of leaves with smooth, unbroken margins.

Entomophilous. Insect-loving, or insect-fertilized.

Entomophily. The fertilization of plants by insects.

Environment. The surroundings and conditions of soil, atmosphere, sun, shade, air and weather under which a plant or organism grows.

Enzyme. An organic substance, produced by living cells, which acts as a catalyst in bringing about chemical reactions, without being changed in itself; apparently a protein of complexity. Plant cells produce many enzymes in their protoplasm, each specific in effecting one type of the chemical reactions, essential to growth.

Eomecon (e-o-me'con. Fam. Papaveraceae). The one species, E. *chionanthum*, E. China, 1 ft, is a lovely herbaceous perennial, with cordate leaves, and large white flowers, summer, for growing in well-drained, leaf-mould enriched soil, in sheltered sunny positions, of borders or rock garden.

Propagation. By division of the rhizomatous roots in spring.

Epacris (e-pak'ris. Fam. Epacridaceae). Beautiful, heath-like, evergreen, winter-flowering shrubs of Australia and New Zealand best grown in pots in the cool greenhouse.

Selection. E. *impressa*, Australia, Tasmania, erect-growing, 3 ft, pure white, shaded red, flowers, December–February, and vs. *grandiflora*, purple-red, and *ceraeflora*, white; *longiflora*, New S. Wales, 4 ft, rose-crimson, and white, May; and *purpurascens*, New S. Wales, 3 ft, white, suffused purple, March–April, are worth while attempting.

Cultivation. Pot about May, standard compost without lime, keeping rather close until established; then give good light, water moderately but regularly, ventilate well, aiming to thoroughly

FIG. 98 Entire leaf.

ripen shoots for winter, when plants need very moderate watering, minimum temp. of 7° C. (45° F.), and sun. After flowering, prune hard back, keep close until growing again; renew some of the top soil of pots, taking care not to injure hair-like roots.

Propagation. By tip cuttings of young shoots, in pans of sandy peat, under a handlight or bell-glass.

Epi-. Prefix of compound words, signifying upon.

Epicarp. The outmost or uppermost layer of a drupe.

Epicattleya. Hybrid orchids of Epidendrum × Cattleya species, to be grown as Cattleya. *See* specialist growers' lists and shows for named forms.

Epicotyl. The portion of the stem immediately above the cotyledons of a seedling plant.

Epidendrum (e-pi-den'drum. Fam. Orchidaceae). A very large genus of beautiful orchids, chiefly epiphytic, of which the following may be grown in a cool greenhouse, minimum winter temp. 7° C. (45° F.).

Selection. E. evectum, Colombia, 30 in., rose-purple flowers, summer; *cochleatum*, W. Indies, maroon-purple, yellowish-green, summer; *radiatum*, Mexico, 1 ft, creamy white, purple-lined, summer; *radicans*, Guatemala, to 5 ft, orange-red, summer; *vitellinum*, Mexico, 12 in., yellow, summer, and v. *majus*, cinnabar-orange, spring; and *xanthinum*, Minas Geraes, 2 ft, yellow, summer.

Cultivation. Pot, and repot, March; well-drained pots, compost of equal parts live sphagnum moss and fibrous peat, with charcoal; watering liberally in active growth, with moist atmosphere; very little during dormant period in winter.

Propagation. By division in March–April.

Epidermis. The outermost superficial layer of cells, covering almost all parts of a plant.

Epigaea (e-pi-gi'a. Fam. Ericaceae). Evergreen creeping shrubs, of which *E. asiatica*, Japan, makes a prostrate mat of bristly stems, cordate, ovate leaves, and racemes of rose-pink, white fragrant flowers in May; *E. repens*, N. America, the May Flower or Trailing Arbutus, with somewhat larger leaves and white,

tinged pink flowers in May, and their hybrid × *intertexta*, are hardy.

Cultivation. Plant September–October or March–April, in porous, lime-free, humus-rich soil in shade from direct sun.

Propagation. By division in early September; detaching rooted stems; by cuttings of stems, July–August.

Epigynous. Descriptive of a flower in which the sepals, petals and stamens grow above the ovary.

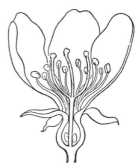

FIG. 99   Epigynous flower (Apple).

Epilobium (e-pi-lo'bi-um. Fam. Onagraceae). Hardy herbaceous perennials, many of which are prone to spread and become weeds.

Selection. E. angustifolium, the French Willow or Rose Bay Willow-herb, 3–6 ft, long racemes of rose flowers, July, is splendid in woodland or wild garden; *hirsutum*, Codlins and Cream or Great Hairy Willow-herb, 3–5 ft, pale pink, July, does well in moist places and by water; and *rosmarinifolium*, to 2 ft, bright pink, summer, for the border, are native species; *obcordatum*, California, is a creeping dwarf of 3 in., with large rose-purple flowers in summer, worth a place in sun and well-drained soil in the rock garden.

Cultivation. Plant October–March in appropriate settings and soil as suggested above, cut down after flowering, unless spread by self-seeding is desired.

Propagation. By division in spring. By seed, sown out of doors, April.

Epimedium (e-pi-me'di-um. Fam.

Berberidaceae). Hardy flowering perennials with creeping rhizomatous roots, useful for shade in the rock garden or border.

Selection. E. *alpinum*, Europe, 6–9 in., Barrenwort, ternate compound leaves, slipper-shaped flowers of crimson and yellow, May; *grandiflorum*, Japan, to 15 in., white, yellow and rose flowers, spring; and v. 'Rose Queen'; their hybrid, × *rubrum*, creeping, many-flowered panicles of crimson flowers, spring; *pinnatum*, Georgia, to 1 ft, large leafed, bright yellow, early summer; and hybrids × *versicolor*, old rose and yellow; × *warleyense*, coppery-red and yellow; and × *youngianum*, to 1 ft, white, spring.

Cultivation. Plant autumn or spring; well-drained, humus-rich loam, in partial shade, borders or rock garden.

Propagation. By division in autumn.

Epipactis (e-pi-pak′tis. Fam. Orchidaceae). Hardy terrestrial orchids or helleborines, which may be easily cultivated in shady woodland.

Selection. E. *gigantea*, N. America, 3 ft, yellowish brown flowers, striped red, July, is pretty; *helleborine*, 2–3 ft, green, marked yellow, white or purple, flowers, July–August; and *palustris*, 12 in., whitish, tinged crimson flowers, July, may be grown, the last in quite boggy ground.

Cultivation. Plant October–March.

Propagation. By division when foliage dies down. By seeds, sown April, where plants are to grow.

Epiphyllum (e-pi-pil′lum. Fam. Cactaceae). The Orchid Cactus, formerly Phyllocactus. Plants with long, thin, flattened leaf-like stems, with crenate margins, angled or ribbed, beautiful large flowers.

Selection. E. *ackermannii*, Mexico, very large crimson flowers; *anguliger*, Mexico, strongly ribbed, white; *crenatum*, Honduras, cream to yellow, scented; *oxypetalum*, Mexico to Brazil, fragrant, white to red; and many hybrids such as 'Adonis', pink; 'Amber Queen', orange; 'Flamingo', scarlet; 'Oriole', yellow, gold and white; and 'Sun Goddess', orange and gold.

Cultivation. Pot in spring, rather large pots, well crocked, compost of equal parts medium loam, leaf-mould and sand, with a little charcoal; water freely, syringe often, in summer, keeping in half shade; no water in winter, temp. 7° C. (45° F.), do well in north windows.

Propagation. By stem cuttings, taken from the broadest part, in summer. By seeds, sown in spring, under glass, in cool greenhouse.

Epiphyte. A plant that grows upon another plant without being parasitic or deriving nutriment from it; e.g. *Vanda* spp. and similar orchids.

Equestris (-e). Of a horse. Ex. *Hippeastrum equestre*.

Equisetum, Horse-tail (e-qui-se′tum. Fam. Equisetaceae). Botanically interesting as the only genus of its kind of non-flowering, vascular cryptogamous plants; perennial with persistent creeping rhizomatous roots, allied to ferns. E. *telmateia*, to 6 ft, may be grown by water in large gardens effectively; but *arvense*, *sylvaticum*, *pratense* and other native species easily become weed problems, calling for repeated treatment with a 2,4-D or 2,4,5-T herbicide; and/or mechanical destruction by hoeing and forking out of roots, to control.

Eragrostis, Love Grass (e-ra-gros′tis. Fam. Gramineae). Pretty annual grasses, grown for their panicles of many-flowered spikelets, for border decoration and drying for winter.

Selection. E. *abessinica*, Teff of Ethiopa, to 3 ft; *interrupta*, Brazil, 1 to 2 ft, are chiefly grown.

Cultivation. Sown in April, where they are to grow, and thinned to 9 in. apart.

Eranthis, Winter Aconite (e-ran′this. Fam. Ranunculaceae). Tuberous-rooted herbaceous perennials, valued for their early cupped yellow flowers borne on short stems, above a ruff of foliage.

Selection. E. *cilicica*, Greece, Asia Minor, 2½ in.; *hyemalis*, W. Europe, 4 in.; and their hybrid × *thunbergeniana*, with larger flowers; all blooming in February–March.

Cultivation. Plant tubers in summer or early autumn, 1½–2 in. deep, in woodland, shrubbery, and allow to naturalize. Take precautions against mice.

Propagation. By division of tubers, summer; or by seeds, sown as soon as ripe.

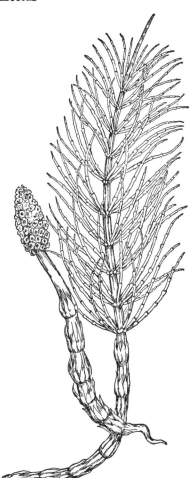

FIG. 100 *Equisetum arvense*, Common Horsetail, a troublesome weed.

Erectus (-a, -um). Erect, upright. Ex. *Prunus serrulata* v. *erecta*.

Eremurus, Foxtail Lily (er-e-mu′rus. Fam. Liliaceae). Stately, herbaceous perennial plants, with magnificent tall spikes of small flowers arising from the crowns of thick, thong-rooted stocks in early summer.

Selection. E. *aitchisonii*, Afghanistan, 3–5 ft, red flowers; *bungei*, Persia, 2 ft, yellow; *elwesii*, to 8 ft, pink; *himalaicus*, 2 ft, white; *olgae*, Turkestan, 5 ft, white; *robustus*, Turkestan, 8 ft, peach; and hybrid strains such as × 'Highdown' and × 'Shelford' in shades of orange, buff, pink, etc.

Cultivation. Plant with crowns 6 in. below surface of porous, deep, loamy soil, 2 ft apart, in warm, sunny positions, sheltered from spring frosts, in August–September, and leave two to four years undisturbed, dressing with rotted manure or compost annually, in spring. Cut down flowered stems.

Propagation. By seeds in spring, under glass, standard compost, bottom heat of 18° C. (65° F.); but take six years to flower. By careful separation of multiple crowns in August.

Erica, Heath (e-ri′ka. Fam. Ericaceae). Evergreen flowering shrubs or small trees, largely of Africa and Europe, for the greenhouse and outdoor garden.

Selection. Greenhouse Heaths consist chiefly of S. African species: *E. campanulata*, 1–2 ft, yellow flowering, June–August; × *cavendishiana*, 2 ft, yellow, May–June; *gracilis*, 1½ ft, rose, September–December, and vs.; *hyemalis*, 1½ ft, rose and white, winter; *massonii*, to 3 ft, red and green, summer; *canaliculata*, 2 ft, white, pink-tinted, March–May; *primuloides*, 1 ft, red and white, summer; *ventricosa*, 2–4 ft, white to rose, June–September, and several vs.; and × *willmorei*, to 2 ft, deep pink, white tipped, summer.

Cultivation. Pot, and repot as necessary, about September, compost of equal parts fibrous peat and sandy loam, or 3 parts peat to 1 part sharp sand; water regularly in active growth, moderately in winter; winter temps. 7–13° C. (45–55° F.); grow rather cool, good light, but shade from sudden bursts of hot sun. Trim after flowering. Propagate by short, non-flowered shoot cuttings, in pans, in propagating case; spring and summer.

Hardy Heaths. These include natives of the Mediterranean region, Europe and Britain, some of which, notably *E. carnea* and vs., *mediterranea* and vs., *terminalis* and *vagans*, tolerate lime in the soil; though all grow well in lime-free, peaty, well-drained soils.

Selection. E. *arborea*, S. Europe, etc., the Tree Heath, to 15 ft, white flowers, March–April, and vs., needs mild locality; as does *australis*, the Spanish Heath, Spain, Portugal, to 8 ft, purplish-red, April–June; v. 'Mr Robert', white,

FIG. 101   *Erica carnea* v. *vivellii* on the left, v. 'Springwood White' on the right.

is hardier. E. *carnea*, C. and S. Europe, and its many vs. *atrorubra*, rose-red; 'Cecilia M. Beale', white; *gracilis*, rose-pink; 'James Backhouse', rose-pink; 'King George', deep pink; 'Queen Mary', rose-red; 'Ruby Glow', ruby-red; 'Springwood Pink', pink; 'Springwood White', best white; *vivellii*, carmine; and 'Winter Beauty', rose-pink, and others; with *mediterranea*, rosy-red, and vs. *alba*, white; 'Brightness', rose-pink; *superba*, pink; 'W. T. Rackliff', white; and × *darleyensis*, pink, and vs., give winter colour November–April. E. *ciliaris*, Dorset

Heath, SW. Europe, and vs. 'Stoborough', white, June–October; *cinerea*, the Scotch or Bell Heath, rosy-purple, and vs. *alba major*, white; 'C. D. Eason', scarlet; 'Apple Blossom', shell pink, etc.; June–September; *tetralix*, the Bell Heath, NW. Europe, 1 ft, rose-red, and vs. *alba*, white; *lawsoniana*, pink; *mollis*, white; 'Pink Glow', *rosea*, rose pink; June–October; *vagans*, the Cornish Heath, 2 ft, rose, and vs. *alba*, white, *kevernensis*, rose-pink, 'Lyonesse', white; and 'Mrs D. F. Maxwell', cherry-pink, July–August; *terminalis*, the Corsican Heath, W. Mediterranean region, to 6 ft, pink, late summer; while *lusitanica*, Portuguese tree heath, to 10 ft, white, March–May; *scoparia*, the Besom Heath of Madeira, to 12 ft, greenish flowers, May–June; *umbellata*, Spain, Morocco, 1–3 ft, pink, May–June, and × *veitchii*, a hybrid tree heath to 6 ft, white, February–March, are only hardy enough for mild localities and shelter.

Cultivation. Plant October or March–April, free-draining soil, enriched with peat or leaf-mould; and lime-free for all except the species noted. Trim to keep compact after flowering.

Propagation. By layers, spring; by cuttings of young growing tips of unflowered shoots in summer; by seeds sown in spring, though slow to come to flower. See also *Calluna* and *Daboecia*.

Erigeron, Fleabane (e-rig′er-on. Fam. Compositae). Hardy herbaceous perennials, flowering profusely in summer with ray flowers strongly resembling those of Michaelmas Daisies.

Selection. E. *auranticus*, Turkestan, 1 ft, bright orange flowers, and vs. *superbus*; *sulphureus*; *macranthus*, Rocky Mts., 2 ft, blue-rayed flowers; *speciosus*, Western N. America, 1½–2 ft, violet-blue, and named forms such as 'Amity', pink; 'Amos Perry', lavender-blue; 'Festivity', lilac; 'Prosperity', semi-double mauve; 'Quakeress', silvery-lilac; 'White Quakeress'; and 'Sincerity', mauve blue, are good for borders. E. *aureus*, Western N. America, 3 in., deep-yellow; *compositus*, Western N. America, 4 in., white or pale blue; *leiomorus*, Rocky Mts, 4 in., violet; and *uniflorus*, Western N. America, 4 in., whitish or purple, are good for the rock garden or alpine house. *E. mucronatus*, Mexico, 6 in., white, flowers freely but needs winter protection.

Cultivation. Plant in autumn or spring, well-drained, ordinary soil, enriched with organic matter, in sun.

Propagation. By seeds sown in April–June, cold frame, or greenhouse. By division in spring. By cuttings in a cold frame in August, to winter.

Erinacea (e-rin-a′ke-a. Fam. Leguminosae). A genus of one species, *E. anthyllis (pungens)*, Spain, France, N. Africa, the Hedgehog Broom, a dome-like evergreen shrub, with violet-blue flowers in May; suitable for well-drained, lightish peaty soil, in a warm sheltered spot in the rock garden; planted in September or April; or in cold districts in a pan in the alpine house. Grows rather slowly. Propagation by cuttings in a propagating frame, July–August; by seeds, in greenhouse, March, bottom heat of 18° C. (65° F.), to plant seedlings out in May.

Erinus (e-ri′nus. Fam. Scrophulariaceae). The sole species grown is *E. alpinus*, a tufted alpine from the mts. of SW. Europe, 6 in., with racemes of purple flowers, May; and two vs. *albus*, white flowering, and 'Dr Hanele', carmine; for planting in well-drained soil, sunny warmth, in the rock garden; or may be established by dropping seeds where they are to develop in March–April.

Eriobotrya, Japanese Loquat (e-ri-o-bot′ri-a. Fam. Rosaceae). The species chiefly grown is *E. japonica*, China and Japan, an evergreen small tree, to 20 ft. with large, strongly ribbed, glossy green leaves, fragrant, yellowish-white flowers in woolly panicles, September; hardy in the south-west, but elsewhere needing a warm, sunny sheltered south wall, and humus-rich, well-drained soil; but unfortunately does not ripen its yellow, pear-shaped edible fruits in Britain. Propagation is by cuttings of young shoots, with a heel, in summer, in frame; by seeds, sown under glass, June.

Eriogonum (e-ri-o-go′num. Fam. Polygonaceae). Only a few of the N. American perennial herbs of this genus are grown, such as *E. jamesii*, New Mexico, a tufted mat of rosetted leaves, 4 in. high, with white or cream flowers,

summer; *racemosum*, W. America, low sub-shrub with white to pink flowers, July; and *umbellatum*, a branching evergreen carpeter, with yellow flowers, September.

Cultivation. Plant March–April, peat-enriched, well-drained soil, full sun, in rock garden.

Propagation. From seeds sown April, in pans, with bottom heat of 18° C. (65° F.). By division in spring.

Eriophorum, Cotton Grass (e-ri-op′or-um. Fam. Cyperaceae). Perennial rhizamatous herbs of which *E. alpinum*, to 10 in.; *angustifolium*, to 18 in.; *latifolium*, to 18 in.; and *vaginatum*, Hare's-tail, to 10 in.; natives of boggy places in the N. hemisphere, including Britain, may be grown in damp places and pool margins for their silky white tufted flower-heads. Planted in March; or propagated by seeds sown where plants are to grow in spring, or by division.

Eritrichium (e-ri-trik′i-um. Fam. Boraginaceae). The species *E. nanum*, a dwarf, tufted alpine of high European Alps, with forget-me-not clear blue, yellow-eyed flowers, June–August, is best attempted in the alpine house, in a pan with compost of 1 part leaf-mould, 3 parts silver sand and a little charcoal, kept moist; as it is not easy to keep out of doors. *E. rupestre*, and v. *pectinata*, Asian mts., 6 in., with blue flowers, yellow-eyed, in sprays, is reputedly easier; in scree, given winter protection with a pane of glass above.

Erodium, Heron's Bill (e-ro′di-um. Fam. Geraniaceae). Hardy flowering perennials, allied to Geranium, which produce summer bloom in the rock garden or border.

Selection. E. absinthoides, SE. Europe, 6 in., soft pink, and v. *amanum*, white, summer; *chamaedryoides*, Majorca, 3 in., white, veined pink, and v. *roseum*, rose; *chrysanthemum*, Greece, 6 in., creamy-yellow (dioecious); *corsicum*, silvery mat, rosy pink flowers, and v. *album*, white; *macradenum*, Pyrenees, 6 in., pale violet; *manescavi*, Pyrenees, 1 ft, carmine; and *supracanum*, Pyrenees, 4 in., white, veined red.

Cultivation. Plant March–April, well-drained, light, leaf-mould enriched soil, sunny positions, in rock garden; or in pans in alpine house.

Propagation. By seeds, sown April, or when ripe, in late July, in pans, cold frame. By cuttings of young stems in May; by root cuttings in April.

Eryngium, Sea Holly (e-ring'i-um. Fam. Umbelliferae). Distinctive herbaceous perennials, with spiny foliage and metallic-blue flower-heads and bluish-green stems and leaves.

Selection. E. alpinum, Europe, 2 ft, pale green foliage, soft thistle-like beautiful blue flowers, summer; *amethystinum*, Europe, to 2 ft, globose heads of amethyst blue; *bourgati*, Pyrenees, 1–2 ft, blue ovate flower-heads; *maritimum*, native Sea Holly, 1½ ft, pale blue roundish heads; × *oliverianum*, 3 ft, deep blue; *planum*, E. Europe, 2 ft, round heads of blue; *giganteum*, Caucasus, to 4 ft, ovate, blue flower-heads; and *tripartitum*, 2½ ft, steel-blue round flower-heads, are hardy and summer-flowering. *E. agavifolium*, Argentine, 6 ft, cylindrical blue flower-heads, spring; *bromeliifolium*, Mexico, 4 ft, round white flower-heads, July; and *serra*, Brazil, to 6 ft, with small white flower-heads, autumn, are half-hardy, and need mild, sheltered quarters, or winter protection.

Cultivation. Plant preferably in March–April; light, well-drained soil, sunny positions.

Propagation. By seeds, sown in spring or early summer, in outdoor seed-bed; by division in March.

Erysimum (e-ris'im-um. Fam. Cruciferae). A rather mixed genus of flowering herbs, related to Cheiranthus. *E. perofskianum*, Afghanistan, 1 ft, is an annual, with reddish-orange flowers, in summer, from spring sowings in good soil, full sun. *E. arkansanum*, Arkansas, Texas, 1½ ft, yellow, and v. 'Golden Gem', are biennial, to sow in June out of doors, and plant in flowering quarters in August for following summer. *E. alpinum*, Scandinavia, 6 in., sulphur-yellow flowers, May, and v. 'Moonlight', soft yellow, and 'Pamela Pershouse', deep yellow; *linifolium* (*Cheiranthus linifolius*), Spain, 1 ft, purple mauve, May–July; *pumilum*, European Alps, 3 in., pale yellow, July–August; and *rupestre*, Asia Minor, 1 ft, sulphur-yellow, spring, are perennials for rock garden or border; planted in early autumn or

March–April; or raised from seeds, in cold frame, summer.

Erythrina (e-ri-thri'na. Fam. Leguminosae). Tropical shrubs and trees of which the most commonly grown is *E. crista-galli*, the Coral-tree of Brazil, growing 4–8 ft, with tri-foliolate leaves, and racemes of bright deep scarlet, pea-like flowers in summer, or shoots that die back to the woody stock in winter; its hybrid × *bidwillii* behaves similarly. They may be grown by a sunny, warm, sheltered wall in the mildest localities, but are usually grown in pots or tubs, planted in April, standard compost, to move outdoors for summer, keeping well watered and syringed, and then to the cool greenhouse in October, for wintering, when very little water is needed, with a temp. of 7° C. (45° F.). Propagation by seeds, spring, under glass, with bottom heat of 18° C. (65° F.), or cuttings of young shoots taken with a heel, in spring, when grown out to 3 in. or so.

Erythronium (e-ri-thro'ni-um. Fam. Liliaceae). Charming bulbous plants, with radical ornamentally mottled leaves, and cyclamen-like flowers in spring.

Selection. E. dens-canis, the Dog's-tooth Violet, Europe, Asia, Japan, 6 in., with 2-in. purple-rose flowers, and vs. *album*, white; 'Lilac Wonder', 'Purple King' and 'Rose Queen'; naturalize freely; American kinds are *americanum*, 6 in., bright yellow; *californicum*, to 18 in., creamy-white; *grandiflorum*, 6 in., bright yellow; *oregonum*, 16 in., creamy-yellow; *howellii*, 6 in., pale yellow, orange spotted; *revolutum*, 1 ft, cream, tinged purple, and vs. 'White Beauty', 'Pink Beauty' and *johnsonii* deep rose; and *tuolumnense*, 1 ft, deep yellow to white; and many fine hybrids are offered by growers.

Cultivation. Plant August–October, well-drained, loamy soil; 3 in. deep, 3–4 in. apart, in rock garden or shrubbery, or front of borders, to flower in March–April. May be pot-grown in cold frames. Do not mind partial shade.

Propagation. Choice kinds by offsets when lifting and dividing in August. Species by seeds, sown in autumn, as soon as ripe, in cold frame, or sheltered seed-bed.

Escallonia (es-kal-lon'i-a. Fam.

Saxifragaceae). Evergreen shrubs from S. America, flowering freely in summer, but imperfectly hardy except in mild districts and near the south and west coasts; apt to lose their leaves in cold winters.

Selection. E. *virgata*, Chile, 4 ft, pure white flowers, June–July, is deciduous and the hardiest sp.; *leucantha*, Chile, to 15 ft, white, July; *macrantha*, Island of Chiloe, 6–9 ft, bright rosy crimson, admirable for seaside gardens; and *pterocladon*, Patagonia, 8 ft, fragrant white flowers, may be tried, but the hybrids are best of all, such as × *iveyi*, to 10 ft, white; × *langleyensis*, to 10 ft, rosy carmine; and the Irish 'Apple Blossom', compact, pink and white; 'C. F. Ball', crimson, tall; 'Donard Beauty', 4 ft, rosy-red; 'Donard Brilliance', large, rose-red; 'Donard Radiance', bright red; 'Donard Seedling', 6 ft, pale pink; and 'Glory of Donard', scarlet, from the Slieve Donard nurseries.

Cultivation. Plant September–October or March–April; well-drained, humus-enriched soil; in sun and warmth, in borders, on walls; some types, especially 'Red Hedger', make fine informal hedges. Prune, when necessary, after flowering.

Propagation. By cuttings of young unflowered shoots, with heel, in July–August, in cold frame or under hand-lights.

Eschalot. *See* Shallot.

Eschscholtzia, Californian Poppy (esk-skolt′zi-a. Fam. Papaveraceae). The plants chiefly grown for their gorgeous, colourful summer flowers are the annual forms of E. *californica*, Californian Poppy, 1–1½ ft, such as *alba flore pleno*, semi-double, white; and a range of colours indicated in their names, 'Carmine King', 'Cherry Ripe', 'Chrome Queen', 'Firedame', 'Orange King', 'Ramona White', 'Mandarin', orange, and others to be chosen in seedsmen's lists; and *caespitosa*, 6 in., yellow, and its v. 'Sundew'.

Cultivation. Sow seeds under glass, March, standard compost, bottom heat of 18° C. (65° F.), to prick off and plant out in early May; or sow in April, thinly, where they are to flower, thinning seedlings; good well-drained soil, sunny positions.

Esculentus (-a, -um). Suitable for food. Ex. *Camassia esculenta.*

Espalier. A term now used to describe a tree trained with one vertical stem, from which horizontal branches are trained, roughly opposite in one plane; particularly fruit trees. Espaliers are useful to line walks or demarcate a vegetable plot from the ornamental garden. *See* Apples, etc.

Etaerio. An aggregate of drupel fruits as in Blackberry.

Etiolation. Blanching of the green colouring matter (chlorophyll) by excluding light, as in forcing vegetables such as rhubarb, and flowers.

Eu-. Prefix meaning good.

Eucalyptus, Gum Trees (eu-ca-lip′tus. Fam. Myrtaceae). Only a few of the more than 500 species of tall evergreen trees can be grown outdoors in Britain.

Selection. E. *coccifera*, Tasmania, to 20 ft; *dalrympleana*, Australia, to 50 ft; *gunnii*, S. Australia, to 60 ft; *niphophila*, Mt Kosciusko, to 20 ft; *nitens*, Australia, 50 ft; *pauciflora (coriacea)*, Australia, Tasmania, to 60 ft; *perriniana*, Australia, 20 ft; *urnigera*, Tasmania, to 75 ft, and *viminalis*, Tasmania, to 50 ft, are grown, chiefly in southern and western areas, including Scotland, where reasonable shelter from wind and sustained cold can be given, particularly while plants are juvenile. E. *globulus*, the Blue Gum, is often grown as a pot plant, or for its foliage for cutting in the cool greenhouse, others for pot culture are E. *citriodora*, Queensland, shrubby, lemon-scented leaves; *amygdaliana*, Tasmania, almond-leaved; and *ficifolia*, SW. Australia, the Red Gum, for its colouring.

Cultivation. Plant outdoors in March–April, deep, well-drained soil, sheltered positions; staking firmly. Juvenile foliage usually differs from that of the mature adult.

Propagation. By seeds, sown in March, under glass, bottom heat 15·5° C. (60° F.), or in frame.

Eucharis (eu-kar′is. Fam. Amaryllidaceae). Bulbous plants of great flower beauty and fragrance, natives of Colombia, to grow in the warm greenhouse.

Selection. E. *grandiflora*, the Amazon Lily, 2 ft, pure white flowers; *sanderi*, 18 in., white; and their hybrids × *lowii*,

2 ft, white, stained green; and *moorei*, 1½ ft, smaller flowers, with yellow line; and *candida*, 2 ft, drooping white flowers.

Cultivation. Pot, and repot triennially, in 2 parts loam, 1 part leaf-mould, with a little JI base fertilizer and charcoal, March. Water liberally in active growth, summer temps. 18–27° C. (65–80° F.), syringing often; give short rest in autumn; moderate watering in winter, temp. 13° C. (55° F.). May be flowered at different times of the year, by resting plants until timely to pot. Grow in large pots, three bulbs to a 7-in. pot.

Propagation. By offsets or dividing bulbs at repotting time; potting and watering little until growth starts.

Eucomis (eu-ko'mis. Fam. Liliaceae). Bulbous plants of S. Africa, with greenish spikes or racemes of flowers, and large ornamental lanceolate leaves, chiefly grown in the cool greenhouse.

Selection. E. comosa, the Pineapple Flower, 2 ft, with green flowers, summer; *bicolor*, pale green, purple-edged; and *regia*, 1½ ft, green.

Cultivation. Pot in March, standard compost, 5-in. pots; water liberally in growth, decreasing in autumn, to keep dry in pots on their sides, under staging during winter; repot every third year.

Propagation. By offsets detached in March when repotting.

Eucryphia (eu-crif'i-a. Fam. Eucryphiaceae). Tall-growing shrubs valued for their handsome white flowers with central brush of golden stamens in late summer.

Selection. E. glutinosa, Chile, to 15 ft, deciduous, pinnate foliage, 4-petalled, 2½-in. white flowers, is the hardiest, but dislikes chalk; × *nymansensis*, evergreen hybrid, fairly hardy, tolerates lime; *billardieri* (*lucida*), Tasmania; *cordifolia*, Chile, make handsome evergreen trees, but only for mild localities; which also applies to the hybrids × *hillieri* and × 'Rostrevor'.

Cultivation. Plant October or March–April, porous, loam soil; sheltered quarters from cold winds; prune in spring to regulate shape. May also be pot- or tub-grown, in cool greenhouse, until too large.

Propagation. By layering in spring; by cuttings of young shoots, July–August, in cold frame or under handlight.

Eulalia. See *Miscanthus*.

Euonymus (eu-on'i-mus. Fam. Celastraceae). Deciduous and evergreen shrubs of ornamental beauty, easily grown.

Selection. Deciduous: E. alatus, Winged Spindle Tree of China, a shrub of 6–9 ft, with four corky wings to branchlets, rich scarlet autumn foliage, purplish fruits; *europaeus*, native and European Spindle Tree, to 25 ft, with lobed rose seed capsules, orange seeds; and vs. *albus*, white-fruiting; *aldenhamensis*, bright pink fruiting; and *atropurpurea*, purple leaved, reddening in autumn; *grandiflorus*, Himalaya, to 25 ft, pale pink fruits; *latifolius*, Europe, 10 ft, rosy red and orange fruits; and *yedoensis*, Japan, to 10 ft, brilliant red autumn foliage, pale pink, orange seeded fruits. *Evergreen:* E. japonicus, Japan, to 15 ft, bright green leaves, with finely variegated vs. in *albo-marginatus*, white margins; *macrophyllus albus*, silvered; *ovatus aureus*, golden; and compact forms in *microphyllus* and *m. aureus*; *fortunei*, Japan, a compact shrub; *radicans*, Japan, makes good ground cover in sun or shade, or a climber; with v. *minimus*, neater and more dainty; and *variegatus*, with whitish variegation of leaves.

Cultivation. Plant deciduous kinds October–March; evergreen October or March–April; any reasonably drained soil, sun or shade.

Propagation. Deciduous kinds by seeds, sown outdoors, April; or by layers, Evergreens by cuttings of shoots, inserted in cold frame, in growing season.

Eupatorium (eu-pa-to'ri-um. Fam. Compositae). A large genus containing herbaceous perennials which are hardy and summer-flowering, and many evergreen shrubs suitable only for greenhouse culture.

Selection. The chief herbaceous plants are E. (*fraseri*) *ageratoides*, N. America, to 3 ft, white, rayed flower-heads, summer; *cannabinum*, the native Hemp Agrimony, to 4 ft, best in v. *plenum*, double reddish-purple flowers, July; and *purpureum*, N. America, 6 ft, purple flowers, autumn; for planting October–March, well-drained soil, sunny borders; and may be raised readily from seeds in spring. In the cool greenhouse, the Mexican *E. atrorubens,* reddish purple flowers, January–February; *ianthinum,* 2 ft, purple; *micranthum,* 2 ft, white, September–November; and *riparium,* 2 ft, white, March, may be grown; with winter temp. 10° C. (50° F.); cutting back plants after flowering, and propagating by cuttings taken in spring, in propagating case. Pot up or repot in September.

Euphorbia (eu-porb′i-a. Fam. Euphorbiaceae). A very large genus of annual and perennial herbs, shrubs and trees, characterized by their milky juice, and often succulent nature.

Selection. Annuals. E. heterophylla, 2 ft, the Mexican Fire Plant, fine foliage, with fiery-scarlet leaves to the end of branches, and *marginata,* N. America, 2 ft, Snow-on-the-Mountain, pale green leaves, white-margined, and flowers with white bracts, used for button-holes, may be grown from seeds, sown March, with gentle bottom heat (15·5° C. [60° F.]), under glass, planting out seedlings in late April or May. *E. lathyrus,* Europe, 4 ft, is the biennial Caper Spurge, with a reputation for deterring moles where it is grown, and seeds itself readily from the first plants.

Hardy Perennials. E. cyparissias, Cypress Spurge, Europe, 1 ft, greenish-yellow spring flowers; good ground cover for wild places; *polychroma,* Europe, 1 ft, attractive, yellow-bracted flowers, early spring; *myrsinites,* S. Europe, trailer, yellow flowers, late spring; *villosa major,* Europe, 1½ ft, golden yellow bracted flowers, spring; *sikkimensis,* Sikkim, 3 ft, red shoots, yellow-bracted flowers, summer; and *wulfenii,* Europe, to 4 ft, shrubby, with bluish-green foliage, and yellow-bracted flowers, April–July. Plant in September–October, or March–April. Propagation by seeds, spring and early summer; or by green cuttings, under handlight, in July–August. All do well in well-drained soils, even poor ones, sun or partial shade.

Greenhouse Shrubs. E. fulgens, the Scarlet Plume, Mexico, 2–3 ft, a leafy slender-branched shrub, with axillary clusters of scarlet-bracted flowers, autumn and winter; *pulcherrima,* the Poinsettia, Mexico, deciduous, 2–6 ft,

with terminal yellow flowers, backed by large vermilion bracts; and *splendens,* Crown of Thorns, Madagascar, 3 ft, spiny brown stemmed shrub with cymes of scarlet-bracted flowers, spring, require warm greenhouse conditions; potted up in spring, well-crocked pots, standard compost, given good light, watered freely in active growth, moderately in winter, temp. 10° C. (50° F.) minimum, syringing in hot weather, but after flowering drying off, until May or June. Propagation is by cuttings, detached in spring, inserted in pots, with bottom heat (18° C. [65° F.]).

Succulents. These are more or less leafless plants, with fleshy stems, reminiscent of cacti but without aeroles, which may be grown in the cool greenhouse, or as house plants: *E. caput-medusae,* Cape Province, to 30 in., low radiating branches, whitish flowers, summer; *echinus,* S. Morocco, branching six- or seven-sided stems, dull green with reddish spines; *globosa,* Cape Province, spineless dwarf, globose stem and branches; *meloformis,* Cape Province, globular with pronounced ribs, deep green with reddish bands; are typical; needing free watering in growing season, very moderate in winter, temp. 7° C. (45° F.), in cool greenhouse or window-sills indoors. Propagation by cuttings, after drying in spring.

Eurybia. See *Olearia.*

Eutoca. See *Phacelia.*

Evening Primrose. See *Oenothera.*

Evergreen. A plant that retains its leaves for at least throughout a full year.

Evergreen Oak. See *Quercus ilex.*

Everlasting Pea. See *Lathyrus.*

Everlastings. Flowering plants which yield flower-heads with coloured bracts and petals that retain their characteristics well after cutting and drying. The genera providing such flowers are Acroclinium, Ammobium, Helichrysum, Helipterum, Rhodanthe, Statice and Xeranthemum. The flowers are best gathered on dry days, before the heads are fully expanded, bunched on small bunches, and hung heads downward in a cool, airy shed, room or outhouse for a few weeks; they may be dried more quickly by laying in dry sand and silica gel.

Evodia (e-vo′di-a. Fam. Rutaceae). Two Chinese species of this genus of trees are sufficiently hardy to grow out of doors in England. *E. daniellii* makes a small ornamental tree, to 20 ft, with long pinnate leaves, flat clusters of dullish white flowers in June, followed by small black fruits; and *hupehensis*, to 40 ft, handsome pinnate leaves, with slender pointed leaflets, whitish flowers in downy clusters in August, which may ripen to reddish brown fruits on female specimens; plants being unisexual.

Cultivation. Plant October–March, well-drained loam soil, does not mind chalk; stake firmly.

Propagation. By seeds in spring, under handlight.

Exacum (ecks'a-kum. Fam. Gentianaceae). Pretty annual or biennial subtropical flowering plants for the warm greenhouse of which *E. affine*, Socotra, 6 in., with salver-shaped, bluish purple fragrant flowers; and *macranthum*, Ceylon, 12–18 in., larger rich purplish-blue flowers, are usually grown; being sown in August, over-wintered in 3-in. pots, temp. 15.5° C. (60° F.), moderate watering, increasing in spring, for summer–autumn flowering; or may be sown in February, with bottom heat, standard compost, to flower the same year.

Exalbuminous. Without albumen, of seeds without a reserve of food (endosperm) outside the embryo, as in peas.

Exaltatus (-a, -um). Lofty. Ex. *Davallia exaltata.*

Excelsus (-a, -um). Very tall. Ex. *Picea excelsa.*

Exfoliation. The peeling off in thin layers, as with the bark of birch trees.

Exo-. Prefix signifying outside. Ex. Exocarp, the outer layer of the pericarp.

Exochorda (eks-o-kor'da. Fam. Rosaceae). Beautiful, spring-flowering, deciduous shrubs of which *E. racemosa* (*grandiflora*), China, to 10 ft, with arching shoots filled with single, open white flowers in May; *giraldii*, NW. China, to 10 ft, large white flowers, May, and its erect v. *wilsonii*; *korolkowii*, Turkestan, to 10 ft, white May-flowering; and *serratifolia*, Manchuria and Korea, 4–6 ft, its shoots crowded with white flowers in May, are all desirable for free-draining, humus-rich soils, preferably non-chalk, and sunny positions, with reasonable shelter from late spring frosts. Plant October–March. Propagation by layers in autumn, suckers in spring; or by seeds, April, sown out of doors.

Exotic. Alien, foreign, introduced from abroad.

Exserted. Projecting: as of protruding stamens. Ex. Fuchsias.

Exstipulate. Without stipules (q.v.).

Extra-. Prefix in compound of words meaning outside or beyond.

Extrose. Facing outwards, of anthers opening towards the outside of a flower and shedding their pollen away from instead of towards the pistil.

Eye. A horticultural term for a bud, especially when undeveloped, as in potatoes; a lateral bud, used in connection with pruning fruits and roses; the centre of a flower.

Eyebright (*Euphrasia* spp. Fam. Scrophulariaceae). Annual hemiparasitic plants with white or purple flowers, forming nodules on the roots of the host plant without injury to it.

F

F₁ and **F₂.** Designations used to indicate hybrids produced by crossing two perfectly true parent strains; F_1 being the first filial generation; F_2 selected offspring of F_1, a second filial generation. The hybrids have greater vigour, improved performance and complete uniformity of colour, form, habit and size; but seeds should not be saved from them, as they will not breed true.

Faba. See *Vicia*.

Fabiana (fab-i-a'na. Fam. Solanaceae). Evergreen, heath-like shrubs from Chile, of which *F. imbricata*, 3–6 ft, with slender branches, bearing numerous short twigs with tubular white flowers at the er d in June; and *violacea*, similar with mauve flowers, may be grown in mild localities, given a porous light soil, and sunny, warm shelter; or as pot plants in a cool greenhouse. Plant in spring. Propagate by cuttings of young shoots, July–August, under handlight or in propagating frame.

Fagopyrum (fa-go-pi'rum. Fam. Polygonaceae). *F. sagittatum*, Buckwheat, Central Asia, 3–5 ft, is an annual which may be sown in ordinary soil, spring, broadcast or in drills, 8 in. apart, for its mealy seeds, good for poultry, birds and pheasants; or for a green manure crop.

Fagus, Beech (fa'gus. Fam. Fagaceae). Tall, hardy deciduous trees, for all soils except heavy, wet ones.

Selection. F. sylvatica, Common Beech, Europe, to 100 ft, has notable vs. in *fastigata*, the Dawyck Beech, symmetrical specimen; *heterophylla*, the Fern-leaved Beech; *pendula*, the Weeping Beech; *cuprea*, the Copper Beech; *purpurea*, the Purple Beech, and *atropunicea*, deep purple; and *rotundifolia*, the round-leafed, dainty erect Beech of small stature. Exotic beeches are not considered any better than these selections.

Cultivation. Plant October–March, any well-drained soil, including lime. *F. sylvatica* forms a good hedge, almost to any reasonable height, retaining brown withered leaves under trimming.

Propagation. By seeds, ½ in. deep, in rows 12 in. apart, warm light soil, March–April; transplanting when two years old. By grafting, varieties on stocks of the common species.

Pests. Woolly Beech Aphis (*Phyllaphis fagi*) disfigure and wither leaves in May–June; and Felted Beech Scale (*Cryptococcus fagi*) may produce masses of white waxy wool on trunks and stems; both pests controllable by applying a DDT/gamma BHC insecticidal spray.

Fair Maids of February. See *Galanthus* (Snowdrop).

Fair Maids of France. See *Ranunculus acontifolius*.

Fairy Rings. Rings or arcs of darker grass in lawns. caused by certain fungi such as the Champignon, *Marasmius oreades*, and fifty-nine others, spreading outward annually. Arcs of other fungi may appear in autumn. Turf should be hollow-tined forked, dressed with a mercurized turf fungicide or sulphate of iron solution (2½ per cent), or of potassium permanganate (1 per cent).

Falcatus (**-a, -um**). Falcate, sickle-shaped. Ex. *Dendrobium falcatum*.

Fallowing. Cultivating ground without cropping it for a season to cleanse it of weeds, etc. It is better to crop with potatoes, even roughly, since this cleanses cultivation with some profit.

False Acacia. See *Robinia pseudacacia*.

Family, Fam. A group of plants embracing related Genera; the name usually terminating in -aceae, excepting Compositae, Labiatae and Gramineae. Related Families form an Order.

Farmyard Manure. F.Y.M. *See* Manures.

Fasciation. When lateral shoots or stems fail to separate normally and produce fused, banded, flattened thickish growths, they are said to be fasciated. It is common among many plants, sometimes hereditary as in the Cockscomb (*Celosia*), but the cause is obscure. It is best to remove the abnormal growth by pruning.

Fasciculatus (-a, -um). Fasciculate, clustered or bundled together. Ex. *Deutzia discolor fasciculata.*

Fastigatus (-a, -um). Fastigiate, erect-growing, narrow, columnar. Ex. *Fagus sylvatica fastigiata.*

Fatshedera (fats-hed′e-ra. Fam. Araliaceae). The plant grown is × *F. lizei,* a bigeneric hybrid of *Fatsia japonica moseri* × *Hedera hibernica.* It is a hardy evergreen shrub, with large palmately lobed lustrous green leaves, with umbels of pale green flowers in October–November; and may be planted in almost any soil, shady places, autumn or spring. Propagation by cuttings of young shoots, July–August.

Fatsia (fats′i-a. Fam. Araliaceae). The chief species, *F. japonica,* Japan, to 12 ft, is a rather lush evergreen spreading shrub, with deeply lobed, leathery, green leaves, and umbels of milky white flowers in October–November; v. *moseri* has even larger leaves, but is more compact, and *variegata* has the leaf lobes tipped white.

Cultivation. Plant in spring, almost any soil, in sheltered shade; not for cold exposures. May also be grown as a pot or tub plant in a cold greenhouse, potted in March–April, standard compost.

Feather Grass. See *Stipa pennata.*

Feather Hyacinth. See *Muscari comosum.*

Feijoa (fay-yo′a. Fam. Myrtaceae). The one species, *F. sellowiana,* Brazil, makes an attractive evergreen shrub or small tree, with oblong, shining green leaves, white beneath, and white, red-centred, flowers in leaf axils, in late summer. Plant at foot of sunny warm walls in mild localities, in March–April, any well-drained soil; but better grown in a large pot, standard compost, with cool greenhouse protection in winter. Propagation by cuttings of young shoots, July–August, in frame.

Felicia (fe-li′ki-a. Fam. Compositae). Annual herbs or sub-shrubs from S. Africa.

Selection. F. bergeriana, the Kingfisher Daisy, 4 in., bright blue flowers, summer, and *fragilis (tenella),* violet-blue, are raised as half-hardy annuals, sowing under glass, March, standard compost, to plant out in May. *F. ammelloides (Agathaea coelestis),* 1–2 ft, the Blue Marguerite, sky-blue flowers, summer, is a favourite pot plant for the cool greenhouse; raised from seeds as for the annuals, and perpetuated by cuttings of young shoots in July–August, under a bell-glass; *echinata,* 1–2 ft, with lilac flowers, can be grown similarly; cut back hard after flowering.

Fences. Where walling of brick or stone is too expensive in enclosing a garden, a fence is a suitable alternative. It can be of lapped larch panelling or woven board where complete privacy is desired. Openwork rustic fencing, rail fencing, or cleft chestnut fencing are alternatives. A height of at least 4 ft is desirable. Posts should be of 4 in. by 4 in. section, or concrete posts can be used. All woodwork should be properly preservatively treated, preferably with an organic solvent (cuprinol). Creosote should not be used where plants are likely to touch or be exposed to the fumes. Strong metal fences can be made with chain-link mesh, galvanized or plastic-covered netting, or plastic mesh itself, given sufficient upright supports. A rabbit-proof fence calls for wire netting at least $3\frac{1}{2}$ ft above ground, with an L-shaped foot of 6 in., buried 6 in. deep, and facing outwards at the base. Temporary hedges can be made with pea-sticks. Utilitarian fences can look stark, and can be softened by planting suitable climbers, shrubs or a hedge alongside.

Fenestralis (-e). With openings; latticed. Ex. *Aponogeton fenestralis.*

Fennel (*Foeniculum vulgare*). A perennial culinary herb, from Southern Europe, growing 3–5 ft tall; used for flavouring sauces, garnishing, and young tender stems in salads. Best grown from seeds, sown in April, well-drained soil, sunny spot, thinning seedlings to 15 in. apart; flower stems are best cut out, as plants are otherwise short-lived; and should be renewed every third or fourth year. Florence Fennel or Finnochio (*F. v. dulce*) is a more dwarf variety, good for stews, used like celery, but needs generous manuring.

Fennel Flower. See *Nigella.*

Fenzlia. See *Gilia.*

Ferns. Ferns belong to the Order Filicopsida (Pteropsida) of the flowerless or cryptogamous plants grouped in the Class Pteridophyta, and are related to the Horse-tails and Clubmosses. About 10,000 species have been identified and described, about forty-seven of them native to Britain. Their structure is as elaborate as that of flowering plants, with readily distinguishable stems, roots and leaves, and a complex internal anatomy. They pass through two distinct stages on their life cycle; first,

FIG. 102 Fern frond (*Dryopteris* sp.) and its parts: a. rachis or stem; b. pinnae; c. pinnules.

FIG. 103 Underside of a fern leaf (*Dryopteris* sp.) showing sori.

the comparatively short-lived one of the prothallus (q.v.), and second, the fern plant itself. The leaves are termed *fronds*, their leaf-stalks *stipes*, the first divisions of divided fronds are *pinnae*, and sub-divisions *pinnules*. Ferns reproduce themselves by cells known as spores, which are formed in stalked cases, *sporangia*, which grow in clusters, *sori*, on the undersides of fronds. In many species, each sorus is covered by a protective membrane or scale, the *indusium*. The fronds arise from stems, often creeping, and known as *rhizomes*. Most ferns have basal stems or rhizomes, some upright, and are known as tree ferns. There are deciduous and evergreen types. Mostly terrestrial, rooting in soil, some are epiphytic.

Selection. Ferns are largely grown for the form and beauty of their fronds, and there is much variation within many species.

Hardy Ferns. Broadly, ferns are tolerant of shade, cool and moist conditions, and therefore grow where few flowering plants thrive. A fernery is best established with a north aspect, where the light is good but not strong, and may take the form of a shady rock garden. Ferns may be planted to mask tree stumps, to grace shaded slopes or ravines; many thrive in woodland, and most hardy kinds will grow in full light, given adequate moisture supplies at the roots. The soil should be enriched liberally with peat, bark fibre, weathered sawdust or similar material, and sub-soil drainage should be adequate. Only a few ferns, such as *Osmunda* spp., revel in bog or waterlogged soils. Planting is best done in early autumn, as rooting starts early, though ferns can be moved during the winter, up to March. Once established, ferns need little attention, though appreciating a good overhead soaking in dry weather. Good ferns for outdoors are: *Asplenium adiantum-nigrum* and vs., *A. ruta-muraria, A. trichomanes, A. viride, Athyrium filix-foemina* and vs., *Blechum amabile, B. spicant, Ceterach officinarum, Crypto-gramma acrostichoides, C. crispa, Cystopteris bulbifera, Dryopteris filix-mas crispa, D. cristata, D. marginalis,* etc., *Onoclea sensibilis, Phyllitis scolopendrium* and vs., *Osmunda cinnamomea, O.*

regalis, Polypodium vulgare and vs., *Polystichum aculeatum angulare* and vs., *P. lonchitis, P. vulgare* and vs., *Pteridium aquilinum, Woodsia ilvensis, W. obtusa, Woodwardia radicans* and vs. For fuller details *see* individual entries.

Cool Greenhouse and Indoor Ferns. Many ferns may be grown in the cool greenhouse with a minimum winter temperature of 5° C. (40° F.). In large houses it may be possible to grow them in a rock fernery, among porous tuffa rock, where shade is adequate. Particular attention must be given to good ventilation, moisture needs, humidity and shading from direct sun. Several ferns make good pot plants for indoors in the house, but a too dry atmosphere and neglect of watering must be avoided, and no draughts.

Ferns may be potted just when new growth is beginning, in early spring, in pots well-crocked for drainage, and a compost of 2 parts loam, 1 part sifted leaf-mould, ½ part coarse sand and a little crushed charcoal. Most of the hardy ferns given above may be grown in a cool greenhouse, augmented by such kinds as: *Adiantum pedatum, Blechnum gibbum, Davallia canariensis, Nephrolepsis exaltata* and vs., *Ophioglossum vulgatum, Selaginella helvetica.*

Indoor Room or House Ferns. To avoid dryness in heated rooms, it is often useful to place pots inside larger containers, packing with moist peat in between and keeping this moist. It is advantageous to rest plants in a cool greenhouse from time to time. Good kinds are: the Maidenhairs: *Adiantum cuneatum, A. pedatum; Asplenium bulbiferum, A. nidus, Davallia canariensis, Dryopteris spinulosa* and vs., *Nephrodium molle, Polystichum lonchitis, Nephrolepsis exaltata* and vs., *Pteris cretica cristata, P. tremula, P. serrulata.*

Basket Ferns. Hanging baskets of ferns are attractive in the greenhouse, conservatory or shaded porch; the basket is lined with moss, filled with fern compost, and may be planted with a selection of: *Adiantum caudatum, A. cuneatum, A. gracillimum, Asplenium longissimum, Cryptogamma acrostichoides, Davallia dissecta, D. pallida, Dryopteris effusa, Hypolepis distans, H. tennis, Nephrolepis cordifolia pluma, N. exaltata, Phyllitis*

scolopendrium fimbriatum, Polypodium pustulatum.

Filmy Ferns. These are ferns with transparent looks about them, requiring dense shade and a cool moist atmosphere, and will be found in the *Hymenophyllum, Leptopteris, Todea* and *Trichomanes* genera (q.v.).

Warm Greenhouse Ferns. Where space, shade and essential moisture and humidity, with a winter temp. above 13° C. (55° F.) can be maintained, the following ferns are rewarding: *Adiantum spp., Asplenium nidus, Ceratopteris thalictroides, Ceropteris peruviana, Cheilanthes spp., Davallia spp., Dicksonia antarctica, Gleichenia spp., Gymogramma spp., Nephrolepis spp., Nothoclaena spp., Pellaea spp., Platycerium spp., Polypodium spp., Pteris spp.,* and the *Selaginella spp.*

Propagation. By division, preferably in February–April, just before growth begins; of rhizomes in the case of ferns with creeping rhizomes; by splitting off crowns of those producing crowns; by small bulbils of those producing them on fronds (e.g. *Asplenium* sp.). By spores when ripe (when the sori turn brown) at any time of the year, particularly spring; sowing in pans half-filled with crocks, topped by compost of finely sifted sterilized loam, and crushed brick or sandstone, levelled firm and even, and moistened throughout; sow spores thinly on top, cover with glass, and stand in water in a close propagating frame or case; shading from direct sun. On germinating the spores form a plate-like organism, the prothallus (q.v.), and when these are discerned, in four to six weeks, they may be lifted with a small forked stick and transferred to small pots, similar soil, to grow on in close frame in the greenhouse, until fronds form; watering by immersion when needed.

Pests. Fern Eelworms (*Aphelenchoides olesistus*) may cause sharply defined brown and black blotches on fronds under glass; as the pests attack begonia, gloxinia and other plants, control is important. All affected fronds should be detached and burnt; and the plants watered with a parathion insecticide; or washed free of soil (which should be resterilized), and immersed in water at a constant temperature of 43° C. (110° F.)

for twenty minutes, and promptly cooled in cold water and replanted in sterilized soil and pot. Fern Mites (*Tarsonemus tepidariorum*) sometimes infest *Aspleniums*, and dusting with sulphur is helpful. Aphids and Thrips can be controlled with malathion or a gamma-BHC insecticide.

Ferocactus (fe-ro-kak'tus. Fam. Cactaceae). Cacti with round or cylindrical bodies, prominently ribbed, strongly spined, with some spines hooked, and growing big, to merit their common name of 'Barrel Cacti'; their bell-shaped red or yellow flowers form at the top of mature plants but are rare in Britain.

Selection. F. acanthoides, round, many-ribbed, pink or reddish spines; *echidne* Mexico, globose, green, wavy ribs, yellow spines; *melocactiformis*, Mexico, cylindrical, bluish-green, yellow, red-tipped spines; and *steinesii*, globular, wavy-ribbed, ruby-red spines, ageing grey.

Cultivation. Chiefly grown for their form, on window-sills or in cool greenhouse, winter temp. 7° C. (45° F.); watering freely in summer, very little in winter. Pot, and repot, March–April, as for terrestrial cacti (*see* Cactus).

Ferox. Very prickly. Ex. *Ilex aquifolium ferox*.

Ferraria, Black Iris (fer-ra'ri-a. Fam. Iridaceae). Dwarf bulbous plants of S. Africa, about 8 in. tall, with large flowers, April–July.

Selection. F. atrata, dark reddish-purple flowers; *ferrariola*, greenish-brown; *uncinata*, brown; and *undulata*, greenish-brown; all with stiff, linear leaves.

Cultivation. Pot in November, standard compost, in cool greenhouse; winter temp. 7° C. (45° F.), watering sparingly until growth begins, more freely to flowering, drying off after June. May be tried outdoors in mildest areas.

Propagation. By offsets when repotting.

Ferrugineus (-a, -um). Ferruginous, rust-coloured. Ex. *Rhododendron ferrugineum*.

Fertilization. The process in which male and female cells of reproduction, gametes, unite. It is effected by a pollen tube forming through a pistil to the female ovule in the ovary and from which a male cell is extruded into the oosphere to fuse with the female cell and form an embryo. When the pollen is from the same plant it is termed self-fertilization; when it comes from another plant it is cross-fertilization. It is often confused with pollination, but this is the transfer of pollen to the style of a plant, and precedes fertilization.

Fertilizers. Although sometimes described as artificial manures, fertilizers are not substitutes for organic manures, but complementary to them. They may be described as concentrated forms of plant nutrient material used to stimulate the growth and improve the performance of plants; and to meet the nutrient deficiencies of a soil. They are not necessarily beneficial to a soil, and wrongful or over use can do more harm than good to soil fertility. They may be of organic or inorganic origin. Organic fertilizers are more expensive, but more sustained in effect. Inorganic fertilizers are chemical, either derived from natural deposits or synthesized. Plants need twelve to fourteen mineral nutrients from the soil; seven in relatively large or major amounts; five to seven in small or trace amounts. In nature these nutrients come from the inorganic mineral particles and the organic matter of which soils are formed. Under cultivation soils tend to lose their soluble nutrient salts more quickly than they can be replaced by natural agency. Fertilizers are used to provide the nutrient elements most subject to deficiency and loss under intensive garden or farm cultivation. As such they may be divided into three groups: (1) those which supply nitrogen; (2) those which supply phosphorus; and (3) those which supply potash; sometimes referred to as N, P and K. A fourth, which is increasingly used, consists of those which supply magnesium. Fertilizers must be appraised on four points: (1) their mineral nutrient content; (2) solubility or action in the soil; (3) residual value; and (4) end reaction, or effect on soil acidity.

FERTILIZERS SUPPLYING NITROGEN (N).

Ammonium Nitrate (35 per cent N), white soluble deliquescent chemical salt, made by combining ammonia and nitric acid; quick-acting; no residual value; acid end-reaction; for late winter to early summer application. Primarily for use in explosives, and should be stored with care, cool and dry.

Ammonium Sulphate (20·6 per cent N), synthetic chemical; soluble, reasonably quick-acting; little residual value; acid end-reaction; use with caution on acid soils; for late winter to early summer application.

Calcium Cyanamide (20·6 per cent N, 60 per cent Ca); inorganic; quick-acting; no nitrogenous residual value; alkaline end-reaction; for spring or early summer use, prior to sowing; caustic to plant foliage and sometimes used as a superficial weed-killer.

Dried Blood (12–14 per cent N); organic; very quick acting; acid end-reaction; for spring and summer application.

Hoof and Horn Meal (12–14 per cent N); organic; slowly but steadily active; residual value about 25 per cent for following year; slightly acid end-reaction; for winter to spring use, prior to planting or sowing.

Nitro-chalk (15·5 per cent N, 48 per cent Ca); inorganic; quick-acting; alkaline end-reaction; for spring and early summer application.

Nitrate of Soda (15·5 per cent N); inorganic; quick-acting; no residual value; neutral end-reaction; for spring and summer use. Not suitable for clay, as it is deliquescent; not for roses.

Nitroform (38 per cent N); inorganic; steady-acting; small residual value; slightly acid end-reaction; for spring or early summer use.

Urea (46 per cent N); synthetic, inorganic; quick-acting; no residual value; acid end-reaction.

Soots (3–6 per cent N); inorganic; fairly quick-acting; no nitrogenous residual value; acid end-reaction; for winter to early summer use; darkens light-coloured soils usefully.

FERTILIZERS SUPPLYING PHOSPHORUS (P, or as P_2O_5).

Basic Slag (9–18 per cent P_2O_5; 30–40 per cent Ca); inorganic by-product of steel-making, for use according to the stated content of phosphoric acid (P_2O_5) and its solubility. Slags of over 80 per cent solubility in citric acid are good;

slow-acting; residual values for up to three years; alkaline end-reaction; for autumn and winter application.

Bone Meal (20–24 per cent P_2O_5; 3–4 per cent N; with calcium); organic; slow-acting; residual values up to three years; alkaline end-reaction; for use in autumn–winter, for all plants, except the lime-intolerant, when planting.

Steamed Bone Flour (27·5 per cent P_2O_5; 0·8–1 per cent N; with calcium); organic; reasonably quick-acting; residual values to three years; alkaline end-reaction; for use in late winter and spring.

Superphosphate (18 per cent P_2O_5); inorganic; quick-acting; residual values up to two years; neutral end-reaction; for use in spring and summer.

Triple Superphosphate (45–48 per cent P_2O_5); inorganic, granular; quick-acting; residual values up to two years; neutral end-reaction; for spring and early summer use, in small amounts only.

Ground Mineral Phosphate (26–38 per cent P_2O_5); inorganic natural mineral rock; slow-acting; good residual values to three years; neutral end-reaction; for use in autumn or winter.

FERTILIZERS SUPPLYING POTASH (K or K_2O).

Muriate of Potash (50–60 per cent K_2O; 15 per cent NaCl [sodium choride]). Slow to steady acting; inorganic; residual values up to two years; acid end-reaction; for use in winter or early spring.

Sulphate of Potash (50 per cent K_2O); inorganic; quick, then steady acting; acid end-reaction; for use in winter and spring; the best chemical source of potash.

Wood Ashes (2–6 per cent K_2O); inorganic, with variable but high proportion of calcium (30–40 per cent); quick-acting; alkaline end-reaction; for spring use; but not for lime-intolerant plants.

FERTILIZERS SUPPLYING MORE THAN ONE NUTRIENT.

Blood, Fish and Bone Meal (6·5 per cent N, 7·7 per cent P_2O_5, 5 per cent K_2O); organic; steady-acting; residual values for three years; acid end-reaction; use in late winter or spring.

Fish Guano (av. 7 per cent N, 6·5 per

cent P_2O_5); organic, steady-acting; residual values for two years; acid end-reaction; for use in late winter or spring.

Chilean Potash Nitrate (15 per cent N, 10 per cent K_2O); inorganic; quick-acting; little residual values; neutral end-reaction; for use in spring and summer, best on light or good loam soils.

Nitrate of Potash; Saltpetre; Potassium Nitrate (12 per cent N, 40 per cent K_2O); inorganic; very quick-acting; little residual values; alkaline end-reaction; for use in spring and summer, chiefly as a supplementary feed, and for pot plants.

Ammonium Phosphates (11–15·6 per cent N, 31–48 per cent P_2O_5); inorganic; no residual values; acid end-reaction; very quick-acting; chiefly used as an ingredient of liquid fertilizers for spring and summer use.

Dried Poultry Manure (av. 4 per cent N, 3 per cent P_2O_5, 1·5 per cent K_2O); organic; steady acting; residual values to two years; acid end-reaction; for use in late winter and spring.

Peruvian Guano (10–14 per cent N, 8–10 per cent P_2O_5, 2–4 per cent K_2O); organic; fairly quick- and steady-acting; residual values up to two years; acid end-reaction; for use in late winter, spring and summer.

OTHER FERTILIZERS. Calcium, as a major element of plant growth, is chiefly provided by periodic liming (q.v.). Salt (sodium chloride) is not a fertilizer, but may be used to liberate potash in light, sandy peat soils; particularly for beet crops; and is also used as a top-dressing for asparagus in spring.

Sulphate of Magnesium (Epsom Salts) is often added to fertilizers, especially those high in potash, and for crops such as tomatoes, fruits and roses, on acid soils. Kieserite is an inorganic crude source of magnesium, which may also be used. Magnesium may also be supplied by the use of a dolomite or magnesian ground limestone as a liming agent.

Sulphate of Iron may be used to provide iron on alkaline soils, though it is rather slow-acting. It may be used as an ingredient of Lawn Sand for weed control and feeding of lawns.

Chelated Compounds. Iron, manganese and magnesium deficiencies in lime-containing soils are most promptly corrected by use of chelated forms of the minerals, sometimes known as Sequestrenes.

Borax is sometimes used to correct a boron deficiency, though the amount required—roughly 1 oz. to 20–30 sq. yds.—is small.

Compound or Complete Concentrated Fertilizers (C.C.F.). In using fertilizers it is wisest to apply a compound or mixture as a base fertilizer just prior to the sowing or planting of a crop or the beginning of the growing season, balanced to meet the nutrient needs of the plants. Such compounds are known as complete concentrated fertilizers. They can be bought under various proprietary names, factory blended or made up to recommended formulae, such as given for various vegetables, fruits, etc., in this work. The mixing must be thorough, and care must be taken not to mix chemicals likely to react with one another; ammonium sulphate, nitro-chalk or fertilizers containing these substances should not be mixed with lime, chalk, basic slag or any substance containing free lime. Superphosphate should not be mixed with chalk, lime, nitro-chalk or chemicals containing much lime. The analysis of a fertilizer may be given as a ratio in terms of N (nitrogen), P (phosphorus) and K (potash). Thus the analysis of 'Growmore' fertilizer is 7 : 7 : 7, implying 7 per cent nitrogen, 7 per cent phosphoric acid and 7 per cent potash.

Liquid Fertilizers. These are usually soluble fertilizer salts in a concentrated solution, needing dilution before application. They act quickly in providing nutrients for plants to take up; and are being increasingly used both for base fertilizing and for supplementary feeding. They may be of high-concentrate chemicals; or of organic derivatives, such as seaweed concentrate; or, oldest of all liquid fertilizers, liquid manure prepared from animal dung.

Ferula, Giant Fennel (fe'rul-la. Fam. Umbelliferae). Tall herbaceous perennials, grown for their fine foliage of much divided leaves.

Selection. F. communis, Mediterranean region, 8–12 ft, the source of gum ammoniac; *glauca*, S. Europe, 8 ft; and *tingitana*, N. Africa, to 8 ft, are nominally hardy, in sunny, sheltered positions, in gardens free of keen spring frosts.

Cultivation. Best grown from seeds, sown under glass, March–April, bottom heat of 18° C. (65° F.); and planted out to permanent stations, in any well-drained soil, in May–June; may bear huge umbels of flowers in June when fully matured. May be propagated best by seeds.

Fescues. See *Festuca.*

Festuca, Fescue (fes-tu′ka. Fam. Graminae). A genus of grasses of which *F. ovina,* Sheep's Fescue, and its vs., *F. rubra,* Creeping Red Fescue, and its vs., are important for making lawns (q.v.).

Feverfew. See *Chrysanthemum parthenium.*

Ficifolius (-a, -um). Fig-leaved. Ex. *Althaea ficifolia.*

Ficus (fi′kus. Fam. Moraceae). A diverse genus of shrubs or trees which includes the edible Fig (*Ficus carica*) (q.v.), and a number of ornamental-leaved Asian species grown as greenhouse or house plants.

Selection. F. elastica, the Indiarubber Tree, tropical Asia, is the easiest to grow in cool conditions, v. *decora,* and variegated leafed *doescheri,* preferred; *benghalensis,* India, the Banyan, branches with large elliptical leaves; *deltoidea,* the Mistletoe Fig, India, Malaya, is shrubby, with bright green leaves, and yellow fruits in pairs in leaf axils; *benjamina,* India, grows with slender drooping branches, and narrowish, grass-green leaves; *lyrata,* W. tropical Africa, the Banjo or Fiddle-leaved Fig, is perhaps the handsomest for foliage; *pumila,* China, Japan, the climbing Fig, adheres by aerial roots, with small, one-inch, heart-shaped leaves, and does well in a cool greenhouse; *radicans,* East Indies, and v. *variegata,* are both charming evergreen creeping or trailing small-leaved plants, good for baskets; there are others.

Cultivation. Pot in March–April, standard compost, water freely during active growth, syringe in hot water and sponge leaves often; water only moderately in winter, with temp. of 10° C. (50° F.) minimum, and some humidity.

Propagation. By cuttings of shoots

taken in April, in a propagating case; by air-layering stems of leggy plants in spring, when overgrown. *See* Layering.

Fig (*Ficus carica*). Reputedly from W. Asia, Figs have been grown in England since 1162. The flowers are monoecious, developing on the inner surface of a hollow fleshy receptacle, the male above the female, and after fertilization the receptacle becomes the fruits. May be grown out of doors in mild localities, given a warm, sunny, south-facing wall, or under glass.

Varieties: Black Ischia; Brown Turkey*; Brunswick*; Castle Kennedy; Osborne's Prolific; White Ischia, White Marseilles.*

*Recommended for outdoors.

Cultivation. The root system needs to be restricted, to a space about 2 ft deep, with a layer of well-packed stone, brick rubble, etc., 1 ft thick at the base, and enclosed by a brick or concrete wall within an area of about 9–12 sq. ft; filled with a loam soil liberally mixed with brick rubble and old lime mortar or limestone grit. Plant October or April, firmly. Under glass, may be grown in restricted border or pots.

Pruning. Train shoots in the shape of a fan; prune to thin out crowded growth, and remove unwanted shoots from which fruits have been gathered, in winter; limit main shoots to those easily accommodated on the wall space.

Fruiting. A fruiting shoot carries three sets of fruits in autumn; the biggest figs at the lowest part of the shoot are the current season's crop; above these are some intermediate immature fruits which would ripen into a second crop under native conditions; and at the top of the shoot will be found the embryo 'figs' or buds for next season's cropping. The intermediate fruits should be rubbed off on outdoor figs; under glass, with moderate heat, they will ripen later. Give frost protection to outdoor figs with netting or hessian in spring.

Propagation. By cuttings of well-ripened shoots, 12 in. long, firmly planted in September, in warm corner, under handlight; transplant two years hence; by suckers lifted in autumn and planted out; by layering in spring or summer.

Fig Marigold. See *Mesembryanthemum.*
Filbert. *See* Nuts.

Filiformis (-e). Filiform, thread-like. Ex. *Veronica filiformis*.

Filipendula (fil-i-pen'du-la. Fam. Rosaceae). Hardy herbaceous perennials, with finely divided foliage, and large corymbs of showy flowers.

Selection. F. hexapetala v. *flore pleno*, 2 ft, ferny foliage, creamy white flowers, fine form of the native Dropwort; *palmata* (*Spiraea digitata*), Siberia, 2 ft, pale pink flowers, July, and v. *nana*, 1 ft; *purpurea*, Japan, to 3 ft, crimson, July; *rubra*, Queen of the Prairie, E. U.S.A., in vs. *magnifica*, 6 ft, peach-pink, autumn; and *venusta*, deep pink, 4 ft, July; and *ulmaria flore pleno*, 4 ft, a fine form of the white flowering native Meadowsweet; are good for most gardens.

Cultivation. Plant October–March, well-drained but moist soil, excellent with waterside plantings; sun or partial shade.

Propagation. By division in autumn or spring.

Filmy Ferns. *See* Ferns.

Fimbriatus (-a, -um). Fimbriate, fringed. Ex. *Primula sinensis fimbriata*.

Finger-and-toe. *See* Club-root.

Finnochio. *See* Fennel.

Fir. The true Firs are species of *Abies* (q.v.). For the Douglas 'Fir' see *Pseudotsuga taxifolia*; for the Scotch 'Fir', see *Pinus sylvestris*; for Spruce 'Firs', see *Picea*.

Fistulosus (-a, -um). Fistular, hollow like a stem. Ex. *Helianthus fistulosus*.

Fittonia (fit-ton'i-a. Fam. Acanthaceae). Evergreen trailing perennials of Peru, valued for their ornamental leaf venation, and for growing in the shade in a warm greenhouse. *F. argyroneura*, with bright green, white veined leaves; and *verschaffeltii*, with dark green, netted red veins, are chiefly grown.

Cultivation. Pot, and repot, March–April, standard compost; water freely in growth; moderately in winter, with minimum temp. 10° C. (50° F.); shade from sun.

Propagation. By cuttings of young shoots, in spring, in propagating case with bottom heat of 18° C. (65° F.), pinch back young shoots to induce a bushy plant.

Fitzroya (fits-roy'a. Fam. Pinaceae). The one species, *F. cupressoides*, Chile, is a very charming evergreen conifer, to 50 ft, for mild localities of the south-west, for light soils, enriched with peat. Plant in September–October or March–April in good shelter from wind, but open. May be propagated by heeled cuttings taken in August, in a frame.

Flabellatus (-a, -um). Flabellate; fan-like. Ex. *Aquilegia flabellata*.

Flag See *Iris*.

Flame Flower. See *Kniphofia*.

Flame Gun. An appliance burning paraffin oil under pressure and throwing a flat flame of 1093° C. (2000° F.), which may be used for the top growth destruction of weeds, and surface sterilization of seed-beds, prior to sowing. Best used on dry days, being passed over the weed vegetation at walking pace to wilt it, and later again to burn the wilted foliage up. Weed seedlings, annual, biennial and surface-rooting weeds are well controlled, but deep rooting perennial weeds are only checked. The flame should be hooded when used to clear hedge bottoms or near garden plants.

Flame Nasturtium. See *Tropaeolum speciosum*.

Flamingo Flower. See *Anthurium*.

Flammeus (-a, -um). Flame-coloured. Ex. *Emilia flammea*.

Flavescens. Yellowish. Ex. *Iris flavescens*.

Flavones. Pigments which impart a yellow colour to flower petals, etc.

Flavus (-a, -um). Almost pure yellow. Ex. *Linum flavuum*.

Flax. See *Linum*.

Flax, New Zealand. See *Phormium*.

Flea Beetles, Turnip Flies. Leaf beetles, chiefly of the *Phyllotreta* genus, which do damage to seedlings of the Cruciferae, especially of brassicas, radishes, turnips, etc., by eating the seed leaves above and below ground in spring. The beetles over-winter in hedge bottoms, rubbish heaps, etc., to emerge in spring and feed on cruciferous weeds and crops; later the females lay eggs in the soil, the larvae feed on plant roots, then pupate and a new generation of beetles emerge in late summer or autumn. Clean cultivation; dressing seeds with a gamma-BHC dust, and prompt application of a gamma-BHC insecticide in spring should give good control.

Fleabane. See *Erigeron*.

Fleur de Lys. See *Iris*.

Flexilis (-e). Pliant. Ex. *Pinus flexilis*.

Feluosus (-a, -um). Zigzag.

Floccosus (-a, -um). Having wool-like tufts. Ex. *Rhipsalis floccosa*.

Flora. The plants that grow in a particular country, region or locality; or a book devoted to them.

Flore Pleno. With double flowers. Ex. *Kerria japonica* v. *flore pleno*.

Florets. Small flowers: e.g. the outer flowers of the Compositae as ray florets, the inner disk florets.

FIG. 104   A floret of a Composite flower.

Floribundus (-a, -um). Flowering freely. Ex. *Rosa* × *floribunda* section.

Floridus (-a, -um). Flourishing with flowers. Ex. *Weigela florida*.

Florist. A cultivator, a dealer or a student of flowers.

Florists' Flowers. Primarily flowers which have been developed or garden-raised by florists or exhibitors for their floral qualities and colour, from relatively few species such as Antirrhinum, Aster, Auricula, Begonia, Callistephus, Carnation, Chrysanthemum, Cineraria, Cyclamen, Dahlia, Delphinium, Fuchsia, Gladiolus, Hyacinth, Iris, Pansy, Pelargonium, Peony, Pink, Polyanthus, Primula, Pyrethrum, Ranunculus, Rose, Tulip, Verbena, Viola and others.

Flos. A flower. Ex. *Lychnis flos-jovis*, Jove's flower.

Flower. The organ of reproduction in the higher plants (Spermaphyta); normally consisting of four parts: the calyx and its sepals; the corolla of coloured leaves or petals; the stamens or androecium; and the pistil of carpels or gynoecium. Any of these parts, however, may be absent. Their numbers and arrangement vary, but are usually constant for all the species of a genus or family, and form the basis on which the Linnaean classification of plants is founded. A flower with stamens but without pistils is male, sometimes termed

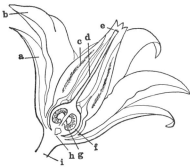

FIG. 105   A flower (diagramatic) and its characters: a. sepal; b. petal; c. stamen; d. pistil; e. stigma; f. ovary; g. ovules; h. receptacle; i. pedicel.

barren or blind since it cannot form fruit or seed; a flower with pistils but without stamens is female, and normally bears fruit when fertilized by pollen from a male flower. Some flowers, notably ray florets of the Compositae, have neither pistils nor stamens and are termed neuter.

Flower Bud. *See* Buds.

Flower de Luce. Old name for *Iris* (q.v.).

Flower of a Day. See *Hemerocallis*.

Flower of the West Wind. See *Zephyranthes*.

Flower Pots. *See* Pots.

Flowering Ash. See *Fraxinus ornus*.

Flowering Currant. See *Ribes sanguineum*.

Flowering Rush. See *Butomus umbellatus*.

Flowers, Cutting. Except when seeds are wanted, it is always wise to cut off the flower-heads of annuals, biennials and perennials in the garden as soon as they fade, so that growth energies are not wasted on seed production. Similarly, with shrubs grown for their flowering, it is helpful to remove faded flowers or forming seed-heads. When cutting flowers for indoor decoration it is sensible to cut in the early morning, if possible, when tissues are fully turgid, choosing young bloom, not fully opened, plunging at once into buckets of water. There are many recipes for making cut flowers last longer; the most successful being the addition of a bacteria-inhibiting substance (Chrysal) to the water. Woody stems may be slit or broken open with a hammer to expose more tissue to imbibe water; hollow stems may be filled with water and carefully plugged with plasticine or stem plugs; stems which exude sap may be sealed by dipping in hot water or passing lightly through a flame. Cut flowers for packing and dispatch on a journey should be cut when buds are swelling and colouring, with surfaces dry, packed in special wrapping papers and boxes, available from specialist florist suppliers; or in tissue, and with damp moss rather than cotton wool. Flowers for identification are best placed in polythene bags, sealed at the base, and placed inside a stout box, large enough to preserve the flowers without crushing.

Fluitans. Floating in water. Ex. *Glyceria fluitans*.

Fly. A gardener's term for an infestation of various insects, e.g. Carrot Fly, Celery Fly, Green-fly (Aphids), Onion Fly, White-fly, etc., discussed further under separate headings or the crops concerned. The House Fly, *Musca domestica*, is not a plant parasite. The gardener is subject to various biting flies, including midges and mosquitoes, best combated by the use of a dimethyl phthalate, cream or oil, repellent.

Fly Orchid. See *Ophrys muscifera*.

Fly Trap, Venus. See *Dionaea muscipula*.

Foam Flower. See *Tiarella cordifolia*.

Foeniculum. *See* Fennel.

Foetidus (-a, -um). Stinking. Ex. *Helleborus foetidus*.

Foliaceous. Leafy or leaf-like.

-foliolatus (-a, -um). Suffix to compound epithets, with a number, indicating so many leaflets; Ex. *trifoliolatus*—with three leaflets.

Foliole. A leaflet.

Foliosus (-a, -um). Leafy. Ex. *Orchis foliosa*.

Follicle. A fruit consisting of an inflated carpel of one cell only; e.g. Fruit of Peony.

Food of Plants. *See* Nutrition.

Forcing. Inducing flowering plants to bloom and vegetables to come into edible condition before their normal seasons. For methods, *see under* plants concerned.

Forcing of Bulbs. The forcing of bulbs into early flowering has become a somewhat specialized and precise operation. Briefly, the bulbs are specially prepared by temperature treatment, and should be obtained and planted at specified times, usually in October. The bulbs are planted in pots or bowls, using bulb fibre or standard compost, plunged in ashes or fibre, or kept cool, at 7° C. (45° F.), until roots are well developed and shoots are showing, usually for six to eight weeks, and then brought into light and heat gradually, according to the grower's instructions. Hyacinths are usually introduced to temp. of 10° C. (50° F.); specially prepared Narcissi to 15·5° C. (60° F.) and full light for four days only, and then grown in temps. of 10–13° C. (50–55° F.). Early Tulips require plunging in September, and to flower at Christmas are removed to 15·5–18° C. (60–65° F.), and kept dark for a week or so, before being forced in the light at 21° C. (70° F.). Only chosen varieties force well. Ordinary unprepared bulbs are kept cool in ashes, fibre, or in dark cool cellars or cupboards, at 7° C. (45° F.), for six to eight weeks, until showing shoots; then introduced gradually to the light and greater warmth, in January, February, March; spending a week or two at 10–13° C. (50–55° F.), before being brought into heated living-rooms.

Foreright (Forthright) Shoots. *See* Breastwood.

Forget-me-not. See *Myosotis.*

Fork. A 4-tined, almost straight-shanked, fork with T, D or Y grip-handle is most useful for working and breaking up the soil. A flat-tined fork is more easily used than a spade in turning over stiff clay. Round- or oval-tined, somewhat dished, forks are useful for handling manures, turning compost heaps and distributing litter or mulching materials. Smaller hand-forks are useful for weeding, working among plants and for planting-out; the two-pronged fork with pointed round tines is invaluable for weeding in rock gardens.

Formalin, Formaldehyde. Formalin is a solution of 38–40 per cent. formaldehyde (H.CHO), used as a fungicide in sterilizing soil and the treatment of empty greenhouses, pots, seed boxes, etc. It is normally used as a 2 per cent solution (1 part to 49 parts of water). *See* Soil Sterilization.

Formosus (-a, -um). Beautiful. Ex. *Dicentra formosa.*

Forsythia (for-sith′i-a. Fam. Oleaceae). Deciduous flowering shrubs, valued for their profusion of yellow bloom in early spring, on leafless shoots.

Selection. *F. ovata*, Korea, 3–4 ft, butter-yellow flowers, February–March; *suspensa*, E. China, 8–10 ft, slender lax growth, golden-yellow, March–April; and vs. *atrocaulis*, dark purplish shoots; *fortunei*, arching shoots; and *sieboldii*, slender shoots; good for banks; *viridissima*, 5–8 ft, stiffly erect, bright yellow, April; and × *intermedia*, in vs. *spectabilis*, to 10 ft, bright yellow, March; 'Lynwood' and 'Beatrix Farrand', both large-flowering; *primulina*, pale yellow, and the dwarf form 'Arnold Dwarf', to 1½ ft.

Cultivation. Plant in any reasonably well-drained soil, October–March; sun or partial shade. Prune, if necessary, after flowering, removing a proportion of the older wood, and shortening flowered shoots.

Propagation. By cuttings of young shoots in July–August, under handlight. By layering in spring.

Fothergilla (foth-er-gil′la. Fam. Hamamelidaceae). Deciduous shrubs from Eastern U.S.A., with spikes of white flowers, May, before the coarsely toothed ovalish leaves appear.

FIG. 106 *Forsythia* × *intermedia* v. 'Lynwood'.

Selection. *F. major* and *monticola* are rather similar, making 6-ft shrubs, with roundish spikes of white flowers, and foliage colouring crimson in autumn; *gardeni*, 2–3 ft, has smaller leaves, and seems a little more tender.

Cultivation. Plant October–March, preferably in warm shelter, and a peat-enriched loam soil; little pruning needed, but after flowering when necessary.

Propagation. By seeds, but slow germinating; by layers in spring; by heeled cuttings in July in frame.

Foxglove. See *Digitalis.*

Foxtail Lily. See *Eremurus.*

Fragaria (fra-ga′ri-a. Fam. Rosaceae). Perennial herbs with runners, to which the Strawberry (q.v.) belongs, and *F. vesca* is the native wild strawberry. *F. indica*, India, Japan, is a pretty trailing plant with golden-yellow flowers in summer, for the rock garden; planted in well-drained soil, with a little peat, in March–April, full sun; propagated by runners.

Fragilis (-e). Fragile, brittle. Ex. *Campanula fragilis.*

Fragrans. Fragrant, sweet-scented. Ex. *Viburnum fragrans.*

Frames, Garden. Frames are low, squat, glazed structures, permanent or portable, with sloping top covers or 'lights', glazed with glass or transparent plastic, which can be opened or removed. They may be unheated or heated, and are most useful in themselves and as complementary equipment to a greenhouse. They may be used for the raising of plants from seeds or cuttings; for the growing of crops, such as lettuce and saladings; or flowers; for the housing of seed-boxes, pans and pot plants; for the hardening-off of greenhouse raised plants; for the sheltering of pot plants; for the growing of melons, cucumbers and other exotics in summer; for storage purposes; for over-wintering frost-sensitive plants; and the growing of bulbs or vegetables for forcing.

Size of Frame. This is dictated by the size of the light. The standard English light measures 6 ft by 4 ft, or 3 ft by 2 ft, but 4 ft to 2 ft square lights are also used. Frames are usually lean-to, the light sloping to the front; though span-roof types are also made, often with the lights hinged at the centre. The pitch of the frame light varies according to purpose. For general use, a frame 18 in. at the back and 12–14 in. at the front is right. Small portable frames are often much shallower. Permanent frames may be built with brick, stone, concrete, asbestos sheeting or preservatively treated timber walls, and should be sited in the open, with a southerly aspect. Portable frames are of wooden, steel or alloy structure; the wood being of rotproof Red Cedar or preservatively treated with an organic solvent (Cuprinol) not creosote. Glazing may be of glass or a heavy-gauge transparent plastic sheet. Dutch lights are more efficient than English lights, since they admit more light, but breakages can be more costly.

Cold Frames. Without heat, the temperature inside a cold frame is only a few degrees above that outside in winter or dull weather. Nevertheless the protection and higher temperatures aid growth. A cold frame may be used for (a) sheltering seedlings for hardening off which have been raised in heat in a greenhouse, prior to planting out in spring; (b) for raising hardy annuals and vegetables in March–April, from seed, for later planting out; (c) for raising hardy perennials and biennials from seed, in June–August; (d) for growing salad crops in early summer and late autumn; (e) for sheltering plants, not reliably hardy, during the winter. In cold frosty weather the frame should be covered with sacks, mats or evergreen boughs, and the sides may be insulated by heaping cinders, leaves or peat against them. Top cover must be removed in the warmth of the day to prevent growing plants being drawn to the light.

Heated Frames. Heat extends the length of the growing season early and late in the year, and permits more exotic plants to be raised and grown. Traditionally, a fermenting hotbed of horse manure was used, on which a frame was placed. This gave bottom heat for two to three months, when properly prepared. In modern gardening this method is largely superseded by soil-heating with electricity, either by means of a high voltage soil-warming cable, or more efficiently by galvanized wires laid in the soil, connected to a transformer, which gives a low-voltage system. The cable or wiring is laid at the level of the surrounding soil, and covered by 6 in. of soil compost in which plants are grown; or if used for propagation only in 2 in. of fine sand, kept moist, on which seed-boxes, pans and pots may be placed, packed around with peat. Heating can be thermostatically controlled with a rod type thermostat. For winter use, space heating will also be necessary, and a tubular heater may be installed, or with space-economizing effect, the core-filled wire system (Pyrotenax) can be used, by which wires are run round the walls on insulator fasteners, and again, heating may be thermostatically controlled. Full details are provided by manufacturers and Electricity Board offices.

Management of Frames. The soil must

be free-draining, preferably 6 in. of a standard compost over well-dug subsoil. Ventilation needs intelligent care, and may be given by tilting or sliding the lights, at first, then propping open with reliable props, as temperatures rise, to removing altogether in summer heat. Draughts must be avoided; opening lights on the side away from the wind, and closing in advance of temperature fall at night. Cuttings and seedlings being hardened off need to be kept fairly close at first, with gradual increase of ventilation. Watering should be regulated by the weather and temperatures; more being needed in bright sunny weather than when cloudy and overcast, and increasing with temperature rise. It is important to water sufficiently early in the day so that plant foliage is dry when the frame is closed for the night. Shading is important, as direct hot sun can soon damage and wilt plants; lath frames or plastic netting can be used to give a dappled shade; or strategically placed wattle hurdles will cast a shadow over frames during midday heat. Removable green plastic sheeting is better than painting the glass itself with shading materials.

Deep Frames. These are portable wooden frames, deep enough to accommodate potted plants such as chrysanthemums, tomatoes, etc., in spring; primulas and cool greenhouse plants in summer; and may be stood on cinders, paths or similar flat surfaces.

Pests. The most ubiquitous are slugs and snails, which do havoc among young plants, but can be controlled by the use of metaldehyde bait pellets in the frame; by a band of equal parts by weight powdered copper sulphate and ground limestone, 12–18 in. wide, round the frame, using ½ lb. per 10 sq. yds; renewing each February. Woodlice can be kept down by using a DDT insecticidal dust at frame bases, inside and out. Frames need to be cleansed and disinfected by formalin or cresylic acid treatment annually, and the glass kept clear with a window-cleaning detergent or hot soapy water. Diseases are discussed under separate headings for plants, but need prompt attention as their spread can be very rapid in the close confines of frames.

Francoa (fran-ko'a. Fam. Saxifragaceae). The chief species grown is *F. ramosa*, Chile, 2–3 ft, known as Bridal or Maiden's Wreath for its long, slender branching panicles of small, white, late summer flowers; *appendiculata*, Chile, 2 ft, with rose flowers; and *sonchifolia*, 2 ft, pinkish flowers, may also be grown as half-hardy perennials.

Cultivation. Sow seeds, March, under glass, bottom heat of 15·5° C. (60° F.), standard compost; transferring finally to 5-in. pots and summering in a cool frame; returning to the cool greenhouse to flower; or plants may be set out in early June in warm, well-drained moisture retentive soil and sun. Best treated as annuals and raised anew each year.

Frankenia (fran-ke'ni-a. Fam. Frankeniaceae). The chief species grown is the native *F. laevis*, or Sea Heath, an evergreen prostrate inch-high, trailing sub-shrub, with rose-pink flowers along wiry shoots in summer, for the rock garden; *thymifolia*, Spain, is similar with rose-red flowers. Plant in March–April, in well-drained, moist soil, in warm sun; or the alpine house. Propagation by careful division in April.

Fraxinus, Ash (fracks-i'nus. Fam. Oleaceae). Mainly deciduous trees, often too large-growing for modern gardens though very hardy and good on heavy soils.

Selection. Ornamentally, *F. bungeana*, N. China, to 15 ft, pretty with white panicles of May bloom; *mariesii*, China, to 20 ft, creamy-white June flowers, deep purple summer fruits; *ornus*, S. Europe, the Manna Ash, to 60 ft, its dull white May flowers heavily scented; and *spaethiana*, Japan, to 30 ft, large white panicles of May flowers, are most distinctive. *F. excelsior*, the Common Ash, Europe and Britain, to 120 ft, excellent for its timber, and wood which burns easily when green, is striking in its golden v. *aurea*, and its weeping form, *pendula wentworthii*; *americana*, the White Ash of N. America, fast-growing to 100 ft, a fine shade tree; *angustifolia*, S. Europe, to 90 ft, is elegant in foliage for mild localities; *pennsylvanica*, Eastern U.S.A., 50 ft, may be grown in v. *aucubaefolia*, with golden mottled foliage, or *lanceolata*, bright green; and *xanthoxyloides*, Afghanistan, to 20 ft, a tall shrub or small tree, is pretty with downy foliage.

Cultivation. Plant October–March in deep loam soils, tending to be heavy; not for chalk.

Propagation. By seeds, sown in April, outdoors or in autumn when ripe. Selected forms by grafting.

Freesia (free′si-a. Fam. Iridaceae). Cormous plants of S. Africa, valued for their fragrant flowers.

Selection. F. refracta, 18 in., and its vs. *alba* and *leichtlinii*, and *armstrongii*, are the chief species, but modern Freesias are their hybrids, available in a wealth of delicate colours, white, yellows, pinks, mauves, orange, to purplish violet or rose; notable named forms being 'Afterglow', red to orange; 'Blue Banner', blue and white; 'Blushing Bride', creamy-white, flushed mauve; 'Goldcup', chrome yellow; 'Margaret', purple; 'Orange Favourite', yellow and orange; 'Pimpernel', salmon pink; 'Princess Marijke', orange and gold; 'Sapphire', blue; 'Souvenir', cream gold; 'White Swan', white; etc. *See* growers' lists.

Cultivation. For late winter and spring flowering, corms are planted 1 in. deep, 2 in. apart in 6-in. pots, August–December; standard compost; placed in a cold frame, lightly covered with sand or fibre, occasionally syringed in warm weather, until seven leaves can be counted, when they may be brought into a cool greenhouse, temp. 10° C. (50° F.), with full light; given liquid feeding weekly; and for flowering may be given 15·5° C. (60° F.) when buds are well formed, watering moderately. After flowering, gradually reduce watering, dry off in a sunny frame when leaves begin to yellow. Specially prepared corms are offered in April for July–October flowering out of doors, being planted 1 in. deep in well-drained soil, full sun, in late April, and watered in dry weather; or may be grown in pots in the greenhouse.

Propagation. By seeds, soaked 24 hours in water, and sown in August–September, standard compost, under glass, and grown on in cool greenhouse or frame, thinning to six plants per pot, to flower next spring. By offsets in August.

Fremontia (fre-mon′ti-a. Fam. Sterculiaceae). Pretty deciduous shrubs, of which *F. californica*, California, to 15 ft, heart-shaped foliage, and bright yellow flowers, April; and *mexicana*, Mexico, to 10 ft, with orange flowers, April, are worth trying in mild localities as wall shrubs or in shelter, in well-drained, lightish soil; planted March–April. Propagation by cuttings of young shoots in spring, under handlight; or by seeds, sown in April.

French Honeysuckle. See *Hedysarum coronarium.*

French Marigold. See *Tagetes.*

French Tree. See *Chionanthus.*

Fritillaria (frit-il-la′ri-a. Fam. Liliaceae), Fritillary. A large genus of rather unusual flowering bulbous plants, with bell-shaped flowers in spring.

Selection. F. meleagris, the Snake's Head, Europe and Britain, to 15 in., with solitary, nodding, purple and white chequered flowers, May, and its vs. *alba*, white, green-veined; 'Aphrodite', white; 'Artemis', grey-purple; 'Purple King', dark purple; 'Sulphanus', sulphur white; and hybrids, may be naturalized in grass, or grown in borders. *F. imperialis*, the Crown Imperial, W. Himalaya, 3–4 ft, with a whorled head of yellow flowers, and vs. 'Aurora', bronzy crimson; *maxima rubra*, red; and others, are majestic for the border, but not long-lived. *F. acmopetala*, Syria, 6 in., single, green, brown-purple streaked flowers, April; *camschatcensis*, 12 in., purple-black, May; *citrina*, Greece, 12 in., pale yellow and green, April; *glauca*, Oregon, 6 in., purple, April; *latifolia*, Caucasus, 12 in., purplish, chequered yellow-green, May; *nigra*, Mediterranean, 6 in., deep red-purple, May; *pudica*, to 8 in., golden-yellow, May; *pyrenaica*, Pyrenees, 12 in., purple, spotted green, May; and *tubiformis*, Alps, to 12 in., reddish-purple and yellow, April, may be tried in the rock garden or alpine house.

Cultivation. Plant September, well-drained soil with humus, sunny positions, at twice the diameter of the bulbs in depth. In the rock garden, do well in scree.

Propagation. By seeds, if available, sown in August, in cold frame, pricking out in second year; take 4 to 6 years to flower. By offsets, when lifting bulbs for division and replanting in September.

Frog-hoppers (*Cercopidae*: *Hemiptera*); small, jumping bugs, related to Aphids and Leaf-hoppers, whose nymphs or larvae are termed the 'Cuckoo-spit' insects, found on many plants in the garden in summer. The commonest is *Philaenus spumarius*; its nymph being yellowish-green. Forceful spraying with a malathion or nicotine insecticide will control these sap-sucking, plant-growth distorting larvae.

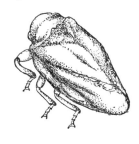

FIG. 107 Frog-hopper (*Philaenus spumarius*): adult insect, and (below) its nymphal form, the 'Cuckoo-spit Insect'

Frond. The leaf of a fern or a palm, or a seaweed.

Frondosus (-a, -um). Leafy, frond-like. Ex. *Primula frondosa*.

Frost. A state of freezing when the air temperature is at or below the freezing point of water (0° C. [32° F.]), and ice is formed. As its temperature falls, the volume of water contracts, but on freezing it suddenly increases; this has the effect of disrupting clay bonds in soil, and helps to break it up. It also accounts for the injury done to frost-sensitive plants. A Rime frost occurs when the air is moisture-laden and deposits its surplus water vapour on plants and other surfaces at freezing

temperatures; a Hoar frost occurs when very cold air affects dew already present; a Black frost when the air contains no surplus moisture and surfaces are dry. Frost benefits soils, its particles being pushed apart by the expansion of the water in them on freezing; thus clods are broken into smaller crumbs, and a good surface tilth results. Frost can do much damage to plants, however; to exotic tender plants in winter or late spring, when air frosts are caused by the movement of polar or cold air from arctic regions; to plants just starting into growth in late winter or spring, by radiation frosts. Radiation frosts usually occur when fine, clear nights follow sunny warming days; as the plant and earth surfaces lose heat, cold air flows in, behaving like water and seeking the lower levels of the terrain. Consequently plants are apt to suffer most in valleys and on the lowest lying ground in relation to the surroundings. A cloud cover checks radiation and the severity of frost. The gardener can prevent much frost damage by interposing a 'ceiling' between plants and the clear sky, even if only of newspapers, netting, hessian, polythene sheeting or litter cover. Frost-touched plants may recover if promptly syringed with cold water and kept cool before the sun is on them and temperatures rise. The practice of 'smoke protection' by smudge fires followed by fruit-growers is impractical for gardens; nor can much be done in small areas by inverting the air flow with air propelling equipment.

Fruit. Botanically the fertilized and ripened ovary and seeds of a seed-plant (Angiosperm); more broadly, it includes the structure surrounding them, such as the fleshy receptacle in apple. Dry fruits are called Achenes, Caryopsis, Capsules, Cypselas, Follicles, Legumes, Nuts or Siliquas. Many-seeded fruits may be called Carcerules; winged fruits Samaras.

Fruit-growing in Gardens. As a rule the amount of fruit that can be grown in a modern garden is limited by the space available. To make the most of this needs careful planning and choice. Although personal preferences will enter largely into the choice of fruits in kind and variety, consideration must be given to suitability for the site and soil, and then to the best forms of trees to be grown. Generally, the farther north or the higher the garden, the more vital it is to choose the more hardy kinds and varieties of fruits. It is not sensible to grow Cox's Orange Pippin, for instance, north of the Midlands and expect good crops. Similarly, damsons are hardier than plums, and both are hardier than gages. Peaches may succeed as bush trees in the open in many localities, but not where much frost is experienced in early spring. The site is important in relation to surrounding ground. If it is low-lying, in a valley or a pocket of soil where cold air drains readily, preference would have to be given to late-flowering varieties, and forms of trees carrying their blossom high, such as standards. Soil is important as few fruits succeed where the soil dries up rapidly in drought, or becomes waterlogged in winter, or where the pH value reflects alkalinity or great acidity, or the humus content is very low. With intensive cultivation, however, most garden soils can be amended and improved for soft fruits and some tree fruits; the prime needs being good drainage, allied with moisture retention, moderate to slight acidity and a build-up in humus-content.

In planning a small fruit garden priority must be given to those fruits which yield heavily in a given space. This affects the ratio of tree fruits to soft fruits. Standard and half-standard forms of trees need much space, and also pose problems in spraying and pruning and tending. They are best used as specimens. On the other hand, trained trees on dwarfing rootstocks, such as cordons, bush, dwarf pyramid and espaliers enable us to plant sufficient varieties, and at the same time are easier to spray, prune and manage, while tending to fruit earlier in their lives than standard types. It is true that there are no dwarfing stocks for the stone fruits, and where these are grown, bush, half-standard or standard forms must be planted in the open; though wall trees need less room for their spread. In the smaller gardens it may be wise to keep mainly to soft bush fruits, with perhaps dwarfed forms of apples.

In planning small fruit gardens, it is wise to keep fruits needing similar treatment grouped together, to facilitate routine attentions such as spraying, pruning, manuring and fertilizing. Dessert apples, red and white currants, and gooseberries need ample potash, and may therefore be planted near one another; while culinary apples, pears, black currants and plums, needing more nitrogen, can occupy adjoining areas. Strawberries, which need renewal every third or fourth year, may be planted as part of the vegetable garden. It is, however, a mistake to attempt to run other fruits and vegetables together, as the surface cultivations required for the latter mean much disturbance of the root system of the former. For the detailed cultivation of each kind of fruit see individual entries.

Fuchsia, Ladies' Ear-drops (fewks'i-a, or few-shi'a. Fam. Onagraceae). Elegant and colourful flowering shrubs, notable for their slender-stalked, hanging flowers, made up of tubular corolla, with four outer segments and petals and protruding stamens.

FIG. 108   *Fuchsia* hybrid 'Pink Ballet Girl'.

Selection. None are perfectly hardy, though *F. magellanica* v. *riccartonii*, to 8 ft, with flowers of scarlet tube and sepals, and violet-purple petals, summer–autumn, forms hedges in mild districts, and is rarely killed outright elsewhere.

F. magellanica, Chile and Argentina, to 12 ft, deep red and purple flowers, and its vs. *alba*, white, and mauve; *macrostemma*, purplish-red; may also be grown. The hybrids, × *exoniensis*, 4–6 ft, with extra large red and purple flowers; × 'Madame Cornellison', red and white; and × 'Mrs Popple', large red and purplish flowers, are nominally hardy for sheltered positions with some winter protection of litter. Plant in March–April, well-drained, ordinary soil, sun or partial shade; prune in February, cutting out winter-killed shoots.

Half-hardy Fuchsias. Of other species, *F. corymbiflora*, Peru, to 6 ft, large, deep red flowers, summer; *fulgens*, Mexico, 4 ft, scarlet, summer; *procumbens*, New Zealand, dark red and green, trailing basket species; *splendens*, Mexico, 6 ft, scarlet, summer; and *triphylla*, Haiti, 1–2 ft, cinnabar red, may be grown in the cool greenhouse, but most fuchsias grown today are of hybrid origin, embracing single and double forms, pendulous trailers and some of ornamental foliage, running into a wide variety of colours and names, best culled from specialist growers' lists and shows, numbering hundreds.

Cultivation. Pot, and repot, plants in March, standard compost, cool greenhouse, in partial shade; or as houseplant, watering with increasing frequency as growth is made, temp. 13–18° C. (55–65° F.); or may be planted out from late May to October; pinch out growing points of shoots frequently when actively growing in spring and early summer to induce bushy growth; syringe in hot sunny weather; and feed with liquid manure weekly when buds show colour. Decrease watering after flowering, and give very little in winter, temp. 7° C. (45° F.) minimum; lift outdoor plants early October, to store in greenhouse.

Propagation. By cuttings of young shoots, 2–3 in. long, in February–March, inserted in small pots, bottom heat of 18° C. (65° F.); potting on in three weeks. By seeds, under glass, with bottom heat of 21° C. (70° F.).

Fugacious. Fleeting, brief, lasting only a short time; such as the flowers of Poppy or Day Lilies.

Fulgens. Shining. Ex. *Lobelia fulgens*, *Fuchsia fulgens*.

Fulvus (-a, -um). Tawny. Ex. *Iris fulva*.

Fumigation of Greenhouses. Fumigation is carried out to control diseases or pests. When fungal disease has been rampant, it is useful to fumigate with sulphur, using a sulphur candle, when the house is temporarily cleared of plants in au umn. The fumigation to control insect pests, such as Aphids, White-Fly, Red Spider Mites, Mealybugs and Thrips is now carried out by means of insecticidal smoke generators, of nicotine or gamma-BHC (lindane); or for Red Spider, azobenzene. For best results, fumigation by smoke should be done in late afternoon or evening, when temps. are at 18–21° C. (65–70° F.), and the house kept closed overnight. The weather should be calm, the house closed, and cracks sealed with paper strips. The dosage should be according to the cubic capacity of the house and the makers' directions. In many cases smokes may be used while plants are growing in the house, but again makers' directions should be followed, as some kinds of plants are sensitive. The cubic capacity of a lean-to house is found by adding the height of the shortest wall to that of the tallest, dividing by two, and multiplying by the width and length in feet. Of a span-roof, the height of one side wall is added to the height to the ridge, divided by two, and multiplied by the width and length in feet; and the capacity to the nearest 1,000 cubic feet is the guide line to dosage.

Fumigation of Soils. *See* Soil Fumigation.

Fungi. A very large division of flowerless plants, differing from all other plants in that they lack the green pigment, chlorophyll, and obtain their carbon and nitrogen from a host plant, dead or alive. Many fungi live on dead or decaying organic animal or plant material, assisting decomposition, and are termed saprophytes. Others feed on living hosts, animals or plants, and are parasites. Some are capable of living on dead and living organisms. Parasitic fungi are responsible for most of the diseases afflicting garden plants. Fungi are divided into three classes: Phyco-mycetes or microscopic Algal Fungi; Basidiomycetes, or Club Fungi, and Ascomycetes, or Sac Fungi; to which must be added the Fungi Imperfecti, or Deuteromycetes.

Fungicides. Chemical compounds used to destroy parasitic fungi on plants. They fall into two groups: those which kill by direct contact, chiefly surface fungi such as mildews; and those which protect plants against the infection by fungi which live inside the plant tissue. The following are the important fungi-cides in present-day use:

Bordeaux Mixture. A copper fungicide, relatively safe to use; prepared from two stock solutions, one of copper sulphate dissolved at 1 lb. per gallon of water; and one of quicklime, at the same rate, slowly slaked with water. To make up to a required dilution, the lime solution is added to water, stirred well, and the copper solution then stirred in, and the solution used fresh. A formula of 8 : 8 : 100 calls for 84 parts water, 8 parts lime solution and 8 parts copper solution, stirred in respectively; a wetting agent may be added.

Burgundy Mixture. A variant of Bordeaux Mixture in which 1¼ lb. of washing soda is used to replace each 1 lb. of quicklime, and the copper sulphate solution is diluted first before adding the washing soda solution.

Calomel (mercurous chloride). As a fungicide it is usually prepared as a 4 per cent dust, and used to protect brassicas against Club-root, and Onions against White Rot disease, and as a turf fungicide.

Captan (SR406). A protective fungi-cide, chiefly used to prevent Scab disease in tree fruits; Black Spot in roses; Blight in potatoes, etc.

Cheshunt Compound. A protective fungicide, prepared by mixing 2 parts by weight copper sulphate and 11 parts ammonium carbonate, after exposure to air, and used in solution with water to prevent damping-off diseases of seedlings; usually at 1 oz. per gallon.

Colloidal Copper. Preparations of copper oxychloride as suspensions, for dilution and use instead of Bordeaux Mixture.

Copper-lime Dusts. May be powdered formulations of cuprous oxide, chiefly used as a seed dressing; or powdered forms of Bordeaux Mixtures.

Copper Sulphate. Sometimes used at 1 lb. per 20 gallons water in winter to spray dormant rose bushes and combat Black Spot infection.

Formaldehyde (Formalin). Chiefly used as a soil disinfectant and fungicide (q.v.).

Lime Sulphur. Prepared by boiling sulphur with lime water, and used as a protective fungicide against apple Scab, and as a control of Mildews.

Liver of Sulphur (potassium poly-sulphide). An alternative to lime sulphur, rarely used today.

Karathane (Dinocap). An organic fungicide—dinitro (1-methyl heptyl) phenyl crotonate—protective and eradicant against Mildews.

Maneb. An organic fungicide, based on manganese ethylene—1 : 2 bisdithio-carbamate—for the control of tomato stem rot and downy Mildews.

Salicicylanilide. Sometimes used to control tomato Leaf-mould disease and Grey Mould on soft fruits.

Sulphur. Prepared as a dusting powder for the control of Mildews, etc., and as colloidal sulphur for spraying.

Thiram (TMTD). An organic fungicide based on tetramethyl thiuram disulphide, effectively used as a seed-dressing and to control Rust Diseases, Tulip Fire and Grey Mould (Botrytis) infection.

Zineb. An organic fungicide based on zinc ethylene bis dithiocarbamate, used to control Downy Mildews, tomato Leaf-mould and Rusts.

Funkia. See *Hosta.*

Furze. See *Ulex europaeus.*

Fuscus (-a, -um). Fuscous, dark, dusky. Ex. *Cyperus fuscus.*

Fusiform. Spindle-shaped, like the root of a parsnip.

G

Gage. A type of plum, with round green or yellow fruits of distinctive flavour. *See* Plums.

Gagea (ga'ge-a. Fam. Liliaceae). Small bulbous plants of which the Europeans *G. pratensis*, 4 in., umbels of pale yellow flowers, March; and *sylvatica*, 6 in., yellow, April, may be grown, planted in sunny borders or shrubbery in autumn, ordinary soil. Propagation by offsets.

Gaillardia, Blanket Flower (gaillard'i-a. Fam. Compositae). Annual and herbaceous perennial plants from America, with showy heads of yellow, orange or red flowers, with purplish disk florets.

Selection. The annuals are forms of *G. pulchella*, Arizona and Southern U.S.A., 1-2 ft, and its vs. *lorenziana* and *picta*; 'Indian Chief', being a single-flowering, coppery-red, and 'Lollipop' a fine double-flowering strain. These are grown as half-hardy annuals, sown under glass, February–March, standard compost, bottom heat of 15·5° C. (65° F.), for planting out in May, and are good for cutting or bedding.

The herbaceous perennials are forms of *G. aristata*, Western N. America, 2 ft, such as 'Monarch Strain' in various colours; 'Yellow Queen'; and 'Dazzler', yellow with maroon centre; flowering well in summer. Plant in April, well-drained ordinary soil, sun; protect in winter with peat litter or ashes in cold districts. May be propagated by cuttings in August in a frame; by division in October; by root cuttings in spring; by seeds in April.

Galanthus, Snowdrop (ga-lan'thus. Fam. Amaryllidaceae). A genus of much beloved bulbous flowering plants originating in the E. Mediterranean region, with white, green or yellow marked, dropping flowers early in the year. Botanists have had a field day sorting out and renaming these plants as indicated below.

Selection. G. nivalis subsp. *nivalis*, the common Snowdrop, naturalized, possibly native, in Britain, 4–8 in., green-tipped white flowers, February–March, has many vs., of which *lutescens*, yellow-tipped flowers; *atkinsii*, larger flowers;

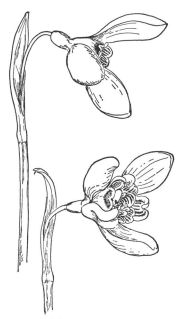

FIG. 109 *Galanthus nivalis*, Snowdrop, and its double-flowering form.

flore plena, double flowers; and 'Allen Seedling', 'Galatea', 'Magnet' and 'Straffan' are good named forms; subsp. *cilicicus*, Lebanon, November–February-flowering; *G. ikariae* subsp. *latifolius*, Asia Minor, flowers February–March, and *ikariae*, Greece, a little later. *G. elwesii*, Asia Minor, is larger in flower,

236

taller and broader-leaved, and has several vs. such as *whittallii* and *maximus*, for February; *alleni*, Caucasus, a dainty alpine for March; and *plicatus*, Crimea, latest to flower in April, are not always easy to keep. *G. nivalis* subsp. *reginae-olgae*, Greece, autumn-flowering; *byzantinus*, Asia Minor, February; *corcyrensis*, Corfu, November; *fosteri*, Asia Minor; and *graecus*, Balkans, January–February, are often difficult and best grown in deep pans in the alpine house, without forcing.

Cultivation. Plant as soon as bulbs are available in late summer, 2 in. deep, to naturalize in grass or shrub borders, well-drained soil, receiving winter and spring sun. Protect against slug damage. Leave undisturbed as long as growth is healthy and vigorous.

Propagation. By division, lifting immediately after flowering, and replanting immediately. By seeds, sown in April, out of doors.

Galax (ga'lacks. Fam. Diapensiaceae). The one species, *G. aphylla*, E. North America, is an evergreen hardy creeping perennial, with cordate, rounded leaves, often bronzed, and spikes of small white flowers, of 1–2 ft, in June–July; useful for rock gardens, in peaty, well-drained soil, partial shade or among shrubs. Plant in March–April. Propagated by division.

Galega (ga-le'ga. Fam. Leguminosae). *G. officinalis*, the Goat's Rue, S. Europe, 3–4 ft, with pinnate foliage, and stalked racemes of blue flowers in summer, has good vs. in *alba*, pure white, *hartlandii*, white and lilac, and 'Lady Wilson', blue and white on long stems for cutting; making fine hardy herbaceous border perennials; *orientalis*, Caucasus, 3–4 ft, with bluish purple flowers, may also be grown.

Cultivation. Plant October–March, well-drained, humus-rich loam, if possible, though doing quite well in most soils, and full sun.

Propagation. By division, October–April. By seeds, sown out of doors, April.

Galingale. See *Cyperus longus*.

Galium, Bedstraw (ga'li-um. Fam. Rubiaceae). A genus of weeds, of which *G. aparine*, Cleavers or Goosegrass, is common in gardens; and *mollugo*, Hedge Bedstraw, and *verum*, Ladies' Bedstraw, running perennials, which should not be allowed to get out of hand; now controlled by mecoprop herbicides (q.v.).

Galls. Abnormal growths on plants, resulting from the activities of insects, mites, fungi or bacteria, or eelworms. Oak-apple, Spangle, and Currant galls, on oak trees, Bedeguars or Robin's Pincushions, and Pea galls on roses are caused by Gall Wasps (*Cynipidae*); Red Bean galls on willow leaves by the sawfly, *Pontania proxima*; nail galls on leaves; Big Bud in currants and leaf-blisters on pears are caused by mites (*Phytoptidae*); Peach Leaf Curl and Blisters and Witches' Brooms on trees by fungi. The growths are best cut out and burnt when seen.

Galtonia, Cape Hyacinth, Spire Lily (gal-ton'i-a. Fam. Liliaceae). The species grown is the S. African *G. candicans*, with long lanceolate leaves and flowers of waxy white, drooping in racemes on stems of 4 ft, in summer. The bulbs are planted 6–8 in. deep, in well-drained soil, in groups of three to twelve, in autumn or spring, and left undisturbed, freshened by annual top-dressings of rotted manure or compost and a base fertilizer after flowering. May be flowered in a cold greenhouse in 6–8-in. pots, and then planted out. Propagation by offsets in autumn when lifting to divide; by seeds sown in April, in the open, sandy loam soil.

Gamma-BHC (Lindane). The gamma isomer of benzine hexachloride, a purer and less-tainting formulation for insecticidal use. *See* Insecticides.

Gametes. The sexual reproductive cells of pollen (male) and ovule (female) in plants.

Gamopetalous. Of flowers more or less united to form a cup or tube. Ex. Canterbury Bells.

Garden, Gardener. A garden may be defined as a piece of ground cultivated and devoted to the growing of plants of the gardener's choice; vegetables, fruits, flowers, ornamental plants, shrubs and trees, by themselves or in congregation; the choice may be specialized or catholic. A gardener is anyone who cultivates a garden; more narrowly, he (or she), if privately and permanently employed, is in law a menial or domestic servant. The professional gardener is one who has been trained in horticulture, with experience of garden management and the cultivation of plants, and with some knowledge of botany, plant chemistry and physics. A useful qualification is the N.D.H., National Diploma in Horticulture, for which examinations are held annually; and details are obtainable through the Secretary of the Royal Horticultural Society, Vincent Square, London, W.1, or the Principals of County Farm Institutes, when training facilities exist.

Gardener's Garters. See *Phalaris*.

Gardenia (gar-de'ni-a. Fam. Rubiaceae). Evergreen flowering shrubs, grown for their white, strongly scented flowers in a warm greenhouse.

Selection. G. *jasminoides*, China, Japan, 1–4 ft, produces single, salver-shaped white flowers June–September in succession; double in v. *florida*, and larger in vs. *fortuniana* and *major*, and *variegata* has cream-margined leaves; others sometimes offered are G. *globosa*, Natal, to 3 ft, terminal white, fragrant flowers in June; and *thunbergia*, S. Africa, 4 ft, large white flowers in spring.

Cultivation. Pot in 6- or 7-in. pots, standard compost without lime, March–April; temp. 15·5–27° C. (60–85° F.), liberal watering and frequent syringing to keep a moist buoyant atmosphere to October, when watering should be only moderate, with winter temp. of 10–15·5° C. (50–60° F.). As young plants flower best, they should be replaced after three years or so.

Propagation. By cuttings of strong, young shoots, taken with a heel in late spring or summer, or in January–February, if a propagating case with bottom heat of 24° C. (75° F.) is available; rooting singly in 3-in. pots.

Garland Flower. See *Daphne cneorum*.

Garlic (*Allium sativum*). Apparently only found wild in the deserts of Central Asia, the pungent garlic, so esteemed by epicurean cooks, was introduced to England from the Mediterranean region in 1548. It is grown by splitting a bulb into segments, termed cloves, setting each clove 1 in. or so deep, at 9 in. apart, in rows 12 in. apart, in well-drained, light sandy loam, and a sunny,

warm position; preferably in November–December in the mildest localities, but by February even in mild localities, as the plant needs to make its roots and leaf growth in the early short days, and begins to ripen off after midsummer when days start to shorten. When leaves yellow, the bulbs should be lifted and dried off in the sun, before storing. Not so suitable for cold districts or heavy damp soils.

Garrya (gar'ri-a. Fam. Garryaceae). Evergreen shrubs of which G. *elliptica*, California, 6–8 ft, is reasonably hardy for mild localities and warm, sheltered walls or positions in western gardens, where it can be grown in well-drained, light humus-rich soil, for its gorgeous silvery-grey catkins, up to 6 in. long if male, the female being much shorter, in November–February; the hybrid G. × *thuretii* may also be attempted, its catkins usually forming in spring; but *macrophylla*, Mexico, to 10 ft, with May–June flowering, is only suitable for the warmest gardens.

Propagation. Preferably by cuttings of young firm shoots, taken in August, in propagating case, with gentle bottom heat (18° C. [65° F.]), as seeds will give male and/or female plants.

Cultivation. Plant September–October or March–April (male plants for the longer catkins), out of pots, in well-drained, organically enriched soil, sun.

Gasteria (gas-te'ri-a. Fam. Liliaceae). Stemless succulents with thickened leaves in two rows, or spirally arranged, prettily marked, and producing tubular, drooping red or pink flowers on tall stems; natives of S. Africa, they make easily grown decorative plants for the cold greenhouses or house window.

Selection. G. *carinata*, 5–6-in. leaves in a rosette, dark green, white-dotted; *colubrina*, leaves spirally arranged, dark green, blotched white; *liliputana*, 2-in. leaves, spirally arranged, heavily marked white; *maculata*, smooth leaves, to 8 in., in two ranks transverse whitish banding; and *verrucosa*, 6-in. leaves in two rows, grey-green, marked white.

Cultivation. Pot March–April, standard compost, good drainage; water freely in warm months; very little in winter, minimum temp. 7° C. (45° F.). Cool greenhouse or window.

Propagation. By offsets; by leaf cuttings, in spring.

Gaultheria (gall-ther'i-a. Fam. Ericaceae). Attractive evergreen shrubs of the Heath family, distinctive for their bell- or urn-shaped spring flowers, and capsular, berry-like fruits; requiring lime-free soils.

Selection. G. cuneata, W. China, 1 ft, white flowers, June, clustered with white fruits in autumn; *micqueliana,* Japan, 1 ft, white, May–June, and white flushed pink in fruit; *nummulaioides,* 6 in., white or pink flowers, July, blue-black fruits; *procumbens,* the Canada Tea Partridge Berry or Spicy Wintergreen, 4 in., white, stained pink, in July flowering, and autumn berrying; *pyrolifolia,* E. Himalaya, 8 in., white or pink flowers, May, blue-black berries; *trichophylla,* W. China, 4 in., white flowers, May, blue fruits; and *veitchiana,* Central China, 1 ft, white flowers, May, dark blue fruits, are good rock garden shrubs, or ground coverers. *G. forrestii,* Yunnan, to 4 ft, white flowers, May, and blue fruits; and *shallon,* Western N. America, 2–4 ft, the Salal or Shallon, pinkish-white flowers, May–June; purple-black fruits, are very attractive spreading shrubs for ground cover; but *fragrantissima,* Himalaya and Ceylon, to 4 ft, white or pinkish fragrant flowers, April–May, and violet-blue fruits, needs a cool greenhouse.

Cultivation. Plant September–October, or March–April, in lime-free, well-drained, peaty soil, partial shade; pruning when necessary after flowering.

Propagation. By layers in spring; by cuttings of young shoots with a heel, July–August, under handlights or in a frame; by seeds, sown April.

× **Gaulthettya** (gall-thet'ti-a. Fam. Ericaceae). A bigeneric hybrid × *G. wisleyensis* (*Gaultheria shallon* × *Pernettya mucronata*), makes a dwarf evergreen shrub, with ovalish leaves, short racemes of pearly white flowers, May–June, followed by maroon or wine-purple berries; for lime-free, well-drained, peaty soils, and conditions similar to those needed for its parents.

Gaura (gaw'ra. Fam. Onagraceae). The chief species grown is *G. lindheimeri,* Texas, Louisiana, a graceful branching plant to 3 ft, with spikes of rosy-white flowers all summer, naturally perennial but usually grown as an annual; *coccinea,* Central N. America, 1 ft, with rose flowers, may also be grown similarly. Sow in March in cool greenhouse or frame, and plant out in well-drained lightish soil, full sun, where they are to flower.

Gaya. See *Hoheria.*

Gazania (ga-zan'i-a. Fam. Compositae). Sometimes called Treasure Flowers, these low-growing, naturally perennial herbs of S. Africa, with their large, showy rayed flower-heads in summer, are chiefly grown in hybrid forms as half-hardy perennials; being sown under glass, March, with bottom heat (18° C. [65° F.]); pricked off, hardened, and planted out in May in well-drained soil, full sun, on rock gardens or borders; or may be pot-grown in the cold greenhouse. *G.* × *splendens,* 6 in., with bright orange flowers, black-and-white ringed at the centre, is very good, but seedsmen usually offer seeds of hybrids yielding white, yellow, orange, pink, red and brown flowers. Outstanding plants may be propagated by cuttings of side-shoots in July–August, rooted in a close propagating case; and over-wintered in a cool greenhouse.

Genista (gen-is'ta. Fam. Leguminosae). Deciduous shrubs with fresh green stems, related to and often confused with Cytisus, commonly known as Brooms, and valued for their racemes of pea-like yellow flowers of late spring and summer.

Selection. G. aethnensis, Mt Etna Broom, Sicily, to 15 ft, golden-yellow, July; *cinerae,* Spain and W. Mediterranean region, to 10 ft, elegant, yellow, June–July; *hispanica,* Spanish Gorse, SW. Europe, 1–3 ft, bright yellow, June–July; *tinctoria,* the native Dyer's Greenwood, to 3 ft, yellow, summer, and vs. *elongata flore pleno,* double flowering and *ovata,* 20 in., yellow, are more or less hardy for most gardens; but *januensis,* Genoa Broom, 1 ft, bright yellow, May–June; *lydia,* SE. Europe, to 2 ft, yellow, May–June, *pilosa,* S. Europe, prostrate growing, yellow, May–July; *sagittalis,* SE. Europe, 1 ft, yellow, June–July; *villarsii,* SE. France, low-growing, yellow, June–July; and *virgata,* Madeira Broom, 6–12 ft, yellow, June–July, need warm corners in mild localities, and shelter from hard frosts, if they are to last.

Cultivation. Plant in March–April, out of pots, in well-drained, porous soil, and sunny positions; prune, if necessary, after flowering, but only to near the base of flowered shoots, not older wood.

Propagation. By seeds, sown March–April, in cold greenhouse or frame, and grown on in pots. Cuttings may be taken of unflowered shoots in July–August.

Gentiana, Gentian (gen-ti-an′a. Fam. Gentanaceae). A genus of alpines, running to over 400 species, of which, however, only a few are relatively easy to grow out of doors in Britain, chiefly European or Asian, and valued for their glorious blue flowers.

Selection. G. acaulis, European Alps, 2–4 in., bell-mouthed, funnel-shaped, deep blue flowers, May–June; has vs. *alba,* white; *angustifolia,* brilliant blue, June; *clusii,* deep blue, with paler throat, May; and *kochiana,* blue, speckled green in the throat, June; requiring a rather heavy, porous, leaf-mould rich soil, with bone meal to feed; *alpina,* European Alps, 2–4 in., deep blue, spotted green, July; *angulosa,* Caucasus, 2–5 in., deep lilac, May–June; *cachemirica,* W. Himalaya, 3 in., soft bright blue, June–July; *verna,* the Spring Gentian, Asia, Europe, Britain, 4 in., azure blue, April–May, and v. *alba,* white; all bloom in spring or early summer, and

tolerate lime in the soil, if given humus in the shape of well-sifted leaf-mould, plus good drainage. *G. farreri,* W. China, 3 in., Cambridge blue, white-throated, flowers, August; *gracilipes,* Kansu, 6–8 in., deep purplish-blue, August; × 'Inverleith', 3 in., deep Cambridge blue, September; × 'Kidbrook Seedling', 6 in., rich deep blue, September; *lagodechiana,* 6 in., Caucasus, deep blue, spotted green and white, August–September; × *macauleyi,* 4 in., deep blue, August–October; *septemfida,* Asia Minor, deep blue, August; and *sino-ornata,* W. China, Tibet, 6 in., royal blue, September–October (needing lime-free soil), are the late summer–autumn glories.

Cultivation. In general terms, plant in March–April or September–October, in rock gardens or borders, where roots will not be disturbed; most spring-flowering kinds have some tolerance for lime; autumn flowering, except *G. farreri,* dislike limy soils; all welcome humus as sifted rotted leaf-mould or good peat; and moisture-retentive but free-draining soil; in sun or partial shade. There are many other species whose needs should be studied with the help of specialists' books.

Propagation. By seeds sown as soon as ripe, in pans, in cold frame or greenhouse; germination may be slow. By very careful division in early spring, when growth is just beginning. By cuttings in July–August, where plants make non-flowered shoots at the base, inserted in a cold frame; but not all Gentians are easy.

Genus (pl. **Genera**). A group of species with like structural characters in flower, fruit and seed, assumed to have derived from a common ancestor long ago.

Geophyte. A perennial plant having buds which over-winter below the surface of the soil.

Geotropism. The growth-response of a plant to the stimulus of gravity, resulting in the positive turning to the earth and growing downwards, as with roots.

Geranium, Crane's Bill (ge-ra′ni-um. Fam. Geraniaceae). Botanically a genus of herbaceous perennials, free-flowering and easily grown; but not to be confused with the florist 'Geraniums', which belong to *Pelargonium* (q.v.).

Selection. For the rock garden: *G. argentum,* N. Italy, 3 in., pink, darker veined flowers, June–July; and vs. *album* and *roseum; cinereum,* Pyrenees, 3 in., purplish-pink, June; and vs. *album* and *subcaulescens; dalmaticum,* Balkans, 3–6 in., light pink, June; *napuligerum (farreri),* W. China, 6 in., rose, June; *sanguineum* v. *lancastriense,* Europe, 3 in., pink, summer; and for borders: *endressii,* Pyrenees, 1 ft, light rose, all summer; *grandiflorum,* Sikkim, to 16 in., blue, red-veined, July; *ibericum,* Caucasus, 1 ft, blue, summer; *pratense,* N. Europe, 3–4 ft, blue, all summer, and vs. *album* and *plenum; psilostemon,* Armenia, 3 ft, magenta, summer; and *wallichianum,* Himalaya, 1 ft, purple, August–September; an added attraction is their lobed or finely divided foliage.

Cultivation. Plant October–March, well-drained, ordinary soil, preferably in sun or partial shade.

Propagation. By seeds sown outdoors in April–June; by division in March.

Gerbera (ger'ber-a. Fam. Compositae). The species chiefly grown is *G. jamesonii,* the Barberton Daisy of Transvaal and Natal, 1–1½ ft, as a half-hardy perennial in the cool greenhouse, for its long-stemmed, large, starry, rayed flowers, now in hybrid form available in colours of red, orange, yellow, cream to white, in summer, lasting well when cut.

Cultivation. Pot, or repot, March–April, standard porous compost, watering freely in active growth, little in winter, temp. 7° C. (45° F.) minimum, or may be grown in the border, under light airy conditions. Only suitable out of doors in the mildest localities, on warm, sunny sheltered borders.

Propagation. By seeds, sown immediately available, under glass, bottom heat of 18° C. (65° F.), and potted on. By cuttings of young basal shoots in April.

German Catchfly. See *Viscaria.*

Germander. See *Teucrium.*

Germination. The development of the embryo plant within the seed until growth. It occurs when the seed is exposed to favourable conditions of moisture, air and temperature. Most seeds also germinate well in darkness, some do better in light; others are adversely affected by light. The seed absorbs moisture through its seed-coat (testa) and the micropyle, with oxygen; this activates chemical and enzyme reactions to liberate growth energies; the seed and embryo swell, rupturing the testa, and the emergence of the radicle (first root) occurs, followed by that of the plumule (stem). *See* Seeds and Sowing.

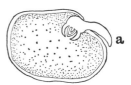

FIG. 111 Germination: emergence of the radicle or first root (a) in a pea.

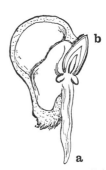

FIG. 112 Germination: radicle (a) well developed; plumule (b) emerged, in a sweet corn seed.

Gesneria (ges-ne'ri-a. Fam. Gesneriaceae). Tuberous-rooted, herbaceous perennials of Brazil, grown for their large, roughish, handsome leaves and showy tubular flowers, loosely borne on stems, in summer and autumn, in the warm greenhouse.

Selection. G. cardinalis, 15 in., bright red; *donkelaeriana,* 2 ft, vermilion; × *exoniensis,* 1½ ft, orange-scarlet; and hybrids with white, yellow, orange and pink blooms are available.

Cultivation. Pot, and repot biennially, 1 in. deep, in 5- or 6-in. pots, compost of equal parts leaf-mould, peat, loam and sand; water freely in growth, shade from bright sun, with pots on moist gravel or ashes; summer temp. not less than 18° C. (65° F.); after flowering, withhold water gradually, and when foliage dies, keep dry, in temp. of not less than 13° C. (55° F.), until spring.

Propagation. By seeds, February, bottom heat of 24° C. (74° F.); by the increase of the tubers; by leaf cuttings in early summer.

Geum (ge′um. Fam. Rosaceae). Hardy, herbaceous perennial plants, with lobed leaves and brilliant flowers on slender stalks in spring and early summer.

Selection. For the rock garden: *G. montanum,* S. Europe, 6 in., yellow; *reptans,* European Alps, 8 in., yellow, July; and × *tirolense,* Carpathians, 6 in., yellow, summer; for borders: *G.* × *boris,* to 12 in., yellow, summer; *chiloense,* Chiloe, 1–2 ft, in its forms 'Lady Stratheden', double, golden-yellow; 'Mrs Bradshaw', double scarlet; and 'Prince of Orange', rich orange; × *heldreichii,* 1 ft, orange-red, summer; and vs. *splendens* and *superbum,* large-flowered; and × *rossii,* Alaska, 1 ft, yellow, summer.

Cultivation. Plant October–March, any well-drained ordinary soil, enriched with humus, in sun or partial shade.

Propagation. Most forms come true from seeds, sown in pans or boxes, in cold frame, early summer, for planting out in autumn; or under glass, early spring, for planting out in summer. By division, October–March.

Gherkin. A variety of Cucumber (q.v.).

Gibbus (-a, -um). Gibbous, swollen, bulging. Ex. *Echeveria gibbiflora.*

Gigas. Giant. Ex. *Haworthia gigas.*

Gilia (gi-li′a. Fam. Polemoniaceae). Annuals and biennials of Western N. America, attractive for their tubular flowers with spreading petals in dense heads in summer, for warm sunny borders or cool greenhouse.

Selection. *G. achilleaefolia,* 1 ft, large blue flowers, with white, rose and a very large flowered *major* forms; *androsacea,* 1–1½ ft, pink, lilac or white, summer; *capitata,* to 2 ft, blue; and *tricolor,* 2 ft, purple, white, yellow; with several vs.; are annuals, for sowing, March–April, standard compost, bottom heat of 15·5° C. (60° F.); pricked off and

planted out or potted in May. *G. aggregata,* 2 ft, red, rose, yellow; and *rubra,* to 4 ft, rich red, are biennials to sow in June, and give winter protection in cool greenhouse, planting out the following May.

Cultivation. Any well-drained, ordinary soil, and full sun, will suit these plants.

Gillenia (gil-len′i-a. Fam. Rosaceae). Fairly hardy herbaceous perennials of central and southern U.S.A., with trifoliolate leaves, and panicles of red to white, strap-petalled flowers in June. *G. stipulata,* to 2 ft, and *trifoliata,* to 4 ft, may be planted, October–April, rather moist, peaty soil, partial shade, in all but the colder localities, and easily increased by division in spring.

Gilliflower, Gillyflower, Gilloflower, Gilofre, Gillyvor. Originally the name for Carnation (*Dianthus caryophyllus*), but also applied to Stocks and Wallflowers in England. From the French, Giroflée; the Gilliflower of Shakespeare was the Carnation.

Ginkgo, Maidenhair Tree (gink′go. Fam. Ginkgoaceae). The sole species, *G. biloba,* N. China, to 100 ft, is a fine deciduous tree, with fan-like, notched leaves, resembling those of a Maidenhair fern, to warrant its common name; and one of the most ancient flowering trees of its kind, with foliage turning bright yellow in autumn. Slow-growing at first,

FIG. 113   *Ginkgo biloba,* its foliage.

but desirable as a specimen tree, especially in its v. *fastigiata* for small gardens, it succeeds in any well-drained, fertile soil, and is quite hardy; planting is done in autumn or spring; propagation by seeds, sown in spring, in a cold frame or cool greenhouse.

Glaber (**-bra, -brum**). Glabrous, smooth. Ex. *Elaeagnus glabra*.

Gladiolus, Sword Lily (glad′i-o-lus. Fam. Iridaceae). A most beautiful genus of charming cormous plants, notable for their long sword-like leaves and tall spikes of flared tubular flowers, often one-sided, in a tremendous range of attractive colouring. Although of some 150 species, only a few of these are garden-grown, and interest centres very largely in the many hybrid strains.

FIG. 114 Gladiolus corm.

Selection. G. byzantinus, Mediterranean region, 2 ft, dark red; *communis*, Mediterranean region, 2–3 ft, rose-pink; *illyricus*, Mediterranean region, to 1½ ft, purplish-pink; and *segetum*, S. Europe, 2 ft, purplish pink, are relatively hardy, and may be planted 4 in. deep in autumn, given little cover for the winter, in well-drained, porous soil, sunny warm positions, to flower in June–July. *G. cardinalis*, 3 ft, scarlet; *cuspidatus*, 1½ ft, white to purple; *grandis*, 1½ ft, white, striped yellowish-brown; *leichtlinii*, 2 ft, bright red; *oppositiflorus*, to 4 ft, white, violet striped; *psittacinus*, 3 ft, bright red and yellow; *saundersii*, 3 ft, carmine-rose; and *tristis*, 1½ ft, yellowish white, tinged red, are S. African species, worth growing for their own merits, being planted in early spring for summer flowering; but have also played their parts as parents of garden hybrids.

Garden Hybrids. The classification of hybrid garden gladioli is becoming more complex as more and more varieties and forms are introduced. For our purposes here, they may be divided or grouped as follows, though the varieties named are only chosen as good representatives of their kind. For fuller and more complete lists, and newer introductions, catalogues, shows and the recommendations of the British Gladiolus Society should be followed.

1. *Early-flowering group:* also known as 'Nanus'. It includes *G.* × *colvillei*, 1½ ft, bright red, and forms such as 'Amanda Mahy', salmon-red; 'Blushing Bride', white, flaked carmine; 'Nymph', white, crimson flakes; 'Peach Blossom', pink; 'Spitfire', vermilion, violet flakes; and 'The Bride', white; the 'Herald' strain, such as 'Comet', poppy red, 3 ft; and 'Fair Lady', soft pink; × *harlemensis*, 2 ft, in vs. 'Blue Gem', lilac; 'Festa', white and lilac; 'Ivory Gem', creamy white; and 'Magent', pink; and × *tubergenii* with forms 'Charm', purplish rose, white centred; and 'Warmunda', soft pink. This group should be planted in autumn, 3 in. deep, in well-drained, humus-rich soil, warm, sunny positions, with litter protection against frost, to flower in June; or they may be grown in pots, standard compost, in cool greenhouse or frame, to flower in March–May, according to the temperature maintained.

2. *Summer- and Autumn-flowering Hybrids*. These may be divided into the following sections:

(a) *Large-flowering*. They grow to 3–4½ ft tall, with stout stems and brilliantly coloured large flowers, well-established favourites being, for early summer flowering: 'Acca Laurentia', orange on yellow; 'Flower Song', golden yellow, frilled; 'Life Flame', red, flecked crimson; 'Maria Goretti', white; 'Scarlet Royal', vermilion-red; for mid season flowering: 'Dr Fleming', shell-pink; 'Firebrand', orange-scarlet, cream marking; 'Forgotten Dreams', primrose, yellow and rose; 'Green Woodpecker', greenish lemon and wine-red; 'General Eisenhower', rosy salmon-pink; 'Picardy', creamy salmon-pink; 'Spoetnik', poppy red; 'Toulouse-Lautrec', apricot-salmon and yellow; 'White

Angel', white; for late-flowering: 'Albert Schweitzer', scarlet to orange and scarlet pink; 'Bloemfontein', apricot-pink; 'Blue Conqueror', violet-blue; 'Elan', pink; 'My Love', 'Ivory', carmine splashed; 'Scarlet Pimpernelle', orange-scarlet; and 'Tigris', vermilion-orange.

(b) *Primulinus Hybrids.* They grow 3–4 ft tall, with slender stems, with smaller, somewhat hooded, flowers than the large-flowering hybrids, finely coloured, as in: 'Blue Bell', lavender blue; 'Chrysantha', yellow, marked scarlet; 'Fiery Knight', reddish orange; 'Ivory and Mauve', ivory, carmine flush; 'Jean', white; 'Katharine', rose-mauve; 'Richard Unwin', deep crimson, cream stripes; 'Rosy Maid', apricot-salmon; and 'Zylpha', salmon. There are also some larger-flowering *primulinus grandiflorus*, with stronger stems, 3–4½ ft tall, such as 'Harmony', cherry-salmon; 'Joyce', cherry-rose and salmon; 'Netty', vermilion-orange; 'Corvair', red; 'Treasure', blood red; and 'White City', cream and white.

3. *Miniature Small-flowered Hybrids.* These varieties are increasingly popular, growing 20–40 in. tall, with strikingly coloured flowers, often frilled, somewhat smaller than those of the Primulinus types. Their culture is similar to that of the large-flowered hybrids. They include 'Butterfly' types, such as 'Blue Goddess', silver blue; 'Capricio', creamy yellow, pink; 'Donald Duck', lemon-yellow, orange-scarlet blotched; 'Gigi', creamy pink; 'Gipsy Love', orange-salmon; 'Ice Follies', ivory white, cream; 'Mde Butterfly', pink, salmon and violet; 'Storiette', salmon-pink, cream; 'Summer Fairy', coppery rose, yellow and maroon; and 'Walt Disney', sulphur-yellow, blood-red blotch; and Miniatures, such as 'Bermuda', lemon-white, scarlet throat; 'Coral Reef', salmon, orange and cream; 'Green Bird', greenish yellow, flushed rose; and 'Southport', ivory, creamy throated.

Cultivation. Garden hybrid gladioli are easily grown; being planted as corms 3–4 in. deep, 6–9 in. apart, in March–May; well-drained, organically rich soil, and sunny positions, though midday shade from hot sun is helpful to sustained flower colour. The taller kinds

need staking. Steamed bone flour at planting is helpful; with liquid feeding when buds show if the weather is dry. The corms should be lifted in mid to late October, cutting the stalks to within 4 in. of the ground; dried off under airy conditions, and then stored in boxes under dry cool conditions ($7°$ C. [$45°$ F.]).

They may also be grown in large pots, in the cold greenhouse or frame, standard compost, watering freely in growth, the Butterfly and Miniature type being rewarding.

Propagation. When corms are lifted, a new large corm will be found formed above the old shrivelled one, which should be detached; and a number of small cormlets (or spawn), which should be detached after drying, and stored for replanting. The cormlets are used to increase stock, being planted separately the following spring, on good, rich, well-drained soil, to grow on and make flowering plants in about two years. They need generous treatment, otherwise the plants deteriorate, and do best in light loam soils, generously fed with rotted manure or compost and organic fertilizers. Species and mixed varieties of hybrids may be grown from seeds, sown in spring, standard compost, in cold frame or greenhouse, in deep pans or boxes, thinly. Grow on in the open in summer, lift the corms in October, and grow on as cormlets the following year to bring to a good flowering size.

Cutting Flowers. The flower stems may be cut when the first four to five flowers are just opening; placed in a bucket of water immediately, until taken indoors for arrangement.

Diseases. Early yellowing of the leaves may be caused by a fungus, *Sclerotinia gladioli*, which infects the corms, causing black spots and blotches and a mummifying of the corm into a black mass. Yellow-brown spotting of the leaves, followed by black sunken patches on corms, is usually caused by the fungus *Septoria gladioli*. It is unwise to save infected plants for propagation, but lift and burn them. Most gladiolus diseases are carried on the corms. It is important to examine them before planting and before storing, rejecting the doubtful, showing any signs of rot or abnormality. Planting should be rotated to fresh ground periodically. Corms may be dressed with a thiram fungicide as a precaution when planting.

Pests. The most damaging specific pest is Gladiolus Thrips, *Taeniothrips simplex*, which multiply rapidly; adults and larvae feeding on foliage, etc., causing silvery streaks and mottling. In summer, control calls for a gamma-BHC insecticide; as the insects overwinter under corm scales, loose scales should be removed, and the stored corms dusted with a gamma-BHC/DDT insecticidal dust. Wireworm damage to roots can be prevented by dressing planting stations with a gamma-BHC dust; and slugs can be defeated with metaldehyde bait pellets.

Gland. In plants, a small sac on or in the green tissue of leaves, stems, etc., secreting oil, resin, aromatic liquid, etc.; when stalked it is known as a glandular hair.

Glandulosus (-a, -um). Bearing glands. Ex. *Aquilegia glandulosa.*

Glastonbury Thorn. See *Crataegus.*

Glaucium (glauk′i-um. Fam. Papaveraceae). The popular species is *G. flavum*, the Horned Poppy of N. Africa, 1–2 ft, with silvery foliage and chrome-yellow flowers, summer; an easily grown perennial, at home in any well-drained garden soil, and sun; from seeds sown in April, and thinned to 9 in. apart; *corniculatum*, 9 in., is an annual, with crimson, black centred, flowers in early summer, easily grown from seeds sown in spring where plants are to flower.

Glaucus (-a, -um). Glaucous, dull bluish or greyish green. Ex. *Rhododendron glaucum.*

Gleditschia, Honey Locust (gledits′ki-a. Fam. Leguminosae). Deciduous trees with handsome pinnate foliage, spiny branches, but insignificant flowers. *G. triacanthos*, the Honey Locust of N. America, to 60 ft, is worth growing for its foliage effect, turning clear yellow in autumn; but rarely ripening its long, sweet fleshy pods reponsible for its common name; v. *bujotii* is an elegant weeping form; *elegantissima*, a slow-growing variety, and *inermis* is without spines. The Persian *caspica*, to 30 ft, he Japanese *japonica*, to 60 ft, are also hardy and sometimes offered.

Plant October or March, in well-drained loam soil, sun and shelter.

Gleichenia (glai-ke′ni-a. Fam. Gleicheniaceae). A large genus of beautiful fronded ferns, creeping by rhizomes over the soil, and forming dense bushes.

Selection. G. circinnata, Australia, New Zealand, fronds to 5 ft, and vs. *mendelli*, silvery beneath, and *speluncae*, with arching fronds; *flabellata*, Australia, New Zealand, 3–4 ft; and *rupestris*, Australia, 2–6 ft, and v. *glaucescens*, with thickish glaucous fronds, may be grown in the cool greenhouse, minimum temp. 7° C. (45° F.), with ample light and ventilation; watering freely in warm weather, and growing in simple shallow pans, with good drainage and a compost of equal parts peat and sand.

Propagation by division is difficult, by spores, very slow.

Globe Amaranth. See *Gomphrena.*

Globe Artichoke. *See* Artichoke.

Globe Flower. See *Trollius.*

Globe Thistle. See *Echinops.*

Globosus (-a, -um). Globose, rounded or spherical. Ex. *Buddleia globosa.*

Globularia, Globe Daisy (glob-u-lar′i-a. Fam. Globulariaceae). Shrub-like, dwarf perennial plants, of cushion-like habit with rounded heads of blue or white flowers in early summer, from the Mediterranean regions.

Selection. G. bellidifolia, 2 in., blue; *cordifolia*, 3 in., bright blue; v. *alba*, white; *incanescens*, 3 in., light blue; and *nana*, 1 in., lilac-blue; and *trichosantha*, 3 in., grey-blue.

Cultivation. Plant March–April, well-drained light soil, with lime, and sunny shelter in the rock garden; or in pans for the alpine house, especially in cold districts; not for heavy or wet soils.

Propagation. By division in April; by cuttings of young shoots, taken in July, under handlight or in frame.

Glomeratus (-a, -um). In a roundish head. Ex. blooms of *Campanula glomerata.*

Gloriosa, Glory Lily (glo-ri-o′sa. Fam. Liliaceae). Highly ornamental bulbous, tendril-climbing plants with showy flowers, native to tropical Africa, and grown in the warm greenhouse.

Selection. G. rothschildiana, Uganda, to 4 ft, vermilion, edged light yellow flowers, is chiefly grown; *abyssinica*,

Ethiopa, 2 ft, branching, is smaller, deep yellow flowers; *carsonii*, tropical Africa, 3 ft, red, yellow centred; *simplex*, Mozambique, 4 ft, orange and yellow; and *superba*, tropical Africa, 6 ft, orange and red, are all good; the flowers resembling thin Martagon lilies.

Cultivation. Pot the tuberous 'bulbs' in February, standard compost, temp. 21° C. (70° F.), watering freely during growth, and syringing on sunny days; allow to dry off after flowering gradually; keep dry in winter, pots on their sides, temp. 13° C. (55° F.) minimum; *G. superba* will grow in a cool house.

Propagation. By offsets, when repotting. By seeds, under glass, bottom heat of 24° C. (75° F.); growth is slow.

Glory of the Snow. See *Chionodoxa*.

Glory of the Sun. See *Leucocoryne*.

Glory Pea. See *Clianthus*.

Gloxinia. See *Sinningia*.

Glucose. Sugar occurring in many fruits.

Glume. The small scale or bract at the base of the flower of a grass or sedge.

FIG. 115 Glumes.

Glutinosus (-a, -um). Glutinous, sticky. Ex. *Mimulus glutinosus*.

Goat Willow. See *Salix caprea*.

Goat's Beard. See *Aruncus sylvestris*.

Goat's Rue. See *Galega*.

Godetia (go-de'ti-a. Fam. Onagraceae). Summer-flowering annuals developed from species native to Western N. America, related to Oenothera, and having much in common with Clarkia, with their profusion of showy flowers, in reds, pinks and white.

Selection. Dwarf forms, derived from *G. grandiflora* (*whitneyi*), include 'Crimson Glow', 9 in.; 'Kelvedon Glory', 1½ ft; 'Scarlet Emblem', 1 ft; 'Sybil Sherwood', 1½ ft, salmon-pink, in single- and double-flowering strains; 'Dawn', 1 ft, pink and white; 'Lavender Queen', 1½ ft; 'Orange Glory', 1 ft; 'White Swan', 1 ft, and others, such as *azaleiflora plena*, 1 ft, coral-pink, blotched crimson. Taller forms, derived from *G. amoena*, 2½ ft, are 'Sutton's Double' in 'Shell Pink', 'Rosy Morn', 'Cherry Red'; and *schamini flore pleno*, 2 ft, salmon-rose.

Cultivation. Sow under glass, March, bottom heat of 18° C. (65° F.), to prick off, and plant out in May to fairly rich soil, well-drained, and in sun; or in April, out of doors, where they are to flower. May also be sown in September in cold frame, to pot for the greenhouse, or plant out the following spring; or outdoors in mild localities.

Gold Thread. See *Coptis*.

Golden Bell. See *Forsythia*.

Golden Chain. See *Laburnum*.

Golden Feather. See *Chrysanthemum parthenium aureum*.

Golden Rod. See *Solidago*.

Golden Willow. See *Salix*.

Goldilocks. See *Aster linosyris*.

Gomphrena, Globe Amaranth (gomfre'na. Fam. Amaranthaceae). Half-hardy annuals of which *G. globosa*, India, 1 ft, in yellow, purple, rose and white forms, and a 6-in. dwarf *nana*, dark red, are grown; from seeds sown in March, under glass, bottom heat of 15·5° C. (60° F.); to plant out in May, or grow on in pots in the cold greenhouse; or may be sown in September to winter in a cool greenhouse (7° C. [45° F.]) for spring bloom. The flower-heads are 'Everlasting' if cut just before reaching maturity.

Good King Henry, All-good, or **Mercury** (*Chenopodium bonus-henricus*). A native perennial, cultivated as a vegetable; the young green axillary shoots with embryo flower-buds at their tips being detached and cooked like asparagus in April–May, and the soft green leaves gathered to June for use like Spinach. It is grown from seeds, sown in spring, $\frac{1}{2}$ in. deep, in drills 9 in. apart, thinning seedlings to 9 in. apart; in well-drained, porous rich soil, keeping free of weeds, and giving annual top-dressings of rotted manure or compost.

Goodyera (good'ye-ra. Fam. Orchidaceae). Fleshy or tuberous rooted terrestrial orchids, with pretty flowers and handsome foliage.

Selection. G. *japonica*, Japan, velvety green, silvery and pinkish leaves; *macrantha*, Japan, dark and light green, with yellow-bordered leaves and pale rose flowers; and *velutina*, Japan, purplish green, white-ribbed leaves and whitish flowers, may be grown in a cool greenhouse, in shade, potted in a mixture of equal parts peat, sphagnum moss and sand, with a little loam; while *pubescens*, N. America, silver-veined leaves, pale yellow flowers, and *repens*, the native Ladies' Tresses, deep green, with spike of yellowish-white flowers, summer, may be attempted outdoors, shady sheltered places, in well-drained soil, enriched with peat and leaf-mould.

Gooseberry (*Ribes grossularia*). A hardy bush fruit long cultivated and developed from the native species of Europe and Britain.

Selection. Green berries: 'Keepsake', 'Lancer', 'Green Gem',* 'Careless'. Red berries: 'Lancashire Lad', 'Whinham's Industry'. Yellow berries: 'Leveller',* 'Golden Drop'.* White berries: 'Langley Gage',* 'Whitesmith'.

*Best for flavour.

Soil. A well-drained, moisture-retentive loam is ideal; but almost any soil, free from waterlogging, well-trenched and enriched from humus-forming organic matter, will suit; light soils need dressing with sulphate of potash, 2 oz. per sq. yd.

Planting. This may be done between October and March, in mild weather. Bushes on a single leg, 2 to 3 years old, are spaced at 6 ft apart; single cordons, 12–15 in. apart; spreading roots evenly, not too deeply, and firming well.

Pruning. Gooseberries produce fruit on one-year-old shoots and on spurs of older shoots. Newly planted bush fruits should have their shoots cut back by about one-half to a suitably placed bud

after planting. For the next two years or so the new leading growths are cut back by one-half each winter, to develop a good branch framework. Thereafter the bushes may be pruned as for black currants, a proportion of the oldest branches being cut out each year, and strong new shoots allowed to replace them; this gives plenty of small berries. A better plan is to prune the new

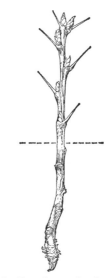

FIG. 116 Gooseberry Cutting, prepared for planting in early winter.

lateral shoots on the main branches to about five leaves in early summer, and to within 2 in. of their base in February; leading shoots are shortened by one-half to two-thirds each winter. With cordon and trained trees, the side-shoots only are shortened to about three buds in winter; and in summer all laterals are pruned to about five leaves; the leading shoot only needs cutting back when it becomes overlong.

Manuring. An annual dressing of rotted organic matter should be given, supplemented by a base fertilizer rather high in potash in February–March, as for red currants and dessert apples, with which gooseberries should be associated. Weeds are best kept down by mulching, as surface roots should not be disturbed.

Propagation. Gooseberries are grown on their own roots, propagated from cuttings of young shoots, taken in autumn, with lower buds removed, except for the top three or four on the part remaining above ground, after firming the shoots in well-drained soil. Subsequent growth from the buds is regulated to give a branching bush on a short clean stem, or for cordons, the growth from the strongest bud is trained as the main stem, and other growths suppressed.

Diseases. American Gooseberry Mildew (*Sphaerotheca mors-uvae*) is the worst, coating leaves, shoots and berries with a white powder which turns brown and felt-like later in summer. Control lies in pruning to permit free circulation of air through the bushes, avoidance of heavy nitrogenous feeding, and spraying, preferably with karathane just before the flowers open, again when fruit is set, and again in a fortnight; or lime-sulphur (1½ per cent solution) may be used except on sulphur-shy easily damaged varieties —'Careless', 'Golden Drop', 'Leveller'. Leaf Spot (*Gloeosporium ribis*) causes dark spotting, yellowing and early fall of leaves. Such leaves should be collected and burnt, and a zineb or colloidal copper fungicide should be applied after harvest. Grey Mould (*Botrytis cinerea*), may attack leaves and shoots, causing extensive die-back, especially on ill-drained soil; infected shoots must be cut out, and if the main stem is involved the whole bush uprooted and burnt. Cluster Cup Rust (*Puccinia pringsheimiana*) causes red or orange blotches on leaves, shoots and fruits; spraying with a colloidal copper fungicide a week or two before flowers open is helpful; but the fungus has an alternative host in Sedges, and any of these in the vicinity should be removed if possible.

Pests. Sawfly caterpillars (*Pterodinea ribesii*) can rapidly defoliate a bush in late April–July; and prompt spraying should be carried out as soon as caterpillars are seen with a malathion or derris insecticide, or in May after fruit set. Magpie Moth caterpillars (*Abraxas grossulariata*) also devour leaves; and it is useful to apply a derris insecticide immediately before flowers open, and malathion or derris three weeks later. Gooseberry Red Spider (*Bryobia praetiosa*) and Aphids (*Aphis grossulariae*) are controlled by winter washing with a tar-oil emulsion; and, if necessary, by malathion in late April–May. The caterpillars of the Currant Shoot Borer (*Lampronia capitella*) are reduced by tar-oil winter spraying, and those of the Currant Clearwing Moth (*Aegeria tipuliformis*) by cutting out infested shoots as soon as seen.

Gordonia (gor-don'i-a. Fam. Theaceae). Beautiful shrubs or small trees with shining leaves and creamy-white flowers with golden stamens freely borne on even young plants; but unfortunately not very hardy.

Selection. G. axillaris, China and Formosa, to 20 ft, evergreen foliage, creamy-white flowers to 5 in. across, in spring; *chrysandra,* Yunnan, to 10 ft, white flowers, February; and *lasianthus,* SE. U.S.A., to 30 ft, evergreen leathery leaves, and white single flowers in July–August; have been likened to white-flowered camellias.

Cultivation. Plant outdoors in lime-free, humus-rich soil in mildest localities only, woodland conditions suit. Otherwise, grow in large pots, lime-free standard compost, in cool greenhouse, winter temp. 7° C. (45° F.) minimum; standing outdoors June–September.

Propagation. By cuttings of young shoots taken in July–August, in propagating frame; by layers in spring.

Gorse. See *Ulex.*

Gourds (*Cucurbita.* Fam. Cucurbitaceae). Most seedsmen offer packets of seeds of Ornamental Gourds, chiefly varieties of *C. pepo,* such as apple-, egg-, Hercules-club-, orange-, pear-, spoon- and warted-shaped; or of *moschata* (Squashes); or *maxima,* large gourds; which are useful to grow up poles, trellis, pergolas or fences, from seeds raised in the same way as for marrows (q.v.), and planted out in May, into well-dug organically enriched soil in sunny positions. When ripe, the gourds can be dried for winter ornament indoors. See also *Lagenaria* and *Luffa.*

Gracilis (-e). Slender, graceful. Ex *Viola gracilis.*

Graft-hybrid. A plant that results from the growing together of the stock of one plant with the scion of another species forming a chimaera; the best example being × *Laburnocytisus adami* (q.v.).

Grafting. The operation by which a shoot, termed the scion, of one plant is united with the rooted part, termed the stock, of another, to form one growing plant. Grafting has been practised from remote times, by Chinese, Greeks and Romans; budding (q.v.) is a comparatively recent development of it. To succeed the scion and the stock must have natural genetical affinity, either being varieties of the same species, species of the same genus, or genera of the same family. A second essential is that the cambium layers or cells of the scion and the stock must be brought into close contact, at a time when active growth can take place.

Outdoor Grafting. This is chiefly practised with fruit trees and ornamental shrubs and trees. It may be used to graft desirable varieties on old trees; to propagate a variety quickly; to repair damage done to the bark and stems of existing trees by gnawing animals or frost injury. The best time to graft is in calm moist weather in spring when the sap is beginning to rise rapidly, March–April; though technically it can be done up to late summer until the sap flow slackens. It is easiest, however, to graft deciduous plants while leafless but when the buds are beginning to swell. When grafting plants in leaf or evergreens it is necessary to keep the growth close or moist to avoid too much loss of moisture in transpiration. The scion should be less advanced in growth than the stock, and it is best to take scions of pencil-thick young shoots in the winter, standing them buried in moist soil until required. When ready to graft with materials at hand, the scion and the stock are cut so that the greatest area of cambiums can be fitted together. The cuts should be made cleanly and smoothly, with a razor-blade or very sharp knife. The method of grafting depends on the size and type of plant to be grafted.

Whip and Tongue Graft. This is used in uniting scions and stocks of about the same diameter, as when using seedling stocks. An upward slanting cut is made of the stock, then a second cut is made downward, beginning almost at the top, to at least half way down the length of the first cut; the scion is then similarly prepared to fit into the cleft and on the plane of the slanting cut (*see* Fig. 117). Alternatively, the *Saddle Graft* may be used, the stock being prepared as an upward pointing wedge, and the scion cleft to fit on it (*see* Fig. 118). When the stock is of much larger size than the

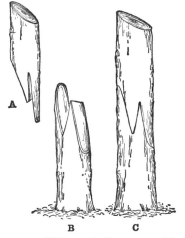

FIG. 117 Whip and Tongue grafting, used in grafting scions on stocks of like size: A. prepared scion. B. prepared stock. C. united scion and stock prior to sealing and taping.

scion, as in top-grafting the branches of old trees, the *Cleft Graft* is often used. The scion is cut downward at the centre, and the scion prepared as a simple wedge, to be inserted in the cleft with the outer cambium in register with the cambium of the stock. In practice, a scion is inserted on each side of the cleft; the weaker being removed later. A variation is *Crown Grafting*, in which the bark of the stock is slit downward to about three inches and gently eased back, and a scion prepared with a slanting cut slipped carefully in so the cambiums are in contact (*see* Fig. 119). *Bark Grafting* is resorted to when

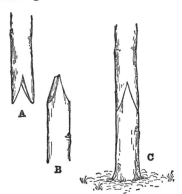

FIG. 118 Saddle grafting, used in grafting seedling rootstocks: A. prepared scion. B. prepared end of stock. C. scion and stock united before sealing and taping.

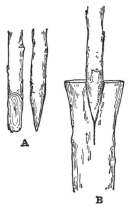

FIG. 119 Simple wedge grafting or crown grafting on older trees: A. prepared scion, face and side view. B. scion placed in split stock, prior to sealing and taping.

additional framework branches are required. One way is to make a vertical cut in the bark, lift it gently with a sacking-needle or bluntish blade and slip a prepared scion with a wedge-cut base behind, and firming it in (see Fig. 120). Alternatively, a piece of bark can be removed, triangular or V shaped, with

FIG. 120 Bark grafting, whereby a scion can be inserted and united under the bark of a stock: A. prepared scion. B. bark of stock cut and lifted to permit scion to enter, prior to sealing and taping.

a chisel, to the cambium, and a scion prepared to fit the incision precisely. When bark has been damaged or removed by gnawing animals so that there is doubt about the survival of a tree, one or more *Bridge Grafts* can be made. Scions are cut long enough to span the barked area, with 'tongues' at both ends to slip beneath the bark, lifted at appropriately placed incisions.

All completed grafts must be tied and secured with raffia and covered with grafting wax to exclude air, at once. Or more easily they can simply be bound with a prepared grafting tape. Once the grafts have taken and growth begins to swell the tissues, any bindings should be cut. It is wise to support grafted seedlings with a cane against wind breakage.

Indoor Grafting. This is chiefly done at nurseries, where plants, particularly evergreens, can be kept close in greenhouses, usually with bottom heat, to speed healing and new growth. The grafts commonly employed are the saddle graft or the veneer graft, especially in the propagation of such plants as young rhododendrons, magnolias and camellias. Grafting may also be practised with non-woody herbaceous plants, such as tomatoes, and is commonly resorted to in propagating choice Cacti.

Gramineae. The monocotyledonous family of Grasses, *Agrostis, Arundo, Bambusa, Briza, Bromus, Cortaderia, Festuca, Lamarkia, Miscanthus, Phalaris, Phyllostachys, Poa, Sasa, Zea* and *Zizania* being genera mentioned in this book.

Gramineus (-a, -um). Gramineous, grassy. Ex. *Ranunculus gramineus.*

Granadilla. Fruit of *Passiflora edulis.*

Grandis (-e). Large, noble. Ex. *Campanula grandis.*

Grape Hyacinth. See *Muscari.*

Grape Vine (*Vitis vinifera.* Fam. Vitaceae). The grape vine is held to have originated in Asia Minor, and to be introduced into Britain by the Romans, possibly via Egypt. Pleasant and of high health-giving nutrient value, grapes are well worth growing and are not difficult.

Grapes Under Glass. Grapes can be grown in any well-sunned greenhouse, though the best form is a lean-to or three-quarter-span on a south wall. The best results are achieved when the house can be devoted to grapes, although plants such as chrysanthemums, winter-flowering shrubs such as camellias, in pots, and plants requiring winter protection can be housed during winter. The vines are quite hardy, and can be fruited successfully in a cold house; but if early fruit is wanted, heat must be available for late winter and spring, though in winter the colder the house the better for the vine.

Varieties. The most easily grown are 'Black Hamburgh', 'Black Alicante' and 'Lady Downes' for black grapes; 'Buckland Sweetwater' and 'Foster's Seedling' for white grapes. 'Cannon Hall Muscat', white, 'Muscat of Alexandria', amber, and 'Gros Colmar', black, yield luscious grapes but need more heat and skill.

Soil. The soil border must be thoroughly well drained, and as wide as possible; bastard-trenched, and enriched with rotted manure or compost, ground limestone or chalk to bring to pH 6·5, crushed bone ($\frac{3}{4}$–1 lb. per sq. yd), bonfire ash and charcoal (or sulphate of potash at 2 oz. per sq. yd),

and well firmed. A subsoil of chalk or limestone is valuable. On heavy clays it is worth adding broken limestone freely to the subsoil. On light soils, a few barrowloads of clay loam would help. Grapes grow on almost any soil, but a soil subject to waterlogging should be avoided.

Planting. The young vines are best planted in autumn or early winter, in the front border of the house, 4 ft apart. They are sometimes planted with roots outside, and the stem led into the house through a hole or pipe in the wall, but this makes for difficulties later on. Planted in the inside border, roots will eventually find their way to the outside under shallow foundations.

Training. After planting, the stem of the vine is shortened to the first bud showing above the house wall, or to $1\frac{1}{2}$–2 ft. This will start into growth to some feet the first year, and is pruned by one-third to one-half its length in early winter. Side-shoots are stopped at 2 ft in growth, and then cut off in the winter. In the second year the new growth of the leader is cut back by about one-half in winter, but side-shoots are pruned to the first strong bud from their base. This gives a strong main stem or rod, with bud laterals that eventually form spurs. The shoots are trained up wires, and when the main stem reaches the topmost point it is stopped there, being cut back each year. The lateral buds make new growth and these will usually bear in their second year. They are allowed to grow out until one or two flower clusters form, and are then stopped by pinching out the soft tip growth at the second leaf beyond the end cluster. Any subsequent secondary growth is pinched after making one or two leaves. Not more than two bunches of fruit should be allowed to develop per lateral, and the laterals should be chosen at about 1 ft apart, weak ones being suppressed. After fruiting, each lateral is cut back by half its length, and after leaf-fall cut back to the strong basal bud. Rods and laterals are tied to the wires as they are made. The wires should be about 9 in. apart, and at least 1 ft, preferably $1\frac{1}{2}$ ft, below the roof glass. Instead of growing a vine to one main rod, it is also possible to let two laterals develop to be trained horizontally and be trained as main rods subsequently, up the roof.

Routine Management. Pruning should be finished before the turn of the year, when it is helpful to remove the main rods from the wires and let them bend downward to encourage even breaking of the laterals. The border should be heavily watered in advance of new growth; when buds begin to break the rods are tied up. For early grapes, heat is given in January–February, to about 10° C. (50° F.), for varieties other than the Muscats, which require 15·5° C. (60° F.) at least. With increasing sun heat, temperatures will go higher, but a minimum of 15·5° C. (60° F.) [21° C. (70° F.) for Muscats], is desirable when the vines are in flower. A buoyant atmosphere must be maintained, with morning watering and syringing of the new growth, and ample ventilation with the daily temperature rise. In dull weather syringing is less necessary, and in cold, ventilation must be done when temperatures rise to their daily peak, shutting down before nightfall. During flowering a somewhat dry atmosphere is best, and shoots should be tapped to dislodge and spread the pollen; in the case of Muscats it is advantageous to pollinate with a rabbit's scut. Over-cropping must be avoided. On young vines one bunch of fruit per lateral is sufficient. The bunches of young fruitlets must be thinned soon after being set. Thinning is something of an art. It is done with pointed grape-thinning scissors and a forked stick to separate the grapelets without impairing their bloom. Briefly, the terminal fruitlets are left and the top shoulders of the bunches can be left fairly full, but the centres are thinned drastically, and adequate room given for expansion of the fruitlets left. Large-berrying varieties can be thinned more than small, but always visualizing the finished ripe bunch in mind. It is better to over- than under-thin. After leaf-fall no heat is required and watering should largely cease, while the vines rest and can be pruned. Bunches of grapes can be kept for some time if cut with a length of lateral stem, which is placed in a bottle or jar of water, in a cool, airy place.

Grapes Out of Doors. Grape vines are quite hardy, but need warmth and sun to ensure properly ripened fruits; consequently they succeed best in southern and sunny, warm localities; grown on wires against a wall, or in the open on wire supports trained to secure posts, and trained horizontally. The best varieties are 'Black Hamburgh', black, and 'Royal Muscadine', white, for fruit. In recent years there has been considerable interest taken in reviving vineyards for wine-making, using such varieties as 'Brant', 'Chasselas Rose', 'Madeleine Royale' and selected strains suited to English conditions. For general culture and amateur growing, the 'Strawberry Grape', with prolific crops of strawberry-flavoured small berries, is to be recommended. General culture of grapes out of doors is along the lines of those laid down for under glass as far as pruning and soil management is concerned. Wine grapes are not thinned.

FIG. 121 A grape vine 'eye' prepared for propagation.

Propagation. Grape vines are grown on their own roots, and plants can be easily raised from eyes or buds, consisting of 2-in. lengths cut from young, newly matured lateral shoots, each with a good bud; a slanting cut of half an inch is made directly under the bud, and it is then planted, buried to bud level, in a 3-in. pot, standard compost, in January, with bottom heat of 18° C. (65° F.) in a warm greenhouse. Alternatively, 8–10-in. cuttings of young laterals, taken with a heel, may be inserted in warm borders, with the buds below soil level rubbed off, in autumn, to give plants for planting out the following winter.

Diseases. Powdery Mildew (*Uncinula necator*) is the commonest disease, covering foliage, shoots and fruit with a white, mealy mould. It is primarily

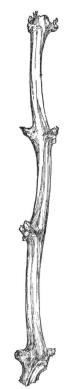

FIG. 122 Grape vine cutting, ready for planting in autumn or early winter.

encouraged by faulty ventilation and inadequate watering and syringing, but may be checked by spraying with karathane or colloidal sulphur fungicide or dusting with sulphur dust. Shanking describes a functional disorder and shows in the berries going flaccid, shrunken and sour, and their stalks shrivelling and discolouring. It can be induced by over-cropping in young vines, by some failure of rooting caused by poor soil conditions or exhaustion. Replacement of the top soil with new soil compost, attention to drainage and meticulous culture will generally cure the trouble. Scalding, or discoloration of the fruits may occur if

ventilation is neglected, while scorched shrivelling foliage suggests too much hot sun under conditions of poor ventilation, and/or impaired drainage at the roots.

Pests. Mealy Bug makes white mealy patches on shoots, rods and fruit. The rods should be scraped and painted with tar-oil wash in winter; vines may be sprayed with malathion immediately after thinning. Red Spider Mites can be troublesome, turning leaves dryish and yellowish, if conditions are too dry; adequate watering and syringing repels this pest; Azobenzene Smoke Fumigation can be carried out in May, and repeated if necessary. Scale insects sometimes line rods, but treatment as for Mealy Bug gives good control. Thrips, small blackish or yellowish insects, and White-fly should be promptly sprayed with malathion when seen.

Grass. *See* Lawns.

Grass of Parnassus. See *Parnassia.*

Grasses, Ornamental. Increasingly popular for flower arranging and floral art, and for drying for the winter, details will be found under *Agrostis, Avena, Briza, Bromus, Coix, Cortederia, Hordeum, Lagurus, Lamarkia, Miscanthus, Panicum, Pennisetum, Phalaris, Stipa* and *Zea.*

Gratus (-a, -um). Pleasing. Ex. *Lonicera grata.*

Gravel. *See* Paths.

Graveolens. Strong-smelling. Ex. *Ruta graveolens.*

Greek Valerian. See *Polemonium.*

Green Manure. *See* Manuring, Green.

Greenfly. *See* Aphis.

Greengage. *See* Plums.

Greenhouse. May be defined as a light-admitting, heat-conserving glass or plastic structure, principally used for the growing of plants and crops ahead or out of season, and of exotic plants, too tender for growing out of doors. It may be used as a gardening entity in itself, or as an auxiliary to the outdoor garden for raising plants from seeds or cuttings in advance, and giving winter shelter to non-hardy stock.

Types. Greenhouses are of three basic types, according to the shape of the roof: lean-to, span and three-quarter span. The lean-to is usually built on a wall, and is useful where space is limited. It is less easily managed in ventilation than a free-standing house, and plants inevitably tend to be drawn to the glass. It is, however, well suited to the growth of such plants as wall trees, peaches, grapes and climbers. With good management and arrangement of shelves, with periodic turning of plants in boxes or pots, it answers well. The installation of an extractor fan for ventilation overcomes the drawback of ventilators which face only one way.

The three-quarter span is an elaboration of the lean-to, with a hipped roof, designed to overcome some of the drawbacks of the lean-to in permitting more even lighting and ventilation, but of more expensive construction.

The span roof greenhouse, admitting light on all sides, is most easily managed. It is available in a wide variety of designs and materials. The plain tent-span is most common, and most economical to construct; but a broken span or an uneven span is more efficient in admitting light, especially in winter months, and the point is worth considering if the house is primarily for winter use.

Structural Materials. The materials used in the construction of a greenhouse affect first costs and also efficiency, and advantages and disadvantages should be carefully weighed.

1. *Timber* is relatively cheap, and wood has a low coefficient of expansion in hot weather. It is easily worked, convenient for wiring and fitting up. The best woods are teak and oak, for durability, but relatively expensive. Western Red Cedar, a softer wood, is much used as it resists decay. It is, however, absorbent of moisture, swelling and shrinking with wetting and drying, and of oil, often taking it from putty used in glazing. This may lead to glass breakages. It splits easily, and care is needed in nailing or screwing fitments to it. It is lightish and its strength is more suited to the smaller compact greenhouses than to long spanned ones. On the whole it does better, lasts longer, if painted. Other woods, such as deal, are satisfactory if kept well-preserved with regular painting or preservative treatment.

2. *Steel* gives a strong house, the narrow section of its components permits maximum light penetration, but its high coefficient of expansion makes it desirable that a puttyless glazing system should be used; and its vulnerability to corrosion compels the use of hot-dipped galvanized steel for long life. A point to look into is the provision of means for wiring or providing supports for growing plants.

3. *Aluminium Alloys* provide great strength with light weight, very low maintenance costs, excellent light admission, and a lower coefficient of expansion than steel, and are ideal for greenhouses, small and large. The glazing system usually does away with putty, but provision for wiring and fixing plant supports should be checked.

4. *Concrete.* Pre-cast concrete structures are strong, durable and economically maintained, though special putty or means of fastening the glass is necessary; and the rather heavy structures tend to exclude light, casting much shadow.

5. *Plastic.* Plastic transparent film, stretched taut on light wooden framework, gives a remarkably cheap greenhouse structure, though it usually needs anchoring against strong winds. Polythene sheeting, of fairly heavy gauge should be used. It transmits the sun's rays readily, but also lets heat rays out just as readily, and so cools more rapidly than a glass house at night, unless a second inner lining is installed. Polythene also deteriorates gradually in sunlight, and has a short life of three years or less, tearing easily as it ages. P.V.C. sheeting is better, with a longer life and slower to lose heat at night, and may last five years or more with good care. Newer plastic materials are being developed which may perform better.

6. *Fibreglass.* Moulded fibreglass structures have been developed, which have the advantages of admitting light, virtually without shadow, even diffused, of being durable and relatively light in weight, and easily erected. They are, however, high in first cost, and internal fittings have to be independent of the structure.

7. *Glass.* Despite the drawbacks of its weight and brittleness, glass is still an efficient, low-cost material for greenhouses. It may be of 21- to 24-oz. grades,

clear or of semi-obscure horticultural quality, for garden purposes. The standard size used is 18 in. by 24 in., though there is a strong welcome tendency towards the use of larger panes which make for greater light admission without shadow. There is no advantage in using a plate glass.

Site. A position permitting maximum light is usually preferable, unshaded by trees, buildings, etc.; and secondly, with accessibility in relation to the garden it serves. Shelter from cold north and east winds is desirable, though much can be done to minimize wind effect by judiciously placed windbreaks or hedges. The lean-to should face south or south-west, unless it is to be devoted largely to ferns. The span house may be orientated to run north–south, with the door at the south end; but for winter use it is better to place it on an east–west line, and let it be of broken or uneven span construction.

Foundations. If the greenhouse is to be movable, a tenant's fixture, it should be made in sections, and rest on a movable foundation too, such as loose bricks. This serves for a cold greenhouse. For a heated greenhouse the foundation must be draught-proof, and should consist of a concrete footing to a double row of mortared bricks to which the basal parts of the frame is fixed.

Base. If plants are to grow in borders, glazing to the foundations is necessary. If staging is to be used, the greenhouse may have a basal wall of brick, asbestos or wood to a height of 30–33 in. It is possible and useful to have glazing to soil level on one side, and a wall and staging on the other. The need to change the soil at four-year intervals should be borne in mind.

Ventilation. The aim of ventilation is to provide a good circulation of air without draughts. This may be by means of roof ventilators or sashes which open at the ridge, to exhaust rising warm air; at least one per 10-ft run of greenhouse, but at least two to every greenhouse, even if small. These ventilators should alternate on opposite sides. Stage ventilators, in the side of the greenhouse, are useful in summer, to provide extra ventilation, from one side or both. Sub-stage ventilators, admitting cool air low down, are needed in the heated

greenhouse, controlled by slides, arranged so that cool air flows in over the heating system. In small greenhouses, one in the end opposite the door and one in the north side are usually sufficient. The basic principle of ventilation is to increase it as temperatures rise, but decrease in advance if temperature falls as night approaches; and some skill and attention to weather conditions is necessary to manage it aright, especially in autumn to spring. More automatic control can be achieved by the installation of an axial-flow extractor fan, usually placed near the top of the wall opposite the door, and controlled by a thermostat; especially useful in lean-to houses, which are difficult to ventilate properly when the wind is on the face of the house. Where electricity is not available an automatic self-powered control, based on a thermoforce device, sensitive to temperature changes, may be used. More elaborately, in large greenhouses the ventilators can be controlled by means of small electric motors operating push-arms, and responsive to thermostatic control. Louvred ventilators have the advantage of admitting air but excluding weather and reducing draughts, and are very useful at the ends of greenhouses.

Internal Lay-out. This will be dictated by the size, purpose and planting scheme to be followed. In the simple rectangular span-roofed greenhouse, a firm, centre path from the door to within 3 ft or so of the opposite end is most practical, flanked by beds, or staging at the sides and one end. In a wide house, the path can go round a centre bed or staging. The path itself should be easily kept clean, and concrete or stone flags, bricks, tiles or gravel between thin copings can be used. Staging should be waist-high, at 30–33 in., no wider than can be reached across with the arms, about 3 ft. It may be of 2-in. by $\frac{5}{8}$-in. wooden slats, nailed to cross-pieces with 2-in. spacing; treated with a good wood preservative, preferably of the metallic salt or organic solvent type; resting on $2\frac{1}{4}$-in. square upright legs and cross-framing; or more durably of the patent slotted metalwork now available. The staging is covered with asbestos or galvanized metal sheeting, to make gravel or soil beds for plants, fitted with a retaining edging board at the front. Space must be left at the back between greenhouse wall and stage covering for warm air to circulate in the heated greenhouse. The space under the staging can be used for storage or hung with opaque plastic curtaining to provide forcing quarters for crops such as rhubarb. Shelves will be needed to place seedlings and plants near the light to promote sturdiness. It is better to keep tools, chemicals, twine, etc., under cool, dry, even conditions than in the greenhouse itself. In the lean-to, staging may be arranged along the front of the house, and a tiered staging against the wall, if the house is to be used for pot plants and display.

Water Supply and Watering. A constant and clean water supply is essential. Except in areas where the atmosphere is polluted by industrial smoke and gases, the rain butt or tank inside or outside the greenhouse, storing water from the roof, is useful, provided it is fitted with a light-excluding lid to prevent contamination by algae, etc. Water drawn from ponds, rivers or springs should be checked for purity. There is no scientific reason to believe that mains or tap water is harmful to plants. Where this is a hard water, high in lime content, however, it is likely to be unsuitable for lime-intolerant plants such as ericas and rhododendrons, though the effect can be offset by the use of a little acid-reacting fertilizer from time to time. It is probably helpful to use water at or near the greenhouse temperature, but not essential when watering plants in large pots or borders. Very cold water could check growth of plants in small pots. When to water and how much to supply requires judgment that is often only gained by experience; so much depends upon the kind of plant, its stage of growth and factors such as temperature, humidity and the moisture retentiveness of the soil. Broadly, watering should increase in frequency and amount as daily temperatures rise and growth develops, from late winter to early autumn; and decrease as temperatures fall to little more than keeping the soil just moist in winter. More water is needed on hot sunny days than on cool

cloudy ones; none at all or very little at low temperatures and high humidity or fog. Pot plants usually need more frequent watering than those in soil borders or beds. The aim in watering is to maintain sufficient water in the water films on soil particles at a tension that plants can easily overcome without overwatering and saturating the soil. Overwatering can be guarded against by a sufficiently porous and free-draining soil. Under-watering can be avoided by learning to recognize the signs of need before an actual shortage develops (*see* Watering). Much guesswork can be eliminated by the use of a tensiometer (q.v.), though the instrument is not cheap. Watering may be done by applying from overhead by means of a watering-can or hose. As far as possible this should simulate the fall of rain, and a rose should be fitted. The aim must be to wet a soil in depth; a free-draining soil requires about half a gallon per sq. ft to wet it to a depth of 12 in.; the denser or heavier the soil, the more water is needed for the same effect, but at less frequent intervals. Much thought has been given in recent years to automatic ways of watering. One of the simplest is what is known as drip or trickle irrigation, whereby small-bore tubing or hose, with holes or nozzles at intervals in it, is laid on the soil, boxes or pots, and feed by gravity from a tank. The nozzles are usually arranged to drip water at the base of plants, at a definite rate. Fertilizers are also to be given through a trickle system. The system permits watering with greater precision and effect and saves much time and effort. An alternative system is to water plants from below by a system of sub-irrigation, but it requires rather elaborate equipment.

Humidity. The humidity of the air in a greenhouse has a bearing upon plant growth and health. Too dry an atmosphere may encourage pests such as red spider mites; too moist is apt to increase trouble from certain diseases such as mildews and grey-mould. Plants vary considerably, however, in their need for humidity; cucumbers for instance require more than tomatoes. Normally, plants create their own humidity by transpiration of moisture vapour, which is added to by evaporation of moisture from the soil. On hot sunny days it is helpful to fine-spray or syringe plants and their foliage to conserve moisture losses, and to damp-down floors and walls by wetting them; but humidity is more effectively influenced by ventilation control and shading. A hygrometer is a useful instrument to have for guidance.

Heating. With heat a greenhouse can be used more fully. Despite rising prices, the most economical permanent heating is provided by 4-in. diameter water pipes, and a solid fuel boiler built into the base wall at one end, to be fed from outside, fired by small coke or anthracite. To estimate the amount of piping required the cubic capacity of the house (length by width by average height in feet) is divided by 30 for a cool house, by 25 for a warm house and 20 for a hot house. The flow and return pipes may be placed along one side, one side and end, or along one side, one end and the opposite side; with a rise of 1 in. in 9 ft from the boiler end. Solid fuel means that the boiler will need regular feeding, ash removal and periodic cleaning of flues. Alternatively, the boiler can be oil-fired, gas-fired, or the water electrically heated by immersion heater, at greater cost but less need for laborious attention, for the heating can be linked to a thermostatic control.

For the small greenhouse, where it is chiefly desired to keep temperatures just above freezing in winter, and to give a little extra heat in spring, portable heaters, electric or paraffin oil, may be used. The paraffin-oil heater, constructed specially for greenhouse use, is relatively cheap to buy, and if suitable in size, effectively maintains temperatures of 5·5–8° C. (10–15° F.), higher than outside temperatures. To avoid fumes, the right type of oil must be used, wicks kept well trimmed, and the heater clean and free of spilt oil which may vaporize into fumes injurious to plants. It is useful to have a pan of water with these heaters to help humidity.

Electrical heating is relatively cheap to install, clean and simple to use. The apparatus must be designed for greenhouse use, and a choice lies between: (1) Tubular heaters, thermostatically controlled, to be placed at the sides of the house. (2) Mineral-insulated cables, strung on insulator saddles, round the walls of the greenhouse, also thermostatically controlled, and having the advantage of taking up little space. (3) Convector heaters, which promote a circulation of warm air through the greenhouse, and may be easily moved about; the electrical equivalent of an oil heater. (4) Fan heaters, which blow air over heating elements, but need to be carefully positioned in relation to plants to avoid pockets of overheating and dryness. (5) Thermal storage heating, as yet not fully developed for greenhouse use, but uses off-peak current usually available at cheap rates. Fuller details of these heaters will be found in *Electricity in Your Garden*, published free by the Electrical Development Association, and usually available from the local office of the Electricity Board.

For serious propagative work it is invaluable to have a soil bed or bench bed fitted with electrical soil-heating, or a simple propagating frame or unit (*see* Propagation).

Heat Conservation. Heat loss through greenhouse walls and glass can be reduced by insulation or lining the glass with sheet polythene on the inside as a form of double glazing. The polythene film may be attached to wooden glazing bars by drawing-pins or tacks with small whale-hide or fibre squares; to metal glazing bars by clips. The sheet polythene should stop short of the ridge by at least 12 in. to avoid troublesome condensation. It is usually placed in position in autumn. Solid walls can be insulated by polystyrene sheeting.

Shading. Too high a temperature can be injurious to plants, and some form of shading is needed in summer. This is best movable and can now be cheaply provided by the use of tinted plastic sheeting, which can be rolled up and down as required; and by its lightness and cheapness supersedes the lath or tiffany blind, and by its efficiency the need to apply semi-permanent shading to the glass which is not always required in our climate, and is often difficult to remove for winter.

Thermometers. A thermometer is an essential piece of greenhouse equipment; the most useful being the maximum and minimum type, registering the highest and lowest temperatures daily, being reset with a magnet. Rotary types are the latest development, and for greenhouse work are made to be very robust and efficient. It is important to place the thermometer correctly, neither over heating apparatus nor in draughts, but in a median position to the plants being grown (*see* Thermometer).

The Cold Greenhouse. Although temperatures in the unheated greenhouse tend to remain a few degrees above those outside, only hardy plants can be grown in it during the winter and early spring; chiefly alpines that appreciate shelter from damp (*see* Alpine House); hardy shrubs such as *Erica carnea* and vs., *Fatsia japonica, Viburnum fragrans, Jasminum nudiflorum,* and for spring *Cytisus beanii, C. × kewensis, Daphne cneorum, Forsythia* sp., and hardy 'Azalea'; and a range of bulbs— Crocus, Galanthus, Eranthis, Narcissus, Iris, Scilla, Tulipa, etc., to bloom earlier than out of doors. In March–April it may be used for the raising of annuals, biennials and plants from seed, both for outdoors and pot growth; and for the propagation of such plants as Chrysanthemum, Dahlia, Pelargonium and other half-hardy perennials. In summer a wide range of flowering plants may be grown, especially Begonia, Crinum, Gladioli, Agapanthus, Iris and Freesia, or it may be devoted to tomato or cucumber cropping. In autumn it may be used to house late-flowering Chrysanthemums, and somewhat tender Primulas to bloom in the winter.

The Cool Greenhouse. With winter temperatures of 7–15·5° C. (45–60° F.), and summer of 13–18°C. (55–65° F.), a much wider range of plants may be grown, and a few of the more outstanding to be added to those given for the cold greenhouse are: for winter— fibrous-rooted Begonias, Bouvardia, Carnations, Cineraria, *Cyclamen persicum*, Epacris, tender Ericas, *Sparmannia africana* and tender annuals such as Schizanthus; for spring—*Acacia dealbata, Camellia* spp., *Cytisus canariensis, Deutzia gracilis,* Hippeastrum, Lachenalia, Lilium, Regal Pelargoniums and Primula. The cool greenhouse is invaluable for the early raising of annual

plants, half-hardy and hardy from seeds, and for the advance cropping with lettuce, tomato, etc. For summer flowering it may shelter half-hardy plants such as Agapanthus, Canna, *Cobaea scandens,* Fuchsia, Nerium, Gardenia and Verbenas; and for autumn, Abutilon, Bignonia, Gerbera, *Lapageria rosea,* Nerines, Streptocarpus, Vallota, Zinnia, etc. Several orchids can also be grown under cool conditions.

The Warm Greenhouse. Here, with winter temperatures of 13–21° C. (55–70° F.), many exotic plants may be grown, including a wide range of orchids, exotic ferns, foliage plants and tropical flowers. Most cool greenhouse plants do equally well, with somewhat softer growth, but the extra heat available is particularly useful in growing such things as exotic 'house' plants such as *Begonia rex,* etc., Monstera, Dieffenbachia; tender Acacia, Arums, Epiphyllums, Eupatorium, Boronia, Calceolaria, Achimnes, Bouvardia, Callistemon, Crassula, Streptosolen, Polianthes, Solanums, Bougainvillea, Cestrum and many others, as indicated throughout this book.

Grevillea (grev-ill′e-a. Fam. Proteaceae). A large genus of evergreen shrubs and trees, native to Australia and New Zealand, mostly too tender except for greenhouse or indoor cultivation.

Selection. G. robusta, the Silk Bark Oak, New S. Wales, is much grown for its ferny foliage, as an elegant pot plant, capable of 6–15 ft, as such, in cool greenhouse or room; *alpina,* Australia, 2 ft, a bushy shrub with small linear leaves; *glabrata,* W. Australia, shrub to 4 ft, coarsely lobed leaves, large panicles of white flowers with pink stigmas, summer; *rosmarinifolia,* Australia, 6 ft, shrubby with linear leaves, clusters of reddish flowers, is near-hardy; as is *semperflorens,* a hybrid, 6 ft, orange-yellow to pink flowers; and *sulphurea,* New S. Wales, to 6 ft, pale yellow summer flowers; while *thelemanniana,* W. Australia, makes a good pot plant of 3 ft, with pinnate leaves, and pink and green racemes of flowers in summer.

Cultivation. Pot, and repot, in April, standard compost, and grown under cool greenhouse conditions. Near-hardy species may be tried out of doors in warm sheltered positions in very mild localities; light, porous, but humus-rich soil.

Grey Mould. Common name of a fungus infection, caused by *Botrytis cinerea*, almost ubiquitous in gardens and greenhouses, under moist conditions, in summer and autumn; saprophytic on dead tissue, but soon attacks the live. Good spacing with free air circulation is helpful; copper or captan fungicides can be used to give control.

Gromwell See *Lithospermum.*

Ground Elder, Goutweed, Bishop's Weed (*Aegopodium podagraria*). A pernicious perennial weed, difficult to eradicate, though the repeated use of a paraquat herbicide greatly inhibits it.

Ground Ivy. See *Nepeta.*

Ground Nut. See *Apios.*

Growth-promoting Substances, Growth-regulating Substances. The scientific description of the so-called plant hormones, or auxins. They consist of synthetic complex organic chemicals which regulate the rate at which the various parts of a plant will grow. Several have been developed for horticultural use and are available in powder, liquid or tablet form, but must be used at correct dilutions and at the right time to achieve proper results. They include: (1) *Root-inducing hormones* (Ex. α-naphthalene-acetic acid; indolyl-acetic acid); used to hasten the development of roots by cuttings, layers, etc. (2) *Fruit-setting hormones* (Ex. dichlorophenoxy-acetic acid; β-naphthoxy-acetic acid), which promote the development of the flesh and tissues of certain fruits without seed formation; especially in tomatoes, cucumbers, melons, and in apples and strawberries. (3) *Pre-harvest-fruit-drop-preventing hormones* (Ex. α-naphthalene-acetic acid), which are sprayed on the stalks of fruit nearing maturity to retard the formation of the abscission layer between stalk and tree and so prevent premature falling to which early ripening apples such as 'Beauty of Bath' are prone. (4) *Bud-retarding hormones* (Ex. α-naphthalene-acetic acid), which retard the opening of vegetative buds, and are chiefly used to stop the sprouting of potatoes, carrots and root vegetables in

store. (5) Selective weed-killing hormones (Ex. phenoxyacetic acids, MCPA, 2,4-D 2,4,5-T; 2-(phenoxy)propionic acids, Mecoprop, Dichloroprop, Fenoprop), which can injure certain types of plants while leaving others unimpaired (*see* Herbicides). Synthetic hormones may also be used to thin blossoms on fruit trees to lessen the tendency to biennial bearing; to retard bud development in spring to escape frost damage; to make sterile plants, notably hybrids, set seeds.

Guano. See Fertilizers.

Guelder Rose. See *Viburnum opulus.*

Guernsey Lily. See *Nerine sarniensis.*

Gum, Blue. See *Eucalyptus.*

Gumming, Gummosis. A condition frequently seen in stone fruit trees, Cherries, Peaches and Plums, when an injury to the bark by tool, insect, bacterial or fungus attack is followed by the exudation of a clear, resin-looking sticky fluid. Such trees should be pruned when in leaf, and as the trouble is worst on wet soils, drainage should have attention, and the soil be reinforced with humus, lime and balanced feeding. *See* the fruits concerned.

Gunnera (gun′ne-ra. Fam. Gunneraceae). Herbaceous perennials from the southern hemisphere, varying from quite small to exceptionally large-leafed, majestic plants, with surprising hardiness.

Selection. G. chilensis, Chile, throws up leaves 4–5 ft, across, lobed and deeply toothed, on prickly stalks of 3–6 ft, and a large panicle of reddish flowers, when established, in summer; *manicata*, Brazil, is similar but with even greater majesty, with leaves to 6 ft across and stalks up to 8 ft; both are excellent waterside plants, in rich, peaty loam. *G. magellanica*, Magellan Straits, on the other hand, is a dwarf, 3 in. high, with small, kidney-shaped crenate leaves, and spikes of reddish flowers, summer, and useful as a carpeter in dampish places.

Cultivation. Plant October–November or March–April, in deep soil unlikely to dry out, as by lakes or streams, covering crowns with litter for winter.

Propagation. By division in spring; by seeds, in standard compost, or outdoors, April.

Guttatus (-a, -um). Covered with small spots or dots.

Gymnocalycium, Chin Cactus (gim-no-ka-li'ki-um. Fam. Cactaceae). Globular, ribbed cacti, characterized by a protuberance or chin below the aerole, with relatively large, many-petalled flowers; summer.

Selection. *G. gibbosum*, Argentina, to 9 in., pink flowers; *platense*, Argentina, small, whitish pink flowers; and *mihanovichii*, round, greyish-green with red bands, yellowish-white flowers, are good.

Cultivation. Pot, and repot March–April, standard cactus compost; water freely in summer, very little in winter, temp. 7° C. (45° F.) minimum.

Gymnocladus, Kentucky Coffee-tree (gim-no-kla'dus. Fam. Leguminosae). The chief hardy species grown is *C. dioica*, E. U.S.A., which grows slowly, making a handsome deciduous tree, with pinnate leaves up to 3 ft long and 2 ft wide, with greenish-white flowers, male and female panicles borne separately in June, but rarely fruiting to yield the podded seeds, at one time used for coffee in America. It may be planted in well-drained, good loam, in the warmer counties in October–March, growing to 30 ft or more eventually.

Gymnogramma (gim-no-gram'ma. Fam. Polypodiaceae). Species now grown include *G. flexuosa*, S. America, with fronds of 3 to 4 ft, and *matthewsii*, Peru, with leathery tri-pinnatifid fronds of 12–15 in., which may be grown in the cool greenhouse in pots or baskets, with compost of 2 parts fibrous peat, 1 part chopped sphagnum moss, and 1 part coarse sand; watering freely in spring and summer moderately in winter, minimum temp. 10° C. (50° F.). Propagation is by spores on above compost, with bottom heat of 15·5° C. (60° F.).

Gymnopteris (gim-nop'ter-is. Fam. Polypodiaceae). Ferns related to Gymnogramma, at one time included in that genus; attractive for the silvery or reddish hairs, covering their fronds.

Selection. *G. hispida*, New Mexico, pinnate fronds, finely cut; *muelleri*, Australia, reddish-brown, fronds to 10 in.; *tomentosa*, S. America, fronds of 1 ft, on tufted rusty-brown stipes; and *vestita*, China, with handsome 6–12 in. fronds, silvery, turning brown, velvety hairs, are usually listed.

Cultivation. Pot, or repot in March–April; compost of 2 parts peat, 1 part sphagnum moss, 1 part coarse sand; to grow in cool or warm greenhouse; watering freely in summer, moderately in winter, minimum temp. 10° C. (50° F.) and propagate by spores.

Gymnospermae. One of the Divisions of flowering or seed-bearing plants, characterized by bearing their seeds exposed or naked, often in cones (conifers), and having unisexual flowers. *See* Angiosperms.

Gynaeceum, Gynoecium. The female organs of a flower, pistil.

Gypsophila (gip-sop'i-la. Fam. Caryophyllaceae). Dainty-flowering annual and perennial plants, related to Dianthus, often called Chalk Plants from their tolerance of lime, and hardy in most districts.

Selection. *G. elegans*, Asia Minor, 1–1½ ft, with pretty branching panicles of white, rose and crimson flowers in summer, and *muralis*, Europe, Asia Minor, 6 in., pink-flowering in summer, are annuals, easily raised from seeds in spring. *G. paniculata*, E. Europe, Siberia, to 3 ft, has very large loose panicles of small white flowers, summer, even finer in its double form 'Bristol Fairy' or 'Snow White'; 'Rosenchleirer', 18 in., double, rosy-pink, and 'Pink Star', 12 in., double, pink, are more compact forms, for the border. *G. aretioides*, Persia, 3 in., a greyish-green cushion of rosetted leaves, with pearl white flowers, July; *cerastioides*, Himalaya, 2 in., white flowers, summer; × *monstrosa*, to 1 ft, white; and *repens*, European Alps, 6 in., white, reddish veined flowers, all summer; with its v. *fratensis*, pinkish, are charming for the rock garden or alpine house.

Cultivation. Plant October–March, well-drained, deepish soil on the light side, full sun.

Propagation. Species by seeds, sown in cool greenhouse or frame, March–April. By cuttings of young shoots, in July–August, in cold frame.

Gypsum (calcium sulphate). The natural hydrated calcium sulphate may be used in various ways in the garden. Sprinkled over a manure heap it helps to conserve its nitrogenous value, by fixing ammonia; it is a useful component of compound fertilizers for roses; it is used as a base-exchange material to displace salt (sodium chloride) in soils which have been flooded by the sea; it may be used as a soil conditioner for sticky sodium clays, its calcium displacing the sodium and rendering the soil more crumbly and more easily worked, being used at $\frac{1}{2}$–1 lb per sq. yd for this purpose.

H

Haberlea (ha-ber'le-a. Fam. Gesneriaceae). Small evergreen perennials with tufted rosettes of leaves, and umbellate heads of tubular, flared petalled flowers on short stems, related to Ramonda, and very eligible for partial shade in rock gardens.

Selection. H. ferdinandi-coburgi, Balkans, soft hairy leaves, pale lilac flowers, with white, yellow-spotted throat, June; and *rhodopensis,* Bulgaria, drooping umbel of deeper lilac flowers, May–June; with *virginalis,* pure white flowering variety.

Cultivation. Plant March–April, well-drained, moist soil, rich in leaf-mould, partial shade, in rock garden, or alpine house.

Propagation. By division in April. May need winter protection in cold localities.

Habitat. The natural surroundings or locality in which a plant grows.

Habranthus (hab-ran'thus. Fam. Amaryllidaceae). Bulbous plants from S. America, related to Hippeastrum and Zephyranthes, producing linear leaves in spring and trumpet-like flowers in early summer, usually singly, on stems of 8–12 in., with a spathe sheathing the base of the flower pedicel. Although easily grown, they are not hardy and need a cool greenhouse or may be grown indoors.

Selection. H. andersoni, golden-yellow flower, leaves appear with the bloom; *brachyandrus,* Brazil, 12 in., pale pink, deepening to dark red at base; *robustus,* Argentine, 10 in., rose pink, greenish white centre; and *versicolor,* Brazil, 6 in., rose and white, flowering in winter.

Cultivation. Pot in October–November, standard compost, growing cool, temp. 7–10° C. (45–50° F.), very moderate watering, until growth shows in late winter–spring, when plants require more light, warmth and watering, to flowering;

rest with little or no water when leaves die down.

Propagation. By offset bulbs when repotting, though this is needed only infrequently.

Hacquetia (hak-kwet'i-a. Fam. Umbelliferae). The only species, *H.* (*Dondia*) *epipactis,* is a compact, tufted, herbaceous perennial of European alps, with trifoliolate leaves, and simple umbels of yellow flowers, to 6 in. high, in early spring; for good loam soil and sun in rock gardens, planted in March. Propagation is by seeds, sown in April–May; or by division of plants in March–April.

Haemanthus, Blood Flower (heman'thus. Fam. Amaryllidaceae). Bulbous plants of Central and S. Africa, producing a pair of broad, fleshy leaves, and a stout floral stem bearing a dense umbel of small tubular flowers with protruding stamens, best grown in the cool greenhouse, or for flowering indoors, as curiously peculiar plants.

Selection. H. albiflos, 1 ft, white flowers, autumn; *coccineus,* 8 in., coral red, autumn, huge 2-ft leaves; *katherinae,* to 20 in., scarlet, August; and hybrid forms.

Cultivation. Pot in early spring, standard compost, water regularly with growth, good light and moderate warmth; resting after flowering, with virtually no water. Do not repot until necessary, when offset bulbs may be taken for propagation.

Ha-ha. A fence or wall sunken in a dry ditch or wide depression, to allow an unrestricted view across parkland and yet prevent livestock entering a garden landscape.

Hail. Raindrops which are frozen through being carried by the updraughts of thunderstorms through freezing layers of air before falling to earth; can do much damage in gardens to tender growth and glass, occurring chiefly in spring and early summer.

Hair Worms, Horsehair Worms (*Gordius* sp., *Mermis* sp.). Long, thread- or hair-like Round Worms (Nemathe-helminthes), parasitic on insects, but sometimes seen after rain writhing and knotting on plants.

Hakea (ha'ke-a. Fam. Proteaceae). Evergreen flowering shrubs of Australia and Tasmania, of which *H. acicularis*, to 12 ft, white or pinkish flowers, July; *microcarpa*, to 6 ft, fragrant yellowish-white clusters of flowers, May; and *saligna*, to 10 ft, highly scented white flowers, early summer, may be grown out of doors in warm, sunny shelter in the mildest localities only; otherwise in tubs or pots to winter in a cool greenhouse. Plant in March–April, well-drained peaty loam; propagate by cuttings of firm shoots, July–August, in cold frame.

Halesia (ha-les'i-a. Fam. Styracaceae). Rather beautiful small deciduous trees, of which *H. carolina*, the Snowdrop or Silver-bell Tree, SE. U.S.A., may grow to 25 ft, producing pure white, dangling, bell-shaped flowers in May, but needs a rather warm, sunny sheltered position, in well-drained, sandy and humus-rich soil, in the warmer counties; *diptera*,

to 10 ft, is less free-flowering, but *monticola*, to 40 ft, with larger flowers, makes a fine tree for mild localities. Propagation by layers, autumn, or by seeds, sown in sandy loam, April, under handlights.

Half-hardy. Descriptive of plants, annual, biennial or perennial, which require winter protection.

Halimiocistus (ha-lim-i-o-kis'tus. Fam. Cistaceae). Hybrids of *Halimium* × *Cistus*, being dwarf shrubs, bearing single cistus-like flowers in late spring, of which × *ingwersenii*, to 3 ft, slender-stalked white flowers in panicles; × *sahucii*, 1½ ft, white flowers in clusters; and × *wintonensis*, 1½–2 ft, white flowers with crimson base and yellow centre, make spreading shrubs in light humus-rich soil and warm sheltered positions in mild localities, but are tender in the north. Propagation by cuttings of firm shoots, July–August, in a cold frame.

Halimium (ha-lim'i-um. Fam. Cistaceae). Evergreen shrubs, related to Helianthemum, native to the Mediterranean region, hardy except in cold areas.

Selection. *H. alyssoides*, SW. Europe, 2 ft, bright yellow flowers, May–June; *lasianthum formosum*, Portugal, to 3 ft, yellow flowers with crimson at the base, June; and *umbellatum*, to 1½ ft, clusters of white flowers, June, are the pick.

Cultivation. Plant October, or March–April, warm, sunny positions, light, well-drained soil with humus.

Propagation by cuttings of young firm shoots, July–August, in cold frame.

Halophyte. A plant which grows naturally where the soil water is salty, by sea coasts, on salt steppes.

Hamamelis, Witch Hazel (ha-ma-me'lis. Fam. Hamamelidaceae). Tall deciduous shrubs or small trees, delightful for their unique ribbon-petalled flowers and surprising hardiness.

Selection. *H. mollis*, China, to 10 ft, deep golden scented flowers, January–February, autumn leaf colour, is the gem, with v. *brevipetala* having shorter petalled flowers, and *pallida*, paler yellow; *japonica*, China, Japan, to 8 ft, dainty, yellow flowers, February–March; and vs. *arborea*, to 20 ft, 'Carmine Red', reddish flowers, and

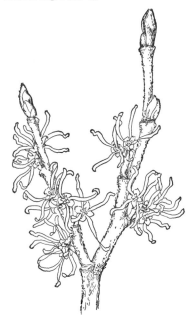

FIG. 124 *Hamamelis mollis,* Witch Hazel, winter flowers.

zuccariniana, to 20 ft, erect growing, lemon-yellow flowers; and hybrids ×
flavo-purpurescens, purple-red flowers; × 'Jelena' ('Copper Beauty'), coppery yellow flowers; while *virginiana,* Eastern N. America, to 15 ft, bears bright yellow, scented flowers in autumn, before the leaves fall.

Cultivation. Plant September–October, in well-drained soil, enriched with peat or leaf-mould, sunny position, with dark background of evergreens. Prune to shape when young, after flowering.

Propagation. By layering in autumn. By grafting selected forms. By seeds, sown in pots, but may take two years to germinate, sinking pots outdoors in sandy loam, under handlight.

Hamburg Parsley (*Carum petroselinum fusiformis*). A variety of parsley, owing its name to its popularity in Germany, grown for its parsnip-like, celery-flavoured roots. Seeds are sown in well-prepared friable soil, at about 6 in.

apart, in March–April, in rows 9 in. apart; and kept supplied with water in dry weather. Lift as required from September onwards; for grating raw in salads, or as a cooked vegetable, while the leaves may be used as a flavouring herb.

Handglass or Handlight. A small glass case, often made with a light movable top for access, useful for protecting half-hardy plants or as a close cover for cuttings being rooted. Plastic transparent covers are also now available.

Haploid. A plant (or organism) with one set of unpaired chromosomes in the nucleus of each cell.

Hardening-off. The operation of gradually adjusting plants to conditions of lower temperatures and drier atmosphere than under which they have been raised; chiefly used in connection with successively transferring seedlings raised in heat to frames, and subjecting them to increasing exposure to the air and outdoor temperatures, to harden growth, prior to planting out.

Hardy. Descriptive of plants capable of growing and living out of doors without protection.

Hardy Perennials. In gardening, usually descriptive of hardy herbaceous perennials or border plants, excluding bulbs, corms, shrubs and trees, though technically they are often hardy perennials too.

Harebell, Hairbell, also Bluebell of Scotland, *Campanula rotundifolia.*

Hare's-foot Fern. See *Davallia canariensis.*

Haricot. The ripe seeds of kidney beans. *See* Beans, French.

Hart's-tongue Fern. See *Phyllitis scolopendrium.*

Hastate. Of leaves formed like a halberd or spear.

Haulm. The stems of crops such as beans, peas and potatoes.

Haustorium. The sucker-like structure of a parasitic plant by which it attaches itself to the plant host to feed; fungi such as Mildews and Rusts, and plants such as Dodder and Mistletoe form haustoria.

Hautbois, Hautboy. A small Strawberry.

Haw. The fruit of the hawthorn, *Crataegus* sp.

Hawkbit. Common weeds of *Leontodon* spp.

Hawkweed. See *Hieracium*.

Haworthia (ha-worth'i-a. Fam. Liliaceae). Small succulent plants of S. Africa, with leaves in rosettes or spirals, chiefly grown for their foliage beauty as house or cool greenhouse plants.

Selection. H. chalwinii, 6 in., spiralling leaves, white tubercles; *coarctata*, 8 in., rosetted, triangular leaves, white tubercles; *cymbiformis*, stemless rosettes of fleshy leaves, windowed at the top; *fasciata*, rosetted, shiny dark green, white tubercled leaves; *papillosa*, rosetted, grey-green, white warted leaves; *sessiflora*, thick, pointed, smooth pale green leaves; and *tessellata*, fleshy, triangular, leaves in rosettes.

Cultivation. Pot and repot March–April, standard cactus compost or JIP No. 1, partial shade, watering freely in warm weather, occasionally in winter, minimum temp. 10° C. (50° F.).

Propagation. By offsets in spring.

Hawthorn. See *Crataegus oxyacantha*.

Hazel. See *Corylus avellana*.

Hazel, Witch. See *Hamamelis*.

Heading-back. The removal of the top growth of the branches of a shrub or tree, to stimulate new growth lower down, or in preparation for grafting.

Heartsease. See *Viola*.

Heath. See *Erica*.

Heather. See *Calluna*.

Heating. *See* Greenhouse.

Hebe. See *Veronica*.

Hedera, Ivy (hed'e-ra. Fam. Araliaceae). Evergreen climbers by means of aerial roots, chiefly grown for their foliage, but producing umbels of small, yellowish-green flowers in summer, followed by berry-like, usually black, fruits, when the plants reach the tops of their supports.

Selection. H. helix, the common Ivy of Europe and Britain, has attractive vs. 'Buttercup', golden and green leaves; *caenwoodiana*, small, finger-like lobed leaves; *cavendishii*, small, silver-veined leaves, slow-growing; *digitata*, deeply lobed leaves; 'Emerald Green', shining vivid green; *marginata major*, creamy white variegated leaves; *marginata rubra* (*tricolor*), white, green and reddish leaves; *purpurea*, bronzy

purple, especially in autumn; and *minima*, smallest leaved of all. Many decorative variegated forms have been developed as house plants, notably 'Chicago', 'Glacier', 'Golden Leaf', 'Jubilee', *lutzii*, 'Pittsburg', *sagittaefolia* and its form 'Shamrock'. *H. colchica*, Caucasus, has leaves up to 8 in. long, very striking in v. *variegata*; *canariensis*, Canary Islands, and vs. *azorica* and *variegata*, are doubtfully hardy except in frost-free gardens; *chrysocarpa*, SE. Europe, distinctive for its yellow berries; *hibernica*, Irish Ivy, with dark green triangular-lobed leaves, makes good ground cover under trees, and *nepalensis*, Himalaya, greyish-green, slender-pointed leaves, and yellow fruits, is unusual.

Cultivation. Plant in October or March–April, almost any soil, shade or sun, any aspect, though variegated forms do best in good light; to clothe walls, rocks, etc., or as ground cover for banks or waste areas. Trim in April. As house plants, succeed potted in March–April, standard compost, with minimum winter temp. 5° C. (40° F.).

Propagation. By cuttings of young firm shoots, spring or summer.

Hederaceus (-a, -um). Hederaceous, ivy-like. Ex. *Ipomoea hederacea*.

Hedgehog Cactus. See *Echinocactus*.

Hedgehog Holly. See *Ilex aquifolium* v. *ferox*.

Hedges. Permanent hedges are formed from shrubs and trees which grow well in close company and stand up to restriction. The choice depends upon purpose, whether the hedge is to be a boundary hedge, for privacy; to keep out animals; to serve as a background to other plants; to give shelter from winds and weather; to divide garden features; or create more favourable micro-climates within the garden; and suitability for the soil latitude and environmental location. First cost should be balanced against maintenance costs in time and effort needed in trimming. Rate of growth depends on the kind of plant chosen, but also on the soil and its preparation. *Evergreen Hedges.* These give perfect privacy and shelter, and submit well to formal shaping. The fastest-growing is the hybrid *Cupressocyparis × leylandii*, making 2–3 ft annually; submitting well to clipping at any height; other conifers for hedging are *Chamaecyparis lawsoni-ana* 'Green Hedger', and vs. *alumii, erecta viridis* and *lanei*, to 6 or more ft; and *Thuja plicata* v. *atrovirens*, planted young. *Cupressus macrocarpa* performs unreliably and is best avoided. The Privet, *Ligustrum ovalifolium*, is the cheapest evergreen for hedging; with *Lonicera nitida* or v. *fertilis* pressing it close, both need to be kept trimmed often. Holly (*Ilex aquifolium*), Box (*Buxus sempervirens*), Yew (*Taxus baccata*) and, for warm localities, evergreen oak (*Quercus ilex*), make the finest, long-lived hedges, with lowest mainte-nance costs; though only holly should be planted where grazing animals have access; the others being poisonous if eaten. The flowering evergreens *Osmarea* × *burkwoodii* and *Viburnum tinus*, make good hedging. *Deciduous Hedges.* The quickest growing and cheapest are Hawthorn (*Crataegus oxy-acantha*) or quick (*C. monogyna*), planted in staggered rows; and kept well trimmed; flowering plums, *Prunus cerasifera* vs. such as 'Blaze', and 'Greenglow', and the Myrobalan, *P. blireiana*, and the Sloe, *P. spinosa* and v. *rosea*, make colourful hedges. Beech, *Fagus sylvatica* and v. *purpurea*, and Hornbeam, *Carpinus betulus*, make sound hedges or tall screens, retaining their brown foliage through the winter. *Flowering Hedges.* Good evergreen kinds are *Berberis darwinii, B.* × *stenophylla*, Firethorns, *Pyracantha* sp., and *Cotone-aster lactea, C. simonsii* and *C. wardii*. Deciduous types are *Forsythia* × *intermedia* vs., *Ribes sanguineum*, and *Berberis thunbergii* and vs. *Escallonia* hybrids do well up to 4 ft, and *Hippo-phae rhamnoides* should be first choice as a windbreak in seaside gardens. Lavenders, *Fuchsia* sp., *Senecio greyii, Choisya ternata* and tall floribunda roses, such as 'Queen Elizabeth', are good for interior hedges; while low edging plants are *Erica carnea* vs., *E.* × *darleyensis, E. mediterraneana* and v. 'W. T. Ratcliff', and the dwarf box, *Buxus sempervirens nana*. These hedges may be grown informally, pruning once annually after flowering; or more formally by pruning again in summer.

Cultivation. Prior to planting, the soil should be bastard-trenched and enriched with humus-forming organic material and bone meal. Deciduous hedges can be planted in October–March; evergreen in September–November or March–early May. Most hedges can be planted in single rows of plants, but for very strong hedges of plants such as hawthorn, quick and lonicera plants should be in two rows, 12 in. apart, and staggered . · . · . · . · . about 18 in. apart. Care should be taken to see that the roots do not dry out in spring; conifers and evergreens often need some shelter in the form of a temporary windbreak from strong cold winds. *Trimming.* Young hedges need more frequent trimming than established ones, and when plants have recovered from trans-planting, side growths may be trimmed in August in the first growing season, and thereafter in June and August. The slower-growing evergreens and hedges of beech or hornbeam may then only need an annual trimming, prefer-ably in August. Central leading shoots may be left unpruned until of the height required. Formal hedges should be trimmed with straight sides or a taper to the top, and the top may be flat, rounded or shaped like a tented roof. Trimming may be done with sharp hand shears or a powered hedge trimmer, and it is easier if a simple profile of laths is used to place against the hedge to check evenness. *Manuring.* A generous top-dressing of an organic based fertilizer (e.g. JI base) and a mulch of organic matter every third year over the roots will keep growth vigorous. Hedge bottoms should be cleared each year of weeds and grasses.

Hedychium, Butterfly Lily (hed-ik'i-um. Fam. Zingiberaceae). Rhizo-matous, subtropical perennials, with striking large lance-shaped leaves, and attractive, sweetly scented, tubular and lobed flowers in spikes in summer, half-hardy in Britain.

Selection. H. gardnerianum, N. India, 4–6 ft, yellow flowers, summer, is the easiest to grow; others include *coccineum*, Burma, orange-red; *coronarium*, India, 3 ft, white; and *greenei*, Bhutan, to 6 ft, red.

Cultivation. Plant in cool or warm greenhouse borders, or in large pots, standard compost, watering liberally during growth; very moderately in winter, temp. 10–13° C. (50–55° F.) minimum.

Propagation. By seeds, under glass, with bottom heat of 21° C. (70° F.), spring. By division when repotting, March–April.

Hedysarum (hed-is-a'rum. Fam. Leguminosae). The species chiefly grown is *H. coronarium*, French Honeysuckle, Europe, a biennial of 3–4 ft, with deep red, fragrant, broom-like flowers in an erect spike, summer, with white v. *album*; from seeds sown in May, out of doors, transplanted to flowering site by August–September, well-drained soil, and sun.

Heeling-in. The practice of placing the roots of fruit and ornamental trees, shrubs and roses in a shallow trench, and covering with soil, pending a favourable time for planting.

Heeria. See *Schizocentron*.

Helenium (he-le'ni-um. Fam. Compositae). The chief species grown is *Helenium autumnale*, the Sneezeweed of Canada and N. America, 3–5 ft tall, an invaluable herbaceous perennial with branching stem bearing yellow rayed flowers, August–October, of which notable vs. are 'Butterpat', 3 ft, rich yellow; 'Coppelia', 3 ft, coppery orange; 'Moerheim Beauty', 3 ft, mahogany red; 'Riverton Gem', 3 ft, yellow and brown; and *striatum*, 5 ft, gold and crimson; *H. bigelovii*, California, 2 ft, yellow; *bolanderi*, 1–2 ft, bright yellow; and *hoopesii*, Rocky Mts, 1–3 ft, large orange flower-heads, are also worth growing.

Cultivation. Plant March–April, well-drained ordinary soil, and sunny position in borders.

Propagation. By seeds in spring outdoors; by division in March.

Helianthemum, Sun Rose (he-li-an'the-mum. Fam. Cistaceae). Dwarf ever-green shrubby plants, for sunny places, banks and rock gardens, and porous light soils, for early summer flowering.

Selection. H. nummularium, Europe, 1–1½ ft, the Sun Rose, single yellow flowers in terminal racemes, has many noteworthy vs. such as 'The Bride', white, 'Fireball', red, 'Wisley Primrose', and 'Ben' vs., in many flower colours;

alpestre, S. Europe, 4 in., bright yellow; *apenninum roseum*, Europe, 18 in., rose; and *lunulatum*, Italy, 8 in., yellow; while *tuberaria*, S. Europe, 4 in., is a pretty herbaceous perennial.

Cultivation. Plant out of pots, 2 ft apart, autumn or spring; excellent for covering dry sunny banks.

Propagation. By seeds sown in March–April, in cold frame or outdoor seedbed; by cuttings of young shoots in July–August, in cold frame or greenhouse.

Helianthus, Sunflower (he-li-an'thus. Fam. Compositae). Annual species of these N. American, large flower-headed plants include *H. annuus*, to 10 ft, in various forms such as 'Autumn Beauty', 3 ft, sulphur yellow; 'Golden Nigger', 4 ft.; *flore pleno*, 5 ft, double flowering, of which 'Dwarf Sungold', 2½ ft, orange, is outstanding; 'Russian Giant', to 12 ft; 'Red' 4 ft, chestnut; and 'Chrysanthe-mum-flowered' vs. in dwarf and tall kinds. 'Pole Star', 'Southern Cross', 'Mars' and 'Jupiter' are semi-dwarf vs., developed for their yield of seeds. Other annuals are *H. argophyllus*, Texas, 4 ft, *debilis*, S. U.S.A., 2–3 ft, and its vs. 'Dazzler', chestnut and orange, and 'Excelsior', yellow, red and purple flowers. The perennials make good herbaceous border plants if not allowed to spread too far, and include *H. decapetalus*, N. America, 4–6 ft, and its v. *multiflorus*, of which 'Loddon Gold', double golden-yellow, *maximus*, 5 ft, single, golden-yellow, are typical; *laetiflorus*, middle U.S.A., 5 ft, in v. 'Miss Mellish', deep yellow; *mollis*, middle U.S.A., 4 ft, yellow; and *salici-folius*, 6–10 ft, deep yellow; all flowering August–October. *H. tuberosus* is the Jerusalem Artichoke (q.v.).

Cultivation. Annuals are sown, ¼ in. deep, well-drained ordinary good soil, sunny position, where they are to flower in spring. Perennials are planted in October or April, good border soil and sun.

Propagation. By seeds, sown April. Perennials also by division in March–April.

Helichrysum (he-li-kri'sum. Fam. Compositae). A large genus which includes annuals, perennials and shrubs, popular for their 'Everlasting' flowers, which dry well when cut freshly open and hung heads down in an airy, cool, dry place.

Selection. *H. bracteum*, Australia, 2–4 ft, pink and yellow, and vs. *album*, white; and golden, red, rose and salmon strains, are grown as half-hardy annuals, sown under glass in March, pricked off and hardened off to plant out in May; *nanum flore pleno*, 2 ft, and *monstrosum*, 4 ft, are double flowering, July–August. *H. arenarium*, Europe, 1 ft, small yellow and orange 'immortelle' flower-heads, August; *angustifolium*, S. Europe, 1 ft, small yellow flowers, summer; *orientale*, SE. Europe, to 1½ ft, tiny golden flower-heads in clusters, August, and *stoechas*, S. Europe, Goldy-locks, to 2 ft, crowded heads of yellow flowers, summer, are reasonably hardy perennials for sunny borders and well-drained soil. *H. bellidioides*, New Zealand, 3 in., white, June; *coralloides*, New Zealand, 6 in., creamy white, June; *frigidum*, Corsica, 4 in., white, June; *selago*, New Zealand, 6–12 in., dullish white, June, may be grown in pans in the alpine house, standard compost, and propagated by cuttings taken with a small heel in May, inserted in propagating frame.

Heliocereus (he-li-o-ke're-us. Fam. Cactaceae). Slender-stemmed with triangled branches, and large funnel-shaped flowers, strongly scented, in summer. *H. speciosus*, Mexico, scarlet-flowering, is a parent with *Epiphyllum* of many fine hybrids; *amecaensis*, Mexico, is similar but white-flowering. Both appreciate warmth, 10–18° C. (50–65° F.), and partial shade, with normal cacti culture.

Heliofila (he-li-o-fil'a. Fam. Cruciferae). Pretty flowering annuals from S. Africa, of which *H. amplexicaulis*, 9 in., white to purplish blue; *coronopifolia*, to 2 ft, blue-violet; and *longifolia*, 1½ ft, blue and white, flowering in late summer, are sown in March–April, under glass or in the open, as half-hardy annuals.

Heliopsis (he-li-op'sis. Fam. Compositae). N. American hardy perennial 'Orange Sunflowers' of which *H. helianthoides*, 3–6 ft, and its v. *pitcheriana*, flower freely in summer; and *scabra*, 2–4 ft, rich deep yellow, has vs. 'B. Ladhams', semi-double, yellow; 'Gold Plume', double, yellow; *gratissima*, 4 ft, pale yellow; *incomparabilis*, 3 ft,

orange-yellow; and *vitellina*, 3 ft, double golden-yellow flowers, July–September.

Cultivation. Plant October–March, well-drained, light soil, full sun.

Propagation. By division in March.

Heliotrope. See *Heliotropium*.

Heliotropism. The blending or growing of plants and their parts in reaction to light; said to be positive when growth is towards the light as with stems; and negative when away from the light as with roots.

Heliotropium (he-li-o-trop'i-um. Fam. Boraginaceae). Of the more than 200 species of the genus only *H. peruvianum*, Common Heliotrope or Cherry Pie, Peru, naturally a shrub to or 6 ft, with highly fragrant violet flowers throughout summer in the cool greenhouse or for summer bedding, but with *H. corymbosum*, Peru, 4 ft, lilac flowers, has given rise to hybrids such as 'Regale' strains, in various rich blue, red, to white colours; and named forms such as 'Madame Bruant', violet with white eye; 'Marine', deep violet; 'Marguerite', dark blue; and 'White Lady'. These plants are grown as half-hardy annuals, being sown under glass, standard compost, with bottom heat (15·5° C. [60° F.]), March, to plant out in late May, or to grow in pots for greenhouse or home decoration.

Pot Culture. Cuttings yield the best plants, and these are taken in August, potted into 3- or 4-in. pots, standard compost, and grown on in a warm greenhouse (10° C. [50° F.]), or the cuttings may be taken in spring to give flowering plants for late summer and autumn. In the greenhouse plants are perennial, and may be trained to form bushes by judicious stopping of shoots; or as standards by growing to a single stem up to the desired height. Water freely in growth; feed when in bud every other week, but keep rather dry in winter.

Helipterum (he-lip'ter-um. Fam. Compositae). Native to warm countries, this genus, which now includes *Acrolinium* and *Rhodanthe*, provides a number of half-hardy annuals grown for their 'everlasting' flowers, such as *H. humboldtianum* (*sandfordii*), to 1 ft, yellow flowers in summer; *manglesii* (*Rhodanthe manglesii*), 1–2 ft, purple, rose and pink; *roseum* (*Acrolinium roseum*), 1–2 ft, pink, and vs. *album*, and semi-double and double forms; all natives of Australia.

Cultivation. Sow seeds, March, under glass, standard compost, bottom heat of 18° C. (65° F.), to pot on and flower in the cool greenhouse, or may be hardened off to plant out in late May, light soil and warm sunny position.

Hellebore. See *Helleborus*, and *Veratrum*.

Helleborine. See *Epipactis*.

Helleborus (hel-leb'o-rus **or** hel-e-bor'-us. Fam. Ranunculaceae). Herbaceous perennials with long-stalked, large finely lobed leaves, and flowers with large coloured sepals and stamens.

Selection. H. niger, the Christmas Rose, central and S. Europe, evergreen pedate leaves, and white or rose-tinted flowers, December–February, is beautiful, with vs. *altifolius*, growing taller; and 'Potter's Wheel', very fine saucer-shaped flowers; *orientalis*, Greece, Asia Minor, the Lenten Rose, large, cream to brownish yellow flowers, February–April, needs a sheltered position; and is available in selected flower colours; and hybrids have white through pink to purple flowers; *atrorubens*, SE. Europe,

FIG. 125 *Helleborus niger* v. Christmas Rose.

dull purplish-green, spring; *argutifolius* (*corsicus*), Corsica, yellowish-green, April; the native *foetidus*, 2 ft, with branching heads of pale green nodding flowers, for March to May, in woodland or waste ground; and *viridis*, Ireland, Britain to Siberia, bright green flowers, February, are hardy for most gardens.

Cultivation. Plant September–October or April; well-drained, humus-rich soil, to be undisturbed; tolerate light shade, but not unmitigated damp. Good crowns may be lifted, potted and gently forced in the cool greenhouse at 10° C. (50° F.) in November.

Propagation. By division in spring. By seeds as soon as ripe, otherwise germination is delayed.

Helxine (Soleirolia), Mind-your-own-business (hel-si'ne. Fam. Urticaceae). *H. soleirolii*, Corsica, is a creeping perennial, with roundish, small, bright green leaves, and inconspicuous flowers, often used as ground in a greenhouse or rock garden, very adaptable to cool damp places, and as a pot plant indoors; but apt to become invasive and a weed with little encouragement. Easily propagated by cuttings in the growing season.

Hemerocallis, Day Lily (he-mer-o-kal'lis. Fam. Liliaceae). Herbaceous perennials of temperate Asia, with long, coarse, grass-like leaves, and funnel-shaped flowers, borne in numbers, on strong stalks, opening successively over a period in summer, although individual flowers last only a day or two, and very adaptable to soils and situations.

Selection. H. aurantiaca, Japan, 2½ ft, orange, and v. *major*, many-flowered; *citrina*, Japan, 2½ ft, pale yellow; *flava*, China, 2 ft, lemon-yellow; *fulva*, 3 ft, orange-red, with double forms *flore pleno* and 'Kwanso'. It is the hybrids that enlarge the flower colour range, such as 'Apricot', 'Black Magic', deep maroon; 'Glowing Gold', 'Garnet Red', 'Hyperion', canary-yellow; 'Imperator', orange-red; 'Margaret Perry', orange-scarlet; 'Marie Ballard', salmon-apricot; 'Painted Lady', yellow, coppered; and 'Pink Damask', and others.

Cultivation. Plant October–March, in any ordinary soil, succeeding in grass, or even quite moist soils as well as free-draining, but need a year to establish themselves, tolerant of some shade.

Propagation. By division in spring, but not too frequently. By seeds, sown in April, outdoors.

Hemi-. Prefix in compound words, meaning half or part.

Hemlock Spruce. See *Tsuga canadensis.*

Hemp. See *Cannabis.*

Hemp Agrimony. See *Eupatorium cannabinum.*

Hepatica. See *Anemone.*

Heracleum (he-rak'le-um. Fam. Umbelliferae). Too coarse for most gardens, but striking for their height, pinnate foliage and huge umbels of white flowers in summer. *H. mantegazzianum.* the Cartwheel flower, Caucasus, to 12 ft, and *villosum,* the Tree Parsnip, Caucasus, to 10 ft, may be grown from seeds, sown in April, for the wild garden or waste places.

Herb. A non-woody vascular plant, annual, biennial or perennial, of which the top growth dies to the ground at the end of the growing season. *See* Herbs.

Herb of Grace. See *Ruta.*

Herbaceous. Descriptive of plants which do not form a persistent woody stem.

Herbaceous Border. Characteristically English in conception, this is in the strictest sense ground devoted to the growing of hardy herbaceous perennials of which the top growth is cut away and removed in early winter; the soil weeded, forked, manured and fertilized during winter, and growth is sustained for the following year on this simple maintenance.

Site. The site for the border should be open, with a sunny aspect, and with shelter from strong winds. It may be backed by a wall, a fence or trellising, an evergreen hedge or screen, and abut a lawn or pathway. It may be straight or curved and as wide as possible, at least 8 ft, preferably up to 12 or 14 ft, for a satisfying array of plants and bloom. Where there is ample room, double borders, separated by a broad grass walk, give ample scope to the enthusiast. Where space is limited there is much to be said for planning corner borders or island borders, to be devoted to flowering perennials. The orientation of the border is less important than a freedom from shade from trees or buildings and reasonably good drainage.

Soil Preparation. This must be thorough since plants will go 2–4 years, often longer, without disturbance. It is sensible to bastard-trench any ground with a dense or hard subsoil; if heavy, it will benefit from grit, sifted clinker and ash or coarse sand forked in; if clayey, ½–1 lb. per sq. yd of gypsum will give long-lasting improvement of soil structure. Whether heavy or light, the top soil needs liberal enrichment with humus-forming organic matter; horse manure, hops, leaf-mould or peat on heavy soils; farmyard manure, sewage, strawy compost or fibrous peat on light. Acid soils will need lime to bring a pH of 6·0–6·5; ground limestone for clayey soils; chalk on light. Pre-fertilization of a mixture of 2 parts by weight hoof and horn meal, 2 parts bone meal, and 1 part sulphate of potash at 2–3 oz. per sq. yd will be helpful before planting.

Planting. Most herbaceous perennials may be planted in mild open weather between November and April, with roots evenly spread, and crowns at soil level. The general plan of planting is to place the tallest plants at the rear and grade to the shortest at the front, but this should not be followed too rigidly; here and there taller plants should be brought forward in the interests of contrast. It is helpful to plan a border to scale on squared paper before actually planting, arranging plants in groups rather than singly for effectiveness, and spacing them to allow for mature development.

Colour Schemes. Unless the border is a large one, it is difficult to plant it to be colourful throughout all the growing season. Where this is not possible, it is better to plant to have dominant shows of colour at definite periods. Again, although there is much to be said for colour schemes in variations on one colour theme, such as white or blue, in practice they are apt to be a little disappointing and insipid. A mixed border, with colours composed in harmony, with the more strident colours used sparingly as accents, is usually most successful. Colours which associate well together are red, yellow and blue; orange and violet; cream, pink and light blue; blue and rose; blue and gold; and yellow and lavender; together with foliage greens and greys. A border can be planned to come into flower within a given period, but with little to show at other times it will be trying to live with. Where the desire is for a long season of bloom, it is sensible to give prominence to certain flowers that flower at certain times; for instance, for early summer, Doronicums, Lupins, Trollius or Pyrethrums may be freely planted; for high summer, Delphiniums, Astilbes, Campanulas and Pinks; and for later summer, Phlox, Gaillardia, Chrysanthemums and Michaelmas Daisies.

A Selection of Plants. Apart from personal preferences, the choice of herbaceous perennials must be subordinated to their suitability for the soils, situations and climatic environment in which they are planted. A short list of hardy plants, needing a minimum of skill and having the capacity to flourish in a fairly wide range of soils and open or partially shaded sites, may be drawn from the following:

Tall, for the rear of border, 4–6 ft. Achillea filipendula v., *Aconitum napellus, Anchusa azurea, Aster novaeangliae, Astilbe* × *ardensii, Delphinium elatum* vs., *Helenium autumnale, Helianthus decapetalus, Macleaya cordata, Monarda didyma, Rudbeckia nitida, Sidalcea, Solidago* × *hybrida, Thalictrum dipterocarpum* and *Verbascum.*

Medium, for middle of border, 2–4 ft tall. Achillea ptarmica, Anemone hupehensis, Aster amellus, Campanula latifolia, C. persicifolia, Chrysanthemum maximum, C. rubellum, Coreopsis, Delphinium belladonna, Doronicum, Eryngium, Gaillardia, Gypsophila paniculata, Lupinus, Lychnis chalcedonica, Lysimachia vulgaris, Nepeta faassenii, Paeonia, Papaver orientale, Phlox paniculata, Scabiosa caucasia, Trollius.

Dwarf, for front of border, ½–2 ft tall. Aquilegia, Aster yunnanensis and hybrids, *Dianthus* (Pinks), *Geum, Helleborus niger, Heuchera, Hosta, Incarvillea delavayi, Linum narbonense, Nepeta mussinii, Potentilla, Pulsatilla vulgaris, Tradescantia, Veronica* and *Viola.*

Other Plants. It is legitimate to add bulbs and corms to give colour in spring and summer; while some of the low-growing shrubby perennials, such as lavenders, santolinas and artemisias are not amiss. Half-hardy perennials such as dahlias, begonias and gladioli are often used to fill gaps, though they add to the work of maintaining a border. Some of the alpine perennials such as Alyssum, Aubrieta, Sedum and Saxifrages make good edge plants, and to avoid complete emptiness in winter, a few groups of *Erica carnea* do not look amiss.

Herbicides. Herbicides, or weed-killers, are not new, but in recent years their numbers have steadily increased with the advance of organic chemistry. Their use in the garden may be justified by their action in eliminating weeds or unwanted plants which compete with garden plants for light, air, moisture and nutrients; their saving of time and effort in weeding, and aesthetic end results. Herbicides, according to their kind and method of use, may be grouped in two kinds: non-selective, which are applied for the total destruction of all vegetation present; and selective, which are used to control weeds among garden plants without affecting them. Non-selective herbicides are chiefly used to clear paths, drives and vacant ground of existing plant growth. They include: *ammonium sulphamate*, used at ½–1 lb. per gallon water to 20 sq. yds, to the weed foliage, being rapidly translocated to the roots, etc., and leaving the soil fit for cultivation in 4–6 weeks; it is also invaluable to kill unwanted trees and their stumps; *sodium chlorate*, used at ¼–1 lb. per gallon water per 10 sq. yds, to plant foliage, according to the character of the weeds and their vigour; but care is needed, and it should not be applied within 1–2 ft of garden plants; treated ground requires 3 to 9 months fallowing before it can be cultivated safely; and there is a fire hazard with this solution if allowed to soak and dry on clothing, etc.; it is best to use a liquid form and dilute it, or use a product with a fire depressant (calcium chloride) added as in atlacide. Both these chemicals are non-toxic to mammals. *Copper sulphate* at ¼–½ lb. per gallon water per 10 sq. yds kills annual weeds and the top growth of perennials, but is acidifying, and the soil should contain lime. The organic chemical, *simazine*, is an effective total weed suppressor, applied to paths, etc., after a clearance of top growth, for a year or more. *Phenols* (DNOC, Dinoseb, etc.) are efficient destroyers of weeds and moss on paths, etc., but toxic to mammals and require careful handling. Of selective herbicides, *Lawn Sand* (3 parts by weight ammonium sulphate, 1 part calcined ferrous sulphate, 15–20 parts lime-free sand or sifted peat) has long been used at 2–4 oz. per sq. yd, to control broad-leaved weeds and moss in lawns in spring, as its action is to adhere to the rougher weed foliage and slide off the finer grass blades. Modern selective herbicides are complex organic chemicals, and may be divided into: (1) Those based on growth-regulating substances, such as 2,4-D, 2,4,5-T, Dicamba and MCPA, chiefly used to control dicotyledonous weeds in lawns. 2,4,5-T is a brushwood herbicide, effective against woody plants. To these may be added the phenoxypropionic acids, mecoprop, dichlorprop and feno-prop, for the control of white clover, chickweeds and pearlwort. (2) Grass herbicides, based on dalapon, which controls couch and other coarse grasses. (3) Pre-emergent herbicides, chiefly based on pentachlorophenols, to control germinating weed seeds in seed beds before plant seedlings emerge. (4) Contact herbicides, based on paraquat, which are selective by application; destroying the chlorophyll in the green parts of growing plants, in sunlight, and must therefore be confined to weed foliage only; any solution falling on the soil is harmless to plants. (5) Residual herbicides, chiefly based on simazine, which at recommended concentrations can be applied to the soil between garden plants to suppress weeds for a period; being particularly useful in rose beds, among ornamental shrubs and trees, and in the orchard. In using any herbicide it is important to read and follow the makers' directions implicitly, and watering-cans, hoses and sprayers should be thoroughly cleansed after use, by washing with a detergent solution, leaving full of the solution overnight, and flushing with clear water afterwards; by flushing well with water immediately after use, and then filling with a washing soda solution (3 oz. per 10 gallons water) overnight; rinsing with clear water in the morning; or wash through with a solution of activated charcoal (1 per cent), and rinse with clear water, which is the quickest way.

Herbs. In a garden sense, herbs are plants which are grown for their culinary, medicinal or aromatic properties. Those whose leaves, etc., are used in cooking are often termed pot-herbs, though the term is also used for vegetables or a mixture of vegetables; while sweet-herbs are those having an aromatic character which makes them valuable for flavouring sauces, soups, stews, etc., and salads. Fragrant herbs are grown for drying and use in pot-pourri. Every garden should have a part devoted to herbs. The most useful herbs are the annuals Sweet Basil, Borage, Chervil, Coriander, Cumin, Dill, Pot Marigold and Summer Savory, and the biennials Angelica, Caraway and Parsley, which are grown from seed sown afresh each year: and the perennials Balm, Burnet, Chamomile, Chives, Clary, Dandelion, Elecampane, Finnochio, Horehound, Hyssop, Lovage, Common Marjoram, Sweet Marjoram, Mint, Rosemary, Sage, Southernwood, Sweet Cicely, Tansy, Tarragon, Thyme and Winter Savory, many of which may be grown from seed but are better started as roots or crowns when early produce is required. Plants are usually available from late September to early May. Most herbs thrive in sunny sites, and a well-drained, lightish soil. Culture and uses are given in more detail under the entries for the individual plants.

Hermaphrodite. A plant with both male (stamens) and female (pistil) organs in the same individual flower. *See* Dioecious and Monoecious.

Herniaria, Rupture Wort (her-ni-ar'i-a. Fam. Caryophyllaceae). The chief species grown is *H. glabra*, a native hardy evergreen perennial trailer with small ovate opposite leaves, greenish flowers in summer, used in carpet bedding and in rock gardens for its green cushions of leaves; succeeding in an ordinary soil, planted in October or April; and being propagated by division at the same times.

Heron's Bill. See Erodium.

Hesperis (hes'per-is. Fam. Cruciferae). The perennial *H. matronalis*, SE. Europe, Dame's Violet, Damask Violet or Sweet Rocket, 2–3 ft, with single fragrant summer flowers, variable in colour, and its vs. *alba plena*, double white; *candissima*, single, white; and *purpurea*, violet-purple, are chiefly grown; thriving in ordinary soil, and easily raised from seeds, sown April–May, out of doors, and being propagated by divisions or cuttings in spring or early autumn.

Hetero-. A prefix in compound words, meaning diverse. Ex. *Heterophyllus*, with more than one kind of leaf.

Heterocentron (het-er-o-ken′tron. Fam. Melastomataceae). From Mexico, *H. roseum* (*Heeria rosea*) is a pretty subshrub of 1–2 ft, with showy bright rose flowers in compound panicles in autumn-winter, for the cool or warm greenhouse, in pots, standard compost. Pot in February–March, standard compost, winter temp. 7–13° C. (45–55° F.); propagation by cuttings of firm young shoots in March, under glass, with bottom heat of 18° C. (65° F.).

Heterostylous. Flowers having differing sizes of styles, long and short, as in Primrose.

Heuchera (heuk′e-ra. Fam. Saxifragaceae). Perennial herbs with close tufts of heart-shaped, crenate, stalked leaves, and tall graceful sprays of small colourful carmine flowers in early summer.

Selection. H. micrantha, E. N. America, 2 ft, flesh-pink flowers; *rubescens*, W. U.S.A., 1½ ft, purplish-red flowers; and *sanguinea*, Coral Bells of N. Mexico and Arizona, 1½ ft, bright red, and vs. *grandiflora*, coral-scarlet; *splendens*, dark crimson, and 'Shere variety', scarlet; are notable species, though the hybrids × *brizoides* 'Coral Cloud', and Bressingham strains, pale pink to blazing red, are perhaps even more oustanding.

Cultivation. Plant October or March, any good soil with lime, sun or partial shade; borders or rock garden.

Propagation. By division in spring. By seeds sown in April, in cold frame or outdoor seed-bed.

Heucherella (heuk-er-el′la. Fam. Saxifragaceae). A hybrid of *Heuchera* × *brizoides* × *Tiarella cordifolia*, *H.* × *tiarelloides*, with tufted evergreen orbicular, lobed leaves, and panicles of small, carmine bell-shaped flowers on 18-in. wiry stems, early summer, makes good ground cover, and 'Bridget Bloom' is a

clear pink form for partial shade, ordinary soil, humus-rich. Propagation by division in spring.

Hibbertia (hib-bert′i-a. Fam. Dilleniaceae). Evergreen trailing shrubs, bearing yellow flowers through spring and early summer, of Australia, for decorative effect in the cool greenhouse, winter temp. 7–13° C. (45–55° F.); of which *H. dentata* and *perfoliata* are usually grown.

Cultivation. Plant September–October, in border or pots, standard compost or peaty loam, water freely in active growth; moderately in winter. Propagate by 3–4-in. cuttings of young stems in May–June, in propagating frame.

Hibiscus (hib-is′kus. Fam. Malvaceae). A genus containing annuals, perennials and shrubs or trees, mostly with large showy flowers and fine foliage.

Selection. The chief annuals are *H. trionum*, Bladder Ketmia, Africa, 2 ft, yellow or white, purplish-brown centred flowers in summer, inflated fruits, and tropical *esculentus*, Okra, 3–6 ft, crimson-centred yellow flowers, and long edible fruits; which are grown as half-hardy annuals, raised from seeds sown under glass to plant out in May in warm localities. *H. manihot*, China, Japan, to 6 ft, sulphur-yellow flowers up to 6 in. across, although naturally perennial, is best grown as a half-hardy annual, from seeds sown under glass in heat. *H. militaris*, SE. U.S.A., 3 ft, rose-pink flowers in summer, and *moscheutos*, Swamp Rose Mallow, 3 ft, pale rose flowers, and v. *roseus*, deep rose, are N. American perennials, hardy for sheltered gardens, planted in October or March, or grown from seeds, sown in April, and given well-drained soil and sun. The deciduous shrub, *H. syriacus*, Syria, to 6 ft, of which there are several named vs. such as 'Coleste', single, mauve blue; 'Hamabo', pink, white, crimson basal blotch; 'Snowdrift', white; 'Woodbridge', rosy crimson, and others, is hardy, but blooms late in summer, and can be disappointing in the north. Plant October–March, well-drained, humus-rich soil, sunny positions; may take two years to start new active growth. Propagation by seeds, in March, standard compost, bottom heat of 15·5° C. (60° F.); by cuttings of mature young shoots in

August, in pots, propagating frame, bottom heat of 15·5° C. (60° F.), kept close and shaded for 2 weeks. *H. mutabilis*, China, is tree-like to 10 ft, with pink flowers deepening to red with age, and may be raised from seeds. *H. coccineus*, Florida, to 6 ft, rose-red flowering perennial, and *rosa-sinensis*, China, to 8 ft, and v. *cooperi*, finely foliaged, and with beautiful reddish flowers, shrubs, are for the warm greenhouse, but not readily obtainable.

Hidalgoa, Climbing Dahlia (hi-dal'go-a. Fam. Compositae). The species grown is *H. wercklei*, a half-hardy climbing perennial of Costa Rica, with pinnately cut foliage and scarlet and yellow, single dahlia-like flowers in summer, to grow in the cool greenhouse up supports around which its long leaf-stalks can twine, in standard compost, potted in spring. Propagation is by cuttings of young shoots in spring; or of shoots taken in August, rooted in warm greenhouse propagating frame.

Hiemalis (-e). Of the winter. Ex. *Eranthis hiemalis.*

Hieracium, Hawkweed (hi-er-ak'i-um. Fam. Compositae). Hardly front-rank garden plants, for the majority of these hardy perennials are weeds, but *H. aurantiacum*, Europe, 1–1½ ft, vivid orange-red flowers, summer; and *villosum*, central Europe, 1 ft, silvery leaves, bright yellow summer flowers, grow readily in ordinary soils and sun, planted October–March; and are attractive, kept in check.

Propagation. By seeds, sown April, out of doors. By division in spring.

Hilum. The scar or point of attachment on a seed where it was joined to the ovary.

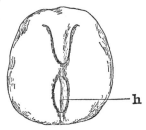

FIG. 126 Hilum in a pea seed, at h.

Hippeastrum (hip-pe-as'trum. Fam. Amaryllidaceae). Large bulbous plants, with strap-like leaves, and magnificent heads of trumpet-shaped flowers on strong stalks, native to subtropical and tropical S. America, and half-hardy perennials for the cool greenhouse or house; apt to be confused with, and called, Amaryllis, a related but S. African genus.

Selection. H. × ackermannii, 1½–2 ft, vermilion; *aulicum*, Brazil, to 2 ft, scarlet; *equestre*, Mexico, 1½–2 ft, red; × *johnsonii*, red and white; *pardinum*, Peru, 1½ ft, cream dotted crimson; *pratense*, Chile, 1 ft, scarlet; *rutilum*, Brazil, 1½ ft, crimson; and *vittatum*, Peru, 2–3 ft, white with red stripes, are noteworthy species and hybrids; to which may be added many beautiful garden-raised hybrids from their crossings to be found in specialists' lists.

Cultivation. Plant the bulbs in early autumn or spring; singly in suitable sized pots, standard compost, well firmed, water sparingly until growth begins, then increase gradually, temp. 13° C. (55° F.). Autumn planting gives winter–early spring flowers; spring planting, late spring or early summer flowers. After flowering, cut out flower scapes, keep plants growing until leaves have grown to the full, then water less, and rest for a month or two, almost dry, before restarting into growth with gentle spraying and watering. Repot only every third or fourth year, saturating afterwards by immersion in water.

Propagation. Usually by seeds, sown when ripe, in pans, bottom heat of 15·5–21° C. (60–70° F.); growing seedlings on as for bulbs for 2–3 years to flowering size, without checking unduly. By offsets at repotting time.

Hippocrepis, Horseshoe Vetch (hippo-kre'pis. Fam. Leguminosae). *H. comosa*, Europe and native, with finely pinnate foliage and yellow umbels of pea flowers in spring, is a trailing perennial for the rock garden, well-drained ordinary soil, and sun. Propagation by seeds, April; or by division at planting time in October or March–April.

Hippophae, Sea Buckthorn (hippof'ai. Fam. Elaeagnaceae). *H. rhamnoides*, Europe to E. Asia, a hardy deciduous shrub, to 20 ft or more, with narrow, simple leaves, white April flowers, and small, round orange-yellow fruits on female plants, untouched by birds, is ornamental, thriving near the sea in sand or poor soils, and as a hedge makes a good windbreak to salt-laden off-sea winds. One male plant to every eight female is sufficient for good berrying. *H. salicifolia*, Himalaya, is not quite so ornamental but quite hardy.

Cultivation. Plant in October–March, ordinary soil, or on the seashore even.

Propagation. By layers of cuttings, summer. By seeds, sown in April, out of doors.

Hippuris, Common Mare's-tail (hippur'is. Fam. Hippuridaceae). The only species, *H. vulgaris*, a native aquatic herb, may be grown in pools as an oxygenating plant, or in damp places. Plant in March–June. Propagated easily by root division, spring or early summer.

Hips or **Heps.** Fruits of the Rose (q.v.).

Hirsutus (-a, -um). Having long soft hairs. Ex. *Rhododendron hirsutum*.

Hirti-. Prefix in compound words, signifying hairiness.

Hispid. Descriptive of plants with stiffish bristly hairs.

Hoary. Having greyish or whitish hairs or down.

Hoe, Hoeing. Hoes are largely used to control weeds, especially between crop rows or plants. The most useful is the Dutch hoe, with flat blade, to push just under the soil surface, cutting weed stems and mixing their remains in the soil; a modern version is the Swoe. A draw hoe or swan-neck hoe is used to chop down older weeds, and to draw wide seed drills; while the triangular hoe is good for weeding in small spaces, and for making single seed drills. Hoeing helps chiefly in breaking up a crusted or cracking soil, in working in top-dressings and keeping down weeds.

Hoheria (ho-he'ri-a. Fam. Malvaceae). *H. populnea*, New Zealand, to 10 ft, is chiefly grown, a bright evergreen shrub, with toothed ovate leaves, and clusters of white flowers in September; and 'Glory of Amlwch' is a notable hybrid.

Cultivation. Plant March–April, well-drained soil, in sunny warm shelter, in the mildest localities; otherwise in large

pots, standard compost, and give cool greenhouse shelter. October–May.

Propagation. By layers in spring; by cuttings of firm young shoots in July–August, in propagating frame.

Holboellia (hol-bo-el'li-a. Fam. Lardizabalaceae). Evergreen twining climbers of which *H. coriacea*, W. China, to 20 ft, trifoliolate leaves, small purplish male flowers, and greenish-white female, finely scented, may be grown outdoors in mild localities; and *H.* (*Stauntonia*) *latifolia*, Himalaya, three to nine leafleted leaves, greenish-white male flowers, and purplish female, fragrant, in spring, may be grown under cool greenhouse or conservatory conditions. Plant in March–April, well-drained ordinary soil. Propagation by seeds, layers or cuttings, under glass.

Holcus (hol'kus. Fam. Gramineae). Tufted tough perennial native grasses, *H. mollis*, Creeping Soft-grass, and *H. lanatus*, Yorkshire Fog, often being troublesome weeds; but *H. l. albo-variegatus* is cultivated for its soft, woolly, silvery-white variegated and margined leaves, growing 9 in., and making tufted clumps in any ordinary soil, from October–March plantings; or divisions.

Holly. See *Ilex*.

Holly Fern. See *Polystichum*.

Holly, Sea. See *Eryngium*.

Hollyhock. See *Althaea*.

Holm Oak. See *Quercus ilex*.

Holodiscus (hol-o-dis'kus. Fam. Rosaceae). Deciduous shrubs of which the form usually grown is *H. discolor* v. *ariaefolia* (*Spiraea ariaefolia*), Western N. America, to 6 ft, with handsome greyish-green foliage, and large drooping panicles of creamy-white flowers in July.

Cultivation. Plant in October–March, any well-drained, humus-rich soil, sun or partial shade.

Propagation. By cuttings of young shoots, July.

Holy Thistle. See *Silybum marianum*.

Homeria (ho-me'ri-a. Fam. Iridaceae). Cormous plants of S. Africa, grown as half-hardy plants in the cool greenhouse; chiefly *H. collina*, 18 in., for its reddish-orange summer flowers, and vs. *aurantiaca*, bright orange; and *ochroleuca*, pale yellow, and narrow linear leaves.

Cultivation. Plant the corms in

October–November, five to a 5-in. pot, standard compost, and place plunged in a frostproof frame until growth is showing; then bring into a cool greenhouse or to a sunny window-sill, watering freely, to flower in July. Dry off after leaves die down. Propagation by offsets.

Homogyne (ho-mo-gi′ne. Fam. Compositae). Stemless perennial herbs of which *H. alpina*, the alpine Coltsfoot of Austria, 6 in., with glossy evergreen kidney-shaped leaves, and clear rose-purple flowers in spring, may be grown in dampish, but drained, soil in the rock garden; planting in September or March; increasing by division.

Honesty. See *Lunaria annua*.

Honeysuckle. See *Lonicera*.

Honeywort. See *Cerinthe*.

Hoodia (hood′i-a. Fam. Asclepiadaceae). Succulent plants from S. Africa, for the cool greenhouse, with large, showy dish-shaped flowers.

Selection. H. bainii, 1 ft, pale yellow, August; and *gordoni*, 1½ ft, buff-purple, July.

Cultivation. Pot in March–April, well-drained standard compost, water moderately in growth, almost none in winter, minimum temp. 7° C. (45° F.). Repot in March. Propagation by careful division.

Hoop Petticoat. See *Narcissus*.

Hop. See *Humulus*.

Hop Tree. See *Ptelea*.

Hops, Spent. Often available from breweries, spent hops are useful as humus-forming organic manure for working into the soil in autumn or winter, though plant nutrient value is small. They form the basis of proprietary hop manures, to which fertilizers have been added to make them balanced organic 'feeds' for plants; used to the makers' directions.

Hordeum (hord′e-um. Fam. Graminae). The genus which includes Barley (*H. sativum*), but in gardens *H. jubatum*, the Squirrel-tail grass, 1 ft, is a hardy American annual, grown for its ornamental feathery spikes; being sown where it is to grow in late March–April, well-drained soil.

Horehound (*Marrubium vulgare*). A native perennial herb of the Mint family (Labiatae), with white, rough leaves and stems from a rhizomatous rootstock, easily grown in poorish, well-drained soil, from seeds, sown in spring, or root divisions, or cuttings in summer. The stems with leaves are cut when plants open their whorls of whitish flowers, to be dried and used as a herbal remedy for coughs; the dried leaves being infused with boiling water as a tea. The stems may be candied.

Horizontalis (-e). Growing horizontally, in line with the ground surface. Ex. *Cotoneaster horizontalis*.

Horminium (horm′in-um. Fam. Labiatae). The sole species, *H. pyrenaicum*, Pyrenees, 1 ft, is a hardy herbaceous perennial, with tufted foliage, and bears bluish-purple flowers in whorls on a short stem in summer; v. *roseum* has rose-purple flowers. Plant October–March, ordinary soil, sunny position, in rock garden or border; propagating by division in spring.

Hormone. From the Greek, *hormōn*, meaning 'to impel or to arouse to activity'; a hormone may be described as a chemical messenger formed in one part of a living organism and effectively active in another. At first it was used to describe the secretions of the endocrine glands in animals; but is now being increasingly used also for growth-regulating substances (q.v.) or auxins in plants. The synthetic products now widely used for root-promotion, weed control, etc., are frequently described as 'hormones'.

Hornbeam. See *Carpinus betulus*.

Horned Poppy. See *Glaucium*.

Horridus (-a, -um). Bristly, prickly, very thorny. Ex. *Genista horrida*.

Horse Chestnut. See *Aesculus*.

Horsehair Worms. See Hair Worms.

Horse-radish (*Armoraica rusticana* (*Cochlearia armoracia*). Fam. Cruciferae). A hardy European perennial, naturalized in Britain, grown chiefly for its roots and their pungent flavour, to be used as a relish and in sauces. It grows about 2 ft tall, with rather rank foliage, and can become an ineradicable weed under neglect. Plant pieces of root (thongs) of 2–3 in. in soil well-dug and liberally enriched with manure or compost, in early spring, 12 in. apart. To keep under control it is wise to lift the plants in autumn, retaining and storing, cool, a few thongs for planting the following year. Generous manurial treatment is the key to good crops of fat roots, which may be stored in moist sand until wanted in the kitchen.

Horseshoe Vetch. See *Hippocrepis.*

Horsetail. See *Equisetum.*

Hortensia. See *Hydrangea.*

Hortensis (-e). Cultivated in gardens. Ex. *Hydrangea* (*hortensis*) *macrophylla.*

Horticulture. The science and practice of gardening.

Host Plant. A plant on which other organisms, fungi, insects or plants are parasitic.

Hosta (Funkia), Plantain Lily (hos'ta. Fam. Liliaceae). Herbaceous perennials with tuberous roots, with handsome, radical, parallel-veined leaves, and spikes of tubular flowers in summer, making superb woodland, shrubbery and border plants; or in pots in the cold greenhouse.

Selection. H. *albomarginata*, Japan, small, matt green leaves, violet flowers; with v. *albomarginata*, white-edged leaves; *elata*, Japan, dark green wavy-edged leaves, pale lavender flowers; *fortunei* v. *albopicta*, Japan, green and yellow leaves, pale purple flowers; *crispula*, Japan, rich green, edged white leaves, pale lilac flowers; *lancifolia*, Japan, dark green leaves, lilac flowers; *plantaginea*, China, Japan, bright green leaves, late white flowers; *sieboldiana*, Japan, blue-grey leaves, lilac white flowers, very beautiful; *tardifolia*, a dwarf species, narrow dark green leaves, mauve flowers; *undulata*, Japan, rich green leaves, variegated creamy white, lilac flowers; and v. *erromena*, the tallest Hosta, rich green leaves, lilac flowers; and *ventricosa*, E. Asia, dark green foliage, bell-shaped deep lavender flowers.

Cultivation. Plant October–March, well-drained or damp soil, sun (for flowers) or shade; in borders, or in woodland or shrubbery; excellent ground cover; welcoming organic top-dressing annually.

Propagation. By division in March.

Hotbed. A bed in which the temperature is raised in the interests of propagation, especially in spring. Traditionally it is made from stable manure and litter, plus an equal quantity of leaves, nicely moistened, and stacked to ferment, turning every other day, top to bottom, for at least a week; and then firmly made into a flat heap, on which one or more frames may be placed, the heap being 2 ft wider on all sides. When the temperature settles to 24–29° C. (75–85° F.), seed boxes or pots or pans containing seeds of half-hardy annuals, vegetables such as Tomatoes, Cucumber, Melon, Vegetable Marrows, etc., may be placed in the frame; or cuttings of such plants as Dahlias brought on. Protection should be given against night frosts. Later the spent heap may be used for Marrows, Cucumbers, etc. More precise heat is given by the electrically soil-heated hotbed, in frames and greenhouses (q.v.).

Hottentot's Fig. See *Mesembryanthemum.*

Hottonia (hot-to'ni-a. Fam. Primulaceae). The chief species grown is *H. palustris*, the native Featherfoil or Water Violet, a beautiful aquatic plant for the garden pool, with finely divided underwater leaves, and lilac flowers, with a yellow eye, primrose-shaped, in whorls on stems above the water in June; *inflata* is a white-flowering N. American plant, less often seen. Plant in spring; propagate by division, or by seeds at the same season.

Hot-water Treatment. One way of controlling certain diseases and pests. It entails immersing the plants (roots and crowns without soil) in water kept at a constant temp. of 43–44° C. (110–112° F.), for 10 minutes, in the case of Mint Rust; for 20 to 30 minutes for eelworms in Chrysanthemum stools or Narcissus bulbs; for 20 minutes in the case of eelworms in Strawberry plants; for 30 minutes in the case of bulb fly maggots, eelworms or mites in bulbs such as Narcissi. After the bath, the plant material is promptly cooled in cold water, and then planted.

Hound's Tongue. See *Cynoglossum.*

House Plants. The range of plants which can be successfully grown in modern houses is steadily increasing. There is a tendency to restrict the definition of house plants to exotics which are largely grown for their foliage beauty first and flowers second; but most gardeners interpret it more catholically, to embrace many flowering plants, and those plants which are only brought into the house for their period of greatest beauty, such as bulbs. The choice of plants must, however, be be governed by the growing conditions that the house provides; taking into consideration the plant's growing needs in light, temperature, humidity and atmosphere. A good rooting medium or compost, proper watering, feeding and disease- and pest-preventing care are important also. Broadly, light, while essential to all plants, is especially important for flowering plants. Foliage plants do better in the partial shade of rooms since they can make the best use of the light available. Plants should not, however, be subject to strong, hot, direct sunshine in a window. *Heat*. Although many house plants tolerate fluctuating temperatures well, the steadier and warmer the heat, the greater and more exotic the choice becomes. Temperatures are a winter problem, and the night level is crucial. Most plants can tolerate temperature drops of 2·8–5·4° C. (5–10° F.) at night; but not rises at night after low daytime temperatures. The steadiness of central heating has enlarged the range of house plants that can be grown. But higher temperatures usually mean drier air, and this has to be guarded against by making provision for humidity by the use of humidifiers or trays of water to evaporate in heated rooms. Few house plants remain unaffected by draughts, although air circulation and changes of the air in rooms are invaluable. *Atmosphere*. Plants breathe and like a clean atmosphere. It is unlikely that the normal concentration of tobacco smoke in a room will affect them adversely, but fumes from gas fires and oil heaters are often toxic and should be avoided; while dust and lint deposits should be removed by wiping the leaves periodically. *Watering*. Over-watering is a principal cause of house plant failures. It can be avoided in the first place by using well-drained, properly crocked pots, and a porous compost. Broadly, plants may be watered more frequently in active growth, and in warm weather or heat, less frequently in cold, dull weather, and when they become dormant or during their rest period, often in winter for most plants. Tepid water is preferable, and it is often more suitable to water by immersing a pot

in a bath of water than overhead. After watering, let the pot drain. *Feeding*. Plants in pots have only limited amounts of soil to draw upon, and those which are grown perennially in the house benefit from some feeding when established and in active growth, usually just before and when coming into flower. A liquid fertilizer in dilute solution can be given at 10–14-day intervals, between May and October. *Repotting*. Plants are usually repotted at the end of their rest period, just before starting into active growth again. Some plants need repotting annually, others at longer intervals; particularly those which like to become rather pot-bound. In potting and repotting, the soil needs of the plant should be studied, though for most house plants, one of the standard composts answers them very well. House plants may be divided into three types: (1) Those grown for a limited period in the house, usually for their flowering; such as pot-grown bulbous and cormous plants, half-hardy herbs such as Calceolaria, Cineraria, and annuals, discarded after flowering. (2) Perennial plants grown as house plants while in flower, and later rested in the greenhouse or out of doors, such as bulbous, cormous and rhizomatous perennials like Achimenes, Hippeastrum, Cyclamen, Gloxinia, Vallota, etc.; and half-hardy deciduous and evergreen shrubs of which Camellia, Erica, Azalea, Sparmannia and Solanum are typical. (3) Permanent house plants which can be grown in the house year after year. Some short selective lists for various conditions are:

Easily grown house plants for cool rooms, minimum temperature at night of 7–10° C. (45–50° F.): *Aechmea fasciata, Aspidistra lurida, Cissus antarctica, Fatsia japonica, Ficus elastica, Haworthia attenuata, Hedera helix* and vs., *Peperomia magnoliaefolia, Philodendron scandens, Rhoicissus rhomboidea, Sansivieria trifasciata, Saxifraga stolonifera, Sygonium podophyllum, Tradescantia fluminensis* and vs., *Vriesia splendens, Zebrina pendula* and vs., *Zygocactus truncatus.*

Easy plants for heated rooms, minimum temperature at night of 10–15·5° C. (50–60° F.): *Adiantum capillus-veneris,*

Agave albicans, Aloe variegata, Anthurium sp., *Aphelandra squarrosa, Begonia rex*, etc., *Belleperone guttata, Bilbergia nutans, Coffea arabica, Coryline terminalis, Crassula* sp., *Davallia canariensis, Codiaeum variegatum, Dryopteris sieboldii; Echeveria* sp., *Epiphyllum* hybrids, *Euphorbia splendens, Hoya carnosa, Maranta* sp., *Nidularium* sp., *Pananndus* sp., *Peperomia caperata, P. sandersii, Philodendron elegans, P. erubescens, Piqueria trinervia, Saintpaulia ioanatha, Scindapsus picta* and vs., *Sedum sieboldii, Spathiphyllum wallsii, Syngonium vellozianum* and *Tetrastigma voinierianum, See also* under individual species.

Houseleek. See *Sempervivum*.

Houstonia (hous'ton-i-a. Fam. Rubiaceae). N. American hardy herbaceous tufted perennials of which *H. caerulea*, Bluets, makes a creeping mat of evergreen foliage, with light blue, salver-shaped flowers on 2-in. stems in May, for the rockery or alpine house; with vs. *alba*, white; and 'Millards variety' with flowers of a richer blue; *serpyllifolia*, with thyme-like leaves, and violet-blue flowers, is also charming.

Cultivation. Plant October or March–April, well-drained soil, in cool shade for summer.

Propagation. By division in March. By seeds in cold frame, when ripe.

Howea (how'e-a. Fam. Palmaceae). Handsome palms with feather-shaped graceful foliage, and highly decorative for the warm greenhouse or in rooms.

Selection. H. belmoreana, Curly Palm, has the more numerous arching leaf segments; and *forsteriana*, Thatch Leaf Palm, fewer and flat leaf segments; both grow to 6–10 ft, in pots; and are natives of Lord Howe Islands, formerly under *Kentia*.

Cultivation. Easily raised from seeds, sown 1 in. deep, standard compost, bottom heat of 27° C. (80° F.), under glass, seedlings being potted when at first leaf stage, temp. 18° C. (65° F.), and grown on in light shade. Water liberally when in active growth, moderately in winter, minimum temp. 13° C. (55° F.). Repot as growth requires it.

Hoya, Wax Flower (hoi'a. Fam. Asclepiadaceae). Evergreen climbing shrubs of warm countries, with leathery leaves, and flowers of waxy-textured petals.

Selection. H. carnosa, Queensland, will climb and cling to a wall with aerial roots like Ivy, or may be grown up supports or trellis to 10 ft, in a cool greenhouse, with pointed, somewhat fleshy leaves, and clusters of pinkish-white tubular flowers; summer; v. *variegata* has creamy variegated leaves; *bella*, India, is a dwarf shrub of 18 in., with waxy white, rose-centred flowers, early summer, and requires a warm greenhouse.

Cultivation. Plant or pot in March, standard composts; water freely in active growth, very moderately in winter, minimum temp. 10–13° C. (50–55° F.); prune in February, cutting straggling and weak shoots back.

Propagation. By layering in early summer; or by cuttings of firm shoots in spring, with bottom heat of 24° C. (75° F.).

Humea, Incense Plant (hu'me-a. Fam. Compositae). The one species grown is *H. elegans*, an Australian biennial, which is highly ornamental with large, stem-clasping lance-shaped leaves, and loosely branched drooping panicles of brownish, pink or red composite flowers, in July–August, reaching 4–6 ft, the whole plant piquantly scented, especially when touched or rubbed. Seed is sown in July, standard compost, in a cold frame, and the seedlings potted singly in 3-in. pots, to grow on in cool greenhouse for the winter; potting on in spring into 4½- or 6-in. pots, and with increased watering, grow on to flower in the greenhouse, or to plant out in June, in borders or beds; light, humus-rich loam, full sun.

Humifusus (-a, -um). Humifuse, spreading out on the ground. Ex. *Veronica humifusa*.

Humilis (-e). Humble, dwarf or low on the ground. Ex. *Carex humilis*.

Humulus (hu'mu-lus. Fam. Cannabinaceae). Perennial herbaceous, clockwise twining climbing plants, with ornamental, palmately lobed leaves, and male flowers in panicles, female in spikes, useful for screening.

Selection. H. lupulus, native, 10–15 ft, yields the hops used in brewing, its golden-leafed v. *aurea* is pleasing in the garden; *scandens (japonicus)*, Japan, to 12 ft, is decorative on trellis or pergolas, and has a bronzy golden v. *lutescens*, and spotted silvery variegated form, *variegatus*.

Cultivation. Often grown as hardy annuals, from seeds sown in March. Plants are set out in March, by walls, trellis, arbours, tree stumps, for rapid cover, cut down in October and given winter cover of organic mulching material. The female flowers (hops) may be dried for herbal use. Propagation by division.

Humus. A complex entity of the soil originating in the decomposition of organic matter, as a blackish-brown amorphous colloidal substance. It ameliorates the physical texture and structure of all soils; is a centre of biological and chemical soil activity, and a vital reserve of moisture and nutrients for plants; in short it is the foundation of soil fertility.

Hunnemannia, Mexican Tulip Poppy (hun-ne-man'ni-a. Fam. Papaveraceae). The only species, *H. fumariifolia*, Mexico, 2–3 ft, with large, yellow, poppy-like flowers in summer, is naturally perennial, but is grown as an annual, raised from seeds, sown March, under glass; or in the open border; or as a biennial, sowing in July, and giving winter protection to seedling plants. Likes a well drained, loam soil, and sun.

Hutchinsia (hut-kin'si-a or hutchin'si-a. Fam. Cruciferae). The species usually grown is *H. alpina*, 3 in., a hardy perennial from the Pyrenees, with clusters of white flowers, May–July; for the rock garden or alpine house; in well-drained, sandy loam, planting in early spring. Propagation by seeds, or division, in early spring.

Hyacinthella (correctly, hi-a-kin-thel'la; popularly, hi-a-sinth'el-la. Fam. Liliaceae). Small-flowered bulbous plants, of which *H. azurea (Hyacinthus azureus)*, Asia Minor, with a spike of tiny bright blue flowers in early spring, 6 in. high, may be grown in a sunny, well-drained position in the rock garden, along with its white v. *alba*. Plant in September. Propagation by offsets; or by seeds, which take five years to build to flowering.

Hyacinthus, Hyacinth (correctly, hi-a-kin'thus, or by usage, hi-a-sin'thus. Fam. Liliaceae). Botanists now tend to treat this genus as of one species, *H. orientalis*, a native of eastern Mediterranean countries, from which, together with its v. *provincialis*, the strains of popular large-flowered hyacinths have been developed. Hyacinths were known to the Greeks and Romans and esteemed for their scent, but were reintroduced to Europe about 1560, and the breeding and development of the large, bulbous plants with their magnificent spikes of closely packed, scented, bell-shaped flowers have been done in Holland by the Dutch.

Roman Hyacinths (H. orientalis v. albulus), bear rather open spikes of white flowers, 6–10 in. tall, and are planted up as soon as available in August–September, in bowls in fibre, in pots, in standard compost or on pebbles, with the bulbs just above the water level, in a deep saucer; and placed in the dark, at temp. not more than 7–10° C. (45–50° F.), for about 8 weeks, being brought to the light gradually, and temp. about 10–13° C. (50–55° F.), to flower in late November and December.

Large-flowered Hyacinths. Bulbs may now be bought specially prepared for forcing into bloom at stated times, and the growers' instructions should be meticulously followed for such bulbs.

Selection. Early Hyacinths or Dutch Miniatures, to be grown along the same lines as for Roman Hyacinths, for Christmas flowering are: 'Autumn Surprise', 9 in., pink; 'Fairy Blue', 9 in., porcelain blue; and 'Rosalie', 7 in., deep rose. Large single-flowering: *Light blue*—'Dr Lieber', 'Gerard Dou', 'Myosotis', 'Perle Brillante', 'Queen of the Blues'. *Sky-blue*—'Côte d'Azur', 'Bismarck', 'Winston S. Churchill'. *Dark blue*—'Delft Blue', 'Duke of Westminster', 'Hindenburg', 'King of the Blues', 'Marie', 'Ostara', 'Paul Veronese'. *Pink*—'Anne Marie', 'Delight', 'Eros', 'Flushing', 'Gertrude', 'Lady Derby', 'Pink Pearl', 'Princess Margaret', 'Queen of the Pinks'. *Red*—'Cyclops', 'Jan Bos', 'La Victoire', 'Madame du Barry', 'Pharos', 'Roi des Belges'. *Purple and Mauve*—'Distinction', 'King of the

Lilacs', 'Lord Balfour', 'Purple King'. *Yellow*—'City of Haarlem', 'Daylight', 'Fleur d'Or', 'Prince Henry', 'Sunburst', 'Yellowhammer'. *White*—'Carnegie', 'Hoar Frost', 'L'Innocence', 'Queen of the Whites'. *Double-flowering*—'Chestnut Flower', blush pink; 'General Kohler', delft blue; 'La Grandesse', white; 'Lauren Koster', blue; 'President Roosevelt', red; 'Sunflower', yellow.

Pot Culture. Plant in late August–September for Christmas and January bloom; October for February and March flowering; in standard compost, well-crocked pots, with neck of bulb at soil level; water thoroughly, and place in cool dark frame, pit or cellar, or plunge in fibre, peat or ashes (at 7° C. [45° F.]). Leave for 8 weeks, and then gradually bring to the light and increasing warmth, to about 18° C. (65° F.) finally. Water with growth, but avoid over-watering. After flowering, cut out flower stalk, grow on with feeding to build up the bulbs for outdoor use next year.

Bulbs in Fibre. Use deep bowls; place a few pieces of charcoal in the bottom, then fibre (fibrous peat, plus one-tenth crushed oyster shell, and charcoal), thoroughly moistened, to a depth of an inch or so, place bulbs on this, just clear of one another, fill and firm with fibre. Stand bowls in dark airy cool cellar, outhouse, frame or under north wall, covered with peat or ashes, for 8 weeks, then bring into light and greater warmth, with roots filling the bowls and shoots about 2 in. high. Keep the fibre moist. *In Glasses.* Special necked glasses are used, filled with soft or rain water, with a piece or two of charcoal in it; the bulbs just touching the water. Place in a cool dark place until roots are well formed, and then bring to the light and greater warmth, gradually; top up the water as required. *In the Open.* Unprepared bulbs may be planted September–November, 6–12 in. apart, at a depth of 4–6 in.; in deep, well-drained, humus-rich soil; lift after leaves die down. To retain good flowering bulbs, the soil must be kept 'fat' with generous organic manuring. Spent bulbs from indoor flowering may be planted out of doors but often deteriorate, unless the soil is porous in depth and generously treated.

Species. H. amethystinus, now classified as *Brimeura amethystina*, the Spanish Hyacinth, 6 in., with loose spikes of bright blue flowers, spring; and its white v. *albus*, may be planted in well-drained soil, in the rock garden or alpine house in September.

Hybrid. A plant resulting from the crossing of two species; indicated by the sign ×. Crosses between genera are more rare, though some orchids yield them freely; such plants are termed bigeneric hybrids.

Hydrangea (hi-dran'ge-a; popularly hi-dran'je-a. Fam. Saxifragaceae). A genus of shrubs and woody climbers of variable hardiness, esteemed for large corymbs or panicles of flowers; usually deciduous.

Selection. Climbers—H. anomala, Himalaya, to 40 ft, yellow-white corymbs of flowers, June; *serratifolia*, Chile, to 45 ft, with evergreen foliage, greenish-white panicles of flowers, June; and *petiolaris*, Japan, to 60 ft, with corymbs of white flowers, June, are self-clinging by aerial roots, ideal for lofty walls, though they can be kept restricted by annual pruning after flowering, and do vigorously in ordinary soils. Propagation by cuttings of firm young shoots, July–August. *Deciduous Shrubs—*Of the species, *H. arborescens* v. *grandiflora*, N. U.S.A., 4 ft, round head of pure white flowers, July–August; *bretschneideri*, China, to 10 ft, white to pink, July; *cinerea.* v. *sterile*, SE. U.S.A., to 6 ft, fine trusses of white flowers, summer needs warm shelter; as does *involucrata*, Japan, 3–6 ft, white and blue flowers, August, and v. *hortensis*, with double flowers; *longipes*, China, 6 ft, spreads with white flowers, July; *paniculata*, Japan, China, to 15 ft, pyramidal, with bracted, sterile white flowers, July; even finer in v. *grandiflora*, splendid garden shrubs; *quercifolia*, SE. U.S.A., to 6 ft, lobed foliage, white turning purplish heads of flowers, July; *sargentiana*, China, to 10 ft, very large leaves, and flattish corymbs of white sterile flowers, rosy-lilac inner fertile flowers, July–August; *serrata*, Japan, Korea, 4–5 ft, small corymbs of vari-coloured flowers, July–August; blue in v. *acuminata*, pinkish in v. *rosabla*; and *villosa*, China, to 9 ft, long hairy leaves, and corymbs of purplish-blue to white flowers, August; all of which are worth trying in any garden, with shelter from freezing winds. The most familiar garden Hydrangeas, however, are those grouped under *H. macrophylla* (*hortensis, opuloides*), Japan, 8–12 ft, of which there are two characteristic forms; (1) Those typical of v. *hortensia*, carrying rounded corymbs of flowers which are of the showy sterile, coloured bracted kinds; and (2) those akin to v. *mariesii*, with flattish corymbs of flowers, with small fertile flowers, margined by showy sterile flowers, usually known as 'Lacecaps'. These Hydrangeas are easily grown in any reasonably well-drained soil, containing moisture-retentive humus, and where frosts or cold winds are unlikely to kill the terminal buds from which the season's flowers develop. Flower colour however, is greatly influenced by the presence or absence of lime in the soil, and consequent availability of aluminium and iron to plants. On strongly limy soils it is wise to be content with red, pink or white bloom, from such forms as 'Princess Beatrix', rose-red; 'Carmen', carmine; 'Vulcain', carmine; 'Ami Pasquier', crimson; 'Mme Mouillière', white; 'Parsifal', rose; and 'Westfalen' crimson. On acid soils of pH 5·5 or less flower colour is likely to be naturally blue or lilac-violet; particularly in forms such as 'Générale Vicomtesse de Vibraye'; 'Hamburg'; 'Maréchal Foch', 'Goliath'; 'Domotoi', 'Kluis Superba' and 'Altona'. On moderately acid soils blue-flowering may be induced or intensified by adding aluminium sulphate in autumn; the amount depends upon the size of the plant, 1–2 lb. for a young recently planted one, up to 7 lb. per plant of 3 ft tall established bushes. Or proprietary blueing agents may be used to instructions. Any inclination to yellow chlorosis of leaves may be countered by applying a chelated iron compound (sequestrene) before growth begins. Of the Lacecap forms, the finest blue is 'Bluewave'; others are the white-flowering 'Lanarth White' and 'Whitewave' and the v. *mariesii*, pinkish, itself. They may be treated similarly to the Hortensias, and make fine garden shrubs.

Cultivation. Most Hydrangeas, being

deciduous, are planted in October–March; preferably in well-drained, humus-rich soils; and with good sheltered conditions from blighting frosts; and should have generous organic feeding with top mulches annually. *Pruning. H. paniculata* may be pruned hard in February–March, shortening last year's flowered stems severely, and feeding generously. Most other Hydrangeas need little pruning, beyond the removal of spent flower-heads in late winter; but overgrown and congested plants may be thinned, and a few older branches cut almost to base, in February–March. Robust shoots with good terminal buds bear the best flowers, and should be left untouched. *Pot and Tub Culture.* The Hortensia types lend themselves well to growth in 6–12-in. pots for the cold greenhouse or indoor flowering; and to tubs or vases. They are potted, February–March, standard compost (omitting lime for blue-flowering kinds), grown cool, with liberal watering, and liquid feeding fortnightly until flowers open. Young plants may be forced by bringing into a warm greenhouse (18° C. [65° F.]) from cold frames in March–September.

Propagation. By cuttings of young shoots of 3 to 4 joints, in April–May, inserted singly in 3-in. pots, standard compost, with gentle bottom heat, or in a frame; by cuttings of young, robust non-flowered shoots, 4–6 in. long, taken in August, to root in a cold frame, and winter there.

Hydrocharis, Frogbit (hi-dro-ka'ris. Fam. Hydrocharitaceae). The one species, *H. morsus-ranae*, the native Frogbit, is a floating aquatic plant with small green roundish leaves, and white flowers, summer, which may be grown in garden pools. Propagation by runners which root at the nodes.

Hydrophyte. A plant that grows in water.

Hydroponics. The art, science and practice of growing plants without soil with the aid of chemical nutrient solutions. Originating in California in 1929, under Professor W. F. Gericke, modern hydroponics (literally from the Greek, meaning water-working) is now an established and practical method of growing crops and plants, particularly in countries where soil resources or rainfall are meagre, but where there is ample sunlight. The basic principles are that the plants are grown in a supporting or anchoring medium of inert material, with their roots growing in a nutrient solution of chemicals, contained in a trough. The original method consisted of growing plants in an aggregate such as wood wool, on wire netting, suspended over a tank filled with a nutrient solution into which the roots could grow and feed. Other methods entail the use of an aggregate (sand or gravel) in a trough, through which a nutrient solution is circulated. Expanded Vermiculite (q.v.) is also an excellent rooting medium. In Britain, hydroponics has found commercial application in greenhouses for the growth of crops such as perpetual flowering carnations. *See* W. F. Gericke, *The Complete Guide to Soilless Gardening*, Putnam, 1940; A. H. Phillips, *The Science of Soilless Culture*, Pearson, 1943; J. Sholto Douglas, *Hydroponics*, O.U.P., 1951.

Hyemalis. See *Hiemalis*.

Hygrometer. An instrument for ascertaining humidity of the air, most useful in the greenhouse. A modern instrument registers humidity on a dial scale, easily read.

Hymenocallis (hi-men-o-kal'lis. Fam. Amaryllidaceae). Large bulbous plants with fragrant white or yellow flowers, related to *Pancratium*, for the cool greenhouse.

Selection. H. amancaes, Peru, 2 ft, bright yellow flowers, spring; × *macrostephana*, 18 in., white flowers, spring; *narcissiflora*, Peru, 2 ft, white with green bands, spring; *ovata*, West Indies, 18 in., white, spring; and × *spofforthiae*, 2 ft, soft yellow, spring.

Cultivation. Pot in October–November, in large pots to accommodate the large bulbs, standard compost, keep just moist, winter temp. 10° C. (50° F.): watering freely as growth increases, rest in autumn.

Propagation. By offsets at potting time.

Hymenophyllum, Filmy Fern (hi-men-o-pil'lum. Fam. Polypodiaceae). Of this very large genus of ferns, mostly of dwarf, creeping habit, liking shade, moisture and warmth, only a few are eligible here.

Selection. H. demissum, New Zealand, etc., 4 in., finely fronded; *dichotomum*, Antarctica, 3 in., to grow in moss, on wood or rock; *pulcherrimum*, New Zealand, 6 in.; may be grown in the cool greenhouse, in shade, or in fern cases or bottle gardens; winter temp. 7° C. (45° F.) minimum. *H. peltatum*, 3 in., and *tunbridgense*, 3 in., are natives, and may be planted in sandstone rock gardens, in sandy peat.

Hypericum, St John's Wort (hi-pe'ri-kum. Fam. Hypericaceae). Hardy perennials of shrubby habit, notable for their late summer yellow flowers, usually with many stamens.

Selection. H. androsaemum, the native Tutsan, to 2 ft, yellow flowering, June–August, good for shade; *calycinum*, SE. Europe, Rose of Sharon, Aaron's Beard, 1 ft, beautiful ground cover, sun or shade; *patulum*, China, Japan, to 3 ft, and vs. *forrestii, henryi*, and 'Hidcote', all free-flowering, large golden flowers; and × 'Rowallane Hybrid', to 6 ft, large flowers; are hardy. Evergreens such as *coris*, S. Europe, 1 ft, golden-yellow; *empetrifolium*, Greece, 12 in., yellow; *olympicum*, SE. Europe, 9 in., yellow, June; *reptans*, Sikkim, 2 in., golden yellow, autumn; and *rhodopeum*, SE. Europe, 6 in., yellow, June, are only hardy for the milder counties, or for the alpine house.

Cultivation. Plant October–March, if deciduous, March–April if evergreen; well-drained ordinary soil.

Propagation. By division in early spring; or by cuttings of young firm shoots in July. By seeds sown April, outdoors or in cold frame.

Hypha (pl. **Hyphae**). A thread of a fungus; collectively the vegetative part of a fungus, cellular and without chlorophyll, from which fructifications arise.

Hypo-. Prefix in compound words meaning under. Ex. Hypocotyl, part of the stem under seed-leaves; Hypogynous, of stamens growing under the pistol; Hypogeal, underground.

Hypoxis (hi-pocks'is. Fam. Amaryllidaceae). Dwarf cormous herbaceous plants, with grass-like leaves and star-shaped yellow flowers, half-hardy and for the cool greenhouse.

Selection. H. hemerocallidea, Natal,

1 ft, golden-yellow flowers, June; *hirsuta*, N. America, 6 in., yellow, June, and v. *alba*, white; and *stellata*, S. Africa, 9 in., white, green striped flowers.

Cultivation. Pot in autumn, standard compost, keeping cool, at 7° C. (45° F.), and rather dry until growth begins, when watering should increase; drying off in late summer.

Propagation. By offsets when re-potting.

Hyssopus, Hyssop (his'so-pus. Fam. Labiatae). The single species, *H. officinalis*, Mediterranean region to 2 ft, is the evergreen bushy herb, with spikes of bluish-purple flowers in whorls in summer; white in v. *alba* and red in *rubra*. The linear leaves have a pleasant minty smell, and are sometimes used as a herbal infusion against phlegm and catarrh.

Cultivation. Plant in Autumn or March–April, well-drained, porous soil, and sun; with shelter in colder localities from frost; prune to shape in March.

Propagation. By seeds sown in April out of doors, in warm sandy loam. By cuttings of young shoots, in April–May in sandy loam, with partial shade at first.

I

Iberis (i-ber'is. Fam. Cruciferae). Annual and perennial sub-shrubs, which are free-flowering.

Selection. I. amara, W. Europe and Britain, 1 ft, white flowering in summer, and its v. *coronaria* is the source of the annuals offered by seedsmen under 'Giant Empress', 'Hyacinth-flowered' in various flower colours, and dwarf 'Little Prince' and 'Tom Thumb'; which with *I. umbellata*, S. Europe, ½–1 ft, in various colours and named forms such as 'Dunnett's Crimson', and dwarf 'Fairy Mixed', comprise the familiar Candytufts; easily grown from seeds sown where they are to flower in March–April, ordinary garden soil; often re-seeding themselves. The evergreen perennials include *I. gibraltarica*, Spain, 1 ft, lilac-blue flowers, May–June; needing full sun and mild sheltered conditions; *saxatilis*, Pyrenees, 4 in., white, late spring; *sempervirens* v. 'Little Gem', S. Europe, 8 in., spreading ground cover, white flowering in spring; and *tenoreana*, Pyrenees, 6 in., purplish white in May; all making good dwarf shrublets in any well-drained soil in the rock garden or border; or may be grown in the alpine house.

Propagation. By seeds, sown March–April, out of doors. By division in early spring, or by cuttings, July–August.

Ice Plant. See *Mesembryanthemum*.

Iceland Poppy. See *Papaver nudicaule*.

Ichneumon Flies (*Ichneumonoidea*). A very large family of parasitic insects which lay their eggs in the eggs or larvae of other insects, destroying their hosts and should be regarded as friendly to the gardener's purposes; *Apanteles glomeratus*, a braconid Ichneumon, parasitizes cabbage white butterfly caterpillars, for instance.

Idesia (i-de'si-a. Fam. Flacourtiaceae). The only species, *I. polycarpa*, Japan, to 15 ft, is a deciduous tree, with attractive large, heart-shaped leaves, and unisexual yellowish-green terminal panicles of flowers in June–July; followed by grapelike bunches of red berries on female trees; v. *vestita*, China, has downy foliage.

Cultivation. Plant October–March, in warm sheltered position, well-drained, humus-rich soil.

Propagation. By seeds, April, in cold frame.

Igneus (-a, -um). Fiery-scarlet. Ex. *Cuphea ignea*.

Ilex, Holly (i'lecks. Fam. Aquifoliaceae). A large genus of trees and shrubs, mostly evergreen, and with unisexual flowers, so only female plants berry when in the vicinity of a male.

Selection. I. aquifolium, common Holly, native, and of Europe, N. Africa and W. Asia, shrub or tree to over 60 ft, with firm, glossy, spine-toothed leaves, red berries; choice vs. being, green-leaved— × *altaclarensis*, large-leaved and male; *camelliaefolia*, almost spineless leaves, female; *ferox*, the Hedgehog Holly, male; *fructu-luteo*, yellow berries, female; *monstrosa*, long slender leaved, male; *ovata*, slow-growing, oval spineless leaves, male; *pendula*, Weeping Holly, female; *pyramidalis*, finely upright, female; *recurva*, small-leaved, dwarf, male; *scotica*, the Dahoon or smooth-leaved Scotch Holly, female; 'W. J.

f   m

FIG. 127 The flowers of *Ilex* sp., Holly, borne on separate trees: f. female; m. male.

285

Bean', compact, wavy leaves, male: gold or silver variegated leaves— *argentea marginata*, silver, female, and its form *pendula*, Perry's Weeping; *aureo-marginata*, yellow, female, and forms; 'Golden King', golden and female; 'Golden Queen', similar but male (!); *handsworthiensis*, creamy-white, female; 'Madame Briot', golden, female; and 'Silver Queen', the best silver variegated form, male (!); *polycarpa* is a hermaphrodite, berrying freely, and suitable for single planting. *I. cornuta*, Horned Holly, China, 8–10 ft, red berries; *crenata*, Japan, to 15 ft, crenate leaves, black berries, and v. *variegata*; *pernyi*, China, to 30 ft, distinctive 5-spined leaves, and v. *veitchii*; *pedunculosa*, Japan, to 20 ft, long-stalked red berries; and *verticillata*, Eastern N. America, 5–10 ft, deciduous, narrow oval leaves, small red berries. *I. insignis*, Himalaya, long, narrow leaves, bright red berries; *latifolia*, to 20 ft, red berries; *perado*, Canary Isles, to 15 ft, large-leaved; and *platyphylla*, Canary Isles, to 20 ft, deep red berries, are only hardy enough for the mildest localities, or tub-growing in a cool greenhouse.

Cultivation. Plant September–October, or preferably April–May, when young; any well-drained soil, sun or shade; syringe and water in dry weather until established; may be propagated by cuttings of firm shoots taken in July–August, in cold frame or under handlights; species by seeds, in spring.

Hedging. Plants of *I. aquifolium* and its vs. form excellent, long-lived hedges, although slow-growing at first; v. *pyramidalis* is commended for this. Plant in well-prepared ground in April–May, 1½ ft apart; prune to shape in late spring; but established hedges only need clipping annually in August.

Illicium, Anise (il-lik'i-um. Fam. Magnoliaceae). Evergreen shrubs, with leathery, entire leaves, aromatic of anise when rubbed, pale greenish-yellow, axillary flowers, spring; but only hardy for mild localities.

Selection. I. anisatum, Japan, Formosa, to 10 ft; *floridanum*, SE. U.S.A., to 10 ft, maroon-purple flowers, May.

Cultivation. Plant April–May, well-drained, acid, humus-rich soil, sheltered sunny positions, mulch with peat.

Propagation by layers or cuttings in July–August, in a propagating frame.

Imantophyllum. See *Clivia*.

Imbricatus (-a, -um). Imbricate, overlapping, like slates or tiles. Ex. *Araucaria imbricata (araucana)*.

FIG. 128   Imbricate; leaves of *Araucaria imbricata (araucana)*.

Impatiens (im-pa'ti-ens. Fam. Balsaminaceae). Annuals, biennials and perennials, notable for their colourful but complicated floral structure.

Selection. The annuals chiefly grown are *I. balsamina*, Balsam, India, Malaya, China, 1½ ft, in forms such as 'Camellia-flowered', 'Rose-flowered', and dwarf vs., white, purple, red, and carmine shades; self-coloured, striped and spotted; raised from seeds sown under glass, standard compost, bottom heat of 18° C. (65° F.), for subsequent planting out in early June, or as greenhouse pot plants; *biflora*, N. America, 2½ ft, orange flowers, spotted reddish brown, as a hardy annual, sowing where it is to flower in moist shady places; and *glandulifera (roylei)*, India, naturalized in Britain, 6–8 ft, and known as the 'Policeman's Helmet', for its purple flowers in summer; 'White Queen' is a white-flowering v., also a hardy annual, which may be sown, March, where it is to flower, with a liking for moist waste places or the water garden, and may re-seed itself. Of the perennials, *I. holstii* is now renamed *I. walleriana*, E. tropical Africa, 2–3 ft, handsome with bright scarlet flowers in summer, to be gᵣwn as a half-hardy annual for bedding, or greenhouse; and *I. sultani*, Chinaman's Pigtail or Busy Lizzie, Zanzibar, 1–2 ft, is regarded as a v. of *walleriana*; but a delightful tender perennial, to grow as a greenhouse or house pot plant, with flowers in various shades of rose, pink, purple and red; and may be raised from seeds, sown under glass, standard compost, with bottom heat (18° C. [65° F.]); or from cuttings at any time in spring to autumn, rooting freely in porous soil; water freely in active growth, with very free air circulation; moderately in winter, minimum temp. 10° C. (50° F.).

Impeditus (-a, -um). Tangled, Ex. *Rhododendron impeditum.*

Imperfect. Of flowers without either stamens or pistils; or unisexual flowers.

Imperfect Fungi. Fungi of which no sexual stage is known.

Imperialis (-e). Highly noble, imperial. Ex. *Paulownia imperialis (tomentosa).*

Inarching. A method of grafting by which a growing shoot of one plant is grafted on to the growing shoot of another; sometimes practised with vines, or with fruit trees.

Incanus (-a, -um). Hoary, grey. Ex. *Statice incana.*

Incarnatus (-a, -um). Flesh-coloured. Ex. *Passiflora incarnata.*

Incarvillea (in-kar-vil′le-a. Fam. Bignoniaceae). Herbaceous perennials with pinnate foliage and beautiful heads of tubular flowers, doubtfully hardy in cold areas.

Selection. I. delavayi, China, Tibet, 3 ft, bright rose trumpet flowers, early summer; and v. 'Bees' Pink'; *grandiflora,* Yunnan, 15 in., rose-red; and v. *brevipes,* crimson; *lutea,* SW. China, 15 in., yellow; *olgae,* Turkestan, 2 ft, pink; and *younghusbandii,* Tibet, 1 ft, rose-purple, summer.

Cultivation. Plant March–April, well-drained, humus-rich soil, in borders, protecting in winter with a good covering of litter.

Propagation. By division in March; by seeds sown under glass, bottom heat of 15·5° C. (60° F.).

Incisus (-a, -um). Deeply cut. Ex. *Prunus incisa.*

Indehiscent. Of fruits which do not burst open when the seeds are ripe.

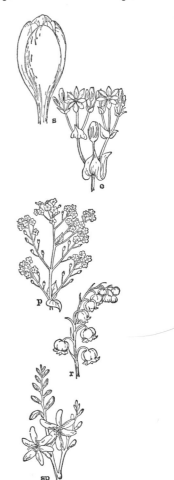

FIG. 129 Inflorescences: s. solitary flower; c. cyme; p. branched panicle; r. raceme; sp. branched spike.

Indian Corn. See *Zea*.
Indian Cress. See *Tropaeolum*.
Indian Fig. See *Opuntia*.
Indian Pink. See *Dianthus chinensis*.
Indian Shot. See *Canna*.
Indiarubber Plant. See *Ficus elastica*.
Indigenous. Native.
Indigofera (in-di-gof'er-a. Fam.
Leguminosae). A large genus of
deciduous shrubs, with pinnate leaves
and slender racemes of broom-like
flowers in summer.

Selection. I. amblyantha, China, to
6 ft, rose pink flowers, July–October;
gerardiana, Himalaya, to 8 ft, rosy-
purple; *hebepetala*, Himalaya, 4 ft, dark
crimson; *potaninii*, China, 4 ft, rosy-
pink, are reasonably hardy, but *I.
incarnata* (*decora*), China, Japan, 1 ft,
white, crimson, and v. *alba*, may be cut
to the base in winter.

Cultivation. Plant in March–April,
well-drained, porous loam, sunny
sheltered positions in wall borders;
prune in March, cutting flowered shoots
back.

Propagation. Cuttings of young shoots,
July–August, in propagating frame or
under handlights. By seeds sown in April,
warm seed-bed, sandy loam.

Indivisus (-a, -um). Undivided. Ex.
Dracaena indivisa.

Indumentum. The hairy or down
covering of a plant.

Indusium. The membrane covering the
spore cases of Ferns.

Inermis (-e). Unarmed, without spines
or thorns.

Inflorescence. The arrangement of the
flowers on the part of the stem above the
last stem leaves, including the branch
stems, stalks (peduncles), bracts and
actual flowers. (*See* Fig. 129, page 287.)

Infundibuliform. Funnel-shaped.

Inodorus (-a, -um). Without smell.

Insecticides. Horticulturally insecticides include substances which destroy
insects, and other pests such as mites,
woodlice, millipedes, slugs and snails,
and are increasingly termed pesticides.
They must not only be lethal to plant
pests, but unlikely to do harm to the
plants, to humans or animals or to
beneficial organisms. Insecticides are
usually designed to kill pests on contact
with them, or by acting as a stomach
poison, or both; and the timing and

mode of application are highly important. Application may be made in the
form of dusts, granules, sprays, aerosols
or smokes, according to conditions. The
important insecticides used in gardening
are:

Azobenzene, an acaricide, used to
control red spider mite eggs and young
active mites in greenhouses; on most
established plants, but not Gerbera, ferns,
roses, Schizanthus, seedlings or young
plants; in aerosol or smoke generators.

* *BHC* (*Benzene hexachloride*); preferably gamma-BHC (lindane); to control
sucking and biting insects (aphids,
capsid bugs, sawflies, thrips, whiteflies,
etc.) as a spray; wireworms, cabbage root
fly, flea beetles, leatherjackets, chafer
grubs in the soil as a dust; as a smoke
under glass; on most plants but not on
currants, cucumbers, hydrangeas,
marrows, melons, potatoes, carrots,
roses, young tomatoes or vines.

Calomel (mercurous chloride), used as
a 4 per cent dust to control cabbage root
fly and onion fly.

* *Chlordane*, a chlorinated hydrocarbon,
which may be used with care to control
earthworms in lawns. Derris is safest.

* *DDT*, persistent chlorinated hydrocarbon, for use early in the season, to
control biting insects, especially beetles,
weevils, capsids, caterpillars, thrips and
whiteflies in dust, spray, smoke or
aerosol; on most plants, except cucumbers, marrows and melons; but not on
food plants near to harvest.

Derris, extracted from roots of
Derris, spp., of which the active ingredient is chiefly rotenone. Used to
control most biting insects, caterpillars,
and red spider mites as a dust or spray;
also to control earthworms in lawns;
non-poisonous to humans and animals.

Dimethoate, systemic organophosphorus insecticide and acaricide, breaking down quickly (Rogor).

DNOC or *DNC* (dinitro-ortho-cresol),
chiefly used in petroleum oil in winter
to control over-wintering aphis eggs,
capsids, winter moths, red spider mites,
scale insects, lichens and mosses, and
check apple mildew, as a spray and
alternative wash to tar-oil.

Kelthane, based on dicofol, a persistent

* Hazardous to wild life if misused.

acaricide, to control red spider mites and their eggs; used as a spray or atomizing solution in greenhouses.

Lead Arsenate, no longer recommended for garden use.

Lime Sulphur, primarily a fungicide, but used in spray form to control currant big bud mites (*see* Currants, Black).

Malathion, an organophosphorus compound, used to control most sucking insects (aphids, apple sucker, leafhoppers, mealy bugs, scale insects, caterpillars, sawflies, red spider mites thrips, weevils and whiteflies) on most plants but not on Antirrhinum, Crassula, Ferns, Petunias, Sweet Peas or Zinnias; in spray, dust or aerosol form.

Menazon, systemic organophosphorus compound, for the control of sap-sucking insects (aphids, etc.), applied as a spray and soil drench; but not within four weeks of harvesting food plants.

Mercuric Chloride (corrosive sublimate), once used to control cabbage root fly and onion fly, but highly poisonous and superseded by calomel.

Metaldehyde, a molluscicide, held to anaesthetize slugs and snails so that they dry off in the open; chiefly used in a pelleted bait form to protect plants, or as an emulsion spray; toxic to humans and animals in its concentrated form.

Nicotine, highly poisonous to humans and animals, but a good contact poison of sucking insects, such as aphids, capsids, leaf miners and thrips in warm weather; volatile and non-persistent; used as a spray; or in greenhouse as a fumigant.

Paradichlorobenzene, chlorinated hydrocarbon, volatile, and chiefly used as a soil fumigant to control wireworms, leatherjackets and soil pests.

Parathion, an organophosphorus compound, not now normally available to gardeners, coming under the Agricultural (Poisonous Substances) Regulations; but effective against chrysanthemum eelworms, as well as many sucking insect pests.

Petroleum Oil Washes, at winter strength used to control red spider mites; at summer strength to control red spider mites, thrips, scale and whiteflies in the greenhouse; except on Asparagus Fern, Carnations, Salvia or Smilax.

Phenatol, 20 per cent phenkapton, an organophosphorus compound, safer to use than parathion in controlling red spider mites on fruit trees in summer.

Pyrethrum, the ground flower-heads of *Chrysanthemum cinerariaefolium* and related plants, containing pyrethrins which have a quick knockdown paralytic effect on many insects, and being non-toxic to animals and humans are useful for use on food plants, in dust or spray form.

Quassia, an extract of *Picrasma excelsa,* a tropical tree, used chiefly to control aphids, being non-poisonous to animals and humans; may be combined to nicotine; used as a spray.

Rogor, 40 per cent dimethoate, an organophosphorus compound, safer to handle than parathion, and used to control red spider mites, aphids, woolly aphids, apple sucker, plum sawfly, leaf hoppers, etc., as a spray.

Tar-oil Washes, distillates of coal tar, used to control aphid eggs, apple sucker, scale insects, lichens and mosses on dormant fruit trees in winter.

Thiocyanate, usually in petroleum oil, and used as an alternative to tar-oil as a winter fruit tree wash for the control of aphid eggs, etc.

Trichlorphon, organophosphorus insecticide, of quick action and breakdown, for sap-sucking and biting pests.

See Sprayers and Spraying.

Insectivorous Plants. These are plants which have developed organs by which they catch insects, and absorb them to obtain nitrogen for their nourishment; they include *Dionaea muscipula,* Venus's Fly Trap; *Drosera anglica, D. intermedia, D. rotundifolia,* the Sundews; *Pinguicula vulgaris,* Butterwort; *Nepenthes* spp., and *Sarracenia* spp., Pitcher Plants; and *Darlingtonia californica.*

Insects. Insecta embraces the most numerous class of terrestrial arthropods. There are over 21,000 species in Britain. They play highly important parts in the garden. Attention tends to be focused on those which feed and are parasitic on plants, but many species are directly or indirectly beneficial, especially the pollinating insects (bees, bumble bees, etc.), the scavenging insects (dung beetles, ground beetles, etc.), and the predatory insects which feed on the parasitic (ichneumon wasps, ladybirds, etc.). Adult insects are characterized by having an external jointed skeleton of hardened cuticle (chitin); a body of three main segments—the head, bearing a pair of antennae or feelers; the thorax, bearing three pairs of legs and usually one or two pairs of wings; and the abdomen, containing part of the alimentary system and reproductive organs. Breathing is tracheal, air entering through spiracles, minute holes along the sides of the body to pass through tubes (tracheae and thraceoles) to all parts, and flowing freely in and out. The typical life cycle passes through three stages, egg, larva and pupa, to adult insect; but some insects (Earwigs, Cockroaches, Aphids, Capsid Bugs, Scale Insects, Mealy Bugs and Thrips) have incomplete or no pupal stage. Of the twenty-seven families, those likely to be encountered in the garden are: *Collembola* (Springtails); *Orthoptera* (Cockroaches, Grasshoppers); *Dermaptera* (Earwigs); *Odonata* (Dragonflies); *Thysanoptera* (Thrips); *Hemiptera* (Bugs, Aphids, Leaf-hoppers, Scales, Mealy Bugs, Whiteflies); *Lepidoptera* (Butterflies and Moths); *Coleoptera* (Beetles and Weevils); *Diptera* (two-winged Flies); and *Hymenoptera* (Ants, Bees, Sawflies, Gall-wasps, Ichneumon Wasps and Wasps).

Insignis (-e). Remarkable, striking. Ex. *Rhododendron insigne*.

Intercellular Space. The space between plant cells, by which air and gases diffuse from one part to another of a plant.

Internode. The space between the nodes or joints on a plant stem.

Introse. Of anthers opening inwards towards the centre or pistil of a flower.

Inula (in'u-la. Fam. Compositae). Hardy herbaceous perennials with ray-petalled, yellow flower-heads in summer.

Selection. I. ensifolia, Caucasus, 9 in.; *oculis-Christi*, E. Europe, 1 ft; *orientalis*, Caucasus, 2 ft; and *royleana*, Himalaya, 2 ft, are the pick. *I. helenium*, the native Elecampane, 3–4 ft, is best planted in the wild garden.

Cultivation. Plant October–March, ordinary soil, sunny positions, in borders, etc.

Propagation. By division in autumn or spring; by seeds, sown out of doors, April–June.

Ivolucre. The leaf-like bracts forming a calyx-like structure round or below the head (capitulum) of a compound flower, as in the Compositae. An Involucel is a secondary or small involucre.

Involutus (-a, -um). Involute, used of leaves rolled inwards or upwards.

Iodine. An element found in plants, particularly maritime, which, although not essential to their economy, is important as a nutrient essential in human dietary, obtainable from food crops.

Ionopsidium, Violet Cress (i-o-nop-sid'i-um. Fam. Cruciferae). From Portugal, *I. acaule*, 2 in., is a pretty hardy annual, with tufted orbicular leaves, and violet tinged white flowers, late summer, to be sown where it is to flower, in March–April, in the rock garden, or as a pot plant for a window-sill; partial shade.

Ipheion (i-pe'i-on. Fam. Amaryllidaceae). A S. American bulbous plant, *I. uniflorum* (*Brodiaea uniflora, Milla uniflora, Triteleia uniflora*), bears starry, violet-blue flowers on 4–6-in. stems from among grassy tufts of leaves, in April; and may be planted in porous, humus-rich soil, in autumn, 2 in. deep, 6 in. apart, in rock garden or border, sheltered position; to increase by offsets.

Ipomea (i-po-me'a. Fam. Convolvulaceae). A large genus of evergreen and deciduous twining herbs, akin to Convolvulus, Pharbitis and Quamoclit, half-hardy in this country.

Selection. I. bonariensis, Buenos Aires, twiner with purplish trumpet flowers in summer; *horsfalliae*, W. Indies, evergreen, showy deep rose flowers, winter, and v. *briggsii*, magenta-crimson; *gerrardii*, evergreen, Natal, white, yellow-throated flowers, highly scented, summer; and *ternata*, W. Indies, evergreen, white flowers; may be grown in the warm greenhouse, winter temp. 13–18° C. (55–65° F.); being planted in the border or large tubs in spring, to climb trellis or poles. *I. decora*, E. Africa, 3 ft, large white flowers, rosy-purple centred, and *leptophylla*, bush Moon Flower, Texas, 3 ft, rose-pink flowers, summer, are herbaceous perennials for similar conditions, and *pes-tigridis*, tropical Asia, a twining annual, pink-flowering in early summer. *I. pandurata*, Wild Potato Vine of U.S.A., white, purple-throated flowers, summer, and × *hardingii*, rose-purple, are hardy enough for outdoors in mild localities, planted in spring, well-drained loam.

Cultivation. As the roots are usually large and tuberous, they need ample room; liberal watering in active growth; moderate in winter. Prune in February.

Propagation. Evergreens by cuttings of sideshoots in July–August, in propagating frame, bottom heat of 21° C. (70° F.). By seeds, in spring, standard compost, under glass.

Iris (i'ris. Fam. Iridaceae). Containing up to 200 species, largely natives of the temperate zones of the northern hemisphere, the genus is one of more or less hardy herbaceous perennials with bulbous, tuberous or rhizomatous rootstocks, with radical linear or sword-like leaves, and lovely flowers, appearing in sheaths, on opening with a perianth of segments in two whorls of three outer reflexed petals, termed the falls, often bearded, and three inner erect petals, known as standards, around a centre style, often crested, and three stamens inserted at the base of the falls; in a glorious array of colours and beautiful markings. Botanists divide the genus into ten to twelve sections, but as this classification is still being modified, and as many species are outside our scope here, it is more simple to consider them according to their flowering period, and as they are offered in catalogues.

Selection. Winter and early spring flowering species and varieties, Reticulata type, bulbs with reticulated or netted tunics, or Xiphion section: *I. bakeriana*, 6 in., mauve and violet, scented flowers, January–February; *danfordiae*, 6 in., lemon-yellow, February; *histrio*, 6 in., lilac-blue, January–February, and vs.; *histrioides*, 4 in., blue, January; *reticulata*, 6 in., purplish-blue, March, and several vs.; all are natives of Asia Minor, and need planting in August–September, 1½ in. deep, in light, well-drained soil, warm sunny positions, in rock garden or border; or in pans to be grown in the alpine house. Increase is by offsets.

To these may be added the bulbous species with perennial tuberous roots, of the Juno section: *I. aucheri*, Syria, Iraq, 8 in., bluish-white, yellow crested, flowers, March–April; *bucharica*, Bokhara, 1–1½ ft, golden, white, April; *graeberiana*, Turkistan, 6 in., mauve, blue-veined, April; and *planifolia* (*alata*), Mediterranean region, 6 in., light blue to violet, November–January (best grown in the alpine house). Plant as soon as bulbs are available in late summer, in light, porous soil, warm sunny positions, taking care not to injure the tuberous roots. Increase is slow, but may be propagated by careful division in time; difficult in the north.

Late Spring and Summer Flowering bulbous species, and varieties, of the Xiphion or Xiphium section: *I. filifolia*, S. Spain, N. Africa, 1½ ft, mauve-purple flower, June; *tingitana*, N. Africa, 1½–2 ft, violet-blue flower, May, are best grown in a cool greenhouse, standard compost, planted in September, as too tender for all but the warmest sunny corners in mild localities outdoors. *I. xiphioides*, Pyrenees, 1–2 ft, deep blue, golden patch, flowers, June, is the parent of the 'English' Iris; *xiphium*, Spain, S. France, 1–2 ft, deep to light purple, yellow striped flower, is the parent of the 'Spanish' Iris; their cross and inter-breeding with other species are the origins of the 'Dutch' Iris; and these cultivated Irises are now grown to the exclusion of the species. The Dutch Irises, 1½–2 ft tall, flower in early June, providing the widest range of flower colours, good kinds being 'Blue Champion', 'Golden Harvest', 'Bronze Queen', 'King Mauve', 'Lemon Queen', 'Princess Irene' (white) and 'Wedgwood'. The Spanish Irises, 1½–2 ft, flower a fortnight later, a token choice being 'Afterglow' (violet, yellow, orange); 'Cajanus', yellow; 'Canary Bird', bright yellow; 'Hercules', purplish blue, bronze; 'King of the Blues'; 'Prince Henry', purple brown, and 'Queen Wilhelmina', white. The English Irises, 1½–2 ft, flower in late June–early July, and include 'Almona', pale violet and blue; 'Delft Blue'; 'Mirabeau', purple; 'Mont Blanc', white; 'Prince Albert', silvery blue; 'Queen of the Blues', and 'The Giant', rich deep blue. Bulbs are best planted in

September, 4 in. deep, porous, well-drained soil, humus-rich; sunny position. When foliage withers, bulbs may be lifted, and dried off until planting time comes again. Propagation by offset bulbils.

The rhizomatous Irises may be divided into the Bearded (Pogon section), Beardless (Apogon section) and Crested (Evansia section). The Bearded may be

FIG. 130 *Iris germanica* v.

further divided into the Tall Bearded, which includes species such as *I. flavescens*, 3 ft, lemon yellow; *florentina*, the Fleur-de-Lis of France, 3 ft, white; *germanica*, the Common Iris, 2–3 ft, bright purple, and v. *kharput*, with red-edged leaves; *mellita*, SE. Europe, 5 in., smoky brown; *pallida*, 2–3 ft, pale purple; and *trojana*, 2 ft, reddish purple; but the bearded Flag or German Irises of our gardens are hybrids of complex breeding, a modern short list being: white—'White City'; cream—'Starshine'; light blue—'Great Lakes', 'Helen McGregor'; medium blue—'Blue Rhythm', 'Pierre Ménard'; deep blue—'Black Hills'; pink—'Cherie',

'Pink Cameo', 'Pink Formal', 'Radiation'; red—'Cordovan', 'Garden Glory'; yellow—'Benton Duff', 'Benton Honey', 'Moonlight Sonata'; variegated —'Gypsy', 'Red Torch'; with many others on specialists' lists. Tall Bearded Irises flower in May–June. Dwarf Bearded, which include species such as *I. flavissima*, Hungary, 3 in., yellow; *pumila*, Austria, Hungary, 4 in., blue, and v. *azurea*; *chamaeiris*, S. Europe, 9 in., blue, purple; and hybrids of which the newer vs. such as 'Blue Mascot', 5 in., lilac-blue; 'Keepsake', 7 in., golden yellow; 'Mist o' Pink', 7 in., mulberry pink; 'Moongleam', 7 in., cream-yellow; 'Tiny Tony', 6 in., wine red; and 'Tiny Treasure', 6 in., golden yellow, are typical; all flowering in April–May. All Bearded Irises are planted in October or March, in well-drained soil, enriched with humus-forming organic material, limed to a pH 6·5, in full sun. The rhizomes are planted half-in, half-out of the soil. After three years, plants should be lifted and divided, and propagated by cutting off the young healthy end rhizomes for replanting, in September–October. Other Bearded Irises are the Cushion Iris (Oncocyclus), natives of Asia Minor and Syria, flowering May–June, from rhizomes planted in October, well-drained, humus-rich soil, warm full sun, given protection from wet; but they are difficult to grow; the easiest is *I. susiana*, the Mourning Iris, 1–1½ ft, brownish black on white; others include *gatesii*, 14 in., silvery white and purple; *lortetii*, Lebanon, 1 ft, dark veined violet; and *sari*, 8 in., yellow; perhaps best attempted in pots, or under cloches after studying their habitat and needs; and Regelia Irises, from Turkestan, more easily grown in well-drained soil, given humus and lime, and full sun; *I. hoogiana*, 1½–2 ft, porcelain blue, May; *korolkowi*, 1–1½ ft, pale white, chocolate markings, May; *stolonifera*, 2 ft, light brownish purple, late May, and *flavissima* is sometimes included here; covering with a cloche after flowering is helpful; inter-crossing of these two groups has resulted in several relatively hardy Regelio-cyclus hybrids, good forms being 'Ancilla', 1 ft, blue; 'Bocena', 1½ ft, deep violet; 'Clara', 1½ ft, purplish black on white; 'Sylphide', 1½ ft, white, brownish grey netted; and 'Mercurius', 1½ ft, deep violet. Propagation by division, September.

The Beardless, Apogon section, Irises are numerous and vary in their requirements. They include *I. crocea* (*aurea*), Kashmir, 3 ft, golden, June; *bulleyana*, W. China, 1½ ft, bright blue, June–July; *chrysographes*, Yunnan, 1½ ft, purple-blue, June; *forrestii*, Yunnan, 1–1½ ft, yellow, June–July; × *ochraurea*, 4 ft, yellow, white, June–July; *ochroleuca*, Asia Minor, 4 ft, white, yellow, June–July; *siberica*, Russia, 3–4 ft, blue-purple, June; and *sanguinea* (*orientalis*), Japan, 2 ft, violet-blue, June, and their hybrids such as 'Caesar', 'Emperor', 'Heron', 'Perry's Blue', 'Pickanock' and 'Snow Queen'; and *tenax*, Oregon, 1 ft, claret and yellow, June; for moisture-retentive soil in borders, September–October planting; dwarfer kinds, such as *douglasiana*, California, 8 in., blue, gold, May; *innominata*, Oregon, 6 in., apricot to mauve, June; and *ruthenica*, Siberia to China, 8 in., creamy-white, violet, May, may be planted in rock gardens, well-drained, humus-rich soil, warm sunny positions; while *I. fulva*, S. U.S.A., 2–3 ft, reddish brown, June–July; *kaempferi*, Japan, 2–3 ft, and its cultivated vs. such as 'Attraction', 'Matsu-No-Ju', 'Purple Splendour', 'Ruby' and 'Violet Queen'; *laevigata*, Japan, 2–3 ft, blue, June–July, and v. *albopurpurea*, and *pseudacorus*, the native Yellow Flag, 2–3 ft, June–July, and its vs., make excellent growth in moist, rich soil, bog garden or the shallows of pools. *I. unguicularis*, Algeria, 1½–2 ft, lilac, scented flowers, November–March, should be planted in April, in poor, porous dry soil at the foot of a sunny wall, in mild localities, and left alone. The Crested Irises (Evansia section) are rather exacting in their needs: *I. cristata*, SE. U.S.A., 6 in., lilac, deep yellow crested flowers, May; *lacustris*, similar but smaller; and *gracilipes*, Japan, 9 in., pinkish-lilac, orange-crested, do reasonably well in a rock garden scree, well watered during active growth, and partial shade; *japonica*, China, Japan, preferably Ledger's variety, 1–1½ ft, lilac, yellow crested, April, needs well-drained, moist

soil, partial shade, in mild localities; while *tectorum*, Japan, 12 in., lilac, white crested flowers, May–June, needs well-drained soil, enriched with humus, and partial shade, being lifted and divided every second year. Alternatively, in the north and cold areas, the crested Irises are best pan-grown in the cool greenhouse.

Diseases. Leaf Spot is a fungus disease (*Didymellina gracile*), causing brown spotting on leaves, and Rust, *Puccinia iridis*, yellow-brown pustules on leaves, sometimes occur in damp, over-shady conditions; but are controlled by a copper fungicide. Rhizomes may suffer Soft Rot, *Bacterium carotovormum*, reducing them to bad-smelling pulp. Affected parts should be cut out, and clean surfaces dusted with copper-lime dust.

Pests. The chief specific pest is the Iris Sawfly, *Rhadinoceraea micans*, the larvae of which eat along the leaf margins of bog Irises, and may be controlled by careful spraying with a malathion insecticide to wet the foliage, but must not fall in water where there are fish. Aphids are sometimes troublesome, and should be painted with malathion insecticide, or wetted with nicotine insecticide in summer.

Irish Heath. See *Daboecia*.

Irish Yew. See *Taxus baccata* v. *fastigiata*.

Isatis, Dyer's Weed, Woad (i'sat-is. Fam. Cruciferae). The biennial, *I. tintoria*, Britain and Europe, 2–4 ft, with long, erect racemes of yellow flowers, may be grown from seed sown, May–June, open ground, at one time grown as the source of the blue dye, Woad.

Itea (i'te-a. Fam. Saxifragaceae). Flowering shrubs of which *I. virginiana*, E. U.S.A., 3–6 ft, with erect, creamy-white racemes of flowers, July, and toothed oval leaves, sometimes turning bright red in autumn before falling, is hardy, for well-drained, rather acid peaty soil; *illicifolia*, W. China, to 12 ft, is evergreen with holly-like leaves, and greenish-white flowers, August, but only for very mild localities. Plant in October or March. Propagation by cuttings of firm young shoots, taken with a heel, July–August, in a frame.

Ivy. See *Hedera*.

Ivy-leaved Pelargonium. See *Pelargonium*.

Ixia (icks'i-a. Fam. Iridaceae). Cormous plant of S. Africa, with linear leaves, and stiff, thin stems, carrying panicles of pretty, open, bell-shaped flowers, up to 2 ft tall, brilliantly coloured, in May–June. Only hardy enough for the warmest, sheltered gardens, they are best grown in pots in the cool greenhouse.

Selection. I. maculata, 1 ft, orange flowering; *paniculata*, creamy white flowers; and *viridiflora*, 1 ft, green flowers, are the chief species offered; and it is more usual to grow named varieties, such as 'Afterglow', orange, amber, dark red centre; 'Artemis', white and carmine; 'Bluebird', blue centre; 'Hogarth', creamy-white, purple centre; 'Hubert', tawny orange, magenta; 'Rose Queen', soft pink; 'Vulcan', scarlet, shaded orange; 'Wonder', double rose-pink, and others.

Cultivation. Plant October–November, six corms to a 6-in. pot, standard compost, plunge in a frame, and when shoots appear move to a cool greenhouse, watering moderately, temp. 7–10° C. (45–50° F.), giving ample light. Rest dry, when foliage withers.

Propagation. By offsets at planting time.

Ixiolirion (icks-i-o-lir'i-on. Fam. Amaryllidaceae). Hardy bulbous plants of W. and central Asia for mild localities, with linear leaves, stiffish stems of 1–1½ ft, trumpet-like star-shaped flowers, in summer.

Selection. I. kolpakowskianum, blue flowering; *montanum*, blue, and vs. *macranthum*, deep blue; and *sintenisii*, pale blue, are good.

Cultivation. Plant October–November, well-drained sunny borders, humus-rich, with protection against frosts, or in pots in a cool greenhouse, standard compost. Propagation by offsets, but slow.

Ixora (icks-or'a. Fam. Rubiaceae). Tropical evergreen flowering shrubs, with corymbs of brilliant flowers, esteemed for the warm greenhouse.

Selection. I. coccinea, E. Indies, 3 ft, bright summer flowers; and vs. *fraseri*, reddish-salmon; *pilgrimii*, orange-scarlet; *lutea*, E. Indies, 3 ft, pale yellow, summer; *macrothyrsa*, Sumatra, 2–3 ft, deep-red; and *splendens*, 2 ft, coppery scarlet.

Cultivation. Pot in March–April, standard compost, water freely in growth and in summer, more moderately in winter, minimum temp. 13° C. (55° F.). Pinch tips to make bushy.

Propagation. By firm, young cuttings in spring or summer, in pots, in propagating frame, bottom heat of 27° C. (80° F.).

J

Jacaranda (jak-a-ran'da. Fam. Bignoniaceae). The chief species grown, *J. mimosifolia* (*ovalifolia*), Brazil, to 8 ft, a deciduous shrub, with fine, fern-like pinnate leaves, and drooping tubular lavender blue flowers in summer, for the warm greenhouse or conservatory, grown in pots or border. Pot in March, standard compost, water freely in growth, very moderately in winter, temp. minimum 10° C. (50° F.). Prune after flowering if necessary. Propagation by cuttings taken in early summer in propagating case.

Jacobaea. Now *Senecio* (q.v.).

Jacobean Lily. See *Sprekelia formosissima*.

Jacobinia (jak-o-bin'i-a. Fam. Acanthaceae). Beautiful flowering shrubby plants of tropical America, grown in the warm greenhouse or hothouse.

Selection. J. carnea, Brazil, to 6 ft, pink, summer; *chrysostephana*, Mexico, 3 ft, leaves red ribbed beneath, yellow tubular flowers, winter; *coccinea*, Brazil, to 5 ft, scarlet, February; *ghiesbreghtiana*, Mexico, 2 ft, scarlet, winter; and *pauciflora*, Brazil, 1–2 ft, scarlet, tipped yellow, summer, are usually grown.

Cultivation. Pot in late March, water freely in active growth, moderately in winter; minimum temp. 10° C. (50° F.). Prune shoots near to base after flowering.

Propagation. By cuttings of young shoots, in propagating case, April–June, bottom heat of 18° C. (65° F.).

Jacob's Ladder. See *Polemonium coeruleum*.

Jamesia (jam-es'i-a. Fam. Saxifragaceae). The species grown is *J. americana*, Western N. America, a deciduous shrub of 4 ft, with coarse-toothed leaves, and cymes of small, white, fragrant, 5-parted flowers, in May; hardy except in the coldest areas, and thriving in any well-drained, porous soil and sun. Propagation by

firm young shoots in July–August, in cold frame.

Japanese Cedar. See *Cryptomeria*.

Japanese Cherries. See *Prunus*.

Japanese Maple. See *Acer palmatum*.

Japanese Yew. See *Taxus cuspidata*.

Japonicus (-a, -um). Of Japan. Ex. *Mahonia japonica*.

Jasione, Sheep's-bit Scabious (ja-si-o'ne. Fam. Campanulaceae). Blue-flowering perennial herbs of neat habit and suitable for the rock garden.

Selection. J. humilis, Pyrenees, 4 in., short-stemmed blue flowers, summer; *jankae*, Hungary, 6 in., tufted, blue, summer; and *perennis*, W. Europe, 9 in., tiny scabious-like blue flowers, summer, are perennial; *montana*, the native Sheep's-bit, 6 in., is normally biennial but may persist as a perennial, or produce its pale blue flowers as an annual.

Cultivation. Plant in October or March, rather light well-drained soil and sun.

Propagation. By division in March. By seeds in spring or autumn (under cloches or in cold frame).

Jasmine. See *Jasminum*.

Jasmine, Box. A common name sometimes used for *Phillyrea* spp. (q.v.).

Jasmine, Rock. See *Androsace*.

Jasminum, Jasmine (jas-mi'num. Fam. Oleaceae). This genus contains climbing, rambling and erect-growing shrubs from temperate and warm regions; some are hardy, others need greenhouse conditions.

Selection. Of the hardy plants, *J. nudiflorum*, China, deciduous rambler to 10 ft, is the indispensable winter-flowering Jasmine, to train on walls, or drape over rocks; *officinale*, Persia, N. China, the common Jasmine, a twining climber, pinnate-leaved, with clusters of white scented flowers, summer, and vs. *affine*, with larger flowers, and *aureum*, yellow-variegated leaves;

FIG. 131 *Jasminum officinale*, Summer Jasmine.

beesianum, China, scented rose flowers, May, and × *stephanense*, to 20 ft, clusters of pale pink flowers, June, are worth while. *J. parkeri*, NW. India, 6 in., evergreen tufted shrub, yellow flowers in June, may be grown in a warm corner of the rock garden; *fruticans*, Mediterranean, 3–5 ft, yellow flowers, June; *humile*, Italy, 3–4 ft, yellow flowers, summer; *revolutum*, Himalaya, spreading shrub, yellow flowers, summer; and *glabrum*, Nepal, to 4 ft, yellow, summer, are usually semi-evergreen, and need warm sheltered position in most gardens. Any well-drained ordinary soil suits the hardy Jasmines, and they are planted in October or March–April; and may be pruned after flowering.

Jasmines for the warm greenhouse include *J. gracillimum*, Borneo, large white, fragrant flowers, winter; *floridum*, China, evergreen, yellow flowering, July–September, trained on a pillar or a wall; *polyanthemum*, China, to 20 ft, climber, highly scented white and rose flowers, summer; and *primulinum*, China, rambling to 12 ft, bright yellow

flowering, March–April. Plant October or March–April, standard compost, large pots, or in beds; water freely in active growth, moderately in winter, temp. 10–13° C. (50–55° F.) minimum.

Propagation. Out of doors by layers spring, or by detached suckers. Greenhouse species by young shoots taken with a heel, and rooted in propagating case, summer.

Jeffersonia (jef-fer-so'ni-a. Fam. Berberidaceae). Small perennial woodland plants for shady positions in the rock garden or alpine house.

Selection. J. diphylla, Tennessee, 4–6 in., reniform, lobed leaves of long stalks, and white, open bell-shaped flowers, April; and *dubia*, Manchuria, 4 in., rounded, two-lobed leaves, and pale blue flowers, May.

Cultivation. Plant in July, sandy soil, enriched with peat, in cool shade.

Propagation. By careful division in July. By seeds sown as soon as ripe, in cold frame.

Jerusalem Artichoke. *See* Artichoke.

Jerusalem Cherry. See *Solanum.*

Jerusalem Sage. See *Phlomis.*

Jessamine. Alias Jasmine. See *Jasminum.*

Job's Tears. See *Coix.*

Joint. A node on a plant stem; the part from which a leaf or leaves are produced.

Jonquil. See *Narcissus jonquilla.*

Jovellana (jo-vel-la'na. Fam. Scrophulariaceae). Two shrubby species, *J. sinclairii*, New Zealand, 2 ft, with panicles of white to lilac, red-spotted, flowers, June, and hairy, coarse-toothed leaves; and *violacea*, Chile, to 6 ft, yellowish white, purple-spotted flowers, July, small evergreen leaves; may be pot-grown in the cool greenhouse, or outdoors in mild localities, in sunny warm sheltered positions, and increased by suckers.

Judas Trees. See *Cercis.*

Juglans (ju'glans. Fam. Juglandaceae). Deciduous trees, characterized by pinnate leaves and male flowers in drooping catkins, female in small greenish pistillate flowers and nutty fruits or drupes; given to leafing out later than most trees, and are slow to start fruiting.

Selection. J. cathayensis, the Chinese

Walnut, to 60 ft, is handsome, with leaves up to 3 ft long, and *sieboldiana*, Japan, to 50 ft, with long leaves and distinctive long catkins, are good big ornamental trees for specimen planting. *J. nigra* is the Black Walnut of E. U.S.A., to 120 ft, grown for timber; and *J. regia*, and its vs., E. Europe, is the common Walnut grown for its nuts and timber; vs. *laciniata*, with finely cut leaves, is very attractive, and *pendula* is a stiffly weeping form. *See* Walnuts.

Cultivation. Plant October–March, in well-drained, deep humus-rich soil, open position. Prune when necessary when in full leaf, June–July.

Propagation. Species by seeds, sown in March, after stratification in damp sand, during winter; varieties by grafting in spring.

Junceus (-a, -um) ; Junci-. Rush-like. Ex. *Narcissus juncifolius.*

June Drop. Descriptive of the premature dropping of fruitlets or immature fruits from apples and stone fruits that often occurs in June, when they fall in fair numbers more or less all at once. It is thought to be caused by fluctuating growing conditions, rainfall, temperature, etc., especially where the soil is not ideal.

Juniperus, Juniper (ju-nip'e-rus. Fam. Pinaceae). Evergreen coniferous shrubs and trees with juvenile awl- or needle-shaped leaves, and scale-like adult leaves.

Selection. Hardy species and vs. are *J. chinensis*, China, to 60 ft, slender, erect, pyramidal; more dwarf and compact in vs. *aurea*, golden-leaved, and *albo-variegata*, creamy variegation; *communis*, the common Juniper, is native, 3–20 ft, with outstanding vs.

compressa, cone-shaped, slow-growing to no more than 2 ft, *cracovia*, Polish Juniper, to 15 ft, weeping at the branch tips; *hibernica*, the fastigiate Irish Juniper, silver foliage; *J. conferta*, Japan, a prostrate dwarf; *coxii*, Burma, to 80 ft, with beautiful pendulous branchlets; *drupaea*, the Syrian Juniper, distinctive, columnar to 60 ft; *horizontalis*, N. America, and vs. *douglasii* and *plumosa* are creeping Junipers, making good ground cover; *recurva*, the Drooping Juniper, Himalaya, to 40 ft; *rigida*, Japan, to 30 ft, attractively drooping; *sabina*, the Savin, Europe, shrubby, to 12 ft, has fine vs. in ' Knap Hill ', *pfitzeriana* and *tamariscifolia*, the spreading Spanish Juniper; *squamata*, Himalaya, etc., is shrubby, but v. *fargesii* makes a fine tree to 40 ft; *meyeri*, an attractive bush, and *wilsonii* grows erectly bushy; *virginiana*, the Pencil Cedar of N. America, to 100 ft, is the tallest of the Junipers, and has variegated silver and golden forms; v. *burkii* is bushy; *cupressifolia* has upright growing branches; *glauca*, silvery or blue-green leaves; and *pendula nana*, an unusual dwarf bush of 2 ft, for the rock garden.

Cultivation. Plant September–October or March–April; almost any soil not waterlogged, and on chalk. On poor soils growth may be stunted.

Propagation. Species by seeds, spring or summer. By cuttings of young shoots, in a cold frame; August–September.

Juvenile. Youthful. Several plants are different in habit and in leaf in their young stages of growth from when mature; e.g. Eucalyptus, Chamaecyparis, Juniperus, etc.

K

Kaffir Lily. See *Schizostyllis*.

Kainit. A crude natural salt containing chloride and sulphate of potash, combined with sodium chloride (salt), magnesium sulphate, etc., roughly 14 per cent potash, 50–60 per cent sodium chloride, 20 per cent magnesium sulphate, and other salts. It may be used in autumn or winter as a potassic fertilizer on sandy or lightish soils or peaty soils, but is less useful on clays, at 2–3 oz. per sq. yd.

Kalanchoe.   (kal-an-ko'e.   Fam. Crassulaceae). Tropical succulent plants with opposite succulent leaves and terminal crowded panicles of colourful flowers in winter for the warm greenhouse or house.

Selection. *K. blossfeldiana*, Madagascar, 12 in., notched green leaves, edged red, and sweetly scented orange-red flowers, late winter; *flammea*, Somaliland, 12–15 in., scarlet, spring; *marmorata*, Eritrea, 2 ft, white, spring; and *teretifolia*, S. Arabia, 3 ft, white, spring, are perennials for the warm greenhouse.

Cultivation. Sow seeds, February–March, standard compost, bottom heat of 18° C. (65° F.); pot on in well-drained pots, watering freely in growth, moderately in winter, minimum temp. 10° C. (50° F.).

Propagation. By cuttings of young shoots, spring or autumn; dried off for a few hours before insertion.

Kale (*Brassica oleracea* v. *acephala*). *See* Borecole.

Kalmia (kal'mi-a. Fam. Ericaceae). Charming, hardy, evergreen shrubs of N. America, with oval leaves, in pairs of threes, and clusters of cup-shaped flowers in June, to grow in association with rhododendrons and other lime-intolerant shrubs.

Selection. *K. angustifolia*, Sheep Laurel, 2–3 ft, purplish-rose flowers; and vs. *ovata*, rose, and *rubra*, crimson;

latifolia, Calico Bush, Mountain Laurel. to 18 ft, rose to pink and white; and *polifolia* (*glauca*), to 2 ft, rosy-lilac, are hardy for all but the coldest areas.

Cultivation. Plant September–October, or April–May; well-drained, lime-free soil, enriched with peat or leaf-mould. May also be pot-grown in the cold greenhouse, to flower a little earlier.

Propagation. By cuttings of young shoots, in a cold frame, August; by seeds in a frame in spring.

Kalosanthes. See *Rochea*.

Kaulfussia. See *Charieis*.

Keel. The two basal petals of a papilionaceous flower, resembling a boat's lower structure.

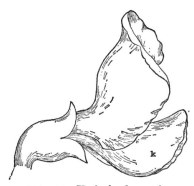

FIG. 132   Keel of a flower: k.

Kelp. The ash obtained from burning seaweed; contains up to 18 per cent potash, and may be used as a fertilizer. *See* Seaweed.

Kentia. See *Howea*.

Kentranthus   (ken-tran'thus.   Fam. Valerianaceae). Pretty, easily grown flowering herbs for ordinary soil, sun or partial shade.

Selection. *K. macrosiphon*, Spain, 2 ft,

compact, large heads of rosy-carmine flowers, July, and v. *alba*, are hardy annuals, easily grown from seed sown in March where they are to grow; *ruber*, Pretty Betsy, Red Valerian, Europe, 2–3 ft, with cymes of red flowers, June–August, is perennial, with vs. *albus*, white, and *roseus*, rose; easily raised from March-sown or autumn-sown seeds, and likely to sow itself if neglected; with fleshy roots, seedlings can be moved in autumn or early spring.

Kentucky Coffee Tree. See *Gymnocladus*.

Kermes Oak. See *Quercus coccifera*.

Kerria, Jew's Mallow (ker'ri-a. Fam. Rosaceae). The one species, *K. japonica*, China, Japan, 6–8 ft, with green branches and alternate, toothed, pointed leaves, single terminal yellow flowers, is elegant, and has vs. *pleniflora*, with double flowers, April–May, and variegated leafed forms. Hardy and easily grown in any loamy soil in wall borders.

Cultivation. Plant autumn or spring. Propagate by cuttings of young shoots, under a handlight, in spring, or by division in March–April. Prune out the older shoots occasionally, and thin after flowering.

Kidney Bean. *See* Beans.

King-cup. See *Caltha*.

Kirengeshoma (ki-ren-ge-sho'ma. Fam. Saxifragaceae). The only species, *K. palmata*, Japan, 2–4 ft, is a herbaceous perennial, with thin palmately-lobed leaves, and stalked, nodding, bell-shaped, yellow flowers in September. Plant in spring, in moisture-retentive soil, enriched with leaf-mould, in partial shade, border or open woodland. Propagation by division in spring, or by seeds sown in April, out of doors.

Kleinia (kleen'i-a. Fam. Compositae). Perennial succulents and sub-shrubs, of the Canary Isles and Africa, suitable for the cool greenhouse or the house.

Selection. K. articulata, the Candle Plant, Cape Province, with jointed stems, ivy-like, long-stemmed leaves, pale yellow flowers in winter; *neriifolia*, Canary Isles, 1–3 ft, stems with linear leaves at the tops in winter, dropping in spring; *pendula*, the Inch Worm, Ethiopia, etc., serpentine stems that bend and enter the soil, brilliant red flowers, October; and *tomentosa*, S.

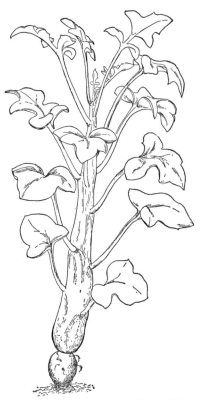

FIG. 133   *Kleinia articulata*, Candle Plant

Africa, 1 ft, cylindrical leaves, clothed in dense, silky white hairs.

Cultivation. Pot in spring, well-drained pots, standard compost, water freely in summer; very little in winter, minimum temp. 10° C. (50° F.). Propagation by detached joints or cuttings, in spring.

Knapweed. Common weed, especially *Centaurea nigra* and *C. scabiosa*.

Kniphofia, Flame Flower, Red Hot Poker, Torch Lily (nip-of'i-a. Fam. Liliaceae). Colourful, herbaceous plants with long, narrow leaves, and showy, cone-like spikes of drooping tubular flowers in summer, at one time listed under Tritoma.

Selection. K. breviflora, S. Africa,

1–1½ ft, yellow-flowering, summer; *corallina*, S. Africa, 2 ft, coral-red, summer; *galpinii*, Transvaal, 1½ ft, flame orange; *macowanii*, S. Africa, 1–1½ ft, orange-red; *nelsoni*, Orange Free State, 1½–2 ft, scarlet; *praecox*, S. Africa, 2 ft, red or yellow; *pumila*, S. Africa, 1½–2 ft, orange-red; and *rooperi*, S. Africa, 2 ft, orange-red, are relatively dwarf; while *leichtlinii*, Ethiopia, 4 ft, vermilion and yellow; *tuckii*, S. Africa, to 5 ft, yellow; and *uvaria*, S. Africa, grows to 6 ft, or more in garden vs. and hybrids, of which 'Autumn Queen', 3 ft, citron yellow; 'Corallina', 3 ft, tangerine red; *grandiflora*, 4ft, orange-scarlet and yellow; 'Maid of Orleans', 3 ft, pale primrose; 'Mount Etna', 5 ft, scarlet; 'Royal Standard', 3½ ft, scarlet and yellow; 'Samuel's Sensation', 5 ft, coral-red; and 'Springtime', 3 ft, buff and red, are selections. *K. longicollis*, Natal, 2 ft, lemon-yellow, late autumn, and *primulina*, Natal, 3–4 ft, light yellow, autumn, are cool greenhouse subjects.

Cultivation. Plant October or March in well-drained, humus-rich soil, in groups; and give litter cover in winter. Or they may be potted in 8–10-in. pots, standard compost, and grown in the cool greenhouse, winter temp. 7° C. (45° F.).

Propagation. By careful division in spring, replanting immediately. By seeds, sown in spring, in cool frame or warm border.

Knot Garden. A formal kind of ornamental bedding of Elizabethan times; with designs outlined by dwarf box, lavender, etc., and planted with flowers.

Knot Grass, Knot Weed. See *Polygonum.*

Kochia (kok'i-a. Fam. Chenopodiaceae). From S. France, etc., *K. scoparia*, Belvedere, 2–3 ft, is grown for its soft feathery fern-like foliage, for the small green summer flowers are insignificant; v. *trichophila*, Summer Cypress, is similar, but the foliage

turns purple-red in autumn; and form *childsii*, Fire Bush, is even more brilliant. They are half-hardy annuals, grown easily from seeds, sown in March, standard compost, bottom heat of 15·5° C. (60° F.), hardened off to plant out in May; or to grow in pots in the cool greenhouse.

Koelreuteria (kol-roo-ter'i-a. Fam. Sapindaceae). Small beautiful trees with pinnate leaves or serrated leaflets, large terminal panicles of bright yellow flowers in summer, and bladder-like capsules containing three seeds; hardy for most gardens.

Selection. K. *apiculata*, Szechwan, 15 ft or more, and *paniculata*, N. China, to 20 ft, the hardier for the north, are usually grown.

Cultivation. Plant October–March, well-drained loam soil, sunny sheltered positions.

Propagation. By seeds in spring; may also be raised from root cuttings, taken about March.

Kohl-rabi, Knol-kohl, Corinthian Turnip (*Brassica oleracea caulorapa*). Literally, a cabbage-turnip, distinctive for its tennis-ball-like swollen stem, bearing leaves, appearing just above ground, that makes good eating. Suitable varieties are 'Earliest White', and 'Early Purple' and 'Model Green'. Seeds are sown in March–July, in rows 12 in. apart, thinning seedlings to 8 in. apart, in well-drained soil, humus-rich from a previous crop. Harvest when young.

Kolkwitzia (kol-kwitz'i-a. Fam. Caprifoliaceae). Represented by one species, *K. amabilis*, W. China, a 5–6-ft deciduous, erect-growing shrub, with opposite, long, pointed and toothed leaves, and corymbs of bell-shaped, pink, yellow-throated flowers in pairs, in May. Plant October–March, well-drained ordinary soil, full sun; and may be propagated by cuttings of young shoots taken with a heel in July–August; inserted in sandy loam under handlight.

L

Labellum. Lip. A term used in describing orchids, referring to the conspicuous front segment.

Labels. Although many gardeners rely on memory and personal knowledge as to the identity of their plants, it is much more satisfactory and helpful to others to use labels. Used fully, a label may provide not only the correct name of a plant, but information on origins, dates of planting and cultural attention. In sowing seeds in batches, raising plants from cuttings, hybridizing and propagative work, labels are essential, and for such purposes small wooden labels are still the most inexpensive, though green celluloid, plastic, aluminium, and anodized metal are more permanent and re-usable. They are available in various sizes, and easily written on, preferably with an indelible, but erasable, plastic or marking ink. One type of plastic label has a prepared dark surface on which the name is scratched with a sharp point. In the garden itself, where permanent labels are required, wooden types should be preservatively treated (preferably with Cuprinol) for long life. Although outdoor labelling should be as unobtrusive as possible, labels need to be easily seen if they are not to be damaged or lost in the soil. For permanence, plastic or metal labels are best. The lead-tape type, with the names punched in, are virtually indestructible, and cast aluminium plates can be obtained for commemorative planting, though perhaps too institutional for private use. The modern trend is to plastic labels, with plant names embossed indelibly on self-adhesive plastic tape by means of a small machine. When labels are attached to stems of shrubs or tress, it is best to use a plastic tie and allow for expansion of the stem in growth. For the serious grower of carnations, chrysanthemums, dahlias, gladioli, etc., plastic record labels on which to inscribe the year's performance and cultural treatment are most useful. The alternative to labelling in the garden is a carefully drawn-to-scale plan, with numbered squares, and a corresponding record book indicating the planting.

Labiatus (-a, -um). Labiate, lipped. Ex. *Cattleya labiata*.

Labrador Tea. See *Ledum*.

Laburnocytisus (la-bur-no-ki′ti-sus.) *L.* × *adami* is a graft hybrid or chimaera, resulting from the grafting of *Cytisus purpureus* on *Laburnum anagyroides* in such a way that the former, the scion, grows within the latter, the stock, together, to form a small tree, curiously interesting though not of great beauty, on which the foliage is usually that of Laburnum, but flowers may be produced in small nodding racemes of purplish-pink, or bud from the outer tissues and be characteristically yellow as of Laburnum, or from the inner tissues and be purple and characteristic of Cytisus, in spring. It first occurred accidentally in a French nursery of M. Adam, after whom it is named; and is propagated by grafting on seedling common Laburnum. Plant October–March, well-drained, ordinary soil, sunny position.

Laburnum (la-bur′num. Fam. Leguminosae). Handsome, ornamental small deciduous trees, with trifoliolate leaves, and fine drooping racemes of yellow, pea-like flowers of spectacular beauty when well grown.

Selection. There are two species, both natives of S. Europe. *L. alpinum*, the Scotch Laburnum, growing well in the north, to 20 ft or more, is the better; with broad-headed, compact growth, and longer, more slender racemes of flowers in June; two weeks later than *L. anagyroides*, the common Laburnum or Golden Chain, of 30 ft, flowering late May–early June, but especially beautiful in the vs. *aureum*, with golden leaves, and *quercifolium*, with wavy-edged leaves. Hybrids of the two species are L. × *vossii* and × *watereri*, both free-flowering, with very long racemes.

Cultivation. Plant October–March, in fairly porous light soil, though any soil except the very wet is acceptable. Little pruning is necessary.

Propagation. Species by seeds, sown in spring in light soil out of doors. Varieties and hybrids by grafting or budding on seedlings of common Laburnum. Note: seeds are poisonous to children, who should be warned against them. All parts are toxic to animals.

Lachenalia, Cape Cowslip, Leopard Lily (lak-en-al'i-a. Fam. Liliaceae). Delightful S. African bulbous plants, with radical thickish linear leaves, and spikes of pretty tubular or bell-shaped flowers, spring or early summer.

Selection. The best of the species are L. *aloides*, 12 in., bright green, red and yellow flowers; and vs. *aurea*, orange-yellow; *nelsonii*, bright yellow, tinged green; and *quadricolor*, red, greenish-yellow, green and reddish-purple; *bulbifera* (*pendula*), to 10 in., purple, red and yellow; *orchioides*, to 9 in., white or yellow, tinged red or blue, scented; *glaucina*, 6 in., pale blue, scented; and *purpureo-caerulea*, to 9 in., purplish blue. There are several notable hybrids in specialists' lists.

Cultivation. Pot in early August, ½ in. deep, six bulbs to a 6-in. pot, standard compost, placing pots in a cool frame, cellar, or plunged in ashes or fibre under north wall, until well rooted and growth showing; bring in to a cool greenhouse temp. 10–13° C. (50–55° F.), gradually increasing watering. After flowering cut out flower stalks, grow on until plants flag, then dry off to ripen bulbs in the sun.

Propagation. By offsets at repotting time. By seeds, when ripe, in pans in cool greenhouse.

Laciniatus (-a, -um). Laciniate, jagged, raggedly cut. Ex. *Rudbeckia laciniata*.

Lackey Moth (*Clisiocampa neustria*). A pest of fruit trees, ornamental trees and roses in the south; this moth lays its eggs in bands on young shoots in autumn, from which bluish-grey, white and reddish striped, slightly hairy caterpillars emerge in spring to feed on leaves,

congregating in silky webbed nests; pupating in cocoons between leaves, on bark, etc., before emerging as adult moths in August. Control lies in cutting away egg-banded shoots in winter; spraying nests with malathion insecticide in spring.

Lacryma-Jobi. Job's Tears (Job xvi. 16). See *Coix*.

Lacteus (-a, -um) ; Lacti-. Milky, milk-coloured. Ex. *Campanula lactiflora*; *Cotoneaster lactea*.

Lactuca (lak-tu'ka. Fam. Compositae). Herbs with a milky sap, of which L. *sativa*, an annual, is the common Lettuce (q.v.); others are grown as hardy ornamental perennials.

Selection. L. *alpina*, Arctic, Siberia, 3 ft, flower-heads of purplish-blue, July; *bourgaei*, Mediterranean region, to 6 ft, pinkish lilac, August; *plumieri*, S. France, 6 ft, handsome leaves, purple flower-heads, summer; *perennis*, S. Europe, 2 ft, light blue flowers, August; and *tenerrima*, S. Europe, to 1½ ft, blue flower-heads, July.

Cultivation. Plant October–March, in woodland or informal parts of the garden, well-drained, deep moist soil; tolerant of shade.

Propagation. By division in March; a few by seeds.

Lacustris (-e). Of lakes or ponds. Ex. *Scirpus lacustris*.

Ladder Fern. See *Nephrolepsis*.

Lad's Love. Alias Southernwood; see *Artemisia*.

Lady Fern. See *Athyrium filix-femina*.

Lady Tulip. See *Tulipa clusiana*.

Ladybirds (*Coccinellidae*). A family of 45 species of small beetles, usually red or yellow and black-spotted; over-wintering as adults. Invaluable to gardeners as the females lay eggs near aphids, etc., which hatch into alligator-like grubs or 'niggers' which feed on greenfly and related insects.

Lady's Ear-drops. See *Fuchsia*.

Lady's Slipper. See *Cypripedium*.

Lady's Smock. See *Cardamine*.

Lady's Tresses. See *Spiranthes*.

Laelia (le'li-a. Fam. Orchidaceae). Beautiful orchids of Mexico to Brazil, related to Cattleya.

Selection. L. *anceps*, Mexico, 4–10 in., pink with purple-lipped flowers, December, with many vs.; *autumnalis*,

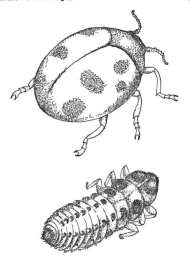

FIG. 134 Ladybird (*Coccinella septempunctata*), and larva.

Mexico, 4–8 in., soft rose, purple, white, January; *gouldiana*, Mexico, 1 ft, crimson, winter; *pumila*, Brazil, 6 in., rose-purple; and vs. *dayana*, and *praestans* and its forms, are comparatively easy to grow in a warm greenhouse, winter temp. 13° C. (55° F.) minimum. *L. cinnabarina*, Brazil, 12 in., orange-red, March; *harpophylla*, Brazil, 6 in., orange-scarlet, February–March; *perrinii*, Brazil, 8 in., crimson-purple, November; *purpurata*, Brazil, 9 in., white, flushed purple, May–June; and *tenebrosa*, Bahia, 6 in., coppery, purple, summer, need hothouse conditions, winter temp. of 15·5° C. (60° F.) minimum.

Cultivation. Pot when new roots begin to form, well-crocked pots, compost of equal parts Osmunda fibre and live sphagnum moss, with charcoal added; ventilate and sun freely, water liberally in growth, syringe on sunny days; water sparingly when resting.

Propagation. By division in March. Laelias cross freely with Cattleyas. See *Laeliocattleya*.

Laeliocattleya (le-li-o-kat′le-ya. Fam. Orchidaceae). Hybrids of *Laelia* × *Cattleya*, some of which have arisen naturally, others by artificial breeding,

and now numbering over 2,000. Outstanding natural hybrids such as *L-c.* × *elegans*, Brazil, to 20 in., rose, white, and purple, summer; *gottioana*, 1½ ft, rose-purple; × *pittiana*, Bahia, 6 in., creamy white, rose, crimson-dotted; × *schilleriana*, Brazil, to 20 in., white, purple and yellow, and many others may be grown as Cattleyas (q.v.).

Laevigatus (-a, -um). Smooth, polished. Ex. *Iris laevigatus*.

Laevis (-e). Smooth. Ex. *Aster laevis*.

Lagenaria (la-gen-a′ri-a. Fam. Cucurbitaceae). The one species, *L. vulgaris*, the Bottle Gourd of tropical Africa and Asia, is an annual, tendril-climbing, 10-ft plant, with hairy, heart-shaped leaves, white starry flowers in clusters, giving way to pale-yellow, inedible, bottle-shaped gourds; grown from seeds, sown March, under glass, bottom heat 21° C. (70° F.), for cool greenhouse, or planting out in warm shelter in May.

Lagurus (la-gur′us. Fam. Graminae). The native Hare's-tail Grass. *L. ovatus*, 1 ft, is an ornamental annual with decorative panicles of bloom, from seeds sown in pots in August, wintered in a cold frame or greenhouse, and planted out the following spring, in well-drained ordinary soil and sun. (*See* Fig. 135, page 304.)

Lamarckia (la-mark′i-a. Fam. Gramineae). The one species is a dwarf annual grass, *L. aurea*, Mediterranean region, 1 ft, with one-sided plume-like panicles in spring; best grown like Lagurus (q.v.), or from April sowings out of doors.

Lamb's Ear, or **Lamb's Tongue.** See *Stachys lanata*.

Lamb's Lettuce. *See* Corn Salad.

Lamina. A thin plant tissue, such as a leaf-blade, a petal or free sepal.

Lamium, Dead Nettle (la′mi-um. Fam. Labiatae). Of this genus of herbs, many are weeds, but some of the perennials make good ground-cover plants.

Selection. L. galeobdolon, v. *variegatum*, the golden-bronze leafed 'Yellow Archangel', of Britain and Europe, 1–1½ ft, spikes of yellow flowers, summer; *maculatum*, native, 1 ft, white-striped leaves, purple flowers; and v. *aureum*, golden-leafed; and *orvala*, Italy, France, to 1½ ft, reddish flowers; are attractive.

FIG. 136   Lanceolate leaf.

FIG. 135   *Lagurus ovatus*, Hare's-tail Grass.

Cultivation. Plant in October–March, well-drained light soil, and propagate by division in spring.

Lanceolatus (-a, -um). Lanceolate, lance-shaped, of leaves, tapering to both ends. Ex. *Coreopsis lanceolata.*

Land Cress, American Cress (*Barbarea praecox*). An annual herb, resembling watercress and used as an alternative salading. Seeds may be sown in drills, $\frac{1}{4}$ in. deep, 12 in. apart, March–August, thinning plants to 8 in. apart; in good humus-rich, moist soil, covering with cloches for winter cropping.

Landscape Gardening, or landscape architecture, is the art and practice of laying out gardens and their amenities. On the largest and most elaborate scale it is perhaps the province of the specialist. What has been achieved in this direction in the past and in the present can be studied in the great gardens of which so many are now open to the public, some still in the hands of private families, others cultivated under authorities such as the National Trust. Landscape gardening and design today is greatly influenced by the need for economy in maintenance. In layout the trend is to simplicity. Garden and house are regarded as a unity, complementary to one another; the garden providing the setting to the home, providing the outdoor counterpart to the indoor living space; complementing its architectural lines and structural materials, blending house and outbuildings with their immediate landscape, and providing beautiful vistas from the main windows and doorways. The qualities sought are restfulness and variety; the former born of the garden as a whole by spacious design in such matters as the open, unbroken sweep of a lawn, the long path taking the eye into the distance, the vista to inviting far-off well-placed plantings, or ornament or pool; the latter in the garden features such as the rose garden, rock garden, walled garden, pergola, pool, herbaceous borders, shubbery, sunken garden, play areas, terrace, orchard, vegetable plot or wild garden, according to personal preference and appropriateness to the garden scene. These features are more fully developed under their separate entries in this book.

Lantana (lan-ta'na. Fam. Verbenaceae). Evergreen tropical flowering shrubs with rather rough, toothed pairs of leaves, and round heads of small, five-lobed flowers that change colour prettily as they age; for growing in pots in the cool greenhouse or home.

Selection. L. *camara*, the Jamaica Mountain Sage, to 6 ft, with pink or yellow flowers, deepening to red or orange, in summer, and vs. in different flower tints; *salvifolia*, Africa, 1 ft, aromatic leaves, lilac or pink flowers; and *selloviana*, S. America, trailing with rosy-lilac flowers in summer. 'Globe D'Or', yellow flowering; 'La Neige', white; and 'Chelsonii', scarlet and yellow, are named dwarf forms.

Cultivation. Pot, and repot, in March, standard compost, 6- or 7-in. pots; water freely in active growth, syringe on sunny days, giving sun; water very moderately in winter, minimum temp. 10° C. (50° F.); prune back in February–March; renew top inch or so or compost; repot every third year.

Propagation. By seeds sown in March, bottom heat of 24° C. (75° F.), standard compost. By cuttings of half-ripe shoots in July–August, in propagating frame.

Lanuginosus (-a, -um). Lanuginose, downy, woolly. Ex. *Androsace lanuginosa.*

Lapageria, Chilean Bell-flower (la-pa-ge'ri-a. Fam. Liliaceae). The only species, L. *rosea*, Chile, is a beautiful evergreen twining climber, with handsome, ovate, dark green leaves, and clusters of large, waxy, bell-shaped, hanging rosy-crimson flowers during summer; and has a white v. *albiflora*, and larger-flowered forms in *ilsemanni*, and *superba*, more brightly coloured.

Cultivation. Pot in large pots, or better still in a bed, enriched with peat, in March, to train up trellis or supports; watering freely in growth, in cool greenhouse, with cool shade; soil compost of 1 part by bulk fibrous loam, 3 parts peat, 1 part sand, is suitable for pots. Protect against slugs and aphids. Water very moderately in winter, temp. 7° C. (45° F.) minimum. Cut away weak shoots and old shoots in March.

Propagation. By seeds, bottom heat of 18° C. (65° F.), spring, in standard compost. By layering in spring or early autumn.

Lapeirousia (Anonomatheca) (la-pi-roo'si-a. Fam. Iridaceae). Bulbous plants of tropical and S. Africa, with small tubular, six-lobed flowers on a branched penduncle in summer, for the cool greenhouse.

Selection. L. *laxa* (*cruenta*), 6 in., carmine-crimson flowers, near-hardy; *corymbosa*, 6 in., blue, May; and *grandiflora*, Zambezia, 1 ft, bright red, autumn, are worth growing.

Cultivation. Pot in March, standard compost, 1 in. deep, keep cool until growth shows, covered with moist peat; then give water freely, and light, cool greenhouse conditions; keep dry after leaves die down until following March. Propagation is by offsets when repotting.

Larch. See *Larix.*

Larix, Larch (la'ricks. Fam. Pinaceae). Hardy, deciduous, coniferous trees of the mountainous regions of the northern hemisphere, important commercially for their softwood timber, and attractive in spring for their fresh green clusters of needle-leaves, and male, yellow-stemmed flowers, and female rosy-red bracted cone-like flowers, in the larger garden.

Selection. L. *decidua*, Europe, to 120 ft, grows pyramidal; with vs. *fastigiata*, stiffly erect, and *carpathica*, with pendulous branches; *leptolepsis*, Japanese Larch, 60 ft or more, reddish bark, fine golden autumn foliage, and their hybrid × *eurolepsis*, the Dunkeld Larch, to 80 ft, are probably the pick.

Cultivation. Plant in autumn or early spring; open situation, well-drained soil.

Propagation. By seeds, sown in sandy loam, in open seed bed, March–April.

Larkspur. See *Delphinium.*

Larva (pl. **Larvae**). The active immature stage of insects undergoing a development from egg through larva and pupa to adult; that of a butterfly or moth being called a caterpillar; of a beetle or weevil, a grub; and of a 2-winged fly a maggot.

Lasiandra. See *Tibouchina.*

Lastrea. A synonym of *Dryopteris* (q.v.).

Latania (la-ta'ni-a. Fam. Palmaceae).

Attractive palms with fan-shaped, bright green leaves for the warm greenhouse.

Selection. L. borborica (commersonii), Mauritius, to 7 ft, with leaf stalks and ribs of crimson; and *verschaffeltii*, Rodriguez Island, to 7 ft, with golden leaf stalks and leaf ribs.

Cultivation. Pot in spring, standard compost, well-drained pots; water freely in warm months, very moderately in winter; sponge leaves regularly; minimum temp. 13° C. (55° F.) in winter.

Propagation. By imported seeds, in spring, with bottom heat of 21° C. (70° F.), moist compost.

Latent Bud. A bud which fails to grow out as a shoot within a year of its formation, but remains capable of growing.

Laterals. Side-shoots or side growths branching from a main stem or branch; particularly of vines and fruit trees.

Latex. The milky fluid, juice or sap, of certain plants, usually white, sometimes yellow or red, such as Euphorbia, Campanula, Dandelion, Poppy, Ficus, Nettle, Convolvulus and Sanguinaria.

Lathyrus (lath'i-rus. Fam. Leguminosae). Decorative tendril-climbers, of which *L. odoratus* is the parent Sweet Pea (q.v.). Several other hardy species are worth growing, and are perennial.

Selection. L. cirrhosus, Pyrenees, many-flowered racemes, rose-pink, summer; *latifolius*, the Everlasting Pea, large rose-purple flowers, summer, and vs. *albus*, white; *roseus*, bright rose, etc.; *magellanicus*, Lord Anson's Pea, Magellan Straits, bluish-purple flowers, summer; *rotundifolius*, Tauria, rose flowers, summer; are hardy perennial climbers. *L. pubescens*, Chile, climber, pale violet flowers, and *splendens*, Pride of California, sub-shrubby, 1 ft, large pale rose flowers, are good plants for the cool greenhouse. *L. sativus*, the Chickling Pea, an annual climber with blue flowers, and a white form *albus*, S. Europe; *tingitanus*, North Africa, 3 ft, purple-red flowers, also annual, may be sown in March where they are to flower. *L. vernus*, perennial, the Bitter Vetch, Europe, 1 ft, purple and blue flowers, summer, has a white and a double-flowering form, sometimes grown for spring-flowering.

Cultivation. All the above are easily raised from seeds sown March–April in any ordinary soil. Perennials may be propagated by division in spring.

Lattice-Leaf Plant. See *Aponogeton*.

Latus (-a, -um), Lati-. Broad. Ex. *Kalmia latifolia*

Laurel. See *Laurus.*

Laurel, Cherry. See *Prunus laurocerasus.*

Laurel, Japan. See *Aucuba japonica.*

Laurel, Mountain. See *Kalmia.*

Laurel, Portugal. See *Prunus lusitanicus.*

Laurel, Spurge. See *Daphne laureola.*

Laurel, Variegated. See *Aucuba japonica.*

Laurus, Bay Laurel, Sweet Bay (lawr'us. Fam. Lauraceae). Evergreen, aromatic, unisexual trees, of which *L. nobilis*, S. Europe, to 40 ft, is hardy for the south and mild western areas, but not for the north or cold districts, to grow as a dense pyramidal tree, in well-drained, humus-rich soil, and warm sun. Otherwise it is grown in tubs, and lends itself to clipping into formal shapes, being moved to frost-free shelter in winter. The leaves may be dried for culinary use. The v. *angustifolia* has narrower, smaller leaves. *L. canariensis*, Canary Island Laurel, has much larger leaves, but is less hardy.

Propagation. By cuttings of young shoots taken in July–August, in cold frame or under handlight.

Laurustinus. See *Viburnum tinus.*

Lavandula, Lavender (la-van'du-la. Fam. Labiatae). Aromatic perennials, chiefly shrubs, valued for their fragrance and long flowering in summer.

Selection. L. spica, Mediterranean region, is the common Lavender, to 3 ft, grey-leaved, grey-blue perfumed flowers, with vs. *alba*, white; 'folgate', deep blue; *gigantea* ('Grappenhall'), very robust; 'Twickel Purple', deep purple; and dwarf forms *nana atropurpurea* ('Hidcote'), purple-blue; *nana* 'Munstead Dwarf', purple-blue; of about 1½ ft, flowering a little earlier than the type. *L. stoechas*, SW. Europe, 2–3 ft, is distinctive for its purple bracted flowers; *vera* is not much different from *L. spica* but with greener leaves.

Cultivation. Plant October or March–April, in well-drained, porous and preferably calcareous soil; full sun. Prune after flowering; or clip if used for hedging, but not into more than year-old wood.

Propagation. By cuttings of unflowered young shoots, taken with a 'heel', in July–August. By seeds, sown in spring, outdoor seed-bed.

The flower spikes may be cut for drying when most of the flowers on a spike are fully out, and hung in small bunches in a line in airy place to dry out steadily, until the flowers rub off readily.

Lavatera, Mallow (la-va-te'ra. Fam. Malvaceae). A genus containing annuals, biennials, perennials and shrubs, esteemed chiefly for their large, single, mallow-like flowers in summer.

Selection. L. trimestris, a Mediterranean annual, makes a bush of 3–4 ft, with large rose flowers, and vs. *alba,* white, *splendens,* bright rose, and 'Loveliness', deep rose; from sowings in well-drained, open soil, in spring, thinning plants to 2 ft apart. *L. arborea,* the Tree Mallow, Europe, 6–10 ft, is grown as a hardy biennial, sown in June, and winter-protected with litter, to flower the following summer, with pale purple flowers; v. *variegata* has yellow variegated leaves. *L. olbia,* S. France, to 4 ft, is shrubby with reddish-purple flowers, summer, and v. *rosea,* rose-pink, for a sheltered border; planted out in October or March. All the Lavateras may be grown from seeds in spring.

Lavender. See *Lavandula.*

Lavender, Cotton. See *Santolina.*

Lavender, Sea. See *Limonium.*

Lawn. A well-constructed and maintained lawn makes a valuable feature of a garden; restful to the eye, a recreational outdoor carpet, an admirable foil to plants. Grass lawns are made (*a*) by sowing seeds, (*b*) by laying turf of established grasses, or (*c*) by inserting pieces of grass plants or their stoloniferous runners or roots.

Site. An open sunlit site is preferable, though well-nurtured grass will grow in partial shade. It may be level, sloping or gently undulating with the surface finished to permit easy mowing. First-class drainage is essential, especially at subsoil level, and must be provided (*see* Drainage). Persistent perennial weeds such as horse-tails (*Equisetum* spp.), thistles (*Carduus* spp.), couch and other coarse grasses must be eradicated by the use of effective herbicides (q.v.) before attempting to make a lawn. *Soil.* A light to medium porous loam soil, overlying a well-drained subsoil, is ideal; with a pH of 5·5 to 6·0. Heavy clay soils need amending and conditioning by the incorporation of gypsum, well-rotted organic matter and coarse materials such as sand, breeze, grit, etc. Light sandy soils, gravels and chalk usually need liberal dressings of sifted peat or rotted manures. On very poor soil, imported top soil, screened and mixed with lawn peat, may be added. Prior to sowing or turfing the soil must be consolidated and firmed, either by allowing it to settle for a period, or by treading it well, walking over it on the heels, or using a compacting roller, raking and repeating. When finally level it may be dressed with a balanced lawn fertilizer, or a mixture such as 2 parts by weight ammonium sulphate, 4 parts superphosphate and 1 part sulphate of potash at 1½–2 oz. per sq. yd.

Sowing. The seasonable times for sowing a lawn are August–September or April–May; the former where the soil is porous and well-drained on light soils; the latter in colder districts, and on the heavy soils apt to be damp in winter. It is possible to sow in summer if watering is no problem in dry weather spells. *Seeds.* The choice of a seeds mixture is important, and it is wise to buy only from a specialist seedsman who will state the composition. Briefly, fine lawns are made from selected strains of fescues (*Festuca rubra* and subspecies) and bents (*Agrostis tenuis, A. canina*). Perennial rye-grass (*Lolium perenne*) in strain S. 23, timothy (*Phleum pratense*) in strain S. 50, and crested dog's-tail (*Cynosurus cristatus*) may be added where hard-wearing, play lawns or general purpose lawns are needed and economy has to be practised. Smooth-stalked meadow-grass (*Poa pratensis*) is useful on light, porous soils, and rough-stalked (*Poa trivalis*) on moist heavy soils; while for shady situations wood meadow-grass (*Poa nemoralis*) is a useful addition. From these varieties of grasses suitable mixtures can be made to suit various purposes and soils. Immediately before sowing on a calm day, the surface is lightly raked into furrows, not more than ½ in. deep, and marked in 6 ft wide strips or squares. With even distribution 1 oz. of seed per sq. yd is adequate. Heavier sowing means a thicker stand of seedlings competing strongly but more vulnerable to damping-off and seedling diseases. To minimize damage by fungal diseases and insect pests, the seed may be dressed with a fungicidal/insecticidal dressing (thiram-gamma-BHC dust). Seed may be distributed by a mechanical seed distributor. To broadcast by hand it is useful to add twice the bulk of dry clean sand, mix thoroughly, and then sow one-half of the seed one way, the other at right angles, covering a 6-ft strip at a time. After sowing, the seeds are just covered by a light raking, or sifting of sand or peat, and lightly firmed in. A bird repellent can then be sprayed over the area, if necessary, and weed seedlings can be inhibited by the application of a pre-emergent herbicide (pentachlorophenol). Seeds germinate in one to three weeks. When seedlings are about 2 in. high a light rolling and a cutting to reduce height by about one-half should be done. Thereafter cutting should be frequent, though not too close. An alternative is to sow by laying down strips of de-composable paper, pre-sown with seeds, and provided with soluble fertilizer and pesticide. It simplifies the operation, and is very useful in grassing down banks, though at greater initial cost.

Turfing. To ensure satisfactory rooting of the turf, laying a lawn with sods of established grasses should be done be-tween September and early March, in mild weather. Much depends upon securing quality turf, weed-free, of good lawn grasses. This is expensive, com-pared with seeds, but gives an 'instant' lawn. Sea-washed marsh turf from Lancashire and Cumberland is esteemed for lawns of bowling or golf green quality, but needs well-drained, porous, lightish soils and meticulous attention to thrive. Local turf from such places as heaths, moorlands, downland, parkland, first-class pasture (not ley or hay fields) are worth considering, since the cost of turf is greatly affected by the transport involved. The sods or turfs are cut 1 ft wide, 1–3 ft long and 1¼ in. thick, and

are laid on the prepared ground in bonded courses like brickwork, working forward from one end or corner. Each turf should be inspected and perennial weeds pulled out, and then placed in an open-ended box of the same measure-ments, inverted, to permit cutting to an even thickness with a flat scythe blade or long knife. Levelling is done by adding or taking away soil underneath. As the laying progresses, a board is placed on the new turf to stand on, and when completely finished a top-dressing of coarse sand may be brushed into the joints. Watering may be needed in dry weather, especially if laying is delayed into spring.

Cuttings. Lawns can be made of cuttings, 4–6 in. long, of stolons or surface rooting stems of certain grasses, chiefly selected strains, such as Z. 103, of *Agrostis stolonifera* v. *stolonifera*, shal-lowly pushed into the soil at 1 ft. distances in autumn or spring. The lawn becomes one of a ground-covering, felt-like sward, reputed to effectively smother weeds, but requiring control at the limits of the lawn area. Lawns may also be made by simply dividing grasses, such as Fescues, in March, and dibbling the pieces in; but the technique is probably more useful in repairing patchy lawns than for making new ones.

Maintenance. To maintain a lawn in smooth, weed-free, even verdure requires skill and regular attention. Lawn grasses are chiefly selected for their fineness of leaf and resilience under the constant dwarfing action of wear and cutting.

Mowing. Removing the foliage of a plant deprives it of some of its capacity to manu-facture food for itself. Although grasses react by budding more shoots with shorter stems and finer leaf-blades, the end effect is debilitating, and has to be offset by good culture. In mowing the closeness of the cut and the frequency are impor-tant. For games lawns it is necessary to cut close, but for more ornamental lawns there is seldom need to cut closer than half an inch. The more frequently a lawn is cut, the less foliage is removed at a time, and on the average throughout a cutting season. Cutting frequency should be geared to growth vigour—occasional in winter and early spring, but much more often in growing weather, except when drought intervenes. Whether a machine with a cylindrical cutting reel or a rotary scything action is used, the direction of mowing should be changed regularly (*see* Lawn-mowers).

Rolling. The purpose of rolling is to true the freshly mown surface, without unduly compressing it. It should not be done to 'iron out' irregularities or ridges or to squash wormcasts. A light roller is best for lawn use, the modern double roller with narrow diameter cylinders being excellent.

Aeration. A periodic piercing or slitting of turf offsets compaction by use and foot traffic, admits air to grass roots, stimulates growth and facilitates the entry of top dressings, fertilizers and water. On heavy soils, hollow-tined forking which removes small cores of soil, followed by gritty top dressings, improves percolation. Spiking or slitting can be usefully carried out at almost any time, especially in autumn and spring, by hand tools or machine.

Scarifying. This can be done with a scarifying tool or sharp-toothed rake, with the intent of loosening dead growth and debris at surface level, prior to mowing, or to prepare sparse areas for re-seeding. It should not be used to eradicate moss, since it only breaks it up and distributes filaments and spores to compound infestation.

Watering. There is no doubt that lawns transpire moisture copiously in dry or hot weather, and water is a constant need. It is preferable to water before the grasses show distress, copiously, 3–4 gallons per sq. yd being little enough. If restrictions are in force, watering with a dilute foliar feeding fertilizer is more helpful.

Fertilizing. Normal modern practice is to give a base fertilizer, providing 5–7 per cent nitrogen, 10–15 per cent phosphoric acid and 3–5 per cent potash, in March, in proprietary form, or to a formula such as 15 parts by weight ammonium sulphate, 15 parts dried blood, 40 parts fine bone meal, 25 parts superphosphate, 5 parts sulphate of potash, recommended by the St Ives Research Station, at 2–3 oz. per sq. yd. This may be followed by an autumn fertilizer, which may simply consist of 4 parts by weight bone meal and 1 part sulphate of potash at 2 oz. per sq. yd,

or a low nitrogen compound such as 1 part by weight sulphate of ammonia, 1 part hoof and horn meal, 6 parts bone meal, 2 parts sulphate of potash at $1\frac{1}{2}$ oz. per sq. yd, or a proprietary lawn fertilizer. During the summer months supplementary liquid feeding may prove helpful, once every 4–6 weeks; or on calcareous soils, $\frac{1}{2}$ oz. ammonium sulphate per sq. yd, bulked with peat, is often given. Normally lawns do not need liming, but where the pH value is below 5·5, basic slag can be applied in autumn at 2–4 oz. per sq. yd.

Top dressings. In autumn or early winter, a top dressing of lawn peat and loam in equal parts may be given to lawns on light soils; on heavy soils, coarse sand should replace the loam fraction. Sifted well-rotted manure or compost may be used instead of peat.

Weeds. Many hairy or rough-leaved weeds may be controlled by applying lawn sand (3 parts by weight ammonium sulphate, 1 part calcined ferrous sulphate, 15–20 parts coarse sand or sifted peat) at 3–4 oz. per sq. yd, in spring or early summer, in mild dewy weather. More sophisticated weed control is given by selective herbicides (q.v.) based on MCPA, 2,4-D or 2,4,5-T, which kill a wide range of broad-leaved dicotyledonous weeds. Weeds such as white clover, pearlwort, chickweeds, yarrow, bedstraws, cleavers, etc., succumb to mecoprop, dichlorprop or fenoprop herbicides; and the trend is to use combinations of these two groups of selective herbicides. These herbicides are most effective when applied in warm temperatures, when weeds and grasses are actively growing, before a mowing, giving the plants a day or two to absorb the solution. Lawn mowings may be composted but not used for immediate mulching of plants. Moss in lawns is inhibited for a year by lawn sand, but is more effectively controlled by the application of a mercurized moss eradicant, based on mercurous chloride and/or mercuric chloride, which prevents re-infestation for up to three years.

Worms. More than twenty species of earthworms are found in British soils, doing invaluable work in aerating, draining and enriching them. Not all species make casts on the surface, but these casts can be unsightly and detrimental to a lawn's appearance. The safest worm control is a 2 per cent rotenone derris dust, applied at ½ oz. per sq. yd, with one gallon water to wash it in, when worms are casting freely at the surface. It is non-poisonous to animal life, and effective for a year. Lead arsenate and chlordane are more drastic as well as highly poisonous, and should be used with great care.

Diseases. The worst is Fusarium Patch, caused by the fungus *Fusarium nivale,* beginning as small, roundish patches of brown-yellow dying grasses, increasing in size, and bearing a pinkish-white mycelium on the leaf blades; particularly in dull, humid weather, autumn or spring. Treatment consists of applying a mercury-based fungicide or a Malachite Green/Bordeaux Mixture, and repeating at 3-week intervals, two or three times. Corticium disease, alias Red Thread or Autumn Rust, caused by the fungus *Corticium fuciforme,* is characterized by irregular patches of bleached grasses, especially fescues, with leaf blades covered by a red thread-like fungus, paling to thin pink needles at the tips. It is not so deadly as Fusarium Patch, but requires similar fungicidal treatment at ten-day intervals. Other diseases such as Brown Patch Disease (*Rhizoctonia solani*), which shows in patches of grass, especially bents, turning brown and sere, and Dollar Spot (*Sclerotinia homeocarpa*), characterized by small 1-2-in. round spots of dying grass, sometimes enlarging and running together, are less common in this country, but respond to treatment with a mercurized turf fungicide.

Pests. The most destructive are Leatherjackets, the cylindrical grey-brown larvae of Crane Flies or Daddy-long-legs. (*Pales* spp., *Tipula* spp.), of which there are at least eight species. Eggs are usually laid in late summer to hatch into grubs which feed on grass roots throughout the winter, leaving dead, browning tufts of grass easily dislodged. Dusting with a gamma BHC/DDT insecticidal dust, bulked with sand, where crane-fly activity has been noted or grubs are found, will give control. Lawns may also harbour wireworms, chafer grubs, cutworm caterpillars and ants, but damage is localized and can be controlled by the gamma BHC/DDT dust.

Fairy Rings. Toadstools, mushrooms and large fungi are apt to appear in lawns in late summer and autumn, often in arcs or annually extending rings. Primarily feeding on dead roots, organic matter or wood in the soil, their mycelium may choke grasses. Thorough hollow-tine forking of the area, and watering with a mercurized turf fungicide promise control. In severe cases it may be necessary to strip, take out the mycelium-ridden soil and replace with fresh soil; or sterilize the soil with a 2 per cent solution of formaldehyde at 1 gallon per sq. yd, returfing after about four weeks.

Lawn Sand. Basically a mixture of ammonium sulphate, calcined ferrous sulphate and dry, lime-free sand, used as a lawn weed-killer and clover and moss control in spring and early summer, which is caustic when freshly applied, burning the foliage of rough-leaved weeds by which it is retained; but later stimulating grass growth by its nutrient content. For the spot treatment of weeds a mixture of 7 : 3 : 10 parts by weight may be used; for overall application one of 3 : 1 : 20 is used at 4-6 oz. per sq yd. On light sandy or chalky soils, some or all of the sand may be replaced by sifted dry peat.

Lawn-mowers. Some type of cutting machine is essential for a lawn since no grasses are truly dwarf-growing. The scythe has long been superseded by the lawn-mower. For small lawns, hand-pushed lawn-mowers answer quite well. They work on the principle of a cylinder or reel of spirally arranged cutting blades, rotating closely to a fixed horizontal blade, and shearing the grass off by a scissor-action, and may be chain or gear driven from the wheels. The simplest and cheapest are side-wheel driven, but the cylinder blades are set far apart and they do not give the finest finish. One type, fitted with flexible blades, is excellent for cutting long grass. The better hand-mower is the roller type, with a land-roller drive, preferably split for manœuvrability, at the rear, and a shaft of small wooden rollers at the front. It rolls as well as mows, and can be used to the edges of lawns where the side-wheel machine cannot. The cuts per foot depend on the number of cutter blades in the cylinder, and this determines the finish. Six blades are usual, but eight or ten may be fitted for bowling-green finish. The more blades, the more effort is needed to push the machine. The width of cut may be 6–12 in., the wider cutting machine needing more effort. Power-driven lawn-mowers save much time and effort. They are available in many sizes, and various types, chiefly side-wheel, roller and rotary-scything, with cutting widths from 10 in. upwards. For the garden, choice lies between the roller machine with cylindrical cutters, and the rotary-scything machine which has either a rapidly rotating disk fitted with renewable blades or a revolving single straight blade, under a shrouding cover. As a rule, the roller machine is self-propelled, gives the better-looking finish, but requires periodic resharpening and adjustment. The rotary-scything machine is only self-propelled in the more expensive models, cuts long and short grass, and needs only inexpensive replacement of worn cutter blades. Machines may be powered by 2-stroke or 4-stroke petrol engines, with some inevitable accompanying noise, and the need for mechanical maintenance; or by electric motor, which gives more silent running, but the machine is more or less tethered by a long flex attached to a mains power outlet. Ingenious reeling devices largely prevent the flex or cable being a hindrance or danger. Roller mowers are now available in the small sizes, self-contained and powered by an electric battery, similar to a car battery, which, provided the battery is properly trickle-charged after use, and maintained in winter, are excellent for small, more or less level, lawns. Battery-powered rotary-scything machines are not yet available. Another type of rotary-scything mower is the wheel-less hovering type ('Flymo') which floats on a cushion of air, like a hovercraft, and is efficient in cutting to ½ in. height, on lawns, and invaluable for slopes or banks, though care is needed at lawn edges to keep the mower level and prevent scalping. Large power-mowers are usually petrol-engined, and may be fitted with a seat for the operator. The scissor-scything machine, akin to the farmer's hay-cutter, is useful where there is long grass or rough vegetation to be cut. Most machines can be fitted with grass-catching boxes or containers, and so gather material for composting. Their continued efficiency depends upon proper maintenance in oiling, greasing, cleaning and periodic overhaul.

Laxus (-a, -um). Lax, loose or not compact. Ex. *Trollius laxus*; *Senecio laxifolius.*

Layering. A method of propagation by which a shoot of a plant is induced to root before being detached. It is most useful with plants which do not root readily from cuttings—shrubs, trees and woody perennials such as carnations. The technique consists of bending

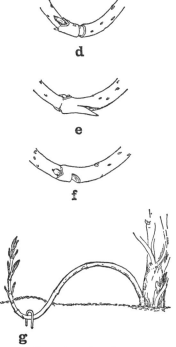

FIG. 137 Layering: d, e, f, ways of preparing the shoots for pegging down at g.

suitably placed low young shoots to the ground, and pegging or weighting them in the soil; at the lowest point, the sap flow is interrupted by notching, slitting, narrowly bark-ringing, twisting, piercing or constricting with a tightly twisted wire; and covering with a moist soil compost. The best times are spring or autumn. The point of restriction may be painted or dusted with a root-inducing hormone to speed root formation; but as a rule the layer is not ready for severance and transplanting until the following year, and is best severed a few weeks before moving.

Layering, Air. When there are no suitable shoots on a shrub or tree for normal soil layering, the technique of air-layering may be used. A young sturdy shoot is chosen; notched, ringed or slit half-through with a slanting cut; treated with root-inducing hormone, and enclosed in a suitable rooting medium. The older method is to use a flower-pot, sawn in half, refitted around the shoot and filled with a cuttings compost, which is kept moist. The modern method is to enclose the point of restriction with a ball of moist sphagnum moss, itself wrapped around in polythene film, secured tightly at the top and bottom. Such plants as camellias, magnolias, hamamelis, rhododendrons, etc., can be air-layered in spring to be detached a year or so later, and carefully transferred to a pot and standard compost.

Layia (lai'i-a. Fam. Compositae). The chief species offered is *L. elegans*, the Tidy-tips Flower, of California, as a showy half-hardy annual of 18–24 in., with many flower-heads of single golden, white-tipped, rayed flowers in summer. Seeds may be sown under glass, March, bottom heat 15·5° C. (60° F.), or in the open in late April.

Laying-in. The tying in of young shoots of wall-trained trees to wires or their supports. Also used for heeling-in (q.v.).

Leader. The terminal extension shoot of the main stem or framework branch of a tree.

Leadwort. A common name sometimes used for *Plumbago* sp.

Leaf. A leaf of a flowering plant is a lateral member or outgrowth of the shoot

differing from it in form and structure and function. Structurally a leaf usually consists of a leaf-base from which it grows, a leaf-stalk or petiole, and a leaf-blade or lamina which is a flat, thin, green, soft tissue of cells supported by a network of veins. The leaf-stalk may be winged, but is often absent. The leaf-

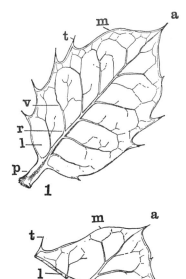

FIG. 138   1. A leaf; 2. A mid-section: a. apex; l. lamina; m. margin; p. petiole; r. mid-rib; t. tooth; v. vein.

base is often flanked by winged structures known as stipules. Leaves vary greatly, however, in shape and form, and arrangement on stems. With the exceptions of seed-leaves (cotyledons) and floral leaves (bracts), leaves grow out at the growing tips of stems in progressive succession. Leaves are vital to plants as the food manufactory organs, particularly of carbohydrates, by photosynthesis (q.v.), assembling water and mineral nutrients as sap from the roots, carbon dioxide and oxygen from the atmosphere to be converted into foodstuffs for the whole plant in the presence of light. Leaves transpire surplus moisture to tne .tmosphere, respire or breathe and perform gaseous exchanges. They may als absorb soluble mineral nutrients directly from rain or water solutions. Leaves are arranged variously on stems, in opposite pairs, alternating, spirally or whorled,

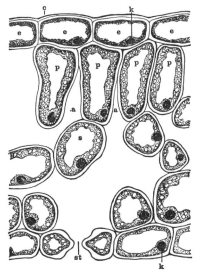

FIG. 139 A section through a leaf: a. air space; c. cuticle; e. epidermis cells; k. chloroplasts; p. palisade cells; s. spongy cells; st. stoma, flanked by guard cells.

to present a large surface area to air and sunlight. Leaves may be modified to suit special environmental conditions such as in the leathery evergreen leaves of many plants, succulent leaves of desert plants, tendril leaves of climbing plants, and spines, scales, etc. Most leaves, however, are thinnish in section. In structure they are covered with a skin or epidermis—a layer of transparent cells, fitting closely together, sometimes secreting a waxy layer (cuticle) from the upper surface, which helps to reduce excessive transpiration. Beneath the

upper epidermis lie one or more rows of tall cylindrical cells, with narrow air spaces between, which contain chloroplasts in their cytoplasm. The chloroplasts contain chlorophyll, the green pigments, which absorb the light energy from the sun and use it to energize the manufacture of carbohydrates. Beneath the palisade cells lies a layer of spongy cells, loosely arranged, containing chloroplasts but fewer than in the palisade cells, and facilitating the circulation of air and gaseous exchange within the leaf. The epidermis is pierced with openings, particularly in the underside of leaves, known as stomata, through which air, gases and water vapour diffuse. The stomata are formed between two guard cells, which regulate the size of the opening of a stoma, according to their internal pressure. The leaf structure is itself supported by the midrib extension of the petiole and veins branching from it, which conduct sap to the leaf cells and food from them to other parts of the plant.

Leaf Cuttings. See Cuttings.

Leaf Miners. Larvae of certain insects which feed inside leaves, causing linear tunnelling, or blotches. See Chrysanthemum, Celery, etc. Apple, cherry, rose, brassicas, aquilegia, cineraria, azalea, laburnum, lilac, privet, pear, celery, holly and beetroot leaves are sometimes attacked, and mined leaves should be detached and burnt, or sprayed with a malathion insecticide.

Leaflet. A part of a compound leaf.

Leaf-mould, Leaf Soil. Leaves which have accumulated and naturally decomposed into tiny, crumbly fragments constitute the traditional leaf-mould or leaf soil; esteemed particularly for its humus nutrient qualities in seed and potting composts, and for enriching soils. The best leaf-mould comes from rotted oak, beech or sweet chestnut leaves, gathered moist, into a compact heap, left to decompose naturally for two to four years. Decomposition can be speeded up by turning occasionally, and activating with an organic agent such as a seaweed derivative, QR herbal compound or bacterial substance (Fertosan). Nutrient value is about 1 per cent nitrogen, 0·6 per cent phosphoric acid, 0·5 per cent potassium.

Leatherjackets. The larvae of Crane Flies (q.v.).

Ledum (le'dum. Fam. Ericaceae). Evergreen spring-flowering shrubs with terminal clusters of open, 5-petalled white flowers, for lime-free soils.

Selection. L. groenlandicum, the Labrador tea, Greenland and N. America, upright-growing to 3 ft, v. *compactum*, 1–1½ ft, a dwarf version; *hypoleucum*, Japan, 9 in., rough-leaved; *palustre*, Arctic Asia and America, 2 ft, cup-shaped flowers; and v. *decumbens*, 1 ft, tiny linear leaves, and loose heads of flowers.

Cultivation. Plant in April–May, lime-free well-drained, humus-rich soil. Prune if necessary, after flowering.

Propagation. By division in spring, by cuttings of young shoots in July–August; by layers, spring or autumn. By seeds in spring, peat-enriched loam, April–May.

Leek (*Allium porrum*). Easily grown, thoroughly hardy, the Leek is a biennial of the Onion family, valuable for winter and early spring cropping, with the lower part of its long bulb-like cylindrical stem and leaves blanched. *Varieties.* The London in strains such as Holborn Model; the Lyon and strains Prizetaker and Marble Pillar; and the Musselburgh.

Culture. The crop succeeds on almost any garden soil, particularly on rich loam, organically manured for a previous crop, open position. Seeds may be sown in drills, ½ in. deep, March–June. Plant out seedlings, late May–early August, either in shallow trenches, as for celery, or in holes, 6–9 in. deep, 12 in. apart, dropping a strong plant in each, and allowing the hole to fill with usual cultivations and hoeing. Plants in trenches are earthed up to blanch the stems periodically; and the crop may be left in the ground until harvest.

Diseases. Leeks are subject to the Soft Rot, Rust and White Rot affecting Onions (q.v.), but are seldom much affected. White Tip, a fungus disease (*Phytophthora porri*), sometimes causes leaf points to turn white, but a copper fungicide or dust may be used to give control.

Pests. The chief pest is the Leek Moth (*Acrolepia assectella*), the young caterpillars making whitish, elongated mines in the leaves in May–June; but timely spraying with malathion usually gives control.

Legume. A dry fruit or pod, two-valved, opening at both sides, with seeds attached to the ventral suture, as in the Pea and plants of the Leguminosae.

Leguminosae. The Pea Family, containing over 7,000 species, sometimes divided into Sub-families of Papilionaceae, Caesalpinioideae and Mimosoideae; characterized by having their seeds in a pod (legume), and a symbiotic association with certain soil bacteria at their roots which furnishes them with nitrogen from the atmosphere, and results in the plant ultimately enriching the soil. Typical genera are *Acacia, Anthyllis, Astragalus, Caesalpina, Caragana, Cercis, Colutea, Cytisus, Galega, Genista, Gleditschia, Glycine, Hedysarum, Indigofera, Laburnocytisus, Laburnum, Lathyrus, Fabia, Lupinus, Medicago, Mimosa, Ononis, Phaseolus, Pisum, Robinia, Spartium, Trifolium, Ulex, Vicia, Wisteria,* etc.

Leio-. Prefix in compound words, meaning smooth. Ex. *Leiophyllum*, smooth-leaved.

Leiophyllum, Sand Myrtle (li-o-pil'lum. Fam. Ericaceae). The only species, *L. buxifolium*, Eastern N. America, 18 in., is an evergreen shrub, with small, glossy, oval leaves, and terminal clusters of pink-tipped white flowers in May–June; v. *hugeri*, 6 in., and *prostratum*, 4 in., being dwarf forms for the rock garden or alpine house.

Cultivation. Plant April–May, in lime-free, peat-enriched soil, cool, partial shade, out of drying winds.

Propagation. By young shoot cuttings in July, in cold frame or under handlight.

Lemna, Duckweed (lem'na. Fam. Lemnaceae). Floating native aquatic weeds, multiplying rapidly in still water. *L. gibba, minor* and *trisulca*, the Ivy-leaved Duckweed, are sometimes introduced into garden ponds to provide food for fish and to keep the water clear, but need to be kept under strict control.

Lemon. See *Citrus.*

Lent Lily. See *Narcissus pseudo-narcissus.*

Lenten Rose. See *Helleborus orientalis.*

Lenticel. A small channel through the cork layer of bark, filled with loose, powdery cork cells, through which oxygen and gases can pass between the atmosphere and living tissue cells beneath.

Lenticular. Lens-shaped.

Leonotis (le-on-o'tis. Fam. Labiatae). S. African shrubs, of which *L. leonorus*, Lion's Tail, 3 ft, may be grown for its whorls of tubular orange-scarlet flowers in October–December, in the cool greenhouse; potted in March–April, standard compost, temp. 13° C. (55° F.), summered outdoors May–September, pinching top growth back to induce bushiness. Propagation is by cuttings of young shoots taken in April, gentle bottom heat.

Leontopodium (le-on-to-po'di-um. Fam. Compositae). The chief species grown is *L. alpinum*, the Edelweiss of European Alps, a 6-in. perennial with tufted, grey-green, woolly leaves, terminal flower-heads, with thick, silvery woolly bracts, June–July; and v. *crassense*, a finer form from the Balkans.

Cultivation. Plant April, in well-drained soil, rock garden or alpine house, where it will be fairly dry in winter.

Propagation. By seeds, sown March–April, in cold frame. By careful division in April–May.

Leopard's Bane. See *Doronicum*.

Leptopteris (lep-top'ter-is. Fam. Osmundaceae). Filmy ferns which may be grown in the cool greenhouse, allied to *Todea*, of much beauty.

Selection. L. hymenophylloides, New Zealand, feathery fronds of 1–2 ft, and *superba*, New Zealand, to 1½ ft, a miniature tree fern.

Cultivation. Pot in mixture of 2 parts peat, 2 parts silver sand, 1 part sphagnum moss, April; grow in close shape, winter temp. 10° C. (50° F.).

Propagation. By spores in March–April.

Leptosiphon. Now included in *Gilia*.

Leptospermum (lep-to-sperm'um. Fam. Myrtaceae). Attractive, small-leaved, Australasian evergreen shrubs, with open, white flowers in summer, only hardy in the mildest localities, and in the cool greenhouse.

Selection. L. pubescens, Australia, Tasmania, to 10 ft, with silvery, silky leaves, white flowers, is the hardiest, and its compatriots *keatleyi*, very large

flowers; *myrtifolium*, and *rodwayanum*, may be tried, given wall shelter; while *L. scoparium*, the Manuka of New Zealand, to 15 ft, white flowering in May–June, and vs. *boscawenii*, pale pink; *chapmanii*, rose-red; and *nichollsii*, carmine, are pretty outdoors in the south-west, in the greenhouse elsewhere; v. *prostratum* is low-growing.

Cultivation. Plant (or pot) March–April; well-drained humus soil or standard compost, sunny warmth. Potted plants may be placed outdoors, June–September.

Propagation. By cuttings of young shoots, in July, in propagating case, bottom heat of 18° C. (65° F.).

Leptosyne. Now *Coreopsis* (q.v.).

Lespedeza (les-ped-e'za. Fam. Leguminosae). Shrubby plants, dying to ground level each winter, sending up new shoots again which are almost bowed down with pea-like flowers along their length in late summer, from the axils of trifoliolate leaves.

Selection. L. thunbergii (*sieboldii*), China, Japan, to 4 ft, racemes of rose-purple flowers, is chiefly grown. *L. japonica* (*bicolor*), Japan, to 8 ft, rose purple, is less often available.

Cultivation. Plant October–March, well-drained, light loam soil, full sun.

Propagation. By seeds sown in April, outdoors, or in pots.

Lettuce (*Lactuca sativa*). This popular, hardy, annual salad vegetable is held to have reached England via Persia, Greece and Italy, and to have been grown in Britain since 1562. There are two main types, the Cabbage and the Cos, with some intermediate strains.

Outdoor Cultivation. It is important to choose appropriate varieties, according to sowing times. Cabbage vs.: for early spring sowing—Attractie, Trocadero Improved, May King; for spring and summer sowing—All The Year Round, Continuity, Feltham King, Unrivalled; and for crisp, curly-leafed types, Iceberg, Sutton's Favourite, Holborn Standard, Webb's Wonderful; for late summer sowing to winter outdoors—Arctic King, Imperial, Stanstead Park. Cos vs.: for spring sowing—Balloon, Lobjoit's Green, Paris White; for autumn sowing—Hick's Hardy Winter White, Density. Intermediate types: for spring and summer sowing—Buttercrunch, Histon Krispie. Novelty vs.: Salad Bowl (fimbriated leaves), Grand Rapids (fringed leaves).

An early sowing may be made in February, in seed boxes, under glass, temp. 13–15·5° C. (55–60° F.), standard compost, to plant out late March. Otherwise sowings may be made at 2- to 3-week intervals, in drills ¼ in. deep, thinly, 12 in. apart, subsequently transplanting 8–12 in. apart, or thinning. Soil should be well-prepared, moisture-retentive and humus-rich, liberally manured in autumn or from a previous crop; limed to pH 6·5. Suitable fertilizer for summer cropping—8 parts by weight hoof and horn meal, 4 parts super-phosphate, 1 part sulphate of potash at 3–4 oz. per sq. yd; for winter cropping—2 parts by weight superphosphate, 1 part sulphate of potash at 2 oz. per sq. yd. Weeds should be well controlled during growth, and watering done in dry weather. Over-wintering lettuce respond to a readily available nitrogenous fertilizer (dried blood or sodium nitrate) in March–April.

Cultivation in Frames and under Cloches. Varieties most suitable are Early French Frame, Cheshunt Early Giant, and Cheshunt 5B; May King under cloches. Seeds are sown in autumn, planted out a month or so after sowing, for winter or early spring cropping. In the cool greenhouse, autumn sowings of the Dutch forcing vs., Kordaat, Kwiek, Kloek, Knap and Korrekt may be made, to give lettuces in the winter and spring months; planted out in soil beds at ground level or on staging, with minimum winter temps. of 10–13° C. (50–55° F.); higher in the daytime.

Diseases. Damping-off of seedlings can be prevented by dressing seeds with a captan dust prior to sowing. Grey Mould (*Botrytis cinerea*) may attack under damp, cold conditions indoors and out, and careful watering is essential without wetting plants, while the use of a captan or thiram fungicide at 2–3 week intervals is preventive. Badly infected plants should be burnt. Downy Mildew (*Bremia lactucae*) may occur under glass or conditions of excessive humidity; a copper fungicide or zineb may be used to prevent its spread. 'Bolting' or the

rapid growth of a flowering stem is not a disease but a growth reaction to dry conditions and high temperatures. It can be minimized by good culture, which assures the plants adequate moisture at all times, especially after transplanting, and dense shading when temperature reaches about 21° C. (70° F.).

Pests. Root Aphids (*Pemphigus bursarius*) may appear in June–July, feeding on roots, and causing wilting and dying. A liquid derris insecticide can be used to water rooting areas. The primary winter host plants are poplars. Weed hosts such as Sowthistle (*Sonchus* sp.) and Goosefoot (*Chenopodium* sp.) should be kept down. Root maggots—larvae of Chrysanthemum leaf miner or Carrot Fly—may attack lettuces in ground previously occupied by these crops; a gamma-BHC soil insecticidal dressing would be preventive. Cutworms, wireworms, millipedes and chafer grubs may attack lettuces in ill-prepared ground. Slug damage is preventable by use of metaldehyde bait pellets.

Leucocoryne, Glory of the Sun (le-u-ko-ko-ri'ne. Fam. Liliaceae). The chief species grown is *L. ixioides*, a charming bulbous plant of Chile, with loose umbels of pale blue flowers on 12-in. stems in spring, which, being half-hardy, is best grown like *Freesia* (q.v.).

Leucogenes (lu-kog'en-es. Fam. Compositae). A genus of two species of New Zealand sub-shrubs, most satisfactorily grown in the alpine house.

Selection. L. grandiceps, 4 in., with short stems and whorls of overlapping small leaves, covered with silvery-white down, and small clusters of light yellow flowers surrounded by woolly white bracts, June; and *leontopodium*, a somewhat taller version to 8 in., silvergrey with fine hairy down, and light yellow flowers, June, suggestive of the Swiss Edelweiss.

Cultivation. Pot in March, compost of equal parts by volume loam, leaf-mould, peat and sand or fine grit, in well-drained pots; water freely in growth, little in winter, shade from hot direct sun. Repot annually.

Propagation. By cuttings of young shoots taken in June.

Leucojum, Snowflake (le-u-koy'um. Fam. Amaryllidaceae). Includes *Acis*.

Pretty bulbous plants, allied to Snow-drops, and resembling them with their drooping, bell-shaped white flowers; hardy except in cold areas.

Selection. L. aestivum, the Summer Snowflake of central and S. Europe, 15 in., white, green tipped flowers, May, and v. *pulchellum; autumnale,* Autumn Snowflake, SW. Europe, Morocco, 6 in., white and pink, autumn; *hiemale,* Winter Snowflake, Alps, 6 in., white, green tinged, spring; *vernum,* Spring Snowflake, Central Europe, 9 in., white,

FIG. 140 *Leucojum vernum,* Spring Snowflake.

tipped green, spring; and vs. *carpathicum,* with white, tipped yellow flowers; and *vagneri,* 12 in., two-flowered.

Cultivation. Plant in September, except *L. autumnale* which is planted in spring; well-drained, humus-rich soil, open site or partial shade, 2 in. deep, 4 in. apart. Or in pots in cold frame, to move to cool greenhouse when in active growth.

Propagation. By offsets on lifting bulbs when foliage withers. By seeds (3–4 years to flowering).

Leucothoe (le-u-ko-tho'e. Fam. Ericaceae). Evergreen flowering shrubs, akin to *Andromeda,* with small racemes of urn-like flowers.

Selection. L. catesbaei, SE. U.S.A., to

6 ft, long lanceolate leaves, flowering April–May; *davisiae,* Oregon, California, 1–3 ft; *keiskei,* Japan, prostrate-growing, with white July flowers, are the pick.

Cultivation. Plant October or April, in lime-free, peat or leaf-mould enriched soil, partial shade.

Propagation. By half-ripe cuttings of young shoots taken with a heel. August; by layering; by seeds sown in April, in cold frame.

Lewisia (le-wis'i-a. Fam. Portulaceae). Beautiful flowering perennial herbs of Western N. America, not dependably hardy where winter temperatures fluctuate too much; but splendid for rock gardens or the alpine house, under equable conditions.

Selection. L. howellii, Oregon, 6 in., cymes of deep rose flowers, May, and its vs.; *cotyledon,* California, 8 in., white, veined pink, flowers, June; and *tweedyi,* Washington, U.S.A., 6 in., apricot or pink, and vs., may be tried outdoors; *columbiana,* Columbia Rockies, 6 in., pink, veined purple, flowers, July, and v. *rosea; heckneri,* California, 6 in., pink and rose, June; and *finchii,* Oregon, 6 in., soft pink, are choices for the alpine house, with rosettes of evergreen leaves. *L. brachycalyx,* Western N. America, white solitary flowers, May; *pygmaea,* Rockies, 2 in., rose-red, May–June; and *rediviva,* W. U.S.A., solitary pale pink, red-veined flowers, July, are stout-rooted and herbaceous, requiring winter-dry positions.

Cultivation. Plant in very well-drained, leaf-mould-enriched soil, sunny dryish positions out of doors, March–April or October; pot for the alpine house in March, well-crocked pots, porous standard compost, with top layer of granite chippings.

Propagation. By offsets detached in June, and potted as cuttings, in cold frame. By seeds, sown April.

Leycesteria (ley-kes-ter'i-a. Fam. Caprifoliaceae). The species usually grown is *L. formosa,* a Himalayan deciduous flowering shrub of 4–6 ft, notable for its hollow-stemmed, sea-green, stout shoots, bearing long-pointed, simple leaves, and drooping spikes of reddish-purple, bracted flowers in late summer, followed by berries appreciated by game birds.

Cultivation. Plant in any reasonably good soil, partial shade or woodland, October–March. Prune in February, cutting away dead shoots and weak growth.

Propagation. By seeds, sown March–April, outdoors. By cuttings of young shoots, July–August, under handlight.

Liatris, Blazing Star, Button Snakeroot (li-at′ris. Fam. Compositae). Hardy herbaceous perennials of N. America, notable for their spikes of summer flowers, attractive to bees.

Selection. L. callilepsis, 2 ft, purple flowers; and v. 'Kobold', deep purple; *pycnostachya,* 3–5 ft, purple-crimson; *scariosa,* 2–5 ft, purple, and fine white form, *alba;* and *spicata,* 2 ft, red-purple.

Cultivation. Plant October–April, humus-rich, light soil, full sun, in borders.

Propagation. By seeds, sown April–July, cold frame. By division in April.

Libertia (li-bert′i-a. Fam. Iridaceae). Rhizomatous rooting, Iris-like, flowering perennials, not reliably hardy except in mild localities.

Selection. L. formosa, Chile, 1½ ft, narrow evergreen leaves, dense clusters of white flowers, May; *grandiflora,* New Zealand, 2–3 ft, white, summer; *ixioides,* New Zealand, 2 ft, white, summer; and *pulchella,* Australasia, 3–6 in., white, spring, are usually offered.

Cultivation. Plant October–March, in well-drained, porous soil, warm, sunny position, with litter protection of roots in winter.

Propagation. By seeds, in frame or cool greenhouse, spring (3 years to flower); or by careful division, April.

Libocedrus, Incense Cedar (li-bo-ke′drus. Fam. Pinaceae). Of these handsome, evergreen coniferous trees, only *L. decurrens,* Oregon, California, 100 ft, is reasonably hardy in Britain, stiffly columnar for formal effect, with fragrant wood; *chilensis,* the Chilean Cedar, 30–40 ft, is attractively pyramidal, but slow-growing and only for mild localities.

Cultivation. Plant in late March–April, well-drained soil and in good shelter from strong winds.

Propagation. By seeds, April, in cold frame; by cuttings, July–August, in cool frame.

Lichen. Lichens (li′kens) are composite plants, consisting of a fungus with hyphae enfolding an alga of the green or blue-green type in symbiotic association of mutual benefit, and producing fruit-bodies like those of the fungus. They are chiefly found on bare surfaces such as rocks, mountains and the ground, where they play a part in disintegrating rocks and so forming soil. They may also grow on walls, tree trunks and branches and among plants, chiefly in clean air, being inhibited in towns, cities and industrial areas where the air is polluted.

FIG. 141 Lichen, *Peltigera canina,* often troublesome on lawns.

Species are very numerous, but may be grouped into three forms: crustose or crusted; foliose or leaf-like; and fruticose, with strap-like or round 'stems'. Some are used for food (e.g. Reindeer Moss, Iceland Moss), many for dye-making (e.g. Lungwort). On tree or shrub stems they are not parasitic, but may interfere with respiration and harbour pests, and are easily controlled by winter tar-oil, DNOC or petroleum oil washes, or a copper fungicide. Leafy lichens on lawns can usually be controlled by painting with a tar-oil wash and improving soil fertility.

Light. Light is indispensable to the growth of green plants. It greatly affects the kind of growth made by the plant. Without light, chlorophyll, the green pigment, is not formed; plant tissue is whitish or yellow, stems elongate and leaves are reduced in size. Light is essential to photosynthesis (q.v.), the process by which plants manufacture food for themselves. Light also plays an important part in the flowering of many plants (see Photoperiodism). The influence of light on plants varies according to its actinic composition, its intensity and its duration.

Ligneous. Woody.

Ligularia (lig-u-lar'i-a. Fam. Compositae). Herbaceous perennials with bold foliage, and handsome flower-heads, allied to *Senecio*, for waterside planting or moist ground.

Selection. L. *dentata* (*clivorum*), China, 3–5 ft, orange-yellow rayed flowers, July–August, and vs. 'Desdemona' and 'Othello'; × *hessei*, 5 ft, orange, autumn; *przewalskii*, Mongolia, 4 ft, deep yellow, July; *veitchiana*, China, golden-yellow, July–September; and *wilsoniana*, China, to 5 ft, yellow, June, are hardy.

Cultivation. Plant October–March, moisture-retentive soil, in water garden or moist border.

Propagation. By seeds, sown early summer. By division in autumn or spring.

Ligulatus (-a, -um). Ligulate, strap-shaped. Ex. *Saxifraga ligulata*.

Ligule. A strap-like growth at the base of a leaf, especially in grasses.

Ligustrum, Privet (li-gust'rum. Fam. Oleaceae). A genus of deciduous and evergreen shrubs of which the hardy species are easily grown.

Selection. For shrub borders, L. *confusum*, N. India, to 20 ft, pale evergreen lanceolate leaves, panicles of white flowers, June–July, followed by small, grape-like clusters of berries, is good for the south and west, or sheltered wall border; *delavayanum*, China, to 6 ft, dark evergreen small leaves, white, June flowers; *japonicum*, Japan, 8 ft, slow-growing glossy evergreen, camellia-like leaves, large panicles of white flowers, late summer; *lucidum*, China, to 20–30 ft, tall shrub or tree, with large, oval, evergreen leaves, white panicles of bloom, August–September, and vs. *excelsum superbum*, fine yellow and cream variegated form, and *tricolor*, variegated pink and white in young leaves; *ovalifolium* v. *aureum*, Japan, to 12 ft, the Golden Privet, valuable for its bright foliage; *quihoui*, China, to 10 ft, deciduous, elegant shaped, valuable for late

panicles of white flowers, September; and *sinensis*, Chinese Privet, to 15 ft, semi-evergreen oval foliage, free-flowering with panicles of clear white flowers, July, and purplish-black autumn berries. L. *ovalifolium*, Japan, to 15 ft, is preferable to L. *vulgare*, Europe, the common Privet, for evergreen, quick-growing hedging, submitting well to a twice-a-year clipping.

Cultivation. Plant October–November or March–April, in reasonably well-drained soil, open sun. Prune or trim, as necessary, in May–June and August.

Propagation. By cuttings, young shoots, July–August.

Lilac. See *Syringa*.

Liliaceae. A large family of about 2,000 species, chiefly herbaceous perennials, among which bulbous, cormous, rhizomatous and fascicled rooted, and woody evergreen plants are to be found. Typical species are: *Asphodelus, Amane, Anthericum, Asparagus, Aspidistra, Bessara, Bulbocodium, Calochortus, Camassia, Chionodoxa, Colchicum, Convallaria, Cordyline, Dracaena, Eremurus, Erythronium, Eucomis, Fritillaria, Galtonia, Gloriosa, Haworthia, Hemerocallis, Hosta, Hyacinthus, Kniphofia, Lachenalia, Lapageria, Lilium, Muscari, Nomocharis, Ornithogalum, Polygonatum, Puschkinia, Rhodea, Ruscus, Sanseveria, Scilla, Smilax, Streptopus, Trillium, Tulipa, Urginea, Veltheimia, Yucca* and others.

Lilium, Lily (li'i-um. Fam. Liliaceae). Bulbous plants of great flowering beauty, originating in warm temperate or temperate regions of the northern hemisphere, but from widely differing habitats, which makes their cultural needs diverse, and often exacting and requiring study. See also *Cardiocrinum*.

Selection. Hardy kinds for outdoors: L. *amabile*, Korea, 3–4 ft, vivid red, black-spotted, flowers, July, stem-rooting; *auratum*, Golden-rayed Lily of Japan, 4–6 ft, ivory white, golden-banded, crimson and brown spotted, August, and vs., stem-rooting; *brownii*, China, 3–4 ft, creamy white, trumpet flowers, brown-tinged without, July, stem-rooting; *canadense*, Eastern N. America, 3 ft, yellow to red drooping bell-flowers, July; *candidum*, the Madonna Lily, E. Mediterranean, to

5 ft, pearl-white trumpet flowers, June; *chalcedonicum*, Greece, to 4 ft, Turk's cap, scarlet, recurving flowers, July; *concolor*, China, to 2 ft, scarlet, starry flowers, June–July, and v. 'Dropmore', orange-red; *bulbiferum croceum*, Orange Lily, S. Europe, tangerine-orange raceme of flowers, June; *dauricum* NE. Asia, 2 ft, red, brown-spotted flowers, June, stem-rooting; × 'Fire King', 3 ft, orange-red, July; *hansonii*, Korea, to 4 ft, orange-yellow Turk's cap flowers, June; *henryi*, China orange-yellow, brown-spotted flowers, August; × *imperiale*, 4 ft, funnel-shaped, fragrant white, greenish tinged, flowers, July; *longiflorum*, Formosa, white, fragrant trumpets, July, stem-rooting; × *maculatum* (*elegans*, *fortunei*, *thunbergianum*), Japan, 2–4 ft, in many fine vs., such as *batemanniae*, dark yellow; 'Golden Fleece', 'Kikak', dwarf, buff orange; 'Red Emperor', and 'Mahogany'; × 'Marhan', 6 ft, yellow, spotted brown, July; *martagon*, Europe, Asia, to 4 ft, Turk's cap, purplish-red, spotted darker, flowers, June–July; and v. *album*, white; *philippinense*, Philippines, to 2 ft, white funnel-shaped flowers, streaked red, August; *nanum*, Sikkim, Tibet, 8 in., bell-like, lilac, spotted reddish-purple, flowers, June; and v. *flavidum*, yellow flowering; *oxypetalum*, N. India, 9 in., yellow bell-flowers, June; *pumilum* (*tenuifolium*), China, Siberia, to 1½ ft, scarlet, nodding flowers, June, stem-rooting; *regale*, China, 3–6 ft, white, yellow-throated, trumpet flowers, July, stem-rooting; *sargentiae*, Szechwan, to 5 ft, white trumpet flowers, brown without, July; *speciosum*, Japan, 2–4 ft, white, spotted red, fragrant nodding flowers, August, and vs. *roseum*, rose-pink, *rubrum*, rosy-red washed; with forms 'Attraction', fine red, 'Melpomene', crimson dots on white, stem-rooting; *superbum*, Eastern N. America, to 8 ft, orange, crimson spotted, recurving flowers, July; × *testaceum*, the Nankeen Lily, 5–6 ft, pale yellow, July–August; *tigrinum*, Tiger Lily, China, Japan, to 4 ft, orange-red, black spotted, recurved flowers, August–September, stem-rooting; and vs. *flaviflorum*, yellow; *fortunei*, orange-scarlet; and *splendens*, salmon-red; *umbellatum* × *hollandi-*

cum [× *maculatum?*]), of garden origin, to 2 ft, in forms *erectum*, red, orange flushed flowers, July; *grandiflorum*, orange; 'Monarch', dark red; 'Orange Triumph', orange-yellow, etc.; *davidii* (*wilmottiae*), 3–4 ft, orange-red, spotted flowers, July, stem-rooting.

Hybrids. Numerous hybrids have been raised in recent years, particularly in U.S.A. and Canada, which are of enhanced garden merit and easy culture, and will be found under names such as *Aurelian* Hybrids ('Golden Clarion', 'Heart's Desire', 'Sunburst'), × *aureliense* Hybrids ('Stooke's'; 'Constance Spry', 'Lady Londonderry), trumpet-flowered; *Backhouse* Hybrids ('Brocade', 'Golden Orb', 'Mrs R. O. Backhouse', 'Sutton Court'), martagon-type flowers; *Bellingham* Hybrids ('Cyrus Gates', 'Kulshan', 'Shuksan',

FIG. 142 Lilium hybrid 'Brandywine', of *Mid-Century* group.

'Star of Oregon'), many-flowered, tall stems; *Fiesta* Hybrids ('Dr Abel'); reflexed petals; *Mid-Century* Hybrids ('Brandywine', 'Destiny', 'Enchantment', 'Joan Evans', 'Valencia'), stem-rooting; *Preston* Hybrids ('Brenda Watts', 'Grace Marshall', 'Lilian Cummings', 'Muriel Condie'; 'Hurricane', 'Spitfire', 'Typhoon', etc.), stem-rooting; and *Olympic* Hybrids, which are trumpet-flowering in white to soft green, and stem-rooting.

Cultivation. Most hardy lilies need well-drained soil, well provided with humus, a cool root run and sheltered quarters from wind, with good sun and light for their foliage, though midday shade from very hot sun is agreeable. The time to plant is preferably as soon as the bulbs go dormant on completion of their annual growth. Lilies which produce roots from the base of the bulb only, very largely those of European and American species, are planted in late summer and autumn. A few, such as *L. candidum, L. × testaceum*, have short dormancy periods and should be planted in August–September. Lilies which root from the base and later from the stem, chiefly Asiatic species and their hybrids, may be planted early autumn to early spring. Basal rooting lilies are planted 4–6 in. deep, though *L. candidum* needs only a bare inch of soil over its top; and the neck of the bulb of *L. giganteum* should be at soil level. Stem-rooting lilies need to be planted 8–10 in. deep. On loam or heavy soils, it is useful to plant on and surround with coarse sand. On calcareous soils, preference should be given to species such as *L. amabile, brownii, bulbiferum croceum, candidum, chalcedonicum, davidii, hansonii, henryii, × maculatum,* × 'Marhan', *martagon, monadelphum, pumilum, pyrenaicum, regale, sargentiae, × testaceum* and *tigrinum*. Lilies for moist, cool conditions, where the soil is well-drained but rich in leaf-mould or peat, or by water, include *L. auratum, canadense, columbianum, grayi, japonicum, pardalinum, parryi, parvum, rubellum, rubescens, superbum, wardii*. Lilies which succeed in the partial, not dense, shade of shrubs and woodland are *L. auratum, brownii, candense, columbianum, distichum, giganteum*, Himalaya,

6–10 ft, *hansonii, henryii, humboldtii*, California, 5–6 ft, *leichtlinii* v. *maximowiczii*, Japan, 6 ft, *japonicum, martagon, monodelphum*, N. Caucasus, 3–5 ft, July, *pardalinum*, California, 3–6 ft, *parryi, parvum, rubellum, superbum, washingtonianum*, California, 3–5 ft, and their varieties, which appreciate the wind and frost shelter afforded by the woody plants.

Lilies under Glass. The lilies most successful for pot culture are the stem-rooting species and hybrids, planted deeply in rather large pots. They include *L. brownii, dauricum, formosanum, hansonii, henryii, longiflorum* and v. *eximum,* × *maculatum, pumilum, regale, speciosum, rubellum tigrinum* and × *umbellatum* (*hollandicum*), which may be potted in autumn for spring and summer flowering. Basal-rooting species which may be grown in pots are *L. bulbiferum croceum; catesbaei*, SE. U.S.A., 1–2 ft, red and yellow; *candidum*, and × *testaceum*; potted in late summer. The size of the pot must be regulated by the size of the bulbs and their top growth. Single bulbs need 5- or 6-in. pots usually, large bulbs 8–10-in. pots. Pots must be well-crocked for good drainage, and filled with a standard compost or one of 2 parts by bulk good loam, 1 part leaf-mould and peat, and ½ part sharp sand. The bulbs must be encouraged to form good roots first, and are best grown like hyacinths, plunged in ashes or fibre, in cold frame or under a north wall, for 6–8 weeks before bringing into a greenhouse at 7–10° C. (45–50° F.), which may be increased if early flowering is required to 15·5–21° C. (60–70° F.). Watering needs care, being done to keep the soil nicely moist; plants may be fed a liquid feed, when in bud, weekly. Stems need staking, and may be cut down only when growth is completed for the year.

Propagation. By seeds in pans, boxes or the cold frame; or outdoors in prepared seed-beds, in spring. Germination varies from a few weeks to up to two years according to species. By bulb scales, taken from the bulb, inserted upright in sandy loam or mixture of sand and peat, for at least three parts their length, with bottom heat of 15·5–18° C. (60–65° F.), in greenhouse or frame. Bulbils form in a few weeks which can be transplanted and grown on. By offsets, removed and planted separately during dormant period. By bulbils where produced in the axils of upper leaves in such lilies as *L. bulbiferum croceum, sargentiae, tigrinum* and forms of × *maculatum*, detached and planted separately when easily detached.

Diseases. Lily Disease, in which round, water-soaked patches appear on leaves, turning grey or white, is caused by *Botrytis elliptica*, a fungus, especially in warm damp weather. *L. candidum, regale* and × *testaceum* are susceptible, also seedlings, but the use of a copper fungicide is helpful. Plants should be lifted when foliage dies, and bulbs replanted on a fresh site. Bulbs store poorly, and scales attacked by green mould (*Penicillium* spp.) or rot (*Rhizopus necans*) should be removed, and bulbs dusted with a thiram fungicide prior to planting. Lilies suffer from two virus diseases, Mosaic and Rosette, which cause degeneration and stunting of plants. It is very important to buy only clean healthy bulbs, especially if imported; and to rogue out any plants showing signs of virus infection promptly.

Pests. Lily bulbs are good food for mice and rats; to be defeated by the use of Warfarin baits. Slugs need to be controlled with metaldehyde; millipedes by use of a gamma-BHC soil insecticidal dust; which should also be used to deter bulb Thrips (*Liothrips vaneeckei*). Aphid attacks on foliage should be countered promptly with malathion, derris or nicotine. The Lily Beetle (*Crioceris lilii*) may be imported with bulbs from abroad, a bright scarlet beetle giving rise to greyish-white, short hump-backed grubs, feeding on the foliage. May be controlled by removal or the use of a derris or nicotine insecticide.

Lily, African. See *Agapathus.*

Lily, Belladonna. See *Amaryllis.*

Lily, Day. See *Hemerocallis.*

Lily, Guernsey. See *Nerine.*

Lily of the Valley. See *Convallaria.*

Lily-Tree. A name sometimes used for *Magnolia* (q.v.).

Lily, Water. See *Nymphaea.*

Lime. Lime is a name somewhat loosely used in gardening for compounds of calcium oxide (CaO). It is important in soil cultivation under temperate conditions as a base or alkali which combines readily with acids to neutralize soil acidity, which is often inhibitory to the growth of many garden plants. In so doing it makes other nutrient elements such as magnesium, potassium and phosphorus more available to plants. It supplies calcium, an essential nutrient of plant growth. Physically, it causes soil particles to flocculate or form aggregated particles, particularly of clay, and tends to make heavy soils more friable, and light ones slightly more moisture-retentive. The presence of lime is favourable to the activity of beneficial soil bacteria, micro-organisms and earthworms. It helps the rapid decomposition of organic matter in the soil. Too much lime, however, inhibits the availability of nutrients such as phosphorus, iron and manganese to plants. Lime normally exists in the soil as calcium carbonate, chalk or limestone and as exchangeable lime, which, combined with the clay and humus fractions, is most active and most needed. The purpose of liming is to assure sufficient soluble and available lime to maintain the acid-alkali balance of the soil solution at a level most favourable to the plants being grown, bearing well in mind that plants differ in this respect. Soil acidity is determined by its hydrogen ion concentration, expressed in terms of the pH scale or value (see pH scale). The tendency in most soils under cultivation is to become more acid as soluble calcium salts are lost in chemical reactions, plant nutrition and drainage. The following forms of lime may be used to correct soil acidity. *Quicklime* (CaO), or burnt lime, made by heating limestone in a kiln. It is caustic, and needs to be slaked to form hydrated lime before use, in autumn or winter. *Hydrated lime* (calcium hydroxide, $Ca(OH)_2$) is powdered and non-caustic, applicable when convenient. *Ground chalk* (calcium carbonate, $CaCO_3$) slightly porous, beneficial on all soils, particularly sand and light ones, is best used in autumn or winter. *Ground limestone* (calcium carbonate, $CaCO_3$) is an alternative to ground chalk for autumn or winter use, preferably finely ground. *Ground dolomite* or *magnesian limestone* is similar but also contains magnesium and is useful on acid, magnesium-deficient soils and for peat-sand propagating composts. *Mortar rubble* is often advocated for soil composts, but it should be derived from the old lime-mortar, and not modern materials, now used in building. The actual amount of a liming material to apply depends on the present acidity and how much it needs correcting for the plants to be grown, the nature of the soil and the kind of lime applied. The more porous and open the soil, the more quickly lime makes its influence felt, and less is needed. Dense heavy clay coils are rather resistant to quick changes in pH and should be limed more heavily, ahead of the growing season.

dendrons, Vaccinium and Zenobia; with a few exceptions such as *Arbutus unedo*, *Erica carnea* and vs., *E. mediterranea*, *E. stricta*, *Rhododendron hirsutum*.

Lime Tree. See *Tilia*.

Limnanthemum. See *Nymphoides*.

Limnanthes (lim-nan'thes. Fam. Limnanthaceae). Californian flowering annuals of which the species chiefly grown is *L. douglasii*, 6–12 in., with yellow and white open flowers, spring and summer, much visited by bees. It may be sown in March–April where it is to flower, almost any garden soil, and sun, and will tend to resow itself.

Limonium, Sea Lavender (li-mo'nium. Fam. Plumbaginaceae), sometimes still listed as *Statice*. Annual and perennial flowering plants from coastal habitats in various countries.

Selection. *L. bonduellii*, N. Africa, 2 ft,

Type of Soil	Amount of hydrated lime* in oz. per sq. yd, needed to correct acidity of pH				
	4·5	5·0	5·5	6·0	6·5
Sands	8	6½	5½	5	0
Silt or Light Loams	10	8	7	6	0
Medium Loams	12	10	8	6½	0
Heavy Loams	14	12	10	7	0
Clay or Peat	16–18	14–15	11–13	9–10	0

* If ground chalk or limestone is used, amounts are increased by about one-third.

Lime is best applied as a top-dressing and raked in, at least a month before or after manure or organic materials. It should not be mixed with fertilizers such as ammonium sulphate, or nitrogenous fertilizers.

Lime Sulphur. *See* Fungicides.

Lime Tolerance in Plants. The majority of garden plants have a tolerance for lime in the soil, and thrive best in soils of slight to strong acidity. A number of plants are intolerant of exchangeable lime in the soil, and only thrive in very strongly acid soils, notably most genera of the *Ericaceae* or Heath family, which includes Andromeda, Calluna, Cassiope, Daboecia, Enkianthus, Erica, Gaultheria, Kalmia, Ledum, Leiophyllum, Pernettya, Phyllodoce, Pieris, Rhodo-

yellow, and *sinuatum*, Mediterranean region, to 15 in., in rose, lavender, blue and many coloured flower forms, are half-hardy perennials, grown as annuals. *L. suworowii*, Turkestan, with poker-like spikes of lilac flowers to 3 ft, is a fairly hardy annual. *L. bellidifolium*, Europe, 9 in., white flowers, late summer; *cosyrense*, S. Europe, violet, June; *gougetianum*, Italy, 10 in., white, red and lavender flowers, July; *incanum*, Siberia, 1 ft, white and crimson, summer; and *minutum*, Mediterranean region, are perennials for the rock garden. *L. elatum*, Russia, 2 ft, blue, July; *eximium*, C. Asia, 2 ft, rosy lilac, July; *gmelinii*, Siberia, to 2 ft, pink, July; *latifolium*, Bulgaria, 2 ft, blue, June; *sinense*, China, 1 ft, yellow, summer; and *tartaricum*, SE. Europe, 1½ ft, ruby-red, July, are useful hardy perennials for borders. *L. vulgare*, the native Sea Lavender 1½ ft, purplish-blue, summer, may be cultivated. *L. imbricatum*, Canaries, 1½ ft, blue, summer; *macrophyllum*, Canaries, to 3 ft, purple-blue, May onwards; × *profusum*, 2 ft, purple, autumn, are perennials for the cool greenhouse.

Cultivation. Plant in well-drained ordinary soils in spring; annuals in May, spacing 6–12 in. apart; sunny positions.

Propagation. Annuals by seeds sown under glass in March, or outdoors in April, warm beds. Perennials by seeds sown outdoors, April–June, or by division in April. Greenhouse perennials are usually grown from seeds sown in March, and make good long-flowering pot plants, minimum winter temp. 7° C. (45° F.), watering very moderately in winter, freely in summer.

Linaria (lin-a′ri-a. Fam. Scrophulariaceae). Pretty annual and perennial flowering herbs; Toadflax.

Selection. L. maroccana, Morocco, to 1 ft, in colour forms such as 'Fairy Bouquet', 'Northern Lights' and 'Excelsior', gives annual colour in red, violet, blue, white, yellow, June–July; *reticulata*, Portugal, 2 ft, white, veined purple, and its v. *aureo-purpurea*, deep purple and gold, are hardy annuals. *L. aequitriloba*, Sardinia, 1 in., dwarf evergreen, purple flowers, June; *alpina*, European Alps, to 4 in., violet and orange, summer, with vs. *alba*, white, and *rosea*, pink; and *supina*, SW. Europe, 6 in., yellow, and v. *nevadensis*, red-purple, summer, are useful for the rock garden or alpine house. *L. cymbalaria*, Kenilworth Ivy, Mother of Thousands, Pennywort, with many vs., is the pretty lilac-flowering, creeping perennial, naturalized from S. Europe, useful for walls, hanging baskets, though apt to become a weed. *L. dalmatica*, SE. Europe, 3 ft, yellow flowering, summer; *purpurea*, S. Europe, 2½ ft, bluish purple, summer, and its form 'Canon J. Went', rose-pink, are good border perennials. *L. triornithophora*, Portugal, to 3 ft, purple and yellow, makes a good cool greenhouse pot plant.

Cultivation. All succeed in well-drained garden soils, enriched with humus, and

sunny positions; annuals being sown where they are to flower, and perennials planted October–April.

Propagation. Perennials by division in autumn or spring; or by seeds in April onwards. Annuals by seeds, sown under glass in February–March, or outdoors, March–April.

Lindane. The insecticide based on gamma isomer of benzene hexachloride (gamma-BHC). *See* Insecticides.

Lindelofia (lin-de-lo′fi-a. Fam. Boraginaceae). The species *L. longiflora*, W. Himalaya, 1½ ft, is a hairy, hardy perennial, with bright blue flowers in summer, for any ordinary humus-rich soil and warm, sunny position. It may be raised from seeds, sown in April–May, and propagated by root division in spring.

Linden. See *Tilia*.

Linearis (-e). Linear, narrow. Ex. *Callistemon linearis*.

Lineatus (-a, -um). Streaked or marked with fine parallel lines. Ex. *Convolvulus lineatus*.

Ling. See *Calluna vulgaris*.

Lingulatus (-a, -um). Lingulate, tongue-shaped. Ex. *Saxifraga lingulata*.

Linnaea (lin-ne′a. Fam. Caprifoliaceae). The one species, *L. borealis*, is a useful hardy trailing evergreen with flesh-pink, scented flowers, May–July, of the northern hemisphere, with v. *americana* deeper coloured; useful for the shade in rock gardens, in peaty soil; planted April. Propagated by division in April.

Linum, Flax (li′num. Fam. Linaceae). Annual and perennial flowering plants.

Selection. L. grandiflorum, N. Africa, 1 ft, is a showy annual, with rose-carmine early summer flowers, and vs. 'Bright Eyes', white-eyed, *caeruleum*, blue, and 'Venice Red', for sowing in March in well-drained, humus-enriched soils, and sun, where they are to flower; *usitatissimum*, Europe, 1½ ft, is the blue-flowered annual common Flax, grown in selected varieties for its fibre used in linen-making, or for its oily seeds (linseed) in the herb garden. *L. alpinum*, European Alps, 6 in., china-blue flowers, July–August; *flavum*, E. Europe, 1 ft, golden-yellow, August; *salsoloides*, SW. Europe, 6 in., pearly white, June, and v.

nanum, a dwarf of 1 in., are hardy for the rock garden; but *arboreum*, Crete, 1 ft, shrubby with golden June flowers; *elegans*, Mount Athos, 8 in., yellow, May, need winter protection or the alpine house. *L. narbonense*, S. Europe, to 2 ft, blue, May–July, and v. 'Heavenly Blue'; *perenne*, v. *lewisii*, N. America, 1½ ft, white, June, are good for the border.

Cultivation. Plant perennials in March–April, good, well-drained soil and sun; sheltered in cold areas.

Propagation. All the above may be grown from seeds in spring, sown in cold frame, March, or outdoors later. Perennials by cuttings of firm young shoots, July–August, under handlight or in cold frame.

Lip. The labellum in Orchids (q.v.).

Lippia (lip'pi-a. Fam. Verbenaceae). The only species much grown is *L. citriodora* (*Aloysia c.*), Lemon Verbena, Chile, to 10 ft, a deciduous shrub with lemon-scented, lanceolate leaves in threes, and slender panicles of pale purple flowers, August; hardy only for very mild localities, by warm walls, or for the cool greenhouse; given humus-rich, free-draining soil, or standard compost. Plant or pot in March–April. Protect in cold weather, if out of doors with litter or matting. Easily propagated by cuttings of young shoots in summer, in a cold frame or under handlight.

Liquid Fertilizers. *See* Fertilizers.

Liquid Manures. *See* Manures.

Liquidambar (lik-wid-am'bar. Fam. Hamamelidaceae). Ornamental, pyramidal deciduous trees with maple-like foliage and fragrant balsam-like resin.

Selection. L. styraciflua, the Sweet Gum of N. America, to 70 ft, colours beautifully in autumn; *formosana*, China, is usually offered in v. *monticola*, to 70 ft, with somewhat larger, 3–5-lobed leaves, tinted in spring, colouring again in autumn.

Cultivation. Plant October–March, good, well-drained loam soil, somewhat sheltered position.

Propagation. By imported seeds, sown April, though often taking two years to germinate. By layering in spring.

Liriodendron, Tulip Tree (li-ri-o-den'dron. Fam. Magnoliaceae). Most handsome, hardy deciduous trees with distinctive, squarish pointed leaves, turning yellow in autumn, and large, greenish-yellow, bell-shaped flowers, like upturned tulips, in summer on well-established specimens in the warmer counties.

Selection. L. tulipifera, N. America, to 100 ft, is perfectly hardy, with v. *aureo-marginatum*, yellow-edged leaves, and *fastigiatum*, narrowly pyramidal, sometimes offered; *chinense*, a Chinese species, is similar but smaller-leafed and flowering.

Cultivation. Plant in October–March, well-drained loam, open situation, not too exposed.

Propagation. By seeds when available in a cold frame, though a percentage will prove infertile.

Liriope (li-ri-o'pe. Fam. Liliaceae). Only *L. muscari* (*L. graminifolia* v. *densiflora*) is now offered, a choice Chinese perennial with evergreen grass-like foliage, and spikes of deep purple, bell-like flowers, 18 in. tall, in autumn. Plant in well-drained, open soil in spring; propagating by division at the same time, April.

Lithops, Pebble Plants (lith'ops. Fam. Aizoaceae). Pebble-like succulent plants from Namaqualand, S. Africa, for pot-growth indoors or in the cool greenhouse.

Selection. Distinctive species are *L. alpina*, brownish; *bella*, brownish-yellow; *comptonii*, olive-green; *fulleri*, dove grey, brownish markings; *kuibisensis*, reddish; *laterita*, brick-red; *lesliei*, rust-brown, greenish markings; *olivacea*, olive-green; *optica*, grey to fawn, and v. *rubra*; and *salicola*, grey; and others.

Cultivation. Pot rather generously or in pans, with well-drained cactus compost, April, keeping moist until after flowering in summer, when water is gradually withheld, keeping dry October–March; good light or sun; minimum winter temp. 7–10° C. (45–50° F.).

Propagation. By seeds, in spring, bottom heat 18° C. (65° F.).

Lithospermum, Gromwell (lith-o-sperm'um. Fam. Boraginaceae). Flowering perennial herbs or sub-shrubs chiefly for the rock garden.

Selection. L. diffusum, S. Europe, evergreen sub-shrub, to 12 in., prostrate habit, notable for its fine deep blue flowers, June, and vs. 'Grace Ward' and 'Heavenly Blue', and *album*, white; must have lime-free soil: others such as *fruticosum*, Spain, to 1 ft, blue, June; *oleifolium*, Pyrenees, 6 in., violet to blue, June; and *purpureo-caeruleum*, Europe, 1 ft, rampant, red to blue flowers, June, are quite lime-tolerant. *L. rosmarinifolium*, Italy, 1 ft, bright blue, lined white flowers, early spring, makes a good plant for the alpine house.

Cultivation. Plant preferably in spring, ex pots.

Propagation. By seeds in spring, in cool frame. By cuttings of young shoots in June.

Liver of Sulphur. Water-soluble, reddish-brown solid, containing potassium polysulphides, at one time used as a fungicide and acaricide, but phytotoxic to many plants and now superseded by lime-sulphur, etc.

Liverwort. A Class, Hepaticae, which with the Mosses form the Order Bryophyta. Liverworts are green lower plants with fat, lobed, leaf-like structures, often in three rows, found under damp conditions; sometimes troublesome on poor damp soils and lawns.

FIG. 143 Common Liverwort, *Lunularia cruciata*: r. reproductive bodies (gemmae) on a leaf.

Lividus (-a, -um). Livid, lead- or greyish-coloured. Ex. *Helleborus lividus*.

Livistona (li-vis-ton'a. Fam. Pal-maceae). Ornamental palms with fan-shaped leaves for the warm greenhouse.

Selection. L. australis, Australia, tall-growing, and *chinensis*, China, are the more hardy, requiring minimum temps. of 13–15·5° C. (55–60° F.); while *humilis*, tropical Australia, and *rotundifolia*, Malaya, need 18–21° C. (65–70° F.).

Cultivation. Pot in April, standard compost; watering freely in April–September, with frequent overhead syringing on hot days; very moderate watering in winter. Repot triennially.

Propagation. By imported seeds, sown with bottom heat of 21° C. (70° F.), in propagating frame.

Lloydia (loid'i-a. Fam. Liliaceae). The one species grown in *L. serotina*, 4 in., a high alpine bulbous plant of European Alps and Welsh mountains; with single, sometimes a pair, of drooping, bell-shaped, white, tinged yellow flowers, June; needing a gritty peaty soil, draining perfectly, in a cool northerly place in the rock garden. Propagated by offsets at planting time, in September.

Loam. Horticulturally a soil in which the sand, silt and clay fractions are in good balance, with some humus. It is termed light if sand predominates; medium when ideally proportioned; heavy if clay is dominant. It is the basis of soil composts, being prepared from turfs cut 4½ in. thick, about 12 in. square, stacked grass-side down, from pasture land, in moist conditions to rot for 6–12 months; and then broken down, sifted and sterilized for use.

Loasa (lo-a'sa. Fam. Loasaceae). Chiefly annuals of tropical America, with stinging hairs and colourful showy flowers.

Selection. L. acanthifolia, Chile, to 4 ft, yellow flowers, summer; *canarinoides*, C. America, to 10 ft, brick-red; and *vulcanica*, Ecuador, 2 ft, white summer flowers, are good.

Cultivation. Sow under glass, March, bottom heat of 18° C. (65° F.); prick off and plant out in May, well-drained soil and sun.

Lobatus (-a, -um). Lobed. Ex. *Clematis indivisa lobata.*

Lobe. A division of a leaf, petal or similar organ of a plant.

Lobelia (lo-be'li-a. Fam. Campanulaceae). A large genus of annuals and perennial flowering plants from warm temperate and tropical regions.

Selection. Although naturally perennial, the dwarf bedding and edging Lobelias stem from *L. erinus*, S. Africa, 6 in., which are grown as half-hardy annuals, and include forms such as 'Cambridge Blue', 'Mrs Clibran', deep blue, white eye; 'White Lady' and 'Rosamond', carmine; seeds being sown under glass, March, standard compost, for planting out in May; *pendula* in vs. 'Blue Cascade' and 'Sapphire' is grown similarly as a trailer for baskets. Fine border perennials are *L. cardinalis*, the Cardinal Flower of N. America, 3 ft, scarlet flowers, July–August, and forms such as 'J. MacMasters', deep purple, 'Purple Emperor', 'Queen Victoria', crimson, and 'Russian Princess', salmon-pink; × *milleri*, 2 ft, blue and purple flowering hybrids; *syphilitica*, E. U.S.A., 2 ft, light blue; and *tupa*, Chile, to 6 ft, reddish-scarlet, autumn; but all should have winter protection in cool areas, or be lifted to winter in a frame. *L. linnaeoides*, New Zealand, a creeping mat-forming perennial, white flowers, violet beneath, July–October, and *tenuior*, W. Australia, 1 ft, deep blue, white-eyed flowers, September, are best pot-grown in the cool greenhouse, standard compost.

Cultivation. Plant perennials in March–April, humus-enriched, well-drained soil, and sunny warmth.

Propagation. By seeds, under glass, in early spring; or on warm seed-beds outdoors, May–June. Perennials may be increased by division in April.

Lobivia (lo-biv′i-a. Fam. Cactaceae). Very spiny, round or cylindrical, ribbed plants, with short-lived, large bell-shaped flowers, opening in the sun only.

Selection. L. aurea, Argentina, lemon-yellow flowers, very free; *famatimensis*, Argentina, small, various coloured forms of yellow to red flowers; *hertrichiana*, Peru, scarlet; *pentlandii*, Bolivia, pink, but several forms; *saltensis*, Argentina, red flowers.

Cultivation. Pot, and repot, March–April; standard cactus compost; water freely to September; very little at other times, winter temp. 10° C. (50° F.); good light.

Propagation. By seeds in spring; by offsets.

Lobularia, Sweet Alyssum (lob-u-la′ri-a. Fam. Cruciferae). The one species, *L. maritima*, Europe, is a grey-leaved hardy annual, 6–9 in., with white, scented summer flowers; 'Little Dorrit', 'Snow Carpet' and 'Snow Quilt' are selected strains. May be easily grown from seeds, sown where plants are to flower, in ordinary garden soil in spring; a good bee plant, tending to re-sow itself.

Locust, Honey. See *Gleditschia*.

Locust-tree. See *Ceratonia*, and *Robinia*.

Loganberry. A hybrid bramble fruit, said to have originated in California from a cross between a Blackberry and a Raspberry in 1881. The Boysenberry is somewhat similar and may be considered here. The plant grows like a bramble, with vigorous shoots to 15 ft long; the fruit is oblong, large, acid and juicy, but comes away with the core or plug, when ripe in mid July–mid August, and is most suitable for jam-making or culinary use.

Varieties. Loganberry E.M. strain, or Thornless Loganberry are suitable for modern gardens.

Cultivation. Plant in October–March, in any reasonable soil, well-dug, organically manured, and limed to pH 6·5; 12–15 ft apart, on walls or wire supports. Cut the canes back to 9 in. after planting. Plants fruit on the previous year's canes, so when established, treatment consists of cutting away the fruited canes at their base after harvest, and training in the new canes in a fan formation. An annual top dressing of organic manure or compost in autumn/winter, and a high potash compound fruit fertilizer should be given in March each year.

Propagation. Tips of shoots, buried firmly in 3 in. of soil in July, root readily, and can be detached for planting out the following spring.

Diseases and Pests. Similar to those affecting Raspberries, and needing similar control.

Loiseleuria, Creeping Alpine Azalea (loi-se-lew′ri-a. Fam. Ericaceae). The only species, *L. procumbens*, common to alpine arctic regions, is a low, evergreen, mat-forming, prostrate shrub, for lime-free, moisture-retentive, peat and granite grit soil, in cool conditions and clear light, when it may bear its clusters of campanulate pinkish or white flowers in July–August. Needs watering thoroughly in dry weather with lime-free water. Propagated by layers, or cuttings of young shoots with a heel, in July.

Lomaria. A genus now grouped under *Blechnum*.

Lomatia (lo-ma′ti-a. Fam. Proteaceae). Fine ornamental evergreen shrubs, doubtfully hardy except in very mild localities, but eligible for cold greenhouse treatment, summering out of doors.

Selection. L. *ferruginea*, Chile, to 12 ft, large, fern-like leaves, deep yellow and rose racemes of flowers, July; *longifolia*, New S. Wales, to 6 ft, long, oak-like leaves, white, scented flowers, July; *obliqua*, Chile, to 12 ft, ovate leaves, white June flowers; and *tinctoria*, Tasmania, 2 ft, pinnate leaves, yellow flowers, July, may be attempted.

Cultivation. Plant in April–May, humus-rich, well-drained loam soil, warm sunny wall shelter in mild localities; in tubs or large pots, which can be moved to a greenhouse for winter, elsewhere.

Propagation. By cuttings of young firm shoots, July–August, inserted in close propagating frame, with bottom heat of 18° C. (65° F.), or mist propagation.

Lombardy Poplar. See *Populus*.

Lonas, African Daisy (lo′nas. Fam. Compositae). The one species, L. *inodora*, Mediterranean region, to 1 ft, with corymbs of small yellow daisy-like flowers in summer, is an annual, easily grown from seeds sown in ordinary soil in spring, and may be dried as one of the 'everlasting flowers'.

London Pride. See *Saxifraga umbrosa*.

Lonicera, Honeysuckle (lon-i′ke-ra; lon-i′se-ra by usage. Fam. Caprifoliaceae). A fairly large genus of shrubs, deciduous and evergreen, which may be divided into Bush Honeysuckles and Climbers; all originating in the northern hemisphere.

Selection. Attractive shrubs of bushy habit include: L. *alpigena*, Central Europe, to 8 ft, yellow tubular flowers in pairs, May, red cherry-like autumn fruits; *angustifolia*, Himalaya, 6 ft, pinkish white fragrant flowers, April, red fruits; *chrysantha*, NE. Asia, to 10 ft, pale yellow flowers, May, red fruits; *korolkowii*, Turkistan, 6 ft or more,

rose-pink flowers, June, red fruits; *maximowiczii* v. *sachalinensis*, Korea, to 10 ft, dark purple flowers, May–June, purple fruits; *myrtillus*, Himalaya, 3 ft, yellowish white flowers, May, orange-red fruits; *rupicola*, Himalaya, 6 ft, pale pink fragrant flowers, May–June; *syringantha*, China, 6 ft, fragrant rose flowers, May–June, red fruits; *tartarica*, v. *latifolia*, Turkistan, to 8 ft, rosy-red flowers, June; *thibetica*, Tibet, 4 ft, fragrant lilac flowers, May–June, red fruits; and *alberti*, Turkistan, 2 ft, fragrant, rose-lilac flowers, May, purplish-red fruits; all being deciduous.

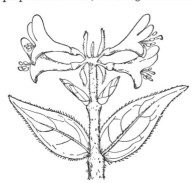

FIG. 144 Flowers and leaves of *Lonicera standishii*, a bush Honeysuckle.

L. *fragrantissima*, China, 6 ft, creamy-white fragrant flowers in winter; *standishii*, China, 6 ft, fragrant white flowers, November–March, and their hybrid × *purpusii*, are semi-evergreen and valuable for their early flowers; while L. *nitida*, China, to 6 ft, and its v. *fertilis*, are evergreens often used for quick-growing hedges, which, however, need frequent trimming. Climbing Honeysuckles which are deciduous are L. × *americana*, creamy-yellow, tinged rose, fragrant flowers, summer; × *brownii*, orange-scarlet flowers, May–August; *caprifolium*, Europe, fragrant, creamy white, June–July; *etrusca*, Mediterranean region, fragrant creamy-white, flushed purplish-red, flowers, July–August; *periclymenum*, native Woodbine, fragrant, yellow-white flowers, June–August, and vs. *belgica*, early Dutch Honeysuckle, deep purplish-red flowers; and *serotina*, late Dutch Honeysuckle, purplish red and yellow flowers, August; × *tellmanniana*, large leaved, rich yellow flowers, tipped red, June–July; and *tragophylla*, China, ornamental leaved, golden-yellow flowers without scent, June–July. Evergreens include *L. alseuosmoides*, China, funnel-shaped, small yellow and purple flowers;

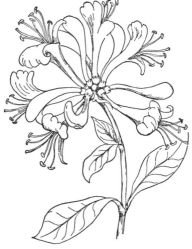

FIG. 145 Flower of *Lonicera pericly-menum*, a climbing Honeysuckle.

giraldi, China, very hairy leaved, small purplish-red flowers in clusters; July; *henryi*, China, small purplish-red flowers, June–July; *japonica*, Japan, China, very fragrant, tubular, creamy-yellow flowers, tinged pink, June–July, and vs. *aureo-reticulata*, leaves with netted golden variegation; *flexuosa*, leaves and flowers tinged purple; and *halliana*, white, changing to yellow flowers; and *similis delavayi*, China, fragrant yellow tubular flowers. August; while *semper-virens*, the Trumpet Honeysuckle of U.S.A., with scentless orange, yellow and scarlet flowers, June–August, and *splendida*, Spain, fragrant yellow flowers, summer, need to be grown in the cold greenhouse, except in the mildest localities.

Cultivation. All honeysuckles do well in well-drained but moisture-retentive loamy soils. Bush kinds like full sun; climbers do not mind shade. Plant deciduous types in October–March; evergreens in September–October or March–April. Prune after flowering when necessary, or in early spring. As the climbers are twiners, they do best up pergolas, tree stumps, etc., and not up choice young trees which may be strangled.

Propagation. By cuttings of young shoots in July–August, under handlights or in cold frame. Species by seeds sown in April on outdoor seed beds.

Loofah. See *Luffa*.

Loosestrife, Purple. See *Lythrum salicaria*.

Loosestrife, Yellow. See *Lysimachia vulgaris*.

Lophospermum. See *Maurandia*.

Loquat. See *Eriobotrya*.

Lord Anson's Pea. See *Lathyrus magellanicus*.

Lorette Pruning. A French system of pruning pears, in which new shoots are pruned hard to base as they attain a certain size and begin to get woody, three or four times in a summer, at intervals of about one month, to stimulate basal fruit buds; leader shoots being shortened in spring when an inch or two long. Under English conditions it is modified, new lateral shoots being shortened to two leaves or buds from the base in late June or early July, and any secondary growth to one bud in the following winter.

Loropetalum (lo-ro-pet'a-lum. Fam. Hamamelidaceae). The species grown, *L. chinense*, China, to 10 ft, is a choice evergreen shrub with oval leaves, and clusters of white, ribbon-petalled flowers, February–March; but only hardy for very mild localities and needing cold greenhouse shelter elsewhere. Plant in April, peat-enriched, well-drained loam. Propagation by layers in autumn, or cuttings of firm shoots, July–August, in a cold frame.

Lotus (lo'tus. Fam. Leguminosae). The chief plants worth growing are *L. corniculatus* v. *flore pleno*, a native double-flowering form of the Bird's-foot Trefoil, an attractive procumbent perennial, with its racemes of golden-yellow, red-tinged, papilionaceous, summer flowers, for the rock garden; and *bertholetii,* the Coral Gem of Teneriffe, silvery foliage, and scarlet May flowers, as a pot plant in the cool greenhouse, or for baskets; minimum winter temp. of 7° C. (45° F.), with minimum watering. Propagation is by seeds, in April, or division in April.

Lotus, Sacred. See *Nelumbo.*

Love Apple. See *Lycopersicon,* and Tomatoes.

Love Grass. See *Eragrostis.*

Love-in-a-mist. See *Nigella.*

Love-lies-bleeding. See *Amaranthus caudatus.*

Lucidus (-a, -um). Clear, shining. Ex. *Arabis lucida.*

Luffa (luf'fa. Fam. Cucurbitaceae). Annual tendril-climbing plants, of which *L. cylindrica,* Tropical Africa, is the Dishcloth Gourd, the fruit of which are prepared as Loofah bath sponges. It may be grown in the warm greenhouse, from seeds sown in February–March, standard compost, bottom heat of 24° C. (75° F.), transferred to 10-in. pots, and trained as a melon plant, to 10 ft, in warm, fairly humid atmosphere, as in a cucumber house, watered and syringed freely. The fully ripe gourds may be softened in a washing soda solution, the soft tissues, seeds, etc., squeezed out, and the fibrous interior bleached and dried.

Lunaria, Honesty (lu-nar′i-a. Fam. Cruciferae). An invaluable annual, usually grown as a biennial, *L. annua,* Sweden, to 2 ft, has violet-lilac flowers in spring, followed by attractive rounded oval seed pods, which, with the papery valves rubbed off when ripe, provide silvery heads for winter decoration; v. *alba,* white-flowering; 'Munstead Purple', rich purple flowering; and *variegata,* with leaves edged creamy-white, are worthy forms. Sow in ordinary soil in May, where plants are to flower; one of the few biennials for shade, and tends to re-seed itself. *L. rediviva,* Europe, 2–3 ft, is an unusual herbaceous perennial, with smaller scented purplish flowers, and lance-shaped seed pods easily raised from seeds, in March–April, on ordinary soils.

Lungwort. See *Pulmonaria.*

Lupin, Lupine. See *Lupinus.*

Lupinus, Lupin, Lupine (lu-pi′nus.

FIG. 146 *Lunaria annua,* Honesty.

Fam. Leguminosae). A large genus of annual or perennial flowering plants, which increase soil fertility in nitrogen.

Selection. Annuals: *L. hartwegii,* Mexico, 2–3 ft, and its forms, with racemes of shades of blue and white flowers, July onwards; *luteus,* S. Europe, to 2 ft, may be broadcast as a soil-improving green-manure crop, but 'Romulus', with pale yellow, sweet scented flowers, is a garden form; × *tricolor,* to 2 ft, has various named colour varieties; 'Tom Thumb' and 'Pixie Delight' are dwarf strains. Herbaceous Perennials: These consist today largely of hybrids (*L. arboreus* × *L. polyphyllus*) and their strains; notably the 'Russell' hybrids, of 3–3½ ft, with magnificent upright racemes of self-, bi- and tri-coloured flowers in summer, available in a wide variety of named forms, embracing colours in almost every shade; 'Sutton Hybrids' embody many excellent forms, and 'Minarette' is a new strain of dwarf Russell lupins, growing 1½ ft. *L. arboreus*, California, the Tree Lupin, is a branching shrub of 5–6 ft, with racemes of yellow flowers, fragrant in summer, with a white 'Snow Queen', and deep yellow 'Golden Spire' and other vs. for mild countries.

Cultivation. Annuals are sown where they are to flower, in well-drained, rather light soils, in spring. Perennials require a well-drained soil, of some depth, enriched with bone meal, and succeed in sun or partial shade, from autumn or early spring plantings.

Propagation. By seeds, sown in spring or early summer; by division in March or April. Seedlings for planting out may be raised in peat-wood fibre pots in a cold frame, obviating root disturbance, which may lead to failure.

Lusitanicus (-a, -um). Portuguese. Ex. *Erica lusitanica.*

Lutescens. Becoming yellow. Ex. *Rhododendron lutescens.*

Luteus (-a, -um). Yellow. Ex. *Chamaecyparis lawsoniana lutea.*

Luxurians. Rapid-growing. Ex. *Robinia luxurians.*

Luzula (lu'zu-la. Fam. Juncaceae). Wood rushes with grass-like leaves; *L. maxima*, Europe, to 2 ft, of evergreen, tufted, surface creeping habit, makes good ground cover in woodland; European Alps, 18 in., has evergreen tufts, non-running, and loose, arching panicles of white flowers in summer; making a good plant for woodland.

Lycaste (li-kas'te. Fam. Orchidaceae). Epiphytic orchids of tropical America, usually with solitary flowers.

Selection. L. aromatica, Mexico, fragrant yellow flowers, spring; *costata* Colombia, cream to ivory, spring; *cruenta*, Guatemala, orange, yellow, April; and *skinneri*, Guatemala, white, flushed rose, and several vs., winter; are relatively easy to grow.

Cultivation. Pot, and repot, when coming into new growth, late spring, well-crocked pots and compost of equal parts Osmunda fibre, sphagnum moss

and loam; give good light, water freely in active growth; rest after flowering; water moderately in winter, minimum temp. 10–13° C. (50–55° F.).

Propagation. By division when repotting.

Lychnis (lik'nis. Fam. Caryophyllaceae). Now a genus of hardy perennial flowering plants, allied to Viscaria, brilliant in summer.

Selection. L. × arkwrightii, 1½ ft, scarlet shades of flowers, summer; *chalcedonica*, E. Russia, to 3 ft, scarlet, summer, and vs. *alba*, white, *carnea*, pink, *rubra plena*, double red; *coronaria*, S. Europe, 2½ ft, purplish, or v. *alba*, white; *flos-cuculi*, Cuckoo Flower, Britain, 2 ft, rose; *flos-jovis*. Central Alps, 1–2 ft, scarlet, June–July; *fulgens*, Siberia, 2 ft, bright red, June–August; × *haageana*, 1 ft, orange, scarlet, July–August; *yunnanensis*, Yunnan, 6 in., white, tinged red, veined green, bell-shaped flowers, summer; and strains such as × *forrestii* hybrids. Other species now listed under *Melandrium, Silene* and *Viscaria*.

Cultivation. Plant October–March, well-drained, moisture-retentive soil, warm, sheltered positions.

Propagation. By division in March–April. By seeds in April, in cold frame or outdoor seed-bed.

Lycium, Box Thorn (li'ki-um. Fam. Solanaceae). A not very distinguished large genus of deciduous shrubs, chiefly useful for hedging or as seaside plants.

Selection. L. chinense, Tea-tree, China, with long arching, rambling branches, purple flowers, summer, reddish fruits; and *halimifolium*, SE. Europe, somewhat similar but smaller, dull purple flowers, summer, scarlet fruits, are chiefly offered.

Cultivation. Plant October–March, any ordinary soil, in sun, on walls or trellises, or for rough hedging.

Propagation. By suckers, detached in winter. By cuttings of young firm shoots, in spring or autumn.

Lycopersicon (Lycopersicum), Love Apple, Tomato (li-ko-pers'i-kon. Fam. Solanaceae). Hairy leaved, annual herbs of which *L. esculentum*, S. America, with its trusses of yellow flowers and 2-celled, many-seeded berry-fruits, and its forms, have given rise to the edible

Tomato (q.v.); while *L. pimpinellifolium*, Peru, Ecuador, is the Currant Tomato.

Lycopodium, Club Moss (li-ko-po'di-um. Fam. Lycopodiaceae). A genus of an ancient group of flowerless plants with branching stems of dense foliage, useful for fern cases, or baskets. *L. alpinum*, *clavatum*, the Stag's-horn or Common Club Moss, and *selago*, Fir Club Moss, are native species, easily grown in a spongy peat, with shade, and ample water, from tips of growing shoots.

FIG. 147 *Lycopodium selago*, Fir Club Moss.

Lycoris (li'kor-ris. Fam. Amaryllidaceae). Attractive bulbous plants of China and Japan, opening their flowers after the leaves have died down, for the cool greenhouse.

Selection. *L. aurea*, Golden Spider Lily, 1 ft, golden-yellow, funnel-shaped flowers, August–September; *radiata*, 1½ ft, deep pink, August; and v. *alba*, white, and *variegata*, crimson and white; and *squamigera*, 2 ft, rose-lilac (almost hardy).

Cultivation. Pot, and repot, September–December, standard compost, water moderately, winter temp. 10° C. (50° F.), increasing with active growth, giving good light without direct sun. Rest after flowering.

Propagation. By offsets when repotting.

Lygodium, Climbing Fern (li-go'di-um. Fam. Schizaeaceae). Handsome twining ferns for the warm greenhouse or conservatory, for pillars and walls.

Selection. *L. japonicum*, Japan and Australasia, 8–10 ft, finely cut, fresh green foliage; *palmatum*, E. U.S.A., to 6 ft, handsome fronds, palmate; and *scandens*, Africa, etc., to 10 ft, are mostly grown.

Cultivation. Plant or pot in March, 2 parts sandy loam, 1 part peat with a little charcoal, water freely in summer, moderately in winter, minimum temp. 10° C. (50° F.).

Propagation. By division in March; by spores in propagating case in greenhouse.

Lyonia (li-on'i-a. Fam. Ericaceae). Flowering shrubs of which *L. ligustrina*, Eastern N. America, 6–10 ft, is deciduous, with panicles of white flowers in late summer, is chiefly grown; planted in September–March, lime-free, peaty soil, and a warm, sheltered position. Propagation by seeds, layering, or firm, young shoot cuttings, July–August.

Lysichitum, Skunk Cabbage (li-si-ki'tum. Fam. Araceae). Hardy perennial bog plants, notable for flowers with large ornamental spathes, and large grey-green leaves.

Selection. *L. camtschatcense*, Japan, white spathe, May; *americanum*, Western N. America, yellow spathe, April.

Cultivation. Plant the rhizomatous crowns in bog-garden or at the waterside, in moist soil, March.

Propagation. By division of the rhizomes, March, or seeds.

Lysimachia (li-si-mak'i-a. Fam. Primulaceae). Beautiful flowering herbaceous perennials for moist soils in borders or the waterside.

Selection. L. *clethroides*, China, Japan, 2½ ft, graceful with long terminal racemes of small white flowers, July–September; *ephemerum*, SW. Europe, to 3 ft, white, tinged purple racemes, summer; *nummularia*, the Creeping Jenny of Britain, a prostrate trailer, yellow flowers, summer, for ground cover on banks and in shade; *punctata*, Asia Minor, 1½ ft, whorls of yellow flowers, July–August; and *vulgaris*, the native Yellow Loosestrife, 2½ ft, showy with yellow flowers in panicles, summer.

Cultivation. Plant October–March, moist, humus-rich soil, sun or shade.

Propagation. By division in autumn or spring. By seeds, sown outdoors in moist loam, April onwards.

Lythrum (lith'rum. Fam. Lythraceae). Flowering herbaceous plants, for moist soils.

Selection. L. *salicaria*, Purple Loosestrife, found in N. temperate regions, Britain and Australia, 4 ft, spikes of red-purple flowers, July–August, and vs. 'Brightness', pink; 'Lady Sackville', rose-red; 'Pritchard's', rose-pink; and 'The Beacon', rose-red; *virgatum*, Taurus, 2–3 ft, purple flowering, and v. 'Rose Queen', bright rose, summer.

Cultivation. Plant October–March, moist soil in borders or at water edges.

Propagation. By division in March. By seeds, sown in April onwards, out of doors.

M

Macartney Rose. See *Rosa bracteata*.

Macleania (mak-le′ni-a. Fam. Ericaceae). Evergreen semi-trailing shrubs of central and S. America, attractive in foliage and flower for the cool greenhouse.

Selection. **M.** *cordifolia*, Ecuador, leathery entire leaves, axillary clusters of scarlet and yellow flowers, April; *insignis*, Mexico, scarlet flowers, June; *pulchra*, New Grenada, red young foliage, scarlet flowers, May; and *punctata*, Ecuador, rosy-red and yellow flowers, June.

Cultivation. Pot, March–April, lime-free compost, water freely in active growth to September, very moderately in winter, temp. 7° C. (45° F.) minimum. Prune straggling shoots back in March.

Propagation. By cuttings of young shoots, in summer, with bottom heat of 18° C. (65° F.) in propagating case.

Macleaya (mak-le-ai′a. Fam. Papaveraceae). Large herbaceous perennials, formerly under *Bocconia*, with glaucous, palmately lobed leaves, and plume-like inflorescences. *M. cordata*, China, Japan, 5–8 ft, flowering in summer; and *microcarpa*, 5–8 ft, China, with bronzed flower plumes, are grown. 'Kelway's Coral Plume', with coral-pink flowers, is an improved form of *M. cordata*.

Cultivation. Plant October–March, in deep loam soil, in large borders, grouped or in large pots or tubs.

Propagation. By division in March; by severing running roots and suckers in summer.

Maclura, Gage or **Osage Orange** (mak-lu′ra. Fam. Moraceae). The species, *M. pomifera*, N. America, is a deciduous small tree, spiny, with ovate, glossy green leaves, and inconspicuous greenish June flowers, giving way to orange-like, inedible fruits if plants of both sexes are planted, in warm-enough gardens. Plant in autumn or spring, ordinary, well-drained soil, warm shelter. May be propagated by seeds in spring, by layer-ing in autumn or by root cuttings, March.

Macro-. Prefix in compound words meaning large or long. Ex. *macranthus*, large-flowered; *macrocarpus*, large-fruited; *macrocephalus*, large-headed.

Macrozamia (mak-ro-za′mi-a. Fam. Cycadaceae). Easily grown Australian evergreen Fern Palms for the greenhouse, with feather-like foliage.

Selection. **M.** *fraseri* 3–4 ft, stem; *pauliguilielmii*, leaves to 3 ft, spirally arranged; and *spiralis*, to 4 ft, shining green leaves.

Cultivation. Pot in April, compost of 2 parts sandy loam, 1 of peat; water freely during growth, rest during winter, minimum temp. 10° C. (50° F.).

Propagation. By imported seeds, when available, standard compost, bottom heat of 18° C. (65° F.).

Maculatus (-a, -um). Spotted, Blotched. Ex. *Nemophila maculata*.

Madonna Lily. See *Lilium candidum*.

Madwort. See *Alyssum*.

Maggot. The larva of a two-winged fly.

Magnificus (-a, -um). Magnificent. Ex. *Lobelia pumila magnifica*.

Magnolia (mag-no′li-a. Fam. Magnoliaceae). Shrubs or small trees with extremely beautiful flowers, mostly deciduous, a few evergreen.

Selection. **M.** *cordata*, N. America, to 15 ft, yellow flowers, May; *denudata* (*conspicua*), the Yulan, China, 30 ft, large, white, cup-shaped flowers, early spring; *kobus*, Japan, to 25 ft, creamy-white flowers, April–May, but slow to start flowering; *obovata*, Japan, upright tree to 45 ft, large-leaved, very large white, cup-shaped flowers, June; *sieboldii*, Japan, shrub to 10 ft, white, cup-shaped, fragrant flowers, May–August; × *soulangiana*, tall shrub to 18 ft, white, purple stained flowers, April–June, and vs. *alba superba*, white; *lennei*, very fine globular rose-purple

334

flowers; *nigra*, dark purple flowers; and *rustica rubra*, rose-red; *sprengeri*, W. China, tree to 50 ft, rose-pink flowers, April; *stellata*, to 10 ft, fragrant, many petalled, white flowers, April; and v. *rosea*, pinkish; and *wilsonii*, Szechwan, to 25 ft, white, cup-shaped, nodding fragrant flowers, May–June; are all

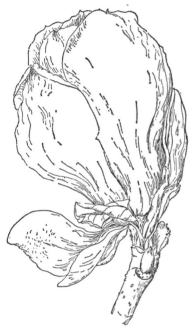

FIG. 148 *Magnolia × soulangiana* v. *lennei*.

deciduous. *M. delavayi*, Yunnan, tree to 30 ft, creamy-white, cup-like flowers, June; and *grandiflora*, to 60 ft, creamy-white flowers, July–September, with v. 'Exmouth' tending to flower at a younger age, are evergreen, and need a mild climate or good warm wall shelter. *M. campbellii*, Sikkim, the tallest tree form, to 70 ft, deciduous, slow to produce its large, cupped pink to rose flowers in March, needs a mild locality.

Cultivation. Plant in late March–May, well-drained loam soil, enriched with leaf-mould or peat liberally. No regular pruning.

Propagation. Layering or air-layering is most successful in the garden: cuttings under mist propagation in summer.

Mahaleb Cherry. *Prunus mahaleb*, used as a rootstock for Cherries (q.v.).

Mahonia (ma-ho′ni-a. Fam. Berberidaceae). Evergreen shrubs, allied and sometimes listed with *Berberis*, but differing in their pinnate leaves and stems without spines.

Selection. M. *aquifolium*, Western N. America, 3 ft, clustered racemes of rich yellow flowers, April; *japonica* (*bealei*), Japan, to 6 ft, long racemes of strongly scented, yellow flowers, January–March; *fortunei*, China, 5 ft, bright yellow erect racemes, autumn; *lomariifolia*, Yunnan, 4 ft, yellow flowers, November, unfortunately a little tender; and *toluacensis*, 2 ft, yellow racemes, spring.

Cultivation. Plant September or March–April; well-drained, loam soil, open or shaded, wind-sheltered situation. Prune after flowering, if needed.

Propagation. By seeds, in spring. By cuttings of young shoots, July–August.

Maianthemum (mai-an′the-mum. Fam. Liliaceae). The chief species, *M. bifolium*, Europe and native, is a dwarf creeping herbaceous perennial, with twin cordate shining green leaves, and up to thirty tiny, white fleshy flowers on spikes up to 6 in. in May. A good carpeter for cool, shady situations, fairly moist soil, planted October–March, and increased by division at the same time.

Maiden Pink. See *Dianthus deltoides*.

Maidenhair Fern. See *Adiantum capillus-veneris*.

Maidenhair Tree. See *Ginkgo biloba*.

Maize. *See* Sweet Corn; *Zea*.

Majalis (-e). Of May. Ex. *Convallaria majalis*.

Malachite Green ($3C_{23}H_{25}N_2Cl$, $2ZnCl_2$. $2H_2O$). A dyestuff, combined with Bordeaux Mixture, 1 level teaspoonful in half a gallon water to 6 gallons Bordeaux Mixture, for use as a turf fungicide on lawns.

Malcomia (**Malcolmia**) (mal-kom′i-a. Fam. Cruciferae). The chief species grown is the pretty hardy annual Virginian Stock, *M. maritima*, Mediterranean region, 1 ft, its vari-coloured flowers blooming from spring to autumn from successional sowings in ordinary soil made in autumn and in early to late spring.

Male. Of flowers having stamens only.

Male Fern. See *Dryopteris filix-mas*.

Mallow. See *Malva*.

Mallow, Musk. See *Malva moschata*.

Mallow, Rose. See *Hibiscus*.

Mallow, Tree. See *Lavatera*.

Malope (mal-lo'pe. Fam. Malvaceae). Easily grown flowering annuals from the Mediterranean region, of which *M. trifida* (*grandiflora*), 2 ft, and its vs., give large, purple, white, pink and red mallow-like flowers in summer; from sowings made under glass in March, or outdoors in late April.

Malus, Apple (ma'lus. Fam. Rosaceae). Deciduous trees or shrubs, esteemed for their clustered spring flowers and handsome pome fruits.

Selection. Fine ornamental Crab apples are: *M. baccata* v. *mandschurica*, E. Asia, to 40 ft, white flowers, April, bright red fruits; *coronaria* v. *charlottae*, N. America, 20 ft, semi-double rose flowers, May, autumn leaf colour; ✕ *eleyi*, to 30 ft, vinous purple leafed, reddish flowers, April, purplish-red fruits; *florentina*, to 12 ft, hawthorn-leafed, white flowers, May, red fruits; *floribunda*, Japan, to 30 ft, pale pink flowers, May, yellowish fruits, and v. *hillieri*, semi-double flowering; *hupehensis*, China, 25 ft, white flowers, May, and v. *rosea*, pink, small greenish yellow fruits; ✕ *lemoinei*, to 30 ft, purple in leaf, flower and fruit; *prunifolia*, NE. Asia, to 20 ft, white flowering, April, and v. 'Cheal's Golden Gem', small yellow fruits; *pumila*, Europe, Britain, Wild Crab and parent of orchard apples, 20–30 ft, provides vs. 'Beauty of Montreal', white flowers, April, conical yellow-red fruits; 'Dartmouth', white flowers, plum-like red-purple fruits; 'John Downie', white blossom, red and yellow fruits, finest for jelly-making; *pendula*, drooping branches, white flowering, large reddish fruits; 'Simcoe', Canadian origin, rose flowers; *sargentii*, Japan, bush to 8 ft, white flowers, May, bright red fruits; ✕ *scheideckeri*, to 15 ft, semi-double white flowers, May; *spectabilis* v. *flore pleno*, double rosy-red flowers, May; and *trilobata*, Syria, 30 ft,

tri-lobed leaves, white flowers, May, yellow fruits, autumn colour.

Cultivation. Plant October–March, in well-dug, free-draining, humus-enriched soil, and full sun. Prune to shape in winter, to induce flowering in summer.

Propagation. Species by seeds, sown outdoors, spring. Varieties and hybrids are grafted on apple rootstocks.

Malva, Mallow (mal'va. Fam. Malvaceae). Hardy, summer-flowering perennials for the border.

Selection. *M. alcea*, Europe, 3 ft, rose-purple satiny flowers, and its v. *fastigiata*, red; *moschata*, the Musk Mallow, Europe and Britain, 3 ft, pink, and v. *alba*, white, and hybrids.

Cultivation. Plant October–April, good loam, soil and sun.

Propagation. By seeds, sown April–June, outdoors. By division in April.

Malvastrum (mal-vas'trum. Fam. Malvaceae). The perennials *M. coccineum*, U.S.A., 6 in., with racemes of round, scarlet flowers, in summer; and *lateritium*, S. America, 6 in., solitary brick-red flowers, autumn, are useful for well-drained soil and sun in the rock garden, with some winter protection in cool areas; *campanulatum*, Chile, 1 ft, clusters of purple-rose flowers, August, is best in the alpine house, and ✕ *hypomadarum*, S. Africa, a branching shrub to 6 ft, with white, flushed pink flowers, summer, is best pot-grown in a cool greenhouse.

Cultivation. Plant in spring, well-drained soil or compost, warm sun. Propagate by cuttings, July–August, inserted in a cold frame.

Mammillaria (mam-mil-la'ri-a. Fam. Cactaceae). Round or cylindrical perennial 'Nipple' cacti, with tubercles in spiral rows, and flowers arising in the axils between the tubercles, to the top of plants.

Selection. *M. bocasana*, clustering round bodies, with bristle-like spines, silky white hair, pinkish flowers; *bombycina*, cylindrical, hairy, light purple flowers; *elongata*, clusters of erect stems, carmine flowers; *gigantea*, large, axils woolly, yellowish green flowers; *glochidata*, clusters of round bodies, showy pink flowers; *haageana*, rounded, small carmine flowers; *hahniana*, globular, flattened stem, small crimson flowers;

mammillaris, round, very woolly, cream flowers; *prolifera*, W. Indies, large clusters, yellow flowers; *rhodantha*, large, cylindrical, variable with pink or carmine flowers; *sempervivi*, cylindrical, flattened top, white, lined red flowers; *wildii*, clustering, white flowers; all of Mexico, except where stated, and many others up to 200 species.

Cultivation. Pot in March–April, well-drained pots, standard cactus compost, repotting every 3 or 4 years; water weekly March–September, very little in winter, temp. 10° C. (50° F.) minimum.

Propagation. By seeds in pans, in spring, bottom heat of 24° C. (75° F.). By cuttings of tops of plants, spring. By offsets when repotting. By grafting on *Cereus speciossimus*, at any time, March–October.

Mammoth Tree. See *Sequoiadendron*.

Mandevilla, Chilean Jasmine (man-de-vil'la. Fam. Apocynaceae). The chief species grown is *M. suaveolens*, Argentine, a half-hardy perennial climber to 15 ft, with long pointed pairs of leaves, attractive, funnel-shaped and flared, fragrant white flowers in summer; for planting in well-drained soil, humus-rich, in cool greenhouse or conservatory, trained up a pillar or rafters. May be grown from seeds, with bottom heat of 18° C. (65° F.), in the greenhouse in spring.

Mandragora (man-dra-go'ra. Fam. Solanaceae). Of legendary interest, hardy perennials with large roots from the Mediterranean region. *M. officinarum*, 1 ft, with long undulate leaves, white or bluish flowers in May, is the Mandrake of Genesis; *autumnalis*, ½–1 ft, has violet flowers in September.

Cultivation. Plant in light loam soil and shade, March. Propagate by seeds in spring, or division.

Manetti. A rootstock used for dwarf roses, especially for dry, gravelly soils. *See* Roses.

Manicatus (-a, -um). Covered with a dense down or hairs. Ex. *Gunnera manicata*.

Manna Ash. See *Fraxinus ornus*.

Manures. Horticulturally, manures are best classified today as the bulky, natural organic materials which are largely used to provide humus-forming

organic matter, essential to soil fertility, and may also contribute small percentages of plant nutrients. Fertilizers, sometimes described as inorganic manures, provide nutrient elements but no humus; and are really complementary to organic manures, not substitutes for them. Organic manures are dead or waste substances of animal or plant origin which must undergo decomposition before they can be of value to the soil and plants. Total decomposition takes place in the soil, but manures may be partially decomposed before application. Fresh unrotted materials, when applied to the soil, need time to decompose and should be used several weeks ahead of the growing season. Pre-rotted, or composted, material integrates with the soil quickly. The important manurial sources to gardeners are:

Cow Manure varies, as do all animal manures, in quality, according to the age and feeding of the animal. It is wet and cold, most valuable on the lighter soils; and best mixed with straw, chaff, leaves, peat, etc., and composted. An average analysis is 0·4 per cent nitrogen, 0·3 per cent phosphoric acid, 0·44 per cent potash; moisture content 83 per cent. Rate of application: 1 cwt. or barrowload per 8–12 sq. yds; 15 to 25 tons per acre. *Farmyard Manure* is a mixed product, variable in character and composition; average analysis of 0·64 per cent nitrogen, 0·23 per cent phosphoric acid, 0·32 per cent potash; 76 per cent moisture. Use much the same as cow manure. *Stable or Horse Manure* is fibrous, decomposes relatively rapidly, and is termed a dry or hot manure, valuable for all soils, particularly clays; and at one time much used for making hotbeds; also for growing mushrooms. Average analysis is 0·76 per cent nitrogen, 0·56 per cent phosphoric acid, 0·65 per cent potash; 62 per cent moisture. Use at 1 cwt. per 10–15 sq. yds; 10–15 tons per acre. *Pig Manure* is a wet, caustic (when fresh) manure preferably composted with absorbent plant waste before use. Average analysis is 0·6 per cent nitrogen, 0·3 per cent phosphoric acid, 0·67 per cent potash; 85 per cent moisture. Use at the same rates as for cow manure. *Sheep Manure* is a fibrous, 'dry', hot material, rotting readily in compost. Average analysis is 2·34 per cent nitrogen, 0·69 per cent phosphoric acid, 1·2 per cent potash; 66 per cent moisture. Use at 1 cwt. per 12 sq. yds, 10–12 tons per acre. *Poultry Manure*, with an analysis of 1–1·5 per cent nitrogen, 1–1·5 per cent phosphoric acid, 0·5–0·75 per cent potash, and a moisture content of about 55 per cent, is a rich, quickly decomposing manure; most useful when composted, at 1 cwt. per 12–15 sq. yds, 8 tons per acre. *Deep Litter* from poultry houses is rich but variable with an analysis of 1·8–2·4 per cent nitrogen, 2·3–3·4 per cent phosphoric acid, 1·4–1·9 per cent potash; 22 to 38 per cent moisture. Peat or chopped straw is the best litter; where sawdust and/or wood shavings have been used, the litter must be well rotted before use: 1 cwt. per 15–18 sq. yds; 6–7 tons per acre. Animal manures, under modern farming practices, are unavailable to an increasing number of urban and suburban gardeners. Alternatives must be found such as *Compost* (*see* Compost and Compost-making) which, when well-made, has higher plant nutrient values than those of farmyard manure, and may be used freely. *Peat*, which is plant matter in an arrested state of decay, is good humus material, but ill-balanced and poor in nutrient content. Horticultural grades of sedge or sphagnum moss peats are clean to handle, and may be used at rates of 1–6 lb. per sq. yd, according to need. *Hops*. Spent hops from the brewery provide humus, and slight nutrient values, and may be used in autumn/winter at 1 cwt. per 10 sq. yds. Prepared hop manures have chemical fertilizers added to furnish complete plant foods, and are used to makers' directions. *Seaweed* is excellent but lacks fibre. It may be used fresh ahead of the growing season, otherwise should be composted. Average analysis is 0·5 per cent nitrogen, 0·1 per cent phosphoric acid, 1 per cent potash; use at 1 cwt. per 6–8 sq. yds. *Sewage* is cheap but variable. Wet raw sewage sludge is useful on light, sandy or chalk soils. Nutrient values vary from 0·3–0·9 per cent nitrogen, 0·4–1 per cent phosphoric acid, 0·1–0·5 per cent potash; 50–84 per cent moisture; and it should be used at

½–1 cwt. per 10 sq. yds, in autumn or winter. Dried digested sewage has values of 1·4–2 per cent nitrogen, 0·7–1·1 per cent phosphoric acid, 0·2–0·7 per cent potash; 8–12 per cent moisture, and may be used at ½–1 cwt. per 15–25 sq. yds. *Shoddy* is wool waste from woollen mills, averaging 5 per cent nitrogen. It rots slowly, but is useful on heavy and light soils, applied in autumn or early winter, ½ lb per sq. yd, or 1 ton per acre. *Municipal Compost.* Several municipal authorities now prepare a form of fertilizer-compost from collected waste materials, which are available cheaply. They usually have a high content of organic matter, 40–50 per cent, 2–3 per cent nitrogen, small amounts of phosphoric acid, but negligible amounts of potash; and should be used as recommended; usually 1 cwt. per 100–120 sq. yds. *Leaf-mould* (q.v.) is humus-forming, and has slight nutrient values in nitrogen, phosphates and potash; an alternative to peat. *Feathers, Hair, Leather Waste and Dust* are sometimes available as waste products of processing works. They are best used in autumn or early winter, at ½–1 lb. per sq. yd; and have a nitrogen content of 6–8 per cent, which is slowly made available. In their application, it is usually better to incorporate organic manures throughout the top soil, rather than as a layer below the top spit of soil; or as a top-dressing when mulching plants.

Manures, Liquid. Strictly, liquid manure consists of the urine and fluids draining from animal dung. It is relatively rich in nitrogen (0·22–0·5 per cent) and potash (0·44–1·4 per cent), but low in phosphates, when freshly collected. It may be diluted to straw colour with 3 or 4 parts water, and used as a liquid feed for growing plants out of doors. In the garden, liquid manure is traditionally made from rotted manures, particularly cow, horse, sheep or poultry, placed in a coarse sack, which is immersed and steeped in a tubful of water for a week or two. Then the liquid is drawn off, further diluted to a pale straw colour, and used to water growing plants in need of a stimulus. Water in the tub may be replaced up to three times before the manurial qualities are deemed exhausted. Liquid nitrogenous manure can be prepared from dried blood ($\frac{1}{2}$–1 oz. per gallon water); one rich in potash and other nutrients may be prepared from a seaweed derivative. *See* Soot Water; Fertilizers, Liquid.

Manuring, Green. An old practice of growing quick-growing catch crops from seed to be turned into the soil and enrich it with humus-forming organic matter and plant nutrients; usually at the beginning or the end of the growing season when ground becomes vacant. The seeds used are the leguminous: Vetch, Field Pea, Clover, Lupin, Alfalfa; and the non-leguminous: Mustard, Rape, Buckwheat, Oats, Ryes, Barley, Wheat and Rye Grass. For a clay soil a mixture of Red Clover, Vetches and Oats is suitable. For a light sand or gravel soil, Lupins, Mustard, Rye; or Field Peas, Barley and Mustard would suit. Loams would benefit from a mixture of Vetches, Oats, Barley, Rye, Clovers and Rape. Mustard and Rape must be avoided on soils which harbour Club-root. The seeds mixture is broadcast on a prepared seed-bed, fertilized with a quick-acting fertilizer if necessary, 1–2 oz. per sq. yd, raked in; to be turned into the soil when flower buds begin to form, or at the first frost, to decompose in the soil. Alternatively, the top growth can be cut and composted.

Maple. See *Acer*.

Maranta (ma-ran'ta. Fam. Marantaceae). Tropical American, rhizomatous rooted perennials, grown for their attractive foliage as greenhouse and house plants.

Selection. M. bicolor, Brazil, 1 ft, with leaves dark green, blotched a lighter green, purple beneath; *leuconeura*, Brazil, 1 ft, of which v. *kerchoveana*, oval leaves, with purple-red blotches, folding at night, known as the Prayer Plant; and *massangeana*, with smaller, whitish-veined, leaves, bright purple beneath, are popular; *arundinacea*, S. America, to 6 ft, the Arrowroot Plant, is less often grown.

Cultivation. Pot, and repot, April–May, 3 parts by bulk leaf-mould, 2 parts peat, 1 part coarse sand, and a little base fertilizer, to grow in partial shade, watering freely in summer, moderately in autumn, little in winter; minimum temp. 13° C. (55° F.).

Propagation. By division when repotting.

Marginatus (-a, -um). Edged in a different colour or texture; of leaves, etc. Ex. *Primula marginata*.

Marguerite. See *Chrysanthemum frutescens*.

Margyricarpus (mar-gi-ri-kar'pus. Fam. Rosaceae). The chief species grown is *M. setosus*, Andes, a pretty little evergreen with awl-shaped leaves, of 1 ft, tiny, axillary greenish flowers followed by small pearl-white berries in autumn, useful for sunny, peaty but well-drained places on the rock garden in mild areas, or as a pot plant in the alpine or cool greenhouse. Propagation by young shoot cuttings, summer, under a handlight, by layering, or by seeds, April.

Marigold (*Calendula officinalis*, q.v.). As a hardy annual herb it is sometimes grown for its flower-heads, picked and dried quickly on trays or sheets of paper, in an airy warm place, for the ray florets, which are rubbed off and stored in bottles, for subsequent use in flavouring soups and stews.

Marigold. African. See *Tagetes erecta*.

Marigold, Cape. See *Dimorphotheca*.

Marigold, Fig. See *Mesembryanthemum*.

Marigold, French. See *Tagetes patula*.

Marigold, Marsh. See *Caltha palustris*.

Mariposa Lily. See *Calochortus*.

Maritimus (-a, -um). Grows by the sea. Ex. *Alyssum maritimum*.

Marjoram. Two kinds are grown for their aromatic leaves as culinary herbs. Knotted or Sweet Marjoram (*Origanum majorana*), N. Africa, naturally perennial, but half-hardy; and Pot Marjoram (*Origanum onites*), Mediterranean region, also perennial, persisting in warm sheltered gardens; may both be raised from seeds, sown in well-drained soil, and sun, April or May. Pot Marjoram may be propagated by division in spring, when established. The top growth of both plants is cut and dried in a warm airy place in July–August, for storing, the rubbed leaves being used for flavouring soups, stews and stuffings; and may be mixed.

Marl. A natural mixture of clay and chalk, or a calcareous clay, occurring in East Anglia, the West Midlands,

Cheshire, Cumberland, etc. It is invaluable to give body to light gravel or sandy soils, silty peats, etc., incorporated after being spread and exposed to frost. It is sometimes used to give a surface finish to cricket pitches.

Marmoratus (-a, -um). Marbled. Ex. *Caladium marmoratum.*

Marrow. *See* Vegetable Marrow.

Marsh Marigold. See *Caltha palustris.*

Martagon Lily. See *Lilium martagon.*

Martynia (mar-ti'ni-a. Fam. Martyniaceae). Semi-tropical plants grown as half-hardy annuals for their Gloxinia-like flowers of late summer in warm, sunny border, or the greenhouse.

Selection. M. *proboscidea fragrans,* Mexico, 2 ft, racemes of crimson-purple, scented flowers, and *louisiana,* the Unicorn or Elephant's Trunk plant, to 3 ft, yellowish-white and spotted flowers, unusual fruits.

Cultivation. Sow under glass, March, bottom heat of 18° C. (65° F.), to transplant to 4½-in. pots, or to plant out in May, well-drained soil and sun.

Marvel of Peru. See *Mirabilis jalapa.*

Mas. Male. Ex. *Cornus mas.*

Masdevallia (mas-de-val'li-a. Fam. Orchidaceae). Tufted epiphytic orchids of cool mountainous parts of S. America with brilliant flowers.

Selection. M. *amabilis,* Peru, orange-carmine, May; *caudata,* Colombia, green and yellow, May; *coccinea,* Colombia, crimson and white, May; *ignea,* Colombia, red, spring; and *veitchiana,* Peru, yellow and vermilion, April; with many others and their varieties.

Cultivation. Pot in August–September, compost of 2 parts sphagnum moss and fibrous peat, with charcoal, well crocked pots; ample ventilation, shade, liberal watering in growth, little in winter, minimum temp. 7–10° C. (45–50° F.).

Propagation. By division when re-potting, September.

Matricaria (mat-ri-ka'ri-a. Fam. Compositae). The plant, M. *eximia,* 9–12 in., with good free-flowering forms 'Golden Ball', small very double flower-heads; 'Silver Ball', milk-white; and 'Snow Dwarf', is grown as a half-hardy annual, from seeds in spring, but botanically belongs to *Chrysanthemum parthenium* (q.v.). M. *maritima,* the native Scentless Mayweed, 1–2 ft, is sometimes

a weed, though its v. *plenissima,* with double pure white flowers, may be grown as a hardy annual.

Matthiola (mat-thi'o-la. Fam. Cruciferae). Stocks. Although there are about fifty species in this genus of cruciferous flowering annual or perennial plants, the only one commonly grown as such is M. *bicornis,* the Night-scented Stock, of Greece, 1 ft, with lilac flowers, closed during the day, opening in the evening and diffusing a powerful sweet scent in summer. It may be sown out of doors, well-drained soil, April. Garden Stocks, formerly Stock Gilliflowers, have originated chiefly from M. *incana,* a native of S. Europe, and its v. *annua*; and *sinuata,* a biennial of Europe and Britain, and possibly M. *fenestralis,* a perennial of Crete, has played a small part. The Stocks fall into two main groups, the Summer or Ten Week, and the Winter.

Summer Stocks include the following classes: (a) *Ten Week Beauty or Mammoth,* 18 in., bushy; for bedding, cutting or pot growth, in named vs. such as 'Abundance', crimson-rose; 'Beauty of Nice', pink; 'Côte d'Azur', light blue; 'Heatham Beauty', rosy-mauve, flushed terra-cotta; 'Monte Carlo', canary yellow; 'Salmon King', salmon-rose; 'Snowdrift', white; and 'Violette de Parme', violet. (b) *Giant Imperial Ten Week,* to 2 ft, in shades of copper, crimson, lavender, mauve, pink, copper and golden yellow, double flowering. (c) *Giant Perfection Ten Week,* 2–2½ ft, in shades of blood red, silvery-lilac, purple, rose, white and yellow. (d) *Hanson's Mammoth Ten Week, All Double,* 1½ ft, in shades of carmine, dark blue, flesh pink, light blue, lilac, rose and white; the flower-doubling factor is linked with the colour of the seed leaves and those showing dark colour will be single flowered and can be rogued out. (e) *Hanson's Dwarf Ten Week,* 1 ft, in shades of apricot pink, crimson, dark and light blue, lilac, rose and white; another strain in which dark-leaved cotyledons indicate single-flowering, and light colour double-flowering. (f) *Ten Week Dwarf,* 1¼ ft, an older strain in shades of blood red, rose, crimson, dark and light blue, salmon-pink, white and yellow. (g) *Ten Week Excelsior,* of upright growth, available in shorter early-flowering forms of 1½ ft, and Giant Excelsior Column of 2–2½ ft, in colours ranging through deep rose, yellow, blue and pink. All the above are usually raised from seeds sown under glass, March, bottom heat of 18° C. (65° F.) standard compost, pricked off, for planting out in May, or potting on for greenhouse decoration.

Winter Stocks consist of hardy bien- nial strains, and are so called because they are normally sown in June or early July one year, to over-winter and flower the next. In mild districts, given well- drained soil and a dryish winter, plants can be placed outdoors where they are to flower; elsewhere they are wintered in pots in the cold greenhouse or frame and planted out in March. The enemy is damp rather than low temperatures. They include: (a) *Brompton Stocks*, upright growth to 1½–2 ft, in shades of crimson, rose-carmine, pink, lavender, purple and white. (b) *Hanson's Brompton Stock, 100 per cent Double*, in deep car- mine, light blue, rose pink and white, 1½ ft, with double-flowering linked to cotyledon-leaf colour, dark green indi- cating singles. (c) *East Lothian or Intermediate Stocks*, 1¼ ft, in shades of crimson, lavender, rose, scarlet, white. Seeds may be sown in January, under glass, for summer flowering; in July for spring flowering the following year. (d) *All the Year Round or Perpetual Flowering*, often perennial in mild localities, of vigour to 2 ft, with green, wallflower-like leaves, and double white flowers; may be sown in summer to flower in spring the following year; in February–March, to flower the same year.

Trysomic Seven Week Stocks, 1 ft, are vigorous dwarfs, flowering in seven to eight weeks from March–April sowings under glass, bottom heat of 15·5° C. (60° F.), and pricking out in late April.

General Cultivation. Plant in well- drained soil, enriched with rotted organic matter, and lime to a pH of 6·5. The greatest enemy is excessive damp, when attacks by various fungi may occur; Black Rot (*Pseudomonas campestris*), Root Rots (*Corticum solani, Thielaviopsis basicola*) and the troubles to which Brassicas fall heir such as Damping-off, Grey Mould (*Botrytis cinerea*) and Downy Mildew (*Perono-*

spora parasitica). It is wise to destroy seriously infected plants, and amend soil conditions, particularly drainage.

Mattock. A tool somewhat like a pick with a narrow pointed or chisel-edged blade on one side, and a broader, round- pointed blade on the other; most useful in breaking up clay and hard ground.

Maurandia (maw-ran'di-a. Fam. Scrophulariaceae). Climbing perennial plants of Mexico, allied to Antirrhinum, which are grown as half-hardy annuals.

Selection. M. barclaiana, to 15 ft, tubular, purple to rose or white flowers, summer; *lophospermum*, rose-purple flowers, summer; and *scandens*, violet.

Cultivation. Sow seeds, March–April, under glass, standard compost, bottom heat of 21° C. (70° F.); potting on to 6-in. pots for the cool greenhouse; or planting out in warm, well-drained loam, to grace trellis or walls in warm localities, in May.

Maxillaria (maks-il-la'ri-a. Fam. Orchidaceae). Epiphytic orchids with fine single flowers, late winter.

Selection. M. grandiflora, Peru, Ecuador, 10 in., white lip, lemon-yellow lobes, crimson inside, March; *lindeniae*, Ecuador, 10 in., milk white and pink, February; *picta*, Brazil, 6 in., creamy yellow, dotted chocolate, winter; *sanderiana*, Ecuador, white, blood red, late winter, best grown in a basket; and *venusta*, Colombia, 10 in., white and yellow, scented, winter.

Cultivation. Pot and repot, in spring, in 2 parts sphagnum moss and fibrous peat, a little sand and charcoal; water and syringe freely in active growth, partial shade, summer temp. to 18° C. (65° F.); water very moderately in winter, temp. about 13° C. (55° F.).

Propagation. By division when new growth shows, May.

Maximus (-a, -um). Very large; largest. Ex. *Narcissus maximus*.

May. See *Crataegus monogyna, C. oxyacantha*.

May Bug. See Chafer.

Mayflower. See *Epigaea repens*.

Mazus (ma'zus. Fam. Scrophulari- aceae). Dwarf creeping perennials with mimulus-like flowers, originating in SE. Asia or Australasia.

Selection. M. pumilio, 3 in., violet- white, yellow centred flowers, summer;

and *radicans*, 3 in., white with yellow-centred flowers, summer, are from New Zealand; *reptans*, 2 in., a trailer with blue and white flowers, July, of the Himalaya.

Cultivation. May be planted in sunny positions in well-drained soils in the rock garden in mild localities; but otherwise are best in the alpine house. Plant in April.

Propagation. By division of plants in April.

Meadow Rue. See *Thalictrum*.

Meadow Saffron. See *Colchicum*.

Meadow Saxifrage. See *Saxifraga granulata*.

Meadowsweet. See *Filipendula*.

Mealy Bugs. Small oval, sap-sucking insects covered with a white, cottony waxy secretion, related to the Scale Insects (q.v.). Most species are pests of plants growing under glass, such as

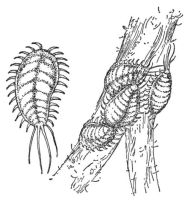

FIG. 149   Mealy Bugs (*Pseudococcus* spp.)

Pseudococcus citri, maritimus, nipae, gahani and *adonidum*, while *Ripersia halophila* and *subterranea* may be found on plant roots. Almond, Apricot, Grape Vines, Nectarine, Rose, Peach, Cacti, Orchids and a range of pot plants are liable to infestation. *Control.* On woody trees, a 4 per cent tar-oil emulsion wash can be given in December. In the growing season, a malathion or nicotine insecticide is most promising.

Meconopsis (mek-on-op'sis. Fam. Papaveraceae). A genus of the Poppy

family which provides some notable herbaceous plants for the modern garden.

Selection. M. *betonicifolia* (*baileyi*), the Blue Poppy of Tibet, 3 ft, blue flowers, May–June; *cambrica*, the Welsh Poppy, 2 ft, yellow or orange, May–July, and v. *flore pleno*, double flowering; *chelidonifolia*, China, 3 ft, yellow, early summer; *dhwojii*, Nepal, 2½ ft, primrose, June; *grandis*, Tibet, 2–3 ft, purple or deep blue, May–June; *integrifolia*, W. China, 1½–3 ft, yellow, June–July, *paniculata*, Nepal, 2½ ft, yellow, June; *quintuplinervia*, the Harebell Poppy of Tibet, 1 ft, lavender blue, June; *regia*, Nepal, to 5 ft, yellow, June, fine winter foliage; × *sheldonii*, 3 ft, blue flowering, May–June; *sherriffi*, Tibet, 1–2 ft, pink to rose, June; *simplicifolia*, Nepal, 2 ft, sky blue to purple, June; *superba*, Tibet, 3 ft, white, May–June, and *villosa*, Upper Burma, Tibet, to 6 ft, yellow, July, are normally perennial, but with strong tendencies to be monocarpic when grown from seed, unless the first year's flowers and stems are pinched out. M. *aculeata*, W. Himalaya, 2 ft, sky-blue, June; *nepaulensis*, Nepal, 6 ft, red, purple or blue, June; *latifolia*, Kashmir, 3½ ft, pale blue, June; and *violacea*, Burma, to 6 ft, bluish-violet, June, are others which may be grown.

Cultivation. Plant March–April, in cool situations, and soil that is porous and well-drained near the surface, but rich in humus and moisture-retentive below. Pinch out flower stems of young plants attempting their first flowering, to ensure perennial performance. Avoid moisture round the crowns.

Propagation. By seeds, thinly, in pans, standard compost, in cold frame, as soon as seeds are available, summer or autumn. A few species such as M. *quintuplinervia* by careful division, April.

Medicago (med-i-ka'go. Fam. Leguminoseae). Only M. *echinus*, Calvary Clover, S. France, 6 in., an annual with leaves marked by blood-red spots, yellow July flowers, followed by coiled spiny fruits likened to a 'Crown of Thorns', is much grown; from seeds sown in March in the cool greenhouse, to plant out in May, or grow as an interesting pot plant.

Medlar (*Mespilus germanica*). Although seldom grown for its fruit today, the Medlar makes a handsome, ornamental deciduous tree, of 15–25 ft, and may be grown in bush, pyramid or half-standard form. Originating in Europe and Asia Minor, good varieties are 'Nottingham', 'Royal' and 'Dutch Monstrous'. Of crooked angular growth, it bears solitary white flowers in late May or June, followed by hard, roundish fruits, with persistent hairy calyces and leafy segments in late October–November. The fruits need to be stored for a few weeks until soft and over-ripe or 'bletted', when they may be eaten with sugar or used for making jelly.

FIG. 150   A Medlar, fruit of *Mespilus germanica*.

Cultivation. Trees may be grafted on Hawthorn, Pear or Quince stocks, and planted in October–March; well-drained, loam soil, sunny, warm open position, with wall shelter in cold districts and the north. Pruning consists of thinning out old and weak shoots in winter. General culture is as for apples. Diseases and pests are few.

Medulla. Pith, the soft internal tissue of plants.

Medullary Rays. Plates of soft cellular tissue, or 'silver grain', radiating from the centre of roots or stems of dicotyledons, between the vascular bundles, often storing food reserves.

Megasea. See *Bergenia*.

Meiosis. The reproductive process in which the nucleus of a cell divides into two with only one division of the individual chromosomes.

Melaleuca (mel-a-lu'ca. Fam. Myrtaceae). Evergreen shrubs with heads or spikes of flowers with stamens in colourful bundles, for the cool greenhouse.

Selection. *M. fulgens*, W. Australia, 6 ft, rich red spikes of flowers, June; *hypericifolia*, New S. Wales, 6–12 ft, red, June; *wilsonii*, W. Australia, 6 ft, red or pink, July.

Cultivation. Pot in March–April, firmly in standard compost; water freely in active growth; may be placed outdoors June–September, syringe on hot sunny days; water very moderately in winter, minimum temp. 10° C. (50° F.); repot every second or third year.

Propagation. By cuttings of young shoots, July–August, in propagating case.

Melandrium (mel-and'ri-um. Fam. Caryophyllaceae). Attractive summer-flowering plants, sometimes listed under *Lychnis* or *Silene*; nominally perennial.

Selection. *M. album*, White Campion, Britain, 2 ft, is best in v. *multiplex* for the garden; *rubrum*, Red Campion, Europe, 1½ ft, may be grown for summer flowers; but *elisabethae*, Tyrol, 6 in., purplish-violet flowers, July–August, is a gem for the rock garden.

Propagation. By seeds, March, in cold frame.

Melia (me'li-a. Fam. Meliaceae). The chief species grown is *M. azedarach*, N. India and China, the Bead tree, 6–30 ft, with feathery pinnate foliage, panicles of highly scented, violet-lilac flowers, June, yellow fruits with bony seeds, threaded as beads in native countries.

Cultivation. Plant outdoors in autumn or spring, by warm, sheltered walls in mild localities, well-drained humus-rich soil; or in pots for cool greenhouse.

Propagation. By seeds, under glass, bottom heat of 18° C. (65° F.); or young shoot cuttings, July–August, in propagating case or frame.

Melissa (me-lis'sa. Fam. Labiatae). *M. officinalis*, Balm, a perennial of S. Europe, 2–3 ft, with foliage of lemon fragrance, and white flowers in summer, is hardy and sometimes grown as a herb, in any well-drained soil, and sun; easily raised from seeds in spring.

Melittis (me-lit'tis. Fam. Labiatae). The one species, *M. melissophyllum*, the Bastard Balm, Europe, 1–1½ ft, scented leaves, creamy white, spotted pink, May flowers, is a perennial for half-shade in border or woodland, and good loam soil. Propagation by seeds, spring, or division, at planting in October–March.

Melocactus. See *Cactus*.

Melon (*Cucumis melo*. Fam. Cucurbitaceae). Introduced from Jamaica, 1570, the Melon has long been cultivated under glass for its large, juicy-fleshed and luscious fruits, in gardens blessed with sufficient warm summer sun. *Varieties*: green-fleshed—'Best of All', 'Emerald Green', 'Honeydew' and 'Ringleader'; scarlet-fleshed—'Blenheim Orange', 'King George' and 'Superlative'; white-fleshed—'Hero of Lockinge'; Canteloupe, orange pink-fleshed—'Ogen', 'Dutch Net'. For frame or cloche culture—Canteloupe Charantais, Tiger or Prescotts, all orange-fleshed; 'Munroe's Little Heath', scarlet-fleshed.

Propagation. Plants are raised from seeds, sown preferably in peat-wood fibre pots, standard compost, bottom heat of 18° C. (65° F.), in the greenhouse or frame, January–April, allowing about 12 weeks from sowing to harvest. In peat-wood fibre pots, root disturbance in transplanting is avoided.

Culture under Glass. A growing temp. of 15.5–21° C. (60–70° F.) is desirable, steadily maintained with good ventilation without draughts. Plants may be set out in mounds of good loam soil, plus one-third rotted manure, and sand, or a standard potting compost; on staging; or in beds, enriched with moist peat and a balanced fertilizer (John Innes Base (q.v.) at 6 oz. per sq. yd, or in rings to be grown on the Ring Culture System (q.v.). Plants should be 2 ft apart, and grown as single cordons, up canes to wires, about 10 in. apart, on which the lateral shoots may be supported. The main stem is stopped by pinching out top growth at 4–6 ft, lateral shoots at 18 in. Regular liberal watering should be given, consistent with growth vigour, and plants syringed on hot sunny days, though humidity should not be as great as for cucumbers. Flowers are unisexual, and female flowers, identifiable by small rounded growths at their base, should be pollinated when fully open by picking a staminous male flower and pressing the stamens into the female flower in early morning, when dry. One fruit per lateral should be allowed to develop; and not more than four per plant. The fruits will need support in nets tied to the wires as they gain in weight, taking four to five weeks to grow and ripen. Growth beyond the fruit on the lateral may be pinched back at two or three leaves. With ripening, watering should diminish.

Culture in Frames. The traditional method is to prepare a hotbed of manure and leaves, turned two or three times, and made up firm, with a mound of soil in the centre, when temp. of 18° C. (65° F.) is reached. A frame is placed on the hotbed, and two plants placed in the centre of each light. Each plant is stopped at its second true leaves, and laterals allowed to grow out to 6–8 leaves, and stopped at the fourth leaf. Sub-laterals then form, which are stopped at the third leaf, and on which female flowers form. After pollination and early development, two evenly developing fruits are selected per plant for the crop. The soil is kept moist, and plants well ventilated. The chief crop is raised from March–April sowings, to fruit in July–August.

Culture under Cloches. This is only practicable in warm sunny localities. Plants raised from vs. Canteloupe Charentais or Tiger strains under glass are planted out in well-prepared humus-manured ground on 3-in. hills, June, under barn cloches, spaced 3 ft apart; stopped as in frame culture, and the two strongest laterals trained along under the cloches, stopping at 18 in. Pollination is sometimes left to bees, but it is safer to carry it out by hand.

Melon Cactus. See *Cactus melocactus*.

Mendel, Mendelism. Abbé Gregor Mendel, an Austrian monk, was the first to show that heredity followed simple statistical laws, by publishing, 1866, his investigations and observations on the mechanism of heredity in the garden and sweet pea; now known as Mendelism, or the Mendel's Laws of Heredity; although not generally recognized and accepted until 1900. These laws became the scientific basis of Heredity. Briefly,

Mendel held that characters in plants could be classified as pairs of alternative characters, Dominant and Recessive. Working with seven different pairs of garden peas he showed that the crossing of two pure races unlike in a pair of alternative characters resulted in a uniform first hybrid filial (F_1) generation. The self-fertilizing of the F_1 generation produces a second hybrid generation (F_2) in which a segregation or separation of the parental characters occurs in such a way as to give rise to plants of the pure paternal type, the pure maternal type and the hybrid type, in the ratio of 1 : 1 : 2 respectively; in the next generation (F_3) the seeds of the paternal and maternal types breed true, while the hybrid type segregate again in the same ratio as for the F_2 generation; and the pattern repeats in the F_4 generation. One of the pairs which Mendel used consisted of tall peas and dwarf peas; the dominant tall character may be represented by the capital T; the dwarf recessive character by the small t., and Mendel's Law of Segregation diagrammed as follows:

are segregated so that half the male gametes and half the female are carriers of the Dominant character, and half of the Recessive character; they are pure in that a single gamete carries one or the other, but not both. Subsequent work has shown that these simple laws apply generally to all organisms, plants and animals, though heredity is still a highly complex study.

Mentha, Mint (men'tha, Fam. Labiatae). Perennial herbs with aromatic leaves, small flowers in whorls or spikes.

Selection. M. citrata (odorata), Bergamot Mint, 1 ft, reddish-purple flower spikes, summer; *piperita*, Peppermint, 1–2 ft, purple, autumn; *pulegium*, Pennyroyal, prostrate, and its v. *gibraltarica*, both good carpeters; *rotundifolia*, Round-leafed Mint, 2 ft, purplish-white flowers, summer; and *spicata*, Spearmint, 2 ft, purplish, August, are natives of Europe and Britain; *requienii*, Corsica, small-leafed, pale purple, summer, is a creeping plant for the rock garden, peppermint-scented.

Cultivation. Plant October–March,

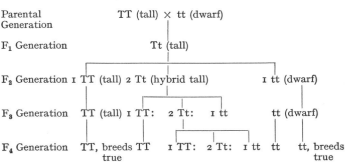

Parental Generation	TT (tall) × tt (dwarf)		
F_1 Generation	Tt (tall)		
F_2 Generation	1 TT (tall)	2 Tt (hybrid tall)	1 tt (dwarf)
F_3 Generation	TT (tall) 1 TT:	2 Tt: 1 tt	tt (dwarf)
F_4 Generation	TT, breeds TT true	1 TT: 2 Tt: 1 tt tt	tt, breeds true

Mendel showed that other characters such as flower colour, forms of the seed and pod, colour of testa (seed coats), etc., were inherited according to the same law. This led him to enunciate his second law, the Law of the Purity of the Gametes. This held that while all cells in a hybrid plant contain both characters of a pair of characters, when cell division leads to the formation of germ cells or male and female gametes, the characters

well-drained, ordinary soil, sun or partial shade.

Propagation. By division, autumn or spring: by cuttings of young shoots, spring or summer. *See* Mint.

Mentzelia (ment-ze'li-a. Fam. Loasaceae). Only *M. lindleyi (Bartonia aurea)*, a Californian annual, 1 ft, with fragrant, golden-yellow, open-faced flowers in summer, is much grown, from seed sown in March–April, in ordinary well-drained soil, where plants are to flower; or in cold districts plants may be raised in the cool greenhouse, to plant out in May.

Menyanthes (men-i-an'thes. Fam. Gentianaceae). The Bog-bean or Buck-bean, *M. trifoliata*, 9 in., natively the Marsh Trefoil, is a useful hardy aquatic perennial, with trifoliolate olive green leaves, white, pink-tinged flowers in spring, for planting at the margins of pools. Easily propagated by division of the rootstock in March.

Menziesia (men-zes'i-a. Fam. Ericaceae). Deciduous low shrubs, related to the Heaths, with small nodding, urn-shaped flowers in clusters.

Selection. M. ciliicalyx, Japan, 1–2 ft, light green to purple flowers, May; *pilosa*, N. America, 1½ ft, white, tinged yellow, May; and *purpurea*, Japan, 2 ft, bright red and purple, May; flowers being on previous year's shoots.

Cultivation. Plant October or March, lime-free, peaty soil, partial shade. Or grow in the alpine house.

Propagation. By cuttings of young shoots in June–July, inserted in cold frame or under handlights.

Mercuric Chloride. Corrosive Sublimate. *See* Fungicides.

Mercurous Chloride. Calomel (q.v.).

Mercury Vapour Lamps. Lamps emitting a strong bluish light by the passage of an electric current through mercury vapour at high pressure, and used in the greenhouse for the irradiation of tomato, cucumber and other seedling plants to quicken development, and give improved vigour with a view to promoting earliness and yield.

Merendera (me-ren-de'ra. Fam. Liliaceae). Pretty hardy cormous plants, with starry shaped flowers in autumn, before the leaves, as with Meadow Saffron.

Selection. M. montana (bulbocodium), Spanish Pyrenees, 3 in., rose-lilac; *robusta*, Persia, lilac or white, February; *sobolifera*, Bulgaria to Persia, pale lilac, flowers in April; and *trigyna*, Persia, rose, May, with leaves.

Cultivation. Plant corms 1 in. deep, 4 in. apart, well-drained soil, warm sunny situations, July–August. Or may be grown in pots in the alpine house.

Propagation. By offsets in July; by seeds, August.

Mericarp. A dry fruit, splitting into one-seeded portions. Ex. *Malva*.

Meristem. A zone of actively dividing and growing cells, forming new tissues, chiefly the apical growing points or stems, and top growth; the cambium of stem and root, and root tips.

Mertensia (mer-ten'si-a. Fam. Boraginaceae). Hardy herbaceous perennials with blue or purplish flowers in terminal racemes, cymes or panicles.

Selection. M. alpina, Rocky Mts, 6 in., light blue, clusters, May; *ciliata*, Rocky Mts, 1–2 ft, bright blue, June–July; *echioides*, Himalaya, 6 in., deep blue, June; *maritima*, the native Oyster Plant, prostrate, racemes of blue flowers, July; *primuloides*, Himalaya, 6 in., indigo-blue, June; *sibirica*, E. Asia, 1 ft, purple-blue, May–July; *virginica*, Virginian Cowslip, 1–2 ft, purple-blue flowers in drooping clusters, April–May.

Cultivation. Plant October–March, in free-draining soil, enriched with peat or leaf-mould, in the rock garden or front of border; *M. virginica* in woodland shade. Apt to be short-lived in colder districts.

Propagation. By seeds, sown in summer as soon as ripe, in cold frame. By careful division, August or spring. May also be grown in the alpine house.

Mesembryanthemum (me-sem-bri-an'the-mum. Fam. Aizoaceae). A very large genus of succulent-leafed plants, with showy flowers, at present subject to taxonomical revision. Being chiefly S. African, with a few exceptions from other warm countries, none are perfectly hardy.

Selection. For gardening purposes, the plants may be grouped: (1) *Mesembryanthemums for Outdoors.* These include *M. (Aptenia) cordifolium* v. *variegatum*, prostrate, half-hardy perennial, with leaves marked creamy white, purple flowers, summer; *crinifolium (Dorotheanthus bellidiflorus)*, the Livingstone Daisy, trailing, buff, apricot, crimson, pink and white flowers, June onwards; *M. (Cryophytum) crystallinum*, the Ice Plant, with leaves glistening with tiny crystals, 6 in., small whitish flowers, summer; *M. (Carpobrotus) edule*, Hottentot Fig, trailing, yellow or purple flowers, early summer, edible fruits; *M. (Dorotheanthus) gramineum*, 3 in., carmine flowers in summer; *tricolor* (*Erepsia mutabalis*), rose, red and yellow flowers; are chiefly raised from seeds sown in March–April, in cool greenhouse or frame, and planted out in porous, free-draining soil and hot sunny positions, in rock garden, terrace or border, or window boxes. (2) *Mesembryanthemums for the Cool Greenhouse*. *M.* (*Lampranthus*) *aurantiacum*, sub-shrubby to 2 ft, bright orange flowers, summer; *M.* (*Lampranthus*) *aureum*, 1½ ft, golden yellow flowers, summer; *M.* (*Lampranthus*) *coccineum*, 2½ ft, scarlet; *M.* (*Lampranthus*) *falciforme*, 1½ ft, pink; *M.* (*Lampranthus*) *roseum*, 2 ft, pale pink; and *M.* (*Lampranthus*) *violaceum*, 1½ ft, small violet flowers. These plants may be potted, and repotted, in early spring, watered freely in active growth, given ample sun; watered very moderately in winter, minimum temp. of 10° C. (50° F.). Propagation by cuttings, spring.

Mesocarp. The middle layer of the fruit (drupe) wall. See Endocarp, Epicarp, Pericarp.

Mesophyll. The tissue between the upper and lower epidermis of a leaf. *See* Leaf.

Mesophyte. A plant which grows under environmental conditions midway between the extremes of water and drought; i.e. most garden plants. *See* Hydrophyte and Xerophytes.

Mespilus (mes'pi-lus. Fam. Rosaceae). *M. germanica*, the only species, is the Medlar (q.v.).

Meta, Metaldehyde. A white, volatile, inflammable solid polymer of acetaldehyde (CH_3CHO), often used as fuel for small heaters, but with excellent molluscicidal properties for the control of slugs and snails in the garden, having an anaesthetic action which immobilizes the pests and leads to their dessication. Most effectively used as a prepared bait in tablet, pellet form, or an emulsion for spraying on plants. Toxic to animals and children.

Metake. Japanese name of *Arundinaria japonica*.

Metasequoia (me-ta-se-quoi'a. Fam. Pinaceae). The one species, *M. glyptostroboides*, a relic of the distant past and known only from fossil remains until 1947 when living plants were found in Hupeh, China, is a deciduous conifer, with linear leaves on opposite sides of shoots, colouring russet in autumn; possibly growing to 100 ft or more.

Cultivation. Plant September–October to April; well-drained deep soil, moisture-retentive with humus-content; open situation but not unduly exposed.

Propagation. By seeds, April, outdoors, prepared well-drained seed-bed. By cuttings of young shoots, June–August, in closed frame or under mist propagation.

Mezereon. See *Daphne mezereum*.

Mice. It is probable that the long-tailed Field Mice (*Apodemus* spp.) do more damage than the House Mice (*Mus musculus*) in the garden, eating bulbs, seeds, berries and fruits; together with the Field Vole, wrongly called the short-tailed Field Mouse. Trapping and baiting with Warfarin pellets may be used to control these rodents; the bait pellets being covered out of reach of children and pets. Corms and bulbs may be protected by chopped gorse or short lengths of rose prunings placed above them after planting. Young tree trunks should be painted with fruit-banding grease, or a repellent to 18 in.

Michaelmas Daisy. See *Aster*.

Microclimate. The climate of a limited habitat, such as that created within a garden, by situation and relationship to nearby plants, etc.

Micromeria (mi-kro-me'ri-a. Fam. Labiatae). Flowering herbs or sub-shrubs of the Mediterranean region, for the mild rock garden or alpine house.

Selection. *M. corsica*, Corsica, Sardinia, 4 in., small, round, grey-green leaves, large purple flowers in July–August; and *graeca*, E. Mediterranean, 9 in., pink flowers, June, are the hardiest; *piperella*, SW. Europe, 3 in., purplish pink flowers, August, needs winter shelter.

Cultivation. Plant (or pot) autumn or spring, well-drained, loam soil, warm position, in rock garden.

Propagation. By cuttings of young shoots taken with a heel, June–July, in cold frame, standard compost.

Micro-organism. An organism of microscopic size, usually alga, some fungi, bacterium, actinomyces, protozoa, amoebae and minute soil organisms.

Micropyle. The narrow opening at the

apex of the ovule through which the
pollen tube enters in fertilization; it
also becomes in the seed the opening
through which moisture enters the
embryo for germination.

Miffy. A gardening term for an ailing
plant.

Mignonette. See *Reseda.*

Mildews. In horticulture, plant diseases
caused by fungi which grow on the leaves
and stems of host plants as greyish or
white powdery or felted deposits. There
are two classes: Powdery Mildews, which
are superficial, tending to smother
plants; to be controlled by karathane
or sulphur fungicides; and Downy
Mildews, which are more serious since
the fungi penetrate deeply into cell
tissues, but may be controlled by copper
fungicides. A wide range of plants are
subject to mildews, indoors and out, and
early action is needed.

Milfoil. See *Achillea.*

Milk Vetch. See *Astragalus.*

Milkwort. See *Polygala.*

Millipedes. A class of myriapods
(*Diplopoda*), hard-bodied, usually with
two pairs of legs on each segment of the
body; curling up when disturbed; slow-
moving, and dark grey or blackish in
colour. The chief types are the Snake
Millipedes, with cylindrical bodies, such
as the Black Millipede (*Tachypodojulus
niger*) and the Spotted Millipede
(*Blanjulus guttulatus*), and the Flattened
Millipedes, with broader bodies, such as
Polydesmus angustus. They feed chiefly
on dead to rotting organic matter,
but attack soft tissues such as germinating seeds, roots and bulbs, and exploit

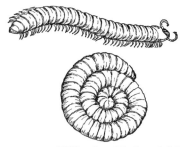

FIG. 151 Millipede (*Tachypodojulus
niger*); curling up when disturbed.

injuries to plants by other agents.
Judicious use of a gamma-BHC soil
insecticidal dust clears infested ground;
and a gamma-BHC seed dressing protects seeds. Good drainage, liming to
bring the pH value to 6·5, and regular
hoeing in the growing season also help.

Miltonia (mil-to′ni-a. Fam. Orchidaceae). Beautiful epiphytic orchids of
tropical America, with showy, large,
velvety textured flowers, for the warm
greenhouse.

Selection. M. *clowesii*, Brazil, yellow,
marked brown flowers, autumn;
phalaenopsis, New Grenada, white, May;
roezlii, Colombia, white, and wine
purple, autumn; and *vexillaria*, Colombia, rose and white, May–June, and
many vs., and hybrids.

Cultivation. Pot, and repot, when new
growth begins, March, well-drained pots,
compost of 2 parts sphagnum moss, 1
part fibrous peat and a little sand and
charcoal; water liberally in active
growth, summer temp. 15·5–24° C.
(60–75° F.); little in winter, temp.
13° C. (55° F.) minimum.

Propagation. By division when
repotting, March.

Mimosa, Sensitive Plant (mi-mo′sa.
Fam. Leguminosae). Only M. *pudica*,
the Humble or Sensitive Plant, tropical
America, 1 ft, with feathery, pinnate
leaves, that droop at a touch, and small
rose-purple summer flowers, is grown
much, chiefly as a half-hardy annual,
raised from seeds, sown under glass,
March–April, with bottom heat of
18° C. (65° F.), standard compost, and
potted on as a pot plant in the warm
greenhouse.

Mimulus, Monkey Flower (mim′u-lus.
Fam. Scrophulariaceae). Free-flowering
annual and perennial herbs of brilliant
flower beauty and diverse character.

Selection. M. *cardinalis*, Oregon, 2 ft,
red or red and yellow flowers, summer;
lewisii, British Columbia, to 2 ft, red or
white flowers, summer; *luteus*, Monkey
Musk, 1–2 ft, bright yellow, and vs.
moschatus, British Columbia to California, the Common Musk, now held to
have lost its scent, 1 ft, pale yellow,
dotted brown, summer flowers, and v.
harrisonii, larger flowered, are hardy
perennials for the border, in moisture-
retentive soils. M. *cupreus*, Chile, 6 in.,

yellow, spotted brown, summer flowers, and vs. 'Red Emperor' and 'Whitecroft Scarlet'; and *primuloides*, California, 4 in., yellow May flowers are suitable for the rock garden. *M. glutinosus*, California, to 4 ft, with orange, salmon or buff flowers, is a half-hardy perennial, largely grown as a pot plant in the cool greenhouse.

Cultivation. Plant hardy kinds in October–March, in moist soil in the border, or by the waterside.

Propagation. By seeds, sown April, under glass, or cold frame. By division, March.

Mina. See *Quamoclit*.

Minimus (-a, -um). Smallest. Ex. *Narcissus minimus*.

Mint (*Mentha* spp.). More than one Mint may be grown for culinary purposes; the Common Green Mint, *Mentha spicata*, 2 ft, is the smooth-leaved mint commonly grown, but the Apple or Round-leaved Mint, *M. rotundifolia*, to 2 ft, is the epicure's choice for flavour, though the foliage is slightly hairy; × *alopecuroides*, to 5 ft, is excellent, with leaves up to 3 in. long. The mint bed is usually planted in autumn or spring, from roots placed 2 in. deep, in well-dug soil, liberally manured. To defeat the invasiveness of the roots, it is wise to enclose the bed in 8-in. strips of asbestos sheeting, or for a small bed, in a sunken bottomless old bucket; lift, thin and replant every third or fourth year. Cut stems before flowering, lay on trays for drying quickly at the back of a stove or in temp. of 32° C. (90° F.); turn often; rub off leaves when dry, store in screwtop jars.

Mint, Cat. See *Nepeta*.

Mint, Horse. See *Monarda*.

Minutus (-a, -um). Very small. Ex. *Bellium minutum*.

Mirabilis (mi-rab'i-lis. Fam. Nyctaginaceae). The chief species grown is *M. Jalapa*, the Marvel of Peru, 2 ft, of tropical America, in forms giving crimson, yellow, white and various spotted and striped flowers, July–September, and a dwarfer strain 'Pygmee'; as a half-hardy annual, raised from seeds, March–April, standard compost, bottom heat of 18° C. (65° F.), under glass, to plant out in May. *M. multiflora*, 3 ft, scented rose flowers, may be grown similarly. Actually

perennial, the tuberous roots may be lifted in autumn and stored under frost-proof conditions like Dahlias.

Miscanthus, Eulalia (mis-kan'thus. Fam. Gramineae). Hardy, ornamental perennial grasses of China and Japan.

Selection. M. sacchariflorus, 3 ft, and *sinensis*, 4–6 ft, blue-green foliage, and vs. *gracillimus*, slender grace; *univittatus*, yellow-striped leaves; and *zebrinus*, with cross bars of yellow on the leaves.

Cultivation. Plant in autumn or spring; moist soil, grouped on lawns or in borders, or in large pots in the cool greenhouse.

Propagation. By division, autumn or spring.

Mistletoe. See *Viscum album*.

Mistletoe Cactus. See *Rhipsalis*.

Mitchella (mit-kel'la. Fam. Rubiaceae). Mat-forming evergreen trailing plants, of which *M. repens*, the Partridge Berry of N. America, may be grown in shade in the rock garden, or in the alpine house, its shining green, white-veined leaves, with scented, white, tinged purplish, June flowers, and oval scarlet berries, being very attractive; v. *leucocarpa* is similar with white berries; *undulata*, a Japanese counterpart; is also worth growing.

Cultivation. Plant September–October or March–April; well-drained soil enriched with peat. In the alpine house a lime-free standard compost is best, and plants need shade in summer.

Propagation. By layers, detached when rooted, and grown on as cuttings.

Mitosis. The process of the division of chromosomes in living and growing cells.

Mitraria, Mitre Flower (mi-tra'ri-a. Fam. Gesneriaceae). A monotypic genus, represented by *M. coccinea*, Chile, an evergreen, semi-climbing shrub of 4 ft, with glossy leaves, and bright scarlet, tubular flowers on long stalks, summer; best grown in the cool greenhouse, in shade, peaty lime-free compost, potted in March–April. Propagation by cuttings, July–August, in propagating case.

Moccasin Flower. See *Cypripedium*.

Mock Orange. See *Philadelphus*.

Mole (*Tala europaea*). Troublesome rather than harmful, the mole disturbs plants by its underground tunnelling and by throwing up hills of soil dis-figures lawns, beds and borders. Trapping with a steel trap, set in the main run, wearing gloves, is most effective. Fumi-gation by means of Smoke Fuses, or the poisonous calcium cyanide (Cymag, Cyanogas) placed in the runs and sealed at once, is sometimes effective. Repel-lents include moth-balls, castor-oil seeds, or lengths of bramble shoots placed down the runs.

Mollis (-e). Soft. Ex. *Hamamelis mollis.*

Moltkia (molt'ki-a. Fam. Boragin-aceae). Perennials of shrubby habit for sunny rock gardens in mild localities, or the alpine house.

Selection. M. caerulea, Asia Minor, 1 ft, spikes of bluish-purple, funnel-shaped flowers, April; *petraea,* Greece, ½–1 ft, pinkish-blue, June; *suffruticosa,* N. Italy, 6 in., violet-blue, June; and hybrids × *froebelli,* 6 in., bright blue, June; and × *intermedia,* 15 in., violet-blue, June.

Cultivation. Plant October–March, any well-drained soil, containing lime and humus; full sun.

Propagation. By cuttings of young shoots, July.

Moluccella, Shell Flower, Bells of Ireland, Moluccella Balm (mo-luk-kel'la. Fam. Labiatae). The species, *M. laevis,* Syria, 1–1½ ft, is grown as an annual for its stems of unusual whorled white flowers with apple-green, bell-like calyces, August, which may be dried as 'everlasting' flowers for winter decora-tion, when cut with flowers freshly open.

Cultivation. Sow seeds, March–April, under glass, bottom heat of 15·5° C. (60° F.), pricking out and hardening off to plant out in sunny positions, well-drained, rather porous soil, early May.

Moly. See *Allium moly.*

Momordica (mo-mord'ik-a. Fam. Cucurbitaceae). Interesting tropical climbers with ornamental palmate foliage, large yellow June flowers, and striking and edible coloured fruits.

Selection. M. balsamina, the Balsam Apple, tropical Africa and Asia, scarlet, roundish, gourd-like fruits; and *charantia,* the Balsam Pear, a larger plant, tropical Africa and SE. Asia, with oblong, pointed yellowish fruit, are usually grown.

Cultivation. Sow seeds, as for marrows,

under glass, bottom heat 21° C. (70° F.), April, to plant out in sunny positions, loam soil, on trellis, etc., or grow in the cool greenhouse to the rafters.

Monarda, Horse Mint (mon-ar'da. Fam. Labiatae). Easily cultivated, aromatic herbaceous perennials of N. America, with coloured bracted flowers in whorled heads, mid to late summer.

Selection. M. didyma, Bee Balm, Sweet Bergamot, Oswego Tea, 2–3 ft, has good forms in 'Cambridge Scarlet', 'Croftway Pink' and 'Blue Stocking'; *fistulosa,* 'Wild Bergamot', 2–5 ft, with purplish flowers is variable, with vs. *media* (*M. menthaefolia*), deep purple, and *violacea superba,* violet-purple.

Cultivation. Plant October–March, massed in fairly moisture-retentive soil, sun or partial shade.

Propagation. By division in spring. By seeds, sown in April, on prepared outdoor seed-beds.

Moneywort. See *Lysimachia nummu-laria.*

Monkey Flower. See *Mimulus.*

Monkey Puzzle. See *Araucaria.*

Monk's Hood. See *Aconitum.*

Mono-. A prefix in compound words, meaning One. Ex. Monocarpic, fruiting only once; Monophyllus, having only one leaf.

FIG. 152   Monocotyledonous flower.

Monocotyledons. Plants having one cotyledon or seed-leaf; one of the two Classes of Angiosperms, with Dicotyle-dons as the other. Important charac-teristics are that the root system is tufted, branching adventitiously from the base, without a tap-root; the vascular bundles of the stem are closed, without cambium; the leaves are usually parallel-veined, and grow singly at each node on

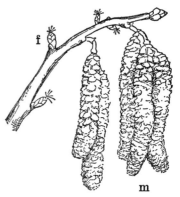

FIG. 154 Monoecious: m. male flower; f. female flower. (*Corylus* sp.).

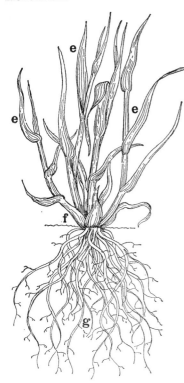

FIG. 153 Monocotyledon: main characters: e. parallel veining of leaves; f. little or no main stem; g. tufted and fibrous root system. Single seed leaf (not shown)

stems; the parts of the flower are usually in threes.

Monoecious. Having separate unisexual flowers, male and female, on the same plant.

Monogynous. Having one style, or pistil.

Monopetalous. Of flowers having all the petals more or less united, in one bundle.

Monotypic. A genus of only one species.

Monstera (mon-ste'ra. Fam. Araceae). Tropical evergreen climbing plants of the West Indies and tropical America, for the hothouse, though also popular for the centrally heated house.

Selection. M. *deliciosa*, the Ceriman, Mexico, to 20 ft, with aerial roots, large shining green, perforated leaves; and *pertusa*, tropical America, the Swiss Cheese Plant, to 16 ft, with oblongish oval leaves, irregularly perforated.

Cultivation. As house plants, pot in April–May, compost of 3 parts leafmould, 2 parts peat, 1 part coarse sand, plus John Innes Base at 4 oz. per bushel, 8–10 in. pots; water very freely in warm weather months, regularly but moderately in winter, minimum temp. 13° C. (55° F.), but will stand up to 27° C. (80° F.). In hothouse, may be pot-grown or in beds.

Propagation. By stem cuttings, spring or summer, in propagating case, with bottom heat of 23° C. (75° F.).

Montanus (-a, -um). Of the mountains. Ex. *Clematis montana.*

Montbretia (mont-bre'ti-a. Fam. Iridaceae). Cormous plants of S. Africa of which M. *laxifolia*, 1–1½ ft, with a spike of slender, funnel-shaped flowers, cream to pink, in autumn, may be grown; corms being planted 2 in. deep, 6 in. apart, in well-drained soil, sunny position, in late autumn to spring. For garden Montbretias see *Crocosmia*.

Monterey Cypress. See *Cupressus macrocarpa.*

Monterey Pine. See *Pinus radiata.*

Monthly Rose. See *Rosa chinensis.*

Moraea (mo-re'a. Fam. Iridaceae). Sometimes known as Butterfly or Peacock Irises, these S. African cormous plants are graceful with narrow leaves, and carry extremely lovely, sweet-scented, though ephemeral flowers on stems of 1–2 ft, in summer; succeeding outdoors in light, sandy loam and warm, sunny shelter, but otherwise in the cool greenhouse.

Selection. M. bicolor, yellow, brown-spotted, flowers; *pavonia,* orange-red, bluish basal spots, June; *robinsoniana,* Australia, 4 ft, white, spotted red and yellow; and *tristis,* 1 ft, brown with yellow basal spot.

Cultivation. Outdoors, plant in autumn or early spring, light sandy loam, full sun. In greenhouse, pot in standard compost, four corms to a 5-in. pot, 3-in. deep, in November; place in dark until growth shows, and grow in light at 10–15·5° C. (50–60° F.); watering increasingly with growth. Dry off when foliage withers.

Propagation. By offsets, when re-potting, November. By seeds sown as soon as ripe, in frame, at 15·5° C. (60° F.).

Moraine. The deposit of debris and ice-worn rock at the foot of a glacier, left behind when the ice melts. In the garden, synonymous with a Scree, an artificially constructed bed of small stones, broken rock and rubble, with smaller stones and chippings mingled with rock sand, soil and a little leaf-mould near the surface; for the growing of alpine plants in the rock garden (q.v.).

Morina (mo-ri'na. Fam. Dipsaceae). Border perennials with thistle-like spiny foliage and elegant habit, with bright summer flowers.

Selection. M. longifolia, Nepal, 2 ft, with whorls of tubular flowers, white, turning pink and crimson, June–July; and *persica,* Himalaya, 3 ft, long spikes of pink flowers, July.

Cultivation. Plant in autumn or spring, well-drained, sandy loam, partial shade or warm sun, with wind-sheltered quarters.

Propagation. By seeds in April, in cold frame. By division, immediately after flowering, or in spring.

Morisia (mo-ris'i-a. Fam. Cruciferae). Only *M. monantha,* Corsica, Sardinia, with its flat rosette of finely serrated leaves, and clear yellow flowers in March–May, is grown; planted in sandy porous loam, and sun, in the rock garden; or in well-drained pans in the alpine house. Propagation by root cuttings taken in June. By seeds, when ripe, if available.

Morphology. The study of the form of plants.

Mortar Rubble. A mixture of lime, sand and crushed brick from old buildings, esteemed as a benign liming and drainage material. The remains of mortar made with cement, breeze, plasticizers are not suitable for garden use.

Morus, **Mulberry** (mor'us. Fam. Moraceae). Deciduous trees of which the Chinese and Asian species have long been cultivated, though in Britain they succeed best in the south and mild localities.

Selection. M. alba, the White Mulberry, 40–60 ft, with heart-shaped, broadly ovate or lobed lightish green leaves, yields clusters of white, tinged pink, insipid blackberry-like fruits, and was long cultivated in Europe for its leaves, fed to silkworms; v. *pendula,* stiffly weeping, needs careful training. *M. nigra,* the Black Mulberry, 20–30 ft, with lobed, heart-shaped, toothed and dark green leaves, bears clusters of dark red, sweet, sub-acid fruits in autumn, and may be used for dessert, wine-making or preserves. This species is now more often grown for ornamental value, and old specimens with their short rugged trunks have a certain grandeur.

Cultivation. Plant, preferably, in November, well-drained, loam soil, open but not unduly exposed position. The Black Mulberry is more hardy than the White for northern gardens. Pruning is not advised, as plants tend to 'bleed', but if necessary it should be done in June–July.

Propagation. By cuttings of young shoots, with a heel of older wood in July–August, under handlights. By layering in spring or autumn. By seeds sown in April–May, though seedlings need several years to reach fruiting size and age.

Mosaic. In horticulture, a term often

used to describe symptoms of virus infections in which leaves develop mottled patches of lighter green or yellow-green scattered in the normal healthy dark green of the leaf tissues. *See* Virus.

Moschatus (-a, -um). Musky. Ex. *Mimulus moschatus.*

Moschosma (mos-kos′ma. Fam. Labiatae). Only *M. riparium*, a perennial sub-shrub of S. Africa, 2–4 ft, with nettle-like foliage, and erect panicles of small creamy-white flowers in winter, is much grown; as a pot plant, in the cool greenhouse. Pot in March–April, standard compost, water freely in active growth, moderately in winter, temp. 10° C. (50° F.); cut shoots back after flowering; use cut shoots as cuttings to propagate the plant.

Moss Campion. See *Silene acaulis.*

Moss Rose. See *Rosa centifolia* v. *muscosa.*

Mosses. A Class of lower green flowerless plants, Musci, which, with the Liverworts, Hepaticae, make up the Order Bryophyta. They grow mostly in damp, summer-shaded places, on impoverished, compacted soils, rock, stone or hard surfaces, where wind-blown dust and soil are caught. In most cases the plants have stems and leaves, spirally arranged, of simple structure, one cell thick, and anchor themselves to the soil by special hairs, rhizoids. They consist chiefly of Acrocarpous Mosses, which are mat-forming, with short stems, few side branches, and develop spore-bearing capsules at the apices of the shoots; and Pleurocarpous Mosses, which have fern or feathery stems and leaves, of prostrate habit, producing spore-bearing capsules on side branches. Mosses may propagate themselves sexually by means of spores, often produced in autumn and again in spring, by broken-off fragments of their leaves, stems and rhizoids. Sphagnum moss has a special 'spongy' structure, and is used, living or chopped up, as an ingredient of the compost for epiphytic plants, such as orchids. In woodland and wild gardening, a ground cover of mosses is not out of place. On paths, driveways, walls, and rock garden stones where it is not wanted, moss can usually be eradicated by wetting with a phenolic herbicide, a 10 per cent tar-oil solution,

or a domestic bleach. See Moss Control in Lawns.

Mother of Thousands. See *Linaria cymbalaria,* and *Saxifraga* v. *stolonifera.*

Mould. Old name for top soil, especially when rich in humus and organic matter. Also used for woolly or furry growth of small fungi on food, clothing, household things and plants, especially on fruits and bulbs in store.

Mountain Ash. See *Sorbus aucuparia.*

Mountain Avens. See *Dryas octopetala.*

Mournful Widow. See *Scabiosa atropurpurea.*

Mowers and Mowing. *See* Lawns and Lawn-mowers.

Mucronatus (-a, -um). Sharply pointed. Ex. *Pernettya mucronata.*

Mulberry. See *Morus.*

Mulch, Mulching. A mulch is a layer of material placed on the soil over the rooting area of plants, with a view to maintaining even soil temperatures, suppressing weeds, conserving soil moisture and, in the case of organic materials, of providing 'food' for the plants. As such a mulch usually consists of organic material such as rotted manure, compost, moist peat, sawdust, spent hops, leaf-mould, chopped straw or lawn mowings. Newspapers, sheet kraft paper and sheet polythene may be used between crop plants. Alpine plants often benefit from a mulch of stone chippings or gravel, and stone may be used for certain shrubs and trees outdoors. Mulching is best carried out after the soil has been provided with fertilizers, or after rain or watering.

Mullein. See *Verbascum.*

Multi-. A prefix in compound words meaning many. Ex. *Multiflorus,* many flowered.

Multifid. Cut into many parts.

Muralis (-e). Growing on walls. Ex. *Campanula muralis.*

Musa, Banana, Plantain (mu′sa. Fam. Musaceae). Very large, tropical tree-like perennials, grown in Britain for their decorative handsome foliage.

Selection. M. basjoo, Japanese Banana, 10 ft, is hardiest sp.; *cavendishii,* China, 5 ft, may be grown for its fruits; *ensete,* Abyssinian Banana, to 12 ft and more; *paradisiaca,* Plantain of the tropics, to 20 ft, and v. *sapientum,* the edible Banana, with several forms; and *superba,*

Cochin-China, 12 ft, but *textilis*, Philippines, source of Manilla Hemp, has no decorative value.

Cultivation. Plant in the bed, large pots or tubs of a warm greenhouse, spring, loam soil, liberally manured; summer temps. of 18–27° C. (65–80° F.); minimum winter temp. 10° C. (50° F.); but for fruiting 18° C. (65° F.) minimum is needed. Water liberally, syringe often in summer; very moderately in winter. *M. basjoo, ensete* and *superba* may be planted out in June in warm sun and shelter, in warm localities.

Propagation. By suckers taken from around the base of plants, potted, and kept close, at 18–24° C. (65–75° F.), and transferred to larger pots when roots are well developed. By seeds, April, bottom heat of 21° C. (70° F.), when available.

Muscari, Grape Hyacinth (mus-ka'ri. Fam. Liliaceae). Pretty bulbous plants, with narrow fleshy leaves, and racemes of small globose or pitcher-shaped flowers in spring.

Selection. M. armeniacum, Asia Minor, 1 ft, blue, May; *botryoides*, Europe, sky blue, May; and vs. *album*, white, *carneum*, pink, and *pallidum*, pale blue, 6–12 in.; *comosum*, 1 ft, blue-green, April, and v. *monstrosum*, the Feather

Hyacinth, loose bluish-violet flowering raceme, May; *latifolium*, Asia Minor, 1 ft, blue, May; *moschatum*, Musk Hyacinth of Asia Minor, 10 in., sweet-scented, greyish-green, May, and v *flavum*, yellow; and *tubergenianum*, Persia, 8 in., light and deep blue, April.

Cultivation. Plant bulbs in any reasonably well-drained soil, 2 in. deep, 3–4 in. apart, in rock garden or shrubbery, August–September.

Propagation. By offsets, August; by seeds, sown autumn or spring; often self-sowing.

Mushroom (*Psalliota campestris*). Commercially, the cultivation of the Field Mushroom is a highly technical and specialized industry. On a small garden scale this edible fungus may be grown in caves, cellars, greenhouses, frames, sheds, etc., or in the open. The chief essentials are a good compost, an even temperature, humidity and good casing soil; plus meticulous care at every stage. The first essential is good compost. The best is stable manure, from corn-fed, healthy horses, fresh and mixed with half as much bulk of chopped straw. One to one and a half tons are needed to make a satisfactory mushroom bed. The material is heaped on to a clean surface, and turned daily for four to five days in the interests of even fermentation, and then heaped squarely to 4–5 ft high, under cover. Allow to heat for 7–8 days until about 82° C. (160° F.); turn top to bottom, sides to middle, shaking out, mixing well, moistening if any parts appear dry, and after another 3–5 days, turn again; repeat the turning and re-heaping at 3–5-day intervals, until the heap is rich brown and has a sweet odour, at 21–27° C. (70–80° F.), when it is ready to make up into beds. Indoors, flat beds are best, about 4 ft wide, 9–12 in. thick, the compost being carefully placed and firmed. Outdoors, ridge beds are made, 2½ ft wide at the base, 2 ft high, tapering to 6 in. wide at the top; preferably in June–July for autumn cropping. Beds will tend to heat, but when the temp. falls to 27° C. (80° F.), they are ready to be spawned. Indoors, a temp. of 7° C. (45° F.) to 21° C. (70° F.) is essential; with 80 per cent humidity, and very good ventilation; and preferably darkness. When the

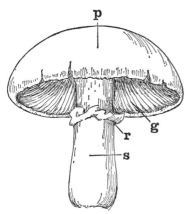

FIG. 156 Mushroom (*Psalliota campes-tris*); and its parts: p. pileus or cap; g. gills; r. ring; s. stipe or stem.

correct type of horse manure cannot be obtained, compost may be made of other materials, such as wheat-straw, together with a special mushroom compost activator, for use according to the makers' instructions.

Spawning. Sterilized pure culture spawn is used exclusively today; small pieces being inserted 3 in. below the surface of the compost when temps. of 21–27° C. (70–80° F.) are assured. Out of doors, the bed is then covered with long litter or straw, and a tarpaulin or plastic perforated sheeting; indoors no cover is necessary. In 8–12 days, when the spawn shows a bluish-grey fluff and whitish threads of mycelium, the bed is cased, with a reasonably friable second-spit soil or sterilized top soil, usually mixed with a little lime or gypsum. An inch-thick layer is placed on indoor beds; two-inch thick on out-door beds, smoothed and covered with straw. Indoors, mushrooms appear in 6–9 weeks; outdoors, 10–12 weeks; and beds go on yielding for 3–4 months, given continuing favourable tempera-tures.

Diseases and Pests. The edible mush-room may be attacked by various parasitic fungi and bacteria, causing symptoms known as Bubbles or White Mould, Brown Blotch and Plaster

Mould. There is little that can be done for the infected mushrooms other than removal and destruction; but future freedom from disease depends upon sterilizing the growing quarters, and giving every attention to the hygienic needs of the crop, seeing that the compost and soil are of first-class quality, and growing conditions strictly controlled. The chief pests are Fungus Gnats or Phorid Flies, their larvae riddling the mushrooms. A DDT/pyrethrum dust gives good control. This insecticide will also control millipedes and woodlice, or derris dust may be used during cropping, after a picking. Slugs are deterred by metaldehyde bait.

Mushroom Growing in the Lawn. Much depends upon weather conditions, but a crop may result from: removing a square foot of turf, taking out 3 in. of soil and replacing it with partially rotted mush-room compost or stable manure, in which a kernel of spawn is placed, and the turf replaced, May–July, for early autumn mushrooms.

Musk. See *Mimulus moschatus.*

Musk Hyacinth. See *Muscari mos-chatum.*

Musk Rose. See *Rosa moschata.*

Mustard. Black Mustard is *Brassica nigra*, of which the seeds yield table mustard; White Mustard is *B. alba.* For these growing as saladings, see Cress. They may also be used for green manuring; *see* Manuring, Green.

Mutabilis (-e). Variable, changeable. Ex. *Hibiscus mutabilis.*

Mutation. Strictly, a change in the genetical composition of an organism or part of an organism; often referred to in gardening as a 'Sport'.

Mutisia (mu-tis'i-a. Fam. Compositae). S. American, tendril-climbing plants with evergreen leaves and star-rayed flowers, July–August, succeeding best in the cool greenhouse.

Selection. M. clematis, Columbia, to 20 ft, pinnate foliage, orange-scarlet nodding flowers; *decurrens*, Chile, to 12 ft, orange or vermilion flowers; *illicifolia*, Chile, to 10 ft, pale pink; *oligodon*, Chile, dwarf, to 2 ft, pink; *retusa*, Chile, to 10 ft, pink; and *speciosa*, Brazil, to 6 ft, red flowers.

Cultivation. Plant in spring, large pots or greenhouse border, lime-free standard compost; water liberally in May–August, syringing overhead, and then moderately to very moderately in winter, temp. of 10° C. (50° F.) minimum. Or may be tried out of doors in very mild, frost-free localities, on warm, sunny sheltered walls.

Propagation. By cuttings of young shoots, in March–April, in propagating case, bottom heat of 18° C. (65° F.).

Mycelium. The vegetative feeding part of a fungus, made up of a web of minute tubular threads or Hyphae.

Mycology. The study of fungi.

Mycorrhiza. A symbiotic association between the mycelium of a fungus and the root cells of a plant, common in epiphytes, including orchids, and in many trees, particularly of the Coniferae and in heaths, and other plants.

Myosotidium, Giant Forget-me-not (mi-o-so-tid′i-um. Fam. Boraginaceae). The one species, *M. hortensia* (*nobile*), Chatham Isles, to 1½ ft, is a hardy perennial with large, fleshy leaves, and corymbs of blue and white Forget-me-not flowers in spring; suitable for cool sheltered damp places in mild localities; for autumn or spring planting. Propagation is best from seeds in spring.

Myosotis, Forget-me-not (my-o-sot′is. Fam. Boraginaceae). Charming flowering perennials or biennials with radical stalked leaves, and terminal scorpioid cymes of small pretty flowers.

Selection. *M. caespitosa,* Europe and Britain, 3 in., blue flowers, summer, and v. *rehsteineri*; *dissitiflora,* Switzerland, ½–1 ft, deep sky blue, spring, and v. 'Perfection'; and *sylvatica,* Europe and Britain, 1 ft, blue, yellow-eyed, spring, may be grown as biennials, sown in summer for background to bulbs in spring; *M. alpestris,* Europe and Britain, 3–6 in., azure blue, summer, and vs. *alba,* white, 'Blue Ball', deep blue, 'Carmine King' and 'Victoria', larger flowered; *rupicola,* European Alps, 2 in., azure blue, early summer; with *caespitosa,* make charming rock garden plants. *M. scorpioides,* Europe, Britain and Asia, 6–12 in., yellow-eyed, blue flowers, spring, and vs. *alba,* white, and *semperflorens,* long-flowering, are good for moist places and by pools and water. The New Zealand *M. australis,* to 1 ft, white or yellow, summer; *explanata,* 6 in., white flowering alpine; *lyallii,* 4 in., white, summer, and others are not long-lived, and need scree conditions.

Cultivation. Plant out in well-drained soils, provided with humus and lime in autumn or early spring, especially useful on limestone or chalk.

Propagation. From seeds sown in early summer, outdoors; the choice sorts can be raised in pans in a cold frame. Many species seed themselves. Perennials may be divided in March–April.

Myrica (mi-ri′ka. Fam. Myricaceae). Aromatic shrubs or trees with unisexual flowers.

Selection. *M. cerifera,* the Wax or Candleberry Myrtle, Eastern N. America, tall, semi-evergreen shrub or small tree, with narrow leaves, white catkins in May, followed by waxy fruits, at one time used for making fragrant-burning candles; *pensylvanica,* the Bayberry, Eastern N. America, deciduous, to 8 ft, scented leaves, grey-white waxy berries in winter; and the native *gale,* Sweet Gale or Bog Myrtle, 3–4 ft, deciduous, with fragrant scented leaves, and greenish-brown flower catkins in summer, are hardy.

Cultivation. Plant in autumn or March–April, in peat-enriched soils, more or less free of lime; good for moist situations, sun or partial shade. No regular pruning is necessary.

Propagation. By layers in late summer.

Myricaria (mi-ri-ka′ri-a. Fam. Tamaricaceae). The species chiefly grown is *M. germanica,* S. Europe and W. Asia, 4–6 ft, a deciduous shrub with plume-like stems set with tiny leaves, and crowded racemes of pink flowers, June–August. Easily grown in well-drained ordinary soils, full sun; planted October–March. Propagation by young firm cuttings of shoots in July–August, inserted and well firmed in the soil.

Myrio-. Prefix of compound words, meaning many or innumerable. Ex. *myriophyllum.*

Myrmechory. The dispersal of seeds by ants; often an unsuspected cause of plants such as Snowdrops, Scillas, Colchicums and Cyclamens appearing in unexpected places.

Myrobalan Plum. See *Prunus cerasifera.*

Myrrhis, Myrrh, Sweet Cicely (mir′ris.

Fam. Umbelliferae). The single species, *M. odorata*, Britain and Europe, 3 ft, is a graceful hairy perennial, with aromatic, finely split thrice pinnate leaves, and umbels of white flowers, summer, and a fleshy, swollen root. Easily raised from seeds, sown in April, ordinary, well-drained soil, and planted September–March in sunny positions.

Myrtle. See *Myrtus*.

Myrtle, Bog. See *Myrica gale*.

Myrtus (mirt'us. Fam. Myrtaceae). Ornamental evergreen fragrant shrubs, with small, usually stalkless, shining green leaves, and white flowers.

Selection. *M. communis*, Common Myrtle, S. Europe, 10–15 ft, is reasonably hardy, with vs. *microphylla*, small-leaved and more dwarf; and *tarentina*, very free-flowering in July; but others are only hardy in warm south-west localities, or may be grown in tubs and given winter shelter, or in the cool greenhouse; such as *M. bullata*, New Zealand, to 10 ft, reddish-brown, puckered leaves, white flowers, July; *lechleriana*, Chile, to 10 ft, bright green, red-stalked leaves, fragrant white flowers, May; *luma* (*Myrceugenia apiculata*), Chile, to 20 ft, reddish shoots and bark, peeling cream, succeeding in Cornwall; and *ugni*, Chilean Guava, 4–8 ft, stiffly erect with flowers followed by edible blue-black juicy fruits, good for jam-making.

Cultivation. Plant outdoors in warm, frost-free, sheltered positions, well-drained, humus-rich soils, September–October or April–May. Or pot in March–April, standard compost, in cool greenhouse or frame; for growing on in large pots or tubs, moving outdoors May–September.

Propagation. By cuttings of young shoots, taken in July–August, in a cold frame.

N

Naegelia (ne-ge'li-a. Fam. Gesneriaceae). Herbaceous perennials with stoloniferous roots, of tropical America, allied to Achimenes, with soft cordate or ovate leaves, showy, foxglove-like flowers in a terminal inflorescence, for the hot greenhouse.

Selection. N. cinnabarina, Guatemala, 2 ft, scarlet flowers, winter; *fulgida*, Vera Cruz, 2 ft, vermilion, September; *multiflora*, Mexico, 2½ ft, white or cream, autumn; and *zebrina*, Brazil, 2 ft, orange-scarlet, dotted red, September.

Cultivation. Pot in spring or early summer, one stolon to a 5-in. pot, 1 in. below surface of a standard compost, temp. 15·5–21° C. (60–70° F.), water increasingly with growth; syringe with clear water on hot sunny days. When foliage withers after flowering, dry off until repotting time and place under the greenhouse bench.

Propagation. By stolons in spring; by seeds in March–April, under glass, with bottom heat of 24° C. (75° F.), to germinate readily.

Names, Plant. *See* Nomenclature, or Pronunciation.

Nandina (nan-di'na. Fam. Berberidaceae). The single species, *N. domestica*, China, is a bamboo-like, decorative shrub, with thrice pinnate evergreen foliage, to 6 ft, large panicles of white flowers in June–July, sometimes followed by red berries; but doubtfully hardy, except in mild localities and sheltered situations, or it may be grown in a cold greenhouse. Plant in autumn or spring, well-drained soil, enriched with peat or leaf-mould. Propagate by cuttings of young ripe shoots in July–August, under a handlight or in a cold frame.

Nanus (-a, -um). Dwarf. Ex. *Betula nana*.

Naphthalene (C₁₀H₈). A white, shiny crystalline substance which volatalizes with a penetrating vapour. Used in gardening as a soil fumigant against wireworms and other insect pests, in the form of flake or whizzed naphthalene grade 16 at about 1 lb. per 10 sq. yds, strewn evenly along the base of the trench when digging, at least 4–6 weeks prior to sowing or planting; and less often now, as a fumigant in the greenhouse for the control of red spider mites.

Narcissus (nar-kis'sus; by usage, nar-sis'sus. Fam. Amaryllidaceae). This genus of bulbous perennial plants, enchanting in their diversity of size, flower form and beautiful colour, consists of some forty species and innumerable sub-species and varieties, to say nothing of hybrids, which do so much for the spring garden scene outdoors, and indoors.

Selection. The great majority of Narcissi grown today are cultivated varieties and hybrids in named forms, raised within the past 150 years. Horticulturally they are classified as follows, with appropriate selections restricted to proven named kinds of garden merit, generally available. For fuller lists and the latest introductions, specialists' catalogues should be consulted.

Division 1. *Trumpet Narcissi*; most commonly known as 'Daffodils'. Singleflowered, with trumpet or corona as long as or longer than the perianth segments.

(a) Coloured perianth, coloured corona, not paler than the perianth: 'Flower Carpet', 'Forerunner', 'Golden Harvest', 'King Alfred', 'Magnificence', 'Rembrandt', 'Winter Gold' and 'Unsurpassable'; all tall-growing, golden-yellow.

(b) White perianth, coloured corona: 'Chatsworth', 'Sincerity', 'Foresight', 'Preamble', 'Queen of Bicolors', 'Spring Glory'.

(c) White perianth, white corona, not paler than the perianth: 'Beersheba', 'Broughshane', 'Mount Hood', 'Mrs

FIG. 157 Large-cupped Narcissus, 'Fortune'.

E. H. Krelage', 'Petsamo', 'W. P. Milner'.

(d) Any other colour combination: 'Spellbinder'.

Division 2. *Large-cupped Narcissi.* Single-flowered, with corona more than one-third, but less than equal to the length of the perianth's segments.

(a) Coloured perianth, coloured corona, not paler than the perianth: 'Armada', golden perianth, orange-red corona; 'Bahram', yellow, marigold-orange; 'Carbineer', yellow, bright orange; 'Carlton', pale yellow, clear yellow; 'Ceylon', canary - yellow, orange; 'Fortune', golden, red-orange; 'Golden Torch', yellow, lemon-yellow; 'Helios', creamy-yellow, yellow-orange; 'Jubilant', sulphur-yellow, buttercup-yellow; 'Killigrew', primrose, orange; 'Krakatoa', canary-yellow, orange; 'Rustom Pasha', yellow, orange; 'Scarlet Elegance', golden-yellow, orange-red; 'St Keverne', yellow, lemon-yellow; 'Sun Chariot', deep yellow, orange-red; 'Thriller', golden-yellow, orange-red.

(b) White perianth, coloured corona: 'Blarney's Daughter', apricot-orange corona; 'Brunswick', lemon-yellow; 'Fermoy', orange-red corona; 'Flamenco', tangerine-orange; 'John Evelyn', apricot-orange; 'Mrs R. O. Backhouse',

shell-pink; 'Penpose' chrome yellow; 'Salmon-Trout', salmon-pink; 'Signal Light', orange-red; 'Selma Lagerlof', orange; 'Tunis', amber.

(c) White perianth, white corona, not paler than the perianth: 'Ave', 'Killaloe', 'Ludlow', 'Silver Bugle', 'Truth', 'White Nile'.

(d) Any other colour combination: 'Binkie', sulphur-yellow, white corona.

Division 3. *Small-cupped Narcissi.* Single-flowered, corona not more than one-third the length of the perianth segments.

(a) Coloured perianth, coloured corona, not paler than the perianth: 'Alight', deep yellow perianth, orange-red corona; 'Chungking', golden-yellow, red; 'Birma', yellow, orange-scarlet; 'Dinkie', pale yellow, orange to scarlet; and 'Market Merry', yellow, orange.

(b) White perianth, coloured corona: 'Blarney', chrome-yellow corona; 'Barret Browning', orange corona; 'La Riante', scarlet corona; 'Mahmoud', orange corona; 'Pomona', orange red corona; 'Snow Princess', yellow, edged orange, corona; 'Verger', orange corona.

(c) White perianth, white corona, not lighter than the perianth: 'Chinese White', 'Foggy Dew', 'Frigid', 'Polar Ice'.

Division 4. *Double Flowers:* 'Camellia', soft yellow; 'Golden Ducat', golden-yellow; 'Inglescombe', lemon-yellow; 'Irene Copeland', white and yellow; 'Mary Copeland', snow-white, orange; 'Mrs Wm Copeland', white; 'Texas', yellow, orange-scarlet; 'Van Sion', golden-yellow.

Division 5. *Triandrus Narcissi.* Flowers one to six, drooping, segments of perianth reflexed, corona cup-shaped, characteristic of *N. triandrus*: 'Hawera', lemon-yellow; 'Horn of Plenty', snow-white; 'Silver Chimes', white; 'Angel's Tears', white; 'Thalia', white; 'Tresamble', white.

Division 6. *Cyclamineus Hybrids.* Flowers drooping, strongly reflexed segments of the perianth, characteristic of *N. cyclamineus*: 'Baby Doll', golden-yellow, 10 in.; 'Beryl', primrose-yellow, 8 in.; 'February Gold', deep yellow, 12 in.; 'February Silver', silvery-white, 12 in.; 'Garden Prince', deep yellow; 'Peeping Tom', deep yellow, 15 in.

Division 7. Jonquilla Narcissi. Flowers two to six, fragrant, with shallow cup-shaped corona: 'Baby Moon', single, soft yellow, 10 in.; 'Golden Goblet', deep aureolin-yellow, 14 in.; 'Golden Perfection', golden yellow, 16 in.; 'Golden Sceptre', buttercup-yellow, 14 in.; 'Lanarth', buttercup-yellow, orange corona, 14 in.; 'Trevithian', lemon-yellow, 16 in.

FIG. 158 Tazetta Narcissus; 'Geranium'.

Division 8. Tazetta Narcissi. Flowers four to eight, normally scented, shallow corona, early flowering: 'Cheerfulness', white and buff-yellow; 'Cragford', white with orange-red corona; 'Early Splendour', white, orange corona; 'Geranium', white, orange-red corona; 'Laurens Koster', white, pale yellow corona; 'L'Innocence', white, orange-yellow corona; 'Scarlet Gem', golden-yellow, orange-scarlet corona; 'Yellow Cheerfulness', soft yellow.

Division 9. Poeticus Narcissi. Flowers solitary, not drooping, scented, white spreading segments, flat corona with

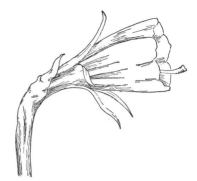

FIG. 159 *Narcissus bulbocodium* v. *conspicuus*; 'Hoop Petticoat Daffodil'.

red edge: 'Actea', large, white, yellow corona, edged fiery red; 'Cantabile', large, white, deep green, edged red, corona; 'Milan', white, green corona, edged pink; 'Red Rim', white, yellow to green corona, red rim; 'Pheasant's Eye', white, red-edged corona; 'Sarchedon', white, yellow corona, edged scarlet; and 'Sea Green', green corona, edged bright red.

Division 10. Wild Species, their forms and hybrids. All species and their natural forms and hybrids. *N. asturiensis*, Spain, 2–4 in., tiny trumpet flowers, March; *bulbocodium*, 'Hoop Petticoat Daffodil', S. France, Spain, etc., to 6 in., funnel-shaped, golden-yellow flowers, March–April, and vs. *conspicuus*, deep yellow; *citrinus*, lemon-yellow; *obesus*, clear yellow; and

FIG. 160 *Narcissus cyclamineus.*

tenuifolius, bright yellow, early; *mono-phyllus*, white; *calciola*, Spain, S. France 6–8 in., golden-yellow, March; *cyclamineus*, Cyclamen-flowered Daffodil, Portugal, 6 in., clear yellow, reflexed perianth; *gracilis*, Spain, 1 ft, sulphur-yellow, April; *jonquilla*, Spain, Portugal, 1 ft, several very fragrant yellow flowers, April; *juncifolius*, Rush-leaved Daffodil, Spain to S. France, 4 in., rich yellow, April; *nanus*, Miniature Trumpet Daffodil, 4 in., yellow, March, and v. 'Little Beauty', white and bright yellow; *odorus*, Mediterranean region, 1 ft, bright yellow, April; *rupicola*, Spain, Portugal, 3 in., bright yellow, May, rush-like leaves; *pseudo-narcissus*, the Lent Lily, W. Europe, Britain, 8–14 inches, the native daffodil, pale yellow perianth, deeper yellow corona, March–April; *recurvus*, Old Pheasant's Eye Narcissus, Switzerland, to 1½ ft' white, greenish, red-rimmed corona, May; *scaberulus*, Portugal, 10 in., several flowers, deep orange, April; *serotinus*, Mediterranean region, 4 in., creamy-white, yellow corona, October, difficult; *tazetta*, Spain to Japan, 1–1½ ft, many flowers, lemon-yellow, January–February; and v. *canaliculatus*, 3 in., white with lemon-yellow corona, April; *tenuior*, Silver Jonquil, origin not known, 4 in., several flowers, cream and yellow, April; *triandrus*, Angel's Tears Narcissus, Spain, Portugal, ½–1 ft, drooping flowers, creamy white, April, and vs. *albus*, pure white, and *aurantiacus*, golden-yellow, *calathinus*, is a rare snow-white form of much larger blooms; *viridiflorus*, Gibraltar, Morocco, 1–1½ ft, very rare green-flowering, November; *watieri*, Morocco, solitary flowers, white, April.

Division 11. *Narcissi of horticultural origin which do not belong to any other division.* Here, perhaps, belong the forms of *N. polyanthos*, 'Grand Soleil d'Or', with many flowers of yellow, with small orange corona; and *N. papyraceus*, 'Paperwhite grandiflorus', with heads of white flowers; grown for December–January blooming.

Cultivation. Narcissi are easy to grow.

Out of Doors. It is usual to begin by planting bulbs of flowering size in beds, borders or grouped in among other hardy plants, or on lawns for which large-flowered forms are most effective. The small and many-flowered species and forms may be planted as edgings or in terraces or rock gardens. Narcissi welcome cool, well-drained, but moisture-retentive soils, of only slight alkalinity, pH 6·0 to 6·5. Most soils can be made suitable by thorough cultivation, the addition of humus-forming matter in the nature of well-rotted manure, compost or peat, and bone meal is a useful fertilizer at planting. On heavy soils planting stations can be lightened with coarse sand or grit. Planting may be done from August to late October, though the earlier the better, especially for early-flowering species or varieties of *N. poeticus*. Bulbs should be spaced 3–6 in. apart, according to size, and at a depth of 1½ times the height of the bulb in heavy soils, twice the height in lightish soils. After flowering, bulbs should be allowed to grow on until the leaves yellow and wither before disturbance. They do best if left undisturbed for 3–4 years, after which clumps should be lifted not later than August, to sort according to size, and replant immediately; large bulbs in flowering stations, smaller offsets in reserve borders and enriched soil to grow on. It is helpful to give bulbs a balanced liquid fertilizer feed after flowering to increase bulb size for future flowering. Most cultivated Narcissi naturalize well in grass, where planting stations are enriched prior to planting, and the plants given a good balanced fertilizer each March. When many bulbs have to be planted, it is worth while using a bulb-planting implement.

Indoors. The varieties 'Soleil d'Or', 'Paperwhite grandiflora' and narcissi of the Tazetta Division may be grown in deep saucers or shallow bowls, wedged among pebbles to keep them upright, and with sufficient water to keep the roots submerged, in September, kept cool and dark until roots are well formed and growth is showing, and then brought to more warmth and light to flower in late December–January. The bulbs are usually exhausted, and should be discarded afterwards. *In Bowls.* Most of the large-flowering narcissi may be once-grown in bulb fibre in bowls. The bulbs are planted from August onwards to give a succession of bloom, well firmed in moist prepared bulb fibre (*see* Bulb) up to their necks, equidistant apart, and placed in cool, dark quarters, temp. 5–10° C. (40–50° F.); such as a cellar, cold cupboard or under a covering of ashes or coco-fibre in a cold frame, or by a north wall for about 8 weeks; when bowls show they are full of roots and the shoots are showing, bring into warmer, lighter conditions gradually, to a room of 10–13° C. (50–55° F.) at first, then to about 15·5° C. (60° F.) where they are to flower, in another week or two. After flowering, they may be planted out in a sheltered place, without disturbing the roots, to finish growing, but the bulbs need nursing for a year or more to build up again. Watering must not be neglected during their growth, but the accumulation of stagnant water at the base of a bowl must also be avoided. *In Pots.* Plant in well-crocked 5- or 6-in. pots, standard compost, or one of 2 parts by bulk loam, 1 part peat, 1 part coarse sand, with bone meal, August–October; place pots in cold frame or under a north wall, covered with ashes or coco-fibre, for about 8 weeks; then bring to light and gradually increased heat, first at 10–13° C. (50–55° F.) for a week or so; and then on to 15·5–18° C. (60–65° F.), in the greenhouse. Water regularly; stake as necessary; remove flower scapes after flowering, and knock out roots in soil ball with a minimum disturbance, to grow on in a sheltered place.

Specially Prepared Bulbs for Forcing. Flowering can be accelerated by placing bulbs in cold store at 9° C. (48° F.) for 6–8 weeks, prior to planting, and such prepared bulbs are generally offered by the end of September and beginning of October. The bulbs must be planted up immediately in pots, and kept cool as described above, until showing good growth development, when they are moved to warmer temperatures in December. Such varieties as ' Actaea', ' Carlton', ' Fortune', ' Geranium', ' Golden Harvest', ' Helios', ' King Alfred', ' Magnificence', ' Scarlet Elegance' and ' Sempre Avanti' are suitable.

In the Alpine House. Most of the dwarf species and their forms may be grown in the alpine house, cold frame or cold greenhouse; potted in well-crocked pots or pans, standard compost,

at twice their height in the soil, preferably in August, and plunged in moist peat or ashes to their rims, in partial shade, being brought under glass in November; and kept moist until after flowering and foliage has died down, when water should be reduced to very little, until it is time to repot.

Propagation. By offset bulbs when dormant plants are lifted, preferably in August. By seeds sown in pans in cold frame, autumn or spring, but require 4–5 years to build up to good flowering bulbs.

Diseases. Basal Rot, caused by the fungus *Fusarium bulbigenum*, with brown rot of the scales: and Green Mould (*Penicillium narcissi*), are storage infections, avoidable by drying off bulbs properly and storing under dry though cool conditions. Smoulder (*Botrytis narcissicola*) may cause rotting of leaves and flowers in cold wet seasons, and affected plants are best dug up and burnt; ' Stripe' is a condition in which leaves are mottled or striped silver-grey, yellow or pale-green, sometimes with roughening and corrugation of the leaves, which is apparently caused by virus infection, and the plants are best destroyed until more is known of better controls.

Pests. Narcissus Flies are of two species: *Meredon equestris*, a large two-winged fly, which gives rise to one dirty-white maggot infesting a single bulb, and *Eumerus strigatus*, and *E. tuberculatus*, small bulb flies, which give rise to several maggots in a single bulb. These flies are actively laying eggs on or near Narcissi (and other members of the Amaryillidaceae) in mid May to late June; which hatch into the maggots that tunnel into bulbs through the base, and feed inside, reducing them to a mass of wet frass and browned rotting scales. Later, the maggots leave to pupate in the soil. The application of a gamma-BHC insecticidal dust to bulb plantings from late April to early July, renewed after rain, is preventive. It is wise to lift every three or four years to check the bulbs. Eelworms (*Ditylenchus dipsaci*) may cause failure of bulbs to grow in spring. Infested bulbs should be lifted and immersed in water kept at 43° C. (110° F.) for three hours, and then cooled quickly, and dried. Slugs and snails may be deterred by metaldehyde bait pellets.

Nasturtium. See *Tropaeolum*.

Naturalized. A term used to describe exotic plants which have escaped from cultivation and established themselves in the wild: or of plants grown in natural surroundings, such as Daffodils in grass.

Navelwort. A tuberous-rooted perennial weed, *Umbilicus rupestris*.

Navelwort, Venus's. See *Omphalodes linifolia*.

Necklace Poplar. See *Populus deltoides*.

Necrosis. The death of circumscribed parts of tissue of organs of plants, such as leaves, stems, etc., usually shown in discoloration, browning or blackening.

Nectar. A sweet sugary solution the specialized cells of the nectary excrete, consisting chiefly of glucose, fructose and sucrose, gathered by bees and converted by them into honey.

Nectarine. A smoothed-skinned variety of the Peach (q.v.).

Nectary. A glandular organ composed of cells through the outer walls of which nectar is excreted, usually situated in the flower and attractive to insects which assist pollination; though sometimes extra-floral on leaves or stipules where ants are the visitors.

Neglectus (-a, -um). Neglected, disregarded. Ex. *Dianthus neglectus*.

Negundo. See *Acer*.

Neillia (neel'li-a. Fam. Rosaceae). Deciduous Chinese shrubs of which *N. longiracemosa*, W. China, 4–6 ft, is chiefly grown, with erect stems, slender-pointed, toothed leaves, and terminal racemes of small rosy-pink flowers, May–June, like a Spiraea. Plant October–March, well-drained, humus-rich soil, in warm shelter. Propagation by cuttings of young shoots in July–August, under handlight.

Nelumbo, Lotus (ne-lum'bo. Fam. Nymphaeaceae). A genus of two aquatic plants, with rhizamatous roots, large roundish leaves, and fragrant flowers in summer, for growing in a pool or tank in a cool greenhouse, or in a tub which may be moved out of doors from June to September.

Selection. *N. lutea*, the American Lotus, Southern U.S.A., has leaves 1–2 ft across, and fragrant yellow flowers to 9 in. across; *nucifera*, the East Indian Lotus, Asia, has the larger leaves, and white, tipped rose flowers; and vs. *alba*, the Magnolia Lotus, *pygmaea alba*, a dwarf form; and double-flowering forms in *roseum plenum*, deep rose-pink, and *pekinensis rubra*, red, and others.

Cultivation. Plant in April–May in rich loam soil, at least 8 in. deep, in water depth of 12 in.; temp. 18° C. (65° F.). Must have winter protection against frost, if necessary.

Propagation. By root division in spring.

Nematodes. Nematoda comprise a class of roundworms, of which terrestrial forms known as eelworms are minute parasites of plants.

Nemesia (ne-me'si-a. Fam. Scrophulariaceae). The chief species grown is *N. strumosa*, a S. African half-hardy annual, of which several strains have been developed, with flowers in a variety of colours for summer bloom; notably *suttoni*, 1 ft, in white, clear yellow, rose-pink, orange, cherry red, blue, scarlet and pink shades; *compacta grandiflora*, 9 in., in named forms 'Aurora', carmine and white; 'Blue Gem', 'Fire King', 'Orange Prince' and others; and dwarf *superbissima grandiflora*.

Cultivation. Sow under glass, standard compost, bottom heat of 15·5° C. (65° F.), February–March, to be pricked off and hardened for planting out in May; or potted for greenhouse decoration; autumn sowings can be made for winter greenhouse bloom.

Nemophila (ne-mof'il-a. Fam. Hydrophyllaceae). *N. menziesii (insignis)*, Baby Blue Eyes, N. America, 4 in., is a spreading hairy hardy annual, with blue to white summer flowers, and vs., easily grown from seeds sown in April out of doors in well-drained soil and sun, where plants are to flower; v. *alba* is pure white; *N. maculata* is somewhat taller growing, with white flowers, veined purple, for similar treatment.

Nepenthes, Pitcher Plant (ne-pen'thes. Fam. Nepenthaceae). Interesting and handsome evergreen, tendril clambering plants of Malaya and Borneo, grown for their urn-like, brightly coloured, lidded pitchers to which insects are attracted, drowned in the liquid at the bottom to decay and yield nitrogen to nurture the plants; in warm greenhouse.

Selection. There are several species and many beautiful hybrids, such as *N. albomarginata*, Singapore, dwarf, pale green and reddish pitchers, white rimmed; *ampullaria*, Malaya, pale green; × *atrosanguinea*, reddish-crimson, yellow-spotted; *rafflesiana*, India, greenish-yellow, brown spotted; *rajah*, Borneo, very large reddish-brown pitchers; × *sedenii*, light green, marked brownish-crimson; and *veitchii*, small yellow-green, ribbed scarlet.

Cultivation. Pot in baskets, or orchid pots, compost of 2 parts peat fibre, 1 part loam, 1 part sphagnum moss, a little sand and charcoal, March, to suspend in warm greenhouse; summer temp. 21–27° C. (70–80° F.), watering liberally, with moist atmosphere; more moderate watering in autumn and winter, minimum temp. 15·5° C. (60° F.). Shade from direct sun. Pinch out growing point of shoots when five or six leaves have formed.

Propagation. By cuttings of sucker shoots or one-year-old shoots, placed through the hole of an inverted 2-in. pot, plunged in sphagnum moss in a closed propagating frame, bottom heat of 27° C. (80° F.). Or by seeds, sown thinly on compost as for plants.

Nepeta, Catmint (ne'pe-ta. Fam. Labiatae). Hardy herbaceous perennials, useful for edging borders, or for ground cover, easily grown.

Selection. N. cataria, the true Catmint, 2 ft, erect-growing, white-flowering in summer, is a native; × *faassenii*, confused with *mussinii*, 1 ft, silver-grey leaves, lavender flowers all summer; *hederacea*, the Ground Ivy, kidney-shaped leaves, blue flowers, spring and summer, makes good woodland cover, and v. *variegata*, creamy white and green leaves, is good for hanging baskets; *marifolia*, Spain, 1 ft, lemon-scented, white flowers, July–August; *nervosa*, Kashmir, 2 ft, clear blue, summer; and × 'Souvenir d'André Chaudron', 1 ft, upright, dark blue flowering, are good for borders.

Cultivation. Plant October–March, any well-drained ordinary soil, sun or partial shade.

Propagation. By seeds, April–June,

outdoors, planting seedlings out in autumn. By cuttings of unflowered shoots, July–August, in cold frame.

Nephrodium. Now included in *Dryopteris* (q.v.).

Nephrolepsis, Ladder Ferns (nep-ro-le'pis. Fam. Polypodiaceae). A genus of handsome tropical ferns, commonly known as ladder or sword ferns owing to their fine fronds, for heated rooms and greenhouses with temperatures of about 10° C. (50° F.) in winter; 21° C. (70° F.) in summer.

Selection. N. acuminata, Malaya, drooping fronds of 2–3 ft; *cordifolia*, 1–2 ft fronds, and its v. *compacta*, neat for pots; *exaltata*, with fronds to 2 ft, and several vs., offered by fern specialists.

Cultivation. Pot in March, compost of 1 part sandy loam, 2 parts leaf-mould, 1 part peat; water freely in active growth, but keep moist otherwise. Tolerate shade.

Propagation. By division when re-potting in March; or by spores whenever available.

Nerine (ne-ri'ne. Fam. Amaryllidaceae). Beautiful bulbous plants of S. Africa for autumn flowering; unfortunately not completely hardy.

Selection. N. bowdenii, 1½ ft, bears a head of several glistening pink flowers, September, before the leaves, and is the hardiest for planting outdoors in mild localities, warm sheltered borders, humus-rich, well-drained soil; *sarniensis* the Guernsey Lily, 2 ft, similar, with pale salmon umbels of flowers, September–October, may be grown outdoors in the mildest areas; and its vs. with white, pink, orange and red flowers. They may also be grown in the cool greenhouse together with *N. curvifolia*, 1½ ft, scarlet flowers, and v. *fothergillii major*, crimson; *flexuosa*, to 2 ft, light pink, and white flowering v. *alba*; *pulchella*, 1½ ft, pink and rose, and *undulata*, 1 ft, flesh pink, leaves evergreen; while *masonorum*, 6 in., pale pink, is also evergreen, and near-hardy in mild localities. There are many beautiful named hybrids to be culled from specialists' lists.

Cultivation. Out of doors, plant bulbs 9 in. deep, late spring, early summer; arrange for winter protection as the leaves

FIG. 161   Flower of *Nerine bowdenii*.

must grow out after flowering. Under glass, pot single bulbs in 5-in. pots, July–August, standard compost, water freely in active growth, liquid-feed occasionally, until May, when water is gradually withheld and plants rested almost dry, in cool conditions; repot only when essential every three or four years; winter temp. 7–10° C. (45–50° F.).

Propagation. By offsets, when re-potting, August. By seeds immediately they are ripe, in cool greenhouse.

Nerium, Oleander, Rose Bay (ne'ri-um. Fam. Apocynaceae). The Oleander, *N. oleander*, is a beautiful evergreen, with narrow, pointed leaves in whorls, grow-ing 6 ft tall or more, with terminal racemes of pink or white flowers in summer, and vs. *album*, white; *luteum plenum*, double yellow; and *splendens*, double, bright red; but is from the warmer regions of the Mediterranean and needs cool greenhouse shelter in this country; while *N. odorum*, Persia, the sweet-scented Oleander, is similar but less vigorous, with rose-white to pink flowers.

Cultivation. Pot February–March, 6–12-in. pots, standard compost, give sunny position, water freely in summer, syringing and sponging leaves; very moderately in winter, temp. 10° C. (50° F.) minimum. Keep free of Aphids by spraying with a malathion insecti-cide immediately the insects are seen.

Propagation. Prune after flowering, reducing flowered shoots to within three buds of their base. Place cuttings of shoots in water in the sun, and when roots form, pot up in standard compost. As flowers, leaves and wood are poison-ous, prunings are best burnt, and children warned of their danger.

Nertera, Bead Plant (ner'te-ra. Family Rubiaceae). Creeping herbs from the antipodes of which *N. granadensis*, S. America, Australasia, is chiefly grown, for its mat-forming stems, carrying small, ovate leaves, minute greenish flowers, which are followed by a profu-sion of pea-sized, bright orange-scarlet berries; in rock gardens in very mild localities, but more often in pots or pans, standard compost, in the alpine house or cool greenhouse. May be grown from seeds, in March–April, bottom heat of 15·5° C. (60° F.), under glass; and propagated by division in March.

Nets, Netting. Demountable nets are invaluable for protecting fruit crops from birds, and should be of 1-in. mesh. Twine or old fish netting is useful for this, and for giving frost protection in spring, draped over vulnerable plants. It is, however, fast giving way to terylene or nylon or ulstron netting, with a longer life. Netting of plastic materials, in various meshes, are most useful for plant supports and various protective functions. To exclude rabbits, a 2-in. mesh galvanized wire netting or plastic netting, with the bottom 9 in. buried in the soil and bent outwards, is needed.

Neviusia (ne-vi-u'si-a. Fam. Rosaceae). The single species, *N. alabamensis*, Alabama, U.S.A., is a deciduous shrub of 4–6 ft, with ovate, pointed leaves, and pretty flowers of creamy-white many stamens, above five-lobed, spread-ing calyces, in cymes, in May; and may be grown out of doors, in well-drained, humus-enriched soil, and sun, in all but cold or exposed gardens. Propagation is by cuttings of young shoots in July–August, in a cold frame, or by layering.

New Zealand Flax. See *Phormium.*

Nicandra, Shoo-Fly Plant (ni-kan'dra. Fam. Solanaceae). The one species, *N. physaloides*, Peru, growing 2–4 ft, with coarsely toothed leaves, and large, solitary drooping blue flowers in summer, is a hardy annual, which may be sown outdoors in April, in ordinary soil, where it is to grow, and thinned. It is held to be repellent to white-fly and toxic to sap-sucking insects.

Nicotiana, Tobacco (ni-ko-ti-a'na. Fam. Solanaceae). Strong-scented annuals and perennials of the tropics, chiefly America, which contain the toxic narcotic alkaloid, nicotine. *N. tabacum* and its vs. are the tobacco-leaf yielding plants (*see* Tobacco). Several species, however, have ornamental merit.

Selection. N. alata, S. Brazil, 2 ft, white fragrant flowers, summer, and v. *grandiflora (affinis)*, with forms 'Daylight', 2½ ft, pure white, 'Lime Green', 2½ ft, greenish-yellow; 'Sensation' in various colours, and 'Dwarf White Bedder' of 1¼ ft; × *sanderae* in forms 'Crimson King', 'Knapton Scarlet' and other shades, 2–3 ft; *suaveolens*, Australia, 2 ft, small white fragrant flowers, purplish without; *sylvestris*, Argentine, to 5 ft, tubular white flowers in panicles, August; and *tomentosa*, Brazil, 7 ft, very large fine leaves, pinkish-white flowers, and v. *variegata*, chiefly grown for their ornamental foliage, are all grown as half-hardy annuals.

Cultivation. Sow seeds thinly under glass, standard compost, bottom heat of 18° C. (65° F.), March–April, pricking off, and hardening off to plant out in May, in well-drained, rather moisture-retentive soil, and full sun, in beds or borders. These plants are liable to Virus infection, and any showing signs of light- and dark-green mottling, mosaic or stunted growth are best removed and burnt.

Nicotine. A useful insecticide, extracted from tobacco waste to contain not less than 95 per cent of nicotine. Soluble in water, volatile and non-persistent, it is used as a quick, contact control for Aphids, Red Spider Mites, Thrips, etc., and is available in various liquid formulations which should be used to makers' directions. It is also prepared as a 3 per cent dust. Nicotine shreds are also used for greenhouse fumigation. As it is highly toxic, nicotine should be used with care, and kept in a safe place. At least two days must elapse before harvesting a food crop after using nicotine. In America and other countries, nicotine sulphate (40 per cent nicotine) is more often used. *See* Insecticides.

Nidus. A nest. Ex. *Asplenium nidus.*

Nierembergia (ne-rem-ber'gi-a. Fam.

Solanaceae). A genus of S. American herbs with pretty flowers, imperfectly hardy in Britain.

Selection. N. caerulea, Argentine, 8 in., erect, fine linear leaves, bell-shaped, blue-violet flowers, June–September; *gracilis*, Argentine, 6 in., white flowers, streaked purple, summer; and *repens*, Argentine, Chile, prostrate, white, tinged yellow flowers, July–August, are half-hardy perennials, excellent for pots in the alpine house or cool greenhouse. *N. frutescens* Chile, 1½ ft, more shrubby, with lightish blue to white flowers, in summer, is also a good pot plant. Or all may be raised as half-hardy annuals from early sowings under glass, to plant out in warm borders or terraces in May.

Cultivation. Plants may be raised from seeds, sown in warm greenhouse, February–March, bottom heat of 18° C. (65° F.), standard compost; or in autumn, to winter in a cool greenhouse, temp. 10° C. (50° F.).

Nigella, Devil-in-a-bush, Love-in-a-mist (ni-gel'la. Fam. Ranunculaceae). Pretty hardy annuals, notable for their finely cut stem-leaves and distinctive blue, white or yellow flowers.

Selection. N. damascena, Mediterranean region, 1–2 ft, blue flowers, summer, and vs. *alba*, white, 'Miss Jekyll', bright blue, 'Oxford Blue', 'Persian Rose', pink, and 'Persian Jewels', of several shades; *hispanica*, the Fennel Flower, Spain, S. France, 1–2 ft, deep blue, red-stamened flowers, and v. *alba*.

Cultivation. Seeds may be sown in March–April, in reasonably good soil, thinned later; or in mild localities, in September, to flower earlier the following year.

Niger, Nigra, Nigrum. Black. Ex. *Helleborus niger.*

Night-scented Stock. See *Matthiola bicornis.*

Nitidus (-a, -um). Smooth, polished; shining. Ex. *Lonicera nitida.*

Nitrates. Salts of nitric acid with a mineral base; soluble in water, and the chief form in which nitrogen is made available and taken in by plant roots from soil.

Nitrification. The process of conversion, by bacterial action, of nitrogen compounds from animal and plant remains into nitrates which plants can take up.

Nitrogen (N). The chemical element,

which exists as an invisible, odourless, tasteless gas, forming four-fifths of the atmosphere; and is vital to all living organisms, as an essential constituent of proteins.

Nivalis (-e). Of snow. Ex. *Galanthus nivalis.*

Nocturnal. Of plants which open their flowers at night, but keep them closed by day.

No-digging Techniques. Based on the theory that much disturbance of the soil by digging and cultivation destroys soil fertility and is unnatural. The basic principle is to obviate digging by regular top-mulching or dressing the soil with composted organic matter in active decay, thereby nurturing the soil and benefiting it by the gradual incorporation of the organic matter by natural agencies, such as bacteria, earthworms, etc. At the same time, plants are kept in good nutrition and health. It is necessary, however, to start with a weed-free surface, and there must be ample resources of organic matter available for composting and application.

Node. A joint, or junction of the stem and one or more leaves, from which buds arise, and at which roots form most readily in cuttings.

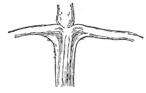

FIG. 162   Node, or joint (*Clematis* sp.).

Nodosum, (-a, -um). Nodose, with swollen joints. Ex. *Geranium nodosum.*

Nolana (no-la'na. Fam. Nolanaceae). Striking, unusual, procumbent annuals with trumpet-shaped flowers in summer.

Selection. N. paradoxa, Chile, with purplish-blue, yellow-throated flowers, and v. *alba,* white; *rupicola,* Chile, blue, white-throated flowers; and × *tenella,* pale purple-blue, white and purple-veined throat, are chiefly grown.

Cultivation. Sow in March–April, standard compost, bottom heat of 18° C. (65° F.), under glass, to plant out in May, or grow in pots in the greenhouse.

Ordinary soil and a sunny position are suitable.

Nolina (no-lin'a. Fam. Liliaceae). Handsome, tall-growing evergreen woody plants, with slender stems, striking rosettes of graceful, long linear leaves, and panicles of small flowers of no importance.

Selection. N. gracilis, Mexico, to 20 ft, glaucous leaves, 2–3 ft long; *longifolia,* Mexico, 6 ft, dark-green, narrow leaves, 3 ft and more long; and *recurvata,* Mexico, to 15 ft, thin, green leaves, up to 6 ft long.

Cultivation. Pot, and repot, in spring, standard compost, water liberally in active growth, summer temp. 15·5° C. (60° F.) and more; more moderately in winter, with minimum temp. of 13° C. (55° F.).

Propagation. By cuttings of young side-shoots, March–April, in propagating case.

Nomenclature. The scientific naming of plants in Latin aims at ensuring that a plant bears only one name that is valid and acceptable the world over. Secondly, the valid name is the earliest given which conforms to the rules of botanical nomenclature. Briefly, these are based on Linnaeus's binominal system, in which a species is given two names, the first being that of the genus to which the plant belongs, written with a capital initial letter; the second the earliest specific or trivial epithet, written with a small initial letter (e.g. *Abelia floribunda*). Technically the specific name should be followed by that of the author responsible for naming the plant, commonly abbreviated. Thus the letter L. after a plant name is for Linnaeus (e.g. *Abelia floribunda* L.), which means that the plant is the one described by Linnaeus in his *Species Plantarum* in 1753. When it is necessary to change the botanical name of a plant it is either because an earlier published, prior description and name has been found, or the plant has been wrongly classified. The name of the author responsible for the revision then follows the earlier authority. In gardening and horticulture, however, the authority designation is usually left out. A hybrid is indicated by ' × ' between the generic and specific names, or for inter-generic hybrids, before the generic name (e.g. × *Heucherella*). Names of graft hybrids or chimaeras are indicated by ' + ' (e.g.

+ *Laburnocytisus*). Species and hybrids are often variable, and the varietal name is indicated by var. or v., though the indication is often omitted. Varieties arise and may be found in the wild or in cultivation when it is known as a cultivar (cult. or cv. for short). A varietal name is usually given in Latin. A cultivated variety is often named in a language other than Latin, and is then written in Roman characters between parentheses and usually with capital first letters; thus the full cultivar name of the Japanese Amanogawa Cherry is *Prunus serrulata* (Amanogawa); its botanical name, *Prunus serrulata* v. *erecta*. Simply personal names of cultivars are retained as written with capital initial letters (e.g. *Mimulus guttatus* 'A. T. Johnson'). The full rules of nomenclature are set out in the International Code of Nomenclature for Cultivated Plants, periodically reviewed and revised at international congresses held from time to time at capital cities of the world.

Nomocharis (no-mo-ka'ris. Fam. Liliaceae). Extremely beautiful flowering bulbous plants, akin to Fritillaria and Lilium, native to open alpine woodland conditions in the Himalaya.

Selection. N. *aperta*, W. China, 1½–3 ft, large, open-saucered flowers, rose-pink, spotted crimson, July; *farreri*, Upper Burma, 1½ ft, soft pink, red blotched, axillary flowers, up to ten per stem, May–June; *mairei*, W. China, white to pink, spotted rose-purple, flowering May–June; and v. *candida*, white flowers, reddish at the base; *pardanthina*, Yunnan, 2 ft, large rose, spotted crimson flowers, May–June; *saluenensis*, W. China, N. Burma, 1½–2 ft, white or pale yellow, flushed purplish-rose, flowers, June–July. N. *nana* and *oxypetala* are now included in Lilium.

Cultivation. Plant ex pots, in early spring, under cool, partially shaded conditions, fairly deep, well-drained, humus-rich and moist soil, 3–4 in. deep. Succeed well in the north, associated with rhododendrons, and like fairly acid soil conditions, with peat or leaf-mould.

Propagation. By seeds, February–March, lime-free standard compost, cool greenhouse; seedlings being moved on at 3 in. high to deep boxes, and grown on in cold frame or greenhouse, to flower when

three or four years old. May also be grown in cool shade in the alpine house.

Norfolk Island Pine. See *Araucaria excelsa.*

Norfolk Reed. See *Phragmites communis.*

Norway Maple. See *Acer platanoides.*

Norway Spruce. See *Picea abies.*

Nothochlaena. See *Notholaena.*

Nothofagus, Southern Beech (no-tho-fa'gus. Fam. Fagaceae). Graceful and attractive trees, differing from other beeches (*Fagus* spp.) in having smaller, more closely set and more or less stalkless leaves; but being natives of Australia, New Zealand and S. America are less hardy.

Selection. The deciduous N. *antarctica*, Chile; *obliqua*, Roblé Beech, Chile, to 100 ft; and *procera*, Chile, to 80 ft, finely veined leaves, and probably the best single choice, are hardy in the south and mild localities; the evergreens N. *betuloides*, Chile, to 80 ft, hardiest; *cliffortioides*, New Zealand, to 40 ft; *cunninghamii*, Tasmania, to 100 ft; *dombeyi*, Chile, to 100 ft; *fusca*, New Zealand, to 100 ft; and *menziesii*, New Zealand, to 60 ft, can only be relied upon in southern counties, and mild sheltered localities; apt to be semi-evergreen in hard winters.

Cultivation. Plant September–October or March–April; deep, loamy, well-drained soil.

Propagation. By imported seed, sown February–March, standard compost, bottom heat of 18° C. (65° F.). By layering in nurseries. N. *dombeyi* and *procera* sometimes succeed from cuttings of young firm shoots, inserted in cold frame, July–August.

Notholaena (Nothochlaena), Gold and Silver Ferns (no-tho-le'na. Fam. Polypodiaceae). Attractive small ferns with graceful light fronds, often covered with a golden or silvery wax-like powder, for the warm greenhouse and light airy conditions.

Selection. N. *bonariensis*, S. America, slim pinnate fronds of 6–12 in., woolly-haired beneath; *hookeri*, California, star-shaped, five-pointed fronds, powdered; *marantae*, S. Europe to Yunnan, two-pinnate fronds, 6–12 in.; *sinuata*, Arizona, etc., simply pinnate narrow 1-ft fronds; *trichomanoides*, Mexico,

narrow fronds of broad pinnae, 6–12 in.;
and *vellaea*, S. Europe to Australia, bi-
pinnate, 6–9 in. fronds, woolly white
beneath.

Cultivation. Pot in spring, equal parts
fibrous peat, silver sand, a little fibrous
loam and charcoal, in pots or hanging
baskets, water liberally in growth, light,
airy positions; minimum winter temp.
10° C. (50° F.).

Propagation. By division in spring.
By spores, when available.

Notospartium (no-to-spar'ti-um. Fam.
Leguminosae). The chief species grown,
N. carmichaeliae, New Zealand, is a
broom-like shrub, to 10 ft, beautiful in
flower with short racemes of purplish-
pink, pea-like flowers, July. Plant in
March–April, at foot of a sunny wall,
porous, humus-rich soil, protected in
winter with brushwood. Propagate by
cuttings of young firm shoots, July–
August, under a handlight; or by seeds,
in spring, in a cold frame.

Nucellus. A body of tissue within the
integuments of the ovule.

Nucleus. A dense mass of a special kind
of protoplasm in the plant cell, that
apparently controls the cell's physiological processes, shape, size and function,
and initiates and controls cell division.

Nuphar (nu'far. Fam. Nymphaeaceae).
Aquatic plants of the temperate regions
of the northern hemisphere, suitable for
slow-running streams and pools.

Selection. N. lutea, the Yellow Water-
lily, or Brandy Bottle, is native, with
large orbicular leaves, and globular yellow flowers, smelling of alcohol, borne just
above the water; v. *sericeum* is the better
for small pools; *advena*, N. America, has
larger yellow flowers, summer; *microphyllum*, E. U.S.A., dwarf, small-leaved,
and 1-in. yellow flowers; and *pumila*,
Europe and Britain, is a dwarf *lutea*, for
shallow small pools.

Cultivation. Plant April–June, firming
well in soil at base of pool; or in plastic
baskets.

Propagation. By division in April–
May.

Nut. A hard indehiscent fruit, usually
one-seeded.

Nutrients, Nutrition, Plant. Apart
from oxygen, hydrogen and carbon
which plants largely obtain from the air
and water, plants need certain mineral

nutrient elements from the soil for
healthy growth and reproduction. These
nutrients fall in two groups: (*a*) Major
nutrient elements, required in relatively
large amounts, which are nitrogen,
phosphorus, potassium, calcium, magnesium, sulphur and iron. (*b*) Minor or
trace nutrient elements, required in
relatively small amounts, which include
manganese, copper, boron, molybdenum,
zinc and chlorine. Other elements may
be absorbed and beneficial, such as
silicon, sodium, aluminium, nickel and
cobalt, but on the other hand excesses
may prove toxic. Plants take up mineral
nutrient elements from their soluble salts
dissolved in the soil solution. The salts
are made available by the complex biological and chemical activities and reactions in the soil. The chief sources of the
mineral elements are the inorganic
particles of the soil and the decomposing
organic matter. Since soils vary considerably in composition, the amounts
and proportions of mineral nutrients
coming available to plants in the soil
solution are also variable. Under cultivation a soil is subject to losses of these
mineral elements, partly in what is
absorbed by the plants grown, and partly
in drainage. It is therefore important to
know the chief effects of the various
nutrient elements on plant growth, and
their availability in various soils.

Nitrogen. This element is an essential
constituent of chlorophyll and proteins,
and of the vital structures of plants, and
is needed in relatively large amounts,
particularly in the active growing stages,
promoting strong stem and shoot formation and strong green leaves. When
deficient, shoot growth is stunted, thin
and stiffish, leaves small, sparse, yellow-
green, often highly tinted, falling prematurely; flower-bud formation is reduced, or weak and delayed. In fruit
trees, bark may show reddish, and any
fruits small, highly coloured and woody
to taste, though sweet. Nitrogen comes
from air (by bacterial action; *see* Leguminosae), organic matter and fertilizers;
but is readily lost on all soils, particularly
the humus-poor. It may be supplied in
organic manures, plus nitrogenous fertilizers in proper balance (*see* Fertilizers).

Phosphorus. Closely concerned with
all vital health and growth processes,

phosphorus is essential to root development, the functioning of cell nuclei, the formation of flowers and seed, and a sturdy, disease-resistant plant. It comes chiefly from the mineral fraction of the soil and decomposing organic matter. Deficiency is most likely under high alkaline or strongly acid soil conditions, which make the element less available to plants. The symptoms are chiefly stunted, thin, upright shoot growth, small leaves, often bluish-green, purplish or bronzed, or brown spotting or marginal fading of soft leaves; poor flower-bud and seed formation; in fruits, tissue is soft, acid, and lacks taste. It is corrected by bringing the pH value to a suitable level, and applying phosphatic fertilizers (*see* Fertilizers).

Potassium. This element is found in all parts of a plant, fosters good development of growing points of leaves, stems and roots; contributes to the building-up of plant substance, and is essential to sap movement and photosynthesis, and weather and disease resistance. It comes chiefly from the mineral part of the soil and decomposing organic matter. Deficiency is most apt to occur on light, free-draining and calcareous soils. The symptoms are restricted growth at growing points of shoots, leaves and roots; with leaves bluey-green, and tending to turn brown or greyish-brown at tips and margins, and shoots easily die back; orchard fruits are small and fall prematurely.

A deficiency is made good by organic manuring and applying potassic fertilizers (*see* Fertilizers).

Calcium. As a nutrient, calcium is a constituent of cell walls, gives strength to a plant, and promotes growth at shoot and root tips; by neutralizing organic acids, it helps to make other nutrients more readly available. It comes from the mineral soil, and deficiency only occurs on non-calcareous acid soils. The symptoms are restricted shoot and root growth, with tip die back, and leaves are distorted, ragged, and often with marginal scorch. It is associated with Bitter Pit in Apples. Correction lies in applying lime (*see* Lime) to bring the soil pH to a level suitable for the plants to be grown, bearing in mind that plants vary in their lime-tolerance. All soils tend to lose

calcium under cultivation, and should be checked periodically for their pH value or acidity.

Magnesium. As a constituent of chlorophyll, magnesium is essential to plants. It plays a vital part in the formation of seeds. It comes from the mineral soil, and is apt to be deficient in strongly acid soils and free-draining sands. A deficiency may be induced by over-fertilizing with potassium on any soil. Deficiency is shown first in the older leaves; by yellowing between the veins, followed by browning, rolling and drooping, to fall prematurely. A deficiency on an acid soil can be made good by the using of a magnesian limestone from time to time; or more quickly by the use of magnesium sulphate as a fertilizer (*see* Fertilizers).

Iron. This nutrient is vital to the formation of chlorophyll and to respiration, functioning as a catalyst. Iron comes from the mineral part of the soil; very few soils are without it, but deficiencies arise from its unavailability, and this is apt to occur in soils rich in calcium carbonate (lime). The chief symptoms are yellowing of the younger leaves between the veins, at the tips of shoots, restricted shoot growth and die-back; particularly when lime-intolerant plants are grown in the presence of lime. Correction lies in organic manuring, and the provision of iron in a chelated form (Sequestrene) unaffected by lime.

Sulphur. As a constituent of plant proteins and oils, sulphur is an essential nutrient. It also plays a part in chlorophyll formation. It comes from the mineral part of the soil, often augmented by atmospheric deposits in industrial and town areas. Deficiency produces symptoms similar to those of nitrogen deficiency but are unlikely to occur in Britain. Powdered sulphur may be used to depress alkalinity in calcareous soils.

Manganese. Closely associated with iron in chlorophyll formation, and a catalyst of reactions promoting growth, manganese is essential to plants. It chiefly occurs in the mineral soil. A deficiency causes chlorosis or yellowing of leaves, which begins near the margins and develops inwardly, and affects older leaves more severely than young tip leaves. In potatoes, brown spotting along the veins occurs; in peas and beans, internal browning known as 'Marsh Spot' occurs in the seeds. These symptoms occur on highly alkaline soils, especially under damp conditions, but can be corrected by the application of manganese sulphate.

Boron. Apparently, this nutrient functions chiefly as a catalyst, enabling the plant to use other elements, such as calcium. It comes from the mineral part of the soil, and deficiencies are not common, but may arise on light sandy and stony soils, and result in failure in meristematic growth, leading to die-back of growing points and deformation of forming tissues. It produces 'Heart Rot' and 'Canker' in beet and turnips; 'Hollow Stem' and 'Brown Curding' in cauliflowers; 'Cracked Stem' in celery; and 'Corky Core' or 'Corky Pit' in apples. It is corrected by applying borax at about 1 lb. per 250 sq. yds.

Copper. This element is essential to plant growth as a catalyst and constituent of enzymes. It occurs naturally in the mineral part of most soils, in the minute quantities needed. Deficiency causes a die-back of growing points, deformation and gumming in stone fruits, with leaves bluish-green or chlorotic, and few or no flowers. It is rare in Britain, but has been noted in parts of Wales, on some sandy soils, and heath, peaty or peat-bog land, but is corrected by marling (*see* Marl), or copper sulphate applications at 1 lb. per 250–1,000 sq. yds.

Zinc. Like copper, zinc is only needed by plants in very small amounts, and apparently the element is similar in effect as a catalyst. It comes from the mineral part of the soil; a deficiency in Britain is rare, but is characterized by shoots being stunted, and the leaves are small, narrow and crowded in a rosette effect at the ends of shoots, with yellow mottling, especially in late summer. Zinc sulphate may be used to correct a deficiency on the lines as for copper at 1 lb. per 250–1,000 sq. yds, though it is wise to get expert confirmation of a diagnosis first.

Molybdenum. Its role in plant nutrition is not fully understood, though there is no doubt that it is essential in very minute amounts. Deficiency symptoms

are yellow mottling of the leaves, and death of growing points in brassicas and lettuce, whiptail of cauliflowers from a failure of the laminae to develop, a failure or chlorosis in legumes as the element is necessary to the nitrogen-fixing root nodule bacteria; but deficiencies are very rare in Britain.

Chlorine. Too little is known about the role of chlorine in plant nutrition, beyond the fact that it may exert a beneficial effect on certain plants, but an excess may produce marginal leaf scorching similar to potassium deficiency. It is commonly found in most soils, and deficiency is rare in Britain.

Sodium. Apparently not strictly essential, sodium has beneficial effects in small amounts, particularly for plants of the beet family; but an excess is harmful.

Other elements may be absorbed which are not essential to plant nutrition but which benefit animals and humans eating the plants, such as cobalt and iodine. In excess, many of the mineral elements have an adverse effect, largely because their presence leads to deficiencies and ill balance among other nutrients. Broadly, good plant nutrition depends on (1) good drainage; (2) adequate soil aeration; (3) the correct degree of acidity or pH value; (4) satisfactory organic manuring; and (5) balanced provision of fertilizers appropriate to the soil and plants grown.

Nuts. Cultivated from very early times, nuts are grown through Europe and N. Africa to central Asia and Siberia. Two species are the parents of the cultivated nuts now grown; *Corylus avellana*, the Hazel or Cob-nut, a native shrub of 12–20 ft, and *C. maxima*, the Filbert, introduced from S. Europe, of equal vigour. The Cob-nut is roundish-oval, with a short husk, only partly covering it; the Filbert is oblongish, with a husk that covers it.

Selection. Good varieties of Cob-nuts are 'Cosford Cob', thin-shelled; 'Webb's Prize Cob'; 'Pearsons's Prolific', thick-shelled, heavy-cropping; and of Filberts 'Lambert's Filbert', often offered as 'Kent Cob' though the nuts are long-husked; 'White Filbert', 'Red Filbert', 'Prolific' and 'Bergeri'. The purple-leaved *C. maxima* v. *atropurpurea* bears Filberts with a red skin and is worth growing where ornamental value is valued as well as fruit. As Filberts set a crop less readily on their own, it is wise to plant two of different varieties to ensure proper pollination. The flowers are unisexual, the male pollen-bearing flowers in catkins, the females are small and reduced to a show of two short red stigmas, and wind-pollinated.

Cultivation. Nuts grow well in almost any soil with good drainage, and may be planted on gravelly or stony soils, with or without lime; preferably in sunny positions, sheltered from east and north-east winds; in October–March, about 12 ft, apart. After planting the main shoots are cut back to two or three buds above the ground, which will result in four to six strong branches to form the basis of a good open bush. The following year, these branches are in turn cut back half way or so, according to vigour, until a good strong framework of branches, forming a basin-shaped shrub, is obtained up to 6 ft. Many short lateral shoots will then form to bear flowers and fruits. These are pruned towards the end of February, after pollen has been shed, cutting back to just above a catkin a few inches from the base of the previous year's growth. Shoots which bore fruit the previous year can be cut back to two or three buds from the base; suckers should be twisted off at the base. In summer strong-growing laterals may be pruned or broken across by hand at about six buds from their base, and pruned to two or three buds or a female flower in winter. The nuts are harvested ripe, when the husks are quite brown about late September, laid on trays to dry off thoroughly, and then may be stored in jars or tubs, in layers with sand between, adding a sprinkling of salt with each layer of sand, under cool conditions.

Pests. Nuts are not subject to much disease, but the Nut Weevil, *Balaninus nucum*, can be damaging, the female adult piercing the young nuts in late May and June to lay an egg, which soon hatches into a maggot that feeds on the kernel, and then leaves to enter the soil and turn into a chrysalis until ready to emerge as a small brown or greyish brown beetle the following spring, and renew the attack. The application of a DDT insecticide in late May, repeated after

three weeks, and cultivation of the soil beneath the bushes in winter to expose the chrysalids will give good control. Or sheet polythene can be spread beneath the bushes in May–June, and the branches shaken to dislodge the weevils, which can then be gathered and destroyed. The caterpillars of the Nut Sawfly, *Croesus septentrionalis*, can soon defoliate bushes in early summer, and shoots carrying colonies of caterpillars are best cut off and destroyed; the DDT insecticide is also helpful.

Nuttallia. See *Osmaronia*.

Nyctocereus (nik-to-ke're-us). Fam. Cactaceae). Night-flowering cacti, natives of Mexico, of which *N. serpentinus*, with long, slender stems, dark-tipped white spines, flowers freely with large white flowers opening at night in summer; *guatemalensis* is similar with thicker stronger stems; and *hirschtianus* has thin yellow-spined stems.

Cultivation. Pot in standard compost, March, water during growth and in summer; very little in winter, minimum temp. 7° C. (45° F.). Propagate by cuttings.

Nymphaea, Water Lily (nimp'e-a. Fam. Nymphaeaceae). Beautiful flowering aquatic plants, with large, heart-shaped or peltate floating leaves, and showy flowers, for pools, tubs, etc., outdoors and indoors, according to hardiness.

Selection. Hardy species and varieties which should be chosen according to the depth of water in which they will be planted, and the size of the pool, include: *N. alba*, Europe and Britain, white flowering in summer, and v. *rubra*, Sweden, rosy-pink, need deep water, 6 ft or more. For water depth of 4–6 in.: *odorata minor*, N. America, white; *pygmaea alba*, white; × *pygmaea helvola*, soft yellow; × *pygmaea* 'Johann Pring', pink. For water depth of 1–1½ ft: 'Aurora', buff-yellow; *candida*, N. Europe, white; 'Ellisiana', garnet red; *froebeli*, blood-red; 'Graziella', coppery red to yellow; × *laydekeri* hybrids such as *fulgens*, crimson; liliacea, soft rose; and *purpurata*, rosy-crimson, spotted white; *odorata* vs. 'Eugenia de Land', pink; 'Wm B. Shaw', creamy-pink'; and *sulphurea*, sulphur-yellow; 'Paul Hariot' apricot- to copper-red; 'Rene Gerard', rose; 'Rose Arey', deep rose-pink;

'Solfaterre', yellow, flushed rose; and 'Sunrise', pale yellow. For water depth of 1½–2 ft: *brackleyi rosea*, rose; 'Conqueror', red, flecked white; *gloriosa*, large red; 'James Brydon', carmine red; *marliaceae albida*, white; *marliacea chromatella*, yellow; *masaniello*, rosy-carmine; 'Rose Nymphe', deep rose, fragrant; and 'Wm Falconer', deep red.

FIG. 163   *Nymphaea* × 'Escarboule'.

For water depth of 2½–3 ft: *amabilis*, salmon-rose; *colossea*, blush pink; 'Escarboule', rich crimson; *gladstoniana*, white; 'Gonnêre, double white; 'Marguerite Laplace', lilac-pink, spotted rose; *marliacea rosea*, rose; 'Col. A. J. Welch', yellow; *tuberosa rosea*, shell-pink; and *virginalis*, snow-white.

Cultivation. Plant, May–June, in bottom of pool, in compost of rotted loam, plus 2–3 oz. coarse bone meal per bushel; or in a basket of withies, wood or plastic, in similar compost; just cover with water, increasing depth as growth is made by adding more water, to correct planting depth; give full sunny position. Overgrown plants may be lifted after four years or more, divided and the old rhizomes cut out and discarded.

Propagation. By division, May–June. By seeds sown in small pots, submerged in shallows, April–June.

Selection for Warm Greenhouse. N. caerulea, the Blue Lotus of Egypt, N. and central Africa, light blue flowers, summer; *capensis*, S. and E. Africa, bright blue; *gigantea*, Australia, blue, summer; and *stellata*, S. and E. Asia, blue, summer; and hybrids such as 'Blue Beauty', 'Henry Shaw', bright blue; 'Mrs C. W. Ward', rose-pink; and

'St Louis', yellow, are good for cool to warm greenhouse conditions, minimum winter temps. 10–13° C. (50–55° F.).

Cultivation. May be planted in tubs, or in pots for placing in an aquarium, compost as for outdoor plants; in April–May. Propagation as for outdoor plants.

Diseases. Leaf-spotting and blotching may be caused by fungus infection (*Ovularia nymphearum*, etc.), and it is best to remove leaves and stalks as soon as seen, as fungicidal control is very difficult.

Pests. Water-lily Beetles (*Galerucella nymphaceae*) cause leaves to be eaten by their grubs, and decay; and the oblong, dark brown beetles, and grubs in clusters, may be found on plants from late June to August. They should be washed off for fish to devour, or in the absence of fish, carefully wetted with a nocotine insecticide. Aphids (*Rhopalosiphum nymphaeae*) may attack leaves, etc., in June–September. They may be washed off by hosing, or carefully wetted with nicotine insecticide. Derris, pyrethrum and other insecticides should not be used, being toxic to fish.

Nymphoides (Limnanthemum) (nymp' oi-des. Fam. Menyanthaceae). The chief species grown is *N. peltatum* (*Limnanthemum nymphaeoides*), the Fringed Water-lily, native to central and eastern England and Europe, with light green, maroon-mottled leaves, and umbels of golden-yellow flowers in summer. Except in mild localities, it requires cool greenhouse shelter; being planted in May–June, ½–1½ ft depth of water, in compost as for Water-lilies (*Nymphaea*).

Propagation. By division of rhizomatous roots, spring.

Nyssa (nis'sa. Fam. Nyssaceae). The only species of these deciduous trees worth considering is *N. sylvatica*, the Tupelo of eastern N. America, 50 ft or more, with glossy, vari-shaped ovate to obovate leaves, colouring well in autumn, to reds and yellow; greenish-yellow June flowers, sometimes followed by small blue-black ovoid fruits. Specimens should be planted young, in deep good loam, containing little lime, and a mild sheltered position, in autumn or spring. Propagation is by imported seeds sown in spring, lime-free compost, in cold frame, in pots.

O

Oak. See *Quercus*.

Oak-leaved Geranium. See *Pelargonium quericifolium*.

Ob-, prefix of compound words meaning inverted or reversed: *Obcordate*, reversed heart-shape; *Oblanceolate*, reversed lance-shape; *Obovate*, reversed egg-shape.

FIG. 164 Obcordate leaf (*Myrtus obcordata*).

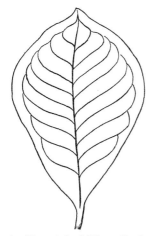

FIG. 165 Obovate leaf (*Magnolia obovata*).

Occidentalis (-e). Western. Ex. *Thuja occidentalis*.

Ocimum (o-ki'mum. Fam. Labiatae). A genus of subtropical herbs, of which *O. basilicum*, Sweet Basil, is chiefly grown (q.v.).

Octa-, Octo-. Prefix of compound words, meaning eight: *Octandrous*, with eight stamens; *Octogynous*, with eight styles; *Octopetalous*, with eight petals.

-odes, -oides. Suffix to words meaning likeness. Ex. *Sempervivum arachnoideum*.

× **Odontioda** (o-don-ti-o'da. Fam. Orchidaceae). Bigeneric hybrids of *Odontoglossum* × *Cochlioda*, of rich and beautiful coloured flowering, offered in named forms and varieties, for culture similar to that for *Odontoglossum* (q.v.).

Odontoglossum (o-don-to-gloss'um. Fam. Orchidaceae). A large genus of Orchids, mostly epiphytic, from the Andes mountains of S. America, many of which may be grown in the cool greenhouse.

Selection. Of species, *O. cervantessii*, Oaxaca, dwarf-growing, white, striped red, flowers, May; *citrosmum*, Guatemala, 6 in., white, flushed pink, June; *crispum*, Colombia, 1 ft. white and pink, May; and many fine vs.; *grande*, Guatemala, 6 in., orange-yellow and brown, autumn, winter; *nobile*, Colombia, 2 ft, white, spring; *rossii*, Mexico, dwarf, white, barred brown, winter; *triumphans*, Colombia, 10 in., golden yellow, and brown, spring, and their vs. are the easiest to grow. There are also many choice hybrids to be found in Orchid specialists' lists, and to be seen at shows.

Cultivation. Pot in September, well-crocked pots, compost of equal parts live sphagnum moss and fibrous peat, with charcoal; grow cool, watering often, but moderately in winter; temps.: winter 10–15·5° C. (50–60° F.); summer 15·5–18° C. (60–65° F.), in fairly humid atmosphere, shade from direct sun, but give good light and ventilation

374

when flowering; with daily watering and syringing in warm weather.

Propagation. By division in September, when repotting.

× **Odontonia** (o-don-to'ni-a). Fam. Orchidaceae). Bigeneric hybrid Orchids with richly coloured flowers, of *Miltonia* × *Odontoglossum*; to be grown as *Odontoglossum* (q.v.) with slightly higher temperatures.

Odoratus (-a, -um). Fragrant Ex. *Reseda odorata.*

Oenothera, Evening Primrose (e-no-the'ra. Fam. Onagraceae). A very large genus of annual, biennial and perennial flowering plants, chiefly from the Americas, of which several make fine border plants, some flowering at night, and many with fragrance.

Selection. O. *biennis*, the Common Evening Primrose, eastern N. America, 2–4 ft, yellow, evening flowers, scented, July–September; *erythrosepala* (*lamarckiana*), of garden origin, 3–4 ft, golden-yellow, nocturnal flowers, July–September; *fruticosa*, eastern N. America, 1½ ft, yellow diurnal summer flowers, and v. *youngii*, very free-flowering; and *trichocalyx*, Rocky Mts, 1 ft, white evening flowers, June–July, are biennials, grown from seeds sown the previous early

summer. O. *odorata*, S. America, 2 ft, yellow night flowers, June; and *speciosa*, S. U.S.A., 2 ft, white to rose diurnal flowers, June–July, are not reliably hardy; but *perennis*, eastern N. America, 2 ft, yellow diurnal flowers, July; *tetragona*, eastern N. America, to 3 ft, yellow, diurnal flowering in summer, and vs. *fraseri*, large flowers; 'Highlight', very large flowers; and *riparia*, long flowering, are useful border perennials; while *acaulis*, Chile, white flowers turning rose; and *missouriensis*, S. U.S.A., yellow evening flowers, are dwarf trailing plants for the border front or rock garden in June–September. O. *bistorta*, California, 1 ft, yellow to green diurnal flowers, summer, is a good annual.

Cultivation. Plant perennials in March–April, any well-drained ordinary soil, sunny positions or sheltered partial shade, in mild localities.

Propagation. Annuals by seed, under glass, March–April, to plant out in May. Perennials by division in spring, or by seeds, sown early summer out of doors, to transplant to flowering quarters by late August.

Officinalis (-e). Of shops (medicinal). Ex. *Galega officinalis.*

Offset. A gardening term often used to describe new bulbs or corms or short runner shoots, typical of the parent plant, produced at the sides, which may be detached and grown on to make new plants.

Okra. See *Hibiscus esculentus.*

Old Man. See *Artemisia abrotanum.*

Old Man Cactus. See *Cephalocereus senilis.*

Old Man's Beard. Common name for the native *Clematis vitalba.*

Olea (o'le-a. Fam. Oleaceae). Evergreen shrubs or trees, of which O. *europaea*, the Olive of the Mediterranean region, to 20 ft, with small white flowers in axillary racemes, nicely scented, and its vs., may be grown in warm sheltered borders, and loam soil, in counties such as Cornwall, though seldom ripening their oil-rich oval fruits. Plant in April; may be propagated by seeds, under glass, sown in March–April, bottom heat of 21° C (70° F.); or by cuttings under handlight in summer.

Oleander. See *Nerium.*

Olearia (o-le-a'ri-a. Fam. Compositae).
A large genus of evergreen Australasian
shrubs, with leathery leaves, white or
buff beneath, and daisy-like flower-heads
in panicles, not reliably hardy.

Selection. O. haastii, New Zealand
Daisy Bush, 4–8 ft, fragrant corymbs of
white flowers, July–August, is hardiest
species; *albida*, 6 ft or more, white-felted
leaves, white flower-heads; *avicenniae-
folia*, 8 ft, long, white-felted leaves, white
flowers, August; *macrodonta*, to 12 ft,
coarsely toothed leaves, white-felted,
large white flower-heads, July; *illicifolia*,
to 10 ft, musky odoured, white flower-
heads, June; and *nummularifolia*, 6 ft,
tiny leaves, and yellowish flower-heads,
July, are all from New Zealand, but only
hardy enough for mild localities and
warm sheltered conditions. *O. erubescens*,
Tasmania, 4 ft, brown-felted leaves,
long panicles of daisy flowers, May–June;
gunniana, Tasmania, 5 ft, large flower-
heads in clusters, white, June; *insignis*,
New Zealand, 3 ft, large leaves, and large
white flowers, August; *semidentata*,
Chatham Is., to 6 ft, pale purple flowers,
July, of much beauty; and *tomentosa*,
Australia, 2–3 ft, rufous felted leaves and
shoots, pale rose flowers, early summer,
may be grown in the cool greenhouse, in
large pots or tubs, and set outside during
summer.

Cultivation. Plant March–May, well-
drained, loam soil, sunny, sheltered
positions, in mild areas. Pot half-hardy
species in March–April, standard compost, water liberally April–October, very
moderately in winter, minimum temp.
10° C. (50° F.), in greenhouse.

Propagation. By cuttings of young
firm shoots, with heel, August, in cold
frame or under handlights; or by layering, spring or autumn.

Oleaster. See *Elaeagnus*.

Oleraceus (-a, -um). Oleraceous, edible,
for culinary use. Ex. *Spinacia oleracea*.

Olive. See *Olea*.

Omphalodes (omp-a-lo'des. Fam. Boraginaceae). Pretty flowering annuals and
perennials, well worth growing, in border
or rock garden.

Selection. O. linifolia, Venus' Navelwort, of SW. Europe, ½–1 ft, with loose
racemes of white flowers, summer, is a
hardy annual, for sowing in March–
April, where it is to flower, in partial

shade. *O. cappadocica*, Asia Minor, 8 in.,
blue flowers, summer; and *luciliae*, Asia
Minor, 6 in., pink buds opening to sky-
blue flowers, summer, are good for the
rock garden or dry wall, or alpine house.
O. verna, Blue-eyed Mary, S. Europe, is a
creeping plant, with blue, white-throated
spring flowers, for shady woodland.

Cultivation. Plant perennials in April–
May, lightish, well-drained but moisture-
retentive loam, with lime present; protect from slugs.

Propagation. By seeds, June–August;
or by careful division in May.

Oncidium (on-kid'i-um. Fam. Orchidaceae). A very large genus of epiphytic
orchids, natives of tropical America, of
which some of the easier to grow in a cool
greenhouse are given here.

Selection. O. concolor, Brazil, 1½–2 ft,
golden-yellow flowers in panicle, June–
July; *crispum*, Brazil, 2–3 ft, panicle of
rich brown flowers, June; *forbesii*, Brazil,
1½–3 ft, chestnut-brown and gold,
autumn; *incurvum*, Mexico, 2½ ft, many-
flowered, white, lilac and rose, autumn;
macranthum, American tropics, 4–7 ft,
golden, tinged purplish, white crested
flowers, spring; *marshallianum*, Brazil,
3–5 ft, many golden-yellow, red-spotted
flowers, June; *ornithorhynchum*, Mexico,
15 in., drooping panicles of small, rose-
purple, scented flowers, autumn; *tigrinum*, Mexico, 3 ft, panicles, brown,
barred yellow, finely scented, winter;
and *varicosum*, Brazil, 3 ft, many-
flowered panicles, yellow-green, banded
brown, autumn, and vs. *charlesworthii*,
insigne and *rogersii*. Others, including
many for the warmer greenhouse, will be
found in Orchid specialists' lists.

Cultivation. Pot in September, when
new bulbs are forming; well-crocked pots,
compost of equal parts live sphagnum
moss and fibrous peat and grain charcoal.
Keep cool and damp, watering more
freely as temperatures rise; ventilate
adequately, shade from hot sun, give
ample light as flowers form, with humidity; water only moderately in winter;
temps.: summer 15·5–18° C. (60–65° F.);
winter 10–13° C. (50–55° F.).

Propagation. By division in September.

Onion (*Allium cepa*). Cultivated since
very ancient times, known to the
Pharaohs of Egypt, the Onion is an

important culinary and salading vegetable in modern diet. The plant is a biennial, the edible bulb forming in the first season of growth; if allowed, it flowers and forms seeds in the second year.

Varieties. These are numerous, but may be grouped as (1) Spanish or Portugal, with more or less flattened bulbs: 'A1', 'Improved Reading', 'Rousham Park Hero' and 'Nuneham Park', with straw-coloured skin; (2) Brown Spanish: 'Brown Globe', 'James's Long Keeping', with brown skin; (3) Dutch Hybrid, with more or less globular bulbs: 'Ailsa Craig', 'Bedfordshire Champion', 'Cranston's Excelsior', 'Giant Zittau', 'Unwin's Reliance', 'Up-to-date' and 'Wijbo'; (4) American: 'Danver's Yellow', 'The Flagon', 'Red Wethersfield'; (5) Italian, well suited to autumn sowing: 'Giant Rocca', 'Golden Rocca', 'White Tripoli'. All the above may be spring or autumn sown. For pickling onions, 'Paris Silverskin', 'The Queen' and 'White Portugal' are sown. For salad onions to be pulled green and immature, 'White Lisbon' or 'White Spanish' are most useful.

Cultivation. A light to medium, well-drained soil, and open sunny situation suit onions best. Sandy, chalky, and heavy soils need amendment. The soil should be well dug, thoroughly enriched in rotted organic matter several weeks before sowing, and brought to a pH 6·0 to 6·5. The soil should be firm and consolidated, and weed-free before sowing or planting. A mixture of 5 parts by weight hoof and horn meal, 6 parts bone meal, 2 parts sulphate of potash at 4–6 oz. per sq. yd, may be given in winter for spring cropping, or sowing. Onions may be grown on the same soil perennially, so long as it remains disease and pest free. Or the crop may be included in a rotation; autumn sowings can follow potatoes, for instance. Autumn sowings are made in early August in the north, and about the third week of August in the south, sowing more thickly than in spring, in rows 9–12 in. apart, thinning seedlings to 6–9 in. apart. Spring-grown crops are sown under glass in January, in boxes, bottom heat of 15·5° C. (60° F.), standard compost, to harden off and plant out in April; *or* in late February–March,

outdoors, in prepared sheltered seedbed, and transplanted when 2–3 in. high, 6–9 in. apart in rows 15 in. apart. Onions are sensitive to day-length and temperature (*see* Photoperiodism) and must be planted out in good time in spring. The crop is ready for harvesting when the leaves begin to yellow; late July if autumn-sown; August onwards if spring-sown; when bulbs should be lifted slightly in the soil to break the roots, with a fork; bent over at the neck; and gathered after a fortnight, dried off, and stored cool.

Pickling Onions. These are sown broadcast, on a firm, well-prepared seed-bed, in March, thinly covered, to harvest in June–July.

Salad Onions. Sow in late summer, on well-drained soil, in rows 1 ft. apart, thinly, for spring use; in March–April for summer use.

Diseases. White Rot, caused by the fungus *Sclerotium cepivorum*, shows in wilting, yellowing foliage and a white fluffy fungus growth at the bulb base; infected plants should be destroyed, and crop rotated to new ground next year. Downy Mildew, caused by the fungus *Peronospora schleideniana*, shows in leaves toppling and shrivelling, under moist conditions; collapsed plants are best burnt, and crop treated with karathane fungicide or a copper fungicide. Smut (*Urocystis cepulae*) is not common, but causes dark blisters on leaves, which split to release black, powdery masses of spores, and is a disease to report to the Ministry of Agriculture. Onions should not be grown on the same soil without official permission and direction. Neck Rot, when sorted bulbs develop a brown rot of the scales from the neck downwards, and grey mould appears, is caused by *Botrytis allii*; good culture, proper ripening and drying of bulbs are preventive.

Pests. The most serious is the Onion Fly, *Delia antiqua*, which lays eggs in spring and early summer at or near bases of plants to hatch into root- and bulb-devouring maggots; dusting seedlings at the 'loop-stage' with 4 per cent calomel dust is preventive; or a gamma-BHC insecticidal dust may be used. Bulb Eelworms sometimes cause leaves to be distorted and puffy, with swollen neck and bloated bulbs, which should be promptly destroyed.

Onion, Egyptian or **Tree.** A variety of *Allium cepa* which produces bulbs at the head of its scape, which may be used as culinary onions, or planted for further increase, as for 'sets'.

Onion, Potato. A variety of *Allium cepa*, which, planted in February–March, as single bulbs, produces several new bulbs or 'cloves', mild flavoured, and may be lifted and stored.

Onion 'Sets'. Small bulblets of certain strains of onions which are set out in early March, 4–6 in. apart, in rows 12 in. apart, to grow on and form large onions by August. Less likely to be troubled by Onion Fly than seed-sown crops. Good strains are 'Stuttgart Giant', 'Stuttgarter Riesen', 'Sutton's'.

Onion, Welsh. An evergreen perennial onion, *Allium fistulosum*, Siberia, which forms a clump of small, oblong, oval bulbs, which may be divided like Chives each spring. Useful as spring onions or for flavouring, and perfectly hardy.

Onoclea (o-nok′le-a. Fam. Polypodiaceae). The one species, *O. sensibilis*, is a hardy, easily grown creeping fern, found in N. America and Asia, with two kinds of fronds, 2 ft, high, which may be grown in moist, cool places in the rock garden, fernery or the cold greenhouse in pots, stood in saucers of water.

Ononis (on-o′nis. Fam. Leguminosae). Plants with pea-like flowers, and simple or trifoliolate leaves.

Selection. O. fruticosa, SE. France, Spain, 2–3 ft, a deciduous spreading shrub with light rose, pea-shaped flowers, summer; *natrix*, Goat-root, S. Europe, E. Mediterranean region, 1½ ft, sub-shrub with yellow, streaked red, flowers, May–July; and *rotundifolia*, S. Europe, 1 ft, sub-shrub with rose flowers, summer, are moderately hardy for warm, sheltered situations. *O. speciosa*, Spain, 3 ft, is lovely with racemes of golden, striped purple flowers, early summer, but best pot grown in a cool greenhouse. *O. procurrens*, the native Restharrow, with rosy-pink or white flowers, summer, a running sub-shrub, is for rough places or the wild garden.

Cultivation. Plant in March–April, well-drained porous soil, sunny position, and mild localities.

Propagation. By seeds, sown April, in cold frame or greenhouse. By cuttings of young shoots, July–August.

Onopordon (on-o-por′don. Fam. Compositae). The species chiefly grown is *O. acanthium*, the Cotton or Scotch Thistle, Europe, doubtfully native, 4–5 ft, with woolly leaves, fine purple flower-heads, July, as a biennial, sown in early summer, to flower the following year; *arabicum*, to 8 ft, with magnificent foliage, and purple-blue flowerheads, is sometimes offered.

Onosma (on-os′ma. Fam. Boraginaceae). A genus of small plants, native to the Mediterranean region and central Asia, providing charming rock plants.

Selection. O. albo-pilosum, Asia Minor, 9 in., tufted, hairy sub-shrub, grey-green leaves, white, ageing pink, flowers, May; *echioides*, S. Europe, ½–1 ft, branched sub-shrub, yellow flowers, June; *stellulatum*, SE. Europe, 6 in., linear leaves, yellow flowers, June; and *tauricum*, SE. Europe, 6 in., yellow flowers in summer.

Cultivation. Plant these evergreens in March–April, well-drained, light soil, sun; with protection against winter damp, in rock gardens, or in alpine house.

Propagation. By cuttings of young shoots in June, in propagating frame, shaded for ten days or so. By seeds in April, sown in pan, standard compost, cold frame.

Onychium (o-nik′i-um. Fam. Polypodiaceae). Ferns with finely cut, elegant and attractive fronds for the greenhouse.

Selection. O. japonicum, Japan, finely divided graceful fronds of 15 in., is excellent for the cool greenhouse, and shade; *siliculosum*, tropical Asia, 12 in., broadly ovate handsome fronds, requires hot-house conditions (15.5° C. [60° F.]).

Cultivation. Pot in March, loosely, in well-drained compost of equal parts sandy loam, peat, leaf-mould and silver sand; water liberally in summer, but keep fronds dry, moderately in winter.

Propagation. By spores, but apt to damp-off easily.

Oospore. An egg spore, of fungi, usually a winter or resting spore. Also describes the fertilized egg-cell of flowering and other plants from which the embryo is developed.

Ophioglossum (o-pi-o-glos'sum. Fam. Ophioglossaceae). Ferns of curious flattened spike-like growth on which sporangia form in two rows. *O. vulgatum,* the native Adder's Tongue, 6–9 in., is hardy for moist, semi-shaded situations in the rock garden, and *lusitanicum,* Mediterranean region, may be tried. Propagation is by spores.

FIG. 167 *Ophioglossum vulgatum,* the Adder's Tongue.

Ophiopogon (o-pi-o-po'gon. Fam. Liliaceae). Attractive half-hardy perennials with grass-like leaves and hyacinth-like racemes of flowers, late summer.

Selection. O. jaburan, Japan, 1–2 ft, white flowers; and v. *variegatus,* green and white striped leaves, violet-blue flowers; and *japonicus,* Japan, 1 ft, lilac flowers; and v. *variegatus,* striped yellow-white and green leaves.

Cultivation. Pot in March, standard compost, watering freely, May–October; cool greenhouse conditions; keeping almost dry in winter (10° C. [50° F.]).

Ophrys (op'ris. Fam. Orchidaceae). Pretty terrestrial orchids.

Selection. O. apifera, Bee Orchid, 6 in.,

pink and green with brownish lip, April–May; and v. *alba,* white flowering; *muscifera,* Fly Orchid, 6 in., green and dark red flowers, June; *sphegodes,* 6 in., yellowish green, April; are native, but should not be dug up and taken from the wild. *O. bombyliflora,* Bumble Bee Orchid, S. Europe, 6 in., greenish, chocolate and black bee-like flowers, May; *lutea,* Wasp Orchid, 4 in., greenish, bright yellow and brown flowers, June; and *speculum,* S. Europe, 9 in., the Looking-glass Orchid, with greenish, purple-brown, blue flowers, June, are less hardy.

Cultivation. Plant tubers 1 in. deep, August–October, very well-drained light soil enriched with leaf-mould and bone meal, in rock garden or terrace of cold frame or greenhouse, in 5-in. pots, minimum winter temp. 7° C. (45° F.).

Propagation. By division, every third year, September.

Opium Poppy. See *Papaver somniferum.*

Oplismenus (o-plis'me-nus. Fam. Gramineae). Only *O. hirtellus,* W. Indies, and v. *variegatus,* leaves striped white and pink, are grown as slender creeping perennial grasses in hanging baskets, and edging staging in the cool greenhouse or conservatory. Propagation is by division or cuttings, spring–summer.

Opuntia (o-pun'ti-a. Fam. Cactaceae), Prickly Pear. A very large genus of succulent cacti with a native range reaching from Utah to Patagonia, and variable from low cushion plants to large bushes and trees, usually flowering only on plants of some size and age.

Selection. Sub-genus *Cylindropuntia,* plants with cylindrical stems, jointed, tall-growing: *O. cylindrica,* Ecuador, Peru, to 6 ft, columnar, red flowers; *subulata,* Argentina, to 6 ft, red; *vestita,* Bolivia, erect, branching, 6 ft, red. Sub-genus *Tephrocactus,* low-growing, oval-jointed, seldom flowering: *platyacantha,* S. America, prostrate, flat spines; *glomerata,* Argentina, globular jointed. Sub-genus *Platyopuntia,* strong-growing, with more or less flattened pad-like stems: *basilaris,* Arizona to Utah, cordate pads, no spines, carmine flowers; *engelmannii,* SW. U.S.A., circular pads, yellow flowers; *ficus-indica,* Indian Fig, oblongish pads, 3 ft, yellow flowers;

gosseliniana, Mexico, circular pads, pliable spines; *leucotricha,* Mexico, oval pads, hair-like curling spines, yellow flowers; *microdasys,* Mexico, roundish, velvety pads, no spines, yellow flowers, several vs.; *monacantha (vulgaris),* Prickly Pear, oval pads, golden yellow flowers; v. *variegata,* pads marbled white and yellow; *polyacantha,* W. U.S.A., thin roundish pads, lemon-yellow; *santa-rita,* Arizona, Texas, round, flat pads, deep yellow flowers; *scheerii,* Mexico, oval large pads, many slender yellow spines; and many others.

Cultivation. Pot, and repot every third year, in March–April; water weekly, May–September, very little in winter, minimum temp. 10° C. (50° F.); give sun or light shade, good ventilation; handle with care.

Propagation. By cuttings of stems, June, standard cactus compost; by seeds, spring, bottom heat of 18° C. (65° F.).

Orache (*Atriplex hortensis*). Sometimes called Mountain Spinach, a hardy annual, which may be grown for its large leaves to be cooked like spinach. Sow seeds in April, rich, well-drained soil, thinning plants to 18 in. apart, to grow 3–5 ft tall. There are green, red and white varieties, of ornamental as well as culinary value.

Orange. See *Citrus.*

Orange Ball Tree. See *Buddleia globosa.*

Orbicularis (-e), Orbiculatus (-a, -um). Orbicular, rounded and flat, particularly of leaves. Ex. *Rhododendron obiculare.*

Orchard. Land cultivated for the growing of hardy fruit trees and bushes. *See* Fruit-growing in Gardens.

Orchids. It is estimated that there are between 25,000 and 35,000 species in the monocotyledonous Family of Orchidaceae, found in most countries throughout the world. Those found in tropical regions are mostly epiphytic; those of temperate regions mostly terrestrial; a few are devoid of chlorophyll and are saprophytic. Although the culture of many orchids is well within the scope of the amateur gardener in a cool greenhouse, serious orchid-growing calls for a separate orchid house, since the plants do not lend themselves well to culture in the same house as other greenhouse plants.

The Orchid House. This can be a lean-

to greenhouse, facing north or north-west; or a span-roof type with north-east to south-west or north to south orientation. The house should have side wall, and top ventilation, and provision for shading in the form of blinds or nets easily manipulated and varied. Staging and inside fittings must be resistant to damp and humidity. The range of plants that may be grown is largely determined by the temperatures to be maintained, and orchid houses are usually designed as follows: (1) The Hot or East Indian House; minimum winter temps. of 15·5–21° C. (60–70° F.), rising by 2·3–3° C. (5° F.) by day; summer 18–24°C. (65–75° F.), rising 3–5° C. (5–10° F.) by day; in which tropical species of low altitudes and their hybrids are grown. (2) The Warm or Intermediate House; minimum winter temps. of 13–18° C. (55–65° F.); summer of 15·5–21° C. (60–70° F.); well suited to Cattleyas, Laelias and their hybrids and high altitude tropical orchids. (3) The Cool House; minimum winter temps. of 7–10° C. (45–50° F.); summer of 13–15·5° C. (55–60° F.); in which Cymbidiums, Cypripediums, some Laelias, Maxi-millarias, Odontoglossums, Oncidiums and orchids of warm temperate regions may be successfully grown.

General Cultivation. Broadly, the aim must be to maintain buoyant, warm atmosphere, free from draughts, with humidity increasing with rising tempera-tures in summer, decreasing as tempera-tures fall to winter. Ventilation should admit fresh air without draughts or undue chilling. Shading is needed against direct hot sun from early spring on-wards to autumn, though by autumn more light can be admitted. Humidity is increased by damping-down of the greenhouse floor, and morning syringing of plants, as daily temperatures rise. Proper regular watering with soft water is essential, liberal during active growth, sufficient only to prevent drying out completely at other times. Potting, and repotting, is usually done when new growth is beginning. The epiphytic or aerial species are grown with roots spread between layers of sphagnum moss, bound with copper wire to teak or hardwood blocks, or in moss in orchid-baskets made of hardwood. Terrestrial kinds are grown in free-draining, well-crocked, pots, pans or orchid pots, in a compost of Osmunda fibre (or peat fibre), fresh sphagnum moss, with a little lump charcoal and coarse sand. Hygienic cleanliness of house, pots, soil, water and feeds is vital if pests are to be kept under control.

Propagation. The simplest way is by division when plants are repotted. Most orchids form pseudo-bulbs, fleshy swellings between the collar and the leaf, which are detached with a piece of root attached, three or four pseudo-bulbs to each piece. Orchids may also be raised from seeds, but this demands special aseptic conditions and control, carefully compounded chemical nutrient media, and expensive equipment outside the scope of amateur work, and a specialist book should be consulted by those interested. See *Orchids and Their Cultivation*, by David Sanders, 1956; *Orchids—Their Culture*, by Bruce Hogg, 1959.

Pests. Ants, aphids, cockroaches, mealy bugs, red-spider mites, scale insects, slugs, thrips and woodlice may attack Orchids, and should be promptly controlled by the use of appropriate insecticides; nicotine or pyrethrum for the sap-sucking insects, a gamma-BHC (lindane) insecticide for ants and woodlice, and metaldehyde for slugs. See Insecticides.

Orchis (or'kis. Fam. Orchidaceae). Interesting terrestrial orchids with tuberous roots for the rock garden, woodland glade or alpine house.

Selection. O latifolia, the Marsh Orchis, Europe, Britain, Asia, 12 in., reddish-purple flower in June, and 'Glasnevin var', the more handsome; *maculata*, Europe, Britain, 1 ft, pale purple, spotted purplish-brown flowers, June; *maderensis*, Madeira, 1½ ft, purple flowers, June; *militaris*, the Military Orchis, Europe, England, 1–2 ft, helmeted-like curious rose flowers, spotted purple; *morio*, Europe, Britain, the Meadow Orchis, purplish, green flowers, June, and white v. *alba*; *purpurea*, the Brown Man Orchis, Britain, rose-lilac, brownish and spotted purple flowers, May; *pyramidalis*, Europe, Britain, 1 ft, deep rose flowers, July; and *ustulata*, Europe, Britain, 6 in., purple, white lip, spotted purple, flowers, May.

Cultivation. Plant with care in early autumn, well-drained, moisture-rententive soil, with lime content, in cool, partial shade.

Propagation. By division in autumn.

Order. A division or group in the classification of living organisms, comprised of related Families; related Orders make up a Class.

Oreocereus (o-re-o-ke're-us. Fam. Cactaceae). Mountain columnar cacti, forming low clusters, very spiny and with long white hairs.

Selection. O. celsianus, Peru, Chile, yellow-spined, brownish red flowers on old plants, summer; *hendriksenianus*, Bolivia, Peru, golden hairs; and *trollii*, Bolivia, whitish-grey woolly hair, red flowers.

Cultivation. Pot in March–April, standard cactus compost; water freely in growth, very little in winter, minimum temp. 10° C. (50° F.).

Propagation. By division in spring.

Oreocharis (o-re-ok'a-ris. Fam. Gesneriaceae). Dainty, charming dwarf evergreen plants with rosetted leaves and May flowers, for the alpine house.

Selection. O. aurantiaca, Yunnan, 5 in., bulbous orange flowers with red calyces, May; and *forrestii*, Yunnan, many, pale yellow flowered cymes, May, on 4-in. hairy stems.

Cultivation. Pot in late May after flowering, well-drained pots, standard compost, and grow in cool, summer-shaded position, out of draughts.

Propagation. By careful division after flowering.

Origanum (o-ri-ga'num. Fam. Labiatae). Herbaceous aromatic perennials of the Mediterranean region.

Selection. O. dictamnus, Dittany, Crete, 1 ft. a sub-shrub, with drooping pink flowers, June, may be grown in warm sheltered rock gardens, or the alpine house. *O. majorana* is the Sweet Marjoram (q.v.).

Cultivation. Plant in spring, light, well-drained soil, warm sunny position; likes chalk.

Propagation. By seeds, sown in April. By division in April. By cuttings, July–August.

Ornamental Grasses. See Grasses.

Ornithogalum (or-nith-og'al-um). Fam. Liliaceae). Pretty flowering bulbous plants with white flowers.

Selection. O arabicum, Mediterranean

region, 1–2 ft, round heads of black-centred, white flowers, summer; *lacteum*, S. Africa, 1½ ft, dense racemes of white flowers, June; *pyramidale*, Mediterranean region, 2 ft, white, green-keeled flowers, summer; and *thyrsoides*, Chincherinchees, S. Africa, 18 in., dense racemes of white to gold, long-lasting flowers, June, are best cool greenhouse-grown. *O. umbellatum*, Star of Bethlehem, Europe, Britain, 12 in., white, green-striped flowers, is hardy, and increases easily.

Cultivation. Pot for the greenhouse in autumn, standard compost, and grow as for Narcissi. Plant *O. umbellatum* in autumn, any ordinary soil, sun or shade.

Propagation. By division of bulbs in autumn. By seeds.

Ornus. See *Fraxinus*.

Orobanche (o-ro-ban'ke. Fam. Orobanchaceae). A genus of over 100 species of root-parasitic herbs, annual and perennial, usually peculiar to definite species of host plants; commonly known as Broomrape. Few are cultivated, but the annual *O. uniflora*, N. America, is sometimes sown by hosts such as Aster, Solidago, or Artemisia.

Orobus. Now included in *Lathyrus*.

Orontium (o-ron'ti-um. Fam. Araceae). The only species, *O. aquaticum*, Golden Club, N. America, with elliptical, glaucous-blue foliage, and yellow fingers of flowers in a long spathe, April–May, may be planted in shallow or deep water in late spring, in the garden pool.

Ortho-. Prefix in compound words meaning straight or upright. Ex. Orthocladus—straight shoots.

Osmanthus (os-man'thus. Fam. Oleaceae). Evergreen shrubs with opposite dark green leaves, and small, tubular white flowers of great fragrance.

Selection. O. delavayi, China, 6–10 ft, pure white clustered flowers, April; and *illicifolius*, Japan, 12 ft, white, September–October, with variegated leafed forms. *O. fragrans*, Himalaya, China, 15 ft, summer-flowering, is only hardy in the south-west or very mild localities.

Cultivation. Plant September–October, or March–April, well-drained, good loam soil, wind-sheltered open position. Prune, if necessary, after flowering.

Propagation. By cuttings of firm young shoots, July–August, under a handlight.

× **Osmarea** (os-mar'e-a. Fam. Oleaceae). A hybrid of *Osmanthus delavayi* × *Phillyrea decora, O.* × *burkwoodii* is a pleasing hardy evergreen shrub, to 8 ft, with leathery, lustrous green leaves, and small tubular, scented white flowers in axillary clusters in May. Plant in March–April, any good ordinary soil, sun or partial shade; makes a good hedging plant. Propagation by firm young cuttings in July–August.

Osmaronia (Nuttallia) (os-mar-o'ni-a. Fam. Rosaceae). The one species, *O. cerasiformis*, western N. America, deciduous shrub to 5 ft, is chiefly grown for its racemes of greenish-white, highly fragrant flowers in early spring, succeeding in any ordinary soil, planted in early autumn or early spring. Propagation by suckers detached in spring.

Osmosis. The percolation and intermixing of different densities through a permeable septa or membrane.

Osmunda (os-mun'da. Fam. Osmundaceae). Ferns of stately beauty, with double pinnate fronds.

Selection. O. cinnamomea, the Cinnamon Fern, eastern N. America, Mexico, to E. Asia, fronds to 3 ft; *claytoniana*, N. America, China, Himalaya, to 2 ft, and *regalis*, the Royal Fern, to 6 ft, do well by pools or waterside.

Cultivation. Plant October–March, moist soil, and propagate by division, March; by spores, July.

Osmunda Fibre. This is chiefly obtained from the roots of *Osmunda claytoniana* and *O. cinnamonea*, for use in orchid culture.

Osteomeles (os-te-om'e-les. Fam. Rosaceae). Evergreen flowering shrubs with alternate, pinnate leaves, and terminal clusters of white flowers.

Selection. O. schwerinae is of graceful habit to 6 ft, with slender shoots, flowering in June; with a dwarf form, *microphylla*; while *subrotunda* is slow-growing with tortuous branches, smaller leaves, and white flowers, June.

Cultivation. Plant March–April, in the shelter of a warm wall, except in mild areas; well-drained, humus-rich soil.

Propagation. By firm young cuttings, July.

Ostrowskia (ost-row'ski-a. Fam. Campanulaceae). A monotypic genus consisting of *O. magnifica*, Turkistan, a fine herbaceous perennial of 5 ft, with whorls of large ovate toothed leaves, and large pale-lilac, broadly bell-shaped flowers, summer. Plant out of pots in spring in well-drained, deep humus-rich loam, sheltered warm position, covering crowns with ashes in winter. Most easily propagated from seeds, in peat-wood fibre pots, though it takes three or four years to reach flowering size.

Ostrya (os'tri-a. Fam. Betulaceae). Hardy, attractive, medium-sized, deciduous trees for small gardens.

Selection. *O. carpinifolia*, the Hop Hornbeam, S. Europe and Asia Minor, round-headed to 50 ft, gets its name from its hop-like fruit clusters; *virginiana*, N. American Ironwood, to 50 ft, is somewhat similar but longer in the leaves and fruit clusters.

Cultivation. Plant October to March, in deep well-drained loam, moist subsoil in all but cold exposed areas. Seldom need pruning.

Propagation. By imported seeds, sown March, in pots in cold frame; or layering can be tried.

Oswego Tea. See *Monarda didyma.*

Othonnopsis (o-thon-nop'sis). Fam. Compositae). The species chiefly grown, *O. cheirifolia*, is a N. African pretty, low, spreading sub-shrub with distinctive grey foliage, yellow, daisy-like flowers, May–June, worth planting in porous light loam, and sun, in mild localities, early autumn or spring.

Propagation. By cuttings of young shoots, July–August.

Ourisia (ou-ris'i-a. Fam. Scrophulariaceae). Moderately hardy low-growing perennials for summer flowering in the rock garden in mild localities.

Selection. O. alpina, Andes, 6 in., rosetted leaves, red to pink flowering; *coccinea*, Chile, 6 in., scarlet, trumpet-like flowers, summer; and *macrophylla*, New Zealand, 8 in., white flowers, July, are good.

Cultivation. Plant March–April, well-drained, moist soil, partial shade.

Propagation. By division, April. By seeds in cold frame, spring.

Ouvirandria. Now included in *Aponogeton* (q.v.).

Ovary. The part of the pistil of a flower which forms the immature seed-vessel containing the ovules.

FIG. 168   Ovary (Tulip), and o. ovules.

Ovatus (-a, -um). Ovate, egg-shaped. Ex. *Forsythia ovata.*

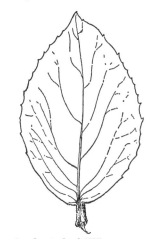

FIG. 169   Ovate leaf (*Viburnum carlesii*).

Ovoid. Egg-like in solid form.

Ovule. A rudimentary or unfertilized seed. (*See* Fig. 168).

Oxalis (ocks'a-lis. Fam. Oxalidaceae). A large genus of annual or perennial herbs, usually stemless and rhizomatous-rooted or bulbous.

Selection. O. acetosella, the Cuckoo Bread or Wood Sorrel, 3 in., white flowering, spring, and its v. *rosea*, rose, purple-veined flowers, for woodlands; *adenophylla*, Chile, 4 in., lilac-pink, May–June; *enneaphylla*, Falkland Is., 3 in., white, and v. *rosea*, pink, May–June; *lobata*, S. America, 4 in., pale yellow, September; *oregana*, Oregon, 3 in., rosy-pink, May; may be attempted in the rock garden in mild localities, or in the alpine house. *O. brasiliensis*, Brazil, 3 in., reddish-purple, May; *chrysantha*, Brazil, 2 in., golden-yellow, June; *deppei*, Mexico, 6 in., reddish-purple, May–June, edible bulb; *hirta*, S. Africa, 9 in., violet with yellow, autumn; *purpurata*, S. Africa, 1 ft, purple, violet, May; and *magellanica*, Bolivia, S. America, 1½ in., white, May, are best grown in pots or pans in the alpine house or cold greenhouse (minimum temp. 7° C. [45° F.]). *O. valdiviensis*, Chile, 6 in., yellow bell flowers, August, may be grown as a half-hardy annual from seed under glass. Some species, notably *O. corniculata* and its vs., *cernua*, the Bermuda Buttercup, *floribunda* (*rubra*), and *stricta* can become troublesome weeds in the garden and are best avoided.

Cultivation. Outdoors, plant September–October, in well-drained, porous soil, sunny warm situations, in the rock garden; giving winter protection of litter. Under glass, pot ½ in. deep in pans, standard compost, good drainage, watering freely in growth, very moderately after flowering, almost dry in winter.

Propagation. By division when repotting.

Ox-eye. See *Buphthalmum*.

Ox-eye Daisy. See *Chrysanthemum leucanthemum*.

Oxlip. See *Primula vulgaris* × *P. vera*.

Oxy-. Prefix in compound words,

meaning sharp. Ex. *oxycarpus*, with sharp-pointed fruit.

Oxycoccus. See *Vaccinium*.

Oxydendrum (ocks-i-den'drum. Fam. Ericaceae). The one species, *O. arboreum*, the Sorrel-tree, to 15 ft or so, deciduous, with serrulate leaves, and drooping panicles of small whitish flowers, July–August, with attractive autumnal red foilage, is a native of the SE. U.S.A., and eligible for well-drained, lime-free, peaty soil, and warm shelter in mild localities; planted in autumn. Propagation is by imported seeds, spring; by cuttings of firm young shoots, July–August, in cold frame.

Oxyria (ocks'i-ri-a. Fam. Polygonaceae). The single species, *O. digyna*, is native, 1 ft, with heart- or kidney-shaped leaves, for salads, and useful as a Mountain Sorrel for rocky soils, being hardy and perennial. Easily raised from spring-sown seeds.

Oxytropis (ocks-i-tro'pis. Fam. Leguminosae). Hardy perennial sub-shrubs with unequally pinnate leaves, and small pea-like colourful flowers in axillary spikes or racemes.

Selection. O. campestris, Europe, Britain, to 6 in., cream, tinged purple flowers, July; *lambertii*, N. America, to 1 ft, rosy-carmine, summer; *montana*, Europe, 6 in., blue and purple, July; *pyrenaica*, Central Pyrenees, 4 in., sky-blue, summer; and *uralensis*, Ural Mts, 4 in., pale purple, summer.

Cultivation. Plant March–April, any well-drained, porous soil in rock garden or terrace.

Propagation. By division in spring; by seeds sown where the plants are to grow, April.

Oyster, Vegetable. See Salsify.

Ozothamnus. Now included in Helichrysum (q.v.).

P

Pachy-. Prefix in compound words meaning thick, Ex. *Pachyphyllous.* thick-leaved; *Pachyphytum*, with thickened leaves and stems.

Pachyphytum (pa-ki-pi'tum. Fam. Crassulaceae). Beautiful Mexican succulents, akin to Echeverias, with thickish stems and leaves, white with meal, flowering freely.

Selection. P. bracteosum, Silver Bract, bright red flowers, spring; *oviferum*, Sugar Almond Plant, carmine and white flowers, June; *uniflorum*, tall-growing, red.

Cultivation. Pot in March–April, standard compost; give sun, air and liberal watering in summer; little in winter; in cold greenhouse or indoors.

Propagation. By cuttings or detached leaves, spring.

Pachysandra (pa-ki-san'dra. Fam. Buxaceae). Evergreen low-growing shrubby plants, useful for ground cover in shady places and under trees.

Selection. P. axillaris, China, 6 in., white flowers, April; and *terminalis*, Japan, 1 ft, greenish-white flowers, April; and v. *variegata*, white marked leaves, good carpeter.

Cultivation. Plant October or March–April, peaty or leafy loam, in shady places.

Propagation. By division in spring.

Paederota. Now included in *Veronica* (q.v.).

Paeonia, Peony (pe-o'ni-a. Fam. Ranunculaceae). A genus of magnificent flowering perennials, hardy and desirable for almost every garden.

Selection. It is convenient to divide the genus into herbaceous and shrubby peonies.

Herbaceous Peonies. Plants with large, much divided leaves, often tinted in autumn, and flowering in May–July. *P. cambessedesii*, Balearic Is., 1½ ft, rose-pink, May; for a sunny wall or among shrubs; *emodi*, NW. India, 2½ ft, white

April; *lactiflora*, China, Siberia, 2 ft, white, June; *mascula*, Europe, 2 ft, deep rose, May; *mlokosewitschi*, Caucasus, 1½ ft, yellow, April; *officinalis*, Europe, 2 ft, red, and double-flowering forms *albo-plena*, white, *rosea plena*, rose, and *rubra plena*, crimson; *obovata* v. *willmottiae*, Siberia, China, 1½ ft, white; *peregrina*, Balkans, 3 ft, red, May; *russi*, Corsica, Sardinia, 1 ft, rose, May; *tenuifolia*, Caucasus, 1–2 ft, fern-leaved, deep crimson, May; *veitchii*, China, magenta, June, and v. *woodwardii*, rose-pink dwarf form; and *wittmanniana*, Causcasus, 3 ft, yellow, April, are, except where stated, single-flowering. The host of garden border peonies in named forms are derived chiefly from *P. lactiflora* and include: double-flowering, 'Adolphe Rosseau', dark red; 'Cleopatra', shell-pink; 'Duchess de Nemours', white; 'Édouard André', carmine; *edulis superba*, silvery pink; 'Felix Crousse', rose-red; *festiva maxima*, white, flecked crimson; 'Jeanne d'Arc', lilac pink; 'Lady Leonora Bramwell', silvery rose; 'Marie Crousse', salmon-pink; 'Mons. Martin Cahuzac', purple-garnet; 'Mrs F. D. Roosevelt', light pink; 'Philomele', satiny rose; 'President F. D. Roosevelt', dark pink; 'Sarah Bernhardt', apple-blossom pink; and 'Solange', white to buff; Anemone-flowering, with a centre of contrasting coloured petaloids, 'Akalu', carmine; 'Ama-no-Sode', rose-pink; 'Geisha', bright red; 'King of England', carmine; 'Lemon Queen', creamy yellow; 'Mikado', red; 'Orion', crimson; 'Ruigegno', light red; and 'Yeso', white; and single-flowering, 'Balliol', maroon-red; 'Defender', claret-red; 'Elena', coral pink; 'L'Étincelante', deep rose; 'Pink Delight', soft rose; 'Pride of Langport', rose-pink; 'The Bride', white; and 'The Moor', deep maroon-crimson. Many others are offered by specialist growers and raisers.

Cultivation. Herbaceous peonies may

be planted October–March; preferably in well-drained, humus-rich loam of pH 6·5. Thin soils need breaking up and liberally manuring; heavy soils opening up with gypsum, lime and organic matter. The plants are better staked in growth, and given liquid manure feeding when in bud. It is wise to clear spent stems and foliage in autumn, top-dress with well-rotted manure or compost and bone meal.

Propagation. By seeds in April, on prepared bed. By division of old crowns in autumn or February–March.

Shrubby Peonies. Mistakenly described as Tree peonies, the deciduous woody species seldom exceed 6–8 ft.

Selection. P. delavayi, China, to 5 ft, dark red, May; × *lemoinei,* yellow, to 4 ft, and vs. 'Alice Harding', double canary-yellow; 'Souvenir de Maxime Cornu', bright yellow, edged carmine; *lutea,* China, Tibet, to 4½ ft, yellow, May, and hybrids 'Argosy', single yellow; 'Chromatella', double, sulphur-yellow; and 'Madame Louis Henry', carmine; and *suffruticosa,* The Moutan Peony, China, Tibet, to 6 ft, rose-pink to white, May, which has given rise to many forms or hybrids such as 'Bijou de Chusan', double white, shaded pink; *fragrans maxima plena,* double salmon pink; 'Madame Stuart Low', double salmon red; 'Souvenir d'Étienne Mechin' china-rose, double; and 'Yano Okima', semi-double white, among many others.

Cultivation. Plant October–February, good loam soil, humus-rich and well-drained, setting grafted plants with the graft union 6 in. below soil level. Although quite hardy, shrubby peonies start into growth rather early, and should be planted on walls or in quarters sheltered from spring frosts and cold cutting winds. Young plants need 3–5 years to come to flowering, but are long-lived and very rewarding later.

Propagation. By cuttings of young shoots, taken with a heel, July–August, in cold frame or pots. Species by seeds sown in April, in pots, cold greenhouse or frame.

Diseases. Herbaceous peonies suffer from a fungus disease (*Botrytis paeoniae*) which rots leaves and young buds. Remove infected growth, mulch plants with sawdust in winter, spray with

copper fungicide as young shoots develop in April–May.

Pagoda-tree. See *Sophora japonica.*

Paliurus (pa-li-u'rus. Fam. Rhamnaceae). The chief species grown is *P. spina-Christi (aculeatus),* a hardy, deciduous shrub of Central Europe and the Middle East, to 10 ft, prickly with pairs of spines, one straight, one curved, greenish-yellow flowers in umbels, July, and winged fruits; by legend the plant from which the Crown of Thorns was made. May be planted in October–March, any ordinary well-drained soil, in full sun. Propagation by seeds in spring; or by layers in summer.

Pallidus (-a, -um). Pale. Ex. *Narcissus pallidus praecox.*

Palm, Date. See *Phoenix.*

Palma-christi. See *Ricinus communis.*

Palmatus (-a, -um). Palmate, handlike, having five lobes. Ex. *Acer palmatum.*

FIG. 170 Palmate leaf (*Acer palmatum* v.).

Palms. Woody perennial plants, of the tropics and sub-tropics, valued ornamentally for their fan-shaped or feather-veined foliage, and grown as pot plants indoors, in warm greenhouses and conservatories. See *Areca, Howea, Livistona, Phoenix, Trachycarpus.*

Palustris (-e). Growing in marshy areas. Ex. *Hottonia palustris.*

Pampas Grass. See *Cortaderia*.

Pan. (1) A shallow type of pot used chiefly for seed-sowing, or for growing certain alpines. (2) A hard layer of soil sometimes formed at cultivation depth by repeated ploughing or pressure of machines, which must be broken in the interests of drainage and fertility.

Pancratium (pan-kra′ti-um. Fam. Amaryllidaceae). Very beautiful white flowering bulbous plants, sometimes called Sea Daffodils.

Selection. P. canariense, Canary Is., 1½ ft, with flowers 3 in. across, May–June, needs a cool greenhouse; *illyricum*, S. Europe, 1½ ft, fragrant flowers, May–June; and *maritimum*, S. Europe, 2 ft, very fragrant umbels of flowers, June; may be attempted out of doors on warm borders in mild districts, but are also greenhouse-grown.

Cultivation. Pot in March, repot every fourth year, 4–5 in. deep, standard compost; water freely in growth, ample sun, dry off gradually after flowering, stand outdoors June–September; water very moderately in winter, minimum temp. 10° C. (50° F.).

Propagation. By offsets when repotting.

Pandanus, Screw Pine (pan-dan′us. Fam. Pandanaceae). A genus of tropical plants, chiefly grown as pot plants for their handsome evergreen foliage, made up of long, linear pointed leaves, which are spirally arranged, to inspire their common name.

Selection. P. baptistii, New Britain, leaves with white lines; *candelabrum* v. *variegatum*, W. Africa, bright green, banded white leaves; *sanderi*, Timor, leaves banded yellow; and *veitchii*, Polynesia, green leaves, bordered silvery-white.

Cultivation. Pot in March, compost of sandy loam and leaf-mould in equal parts, with a little charcoal; water freely during growth in sunny position, but little in winter, minimum temp. 10° C. (50° F.).

Propagation. By offsets or suckers detached in spring, inserted in a propagating frame and kept close until rooted; gentle bottom heat of 15·5° C. (60° F.).

Panicle. A raceme or corymb that branches.

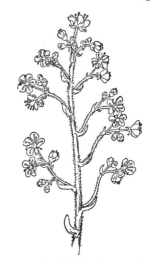

FIG. 171   Panicle (*Saxifraga umbrosa*).

Paniculatus (-a, -um). Pamiculate, arranged in panicles. Ex. *Campanula paniculata*.

Panicum (pan′ik-um. Fam. Gramineae). A large genus of grasses, some of ornamental grace.

Selection. P. capillare (*violaceum*), northern hemisphere, 1–1½ ft, is a hardy annual with long, silky spikelets, to be sown, March–April, where it is to grow; *virgatum*, U.S.A., 2–6 ft, a perennial hardy for all but the coldest localities, is stiff-stemmed with branched purplish spikelets, for sun and well-drained soil; but *palmifolium*, E. Indies, 4–6 ft, with inch-wide, lanceolate leaves, and long narrow panicles, and v. *niveo-vittatum*, with white-striped leaves, are evergreen perennials requiring a warm greenhouse; being potted in 8-in. pots, standard compost, in spring; watered freely in warm weather months; very moderately in winter, minimum temp. 10° C. (50° F.).

Propagation. Of perennials by division in spring; in a propagating case or frame.

Pansy. See *Viola*.

Papaver, Poppy (pa-pa′ver. Fam. Papaveraceae). The Poppies include easily grown annuals, biennials and perennials, distinctive for their crinkled, papery petalled flowers, bright colours, and milky sap.

Selection. Annuals are hardy and include *P. commutatum*, Asia Minor, to 1½ ft, red flowers with black blotch, summer; *glaucum*, Tulip Poppy, Asia Minor, 1½ ft, scarlet, May–July; *pavoninum*, Peacock Poppy, Central Asia, 1 ft, scarlet, summer; *rhoeas*, Corn Poppy, 1½ ft, and its single-flowering 'Shirley' strain in various shades, the double-flowering 'Ryburgh' hybrids, and 'Begonia-flowered' forms; and *somniferum*, the Opium Poppy, 1–2 ft, finely developed in the forms 'Daneborg', scarlet with white central cross; 'Carnation-flowered' and 'Peony-flowered' in various colours; 'Pink Beauty' is a fine selection. Strictly perennial, *P. nudicaule*, the Iceland Poppy of sub-arctic regions, 6 in., is usually grown as a biennial for the rock garden, and has good forms in 'Coonoara', 'Golden Monarch', 'Kelmscott', 'Red Cardinal' and 'Tangerine'; while *P. triniifolium*, Asia Minor, 1 ft, is truly biennial, with pale scarlet summer flowers. The chief perennials include *P. alpinum*, Carpathian Alps, 8 in., in white, yellow, red summer flowering forms for the rock garden; *orientale*, Oriental Poppy of Armenia, 2½–3 ft, large scarlet flowers, May–June, and its forms 'Enchantress', crimson-pink; 'Marcus Perry', orange-scarlet; 'Mrs Perry', shrimp pink; 'Perry's White' and 'Salmon Queen'; *pilosum*, Asia Minor, 3 ft, orange-scarlet, summer; and *rupifragum*, Spain, 1½ ft, brick-red, early summer.

Cultivation. Annuals are sown where they are to flower, well-drained lightish loam, and sun, and thinned; early spring; biennials may be sown in June–July, and perennials at the same time, on seedbeds of light loam, to transplant to flowering positions in September.

Propagation. Perennials may be propagated by root cuttings, about 3 in. long, taken in autumn.

Paradichlorbenzene. A white crystalline solid used as a soil insecticide or fumigant to control Wireworms, Slugs, Springtails and soil-frequenting insects; dropped in holes 12 in. apart, 9 in. deep, at 1 teaspoonful per 6 holes, six weeks prior to sowing or planting.

Paradisea(pa-ra-dis'i-a.Fam.Liliaceae).

The one species, *P. liliastrum*, St Bruno's Lily, S. Europe, 1–2 ft, is reasonably hardy, perennial, with a short rhizome-root, and carries white, scented, bell-shaped flowers in a loose spike in June; v. *major*, to 4 ft, is larger in every way. Plant in October, light, well-drained, humus-rich soil, cool sun or partial shade; and propagate by division.

Paraffin. *See* Petroleum Oils.

Paraquilegia (pa-ra-kwi-le'gi-a. Fam. Ranunculaceae). The species chiefly grown, *P. anemonoides* (*grandiflora*), 3 in., is a Chinese perennial of rare beauty, with large, cupped, white to lavender flowers on slender stalks from rosettes of ternatisect leaves in May; for the alpine house; potted in spring, standard compost, very good drainage, watered with care to avoid waterlogging; and propagated by seed when ripe.

Parasite. An animal or plant that lives on or in another animal or plant, feeding on its host.

Parasitic Plants. Plants which grow on and in other plants (hosts) to derive their food in whole or part. Usually such plants are devoid of chlorophyll. They include bacteria and fungi, and flowering parasites such as Dodder (*Cuscuta*), Broomrape (*Orobanche*) and Toothwort (*Lathraea*); while other plants, possessing some chlorophyll, are only partially parasitic, such as Mistletoe (*Viscum*) and Yellow-rattle (*Rhinanthus*).

Parathion. The first organophosphorous insecticidal compound formulated, but unfortunately highly toxic, and of limited use, under strict conditions, in the garden, chiefly to control leaf miners and Chrysanthemum Eelworm infestation. Protective clothing, rubber gloves and a face-shield or mask should be worn during application.

Parenchyma (pa-ren-ki'ma). A tissue composed of cells containing protoplasm, nuclei and watery sap.

Pari-. A prefix in compound words meaning equal. Ex. paripinnate, with an even number of pinnae.

Parietal. *See* Placenta.

Paris Daisy. See *Chrysanthemum frutescens.*

Paris Green. Copper aceto-arsenite, is a highly toxic arsenical compound, may be used as a powder-bait, mixed with dried blood or fine bran, to control slugs and soil-frequenting insects; but is largely superseded by metaldehyde, gamma-BHC and preparations less toxic and dangerous to humans and animals.

Parnassia (par-nas'si-a. Fam. Saxifragaceae). Perennial herbs for moist, boggy places. *P. palustris*, Common Grass of Parnassus, northern hemisphere including Britain, 6 in., with white, green-veined, single flowers, summer, may be grown from seeds sown in April–July in moist, peaty soil, and propagated by division in spring.

Parochetus, Shamrock Pea (pa-ro'ketus. Fam. Leguminosae). The one species, *P. communis*, Himalaya, is a prostrate trailing perennial, with clover-like leaves, and pea-like, azure-blue flowers, summer and autumn, for moist, warm, well-drained soil and sun in the rock garden of mild localities or as a pot or basket plant in the cool greenhouse or alpine house. Propagation by cuttings or rooted pieces, July.

Paronychia (pa-ro-nik'i-a. Fam. Caryophyllaceae). Small carpeting perennials of the Mediterranean region, notable for the silvery-white bracts surrounding their inconspicuous flowers.

Selection. P. argentea, mat-forming, 2 in., silvery bracts, July; *capitata*, similar with green foliage, and white bracted flowers; *kapela*, 3–4 in., silver-white bracts, May–June; and *serpyllifolia*, roundish leaves, silvery bracted flowers, June.

Cultivation. Plant April, light, well-drained soil, sunny warm positions in rock gardens; or alpine house.

Propagation. By division in April.

Parrotia (par-rot'i-a. Fam. Hamamelidaceae). A genus of two small, hardy, deciduous trees, with strongly parallel-veined leaves, handsome for modern gardens.

Selection. P. jacquemontiana, Himalaya, 16–20 ft, roundish, ovate leaves, and yellow-stamened flowers, surrounded by white bracts, April–June; and *persica*, N. Persia, 30 ft. distinctive for its autumnal golden, crimson and yellow foliage, and small, red-anthered, clustered early spring flowers.

Cultivation. Plant October–March, well-drained loam soil, with some lime, sunny position. Prune to shape only, after flowering.

Propagation. By air-layering in spring. By seeds sown in April, out of doors; slow-growing.

Parrot's Bill. See *Clianthus puniceus.*

Parsley (*Petroselinum crispum*). A hardy biennial herb, extremely rich in ascorbic acid (vitamin C), iron and other health-protective nutrients; native to the Mediterranean region, but introduced to Britain about 1500.

Varieties. 'Imperial', 'Moss-curled' and 'Giant-curled' give largest, long-stalked leaves; 'Dwarf Perfection', 'Myatt's Garnishing' are hardy; 'French', the best flavoured.

Cultivation. Sow out of doors in well-dug, humus-rich soil, provided with lime (pH 6–6·5), and light dressing of a complete fertilizer, in March for summer use; in July for winter; ½ in. deep, in drills 1 ft apart, thinning seedlings to 6 in. apart; germination may take 3–4 weeks. May also be sown in boxes under glass in February to transplant outdoors in April, taking care to preserve the tap-root intact. Pick leaves for drying in July–September, fairly quickly at 44° C. (120° F.).

Parsley, Hamburgh (*Petroselinum crispum* v. *fusiformis*). A variety of Parsley grown for its fleshy, tapering, parsnip-like roots, in the same way as for parsnips (q.v.), for culinary use in the same manner; wrongly termed turnip-rooted.

Parsnip (*Peucedanum sativum*). A hardy biennial vegetable, native to Siberia, Europe and Britain, and grown for its highly nutritious, sweet, fleshy tapered roots.

Varieties. 'Improved Hollow Crown' and 'Tender and True' for long exhibition roots; 'Lisbonnais', 'Offenham', 'The Student' for medium-sized roots; 'Intermediate' for shallow soils.

Cultivation. Sow February–April, well-dug, humus-rich (but not recently manured), soil, with lime (pH 6·5); ½ in. deep, drills 15 in. apart, thinning plants to 9 in, apart: *or* make 3-ft. deep holes with a crowbar, fill with good sifted soil or sandy loam, sow with three seeds, removing the two weaker seedlings later, leaving single plants about 15–18 in. apart. Roots may be lifted as required in winter; or lifted in October and stored cool in boxes, layered in sand. Diseases are seldom serious, but Canker or splitting of the shoulders of the roots suggests unsuitable soil conditions, such as too rich, too little lime, or too much variation in moisture conditions. Celery Fly or Leaf Miner (*Acidia heraclei*) may attack parsnips, and attacks should be checked by the use of a malathion insecticide.

Parterre. A French way of planting flower-beds on level ground to embroidery or tapestry patterns, or a formal garden of patterned beds.

Parthenocarpy. The production of fruits without the fertilization of the ovules, as in Cucumbers.

Parthenocissus (par-then-o-kis′sus. Fam. Vitaceae). Deciduous ornamental-leaved climbing plants, with tendrils either self-clinging by their tips or twining; often listed under *Ampelopsis* or *Vitis* to which they are closely related.

Selection. P. (Vitis) henryana, China, tall, self-clinging, purplish-green, marked silver and pink, leaves; *himalayana* (*Ampelopsis himalayana*), Himalaya, China, very tall, self-clinging, dark green, rich red in autumn, leaves; *quinquefolia* (*Ampelopsis q., Vitis q.*), true Virginia Creeper, eastern N. America, very tall, self-clinging, large leaves, crimson in autumn; *thomsonii* (*Vitis t.*), slender, tendril twining, China, purplish leaves, reddening in autumn; *tricuspidata* (*Ampelopsis veitchii, Vitis inconstans*), China, Japan, tall, quick-growing, self-clinging, most popular for autumnal red and scarlet tints; v. *lowii* with elegant palmate leaves, and 'Beverley Brook', dainty and small leaved; and *vitacea*, Virginia Creeper, N. America, twining, and large-leaved.

Cultivation. Plant October–March, any reasonably well-drained soil, humus-enriched; self-clinging kinds on walls, any aspect; twining kinds on pergolas. Prune after planting to induce branching low down.

Propagation. By layering in spring; by cuttings of young firm shoots, July–August, under handlight.

Parthenogenesis. The production of seeds in a plant without fertilization (e.g. Dandelions); or the reproduction in animals without fertilization as with certain Aphids, when males are absent.

Partridge Berry. See *Gaultheria procumbens.*

Parvus (-a, -um); Parvi-. Small. Ex. *Aesculus parviflora.*

Pasque Flower. See *Pulsatilla vulgaris.*

Passiflora, Passion Flower (pas-si-flo′ra. Fam. Passifloraceae). A large genus of tropical or subtropical plants, chiefly climbing by tendrils.

Selection. P. caerulea, central and western S. America, when introduced in 1699, had some religious significance imparted to it, in that the parts of the plant were likened to the articles used at the crucifixion of Jesus Christ, the leaf, the Roman soldier's spear; the tendrils, the cords and scourge; the ovary column (gynophore), the pillar of the Cross; the anthers, the hammer; the styles, the

FIG. 172 The flower of *Passiflora caerulea*, Passion Flower.

nails; the corona of filaments or rays, the Crown of Thorns; the white of the petals representing purity, and the blue, heaven; it is hardy, and semi-evergreen on warm, sheltered, sunny walls in the south and west; with fragrant flowers from June to September; 'Constance Elliott' is an ivory-white flowering form; and has a hybrid × *allardii*, with pink-shaded, white flowers. In favourable years they may ripen orange, oval fruits. Other species need warm greenhouse shelter, and include *P. antioquiensis*, Colombia, large rose-red flowers, summer; *edulis*, the Granadilla, greenish, white flowers, with edible sweet yellow or purple fruits to follow; *incarnata*, May Apple, or May

Pops, SE. U.S.A., white and pale blue flowers, summer, yellow oval fruits; *quadrangularis*, the Granadilla of tropical America, white, pink, and violet flowers, late summer, and large ovoid, sweet-acid fruits; and *racemosa*, Brazil, rose-crimson racemes of flowers, June–July; and hybrids.

Cultivation. Out of doors, plant October or April, well-drained, warm, humus-rich soil, sunny, sheltered walls. In the warm greenhouse, plant in March, large pots or borders, well enriched with rotted manure, compost or peat, and organic fertilizer; water liberally, syringe often in active growth; keep fairly dry in winter, minimum temp. 10° C. (50° F.); pollinate flowers for fruit.

Propagation. By cuttings of young firm shoots in July, in a propagating frame, potting when rooted. By seeds in pots, standard compost, bottom heat of 18° C. (65° F.), in spring, under glass.

Passion Flower. See *Passiflora*.

Patens, Patenti-. Spreading. Ex. *Salvia patens*.

Pathology. The study of diseases.

Paths. Being permanent, paths need planning with care, not only to give ready access to a garden but to befit its design and be aesthetically pleasing. Simple directness, and gentle curves, free from tortuousness, are best. A width of at least 33 in. is desirable for use by barrow, and 5 ft for two people walking side by side. Basic construction calls for a firm foundation suited to the traffic to be borne. An excavation 3–6 in deep, which is then packed with hard-core (broken brick, stone, clinker, etc.), firmed and levelled to receive the surface finish. Drainage on heavy soils can be arranged by sloping the foundation aggregate to the centre, where a line of 4-in. soil drainage pipes is laid with a fall of 1 in 200 to a suitable outlet. *Gravel paths* are cheap, long-lasting, good-looking, easily maintained, and made of pea-sized gravel or stone chippings, 1½–2 in. thick, well tamped down. For greater firmness, the top layer can be secured with a cold bitumen emulsion. *Asphalt paths* of the old-styled tar-macadam or tarred stone chippings, or the modern product of a petroleum bitumen and stone chippings, are neat, but suggestive of the municipal park, and usually need

surface renovation every few years. *Concrete paths* can be bare and harsh-looking, unless broken by pigmenting, pattern or strip-insertions, but a pleasing variant is to set suitable stone flints or pebbles in the concrete. *Paved paths* call for a hard-core foundation, topped by sand, on which such materials as stone-flags, concrete slabs, bricks or crazy paving may be laid. In actual laying, a cement mortar (3 parts by volume clean sand, 1 part cement, well mixed, with water added, to form a plastic mixture) is used, a small heap being placed at the corner of the flag before firming and levelling in position with straight-edge and spirit level. The interstices, except where space is left for suitable dwarf plants, may be pointed with the cement mortar. It is always advantageous to line paths at each side with edging boards of inch-thick preservatively treated boards, precast concrete kerbing, slates, tiles or metal. See *Concrete in Garden Making*, by the Cement and Concrete Association, 52 Grosvenor Gardens, London. S.W. 1. *Grass paths* may be made to connect different parts of the garden, but where traffic is heavy it is often more practical to sink stone flags or concrete slabs in stepping-stone fashion, with centres 33 in. apart, in the grass at surface level to take the weight of the traffic and avoid bare earth patches.

Patulus (-a, -um). Somewhat spreading, open. Ex. *Tagetes patula*.

Paucus (-a, -um), Pauci-. Few. Ex. *Polemonium pauciflorum*.

Paulownia (paw-low'ni-a. Fam. Scrophulariaceae). Deciduous trees from China, notable for their June panicles of foxglove-like, drooping flowers, formed in the bud in autumn, and all too apt to be injured in capricious winters, though the trees are hardy.

Selection. *P. lilacina*, to 40 ft, large ovate leaves, pale lilac, yellow-throated flowers; *tomentosa*, to 45 ft, long-stalked, tri-lobed leaves, heliotrope flowers; and *fargesii*, to 60 ft, fragrant heliotrope flowers, from youth.

Cultivation. Plant October–March, good loam soil, sheltered position out of the wind, but in full sun.

Propagation. Usually by seeds sown in April, warm seed-bed.

Paving. *See* Paths.

Pavoninus (-a, -um). Peacock-like, peacock-blue. Ex. *Tigridia pavonia.*

Pea (*Pisum sativum*). The origins of the edible green pea are not precisely known, though thought to be in western Asia and to go back some 4,000 years. Its development as we know it today, however, only began in the seventeenth to the nineteenth century, especially at the beginning of the latter when the first wrinkled marrowfat variety was raised.

Varieties. These are numerous, and may be divided into round and semi-round seeded varieties, considered the more hardy for early sowings; and the wrinkled-seeded, yielding the sweeter and heavier crops. Dwarf Early, round-seeded: 'Feltham First', 1½ ft; 'Feltham Advance', 2 ft; 'Forward', 2 ft; 'Meteor', 1½ ft; 'Early Superb', 2 ft. Dwarf Early, wrinkled-seeded: 'Cloche Wonder', 2 ft; 'Little Marvel', 1½ ft; 'Kelvedon Wonder', 1½ ft; 'Kelvedon Triumph', 1½ ft; 'Progress', 1¼ ft. Tall Early, round-seeded: 'British Lion', 4 ft; 'Improved Pilot', 3 ft; 'Foremost', 3 ft. Tall Early, wrinkled-seeded: 'Provost', 3½ ft. Second Early, wrinkled-seeded: 'Giant Stride', 2½ ft; 'Kelvedon Monarch', 2¼ ft; 'Kelvedon Spitfire', 2 ft; 'Onward', 2 ft; 'Senator', 4 ft; 'The Lincoln', 2 ft. Maincrop: 'Alderman', 5 ft; 'Chancelot', 3 ft; 'Quite Content', 5 ft; 'Histon Maincrop', 2½ ft; 'Senator', 4 ft. Late Crop: 'Autocrat', 4 ft; 'Gladstone', 4 ft. Edible-podded, Sugar Varieties: 'Dwarf Sugar', 2 ft; 'Pois Mangetout', 5 ft; 'Sweetpod', 1½ ft; 'Asparagus Pea', 1¼ ft.

Cultivation. Peas need a well-dug soil, rich in humus from a previously organic-manured crop; containing lime to give a pH of about 6·5, and to be pre-fertilized with a high phosphate compound such as 1 part by weight dried blood, 3 parts superphosphate, 1 part sulphate of potash, at 2 oz. per sq. yd, and should not lack moisture in growth, being well mulched. Seeds are sown outdoors in flat-bottomed drills, 2 in. deep, 2–3 in. apart. Early sowings in February in mild localities; mid March for other districts; with successional sowings of Second Early and Maincrop varieties in May; Late varieties in June. Autumn sowings of early round-seeded varieties

may be tried in mild localities. With cloches, January sowings are often possible. It is wise to dress seeds with a 'Thiram' fungicidal, and 'Lindane' insecticidal dust, to avoid trouble from soil fungi and pests. Birds can be kept away from the vital germinating period by stringing twine soaked in a modern bird repellent over the sowings. Slugs may need deterring with a metaldehyde bait; mice by the use of Warfarin. Plants should be staked when about 4 in. high, with brushwood pea-sticks, or plastic netting, well secured to supporting stakes After cropping, the top haulms should be cut away; the roots left to rot and en-rich the soil with nitrogen.

Peas Under Glass. Varieties such as 'Cloche Wonder', 'Little Marvel', 'Eight Weeks' and 'Kelvedon Wonder' may be sown, 8–10 seeds per 10- or 12-in. pot, filled with a compost of 2 parts by vol-ume loam, 1 part rotted manure or leaf-mould and a little sand and pea fertilizer; from mid November to February; though higher yields would come from sowings of 'Improved Pilot', 'Gradus' or 'Thomas Laxton' made in the soil borders; with minimum winter temp. of 10° C. (50° F.).

Diseases. Poor germination is avoided by not sowing under wet conditions, and dressing seeds against damping-off and foot-rot infections. Powdery Mildew (*Erysiphe polygoni*) may attack late in the season, but may be controlled by applying a karathane or colloidal sulphur fungicide. Virus infection may cause a mosaic or yellow mottling of leaves, and affected plants should be promptly destroyed. The presence of dark reddish spots in the centre of a ripe peas indicates a manganese defi-ciency, and is termed Marsh Spot; calling for the application of manganese sul-phate at 1½ oz. per gallon water, and a watering of plants before they come into full flower.

Pests. Weevils (*Sitona* spp.) may scallop the edges of seedling leaves, and should be countered by applying a gamma-BHC insecticide. Thrips (*Kako-thrips pisivorous*) cause silvery marks on pea pods under dry conditions, and may be controlled by a malathion or Derris insecticide, but not within two days of picking. Aphids (Greenfly) should be promptly wetted or dusted with a derris insecticide. The Pea Moth (*Cydia nigricana*) lays her eggs on the sepals of developing pods to hatch into larvae which bore into the pods to feed on the peas; an infestation which may be averted by spraying with wettable Derris a week after flowering begins. Where birds raid ripening crops, netting is the sure preventive; scares are of initial but limited success.

Pea, Everlasting. See *Lathyrus latifolius*.

Pea, Glory. See *Clianthus*.

Pea, Lord Anson's. See *Lathyrus magellanicus*.

Pea, Sweet. *See* Sweet Pea.

Peach and Nectarine (*Prunus persica*). The Peach is now held to have its origins in China, and the Nectarine a variety of it differing in having smooth-skinned, slightly different flavoured fruits and a rather less vigorous constitution. Horticulturally they require similar culture. They are hardy enough for outdoor growth in many gardens, but as they flower early they are vulnerable to frost and low temperatures which damage the flowers or prevent fertilization; and need either the shelter of a warm wall or glass in areas susceptible to frosts in the early months of the year. Experience has shown that they can often be grown in the open as bush trees in many areas, given freedom from blossom-impairing early spring frosts.

Varieties. Peaches—early, July–early August: Alexander, Amsden June,* Dr Hogg, Duke of York,* Hale's Early,* Peregrine,*: mid season, August–early September: Crimson Galande,* Dymond, Prince of Wales, Royal George, Violette Hative; late, mid September–early October: Barrington,* Bellegarde,* Golden Eagle, Princess of Wales, Sea Eagle*. Nectarines–early, July–mid August: Early Rivers,* John Rivers,* Lord Napier,* Late, late August–September: Elruge,* Hardwicke,* Pineapple,* Pitmaston Orange,* Victoria*.

*Denotes varieties suitable for outdoors.

Propagation. Selected varieties are budded on to rootstocks of Plum; Brompton for large vigorous trees; Common Mussel for medium-sized trees; but it is becoming more popular to use seedling peach rootstocks as giving the more robust and healthy trees, especially for outdoor bush specimens.

Planting. Both outdoors and under glass, the best time to plant is October–December.

Cultivation: Bush Trees Out of Doors. Plant trees 15–18 ft apart in rows 30 ft apart, in sunny, open position, out of frost-reach and on eastern, northern or western slopes, if possible. There is no greater virtue in a southern slope if its sunny aspect brings the flowers out too early. A well-drained soil, well stocked with humus-forming organic matter, of pH 6·0–6·5, is desirable. A pre-planting dressing, of 4 parts by weight bone meal and 1 part sulphate of potash at 2 to 3 oz. per sq. yd, is helpful. The newly planted bush tree should be pruned in February, shortening all shoots by one-half their length; and again in late May–early June to remove any die-back. In the second and subsequent years, pruning is done only in late May–early June, to shape the tree to a cup-like formation, removing die-back, weak shoots, inward growing shoots, and curtailing others according to vigour and the fruitlets they carry. Older trees, flagging in vigour, may be pruned hard, but in spring, never in winter. When fruiting, the crop must be thinned, to leave single fruitlets spaced 4–8 in. apart, after pruning.

Fan-shaped Trees on Walls. The training of peach and nectarine trees requires not only skill but much time each year. Trees tend to flower earlier in the shelter of walls, and protection from possible frost damage is often needed. Tradition rules that planting on south or west walls is best; experience indicates that these are the most frost-susceptible, and there is no practical reason why east or northerly walls should not be utilized, given some wind-shelter. Plant in well-dug, free-draining soil, enriched as for bush trees, spacing trees 18 ft apart. Make provision for training by wires, fixed horizontally, 6 in. apart, 4 in. from the wall surface, on vine-eyes. Plant October–December, placing base of tree 9 in. from the wall, slightly tilted to the wall. It is best to plant a 2- or 3-year-old tree with two or more lateral shoots of the fan in being, which are tied to canes, in turn fastened fanwise to the support wires. In late February, the branching shoots are cut back to a triple bud, about half way along their length or 20–30 in. from their base. In summer, the end bud is allowed to make the extension growth of the branch, and two suitably placed shoots may be allowed to develop to increase the branches of the fan, all other buds being rubbed off. The new branches are shortened again the following February if further extension of the fan is required. Thereafter, when the fan is established, pruning is only in spring and summer, bearing in mind that the fruit is borne on shoots of the previous year's growth; fruit buds can be distinguished by their full rounded shape from wood or shoot buds, which are pointed, but triple buds consisting of two blossom buds and a shoot bud are often formed. As soon as buds begin to grow, shoot buds facing to or away from the wall may be rubbed off; young shoots of the previous year's growth, carrying both blossom and shoot buds, then need attention; the end buds are allowed to grow out, the wood buds near the base are thinned to one or two which will give a replacement shoot; the blossom buds are left intact, and shoots growing out adjacent to them are pinched back to two leaves and any secondary growth to one leaf later. This disbudding and pinching-back is done over two to three weeks as the tree is making fresh active growth in spring. Shoots developing where there are no fruits should have the growing tips removed when about an inch long. Fruitlets should be thinned to one per station when about thumbnail size, and again after stoning to 8–9 in. apart, when walnut-size, choosing fruits well placed to the front of shoots with room to swell. In summer, if necessary, the extension shoot can be curtailed at the fifth leaf, and secondary growth at the first leaf. After harvest, the shoot that has borne fruit is cut away at its base and the replacement new shoot trained to take its place.

Pollination. Normally peaches are self-fertile and set their own fruit, but where wall trees are given frost protection with nets, tiffany or covers, it is useful to pollinate when flowers are wide open about midday, by transferring pollen from one flower to another with a camel-hair brush or rabbit's scut.

Trained Trees Under Glass. It is doubtful whether it is really worth while devoting limited greenhouse space, time and labour to peaches and nectarines in the small garden, but where desired, the fan-shaped tree with short stem is best, trained on wires on the back wall of a tall lean-to or three-quarter span house, or a strong wire framework that parallels the glass at 9–12 in. from it. The training of the fan and the cultivation of the tree is similar to that given for the wall-trained outdoor tree. No great heat is required until February, when a temperature of 7–10° C. (45–50° F.) is adequate, and the soil border should be adequately watered. By early March, 10–15·5° C. (50–60° F.) may be maintained, with good ventilation during flowering, when plants should be pollinated as flowers become fully open. After fruit-setting, more heat (18° C. [65° F.]) may be given; the border watered and the tree syringed on hot days, until fruits are ripening, when syringing is discontinued. Ample ventilation is needed throughout summer, and moisture can be conserved with an organic mulch. Fruits should be picked perfectly ripe from the tree, lifting to sever with the fruit well held and cradled in the fingers and palm of the hand, without pressure on the flesh. In autumn, borders should be refurbished with a slow-acting organic fertilizer (bone meal, hoof and horn meal) and rotted manure or compost; and the trees wintered without heat, and only enough watering to prevent the soil border becoming dried out.

Diseases. The commonest disease is Leaf Curl, caused by a fungus, *Taphrina deformans*, which swells, puckers and discolours leaves yellowish and red in spring. Control calls for forceful spraying with either a sulphur or a copper fungicide in February–March when the buds are beginning to burst, so as to kill the spores which over-winter in the bud scales. Infected foliage should be burnt. Brown Rot (*Sclerotinia* spp.) may infect flowers and cause Blossom Wilt and Twig Blight, and/or fruits, but prompt destruction of infected parts will usually give adequate control. Silver Leaf (q.v.)

sometimes infects Peaches and Nectarines.

Pests. Aphids (*Anuraphis amygdali, Myzus persicae*) cause leaf-curling and damage foliage and flowers. Their over-wintering eggs should be destroyed by spraying with a tar-oil wash in December; and the insects by direct application of derris or nicotine or malathion. Peach Scale insects (*Lepidosaphes ulmi, Lecanium corni, Aspidiotus ostreaeformis*) sometimes infest the bark, but winter tar-oil washing controls them effectively. Red Spider Mites (*Tetranychus telarius*) infest peaches under glass in too dry conditions; requiring fumigation with an azobenzene insecticidal smoke.

Peacock Tiger Flower. See *Tigridia pavonia.*

Peanut. See *Arachis.*

Pear (*Pyrus communis*). The parent deciduous tree species from which the delectable European pears have been developed is a native of Britain, Europe and western Asia. Although long cultivated, pears are not so easily grown as apples; blossoming earlier, they need more careful placing, and require rather warmer, sunnier conditions to mature their fruits to perfection.

Site. Pears prefer well-sunned and warm sites, sheltered from strong winds, especially from the east and north; out of valleys or frost pockets. Fine quality, late-keeping dessert pears need shelter and warm sun, especially when ripening; and therefore do best in mild areas of the south, south-east and west of Britain. Under conditions of high rainfall, much cloud and cool temperatures only the hardier varieties of pears should be attempted.

Soil. Pears like a well-drained medium loam of some depth. Light porous soils need stiffening with clay and organic matter. They are least successful on thin light soils, over chalk or gravel, which dry out quickly; and on heavy clay soils or damp soils are prone to canker, and should not be planted where the ground is subject to winter waterlogging. Many soils can be amended by judicious cultivation, drainage, organic-manuring and liming to pH 6·0–6·5.

Rootstocks. Pear varieties are propagated by budding or grafting on quince rootstocks; East Malling Quince A (Angiers Quince) and Quince B (Common Quince) are used for trees of moderate vigour on most soils; and Quince C, which is moderately dwarfing, is suitable for good rich soils, strong-growing varieties and shy cropping varieties, but not for poor soils. Some pear varieties, notably Marie Benoist, Marie Louise, Joséphine de Malines, Dr Jules Guyot, Thompson's, Souvenir du Congrès and Williams's Bon Chrétien, are not fully compatible with quince stocks, and need to be double-worked, the rootstock first being united with a compatible variety (Beurré Hardy is often used) and this variety budded with the incompatible one. Selected seedling pear rootstocks may also be used.

Pear Tree Forms. Although the rootstocks used for pears are not as dwarfing as those used for apples, pears may be grown in the restricted trained forms of *Cordons,* the obliquely trained single cordon being most easily managed; as *Espaliers,* with three or four tiers of horizontal branches; as *Pyramids,* and as *Bush* trees for the small garden. The *Half-Standard* and *Standard* are more suited to orchard use. On the whole, pears tend to make larger plants than apples, to come into bearing less readily, to give lower yields of fruit, but to have longer fruiting lives.

Yields. Cordons may yield from 3 to 6 lb., on the average, more if conditions are very favourable and culture expert; pyramids from 12 to 15 lb.; and bush trees should average 30 to 40 lb., more with age and good culture.

Planting. Trees may be planted between October and March, given favourable soil and weather conditions; cordons 2–3 ft apart, in rows 6 ft apart; espaliers 12–18 ft apart, according to vigour of the rootstock; pyramids 3 ft apart, in rows 6 ft apart; and bushes 10–15 ft apart; in the same manner as for apples; with roots well spread, and soil firmed to them.

Choice of Varieties. Although pear varieties are numerous, the commercial grower in this country confines himself to less than half a dozen. The gardener's choice is wider, but should be guided by the suitability of varieties for his locality and soil, and their fertility. A selected short list of pears recommended for modern gardens is: *Dessert:* Early, ripening August–early September— Clapp's Favourite, Doyenne d'Été, Dr Jules Guyot, Jargonelle, Souvenir du Congrès, Williams's Bon Chrétien. Mid season, October–November—Beurré Hardy, Beurré Superfin, Bristol Cross, Conference, Comte de Lamy, Doyenne

or more diploid varieties of the same flowering period should be planted. When a triploid variety is planted, two or more diploid varieties should accompany it. Tetraploids, chiefly 'Double Williams' and 'Fertility Improved', are self-fertile. Recorded flowering periods are:

Early Flowering	Mid-season Flowering	Late Flowering
DIPLOID		
Beurré Giffard	Beurré Clairgeau	Beurré Hardy
Louise Bonne of Jersey	Beurré Superfin	Bristol Cross
Marguerite Marillat	Conference	Clapp's Favourite
	Durondeau	Dr Jules Guyot
	Émile d'Heyst	Doyenne du Comice
	Joséphine de Malines	Glou Morceau
	Souvenir du Congrès	Marie Louise
	Williams's Bon Chrétien	Winter Nelis
TRIPLOID		
Beurré Diel	Jargonelle	Catillac
Vicar of Winkfield		Pitmaston Duchess

du Comice, Durondeau, Émile d'Heyst, Fondante d'Automne, Louise Bonne of Jersey, Marie Louise, Thompson's. Late, November–January—Beurré Easter, Glou Morceau, Joséphine de Malines, Packham's Triumph, Winter Nelis. *Culinary:* Bellissime d'Hiver (late), Catillac (late); Hessle (mid season), Pitmaston Duchess (mid season).

Fertilization. Only a few pear varieties are self-fertile and capable of setting fruit with their own pollen, chiefly Conference and Durondeau, while Beurré Superfin, Bellissime d'Hiver, Louise Bonne of Jersey, Marguerite Marillat, Marie Louise, Dr Jules Guyot, Pitmaston Duchess and Williams's Bon Chrétien may set some fruit on their own and are partially self-fertile. All pears, however, bear better crops when cross-pollinated by compatible varieties, which flower at the same time, and which carry compatible sets of chromosomes. As with apples, pears vary in kind into diploid varieties, which have two sets of chromosomes (34 altogether), and with the exception of Marguerite Marillat carry good pollen; triploid varieties, with three sets of chromosomes (51); and tetraploids, with four sets (68). For cross-pollination, two

Manuring. For the first year after planting no feeding is necessary other than watering and an occasinal foliar feed-spraying. Pears need rather more nitrogen than apples, a little less potash. A top-dressing of rotted organic matter in autumn/winter can be followed by a mixture of, say, 1 part by weight hoof and horn meal, 1 part ammonium sulphate, 2 parts superphosphate and 1 part sulphate of potash at 2 oz. per sq. yd, in late winter; may be given annually. Too much vigorous growth can be checked by grassing over the roots.

Pruning. Pears are pruned on the same principles and in the same way as already given for Apples (q.v.). This means that winter-pruning is largely devoted to regulating the shape and branch framework; while summer pruning is largely concerned with fruitfulness. If anything, pears can be pruned somewhat more severely without stimulating over-vigorous growth reactions. The Lorette system of pruning is one of intensive summer pruning developed chiefly for warmer French conditions; and in this country its principles are modified and followed out in the summer pruning as laid down under Apples (q.v.).

Cropping. Pears are often able to carry heavier crops to maturity without impairing future fertility than apples. Nevertheless, for quality fruits it is best to thin a heavy crop in June–July to single fruits, spaced 6 in. apart.

Harvesting. Greater judgment is needed in harvesting pears than apples. Ripening varies according to the locality and the season, but normally early and mid season varieties should be gathereed a little before they become completely ripe on the tree, as soon as the fruit parts readily from the tree when lifted to the horizontal and given a slight twist. They are then placed under cool conditions for a few days until they colour and are ripe. Late varieties are picked when they can be easily parted from the tree, to be stored under cool, well-ventilated conditions at 5–7° C. (40–45° F.); preferably laid in single layers on slatted trays or shelves, unwrapped. They need watching as ripening proceeds, as they are at their best for only a short period.

DISEASES. On the whole, pears are less susceptible to diseases than apples, the chief being:

Bacterial Blossom Blight (Pseudomonas spp.) causes a wilting and withering of flower trusses when opening, and infected trusses should be promptly cut out, as there is no known chemical control.

Brown Rot (Sclerotinia laxa) may cause blossoms to wilt, or infect fruits, but is less prevalent when trees are winter-washed annually. Infected parts should be burnt, and a captan fungicide applied in spring.

Cankers (Nectria galligena, Phacidiella discolor). Badly cankered shoots should be cut out and burnt; cankers may be painted with a Canker Paint, and routine spring spraying helps.

Fire Blight (Erwinia amylovora). This bacterial disease is usually fatal to pear trees, and is notifiable to the Ministry of Agriculture. 'Laxton's Superb' is so susceptible that it is no longer recommended for planting. Symptoms are infected collapsing blossom trusses and spurs, cankered branches, leaves turning brown or black; trees look as if scorched by fire by midsummer, and must be burnt.

Mildew (Podosphaera leucotricha).

Whitens shoots and leaves in spring or summer; infected shoots should be cut away, and spraying carried out with karathane.

Scab (Venturia pyrina). Although caused by a different species than Apple Scab, Pear Scab requires similar control to prevent shoots, foliage and fruits becoming spotted olive-green to dark brown spotted and blotched, preferably by spring spraying with a captan or thiram fungicide, instead of lime-sulphur.

PESTS. The most common parasites of pears are:

Aphids or *Greenfly (Aphis pomi, Dysaphis mali, Anuraphis kochi).* Less important than on apples, pear aphids may be controlled by winter tar-oil washing every second year to kill their eggs, or spring spray at bud burst.

Blossom Weevil (Anthonomus pomorum) causes capped brown blossoms as in Apples (q.v.), and is controlled by DDT at bud burst (March) in the same way.

Capsid Bug (Lygus pabulinus) causes brownish-black spots on young leaves, and pitted corky tissue in fruits; but may be controlled by gamma-BHC insecticide in spring, or nicotine later as on Apples (q.v.).

Caterpillars of Gold Tail Moth *(Leucoma chrysorrhoea),* Lackey Moth *(Malacosoma neustria),* March Moth *(Erannis aescularia),* Winter Moth *(Operophtera brumata)* and Tortrix Moths *(Cacoecia* spp.) may eat leaves and blossoms as on Apples (q.v.), but may be controlled by Derris insecticide at the green bud and white bud stages of blossom development.

Codling Moth (Cydia pomonella) damages pears as well as Apples (q.v.), and is similarly controlled.

Pear Leaf Blister Mite (Phytoptus piri). A tiny pest which causes greenish-yellow, turning red and brown, blisters on leaves, and may distort fruitlets. Controlled by a sulphur fungicide at bud-break.

Pear Leaf Curling Midge (Dasyneura pyri). A pest which feeds on young leaves, causing them to roll inwards tightly, but susceptible to nicotine dust applied in late May and repeated if necessary in summer.

Pear Midge (Contarinia pyrivora). A tiny fly, emerging from the soil to lay eggs in blossoms which hatch into larvae that feed on fruitlets, turning them blackish inside and causing premature falling. Derris or nicotine at the white bud stage of blossom development is helpful.

Pear Sawfly (Hoplocampa brevis). The caterpillars of this insect, hatching from eggs laid in the receptacle of flowers, feed on the fruitlets until early June, but may be controlled by including a gamma-BHC insecticide in the petal-fall spray.

malathion or rogor insecticide after petal-fall and later where infestation is heavy.

Red Spider Mite (Metatetranychus ulmi). This pest may attack Pears as well as Apples (q.v.) and requires the same control. A somewhat similar mite, *Bryobia rubrioculus,* is sometimes trouble-some, and requires similar control.

Wood-boring Moths, such as the Goat Moth *(Cossus cossus)* and the Leopard Moth *(Zeuzera pyrina)* may attack Pears

ROUTINE DISEASE AND PEST CONTROLLING SPRAYING SCHEDULE

Stage of Growth	Approx. Date	Disease or Pest controlled	Material to use and concentration	Remarks
Dormant*	Dec.– Feb.	Aphids, Sucker, Scale, Lichens, Moss	5–7½% tar-oil wash	May only be needed biennially
Bud-Burst	early April	Scab	Captan or Thiram or 3% lime-sulphur	
Green Bud	mid April	Scab Moth caterpillars	Captan or Thiram or 2½% lime-sulphur Derris emulsion	
White Bud*	late April	Scab Winter moth caterpillars	Captan or Thiram Derris emulsion	also for Pear Midge and Sawfly
Petal Fall*	mid May	Scab Pear Sucker	Captan or Thiram Rogor	if necessary
Fruitlet	early to mid June	Scab Codling Moth	Captan or Thiram Derris or DDT emulsion	if serious if necessary

* The essential routine applications: others as required.

Pear Slugworm (Caliroa limacina). The description applies to the small slug-like caterpillar of this Sawfly, which skele-tonizes leaves by feeding on the upper surface, but is easily controlled by mala-thion or derris insecticide in June, where damage is noted.

Pear Sucker (Psylla pyricola). Ap-parently increasing, with three to four generations annually, the nymphs of this insect may feed on and kill flower buds in spring, and disfigure leaves and fruits with a sticky secretion that attracts sooty moulds later. Tar-oil washing in winter is needed to control over-wintering adult insects on trees; and a

in the same manner as Apples (q.v.) and require similar control.

Algae, Lichens and Moss. These plants may grow superficially on the bark, and harbour pests, but are readily controlled by tar-oil winter washes.

Damage by hares, rabbits and mice can be prevented in the same way as for Apples (q.v.).

Pear, Alligator. See *Persea.*

Pear, Avocado. See *Persea.*

Pear, Prickly. See *Opuntia.*

Pearl Bush. See *Exochorda.*

Pearlwort. A mossy-like weed of lawns, *Sagina procumbens,* controlled by meco-prop herbicides. *See* Lawns.

Pearly Everlasting. See *Anaphalis margaritacea.*

Peat. Naturally compressed and accumulated remains of moisture-loving plants, chiefly cotton grass, sphagnum mosses and sedges, from boglands or moors, in an arrested state of decomposition. For garden use, peat is invaluable as a more or less sterile humus-forming organic material, with a moisture-holding bulk capacity of 90–95 per cent. Properly prepared it is uniform in texture and composition, and the modern alternative to leaf-mould for the making up of seed and potting composts. It may also be used to substitute for farmyard manures, compost, etc., as a humus material, supplemented by balanced fertilizers, in the garden. It has only small nutrient values, however, of nitrogen, potash and phosphoric acid, and is acid-reacting (pH 4–5). Horticulturally peats are now milled and prepared for specific uses, but are usually available as Sedge Peats, and Sphagnum Moss Peats; the latter are perhaps a little more acid, slightly less rich in nutrients, but more persistent in soils. For garden use, peat is best applied well-moistened, as an organic manure or mulch, and may be used at 2–6 lb. per sq. yd. Surface peat, often contaminated by weed seeds, roots, etc., peat-moss litter, used on poultry farms and in stables, should be used with caution. Peat Blocks, somewhat similar to peat cut for burning, are often used for the making of peat gardens for acid-loving plants. Peats also lend themselves to the making of soilless composts; usually combined with sand. *See* Composts.

Pecan-nut Tree. See *Carya pecan.*

Pectinatus (-a, -um). Pectinate, comb-like with closely packed leaves or segments. Ex. *Saxifraga pectinata.*

Pedatus (-a, -um). Pedate, like a bird's foot. Ex. *Viola pedata.*

Pedicel. The stalk of a flower.

Peduncle. The flower-stalk, usually the main stalk of an inflorescence.

Pelargonium, Stork's Bill (pel-ar-go'-ni-um. Fam. Geraniaceae). A fairly large genus of perennial, often almost shrubby, flowering herbs, distinctive for their beak-like styles and fruits, which includes the hybrids popularly known as 'Geraniums', though there are also some

distinguished species. Few Pelargoniums, originating in S. Africa, are really hardy, except under the mildest conditions.

Selection. The hybrid Pelargoniums or Geraniums naturally claim most attention, and horticulturally may be grouped as follows:

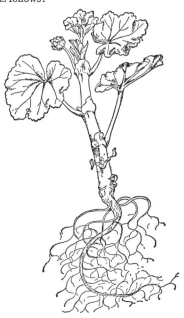

FIG. 173 *Pelargonium zonale* (Geranium); rooted cutting.

1. *Zonal* (*Pelargonium inquinans* × *P. zonale*, etc.), grown as pot plants and for summer bedding, leaves usually marked with a horseshoe zone of darker colour: notable older vs. are 'Flesh Pink', white, flushed pink; 'Gustav Emich', vermilion; 'King of Denmark', salmon-pink; 'Paul Crampel', vermilion; 'Rycroft White'; and 'Skelly's Pride', salmon; newer vs. are 'Cavalier', crimson; 'Empress', scarlet; 'Orange Fizz', orange; 'Show Girl', red; and 'Treasure Chest', brick red.

2. *Variegated-leaved Zonal*, with leaves highly coloured, such as 'Caroline Schmidt', green and pale yellow leaf,

geranium-red flower; 'Dollar Princess', gold and green, rose-pink; 'Happy Thoughts', pale green, ivory butterfly centre zone, cherry-red; 'Mrs Henry Cox', purple-black, red, cream and green, orange-red; 'Mrs Parker', silver and green, double, rose-pink; 'Mrs Strang', reddish, black, green and yellow, vermilion; and others.

3. *Ivy-leaved*, somewhat trailing plants, most suitable for hanging baskets, forms of *P. peltatum* and hybrids with Zonal Pelargoniums; notable vs. are 'Ailsa Garland', double, cerise and rose-pink; 'Apricot Queen', double, apricot-pink; 'Blushing Bride', white, flushed pink; 'Galilee', salmony pink; 'L'Elegante', silver and green leaves, single white, maroon markings; 'Mme Crousse', pale pink; 'Santa Paula', lavender; 'Sussex Lace', white-veined leaves, rose-pink.

4. *Scented-leaved Geraniums*, with fragrant foliage, but rather insignificant flowers, chiefly species: *P. crispum*, melissa-scented; × *fragrans*, nutmeg-scented; *odoratissimum*, apple-scented; *quercifolium*, oak-leafed scented; *tomentosum*, peppermint-scented; and 'Clorinda', a form with large cerise flowers, pungent leaves.

5. *Regal or Show Pelargoniums*, largely of American breeding, of which 'Autumn Haze', salmon-orange; 'Carisbrooke', rose-pink; 'Country Girl', pink, deeper blotches; 'Grand Slam', rose-red, carmine blotch; 'Minuet', ruffled salmon, and white; 'Souvenir', salmon-red, and maroon; 'Rouge', crimson; 'Snowbank', white; and 'Waltztime', lavender, represent older sorts; and 'Clown', blush pink with red blotching; 'May Magic', orange-salmon; 'Pompeii', mahogany with whitish edging; and 'White Chiffon' white, are newer introductions, among a rapidly increasing group.

6. *Miniature Geraniums* constitute a charming group of selected forms of Zonal Geraniums, notable for their dwarf stature and free-flowering; typical vs. are 'Anglia', salmon-scarlet, white eye; 'Caligula', geranium lake; 'Christine Read', orange; 'Gay Baby', ivy-leafed, lilac; 'Granny Hewitt', scarlet; 'St Helen's Favourite', salmon-pink; 'Sweet Sue', red with white eye; 'Venus', shell-pink; and 'White Gem', white. As there are over 5,000 forms of Geraniums

recorded, the lists of specialist nurserymen should be consulted and shows attended to keep up with the latest developments. Of other species, *P. echinatum*, to 1½ ft, white, red-spotted flowers, may be pot-grown, while *endlicherianum*, Armenia, 1–1½ ft, rose, carmine-veined flowers, July, is a herbaceous perennial, hardy for mild localities or the alpine house.

Cultivation. The basic requirements, when pot-grown, are a standard compost, such as JIP 2, light airy positions in cool greenhouse or rooms, moderate to liberal watering in active growth, but little in winter or the rest period, minimum winter temp. 7–10° C. (45–50° F.); feeding with a dilute liquid manure weekly from formation of flower-buds is helpful. Zonal, Variegated-leaved and Miniature Geraniums may be pot-grown to be in flower almost all the year; but are also largely grown to be bedded out of doors in summer. Ivy-leafed are usually grown for indoors, or hanging baskets, vases, window-boxes or tubs, or as climbers trained up greenhouse pillars or walls. Regal or Show Pelargoniums, including the 'Irene' strains, are for culture indoors or under glass, chiefly for spring and early summer flowering. Scented-leafed kinds may be grown indoors or summer-bedded, but need fairly frequent propagation to keep vigorous and shapely.

Propagation. Broadly, all types do best when grown pot-bound, and should therefore be under-potted; 3½–4½ in. pots for miniatures; 5–6 in. pots for strong plants, only. Zonal types are chiefly propagated by cuttings. To flower in summer, take cuttings of young, non-flowered, short-jointed, sturdy shoots, 2–3 in. long; cut beneath a node cleanly; remove lower leaves, allow cut surface to dry for a few hours, insert firmly in 2-in. pots singly, standard compost, or, for bedding, in shallow boxes, and root in cool frame or greenhouse; shaded from hot sun, winter at 7° C. (45° F.) minimum, watering only a little; move to 4-in. pots in March, temp. 10–13° C. (50–55° F.), and later to 6-in. pots; or for bedding out to cold frame, until planted out in June. Pinch out growing points of main shoots in April to make bushy plants; water increasingly, and begin feeding when flower-buds show. After flowering, plants may be plunged outdoors until September, cutting back stems, and brought indoors to over-winter; bedding plants are lifted in September, cut back, potted or boxed to winter under frostproof cover. For winter flowering, take cuttings in February–March, under glass, temp. 13° C. (55° F.), and grow on to 4-in. pots when well rooted. For autumn-flowering, cuttings may be taken in April–May. Ivy-leaved plants may be increased by cuttings taken in August, in the same way, to grow on in cool greenhouse, minimum winter temp. of 7° C. (45° F.), with very moderate watering. Scented-leafed plants are propagated as for Zonals. Regal Pelargoniums are increased by taking cuttings of firm shoots, 2–3 in. long, after flowering in July–August; in 2-in. pots, transferring to 4-in. pots when rooted, to winter at 10° C. (50° F.), very moderate watering, pinch out growing points, February, feed liberally from bud formation. After taking cuttings or after flowering, cut plants hard back, remove from pots, shorten roots, and repot and grow on as for new plants. It may be noted that Pelargoniums can be grown on year after year and improve in flowering with age, if judiciously cut back and repotted after flowering.

Pelargoniums, Succulent. These consist of a few S. African species, quite different from the Geranium types, with smaller leaves, somewhat warty stems, and open flowers, and of interest as pot plants. They include *P. carnosum*, 6 in., deeply crenate leaves, rose flowers, May; *gibbosum*, the Gouty Geranium, swollen jointed stem, lobed leaves, greenish-yellow flowers, June; and *tetragonum*, 15 in., heart-shaped, lobed leaves, rose-pink flowers, June. Easily grown in porous compost, little watering in winter and after flowering. Propagated by stem cuttings taken in early spring, temp. 10° C. (50° F.).

Pelecyphora, Hatchet Cactus (pe-le-kip'-or-a. Fam. Cactaceae). The only species, *P. asselliformis*, Mexico, globular with hatchet-like tubercles and comb-like spines, purple flowers, summer; may be grown in standard cactus compost, in cool greenhouse or sunny windows,

winter temp. 10° C. 50° F.); pot or repot in March.

Propagation. By seeds, sown very shallowly, with bottom heat of 24° C. (75° F.), spring. By cuttings of the tops of plants, April.

Pellaea (Pel'le-a. Fam. Polypodiaceae). Small pretty Brake ferns for the cool greenhouse.

Selection. P. atropurpurea, N. America, to 1 ft, leathery much-divided fronds; *falcata*, tropical Asia to New Zealand, ½–1½ ft, pinnate fronds; *hastata*, S. Africa to Yunnan, ½–2 ft, bi- or tri-pinnate fronds, and *rotundifolia*, New Zealand, ½–1 ft, pinnate, rounded pinnae, are usually grown; *nivea*, Mexico, Peru, 3–6 in., is a dainty subtropical kind, tri-pinnate fronds.

Cultivation. Best grown in hanging baskets, or pots, light, porous compost of 2 parts bulk loam, 1 part each sand and leaf-mould, with charcoal; water liberally from below, not wetting fronds, in summer; moderately in winter, minimum temp. 10° C. (50° F.).

Propagation. By division of rhizomes in March. By spores with bottom heat of 21° C. (70° F.).

Peloria. A monstrosity; applied to abnormal flowers.

Peltandra, Arrow Arum (pelt-and'-ra. Fam. Araceae). A genus of two species of aquatic perennial herbs of N. America, with large, arrow-shaped leaves, and white, arum-like flowers, June–July, red-berried later.

Selection. P. alba, 1–1½ ft, and *virginica*, 2 ft, greenish flowers.

Cultivation. Plant March–April, in pool margins or boggy ground, in clumps.

Propagation. By division of roots in spring.

Peltatus (-a, -um). Peltate, shield-like, with leaf-stalk attached to the lower surface, not the edge of the leaf. Ex. *Pelargonium petatum*. (*See* Fig. 174, page 402.)

Peltiphyllum, Umbrella Plant (pel-ti-pil'lum. Fam. Saxifragaceae). The one species, *P.* (*Saxifraga*) *peltatum*, California, is an entertaining hardy perennial for the waterside, with a corymb of pale pink flowers, April, before the large rounded leaves appear; for planting in moist soil, March; and propagating by simple division.

FIG. 174 Peltate leaf (*Pelargonium* sp.).

Pendulus (-a, -um). Pendulous, drooping. Ex. *Betula pendula*.

Pennatus (-a, -um). Pinnate, of leaves with leaflets arranged feather-like. Ex. *Stipa pennata*.

Pennisetum (pen-ni-se'tum. Fam. Gramineae). Ornamental grasses with elegant long-bristled, plume-like spikes of flowers in summer.

Selection. P. *latifolium*, Argentina, 3 ft, is perennial but only hardy in mild localities. P. *ruppelii*, Ethiopia, 2–6 ft, and *villosum*, Ethiopia, 1–2 ft, are half-hardy annuals.

Cultivation. Sow seeds under glass, March–April; standard compost, 18° C. (65° F.), to plant out in May. P. *latifolium* can be lifted in autumn to winter in a cool greenhouse.

Pennyroyal (*Mentha pulegium*). A prostrate-growing native perennial herb, of Britain, Europe and N. Asia, sometimes grown for its leaves and tips for culinary and herbal use; in humus-rich, well-drained soil; increased by division in autumn or spring; and may be grown as a carpeting plant or non-grass lawn.

Penstemon (pen-ste'mon. Fam. Scrophulariaceae). Commonly the Beard Tongues, perennial herbs, with showy tubular, lipped flowers, very largely of N. America, but unfortunately not very reliably hardy.

Selection. Taller plants for borders are P. *barbatus*, 3 ft, pinkish-red, summer; and vs. *coccineus*, scarlet, and *torreyi*, red; *confertus*, 2 ft, cream to yellow, July; *diffusus*, 1½ ft, pale purple, September, and v. *albus*, white; *eatonii*, to 2 ft, crimson-scarlet, August; *glaber*, to 2 ft, blue, August, and v. *roseus*, pink; *heterophyllus* 'Blue Gem', 1½ ft, brilliant blue, July; *isophyllus*, shrubby, to 6 ft, crimson, July; *hartwegii*, 2 ft, scarlet, June, and forms 'Garnet', deep red, 'Newbury Gem', pillar-box red, and hybrid strains; *ovatus*, 2 ft, blue to purple, July; while dwarfer species suitable for the rock garden in mild localities, or alpine house are P. *barrettae*, sub-shrub, 1 ft, bright purple flowers, May; *fruticosus* v. *cardwellii*, 9 in., evergreen, bright purple, July; *menziesii*, 1 ft, violet-blue, June, and vs.; *newberryi*, 1 ft, scarlet, July, and v. *rupicola*, rose-carmine, July; *pinifolius*, 3 in., evergreen, mandarin-red, June; *scouleri*, 1 ft, rose-purple, July, and vs. *albus* and *roseus*; and × 'Six Hills Hybrid', 6 in. evergreen, pale mauve, June.

Cultivation. Plant out of pots in May–June, out of doors, in humus-rich good loam, well-drained, pH 6·0–6·5, and warm, sunny positions; feed occasionally in summer. Protect from excessive damp and frost.

Propagation. By seeds, sown under glass, standard compost, February–March, bottom heat of 18° C. (65° F.); to prick off into pots or boxes, hardening for outdoor planting in May–June. By cuttings of reasonably firm shoots, June–September, in cold frame or under hand-lights; wintering rooted plants in cold frame.

Pentstemon. Alternative spelling of *Penstemon*, now assigned priority.

Peony. See *Paeonia*.

Peperomia (pe-pe-ro'mi-a. Fam. Piperaceae). A very large genus of exotic subtropical herbs, largely of northern S. America, of which a few are grown as warm greenhouse or house plants, for their foliage.

Selection. P. *argyreia* (*sandersii*), Brazil, 8 in., orb-shaped, pointed, fleshy leaves on dark red stalks; *caperata*, Brazil, dwarf, oval, ribbed leaves; *hederifolia*, cordate leaves, ribbed, grey; *maculosa*, tropical America, ovate, shining green leaves; *marmorata*, S. Brazil, thick fleshy ovate leaves, marbled white; and others in specialists' lists.

Cultivation. Pot in April, compost of 2 parts by bulk loam, 1 part each moss peat, leaf-mould and sand, and a little organic fertilizer; give light, airy conditions, watering moderately in summer; very sparingly in winter, minimum temp. 10° C. (50° F.); repot in April, when necessary; shade from direct sun.

Propagation. By cuttings of stems; by leaf cuttings, inserting stalks in the rooting compost; late spring and summer, with bottom heat of 18° C. (65° F.). By seeds, April–May, under glass, bottom heat of 18° C. (65° F.).

Pepper, Red. See *Capsicum*.

Peppermint. See *Mentha piperita*.

Perennate. Of a plant surviving the winter after flowering.

Perennial. A plant that lives for more than two years, usually flowering year after year. A herbaceous perennial is a plant of which the top growth dies down each winter.

Pereskia (per-esk'i-a. Fam. Cactaceae). Spiny shrubby cacti with woody stems, and evergreen leaves, native to tropical America.

Selection. P. aculeata, American or Barbados Gooseberry, Argentina, Mexico, W. Indies, grows quickly, to 30 ft or more, large, creamy white flowers, autumn, on mature plants, spiny edible fruits when grown natively; used as a stock for grafting on Epiphyllum, Schlumbergera, Zygocactus, etc; v. *godseffiana* has reddish, variegated leaves. *P. bleo,* Colombia, Panama, to 20 ft, with thin, yellowish green leaves, pink flowers, and *grandiflora,* Brazil, to 15 ft, shrubby, with pink flowers in clusters, summer.

Cultivation. Pot and repot March–April, standard cactus compost; water freely in active growth, very moderately in winter, minimum temp. 10° C. (50° F.).

Propagation. By stem cuttings, March–April.

Perfect. Descriptive of a flower containing both male organs (stamens) and female (pistil).

Perfoliatus (-a, -um). Perfoliate, with a stem appearing to grow through a leaf, often two opposite cohering leaves, or a leaf with basal parts joined. Ex. *Uvularia perfoliata*.

FIG. 175 Perfoliate.

Pergola. An open framework connecting and resting on posts or pillars to provide a continuing archway over a path or walk, up and over which climbing plants, such as roses, clematis, vines, wistaria, honeysuckles, jasmines, etc., may be trained. It may be constructed entirely of wood, preservatively treated, or of a wood framework resting on pillars of stone, or brickwork, preferably to give 7 ft headroom, with supports spaced about 6 ft apart.

Peri-. Prefix meaning around. Ex. *Perianth,* the outer surrounding parts of a flower, including sepals and petals. *Pericarp,* the rind, shell or outer covering of a fruit. *Periclineum,* the involucre of a flower-head of a Compositae. *Periderm,* the outer covering of a stem. *Perisperm,* the reserve food tissue surrounding the embryo in a seed.

Perilla (pe-ril'la. Fam. Labiatae). The species chiefly grown, *P. frutescens,* India, China, 1½ ft, is a half-hardy annual and its vs. *nankinensis,* purple foliage, small white summer flowers, and *laciniata,* finely cut foliage, are usually offered; being grown from seeds, under glass, March, bottom heat of 18° C. (65° F.), pricked off and hardened for planting out in May.

Periploca, Silk Vine (pe-ri-plok'a. Fam. Asclepiadaceae). The one species grown, *P. graeca,* a deciduous twining climber, 20–30 ft, with ovate, dark shining green leaves, and corymbs of greenish-brown flowers, summer, is a native of SE. Europe, reasonably hardy, for training on pergolas, in any well-drained soil. Propagation is by layers, in autumn, or by cuttings of firm young shoots, under a handlight, in July–August.

Periwinkle. See *Vinca*.

Pernettya (per-net'ti-a. Fam. Ericaceae). Dwarf evergreen shrubs of S. America, with unisexual or self-fertile hermaphrodite white urn-shaped flowers, hardy except in cold exposed localities.

Selection. P. ciliata, Mexico, 1–2 ft, flowers in white racemes, summer, followed by brownish-red berries; *mucronata*, Prickly Heath, charming for its profusion of globular berries, following June flowers, especially in the hybrid self-fertile forms of 'Bell's Seedling' and 'Davis's Hybrids', the berries being in white, rose, carmine to purple shades; and vs. *alba, lilacina* and *rosea*.

Cultivation. Plant in October or March–April, lime-free, peat-enriched soil, sun or shade, preferably in groups; with, in the case of species and vs., one male to several females. Apt to spread by suckers. Prune in March, if needed.

Propagation. By seeds, April, lime-free soil, outdoors. By cuttings of young shoots, July–August. By layers.

Perovskia, Afghan Sage (per-ows'ki-a. Fam. Labiatae). The species chiefly grown, *P. atriplicifolia*, Afghanistan to Tibet, 3–4 ft, is a semi-woody, hardy deciduous perennial, with silvery white foliage, sage scented, and panicles of violet-blue flowers in August–September.

Cultivation. Plant in autumn or early spring, well-drained, ordinary soil, and sun. Propagated by cuttings of firm shoots with heel, July–August.

Persea (per-se'a. Fam. Lauraceae). Only *P. gratissima*, the Alligator or Avocado Pear, W. Indies, is likely to be grown, as an evergreen shrub or tree, with long, deep-green elliptical leaves, but unlikely to yield its pear-shaped fruits without hothouse culture. A plant may be grown from the 'stone' seed set pointed end upwards, 2 in. deep, in a 5-in. pot, standard compost, with bottom heat of 18° C. (65° F.); and cultivated as an ornamental warm greenhouse or house plant, minimum winter temp. 10° C. (50° F.); watered freely in summer, very moderately in winter.

Persimmon. The name given to the plum-like fruits of species of *Diospyros,* Fam. Ebenaceae.

Selection. D. virginiana, N. America, to 45 ft, deciduous tree, ovate shining leaves, unisexual pale yellow flowers, summer, and round, yellow fruits; *kaki,*

Chinese Persimmon, to 30 ft, and vs. bear fine, large fruits, the cultivated Persimmons; *lotus*, China, Japan, etc., to 40 ft, bears small fruits, known as Date Plums; *armata*, China, to 15 ft, has small, bristly yellow fruits.

Cultivation. Reasonably hardy, plant October–March, well-drained, humus-rich soil, and sun; on south walls or in shelter in cold districts. For certain fruiting, however, must be grown in a cool greenhouse. Propagated by seeds, under glass, April, bottom heat of 18° C. (65° F.).

Peru, Marvel of, See *Mirabilis jalapa.*

Peruvian Lily. See *Alstromeria.*

Pesticide. A chemical substance used in the control of parasitic insects or pests; an insecticide. Sometimes used to include fungicides and herbicides (q.v.).

Pests. Horticulturally, organisms which live on and off garden plants and threaten their destruction.

Petal. A division of the corolla of a flower.

Petalody. The conversion of other organs into petal-like parts.

Petaloid. Petal-like in colour and character.

Petasites (pet-a-si'tes. Fam. Compositae). Hardy herbaceous perennials of which the flowering stems appear before the leaves, deep-rooting and apt to become ineradicable weeds.

Selection. P. albus, France, 1 ft, white flowers, May; *fragrans*, Winter Heliotrope, Europe, 6 in., vanilla-scented white flowers, February; and *japonicus* v. *giganteus*, Japan, to 6 ft, white, February, thick-stalked, magnificent waterside plant; and *hybridus*, Bog Rhubarb, or Butterbar, native, to 1½ ft, white flowers, March–May.

Cultivation. Plant October–March, moist ordinary soil, or water garden. *P. fragrans* may be pot-grown in a cold greenhouse.

Propagation. By root division in autumn.

Petiolatus (-a, -um). Petiolate, having a petiole or leaf-stalk. Ex. *Hydrangea petiolaris.*

Petiole. The stalk of a leaf.

Petraeus (-a, -um). Of rocky places. Ex. *Arabis petraea.*

Petrocallis (Draba) (pet-ro-kal'lis. Fam. Cruciferae). The chief species, *P. pyren-*

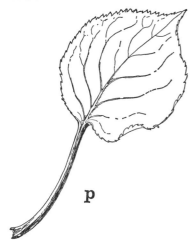

p

FIG. 176   Petiole of a leaf (leaf stalk); p.

aica, Pyrenees, Carpathian Alps, is a dwarf, cushion-like plant, with fragrant, pale lilac flowers in May on 2-in. stems; suitable for the rock garden; planted in spring, in poor, stony soil, or scree, and full sun; or in the alpine house. Propagation is by cuttings taken in August, rooted in a close frame.

Petroleum Oils, White Oils. Refined mineral oils chiefly used as acaricides to control mites, especially Red Spider on dormant fruit trees; and in summer, on foliage.

Petroselinum (pet-ro-se-li'num. Fam. Umbelliferae). The only important species is *P. crispum*, a biennial herb, of central and southern Europe. *See* Parsley.

Petteria (pet-ter'i-a. Fam. Leguminosae). *P. ramentacea*, Dalmatia, 3 ft, the one species, is a deciduous shrub, with fragrant dense racemes of yellow flowers, May–June, quite hardy for ordinary garden soils, and sunny position; planted October–March; and easily raised from seeds, in much the same way as for Cytisus.

Petunia (pe-tu'ni-a. Fam. Solanaceae). Of South American origin, the Petunias are chiefly grown in hybrid form as half-hardy annuals, for their brilliant showy flowers, and ability to thrive in poorish soils.

Selection. Modern Petunias stem from crosses of *P. integrifolia* × *P. nyctagini-flora* and selected and reselected strains; and are offered in single-flowered bedding and dwarf 9-in. strains; semi-double, to 1–1½ ft, fringed flowering forms (*fimbriata*); double flowering 'Canadian Wonder' strains, and large-flowering F_1 and F_2 hybrids, exceptionally suited to bedding, window-box, pot or tub culture; and a cascading form, *pendula*, in a colour range from white, through blue, violet, purple, to pinks, red and scarlet; many in named coloured forms.

Cultivation. Plants are now raised from seeds, sown under glass, February–March, standard compost, bottom heat of 18° C. (65° F.); to prick off, and harden for planting out in May; or may be grown in pots for greenhouse decoration in a cool greenhouse. Fine plants may be propagated by cuttings of unflowered shoots in September, in a warm greenhouse.

Peucedanum (pu-ke-da'num. Fam. Umbelliferae). Of over 100 species, only *P. sativum*, the Parsnip (q.v.), is of horticultural importance.

pH Scale. A quantitative measurement by which the acidity or alkalinity of a solution may be expressed, in terms of its hydrogen ions (H^+) and hydroxyl ions (OH^-). $pH = \log_{10} \frac{1}{[H]}$, where [H] is the hydrogen ion concentration. The pH Scale is from 0 to 14, on which pH 7 represents neutrality (the pH of pure water); less than pH 7 indicates acidity; more than pH 7 alkalinity. The concentration of hydrogen ions increases (or decreases) ten times for each full unit in the pH scale. In gardening, the pH of the soil solution is important as a guide to a soil's chemical balance, and availability of nutrient elements to plants; and is important as a guide to what plants are likely to grow well. Very few soils have an acidity below pH 4 or an alkalinity above pH 8. Most garden plants grow best in soils of slight acidity (pH 6·0–6·5). There is no fixed optimum pH value for particular species or plants, but there is a range outside which they grow les well, if at all. Increasing alkalinity reduces the availability of phosphates, potassium, manganese, iron and several trace nutrient elements to plants, and tends to induce chlorosis, in plants although several plants, shrubs and trees are tolerant of some alkalinity. With increasing acidity, phosphates become unavailable to plants, calcium magnesium, potassium and trace elements are readily lost by leaching, and under very strongly acid conditions soluble aluminium tends to occur in toxic proportions. Only members of the Ericaceae, Rhododendrons, Heaths and certain alpines thrive under strongly acid conditions of pH 5 or less. The pH of a soil may be precisely measured electrically. For gardening purposes it can be ascertained with sufficient accuracy by colorimetric testing, and the reaction of indicator dyes in simple soil-testing outfits. Soil acidity is reduced by adding calcium in the form of lime, chalk or limestone. Alkalinity may be reduced by adding sulphur, aluminium or ferrous sulphates, the use of acid-reacting fertilizers, such as sulphate of ammonia, and adding peat.

Phacelia (pa-ke'li-a. Fam. Hydrophyllaceae). A genus of hardy annual flowering herbs of N. America, for ordinary garden soils.

Selection. P. campanularia, California, 6 in., deep blue bell-like flowers, summer; *parryi*, California, 1½ ft, purplish-blue, summer; *sericea*, Idaho, perennial, 8 in., bright blue, June; *tanacetifolia*, 1½ ft, lavender-blue, summer; *viscida*, in Musgrave Strain, 2 ft, blue with white centre; and *whitlavia*, California, 1 ft, blue, bell-shaped, June.

Cultivation. Sow seeds outdoors, where plants are to grow in March–April, thinning to 9 in. apart; in ordinary well-drained soil and full sun. Or, in mild localities, in autumn.

Phaius (pai'us. Fam. Orchidaceae). Orchids of tropical origin, with pleated leaves, and requiring warm greenhouse conditions.

Selection. P. humblotii, Madagascar, 1½ ft, white, flushed rose-purple, flowers, spring; *mishmiensis*, Assam, 1½ ft, rose to buff, spotted white, spring; *tankervilliae (grandifolius)*, China to Australia, to 4 ft, brown and white, March–April; *wallichii*, Khasia Hills, 2½ ft, yellow, reddish and white flowers, spring.

Cultivation. Pot, and repot, in April,

compost of three parts by bulk fibrous peat, 1 part lightish loam, and a little Osmunda fibre; summer temps. 18–21° C. (65–70° F.), damp atmosphere; water sparingly at rest period, temp. 13° C. (55° F.) minimum.

Propagation. By division in April.

Hybrids are × *Phaio-Calanthe (Phaius × Calanthe)* and × *Phaio-Cymbidium (Phaius × Cymbidium)*.

Phalaenopsis, Moth Orchid (pal-en-op'-sis. Fam. Orchidaceae). Very beautiful epiphytic orchids, with short leafy stems, and long flower spikes.

Selection. P. amabilis, Java, white, yellow, spotted red, flowers, autumn; and vs. *aurea*, yellow; *dayana*, dotted carmine; *aphrodite*, Manila, white, streaked yellow and red; *lueddemanniana*, Philippines, 2 ft, white and violet; *sanderiana*, Philippines, 1 ft, rose-pink, and vs. *alba*, white, and 'Wigan's', rose; *schilleriana*, Manila, rose, white and yellow; and *violacea*, Sumatra, white, violet-crimson, and vs. There are several hybrids.

Cultivation. Plants are grown in teak baskets or on rafts, in a mixture of equal parts by bulk sphagnum moss, Osmunda fibre, a few oak leaves, and crocks; hung near the top of a warm greenhouse, summer temps. 21–29° C. (70–85° F.), watered freely, spring to after flowering in autumn, moist atmosphere, shade from direct sun; in winter, water more sparingly, keeping atmosphere moist and buoyant, minimum temp. 18° C. (65° F.).

Propagation. Rather difficult, but when possible by division in late winter.

Phalaris (pa'la-ris. Fam. Gramineae). Ornamental grasses, with graceful plume-like spikes.

Selection. P. arundinacea, northern hemisphere, 2–4 ft, is perennial, and finest in v. *picta*, Ribbon Grass, or Gardener's Garters, with leaves striped white; *canariensis*, Mediterranean region, 1–3 ft, is an annual, and yields the canary-seeds for cage birds in ornamental spikes.

Cultivation. Plant perennials in March–April, any good ordinary soil, propagating by division. Sow the annual where it is to flower in April, thinning seedlings to 6 in. apart.

Phanerogams (Phaenogams). The division of plants which have stamens and ovules in their flowers, and seeds containing embryos; flowering plants; now called Spermaphytes.

Pharbitis (par-bi'tis. Fam. Convolvulaceae). Twining climbing plants of the tropics, often listed as *Ipomoea*.

Selection. P. *learii*, the Blue Dawn Flower, of tropical America, is an evergreen perennial, with cordate to entire, pointed leaves, and brilliant blue trumpet flowers in clusters, June–October; for a warm greenhouse, or as a pot plant in rooms. P. *purpurea*, tropical America, to 10 ft., purple flowers, summer, and vs. in various shades, are half-hardy annuals; as is *tricolor*, tropical America, to 10 ft, with flowers white, changing to red and blue, in autumn–winter, and grown as a pot plant.

Cultivation. Sow seeds, March, under glass, standard compost, bottom heat of 21° C. (70° F.); seedlings may be potted on to grow in the greenhouse, or hardened to plant out in late May or June, ordinary soil and sun.

Propagation. Perennial by cuttings, July–August.

Phaseolus (pa-se-o'lus. Fam. Leguminosae). A large genus of twining climbing annual and perennial herbs. P. *multiflorus* (*coccineus*) is the Scarlet Runner, and *vulgaris* the Dwarf or French Bean. *See under* Beans.

The only species much grown ornamentally is P. *caracalla*, the Snail Flower, tropical America, a tender perennial, to 6 ft, with racemes of fragrant purple and yellow flowers, contorted and striking, summer; which may be raised from seeds sown in February–March, bottom heat of 21° C. (70° F.), to grow up posts or trellis in a warm greenhouse; winter temp. 13° C. (55° F.).

Pheasant's Eye. See *Adonis*; *Narcissus poeticus*.

Phellodendron (pel-lo-den'dron. Fam. Rutaceae). Small deciduous trees with handsome pinnate foliage and graceful habit, hardy except for areas where late spring frosts are damaging.

Selection. P. *amurense*, Manchuria, 30 ft, corky-barked; *chinense*, Hupeh, to 35 ft, and *sachalinense*, Japan, Korea, to 45 ft, are good.

Cultivation. Plant October–March, well-drained humus-rich soil, out of reach of late spring frosts.

Propagation. By seeds, sown April, out

of doors. By cuttings of young shoots, taken with a heel, July.

Phil-. Prefix meaning 'fond of'.

Philadelphus (pil-a-del'pus. Fam. Saxifragaceae). Deciduous hardy shrubs, esteemed for their early summer, white flowers, sometimes called Mock Orange, and Syringa.

Selection. P. *argyrocalyx*, New Mexico, to 8 ft, single white flowers, July; *coronarius*, SE. Europe, to 12 ft, oldest known, fragrant creamy-white, June,

FIG. 177   *Philadelphus* × *lemoinei*.

and v. *aureus* with yellow leaves; *delavayi*, China, to 12 ft, pure white, June; *grandiflorus*, SE. U.S.A., to 12 ft, scentless white, July, and form 'Conquête', large-flowering; *incanus*, China, fragrant, late flowering in July; × *insignis*, 10 ft, fragrant, white, July; × *lemoinei*, to 6 ft, well scented, white, June, and v. *erectus*; and forms 'Avalanche', 'Innocence' and 'Velleda', which bear single flowers; and 'Boule d'Argent', 'Enchantment', 'Manteau d'Hermine' and 'Virginal', with double flowers; *microphyllus*, Western N. America, 4 ft, very fragrant, white, June; *pubescens* (*latifolius*), SE. U.S.A., to 15 ft, white, late June; × *purpureomaculatus*, 6 ft, and vs. 'Beauclerk', 'Belle Étoile', 'Fantaisie' and 'Sybille', distinctive with white flowers having central rose-purple spotting, June; and *satsumanus*, Japan, 6 ft, erect growing, white, scented, June.

Cultivation. Plant October–March, almost any cultivable soil, indifferent to lime, sun or partial shade, where lower growth may be masked by other shrubs. Prune after flowering.

Propagation. Species by seeds, sown March–April, out of doors. By cuttings of previous year's shoots in February in propagating frame; or by layers, autumn.

Philesia (pil-e′si-a. Fam. Liliaceae). The only species, *P. magellanica*, Chile, is a dwarf, evergreen shrub, with rose-crimson, tubular flowers, June; eligible for warm, sheltered gardens, peaty soil and partial shade; easily increased by suckers, detached in spring.

Phillyrea (pil-lir′e-a. Fam. Oleaceae). Hardy, evergreen shrubs, densely leaved, with clusters of small flowers on previous year's growth.

Selection. P. angustifolia, Mediterranean region, to 8 ft, fragrant, white, May; *decora*, Lazistan, to 10 ft, white, May; *latifolia*, SE. Europe, to 15 ft, white, April–May, and vs. *illicifolia*, narrow-leaved, and *rotundifolia*, rounded leaves.

Cultivation. Plant October or March–April; ordinary soil, prune after flowering; useful for screening.

Propagation. By cuttings of young shoots, July–August.

Philodendron (pil-o-den′dron. Fam. Araceae). Evergreen climbing shrubs of tropical America, notable for their ornamental foliage, and grown increasingly as house plants or warm greenhouse plants.

Selection. P. andreanum, Colombia, pendulous long leaves; *bipinnatifidum*, Brazil, short-stemmed, divided, 2 ft long leaves; *erubescens*, Colombia, arrow-shaped leaves, coppery beneath; *fenzlii*, Colombia, lobed dark green leaves; *imbe*, Brazil, deeply lobed leaves, purpled stems; *melanocchrysum*, Colombia, dark green and gold leaves; *scandens*, Vera Cruz, Panama, perhaps the easiest to grow, heart-shaped, pointed leaves; and *verrucosum*, Ecuador, heart-shaped satiny-green leaves; and others in specialists' lists.

Cultivation. Pot in February–April,

compost of 3 parts by bulk leaf-mould, 2 parts moss peat, 1 part sand, plus John Innes Base fertilizer; to climb up bark or a netting cylinder packed with sphagnum moss; in shade, keep moist, water frequently in growth, moderately in winter, minimum temp. of 13° C. (55° F.).

Propagation. By cuttings of stems, spring, bottom heat of 23° C. (75° F.), compost as above.

Phloem. The soft bast, consisting of sieve-tissue of the vascular system of plants.

Phlomis (plo′mis. Fam. Labiatae). Herbaceous and shrubby plants with wrinkled leaves and whorled flowers.

Selection. P. chrysophylla, Lebanon, hairy shrub to 2 ft, golden-yellow flowers, summer; *fruticosa*, the Jerusalem Sage, Mediterranean region, 2–4 ft, woolly shrub, yellow flowers, June; *herba-venti*, Mediterranean region, 1½ ft, purplish-violet flowers, July–August; and *italica*, Balearic Is., sub-shrub of 1 ft, pale rose flowers, summer.

Cultivation. Plant March–April, well-drained, porous soil, and sun; giving protection in severe winters.

Propagation. By seeds, sown April, out of doors. By cuttings of young shoots, July–August, under handlight or in cold frame.

Phlox (ploks. Fam. Polemoniaceae). Largely a genus of American plants, valued for their thyrses of colourful and handsome flowers, as garden plants.

Selection. Half-hardy Annuals. These are the cultivated varieties developed from *P. drummondii*, Texas, New Mexico, and offered in three types: *grandiflora*, 1 ft, large-flowered, in colours of white, pink, rose, red, to carmine; *nana compacta*, 6–8 in., in strains such as 'Cecily' and 'Beauty', various colours, white, pink, crimson, to blue; *cuspidata*, 6–8 in., in 'Twinkle' star-like flowers, of similar colour range. These are grown from seeds sown in February–March, under glass, standard compost, bottom heat of 18° C. (65° F.), pricked off, and later hardened off to plant out in May; or out of doors from early May in warm districts.

Hardy Border Perennials. Largely developed from selected vs. and hybrids of *P. paniculata*, eastern N. America,

2–4 ft, in named forms such as: 'A. E. Amos', scarlet; 'Balmoral', pink; 'Border Gem', violet; 'Brigadier', orange-red; 'B. Simon-Jeune', rose-pink and carmine eye; 'Europa', white, red eye; 'Elstead Pink', rose-pink; 'Mia Ruys', dwarf white; 'Mother of Pearl', creamy white; 'Olive Wells Durante', rose pink, carmine eye; 'Starfire', crimson scarlet; 'Sweetheart', salmon-rose, white eye; and many others. Flowering in July–August, these may be planted in autumn–March, well-dug soil, humus-enriched, pH 6·5, and protected against slugs; sun or partial shade; most effective in groups. *P. maculata*, Eastern N. America, 3 ft, violet-purple flowers, summer, and its v. *purpurea*, purple on white, are useful for damp sites.

Alpines. Dwarf species and their vs., suitable for the rock garden, are: *P. alyssifolia*, N. U.S.A., procumbent, rose or white flowers, June; *amoena*, SE. U.S.A., 8 in., purplish pink, June; *caespitosa*, NW. America, 4 in., pale lilac, May–June, and vs. *bryoides*, and *condensata*, white; *divaricata*, Eastern N. America, 9 in., lilac, and v. *laphamii*, lavender-blue, June; *douglasii*, Nevada, 3 in., bright pink, June; and v. 'Booth-man's', mauve; 'May Snow' and 'Rose Queen'; *nana*, 6 in., New Mexico, Texas, purple, early summer; and v. *ensifolia*, 3 in., deep rose, June; × *procumbens*, 6 in., lilac, summer; *stolonifera* 'Blue Ridge', 6 in., soft blue, May; *subulata*, the Moss Phlox, 3–6 in., E. U.S.A., lilac, April–May, and named varieties: 'Apple Blossom', rose-white; 'Betty', clear pink; *atropurpurea*, red-purple; 'Fairy', lilac; 'G. F. Wilson', mauve; and 'Sensation', pink. Plant autumn or spring, well-drained soil, and sun.

Propagation. Border perennials by division in autumn or February–March. By cuttings in late March–April, rooted in a cold frame. By root cuttings in spring. Species only by seeds, March–April, in a cold frame or outdoors. Alpine perennials by green cuttings of young shoots taken at the base in May–July. Species by seeds, in cool frame or greenhouse, March–April.

Phoenix (pe′niks. Fam. Palmaceae). Beautiful feather-leaved palms, of tropical and subtropical Africa and Asia, to grow as house or warm greenhouse plants.

Selection. P. canariensis, Canary Is., slender-leaved and graceful; *dactylifera*, the Date Palm, grey-green leaves; and *rupicola*, N. India, bright green leaves, may grow too tall for rooms in time, but *acaulis*, India, short-stemmed, and *roebelinii*, bulbous-stemmed, are dwarf-growing.

Cultivation. Pot in March, standard compost, water freely, syringe and sponge leaves in warm months, moderately in winter, minimum temp. 13° C. (55° F.); repot March–April infrequently.

Propagation. By seeds (stones) sown in pots, bottom heat of 23° C. (75° F.).

Phormium (por′mi-um. Fam. Liliaceae). Handsome perennials with tough, tall, slender evergreen leaves, and erect panicles of flowers, summer, natives of New Zealand.

Selection. P. colensoi, Wharariki, 3 ft, yellowish flowers; and *tenax*, New Zealand Flax, to 9 ft, dull red flowers in very tall panicle; and vs. *atropurpureum*, bronzy-purple leaves; *variegatum*, leaves striped yellow; and *veitchii*, creamy-white striped leaves.

Cultivation. Plant crowns with their fleshy, fibrous roots in March, rich loam, moist soils, sun or light shade, by water or in woodland, well-sheltered, and winter-mulched, in mild localities; not for cold or exposed gardens.

Propagation. By division, March. By seeds, sown outdoors, April, warm seedbed.

Phosphate Insecticides. Insecticides based on organo-phosphorus compounds are now numerous and effective against a wide range of insect pests, but they are toxic to humans, animals and wild life, and need to be used intelligently and carefully. The application of the more highly toxic is governed by the Agricultural (Poisonous Substances) Act of 1952, and Agricultural (Poisonous Substances) Regulations, 1963 to 1965. These include Demeton, Dichlorvos, Dimefox, Mecarbam, Parathion, Phorate, Schradan, TEPP and Thionazin. These are not usually offered now for garden use, but if used must be handled with great care, wearing protective clothing—rubber boots and gloves, overall, rubber apron or mackintosh, and face shield or goggles. For garden use malathion and Rogor 40 are very much less poisonous and preferable, and are not subject to the regulations given. *See* Systemic Insecticides.

Phosphates. *See* Fertilizers.

Photinia (po-ti'ni-a. Fam. Rosaceae). A genus of deciduous and evergreen shrubs or small trees, related to the Hawthorns, natives of China or Japan.

Selection. P. beauverdiana, deciduous, China, to 20 ft, white clusters of flowers, May, giving way to dark red berries, and scarlet foliage in autumn; *villosa*, to 15 ft, white May flowers, scarlet berries, and scarlet and gold leaf tints in autumn; and v. *flava*, leaves turning clear yellow. The evergreens are not quite so hardy, and include *P. davidsoniae*, to 30 ft, glossy leaves, large clusters of white May flowers, orange-red berries; and *serrulata*, to 40 ft, long, oblong leaves, white flower clusters to 5 in. across, May, red, ovalish berries, but needs a sheltered position.

Cultivation. Plant deciduous kinds November–March; evergreens October–November or March–April; well-drained humus-rich soil, to pH 6·0.

Propagation. By cuttings of firm young shoots, July–August, under handlights. By seeds in spring.

Photoperiodism. The reaction or response of plants to relative day- and night-lengths. Plants fall into three categories: (1) Short-day plants which normally flower only in response to day-lengths shorter than a certain critical length in each 24 hours (or inductively to a long night-length). (2) Long-day plants which flower normally only in response to day-lengths longer than a certain critical length in each 24 hours (or inductively to a short night-length). (3) Day-neutral plants, the flowering of which is virtually unaffected by the day- or night-length. Typical short-day plants are Chrysanthemums and Cosmos; long-day plants are Lettuce, Radish and Calceolaria; day-neutral plants are Carnations, Lilacs and many others. There are many gradations between short- and long-day species. Photoperiodic response may also be influenced by age and factors such as temperature. Photoperiodism may also influence other aspects of growth. Flowering of photoperiodic sensitive plants can be controlled by varying the day-length artificially. Short-day plants may be delayed in their flowering by interrupting the dark period by a short period of low intensity light, or by lengthening the day-length with supplementary light. Commercially, this has made it possible to flower chrysanthemums the year round. Long-day plants can be brought to flower in winter by prolonging the day-length with artificial light.

Photosynthesis. The process by which green plants manufacture or synthesize organic compounds, particularly carbohydrates, from atmospheric carbon dioxide and water in the presence of sunlight, using the light energy absorbed by chlorophyll; it takes place in the chloroplasts (q.v.). It is basic to the life and existence of almost all other forms of life.

Phototaxis. The response of certain parts of a plant to the stimulus of light.

Phototropism (also **Heliotropism**). In plants the bending of stems to the stimulus of light.

Phragmites (prag-mi'tes. Fam. Gramineae). Perennial grasses of which *P. communis*, the Common Reed, 4–12 ft, which is cosmopolitan in nature, may be planted in the margins of lakes or large ponds, for its large plume-like panicles of bloom in summer; the stems are used for thatching and may be used for cover mats.

Phygelius (pi-ge'li-us. Fam. Scrophulariaceae). S. African semi-herbaceous sub-shrubs, with opposite, ovate, toothed leaves, with showy tubular hanging scarlet flowers from the axils in summer.

Selection. P. aequalis, 2 ft, crimson flowers, purplish within; *capensis*, the Cape Figwort, 2½ ft, scarlet, yellow within; and v. *coccineus*, bright rose.

Cultivation. Plant in March–April, light, humus-rich soil, warm, sunny sheltered position, in mild localities.

Propagation. By cuttings of young shoots, July–August, in cold frame, or under handlight. By seeds, spring, in pans in cold frame; slow-germinating.

Phyllitis (pil-lit'is. Fam. Polypodiaceae). Ferns with entire simple fronds, formerly listed as *Scolopendrium*.

Selection. P. scolopendrium, the Hart's Tongue, with strap-like leaves, 6–18 in. long, and its many frilled and tasselled forms, is native and common to the northern hemisphere; *sibirica*, with small fronds, and *hemionitis*, S. Europe, fronds 4–6 in., heart-shaped at base, are hardy.

Cultivation. Plant October–March, in cool shade and shelter, soil enriched with leaf-mould or peat. May be pot-grown in compost of 2 parts by bulk peat or leaf-mould, 1 part loam, 1 part sand, in cold greenhouse.

Propagation. By division of crowns when dormant. By spores in spring.

Phyllocactus. See *Epiphyllum*.

Phylloclade. *See* Cladode.

Phyllodes. Flattened leaf-stalks; seen in many Acacias.

Phyllodoce (pil-li-do′ke. Fam. Ericaceae). Dwarf, hardy, heath-like, evergreen flowering shrubs of the northern hemisphere.

Selection. P. aleutica, NE. Asia, 6 in., urn-shaped, yellow flowers, May; *alpina*, Japan, 3 in., reddish-blue, May; *breweri*, Cascade Mts, 8 in., pinkish open flowers, May–June; *caerulea*, N. Europe, Scotland, 6 in., reddish purple, May; *empetriformis*, Western N. America, 8 in., purple, bell-shaped, April–May; × *intermedia*, 6–9 in., rose-pink, May; and *nipponica*, N. Japan, 6 in., white.

Cultivation. Plant October or March, in cool, moist conditions, lime-free, humus-rich, well-drained soil, partial shade, on rock gardens, or in the alpine house.

Propagation. By cuttings of young shoots in June–July, rooted in a propagating frame. By seeds, April, in pans in the cold frame.

Phyllostachys (pil-lo-sta′kis. Fam. Gramineae). Evergreen grasses or bamboos for moist situations but only hardy enough for southern England and Ireland; allied to *Arundinaria*.

Selection. P. boryana, Japan, to 12 ft; *henonis*, Japan, to 12 ft, very attractive; *nigra*, China, Japan, 8–12 ft, black-stemmed; bambusoides Japan, 10 ft, and *viridi-glaucescens*, China, to 20 ft, very graceful: plants are apt to die after flowering.

Cultivation. Plant March–May, deep sandy soil, moist sheltered positions, mild localities only.

Propagation. By division in spring.

Phyllotaxis, Phyllotaxy. The arrangement of leaves on a stem; alternate, opposite, spiral or whorled.

-phyllus (-a, -um). Suffix in compound words, meaning leaf, as *Ilex platyphylla* —broad-leaved holly.

Phylum. A term sometimes used for a major group of organisms in Classification; Division is more common in Plants.

Physalis (pi-sa′lis. Fam. Solanaceae). A large genus of which only a few are of garden interest.

Selection. P. alkekengi, Bladder Cherry, Caucasus to China, 1 ft, and *franchetii*, Chinese Lantern, Japan, 1½ ft, are hardy perennials, white flowers, July, followed by scarlet, bladder-like calyces enclosing fruits, worth drying for winter decoration; × *bunyardii* is a hybrid of the two species. Plant in ordinary soil and sunny border, apt to be invasive in congenial quarters; propagated from seeds, in spring, or by division.

P. ixocarpa, Tomatillo or Jamberry, Mexico, 3 ft, is a half-hardy annual to grow like a tomato for its fruits, useful for cooking. *P. peruviana*, Cape Gooseberry, S. America, 3 ft, may be grown in v. *edulis* 'Golden Nugget' for its yellow fruits as a perennial in the cool greenhouse, in pots, standard compost, like tomatoes.

Physiology, Plant. The study of living processes and functions in plants.

Physostegia (pis-o-ste′gi-a. Fam. Labiatae). The species chiefly grown, *P. virginiana*, Obedient Plant, 2 ft, is a hardy herbaceous perennial of N. America, with erect racemes of rose-pink tubular flowers, summer; with vs. *alba*, white; *nana*, dwarf; and *speciosa*, sharply toothed leaves, and forms 'Summer Snow', white, and 'Vivid', rose pink. May be raised from seeds, sown in June, out of doors, planted in flowering stations in September; reasonably well-drained, humus-rich soil; and propagated by division in March–April.

Phyteuma (pi-tu′ma. Fam. Campanulaceae). Perennial flowering alpine herbs for the rock garden, European in origin.

Selection. P. comosum, Horned Rampion, 3 in., delightful for its tubular, flask-like lilac to purple flowers, June; and v. *album*, rare white-flowering form; *hemisphaericum*, Alps, 3 in., globular heads of bright blue, June; *orbiculare*, Alps, 1 ft, round heads of deep blue; *scheuchzeri*, Alps, 1 ft, deep blue, May; and *spicatum*, Europe and Britain, 1½ ft, for borders with white, cream and blue spikes of flowers, July.

Cultivation. Plant in well-drained ordinary soil, March–April; dwarf kinds in rock garden or alpine house in pans.

Propagation. By seeds, March–April, cool greenhouse or frame. By division in spring.

Phytolacca (pi-to-lak′ka. Fam. Phytolaccaceae). Only the hardy herbaceous perennials are grown.

Selection. *P. acinosa*, Himalaya, 3–5 ft, small pink to white flowers in erect racemes, summer, long, pointed, edible leaves; *americana*, Virginian Poke Weed or Red-ink Plant, Florida, 4 ft or more, white flowers, summer, followed by purple berries with crimson juice, poisonous seeds; and *clavigera*, China, 4 ft, more compact racemes of purple flowers, black berries.

Cultivation. Plant in autumn or spring, in borders, ordinary well-drained soil, and sun.

Propagation. By seeds, sown April–June, outdoors; by division, autumn or spring.

Phytopathology. The study of plant diseases.

Picea (pi′ke-a. Fam. Pinaceae). Spruce. Evergreen coniferous trees of the northern hemisphere, leaves spirally arranged, male flowers in short catkins, female separately, brightly coloured, giving way to pendulous cones; usually pyramidal in habit.

Foliage of Spruce (*Picea abies*).

Selection. *P. abies* (*excelsa*), Common or Norway Spruce, Christmas Tree Spruce, central and N. Europe, 100 ft or more; and vs. *clanbrassiliana*, 6 ft, slow-growing leaves; *gregoryana*, 2 ft, cushion-like shrub; *humilis*, dwarf bush; *nidiformis*, dwarf, spreading; *pendula*, stiffly drooping, 60 ft; *pumila*, low, flat-topped growth; *repens*, creeping, wide-spreading; and *virgata*, Snake Spruce, 90 ft, long, pendulous branchlets. *P. albertiana* v. *conica*, slow-growing, to 6 ft, densely leaved, conical form; *breweriana*, Weeping Spruce, Oregon, 80 ft; *glauca*, White Spruce, N. America, 60 ft, v. *echiniformis* dwarf, blue-leaved; *omorika*, Serbian Spruce, Yugoslavia, to 100 ft, slender and graceful; *pungens*, Colorado Spruce, to 80 ft, finest in blue-leaved vs. *kosteriana*, or *moerheimii*; *sitchensis*, Sitka Spruce, Western N. America, to 150 ft.

Cultivation. Plant September–October or March–May; well-drained but moisture-retentive soil, open positions, but not exposed to strong winds.

Propagation. Species by seeds, sown when ripe, out of doors in light loam beds, to plant out when 1 ft high.

Picotee. See *Dianthus.*

Pictus (-a, -um). Painted. Ex. *Gaillardia picta.*

Pieris (pi-e′ris. Fam. Ericaceae). Ornamental evergreen shrubs, with panicles of white, urn-shaped flowers, March–May.

Selection. *P. floribunda*, SE. U.S.A., 4–6 ft, abundant flowers, March–April; v. *grandiflora*, longer panicles; *formosa*, E. Himalaya, to 12 ft, rather tender, slow to flower; v. *forrestii*, notable for fiery red colour of young foliage in spring; *japonica*, Japan, to 10 ft, drooping panicles; v. *variegata*, pretty yellowish-white margined leaves; and *taiwanensis*, Formosa, to 10 ft, large panicles of bloom, April–May.

Cultivation. Plant September–October, or March–April; lime-free, peat or humus-rich soil, in well-sheltered positions, light shade.

Propagation. By seeds sown outdoors, April. By layers spring; by cuttings with a heel, July–August, in cold frame or under handlight.

Pig-a-back Plant. See *Tolmiea.*

Pilea 413 Pinks

Pilea (pi'le-a. Fam. Urticaceae). A genus of over 200 species, of which only a few tropical American plants are grown for their ornamental foliage as house or warm greenhouse plants.

Selection. P. cadierei, Indo-China, 10 in., bushy, with ovate leaves, three-nerved, dark green, blotched silvery between the veins; *microphylla* (*mucosa*), the Artillery, Gunpowder or Pistol Plant, 6 in., small-leaved, with tiny flowers that discharge clouds of pollen when watered or shaken; *spruceana*, Peru, Venezuela, 3 in., bronze-green leaves.

Cultivation. Pot in April, standard compost, water regularly in active growth, light airy conditions, moderately in winter, temp. 13° C. (55° F.).

Propagation. By seeds, bottom heat of 21° C. (70° F.). By cuttings of stems, July. By division when repotting, April.

Pileostegia (pi-le-o-ste′gi-a. Fam. Saxifragaceae). The chief species grown is *P. viburnoides*, the evergreen climbing Hydrangea, China, Formosa, with glossy leaves, self-clinging, and panicles of creamy-white flowers in autumn; suitable for sunny warm walls in mild localities; planted March–April; well-drained loam soil.

Propagation. By stem cuttings, July–August.

Pileus. The cap-like structure of Mushrooms and Toadstools (*Agaricaceae*).

Pilosus (-a, -um). Hairy. Ex. *Sedum pilosum*.

Pimelea (pi-me′le-a. Fam. Thymelaeaceae). Evergreen, half-hardy shrubs of Australasia, chiefly grown as house or warm greenhouse plants.

Selection. P. ferruginea, W. Australia, 2 ft, round heads of rose-pink flowers, spring; *hypericina*, to 6 ft, white, spring; *rosea*, to 2 ft, rose-pink, June–July; *spectabilis*, 3 ft, pink, May; and *traversii*, dwarf, New Zealand, white, May.

Cultivation. Pot firmly, standard compost, March, water freely, good light and air in growth; cut back after flowering, and syringe daily to encourage new growth; very little water in winter, minimum temp. 10° C. (50° F.).

Propagation. By cuttings of young shoots, April, with bottom heat of 18° C. (65° F.).

Pimpernel. See *Anagallis*.

Pimpinella (pim-pin-el′la. Fam. Um-

belliferae). The chief species, *P. anisum*, Anise or Aniseed, of Greece, is sometimes grown as an annual, sown in ordinary soil, full sun, March–April, in warm gardens, for its aromatic seeds. *P. major*, Europe and Britain, to 4 ft, is a hardy perennial with umbels of rose-tinted small flowers in summer, for the wild garden.

Pinching. The operation of nipping out the soft growing tips of shoots between finger and thumb, to induce branching, bushy growth.

Pine. See *Pinus*.

Pineapple. See *Ananas*.

Pin-eyed. Of flowers of Primula having the style longer than the stamens. *See* Thrum-eyed.

Pinguicula, Bog Violet, Butterwort (pin-gwik′u-la. Fam. Lentibulariaceae). Insectivorous plants which capture insects by clammy exudations from glands on their leaves, and herbaceous perennials.

Selection. P. alpina, Europe and Britain, 3 in., white flowers, May; *grandiflora*, W. Europe, SW. Ireland, 6 in., violet-blue, summer; and *vulgaris*, Europe, Britain, 4 in., violet-purple flowers, May, may be grown in the cool bog garden, or in the alpine house, in well-crocked pans, compost of equal parts sphagnum moss and standard soil compost, standing in a saucer, filled with rain water in summer; emptying the saucer for winter, and keep the compost just moist. Propagate by division in April.

P. bakeriana (*caudata*), Mexico, beautiful deep carmine flowers, autumn; *gypsicola*, Mexico, 3 in., purple, summer; and *lutea*, SW. U.S.A., 6 in., yellow, summer, need warm greenhouse conditions, grown in pans (as for alpine house culture), with winter temp. of 13° C. (55° F.).

Propagation. By division, April; by leaf cuttings, on sand, in propagating case.

Pink, Sea. See *Armeria maritima*.

Pinks. The hardy Pinks apparently descend from *Dianthus plumarius*. They produce smaller flowers, more abundantly, than Carnations, make slighter plants, of more dwarf habit, and are trouble-free garden plants for most gardens.

Selection. For a full list of Dianthus grown as Pinks, *The Pinks Register*, published by the British National Carnation Society, should be consulted. Only token recommendations are made here.

Garden Pinks. Of compact habit, flowering mainly in June, often strongly scented: 'Dusky', double, pink; 'Her Majesty', double, white; 'Inchmery', double, shell-pink; 'Mrs Sinkins', white; 'Pink Mrs Sinkins', rose-pink; 'Sam Barlow', double, white, dark crimson eye; 'Red Emperor'; 'Woodpecker', double, salmon, maroon eye. 'Little Jock' hybrids.

Laced Pinks. Distinctive for the marking or lacing of the flower colours: 'Dad's Favourite', white, laced ruby-red; 'Laced Joy', rose-pink, laced crimson; 'Robin', light pink, laced carmine; 'Victorian', white, laced chocolate; 'London' pinks, various.

Herbert's Pinks. Strong-growing, resembling border carnations: 'Bridesmaid', double, pink, carmine eye; 'Fire King', double, salmon-scarlet; 'Mrs G. Woolley', double, salmon; 'Queen Mary', double, rose-pink; 'The Bride', double, white; 'Victory', double, ruby-crimson.

Allwoodii Pinks. These stem from the crossing of the Old Fringed white *D. plumarius* and the perpetual-flowering Carnation, and give flowers, strongly scented, from June to early autumn: 'Alice', semi-double, white; 'Barbara', double, crimson; 'Denny', single, pink; 'Ian', double, crimson; 'Monty', semi-double, rose-pink, chocolate centre; 'Rebecca', double, maroon-pink; 'Ruth', semi-double, brick-red, maroon centre; and many others.

Laced Allwoodii. Similar to the above, but with laced flowers: 'Esther', semi-double, white, laced fuchsia purple; 'Faith', double, old rose, laced red; 'Hope', double, white, laced crimson.

Allwoodii Alpinus Pinks. Very compact, dwarf forms, with usually single flowers, strongly scented: 'Goblin', salmon, maroon eye; 'Mars', double, scarlet; 'Tinkerbell', pale pink; 'Wink', white, purplish eye.

Imperial Pinks. Originating in crosses of Allwoodii and Herbert's pinks, these are large, 1½–2 ft tall, plants: 'Carlotta',

double, claret; 'Crimson Glory', double, ruby-crimson; 'Fortune', semi-double, rose-pink; 'Snow Queen', double, white; 'Winsome', semi-double, rose.

Allwood's Show Pinks. A group similar to Imperials, tall to 2 ft, 'perpetual' flowering, in white, and all shades of pink to crimson and red, varieties being prefixed by the appellation 'Show'; and excellent for exhibition.

Allwood's Golden Hybrids stem from a cross of an *Allwoodii* seedling × *Dianthus knappi*, and are compact plants, distinctive for yellow, apricot and scarlet flowers, but of poor scent.

Lancing Pinks (Allwoodii vs. × *D. winteri*) are compact, free-flowering selections in a good colour range, which can be grown from seeds. For alpine Pinks and species, and Chinese or India Pinks, see *Dianthus.*

Cultivation. Plant, preferably, in early autumn or March–April; well-prepared soil, draining freely, enriched with humus-forming rotted organic matter, and limed to a pH 6·5; in borders, beds or as edgings; preferably in open sunlit positions. Tall-growing Pinks gain from being staked, preferably by 'growthrough' supports. All Pinks with *Allwoodii* in their breeding benefit by being stopped, pinching out the centre crown bud at the top to induce fine flowering sprays; but Garden Pinks and Herbert's Pinks are best left unstopped. A top mulch of limestone chippings for winter is useful on heavy soils or soils not rich in lime.

Propagation. Selections of most groups of Pinks may be raised by seeds, sown in spring, in cold frame or greenhouse, or outdoors, in April. Named varieties, however, are best propagated by cuttings, consisting of 'pipings' or the tops of non-flowered, young shoots, gently but firmly detached at a node, and firmed into good soil in a frame or under handlights. Herbert's Pinks are increased by layering as for Carnations.

Pinna. A primary division or leaflet of a pinnate compound leaf or frond.

Pinnate. Of a compound leaf, having leaflets on each side of a common axis, stalk or petiole.

Pinnatifid. Deeply divided into lobes or segments from the margin almost to the midrib.

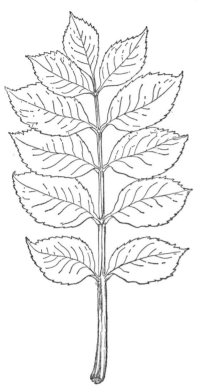

FIG. 179   A pinnate leaf (*Fraxinus* sp.).

Pinnatisect. With pinnate divisions to the midrib, but not into leaflets.

Pinnule. A secondary division of a compound pinnate leaf.

Pinus, Pine (pi′nus. Fam. Pinaceae). Evergreen coniferous trees of the northern hemisphere, usually with branches in whorls, long, needle-like, adult leaves in bundles of two, three or five, monoecious flowers, and woody cones, taking two years to ripen, pyramidal habit.

Selection. Only the more ornamental species are really eligible for gardens. *P. ayacahuite*, Mexican White Pine, to 70 ft, for the south-west and west; *banksiana*, Canadian Jack Pine, to 60 ft, narrowly erect; *cembra*, Arolla Pine, Alps, to 70 ft, × *holfordiana*, fast-grow-

ing to 60 ft; *mugo*, Mountain Pine of Europe, shrubby to 12 ft, vs. 'Gnome' and 'Mops', entertaining dwarfs; *nigra*, Austrian Pine, to 120 ft, and v. *calabrica*, Corsican Pine, to 100 ft, make good shelter trees; *parviflora*, Japanese White Pine, to 40 ft, charming, with short leaves; *peuce*, Macedonian Pine, to 50 ft, slow-growing, glaucous-green foliage; *pinaster*, Cluster or Maritime Pine of Mediterranean region, to 120 ft, for coastal sands; *pinea*, Stone or Umbrella Pine, Mediterranean region, to 60 ft, seeds are edible pine kernels, but needs mild conditions; *ponderosa*, Western Yellow Pine, Western N. America, to 100 ft, for the south and west; *pumila*, Dwarf Siberian Pine, shrubby to 10 ft, quite hardy; *radiata*, Monterey Pine, California, to 120 ft, for southern counties, rich green foliage; *strobus*, Weymouth Pine, Canada, Eastern N. America, to 120 ft, handsome, but needs protection against pests; *sylvestris*, the native Scots Pine or Scotch Fir, Europe and N. Asia, to 120 ft, with fine reddish bark colour; and the autumn-gold v. *aurea*; and *viridis compacta*, distinctive miniature tree; *tabuliformis*, Chinese Pine, to 30 ft, distinctive in v. *yunnanensis*, with long leaves; and *wallichiana*, Bhutan Pine, Himalaya, to 100 ft, bluey green foliage, very fine and hardy.

Cultivation. Plant September–October, or March–April, in open, clean air, and

FIG. 180   Foliage of a two-needle *Pinus sylvestris*, Scotch Pine or Fir.

sun; usually well-drained, rather light soil; preferably when young.

Propagation. By seeds, outdoor seed-beds of sandy loam, spring.

Disease. Rusts are sometimes trouble-some; especially Weymouth Pine Rust (*Cronartium ribicola*), which may also attack Currant bushes, and may be controlled by spraying with a copper fungicide.

Pests. Infestation by the Pine Shoot Moth, *Evetria buoliana*, shows in dis-torted leading shoots, which should be pruned away and burnt in early spring, and a malathion insecticide applied, if practicable. Sawfly caterpillar colonies (*Diprion pini, Neodiprion sertifer*) may sometimes be seen in summer, and should be removed or dusted with nicotine dust or malathion. Pine weevils, *Hylobius abietis*, may bore young stems in spring, calling for a gamma-BHC insecticidal application when seen.

Pip. A seed of a Pome or Citrus fruit. A single flower in the flower truss of Auricula, etc.

Piper (pi'per. Fam. Piperaceae). A very large genus of tropical shrubs, of which a few are grown as ornamental house or warm greenhouse plants.

Selection. *P. ornatum*, Celebes, attrac-tive climber, with shield-like leaves, spotted pinkish; and *porphyrophyllum*, Malaya, with bronzy-green, heart-shaped leaves, are chiefly offered. *P. nigrum*, Malaya, E. India, whose fruits are the source of the black and white peppers of commerce, may be grown under stove conditions.

Cultivation. As pot plants, potted in spring, compost of sandy loam and leaf-mould, to grow up a cylinder of netting filled with sphagnum moss, kept moist; liberal watering from April to Septem-ber; syringing on sunny days; partial shade; only very moderate watering in winter; minimum temp. 15·5° C. (60° F.).

Propagation. By cuttings of young firm shoots, summer, in sandy loam, bottom heat of 18° C. (65° F.).

Pipe-tree. See *Syringa vulgaris*, the wood having been used for pipe-stems.

Pipings. Young tip shoots drawn from the nodes or axils for propagating, as with Pinks (q.v.).

Pippin. An old name given to Dessert Apples, bred from seeds.

FIG. 181 Piping; prepared cutting of a Pink or Dianthus plant.

Piptanthus (pip-tan'thus. Fam. Legu-minosae). Semi-evergreen shrubs, doubt-fully hardy, of which *P. laburnifolius*, Himalaya, 6–8 ft, may be grown on a warm, sheltered wall in mild localities, for erect racemes of bright yellow, May flowers, and three-leafleted leaves, earn-ing it the doubtfully accurate name of the evergreen Laburnum. Plant March–April, light, well-drained, humus-en-riched soil.

Propagation. By seeds, April; or by cuttings of short side-shoots taken with a heel, and firmed in sandy loam, in a cold frame.

Pistacia (pis-ta'ki-a. Fam. Anacardi-aceae). Handsome trees with unisexual flowers, chiefly grown for their attractive foliage.

Selection. *P. chinensis*, China, to 60 ft, is hardy for mild localities, foliage colour-ing brilliantly in autumn before falling; *vera*, Pistachio, W. Asia, 10–20 ft, yields the edible pistachio nuts used in con-fectionery; but requires cool greenhouse conditions. Both may be planted in November–March, well-drained soil, and propagated from seeds.

Pistil. The female organ of a flower; a separate carpel; or the gynoecium comprised of ovary, stigma and style, as a whole.

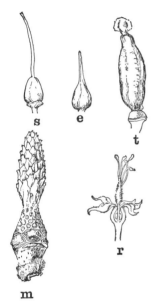

FIG. 182 Pistil: s. *Scilla* sp.; e. *Endymion* sp.; t. *Tulipa* sp.; m. *Magnolia* sp.; r. *Rosa* sp.

Pistillate. Of flowers with carpels (pistils) but not stamens. Cf. Staminate.

Pistol Plant. See *Pilea muscosa*.

Pisum, Pea (pi'sum. Fam. Leguminosae). Noted as *P. sativum*, S. Europe, is the parent species of green peas. *See* Peas.

Pit. A glazed structure with walls below ground level. The simplest form is an excavation, walled, and covered by frame lights at or just above surface level, which means higher temperatures can be maintained in the 'pit' for propagation purposes. More elaborate and larger pits have span-roof greenhouse tops, and may be made with access by a door and path, to beds for cucumber and melon growing, and propagative work; and are heated. The chief advantages are minimum exposure to wind and weather, and greater ease in maintaining even temperatures and good growing conditions.

Pitcher Plants. See *Cephalotus, Darlingtonia, Nepenthes* and *Sarracenia*.

Pith. The central core of cylindrical plant stems, usually of thin-walled parenchymatous tissue; medulla.

Pittosporum (pit-tos'por-um. Fam. Pittosporaceae). Evergreen shrubs, attractive for their foliage and scent when in flower, but not hardy except for mild, south-west and sheltered gardens.

Selection. P. bicolor, Tasmania, 15 ft, maroon-crimson flowers, March–April; *coriaceum*, Madeira, to 6 ft, white, jasmine-scented flowers, May; *dallii*, New Zealand, to 12 ft, white, spring, perhaps the hardiest; *daphniphyllum*, China, to 18 ft, greenish-yellow, May–June; *eugenioides variegatum*, New Zealand, to 20 ft, yellow, honey-scented, May; *ralphii*, New Zealand, to 10 ft, dark crimson, May; *tenuifolium*, New Zealand, to 20 ft, dark purple, May, and vs. *purpureum* and 'Silver Queen', with coloured foliage; *tobira*, China, Japan, to 20 ft, creamy-white, fragrant, summer; and others.

Cultivation. Plant September–October or April–May, well-drained, humus-rich soil, warm shelter, on walls, in mild localities; or may be grown in a cold greenhouse in large pots or tubs. Prune after flowering.

Propagation. By cuttings of firm young shoots, July–August, in propagating frame, bottom heat of 18° C. (65° F.), standard compost.

Placenta. In plants, the part of the ovary wall on which the ovules are borne.

Placentation. Type of arrangement of placentas on the ovary walls; may be (a) parietal, on the walls of the ovary; (b) axile, on the column made by carpellary margins joined together in the centre of the ovary; (c) free-central, arising as a central, erect growth from base of ovary; (d) basal, at the base of the ovary; and (e) suspended, when the ovule hangs down from the top of the ovary.

Plagianthus (pla-gi-an'thus. Fam. Malvaceae). Shrubs or trees of Australasia, graceful in habit, but not reliably hardy except in very mild localities.

Selection. *P. betulinus*, New Zealand, deciduous tree to 30 ft, or more, small, ovate toothed leaves, dull white, unisexual flowers, June; *divaricatus*, New Zealand, branching shrub to 6 ft, small linear leaves, creamy-white flowers, June, are usually offered.

Cultivation. Plant October–March, well-drained and humus-rich soil, sheltered, sunny positions.

Propagation. By cuttings of side-shoots taken with a heel, July–August, in frame with bottom heat (18° C. [65° F.]). By layering, spring.

Plane-tree. See *Platanus*.

Plant. A living organism capable of living wholly on inorganic substances, and possessing no power of independent locomotion, nor specialized organs of digestion or sensation. A member of the Vegetable Kingdom.

Plantago, Plantain (plan-ta'go. Fam. Plantaginaceae). Many of the species are troublesome rosette-leaved weeds, controlled, however, by selective herbicides based on 2, 4-D, 2, 4, 5-T, etc., in lawns, or paraquat among garden plants. *P. major rosularis*, the Rose Plantain, a hardy perennial, 6 in., is sometimes grown from seeds for its curious rose-like rosette of leaves borne on a stout stalk.

Plantain. See *Plantago*.

Plantain Lily. See *Hosta*.

Plantain, Water. See *Alisma*.

Plant-breeding. The art and science of producing new forms of plants with enhanced characteristics for particular purposes or growing conditions. The basis is the selection (and re-selection) of plants providing the male:female gametes or sex cells likely to contribute the desired characteristics to their progeny. Modern plant-breeding is more and more firmly based on the application of the principles of Genetics and the Laws of Heredity; starting with Mendel's Laws (*see* Mendel, Mendelism), which led to our present understanding of chromosomes and gene heredity. For the gardener interested in plant breeding, *Practical Plant Breeding*, by W. J. C. Lawrence, latest edition, Allen & Unwin, is suggested as a basic guide.

Planting. The operation of setting plants in their growing quarters, and vitally important to their survival and future performance. Success depends upon soil conditions suitable to the ready formation of new roots. They must be aerated, moist, sufficiently warm and contain root-promoting nutrients. In general the conditions are assured by proper preparation of the planting station, which should be large enough to accommodate the roots easily, with the subsoil well broken, and the top soil amended suitably with rotted organic matter, and/or coarse sand or conditioning materials, and provided with phosphates, potash and lime to bring to the optimum pH for the plants concerned. Fresh unrotted manure or quick-acting stimulatory fertilizers are not conducive to good rooting.

Annuals, whether half-hardy or hardy, normally recover well from planting out when in active early growth, into friable soil, of sufficient warmth, and are usually set out with roots in a soil ball.

Herbaceous Perennials. Many species of herbaceous plants may be planted in September–November, and indeed throughout the winter, given mild weather and free-draining soil; some, however, are better planted in early spring, notably Amellus Asters, Delphinium, Echinacea, Gaillardia, Kniphofia, Penstemon, Pyrethrum, *Scabiosa caucasia*, Stokesia and Zauschneria.

Evergreen Perennials. These may be planted in September–October, or March–April. Some kinds, such as Primula, may be divided and planted after flowering.

Alpine Plants. When they have been raised in pots, alpine plants may be planted at any time of the year when soil and weather conditions are favourable; though the most favourable times are September–October, or March–May.

Shrubs and Trees. Normally deciduous shrubs and trees are best planted when dormant, broadly between late October and late March. Plants which are more vulnerable to frost when young, such as Magnolia, Eucryphia, Hydrangea, Indigofera, Halimium and Chimonanthus, are better planted in late March–May. It is advantageous to plant fruit trees, roses and early leafing or flowering shrubs in autumn or before the turn of the year if possible. Evergreen shrubs, trees, including conifers, may be planted in September–early November, or late March–May. In cold localities, on heavy soils, subject to winter waterlogging, planting should be done in the spring. Most evergreens and conifers need shelter from drying cold winds when young. Care must be taken to see that plants are placed at the right depth. Trees should be staked at planting.

Container-grown Plants. In theory, all kinds of plants grown in containers may be planted at any time of the year. In practice this is only true if the root system has not been cramped, and conditions are favourable to continued growth. Even such plants should not be set out in drought or under waterlogged conditions. Wet conditions and sticky soil are more inimical to plant recovery than any other. Frost need not deter planting unless it is severe and has penetrated the soil in depth. The frozen surface soil should be placed on one side; the plants top-mulched and the frozen soil then replaced on top.

Planting Growing Plants. When it is necessary to lift and plant specimens in active growth, it is best to spray leaves and stems with a plastic transpiration-reducing spray; then lift with roots in a soil ball; replant as soon as possible, giving shade and careful watering until recovery.

Planus (-a, -um). Flat. Ex. *Eryngium planum.*

Platanus, Plane (pla'ta-nus. Fam. Platanaceae). Handsome deciduous trees, with lobed leaves, and bristly fruit-balls on hanging stalks in autumn, and trunks that shed bark in patches in winter.

Selection. P. × *acerifolia*, 80 ft or more, is the London Plane, thriving in cities and smoke and dust-polluted atmospheres; v. *pyramidalis* being of erect growth; *orientalis*, Oriental Plane, SE. Europe, Asia Minor, 80 ft or more, a more attractive tree for gardens, surprisingly hardy.

Cultivation. Plant November–March, any ordinary soil, staking well. Little pruning needed.

Propagation. By seeds, sown outdoors, spring. By cuttings of firm shoots with a heel, in cold frame or under handlights,

July–August. By layers, spring or summer.

Platy-. Prefix in compound words meaning broad; Ex. *Platyacanthus*, broad-spined; *Platyclados*, broad, flattened stems; *Platyphyllus*, broad leaves.

Platycerium, Elk's-horn or **Stag's-horn Fern** (pla-ti-ke'ri-um. Fam. Polypodicaeae). Beautiful and intriguing epiphytic ferns, with bold, forking fronds, likened to the antlers of Elks and Stags.

Selection. P. *bifurcatum* (*alcicorne*), Australia, rounded barren fronds, forked fertile fronds, and v. *majus*, much larger fronds, are the most easily grown in a cool greenhouse or indoors. P. *grande*, Malaya, N. Australia, fronds to 6 ft; *hillii*, Queensland, 1½ ft; *wallichii*, Malaya, very deeply lobed; and *willinckii*, Java, narrow-lobed, need warm greenhouse conditions.

Cultivation. Grow on blocks of wood, with roots encased in mixture of equal parts of rough fibrous peat and sphagnum moss, wired in position with copper or plastic wire; *or* in baskets or pans, in similar compost with good drainage; water liberally in summer, moderately in winter, with partial shade; minimum temp. 10° C. (50° F.) for P. *bifurcatum*; 15·5° C. (60° F.) for others.

Propagation. By basal buds or suckers at the roots, April or summer; by spores as soon as ripe, especially P. *grande*, which forms no buds.

Platycodon, Chinese Bell-flower (pla-ti-ko'don. Fam. Campanulaceae). The only species, P. *grandiflorus*, China, Japan, to 2 ft, with large, bell-like, blue flowers, singly from leaf axils, June, is a fine hardy herbaceous perennial, with vs. *japonicum flore plenus*, double-flowering; *mariesii*, 1–1½ ft, with white flowering form *album*; and 'Homestall', very large-flowering; *roseum*, has soft pink flowers.

Cultivation. Plant October–March, in sunny border, ordinary soils with humus, protected against slugs. May be grown easily from seeds in spring; and increased by division, autumn or spring.

Platystemon (pla-ti-ste'mon. Fam. Papaveraceae). The species, P. *californicus*, Cream Cups, California, 1 ft, with linear leaves, and yellow flowers, summer, is chiefly grown as a half-hardy annual, from seeds sown under glass, March, with slight bottom heat, or outdoors in April.

Pleaching. The interlacing of branches and shoots to form a flat-like 'wall' and 'roof' for alleys, practised with Lime trees (*Tilia* sp.).

Pleioblastus (ple-o-blas'tus. Fam. Gramineae). A genus of short-stemmed bamboos, formerly in *Arundinaria*.

Selection. *P. pumilus*, Japan, 2 ft; *vagans*, Japan, 1½–3 ft; *variegatus*, Japan, to 4 ft; and *viridi-striatus*, Japan, 3–6 ft, may be grown in all but very cold localities.

Cultivation. Plant in March–April, moisture-retentive soil, in isolation as they can be invasive.

Propagation. By division, April–May.

Pleione, Indian Crocus (ple-i-o'ne. Fam. Orchidaceae). Outstandingly beautiful dwarf orchids, flowering on short stems, and easily grown in a cold greenhouse or frame.

FIG. 183 *Pleione formosana.*

Selection. *P. formosana*, Formosa, 2 in., mauve, cream, spotted brown, April–May, v. *alba*, white; *forrestii*, W. China, 3 in., yellow, April–May; *hookeriana*, Himalaya, 2 in., white, orange and mauve, May; *maculata*, Khasia, Assam, 2 in., white, striped purple, April–May; v. *virginea*, pure white; *pogonioides*, China, 2 in., purple, April–May; *praecox*, Burma, N. India, 2 in., rose to purple, April; v. *alba*, white; and *wallichiana*, India, larger flowers; and *yunnanensis*, Yunnan, 3 in., rose-purple to dark purple, April–May.

Cultivation. Pot fresh pseudo-bulbs, which are renewed annually, in shallow pans, very well crocked, and compost of equal parts loam soil, coarse sand, leafmould and peat, late March; water increasingly as active growth is made, but withhold when foliage dies down; plunge pans in a cold frame until coming into flower, when they may be brought into the cold greenhouse or alpine house.

Propagation. By pseudo-bulbs taken from mature plants, after flowering, and potting as above.

Pleiospilos (ple-i-o-spi'los. Fam. Aizoaceae). Squat succulents of S. Africa, with thick leaves in pairs, and stemless rayed yellow flowers, September–October, related to Mesembryanthemum.

Selection. *P. bolusii*, golden-yellow; *magnipunctatus*, yellow; *nobilis*, clumpforming, yellow; and *simulans*, granitelike leaves, large, yellow flowers.

Cultivation. Pot in March, standard cactus compost, to grow in cool greenhouse or frame; water regularly in summer, very little in winter, minimum temp. 7° C. (45° F.); sunny positions. Useful house plants.

Plenus (-a, -um). Full, double, usually of flowers with extra sepals or petals. Ex. *Bellis perennis* v. *flore plenus*.

Plicatus (-a, -um). Plicate, pleated, folded lengthwise. Ex. *Thuja plicata*.

Plum, Cherry. See *Prunus cerasifera*.

Plumbago (plum-ba'go. Fam. Plumbaginaceae). The species chiefly grown is *P. capensis*, a S. African climbing shrub, to 8 ft, with short spikes of pale blue flowers, summer, and a white v. *alba*; in the border of a warm greenhouse; the current year's growth being cut back almost to its base after flowering. May also be grown in large pots or tubs, standard compost, minimum winter temp. 7° C. (45° F.). Propagation is easy by cuttings of firm young shoots, summer.

Plums. Botanically, cultivated plums are regarded as varieties of the species *Prunus domestica* (*communis*), the origins of which are obscure, and possibly hybrid. Horticulturally, this important group of stone fruits falls into two groups; the plums proper and the gage plums. Damsons and Bullaces, sometimes considered plums, have their parentage in *P. insititia*, and are considered separately under Damsons (q.v.). Plums are hardy enough to be grown throughout Britain, but are commercially important in Kent and the south-east, East Anglia, and the midlands of Worcestershire and adjoining counties. They succeed on most soils, given reasonable drainage, depth and freedom from over-acidity. Since they flower relatively early, they need to be grown away from low-lying sites or situations to which cold air drains readily. Plums yield much more heavily than gages, and are preferable for planting in the north or in cold localities. Bush and standard trees take 5–7 years to come into bearing and then may yield 40–200 lb; gages yield about half these quantities or less.

Varieties. Culinary: Early Laxton, mid July; Rivers's Early Prolific, end of July; Czar, early August; Gisborne's Prolific, mid August; Purple Egg or Pershore, mid August; Belle de Louvain, end of August; Pershore (Yellow Egg), end of August; Victoria, mid August; Blaisdon Red, end of August; Giant Prune, mid September; Monarch, mid September; Warwickshire Drooper, mid September; Marjorie's Seedling, September. Dessert: Early Laxton, end of July; Denniston's Superb Gage, mid August; Early Transparent Gage, mid August; Oullin's Golden Gage, mid August; Greengage, end of August; Cambridge Gage, end of August; Laxton's Goldfinch, end of August; Jefferson's Gage, early September; Kirke's Blue, mid September; Count Althann's Gage, mid September; Coe's Golden Drop, end of September; Severn Cross, end of September; Golden Transparent Gage, early October.

Pollination. Of the above plums, the varieties which can be expected to set a good crop with their own pollen, being self-fertile, are Belle de Louvain, Czar, Denniston's Superb, Early Laxton, Early Transparent Gage, Giant Prune, Gisburn's Prolific, Golden Transparent Gage, Oullin's Gage, Marjorie's Seedling, Pershore, Victoria and Warwickshire Drooper. Other varieties are either self-sterile or only partially self-fertile, and therefore need a compatible variety, flowering at the same period, to be

planted with them. Plums may be divided into four groups:

Early-flowering Varieties: Coe's Golden Drop, Count Althann's Gage, Crimson Drop, Diamond, Denniston's Superb, Early Transparent Gage, Early Laxton, Jefferson, Monarch, Rivers's Early Prolific, Warwickshire Drooper. Any two or more of these varieties may be planted to cross-pollinate one another; except Coe's Golden Drop, Crimson Drop and Jefferson, which are incompatible to one another.

Mid-season Flowering Varieties: Bryanston Gage, Blaisdon Red, Old Greengage, Yellow Egg, Transparent Gage, Victoria, all of which cross-pollinate well.

Late-flowering Varieties: Belle de Louvain, Czar, Gisborne's Prolific, Golden Transparent Gage, Laxton's Goldfinch, Kirke's Blue, Oullin's Golden Gage, Marjorie's Seedling, Purple Pershore, Severn Cross, all of which are compatible and cross-pollinating. Alternatively, damsons can be used: Frogmore to cross-pollinate early-flowering plums; Merryweather for mid season; and Farleigh or King of the Damsons for late-flowering.

Propagation. Plums are propagated vegetatively; selected varieties being budded on forms of *Prunus domestica* such as Common Mussel, slightly dwarfing, suitable for all varieties; Common Plum, partially dwarfing, most suitable for gages and Victoria; Brompton, for vigorous trees, but susceptible to suckering; Myrobalan B for vigorous plums, but not gages; and St Julien A, a selected form of *Prunus insititia*, for all plums, giving medium-sized trees coming into fruit early. Trees may be grown in bush, half-standard, standard or fan-trained forms.

Planting. Ideally, plums should be planted in October–early January, though may be planted until March; bush trees 12 ft apart, half-standards 15 ft, and standards 18–20 ft, in well prepared stations; in sunny, open positions out of reach of early spring frosts.

Soil Preparation. The soil should be cultivated in depth to give good drainage, with subsoil well broken; dressed with gypsum if clayey; top-soil may be enriched with rotted organic matter and bone meal, and limed to a pH 6·5.

Cultivation. When 2- or 3-year-old trees are planted, and staked if standards, no pruning is needed the first year after planting. In second year select three to five robust, healthy, well-spaced shoots for permanent branches; cut back by half their length; remove other shoots, in spring. The following year, shorten leading shoots by about half, cut out very thin weakly growth. Thereafter, no severe pruning is needed, other than removing dead or weak wood, and cutting leaders to induce shapeliness, and removing overcrowding wood, each spring.

Plums do best in arable conditions; with annual top-dressing of manure or compost, and a fertilizer adequate in nitrogen (say 3 parts by weight ammonium sulphate, 2 parts superphosphate, 1 part sulphate of potash at 2 oz. per sq. yd), in March. Liming may be necessary occasionally on acid soils.

Heavily cropping branches should be supported in bearing; and it pays to thin the fruits in June if possible. Fruits are gathered ripe for use. Some varieties keep a while, stored in cool airy conditions.

Fan-shaped Trees. With blossom protection from spring frost damage, the finest dessert plums and gages are grown on walls, preferably south, east or west, on fan-shaped trees on Common Mussel or St Julien A rootstocks. Trees should be spaced 15–18 ft, apart, and planted about 8 in. from the wall to slope towards it, to train branches on wires, spaced 6 in. apart. The branch framework is built up in the same manner as for Peaches (q.v.), cutting the growth back each March, until the fan is established. Thereafter, leading shoots can be trained to extend the framework if necessary, and new shoots trained in to fill empty space. Shoots growing into or straight away from the wall are cut away in spring. Other side-shoots are tip-pruned when they reach to six leaves, and fruiting laterals can be left closer and longer than with peach since the plum fruits on both old and new wood. After harvest, shoots can be shortened by about half, and strong vertical shoots bent and tied down to the wires.

Diseases. Root Rot may be caused by infection by the Honey Fungus, *Armillaria mellea*, which cannot be cured; both tree and roots and the 'bootlace' rhizomorphs of the fungus must be removed and burnt. 'Die-back' of shoots and branches may be caused by waterlogging of the soil, lack of lime, or roots weakened by fungus attacks. Bacterial Canker (*Pseudomonas morsprunorum*) causes yellowing of leaves, stunted shoot growth, and cankered bark on stems; dead and cankered growth must be cut out and burnt, cuts dressed with a tree paint, and it helps to spray with a copper fungicide after leaf-fall in autumn. Powdery Mildew (*Podosphaera oxyacanthe*) coats undersides of leaves with white powdery patches, and needs treatment with a karathane or sulphur fungicide. The Brown-rot fungi, *Sclerotinia laxa, S. fructigena,* which attack other tree fruits, may cause Wither Tip and Spur Blight, Blossom Wilt and Brown Rot of fruits in plums; affected parts should be cut out and burnt, and routine winter tar-oil wash and a spring fungicide applied at budburst. Silver Leaf, *Stereum purpureum,* shows in a silvery appearance of the leaves on infected branches; the fungus staining the wood beneath the bark brown. All dead wood, on which the fungus can fructify and spore, must be cut out, preferably as soon as seen; the bark of the main trunk must then be slit from top to bottom with a sharp knife in one continuous cut from branch or branches affected, and the roots dressed with a fruit fertilizer and organic matter, in May–June. This stimulates growth and helps the tree to overcome the infection. The cutting can be repeated the following year, if necessary. Sooty Blotch (*Glaeodes pomigena*) may disfigure fruits in wet seasons, and a post-blossom application of colloidal copper is preventive. Disfigured fruits, known as Pocket Plums or Bladder Plums, reflect a fungus infection (*Taphrina pruni*), and should be removed and burnt.

Pests. Aphids (*Anuraphis padi, Hyalopterua arundinis, Phorodon humuli*) infest the leaves in spring and summer, but are controlled by the routine winter tar-oil wash, and a malathion or nicotine insecticide in summer. The Red Plum Maggot, *Cydia funebrana*, feeds in maturing fruit from mid June, the red caterpillar and its frass being found inside; tar-oil winter wash and an application of derris in June give good control. Various moth caterpillars— Winter Moth, Mottled Umber, March Moth, Tortrix Moth, Early Moth, Green Moth—may feed on blossoms and leaves, as on other tree fruits, and call for the addition of a gamma-BHC or malathion insecticide to the routine spring spraying, Plum Sawfly (*Hoplocampa flava*) gives rise to brownheaded, creamy white caterpillars which feed in fruitlets, causing them to drop with a wet black frass exuding; gamma-BHC applied at the cot-split stage or 7–10 days after blossom fall is helpful, or derris can be used, and repeated a week later. Red-legged Weevil (*Otiorrhynchus clavipes*) feeds on foliage, blossoms and fruitlets, and bark in April–June; Derris or DDT control, though weevils can be trapped at night by tapping shoots and catching them on a sheet as they fall. Scale insects on shoots are controlled by winter tar-oil wash. Wasps (*Vespula* sp.) can do much damage to ripening fruits; *see* Wasps. Red Spider Mites (*Metatetranychus ulmi*) are best controlled by spraying with a Rogor 40, kelthane or liquid derris in June, and repeat as necessary. Thrips (*Taeniothrips inconsequens*) damage flowers and cause rough russeting on fruits; malathion at white bud stage is useful, or Rogor 40 at cot-split stage.

The routine preventive sprays for Plums are: (1) A winter wash with tar-oil at 5 per cent in December–January to control Aphids and the Red Plum Maggot, and keep Blossom Wilt in check, annually; and (2) a copper fungicide, plus a malathion insecticide for caterpillars, at bud-burst to white bud stage of blossom development; and (3) Rogor 40 at cot-split if sawfly is troublesome. Other sprays according to the need revealed by experience.

Plumule. The undeveloped aerial stem of the embryo of a seed. *See* Radicle.

Poa (po'a. Fam. Gramineae). A large genus of grasses, annual or perennial; of which *P. annua*, an annual that seeds freely, is found often in lawns; *nemoralis*,

woodland meadow grass, is useful for shade; *pratensis* and vs., smooth-leaved Meadow Grass, and *trivialis*, rough-stalked Meadow Grass, are perennials often used for lawns (q.v.); all are native to Britain and the northern hemisphere.

Pod. A dehiscent, dry fruit, containing several seeds; characteristic of the Legumes.

Podocarpus (po-do-karp'us. Fam. Taxaceae). Evergreen trees and shrubs of warm countries, not hardy enough for Britain except for a few species which may be grown in mild, frost-free localities. *Selection. P. andinus*, the plum-fruited Yew of Chile, yew-like in growth and foliage, to 40 ft, with yellow fruits, with light green leaves, thrives in S. England; *alpinus*, Victoria, Tasmania, a decorative, spreading bush, for sheltered rock gardens; *macrophyllus*, the Kusa-maki of China and Japan, small tree, very long leaves; *nubigenus*, Chile, to 30 ft, bright deep green; *salignus*, Chile, to 40 ft, narrow leaved; and *nivalis*, New Zealand, Alpine Totara, a spreading bush of 3 ft, may be tried.

Cultivation. Plant September–October or March–May, humus-rich, well-drained soil, sheltered, frost-free positions.

Propagation. By seeds, April, in cold frame. By cuttings of young shoots, July–August, in propagating frame, slight bottom heat of 15·5° C. (60° F.).

Podophyllum (po-do-pil'lum. Fam. Podophyllaceae). Rather curious perennials, with peltate, lobed leaves, nodding flowers, sometimes followed by edible berry fruits.

Selection. P. emodi, India, 1 ft, white spring flowers, scarlet, tomato-like fruits, and v. *chinense*, rose flowers; *peltatum*, American Mandrake or May Apple, white spring flowers, and edible yellow fruit in July; *versipelle*, W. China, much divided leaves, and deep crimson flowers in umbels, late spring.

Cultivation. Plant October–March, in rather peaty moist soil, partial shade, and shelter.

Propagation. By division of creeping rootstock in March–May; by seeds, sown April, out of doors.

Podsol. A type of soil, consisting of a layer of acid decomposing organic material, over a leached layer of impoverished sandy earth, which overlies a hard pan of mineral-laden soil; characteristic of sandy heaths, or moorlands.

Poeticus (-a, -um). Of the poets. Ex. *Narcissus poeticus*, the Poet's Narcissus.

Pogon. A beard; Pogoniris is the group of Bearded Irises (q.v.).

Poinsettia. See *Euphorbia pulcherrima.*

Poison Ivy. *Rhus radicans.*

Poison Oak. *Rhus toxicodendron.*

Poisonous Berries. The berries or fruits of the following garden and native plants are toxic if eaten: Buckthorn (*Rhamnus* spp.), Baneberry (*Actaea spicata*), Black Bryony (*Tamus communis*), White Bryony (*Bryonia dioica*), Cuckoo Pint (*Arum maculatum, italicum*), Caper Spurge (*Euphorbia lathyrus*), Cherry Laurel (*Prunus laurocerasus*), Cotoneaster spp., Herb Paris (*Paris quadrifolia*), Colchicum autumnale (seeds), Ivy (*Hedera helix*), Holly (*Ilex* spp.), Laburnum spp., Lily of the Valley (*Convallaria* sp.), Lupin (*Lupinus* spp.), Mezereon (*Daphne mezereum*), Mistletoe (*Viscum album*), Privet (*Lingustrum vulgare*), Deadly Nightshade (*Atropa belladonna*), Woody Nightshade (*Solanum dulcamara*), Black Nightshade (*Solanum nigrum*), Jerusalem Cherry (*Solanum pseudocapsicum*), Solomon's Seal (*Polygonatum* spp.), Spurge Laurel (*Daphne laureola*), Spindle (*Euonymus europaeus*) and Yew (*Taxus baccata*).

Poisonous Fungi. These are few, and are best recognized by their appearance and characteristics. The most lethal is the Death Cap (*Amanita phalloides*); others are the False Death Cap (*Amanita mappa*), Fly Agaric (*Amanita muscaria*), Panther Cap (*Amanita pantherina*), Crested Lepiota (*Lepiota cristata*), Livid Entoloma (*Entoloma lividum*), Redstaining Inocybe (*Inocybe patouillardii*), Yellow-staining Mushroom (*Psalliota xanthoderma*) and Verdigris Agaric (*Stropharia aeruginosa*). See *Edible and Poisonous Fungi*, Bulletin No. 23. (Min. of Agriculture).

Poisonous Plants. Many native and several garden plants have toxic properties of leaf, stem, root and fruit, when ingested; but the danger is greatest to grazing animals and children. Many poisonous plants are avoided because they have an unpleasant odour or taste. In general, it is wise to deter children

from sampling the flowers or the seedheads of plants of the *Ranunculus* family, such as Buttercups, Clematis, Hellebores, Aquilegia, Aconitum and Delphinium; the *Papaver* family (Poppies); the *Caryophyllaceae* family, including Carnations, Pinks, Dianthus; *Hypericum* spp., and the weeds such as Hemlock, Cowbane, Dropworts, Henbane, Foxglove and False Caper Spurge and other Spurges (*Euphorbia*). It is worth noting that the nectar of Rhododendrons is poisonous.

Poke Weed. See *Phytolacca.*

Polemonium (po-le-mo'ni-um. Fam. Polemoniaceae). Hardy herbaceous perennials for the border or rock garden, showy, bell-like flowers in summer.

Selection. *P. carneum*, N. America, 2 ft, corymbs of blue flowers; *coeruleum*, Charity, Greek Valerian or Jacob's Ladder, northern hemisphere, 2½ ft, blue; and v. *album*, white-flowering; *flavum*, Arizona, 2 ft, yellow; *foliosissimum*, Rockies, 2 ft, white or blue flowers; and *pauciflorum*, Mexico, 1½ ft, drooping yellow flowers, are good border plants: while *confertum*, Wyoming, 6 in., clustered blue flowers, June; *lanatum*, Arctic, 6 in., blue, July; and *mellitum*, Rockies, 6 in., pale blue to white, are useful for the rock garden or the alpine house.

Cultivation. Plant September–October, or April–May; well-drained, humus-rich soil; pH 6, alpine species with scree drainage.

Propagation. By division in September. By seeds, April, in cool greenhouse or frame, to plant out later.

Polianthes (pol-i-an'thes. Fam. Amaryllicaceae). The one species, *P. tuberosa*, Tuberose, Mexico, to 3 ft, is a half-hardy bulbous plant, with very fragrant white, tubular flared flowers in autumn, for the warm greenhouse. Bulbs are planted deeply in 4- or 5-in. pots, singly, standard compost, and plunged with bottom heat of 15·5–21° C. (60–70° F.), in late autumn or early spring; watered increasingly from when the leaves show. Fresh bulbs are bought each year, preferably double forms such as 'Double American' or 'The Pearl', and old ones discarded.

Pollard. A tree with its trunk cut off at 6–8 ft, so as to produce a rounded head of thin branches, usually practised with Hornbeam and Willow.

Pollen. The dust-like minute spores produced in the anthers of flowers as pollen-grains, each grain consisting of a single cell with nucleus, and nutritive material, within two outer coats. In orchids, the grains are in groups or masses (pollinia); in aquatic plants, they may have only one outer coat. The colour is often yellow, but orange, red, green, blue, purple to black and shadings in between are known, according to species. The form, shape and markings of the outer coat are typical of the genus, and so persistent that pollen grains found buried in geology are reliable guides to the nature of former vegetation of ages ago.

Pollination. The deposition of (male) pollen grains on the (female) stigma or organ of a flower. The grains may be transferred by movement, wind, or insects. See Fertilization.

Poly-. Prefix in compound words meaning many. Ex. *polyandrus*, many-stamened; *polygamus*, having male and hermaphrodite, female and hermaphrodite, or male, female and hermaphrodite flowers on one plant; *polymorphus*, having many forms; *polypetalus*, having many petals; and *polyphyllus*, having many leaves.

Polyanthus. See *Primula*.

Polygala (po-lig'a-la. Fam. Polygalaceae). Milkwort. Although a large genus, only a few are grown for their showy flowers.

Selection. P. calcarea, Europe and Britain, evergreen prostrate perennial, with short racemes of blue, pink or white flowers, summer; *chamaebuxus*, Central Europe, 6 in., evergreen shrublet, with pea-like, white, yellow-tipped purple flowers, June; and v. *purpurea*, purple-red and yellow; *paucifolia*, N. America, 3-in. evergreen shrublet, rose-purple to white, summer flowers; and *vayrede*, Spain, evergreen prostrate shrublet of 3 in., reddish-purple to yellow flowers, June, are choice for the sheltered rock garden in mild localities; the alpine house elsewhere. *P. myrtifolia* v. *gradiflora*, S. Africa, 4 ft, and *virgata*, S. Africa, 4 ft, are shrubs for the cool greenhouse, with purple flowers, summer.

Cultivation. Plant (or pot) in March–April, well-drained, humus-rich soil, partial shade. When pan-grown may be placed outside for summer. Greenhouse plants require regular watering in growth, only very moderate watering in winter, minimum temp. 7° C. (45° F.).

Propagation. By cuttings of rooted runners, taken in June–July; or shoot cuttings in June.

Polygonatum, Solomon's Seal (po-li-go-na'tum. Fam. Liliaceae). Fleshy-rooted herbaceous perennials, distinctive for graceful arching stems, bearing pendulous, tubular, bell-mouthed white or greenish-white flowers.

Selection. P. multiflorum, also known as David's Harp and Lady's Seal, native to Britain, Europe, and temperate Asia, 2–4 ft, white, June; × *hybridum* (*P. multiflorum* × *P. odoratum*), often sold as *P. multiflorum*, 3–4 ft, with double-flowering forms, and finely variegated in 'Barker's variety'; *odoratum* (*officinale*), Britain, Europe, Asia, 1 ft, white, June; *latifolium*, Europe, 2–4 ft, greenish-white, June; and *verticillatum*, with whorls of leaves and flowers, rare native, Europe, Asia Minor, 2–4 ft, greenish, June.

Cultivation. Plant September–October, any good soil, open ground or woodland. Mature roots may be potted in 6-in. pots, for forcing in a cool greenhouse, in early autumn.

Propagation. By division in September; by seeds, April.

Polygonum (po-lig'o-num. Fam. Polygonaceae). A genus of many species of annuals and perennial herbs from temperate regions of the world; including native weeds such as annual Knotgrass, *P. aviculare*, and Black Bindweed, *P. convolvulus*, and Persicaria, *P. persicaria*. The tall-growing herbaceous perennials of Japan, *P. cuspidatum* and *P. sachlinense*, naturalize readily and may also become almost ineradicable weeds.

Selection. P. affine, Nepal, 5–9 in., mat-forming, with spikes of rose-red flowers, autumn, and v. 'Darjeeling Red'; *tenuicaule*, Japan, 4 in., white fragrant flowers, April; and *vaccinii-folium*, Himalaya, 6 in., bright rose spikes. autumn, may be grown on rock gardens, *P. amplexicaule*, Himalaya, 2–3 ft, bright crimson spikes, late summer, and vs. *album*, white, *oxyphyllum*, scented, and *speciosum*, claret; *bistorta superbum*, 2 ft, rosy pink, summer-flowering form of the native Bistort; and *campanulatum*, Himalaya, 2–3 ft, pink branching flower-heads, summer, are useful border perennials. *P. baldschuanicum*, Turkistan, is a quick-growing, twining, deciduous climber to 40 ft, cascading panicles of pink-tinged, white flowers, summer and autumn, to cover stumps, sheds and unsightly objects.

Cultivation. Plant October–April, any reasonably good soil, sun or partial shade.

Propagation. By division in March. By seeds, April, out of doors, or in pans in cold frame.

Polyploid. A plant having three or more times the haploid or basic number of chromosomes in the cell nucleus.

Polypodium (po-li-po′di-um. Fam. Polypodiaceae). A genus of over 1,100 species of ferns, mostly evergreen, with leathery fronds.

Selection. Hardy kinds are the native *P. interjectum*, Polypody, fronds lobed in pairs; *australe*, triangular fronds with paired lobes; and *vulgare*, Adder's Fern, Wall or Wood Fern, and fine vs. *cambricum* (*australe cambricum*) and × *schneideri*, which make fine pot plants. *P. aureum*, tropical America, Australia, and vs., *mayi*, fronds of 3–5 ft; *caudiceps*, Formosa, 6-in. fronds, for baskets; *chnoodes*, W. Indies, 2 ft arching fronds; *enerve*, Java, small, elegant fronds; *fossum*, Easter Is., 12-in. fronds; *pectinatum*, Mexico, 1–3 ft fronds; *picoti*, Brazil, arching, wavy 3-ft fronds; *pustulatum*, Scented Polypody of New Zealand, 6-in. fronds; require cool to warm greenhouse conditions.

Cultivation. Hardy kinds may be planted September–October, or March–April, in shade, moisture-retentive soil, cool positions with rhizomes at surface level. Greenhouse kinds require a compost of 2 parts by bulk fibrous or peaty loam, 1 part leaf-mould, 1 part coarse sand; in shallow pots, or epiphytes in baskets; cool, shade; minimum winter temp. 7–10° C. (45–50° F.).

Propagation. By division March–April, by spores when available.

Polystichum (po-lis′tik-um. Fam. Polypodiaceae). A genus of ferns, often referred to as Aspidium, with somewhat leathery fronds, easily cultivated.

Selection. Hardy evergreen native species are *P. aculeatum*, Hard Shield Fern, stiff fronds to 3 ft; *lonchitis*, Holly Fern, fronds of 2 ft; *setiferum*, Soft Shield Fern, to which may be added *acrostichoides*, N. America, 2 ft fronds, and vs. *grandiceps* and *incisum*, and *munitum*, N. America, 1–2-ft fronds, as hardy for Britain. Exotic species requiring greenhouse conditions are *P. adiantiforme*, S. America, etc.; *aristatum*, Japan, China, Australasia; *drepanum*, Madeira; *echinatum*, W. Indies; *falcinellum*, Madeira; *lentum*, India; and *triangulum*, W. Indies; all with toothed, pinnae on fronds of 1–2 ft.

Cultivation. Hardy kinds, plant September–October or March–April, well-drained, peat-enriched soil, cool, moist places, partial shade. Exotics in compost of sandy loam and peat, in cool greenhouse, with ample moisture and shade, minimum winter temp. 10° C. (50° F.).

Propagation. Preferably by spores when ripe.

Polythene, Polyethylene. A tough, waxy, flexible, chemically resistant, thermoplastic material, which is widely used in gardening. In translucent or clear film or sheeting to substitute for glass in frames, lights and greenhouses; to line greenhouses in winter and early spring against heat losses; in black sheeting to mulch crops, to exclude light for forcing techniques or photoperiodic regulation of flowering; as green sheeting to shade greenhouses; as coloured sheeting for making pools; though under outdoor light its life is limited, tending to become brittle and tear after a few years. It is used to provide inexpensive plant pots in black polythene; and as cold-water piping is used widely for watering and irrigation purposes. Polypropylene is a similar colourless thermoplastic material of greater strength. *See* Polyvinyl Chloride.

Polyvinyl Chloride, PVC. A colourless thermoplastic material, more light transmitting, stronger and longer lasting than polythene, and more expensive. It is superior for cloche, frame and greenhouse use, and for the lining of pools or water reservoirs, where long life is desirable. It is available in flexible sheeting or semi-rigid form; in various gauges or thicknesses.

Pome. A succulent fruit with a firm fleshy layer enclosing carpels or seeds, forming the core. Ex. Apple, Pear, Quince.

Pomegranate. See *Punica granatum*.

Pomology. The study of fruits.

Poncirus (pon-ki'rus. Fam. Rutaceae). The one species, *P. trifoliata*, N. China, is a deciduous stoutly spined shrub, to 10 ft, with white orange-blossom flowers, April–May, and small bitter orange fruits; related to Citrus, but hardy, except for cold districts, in well-drained, reasonably rich soil, and sun. Propagated by seeds, in April.

Pond. *See* Water Garden.

Pondweed. See *Potamogeton*.

Pondweed, Cape. See *Aponogeton*.

Pontederia (pon-te-de'ri-a. Fam. Pontederiaceae). The species chiefly grown is *P. cordata*, a handsome aquatic plant with bright green, cordate leaves, and spikes of sky-blue or white flowers, summer; and v. *angustifolia*, narrower leaves, bright blue flowers; for shallow water and pool margins.

Cultivation. Plant in 6–12 in. of water, autumn or spring.

Propagation. By division, March–October.

Pool. *See* Water Garden.

Poplar. See *Populus*.

Poppy. See *Papaver*.

Poppy, American Prickly, Mexican. See *Argemone*.

Poppy, Blue Himalayan. See *Meconopsis betonicifolia*.

Poppy, Californian. See *Eschscholtzia*.

Poppy, Corn. See *Papaver rhoeas*.

Poppy, Horned. See *Glaucium*.

Poppy, Mallow. See *Callirhoe*.

Poppy, Opium. See *Papaver somniferum*.

Poppy, Welsh. See *Meconopsis cambrica*.

Poppy, White Californian Tree. See *Romneya*.

Populus, Poplar (pop'u-lus. Fam. Salicaceae). Quick-growing deciduous trees with simple leaves and dioecious flowers, especially useful for heavy cold soils, but because of the water-avid, far-reaching roots not suitable for small gardens or for planting near to the house or buildings.

Selection. P. alba, the Abele, White Poplar, Europe, to 100 ft, leaves white-woolly beneath; v. *pyramidalis*, erect-growing; × *berolinensis*, Berlin Poplar, to 60 ft, slender, columnar; *candicans*, Balm of Gilead, to 80 ft, spicy balsam fragrance in spring, but suckers freely; × *eugenei*, to 100 ft, large-leaved, columnar; *lasiocarpa*, China, to 60 ft, very large leaves; *nigra*, the Black Poplar, Europe, best in vs. *betulifolia*, the Manchester Poplar, to 100 ft; *italica*, fastigiate Lombardy Poplar; × *robusta*, to 100 ft, upright, timber tree; × *serotina* v. *aurea*, Golden Poplar, Italy; *tremula*, Aspen, Europe, etc., to 50 ft, with ever quivering leaves, and v. *pendula*, stiffly weeping; *trichocarpa*, N. America, to 150 ft, fast-growing Western Balsam Poplar, fragrant in spring: *deltoides*, American Cottonwood, or Necklace Poplar, 100 ft.

Cultivation. Plant young trees, October–March, in any ordinary soil, including moist, cold ground, open situations. The Lombardy Poplar is good for a tall screen, or hedging if trimmed annually, which restricts root extension.

Propagation. By leafless shoot cuttings, firmed into open ground, autumn–March.

Pore. A term sometimes used for the minute opening or stoma in plant leaves. *See* Stomata.

Portugal Laurel. See *Prunus lusitanica*.

Portulaca (por-tu-la'ka. Fam. Portulaceae). The species chiefly grown is *P. grandiflora*, the Sun Plant of Brazil, 6 in. high, for its single summer flowers, in yellow, red, pink and purple; with vs. *flore pleno*, double; 'Jewel', pink; *thellusonii*, orange-scarlet; and *thorburnii*, yellow, as half-hardy annuals, sown under glass, March–April, standard compost, bottom heat of 18° C. (65° F.); to plant out in May. *P. oleracea*, the common Purslane, S. Europe, may be grown as a hardy annual, sown in March–April, for its young shoots to be used in salads. Both plants like well-drained, light soil, and sun.

Potamogeton (po-ta-mo-ge'ton. Fam. Potamogetonaceae). Rhizomatous-rooting, perennial, submerged aquatic herbs, useful as underwater oxygenating plants in pools, but needing control.

Selection. P. natans, broad-leaved

Pondweed; *crispus*, Curled Pondweed; *densus*, opposite-leaved Pondweed; *lucens*, Shining Pondweed; and *pectinatus*, Fennel-leaved Pondweed, are hardy natives which may be planted in April–May, in pools or streams.

Potash. In gardening, a term loosely applied to potassium oxide (K_2O) or potassium salts.

Potassium, Kalium (K). As an element potassium is an essential constituent of plants, absorbed by the roots from the soil, and necessary to normal growth particularly at growing tips of shoots and roots, and is held to promote sturdiness and vigour, and therefore ressistance to disease. Most soils contain some potash, but it is least in free-draining soils and sands. It is provided in the plant remains, manures, wood and plant ash, or in mineral form by fertilizers such as potassium chloride, potassium sulphate, kainite, potassium nitrate, potassium carbonate and flue dusts.

Potassium Permanganate, Permanganate of Potsh ($KMnO_4$). A purple, crystalline salt, soluble in water, used in gardening as (*a*) a disinfectant to wash pots, tools, etc.; (*b*) a weak algaecide, added to the water for plants to deter 'greening' of the soil under glass; (*c*) an oxidant, chiefly to water fungus-infested lawns, and hasten the decomposition of organic matter.

Potato (*Solanum tuberosum*, Fam. Solanaceae). Introduced from S. America, the potato probably reached Spain about 1570, and England in 1586, being described by John Gerard in his *Herbal* in 1597, and apparently first grown in Ireland in 1587 by Sir Walter Raleigh; since when it has become a food crop of first importance in the British Isles.

Varieties. Since the potato is propagated vegetatively, there is a strong tendency for varietal stocks to deteriorate, and new varieties are constantly being bred. Although it is usually safe to reserve 'seed tubers' from home-grown healthy crop plants for one or two years, it is wise thereafter, in England at least, to bring in certificated seed tubers from the aphis-free, seed-raising areas of Scotland, Northern Ireland and Wales, where virus infections are minimal. Selection:

First Early, to crop in June–July:

'Arran Pilot'*, 'Craig's Alliance'*, 'Duke of York', 'Epicure', 'Sutton's Foremost'*, 'Home Guard'*, 'Sharpe's Express', 'Ulster Chieftain'*, 'Ulster Premier'*, 'Ulster Prince'*.

Second Early, to crop July–September: 'Craig's Royal Red'*, 'Dunbar Rover'*, 'Maris Peer', 'Pentland Beauty', 'Sutton's Ben Lomond'*, 'Ulster Dale'*, 'Ulster Emblem'*.

Maincrop, for keeping: 'Arran Banner'*, 'Arran Consul'*, 'Arran Victory'*, 'Dr Mackintosh'*, 'Dunbar Standard'*, 'Golden Wonder'*, 'Majestic'*, 'King Edward VII', 'Pentland Crown'*, 'Pentland Dell'*, 'Redskin', 'Sutton's Angus Gem'*, 'Ulster Supreme'.

Epicurean Varieties. Esteemed for frying and for salads: 'Belle de Juillet', 'Kipfler', 'Blue Eigenheimer', 'Pink Fir Apple', 'Red Star'.

*Immune to Wart Disease.

Cultivation. Potatoes crop in almost any soil made friable by liberal organic manuring; though the ideal is a lightish, humus-rich soil, well dug in autumn, organically manured, and of pH 5·5 to 6·5. Potatoes, however, are one of the few crops that may be planted in freshly prepared soil, manured prior to planting, though the more rotted the manure the better. Earlies require a warm sheltered site, and may be planted in late February–March in mild districts; mid March to early April elsewhere. Second earlies are planted in first half of April; maincrops before April is out. Seed tubers, about egg-size, are chitted or sprouted by placing eye- or rose-end up, in shallow boxes or papier-mâché egg-trays, in light, frostproof quarters as soon as possible in the year; all but the two strongest sprouts are rubbed off when planting.

Planting. Prepare V-drills, 6–8 in. deep, 20–24 in. apart for earlies, 24–28 in. for second earlies, 30 in. for maincrops; strew with organic matter (manure, compost, peat, spent hops, grass mowings, etc.), set tubers upright in this; earlies 12–14 in. apart, second earlies and maincrops 16–18 in.; cover lightly with soil and dress with a complete potato fertilizer (4 parts by weight ammonium sulphate, 4 parts superphosphate, 2 parts sulphate of potash, at $1\frac{1}{2}$–

2 oz. per linear yd of drill. Finish covering with soil to surface level. If large tubers are used, cut immediately before planting with two good sprouts per piece. Earth up when haulms are 6–8 in. high, and again three weeks later, to give cool rooting, and protection against scab disease; preferably when soil is moist but workable. Earlies are lifted in late June–August as tubers are of good size; second earlies and maincrops when haulms wither, September–October, preferably when the soil is reasonably dry, and tubers can be gathered clean. Store in dry, cool, dark conditions, protected against frost. Reject diseased or slug-ridden tubers.

Potatoes Under Glass. For very early supplies, seed tubers from a dwarf variety such as 'Duke of York' are sprouted beforehand, and set one to an 8-in. pot, three to a 12-in. pot, in a compost of two parts loam, 1 part rotted manure, compost, or leaf-mould, 1 part sand, plus a teaspoonful superphospate and ½ teaspoonful sulphate of potash per 2-gallon measure of soil; or in 12-in. deep boxes 10 in. apart; half-filling the pots, then planting the tubers, and just covering with the compost; water sparingly at first; add more compost as growth is made, stake the haulms; temp. 15·5° C. (60° F.) for first week or two, then about 10° C. (50° F.) for future growth, increasing watering. To gather the crop, turn plants in their soil ball out of the pots carefully, remove largest tubers, then replace plants in pots with a little extra compost to grow on. Alternatively, early potatoes may be grown in a frame, 3 in. deep, 10 in. apart, in similar compost, bottom heat of 10° C. (50° F.), and watered regularly but moderately, from January onwards.

Diseases. Blight (*Phytophthora infestans*) is the worst disease, destroying foliage in brown to black patches, with the risk of tubers being infected by spores washed into the soil; being most severe in wet weather and the wetter western regions. It is controlled by protective preventive sprays or dusts, applied just before infection is expected —about mid to late June in the south-west; early to mid July in the Midlands; late July in the north and Scotland, and renewed as necessary at 2–3-week intervals, according to weather and susceptibility of the area concerned. Forecasts are given by the Ministry of Agriculture to farmers (and gardeners) in the press, and on the radio. Appropriate fungicides are Bordeaux Mixture, and similar copper compounds in spray or dust form.

Scab (*Streptomyces scabies*) shows in skin-deep spots of roughish, corky tissue on tubers, but is largely prevented by liberal organic manuring, adequate earthing-up and clean seed, and is worst on dryish chalky or lime-rich soils. Powdery Scab is a fungus infection (*Spongospora subterranea*), difficult to cure but usually experienced under wet conditions and on poorly drained soils, which need correction. Black Scab or Wart disease (*Synchytrium endobioticum*) is avoidable by growing the varieties indicated as immune in susceptible soils. Dry Rot (*Fusarium caeruleum*) affects stored tubers, causing the ends to shrivel with the appearance of pinkish or bluish-green pustules, and infected tubers should be promptly destroyed. *Virus* infection takes many forms— Leaf Roll or Curl, accompanied by stunted growth; Mosaic, a bright yellow mottling of leaves; Curly Dwarf, very stunted growth with cauliflower-like foliage; Crinkle, leaves slighty mottled, puckered or crinkled and stunted; Leaf-drop Streak, when small angular, blackish-brown spots appear elongating along the veins and leaves drooping brown and withered. Although virus-infected tubers may be used for food, none should be saved for seed. There is no cure, and early and severely infected plants are best lifted and burnt. Viruses are largely transmitted by sap-sucking insects or aphids which need effective control.

Hollow-heart, Second-growth and malformation in tubers are usually caused by very moist growing conditions following a dry period. Similar conditions on heavy soils sometimes cause all top growth and few and small tubers.

Pests. Aphids or greenfly (*Macrosiphum euphorbiae, Myzus persicae,* etc.) damage plants, carry virus infections and make plants susceptible to damage by copper fungicides, and should be promptly controlled by the use of malathion, gamma-BHC or nicotine insecticide. Angleshades moth caterpillars (*Phlogophora meticulosa*), which bite holes in leaflets, Cutworm caterpillars of Noctuid moths, which bite stems and surface roots; Flea Beetles (*Psylliodes affinis*), and Swift Moth caterpillars (*Hepialus humuli, H. lupulinus*), which feed on roots, can be controlled by gamma-BHC applied in late spring. Chafer grubs, leatherjackets, wireworms millipedes, and black slugs which attack tubers, particularly in newly cultivated grassland soil, are best controlled by soil fumigation with flake naphthalene the previous winter. The Colorado Beetle, *Leptinotarsa decemlineata*, is to be feared in southern and eastern areas as an invader from Europe. The beetle is oval, yellowish with black stripes, and lays masses of orange-yellow eggs on potato leaves, hatching into brick-red larvae, which feed voraciously. An outbreak should be promptly reported to the police, or the Ministry of Agriculture. Eelworms (*Heterodera rostochiensis, Ditylenchus destructor*) cannot yet be easily controlled. Infestation shows in pinhead-size whitish cysts on the plant roots and tubers. Infested soil is best rested from potato cropping for 3–4 years, and liberally enriched with actively rotting organic matter; a green mustard crop being very helpful.

Potato Onion. *See* Onion.

Potentilla, Cinquefoil (po-ten-til'la. Fam. Rosaceae). A large genus of flowering plants, mostly herbaceous perennials, but also some fine shrubs, native to the northern hemisphere.

Selection. Herbaceous border plants are *P. argyrophylla*, Kashmir, 2–3 ft, palmate, silvery leaves, yellow flowers all summer; *atrosanguinea*, Himalaya, similar with purplish-red flowers; *nepalensis*, W. Himalaya, to 2 ft, crimson, July–August, and v. *willmottiae*, brilliant rosy-crimson; and *roxana*, orange-scarlet; their named hybrids—'Gibson's Scarlet', 1½ ft, July–September; 'Mons. Rouillard', double, blood-red; 'Yellow Queen', bright yellow, July–August; and 'Wm Rollisson', semi-double, dark orange, July–September; *hirta*, S. Europe, etc., 1½ ft, yellow, May–July; *megalantha*, Japan, 1 ft, yellow, summer; *recta*, S. Europe, 1½ ft, pale yellow,

June–July, and v. *warrenii*, bright yellow; while more dwarf species for the rock garden or alpine house are: *P. alchemilloides*, Pyrenees, 6 in., white, July–August; *aurea*, Alps, 4 in., rich yellow, July–August; *clusiana*, E. Alps, 6 in., white, June–August; *fragiformis*, NE. Asia, 6 in., yellow, summer; *nevadensis*, Spain, 8 in., evergreen, yellow, July–August; *nitida*, Alps, 3 in., pink, July–August; *verna* (*tabernaemontani*), W. Europe and Britain, 6 in.,

FIG. 184 *Potentilla fruticosa* 'Katherine Dykes'.

yellow, April–August, and v. *nana*, a 1-in. dwarf. The shrubby Cinquefoils are hardy, with flowers like small single roses, often from May to October, and include *P. arbuscula*, Himalaya, 1 ft, white flowers; *fruticosa*, northern hemisphere and Britain, 3–4 ft, golden-yellow; *glabra*, N. China, 2–4 ft, white; and their hybrids, of which 'Farrer's White', white flowering; × *friedrichsenii*, 3 ft, light yellow; 'Katherine Dykes', bright yellow; 'Donard Orange' ('Tangerine'), orange-yellow; *grandiflora* (Jackman's variety), yellow; 'Manelys' ('Moonlight'); 'Primrose Beauty', primrose-yellow; × *vilmoriniana*, cream-yellow; and *rigida*, bright yellow, are outstanding; *parvifolia*, N. China, 3 ft, golden-yellow; × *sulphurascens* 'Logan form', creamy yellow; and *tridentata*, Greenland, 1 ft, white flowering.

Cultivation. Plant border and rock garden perennials in October–November or March–April, well-drained loamy soil, partial shade or sun. Plant shrubs in October–March, well-drained soil, with humus, pH 6·0–6·5, sun or shade.

Propagation. Species and vs. by seeds, April, in cold frame or nursery bed. By division in autumn or spring. Shrubs by cuttings of young firm shoots, July–August, well-firmed in sandy loam.

Pots. In gardening, round containers, tapering from rim to base, largely used in propagating and growing plants in the greenhouse or indoors; now made in various materials, as follows:

Clay Pots are traditional and still widely used, for their sturdiness, economy, variety and suitability for balanced plant growth. Bad points are their heaviness, porosity and absorption of salts from the soil, difficulty in keeping clean, and breakability when roughly handled. They are graded according to the number made from a definite quantity of clay, known as a cast; though it is becoming more common to refer to pots by the diameter in inches at the top. The sizes most commonly in use today are:

Top diam. in inches	Height in inches	No. in cast	
$1\frac{1}{2}$	2	72	
2	3	72	(Thimbles)
$2\frac{1}{2}$	3	72	(Thumbs)
3	$3\frac{1}{2}$	60	(Mid Sixties)
$3\frac{1}{2}$	4	60	(Lge. Sixties)
4	$4\frac{1}{4}$	54	
$4\frac{3}{4}$	$4\frac{3}{4}$	48	(Small 48s)
5	5	48	
6	6	32	
$7\frac{1}{2}$	$7\frac{1}{2}$	24	
$8\frac{1}{2}$	$8\frac{1}{2}$	16	
10	10	12	
11	11	8	
$12\frac{1}{2}$	$12\frac{1}{2}$	6	
14	14	4	
$15\frac{1}{2}$	$15\frac{1}{2}$	2	
18	18	1	

There are also half-pots or pans in similar diameters, but half or less in height, chiefly for seed-raising and growing alpines and pot plants. All new clay pots need soaking thoroughly before use.

Plastic Pots. Manufactured in toughened polystyrene or a thermo-plastic, these pots are increasingly available in various colours, in sizes of an equal top diameter and depth of 2–$12\frac{1}{2}$ in., and pots and pans of useful sizes of lesser depth. Extremely light in weight, unbreakable in normal use, resistance to contamination, easily cleaned and non-porosity are the claimed advantages, together with greater and longer moisture retention, reducing watering needs. They do knock over more readily, however.

Whalehide or Bituminized Paper Pots. Cheap in first cost, light in weight, and designed for one-season use only, in sizes of 3–$6\frac{1}{4}$ in. top diameter, these pots make good plant containers.

Papier Mâché Pots. Cheapness, light weight and easy handling are the chief recommendations of these pots, though their use is usually for a single season.

Peat-Wood Fibre Pots. Made in a variety of sizes, square and round, and in strips, and usually impregnated with plant nutrients, these pots are excellent for propagative work, for plant roots grow naturally, through the walls of the pots, and plants can be potted on or transplanted without root disturbance at all, and growth is unchecked.

Polythene Pots. These are made of black polythene film, very cheaply, and being very light in weight are widely used by nurserymen in propagative work and in sending out plants grown in more rigid pots. They are less suitable for continued plant growth in pots.

Special Pots. Pots with extra depth, known as 'Long Toms' are made in various materials for raising sweet peas and deep-rooting plants. Ring Culture pots, without bottoms, are made in clay, plastic and whalehide. Orchid pots are made in clay.

Potting. The operation of transplanting seedlings or newly rooted cuttings to pots. The aim must be to disrupt or break the root system as little as possible. Small pots of 2–3 in. are usually sufficient; the seedling is held by its seed leaves, the cutting by its lower stem, as a rule, central in the pot, and the compost trickled in evenly to surround the root system, after which it can be carefully firmed, and watered.

Potting On. The operation of transferring a potted plant to the next larger size of pot as the root system development demands. Plants to be potted on should be watered a few hours beforehand, and transferred before the roots begin to grow and mat around the base or walls of the pot.

Potting Up. The lifting of a plant growing in open ground and potting it with roots enclosed in a soil ball.

Praecox. Precocious, early, developing earlier than other plants of a genus. Ex. *Cytisus praecox.*

Pratensis (-e). Of meadows. Ex. *Poa pratensis.*

Pratia (prat'i-a. Fam. Campanulaceae). The chief species grown is *P. angulata*, a creeping, mat-forming plant of New Zealand, with white lobelia-shaped flowers, June–July, and purplish berries; nominally hardy for sheltered rock gardens or the alpine house; with v. *treadwellii.*

Cultivation. Plant April–May, well-drained, light, humus-rich soil, and sunny warmth.

Propagation. By seeds, sown March, in cool greenhouse or frame. By cuttings of young shoots, June.

Pre-emergent Herbicides. Weed-killers designed to kill germinating weed seedlings in seed-beds before the plant seedlings appear. Herbicides based on pentachlorophenol may be used on seed-beds of most sown plants, and on newly sown lawns; usually being applied within two to three days of sowing, or immediately prior to sowing. Paraquat may be used to destroy germinated weeds prior to sowing, but several days should elapse between treatment and actual sowing with garden plant seeds.

Pricking Off, Pricking Out. A gardening term for the transplanting of seedlings from a seed box, pan or bed to more generous spacings where they are to be grown on. Recovery is aided by removing seedlings as soon as large enough to handle, usually immediately the first true leaves appear, with as little handling as possible. The younger the seedling, the more easily it is moved with least damage to its roots. It is best to handle seedlings by their seed leaves when possible.

Prickly Pear. See *Opuntia.*

Prickly Thrift. See *Acantholimon.*

Primrose. See *Primula vulgaris.*

Primrose, Cape. See *Streptocarpus.*

Primrose, Evening. See *Oenothera.*

Primula (pri-mu'la. Fam. Primulaceae). A large genus of perennial or monocarpic flowering plants, chiefly alpine though some come from lowland meadows, bogs and woodlands, largely of the northern temperate zones, with few from warm countries; characterized by stocky rhizomatous rootstocks, radical leaves and hermaphrodite flowers in handsome inflorescences.

Selection. Botanists divide the genus into no less than thirty sections. Horticulturally, the most important sections are: Auricula (for the Florist's Auricula, *see* separate entry under Auricula); Candelabra, Denticulata, Farinosae, Malacoides, Obconica, Petiolares, Sikkimensis, Sinenses, Soldanelloideae and Vernales. The gardener may select his plants according to where they are to be grown, as follows:

For the Rock Garden. Hardy European Primulas: *P. allionii*, Maritime Alps, rose-pink, March–April, and v. *alba*, white; *auricula*, Alps, 6 in., yellow, spring, and vs. *ciliata*, golden, May; *carniolica*, Maritime, Julian Alps, 4–10 in., rose with white throat, May; *clusiana*, Tyrol, 3 in., carmine, May; *marginata*, Maritime Alps, 4 in., lavender, May, and vs. *caerulea*, light blue; 'Linda Pope', lavender, white eye; and 'Prichards', bright light blue; × *pruhoniciana (juliana)* and vs., × *pubescens*, 6 in., rose-purple, May, and vs., *alba*, white; 'Faldonside', crimson; and 'Mrs J. H. Wilson', lilac, cream eye; *rubra (hirsuta)*, Alps, Pyrenees, 2½ in., rose, March, and vs.; *villosa*, Tyrol, Alps, 4 in., lilac-rose, May; *viscosa*, Switzerland, 3 in., violet, May; all of the Auricula Section; to which may be added *P. elatior*, Europe, Britain, Asia Minor, 6 in., sulphur-yellow, spring, and its forms; and *wulfeniana*, Austria, 3 in., deep rose, April. Hardy Asiatic Primulas: *P. capitata mooreana*, E. Himalaya, 8 in., violet, July–August; *farinosa*, N. Asia, N. Pacific America, Europe, Britain, the Bird's-eye Primrose, lilac, April–May; *polyneura*, N. China, 9 in., rose, May; *secundiflora*, Yunnan, 1–2 ft, reddish-purple, June; and *sikkimensis*,

Nepal, Burma, Yunnan, etc., 1–2 ft, yellow, May–June, and vs.

For the Alpine House. To the above may be added the Europeans: *P.* × *berniae*, 3 in., blue-mauve, May, and v. 'Windrush'; × *biflora*, 2 in., rose-purple, May; *cortusoides*, Siberia, 9 in., rose, May; *frondosa*, Balkans, 4 in., rose, April; *glutinosa*, Tyrol, 3 in., blue-violet, May; *minima*, S. Europe, 1 in., rose with white eye, April, and hybrids × *forsteri*, 2 in., rose-purple, and × *floerkeana*, 3 in., rose, April; and the Asiatics: *edgeworthii*, NW. Himalaya, 1 in., mauve, white eye, March; and v. *alba*; *forrestii*, Yunnan, 9 in., yellow, orange eye, June; *gracilipes*, Sikkim, mauve, yellow eye, April; × 'Pandora', 2 in., mauve, yellow eye, April; *scapigera*, W. Himalaya, 2 in., rose-mauve, yellow eye, March, and v. *alba*; *sessilis*, Himalaya, ½ in., mauve, yellow and white, April; *sieboldii*, Japan, 1 in., white, rose or purple, May, and its forms; *sherriffae*, Bhutan, 3 in., pale violet, April and *sino-plantaginea*, Yunnan, 6 in., violet-purple, April.

For Bog, Waterside and Moist Places. *P. alpicola*, Tibet, Bhutan, to 20 in., and vs., white, yellow, purple or violet flowers, May–June; the Candelabra species such as *beesiana*, China, 2 ft, rose-carmine, June, and hybrids × 'Edina', × 'Asthore'; *chungensis*, Yunnan to Assam, 2 ft, pale orange, June; *cockburniana*, SW. Szechwan, 1 ft, orange-red, June; *helodoxa*, Yunnan, Burma, to 3 ft, golden-yellow, June; *japonica*, Japan, 1½ ft, purplish-red, May–June, and hybrids 'Miller's Crimson' and 'Postford White'; *pulverulenta*, Szechwan, to 3 ft, deep red, June; and v. 'Bartley', rose-pink; and hybrids 'Aileen Aroon'; 'Red Hugh', 'Ladybird', etc.; *P. denticulata*, Himalaya,' ½–1 ft, purplish-blue, spring, and vs. *alba*, white, *rosea*, rose-pink, do well, also *florindae*, Tibet, to 3 ft, sulphur-yellow, June–July; *rosea*, Himalaya, 5 in., April, and v. 'Micia de Geer', carmine-pink; and *yargongensis*, Tibet, 1 ft, pink or mauve, May.

For Borders and Beds. Given moisture-retentive soil Primulas of the Candelabra Section given above make good border flowers, to which may be added *P. bulleyana*, Yunnan, 2 ft, deep orange,

denticulata, and its vs., Border Auriculas, and at the front of borders, several of the rock garden primulas do well. *P. vulgaris*, the Primrose of Britain and Europe, 4 in., sulphur-yellow flowers, March–April, may be grown in blue, white, pink, red and purple strains, and such abnormalities as 'Hose in Hose', double-flowering forms. *P. veris*, the Cowslip, Europe, Britain, Asia, to 9 in., deep yellow, April–May, has orange and reddish flowering forms, and hybridizes with *vulgaris* to give the Oxlip, with characters intermediate between the parents. This cross is now held to be the source of the popular Polyanthus or bunch-headed Primrose, and by selection and further cross-pollinations been raised to give several strains of superb long-flowering spring plants, such as the Pacific Hybrids, in white, yellow, pink, red, and blue shades; Gold-laced; Giant Bouquet; Munstead Strain in white and yellows; and Giant Fancy Shades, with combinations of colours. Plants of Primroses and Polyanthus are best raised from seeds sown in February–March, under glass, standard compost, bottom heat of 15·5° C. (60° F.); to prick off and harden in a cold frame before planting out in May–June; or in a nursery bed out of doors, April–June, to plant out by September. May also be grown as pot plants in a cold greenhouse.

For the Greenhouse. P. malacoides, Yunnan, the Fairy Primrose, with flowers in whorls on slender scapes, 8–12 in. tall, above a rosette of shallowly lobed leaves, has superior forms in large-flowered strains such as 'Jubilee', cherry-red; 'Fire Chief', 'Pink Sensation', 'Queen of the Whites', 'Rose Bouquet' and the 'Pearl' strain in various colours, growing 6 in high; and although perennial, they are grown as annuals, from seed each year. *P. obconica*, Ichang, China, is valued for its long flowering, with umbels of colourful blooms on 6–8 in. scapes, outstanding in the large-flowered strain, *gigantea*, and vs. such as 'Fasbender Red', 'Red Chief', 'Salmon King', 'Wyaston Wonder', crimson, and 'Giant Blues', 'Giant White' and 'Giant Pinks'. The broadly ovate leaves, however, have glandular hairs underneath, which may cause an irritating rash on the skin of susceptible persons handling them, which may be avoided by wearing gloves when tending the plants. *P. sinensis*, the Chinese Primrose, with flowers borne in whorls on 6-in. scapes, is grown as an annual, and cultivation has given improved strains of single-flowering Giant Hybrids in white, pink, scarlet and blue, 'His Excellency', vermilion, 'Dazzler', orange-red, and 'Pink Enchantress' being outstanding named forms; and double-flowering in 'Charm', salmon-pink; 'Purity', white; and 'Queen of Pinks'; while in its v. *stellata*, the Star Primrose, with tiers of starry flowers on 10-in. scapes, 'Beacon Star', orange-scarlet; 'Crimson Star'; dark and light 'Blue Star'; 'Enchantress', pink; 'Fire King', crimson; 'Orange Glow Star'; 'White Star' and improved forms should be sought. *P. floribunda*, W. Himalaya, with whorls of golden-yellow flowers on 6-in. scapes, and its v. *isabellina*, prim-rose-yellow; *verticillata*, S. Arabia, sulphur-yellow flowers in whorls, and their hybrid × *kewensis*, buttercup-yellow flowers in whorls on tall scapes, are all worth growing in the cool greenhouse for autumn, winter, spring display.

Cultivation. Hardy Rock Garden Species —plant September–October, or March–April, in light porous soil, enriched with moisture-retentive good leaf-mould or sifted peat. Asiatic Primulas prefer the cooler moist atmospheric conditions of the north and west, given perfect drainage. None like arid conditions, and positions where they would be scorched by hot sun. Species by seeds, sown in spring, standard compost, in cold frame. Hybrids may be propagated by division, usually after flowering, or by cuttings, June–August; but in doubt specialist publications should be consulted: *Primulas in the Garden*, by K. C. Corsair.

Alpine House Species—pot firmly September–October; repot after flowering, when necessary; in compost of equal parts by bulk well-broken, medium fibrous loam, leaf-mould and coarse sand, over ample drainage crocks; extra leaf-mould or peat can be added for the moisture lovers. Water with care, not leaving water lodged on leaves; keep soil just moist in winter, temp. 7° C. (45° F.) minimum. Propagation by seeds

for species, by cuttings or offsets in June–July.

In borders or beds, plant September–October, or spring, in well-draining loam soil, liberally enriched with organic matter or peat; cool shade, or partial sun. Propagation of species is by seeds, sown March–April, in cold frame or greenhouse, to plant out in May. By division after flowering.

Greenhouse Primulas. Sow seeds in late April–May, in cool greenhouse, standard compost, with bottom heat of 15·5° C. (60° F.), prick off into 3-in. pots, potting compost, June–July; grow on in cold greenhouse or frame in cool, airy conditions, watering regularly but moderately without wetting leaves or crowns, partial shade; pot on to larger 4½–5-in. pots, September, and feed occasionally when coming into flower; watering moderately, with winter temperatures of 10–13° C. (50–55° F.), in greenhouse or indoors, for flowering. Choice specimens may be repotted and grown on after flowering, but it is usual to raise new plants each year.

Diseases. Crown Rot, affecting crowns and leaf bases of plants, is sometimes aggravated by over-wet conditions, under which soil-harboured fungi such as *Phytophora* spp., or *Thielaviopsis basicola* infect tissues; dusting with copper-lime dust checks such rots if not too far gone. A Soft Slimy Rot (*Bacterium carotovorum*) occurs too quickly for remedial measures, and plants should be lifted and burnt. A thinning, paling or yellowing of older leaves in pot Primulas suggest that the soil is either over-wet or stagnant. The chief pests are aphids, which can be prevented by use of a systemic insecticide or contact-applications of gamma-BHC in aerosol form.

Prince Albert's Yew. See *Saxegothaea*.

Princeps. Chief. Ex. *Narcissus princeps*.

Prince's Feather. See *Amaranthus hypochondianus*.

Privet. See *Ligustrum*.

Procumbens. Procumbent, trailing flat on the ground. Ex. *Cytisus procumbens*.

Profusus (-a, -um). Profuse, very abundant. Ex. *Limonium × profusum*.

Proliferation. The continued active cell-division in new growths beyond the normal stage of growth development. A term applied to such abnormalities as the Hen-and-Chicken Daisy; and flowers forming axillary buds through and beyond the normal flower, or in the axils of sepals or leaf-carpels; king pears, etc.

Pronunciation of Plant Names. Botanically, any plant has only one name in Latin. Pronunciation is apt to vary, however, according to usage and country. This does not matter greatly, provided it is intelligible and understood. While there are no inflexible rules, the universal trend is to use the Reformed Academic methods of pronunciation of which the main features are: all vowels are pronounced (*co-to-ne-as-ter* not *cot-on-easter*; *pe-ta-si-tes* not *pet-a-sites*). Diphthongs (ae, au, ei, eu, oe, ui) are pronounced as one vowel. Words containing more than one vowel or diphthong are split into syllables and all syllables are pronounced (*tra-des-can-ti-a*; *si-le-ne*; *a-tro-pur-pur-e-um*). Vowels are pronounced—ā (long) as in *fa*ther; ă (short) as in *a*ware; ae as *ai* in *ai*sle; au as *ou* in m*ou*se; ē (long) as in wh*ey*; ĕ (short) as in b*e*t; ei as in r*ei*n; ī as *ee* in t*ee*n; ĭ (short) as in b*i*t; ō (long) as in d*o*te; ŏ (short) as in d*o*t; oe as *oi* in b*oi*l; ū (long) as in c*u*te; ŭ (short) as in d*u*ll; ui as *we* (French *oui*); y as in French *u*. Consonants are pronounced as in English with the following exceptions: c is always hard, as in c*o*t; *ch* is *k*; g is hard as in g*o*; j is *y* as in *y*ell; ph as *p* or *p-h* (*f* permissible by usage); t as in *t*ap; and v as *w*. The endings -ii and -iae are pronounced as -*i* and -*ae* respectively. See *Latin Names of Common Plants*, J. D. Drewitt, 1927; and *Glossary of British Flora*, H. Gilbert Carter, 1952.

Propagation. In gardening, the multiplication of plants by sexual or asexual methods. Plants are propagated sexually by seeds (or spores), which may yield plants more or less identical with the parents in the case of species and varieties which are self-fertile, or grown in isolation. The seeds of many plants which are themselves the progeny of cross-fertilization or hybrids may not, however, breed true. *See* Mendelism, Plant-breeding, and Seeds and Sowing.

Asexual or vegetative propagation means the reproduction of a plant by taking a part of it and growing it separately; and means that the plants so raised are normally identical in their characters; and may be carried out by Budding, taking and rooting Cuttings, Division of rootstocks, bulbs, corms or tubers, Grafting, Layering; dealt with under separate entries (q.v.); while the appropriate methods are also given under the separate entries of Plants.

Propagation, Mist. A modern method of greenhouse propagation by which cuttings of plants, especially those normally difficult to root (e.g. Camellia, Hamamelis, Magnolia, and many evergreens such as Rhododendron, Conifers, etc.), may be rooted readily under automatically electronically controlled growth conditions. The equipment consists of a suitable propagating bed, with porous rooting medium, provision for irrigation (preferably automatic), and stand pipes, fitted with atomizer mist jets (approximately one to each 12 sq. ft), connected to an electrical controller, and filter, fed by connection to the main water supply. The jet dispenses a fine mist over the propagating bed in response to an electronic 'leaf' device, which, on becoming dry, breaks an electrical circuit, causing the control unit to open an electrically controlled valve, admitting water to the mist jet. As the leaf becomes wetted, the circuit closes, and misting ceases. In this way the leaf surfaces are moistened at need, transpiration losses are minimized and, other things being equal, the cutting roots more quickly. Where the fully automated electronic apparatus is too expensive, a smaller, automatic non-electric Mist use for amateur use is available.

Propagator. In gardening, a relatively small structure, in which growing conditions of humidity, aeration and temperature may be controlled, to enable plants to be raised from seeds and cuttings, especially half-hardy or difficult kinds, and in some defiance of climatic conditions. It can take the form of a small, shallow propagating frame, placed over the source of heat in the greenhouse. A simple home-made propagator can be constructed from a deep box, bisected by a shelf of slotted metal; in the base heat can be provided by a flat car oilheater, or by one or two 25- or 40-watt electric light bulbs, connected to the mains; a refinement is to insulate the walls with sheet polystyrene. Plants to be

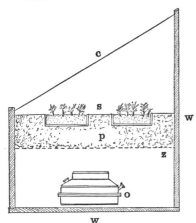

FIG. 185 A simple propagating frame:
w. wood sides and base; o. flat car-type
oil-heater; z. perforated zinc or metal
shelf; p. damp peat; s. seeds or cuttings
boxes; c. clear plastic cover.

raised may be placed in containers, such
as peat-fibre square pots on the metal
shelf, and covered by a glass or PVC
light. Alternatively, electrically heated
propagating units may be bought ready-
made. For serious work, a bench propagator, in which bottom heat is provided by bare wires sunk in sand, and
connected through a transformer to the
main supply, is almost indispensable.

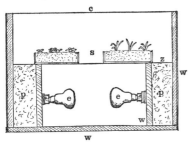

FIG. 186 A heated propagating case: w.
wood sides, base and partitions; p. peat;
e. 15-watt electric bulbs in pattressed
holders; z. perforated zinc or metal shelf;
s. seeds or cuttings boxes; c. clear plastic
cover.

Propagule. A part of a plant—bud,
leaf, cutting, seed, etc.—capable of
growing into a new plant.

Prostratus (-a, -um). Prostrate without rooting. Ex. *Ceanothus prostratus.*

Protandrous. Of flowers with anthers
maturing ripe pollen before the stigma
is receptive. Ex. Dandelion.

Protea (pro'te-a. Fam. Proteaceae).
Evergreen S. African shrubs with
leathery leaves, and curiously structured
terminal flowers with heads surrounded
by coloured bracts, and long-lasting.

Selection. P. cynaroides, 2–6 ft, white,
artichoke-like flowers with pink bracts,
May–June; *latifolia,* 6 ft, large, carmine
flowers, greenish bracts, June–August;
and *mellifera,* 6 ft, white to pink flowers,
whitish bracts, August–September.

Cultivation. Pot in April, standard
compost, and grow in sunny airy conditions, watering regularly but not too
heavily; moderately in winter, with
temp. 10° C. (50° F.). Resents root disturbance, and needs care in repotting.

Propagation. By cuttings of young
shoots, July, in propagating frame. By
imported seed.

Protein. Highly complex organic compound, composed of amino-acids. Proteins are present in all living things, but
differ almost infinitely according to the
kinds and arrangements of the amino-
acids of which they are composed; there
being twenty different amino-acids
occuring in proteins.

Prothallus. A stage in the life cycle of
many ferns and their allies, consisting
of a flat, bright green, leaf-life structure
formed from a germinating spore and on
which male and female organs are formed
to ultimately give rise to a tiny plantlet
which develops roots and becomes
independent.

Protoplasm. The gelatinous matter
found in all living cells; the physical
basis of life, usually divided into the
cytoplasm and the nucleus.

Pruinosus (-a, -um). Pruinose, having
a waxy covering. Ex. *Berberis pruinosa.*

Prumnopitys. Now *Podocarpus* (q.v.).

Prunella (pru-nel'la. Fam. Labiatae).
Hardy perennials with whorls of flowers
on decumbent stems.

Selection. P. grandiflora, 6 in., violet
or purple flowers, July; and *webbiana,*
8 in., bright purple, summer, with white

v. *alba*, and pink *rosea*, are Europeans for the rock garden. *P. vulgaris*, the native All-heal or Self-heal, can become a troublesome weed in lawns though curbed by the use of a selective herbicide.

Cultivation. Plant in September–October or March, any well-drained soil, sun or partial shade.

Propagation. By division in March–April.

Pruning. The cutting away of a part of a plant, usually of woody perennials. The purposes of pruning are (*a*) to regulate their growth to a desired shape; (*b*) to restrict their size to space available; (*c*) to bring about regeneration in ailing plants by removing diseased, pest-ridden and moribund growth; (*d*) to regulate growth to produce a finer performance in flowers, foliage or fruit. Pruning is an art as well as a skill, and its effect upon growth needs careful study, for growth cannot be removed without affecting the whole economy of the plant. Broadly, removal of top growth tends to check root extension and development. Severe or hard pruning provokes the reaction of stronger growth, usually in shoot or wood production. Light pruning, properly timed, fosters flower-bud formation and fruiting. Pruning concerns chiefly fruit trees and bushes, which are dealt with under their entries (*see* Apple, Cherry, Currant, Gooseberry, Pear, etc.); flowering and ornamental shrubs and trees. In the case of the latter many trees and shrubs need little or no pruning beyond the removal of weak growth and dead shoots, where growth is healthy, and the plants have room to display their natural habit and form. For pruning purposes, however, they may be divided into two classes: (1) those which flower in the first half of the year on shoots or wood growth of the previous year; and (2) those which form flowers on shoots of the current season's growth, usually in the second half of the year after midsummer day. The first class are pruned, when necessary, immediately after flowering, removing the flowered or older shoots. The second class are pruned in late winter and early spring, cutting the flowered shoots hard back. The same ruling applies to Evergreens, but when it is desired to reshape an evergreen shrub or tree, the

hard pruning is done just before new growth begins in spring. For the pruning of Roses, *see* Roses.

All pruning cuts should be made smooth and clean, at points where healing can take place quickly; such as immediately above a bud or node or leaf, or, when complete shoots or branches are removed, flush with their junction with other branches or main stem. Dead or diseased growth is cut back to where sound, healthy wood is met, and it is wise to paint cut surfaces of much size with a fungicide or antiseptic paint. Pruning may be done with suitable pruning knives; secateurs, chosen to keep bruising of bark to the minimum; or a pruning saw for large cuts; all being well sharpened and clean-cutting.

Prunus (pru'nus. Fam. Rosaceae). A highly important genus of deciduous shrubs and trees, which includes the stone fruits, Apricot, Cherry, Damson, Nectarine, Peach, Plum, dealt with under their separate entries. Ornamentally, it contains many beautiful flowering, and autumn-foliage shrubs and trees, and a few evergreens. They are natives of temperate parts of the northern hemisphere, and mostly hardy in Britain.

Selection. P. avium, native Gean, Mazzard or Wild Cherry, in v. *flore pleno*, to 40 ft, double white flowers, April–May; *cerasifera*, Myrobalan, W. Asia, white, March; in vs. *atropurpurea* (*pissardii*), Persia, pale rose, purple-leafed, March; *blireiana*, pink, purple-leafed, March; and *lindsayae*, almond-pink; *cerasus*, Cherry, SE. Europe, to 20 ft, double, white, May; *communis* (*amygdalus*), Almond, Mediterranean, 10–20 ft, white or pink, March; and vs. *macrocarpa*, white; *pollardii*, rose-pink; *praecox*, February-flowering; *conradinae*, China, to 35 ft, white, February; and v. *semi-plena*, pink; *Davidiana*, David's Peach, China, to 30 ft, rose, February; *glandulosa*, China, Japan, shrubby to 4 ft, and vs. *alba*, white, and *rosea*, rose, with double-flowering forms, May; *incisa*, Japan, 4–15 ft, white, April; and vs. 'February Pink', and *praecox*, winter-flowering; × *hillierii* 'Spire', 25 ft, soft pink, May; *laurocerasus*, Common or Cherry Laurel, evergreen, E. Europe, Asia Minor, to 15 ft, white racemes of flowers, April, blackish fruits; and vs.

magnoliaefolia, fine-leaved; and *zabeliana*, narrow leaved; *lusitanica*, Portugal Laurel, Spain, Portugal, evergreen, to 15 ft, white, June, and v. *albo-marginata*; *mume*, Chinese Apricot, 12 ft, pale rose, April, and vs.; *nipponica* v. *kurilensis*, Japan, 6 ft, white, May; *padus*, the

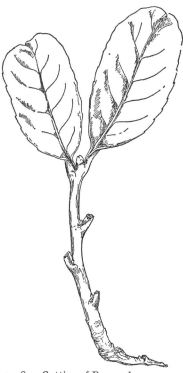

FIG. 187 Cutting of *Prunus laurocerasus*, Laurel, taken with a heel in late Summer.

native Bird Cherry, to 50 ft, best in v. *watereri*, long racemes, white flowers, May; *persica*, Peach, China, to 15 ft, pale rose, April, and vs. 'Clara Meyer', double pink; 'Helen Borchers', semi-double pink; 'Russell's Red'; and 'Windle's Weeping', weeping form, double-pink; *prostrata*, E. Mediterranean, 2 ft, bright-rose, April, for sheltered rock gardens; *sargentii*, Japan, to 20 ft, rose-pink, April, autumn leaf colour; *serrula*,

China, to 20 ft, white, April, fine shining, red-brown, peeling bark; *serrulata*, the 'Japanese Cherry', under which the hybrids of which it is a parent, with *P. speciosa*, are now listed by their Japanese names: 'Amanogawa' (*erecta*), fastigiate poplar-like growth, semi-double, soft pink, May; 'Fugenzo', double, rose-pink, May, spreading head; 'Hisakura', single rose-pink, April–May; 'Hokusai' (*spiralis*), to 30 ft, semi-double pale pink, March–April; 'Horinji' (*decora*), to 16 ft, semi-double, soft pink, April–May; 'Jo-nioi' (*affinis*), white, very fragrant, April; 'Kanzan' ('Sekiyama'), to 40 ft, double, purplish pink, May; 'Kiku Shidare Zakura' (*rosea*), Cheal's Weeping Cherry, double, pink, March–April; 'Ojochin' ('Senriko'), to 25 ft, single, light pink, April; 'Pink Perfection', to 30 ft, double, rose-pink, April; 'Shimidsu Sakura' ('Oku Miyako') (*longpipes*), to 15 ft, semi-double, pink to white, May; 'Shirofugen' (*albo-rosea*), to 30 ft, double, white to pink, May; 'Shirotae' ('Kojima', 'Mount Fuji'), to 18 ft, snow-white, single to semi-double, March–April; 'Tai-haku', to 25 ft, snow-white, single, April; 'Ukon', to 24 ft, semi-double, greenish-yellow, April; *sieboldii* ('Takasago'), slow-growing to 15 ft, downy leaves, semi-double, pale pink. April; *spinosa*, the native Sloe, in v. *plena*, bush to 10 ft, double, white, April; and *purpurea*, bronzy-red leaves, pinkish flowers; *subhirtella*, Spring Cherry, Japan, to 50 ft, white to pink, April, and vs. *ascendens*, upright branching; *autumnalis*, semi-double, white, autumn to spring; 'Fukubana', bright pink, April; and *pendula rubra*, weeping habit, deep rose-pink, April; *tenella*, SE. Europe, shrubby to 4 ft, rose-red, April; and white v. *alba* and *gessleriana*, rose-crimson; *triloba*, China, to 10 ft, pinkish white, April, and double form 'Multiplex'; and *yedoensis*, Yoshino Cherry of Japan, to 15 ft, spreading, white, April. *P. cistena* 'Crimson Dwarf'; *P. cerasifera atropurpurea* 'Blaze'; and 'Greenglow', v. *blireiana* 'Pink Paradise'; and *P. spinosa* 'Sloepink', are forms developed to give quick-growing, hedges of good leaf colour; to 6 ft.

Cultivation. Plant October–March; evergreens autumn or spring; in reasonably well-drained soil, enriched with organic matter, and lime to bring to about pH 6·0–6·5; open sunny situations; but with shelter from cold winds for the early-flowering kinds. Prune, when necessary, immediately after flowering or in June. Unfortunately, subject to Leaf Curl disease and other troubles affecting Cherries and Plums (q.v.), though the same remedies apply.

Propagation. Species by seeds, sown April, after stratification (q.v.) for winter, gently cracking the stones. Varieties and hybrids by budding or grafting on related species seedlings. By layering, spring. *P. laurocerasus* and *lusitanica* from cuttings of firm young shoots July–August; and *subhirtella* may be tried in this way, under hand-light or in cold frame.

Pseudo-. A prefix meaning false. Ex. *Pseudobulb*, the thickened internode in epipthyic orchids; *Pseudocarp*, a fruit consisting of the ripened ovary combined with some other part of the plant; as in pome fruits, strawberries, etc.

Pseudolarix, False or Golden Larch (su-do-la′riks. Fam. Pinaceae). The only species, *P. amabilis* (*fortunei*), E. China, to 50 ft, is deciduous, with larch-like, bright green foliage, whorled, turning golden in autumn, rather slow-growing, reasonably hardy, for planting autumn or early spring, in good loam soil, pH 6, as a specimen with wind-shelter. Propagated by seeds.

Pseudotsuga, Douglas Fir (su-dot-su′ga. Fam. Pinaceae). Evergreen coniferous trees, of N. America and N. Asia.

Selection. P. glauca, Colorado Douglas Fir, Rocky Mts, to 150 ft, slow-growing, glaucous attractive foliage; *japonica,* Japan, to 25 ft, bushy, pale green foliage; (*menziesii*) *taxifolia,* Douglas Fir, to 150 ft or more, stately timber tree, and vs. *caesia,* glaucous foliage; *fretsii,* bush-like, and *pendula,* drooping branchlets.

Cultivation. Plant October or March–April, lightish, deep loam, moisture-retentive but draining readily; pH 5·5.

Propagation. Species by seeds, sown outdoors, spring. Varieties by grafting on seedling species stocks in cold greenhouse, April.

Ptelea (te′le-a. Fam. Rutaceae). The species chiefly grown is *P. trifoliata,* eastern N. America, deciduous, the Hop-tree, so called for its persistent clusters of hop-like seed-vessels, preceded by greenish-white flowers in June; tri-foliolate foliage, yellowing in autumn; permanently yellow in v. *aurea.* Quite hardy, and may be grown in any well-drained ordinary soil, planting October–March. Propagation is by layers, made in spring or summer.

Pteridium, Adder-spit, Bracken, Brake Fern (te-rid′i-um. Fam. Polypodiaceae). If grown at all, *P. aquilinum,* native and cosmopolitan Bracken, should be confined in root run, otherwise becomes invasive and difficult to eradicate; although its fern-like, 2–4-ft fronds are handsome, and make good compost, cut young and rotted down; while dead fronds make good litter cover for wintering plants.

Pteris (te′ris. Fam. Polypodiaceae). A large genus of relatively easily grown ferns for the greenhouse or indoor decoration.

Selection. P. cretica, temperate zones, 6–12-in. fronds, and vs. *mayii,* silver-variegated, and crested; *sempervirens,* crested; and *wimsetti,* 2-ft fronds, chestnut-striped; *ensiformis victoriae,* India, variegated, 1–1½ ft fronds; *multifida,* Spider or Ribbon Fern, China, finely formed fronds to 1½ ft; *tremula,* Australia, 2–4-ft fronds, with crested forms, and *variegata,* silver-banded; and *umbrosa,* Australia, 1–2-ft fronds; and *cristata,* a graceful variety.

Cultivation. Pot in March, equal parts sandy loam and peat; water freely in summer; moderately in winter, minimum temp. 10° C. (50° F.); and light shade.

Propagation. Preferably by spores, when available, with bottom heat of 18° C. (65° F.), as plants do not recover well from division.

Pterocarya, Wing-nut (te-ro-ka′u-a. Fam. Juglandaceae). Reasonably hardy, deciduous trees, with pinnate foliage, unisexual flowers in catkins, and fruits consisting of winged nuts.

Selection. P. fraxinifolia, Caucasus, Persia, to 80 ft, long catkins; *rhoifolia,* Japan, to 80 ft; *stenophora,* China, to 50 ft, and its hybrid × *rehderiana,* to 80 ft, make vigorous specimen trees.

Cultivation. Plant November–March, in fertile, moisture-retentive soils, and sun; do well by water.

Propagation. By seeds, sown April. By layers in spring or summer.

Pterocephalus (te-ro-kep'al-us. Fam. Dipsaceae). The species chiefly grown is *P. parnassi* (*Scabiosa pterocephalus*), Greece, 4 in., a dwarf, prostrate mat of woody stems, grey-green elliptical leaves, and large scabious-like purple-pink flower heads on 2-in stalks, July–August.

Cultivation. Plant March–April, in well-drained soil with leaf-mould, sunny position in rock garden.

Propagation. By division in April.

Pterostyrax (te-ros'tu-raks. Fam. Styracaceae). The species grown, *P. hispida*, Japan, is a deciduous tall shrub, to 15 ft, with long ovate leaves, and drooping panicles of white, scented staminous flowers, June–July, followed by spindle-shaped and ribbed seed vessels. It is quite hardy for any well-drained, humus-rich soil, and a warm sunny position, and is propagated by seeds, in spring.

Pubescens. Pubescent, clothed with soft dense hair or down. Ex. *Primula pubescens.*

Pulcher (-chra, -chrum). Beautiful. Ex. *Senecio pulcher.*

Pulcherrimus (-a, -um). Very beautiful. Ex. *Euphorbia pulcherrima.*

Pullus (-a, -um). Nearly black, russety. Ex. *Campanula pulla.*

Pulmonaria, Lungwort (pul-mon-a'ri-a. Fam. Boraginaceae). Perennial, spring-flowering hardy herbs, easily grown.

Selection. P. angustifolia, central Europe, 3 in., pink, turning blue, flowers, with v. *alba,* white, and 'Mawson's', a selected form; *officinalis,* Bethlehem Sage, Jerusalem Cowslip, 9 in., pink to purplish blue; and *rubra,* Europe, red.

Cultivation. Plant autumn or early spring, any well-drained soil with humus, sun or partial shade.

Propagation. By division in early spring.

Pulsatilla (pul-sa-til'la. Fam. Ranunculaceae). A delightful genus of spring-flowering perennials, formerly included under Anemone.

Selection. P. alpina, European Alps, 4–12 in., white with central boss of yellow stamens, May–June; v. *burseriana,* white, to 16 in.; and *sulphurea,*

sulphur-yellow; *halleri,* Austria, Switzerland, 1 ft, deep violet, April–May; *vernalis,* evergreen, Lady of the Snows, European Alps, 2 in., white, silky brown outside, April; and *vulgaris* (*Anemone pulsatilla*), the Pasque Flower, 6 in., violet, April; v. *alba,* white, and various red forms.

Cultivation. Plant October or March, open sunny places, well-drained, lightish soil, pH 6·5.

Propagation. By seeds, as soon as ripe, outdoors. May also be grown in the cool alpine house.

Pulverulentus (-a, -um). Dusted with powder. Ex. *Primula pulverulenta.*

Pumilus (-a, -um). Low or Dwarf and dense. Ex. *Sempervivum pumilum.*

Pumpkin (*Cucurbita pepo* v.). A native of tropical America, cultivated for its rounded, large, fleshy fruits, beloved by Americans, for making pies with fruit.

Cultivation. Sow seeds of a good strain singly in 3-in. pots, under glass, standard compost, bottom heat of 18° C. (65° F.), April; harden seedlings off to plant out in soil liberally enriched with rotted organic matter, or on mounds of rotted manure, covered by a frame, or cloche. Water freely, shade from hot sun; remove glass in June. Fertilize first female flowers by pressing male flowers to them; pinch out growing points at 1½–2 ft, and allow only the steady-growing fruits to grow on. Harvest in August–September.

Punctatus (-a, -um). Dotted. Ex. *Hypericum punctatum.*

Pungens. Sharply pointed. Ex. *Picea pungens.*

Punica, Pomegranate (pu'ni-ka. Fam. Punicaceae). The Pomegranate, *P. granatum,* SE. Europe to India, to 15 ft, is a deciduous shrub, with spiny branches and clustered entire leaves, bright red flowers in July–September; double in v. *flore pleno,* and orange-scarlet in the charming dwarf form *nana;* but the familiar many seeded fruits seldom mature.

Cultivation. Out of doors it requires a warm, sunny, sheltered wall, in the mildest localities, with well-drained loam soil. Elsewhere it may be grown in large pots or tubs in a cold greenhouse.

Propagation. By cuttings of young shoots, taken July–August, in a propagating frame, with bottom heat.

Puniceus (-a, -um). Bright red, crimson. Ex. *Clianthus puniceus.*

Purple Loosestrife. See *Lythrum salicaria.*

Purpurescens. Becoming purple. Ex. *Arenaria purpurescens.*

Purpureus (-a, -um). Purple. Ex. *Cistus purpureus.*

Purslane. See *Portulaca.*

Puschkinia (pusk-kin'i-a. Fam. Liliaceae). The species grown, *P. scilloides,* Striped Squill, Asia, 6 in., is a pleasing bulbous plant with bluish-white, bell-shaped flowers, March, for any well-drained soil, enriched with leaf-mould, in rock garden or border; or in pots in a cold greenhouse; planted in September, 2 in. deep. Propagation is by seeds, sown August, preferably in pans in cold frame, or by offsets, September.

Pusillus (-a, -um). Small, slender. Ex. *Campanula pusillus.*

Pycnostachys (pik-no-sta'kus. Fam. Labiatae). African flowering perennials grown in the cool greenhouse, for their winter bloom.

Selection. P. dawei, Uganda, 4 ft, spikes of whorled, cobalt-blue, lipped flowers, winter; *urticifolia,* tropical Africa, 3 ft, dark blue.

Cultivation. Pot in March, large pots, standard compost, or grow in border of cool greenhouse; liberal watering in growth; little after flowering, minimum temp. of 10° C. (50° F.).

Propagation. By division in March. By seeds, March–April, with bottom heat of 18° C. (65° F.).

Pyracantha, Firethorn (pi-ra-kan'tha. Fam. Rosaceae). Evergreen, thorny shrubs, reasonably hardy, and valued for their brilliant berrying in autumn.

Selection. P. angustifolia, China, 10 ft, white clustered flowers, June–July, orange berries; *atalantioides,* China, to 15 ft, white flowers ,June, scarlet berries; *coccinea,* S. Europe, to 15 ft, white, June, bright red berries, and v. *lalandei,* orange-red berries; *rogersiana,* China, 10 ft, white, June, reddish-orange berries; and vs. *flava,* yellow berrying; and *watereri,* 7 ft, orange-red berries.

Cultivation. Plant October, or March–April; well-drained, humus-rich soil, pH 6·0–6·5; in the open, or trained on walls. Prune after flowering.

Propagation. By seeds, March–April,

after stratification of berries. By cuttings of young firm shoots, July–August, under handlight.

Pyramidalis (-e). Cone-like shape. Ex. *Campanula pyramidalis.*

Pyrethrum. An insecticide prepared from the powdered heads of *Chrysanthemum cineracia* and *C. roseum,* effective against many insects, but non-poisonous to mammals and humans.

Pyrethrum, Feverfew. See *Chrysanthemum.*

Pyrola (pi'ro-la. Fam. Pyrolaceae). Perennial, stoloniferous herbs with racemes of nodding, cupped flowers, for rock gardens.

Selection. P. media, Europe, Britain, 4 in., white, red-tinged flowers, July–August; *minor,* Europe, Britain, N. America, 8 in., white, tinged rose, June–August; and *rotundifolia,* Europe, Britain, N. America, 6 in., white, summer.

Cultivation. Plant March–April, cool positions, partial shade, in rock garden; light, leaf-mould-enriched soil; rather difficult to establish.

Propagation. By careful division, April; by seeds, sown when ripe, in cold frame.

Pyrus (pi'rus. Fam. Rosaceae). Deciduous hardy trees, tending to be thorny, with flowers in umbel-like clusters of white flowers in spring, and top-shaped fruits, known as pears.

Selection. P. communis, Europe, is the parent Wild Pear from which edible garden pears are derived, and several vs. are of no mean ornamental flowering beauty. *P. amygdaliformis cunefolia,* Mediterranean region, to 20 ft, with narrow pretty foliage; *nivalis,* Asia Minor, to 15 ft, white flowers, with white downy leaves, is charming in spring; *pyrifolia,* the Sand Pear of China, and v. *stapfiana; salicifolia,* SE. Europe, to 20 ft, is most attractive in its weeping v. *pendula.*

Cultivation. Plant November–March, well-drained loam soil and sun. Prune to shape only.

Propagation. By seeds, sown March–April, out of doors. By grafting on wild pear rootstocks.

Pyxidanthera (piks-i-dan'the-ra. Fam. Diapensiaceae). The only species, *P. barbulata,* Pyxie, or Flowering Moss, is a rare evergreen, moss-like, creeping shrublet, from New Jersey, U.S.A., an inch or so high, with pinkish white, solitary flowers March–May, but exacting in its needs; a well-drained, sandy or gravelly, soil, with leaf-mould but no lime, and partial shade, out of reach of cold drying winter winds. Propagation is by careful division in April, in cold frame. May also be grown in deep pans to bring into the alpine house for flowering.

Q

Quadrangularis (-e). Four-angled. Ex. *Passiflora quadrangularis.*

Quaking Grass. See *Briza.*

Quamash. See *Camassia.*

Quamoclit (kwa′mo-klit. Fam. Convolvulaceae). Annual twining climbers, though perennial in their native Mexico, sometimes listed under Ipomoea.

Selection. Q. coccinea (Mina sanguinea), to 8 ft, fragrant, yellow-throated scarlet flowers, summer, and v. *hederifolia,* lobed leaves; *lobata,* to 12 ft, salver-shaped crimson, turning orange to yellow, summer flowers; *pennata,* Cypress Vine, to 6 ft, scarlet, funnel-shaped flowers, summer; and × *sloteri,* 6 ft, crimson.

Cultivation. Cultivated as half-hardy annuals, from seeds sown under glass, bottom heat of 18° C. (65° F.), March–April, to harden off and plant out in May, in any ordinary garden soil, and sun.

Quassia Chips. Prepared from the wood of a tropical tree, *Picrasma excelsa,* quassia chips, boiled in water, plus soft soap (¼ lb. each to 1 gallon water), for ¼ hour, and strained and cooled, give a bitter insecticide to control aphids; or may be bought as an extract; non-poisonous.

Queen of the Night. See *Selenicereus grandiflorus.*

Quercifolius (-a, -um). Oak-like leaves. Ex. *Hydrangea quercifolia.*

Quercus, Oak (kwer′kus. Fam. Fagaceae). A genus of over 240 species of long-lived, noble forest trees, of which only a choice of those of garden value are given here.

Selection. Q. borealis maxima, Red Oak, N. America, to 90 ft, brownish-red foliage in autumn; *castaneifolia,* Chestnut-leaved, Caucasus, to 100 ft; *cerris,* Turkey Oak, S. Europe, Asia Minor, to 120 ft, fast-growing; *coccinea,* Scarlet Oak, N. America, to 80 ft, finest autumn colour; *coccifera,* Kermes Oak, S. Europe,

N. Africa, 10–20 ft, evergreen for warm localities; × *hispanica* v. *lucombeana,* Lucombe Oak, to 100 ft, semi-evergreen; *libani,* Lebanon Oak, Asia Minor, to 30 ft; *palustris,* Pin Oak, N. America, to 80 ft, small leaves; *petraea,* Durmast Oak,

FIG. 188   Leaf of *Quercus robur,* Common Oak.

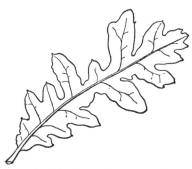

FIG. 189   Leaf of *Quercus robur* v. *asplenifolia,* Fern-leaved Oak.

443

FIG. 190   Leaf of *Quercus velutina*, Black Oak.

FIG. 191   Young leaf of *Quercus ilex*, the Holm Oak, becoming entire in adult trees

Europe, to 100 ft; *phellos*, Willow Oak, N. America, to 60 ft, narrow leaves, yellow in autumn; *robur* (*pedunculata*),

Common Oak, Europe, Britain, Asia Minor, to 100 ft, has fine vs. *asplenifolia*, Fern-leaved Oak; *atropurpurea*, Purple-leaved Oak; *fastigiata*, a columnar form; and *pendula*, weeping; *variabilis*, China, Japan, to 70 ft, bristle-toothed leaves; and *velutina*, Black Oak, N. America, to 70 ft, large-leaved; all being deciduous, but with a tendency to hold their withered leaves long, when young or clipped. *Q. ilex*, the Holm Oak, Mediterranean region, to 60 ft, is the best of the evergreens, for all but very cold localities; *alnifolia*, Golden Oak, Cypress, to 20 ft, is slow-growing.

Cultivation. Plant November–March; evergreens in March–April, any reasonably good soil of some depth, about pH 6, though many species do well on chalk.

Propagation. By seeds (acorns), sown out of doors, October–November, when ripe, 2 in. deep. Evergreen oaks often root from cuttings, July–August.

Quick. Country name for the Thorn, *Crataegus monogyna* (q.v.).

Quinatus (**-a, -um**). Quinate; five-parted. Ex. *Akebia quinata*.

Quince. The quinces grown for their aromatic, acid, pear-shaped fruits for jelly and preserve making are *Cydonia oblonga* varieties, See *Cydonia*.

Quince, Flowering. See *Chaenomeles*.

Quincunx. A method of planting, often used by fruit-growers, which amounts to planting trees alternately spaced in equidistant rows.

Quitch. A country name for Couch Grass (*Agropyron repens*).

R

Rabbits (*Oryctoloagus cuniculus*). Although reduced in numbers by the virus infection, myxomatosis, since 1953, rabbits are still troublesome in many gardens. Their exclusion calls for 1¼-in. strong wire netting, 3 ft high, with the foot buried 9 in. and turned L-shape outwards in the soil. De-barking of shrubs and trees can be prevented by netting sleeves, turned outward at the top; or by smearing the bark with fruit-tree banding grease, or a proprietary repellent. Other plants may be given temporary protection by ringing with repellent-impregnated twine on low stakes. Nominally rabbit-proof plants are: *Asters, Bergenia, Echinops, Epimedium, Eryngium, Erythronium, Eschscholtzia, Euphorbia, Fritillaria, Geranium, Helenium, Helianthus, Helleborus, Hemerocallis, Hypericum, Iris, Kentranthus, Kniphofia, Nepeta, Narcissus, Papaver, Pelargonium, Polygonum, Potentilla, Rudbeckia, Limonium, Stachys, Tradescantia* (Spider-wort), *Verbascum.*

Race. A variety of sub-species which will reproduce itself by seed.

Raceme. An inflorescence with a non-branching main stem, on which the flowers are borne on pedicels, the youngest nearest the top.

Racemosus (-a, -um). Racemous, raceme-like. Ex. *Cytisus × racemosus.*

Rachis. The axis or main stem of an inflorescence or a compound leaf.

Radiatus (-a, -um). Radiate, spreading from a common centre, like the spokes of a wheel. Ex. *Pinus radiatus.*

Radical. Of leaves arising from the base of the stem or from a rhizome; as in *Primula.*

Radicans. With root-producing stems. Ex. *Verbena radicans.*

Radicle. The first root from the embryo of a plant, cf. Plumule.

Radish (*Raphanus sativus*, Fam. Cruciferae). This succulent-rooted, hardy annual vegetable has long been culti-

FIG. 192   Flower raceme (*Laburnum* sp.).

FIG. 193   Radicle, just developing from a seed.

445

vated in China, Japan and Europe, and in Britain from about 1500 or before.

Varieties. Long-rooted: white 'Icicle', 'Long Scarlet', 'Wood's Early Frame'. Round-rooted: 'Saxa', 'Scarlet Globe', 'Red and White Turnip'. Oval-rooted: 'French Breakfast', 'French Breakfast Forcing', 'Sutton's Succulent'. Winter Radishes: 'Black Spanish', 'China Rose'.

Cultivation. Radishes need to be grown quickly; in friable soil, well-enriched with leaf-mould, or sifted rotted manure or compost, or a sifted peat, limed to about pH 6·5, and plus a balanced fertilizer (3 parts by weight hoof and horn meal, 1 part steamed bone flour, 1 part sulphate of potash, at 4 oz. per sq. yd). First sowings of frame or forcing varieties can be made in frames, with bottom heat (15·5° C. [60° F.]), January–February; outdoor sowings from late February to early June, at fortnightly intervals, preferably in rows thinly, ½-inch deep, 4 in. apart; and again from mid August to October, with cloche protection. Summer sowings are not very rewarding. Winter radishes are sown in July–August, in drills 6 in. apart.

Diseases. As cruciferous plants, radishes are susceptible to the same diseases and pests as Cabbage, etc. (q.v.); but trouble can usually be avoided, by dressing seeds with a fungicidal/insecticidal seed-dressing prior to sowing.

Radix. A root.

Raffia (Raphia). Flexible, fibrous, tying material, obtained from palms (*Raphia pedunculata* [ruffia]), in colour or natural buff or straw shade; also now made in plastic substitute.

Ragweed, Ragwort. See *Senecio.*

Rain. Moisture vapour condensing on minute particles of dust in a cloud which coalesce together to form drops that fall through the atmosphere. In its fall rain becomes of the same temperature as that of the atmosphere, acquires oxygen, a certain amount of nitrogen (especially after lightning) and ammonia, and may also carry atmospheric impurities down with it, including the by-products of atomic radiation. Obviously, the rainfall of where we garden has an important influence on plants and their growth both by its amount and its incidence or frequency. Normally, rain is the ideal source

of water to plants, and rain-water is preferred for plant-watering, outdoors or under glass. As normally collected into water butts or tanks as the run-off from roofs, light should be excluded to discourage algae growth.

Rainbow Flower. A common name for *Iris.*

Rakes. A comb-like toothed implement with a long handle. Iron or steel toothed rakes in sizes of 6–12 in. across are most useful for preparing soil seedbeds, gathering weeds, etc. A springtoothed rake or rubber-toothed rake is useful on lawns to loosen stoloniferous weeds prior to mowing or remove moss after moss-killer treatment. A woodentoothed rake may be used for grass or hay gathering, leaf gathering, and breaking down soft lumpy soils.

Ramonda (ra-mon′da. Fam. Gesneriaceae). Pretty, flowering alpine plants for the rock garden or cold alpine house.

Selection. R. myconi (*pyrenaica*), Pyrenees, 4 in., with a rosette of ovate, rugose leaves, and heads of open-face, 5-petalled violet flowers, May–June; with vs. *alba*, white, and *rosea*, deep pink; and *nathaliae*, Bulgaria, Yugoslavia, 4-petalled lavender-blue, orange-throated flowers, with white v. *alba*; and *serbica*, Balkans, 4 in., lilac-blue, cupped flowers, May–June.

Cultivation. Plant in early spring, in north-aspected crevices of a rock garden, well-drained soil; or pot and grow in cool shade in the alpine house or frame, plunging out of doors for summer.

Propagation. By seed, cold frame or greenhouse, March–April, standard compost. By division, April.

Ramosus (-a, -um). Much branched. Ex. *Lobelia ramosa.*

Rampion (*Campanula rapunculus*, Fam. Campanulaceae). A hardy biennial of Europe, sometimes grown for its fleshy roots, used scraped and raw (or boiled), and its leaves in winter salads. Seeds are sown in May, shallowly, in drills 6 in. apart, thinned to 4 in., preferably in lightish, humus-rich soil, partial shade, and liberal watering.

Rampion, Horned. See *Phyteuma.*

Ranunculus (ra-nun′ku-lus. Fam. Ranunculaceae). The large genus of Buttercups contains various weeds—*R. acris, bulbosus, ficaria* and *repens*—but also several decorative flowering plants for the garden.

Selection. R. aconitifolius, White Bachelor's Buttons, Europe, 1½ ft, and vs. *flore pleno*, Fair Maids of France, double flowers; and *grandiflorus*, very large flowers, bloom in May–June; *acris* v. *flore pleno*, 2 ft, double Yellow Batchelor's Buttons; and *psilostachys*, Balkans, 1½ ft, large yellow flowers, May, are good border plants; *lingua*, Greater Spearwort, 2 ft, and v. *grandiflorus*, native, are summer-flowering for bog gardens; *alpestris*, European Alps, 4 in., white, May—June, and its smaller form, *traunfellneri*; *amplexicaulis*, Pyrenees, 6 in., white, April–May; *calandrinioides*, Morocco, 4 in., white, March; *geraniifolius*, Europe, 6 in., yellow, May–July; *glacialis*, European Mountains, Arctic, 6 in., white to red, June; *gramineus*, SW. Europe, to 9 in., citron, April–June; *parnassifolius*, Alps, Pyrenees, 6 in., white, May–June; *pyrenaeus*, Alps, Pyrenees, 1 ft, white, summer; and *seguieri*, Alps, 3 in., white, June–July, are fine forms for rock gardens; *asiaticus*, Orient, 9–15 in., various colours, is the source species of Garden Ranunculus, of which there are several strains—French (v. *superbissimus* forms), double-flowering; Peony-flowered Hybrids, double and semi-double; Persian, rather small, single or double flowers; Turban (v. *africanus* forms), full globular flowers, perhaps the hardiest; Florentine; and Palestine with large double flowers; offered in named varieties by specialist growers; colours ranging from white, through pale to deep yellow, pinks, reds and scarlets to deep carmine.

Cultivation. Plant border and rock garden kinds in early autumn to spring, free-draining, but moisture-retentive, humus-rich soil; sun or partial shade. Assure rock garden kinds good drainage with top-dressing of stone chippings for winter; may also be grown in pans in the alpine house. Garden Ranunculus are usually grown by planting the claw-like, dry roots in well-prepared, porous, free-draining soil, enriched with leaf-mould or sifted rotted organic matter; 1½–2 in. deep, 6 in apart, claws downward; in autumn or February–March.

Propagation. Border and rock garden kinds by division in August–September.

Species by seeds, sown in March–April, standard compost, cold frame or on outdoors seed-bed. In case of Garden Ranunculus, it is best to lift roots when foliage dies, and store dry until planting time arrives again.

Raoulia (ra-oo'li-a. Fam. Compositae). Creeping, carpeting evergreen alpines, with woolly leaves, small, tubular flowers, for mild localities or the alpine house.

Selection. R. australis, New Zealand, 1 in., pale yellow, July; *glabra*, New Zealand, 1 in., white, June–July, are the easiest; *exima*, the Vegetable Sheep, New Zealand, makes a mound of greyish-white foliage, without flowering, but is very difficult to grow in captivity.

Cultivation. Plant in free-draining soil, with leaf-mould, September or March–April, warm sun.

Propagation. By division in August. By seed, April, in cold frame.

Rape (*Brassica napus*, Fam. Cruciferae). Also Cole or Coleseed, the seeds being a source of Colza oil. A biennial native plant, sometimes grown to provide mustard-like leaves for salads, or for its edible, white, carrot-like roots, as a winter vegetable, scraped and cooked like turnips. Sow seeds, February–March, on porous, light soil, not recently manured, ½ in. deep, in drills 6 in. apart, or broadcast if for salading.

Rape Dust. A waste product of rapeseed processing for oil, sometimes available, and useful as a humusorganic dressing, especially for soil infested by eelworms or wireworms.

Raphanus. *See* Radish.

Raphides. Crystals, often oxalates, in the cells of plants; sometimes cause skin irritation from handling plants. Prevented by using a barrier cream.

Raphiolepis (rap-i-o-le'pis. Fam. Rosaceae). Evergreen shrubs, with firm-textured leaves, and clusters of flowers, hardy for mild localities only.

Selection. R. × delacourii, to 6 ft, panicles of rose-pink flowers, intermittently, February–August; and *umbellata*, Japan, 6 ft, white flowers, outstanding in v. *ovata*, for its entire leaves.

Cultivation. Plant September–October, or April–May, well-drained, peaty soil, pH 5·5 to 6, warm sun.

Propagation. By cuttings of young

shoots, July–August, in sandy loam, under handlight or frame.

Raspberry (*Rubus idaeus*, Fam. Rosaceae). Native to Britain and Europe, the Raspberry is a deciduous perennial which produces biennial woody stems (canes) making vegetative growth in their first year, on which they produce flowering and fruiting lateral shoots in their second year, and then die back, while new canes from the roots take their place. Raspberries are notable for readiness in coming into fruit (second year after planting), and heavy yields, $\frac{1}{2}$–$1\frac{1}{2}$ lb. per foot of row.

Varieties. It is important to begin with healthy virus-free strains, now offered by reputable nurseries. Red Fruits: 'Lloyd George', mid season; 'Malling Enterprise', tall, mid season; 'Malling Exploit', early; 'Malling Jewel', early to mid season; 'Malling Promise', early, tall; 'Newburgh', mid season; 'Norfolk Giant', tall, late; 'Pyne's Royal', 4–5 ft, mid season; 'Red Cross', 5 ft, mid season; 'St Walfried', tall, mid season. Yellow Fruits: 'Antwerp', mid season. Autumn-fruiting: 'Hailsham'; 'November Abundance'. 'Lloyd George' will fruit in autumn if all canes are cut to ground level in February.

Soil and Preparation. Raspberries like a deepish light to medium soil, well provided with rotted organic matter, adequate potash, and about pH 5·5–6. Less suitable are heavy soils, subject to waterlogging, or very alkaline soils. Preparation calls for bastard trenching, organic manuring, early in autumn. On poor soils hoof and horn meal at 2 oz. per sq. yd, bone meal at 2 oz. per sq. yd and sulphate of potash at 1 oz. per sq. yd are useful additions.

Planting. Canes are best planted in October–November, 18 in. apart, in rows 6 ft apart, with bases 3 in. below the soil; but may be planted up to April; in open situations or partial shade.

Pruning. Newly planted canes are cut off at about 4–6 in. above soil level in February, or when planted, if set out later. This will give strong canes to fruit the second year after planting. When these canes have fruited, they are cut to soil level as soon as convenient, and the strongest new canes left intact. This procedure is followed annually, though it

is usually best to leave only four canes for the following year on established plants or stools. The raspberry tends to produce canes (suckers) away from the original stool; and where these are not wanted for propagation they should be removed.

Training. Canes may be trained and tied to a wire strained between posts, at about 4–5 ft high; or to grow between two parallel wires, nailed to cross-bars, 12 in. apart, on posts. Or plants may be grown in groups of three and trained to a central stake.

Manuring. An annual top-dressing of the base fertilizers already given, at half the rates stated, in March, followed by a mulch of organic matter in May, will keep the canes vigorous and heavy cropping.

Propagation. Strong sucker canes may be cut off and lifted in November and planted out.

Diseases. The most troublesome fungus diseases are Cane Spot (*Elsinoe veneta*), in which canes are spotted with white-centred, purple-bordered spots, elongating and becoming sunken, from May onwards. Infected canes must be cut out and burnt, plants sprayed with copper, lime-sulphur or thiram insecticide at bud burst, and at white bud stage of blossom development the following year. Cane Blight (*Leptosphoeria coniothyrium*) causes leaves to wilt and wither, and canes to become brittle; the infected canes must be cut out at base and burnt; and as the disease is apparently spread by a midge, a preventive treatment is an application of DDT in early May. Virus infection usually dwarfs the canes and causes the foliage to become mottled with a mosaic of yellow and green, and it is wise to remove infected stock immediately the symptoms are seen.

Pests. Aphids of various species may infest raspberries, and as they may carry virus infections, should be controlled by (*a*) a winter tar-oil wash in December–January; (*b*) malathion or Rogor 40 for summer attacks. The Raspberry Beetle, *Byturus tomentosus*, gives rise to larvae which eat and impair the fruit, and are most safely controlled by a derris insecticide applied immediately flowering is over, about mid June, and again two weeks later. Raspberry Moth, *Lampronia rubiella*, gives rise to caterpillars, which tunnel young shoots in April; but may be controlled by an 8 per cent tar-oil wash to the soil and base of canes in late February or March, or derris in early April. The Raspberry Blossom Weevil, *Anthonomus rubi*, can be damaging, but derris applied at green bud stage gives a good control. Cane Midge, *Thomasiniana theobaldi*, feeds under the rinds of canes in May, to admit fungal diseases such as Cane Blight, but spraying lower parts of canes with gamma-BHC in the first week of May and a fortnight later should give good control.

Weed Control. Couch and coarse grasses may be defeated by dalapon herbicide, when plants are dormant. Other weeds by timely application of a paraquat herbicide in late spring.

Rats. These rodents do more damage to stored crops, greenhouse fruits and buildings than to garden plants themselves, They are, however, omnivorous, and their presence is unwelcome. Rodenticides based on 'racumin' or 'warfarin', in bait form, are usually effective, used regularly and consistently until the rats stop coming are less harmful to humans and animals than other rodenticides but must be used with care, where animals and children are unlikely to find it.

Ray Florets. The outer strap-shaped flowers of the inner cluster of flowers forming the disk in flowers of Compositae.

FIG. 194   Ray Floret.

Rebutia (re-but′i-a. Fam. Cactaceae). Small, round-shaped cacti of Argentina, which flower readily from early youth, bearing funnel-shaped flowers in red, orange and yellow.

Selection. R. aureiflora, golden-yellow, summer; *deminuta*, orange-red; *fiebrigii*, Bolivia, red; *minuscula*, scarlet; *senilis*, bright red; and v. *violaciflora*, pale violet; *steinmannii*, Bolivia, rose red; and *stuemeriana*, scarlet.

Cultivation. Pot, and repot, March, water freely to autumn, sun or partial shade, indoors or in a cool greenhouse, little water in winter, minimum temp. 7° C. (45° F.).

Propagation. By offsets; or by seeds, summer.

Receptacle. The flat, concave or convex part at the top of a stem from which the parts of a flower—sepals, petals, stamens and pistils—arise.

Reclinatus (-a, -um). Reclining or bending backwards. Ex. *Phoenix reclinata.*

Rectus (-a, -um). Straight. Ex. *Clematis recta.*

Recurvus (-a, -um). Bent backwards. Ex. *Juniperus recurva.*

Red Buckeye. See *Aesculus pavia.*

Red Cedar. See *Juniperus virginiana.*

Red Horse-chestnut. See *Aesculus* × *carnea.*

Red Hot Poker. See *Kniphofia.*

Red Pepper. See *Capsicum.*

Red Spider Mites. These insects are not true spiders but sap-sucking mites which feed on the undersides of plant leaves, causing mottling, yellowing and bleached tissue. The Greenhouse Red Spider (*Tetranychus telarius*) over-winters as an adult and is bright-red, but immature mites are pale, and females straw-coloured. May be controlled by fumigating with azobenzene smoke acaracide; by spraying with derris or malathion or Rogor 40. As a dry atmosphere favours the pest, growing plants should be frequently syringed and kept properly watered. The Fruit Tree Red Spider (*Metatetranychus* [*Panonychus*] *ulmi*) may infest fruit trees under glass and out of doors; over-wintering in the egg stage. Spraying with a DNOC winter wash destroys the eggs; with liquid derris, malathion or Rogor 40 at petal-fall stage.

Reed. See *Arundo*.

Reed Mace. See *Typha*.

Reflexus (-a, -um). Reflexed, bent back sharply or abruptly. Ex. *Sedum reflexum.*

Refractus (-a, -um). Refracted, bent sharply backward from the base. Ex. *Freesia refracta.*

Regalis (-e). Royal, regal. Ex. *Osmunda regalis.*

Rehmannia (re-man′ni-a. Fam. Scrophulariaceae). Herbaceous perennials of China or Japan, with showy, foxglovelike flowers, half-hardy in Britain.

Selection. R. angulata, China, 1–3 ft, red, orange-dotted, showy flowers, summer, and v. 'Pink Perfection'; *elata*, China, 3 ft, rose purple, red; *glutinosa*, China, 1–2 ft, buff or purple; and × *kewensis*, 2 ft, yellow, crimson blotch.

Cultivation. Sow in spring, cool greenhouse, bottom heat of 18° C. (65° F.), standard compost; to pot on progressively to 6-in. pots, to flower the following spring–summer, with regular watering to October, keeping just moist in winter.

Propagation. May be increased by cuttings taken in April, under glass.

Reineckia (rein-ek′i-a. Fam. Liliaceae). The only species, *R. carnea*, China and Japan, is a dwarf, hardy, rhizomatous perennial, with sword-like leaves, and a loose spike of fragrant, pink flowers, April, leaves striped in v. *variegata.* Plant September–October, any ordinary soil, and sun; easily propagated by division in March.

Religiosus (-a, -um). Of holy, religious or sacred import. Ex. *Ficus religiosus.*

Reniformis (-e). Reniform, kidney-shaped. Ex. *Synthyris reniformis.*

Repens. Prostrate, creeping. Ex. *Linaria repens.*

Reptans. Creeping on the ground. Ex. *Primula reptans.*

Reseda, Mignonette (re-se′da. Fam. Resedaceae). The chief species grown is *R. odorata*, N. Africa, 1–1½ ft, in vs. such as 'Goliath', 'Orange Queen', 'Crimson Giant' and 'White Pearl'; as hardy annuals, from seeds sown where plants are to flower, in March–April. There is a shrubby form, v. *frutescens*, suitable for pot growth in a cool greenhouse; *R. alba*, S. Europe, 2 ft, is a white, summer-flowering biennial, to grow from seeds

sown out of doors in May, in mild localities. Ordinary, well-drained soil, and sun, suit the Resedas.

Resin. An organic compound secreted by certain plants, notably conifers, and members of the Rose family (Rosaceae), often exuding from wounds and promoting their healing.

Resistance. Resistance to certain diseases troublesome to their kind sometimes appears in individual plants, from which varieties or strains may be bred. Instances are potato varieties resistant to Wart Disease; rust- resistant strains of Antirrhinums; and leaf-mould resistant tomatoes.

Respiration. The conversion of organic compounds (carbohydrates) and oxygen to carbon dioxide and water by living cells; whereby energy for the functions of living protoplasm is liberated. In plants, it goes on continually, increasing with rises of temperature. Respiration is the converse of Photosynthesis (q.v.), the process by which carbohydrates (starches, sugars) are formed and oxygen liberated. In the daylight, these substances are formed more rapidly than they are consumed in respiration. In the dark, however, when photosynthesis ceases, respiration tends to lead to a loss of dry weight; and a fall in temperature at night-time minimizes this loss. Respiration at night, although consuming oxygen and releasing carbon dioxide, should not be overrated in the case of plants or flowers in a room, as the amounts are unlikely to have any appreciable effect on the atmosphere of a room.

Rest Harrow. See *Ononis*.

Resting. A term used of perennial plants in their cyclical period of least growth activity, usually coinciding with completion of flowering/fruiting; when nutrient and water needs diminish. The rest period is more pronounced in deciduous species, and plants subject to annual periods of drought, such as Cacti, in their natural habitats.

Resurrection Plant. See *Selaginella lepidophylla.*

Retarding. The process of retarding or delaying the flowering of plants by keeping them in artificially cooled chambers during their rest period, particularly dormant crowns (e.g. Lily-of-the-Valley) and bulbs; often used to arrest flowering of plants to meet particular dates, such as shows.

Reticulatus (-a, -um). Netted. Ex. *Iris reticulata.*

Retinospora, Retinispora. A genus name mistakenly given to juvenile forms of *Chamaecyparis* (q.v.).

Retusus (-a, -um). Retuse, applied to a leaf with a notch at its blunt tip. Ex. *Schizanthus retusus.*

Reversion. A term usually used to imply changes in plants causing them to 'revert' to older forms; but except in very rare instances, mistakenly. Variegated leafed plants may 'revert' when a green-leafed shoot forms to develop and swamp the rest of the foliage; budded or grafted varieties may 'revert' if shoots from the rootstock are allowed to grow unchecked, as in roses or rhododendrons. 'Reversion' in Black Currants when simpler leaf shapes or 'Nettleheads' develop is the result of a virus infection.

Revolutus (-a, -um). Revolute, rolled back at leaf margins. Ex. *Cycas revoluta.*

Rhamnus, Buckthorn (ram'nus. Fam. Rhamnaceae). A genus of shrubs or small trees, of which only a few are of garden merit for their foliage chiefly.

Selection. R. alaternus, SW. Europe, 8–10 ft, ovalish, evergreen leaves, yellowish spring flowers; and v. *argenteovariegata; cathartica,* the native Buckthorn, 6–9 ft, deciduous, black purging fruits; *costata,* Japan, to 12 ft, many-veined leaves; *frangula,* native deciduous Alder Buckthorn, to 18 ft, green June flowers, followed by red-purple berries; *imeritina,* Caucasus, to 10 ft, very handsome large deciduous leaves, green June flowers, colouring in autumn; and *purshiana,* Cascara Sagrada, N. America, tree-like to 35 ft, deciduous oval leaves, green July flowers, dark purple fruits.

Cultivation. Plant October–March, any well-drained loam soil; open situation, except *R. alaternus,* which is best planted in March–April.

Propagation. By layering, spring. By firm cuttings, July–August. By seeds, April, outdoors.

Rhapis (ra'pis. Fam. Palmaceae). Palms with fan-like leaves on reed-like slender stems, of which *R. excelsa,* the Ground Rattan Cane of China and Japan, to 6 ft, is chiefly grown.

Cultivation. Pot in March, standard compost, 3-in. pot; water freely in spring and summer; syringe on hot days; very moderately in winter, minimum temp. 10° C. (50° F.); in cool greenhouse or light airy indoor rooms, or corridors.

Propagation. By suckers, detached and potted in August.

Rheum (re'um. Fam. Polygonaceae). Hardy rhizomatous rooted perennials, with large handsome leaves, and erect panicles of summer flowers, of which *R. palmatum,* China, 5 ft, deep red flowers, and its vs. 'Bowles Crimson' and *tanguticum,* deeply lobed leaves, are chiefly grown ornamentally in the wild garden or by water. *R. rhaponticum* is the edible Rhubarb (q.v.). Plant in November–March, in almost any soil, sun or partial shade, given sufficient space. Propagation is by division in March.

Rhipsalis (rip-sa'lis. Fam. Cactaceae). Epiphytic cacti, with shrubby, twig-like stems or leaf-shaped, small, cream or white flowers, followed by semi-transparent berries.

Selection. R. baccifera (cassutha), the Mistletoe Cactus, Mexico to Peru, Ceylon and Africa, with pendent stems, cream flowers, white berries; *cereuscula,* Brazil, erect stems, branching shortly, white flowers and berries; *paradoxa,* Brazil, drooping branching stems, aerial roots, large white flowers, and *prismatica,* Brazil, prostrate stems, white flowers and berries.

Cultivation. Pot in April, very porous compost, equal parts by bulk loam, leaf-mould, crushed brick and charcoal; watering freely in growth; moderately in winter; minimum temp. 10° C. (50° F.); in fairly cool shade.

Propagation. By stem cuttings, June. Sometimes grafted on stocks of *Selenicereus.* By seeds, summer.

Rhizome. An underground or nearly underground stem, from which roots and leafy shoots bud readily. (*See* Fig. 195, page 452).

Rhodanthe. Now included in *Heliptrum* (q.v.).

Rhodo-. A prefix in compound words, meaning red.

Rhodochiton (ro-do-ki'ton. Fam. Scrophulariaceae). The one species, *R.*

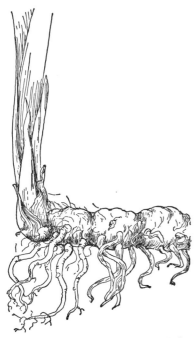

FIG. 195   Rhizome (*Iris germanica*).

atrosanguineum (*volubile*), Mexico, to 10 ft, is a graceful climbing herb, with cordate, pointed leaves, and bell-shaped, pendulous, blood-red flowers, June, for the cool greenhouse; blooming from seed sown in February–March, with bottom heat of 18° C. (65° F.), and grown as an annual.

Rhododendron (ro-do-den'dron. Fam. Ericaceae). The species of this important genus of shrubs and trees run to well over 500, but with varieties and hybrids innumerable provide a tremendous range of handsome plants, of exceptional flowering beauty, with simple, alternate, entire leaves, largely evergreen, and flowers which may be bell-, trumpet-, funnel- or saucer-shaped in spectacular clusters. The vast majority are Asiatic in origin, a few European or N. American, and a few from the tropics of Australasia. Botanically, the genus includes Azalea (q.v.), treated separately for gardening

convenience; and is divided into two great sections—Lepidote, those with scales on their plant parts; and Elipidote, those without scales; and subdivided into no less than forty-one series, or groups of species which are nearly related in characteristics and origins; many of the series being broken up into sub-series. The cultivation of Rhododendrons, however, is dictated by one vital factor; they are intolerant of the presence of lime in the soil.

Selection. Only a representative selection of what are considered the finer plants is given here, that may be planted in confidence by beginner or expert to succeed in gardens throughout the British Isles, where their cultural needs are met.

Tall-growing Hardy Species. R. *augustinii*, China, to 10 ft, lilac-blue; *auriculatum*, China, to 18 ft, white, July–August; *calendulaceum*, N. America, deciduous, to 10 ft, orange-yellow; *calophytum*, China, 10–30 ft, white, blotched crimson, March–April; *campylocarpum*, Himalaya, to 8 ft, yellow; *cinnabarinum*, Himalaya, to 8 ft, tubular, red; *croceum*, China, to 12 ft, yellow; *davidsonianum*, China, 10 ft, rose; *discolor*, China, 10–20 ft, white, June–July; *falconeri*, Himalaya, to 36 ft, cream, April; *fargesii*, China, to 12 ft, rose-pink, April; *fortunei*, China, 10 ft, rose-pink, fragrant; *neriiflorum* v. *euchaites*, China, 8 ft, scarlet, March–April; *ponticum*, Spain, Asia Minor, to 20 ft, purple-pink; *sinogrande*, China, Tibet, 30 ft, creamy-yellow, April, very large leaves; and *wardii*, China, 12 ft, yellow. R. *arborescens*, E. U.S.A., to 18 ft, deciduous, reddish purple, fragrant, June–July; *arboreum*, Himalaya, 20 ft, red, March–April; *souliei*, China, to 10 ft, white; *sutchuenense*, China, to 12 ft, rose-pink, March; and *thomsonii*, Himalaya, 10 ft, blood-red, are admirable for sheltered mild localities.

Compact, Small-leaved, Medium to Dwarf Species. R. *aberconwayi*, Yunnan, 4 ft, white; *albrechtii*, Japan, 5 ft, deciduous, purple-rose; *beanianum*, Tibet, Burma, 5 ft, blood-red; *campylogynum*, China, 1½ ft, rose-purple; *charitopes*, Burma, 1½ ft, pink; *dichroanthum*, China, 4 ft, orange; *edgarianum*, China, 3 ft, white; *fastigiatum*, Yunnan, 1½ ft, light purple, April; *ferrugineum*, the Alpine Rose, central Europe, 3 ft, rose-scarlet, June; *flavidum*, China, 1½ ft, primrose, April; *forrestii*, China, prostrate, crimson, April–May; *haematodes*, China, 3 ft, scarlet; *hippophaeoides*, China, 4 ft, purplish, April; *hirsutum*, Europe, 2 ft, deep pink, June; *impeditum*, China, 1 ft, mauve; *imperator*, Burma, 6 in., pinkish-purple; *intricatum*, China, 1 ft, mauve-lilac; *keiskei*, Japan, prostrate, yellow, April; *keleticum*, Tibet, 1 ft, purple-crimson; *ludlowii*, S. Tibet, 1 ft, primrose; *moupinense*, Tibet, China, 2 ft, white or pink, February–March; *myrtilloides*, Burma, 6 in., deep purple; *obtusum*, Japan, 2 ft, in v. *amoenum*, rose-purple and *japonicum*; *oreotrephes*, China, 5 ft, lavender-rose; *orthocladum*, China, to 4 ft, lavender-mauve, April; *nitens*, NE. Burma, 6 in., magenta, July; *pemakoense*, Tibet, 1 ft, light purple, April; × *praecox*, 3–5 ft, semi-evergreen, bright rose-purple, February–March; *primulaeflorum*, Tibet, 4 ft, yellow to white, April; *prostratum*, China, 6 in., rosy-purple, April; *racemosum*, Yunnan, to 5 ft, pink, March–May; v. *forrestii*, 2 ft, dwarf; *radicans*, Tibet, 4 in., purple; *rubiginosum*, China, 6 ft, rosy-lilac, April; *russatum*, China, 2 ft, violet-purple, April; *saluenense*, Yunnan, 1 ft, rose-purple; *sargentianum*, China, 2 ft, pale yellow; *scintillans*, China, 2 ft, blue, April; *uniflorum*, Tibet, 4 in., purple, April; *williamsianum*, China, 1½ ft, rose-red, April–May; the dwarf species are suitable for pans in the alpine house; as well as for the rock garden. All evergreen, flowering May–June, except where stated.

Hardy Hybrids. For general garden cultivation: 'Aladdin', tall, salmon-cerise, June; 'Albatross', tall, fragrant, white; 'Angelo "Solent Queen"', large, fragrant, white; 'Adrian Koster', creamy-white; 'Alice', rose-pink; 'Betty Wormald', pink; 'Beau Brummell', tall, scarlet; 'Beauty of Littleworth', white, crimson-spotted; 'Blue Peter', lavender blue; 'Bodartianum', tall, white, crimson ray; 'Britannia', crimson-red; 'Corona', coral-pink; 'Cynthia', rose-crimson; 'Dairy Maid', lemon-yellow; 'Dr Stocker', ivory white; 'Doncaster', deep red; *fastuosum plenum*, double mauve; 'Goldsworth Orange'; 'Golds-

worth Yellow'; 'Gomer Waterer', white, blush pink; 'Harvest Moon', cream, blotched carmine; 'J. G. Millais', deep blood-red, tall; 'Lady Bessborough, v. Roberte', pink; 'Lady Clementine Mitford', peach-pink; 'Madame de Bruin', cerise; 'Moser's Maroon'; 'Mrs J. C. Williams', white, spotted red; 'Mrs R. S. Holford', rose-salmon; *nobleanum*, rosy-scarlet, and vs. *album*, and *venustum*, pink, March–April; 'Pink Pearl', rose pink; 'Purple Splendour', purple; 'Peter Koster', crimson; 'Sappho', white, purple-spotted; 'Souvenir de A. Waterer', salmon-red; 'Susan', lavender; 'Sweet Simplicity', blush white; 'Yellow Hammer'.

Dwarf Hardy Hybrids. For rock gardens and small borders: 'Blue Bird', violet blue, April; 'Blue Diamond', lavender-blue; 'Blue Tit', soft blue, April; 'Carmen', 6 in., dark red; 'Elizabeth', orange-red; 'Ethel', crimson-scarlet; 'Humming Bird', pinky crimson, April; 'Intrifast', lavender-blue; 'Racil', shell-pink; April; 'Sapphire', blue, April; *spinulosum*, deep pink; 'Temple Belle', pale rose; and 'Winsome', rose pink. May flowering except where stated differently.

Rhododendrons for the Cool Greenhouse. R. *bullatum*, China, to 4 ft, fragrant, white, April–June; × 'Countess of Haddington', fragrant, blush white, April–May; × *fragrantissimum*, scented, white, tinged pink, April–May; × 'Lady Alice Fitzwilliam', white, fragrant, April–May; × 'Princess Alice', white, April–May; × *sesterianum*, creamy white, April–May; × *tyermanii*, cream, April; *valentinianum*, China, yellow, April; *veitchianum*, Burma, Thai, 3 ft, white, April–May.

Rhododendrons for the Warm Greenhouse. R. *jasminiflorum*, Malacca, to 8 ft, white tubular flowers; summer; *javanicum*, Java, 4 ft, orange-yellow, May–September; *retusum*, Java, Sumatra, to 4 ft, scarlet and yellow, May; and vs.

Cultivation. Plant out of doors, September–October, or March–May; in lime-free, well-drained sandy to medium loams, enriched with peat or leaf-mould; in light or partial shade, with shelter from cold, cutting or drying winds and draughts. On lime-containing soils, rhododendrons may be grown, planted shallowly in stations prepared by dusting subsoil with powdered sulphur, enriching top soil with at least 50 per cent moist peat, and subsequently feeding annually with a chelated iron compound, to provide the iron that lime normally denies to the plant. Normally, little pruning is needed, beyond removing spent flower-heads. When overgrown, however, rhododendrons may be pruned fairly hard in April–May.

Greenhouse Cultivation. Pot in early spring, 4 parts by bulk oak leaf-mould, 1 part medium loam, 1 part coarse sand and a little charcoal, watering fairly freely in active growth, moderately in winter; minimum temp. 7° C. (45° F.) for cool greenhouse; 13° C. (55° F.) for warm greenhouse. Syringe foliage on hot days, give light shade from direct sun; prune, when necessary, immediately after flowering.

Propagation. By seeds, sown March, in pans, cool greenhouse or frame, for species, but rather slow. By cuttings of firm, young shoots, July–August, inserted in lime-free compost, in propagating frame, with bottom heat (15·5° C. [60° F.]) at least. Choice hybrids by grafting on stocks of *R. ponticum*. By layering, spring–summer. Cuttings of large-leafed and elepidote species require mist propagation.

Diseases. Leaf Spots—brown with greyish-white discoloration—may be caused by fungi *Lophodermium rhododendri* or *Pestalozia rhododendri*, but seldom serious if infected leaves are promptly removed. Bud Blast and Twig Blight (*Sporocybe azaleae*) is more serious, browning buds and causing dieback; infected growth must be cut and burnt, and a copper fungicide then applied.

Pests. A 'rusty' appearance, with marbling or mottling of leaves, is caused by the Rhododendron Bug, *Stephanitis rhododendri*, a sucking insect. Infested leaves should be removed and burnt, and plants sprayed with nicotine, derris or malathion insecticide. Whitefly (*Dialeurodes chittendeni*) may appear in mild localities in June–July, but can be controlled by spraying with nicotine and white petroleum oil emulsion.

Rhodohypoxis (ro-do-hi-poks'is. Fam. Hypoxidaceae). The only species, *R. baurii*, is a rhizomatous-rooted herb from S. Africa, with strap-like, radical leaves, and solitary rose-red, six-petalled flowers on 3-in. stems in summer, with a white form, *platypetala*. Not quite hardy, it is best grown in deep pans, in the alpine house, well-draining compost, plenty of water in active growth, none during winter dormancy. Propagation is by division when starting into growth.

Rhodothamnus (ro-do-tham'nus. Fam. Ericaceae). *R. chamaecistus*, Tyrol and E. Siberia, 9 in., an evergreen, slender-stemmed shrub, small ovalish leaves, and terminal clusters of shell-pink flowers in April–May, is the one species, for planting in the rock garden, partial shade, lime-free soil, humus-rich, in March–April. Propagation is by seeds, sown August, in cold frame; by careful division in April. May be grown in the alpine house also.

Rhodotypos (ro-do-ti'pos. Fam. Rosaceae). A monotypic genus represented by *R. kerrioides* (*scandens*), the White Kerria, a twiggy deciduous hardy shrub, China, Japan, 5 ft, with four-petalled white flowers, May–July, which may be grown in any well-drained, loam soil, sunny position, planting in November–March. Propagation is by seeds, in spring, or by firm, young shoot cuttings, July, under handlights.

Rhoeo, Boat Lily (ro-e'o. Fam. Commelinaceae). The sole species, *R. discolor*, Florida to Mexico, with a thick fleshy stem, producing broad, thick-bladed and pointed leaves, to 1 ft long, in rosette formation, olive green, enpurpled beneath, and tiny, white or blue flowers in boat-shaped involucres at the base of the leaves, makes a striking indoor or warm greenhouse plant.

Cultivation. Pot, and repot, in March–April, standard compost, to grow in partial shade, and good ventilation; liberal watering in warm months, very moderate in winter; minimum temp. 10° C. (50° F.). Propagation is by young offset cuttings from near base of plant in spring and summer.

Rhoicissus (ro-i-kis'sus. Fam. Vitaceae). The chief species grown is *R. rhomboidea*, Natal, a moderate erect climber, with rhomboid toothed leaves, cultivated chiefly as a foliage pot plant, for indoor rooms or the cool greenhouse; in the same way as for *Cissus* (q.v.).

Rhubarb (*Rheum rhaponticum*). Rhubarb is known to have been cultivated in China over 4,500 years ago. In this country it is only since the eighteenth century that it has been grown for its edible stalks. The leaves contain soluble oxalates and are poisonous if eaten.

Varieties. Outdoors: 'Prince Albert', early; 'The Sutton', maincrop; 'Victoria', late. For forcing: 'Champagne', 'Dawes Champion'.

Cultivation. Plants may be raised from seeds, sown under glass in February–March, or outdoors in April, pricking out, or singling to 4–6 in. apart, to plant in permanent quarters in the following spring, and to crop in their second year. It is more customary to plant roots in November or March; in well prepared soil, heavily enriched with organic matter and a balanced organic fertilizer, pH 5·5–6, spacing 3 ft apart, with crowns 2 in. below the surface; but no stalks should be pulled in the first year. Stalks are pulled with a slight twist, detaching at base, but leave plants furnished with at least four leaves always; stopping pulling in mid June. Remove flowering stems, if formed. Water freely in dry weather, feed with liquid manure. Top-dress annually with stable manure or good compost, and a complete fertilizer each February.

Forcing. Outdoors, a covering of straw, and the inversion of a bottomless bucket, seakale pot, large drainpipe, in February, over the crown of a plant will give tender blanched stems. For early forcing, lift established, 3-year old roots, December onwards; leave exposed on surface to frost, etc., for two to three weeks; place in box, closely, planted in old moist potting compost, or in damp rotted organic matter, or peat; exclude light with another box on top, or tented black polythene, and keep in temp. of 10–15·5° C. (50–60° F.), in sheds, greenhouse or indoor room, watering with tepid water. Discard roots afterwards.

Propagation. By division, March. By seeds.

Rhus, Sumach (rus. Fam. Anacardiaceae). Deciduous shrubs or small trees, chiefly grown for their foliage colours and autumnal effects.

Selection. R. cotinoides (*Cotinus americanus*), SE. U.S.A., tall shrub to 20 ft, with oval leaves, dioecious flowers in large panicles, unusual red, orange and purple autumn tints; *continus* (*Cotinus coggyria*), the Smoke Tree, S. Europe, 6–10 ft, fine for its panicles of small flowers, turning feathery-grey in autumn, and leaf tints; v. *atropurpurea*, with inflorescence rosy-purple; and 'Notcutt's variety', one of the finest purple-red-leaved shrubs; *glabra*, the Smooth

FIG. 196 Foliage of *Rhus cotinus* v. *atropurpurea*.

Sumach, N. America, 4–6 ft, with long pinnate leaves; deep lobed in v. *laciniata*, unisexual panicles of flowers, July, autumn colour; *potaninii*, China, to 25 ft, long pinnate leaves, rich red in autumn; and *trichocarpa*, Japan, 20 ft, very long pinnate leaves, orange-scarlet in autumn, make good small trees; *typhina*, eastern N. America, the Staghorn Sumach, to 20 ft, with thick, hairy branches, pinnate-leaved, colouring gloriously early in autumn, tending to sucker, and v. *laciniata*, finely cut foliage; has hairy panicles of female flowers; and crimson, hairy fruits; greenish in the male.

Cultivation. Plant November–March, any ordinary soil, sun or light shade, pH 6·0–6·5.

Propagation. By cuttings of firm young shoots, July–August, under handlights. *R. typhina* by detaching rooted suckers and planting separately.

Rib. A main vein of a leaf.

Ribbon Fern. See *Pteris multifida*.

Ribes (ri'bes. Fam. Saxifragaceae). A genus of deciduous and evergreen shrubs which includes the Black Currant (*R. nigrum*), Red and White Currant (*R. sativum*), and the Gooseberry (*R. grossularia*), treated separately; and a few worth-while ornamental flowering kinds, here.

Selection. R. odoratum (*aureum*), the Golden Currant, western N. America, 6 ft, tri-lobed leaves, small racemes of golden-yellow, clove-scented, flowers, April, black fruits later; *sanguineum*, western N. America, to 8 ft, scented leaves, rosy-red flowers in drooping racemes, April–May, and vs. *atrorubens*, deep red; *carneum*, pink; 'King Edward VII', deep crimson, compact growth; and 'Pulborough Scarlet', rich red, tall-growing; × *gordonianum*, sterile hybrid with red and yellow flowers, are deciduous; *laurifolium*, China, 4 ft, greenish-yellow flowers, March; *gayanum*, Chile, 4 ft, honey-scented yellow flowers, June; and *speciosum*, California, 6 ft, clusters of bright red flowers with protruding stamens, May–June, are evergreen, and best suited to mild localities.

Cultivation. Plant deciduous species November–March; evergreen October, or March–April; well-drained soil, humus enriched, pH 6·0–6·5, sun or partial shade. Prune after flowering when necessary.

Propagation. By cuttings of firm, heeled shoots, July–August, under handlight or frame.

Rice, Canada. See *Zizania aquatica*.

Ricinus, Castor-oil Plant, Palma Christi (rik'i-nus. Fam. Euphorbiaceae). The one species, *R. communis*, of tropical Africa, 3–5 ft, yields castor oil from its seeds, but is grown ornamentally for its large, handsome, coloured, palmate-lobed leaves, as a half-hardy annual; sown under glass, February–March, standard composts, bottom heat of 18° C. (65° F.); singly in 3-in. pots, and grown on to plant out in early June, in beds; well-drained, humus-rich soil, and sun. The seeds are large, distinctive for their

caruncles (q.v.), but highly poisonous if eaten.

Ridging. Digging and throwing up stiff, heavy clay soils into rough ridges in autumn or early winter to expose as much surface as possible to frost action. The clods of soil are readily broken down and levelled as a result by forking and raking in early spring.

Rigidus (-a, -um). Rigid, stiff. Ex. *Ceanothus rigidus*.

Ring Culture. A system of growing plants in bottomless containers or 'rings', filled with a standard compost, and standing on a sterile moist aggregate, usually under glass, and now used for cucumber, tomato, chrysanthemum and similar annual cropping. The Rings can be of clay, wood, plastic, whalehide or bituminized composition, usually of 8–10-in. diameter. The aggregate is a 4–5-in. layer of weathered and washed clinker and ash; fine gravel and coarse

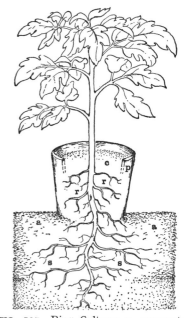

FIG. 197 Ring Culture: a. aggregate; c. compost; p. bottomless ring pot; r. feeding roots; s. secondary roots.

sand; equal parts vermiculite and sand; or a 2-in. layer of moist granulated peat, placed in an excavated bed, level with the surface. Where a soil-borne disease or pest such as eelworm has been previously experienced, the aggregate is isolated from the soil by lining the bed with polythene sheeting, drained by a line of porous drainage pipes sloping gently to one end, down the centre. The aggregate is wetted and kept moist by daily watering. Plants are placed in the rings, spaced a few inches apart on the aggregate, and watered only to keep the roots just moist, for 2–3 weeks, until roots grow into the moist aggregate below the rings. Thereafter the rings are moistened as the aggregate is drenched daily. Feeding is confined to the soil compost in the Rings as in normal culture. It is claimed that the sytem gives steadier, healthier growth, with heavier yields, and obviates the need for laborious soil changes or sterilization. The system is adaptable for use out of doors.

Ringing. The simple cutting of a girdling ring through the bark of the stem of a plant to check the downward flow of sap, with a view to checking vigour and inducing flower bud formation. Often practised when layering shoots, to induce rooting at the point of burial. See Bark-ringing; Layering.

Riparius (-a, -um). Of the banks of streams. Ex. *Oenothera riparia.*

Rivalis (-e). Growing by streams, or water. Ex. *Geum rivale.*

Rivina (ri-vi'na. Fam. Phytolaccaceae). The Rouge Plant or Bloodberry, *R. humilis,* of Caribbean Islands, a shrubby evergreen perennial of 2 ft, is grown for its racemes of white-pink early summer flowers, followed by scarlet berries, in the warm greenhouse, from seeds sown in March, bottom heat of 21° C. (70° F.)., in small pots, standard compost; watered freely until October, moderately in winter, minimum temp. 10° C. (50° F.); may be propagated by cuttings in April.

Robinia (ro-bin'i-a. Fam. Leguminosae). Deciduous shrubs and trees of N. America, with pretty, pinnate foliage and drooping racemes of pea-like flowers in June.

Selection. R. hispida, the Rose Acacia, to 6 ft, rich rose-pink flowers, and *kelseyi,* to 10 ft, lilac-pink, are graceful shrubs; *luxurians,* (*neo-mexicana*), to 35 ft, pale rose; *pseudacacia,* the False Acacia, Black Locust or Locust Tree, to 70 ft, white, make handsome trees, and vs. *angustifolia,* ferny foliage, slow-growing; *bessoniana,* more compact; *decaisneana,* deep rose flowers; *inermis,* to 40 ft, virtually non-flowering; *pyramidalis,* upright-growing; and *semperflorens,* flowering through the summer, are notable forms.

Cultivation. Plant October or March–April; well-drained, porous soils, in sunny, wind-sheltered positions as the wood is brittle.

Propagation. Species by seeds, sown March–April, in cold frame or greenhouse, in pots, to transplant without root disturbance. Varieties by grafting on seedling stocks of *R. pseudacacia,* spring.

Robustus (-a, -um). Strong. Ex. *Grevillea robusta.*

Rochea (Kalocanthes) (rok'e-a. Fam. Crassulaceae). Evergreen succulents from S. Africa, with showy flowers, allied to Crassula.

Selection. R. coccinea, 12 in., scarlet, summer; *jasminea,* prostrate, white; and *versicolor,* 1 ft, white, pink, yellow flowers.

Cultivation. Pot in March, standard compost, for indoor or cool greenhouse decoration; watering freely in summer; moderately in winter, minimum temp. 10° C. (50° F.); good light.

Propagation. By cuttings of shoots, taken in June–August.

Rock Broom. See *Genista.*

Rock Cress. See *Arabis; Aubrieta.*

Rock Garden. This is a feature designed chiefly to enable alpine and dwarf plants to be cultivated. It is best designed to simulate a natural outcropping of stone in the garden landscape, and most successful when advantage can be taken of a natural slope or undulation in the garden.

Site. This should be open, well-lighted, away from trees and dense shade cast by buildings; ideally with a south-west aspect, though other aspects can be used, the worst being due east. The site must be well drained, and thoroughly prepared. A draughty site is unsuitable.

Stone. Natural local stone is best and most economical. Weathered Westmorland or Yorkshire limestone is admirable, except for areas where air pollution with sulphurous compounds react with the stone and spoil its appearance. Tufa, a spongy cellular type of rock, yellowish or brownish grey, is light, well-liked by plants, and comes from Derbyshire. Sandstone, in various forms, suits most alpine plants, especially for southern gardens. Kentish Ragstone, Freestones, Purbeck Stone are amenable to good design; Slate, Granite and Basalt are hard, harsh, difficult stones, unsympathetic to plants unless available in weathered pieces and used boldly. Simulated stones made with cement tend to release chemicals into the soil and are not so satisfactory as natural stones. Rough masonry stone from old demolished buildings can sometimes be exploited, if not too hard in line and uniform in texture. Stone is sold by weight or by bulk, and is best bought by the cubic yard. A cubic yard weighs 1–$1\frac{1}{4}$ tons, according to kind, and roughly will furnish $1\frac{1}{2}$–3 square yards of rock garden area.

Construction. This can be undertaken at any time of the year, given favourable weather and workable soil. The site must be cleared of rubbish and weeds; and good drainage assured. In most instances, where the underlying soil is naturally porous, it will be sufficient to see that the rock garden soil is constituted to facilitate the percolation of rain. Where the soil is clayey or the site low-lying, supplementary drainage may be needed (*see* Drainage). It is unwise to use a site subject to winter waterlogging.

Weeds. It is vitally important to eliminate perennial weeds and their roots, particularly those of couch grass, nettles, ground elder, convolvulus, coltsfoot and horse-tails beforehand, by using appropriate herbicides (*see* Weeds), and forking.

Layout. This will be largely dictated by the nature of the site. When possible, it is advisable that the main orientation of a rock garden in the north should be on an east–west axis, sloping south; in the south and east, a north–south orientation is usually the most satisfactory. This gives the most desirable

micro-climates for the widest range of alpine plants. Where water is to be introduced, there must be adequate fall and pool space.

Design. There are three basic designs: (1) The simulation of a natural outcrop of rock, usually seen on lower slopes of hills or mountains; which is well suited to gentle slopes, or flat sites where ground is raised slightly artificially. (2) The simulation of more rocky, higher landscapes, with bluff or cliff-like formations; excellent for steep rises, high banks, ravines, and where waterfalls are wanted. (3) The terrace rock garden in which rocks are irregularly aligned, at different levels, to give terrace or pocket beds, in which alpine plants in variety may be grown; adaptable to banked corner structure or an island rock garden.

When the layout and design are decided, the site should be marked out with its principle features, and construction begun from the base. The stones must be placed to suggest their natural growth out of the soil from a vast bed of rock beneath. The stones must be placed with their faces upright or slightly tilted backward; with their grain or strata running horizontally, and well firmed, with sufficient bulk in the soil to hold them securely in place, though there is no need to place the greater part of the stone underground. It is usually best to build up the stone framework first, before soiling. Dominant features should not be completely central, whether a stream, fall or scree, and if steps are included, these should wind across the rock garden face.

Soil. Alpines like well-drained top or surface soil, over porous subsoil, and like to make longish roots into cool rooting conditions, where a reserve of moisture can be found. Very open subsoils may need organic matter added, even a little clay; but close impermeable ones need coarse grit, gypsum and peat to open them up. The top soil can be adapted to suit the plants to be grown. Some alpines, for instance, dislike lime; others grow natural on limestone mountains and need lime. Others need dry very porous surface soil. These needs can be met in individual beds or terraces. But by and large, the basic needs are for a soil through which rain can percolate readily; a moisture-retaining capacity furnished by well-rotted organic matter such as leaf-mould or peat; and not over-rich, such as would be afforded by a mixture of equal parts by bulk, medium loam, leaf-mould (or peat) and coarse sand and grit. This can be amended to suit individual plant needs. When the soiling-up of terrace beds and pockets is done, the soil should be firmly rammed to the stones, to ensure no slug-harbouring hollows are left, and the stones should be firm enough not to move or rock when stood upon. The whole may then be thoroughly watered prior to planting.

The Scree, or Moraine. Geologically, a scree is formed of the detritus and rock fragments of varying size at the foot of a cliff, established by weathering, and a moraine is a similar aggregation of rock debris deposited by glacial action. In rock gardening, the scree and moraine are more or less terms for the same thing —a feature where a stony, gritty rooting medium of some depth is provided for alpines thriving in rather loose soils, which dislike moisture around their crowns. A scree is constructed by re-moving 1–2 ft of soil; placing a 3-in. layer of broken stone in the bottom, a thin layer of leaves, coconut fibre or fibrous peat, and filling with a mixture of 4 parts by bulk small stones, ½ in. to dust grading, 1 part loam, and 1 part leaf-mould, well mixed and moistened. For lime-tolerant alpines, limestone grit can be used, for acid-loving alpines, crushed sandstone or granite.

Planting the Rock Garden. Most alpine plants are grown in pots, and, in theory, can be planted at any congenial-to-work time of the year, out of the pots with little or no root disturbance. In practice, the best planting times are March–June. The choice of plants is a matter of indi-vidual preference, tempered by the climatic and soil conditions afforded. The range is wide, but the smaller the rock garden, the greater attention should be paid to the eventual height and spread of the mature plant, as a few rampant specimens of, say, Arabis, Aubrieta, Sedum, *Campanula posharskyana*, can soon overwhelm choice small alpines; and while certain shrubs, trees and coni-fers are very attractive, the word 'dwarf'

should not be taken too literally. *See* Alpines.

Rock Garden Maintenance. Inevitably, rock gardens are catch-alls for airborne weed seeds, which must be dealt with when juvenile. Spot-treatment with a brush or sponge dipped into a suitable herbicide, in May–June and again in August–September, can save much grief and weeding labour. Slugs and snails must be combated with metaldehyde or methiocarb in moist weather. Wood-lice can be kept down with a DDT powder. A top-dressing of grit or stone chippings around alpines intolerant of surface moisture is helpful in autumn; while woolly- or hairy-leafed alpines, and alpines from high altitudes, tolerant enough of low temperatures, but not of cold damp or rain, need the winter pro-tection of glass or plastic cover.

Rock Rose. Common name for *Cistus* (q.v.).

Rocket, White. Common name for *Hesperis matronalis* (q.v.)

Rocket, Yellow. See *Barbarea*.

Rockfoil. Common name for *Saxifraga* (q.v.).

Rodgersia (rod-gers'i-a. Fam. Saxi-fragaceae). Flowering herbaceous peren-nials, with large divided leaves, and small flowers in large panicles in summer.

Selection. R. *aesculifolia*, China, 4 ft, digitate leaves, white; *pinnata*, China, 4 ft, pinnate leaves, reddish to white; *podophylla*, Japan, 3 ft, yellowish-white; and *sambucifolia*, China, 3 ft, white flowering.

Cultivation. Plant November–March, moist, peaty soil, in sunny, wind-sheltered positions.

Propagation. By seeds, sown April, outdoors. By division of rhizomatous roots, March.

Roller. A garden roller is most useful in keeping gravel paths smooth and firm, being used preferably when the surface is dry, but the gravel damp underneath. It is sometimes used in preparing seed-beds, but is apt to leave an undulating surface, apt to cake when wetted. For such purposes, the cast-iron, divided roller, or a water-ballasted roller, or concrete roller may be used. On lawns, however, care is needed. The function of the roller is to give a true surface, particularly for games; and is not strictly essential for well-maintained ornamental lawns. The best modern type of lawn roller is the wide, narrow-cylinder type, of light weight, used after mowing, when the surface is dry. Turf on light soils probably benefits most, but the tendency of rolling to compact a soil must be offset by spiking or aerating with a forked tool or slitter. Turf-aerating spiked rollers, or slitters, are most useful in lawn culture, to aerate the grasses and permit moisture and top-dressings to be incorporated more readily.

FIG. 198   A modern lawn roller.

Romneya, White Californian Tree Poppy (rom′ne-ya. Fam. Papaveraceae). Beautiful herbaceous sub-woody branching plants with pinnatifid leaves and large solitary white flowers, through summer.

Selection. R. coulteri, to 6 ft, branching freely; *trichocalyx*, to 7 ft, more erect growing.

Cultivation. Plant April–May, well-drained, humus-rich loam, sunny, warm positions in reasonably mild localities. Cut old stems to base in April.

Propagation. By seeds, sown April, warm greenhouse or frame, to plant out in June. By root cuttings, taken August–September. By careful division, May.

Room Plants. *See* House Plants.

Root Cuttings. Many plants have roots which readily form adventitious buds, and this faculty may be exploited in propagating them. The method is to cut a length of root of 2–3 in. and insert in a suitable rooting medium, kept moist, at a favourable temperature. Thick roots, such as of Anchusa, *Anemone hupehensis, Acanthus mollis,* Arnebia,

Bouvardia, Borago, *Echinops ritro, Gypsophila paniculata,* and vs., *Incarvillea delavayi, Papaver orientale,* Romneya and Seakale, are cut straight across at the top, slantingly at the base, and inserted vertically, just under the soil surface; thin root cuttings of such plants as Gaillardia, and *Phlox paniculata* and vs., one inch long, can be simply covered with the soil. Root cuttings are usually taken in September, placed in a cold frame or under handlights. Many weeds such as Couch Grass, Convolvulus, Ground Elder, Dandelions, Docks, etc., also bud freely from severed pieces, unfortunately.

Root Grafting. A method of propagation in which a shoot of the current year's growth of a plant is cleft or whip-grafted on to a piece of root used as the stock, which is then buried in the soil. Hybrid Clematis, Tree Peonies, and Rhododendrons may be propagated in this way.

Root Hairs. See Roots.

Root Pruning. *See* Pruning of stone fruits.

Roots. Collectively, roots make up that part of vascular plants that descends and grows first from their seeds, downward into the soil, anchoring the plants and absorbing water and nutrient salts for their growth from the soil. Roots differ from stems in having no leaves or buds, and are normally not green; internally, their tissues are arranged in a central core. The root system of Dicotyledons becomes a main tap-root from which other roots branch; of Monocotyledons the root system develops adventitiously from the base and is tufted in habit. The actively growing parts of the system are the ends or meristems of the fine roots and rootlets at the periphery, which penetrate through the pore spaces of the soil. They are equipped at the tip with a sheath of protective scale-like cells, the root cap, which is constantly abraded by friction with soil particles, but renewed from behind. Behind the root cap, there is a zone of root hairs, tubular fine outgrowths which maintain intimate contact with the water films and soil particles, which, with their great absorbing surface, take up moisture and nutrient salts. Root hairs are themselves short-lived, but constantly replaced from new root tissue as the root extends and grows through the soil. Some plants, as in members of the Orchid and Arum family, develop aerial roots readily. In biennial and perennial plants roots become storage organs.

FIG. 199 Root and Root Hairs, on germinating Bean seedling.

Rootstock. The plant or stock on which a scion is grafted. *See* Apple, etc.

Rorippa. *See* Watercress.

Rosa, Rose (ro′sa. Fam. Rosaceae). A genus of noteworthy flowering shrubs, largely found in the northern hemisphere, largely in Asia, some in America, and a few in Europe and N. Africa. They are mostly prickly-stemmed shrubs, some climbing, with alternate deciduous leaves, pinnate and stipulate, bearing flowers on shoots of the current year from May onwards, followed by fleshy fruits or hips, enclosing hard achenes or seeds.

Selection. For garden virtues, the more outstanding species and varieties are: *R.* × *alba semi-plena*, White Rose of York, to 8 ft, white, fragrant, semi-double, June; *banksiae*, Banksian Rose, China, climber to 20 ft, white, fragrant, May–June, and vs. *banksiae*, double white; and *lutea*, double yellow; *bracteata*, Macartney Rose, rambler, China, 10 ft, rather tender, large white, July–

August; *britzensis*, Kurdistan, to 6 ft, single pale pink, May–June; *brunonii*, climber, Himalaya, to 20 ft, single creamy white, June–July; *californica*, California, to 8 ft, single pink, and v. *plena*, semi-double pink; *canina*, Dog Rose, Europe and Britain, to 10 ft, white to pink, June, with good forms, but important as a rootstock; × *cantabrigiensis*, to 8 ft, yellow, semi-double, June; *centifolia*, Cabbage or Provence Rose, Caucasus, to 5 ft, fragrant, rose-pink, double, June–July; and vs. 'Fantin Latour', pink; 'Juno', blush pink; 'Petite de Hollande', small, pink; and 'Reine des Centfeuilles', very large clear pink; *c. cristata*, Crested Moss, pink; *c. muscosa*, Moss Rose, very fragrant, rose, with moss-like growths on calyx and stems of flowers, and vs. 'Blanche Moreau', white; 'Deuil de Paul Fontaine', dark crimson; 'Gloire des Mousseux', bright pink; 'Nuits de Young', deep purple; *chinensis*, China or Monthly Rose, China, 4 ft, crimson to pink, June–September, and vs. *minima*, the Fairy Rose, 1 ft, in various forms; and hybrids 'Cécile Brunner', blush pink; 'Cramoisie Supérieure', fragrant dark crimson; 'Fellemberg', to 8 ft, bright crimson; 'Hermosa', 2–3 ft, fragrant, blush pink; 'Perle d'Or', 3 ft, yellow; and v. *viridifolia*, the Green Rose, 3–4 ft, green flowers, summer; *damascena*, Damask Rose, Asia Minor, fragrant white to red, June–July, and v. *versicolor*, York and Lancaster Rose, 3–5 ft, semi-double, white splashed pink; *davidii*, Tibet, China, to 8 ft, corymbs of rose flowers, June–July, red, flask-shaped hips; × *dupontii*, 8 ft, single large, white to pink, fragrant, June; *ecae*, Afghanistan, Turkistan, 4 ft, single, golden yellow, May–June; *eglanteria*, Sweet Brier, Europe, Britain, to 7 ft, fragrant, pink, June; parent of the Penzance Briers such as 'Amy Robsart', semi-double, rose pink; 'Anne of Geierstein', single, crimson; 'Florence Mary Morse', semi-double, orange-scarlet, to 4 ft only; 'Janet's Pride', white, pink edged; 'Lord Penzance', single, fawn yellow; 'Meg Merrilees', to 10 ft, single, fragrant, crimson; 'Refulgence', semi-double, scarlet-crimson; *farreri*, NW. China, to 6 ft, single, pale pink, May–June, and v. *persetosa*, Threepenny-bit Rose, tiny, single, salmon-pink; *foetida*, Austrian Brier, Armenia, Persia, to 5 ft, single, rich yellow, June, and vs. *bicolor*, Capucine or Austrian Copper Rose, orange-copper and yellow; and *persiana*, Persian Yellow Rose, double, golden-yellow, fragrant; *gallica*, S. Europe, W. Asia, 2–3 ft, pink to crimson, June; and vs. *officinalis*, double bright pink, Apothecary Rose; and *versicolor* (*Rosamundi*), semi-double, striped red and white; × *harisonii*, 2–3 ft, semi-double, light yellow, June; *helenae*, China, climber to 20 ft, panicles of single, fragrant white flowers, June–July; × *highdownensis*, to 10 ft, single, deep pink, June, scarlet flask-shaped hips; *holodonta*, China, to 6 ft, umbels of single rose flowers, June; *hugonis*, China, 6–8 ft, single yellow, May–June, dark red hips; × *macrantha*, 4–5 ft, single, pale pink, June–July, and form 'Daisy Hill'; *moschata*, Musk Rose, Persia, Central Asia, climber to 30 ft, fragrant, creamy-white in corymbs, July–August; best in its hybrids such as 'Berlin', 5 ft, single, orange-scarlet; 'Bonn', 5 ft, semi-double, orange-scarlet; 'Callisto', 3–4 ft, double, golden-yellow; 'Cornelia', 5–6 ft, semi-double, pink, flushed yellow; 'Elmshorn' 5 ft, bright crimson; 'Erfurt', 5 ft, semi-double, yellow and carmine; 'Felicia', 5 ft, salmon-pink; 'Grandmaster', semi-double, yellow, apricot; 'Moonlight', 6 ft, semi-double, pale lemon; 'Pax', 4–5 ft, semi-double, white; 'Penelope', 5 ft, semi-double, creamy salmon; 'Prosperity', 6 ft, double, white; 'Vanity', single, deep pink; and 'Will Scarlet', semi-double, scarlet; *moyesii*, China. 6–12 ft, single, blood red, June, red flask-shaped hips, and vs. 'Geranium', fine red form; 'Nevada', creamy white; *multibracteata*, W. China, to 10 ft, small, single pink, July; *multiflora*, Korea, Japan, climber to 15 ft, white or pink, small, single flowers in corymbs, July; and v. *platyphylla*, Seven Sisters Rose, double, purple; *nitida*, eastern N. America, 2–3 ft, single, bright red, July; × *noisettiana*, climbers to 10 ft, Noisette Roses, semi-double, white or pink, in corymbs, June–July, and vs. 'Alister Stella Gray', creamy yellow; 'Mme Plantier', creamy white; 'Marechal Niel', fragrant, golden-yellow; and 'William Allen Richardson', orange to

FIG. 200 *Rosa moyesii* 'Geranium'.

buff; *odorata*, Tea Rose of China, in v. *major*, climber to 12 ft, semi-double, light pink; *omeiensis*, China, to 12 ft, single, white, May–June, and v. *pteracantha*, 15 ft, white, decorative red-thorned shoots; *primula*, Incense Rose, Turkistan, to 7 ft, single, pale yellow, fragrant, May–June; *rugosa*, Ramanas Rose, China, Japan, 5–8 ft, red or white, fragrant, June–July; and vs. *alba*, white; *fimbriata*, flesh pink, fringed; *rubra*, crimson; and hybrids 'Blanc Double de Coubert', 5 ft, double, white; 'Conrad F. Meyer', fragrant, silvery pink; 'Frau Dagmar Hastrup', 4 ft, single, rose-pink; 'F. J. Grootendorst', double, crimson; 'Mrs A. Waterer', semi-double, deep red; 'Parfum de l'Hay', 4 ft, fragrant, double, carmine; 'Pink Grootendorst', fringed, clear pink; 'Roseraie de l'Hay', 7 ft, semi-double, fragrant purple-crimson; and 'Schneezwerg', 3 ft, semi-double, white; *roxburghii*, Burr or Chestnut Rose, China,

6 ft, pink, June, spiny hips; *sinowilsonii*, SW. China, to 20 ft, white in corymbs, July; *spinosissima*, Burnet or Scots Rose, Europe, Asia, to 3 ft, suckering, best in forms 'Frühlingsgold', semi-double, pale yellow; 'Frühlingsmorgen', single, pink, yellow; 'Frühlingszauber', semi-double, rosy pink; *harisonii*, double, sulphur yellow; and 'Stanwell Perpetual', double pink to white; *sempervirens* v. 'Félicité et Perpétue', rambler, semi-evergreen, creamy white to pink; *slingeri* (*xanthina*), N. China, Korea, to 8 ft, semi-double, yellow, May–June, and v. 'Canary Bird' (*spontanea*), single, deep yellow; *villosa* (*pomifera*), Apple Rose, Europe, 3–6 ft, pink, June, dark red bristly hips, and v. *duplex*, Wolley Dod's Rose, semi-double, purple-red; *webbiana*, Himalaya, to 6 ft, single, pale pink, June, bottle-shaped, red hips; *wichuraiana*, Memorial Rose, semi-evergreen, trailer to 20 ft, single, white, July–August; parent of many climbing roses (*see* Roses); and *willmottiae*, W. China, to 6 ft, single, rose-purple, June, small orange-scarlet hips.

Cultivation. As shrubs, the species and their forms often have a single flowering season, and are best used informally for garden decoration, with an eye to their foliage merits as well as flowers and hips. Plant October–March, in almost any soil made amenable by thorough digging, enrichment with humus-forming matter, basic fertilizing, and brought to a pH 6·0–6·5, to be well-drained and yet moisture-retentive. Pruning in most cases is simply a matter of cutting out dead or weak wood, and shaping growth, in February–March.

Propagation. Species by seeds, sown March–April, outdoor beds or cold frame. By cuttings of young firm shoots, in July–August, inserted in cold frame. Hybrids may be propagated by budding in July, or grafting in early spring, on common stocks, under glass.

Roscoea (ros-ko'e-a. Fam. Zingiberaceae). Herbaceous, rhizomatous-rooting, flowering perennials with lanceolate leaves, and tubular, tri-lobed somewhat hooded flowers in summer.

Selection. R. cautleoides, China, 1 ft, clear yellow flowers; *humeana*, W. China, 8 in., violet-purple flowers; and *purpurea*, Sikkim, 1 ft, purple.

Cultivation. Plant 6 in. deep, October–November or March; light, well-drained, humus-rich soil in warm sunny positions, or protected light shade.

Propagation. By division in spring.

Rose Acacia. See *Robinia hispida*.

Rose, Alpen, Alpine. See *Rhododendron ferrugineum*.

Rose Bay. See *Epilobium angustifolium*.

Rose Campion. Common name of *Lychnis coronaria*.

Rose Mallow. See *Hibiscus*.

Rose of Sharon. See *Hypericum calcycinum*.

Rose, Sun. See *Helianthemum*.

Rosemary. See *Rosmarinus officinalis*.

Roses (*Rosa*). There is no doubt that of all garden flowers, the rose, in its almost infinite variety of colour, is the most popular and widely planted. Apart from the species and their forms, dealt with under Rosa, interest and enthusiasm are overwhelmingly centred on hybrids and varieties of horticultural distinction and of man's breeding. Their history goes back to about the sixteenth century, when sixteen forms of Roses were described by John Gerard (1597), but not until the late eighteenth century did the pace accelerate. Josephine of France (1763–1814) is stated to have planted 1,000 varieties in her garden at Malmaison, and French and continental breeders were increasingly active, and as the cult of the rose spread to Britain, America and other countries, new roses were raised in ever-increasing numbers, and it is probable that over 20,000 named varieties are now known. Early development began with the introduction of the Monthly China Rose, *Rosa chinensis*, 1768, and its crossing with *R. gallica*, to provide the Bourbon Roses of which 'Commandant Beaurepaire', 'La Reine Victoria', 'Souvenir de la Malmaison' and 'Zéphirine Drouhin' are still grown. The Bourbons crossed with China or Monthly Roses and *R. damascens* gave the more frequently flowering Hybrid Perpetuals, which, in turn, crossed with Tea-scented Roses (*R. odorata* and vs.) resulted in the Hybrid Tea Roses from which other types such as the Pernetianas and Floribundas were developed. For garden purposes, it has been customary to classify modern garden roses according to their pedigree and descent, but today interbreeding tends to blur distinctive lines, and it is now more convenient to group according to type.

Selection. Only a representative selection of roses of proven good performance is attempted here. New varieties are introduced every year, and growers' catalogues, and the trials awards of the Royal National Rose Society, Bone Hill, Chiswell Green Lane, St Albans, Hertfordshire, should be consulted to keep up to date.

Hybrid Tea Types. Hardy, strong growth, prickly stems, flowers pointed in bud, tea-scented, June–November; including pernetianas. (H.T.)

Variety	Intro- duced	Fra- grance	Colour of Flower	Remarks
Allegro	1962	*	Geranium red	For cutting
Anne Watkins	1963	*	Apricot, cream	Tall
Bayadere	1954	**	Pink, orange	Tall
Beauté†	1954	*	Orange yellow	
Belle Blonde	1955	**	Golden yellow	Blackspot?
Bettina	1953	**	Orange, bronze red	
Buccaneer	1953	*	Buttercup yellow	
Casanova†	1964	**	Yellow, buff	Tall
Charles Mallerin	1947	***	Crimson	Mildew?
Chicago Peace†	1962	*	Phlox pink	Tall
Christian Dior	1959		Velvety scarlet	Mildew?
Cleopatra	1955	**	Scarlet and yellow	Blackspot?
Crimson Glory	1935	***	Velvety crimson	Mildew?
Dr A. J. Verhage	1960	**	Golden yellow	
Eden Rose†	1950	***	Deep pink	
Ena Harkness†	1946	***	Crimson scarlet	
Ernest H. Morse	1965	***	Turkey red	Tall
Evensong	1963	*	Rose-pink, salmon	Tall
Flaming Sunset	1947	**	Orange, vermilion	
Fragrant Cloud†	1964	***	Geranium lake	
Frau Karl Druschki†	1900	*	White	Very vigorous
Fritz Thiedemann	1960	**	Vermilion	
Gail Borden†	1956	*	Deep rose-pink	
Garvey†	1960	*	Pink to salmon	Tall
George Dickson	1912	***	Velvety crimson	Mildew?
Gertrude Gregory	1956	**	Golden yellow	Free
Gold Crown†	1960	**	Deepest yellow	Tall
Golden Giant	1960	**	Light yellow	Very tall
Grace de Monaco†	1956	***	Rose-pink	Tall
Grand Gala†	1955	*	Scarlet, pink reverse	Tall
Grandpa Dickson	1966	*	Yellow, edged pink	Tall
Hugh Dickson†	1904	***	Scarlet crimson	Tall
Isabel de Ortiz	1962	**	Deep pink, silver	Tall
Josephine Bruce†	1952	***	Crimson scarlet	Mildew?
June Park	1958	***	Deep pink	Tall
King's Ransom	1961	**	Rich yellow	
Kronenbourg†	1965		Red, crimson, old gold	Exhibition var.
Lady Belper	1948	**	Light orange, bronze	
Liberty Bell	1963	**	Claret, cream	
Lydia†	1949	**	Golden yellow	Black Spot?
Marcelle Gret	1947	*	Deep yellow	

* slightly fragrant   ** fragrant   *** very fragrant   † highly suitable for standards

Variety	Intro-duced	Fra-grance	Colour of Flower	Remarks
Margaret†	1954	**	Bright pink	Black Spot?
McGredy's Yellow	1933	**	Buttercup yellow	Black Spot?
Memoriam†	1960	**	White, tinted pink	
Message	1956	*	White	Black Spot?
Mischief†	1960	***	Coral salmon	Tall
Miss Ireland†	1961	*	Vermilion, orange	Black Spot?
Mme Caroline Testout	1890	*	Pink	
Mojave	1954	*	Orange, red	
Montezuma†	1956	*	Salmon-red	Mildew?
Mrs Sam McGredy	1929	**	Scarlet, deep orange	Black Spot?
My Choice†	1958	***	Pink, yellow	Tall
Opera†	1949	**	Orange-red, carmine	Black Spot?
Ophelia†	1912	***	Pale pink	Thrips?
Papa Meilland	1963	***	Dark crimson	Mildew?
Pascali	1963		White	
Peace†	1942	*	Yellow, edged pink	Tall
Perfecta	1957	**	Cream, crimson	Tall
Piccadilly†	1959	*	Scarlet, yellow	Tall
Pink Peace†	1959	**	Deep pink	Tall
Prélude	1955	**	Lavender mauve	
Prima Ballerina	1958	***	Deep pink	Tall
Red Devil	1967	**	Scarlet	Tall
Rose Gaujard†	1958	**	White, pink, silver	Tall
Sarah Arnott†	1956	**	Rose-pink	Tall
Silver Lining	1958	***	Silvery rose	
Spek's Yellow†	1947	*	Rich yellow	Tall
Stella†	1959	*	Cream, pink	
Sterling Silver	1957	***	Silvery lilac	Black Spot?
Super Star†	1960	**	Vermilion	Tall
Sutter's Gold	1950	***	Orange, red	Tall
Tzigane	1951	**	Vermilion, yellow	
Uncle Walter†	1963	*	Scarlet, crimson	Tall shrub
Virgo	1947	*	White	
Wendy Cussons†	1959	***	Cerise, scarlet	Tall
Westminster	1959	***	Cherry red, yellow	
Winifred Clarke	1965	*	Yellow to cream	

* slightly fragrant   ** fragrant   *** very fragrant   † highly suitable for standards

Hybrid Perpetual Roses. Often now merged in with the hybrid teas but worth citing separately for they are hardy, exquisitely scented, and still worth growing in such vs. as: 'Henry Nevard', crimson-scarlet, tall; 'Julien Potin', double clear yellow; 'Li Bures', double rose-pink, shaded scarlet and gold; 'Luis Brinas', orange-gold; 'Mme Jean Gaujard', golden yellow; 'Mrs John Laing', rose-pink, tall; 'Ulrich Brunner', carmine-red.

Floribunda Roses; Flori. Formerly Hybrid Polyanthas. Shrub roses which bear their flowers in clusters or trusses, many opening at the same time. There are also Floribunda-Hybrid Tea types (Grandifloras in America), and Floribunda Dwarfs which are low-growing bushy plants of about 15 in. high, between the Floribundas and the Miniature China roses.

A Selection is:

Variety	Intro-duced	Fra-grance	Colour of Flower	Remarks
Floribunda Type				
Alison Wheatcroft†	1959	**	Apricot, crimson	
Allgold†	1956	*	Golden yellow	Semi-double
Anna Wheatcroft	1959	*	Vermilion	
Apricot Nectar	1965	*	Apricot yellow	Tall
Arabian Nights	1963	**	Scarlet orange	Tall
Arthur Bell†	1965	***	Golden yellow	Tall
Chanelle†	1958	**	Cream, pink	Very free
Chinatown	1963	**	Yellow	Shrubby
Circus†	1955	**	Yellow, red	Fades paler
City of Leeds†	1966		Salmon	
Dearest†	1960	**	Rosy salmon	Dislikes rain
Dickson's Flame	1958	*	Vermilion	Dwarf
Dorothy Wheatcroft	1960	*	Bright red	Tall, shrubby
Dusky Maid	1947	*	Scarlet maroon	Semi-double
Elizabeth of Glamis†	1964	**	Light salmon	Upright
Evelyn Fison†	1962	*	Vivid red	
Fashion†	1947	**	Orange-salmon	Mildew?
Firecracker	1955	*	Carmine, yellow	Semi-double
Frensham†	1946		Scarlet	Tall
Garnette	1947	*	Garnet red	Bushy
Geisha Girl	1962		Golden yellow	Tall
Goldgleam†	1966	*	Deep yellow	
Heidelberg	1958	*	Bright red	Tall
Highlight	1956	*	Orange scarlet	
Iceberg†	1958	*	White	Tall
Ivory Fashion	1957	*	Ivory White	
Jan Spek†	1966	*	Yellow	Dwarf
Korona†	1954	*	Orange-scarlet	Black Spot?
Lili Marlene	1959	*	Scarlet-red	
Masquerade†	1950	*	Yellow-red	Semi-double
Meteor	1958		Orange-red	Bushy
Moulin Rouge	1952	*	Scarlet	Vigorous
Orangeade†	1959	*	Orange-vermilion	Semi-double
Orange Sensation	1960	**	Vermilion, orange	
Paddy McGredy†	1962	*	Coral-pink	Mildew?
Paint Box	1963	*	Red and gold	
Paprika	1958		Turkey red	
Pernelle Poulsen†	1965	**	Salmon-pink	
Poulsen's Bedder	1948	*	Rose-pink	Upright
Rumba	1959	**	Yellow, pink, red	Upright
Scented Air	1965	**	Salmon-pink	Tall
Shepherd's Delight†	1958	**	Orange-yellow	Black Spot?
Spartan†	1954	**	Salmon-orange	Dislikes rain
Sundance	1954	*	Yellow, pink	Tall
Toni Lander†	1959	*	Salmon, scarlet	
Travesti	1965	*	Yellow, red	
Zambra	1961	*	Orange, yellow	Mildew?
Floribunda: H.T. Type				
Charlotte Elizabeth	1965	*	Rose-pink, red	Upright

* slightly fragrant   ** fragrant   *** very fragrant.   † highly suitable as standards.

Variety	Intro-duced	Fra-grance	Colour of Flower	Remarks
Charm of Paris	1966	**	Pink, double	
Daily Sketch†	1960	**	Pink, silver	Tall
Faust†	1956		Golden yellow	Tall, Mildew?
Golden Fleece	1956	**	Light yellow	
King Arthur	1967	*	Salmon-pink	
The People	1954	*	Orange-scarlet	
Pink Parfait	1962	*	Pink, shaded	Tall
Queen Elizabeth	1955	*	Pink	Tall
Red Dandy†	1960	*	Scarlet-crimson	Tall
Red Lion	1966	**	Cerise	Tall
Sea Pearl	1964	*	Orange, pink	Tall
Floribunda Dwarf				
Baby Masquerade†	1956	*	Yellow, red	12–15 in.
Jean Mermoz	1937		Pale pink	

Polyantha Pompon Roses. Largely hybrids of *R. multiflora*, and dwarf-growing bush roses of floribunda habit, with clusters of small individual flowers, very hardy.

Variety	Intro-duced	Fra-grance	Colour of Flower	Remarks
Cameo	1920		Salmon-pink	
Baby Faurax	1924	**	Violet-blue	15 in.
Coral Cluster	1920		Coral-pink	
Ellen Poulsen	1912		Deep pink	Spreading
Gloria Mundi	1928	*	Orange-scarlet	
Little Dorrit	1922		Coral-salmon	Mildew?
Miss Edith Cavell	1917		Scarlet-crimson	Dwarf
Paul Crampel	1930		Orange-scarlet	Very free
The Fairy	1932		Pink	Very free

Miniature Roses (Min.). Mostly hybrids of *R. chinensis* v. *minima* (*roulettii*), these are very dwarf, 6–12 in. high, blooming freely and recurrently, with tiny well-formed flowers, charming for rock gardens, border edging or grouping, and quite hardy.

Variety	Intro-duced	Fra-grance	Colour of Flower	Remarks
Baby Gold Star	1940	*	Golden yellow	
Cinderella	1952		White, tinted carmine	
Colibri	1959	*	Orange-yellow	Double
Coralin	1955		Coral-red, full	
Dwarf King	1957	*	Velvety crimson	
Eleanor	1960	*	Coral-pink	Dwarf

* slightly fragrant   ** fragrant   † highly suitable as standards.

Variety	Intro-duced	Fra-grance	Colour of Flower	Remarks
Little Flirt	1961	**	Orange-red, yellow	Bicolor
New Penny	1962	**	Salmon to pink	
Perla de Alcanada	1944		Carmine-red	
Perla de Montserrat	1945	*	Clear pink	Dwarf
Pour Toi	1946		White, semi-double	Dwarf
Rosina	1951	*	Golden yellow	(Josephine Wheatcroft)
Sweet Fairy	1946	**	Lilac pink	Dwarf
Tinker Bell	1954		Bright pink	Dwarf
Yellow Doll	1962	**	Light yellow	Dwarf

Garnette Roses. A race of Floribunda type bush roses, of 2–3 ft, developed in France, and yielding blooms which resemble double Camellia flowers, lasting well when cut, now available in a range of colours of red, pink, orange, yellow and white.

Climbing Roses. These are roses suitable for adorning arches, pillars, pergolas, fences and walls. They may be divided into Ramblers, which are hybrids of *R. wichuraiana* or *R. multiflora*, of lax vigorous growth, having somewhat small flowers usually in clusters in summer, and Large-flowered Climbers of very vigorous, stiffer growth, bearing larger flowers, and embracing the climbing mutations or forms of Hybrid Tea and Floribunda varieties, and newer Kordesii Climbers.

Variety	Intro-duced	Fra-grance	Colour of Flower	Remarks
Wichuraiana Ramblers				
Alberic Barbier†	1900	**	Yellow to white	Semi-evergreen
Albertine†	1921	***	Coppery pink	Very vigorous
American Pillar†	1902		Rose; white eye	Single, Mildew?
Chaplin's Pink	1928		Bright pink, semi double	
Crimson Shower†	1951		Crimson, semi-double	Long-flowering
Dorothy Perkins†	1901		Rose-pink, double	July flowering
Dr W. Van Fleet	1910	**	Flesh-pink	Very vigorous
Easlea's Golden	1932	**	Yellow, tinted crimson	Vigorous
Emily Gray†	1916	**	Golden buff	Semi-evergreen
Excelsa†	1909		Rosy crimson	Mildew?
François Juranville†	1906	**	Deep fawn-pink	Very vigorous
Minnehaha†	1905	*	Deep pink	Very vigorous
Sanders' White†	1915	**	White	Very vigorous
Seagull	1914	***	White	Very vigorous
Thelma	1916	*	Soft pink, semi-double	Long in flower
The New Dawn†	1930	**	Shell-pink, double	Long in flower
Large-flowered Climbers				
Allen Chandler	1923	**	Scarlet, semi-double	Perpetual
Aloha	1955	**	Deep pink, double	Pillar Rose
Casino	1963		Soft yellow	To 9 ft
Copenhagen	1964	**	Scarlet	6–8 ft

* slightly fragrant   ** fragrant   *** very fragrant   † highly suitable as standards.

Variety	Intro-duced	Fra-grance	Colour of Flower	Remarks
Coral Dawn	1952	**	Pink, clustered	To 10 ft
Danse de Feu†	1954		Orange-scarlet	To 8 ft
Elegance	1937	*	Pale yellow	To 6 ft
Étude	1968	*	Deep salmon-pink	To 8 ft
Golden Showers	1957	**	Yellow, semi-double	To 6 ft
Guinée	1938	***	Maroon-crimson	To 8 ft
High Noon†	1946	**	Deep yellow	To 8 ft
Lady Hillingdon	1917	***	Apricot-yellow	Very vigorous
Maigold	1953	**	Yellow, double	To 11 ft
Meg	1954		Pink, single	8 ft Pillar
Mermaid	1917	**	Primrose, single	× *bracteata* **v.**
Mme G. Straechelin	1927	***	Coral-pink, large	To 10 ft
Parade	1957	**	Carmine crimson	To 10 ft
Paul's Lemon Pillar	1915	**	Pale lemon	To 8 ft
Pink Perpetué	1965	*	Pink, carmine	To 6 ft
Reveil Dijonnais	1931	**	Carmine, gold	To 8 ft
Royal Gold	1957	**	Deep yellow	To 6 ft
School Girl	1964	**	Orange-apricot	To 9 ft
Soldier Boy	1955		Scarlet, single	6 ft
Gloire de Dijon	1853	**	Cream to buff-pink	To 8 ft
Mme Alfred Carrière	1879	***	Pink to white	To 8 ft
Kordesii Climbers				
Dortmund	1955		Red, white eye, single	To 7 ft
Hamburger Phoenix	1955		Crimson, semi-double	To 9 ft
Leverkusen	1955		Pale yellow, semi-double	To 10 ft
Parkdirektor Riggers	1957		Blood red, semi-double	To 8 ft
Ritter von Barmstede	1960		Deep pink	To 8 ft

* slightly fragrant   ** fragrant   *** very fragrant   † highly suitable as standards.

Climbing Hybrid Tea Roses. (Cli. H.T.)

Bettina (1958)
Crimson Glory (1941)
Étoile de Hollande (1931)
Josephine Bruce (1954)
Mme Butterfly (1926)
Mrs Sam McGredy (1937)
Spek's Yellow (1956)

Crimson Conquest (1931)
Ena Harkness (1954)
Golden Dawn (1947)
Lady Sylvia (1933)
Mme. Edouard Herriot (1921)
Ophelia (1920)
Shot Silk (1924)

Climbing Floribunda Roses (Cli. Flori).

Allgold (1961)
Fashion (1951)
Korona (1957)

Circus (1961)
Goldilocks (1954)
Masquerade (1958)

Roses in Gardens. Ideally, roses should have a garden devoted exclusively to them, with bush roses grown in beds, climbers and ramblers on pillars, pergolas and archways, or walls, and shelter given by a boundary rose hedge. In most gardens today, some compromise has to be made on account of limited space. Consequently there is a strong tendency to introduce roses into other garden features and associate them with other plants. For practical convenience in culture, however, it is wise to bed or group the bush hybrid tea and floribunda roses together. Varieties can be interplanted for colourful harlequin effect, but individual varieties differ in growth habit and stature and their association needs blending and care. It is more effective to group like varieties together; and beds of one variety are most effective of all.

Some of the shorter growing Floribunda roses, such as 'Allgold', 'Anna Wheatcroft', 'Dickson's Flame', 'Dusky Maiden', 'Fashion', 'Ivory Fashion', 'Jan Spek', 'Lili Marlene', 'Meteor', 'Orange Sensation', 'Paddy McGredy', 'Pernille Poulsen', 'Travesti', 'Yellowhammer' and 'Zambra'; the Floribunda Dwarfs and Polyantha Pompons may be introduced into mixed borders; while Miniature Roses are delightful used judiciously in rock gardens.

Standard Roses. These are rose varieties budded and growing at the head of clean stems; half-standards at $3-3\frac{1}{2}$ ft, full standards at $4-4\frac{1}{2}$ ft, and tall standards at 6 ft or more. Suitable varieties are indicated in the lists given. Weeping standards are formed with the Climbers similarly indicated. Standard roses are useful to flank paths, to serve as specimen plants in rose-beds or features or in tubs.

Rose Hedges. For hedges of 4–6 ft some of the strong-growing Floribundas are excellent, planted $2\frac{1}{2}-3$ ft apart, such as 'Chicago Peace', 'Chinatown', 'Dorothy Wheatcroft', 'Frensham', 'Heidelberg', 'Iceberg', 'Scented Air', 'Charlotte Elizabeth', 'Queen Elizabeth', 'Red Dandy'; and for taller hedges Penzance Briers, particularly 'Zephirine Drouhin', are useful. They may be planted in single rows as divisional hedges within the garden, or in double staggered rows, 3 ft apart, to provide a thick, strong boundary hedge.

Roses for Pillars. Climbers of moderate vigour and recurrent flowering are best for pillars, and can be chosen from the list of large-flowered and Kordesii Climbers given, the Climbing Floribundas, and ramblers such as 'Chaplin's Pink', 'The New Dawn'.

Roses for Arches and Pergolas. The Wichuraiana Ramblers are best for training up and over arches and pergolas, although they are only summer flowering. The vigorous varieties of Climbing Hybrid Teas are also used, though apt to become less attractive in age.

Roses for Walls. For the less clement north, north-east and east walls, suitable Climbers are 'Allen Chandler', 'Danse du Feu', 'Gloire de Dijon', 'Guinée', 'Mme Alfred Carrière', 'Mme G. Staechelin', 'Maigold' and 'Paul's Lemon Pillar'. On south and west walls all the above are suitable, together with 'Elegance', 'Meg', 'Mermaid', 'Royal Gold', the Kordesii Climbers, and the Climbing Hybrid Teas, and Floribundas. With possible exceptions in 'Alberic Barbier', 'Albertine' and 'The New Dawn', the Wichuriana Ramblers are less suitable for training on walls.

Soils and their Preparation. The ideal soil is a well-drained, medium to heavy loam, humus-rich, and of pH $6 \cdot 0 - 6 \cdot 5$. Clay is not desirable in excess, but a brick earth grows good roses. Roses, however, can be grown on most soils, suitably amended, and given good subsoil drainage. Clay soils need improving by cultivation, the incorporation of gypsum, organic matter and liming, if acid. Light sandy or gravelly soils need claying, and organic matter with organic fertilizers, with chalk to correct undue acidity. Calcareous soils require generous manuring, acid-reacting fertilizers and peat. Sandy peat soils benefit greatly from the addition of marl. In cultivation it is essential to break up the subsoil well, especially where a hard layer or pan has formed, and the soil should be prepared at least a month ahead of planting.

Site. Roses need sun and air and should be sited in the open, avoiding draughty places near or under trees, low-lying frost pockets and places subject to waterlogging. With good air circulation trouble from diseases and pests is less, but shelter from drying cold east winds is desirable.

Planting. Roses may be planted from late October to March, when the weather is mild and the soil easily worked. Where winter conditions are hard, or the soil likely to be wet and sticky, March planting is best. The planting station should be taken out about 15 in. deep, and large enough to accommodate the spread-out roots without cramping. In the case of bush and base-budded plants, the point of union must be placed about an inch below the soil surface. Spacing depends upon vigour, and may be from 1½–2½ ft apart, and staggered where more than one row is planted. Standards are set at the same level as grown in the nurseries, and staked when planted. Climbing roses should be placed 8–12 in. forward of fences or walls, and 8–10 ft, apart, according to vigour. Before planting, coarse roots may be trimmed cleanly, but fibrous roots left untouched.

Pruning. All bush types, Hybrid Tea, Floribunda, Polyantha Pompon and Miniature Roses, are pruned hard, to a robust bud near the base, facing the direction in which new growth is desired, in March–April, after planting. Thereafter, pruning is guided by the vigour of the plant and the flowering result desired. Annual pruning may be done in November–December, or March–April. Winter pruning tends to be successful in lightish porous soils and mild localities, but in cold districts, damp soils and areas subject to late frosts, early spring pruning is usually preferred. Basic rules in pruning are: (1) remove all dead and weakly shoots at their base, (2) cut back hard when strong shoots bearing large exhibition blooms are desired; (3) cut lightly when more blooms are wanted, as for garden decoration; (4) cut back moderately to give a balance of roses for cutting and bloom for the garden; (5) prune strong, vigorous shoots rather less severely than thinner shoots. Pruning must always be balanced by proper feeding for shoot renewal.

Hybrid Tea Pruning. After removing the dead, weak, unripe shoots, prune out twiggy ingrowing shoots; and then prune the previous year's shoots according to the rules given above, to give a balanced plant.

Floribunda Roses. Although usually pruned less severely than hybrid teas, floribunda roses should have weak thin shoots cut out, and the previous year's shoots cut back to robust buds; while it is often helpful to cut back some of the two-year-old shoots hard. Tall growers, used as specimens or hedges, should have spent flowered shoots removed, and a proportion of older shoots cut hard back to a suitable lateral or bud.

Polyantha Pompons. Flowered shoots may be pruned fairly hard, but where thin shoots are characteristic they only need shortening; a few older shoots can be cut hard back.

Miniature Roses. These are pruned on similar lines to floribunda roses, having due regard to their smaller size, without cutting into older wood too much.

Standard Roses. After planting, in early spring, the shoots at the crown may be reduced by one-third to one-half their length. Subsequently the ripe shoots of the previous year are cut back according to their vigour, but never so severely as with bush roses, and never to their base, unless dead.

Wichuraiana Ramblers. After planting, all climbers and ramblers of Wichuraiana-multiflora breeding should have their shoots cut back to strong buds, 1 ft from ground level, in early spring; and thereafter be pruned according to habit. Strong growers ('Dorothy Perkins', 'Excelsa', 'François Juranville', 'Minnehaha', 'Sander's White'), which bloom on shoots of the previous year thrown up from or near the base, are pruned after flowering in September, when the old flowered shoots are cut out, and the new trained in.

Other hybrid Wichuraiana Climbers such as 'Albertine', 'American Pillar', 'Dr Van Fleet', 'The New Dawn', need less drastic pruning in early autumn; cutting one or more of the three-year-old shoots severely, but only shortening others lightly.

Kordesii Climbers. Shoots of newly planted stock are reduced by one-half after planting to induce branching from near the base; but subsequently little severe pruning is needed, beyond the removal of dead or moribund growth, and one or more older stems each autumn.

Large-flowered Climbers. These require pruning after being planted, reducing their shoots by about one-half to induce branching; but thereafter little severe pruning, beyond shortening of lateral shoots by one-third to one-half, and as the plants get older, rejuvenation by the severe cutting back of one or two older shoots, in autumn.

Feeding. To produce abundant blooms of quality and renew its shoots freely, a rose plant needs fairly generous feeding.

This may consist of a basic rose fertilizer immediately after pruning (proprietary or a mixture of 12 parts by weight super-phosphate, 1 part nitroform, 9 parts nitrate of potash, 2 parts sulphate of magnesium, 1 part sulphate of iron at 3 oz. per sq. yd); topped by a mulch of rotted manure, compost or moist peat. This may be supplemented by a lighter application of fertilizer in late June, or foliar feeding in summer; and a late autumn application of bone meal.

Weeding. Roses are essentially surface-soil feeders, and cannot do well where weeds are allowed to thrive. A residual simazine herbicide is available to keep beds clear of weeds in summer, though weed smothering by mulching is a better practice. Alternatively, carpeting plants such as Violas, Double Daisies, Alyssum or Aubrietas.

Roses in the Greenhouse. Most hybrid tea, floribunda, and miniature roses can be successfully grown in pots, in a cold or cool greenhouse. Plants are best potted in 8–10 in. pots, in autumn, using a compost of 4 parts by bulk medium heavy loam, 2 parts moist peat, 1 part coarse sand, plus $1\frac{1}{2}$ oz. ground lime-stone and $\frac{1}{2}$ lb. compound rose fertilizer per bushel, or of a standard compost such as JIP 3, and placed out of doors plunged in ashes of fibre to the rim, in a sheltered part of the garden, covered with litter. They are watered in Decem-ber, moved into the greenhouse, and pruned hard, each shoot to within two to four buds of its base, watered suffi-ciently to keep the soil nicely moist, night temp. minimum of $7°$ C. $(45°$ F.); by March, plants will be growing well; and should be given judicious ventilation and a liquid feeding every 7–10 days from the appearance of buds to open flowering. If desired, they can be forced by gradually raising the temp. by $3°$ C. $(5°$ F.) each month for April flowering; though without heat, they will flower in May. Flower stems may be disbudded to give a single bloom per stem. After flowering, the plants are placed out of doors again, replacing the top two inches of the pot soil with new compost; and they may be rehoused under glass the following December–January to flower again. Half-standard on *R. rugosa* stocks can also be grown in this way.

Propagation. By Budding. Most garden varieties and types of Roses are pro-pagated by budding, as the quickest and most rapid way of increase. Budding consists of inserting a bud of the chosen variety, or scion, within the bark of a growing rose, or stock. The stocks chiefly used are *Rosa canina, rugosa, laxa* or *multiflora*, or chosen strains of them. The seedling stocks are planted in November–February 1 ft apart, in rows $2\frac{1}{2}$ ft apart, and budded in June–August in weather which is neither too wet nor too dry, when the outer bark lifts readily from the wood of the stem. For bush roses, the stocks are budded low down on the stem; for standards high on the stem.

The buds should be firm and plump, and are taken from a shoot that has just flowered, cut the previous day, with leaves cut off, prickles rubbed off and kept, labelled, in a bucket of water over-night. A bud is then cut out with a razor-sharp budding knife, with a shield of bark, $\frac{1}{2}$ in. above, to an inch below the bud. The thin strip of wood is then carefully removed from behind the bud, leaving bud and bark intact, to be kept moist by placing on moist blotting paper or cloth, while the stock is prepared. This is done by making a T-shaped cut in the bark of the stock, to the wood, and then lifting the bark at each side with the wedge-shaped end of a budding knife sufficiently for the scion to be slipped inside so that the greenish cambiums of scion and stock are in intimate contact. The bud is then firmed in with grafting tape, trimming the bark to leave the bud just exposed to light. In about six to eight weeks the bud will show growth if it has taken. In March the budded stocks are shortened to within half an inch of the point of union.

The budding of standard roses is similar, except that two buds are im-planted at either side of the main stem of the *rugosa* stock, at the height desired. If *R. canina* stocks are used, the buds are inserted on lateral shoots formed at the top of the main stem, as close to the stem itself as possible.

By Cuttings. Cuttings consist of well-ripened, firm, healthy shoots of the cur-rent year's growth, 8–10 in. long, cut off below a bud, or taken with a heel of older wood, in late July–November. Stripped of their lower leaves, these shoots are inserted 6 in. apart, 6 in. deep, in a trench with 2 in. of coarse sand at the bottom, and well-firmed. By the following autumn they can be lifted and planted out to flower at two or three years. Species and their varieties, and strong-growing hybrids respond best, but hybrid teas of complex breeding, particularly bicolours and yellow-flowering, are not so satisfactory as when propagated by budding.

By Layers. Climbers, Ramblers and roses producing young shoots easily bent to the soil can be propagated by layering in June–September. The shoots should be young and flexible; an upward slanting cut is made about 15 in. from the free end on the underside, not more than half way through the shoot; the free end is bent carefully upwards, the cut part pegged to the soil and mounded over with a good soil compost in which to root. The rooted layer can be severed the following spring, as a rule, for planting out.

By Seeds. It may take two to three years to get a flowering plant. Ripe hips are gathered in autumn, and dried so the seeds may be rubbed out for sowing. The seeds may be sown, February–March, in outdoor seed-beds or cold frames, after storing in sand during the winter, intact in the hips. They may take a year to germinate. The method is best for raising seedlings of *R. canina*, *R. rugosa*, etc., for rootstocks. Although hips from garden roses may be saved, the seedlings raised are unlikely to be true to the variety from which the hips were taken, unless fertilization has been controlled.

Diseases. The most common and worst diseases are:

Black Spot (Diplocarpon rosae). A fungus infection which causes small brownish-black spots on leaf top surfaces, which enlarge, often becoming yellow-edged, and cause leaves to fall. The fungus over-winters on stems or fallen leaves, and is difficult to cure; though less prevalent in built-up and industrial areas, where sulphur compounds in the air tend to inhibit it. Control lies in removing and burning fallen leaves in autumn–winter; spraying with copper sulphate solution ($\frac{1}{2}$ oz.

per gallon water, plus wetting agent) to bare stems while dormant; and repeat spraying with a captan or phaltan fungicide in April and afterwards, especially in wet seasons, at 14-day intervals, where disease is serious. Some varieties are more susceptible than others as marked in the lists given.

Mildew (Sphaerotheca pannosa v. *rosae).* Powdery mildew starts with whitish-grey spots on young leaves and shoots, spreading to cover surfaces with its powdery layer, distorting leaves, dwarfing shoots and killing young buds. It is apt to be prevalent where air circulation is poor, in draughty or damp conditions, against walls and hedges; in fluctuating temperatures and high humidity; more in spring and late summer than in high summer. Control calls for cutting out and burning of severely infected growth, and then spraying or dusting with a karathane, thiram or sulphur fungicide; repeated if necessary, especially with susceptible varieties indicated in the lists.

Rust (Phragmidium mucronatum). The symptoms are yellow-orange spots on the undersides of leaves in early summer and darker ones in autumn. Infected leaves are best collected and burnt, and the plant sprayed with a liquid copper or thiram fungicide.

Anthracnose (Sphaceloma rosarum). A fungus disease that causes dark brown to blackish-brown spots, with a purplish rim and greyish centre; more worrying than serious. Leaves are chiefly affected, and it is usually sufficient to remove badly infected and fallen leaves, and see that the plants are well watered. A copper fungicide can be applied.

Stem Canker (Leptosphaeria coniothyrium). This disease shows in blackish-brown, sunken and cracked areas of bark on stems, which, unchecked, may encircle the stems and kill the growth above. It is best to cut the stems back to healthy wood, and paint cuts with a fungicidal paint.

Pests. Unfortunately, the highly bred rose may play host to a number of parasitic pests, though their numbers can be kept down by early action.

Aphids or Greenfly (Macrosiphum rosae, etc.). Several species of these sap-sucking insects may feed on the foliage, shoots and buds, stunting and distorting growth. Spray or dust with a malathion, pyrethrum/gamma-BHC, nicotine or derris insecticide in growing season. A systemic insecticide may be used to give protection for 3–4 weeks. Spray with a tar-oil wash in winter to destroy over-wintering aphid eggs on stems.

Thrips (*Thrips fuscipennis*). Tiny, longish, yellowish to brown insects which feed on foliage, causing silvery mottling, and on petals to streak them brown. May be controlled by the same insecticides as for aphids in summer.

Capsid Bug (*Lygus pabulinus*). Green, shield-like insects causing the leaves to be brown-spotted and later holed, May–September; best controlled by a pyrethrum/DDT insecticidal application immediately they are seen.

Caterpillars of various moths—Tortrix (*Archips oporana, Pandemis heparana, Hedya nubiferana*), Buff-tip (*Phalera bucephala*), Lackey (*Malacosoma neustria* and Vapourer (*Orgyia antiqua*)—attack rose leaves from time to time; rolling them, eating or skeletonizing them and defoliating the plants. Hand-picking suffices if attacks are spotted early enough; otherwise a DDT application or nicotine insecticide is needed.

Sawfly Caterpillars. There are several species of sawflies which attack roses. The commonest is the Leaf-rolling saw-fly (*Blennocampa pusilla*), attacking June–August. Rolled leaflets are best hand-picked, and DDT or nicotine applied. The Slug sawfly, *Endelomyia aethiops*, skeletonizes leaves and needs DDT, gamma-BHC or nicotine applications to control it. Antler sawfly (*Cladius* spp.). Banded Rose sawfly (*Allantus cinctus*), and the Large sawfly (*Arge ochropus*), have yellowish-green or grey-ish-green caterpillars which eat and chew holes in leaves, but can be controlled by the insecticides already given for Slug sawfly.

Red Spider Mites (*Tetranychus telarius*). These spider-like mites attack under dry conditions, causing mottling and yellow drying up of leaves. Malathion or derris insecticides give good control; a systemic insecticide protects for up to four weeks.

Leafhopper (*Typhlocyba rosae*). Pale yellow, active jumping insects feed on undersides of leaves, causing a yellow spotting to appear, and disfiguring by honeydew and sooty moulds, from May onwards, but DDT or gamma-BHC insecticides give good control.

Frog-hopper or Cuckoo Spit Insects (*Philaenus leucophthalmus*). The yellowish-green nymphs in the froth-like spittle are sap-sucking and weakening, but controlled by a forceful application of nicotine or gamma-BHC.

It is doubtful that the Leaf Cutter Bees (*Megachile contuncularis*, etc.), responsible for circular scallops cut out of the leaves; or the Gall Wasp (*Rhodites rosae*), causing the moss-like galls known as Bedeguars or Robin's Pin-cushions, do crippling damage.

Chlorosis. A nutritional deficiency, shown in pale yellowing leaves, on calcareous soils, traceable to the inavail-ability of iron, and corrected by feeding with a chelated iron compound.

Roseus (-a, -um). Rose-coloured. Ex. *Primula rosea*.

Rosmarinus, Rosemary (ros-ma-ri'nus. Fam. Labiatae). The chief species grown is *R. officinalis*, S. Europe, Asia Minor, an evergreen shrub of 3–6 ft, with linear leaves and axillary pale violet flowers, May, of fragrant aroma; and its vs. 'Miss Jessop's Upright', 'Beneden Blue'; *pyramidalis, roseus* and 'Tuscan Blue'; reasonably hardy in sun, and on well-drained soils; and propagated by cuttings of young shoots, in July–August, in the cold frame.

Rostellum. A little beak; of the stigma of some orchids.

Rotation of Crops. *See* Vegetables.

Rotundus (-a, -um). Rotundi-. Round. Ex. *Drosera rotundifolia*.

Rowan. See *Sorbus aucuparia*.

Royal Bay. See *Laurus nobilis*.

Royal Fern. See *Osmunda regalis*.

Rubber Plant. See *Ficus elastica*.

Ruber (Rubra, Rubrum). Red. Ex. *Centranthus ruber*.

Rubiginosus (-a, -um). Brownish red, rusty, Ex. *Rosa rubiginosa*.

Rubus, Bramble, Raspberry (ru'bus. Fam. Rosaceae). A large genus of shrub-by, sub-shrubby and herbaceous plants to which the Blackberry and Raspberry (q.v.) belong. A few are useful ornamen-tally, especially for poor soils and difficult conditions.

Selection. R. amabilis, China, 4 ft, dark purple stems, pinnate laves, large white solitary flowers, June, edible red fruits in autumn; *biflorus,* Himalaya, to 8 ft, the Whitewashed Bramble, with stems coated with a waxy white surface, white July flowers, yellow fruits; *cockburnianus,* China, 8 ft, the best Whitewashed Bramble, panicles of small purple flowers, June; *deliciosus,* Rocky Mts, 6 ft, rose-like, solitary white flowers, May–June; *odoratus,* N. America 6 ft, handsome, with panicles of fragrant purple flowers, July–September; *parviflorus,* the Salmon Berry, western N. America, 6 ft, clusters of pure white flowers, June–July; *phoenicolasius,* China, Japan, to 10 ft, red bristled stem, racemes of pink flowers, July; *spectabilis,* western N. America, to 6 ft, scented, purple-red flowers, July; *thibetanus,* China, 6 ft, handsome finely cut foliage, small purple flowers, June; and *ulmifolius* v. *bellidiflorus,* Europe, 2 ft, spreading double rosy-red flowers, July–August, are all good for informal use, under trees, and in woodland. *R. arcticus,* northern hemisphere, 6 in., rose flowers, June; *chamaemorus,* the Cloudberry, N. Europe, Britain, to 10 in., white solitary flowers, June, edible orange fruits, are herbaceous, for the wild rock garden or woodland borders.

Cultivation. Plant November–March, reasonably well-drained soil, poor conditions well tolerated, sun or shade.

Propagation. By seeds, spring; by division in March; or by layering in spring.

Rudbeckia, Cone Flower (rud-bek'i-a. Fam. Compositae). Hardy herbaceous perennials with ray petalled flowers and a central cone-like disk of florets, from N. America.

Selection. R. deamii, 2 ft, deep yellow flowers, summer; *fulgida,* 3 ft, orangeyellow, and v. 'Goldsturm', orange with black centre; *laciniata,* 4 ft, yellow, and vs. 'Goldquelle', double chrome yellow, and 'Gold Glow', double yellow; *nitida* v. 'Herbstonne', primrose-yellow; *speciosa,* 3 ft, orange, deep purple centre; and *tetra gloriosa* vs., 3 ft, yellow, orange, orange-red, are perennial. *R. bicolor superba* 'Golden Flame', 'Kelvedon Star' and 'My Joy', 2–3 ft, goldenyellow flowering; *hirta,* Black-eyed

Susan, 1½ ft, golden-yellow, and 'Autumn Forest' vs., are grown as halfhardy annuals.

Propagation. Plant perennials in welldrained, humus-rich soil, and sun, November or early April. Sow tender kinds under glass in March, to plant out in June. Divide perennials in March.

Rue. See *Ruta.*

Ruellia (ru-el'li-a. Fam. Acanthaceae). The species chiefly grown are pretty, evergreen, flowering shrubs for the warm greenhouse or indoors.

Selection. R. macrantha, Brazil, 3 ft, long lanceolate leaves, trumpet-shaped flowers rose-purple, darker veined, in winter, sometimes called Christmas Pride; *macrophylla,* Colombia, 3 ft, bright scarlet flowers, summer; and *formosa,* Brazil, 2 ft, scarlet flowers, summer, are grown.

Cultivation. Pot, and repot, in March, standard compost, grow in light shade, water freely to October, more moderately in winter, minimum temp. 13° C. (55° F.). Syringe in hot sunny weather.

Propagation. By cuttings of young shoots, early summer, in propagating case, bottom heat 21° C. (70° F.).

Rugosus (-a, -um). Wrinkled. Ex. *Rosa rugosa.*

Runcinatus (-a, -um). Runcinate. Pinnately lobed with the lobes turned backward, in a leaf.

Runner. A procumbent shoot rooting at the end to form a new plant. Ex. the Strawberry.

Rupestris (-e). Growing on rocks. Ex. *Abelia rupestris.*

Ruscus (rus'kus. Fam. Liliaceae). Low-growing evergreen shrubs with leaflike branches (cladodes), with small, scale-like bracts from the middle, in the axils of which dioecious flowers are produced; the female giving way to bright red berries; native to the Mediterranean region.

Selection. R. aculeatus, Butcher's Broom, native and Mediterranean, 2–3 ft, small greenish flowers in April; *hypoglossum,* 1–1½ ft, yellow flowers, April–May; and *hypophyllum,* 1 ft, white flowers, April, not quite so hardy.

Cultivation. Plant October–November or March–April, almost any garden soil, sun or shade, useful under trees; one male plant to three female to ensure berrying. Propagate by division in spring, or by seed.

Rush, Flowering. See *Butomus*.

Russian Comfrey. See *Symphytum*.

Russian Vine. See *Polygonum baldschuanicum*.

Rustic Work. Ornamental garden furniture, such as open fences, trellis, arches, pergolas, bridges, seats and tables, constructed of natural branch wood. Larch poles, spruce and coniferous forest thinnings are used for straight or angular work; oak for quainter shapes. The branches may have the bark left on, but it is more usual to strip the bark. The wood should be thoroughly treated with a preservative, either a refined tar distillate product or an organic solvent, not creosote, to give long life.

Ruta, Rue (ru'ta. Fam. Rutaceae). The chief species grown is *R. graveolens*, Rue, Herb of Grace, S. Europe, an evergreen shrub to about 3 ft, with glaucous pinnately compound foliage, and dullish yellow flowers in summer; with foliage strikingly blue-green in ' Jackman's variety'.

Cultivation. Plant October or March–April; any well-drained soil, out of frosty areas; chiefly for its foliage beauty. May be pruned in March.

Propagation. By cuttings of young shoots taken with a heel, July–August, under handlight.

Rutilans, Rutilus (-a, -um). Glowing orange-red. Ex. *Thyrsacanthus rutilans.*

S

Sabal (sa'bal. Fam. Palmaceae). Palms with fan-like leaves of subtropical America.

Selection. S. blackburnia, the Thatch Palm of W. Indies, to 30 ft; *minor*, Dwarf Palmetto of S. U.S.A., to 3 ft; and *palmetto*, the Cabbage Palm, S. U.S.A., to 30 ft, may be grown in the cool greenhouse as pot or tub plants.

Cultivation. Pot in March–April, standard compost, water freely to September, very moderately in winter months, minimum temp. 7° C. (45° F.). May be placed out of doors in summer months.

Propagation. By imported seeds, spring, with bottom heat of 21° C. (70° F.). By suckers, when formed.

Sacred Lotus. See *Nelumbo nucifera.*

Saddle-tree. See *Liriodendron tulipifera.*

Saffron. See *Crocus sativus.*

Saffron, Meadow. See *Colchicum.*

Sage (*Salvia officinalis*). The culinary Sage, S. Europe, 1–1½ ft, is normally hardy, and a most useful herb. Plant in almost any free-draining soil, warm position, in March–April, 18 in. apart.

Propagation. By cuttings of young shoots, July, which root readily under cloches in shade. May also be raised from seeds sown in April. Rooted shoots from round the base may also be detached for planting out in spring. Gather leafy shoot tips for drying at 38° C. (102° F.), for herb store.

Sage, Jerusalem. See *Phlomis fruticosa.*

Sagina, Pearlwort (sa-gi'na. Fam. Caryophyllaceae). Tufted, mat-forming dwarf herbs, with small white flowers, sometimes used for carpeting or for lawns as alternative to grass; but apt to be invasive weeds.

Selection. S. procumbens, native and northern hemisphere, and *nodosa*, native, are perennial weeds, controlled by mecroprop herbicides; *boydii*, Scotland, *pilifera*, Corsica, and v. *aurea*, yellow-leaved,

are sometimes used for carpeting in rock gardens, planted in March, and tending to be self-propagating.

Sagittaria, Arrow-head (sa-git-ta'ri-a. Fam. Alismataceae). Perennial herbs with handsome large leaves and spikes of whorled flowers, for waterside planting, or margins of pools.

Selection. S. sagittifolia (japonica), native and European, narrow arrowhead leaves, snow-white flowers on 18-in. stems, late summer, and v. *flore pleno*, are hardy; *latifolia*, Duck Potato, N. America, 3 ft, only nominally so. *S. graminea*, N. America, 1½ ft, grass-like foliage, white; *macrophylla*, Mexico, large bronze to yellow leaves, white flowers; and *montevidensis*, S. America, to 4 ft, large, arrow-like leaves, white, purple-blotched flowers, need the shelter of a cool greenhouse.

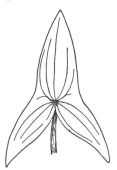

FIG. 201 Sagittate leaf (*Sagittaria* sp.).

Cultivation. Plant hardy species April–May, in shallow water or bog garden, propagating by spring division. Plant greenhouse kinds in shallow water or tubs with very moist soil; may go outdoors for summer.

Sagittatus (-a, -um). Sagittate, arrow-shaped. Ex. *Sagitaria sagittifolia.*

477

St Bernard's Lily 478 Salpiglossis

St Bernard's Lily. See *Anthericum liliago.*

St Bruno's Lily. See *Paradisea liliastrum.*

St Dabeoc's Heath. See *Daboecia cantabrica.*

St John's Wort. See *Hypericum.*

St Joseph's Lily. See *Lilium candidum.*

St Patrick's Cabbage. See *Saxifraga umbrosa.*

Saintpaulia (saint-pawl'i-a. Fam. Gesneriaceae). The chief species grown is *S. ionantha*, the African or Usambara Violet of E. tropical Africa, a tender perennial with fine hairy ovate leaves, cymes of violet-blue flowers to 4 in. high, borne almost continuously, particularly summer–early spring, and now available in many varieties, blue, purple, pink and white, single and double flowers; to be grown as a pot plant in the warm greenhouse or cool heated rooms indoors. Plants do best in small pots, and may be potted or repotted in early spring, standard compost, and given ample sun and light without scorching, and humidity and warmth. Plants are stood on saucers of pebbles, kept watered, and plants watered to keep the soil nicely moist without wetting foliage or crowns, temperatures tolerated are 10–27° C. (50–80° F.), but a drop below 15·5° C. (60° F.) checks flowering. Propagation is by stalked leaves, inserting stalks in moist sand, compost or vermiculite, or water, temp. 21° C. (70° F.), preferably in propagating frame. By seeds, sown April, bottom heat 24° C. (75° F.).

Salad. A combination of vegetables, usually raw, sometimes cooked, with fresh herbs, seasoned and dressed with oil or mayonnaise, and combined with a proteinous savoury or dish to make a balanced course. Most vegetables lend themselves to salad-making, but the essence of their crisp tenderness must be fostered by good even growth. *See* under Beet, Carrot, Celeriac, Celery, Chervil, Chicory, Chives, Corn Salad, Cress, Cucumber, Dandelion, Endive, Lettuce, Mustard, Onion, Radish, Salsify, Shallot, Tarragon, Tomato, Watercress, etc.

Salicifolius (-a, -um). Willow-like leafed. Ex. *Pyrus salicifolia.*

Salix, Willow (sa'liks. Fam. Salicaceae). Hardy deciduous shrubs and trees of the northern hemisphere; usually unisexual with flowers in catkins.

Selection. S. alba, White Willow, native, Europe, to 70 ft, pyramidal, and v. *argentea,* silver-leafed; v. *tristis* (*babylonica, chrysocoma, vitellina pendula*) is the Weeping Willow, to 50 ft; *bockii,* China, shrub of to 10 ft, small-leaved, late September flowering; *caprea,* the native Goat Willow, 10–25 ft, large catkins, the 'Palm' of Easter; v. *pendula,* the Kilmarnock Willow; × *coerulea,* the Cricket Bat Willow, to 70 ft; *daphnoides,* Violet Willow, Europe, to 30 ft; *gracilistyla,* Japan, Korea, shrubby to 6 ft, finely coloured early April flowers; *lanata,* N. Europe and Asia, 2 ft, silvery-haired leaves; *magnifica,* China, to 20 ft, large magnolia-like leaves, long catkins; *matsudana,* China, Korea, to 50 ft; *pentandra,* Europe, Asia, the Bay-leaved Willow, to 40 ft, golden catkins in May, bright foliage; *purpurea,* the Purple Osier, native and Europe, Asia, to 10 ft, the Dicks or Kecks of basket-makers, v. *pendula* makes a small weeping tree; *reticulata,* Scotland, Europe, dwarf, roundish leaves; and its hybrid × *boydii,* to 3 ft, grey-white downy foliage; and *retusa,* Europe, prostrate, tiny downy leaves, for rock gardens.

Cultivation. Plant October–March, any moisture-retentive soil, especially in wet situations.

Propagation. By firm cuttings of shoots taken in November, inserted firmly in soil, and kept moist. Dwarf kinds in pots, in cold frame.

Sallow. An alternative name for the Goat Willow, *Salix caprea* (q.v.).

Salpiglossis (sal-pi-glos'sis. Fam. Solanaceae). The lovely flowering plants grown under this name are largely selected half-hardy annuals, forms of *S. sinuata,* a native of Chile; making graceful plants with large tubular flowers, orchid-like in texture and veining, and usually offered in various colours, large-flowered, and Gloxinia-flora strains, and a F_1 hybrid 'Splash', $1\frac{1}{2}$ ft, more compact, and vividly coloured in shades of red, pinks, purples, orange and yellow, summer.

Cultivation. Sow seeds under glass, March, standard compost, bottom heat of 18° C. (65° F.), to prick off, and harden off for planting out in May. May also be grown as a pot plant in the greenhouse.

Salsify, Vegetable Oyster (*Tragopogon porrifolius*). A hardy biennial of N. Europe, grown for its long, white fleshy roots as a winter root vegetable to which is ascribed a taste similar to that of oysters when cooked. It grows with long linear grass-like leaves.

Cultivation. Sow seeds in late March or April, in well-worked, deep, readily drained soil, humus-manured from a previous crop; ½ in. deep, in rows 1 ft apart, thinning seedlings to 8 in. apart. Fertilize as for parsnips. Alternatively, sow by the crowbar method as for parsnips (q.v.). Roots may be lifted from late October onwards, with care. Protect with litter from frost if roots are left for later lifting in winter; or lift and store in moist sand. Roots left in the ground are likely to send up flowering shoots to 3 ft, next year with bracted, rose-purple flower-heads; but if the shoots are blanched by covering with pots or tubs and litter, they can be cut as 'Chards' and cooked in the same way as Asparagus as a spring vegetable.

Salt. Sodium chloride (NaCl). Common salt has some indirect fertilizer value on light soils and for certain crops such as beet, but only in small amounts. On heavy or clay soils it tends to make the soil more sticky owing to its deliquescent nature. It is held to release potash as a nutrient from soils. Asparagus and Seakale probably benefit from spring dressings on light porous soils. In excess, salt is harmful, as when sea floods land. It occurs as an impurity in some fertilizers such as nitrate of potash, nitrate of soda and muriate of potash, but not to a harmful degree. In strong doses, of about 1 lb. per 10 sq. yds, it is sometimes used as a superficial weed-killer on paths, chiefly of weed seedlings, weed top-growth and moss.

Saltpetre. See Potassium Nitrate, under Fertilizers.

Salvia (sal'vi-a. Fam. Labiatae). A very large genus of annual, biennial, perennials herbs and shrubs; all various in habit, but characteristically with opposite leaves and showy flowers in whorls, forming racemes, panicles or spikes.

Selection. S. guaranitica, S. America, 4 ft, blue to rose flowers, September; *azurea grandiflora,* Mexico, 3 ft, deep blue, August; *coccinea,* central and S. America, and vs., 2 ft, red, summer; *farinacea,* Texas, 3 ft, violet-blue, and vs. *alba* and 'Blue Bedder'; *patens,* Mexico, 2½ ft, blue, September, and vs. *alba,* white; 'Cambridge Blue' and 'Lavender Lady'; *splendens,* Brazil, to 1¼ ft, scarlet, summer, and vs. such as 'Blaze of Fire', dwarf bright scarlet; 'Gypsy Rose', 1 ft, dusky-rose; 'Purple Blaze', 1 ft, reddish-purple; 'Salmon Pygmy', 6 in.; and 'Violet Crown', 1 ft, violet-purple, are naturally perennial but are grown as half-hardy annuals, from seeds sown under glass, March, with bottom heat of 18° C. (65° F.), to be pricked off, hardened and planted out in May. *S. horminum,* S. Europe, a Clary, 2 ft, and vs. 'Bluebeard', deep blue bracted flowers; 'Oxford Blue', 'Pink Sundae'; and 'Art Shades' are grown as hardy annuals for their late summer colour, sown where they are to flower in March. *S. aethiopis,* Mediterranean region, 6 in., white-woolly foliage, white, tinged red, flowers, summer; *argentea,* Mediterranean region, to 3 ft, silvery foliage, pinkish-white flowers, summer; *glutinosa,* Europe, 3 ft, yellow flowers; *jurisicii,* Serbia, 1 ft, violet-blue, July; *nutans,* E. Europe, 3 ft, violet, July; *pratensis,* Europe, 2 ft, bright blue, and vs. *alba,* white; *rosea,* rose pink; and *tenorii,* deep blue; × *superba,* 3 ft, bluey purple, summer; *uliginosa,* E. S. America, to 6 ft, blue, summer; and *verticillata,* Europe, Asia Minor, 3 ft, lilac-blue, July–August, and v. *alba,* white, are herbaceous perennials, hardy except in the coldest areas of Britain. *S. haematodes,* Greece, 3 ft, blue-purple flowers, and *sclarea,* Clary, Europe, to 3 ft, bluish white; and v. *turkestanica,* white, tinged pink, are usually biennial and effective. Of the shrubby perennials, *S. grahamii,* Mexico, 3 ft, apple green foliage, crimson flowers, summer, may be tried as a sunny wall plant in mild localities; and the forms of the culinary Sage, such as *S. officinalis* v. *albiflora,* 2–3 ft, white flowering; *aureo variegata,* leaves flushed gold; *hispanica,* narrow leaves, bright blue flowers, June; and *purpurea,* with leaves suffused purple, are good border plants, hardy except in the colder localities. The sub-shrubby perennials, *S. azurea* v. *grandiflora*, Mexico, to 4 ft, deep blue flowering, August; *fulgens*, Mexico, 2 ft, scarlet, July; closely resembled by *gesneraeflora*, Colombia, 2 ft, scarlet, more showy flowers; *involucrata* v. *bethellii*, Mexico, 3–6 ft, large cordate leaves, rosy-crimson flowers, August; and *rutilans*, S. America, 2–3 ft, pineapple-scented, cordate downy leaves, scarlet flowers, summer, may be grown in the cool greenhouse.

Cultivation. Out of doors, plant in well-drained, porous but humus-rich soil, pH 6·0–6·5, in May, whether seedlings or perennial stock. Under glass, pot in April–May, standard compost, water and syringe freely in growth, giving ample sun; water little in winter, minimum temp. 10° C. (50° F.).

Propagation. By seeds, sown in early spring, bottom heat of 18° C. (65° F.), to plant out in May. Perennials by cuttings of firm young shoots, July–August, in cold frame; tender kinds in greenhouse with gentle bottom heat of 15·5° C. (65° F.).

Samara. A winged indehiscent fruit or seed vessel. Ex. seeds of Maple, Sycamore (*Acer* spp.).

Sambucus, Elder (sam-bu′kus. Fam. Caprifoliaceae). Deciduous shrubs and small trees, some of which make good ornamental foliage specimens.

Selection. S. canadensis, Canada, U.S.A., 12–18 ft, is notable in vs. *aurea*, golden-leaved, red-fruiting; *laciniata*, graceful and finely cut foliage; and *maxima*, long-leaved, and very broad cymes of white flowers, July; the native *nigra* is best in v. *aurea*, golden-leaved; *laciniata*, deeply divided leaves; *pendula*, a weeping form; and *pyramidalis*, upright-growing; all growing 15–30 ft, with white June flowers, and black berry-fruits; *racemosa*, Europe to China, 8 ft, a shrub, flowers yellowish white, April, and v. *plumosa aurea*, yellow-leaved; while *ebulus*, Dane's Blood, Europe and Britain, is a stout perennial, to 4 ft, for cover in wild parts.

Cultivation. Plant November–March in any garden soils retentive of some moisture; sun or light shade. Prune, if necessary, in March.

Propagation. By cuttings of young shoots, July–August, or firm ripe shoots in autumn. Herbaceous perennials by division in March.

Sanctus (-a, -um). Sacred. Ex. *Saxifraga sancta.*

Sand. Small mineral particles of silica or quartz; fine sand 0·02–0·2 millimetres diameter (1/1200–1/120 in.); coarse 0·2–2·0 millimetres (1/120–1/12 in.). Valuable for lightening soils and compost for drainage and root penetration. Coarse sand is preferred for soil composts (i.e. John Innes); fine sand for soilless composts. For garden use, silver sand, Bedfordshire, river sand or sharp sand are descriptive of the material, but any sand should be clean and graded for its purpose. Brown sand, contaminated with iron oxide, seashore sand, contaminated with broken shell and limy, are not suitable for seed or potting composts. Clean moist sand is often a good rooting medium for cuttings, to be transferred to a richer medium later.

Sand Myrtle. See *Leiophyllum.*
Sand Verbena. See *Abronia.*
Sandwort. See *Arenaria.*
Sanguinaria, Bloodroot, Red Puccoon (san-gwen-ar′i-a. Fam. Papaveraceae). The only species, *S. canadensis*, E. N. America, 9 in., is a herbaceous perennial, with 3-in. white flowers in April, before its heart-shaped, lobed leaves, with vs. *grandiflora*, extra large flowers, and *plena*, double flowers.

Cultivation. Plant the thick rootstocks in August, well-drained soil, sun or shade.

Propagation. By seeds in spring; by division in August.

Sanguineus (-a, -um). Blood-red. Ex. *Ribes sanguineum.*

Sanguisorba (san-gwis-orb′a. Fam. Rosaceae). Hardy perennials, striking with large pinnate leaves, and flowers in cylindrical spikes, summer.

Selection. S. canadensis, E. N. America, 5 ft, whitish flowers; *obtusa*, Japan, 4 ft, rose-purple; *officinalis*, northern hemisphere, 2 ft, brownish-red; while *minor*, 2 ft, purple, is the native Burnet.

Cultivation. Plant November–March, any ordinary garden soil, sun or light shade.

Propagation. By seeds, sown April, or by division in March.

Sansevieria (san-sev-er'i-a. Fam. Haemodoraceae). Rhizomatous-rooted tropical perennials, chiefly grown for their attractive, finely marked, tough fleshy leaves, growing stiffly upright from the soil.

Selection. *S. cylindrica,* S. tropical Africa, to 3 ft, curved leaves, marked pale yellow, creamy white flowers; *trifasciata* v. *laurentii,* Snake Plant, Mother-in-law's Tongue, W. tropical Africa, to 3 ft, most popular for its sword-like leaves, banded green colours, marginally yellow; and *zeylandica,* Bowstring Hemp, E. Indies, 2 ft, falcate leaves, marked white.

Cultivation. Pot, and repot, in April, to grow indoors, light or shade, so tolerant of conditions as to be known as Cast-iron plants; water moderately in summer; very little in winter, minimum temp. 10° C. (50° F.). Propagation is best by division, April.

Santolina (san-to-li'na. Fam. Compositae). Small, quick-growing, evergreen aromatic shrubs of the Mediterranean region, hardy except in very cold localities.

Selection. *S. chamaecyparissus,* Lavender Cotton, 1½–2 ft, pinnatisect, silvery-grey, down leaves, yellow button flowers, July; and v. *nana,* 1 ft; *neapolitana,* S. Italy, 2 ft, white felted leaves, bright yellow, July; *pinnata,* Italy, 2 ft, green leaves, white flowers, July; and *virens,* S. Europe, to 2 ft, dark green foliage, yellow flowers, July.

Cultivation. Plant March–May, welldrained, lightish soil, sun. Useful for small hedging, ground cover, shelter plants and foliage contrast.

Propagation. Very easy by cuttings of firm shoots, inserted in soil, July–August. By seeds, April.

Sanvitalia (san-vi-ta'li-a. Fam. Compositae). The species chiefly grown, *S. procumbens,* 6 in., Mexico, with single, bright yellow rayed, flowers, summer, and its v. *flore pleno,* double flowers, may be sown, March–April, under glass, standard compost, bottom heat of 18° C. (65° F.); to be planted out in May, in well-drained soil and sun.

Sap. The fluid contained in living plants, in the cells or flowing up the xylem (wood vessels) and down the phloem (sieve tubes of the bast). The ascending solution is a very dilute one of water and nutrient salts absorbed by the roots from the soil; the descending fluid, after water has been lost in transpiration, is one of soluble food, sugars, proteins, etc., sometimes called 'elaborated sap'; which is distributed to growing points and actively dividing cells in the plant.

Sapling. A young tree.

Saponaceus (-a, -um), Saponarius (-a, -um). Saponaceous, soapy. Ex. *Saponaria.*

Saponaria, Soapwort (sa-pon-a'ri-a. Fam. Caryophyllaceae). A genus of annual and perennial flowering herbs, related to Dianthus.

Selection. *S. calabrica,* Italy, Greece, 1 ft, cymes of pale rose flowers, August, and vs. *alba,* white, and 'Scarlet Queen', red, are grown as hardy annuals, sown in light soil and sun, where they are to flower, in March, or September to bloom next spring. *S. officinalis,* Bouncing Bet, Europe, Asia, to 2 ft, white or pink flowers, August, with double flowering forms, is a useful border perennial. *S. caespitosa,* Pyrenees, 1–2 in., tufted, evergreen, linear leaves, umbels of starry pink flowers, June; *ocymoides,* Alps, 3 in., rose-purple flowers, June; and hybrids × *boissieri,* clear pink; and × *peregrina,* pale yellow, rose flush, are good rock garden plants.

Cultivation. Plant perennials March–May, well-drained soil, with some humus, and sunny warm positions, pH 6·0, or pH 5·5 for rock gardens.

Propagation. Species by seeds, sown March–April, in cool greenhouse or frame. Perennials—*S. officinalis,* by division, March; others by cuttings of firm shoots, July–August.

Saprophyte. An organism which lives and feeds entirely upon the dead tissues of plants or animals; and by its activities make their elements of use to living plants. Innumerable bacteria and fungi are constantly engaged in this vital process.

Sapwood. The most recently formed tissue of the xylem of trees within the cambium, containing living cells active in water conduction and food storage.

Sarcococca (sar-ko-kok'ka, Fam.

Buxaceae). Low-growing hardy evergreen shrubs, spreading by suckers, useful as ground cover under trees or in shade, with small, fragrant white flowers.

Selection. S. confusa, China, to 4 ft, dense elliptic foliage, very fragrant winter flowers; *hookeriana*, Himalaya, to 6 ft, fragrant autumn flowers, black berries; and v. *digyna*, China, purple-stemmed; *humilis*, China, 1–2 ft, very fragrant, January–March; and *ruscifolia*, 2 ft, China, glossy ovate leaves, milk-white, fragrant flowers, December–March.

Cultivation. Plant October or April–May, well-drained, humus-rich soil; shade.

Propagation. By division, April; by cuttings of firm shoots, in cold frame, July–August.

Sarmentosus (-a, -um). Sarmentose, forming runners. Ex. *Saxifraga sarmentosa.*

Sarothamnus (sa-ro-tham'nus. Fam. Leguminosae). The chief species of interest is *S. ingramii*, a Broom of N. Spain, to 8 ft, erect growing, with yellow and cream, small flowers in racemes, June; for spring planting, out of pots, in well-drained, lightish soil, full sun, and sheltered.

The native Broom, *Cytisus scoparius*, is transferred to this genus by some authorities.

Sarracenia, Side-saddle Flower (sar-ra-ke'ni-a. Fam. Sarraceniaceae). Curious herbaceous perennials, with clusters of pitcher-like, fly-trapping leaves, and single, nodding flowers on stalks in spring; sometimes known as Pitcher Plants, Trumpet Leaf and Indian Cup.

Selection. S. drummondii, SE. U.S.A., 2 ft, purple, April; *flava*, SE. U.S.A., 2 ft, yellow, and vs. *catesbaei* and *gigantea*; *psittacina*, SE. U.S.A., 1 ft, purple, April; and *purpurea*, E. U.S.A., 1 ft, purple, May, are hardy enough for sheltered positions in bog gardens of mild localities. *S.* × *chelsonii*, × *courtii*, × *stevensii*, and × *wilsoniana*, are good hybrid forms.

Cultivation. Plant in April, cool, moist, humus-rich soil, mild localities. May also be potted in compost of fibrous peat, chopped sphagnum moss and charcoal,

for cool greenhouse culture, watering freely in growth, very moderately in winter, minimum temp. 7° C. (45° F.), moist shade.

Propagation. By division in March–April.

Sasa, Dwarf Bamboo (sa'sa. Fam. Gramineae). Slender-stemmed, rather rampant dwarf bamboos, for wild gardens or where they can be grown in isolation. Formerly under *Arundinaria*.

Selection. S. chrysantha, Japan, 3–6 ft, leaves striped yellow; *senanensis* v. *nebulosa*, Japan, to 6 ft, purple-leaved; and *tessellata*, Japan, 4 ft, very large-leaved.

Cultivation. Plant April–May, in isolation, ordinary soils or moist ground.

Propagation. By division, April–May.

Satin Flower. See *Sisyrinchium.*

Sativus (-a, -um). Cultivated. Ex. *Crocus sativus.*

Satureia. *See* Savory.

Satyrium (sa-tu'ri-um. Fam. Orchidaceae). Terrestrial orchids of S. Africa.

Selection. S. candidum, 1½ ft, sweetly scented white flowers, September; *coriifolium*, 1 ft, yellow, shaded crimson in v. *aureum*, September; and *erectum*, 18 in., orange, autumn.

Cultivation. Pot, and repot, when growth begins, spring, well-crocked pots, sandy loam, with leaf-mould; grow near glass, warm and moist, shaded from direct sun, watering freely; withhold water after flowering, gradually, and rest in winter, at 10° C. (50° F.) minimum.

Propagation. By division, spring.

Sauromatum (saw-ro-ma'tum. Fam. Araceae). The species, *S. venosum* (*guttatum*), Asia, central E. Africa, is the tuberous perennial sold as Monarch of the East. The tuber may be flowered indoors without soil, placed on a saucer, when it will produce its flower spathe, purplish, green and yellow in a few weeks. After flowering it may be potted and allowed to produce its leaves in a cool greenhouse or shelter out of doors, and when the leaves wither, lifted, and kept cool until brought again into a warm room for flowering. Or the tubers may be pot-grown throughout, in a compost of equal parts sandy loam and peat. Propagation is possible by means of offsets.

Saururus (saw-rur′us. Fam. Saurur-aceae). Aquatic perennial herbs, with cordate leaves, and flowers in spikes, late summer.

Selection. S. cernuus, American Swamp Lily, N. America, 2 ft, white nodding flowers; and *chinensis*, Lizard's Tail, China, 1–1½ ft, yellowish-white flowers, are chiefly grown.

Cultivation. Plant in shallow water or very wet soil, April–May. Propagated by division.

Savin. See *Juniperus sabina*.

Savory, Summer (*Satureia hortensis*. Fam. Labiatae). An annual aromatic herb of S. Europe, 6 in., used for flavouring purposes, fresh and dried. Sow seeds, April, ½ in. deep, rows 8 in. apart, light, humus-rich soil, sun. Cut stems when in bud for drying, and to produce a second crop of shoots.

Savory, Winter (*Satureia montana*, Fam. Labiatae). Aromatic sub-shrub, of S. Europe, 12 in., pale purple flowers, June; an alternative to Summer Savory for culinary uses, but considered inferior. Easily grown from seeds in the same way, and propagated by cuttings in July–August.

Savoy (*Brassica oleracea* v. *bullata sabauda*). The Savoy Cabbage is simply a form of cabbage with wrinkled or puckered foliage, and very hardy.

Varieties. Early: 'Best of All', 'Drumhead Early', 'Ormskirk Early', 'Dwarf Green Curled', 'Tom Thumb'. To be sown in March for September–October cutting. Mid Season: 'Dwarf Green Curled', 'Autumn Green', 'Tom Thumb'. To be sown in April for October–November cutting. Late: 'Omega', 'Ormskirk Late', 'Sutton's New Year', 'Rearguard'. To be sown late April for January–March cutting.

Cultivation. Sowings planting out, soil preparation and general culture as for Cabbage (q.v.).

Sawdust. As a woody waste, sawdust rots slowly, but can be useful as a weed-suppressing mulch and moisture-retaining material. Used fresh, it depletes the soil of nitrogen temporarily, and should be mixed with ammonium sulphate (1 lb. per cwt.) before application; or exposed to weather for 4–6 months. In small quantities, it may be added to general compost heaps.

Saxatilis (-e). Growing on rocks. Ex. *Alyssum saxatile*.

Saxegothaea, Prince Albert's Yew (saks-e-goth′e-a. Fam. Taxaceae). The one species, *S. conspicua*, introduced in 1847 from Chile, and named in honour of the Prince Consort, is a small evergreen tree, to 40 ft, with yew-like foliage, monoecious flowers, and a link between the Taxaceae and Pinaceae botanically. Hardiness is doubtful, but it survives in south-western counties and S. Ireland. Plant in April–May, well-drained humus-rich soil, sheltered position. Propagation is by cuttings taken with a heel, July–August, inserted in a propagating frame.

Saxifraga (saks-i-fra′ga. Fam. Saxifragaceae). A large and varied genus of mostly hardy perennials, usually alpine, widely distributed in northern and southern and arctic zones of the world; providing many species, varieties and hybrids for the rock garden and alpine house, of which only the most outstanding can be selected for mention here. Botanically, the genus is divided into sixteen sections, grouped according to characters, habit and occurrence. Those of garden value are:

Hirculus Section. Mat-forming, deciduous leaves, orange or yellow flowers on leafy stems, summer–autumn.

Selection. S. brunoniana, Himalaya, 3 in., rich yellow flowers, summer; *hirculus*, Britain, etc., 9 in., golden, summer; and v. *major*, 1 ft, larger flowers; and *nutans*, India, China, 4 in., yellow nodding flowers, June; *chrysantha*, Rockies, yellow, May.

Cultivation. Plant in March–April, bog or damp scree. Propagate by division.

Robertsonia Section. Leaves more or less leathery in basal rosette, flowers in open panicles.

Selection. S. geum, SW. Europe, 1 ft, white flowers, June–July; *umbrosa*, London Pride, St Patrick's Cabbage, 1–1½ ft, pink, June–July; and v. *primuloides*, Ingwersen's, 4 in., red.

Cultivation. Plant April, any soil, damp shade. Propagate by division, after flowering.

Dactyloides Section. The Mossy Saxifrages, with moss-like evergreen cushions of rosetted leaves, and flowers on stems, freely borne, usually in April–June. The best forms are chiefly hybrids.

Selection. S. amoena, Europe, pink, May; × 'Avoca Gem', 6 in., rose-crimson; *cebenensis*, French Alps, 1 in., white; × 'Elf', 3 in., carmine; × 'Flower of Sulphur', 4 in., pale yellow; × 'Four Winds', 9 in., ruby-crimson;

FIG. 202 *Saxifraga moschata* v., Mossy Saxifrage, in flower.

'James Bremner', 6 in., large white; *moschata*, Pyrenees, 2–3 in., vs. 'Fairy', pink, and 'Stormonth's', rose-crimson; × 'Red Admiral', 4 in., red; × 'Sir D. Haig', 6 in., velvety crimson; *hypnoides* v. *whitlavei*, 4 in., white; and × 'Winston Churchill', pink.

Cultivation. Plant March–April, well-drained soil, moisture retentive beneath, partial shade. Propagation by division in early spring, or after flowering.

Euaizoonia Section. Strap-leaved, silver saxifrages, compact rosettes of stiffish leaves, encrusted with lime pits; each rosette producing its flower on a stem, and dying afterwards, to be replaced by offsets of younger leaf rosettes, flowering in later years, April–June.

Selection. S. aizoon, Europe, N. America, 3–6 in., white; and vs. *hirsuta*, 6 in., creamy, red-spotted; *lutea*, 6 in., soft yellow; *minor*, 3 in., creamy white; *minutifolia*, 2 in., creamy white; *rosea*, 9 in., deep pink; and *venetia*, 3 in., white; × *burnattii*, 6 in., white; *callosa* (*lingulata*), Maritime Alps, 12 in., white; and vs. *bellardii*, *catalaunica*, *lantoscana*; × 'Cecil Davis', 6 in., white; *cochlearis*, Maritime Alps, 6 in., white; and vs. *major*, *farreri* and *minor*; *cotyledon*, Pyrenees, Alps, Iceland, 1½–2 ft, red-stemmed, white, June; and vs. *caterhamensis*, white, spotted red; *icelandica*, 3 ft, white; *crustata*, E. Alps, 6 in., white; × 'Dr Ramsey', 1 ft, white; × 'Esther', 6 in., soft yellow; *hostii*, Alps, 1 ft, white; and v. *altissima*, to 1½ ft; *longifolia*, Pyrenees, 1–1½ ft, long panicles, white flowers, monocarpic; and vs. *imperialis*, and 'Walpole', producing offsets; × *macnabiana*, 1½ ft, white, spotted red; × *pectinata*, 6 in., creamy-white; × 'Tumbling Waters', 2 ft, very long sprays of white; and *valdensis*, French Alps, 2 in., white.

Cultivation. Easily grown in well-drained soil with lime and leaf-mould, full sun in the north, partial shade in the south or sunny gardens; planting October or March–April. Propagation by division in spring, or offsets in July; by seed for species.

Kabschia Section. Very pretty plants, forming tight compact mounds or cushions of minute, silvery foliage, with short-stemmed, dainty clusters of flowers, March–April.

Selection. S. × 'Ada', 2 in., white; × 'Amitie', 2 in., lilac; × *apiculata*, 4 in., primrose; × *borisii*, 2 in., lemon-yellow; × *boydii*, citron yellow; *burseriana*, E. Alps, 2 in., white; and vs. *crenata*, 1 in.; 'Gloria', 4 in., white; 'His Majesty', 3 in., white, flushed pink; *sulphurea*, pale yellow; and *tridentina*, large white flowers; × 'Buttercup', 2 in., bright yellow; × 'Cranborne', 1 in., deep pink; × *elizabethae*, 3 in., soft yellow;

× 'Faldonside', 2 in., lemon; *ferdinandi-coburgii*, Bulgaria, 4 in., bright yellow; × *geuderi*, 2 in., deep yellow; × *godseffiana*, 2 in., lemon; × *haagii*, 3 in., golden; × *jenkinsae*, 2 in., pink; *lilacina*, Himalaya, 1 in., amethyst; *marginata*, Italy, 3 in., white, and vs. *coriophylla*, more compact; *rocheliana*, May flowering; and *r. lutea*, pale yellow; × *megasaeflora*, 2 in., clear pink; × *obristii*, 2 in., white; × 'Primrose Bee', 3 in., primrose yellow; *scardica*, Macedonia, 4 in., white, May, and v. *obtusa*, more compact; *spruneri*, Balkans, 3 in., white, May; × *suendermannii*, 2 in., large white, and vs. *major* and *tombeanensis*, Alps, 2 in., white, May.

Cultivation. Plant in March–April or September; well-drained, gritty soil, with lime, moisture-retentive below, surface mulch of stone chippings; good light and sun, but not scorching heat. Propagation is easiest by rosettes, detached in May–June, rooted in cold frame; or division.

Engleria Section. Flattish rosettes of silvery grey leaves, with stems carrying spikes or racemes of small flowers with large, highly coloured, hairy calyces, February–April. Somewhat temperamental.

Selection. × *anormalis*, 2 in., yellow; × *frederici-augusti*, 6 in., pink; *grise-bachii*, Greece, 9 in., pink; and 'Wisley variety'; × *kellereri*, 6 in., soft pink; *media*, Pyrenees, 4 in., pink; *porophylla*, Italy, 6 in., pink; and vs. *montenegrina*, purplish; *sibthorpiana*, pale purple; and *thessalica alpina*, 2 in., pink, purple; × *prosenii*, 3 in., orange; and *stribrnyi*, Bulgaria, 4 in., pink.

Cultivation. Plant March–April or September, very well-drained, gritty or scree soils, with lime, enriched with leaf-mould beneath, and sunny crevices. Propagation by cuttings in May; or by seeds of species.

Porphyrion Section. Attractive, prostrate, mat-forming plants, with opposite leaves, and almost stemless flowers, sometimes classed as Oppositifolia.

Selection. S. biflora, Alps on granite, 2 in., purple, May; *blepharophylla*, Alps on granite, 2 in., starry, purple, are high alpines requiring skill; *oppositifolia*, Britain, Europe, Asia, N. America, is best in vs. *latina*, 1 in., rose-pink; *pyrenica splendens*, purple; 'R. M. Prichard', lilac; 'W. A. Clark', crimson rose; and 'Wetterhorn', crimson; and *retusa*, Pyrenees, 2 in., ruby-red; April-flowering.

Cultivation. Plant September or March–April, ex pots, in gritty, scree soil, cool, moist beneath; good light without scorching in summer. Propagation is by division in August–September.

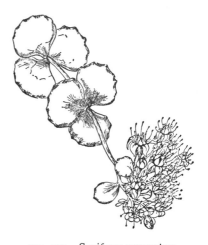

FIG. 203 *Saxifraga sarmentosa.*

Trachyphyllum Section. Small, mat-forming plants, narrow, undivided leaves, large white, pale to deep yellow flowers on branched stems, about 4 in. high.

Selection. S. aspera, Alps, straw-yellow, orange-spotted flowers; and vs. *bryoides*, more compact, and *hugueninii*, sessile flowers; *azorelloides*, Azores, 6 in., white, spotted yellow.

Cultivation. Plant September or March–April, lime-free, well-drained soil, sun, propagating by division in spring; by seeds, February–March.

Other sections may be represented by such garden-worthy plants as: Xanthizoon Section by *S. aizoides*, Europe, Asia, mat-forming, orange, June–July,

Saxifrage

and vs. *atrorubens*, blood-red; and *autumnalis*, orange, August. The Nephrophyllum Section of small deciduous herbs, persisting by resting bulbils, is represented by *S. granulata*, the Meadow Saxifrage or Fair Maids of France, Britain, Europe, with kidney-shaped leaves, panicles of white flowers, June–July, and its v. *plena*, 'Pretty Maid'. The Diptera Section of tufted plants, with deciduous, broad-bladed and stalked leaves and late bloom, yields *S. fortunei*, China, Japan, panicles of white flowers, autumn; *stolonifera* (*sarmentosa*), Mother of Thousands, Roving Sailor, etc., white flowering, July–August, and vs. *tricolor*, often grown as window or greenhouse plants; and *veitchiana*, China, 9 in., white, autumn. From the Miscopetalum Section of tufted plants with leathery leaves, *S. rotundifolia*, northern hemisphere, 1–2 ft, loose panicles of white starry flowers, June–July, and vs., are easily grown in shade. *S. huetiana*, Carpathia, is grown as a half-hardy annual, for its mound of crenulate leaves, and starry yellow flowers produced all summer.

Saxifrage. See *Saxifraga*.

Scaber (**Scabra, -um**). Rough, scabrous. Ex. *Eccremocarpus scaber*.

Scabiosa, **Scabious** (ska-bi-o'sa. Fam. Dipsaceae). Pretty flowering annual or perennial plants.

Selection. *S. atropurpurea*, Sweet Scabious, Mournful Widow, SW. Europe, 3 ft, is a hardy annual, offered in named forms such as 'Azure Fairy', double blue; 'Blue Moon', pale blue; 'Monarch Cockade', in blue, pink, red and white; and 'Tom Thumb', a dwarf mixed colour strain, 1½ ft. *S. caucasica*, Caucasus, 1½–2 ft, hardy border perennial, and vs. 'Bressingham White', 'Clive Greaves' and 'Goldingensis', lavender-blue forms. *S. graminifolia*, S. Europe, 9 in., mauve, summer; and *silenfolia*, Hungary, 6 in., violet; and *lucida*, E. Alps, 4 in., rosy-lilac, are good for rock gardens.

Cultivation. Annuals are sown in March–April, out of doors, or February–March, under glass for subsequent planting out; or in June–July, for winter flowering in a cool greenhouse. Perennials may be planted in October or March–

April; well-drained ordinary soils, and sun; and are best propagated by division. Seeds can be sown in April, but not all the seedlings will be true to variety and shade.

Scabious, Sheep's Bit. See *Jasione*.

Scabious, **Sweet.** See *Scabiosa atropurpurea*.

Scale Fern. See *Ceterach officinarum*.

Scale Insects. Small plant bugs of the Family Coccidae and Homoptera Order; the males being tiny, mouthless and winged, the females wingless, covered by a scale, attached to the plant host, under which eggs are laid and the young develop; the scales becoming small horny bumps or soft and flat. Common and serious infestations are: Mussel Scale (*Leoidosaphes ulmi*) and Oyster Scale (*Aspididiotus ostreaformis*) on fruit trees, felted Beech Scale (*Cryptococcus fagi*) on beeches; and Soft Scale (*Lecanium hesperidum*) on greenhouse plants. Yews, roses and vines may also be hosts to Scale.

Scale Leaves. Rudimentary leaves, such as enclose and protect winter buds of plants.

Scallions. A name for young onions, which have not formed bulbs; salad onions.

Scandens. Climbing. Ex. *Cobaea scandens*.

Scape. A leafless, flowering stem arising from the base of a plant, as in Narcissus.

Scar. The mark left on stems after the fall of a leaf; or on a detached seed.

Scarborough Lily. See *Vallota speciosa*.

Scarlet Runner. See Beans.

Schima (ski'ma. Fam. Theaceae). Related to Camellia, *S. argentae*, China, is a pretty evergreen shrub of 4–6 ft, with narrow, glossy leaves, and 2-in., saucer-like, creamy-white flowers in August–September; worth trying in a well-drained, peaty soil, in mild sheltered quarters; planted in April–May. Propagation is by cuttings of young shoots, July, in propagating case.

Schivereckia (ski-ver-ek'i-a. Fam. Cruciferae). Dwarf perennial alpine plants, with silvery leaves, of which *S. doerfleri*, Asia Minor, Balkans, 2 in., white clustered flowers, May; and *podolica*, E. Europe, 5 in., white, April, may be planted in sunny, sheltered positions, well-drained soil, in September–October, or early spring. Propagation by cuttings taken with a heel, August.

Schiz-. Prefix in compound words, meaning split or divided. Ex. *Schizanthus*, in reference to the split corolla of the flower.

Schizandra (ski-zan′dra. Fam. Magnoliaceae). Deciduous, twining climbers for warm sheltered walls.

Selection. S. glaucescens, China, to 20 ft, obovate leaves, orange-red flowers, May–June, followed by spikes of scarlet berries; *henryi*, China, to 15 ft, white, May, red berries; *propinqua* v. *sinensis*, China, to 20 ft, yellow, June, scarlet berries; and *rubriflora*, China, to 15 ft, deep crimson, May, red berries.

Cultivation. Plant March–April, well-drained, peat enriched soil, in mild localities.

Propagation. By cuttings, July–August, under handlights or in a frame.

Schizanthus, Butterfly Flower (ski-zan′thus. Fam. Solanaceae). Beautiful flowering annual plants from Chile, grown as half-hardy annuals.

Selection. The plants chiefly grown are hybrids of which named forms under *hybridus grandiflorus* are 'Brilliant', 1½–3 ft, reds and rose shades; 'Dr Badger's Hybrids', 1 ft, white, yellow to rose-reds; 'Dwarf Bouquet', 1 ft, crimson to pink; 'Angel Wings', 1 ft, rich pink; 'Improved Danbury Park' or 'Pansy-flowered', 1½–2 ft, self-coloured pinks, crimson to white; 'Sutton's Giant Cattleya Orchid', 2–4 ft, heavily veined, apricot, yellows, pink to purple; and *S.* × *wistonensis* strains such as 'Monarch', 1 ft, many shades; 'Crimson Cardinal', 1 ft, deep crimson; and 'Snowflake', 1½ ft, white.

Cultivation. For outdoors, sow seeds under glass, March, standard compost, bottom heat of 18° C. (65° F.), to prick off and plant out in May. For pot plants, sowings may be made in spring for summer flowering; in summer for winter flowering in a warm greenhouse; in August–September for spring flowering in a cool greenhouse.

Schizocarp. A fruit splitting into one-seeded pieces. Ex. Fruits of *Malvaceae*.

Schizocentron (ski-zo-ken′tron. Fam. Melastomataceae). The single species,

S. (*Heeria*) *elegans*, Mexico, is a creeping mat-forming herbaceous perennial, with deep purple, four-petalled flowers in May–June; for growing in pots, standard compost, in the cool greenhouse or house, watering freely in growth, very moderately in winter, minimum temp. 10° C. (50° F.). Propagation is by rooted pieces of stem, spring; or by seeds.

Schizocodon (ski-zo-ko′don. Fam. Diapensiaceae). The sole species, *S. soldanelloides*, 2 in., is an evergreen sub-shrub, Japan, with open bell-shaped, rich rose flowers, April–May; with vs. *alpinus*, 1 in., deep rose; *ilicifolius*, deep pink, and its white form *albus*; and *magnus*, 2 in., rich pink.

Cultivation. Plant September–October or March–April, ex pots, well-drained, peaty soil, cool position, partial shade in rock garden or alpine house; top-dress annually with soil compost, rather than disturb roots. Propagation by seed, April.

Schizopetalon (ski-zo-pet′a-lon. Fam. Cruciferae). The species chiefly grown, *S. walkeri*, Chile, 1½ ft, is a pretty annual, with pinnatifid leaves, racemes of white flowers, summer; to be grown from seeds, sown March–April, in the cool greenhouse, and reared as a pot plant, or carefully transplanted out of doors in May.

Schizophragma (ski-zo-prag′ma. Fam. Saxifragaceae). Deciduous climbers, by aerial roots, with large cordate leaves, and cymes of yellowish-white flowers, July, akin to Hydrangea, for walls or tree trunks, mild aspect.

Selection. S. hydrangeoides, Japan, to 30 ft, leaves coarsely toothed; and *integrifolia*, to 40 ft, leaves slender pointed to 7 in. long.

Cultivation. Plant October–April; moisture-retaining soil, on walls, fences, tree trunks, etc.

Propagation. By cuttings of young shoots taken with a heel, July–August, under handlight; or layers.

Schizostylis (ski-zo-sti′lis. Fam. Iridaceae). Known variously as Crimson Flag, Kaffir Lily or Winter Gladiolus, *S. coccinea* is a S. African, bulb-like rhizomatous herb, to 3 ft, with a spike of scarlet gladiolus-like flowers in autumn and early winter; pink in the v. 'Mrs Hegarty', and rose-pink in 'Viscountess Byng'.

Cultivation. Plant in spring, 3 in. deep, in well-drained, humus-rich soil, on warm sheltered border in mild localities; 9 in. apart; or in 5-in. pots, three to a pot, to grow and flower in a cool greenhouse, winter temp. 10° C. (50° F.); withholding water when leaves flag.

Schlumbergera (sklum-berg'e-ra. Fam. Cactaceae). This genus now includes Zygocactus and consists of epiphytic flat-jointed stems with spectacular long tubular flowers, having spreading segments in winter, and are commonly called Christmas Cacti.

Selection. S. *bridgesii*, Brazil, arching stems, bright rose, December–February; *truncata* (*Zygocactus truncatus*), 3-in. carmine flowers, and its colour-forms. S. *gaertneri* is now *Rhipsalidopsis gaertneri*, scarlet flower, April.

Cultivation. Pot in May, equal parts fibrous loam, leaf-mould, coarse sand and a little charcoal, well-crocked pots. Keep more or less dry to late autumn, water moderately, increasing as plants come to bud and flower, minimum winter temperature of 10° C. (50° F.), in good light, airy conditions, cool greenhouse or house.

Propagation. By stem cuttings in summer; or may be grafted on *Pereskia aculeata* stock.

Sciadopitys, Parasol or Umbrella Pine (ski-a-dop'i-tis. Fam. Pinaceae). The only species, S. *verticillata*, Japan, to 60 ft, pyramidal, with whorled branches, and two kinds of leaves, small and scale-like on lower parts of shoots, and long, leaf-like cladodes in bunched whorls to the apex of shoots, spreading umbrella-rib-like; terminal monoecious flowers, egg-shaped cones on established trees.

Cultivation. Plant March–May, well-drained loam soil, sheltered position in mild gardens.

Propagation. By seeds, April, sandy loam seed bed.

Scilla, Squill, Wild Hyacinth (skil'la. Fam. Liliaceae). A large genus of bulbous plants, valued for their spring flowers, hardy kinds being given below.

Selection. S. *bifolia*, Mediterranean region, 4–8 in., racemes of starry, gentian blue flowers, March, and vs. *alba*, creamy-white; *rosea*, pink; *lilio-*

hyacinthus, W. France, Spain, 1 ft, blue-lilac, May–June; *pratensis*, Dalmatia, 1 ft, blue, May; *siberica*, Siberia, 6 in., deep blue, March, and vs. 'Spring Beauty', very rich blue; and *taurica*, clear blue, early March; *tubergeniana*, NW. Persia, light blue, darker stripes, March. S. *peruviana*, Mediterranean region, miscalled the Cuban Lily, to 1 ft, lilac, May, and its v. *alba*, are best grown in the cool greenhouse.

Cultivation. Plant September–October, ordinary garden soils, 3 in. deep, 4 in. apart, in shrubbery or rock garden. Also do well in deep pans in the alpine house.

Propagation. By offset bulbs in September; by seeds, but they take 4–5 years to flower. See also *Endymion*.

Scindapsus (skin-dap'sus. Fam. Araceae). Climbing, stem-rooting tropical plants with large, ovate leathery leaves, resembling Philodendron, and grown as warm greenhouse or indoor house plants.

Selection. S. *aureus*, Solomon Is., branching, stalked, heart-shaped leaves, marbled yellow; and *pictus*, Silver Vine, leaves marked paler green, or silvery.

Cultivation. Pot in March, compost of one part fibrous loam, 2 parts leaf-mould, 2 parts moss peat, 1 part coarse sand, with cylinder of bark or netting filled with moist sphagnum moss up which to climb; give partial shade, moderate watering, syringe in sunny weather; winter temperatures of 10–18° C. (50–65° F.). Propagate by stem cuttings in spring.

Scion. A shoot used for grafting on a rootstock; also used for Buds, used in budding.

Scirpus (skirp'us. Fam. Cyperaceae). Perennial ornamental rushes for water gardening. Botanical naming rather confused.

Selection. S. *cernuus* (S. *gracilis*, S. *riparius*, *Isolepsis gracilis*, *I. cernua*), native Club-rush, for the bog garden but often grown as a cold greenhouse pot plant for its ½–1-ft spikelets; *lacustris* (*Schoenoplectus lacustris*), the native Bulrush, to 8 ft, and *tabernaemontani* (*Schoenoplectus tabernaemontani*), 3–5 ft, the glaucous Bulrush, and v. *zebrinus*, leaves banded white and green, are good for marginal pool planting in shallow water.

Cultivation. Plant in November–March, any moisture-retentive soil, or in shallow water.

Propagation. By division in winter.

Sclerotium (pl. **Sclerotia**). A tissue-like mass or resting body of many fungi, tiding them over unfavourable growing periods.

Scolopendrium. See *Phyllitis*.

Scolymus (sko-lu'mus. Fam. Compositae). Flowering, thistle-like herbs of the Mediterranean region.

Selection. S. hispanicus, the Golden Thistle, or Spanish Oyster Plant, is a biennial of 3 ft, which may be grown for its edible roots, or yellow thistle-like flowers, August, from seeds sown, April, in deepish good, well-drained loam, and sun, thinning plants to 1 ft apart. Roots are lifted from October onwards.

S. grandiflorus, to 3 ft, perennial, has yellow thistle heads in May–June; planting in autumn, or raising from seeds.

Scorpoid. Coiled like a scorpion's tail, as the cymes of *Myosotis scorpioides*.

Scorzonera (skor-zo-ne'ra. Fam. Compositae). The species chiefly grown is *S. hispanica*, Common Viper's Grass, S. Europe, a biennial, for its carrot-shaped, white-fleshed, sweet roots, in the same way as for Salsify (q.v.).

Scotch Elm. See *Ulmus glabra*.

Scotch Fir or **Pine.** See *Pinus sylvestris*.

Scree. *See* Rock Garden.

Screw Pine. See *Pandanus*.

Skrophularia (scro-pu'la-ri-a. Fam. Scrophulariaceae). Only *S. chrysantha*, a biennial from the Caucasus, of 1–1½ ft, with golden drooping flowers is much grown ornamentally; from seeds sown in May–June, plants over-wintered in a cold greenhouse or frame, and planted out in ordinary soil and sun, the following March–April. *S. nodosa* v. *variegata*, 2 ft, a yellow-spotted leaf form of the native perennial Figwort, with small greenish and brown flowers, in summer, is sometimes grown in damp places.

Scutellaria, Skull Cap, Helmet Flower (sku-tel-la'ri-a. Fam. Labiatae). Beautiful herbaceous perennials with lipped and pouched flowers, hardy and tender.

Selection. S. alpina, Europe, Asia, 1 ft, purple, August, and vs.; *baicalensis*, E. Asia, 1 ft, blue, August; *indica japonica*, Japan, 6 in., blue, August;

may be grown in borders or rock gardens, sunny positions, well-drained friable soil; being planted in October–March; and propagated by simple division in March.

S. costaricana, Costa Rica, 1½–3 ft, golden-scarlet flowers, June; *mociniana*, Mexico, 1½ ft, bright scarlet, summer; and *splendens*, Colombia, 1 ft, scarlet, August, are good for the warm greenhouse; potted in spring, 5-in. pots, watered freely in active growth, very moderately at other times, minimum winter temp. 10° C. (50° F.). Repot in spring. Propagation by cuttings, July; or by seeds in spring.

Scutellatatus (-a, -um). Shield- or saucer-shaped.

Sea Buckthorn. See *Hippophae*.

Sea Holly. See *Eryngium*.

Sea Lavender. See *Limonium*.

Sea Pink. See *Armeria maritima*.

Seakale (*Crambe maritima*). Developed from a native coastal plant, seakale is grown for its young growths forced and bleached in darkness in winter. A good variety is 'Lily White'.

Cultivation. Plants may be grown from seed, sown March–April, 1 in. deep, in drills 12 in. apart; thinned to 6 in., and planted out the following March, to grow on for a further year or two to forcing size. Alternatively, planting 'crowns' can be bought, and planted 2 ft apart, with pointed buds removed, in spring. These can be forced the following winter. Another method is to take side roots or thongs of established plants, cut into lengths of 4–6 in., cut square at the top, slanted at the bottom, and about ⅜ in. thick; store in damp sand or ash, and plant in March, 2 ft apart. Seakale needs a sunny site, well-drained soil, liberally enriched with rotted manure, compost or seaweed, and JI base fertilizer at 4 oz. per sq. yd prior to planting; and benefits from monthly feeding with a liquid seaweed derivative solution. To blanch out of doors, top growth is cut away in November, the plants covered with seakale pots, large plant pots or boxes, packed with rotted manure or clean leaves, to give blanched shoots in six to eight weeks; after which the plants are gradually exposed to air and light and allowed to grow on normally, being manured and fed to benefit them. To force seakale, however, the roots are lifted from November onwards, potted in 9–10 in. pots, or boxes, with crowns just above the soil surface, in potting compost, leaf-mould or half-rotted manure, and grown in complete darkness, under a greenhouse stage or indoor room, with temperatures of 7–13° C. (45–55° F.); light being excluded by inverted pots, boxes or a tent of black sheet polythene. The shoots are cut when 6–9 in. high, with a little of the basal tissue, at six to seven weeks. The roots are discarded after forcing.

Seaside Gardening. The initial problem in gardening on or near the coast is to establish shelter from strong winds, with plants resistant to salt spray, and able to grow in the often poor, sandy soil. Useful wind-hardy, first-line shrubs are Buckthorn (*Hippophae rhamnoides*), *Berberis darwinii*, *Cotoneaster lactea*, *Crataegus monogyna*, *C. oxycantha*, *Lycium chinense*, *Rosa rugosa*, *Salix caprea*, *S. daphnoides*, *Skimmia japonica*, *Ulex europaeus*; and for mild localities, *Buddleia globosa*, *Escallonia* spp., *Fuchsia* × *riccartonii*, *Hydrangea macrophylla*, *Olearia* spp., *Phormium tenax*, *Pittosporum* spp., *Senecio rotundifolius*, *Stranvaesia salicifolia* and *Veronica* spp., Trees likely to succeed for screening and wind-breaks include *Alnus glutinosa*, *Cupressus macrocarpa*, *Fraxinus excelsior*, *Ilex aquifolium*, *Larix leptolepsis*, *Pinus laricio*, *P. laricio nigricans*, *Populus trichocarpa*, *Quercus ilex*, Sycamore (*Acer pseudoplanatus*) and Cornish Elm (*Ulmus stricata*, *U. wheatleyi*). In the lee of shelter so created, a wide range of plants, suitable for the soil and aspect, can be readily grown.

Seaweed. Marine Algae of brown, green or red colouring, found near the coast and on shores, which form a valuable potassium-rich, organic manure for most soils, especially light sands. Average analysis is ½ per cent nitrogen, 1 per cent potassium, 0·1 per cent phosphorus, plus many minerals in trace amounts, and iodine (invaluable for food crops). Fresh seaweed as gathered may be incorporated into the top soil in Autumn–early Winter, at 1 cwt. per 6–8 sq. yds. Seaweeds may also be added to general compost heaps, or composted on their own. Dried and burnt, the ash makes a very good potassic fertilizer for use at 3–4 oz. per sq. yd. Powdered seaweed manure is an excellent soil conditioner and fertilizer. Liquid seaweed fertilizer is a feed for growing plants; and as a foliar feed is claimed to have an insect pest deterrent effect.

Secateurs. Small, hand-pruning shears, more easily used than a pruning knife, and efficient provided the cutting blades are kept sharp and make a clean cut without bruising. First-class modern types are those which cut with a slicing action, or against a soft metal anvil.

Secundus (-a, -um). One-sided. Ex. *Echeveria secunda*.

Sedge. See *Carex*.

Sedum (se'dum. Fam. Crassulaceae). A large genus of fleshy succulent plants, chiefly perennial but some annual or biennial, as valuable for their foliage, often coloured, as for their bright flowers, and for growing on rock gardens, walls and dryish borders.

Selection. S. cepaea, S. Europe, 12 in., starry white flowers, June–July; and *coeruleum*, S. Europe, Algeria, 3 in., cymes of pale blue, summer, are half-hardy annuals, to raise from seeds, and plant in May, in rock garden or border, or grow in pots. Hardy perennials include *S. acre*, the native Stonecrop, 2 in., yellow, summer, and v. *aureum*, golden-leaved; *adenotrichum*, Himalaya, 3 in., white, April; *aizoon*, Japan, 9 in., herbaceous, yellow, July; *album*, Europe, Britain, 4 in., white, July; *anglicum* v. *minus*, Europe, 1 in., white, tinted rose, summer; *brevifolium*, SW. Mediterranean region, prostrate, white, June; *dasyphyllum*, S. Europe, 2 in., white, June, and vs.; *ellacombianum*, Japan, 6 in., yellow, June; *ewersii*, Himalaya, 6–12 in., herbaceous, pink, August–September; *hobsonii*, Tibet, 4 in., rose-pink, July; *kamtschaticum*, N. China, Siberia, 9 in., orange-yellow, summer; *lydium*, W. Asia Minor, 2 in., white and pink; *middendorfianum*, Siberia, Manchuria, 6 in., yellow, July–August; *oreganum*, W. N. America, 6 in., yellow, July–August; *populifolium*, Siberia, 1–1½ ft, shrubby, white to pink, hawthorn-scented cymes, July; *primuloides*, Yunnan, deciduous sub-shrub to 3 in., white, August; *reflexum*, central and W. Europe,

Stone Orpine, to 1 ft, bright yellow, trailing, summer; *sarmentosum*, China, Japan, prostrate, to 1 ft; *spathulifolium* W. N. America, hummocky, cymes of yellow stars, June–July, and vs. *purpureum*, purple; and 'Cassa Blanca', more dwarf and mealy-foliaged; *spectabile*, China, 1–1½ ft, herbaceous border plant, flat corymbs, pink, September–October, and vs. 'Brilliant', deeper pink; *album*, whitish-pink; *spurium*, N. Persia, Caucasus, 6 in., pink, August–September, and v. *coccineum*, crimson; *telephium*, the native Orpine or Live for Ever, 1½ ft, has a good form in 'Munstead Dark Red', August–September; all of which are evergreen except where stated. Not quite hardy and therefore best as pot plants in the alpine house or cool greenhouse are *S. bourgaei*, Mexico, sub-shrubby, 1 ft, red-tipped white flowers, July–August; *cauticola*, Japan, herbaceous, deep purple, red, September; *multiceps*, Algeria, 3–4 in., yellow, July, deciduous; *oaxacanum*, Mexico, 1 in., yellow, June; *sieboldii*, Japan, herbaceous, 9 in., pink, October; and v. *mediovariegatum* for yellow, centrally blotched leaves; and *stahlii*, Mexico, 6 in., reddish-leaved, yellow, July. A few are biennial and monocarpic, such as *S. pilosum*, Caucasus, Asia Minor, cymes of deep pink from hairy rosettes of leaves, May–June; *hispanicum*, Caucasus to Italy, 4 in., pinkish-grey foliage, pink, June, and v. *aureum*; and *sempervivoides*, Asia Minor, 6 in., crimson, June–July; to be grown from seeds sown in early summer.

Cultivation. All Sedums welcome well-drained soils, enriched with leaf-mould; sun or light shade; and may be planted best in March–April.

Propagation. Species by seeds, sown March–April, out of doors. Perennials by division in spring; or by fleshy leaves shallowly inserted, spring–autumn.

Seed Dressings. Germinating seeds may be given protection from various soil fungi, such as those responsible for 'Damping-off' and 'Foot Rot' diseases if dressed with a thiram fungicidal powder before sowing; and from soil pests such as wireworms, if dressed with an insecticidal seed dressing (based on gamma-BHC). The amount needed is small, and combined seed dressings are offered by several firms.

Seedling. Horticulturally, a plant raised from a seed, usually with its first true leaves forming.

Seeds and Sowing. A seed is the means by which a flowering plant reproduces itself sexually, being the product of the female ovule fertilized by the male (pollen) cell. It consists of a dormant embryo plant enclosed by protective seed coats (testa). The embryo consists of a rudimentary root (radicle) and shoot (plumule), and one or more rudimentary leaves (cotyledons). The seed contains a reserve of food material which may be stored in the cotyledons (e.g. Pea) or separately within the embryo sac as endosperm, or surrounding it as perisperm. The seed coat or testa is usually double, pierced by a minute pore (micropyle), with a scar (hilum) where it was attached to its parent plant; and sometimes with appendages such as wings, or hairs to aid distribution. The shape and size of seeds are very varied, though characteristic of their kind. Seeds provide the most economical means of propagating plants and of producing hybrids. For successful germination seeds need air, moisture and warmth to start the complicated biochemical reactions that mean growth, and these are regulated by the manner and timing of their sowing. Soon after emergence germinated seedlings need soluble nutrients available in the rooting medium, particularly phosphates. Seeds germinate satisfactorily in moist sand, perlite, vermiculite or sphagnum moss, but it is usually wise to use blended seed composts of nutrient value (*see* Composts) for indoor sowing.

Timing. Seeds germinate best in soils of somewhat higher temperatures than that of the atmosphere above. Broadly, tropical or tender species need soil temperatures or bottom heat of 24–29° C. (75–85° F.); subtropical, warm temperate or half-hardy species 21–24° C. (70–75° F.); temperate or hardy species 21–15·5° C. (70–60° F.), to germinate quickly. Under glass, where temperatures can be artificially maintained, sowing can be carried out throughout the year. In practice, early spring is the chief sowing time, though biennials and many perennials are sown in summer, and seeds of many temperate plants in autumn. Out of doors, the main sowing period is March–May; though hardy biennials and perennials may be raised from summer–autumn sowings. It is important that the seed-bed should be well prepared, and of good tilth.

Sowing Depth. The depth at which seeds are sown affects their temperature and access to moisture and air, and therefore their germination speed. The larger the seed, the deeper it may be sown. A good rule of thumb is to sow at twice the seed's diameter; a little deeper in light soils, but never more than four times the diameter.

Viability. This concerns the capability of seeds to germinate and grow. In some seeds (e.g. *Salix* spp.) it lasts only a few weeks. In most seeds it tends to diminish with age, though much depends upon the conditions under which the seeds are stored. It is wise to test 'old' seed by germinating a number on moist blotting paper or flannel in appropriate temperatures, and ascertain the percentage of germination to guide the amount of seeds to sow.

Dormancy. Some seeds have a longer dormant period than others. Some seeds (e.g. those of *Viola* spp., many *Primula* spp. and certain alpines) germinate most quickly when freshly ripe and shed by the plants. If stored and sown later, germination often takes longer. Many seeds undergo changes in the dormant stages before being ready to germinate; this is called 'after-ripening', and takes place in many seeds of species fruiting in autumn, to yield seeds that germinate the following spring. Some seeds need to be subject to low temperatures in moist conditions before germinating readily (e.g. seeds in berries, such as *Ilex*, *Crataegus*, etc.) prepared by stratification (q.v.).

The permeability of the testa to moisture and air affects germination seed. Seeds with hard coats (e.g. most species of the Leguminosae) need to have the seed coats made more permeable by abrasion with sandpaper or a file, or pre-soaking in water prior to sowing. Some seeds may form a root one year, and a shoot the next. Most seeds germinate readily in darkness, but a few do better in light (e.g. Lettuce seed). Where special conditions are needed, these have been noted in the propagation notes for plants throughout this book.

Seed-sowing under Glass. Seeds may be sown in boxes, pans or pots, which must be clean, or, after previous use, chemically sterilized by treatment with a 2 per cent solution of formaldehyde. The container must then be crocked with clean broken clay plant-pot shards, coarse grit, washed broken clinker, covered by a thin layer of leaves or fibrous peat, and then the rooting medium or compost, nicely moist and firm. After sowing, seeds may be covered with sharp sand or finely chopped sphagnum moss. Moisture loss is minimized by covering with a sheet of glass, or a plastic bag, preferably turned daily; and light excluded by a sheet of opaque paper or sheet plastic, until the seedlings break through the surface, when the covers are best removed. Many gardeners find it easiest to raise small sowings in peat-wood fibre pots.

Segment. A division of a plant organ, such as a leaf, or a petal.

Selaginella (sel-a-gin-el'la. Fam. Selaginellaceae.) A very large genus of elegant, evergreen plants, non-flowering relations of the Club-mosses, grown for their freely branching stems and foliage.

Selection. S. helvetica, central Europe to Japan, 2 in., and *selaginoides,* Britain, N. America, are mat-like, hardy, trailers for the rock garden. *S. apoda,* N. America, slender-stemmed dwarf; *braunii,* W. China, to 1½ ft, erect, straw-coloured fronds; *kraussiana,* S. Africa, pinnate trailer, and v. *aurea,* yellow-leaved; *martensii,* Mexico, 6–12 in., bright green; *lepidophylla,* Texas, etc., the Resurrection Club-moss, often sold dry, with densely tufted, curled-up stems that unroll and freshen when placed in water; and *uncinata,* China, trailing stems to 2 ft, may be grown in the cool green-house, winter temp. 10° C. (50° F.); while *S. delicatula (canaliculata),* E. Himalaya, 3–4-ft fronds; *erythropus,* tropical America, 9 in., crimson-stemmed; *galeottei,* Mexico, to 2 ft, graceful fronds; *haematodes,* Andes, 2 ft, crimson-stemmed, bright green leaves; *pallescens (cuspidata, grandis),* Borneo,

1½ ft, erect fronds; *plumosa* (*biformis*, *flagellifera*), Himalaya, 1 ft, trailer; and *willdenovii*, Cochin China, climbing to 15 ft, may be grown in the warm greenhouse, winter temps. 13° C. (55° F.)–18° C. (65° F.).

Cultivation. Out of doors, plant March–April, shade, in humus-rich soil, rock garden or border edging. For greenhouse culture, pot in March–April; compost of 2 parts each of peat, chopped sphagnum moss and sandy loam, with broken charcoal; well-crocked pans or pots; shade; keeping moist, and out of draughts.

Propagation. By cuttings of stems, taken at a joint, February–April, or when convenient.

Selenicereus (se-le-ni-ke're-us. Fam. Cactaceae). Slender-stemmed, climbing cacti, with long aerial roots, and large, white, nocturnal flowers.

Selection. S. *grandiflorus*, Queen of the Night, Jamaica, to 15 ft, flowers vanilla-scented, to 1 ft across, yellow-stamened, June, a parent of modern Epiphyllums; *macdonaldiae*, Uruguay, Argentina, to 20 ft, flowers larger but not scented; and *spinulosus*, Mexico, flowers about 6 in. across, white tinged pink.

Cultivation. Pot, and repot every third year, March, in large pots, standard cactus compost, to train up the wall or pillar of a cool greenhouse, minimum winter temp. 10° C. (50° F.). Water freely in growth, very little in winter.

Propagation. By stem cuttings, April–May.

Self, Self-coloured. Descriptive of a flower or plant of one colour only.

Self-fertilization. The fertilization of the ovule by pollen of the same flower.

Self-heal, All-heal. A native plant, *Prunella vulgaris*, sometimes a troublesome weed.

Self-sterile. Descriptive of plants bearing flowers of which the pollen is incapable of fertilizing the ovules of the same or of any flowers on the plant.

Semi-evergreen. A plant which is evergreen in its native habitat, but not completely so in Britain.

Semper-. A prefix implying continuity; e.g. *semperflorens*, ever-flowering; *sempervirens*, evergreen.

Sempervivum, House Leek (sem-per-vi'vum. Fam. Grassulaceae). Hardy,

succulent herbs, with fleshy leaves, in crowded rosettes, with starry flowers in cymes at the head of leaf-clasping stalks.

Selection. S. altum, Caucasus, hairy leaves, red, yellow-stamened flowers, summer; *andreanum*, N. Spain, pink, summer; *arachnoideum*, Cobweb Houseleek, European Alps, leaves connected by cobwebby hairs, rose, July; and vs. *fasciatum*, and *tomentosum*, much webbed; *arenarium*, E. Alps, small rosettes, greenish, August; *ciliosum*, Bulgaria, grey-green, yellow, summer, and vs. *borisii*, very hairy; × *funckii*, purple-red, summer; *giuseppii*, N. Spain, white-woolly rosette, rose-red, summer; *grandiflorum*, Switzerland, large, white to yellow, June; *heuffelii*, Bulgaria, rosettes dividing, yellow, August; *hirsutum* (*allionii*), Maritime Alps, yellow-green rosettes, cream flowers; × 'Jubilee', water-lily-like rosettes; *kosaninii*, Montenegro, large, dull green, red-green, summer; *macedonicum*, Macedonia, downy leaves, red, summer; *montanum*, European Alps, small, violet-purple, summer; and v. *rubrum*, red-leaved; *nevadense*, Spain, leaves reddening, rose-red, summer; *marmoreum* (*schlehanii*), SE. Europe, deep red, white flowers, August; *pittonii*, Styria, greenish-yellow, July; *soboliferum*, Hen and Chicken Houseleek, Europe, Asia, greenish-yellow, July; *reginae-almaliae*, Greece, purplish, red flowers, summer; *tectorum*, Pyrenees, Alps, etc., is the Houseleek or St Patrick's Cabbage, of walls, roofs, etc., purplish-red flowers, July; and vs. *alpinum*, small; *calcareum*, c. 'Monstrosum', and *glaucum*, blue-green; *robustum*, large; and *triste*, coppery-red; *thompsonianum*, Austria, apple green, yellow flowers, summer; and *zeleborii*, Serbia, open rosettes, yellow-crimson, August.

Cultivation. Hardy and almost indestructible, Sempervivums are excellent for rock gardens, crevices in walls, or alpine house pans, in free-draining, sandy soil, provided with leaf-mould; planted October–November or March–April. Flowering rosettes die after flowering, and if no gaps are wanted, remove flowering rosette early.

Propagation. By offsets, at almost any period of mild weather. S. *heuffelii* by division in July. By seeds, sown April, though plants are likely to be a mixed lot owing to readiness in inter-crossing.

Senecio (sen-ek'i-o. Fam. Compositae). Believed to be the largest genus of the Plant Kingdom, though relatively few are of great garden merit, though varied.

FIG. 204   *Senecio laxifolius.*

Selection. S. *arenarius*, S. Africa, 1 ft, lilac, yellow-centred, daisy-like flowers; *elegans*, the Jacobaea of catalogues, S. Africa, 1½ ft, in single and double flowering forms, white, purple, pinks to red, and a dwarf strain *nana*, 9 in., are grown as half-hardy annuals, from seeds sown under glass, March, bottom heat of 18° C. (65° F.), to plant out in May. S. *cremeiflorus*, Chile, Argentine, 2 ft, clustered heads of pale yellow, June; *doronicum*, Europe, to 2 ft, orange-yellow, summer; *macrophyllus*, Caucasus, 3 ft, large-leaved, yellow, summer; *pulcher*, Uruguay, 1–2 ft, purple, autumn; and *tanguticus*, China, to 6 ft, rampant, panicles of yellow flowers, September, are herbaceous perennials for

sheltered borders. S. *adonidifolius*, S. France, Spain, 8 in., orange, summer; *incanus*, European Alps, 4 in., silver foliage, small yellow flowers, May; and *uniflorus*, Alps, tufted, silvery, orange-yellow, May, may be planted in the rock garden. Some of the hardy shrubs are desirable, such as *abrotanifolius*, central Europe, to 2 ft, orange-yellow, July–September; *greyii*, New Zealand, to 8 ft, white-felted leaves, clear yellow, summer, for mild localities; *laxifolius*, New Zealand, to 4 ft, grey downy leaves, golden-yellow flowers, summer; and *rotundifolius*, New Zealand, 6–12 ft, white-felted leaves, yellowish flower-heads, summer, for seaside planting. Other New Zealand evergreens, S. *compactus*, 2–4 ft, *elaeagnifolius*, to 12 ft, *kirkii*, to 12 ft, *monroi*, 3–6 ft, are only hardy for the mildest southern gardens. For the cool greenhouse, S. *grandifolius*, Mexico, to 6 ft, magnificent for winter clusters of yellow flowers; *magnificus*, Australia, 3 ft, golden-yellow corymbs, October; *pyramidatus*, S. Africa, succulent shrub of 2 ft, yellow racemes in June; and the climbers, *auriculatissimus*, central Africa, evergreen, to 12 ft, golden-yellow, spring; and *macroglossus*, the Cape Ivy, S. Africa, rich yellow flowering, winter, should be considered.

Cultivation. Hardy plants are easy to grow in any well-drained loamy soil, but do best in wind-sheltered, warm positions, not cold exposures; planted in March–April. Greenhouse kinds need to be potted in March–April, standard compost; watered freely in active growth, moderately in winter, with minimum temperature in winter of 10° C. (50° F.). S. *cruentus* is the parent of modern Cineraria (q.v.).

Senilis (-e). Appearing old, often grey-haired. Ex. *Cereus senilis.*

Sensitive Plant. See *Mimosa pudica.*

Sepal. One of the parts forming the outer protective calyx of a dicotyledonous flower, usually green and leaf-like.

Sepaloid. Sepal-like.

Septum (pl. **Septa**). A partition, or wall of tissue; septate, separated by a septum.

Sequestrene. A chelated compound of a mineral element, usually iron, manganese, magnesium, used chiefly in

FIG. 205   Sepals (s).

making such elements available to lime-intolerant plants grown in calcareous soils.

Sequoia (se-kwoy'a. Fam. Pinaceae). The only species is *S. sempervirens*, the Redwood, California, to 130 ft (340 ft is the tallest native); with thick red bark, dense, branches drooping, but pyramidal habit, small cones; for planting in March–April, in good, moist loams, in valleys with wind shelter. Propagation is by seeds, sown March–April; or cuttings of erect shoots, in late summer, in cold frame or under handlight. See *Sequoiadendron*.

Sequoiadendron (se-kwoy'a-den-dron. Fam. Pinaceae). A genus of one species, *S. giganteum* (*Sequoia wellingtonia*, *Sequoia washingtonia*), the Big Tree or Mammoth Tree of California, where specimens of to 320 ft, grow, variously estimated at 1,500 to 4,000 years old. In Britain it reaches to 150 ft, and is grown similarly as for the Redwood, *Sequoia sempervirens*; and has a golden-leaved form *aurea*, and a curious weeping form, *pendula*, with branches close to its trunk. Propagation is usually by imported seeds, sown March–April.

Serotinus (-a, -um). Late, as of flowering. Ex. *Cotoneaster serotinus*.

Serra-, prefix in compound words, indicating saw-like; serrate, edged with forward-pointed teeth; serratulate, edged with small teeth; serrulate, finely saw-toothed.

Service Tree. See *Sorbus domestica*.

Sessile. Stalkless, of leaves and flowers.

Setaceus (-a, -um). Setaceous, bristly. Ex. *Scirpus setaceus*.

Sets. A term sometimes used for seed potato tubers.

Setting. The fertilization of a flower; done artificially by transferring pollen from male to female flowers by camel-hair brush or rabbit's scut, as with melons, peaches, etc.

Shaddock. See *Citrus maxima*.

Shade. By restricting the amount and intensity of the light reaching a plant, shade diminishes photosynthesis, and thus tends to check growth, particularly of flower formation and development in garden plants. Nevertheless, plants vary in their tolerance of shade. Many of them, especially those grown under glass, welcome light shade against the direct hot sun in summer. Plants highly tolerant of shade tend to have deep green foliage, few or no flowers, and include many house plants, native to semi-tropical or tropical forests. Flowering plants grown in shade tend to elongate in stem growth to reach the light, and bear fewer flowers.

Shading. See Greenhouse.

Shallot (*Allium ascalonicum*). Mildly onion-flavoured, this hardy bulbous perennial of Syria, introduced by Crusaders in the Middle Ages is easily and rewardingly grown for culinary use.

Varieties. It is usually grown from small bulbs, of which 'Jersey Shallot', round with violet-tinged flesh; 'Red Shallot', with coppery red skin; and 'Yellow Shallot', straw-yellow skin and white flesh, are good kinds. From seeds it takes two years to give a crop, and a fair proportion of the seedlings are useless as they bolt or run to flower when propagated as bulbs.

Cultivation. Shallots require a friable soil, light to medium loam, humus-rich from previous organic manuring, with a dressing of bone meal and dried sea-weed manure. Traditionally, the bulbs are planted on the shortest day, and lifted on the longest. This may serve in mild localities, but elsewhere February–March are more appropriate to ensure good soil conditions. The bulbs are planted, not pushed in, to half their height, 6 in. apart, in rows 12 in. apart; kept weed-free, and develop into close-packed clusters of bulbs with narrow leaves. They are lifted when leaves yellow, in July, air-dried in the sun, and stored, bunched or in trays, under dry, cool, frostproof conditions for use.

Shamrock. The Irish Shamrock is the Lesser Yellow Trefoil, *Trifolium dubium*, with its trifoliolate leaves; four- or five-leaved forms are the Shamrocks of Luck and Blessing. White Clover, *T. repens*, is also esteemed. But no Irishman would pick the trifoliolate leaves of Wood Sorrel, *Oxalis acetosella*, as Shamrock.

Shamrock, Pea. See *Parochetus communis*.

Shanking. A functional disorder of the Grape Vine (q.v.).

Shears. Short-handled, 8–10 inch bladed shears are useful for hedge-clipping and topiary work. Long-handled, lazy-back shears, with blades at right angles, are used for cutting grass edges of lawns and verges. Shears with a cutter bar, driven by electric motor, cable or small petrol engine, are invaluable where there is much clipping to be done. Edges must be maintained sharp, and the blades well oiled, and rust-prevented with a modern solution.

Sheath. The part of a plant, leaf-base or spathe rolled round a stem.

Sheep Laurel. See *Kalmia angustifolia*.

Shell-flower. See *Moluccella laevis*.

Shells. Finely broken shells are a slowly available source of calcium (lime) and can be used to lighten heavy soils. Some seashore sands contain much shell and are sometimes used for liming.

Shield Fern. See *Dryopteris filix-mas*.

Shirley Poppy. A race of *Papaver rhoeas* (q.v.).

Shoo-fly Plant. See *Nicandra*.

Shoot. The developed half-woody stem from a bud.

Shooting Stars. See *Dodecatheon*.

Shortia (short'i-a. Fam. Diapensiaceae). Pretty, spring-flowering perennial sub-shrubs for the rock garden or alpine house.

Selection. S. galacifolia, N. Carolina, tufted, wiry stems, to 6 in., leathery, glossy evergreen, orbicular leaves, solitary, tubular lobed white flowers, April, and v. *rosea*, pink; and *uniflora*, Japan, prostrate, rounded, sinuately toothed, stalked leaves, pale pink, white stamens, flowers, April, and vs.

grandiflora, bolder flowers, and *rosea*, deep rose-pink.

Cultivation. Plant March, well-drained soil, with leaf-mould or peat, cool shade; or pot for alpine house in lime-free compost, for flowering, removing to cool shady frame afterwards.

Propagation. By careful division in March, preferably in a cool shady frame until re-established. By seeds, in pans, cool frame, March–April, if available.

Shrub. A perennial plant with woody stems growing from or near the base.

Shrubs. The range of garden-worthy shrubs is now very wide, and as permanent plants, providing beauty in flower, foliage and/or fruit, are labour-saving. Most of them are chosen for their flowering, but as this is seasonal and seldom prolonged, their appearance at other times must also be carefully considered. Apart from individual preferences, a choice of shrubs must be regulated by their hardiness and suitability for the soil and environment in which they are to be grown. Important factors are:

Soil. Broadly, a vital distinction must be drawn between shrubs which are lime-tolerant and lime-intolerant; the latter being truly eligible for acid lime-free soils of pH 5·5 or less.

Lime-intolerant shrubs.

Andromeda, Arbutus (except *A. unedo*), *Arctostaphylos, Calluna, Cassiope, Chamaedaphne, Daboecia, Enkianthus, Epigaea, Erica* (except *E. carnea, E. mediterranea, E. terminalis, E. vagans,* and vs.), *Gaultheria, Gaylussacia, Kalmia, Leiophyllum, Pernettya, Phyllodoce, Pieris, Rhododendron* (including *Azalea*), *Rhodothamnus, Vaccinium* and *Zenobia.*

There are several shrubs, which, although not so intolerant of lime as the above, grow best in definitely acid soils, and include *Camellia, Eucryphia, Halesia, Lithospermum prostratum, Magnolia, Skimmia* and *Stuartia*, which are tolerant of lime up to about pH 6·2, provided leaf-mould or peat is added liberally. Under such conditions, with the use of chelated iron compounds (Sequestrenes), it is also possible to grow the lime-intolerant groups, with fair success.

The majority of shrubs may be grown in soils of pH 5·5–6·5, but the gardener should give preference to certain shrubs on calcareous soils and extreme soils.

Shrubs for Calcareous Soils (Chalk or Limestone).

Acacia, Aucuba, Berberis, Buddleia, Ceanothus, Chaenomeles, Choisya, Cistus, Clematis, Clerodendron, Cornus, Cotinus, Cotoneaster, Crataegus, Cytisus, Deutzia, Escallonia, Euonymus, Forsythia, Hibiscus, Hypericum, Ilex, Jasminum, Kerria, Ligustrum, Lavendula, Leycesteria, Lonicera, Malus, Philadelphus, Potentilla, Prunus, Rhus, Ribes, Senecio, Spiraea, Stranvaesia, Syringa, Viburnum and *Weigela.*

Shrubs for Dry or Sandy Soils.

Acacia, Berberis, Caryopteris, Chaenomeles, Cistus, Colutea, Cytisus, Elaeagnus, Genista, Helianthemum, Helichrysum, Hippophae, Hypericum, Indigofera, Lavendula, Phlomis, Potentilla, Rhus, Rosmarinus, Rubus, Santolina, Sarococca, Senecio, Spartium, Tamarix, Ulex, Veronica, Vinca and *Yucca.*

Shrubs for Damp Soils and the Waterside.

Alnus spp., *Cornus alba, C. stolonifera, Hippophae, Forsythia, Philadelphus, Salix, Sambucus, Sorbaria, Spiraea bumalda* and vs., *Viburnum opulus* and vs., *Weigela.*

Shrubs for Shade.

Acer palmatum and vs., *Aucuba, Berberis, Buxus, Camellia, Choisya, Cornus, Cotoneaster, Daphne, Euonymus radicans, Garrya elliptica, Hedera, Hypericum, Ilex, Leycesteria, Ligustrum, Mahonia, Osmanthus, Osmarea, Pachysandra, Pernettya, Phillyrea, Pyracantha, Ribes, Rubus, Sambucus, Sarcococca, Skimmia, Symphoricarpos, Viburnum fragrans,* hybrids and vs., and *Vinca.*

Shrubs for Winter Flowering.

Azara microphylla, Daphne, Erica carnea and vs., *E. × darleyensis, E. mediterranea* and vs., *Garrya elliptica, Hamamelis mollis, Mahonia japonica, Rhododendron praecox, Viburnum × bodnantense, V. fragrans.*

Shrubs for Spring Flowering.

Amelanchier canadensis, Azalea, Camellia, Berberis, Choisya ternata, Corylopsis, Cotoneaster, Cytisus, Chaenomeles,

Deutzia, Enkianthus, Escallonia, Exochorda, Forsythia, Kerria, Kolkwitzia, Magnolia, Mahonia aquifolium, Osmarea, Paeonia (tree), *Philadelphus, Pieris, Pyracantha, Prunus, Rhododendron, Ribes, Salix, Skimmia, Spiraea, Syringa, Viburnum burkwoodii, V. carlesii, V. opulus* and vs., *Weigela.*

Shrubs for Summer Flowering.

Abelia, Buddleia, Ceanthus veitchianus, Cistus, Daboecia, Deutzia scabra and vs., *Genista, Helianthemum, Hibiscus, Hydrangea, Hypericum, Lavendula, Magnolia grandiflora, Olearia haastii, Potentilla fruticosa* and vs., *Rhus, Rosa, Romneya, Senecio laxifolius, Spiraea ×* 'Anthony Waterer', *Tamarix, Veronica, Yucca.*

Shrubs for Autumn Flowering.

Caryopteris, Ceratostigma wilmottianum, Clethra, Cortaderia, Calluna, Erica cinerea, E. vagans, E. terminalis, Fuchsia, Hibiscus syriacus, Hydrangea sargentiana, H. villosa, Veronica × 'Autumn Glory', *Viburnum tinus.*

Shrubs for Autumn–Winter Berries.

Amelanchier, Arbutus unedo, Berberis × 'Buccaneer', *B. aggregata* and vs., *B. darwinii, B. rubrostilla, Callicarpa giraldiana, Clerodendron trichotomum, Cotoneaster, Crataegus, Daphne mezereum, Euonymus europaeus* and vs., *E. planipes, Hippophae, Ilex, Leycesteria, Malus, Mahonia, Pernettya, Pyracantha, Rosa moyesii, R. pomifera, Stranvaesia, Symphoricarpos, Viburnum davidii, V. opulus* and vs.

Shrubs for Foliage Colour.

Cornus alba v. *elegantissima, C. spathi aurea, Corokia virgata, Corylus purpurea, Eleagnus pungens* v. *variegata, Berberis thunbergii* v. *atropurpurea, Ilex,* variegated vs., *Rhus continus* and vs., *Santolina, Sambucus nigra* v. *aurea.*

Shrubs for Autumn Foliage Colour.

Amelanchier, Aronia, Azalea, Berberis thunbergii, B. aggregata and vs., *Cornus florida, C. kousa, C. mas, Enkianthus, Eucryphia, Euonymus europaeus* and vs., *Fothergilla, Hamamelis mollis, Rhus, Ribes aureum, Viburnum opulus, V. lanatum.*

Shrubs for Colourful Bark.

Cornus alba and vs., *C. stolonifera,*

Kerria japonica, Rubus cockburnianus, R. thibetanus, Salix alba v. *chermesina,* and others.

For the cultivation, planting, pruning and propagation of the species, see individual entries.

Siberian Crab. See *Malus prunifolia.*

Sibthorpia (sib-thorp'i-a. Fam. Scrophulariaceae). Prostrate, creeping perennial herbs with tiny flowers.

Selection. S. europaea, Cornish Moneywort, W. England, Ireland, SW. Europe, pink and yellow flowers, July, and v. *variegata,* pretty leaves; and *peregrina,* Madeira, yellow flowers.

Cultivation. Best grown in a cool greenhouse, in pots or hanging baskets, standard compost, planted March–April; easily propagated by division or cuttings, spring or early summer.

Sidalcea, Greek Mallow (si-dal'ke-a. Fam. Malvaceae). Pretty, summerflowering perennials of western N. America for the herbaceous border.

Selection. The chief plants grown are selected forms of *S. malvaeflora,* California, for their 3–4 ft, graceful tapering spikes of mallow-like flowers, such as 'Brilliant', crimson red; 'Croftway Red', deep red; 'Elsie Heugh', satinpink; 'Interlaken', silver-pink; 'Rev. Page Roberts', pale pink; 'Rose Queen', rose-pink; and 'William Smith', salmon pink. *S. candida,* white, is sometimes offered.

Cultivation. Plant November–April, well-drained ordinary soil, humusenriched, and sun.

Propagation. By division in March; by cuttings, summer.

Side-saddle Flower. See *Sarracenia.*

Signatus (-a, -um). Well-marked. Ex. *Tagetes signata.*

Silene (si-le'ne. Fam. Caryophyllaceae). A large genus, containing annuals, biennials and herbaceous and evergreen perennials, of floral merit.

Selection. The chief annual, *S. pendula,* S. Europe, bright rose flowers, May–September, is hardy, and vs. *alba,* white, *ruberrima,* ruby-red, and 'Peach Blossom', pink, are trailing, to 6 in. high, and *compacta,* a dwarf rose cushion; may be sown where they are to flower in March, or the previous September, ordinary well-drained, sunwarmed soil. *S. ameria,* Europe, 1 ft,

purple, rose or white, summer; and *compacta,* Asia Minor, S. Russia, 1 ft, rose, are biennials to be sown in late summer, well-drained soil.

The evergreen hardy perennials include *S. acaulis,* the native Moss Campion, 2 in., reddish-purple, pink or white corolla, May–June; and vs. *alba,* white, and *exscapa,* Pyrenees, light pink; *cretica,* Mediterranean region, 6 in., notched petals, pink; and *elongata,* Alps, 2 in., bright pink; while herbaceous kinds are *S. hookeri,* California, 3 in., cut-petalled pink flowers, May–July; *keiskei,* Japan, 2 in., pale purple, July–August; *saxifraga,* S. Europe, 8 in., white to red, summer; and *schafta,* S. Europe, Asia Minor, 6 in., magentarose, July–October.

Cultivation. Plant evergreen perennials in March–April, well-drained, humus-rich scree in rock garden, herbaceous perennials October–November or March–April. May also be grown in the cold alpine house.

Propagation. By seeds, when ripe. By division in early April. By cuttings of young shoots, July, in cold frame or under handlight.

Silica (silicon dioxide [SiO$_2$]). A hard insoluble mineral very abundant in soils as flint, quartz and rock-crystal; and in combination with other elements as silicates. Although found in all plants, especially in grasses and horse-tails, its role as a nutrient is not well understood or apparent. Silicates formed with potassium and sodium are important sources of these nutrients to plants.

Siliqua. The long, pod-like fruiting capsules of Cruciferae. A siliqua as broad, or more, as long is termed a Silicula.

Silk Bark Oak. See *Grevillea robusta.*

Silk Vine. See *Periploca gracea.*

Silphium (sil'pi-um. Fam. Compositae). Tall, rather coarse growing hardy perennials with resinous sap, from N. America, with large corymbose panicles of yellow flowers, July–August.

Selection. S. laciniatum, the Compass Plant, or Pilot Plant, to 6 ft, interesting because its young leaves turn to face north and south; and *terebinthinaceum,* the Prairie Dock, to 10 ft, Canada, are possible back-of-the-border subjects.

Cultivation. Plant October–March, well-drained, ordinary soil in borders or wild garden.

Propagation. By seeds, outdoors, in March–April. By division in March.

Silt. Technically, soil particles between 0·02 and 0·002 millimetres (1/1200 and 1/12000 in.) in diameter; smaller than sand, larger than clay particles; usually of alluvial deposits, relatively inert. Silt soils benefit from marling and humus manuring.

Silver Cedar. See *Juniperus virginiana glauca*.

Silver Fir. See *Abies*.

Silver Leaf. A fungus disease caused by *Stereum purpureum*, the spores of which gain entry to trees, particularly Apples, Pears, Cherries, Peaches, Plums and Stone Fruit trees, Poplars, and other ornamentals, through wounds or lesions, and grow under the bark, causing the foliage to appear glazed and silvery. The fungus itself does not develop until the attacked branches die, when ranges of purple, overlapping fungus scales break through the bark. Current treatment consists of (*a*) cutting away all dead wood on an affected tree and burning it, preferably before mid July; (*b*) heavy, balanced manuring of the roots with a compound fertilizer and rotted manure or compost; (*c*) if possible, slitting of the bark of the tree in May or early June, on the north side of main branches and stem, in single joining cuts to ground level; (*d*) no removal of silvered branches for a year until the results of the treatment can be assessed. Pruning cuts should be painted with a tree paint.

Silver Sand. *See* Sand.

Silybum (sil'i-bum. Fam. Compositae). The chief species grown is *S. marianum*, S. Europe, N. Africa, The Blessed, Holy or Our Lady's Milk Thistle, 1–4 ft, a hardy annual, with large, white-spotted, spiny lobed leaves, and purple flower-heads, summer; to be grown from seeds, sown in March, any well-drained, sun-warmed soil, thinned to 18 in. apart.

Sinapis (sin'ap-is. Fam. Cruciferae). Annual herbs of which *S. alba*, Mustard, Mediterranean region, 1–2 ft, may be grown as a green manure crop on soils free of Club-root disease. *S. arvensis*, Charlock, Europe, is a persistent weed.

Sinarundinaria (sin-a-run-din-ar'i-a. Fam. Gramineae). A genus of woody-stemmed grasses of the bamboo type, native to China; leafless erect stems the first year, heavily foliaged at the top the second. Formerly grouped under *Arundinaria*.

Selection. *S. murielae*, 6–13 ft, rich green leaves, and *nitida*, 4–10 ft, are attractive and reasonably hardy.

Cultivation. Plant April–May, in humus-rich, loam soil, partial shade and wind shelter, with fairly moist soil.

Propagation. By division, April–May. Stems may be cut for garden canes in early winter, when mature.

Sinensis (-e). Chinese. Ex. *Corylopsis sinensis*.

Sink Gardens. Small gardens usually made in discarded domestic stone sinks or animal feeding troughs. Construction entails scouring the base with drainage channels to the outlet, covering the base with drainage crocks, broken stone or clinker; a layer of leaves or fibrous peat, and then a porous soil medium (say 2 parts by bulk sandy loam, 1 part peat or leaf-mould, 1 part grit or coarse sand) and a mixture of 3 parts by weight bone meal and 1 part sulphate of potash at 4 oz. per bushel, in which are set chosen small rocks to simulate an alpine outcrop or ravine. Dwarf alpines may then be planted in spring. *See* Alpine House, Alpine Plants.

Sinningia, Gloxinia (sin-ning'i-a. Fam. Gesneriaceae). A genus of tuberous-rooted, herbaceous plants, native to Brazil, and esteemed for their richly textured, beautiful, coloured tubular flowers, arising from among magnificent, stalked, often velvety leaves. Modern Gloxinias are largely hybrids of *S. speciosa* and *S. barbarata* and other species, and are offered in named forms such as 'Étoile de Feu', crimson red; 'Mont Blanc', white; 'Prince Albert', blue-purple; 'Princess Mary', ruby red, white-edged; 'Queen Wilhelmina', orchid purple; and 'Scarlet Pimpernel', scarlet red; or in vari-coloured strains such as 'Sutton's Perfection', 'Blackmore and Langdon' or 'Triumph', which may be raised from seeds.

Cultivation. Start tubers into growth in January–March, in warm greenhouse, at 18° C. (65° F.), in a mixture of equal parts moist peat and sand; pot singly in 5- or 6-in. pots, when growth has begun, standard compost, well-drained pots, to grow on at 15·5° C. (60° F.), fairly near to the glass, watering increasingly with growth. Shade from hot direct sun. Give dilute liquid feed when coming to flower, weekly. After flowering, gradually withhold water, and when foliage withers, withhold water, keep dry (10° C. [50° F.] minimum), until time to restart.

Propagation. By seeds, sown February–March, standard compost, bottom heat of 18–21° C. (65–70° F.); transplanting to small 3-in. pots, and then to larger pots as growth warrants. By cuttings of shoots, 1–2 in. long, in summer, under bell-glass. By young leaves, with stalks inserted in a sandy-loam-peat compost under bell-glass; by matured leaves, with midribs cut at junctions on the undersides, with a razor-blade, laid and pegged on the surface of a sand-peat soil; in all cases with temperatures of 18–24° C. (65–75° F.), watering with care, until plantlets are in being; transferring when of easily handled size to pots.

Sino-. Prefix of compound words, signifying Chinese. Ex. *Gentiana sino-ornata.*

Sinus. A recess between two lobes. Sinuate, with recessed margin, Ex. *Statice sinuata.*

Sisyrinchium (si-si-rink'i-um. Fam. Iridaceae). Slender-stemmed, tuberous-rooting, linear-leaved perennials, known as the Satin Flowers of N. and S. America, with open, bell-like flowers in clusters.

Selection. S. angustifolium, Blue-eyed Grass, easily naturalized, 9 in., bright blue, summer; *bellum,* 6 in., evergreen, violet-blue, yellow throated, summer; *bermudiana,* 1 ft, violet-blue, May–June; *douglasii,* Spring Bell, herbaceous, 8 in., deep purple, and v. *alba,* white, March; *filifolium,* Falkland Is., 8 in., white, with pink, May; *striatum,* Chile, to 2 ft, yellow, June.

Cultivation. Plant October–November, or March, well-drained, lightish soil, with humus, sun; in rock terrace or small border. May also be grown in pots in the alpine house.

Propagation. By seeds, when ripe if possible, or in March–April, sandy loam

seed-bed, out of doors. By division in late March or April.

Sium. The only species grown is *S. sisarum,* or Skirret (q.v.).

Skimmia (skim'mi-a. Fam. Rutaceae). Hardy evergreen shrubs, with sweetly scented clusters of small white flowers, spring, followed by red berries, persisting all winter, on female or bisexual hybrid plants.

FIG. 206 *Skimmia × foremanii.*

Selection. S. japonica, Japan, 3–5 ft, unisexual flowers; highly scented in male vs. *fragrans* and *macrophylla;* × *foremanii,* 3 ft, reputedly bisexual berrying form; *reevesiana,* Japan, China, 2 ft, bisexual, crimson berries; and v. *rubella,* red-stalked, male; × *rogersii,* 3 ft, bisexual, crimson berries.

Cultivation. Plant October–November, or March, well-drained, peat-enriched soil, sun or shade; accompanying female plants with a male if berrying is wanted.

Propagation. By cuttings of young firm shoots, July–August, in a shady corner, or under handlight. By seeds, March–April, but slow to make good plants.

Skipjack. Common name for Click Beetles (*Agriotes, Athous* spp.), which are wireworms in larval form.

Skirret (*Sium sisarum*, Fam. Umbel-liferae). A hardy perennial of Altai, Siberia, sometimes grown for its clusters of white, cylindrical, tuberous roots, with sweet, earthy flavour, cooked like Salsify. Seeds are sown in March, in a porous, lightish soil, ½ in. deep, in drills 18 in. apart, and thinned to 12 in. apart; to lift the roots from September onwards. The outer roots can be kept under cool conditions (7° C. [45° F.]) for replanting like dahlia tubers.

Slater. See Woodlice.

Slime Fungi or Moulds (Myxomycetes). A division of flowerless plants, once classed in the Animal Kingdom, charac-terized by a motile mass of protoplasm, the plasmodium, producing spores. The majority are saprophytic, living in damp or wet places, and soils. An exception is *Plasmodiophora brassicae*, the slime fungus responsible for Club-root disease in Cruciferae.

Slipper Flower. See *Calceolaria*.

Slips. Pieces of a plant removed for propagation; usually reserved for stems, etc., with a few roots.

Sloe. See *Prunus spinosa*.

Slow-worm, Blind-worm (*Anguis fragilis*). A legless, harmless, viviparous lizard, to be welcomed in the garden as it feeds on slugs, insects and worms.

Slugs. Terrestrial mollucs, related to the land snails, limpets and whelks, of the class Gastropoda. Although scaveng-ing and living on rotting organic matter, they are also destructive of garden plants, especially the more succulent and tenderly young. There are seventeen British species, the commonest being the Black Slug, *Arion ater*; the Garden Slug, *A. hortensis*; the Field Slug, *Agriolimax agrestis*, *A. reticulatus*; though colouring may range from mottled greys, browns, yellows, to red and black. The Keeled or subterranean soil-frequenting black Slugs, *Milax gagates*, *M. sowerbii*, do much damage to potatoes, roots and tubers. Their natural enemies are hedgehogs, slow-worms, shrews, moles, toads, certain birds (ducks, rooks, starlings, for instance) and the carnivorous snail-slugs (*Testacella* spp.), distinguished by a small, ear-shaped, flat shell at the rear end. They are nevertheless difficult to eradicate completely, especially on damp soils, under moist conditions and where organic rubbish accumulates. They are nocturnal in habit. On vacant ground, a dressing of equal parts by weight powdered copper sulphate and ground limestone, at 1 lb. per 20 sq. yds, a fortnight before cropping, is helpful. The same mixture can be laid at the base of walls, fences or boundaries where slugs hide. Newly planted seedlings and growing plants may be protected by using metaldehyde or 4% methiocarb (Draza) bait pellets, or watering plants and soil with a metaldehyde suspension solution. Trapping with halves of grapefruit or orange skins is useful, if the traps are emptied each morning. Older controls are rings or bands of ground lime, soot or dry ashes, as barriers to slug invasion.

Slugworms. The larvae of Sawflies of the *Eriocampa* genus, which skeletonize leaves, especially of Cherry, Pear and Rose (q.v.).

Smilacina (smi-la-ki'na. Fam. Lili-aceae). Hardy herbaceous perennials, related to Polygonatum, from N. America.

Selection. S. *racemosa*, False Spikenard, 2–3 ft, lanceolate leaves and panicles of creamy white flowers, May; and *stellata*, Star-flowered Lily-of-the-Valley, 1–2 ft, white dense racemes of May flowers.

Cultivation. Plant September–October in moist loam, humus-rich, and shade.

Propagation. By division of the roots, autumn. By seeds, sown April, outdoors.

Smilax (smi'laks. Fam. Liliaceae). Hardy perennials which climb by means of tendrils, with prominently veined ornamental leaves, and umbels of green-ish, unisexual flowers.

Selection. S. *excelsa*, Far East, to 40 ft, with thorny stems; *hispida*, E. N. America, to 50 ft, deciduous; and *rotundifolia*, the Horse Briar of N. America, to 40 ft, deciduous. S. *aspera*, evergreen, S. Europe, zigzag stems, narrow leaves, fragrant, pale-green flowers, August–September, may be grown in a cool greenhouse.

Cultivation. Plant October–March, to climb into tall trees, almost any soil.

Propagation. By division, autumn or spring.

For 'Smilax' of the Florist, see *Asparagus medeoloides*.

Smoke Tree. See *Rhus cotinus*.

Smoke Wood. See *Clematis vitalba*.

Smokes, Insecticidal. The control of insect pests in greenhouses by the use of smoke-generating candles or pellets is simple, economical and efficient. The smoke, impregnated with a chosen insecticide, penetrates freely and deposits a fine film of the insecticide on plant surfaces.

Azobenzene Smokes are used to control Red Spider Mites and their eggs on Tomatoes, Beans, Nectarines, Peaches, Carnations, Cucumbers, Melons, Arum Lilies, and Bulbs, but not on Gerbera, Asparagus Ferns, Pilea, Roses, Schizanthus, seedlings or young plants.

Gamma BHC (Lindane) Smokes may be used to control Aphids, Capsid Bugs, Caterpillars, Leaf-miners, Moths, Thrips and White-fly, except on Roses, young Tomatoes, Hydrangea, Vines and Cucurbits (Cucumbers, Melons, etc.), or food plants within two days of harvesting.

Gamma BHC/DDT Smokes may be used similarly for the above pests, but not within two days of harvesting from food plants.

Nicotine Smokes have a high, short-lived toxicity to most insect pests, but should be used carefully and strictly to the maker's instructions. The Smoke Generators, Candles or Pellets are placed on the greenhouse floor, in numbers calculated according to the cubic capacity of the house, at regular spacings, the ventilators closed, and after igniting, left with door closed overnight.

Smut. A term used for diseases caused by parasitic fungi of the *Ustiginales* group, from the mass of black spores released. Ex. Onion Smut (q.v.).

Snail Flower. See *Phaseolus caracalla*.

Snails. Gastropod relations of Slugs (q.v.) with similar general habits, but less damaging to plants since they are less abundant and less active, tending to withdraw and seal themselves in their shells in cold or dry weather. Their natural enemies are birds (especially Thrushes), Ground Beetles, etc. The more common are the Garden Snail, *Helix aspersa*, and smaller Strawberry Snail, *H. rufescens*, and Banded Snails, *H. hortensis* and *H. nemoralis*. Control measures are similar to those for slugs,

though hand-picking with a torch after dark is useful on rock gardens.

The Fresh-water Snail, *Limnaea stagnalis*, and the Ramshorn Snail, *Planorbis corneus*, are useful scavengers for the ornamental pool.

Snake's Head. See *Fritillaria meleagris*.

Snapdragon. See *Antirrhinum*.

Sneezewort. See *Achillea ptarmica*.

Snow. Ice crystals formed at high altitudes and falling to earth by gravity. In the garden, snow in winter is basically beneficial, providing a cover to plants against frost damage. Under conditions of thaw and re-freezing, however, a surface ice-crust may form and hinder soil and plant air supply. The weight of snow on tree branches, especially conifers, can cause breakage, unless the snow is shaken off. There is evidence that winter snowfalls subsequently benefit plant growth.

Snow Glory. See *Chionodoxa*.

Snow in Summer. See *Cerastium tomonetosum*.

Snowball Tree. See *Viburnum opulus*.

Snowberry. See *Symphoricarpos*.

Snowdrop. See *Galanthus*.

Snowdrop Tree. See *Halesia carolina*.

Snowflake. See *Leucojum*.

Soap. In the forms of soft soap, a soap solution makes a useful spreading agent to improve the effectiveness of insecticidal sprays. Its use as an insecticidal wash in itself is less effective than modern insecticides.

Soapwort. See *Saponaria*.

Sobralia (so-bra'li-a. Fam. Orchidaceae). Non-tuberous, terrestrial Orchids, with reed-like leafy growths and large showy flowers, resembling those of Cattleya; for the warm or intermediate house.

Selection. S. leucoxantha, Costa Rica, 2½ ft, white, yellow-throated flowers, August; *macrantha*, Mexico, 6 ft, purple and crimson, scented, summer, and several vs.; *ruckeri*, Colombia, 3–6 ft, rose-purple and crimson, summer; *xantholeuca*, central America, to 8 ft, yellow, summer, and vs.; and hybrids such as × *veitchii*, purple, and × *wiganiae*, soft yellow.

Cultivation. Pot in March, rather large pots, well-crocked, compost of 2 parts by bulk fibrous loam, 1 part peat, 1 part charcoal and grit; and give ample li'ʇɥᵷ keeping moist; with winter temp. 13° C. (55° F.) minimum.

Propagation. By division in March.

Soda, Washing (sodium carbonate, $Na_2CO_3.10H_2O$). Sometimes advocated as a Mildew control in solution with water, but copious use may impair the structure of a clay soil. *See* Sodium.

Sodium (Na). Although present in plants in varying amounts, sodium is not considered an essential nutrient of plant growth. In some species, however, it does improve growth, especially when potassium is not sufficiently available, indicating that sodium may replace potassium to some extent for plants such as beet. Soil deficiency of sodium is unlikely, but in excess it increases the stickiness of clay, and leads to some deficiency in calcium.

Sodium Chloride (NaCl). *See* Salt.

Softwood. The timber of coniferous trees.

Soil. The surface layer of the earth in which plants grow, formed by the erosion and disintegration of the rocks of the earth's mantle under the action of weathering forces such as heat, air, water and wind, and the accumulation of decaying plant and animal organic matter, with the organisms that live in and off it. As such, soil consists of five things: inorganic mineral particles; organic matter, air, moisture and a population of living organisms (bacteria, fungi, worms, etc.). From their inter-actions arise the nutrient salts of plant life or fertility. The nature and proportions in which these soil constituents exist determine the degree of fertility and the quality of a soil as a rooting medium for plants.

The inorganic mineral fraction of the soil is the least destructible and most permanent, and as such determines its texture. It is made up of particles which are measured and graded in Britain as follows:

Stones and gravel:	*Diameter* 2 millimetres or more
Coarse Sand:	between 2 and 0·2 mm.
Fine Sand:	between 0·2 and 0·02 mm.
Silt:	between 0·02 and 0·002 mm.
Clay:	less than 0·002 mm.

(1 millimetre = 1/24 in.).

Most soils contain particles of all sizes and different shapes, in varying proportions. They lie with small spaces between them, known as *pore space.* The pore space is important. Through it circulates and moves water and air, and it is penetrated by plant roots, and inhabited by micro- and macro-organisms of the soil. It is here, and on the surfaces of soil particles, that the biochemical activities of the soil take place. The spaces between the larger particles are correspondingly large, and where such particles predominate, a soil tends to be light and easy to work, to be well aerated and to drain freely. Where the smaller particles are pre-dominant, spaces may be smaller too, but the total volume of pore space per cubic inch of soil is greater; and the soil tends to be dense, heavy and hard to work, sticky and moisture-retentive. Although the mineral particles are sources of many plant nutrients, they are only very slowly made soluble and available, though more readily the smaller the particle. Soils are classified according to the dominance of their kinds of particles. Sandy soils are those containing at least 80 per cent sand by weight; they may be light (coarse) or heavy (fine) sand, and gravel or stones. Soils containing 30 per cent or more clay are heavy sticky clay soils. Between the two extremes comes a range of loams; light where there is 15–20 per cent silt and clay; heavy loam where the clay is about 20–30 per cent. Soils containing 30 to more than 50 per cent silt, with sands and little clay, are termed silt soils. To these may be added the calcareous soils, dominated by chalk or limestone; and peat soils formed from bogs or moorlands. Gardeners may also find themselves faced with 'soils' made by municipal tipping or filling-in of waste ground.

The organic matter in a soil provides food and energy for the various organisms engaged in its decomposition. It consists of the remains of plants and animals. As it is rotted, its mineral elements are released to become plant nutrients, and in the process it is trans-formed into tiny fibrous particles and a complex amorphous entity, known as humus, which has profound effects upon the mineral fraction of the soil. Physically it acts as a weak cement, to hold soil particles together, particularly those of clay, in a crumb-like or granular structure; it swells when wetted and acts like a sponge, retaining moisture to the advantage of free-draining light soils; it darkens the soil to make it more absorbent and retentive of the sun's heat, and makes it more resistant to the effects of extreme heat and cold. It is a centre of intense biochemical reactions, resulting in the release of soluble mineral elements from the organic matter from which humus forms, and from other particles of the soil, and acts as a reservoir of plant nutrients. Although humus itself is subject to disintegration to simple end-products, and is a fluctuating and unstable content of a soil, it rarely disappears entirely, since the remains of organisms feeding upon it renew the raw material. Nevertheless, under intensive cultivation the breakdown of organic matter and humus goes forward much more rapidly than in a fallow soil. Humus is the prerequisite to fertility in all soils, and the provision of actively decaying organic matter is vital to gardening success. Humus particles become so fine as to become colloidal; and the humus colloids together with the clay colloids are invaluable to soil fertility, and profoundly influence soil structure. A further factor in influencing soil fertility in terms of the availability of nutrients to plants is soil acidity (*See* pH value). This is chiefly affected by the absence or presence of lime. Lime has also a conditioning effect on soils, in that it causes soil particles to temporarily flocculate or form aggregates, several particles clumping around a particle of lime, for as long as the lime persists. In Britain, especially in regions of high rainfall, the tendency is for soils to become more and more acid, as lime salts are readily soluble and easily lost in drainage. Since the constituents of the soil come together in the greatest concentration and proportions near the surface, fertility tends to be greatest in the top soil, and diminishes with soil depth. Cultivation is therefore chiefly devoted to the top soil. Gardeners are apt to refer to the top soil as the top spit, and the soil beneath as the subsoil

or second spit; though the terms have no scientific significance, for there is no arbitrary or actual division. Air and moisture occupy the pore spaces between soil particles and their crumbs, and must have freedom of movement without one excluding the other. Water is chiefly held as a film on the surfaces of particles, and excess water breaks away drop-like to percolate through the soil and escape in drainage. Without good drainage a soil becomes waterlogged and air is driven out, to the detriment of soil activity and plant root growth. It follows that drainage at depths under the top soil is essential to fertility and plant life, and the first thing to see to when taking a soil into cultivation. Further steps to take when bringing a soil into cultivation are: (1) Check the soil acidity or pH value by test, and amend, if necessary. (2) Improve crumb structure by adding humus-forming organic matter, and for clays, gypsum. (3) Amend texture by adding coarse grit or sand to dense heavy soils, though the effect is limited and best confined to surface soil; and by adding clay or marl to light sandy, gravelly or chalky soils. (4) Apply base fertilization to amend soil weaknesses or deficiencies in plant nutrient material. For fuller information on these points see Chalk, Clay, Drainage, Lime, Peat, pH Scale, Sand, Silt, Soil Analysis.

Soil Analysis. A rough estimate of the physical components of a soil can be obtained by shaking a sample of soil thoroughly with ten times its volume of water in a measuring cylinder and allowing to settle. The mineral particles separate out in layers, small stones and grit at the bottom, then sand, silt and clay, with finer particles of clay in suspension in the water, and organic matter floating at the top. The acid-alkaline balance can be ascertained by testing with a simple colorimetric Soil Testing Outfit. A guide to the nitrogen, potash and phosphorus status can be similarly obtained with a Soil Analysis kit, but where trace mineral deficiency is suspected, it is better to have a soil sample tested professionally. Soil samples should be taken at 2–4 in. below the surface, and be typical of the soil; and if necessary consist of several samples mixed, though a dessertspoonful is ample for testing. A free soil analysis can be obtained through the National Agricultural Advisory Service at County Institutes.

Soil Blocks. Moulded blocks of soil compost for the propagation of plants, dispensing with the use of pots. Composts to the John Innes formulae (*see* Composts) are suitable, moistened to cling and mould under moderate compression in a manual or machine soil-block making apparatus. Properly made, they answer well, and enable plants such as annuals, tomatoes, etc., to be raised without any checks in the greenhouse and frame.

Soil Fumigation. With the intent of eradicating soil-frequenting pests such as Chafer Grubs, Leatherjackets, Wireworms, etc., this may be carried out in autumn or early winter on vacant ground. A simple method is to strew Grade 16 Flake Naphthalene along the base of the trench when digging, at 3–6 oz. per sq. yd (the heavier the rate, the denser the soil), and covering immediately with soil. Paradichlorbenzene crystals may also be used, in early autumn, making holes 9 in. deep, 12 in. apart, and using one level teaspoonful to every six holes, covering with soil at once. Carbon bisulphide as a colourless, inflammable, odorous liquid may be used among plants, to clear root aphids and other soil pests, at one teaspoonful per hole, 12 in. deep and apart, sealing at once.

Soil Sterilization or **Pasteurization.** This implies partial, not complete, sterilization of soil to destroy harmful organisms, fungi, insects, eelworms and weed seeds, without impairing its growing properties for plants. It may be done (*a*) by heat, or (*b*) by chemicals. Heat is the more efficient, and consists of raising the soil temperature to at least 82° C. (180° F.) but not more than 100° C. (212° F.), throughout for ten minutes, as quickly as possible, and then cooling at once. Gardeners can do this best by (*a*) low-pressure steaming, or (*b*) electrical heating. Small quantities of soil can be sterilized by placing ½ in. of water in a large saucepan, which is then filled loosely with sifted, dust-dry soil, brought quickly to the boil, sim-

mered for fifteen minutes, and then the soil is tipped out on to a clean surface to cool and lose excess moisture. Larger quantities can be treated by placing in a perforated bucket, or coarse sack, to be suspended in a domestic wash-boiler, containing up to 3 in. of water. With lid down, the water is boiled for 30–40 minutes, and the soil then tipped out to cool and dry. Proprietary steam sterilizers of various designs may be bought and used to the maker's instructions. The most suitable electric sterilizers are the electrode type, in which the soil is placed between two metal plates in a *moist* condition and current passed through. Baking is not recommended, since it is difficult to heat the soil at the required temperatures without overheating in part. Nor can soil be sterilized satisfactorily in a cooking oven.

Chemical soil sterilization calls for the use of 38–40 per cent formaldehyde (formalin) solution, diluted to a 2 per cent concentration at 1 part to 49 parts of water; or cresylic acid, 97 per cent purity, diluted to 2½ per cent concentration at 1 part to 39 parts water. Both solutions are used similarly, but formaldehyde is most effective in preventing fungus diseases and retarding weed seed germination, and cresylic acid for the control of soil pests. The soil is spread thinly on a clean surface, watered thoroughly with the chosen solution at 1 gallon per bushel of soil, and then heaped, covered with polythene sheeting, or wet sacks, for 25–48 hours; and finally spread again to allow excess moisture to evaporate and fumes to disperse, and the soil is usually ready for use in three weeks, being prepared in an open shed. Only the soil or loam fraction of John Innes composts is sterilized; as peat and sand are sterile enough in themselves.

Soil is sterilized in greenhouse beds *in situ*, first flooding the soil with formaldehyde or cresylic acid solution at 3 gallons per 2 sq. yds; then covering with wet sacks or sheet polythene for 24 hours; after which the soil must be aired and allowed to dry out for three weeks or so before being cultivated and planted. The same method can be used for soil out of doors known to be in need of sterilization. Proprietary soil sterilants are also available, but should be used to the maker's instructions.

Soil-less Gardening. The growing of plants without soil has a history going back to the seventeenth century; but modern soil-less gardening or hydroponics (q.v.), is of the present century. There are broadly two methods: the Hydroponic system developed by Dr F. Gericke of California, in which plants are grown on a wire grid or netting, covered with a 2-in. layer of fibrous peat, wood shavings or similar medium, over shallow, waterproof tanks or troughs, filled with a nutrient solution to within 2 in. of the base of the netting. The plants, from seeds or rooted cuttings, develop roots which enter into and feed on the solution, which in turn is kept refreshed or changed periodically according to the needs of the plant. In Britain this system is little used. The second method is to grow the plants in a suitable inert rooting medium to which a nutrient solution is added, and periodically refreshed. It is simpler and more adaptable. A simple system for the gardener is: Use clean containers or pots, wooden, plastic, concrete or metal construction, about 8 in. deep, with ¼-in. diameter drainage holes, at 6-in. distances, in the case. Fill with an aggregate of about 3 parts by volume gravel, grit, pebbles *or* washed and crushed clinker, graded ¼–⅛ in., to 2 parts by volume clean sand, vermiculite, perlite *or* sifted sedge or moss peat, thoroughly moist by soaking for 24 hours; to within ½ in. of the top. It is most useful to place the containers on trays or strong polythene film, to catch the water for re-use. Seedling plants are simply dibbled into the aggregate after watering well, or may be grown from seeds directly in it, if large. The containers may be placed out of doors, in warm sunny sheltered places, or in a greenhouse. The aggregate is then watered regularly to keep the rooting medium moist. Feeding is done about once weekly, using either a proprietary complete liquid fertilizer, liquid seaweed derivative, or a mixture of 1½ lb. sulphate of ammonia, 1 lb. superphosphate, ¾ lb. sulphate of potash, 7 oz. magnesium sulphate, ⅛ oz. ferrous sulphate, at

1½–2 oz. per gallon water, watered evenly over each square yard of bed. This works well with tomatoes, salad vegetables and most flowers, such as annuals, Chrysanthemums, Fuchsias, Primulas and greenhouse plants. Water and feeding solution draining through the aggregate can be collected and re-used. A more sophisticated system is to arrange for the more or less constant circulation of water and a dilute nutrient solution through the rooting medium, by sub-irrigation or overhead watering, controlled automatically.

Solanum (so-la'num. Fam. Solanaceae). A very large genus which contains the Potato (*S. tuberosum*) and the Aubergine (*S. melongena* v. *esculentum*), and a few ornamental species for the greenhouse or mild garden.

Selection. S. aculeatissimum, Tropics, 1 ft, tender greenhouse annual may be grown from seeds, sown in early spring, in the warm greenhouse, to carry large, scarlet, tangerine-size, glossy fruits, among lobed green leaves, in summer. *S. capsicastrum*, Winter Cherry, Brazil, 1–2 ft, a branching sub-shrub, with orange-red or scarlet berries, and vs., *melvinii*, and *nana*, and strains giving fruits in various colours and shapes; and *pseudocapsicum*, Jerusalem Cherry, Madeira, to 3 ft, scarlet fruits, and v. *weatherillii*, orange, oval pointed fruits, and their hybrids, are grown from seed for winter decoration as pot plants. Seeds are sown in March, bottom heat of 18° C. (65° F.), to be potted in 4½-in. pots by June, standard composts, syringed in bright hot weather, and watered freely, pinching back to promote bushiness; may be placed out of doors to late September in sheltered position; and brought into a cool greenhouse to form fruits, with judicious feeding at 10-day intervals. May be raised afresh from seeds each year; or old plants may be pruned fairly hard in spring and repotted to grow on. Cuttings of young shoots root readily.

S. crispum, the Potato Tree, Chile, to 12 ft, semi-evergreen, blue and yellow flowers, summer; *jasminoides*, the Potato Vine, S. America, deciduous twining climber to 15 ft, bluish white flowers, summer, and v. *floribundum*, freer flowering; *wendlandii*, Costa Rica, climber to 20 ft, with hooked prickles, large lilac-blue flowers, August, may be grown in the cool greenhouse; or attempted as wall plants on sunny, warm south walls in very mild localities. *S. aviculare*, the Kangaroo Apple, Australia, New Zealand, to 6 ft, is a shrub with long lance-shaped leaves, and large yellowish green fruits, autumn.

Cultivation. The climbers and shrubs are planted March–April, in pots or borders of well-drained, humus-rich soils, full sun, and watered freely in growth.

Propagation. By seeds, spring, bottom heat of 18° C. (65° F.). By cuttings of young shoots, spring.

Soldanella (sol-dan-el'la. Fam. Primulaceae). Rhizomatous-rooting, pretty spring-flowering alpine plants for the rock garden or alpine house.

Selection. S. alpina, Blue Moonwort, Pyrenees, E. European Alps, 3 in., wide, bell-shaped, blue, crimson-streaked flowers, April; *minima*, S. Alps, 2 in., pale blue, April, and v. *alba*; *montana*, Alps, 5 in., lavender-blue, April; *pindicola*, Albania, 3 in., rose-lilac, April; and *pusilla*, European Alps, 4 in., lavender-blue, March, are chief species; × *ganderi*, 3 in., pale lilac, March, a fine hybrid.

Cultivation. Plant May or October, well-drained, humus-rich, cool soil, in an open, cool, rather moist spot, light shade in the south; largely free of lime.

Propagation. By careful division after flowering. By seeds as soon as ripe, in summer.

Solidago, Golden Rod (so-li-da'go. Fam. Compositae). Perennial flowering herbs, useful for their late summer and autumn flowering.

Selection. S. canadensis, eastern N. America, 3–6 ft, naturalized in Britain, and *virgaurea*, European and native, to 2 ft, are parents of named forms of Golden Rods, such as *ballardii*, 5–6 ft, golden-yellow; 'Golden Gate', 1½–2 ft, lemon-yellow; 'Goldenmosa', 2½ ft, mimosa yellow; 'Golden Wings', 5–6 ft, deep yellow; 'Lemore', primrose, 2½ ft; and 'Leraft', 2½ ft, bright yellow, for the border; while 'Golden Thumb', 1 ft, deep yellow; and 'Laurin', 1 ft, rich yellow, are dwarf compact forms. *S.*

virgaurea v. *brachystachys*, 6 in., is useful for late colour in the rock garden.

Cultivation. Plant October–April, ordinary garden soil in sun or partial shade.

Propagation. By division, November–March. Species may be raised from seeds, sown in spring, outdoors.

Solitary. Growing singly. Ex. Tulip flower.

Sollya (sol'li-a. Fam. Pittosporaceae). The species, *S. fusiformis*, the Australian Bluebell Creeper, is a twining evergreen climber, to 6 ft, with ovate leaves and drooping cymes of sky-blue, bell-shaped flowers, July; while *parvifolia* is smaller in leaf and flower, deep blue; suitable for the cool greenhouse.

Cultivation. Pot or plant in March, standard compost, or well-drained, peat-enriched bed, in cool greenhouse, watering and syringing freely in active growth; keeping soil just moist in winter, minimum temp. 10° C. (50° F.).

Propagation. By cuttings of young shoots, summer; or by seeds, sown spring, bottom heat of 18° C. (65° F.), in greenhouse or frame, standard compost.

Solomon's Seal. See *Polygonatum.*

Soot. The carbonaceous deposit from chimneys serving coal fires, valued by old-time gardeners as a fertilizer, chiefly containing variable amounts of nitrogen (average is 4 per cent) as salts of ammonia, and a little potash. Somewhat caustic when fresh, but may be applied to vacant soil. After standing for 2–3 months under cover, it may be used to feed growing plants at 6 oz. per sq. yd. Its odour tends to deter insect pests such as Fly from Brassica, Carrot and Onion crops, if applied in late April–May. Ringed around plants, it deters slugs. Should not be mixed with lime, except when used as a mild soil fumigant, strewn down the digging trench liberally, topping with a good sprinkling of lime and the soil. Helpful on chalk and light-coloured soils for darkening them, and making more absorbent of sun warmth; while the absorbent carbon is beneficial on clays. *Soot Water*, made by suspending soot in a sack in a tub of water for a few days, is a useful liquid 'feed' for growing plants.

Sophora (sop'or-a. Fam. Leguminosae). A genus of shrubs or trees with unequally pinnate leaves, and racemes or panicles of papilionaceous flowers.

Selection. S. *japonica*, the deciduous Pagoda Tree, China, Japan, to 30 ft, with creamy-white flowers, September, and its vs. *pendula*, a picturesque weeping form; *pubescens*, small-leaved; *variegata*, creamy-white edged leaves; and *violacea*, flowers rose coloured, are hardy; but *macrocarpa*, Chile, evergreen tree to 30 ft, yellow flowering, May; *tetraptera*, Chile, New Zealand, semi-evergreen, 20–30 ft, golden yellow, May; and vs. *grandiflora*, larger flowers; and *microphylla*, smaller leaves; are sometimes placed under *Edwardia* and are only hardy for warm, sunny, sheltered quarters in frost-free, mild localities, though sometimes pot-grown in a cold greenhouse.

Cultivation. Plant October–November or March–April, in well-drained, humus-rich loam; warm sun; dressing soil with bone meal or basic slag.

Propagation. By seeds, sown April, with slight bottom heat of 15·5° C. (60° F.).

Sophrocattleya (so-pro-kat'leu-a. Fam. Orchidaceae). Dwarf hybrid orchids between *Sophronitis* and species of *Cattleya*, winter-flowering.

Selection. S. *batemanniana*, scarlet, rose, crimson and white flowers; *calypso*, yellow and rose-purple; *hardyana*, red, purple and yellow; and 'Queen Empress', rose, crimson and purple.

Cultivation. As for *Cattleya* (q.v.).

Sophronitis (so-pro-ni'tis. Fam. Orchidaceae). Dwarf, tufted, epiphytic orchids of the Organ Mts, Brazil, of which S. *coccinea* (*grandiflora*), with brilliant scarlet flowers in winter, and its vs., are chiefly grown.

Cultivation. Pot in March, in a shallow pan, using equal parts fibrous peat and live sphagnum moss, with charcoal, over crocks; water freely in summer, shade from hot sun; keep just moist in winter, minimum temp. 13° C. (50° F.).

Propagation. By occasional division in March–April.

Sorbaria (sor-ba'ri-a. Fam. Rosaceae). Hardy deciduous shrubs with long pinnate leaves, and large panicles of small white flowers, July–August; akin to Spiraea.

Selection. S. *aitchisonii*, Afghanistan, Kashmir, to 10 ft; *arborea*, China, to

20 ft; *assurgens*, China, to 10 ft; and *sorbifolia*, Asia, 4 ft, are hardy.

Cultivation. Plant November–March, ordinary loam soil, full sun. Flowered shoots may be cut back hard in February–March, to keep plants compact.

Propagation. By seeds, sown April, outdoor seed-bed. By suckers, when produced.

× **Sorbaronia** (sor-ba-ro'ni-a. Fam. Rosaceae). Hybrid shrubs of *Sorbus aria* with species of *Aronia*.

Selection. × S. *alpina*, to 6 ft, leaves white underneath, white flowers, May, red fruits; × S. *dippelii*, to 6 ft, grey-felted shoots, white flowers, rosy anthers, May, purple fruits.

Cultivation. Plant November–March, ordinary soil of loam quality, sun.

× **Sorbopyrus** (sor-bo-pi'rus. Fam. Rosaceae). Hybrids of *Sorbus aria* and *Pyrus communis*, of which × S. *auricularis*, the Bollwyller Pear of Alsace, deciduous tree of 30 ft, ovalish leaves, grey-felted beneath, clusters of white, rose-red anthered flowers, May, followed by small red pears, is best known. Cultivation as for *Sorbus* (q.v.).

Sorbus (sorb'us. Fam. Rosaceae). Deciduous shrubs and trees, formerly under Pyrus, falling into two groups: (1) Aria, Whitebeam, with simple alternate leaves; and (2) Aucuparia, Rowan, with pinnate leaves; both handsome in leaf and fruit.

Selection. Aria Group: S. *alnifolia*, Korea, erect, to 40 ft, bright red fruits, autumn leaf colour; *aria*, Whitebeam, Europe, Britain, to 50 ft, leaves white beneath, red fruits, and vs. *chrysophylla*, yellow-leaved; *decaisneana* (*majestica*), fine large-leaved; *domestica*, Europe, to 60 ft, large fruits; *lutescens*, yellow-leaved; and *pendula*, a weeping form; *folgneri*, China, to 25 ft, narrow leaved, white felted; × *hybrida*, 30–40 ft, fine-leaved; *intermedia*, Swedish Whitebeam, to 40 ft, good for exposed places; and *torminalis*, Wild Service Tree, Europe, Britain, to 70 ft, handsome foliage, autumn colours, brown speckled fruits. Aucuparia Group: S. *americana*, American Rowan or Mountain Ash, to 25 ft, autumnal leaf colours; *aucuparia*, Rowan, Mountain Ash, Europe, Britain, to 50 ft, bright red fruits, beloved by birds, and vs.

asplenifolia, leaflets deeply toothed; *edulis*, large edible fruits; and *xanthocarpa*, yellow berries; *cashmiriana*, Himalaya, to 35 ft, fern-like leaves, glistening white berries; *discolor*, China, to 35 ft, red autumnal colour, whitish fruits; *esserteauiana*, China, to 50 ft, long leaves, downy beneath, colouring in autumn, fine pillar-box red fruit clusters; *hyphensis*, China, to 40 ft, autumn colour, pink-tinted white fruits; *matsumurana*, Japanese Mountain Ash, to 25 ft, autumn colour, orange-red fruits; *pohuashanensis*, N. China, to 30 ft, for its orange-red fruits; *prattii*, China, 25 ft, fine, fern-like leaves, creamy white fruits; *rufo-ferruginea*, Japan, to 40 ft, pyramidal for avenue planting; and *sargentiana*, China, to 30 ft, large leaves, scarlet fruits. *S. tianshanica*, central Asia, tall shrub or small tree to 14 ft, highly attractive in flower in May, bright red fruits; and *vilmorinii*, China, many leafleted leaves, rosy-pink fruits, may be grown as shrubs or small trees, while *S. reducta*, W. China, 6–24 in., is a dense shrub, with pinnate leaves, terminal flowers in May and crimson fruits worth trying.

Cultivation. Plant in November–March, in any well-drained soil, limy or not, in sun to flower and fruit well.

Propagation. Species by seeds, sown in March, after stratification, in outdoor seed-bed. Varieties and hybrids by grafting of seedling stocks of *S. aucuparia*.

Sorrel (*Rumex acetosa*). A broad-leafed form of this herb may be grown to provide tangy leaves for salads or a spinach substitute, from seeds sown in drills, 15 in. apart, March–April, thinned to 9 in. apart, in reasonably rich loam soil, cutting back flower stems to encourage leafing. A perennial, the plant may be propagated by division in March.

Sorus. A group of spore-heaps (sporangia) on the frond of a fern. Plural: Sori.

Southernwood. See *Artemisia abrotanum.*

Sowbread. See *Cyclamen.*

Sow-Bugs. *See* Woodlice.

Sowing. The placing of seeds in a rooting medium to germinate and grow. Seeds may be sown by placing in prepared holes, in lines in drills, or broadcast, and covering with soil or sand to the required depth. The sowing of fine seeds may be facilitated by mixing with fine dry sand, or using a seed-sowing device that can be set to mete out the seed according to its size. In drilling seeds, it is useful to use a seed-drill machine where many seeds have to be sown. Broadcasting seeds to sow an area such as a lawn by hand needs a little skill, and for large areas a 'fiddle sower' is helpful. For gardeners, the growing practice of pre-sowing seeds in paper tape or sheeting promises precision, since the seeds are placed correctly spaced, and may be accompanied by fertilizer in the readily decomposed paper, which is placed in or on the soil.

Spade. The most useful tool for digging, consisting of a broad steel blade, with bottom cutting edge, attached to a handle, fitted with a T, D, or Y-shaped handgrip. There are various sizes and patterns, and time and trouble should be taken in choosing a tool of the right feel, size and weight. A stainless steel blade obviates a lot of cleaning; a steel blade should be scraped, cleaned and oiled after use. Continental and American gardeners prefer a long-handled spade, providing good leverage, and there is much to be said for it. Spring-loaded spades take some of the labour out of digging, but do not permit the breaking up of the soil thoroughly. See Digging.

Spadix. A spike-like fleshy inflorescence, usually bearing male and female flowers, within a spathe, as in the Arum. (*See* Fig. 207, page 510.)

Spanish Broom. See *Spartium junceum.*

Spanish Chestnut. See *Castanea sativa.*

Spanish Iris. See *Iris xiphium.*

Sparaxis (spa-raks'is. Fam. Iridaceae). A small genus of cormous plants from S. Africa, with showy flowers in spring.

Selection. S. grandiflora, 1–1½ ft, violet-purple star-petalled flowers, April, and vs. *liliago*, white; *stellaris*, purple; *tricolor*, 1–1½ ft, brown, orange red and yellow, and vs.; and vari-coloured forms. May.

Cultivation. Plant 2–3 in. deep, well-drained, humus-rich light soil, in rock gardens, very mild localities, in September; otherwise in pots in the cool greenhouse.

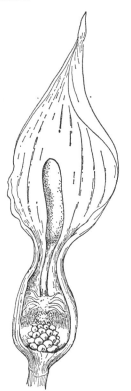

FIG. 207   Spadix, and spathe (*Arum* sp.).

Propagation. By offsets, September.

Sparmannia (spar-man'ni-a. Fam. Tiliaceae). The species grown, *S. africana*, the African Hemp or Linden, S. Africa, is a quick-growing, handsome-leaved shrub, 4–15 ft, with conspicuous cymous umbels of white flowers, finely staminate, April–May, for pot growth, in the cool greenhouse or indoor room; potted, and repotted, in June, standard compost, to stand outdoors to September. Propagated by cuttings of firm shoots in spring, rooting readily, with bottom heat of 18° C. (65° F.).

Spartium (spar'ti-um. Fam. Leguminosae). The only species, *S. junceum*, the Spanish Broom of the Mediterranean and Canaries, 6–9 ft, green rush-like shoots, bright yellow, fragrant flowers, summer, and paler v. *orchroleucum*, do well in porous, lightish soil and sunny shelter, except in cold districts, with protection against rabbits. Prune in March to induce bushiness. Propagate from seeds, in March, to plant out from pots.

Spathe. A large bract enclosing one or more flowers (*see* Fig. 207). Ex. Narcissus, Arum and Cocos.

Spathiphyllum (spa-thi-pil'lum. Fam. Araceae). Stemless evergreen herbs of tropical America, of which *S. wallisii*, Peace Lily, Colombia, with broad, lance-shaped, glossy green, stalked leaves, and 12-in. flower-stem with a white spathe and flower spadix, summer; and *patinii*, Colombia, similar but larger leaved, are grown as warm greenhouse or house plants.

Cultivation. Pot, and repot, March, standard compost, to grow in shady position, with humidity, summer temp. 23° C. (75° F.); watering copiously, and feeding fortnightly; more moderate watering in winter, temp. 18° C. (65° F.).

Propagation. By division in March.

Spathulatus (-a, -um). Spatulate; oblong, narrowing at the lower end. Ex. *Iris spathulata* (*spuria*).

Spawn. The mass of hyphae that make up the mycelium of a fungus. The term is used to describe pieces of the mycelium

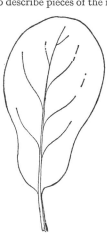

FIG. 208   Spathulate leaf.

of the cultivated Mushroom, now propagated in pure culture form. Spawning is the act of placing the pieces in the bed.

Spearmint. See *Mentha*, Mint.

Spearwort. See *Ranunculus lingua*.

Species. The smallest group of individuals in the Classification of living things, which have the same constant and distinctive characters, and most able to breed among themselves; collectively the species comprise the genus (q.v.).

Specific Epithet. The part of the botanical plant name which is peculiar to the species; following the name of the genus, and now written with a small, not a capital, letter.

Speciosus (-a, -um). Showy, beautiful. Ex. *Lobelia speciosa*.

Spectabilis (-e). Admirable, showy. Ex. *Sedum spectabile*.

Specularia (spek-u-la′ri-a. Fam. Campanulaceae). The species chiefly grown, *S. speculum*, Venus's Looking Glass, Europe, 1 ft, purple, bell-like flowers, summer, and its vs. *alba*, white; *grandiflora*, blue, are hardy annuals, to be sown in March–April, in light, porous soil and sun, where to flower.

Speedwell. See *Veronica*.

Spermaphyta. Seed plants; a division of the Plant Kingdom that includes the Gymnosperms (q.v.) and the Angiosperms (q.v.). *See* Classification.

Sphagnum (spag′num, Sphagnales). A genus of many species of bog mosses, found in swampy, stagnant water and cold conditions throughout the cold temperate zones, including north and west Britain. Accumulations over innumerable years have led to the formation of peat beds, a source of humus-forming material to the gardener. Because of its moisture-absorbent and retentive properties, sphagnum is also much used in Orchid-growing, and as a material for packing living plants; may also be used as a germinating medium for seeds, finely chopped.

Spicatus (-a, -um). Spike-like. Ex. *Lavendula spicata*.

Spider Flower. See *Cleome*.

Spider Orchid. See *Ophrys*.

Spiders. Zoologically spiders belong to the Class Arachnida (Order Araneae), which also includes Gall-mites, Mites and Scorpions. True Spiders are predatory on insects, and therefore beneficial in a gardening sense. Red Spiders, parasitic on plants, are Mites. *See* Red Spider Mites.

Spiderwort. See *Tradescantia* × *andersoniana*.

Spigelia (spi-ge′li-a. Fam. Loganiaceae). Only *S. marilandica*, Indian Pink, Pink Root, Worm Grass, N. America, 1–1½ ft, is much grown as a hardy perennial with handsome red and yellow, salver-shaped flowers, July; planted in peaty, well-drained soil, partial shade, in March; and propagated by cuttings in spring.

Spike. An inflorescence bearing stalkless (sessile) flowers on an unbranched stem (axis). Ex. Hyacinth.

Spikelet. A secondary spike, usually of florets on grasses and sedges.

Spinach (*Spinacia oleracea*). Introduced from East Mediterranean and Iranian regions in the sixteenth century, Spinach is an annual, grown for its leaves, and highly rated for its vitamin and mineral contents.

Varieties. There are two kinds, the round-seeded, for spring and summer sowings, such as 'Monstrous Viroflay', 'Reliance', 'Monarch Long Standing', and 'Cleanleaf'; and the prickly-seeded, for late summer sowing for winter crops, such as 'Sutton's Greenmarket', 'Long-standing Prickly'; all varieties with some resistance to bolting or premature flowering.

Cultivation. Sow for summer crops in late February–July; for winter crops in July–September; ½ in. deep, in drills 12–15 in. apart, thinned to 8 in. apart; in soil that is humus-rich, and unlikely to dry out, dressed with JI base fertilizer, pH 6·0–6·5. Water freely in drought. Harvest by gathering a few leaves from each plant at a time. Protect by cloches in hard winter districts.

Diseases. Downy Mildew (*Peronospora effusa*) may cause yellow patches with greyish mealy down beneath on leaves; best controlled by prompt destruction of leaves, and dusting of plants with a sulphur dust.

Spinach, New Zealand (*Tetragonia expansa*, Fam. Aizoaceae). No relation of Spinach, but a somewhat spreading plant, producing side-shoots with thick fleshy leaves, which are cut to cook as a spinach substitute; esteemed for its ability to grow in dry weather and in soils too hot and porous for Spinach.

Cultivation. Sow seeds under glass in late March, or outdoors in May; spacing plants 2 ft apart in rows 3 ft apart, watering and mulching to induce succulent growth, though the plants stand drought well.

Spinach Beet (*Beta vulgaris* v. *cicla*), also known as Perpetual Spinach, is the plant is a perennial leafy beetroot, producing large, well-ribbed, fleshy leaves, less troublesome to cook and less bitter than Spinach itself.

Cultivation. Sow seeds ½ in. deep, 6 in. apart, in March or August; well-drained, humus-rich soil, prepared as for Beetroot (q.v.); a no-trouble vegetable.

Spindle Tree. See *Euonymus europaeus.*

Spinosus (-a, -um). Spiny. Ex. *Acanthus spinosus.*

Spiraea (spi-re'a. Fam. Rosaceae). A genus of deciduous shrubs which may be divided into two groups: (1) those with white flowers in umbels or racemes, from branches of the previous year's growth, in April–June; and (2) those with pink to crimson, or white, flowers in panicles, produced on the shoots of the current season's growth, June–September.

Selection. Of the first group: *S.* × *arguta,* Bridal Wreath, Foam of May, to 7 ft, white, April–May; *canescens,* Himalaya, 6–12 ft, white, June–July; *hacquetii,* Italy, 8 in., white, June; *henryi,* China, 6–10 ft, white, in rounded clusters, June; *media,* E. Europe, 4 ft, white, April–May, may be forced under glass; *nipponica,* Japan, 6–8 ft, white clusters, June, and vs. *rotundifolia* and *tosaensis; prunifolia* v. *plena,* Japan, 6 ft, double white, May, autumn leaf colour; *thunbergii,* China, 5 ft, white, April, autumn colour; × *vanhouttei,* to 6 ft, white clusters, May; and *veitchii,* China, to 10 ft, white, June. Prune after flowering.

Of the second group; *S.* × *billiardii,* 6 ft, bright rose, summer; *bullata,* Japan, 1 ft, scarlet-rose, July; × *bulmalda,* 1–2 ft, and v. 'Anthony Waterer', carmine, July; *japonica,* Japan, 3–5 ft, rose-red, July, and vs. *fortunei,* pink, and *ruberrima,* deep rose; × *margaritae,* rose-pink, July–August, are garden

worthy, and are pruned severely when dormant.

Cultivation. Plant October–March, in well-cultivated ordinary soil, organically enriched, and in sunny positions. Prune as suggested.

Propagation. By cuttings of firm young shoots, July–August; by layers, or suckering species by division in winter; species by seeds, spring.

For herbaceous Spiraea *see* Astilbe, Neillia, Aruncus, Filipendula; also Sorbaria.

Spiranthes (spi-ran'thes. Fam. Orchidaceae). Lady's Tresses. Terrestrial orchids of which the native *S. aestivalis, spiralis,* etc., are not strictly suitable for modern gardens and are best left in the wild. *S. cernua,* N. America, 1 ft, white, sweet-scented, flowers, September, and *romanzoffiana,* N. America, to 10 in., white, August, are sometimes offered, for limy turf.

Spire Lily. See *Galtonia.*

Spit. A gardener's term for a spade depth of soil in digging.

Spleenwort. See *Asplenium.*

Splendens. Brilliant, gleaming. Ex. *Salvia splendens.*

Sporangium (pl. **Sporangia**). A spore case, or receptacle containing spores. *See* Sorus.

Spore. The reproductive cellular body of a fungus, or flowerless plant (Moss, Fern).

Sport. A somatic mutation, or variation in a shoot or bud growth from the typical growth of the parent plant. A source of many horticultural varieties by vegetative propagation.

Spraguea (spra-gu'e-a. Fam. Portulacaceae). The one species, *S. umbellata,* California, 2 in., a dwarf, half-hardy perennial, with white and rose flowers, July, to be raised from seeds, sown under glass, bottom heat of 21° C. (70° F.), March, planted out in May; and propagated by cuttings, in summer, to overwinter in a cool frame. Any well-drained garden soil, and sun, suit.

Sprayers. Appliances used for chemicals in solution or powder form for fungicidal, insecticidal or feeding purposes should be chosen, not only for their reliability and efficiency, but with regard to the scale on which they will be used, and their purpose. Broadly, the types available to the gardener are: (1) Hand Syringes, useful for small-scale spraying, but tiring for a long-time use. (2) Double-action, Continuous Sprayers, which give a continuous spray with steady pumping, and being fitted with a length of suction hose provide some mobility. (3) Bucket Sprayers, with a pump, provide greater capacity (4) Knapsack Sprayers, giving mobility, but requiring continuous arm-pumping, and becoming tiring. (5) Pneumatic or Compressed-air Sprayers, equipped with a pump whereby pressure is built up in the spray container to give a continuous spray for a time, liberating both hands for manipulation of plants and branches; available in small ½–2-pint hand-held types to 1–3-gallon capacity knapsack or shoulder-carried types. (6) Atomizer Sprayers, usually consisting of glass or plastic containers for attachment to a suitable syringe or air hose or water hose-pipe. Large tank or power sprayers are available for estate gardens and commercial work. The trend is to use plastic materials increasingly in sprayer design, but it is highly important to thoroughly cleanse sprayers after use, to remove toxic residues and to protect metal parts from wear. *See* Spraying. Powder Spraying or Dusting Appliances consist chiefly of (1) Hand Powder Blowers, operated by a bellows action or squeezing operation, useful for small-scale use; (2) Rotary Blowers, which may be hand- or power-operated to give a more or less continuous cloud of dust.

Spraying. The act of applying a solution in finely divided form to plants and/or the soil; either to control parasitic fungi or bacteria, insect parasites, or weeds; or to foliar-feed, or for watering purposes and increasing humidity. It is very important to use sprays correctly and at the proper strength, with full regard to the aim of the spraying. Fungicides should be applied to cover all plant surfaces in fine mist form, and renewed to cover new growth or replace rain-leached material. Insecticides usually need to be applied to come into contact directly with the pests, their larvae or their eggs, and need more forceful application as a rule. Herbicides should be confined to the weeds they are to kill, except where they can be used

with selective action, as on lawns. Foliar feeds are applied to wet foliage and stems. It is wise to wear old or protective clothing and, under glass, a respirator, when much spraying has to be done or a toxic substance used. After use, sprayers and ancillaries should be thoroughly cleaned; filling with a solution of synthetic detergent to stand overnight, and then flushing through with clean water. After using a herbicide, however, a solution of household ammonia (1 tablespoonful per gallon water) is better, or a solution of 1 per cent activated charcoal, followed by washing with clear water. If possible, it is best to use a separate sprayer for herbicides, kept for the purpose.

Spreaders, or **Wetting Agents.** Chemicals added to spray solutions to increase their covering and adherent power as films on plant surfaces. Soft soap is such an agent, but modern spreaders based on saponin, calcium caseinate, etc., are available under proprietary names.

Sprekelia (spre-kel'i-a. Fam. Amaryllidaceae). The only species, *S. formosissima*, the Jacobean Lily, St James's Lily, Mexico and Guatemala, is a bulbous plant with a striking cross-like, crimson flower of six segments, the lower three rolled together, with stamens protruding through, March–April, on 12–18-in. pink stems, and linear leaves developing later. The black-tunicated large bulbs are potted in February–March, standard compost, two-thirds their depth, in 5-in. pots, temp. 18° C. (65° F.), watering freely with growth, in good light and airy conditions, in greenhouse or house. When leaves flag in September, allow to dry off, keeping through the winter at about 10° C. (50° F.). Propagation by offsets, when repotting, February–March. (*See* Fig. 209, page 514.)

Springtails (Ord. *Collembola*). An Order of minute wingless insects, which take sudden leaps into the air; found abundantly in the soil. They live chiefly on decaying organic matter, but under moist conditions may do damage in mushroom beds and to plants already injured by other insects, eelworms or fungi. Pyrethrum dust helps to give control, or gamma-BHC.

Spruce. A common name for certain

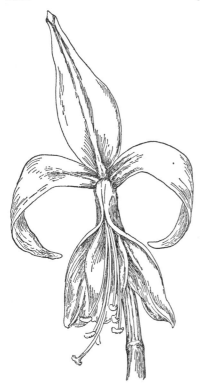

FIG. 209 *Sprekelia formosissima*, Jacobean Lily.

conifers, chiefly of the *Picea* genus. *Picea abies* is the Common Spruce; *P. albertiana*, Alberta Spruce; *P. glauca*, White Spruce; *P. mariana*, Black Spruce; *P. omorika*, Serbian Spruce; *P. pungens*, Colorado Spruce; *P. sitchensis*, Sitka Spruce, and *P. spinulosa*, Sikkim Spruce.

Spur. A tubular extension of certain flowers, such as Aquilegia, Delphinium or Viola. The short lateral shoot carrying fruit buds on fruit trees.

Spurge. See *Euphorbia*.

Spurge Laurel. See *Daphne laureola*.

Spurius (-a, -um). Spurious, false. Ex. *Iris spuria*.

Spurring. The pruning of lateral shoots of fruit trees to a few buds to induce

the formation of spurs and flower-buds; chiefly of pome fruits, Gooseberry and Red Currant.

Squama (pl. **Squamata**). A scale, often a modified leaf.

Squash. *See* Gourd (*Cucurbita pepo*).

Squill. See *Scilla*.

Squirting Cucumber. See *Ecballium*.

Stachy-, Stachys-. Prefix in compound words meaning spike-like. Ex. *Stachys lanata*.

Stachys (sta'kis. Fam. Labiatae). A genus of which *S. affinis*, the Chinese Artichoke (*see* Artichoke, Chinese), is grown as a vegetable, and the following are of ornamental value for the garden.

Selection. *S. lanata*, Lamb's Tongue, Caucasus, 1–1½ ft, stems and leaves white woolly, or silvery grey, small purplish flowers, in a whorled spike, summer; *macrantha*, Caucasus, 1–2 ft, roughly hairy, whorled heads of violet flowers, May, and v. *rosea*, rose; *lavendulifolia*, Armenia, procumbent, with grey-velvety leaves, rose-purple flowers, summer, are herbaceous perennials; *corsica*, Mediterranean region, mat-forming, sub-shrub, bright green leaves, pinkish-white, summer, and *spinosa*, Crete, silvery-grey, white, tinged pink, flowers, June, may be tried in the rock garden or alpine house.

Cultivation. Plant October or March–April, well-drained, ordinary soil, in sun and warmth.

Propagation. By division in March–April; by seeds, April, in outdoor seed-bed or in cold frame.

Stachyurus (sta-ki-u'rus. Fam. Stachyuraceae). Deciduous shrubs of the Far East with pendent racemes of late winter flowers, before the alternate, tapering saw-toothed ovate leaves; hardy but needing warm sun to ripen flowering wood well.

Selection. *S. chinensis*, China, to 10 ft, pale yellow flowers, March; and *praecox*, Japan, 5–10 ft, pale yellow flowers, February–March.

Cultivation. Plant November, free-draining sandy loam or peat-enriched well-drained soil, pH 6, warm sunny position; by a wall in northern gardens.

Propagation. By cuttings of young shoots, July–August, in cold frame, or under handlight.

Stag's-horn Fern. See *Platycerium*.

Stag's-horn Sumach. See *Rhus typhina*.

Stalk. A stem or support of an organ of a plant; a leaf-stalk is a petiole; the stalk of a flower is a pedicel and that of a cluster of flowers a peduncle.

Stamen. The male organ of a flower, including a filament or stem, bearing an anther in which pollen is produced. Collectively a flower's stamens form the androecium.

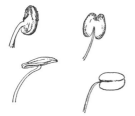

FIG. 210   Stamens, comprising anthers and filaments.

Staminate. Of flowers having stamens only (male).

Staminode. A barren stamen without pollen.

Standard. (1) A plant with a clean, upright, tall stem before branching begins. (2) The large, upright back petal of a leguminous flower. Ex. Pea.

FIG. 211   Standard tree.

Stanhopea (stan-hop'e-a. Fam. Orchidaceae). Epiphytic orchids with beautiful, showy, but short-lived flowers from tropical America.

Selection. S. *bucephalus*, S. Mexico, 16 in., yellow, dotted purple, summer; *devoniensis*, Guatemala, Mexico, 16 in., creamy-yellow, spotted crimson, fragrant, summer; *grandiflora* (*eburnea*), Guiana, Brazil, 12 in., ivory white, fragrant, summer; *hernandezii* (*tigrina*), Mexico, 10 in., orange-yellow, blotched purple, scented, summer; *insignis*, Brazil, 9 in., yellow, spotted purple, scented, summer; *oculata*, Mexico, lemon, spotted brown, summer; and *wardii*, Guatemala, 12 in., golden-yellow, dotted purple, scented, summer.

Cultivation. Pot, and repot, spring; in 3 parts Osmunda fibre, 1 part sphagnum moss and a little charcoal, in teak baskets; water freely in active growth, near the glass, shaded from hot sun; very moderately in winter, minimum temp. 15·5° C. (60° F.) at night.

Propagation. By division, March–April.

Stapelia, Carrion Flower (sta-pe'li-a. Fam. Asclepiadaceae). Leafless succulents, with fleshy four-angled stems, bearing bell-shaped flowers at the base of young stems, fleshy and rather fetid, in summer; natives of S. Africa.

Selection. S. *asterias*, Karroo, 10 in., dull purple, striped flowers, star-shaped; × *bella*, 6 in., yellow, reddish-brown cross-striping; *gigantea*, 8 in., large, star-fish, ochre, crimson cross-lined flowers; *grandiflora*, Cape, 12 in., brown; *hirsuta*, Cape, 8 in., cream, deep red stripes, hairy flowers; and *variegata*, Cape, 6 in., pendent stems, ochre-marbled purple, and v. *bufonia*, brown with black markings.

Cultivation. Pot, and repot, March, well-crocked pots, porous compost of loam, coarse sand, crushed brick and peat; water regularly in active growth, in greenhouse or house, with good light and warmth; very moderately in winter, with minimum temp. 10° C. (50° F.). Repot biennially.

Propagation. By stem cuttings, dried off for a day, in spring–autumn. By seeds, May–June, under glass, at temps. 18–21° C. (65–70° F.).

Staphylea (sta-pi-le'a. Fam. Staphyleaceae). Hardy deciduous flowering shrubs, with terminal panicles of white attractive flowers in spring, followed by inflated, bladder-like seed capsules.

Selection. S. colchica, Caucasus, 8–12 ft, pure white, May; *coulombieri*, to 6 ft, hybrid?, white, May; × *elegans hessei*, to 8 ft, flowers tinted red, May; and *pinnata*, Bladder Nut, Europe, Asia Minor, to 12 ft, white, May–June, fine seed capsules.

Cultivation. Plant November–March, humus-rich loam, sunny position, with wind shelter.

Propagation. By seeds, spring, outdoor bed. By cuttings of young firm shoots, July–August, in cold frame or under handlight.

Star of Bethlehem. See *Ornithogalum umbellatum*.

Star of the Veldt. See *Dimorphotheca*.

Starch. The principal non-nitrogenous reserve food material of green plants; found in all parts, particularly in seeds, roots and tubers, and over-wintering perennials. It is stored in the form of granules or grains, of various, but usually oval, shapes, laid down in concentric layers, in plastids (leucoplats) in storage tissues, and in stroma of chloroplasts, being a product of photosynthesis (q.v.). It is insoluble in water, however, and is converted into soluble sugars in the plants by an enzyme, diastase, to be carried in the sap stream to energize growth; the surplus being reconverted by leucoplasts into starch for storage in the tissues. This process takes place chiefly in darkness, at night. Starch is a polysaccharide carbohydrate, usually a mixture of amylose and amylopectin in plants, and stains blue with iodine.

Starwort. A name sometimes used for Aster (q.v.).

Statice. See *Limonium*.

Stauntonia. See *Holboellia latifolia*.

Stellaria (stel-la'ri-a. Fam. Caryophyllaceae). A genus that includes the Chickweeds and Stitchworts, often troublesome weeds, and only *S. graminea aurea*, Europe, etc., is much grown for its golden foliage, 3 in. high, in carpet-bedding, or for ground cover in the rock garden, planted in April, ordinary soil and propagated by cuttings or division.

Stellatus (-a, -um). Star-like. Ex. *Magnolia stellata*.

Stem. The part or axis (normally aerial) of vascular plants, supporting leaves and buds at definite positions or nodes, and in flowering plants, the flowers. Some stems are acaulescent, others subterranean (rhizomes), but distinguished by having leaves or scale-leaves and axillary buds and, internally, vascular bundles.

Sten-, Steno-. Prefix in compound words, meaning narrow. Ex. *Berberis stenophylla* (narrow-leaved).

Stenomesson (ste-no-mes'son. Fam. Amaryllidaceae). Bulbous plants of tropical America, with linear leaves, appearing with flower-heads of drooping funnel-shaped flowers, vividly coloured, for the cool greenhouse.

Selection. S. coccineum, Peru, 1 ft, bright crimson, May; and *incarnatum*, Peru, Andes, 18 in., large red flowers, August, variable.

Cultivation. Pot and cultivate as for Hippeastrum (q.v.).

Stephanandra (step-an-and'ra. Fam. Rosaceae). Hardy deciduous, graceful shrubs, akin to Spiraea, with elegant foliage, and panicles of white flowers.

Selection. S. incisa, Japan, Korea, 4–6 ft, very graceful habit, greenish-white, June, bright brown stems for winter; *tanakae*, Japan, to 6 ft, slender and twiggy, dull white, June–July, orange autumn foliage, and bright brown stems, winter.

Cultivation. Plant November–March, well-drained, humus-enriched soil, sun or light shade.

Propagation. By division, March–April.

Stephanotis (step-a-no'tis. Fam. Asclepiadaceae). A genus of tropical, evergreen twining climbers, of which *S. floribunda*, Clustered Wax Flower or the Madagascar Jasmine, to 10 ft, is chiefly grown, for its pure white, highly fragrant, flowers produced in bunches in May, and v. 'Elvaston', equally free-flowering but more compact; in the warm greenhouse.

Cultivation. Plant October–November, in large pot or border, to train up to rafters. Water freely in active growth, very moderately in winter, minimum temp. 13° C. (55° F.); prune away weak shoots in spring.

Propagation. By cuttings of previous

year's shoots in spring, bottom heat of
18° C. (65° F.), in propagating frame.

Stereum Purpureum. *See* Silver Leaf.

Sterilis (-e). Barren. Ex. *Viburnum
opulus* v. *sterile.*

Sternbergia (stern-berg'i-a. Fam.
Amaryllidaceae). Bulbous plants with
large crocus-like, yellow flowers, for
the rock garden or border.

Selection. S. lutea, Autumn Daffodil,
central Europe, 4–6 in., yellow, autumn,
is reasonably hardy; *colchiciflora,*
Hungary, Rumania, 4 in., pale yellow,
autumn, may also be tried; leaves
forming later.

Cultivation. Plant bulbs June–July,
6 in., deep, in well-drained, humus-rich
loam, in sun and warmth, to leave
undisturbed. May also be grown in pots,
standard compost, 1 in. deep, in cool
greenhouse or alpine house.

Stewartia. See *Stuartia.*

Stigma. The sticky part of the carpel
or pistil of a flower which receives the
pollen, usually at the tip of the style or
ovary. (*See* Fig. 214, page 522.)

Stigmatic. Belonging to the stigma.

Stipa (sti'pa. Fam. Gramineae). A
genus of grasses, some of which are
grown for their ornamental flowering
panicles and for drying.

Selection. S. pennata, Feather Grass,
Europe, Siberia, 2½ ft, is hardy and
perennial; *calamagrostis,* S. Europe, 3 ft,
violet tinged panicles, and *elegantissima,*
Australia, to 3 ft, feathery-haired
panicles, are for mild localities. *S.
tenacissima,* Esparto Grass, Spain, N.
Africa, 2–3 ft, needs winter protection.

Cultivation. Plant March–April, well-
drained, ordinary soil, sun; cut stems
when newly opened.

Propagation. By division in March–
April. By seeds, out of doors, April–
May.

Stipe. (1) The leaf-stalk of Ferns.
(2) The stalk of a seaweed frond. (3) The
stalk of a toadstool or mushroom fungus.

Stipulary Bud or Eye. The accessory
buds in the axil of a stipule, in Apple,
Pear, etc., extra to the usual leaf axillary
bud.

Stipule. Small, leafy outgrowth from
the base of a leaf stalk. They protect the
axillary bud; being shed as the bud
expands in some plants (as in Beech);
persisting in others to augment leaf

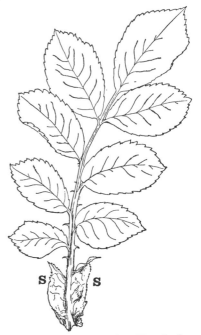

FIG. 212   Stipules (s) on Rose leaf.

functions in photosynthesis, etc. (as in
Roses); sometimes becoming very large
(Viola).

Stock. The part of a plant, usually a
rooted stem or part of the stem on which
a part of another plant (Scion) is budded
or grafted.

Stocks. See *Matthiola.*

Stokesia (sto-kes'i-a. Fam. Compositae). The only species, *S. laevis,* N.
America, 1–1½ ft, is a hardy perennial
with handsome blue flower-heads,
August, and varieties in white and
purple. May be grown from seeds, sown
in spring, out of doors, ordinary soil,
and propagated by division in March;
for the border.

Stolon. A basal horizontal-growing
branch that roots at the tip and nodes.
Ex. Strawberry. Hence, stoloniferous—
propagating by stolons.

Stoma (pl. **Stomata**). A small opening
or pore in the epidermis of leaves and

young stems through which gaseous exchange of air and water vapour takes place. Each stoma is flanked by two specialized crescent-shaped guard cells, which, controlled by the turgidity of the cells, regulate the opening and closing of the pore.

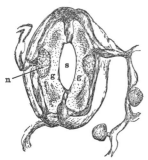

FIG. 213   Stoma, open: g. guard cells; n. nucleus; s. stoma.

Stone. The hard case enclosing the seed in the fruits of certain plants, such as *Prunus* spp., sometimes known as Stone Fruits.

Stone Pine. See *Pinus pinea*.

Stonecrop. See *Sedum acre*.

Stool. (1) The basal crown of a plant from which new stems grow each year, as with Raspberries. (2) A plant, usually earthed up, set aside for the production of rooted stems, or layers for propagation.

Stopping. A gardener's term for the pinching out of the growing tips of shoots of plants to induce the formation of side shoots, or to foster the formation of flower buds and check shoot growth.

Storing. *See* notes under individual fruits and vegetables.

Stove. A greenhouse devoted to plants requiring a high temperature. *See* Greenhouses.

Strain. A selected stock of a particular variety, developed and bred to preserve some desirable character(s).

Stranvaesia (stran-ves'i-a. Fam. Rosaceae). Tall-growing, evergreen shrubs or small trees, with corymbs of white flowers in June–July, and haw-like fruits later.

Selection. S. davidiana, China, 10–20 ft, crimson fruits; and *undulata*, China, 10 ft, wide spreading, red fruits, and v. *fructu-luteo*, yellow fruits, hardy for mild localities, and warm walls; *nussia*, Himalaya, to 20 ft, orange fruits, needs frost-proof quarters and very mild conditions in the south.

Cultivation. Plant March–April, deep, humus-rich, well-drained loam; pH 6·0–6·5, full sun, and wind-sheltered.

Propagation. By seeds, April, in cold frame, or outdoor seed-bed; rather slow.

Stratification. A method of preserving the viability or power of germination in vulnerable tropical or subtropical plant seeds; and of maturing and preserving berried seeds (haws, hips, etc.) over winter for spring planting. It entails placing the seeds or berries in a layer, on sand, in a box, pan or pot, provided with slight drainage, covering with sand, and repeating, until the container is filled, when it is stored somewhere cool or slightly moist, as by a north wall, protected against mice. The seeds are more readily rubbed out for sowing in spring.

Stratiotes (stra'ti-o-tes. Fam. Hydrocharitaceae). The only species, *S. aloides*, Water Soldier or Crab's Claw, Europe and native, is a useful underwater oxygenating aquatic plant, with white flowers in summer, for garden pools; planted in April–June, and easily propagated by cuttings or division.

Straw. The matured stems of cereal crops from the farm, useful for protecting plants against frost; to protect fruits such as strawberries from being soiled, and for covering frames, etc. Also used to cover potatoes and root vegetables stored out of doors in clamps, and to insulate mushroom beds. When rotted, straw makes an invaluable humus-forming material, and for this purpose should be shaken out, bruised, wetted and treated with a straw compost activator (Fertosan S), or composted with fresh manure. Driven upright with the spade into clay soils, it acts to improve aeration, while steadily decaying. Straw used in the garden must be clean, and from crops which have not been treated with persistent herbicides such as 2,3,6-TBA and picloram.

Strawbale Culture. A method of

growing greenhouse crops of cucumbers and tomatoes developed at the Lee Valley Horticultural Experimental Station, Hertfordshire. Bales of clean, herbicide-residue-free straw are placed in line, in trenches, lined with sheet polythene against possible soil-borne diseases and pests, about half-buried. The bales are watered at intervals for 2–3 days until thoroughly soaked, and then sprinkled with a dressing of 8 parts by weight nitro-chalk, 5 parts triple superphosphate, and 9 parts potassium nitrate, at 5½ lb. per cwt. of straw, thoroughly washed by watering (or 8 parts by weight nitro-chalk and 14 parts of a balanced tomato fertilizer may be used). This causes decomposition to start, and the straw will heat. Cover to 6 in. deep with a mixture of equal parts sterilized loam and moist peat, or better still, a standard compost; and after 24 hours, plant up, at 15 in. apart, for training in the normal way. Planting time will be dictated by greenhouse temperatures, which should be not less than 15·5° C. (60° F.). The bales must be watered well each day, and plants are fed as in normal practice, every 10–14 days, after the setting of the first truss. Plants are apt to be very vigorous and grow large, with high yields. After cropping, what remains of the rotted bales makes good humus material for the garden. Cucumbers are grown similarly, with attention to their need for extra humidity.

Strawberry (*Fragaria* ×). Modern large-fruiting strawberries are hybrids, developed after the introduction of American species *Fragaria virginiana* and *F. chiloensis*, in the seventeenth century, though the breeding of important varieties in England began only in the nineteenth century.

Varieties. Since strawberries are propagated vegetatively by runners, it is vital to begin with stocks that are virus-free. A selection can be made from: *Early*—Cambridge Vigour C.I., Cambridge Rival, 632, Cambridge Favourite; *Mid Season*—Royal Sovereign E.M. 50 (still the finest flavoured), Oberschlesien E.M. 42, Red Gauntlet, Talisman, Sir Joseph Paxton; *Late*—Cambridge Late Pine, 490, Huxley Giant E.M. 44, and Waterloo. Newer varieties

from the Continent are 'Hummi Grundi' and 'Hummi Gento'.

Soil. Strawberries can be grown on most soils provided they are well-drained, humus-rich and about pH 6. Very dry or chalky soils need considerable amendment. Soils should be bastard-trenched, copiously manured with rotted manure, compost, peat, leaf-mould, etc., and a heavy dressing of JI base fertilizer; repeated annually.

Site. An open or lightly shaded site, with freedom from spring frosts, is essential; avoiding low ground.

Planting. Plants are usually available as pot-grown from early August, one-year bedded plants from mid August, and as hand-laid runners from September onwards. When possible, it is best to plant in August or September, though planting can go on to late October; or be done in March–April, though no crop should be expected in the first year. Plants may be set 1–1½ ft apart, in rows 2–2½ ft apart, according to vigour, taking care to see that the crown of the plant is at surface level, and roots well firmed.

Management. Weeding should be carried out regularly. In late April a Rogor 40 insecticide may be applied to control Aphids and Red Spider Mites; combined with karathane if Mildew is feared. After petals fall, plants may be strawed with loose clean straw, or straw mats, black polythene sheeting, or peat, or sawdust, to keep fruit clean. In a wet season, it may be worth while spraying with thiram or captan fungicide against Grey Mould (*Botrytis cinerea*) while fruits are green. After harvest, loose straw may be swiftly burnt, or mats taken up. In autumn an organic mulch should be given; in March a complete strawberry fertilizer (JI base answers very well).

Propagation. Strawberry beds are usually cropped for four years, and then renewed. Healthy, vigorous, first-year plants should be marked for runner production for propagation, and not allowed to flower. Four to six runners may be formed from each plant, trained to root at their tips in pots sunk to the rim in the soil, or in 4-in. drills alongside the parent plants, filled with a compost of equal parts loam and peat or leaf-mould. Allow one plant per runner, and stop the free end beyond the rooting plantlet. Sever from the parent plant when rooted.

Forcing. Slightly earlier fruiting can be secured by covering plants with cloches. To force under glass, strong two-year-old plants are lifted, in August–September, potted into 6-in. pots, standard potting compost, and kept cool in a cool frame, or by a north wall, sunk in the soil, until January, when they are brought into a heated house $(13–15 \cdot 5°$ C. $[55–60°$ F.$])$, and placed near the glass. Flower trusses should be thinned to allow 12–15 fruits per plant; supporting trusses on small sticks or twigs; watering to keep moist, and feeding with liquid manure when fruits begin to swell. Plants are best discarded afterwards.

Alpine Strawberries. Small-fruiting varieties, which can be readily grown from March-sown seeds, planted in humus-rich soil, partial shade, or as pot plants in a cool greenhouse, fruiting July–September. 'Baron Solemacher' is excellent; others are 'Harsland Alpine', 'Alpine Yellow', 'Belle de Meaux', 'Gaillon Rouge' and 'La Brillante'.

Perpetual Strawberries. Less exacting in soil requirements, these strawberries yield from July to October, from autumn planting; producing runners which are transplanted next spring, and parent plants are then discarded, as the best yield is from plants in their first year. Suitable varieties include 'Red Rich', 'Sans Rivale', 'St Claude' and 'Hampshire Maid'.

Climbing Strawberry. A type which produces strong, stout runners, which fruit, and needs to be trained up a trellis or netting; and very generous liquid feeding, to yield fair crops of dark-coloured fruits, summer to autumn; 'Sonjana' is a typical variety.

Diseases. Grey Mould (*Botrytis cinerea*) affects fruits, but good strawing, aeration and sunning with rows running north and south, deter, while a timely captan or thiram fungicidal spraying will check the disease, after removing infected berries. Mildew (*Sphaerotheca humili*), showing in dark blotches, greyish underneath, on leaves, and dried-up fruits, is best controlled by karathane fungicide, just before flowering, and ten

days later, and then after fruiting. Leaf Spot (*Mycosphaerella fragariae*) causes small spots, reddish, then turning grey to white in the centre; affected leaves are best removed, or burnt. Red Core (*Phytophthora fragariae*) is a problem in some areas. No control is known, and plants are best destroyed, and replaced with resistant varieties, such as 'Cambridge Vigour C.I.' Hard Rot (*Septogloeum fragariae*) causes berries to have hard, sunken dry patches; fruits should be collected and burnt, plants tar-oil washed in January. The worst diseases are the virus infections: 'Yellow Edge', causing young leaves to be small and yellow-edged, especially in autumn; and 'Crinkle', causing leaves to be dwarfed, crinkled and spotted purple; plants must be destroyed.

Pests. Aphids: no less than four species attack strawberries, but good control is possible with a Rogor 40 insecticide applied just before flowering (mid–late April), and after harvest; or malathion may be used. The same treatment controls Red Spider Mites (*Tetranychus telarius*). Tarsonemid Mites (*Tarsonemus pallidus*) are best controlled by applying kelthane after fruit picking. Damage by slugs and snails can be minimized by putting down metaldehyde bait pellets immediately before strawing. Root Lesion Eelworms (*Pratylenchus penetrans*) weaken plants, while *Xiphinema* species spread the virus disease Arabis Mosaic; a DD soil fumigant may be used in autumn under expert advice, and strawberry planting rotated to fresh soil.

Strawberry Tomato. A name sometimes given to *Physalis peruviana* (q.v.).

Strawberry Tree. See *Arbutus unedo*.

Strelitzia, Bird of Paradise Flower, Bird's Tongue Flower (stre-lits'i-a. Fam. Musaceae). Striking, evergreen perennials, with rhizomatous roots, long-stalked leaves, and large, pointed, boat-shaped flowers, reminiscent of the head of a Crested Grebe; natives of S. Africa.

Selection. S. reginae, to 3 ft, orange and blue-purple flowers, April–May, and vs. *augusta*, 4–6 ft, purple and white; and their hybrid × *kewensis*, 4 ft, yellow and lilac-pink.

Cultivation. Pot in spring or autumn, 6-in. pots, standard compost, water freely in active growth, full sun, and good ventilation in warm greenhouse, very moderate watering in winter, minimum temp. 10° C. (50° F.).

Propagation. By offsets or suckers, spring. By seeds, standard compost, plunged in propagating case, bottom heat of 18–21° C. (65–70° F.).

Strept-, Strepto-. Prefix of compound words, meaning twisted. Ex. *Streptocarpus,* twisted fruit.

Streptanthera (strep-tanth'er-a. Fam. Iridaceae). A genus of two species of dwarf bulbous plants, S. African, for the cool greenhouse.

Selection. S. *cuprea,* 9 in., six-petalled, yellowish-copper and purple, flowers, June; and v. *coccinea,* vivid orange; and *elegans,* 9 in., white, purple-centred, June.

Cultivation. Plant in autumn, pots of porous compost; growing cool; watering increasingly with growth; withholding to dry off when leaves yellow; minimum temperature of 10° C. (50° F.).

Propagation. By offsets, when repotting, autumn.

Streptocarpus, Cape Primrose (strepto-karp'us. Fam. Gesneriaceae). Perennial flowering herbs of subtropical Africa, with flared tubular flowers of colourful distinction for the cool greenhouse.

Selection. S. *caulescens,* E. Africa, 1½–2 ft, cymes of blue-violet flowers from stems, autumn; *holstii,* E. tropical Africa, 1½ ft, white-throated purple flowers, autumn; make bushy branching plants. S. *dunnii,* Transvaal, solitary leaves to 3 ft long, brick-red flowers; *gardenii,* Natal, rosette-leaved, with mauve and green flowers; *galpinii,* Transvaal, solitary leaves to 8 in., violet-mauve and white; *rexii,* S. Africa, rosette leaves, white, mauve and purple-striped; and hybrids such as 'Peed's Strain' and 'Giant Flowered', in a variety of colours, are stemless, rivalling Gloxinias in beauty.

Cultivation. May be raised from seeds, sown February, standard compost, bottom heat of 15·5° C. (65° F.), pricked off singly to small pots, and potted on successively to 6-in. pots; keeping well watered, cool and shaded from hot sun,

to flower in late summer or autumn, or over-wintered to the following year, minimum temp. 7–10° C. (45–50° F.). Feed weekly when buds are formed.

Propagation. By leaf cuttings, summer, as for Begonia. By division in March.

Streptosolen (strep-to-so'len. Fam. Solanaceae). The only species, S. *jamesonii,* Colombia, is an evergreen climbing shrub, to 8 ft, with somewhat hairy ovate leaves, and pleasing panicles of trumpet, orange flowers at the ends of shoots, in early summer; for planting in the cool greenhouse border, sandy loam, enriched with peat or leaf-mould; watering freely in growth, very moderately in winter, temp. 10° C. (50° F.).

Propagation. By seeds, March, under glass, bottom heat of 18° C. (65° F.), standard compost; by stem cuttings, July.

Stria-. Prefix in compound words, meaning striate, or marked with parallel lines, streaks or grooves.

Strictus (-a, -um). Straight and erect. Ex. *Erica stricta.*

Strike, Striking. Of cuttings, to root; the rooting of cuttings by propagation.

Striped Squill. Common name of *Puschkinia scilloides.*

Strobilanthes (stro-bi-lan'thes. Fam. Acanthaceae). A very large genus of subtropical plants, many monocarpic, of which the following sub-shrubs may be grown for foliage and summer–autumn flowering.

Selection. S. *anisophyllus,* India, 2–3 ft, cone-like heads of lavender flowers, June; *dyerianus,* Penang, 1 ft, pale blue, July; and *isophyllus,* India, 1–2 ft, lavender, August.

Cultivation. Pot in March, standard compost, watering freely in active growth, more moderately in winter, minimum temp. 15·5° C. (60° F.). Syringe often in warm weather.

Propagation. By cuttings of firm shoots, 3 in., spring, in propagating case, bottom heat of 24° C. (75° F.).

Strobilus. A cone or cone-like fruit, as of conifers, and Hops.

Struma. A cushion-shaped swelling.

Strumose. Bearing a swelling or tumour.

Stuartia (Stewartia) (stu-art'i-a. Fam. Theaceae). Deciduous shrubs, sometimes small trees, akin to Camellia, with open, saucer-shaped, white, finely stamened flowers in succession on the current year's shoots, July–August, for mild localities; the ovate, toothed leaves colouring well in autumn.

Selection. S. *malacodendron*, SE. U.S.A., to 15 ft, white, blue stamens, July; *monadelpha*, Japan, to 30 ft or more, white, violet stamens, June; *ovata*, S. U.S.A., to 12 ft, creamy-white, July–August; *pseudocamellia*, Japan, to 20 ft or more, white, orange stamens, July–August, and v. *koreana*; and *sinensis*, China, to 30 ft, white, scented, July.

Cultivation. Plant November–March, humus-rich, lime-free, deep, well-drained soil, and partial shade, in frostproof quarters, mild localities; to be left undisturbed, as they do not move well.

Propagation. By seeds, April, after soaking seeds a few days. By cuttings of firm shoots with a heel, July–August, in propagating case.

Style. The extension stem of a carpel which carries the stigma.

Styrax (sti'raks. Fam. Styracaceae). A large genus of beautiful flowering

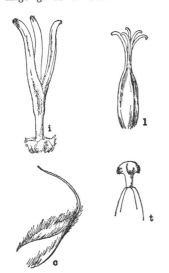

FIG. 214   Styles and stigmas: i. *Iris* sp.; l. *Lychnis* sp.; c. *Clematis* sp.; t. *Tulipa* sp.

shrubs of which only a few are sufficiently hardy for mild localities.

Selection. S. *hemsleyana*, China, to 20 ft, racemes of pure white flowers, June; *japonica*, Japan, to 20 ft, starry white flowers, June; *obassia*, Japan, to 20 ft, fragrant, white racemes, June; and *wilsonii*, China, to 10 ft, nodding white flowers, June, are deciduous and distinguished.

Cultivation. Plant November or March, light, humus-rich soil, light shade, in sheltered positions or by a wall, in southern or south-western gardens.

Propagation. By seeds, April, under cloches.

Suavis (-e). Sweet. Ex. *Vanda suavis.*

Sub-. A prefix meaning nearly, semi- or somewhat, as sub-cordate, somewhat heart-shaped; sub-shrub, nearly shrubby.

Subsoil. A gardener's term for the layer of earth or rock below the cultivated surface layer, usually from about 9 in. downwards. As such, it may be similar in texture and composition to the top soil, but contains less organic matter, fewer micro-organisms, less air, but tends to accumulate more mineral salts, washed down into it. As such, the subsoil requires mechanical cultivation to break it up, especially where it consists of hard impermeable material or a pan, to improve aeration, drainage and facilitate its penetration by plant roots.

Sub-species. A division of a species, above varietal rank.

Subulatus (-a, -um). Awl-shaped. Ex. *Phlox subulata.*

Succulents. Plants with very fleshy leaves and/or stems, made up of water-storing tissue. They include genera such as Aeonium, Agave, Aloe, Apicra, Bryophyllum, Cotyledon, Crassula, Echeveria, Echidnopsis, Euphorbia, Gasteria, Haworthia, Mesembryanthemum, Huernia, Kalanchoë, Kleinia, Monanthes, Pelargonium, Rochea, Sedum, Sempervivum, Stapelia, Tillaea (q.v.), Cacti are also succulents. but distinguished by the possession of areoles.

Sucker. A shoot or branch from the base of a plant below the soil surface. In some plants, such as Blackberry, Raspberry, they are welcome as replacement shoots, essential to survival. In others, notably from rootstocks of grafted or budded plants, such as Roses, Prunus and Syringa, they are undesirable and should be suppressed.

Suffruticosus (-a, -um). Partly shrubby, partly herbaceous. Ex. *Phlox suffruticosa (carolina).*

Sugars. Sweet, soluble monosaccharides, such as glucose (grape sugar) and fructose (fruit, sugar), and disaccharide or sucrose (cane sugar), occur in plants, and form highly important energy foods.

Sulcate. Of stems, channelled, furrowed, grooved.

Sulphate of Ammonia, Ammonium Sulphate [$(NH_4)_2SO_4$]. A major nitrogenous fertilizer, containing 20·6 per cent nitrogen. *See* Fertilizers.

Sulphamate of Ammonia, Ammonium Sulphamate ($NH_4SO_3NH_2$). A water-soluble, white, crystalline salt, used as a total weedkiller, especially for woody plants and trees; non-toxic to animals; with residual fertilizer properties after 5–6 weeks.

Sulphate of Iron, Ferrous Sulphate ($FeSO_4.7H_2O$). Pale green, water-soluble salt, sometimes added to fertilizers to provide iron. Combined in calcined, powder form with ammonium sulphate as a broad-leaved weedkiller on lawns (*see* Lawn Sand).

Sulphate of Potash, Potassium Sulphate (K_2SO_4). A major potassic fertilizer, obtained from natural deposits, containing 50–54 per cent potassium as K_2O. *See* Fertilizers.

Sulphur (S). A mineral element essential for plant growth; naturally abundant in most soils in the form of sulphates. As an acid, powdered sulphur is sometimes used to neutralize calcium in chalk and lime soils. Important also as a fungicide; particularly to control Mildews; and used in powdered form as flowers of sulphur or preferably green precipitated sulphur on plants; in colloidal and dispersible forms as a spray; or combined with calcium as lime-sulphur for spraying. May also be used as a fumigant, vaporized or burnt, in the greenhouse, a convenient form being the Sulphur Candle. May also be used to control Big Bud Mites on Currants, and Red Spider Mites. *See* Fungicides.

Sulphureus (-a, -um). Sulphur-coloured, pale yellow. Ex. *Pulsatilla alpina* v. *sulphurea,*

Sumach. See *Rhus.*

Summer Snowflake. See *Leucojum aestivum.*

Sun Plant. See *Portulaca grandiflora.*

Sun Rose. See *Helianthemum.*

Sundew. See *Drosera.*

Sundials. On pedestals, horizontal sundials are appropriate garden ornaments, as points of focal interest at interesections of walks, on terraces or at the end of a vista. Although contrived in various materials, the essentials for time-telling are that the dial should be level and calibrated for the latitude of the garden; the gnomon or style must be perpendicular to the dial, at an angle equivalent to the latitude in degrees, and on the true north–south line, if the dial is to register true sun-time, which is not necessarily clock-time, especially with daylight-saving manipulations.

Sunflower. See *Helianthus.*

Superbus (-a, -um). Superb, magnificent. Ex. *Dianthus superbus.*

Superphosphates. Normal superphosphate ($Ca(H_2PO_4)_2$), chemically calcium dihydrogen phosphate, sometimes termed superphosphate of lime, is made by treating phosphate rock with sulphuric acid, and is an important phosphatic fertilizer, providing 18–20 per cent phosphorus in terms of P_2O_5. Triple superphosphate is made by treating phosphate rock with phosphoric acid, and is more concentrated, with an analysis of 44–47 per cent of P_2O_5, and is being increasingly used, especially in high concentrate granular and liquid fertilizers. *See* Fertilizers.

Surface Caterpillars or Cutworms. The larvae of various moths, such as the Dart (*Euxoa exclamationis*), the Turnip (*E. segetum*) and the Yellow Underwing (*Graphiphora pronuba*). They feed nocturnally on the basal stems and lower leaves of plants just above, on and below the surface. Dusting with a powder or gamma-BHC insecticide gives good control.

Suture. A line of junction in flowering plants marking the fusion of the edges of a carpel, to be seen in such fruits as peach and plum.

Swainsona (swain-so'na. Fam.

Leguminosae). Evergreen sub-shrubs of the Antipodes of which *S. galegifolia*, Queensland, New South Wales, is a semi-climbing, pinnate-leaved evergreen, bearing large, orange-red, sweet-pea-like flowers in racemes on long stalks, July, reaching 2–4 ft, in a cool green-house; grown in pots, standard compost, and repotted annually in March. Water freely, syringe on hot days, in active growth; very little in winter, temp. 7–10° C. (45–50° F.). Prune after repotting, reducing last year's shoots by one-half to two-thirds, and trimming straggly shoots.

Propagation. By seeds, March, bottom heat of 21° C. (70° F.), but takes three years to flower. By cuttings of young shoots, March, in propagating case, bottom heat of 21° C. (70° F.).

Swamp Cypress. See *Taxodium distichum.*

Swamp Lily. See *Zephyranthes candida.*

Swan River Daisy. See *Brachycome.*

Swede. *See* Turnip.

Swedish Whitebeam. See *Sorbus intermedia.*

Sweeping. For the sweeping up of fallen leaves from lawns and paths, and the scattering of worm casts, the old-fashioned besom or birch broom is reasonably good in calm weather. The modern equivalent is the rubber- or spring-toothed rake, but for efficiency and time-saving the wheeled lawn sweeper with rotary brush is best, especially for collecting the leaves for compost.

Sweet Alyssum. See *Lobularia.*

Sweet Amber. See *Hypericum androsaemum.*

Sweet Bay. See *Laurus nobilis.*

Sweet Buckeye. See *Aesculus octandra.*

Sweet Chestnut. See *Castanea sativa.*

Sweet Cicely. See *Myrrhis odorata.*

Sweet Corn, Indian Corn, Maize (*Zea mays.* Fam. Gramineae). The origin of the species, presumably subtropical, is unknown, but it has long been grown as human food (mealies) and for animals and poultry, especially in the Americas. The breeding of hybrids particularly suited to the British climate has made it possible to grow this cereal for its suc-culent 'ears', served as a vegetable or 'Corn on the Cob'.

Varieties. 'Earliking', 'Golden

Bantam', 'John Innes Hybrid F_1', 'Kelvedon Glory Hybrid F_1', and 'Sutton's First of All' are all early maturing.

Culture. To give as long a summer-growing season as possible, seeds are best sown in March–April, under glass, temp. 15·5° C. (60° F.), in peat-wood fibre pots to avoid transplanting setbacks; and planted out in late April–early May, in blocks of three or four, spaced 9–12 in. apart. Plants are rather gross-feeding, and need a soil rich in humus, and pre-fertilizing with a complete fertilizer, moderate in nitrogen; and to be watered in dry weather. Covering with cloches to the end of May helps to bring on plants and protects from bird damage. Plants grow 3–4 ft tall, may need staking, with male staminate flowers appearing at the top as tassels, and the female pistillate flowers form on the stems in leaf axils, with long silky hairs or silks, late June–early July. In 2–3 weeks after pollination the ears or cobs form, fat-cigar-like, sheathed in green, with the silks persisting at the ends; when the silks turn golden and tend to wither it is time to harvest for cooking as a vegetable.

Sweet Flag. See *Acorus calamus.*

Sweet Gale. See *Myrica gale.*

Sweet Gum. See *Liquidambar styraciflua.*

Sweet Marjoram. See *Origanum majorana.*

Sweet Maudlin. See *Achillea ageratum.*

Sweet Pea (*Lathyrus odoratus*, Fam. Leguminosae). The parent species, an annual, was introduced to Britain in 1699 from Sicily, but its development into the richly coloured, finely sculptured and often sweet-perfumed range of flowers of today has taken place over the past century. Variations occurred, and by selection and cross-breeding large-flowered, fragrant, vari- and self-coloured blooms with erect standards were to the fore, until in 1900 varieties arose, chiefly 'Countess Spencer' and 'Gladys Unwin', from which new colour varieties with waved or frilled standards to their flowers followed. The capacity of the Sweet Pea for variation has led to new varieties being introduced every year, from tall-climbers to dwarf and bush forms, and the interests of the flower are now served by the National Sweet Pea Society. Fortunately Sweet Peas may be grown with relative ease in most types of soil throughout the British Isles, granted a reasonable amount of sun and warmth and adequate moisture in the growing season.

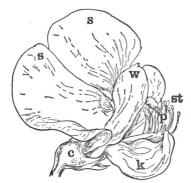

FIG. 215   Sweet Pea Flower: s. standard; w. wing; k. keel; st. stamens; p. pistil; c. calyx.

Varieties. Only a short selection of the best established varieties are given here; growers' lists should be consulted on new introductions annually.

Standard: White—'Albatross', 'Gigantic',* 'Swan Lake'.*† Cream Picotee—'Ballerina',* 'Cream Delight',* 'Rosy Frills'.* Cream and Ivory—'Cream Gigantic',* 'Margot'.* Pink, Cream Ground—'Lady Grace', 'Mischief',* 'Pink Suffusion', 'Princess Elizabeth'.*† Pink, White Ground—'Monty',* 'Mrs R. Bolton',*† 'Pink Magic'.* Rose Pinks—'Elizabeth Arden',* 'Shillingford',*† 'Blossom Time',* 'Geranium Pink',*† 'Norah',* 'Piccadilly'.* Salmon and Orange/Cream—'Cynthia Davis', 'Flare', 'Radar'. Cerise and Scarlet—'Air Warden',*† 'Air Marshal',† 'Brigadier', 'Percy Izzard'.* Carmine Rose—'Carlotta',*†, 'Red Crusader'.* Crimson—'Crimson Excelsior',* 'Red Admiral', 'Winston Churchill'.*† Lavender—'Gertrude Tingay',* 'Lavender Lace',* 'Leamington',* 'Mrs C. Kay',* 'Mrs R. P. Butchard'. Mauve—'Bouquet',* 'Brocade',* 'Elizabeth Taylor"*† Blue—'Blue Bell', 'Blue Veil',* 'Flagship',* 'Mabel Gower',* 'Nocturne',* 'Stylish', 'Velvet Knight'. Purple—'Royalty',* 'Zeta'.*† Maroon—'Black Diamond', 'Mahogany', 'Midnight',* 'Jupiter'.* *Early Multiflora Gigantea* vs., 5–8 flowers per stem, do well under glass, and include named forms in white, pinks, rose, carmine, crimson, lavender, blue and purple. *Cuthbertson Floribunda* vs. are early-flowering, with five or more blooms per stem. *Galaxy Multiflora* * are an American race, with large blooms, five to seven to a stem, nicely scented, in such forms as 'Blue Swan', ice blue; 'Fireglo', cerise-scarlet; 'Gigi', salmon pink; 'Love Song', pink, cream; 'Purity', white; 'Great Britain', rose on cream, etc. Old-fashioned, highly fragrant varieties are usually available in mixtures, their flowers being relatively small. Recent years have seen the development of Dwarf and Semi-dwarf races, suitable for beds and borders, which include 'Burpees Early Dwarf Bijou', 12 in. high, spreading to 20 in., frilled flowers, in pink, rose, cerise and blue; 'Cupid or Tom Thumb', 4 in. high, 12 in. spread, various colours; 'Knee-Hi', to 3 ft, five to seven blooms per stem, good range of colours; and 'Americana', 2 ft, bushy, with good range of colours.

Site. This should be chosen to give the plants airy, mild moist conditions, well sheltered from drying or cutting winds, and away from exposure to spring frosts. Sun warmth is needed, but partial shade or light shade well tolerated.

Soil. With a deep and extensive root system, the Sweet Pea plant needs a well-prepared soil, draining well and yet moisture retentive, adequately provided with phosphates, and potash, and of a pH 6·0–6·5. Traditionally it is customary to deep-trench the soil, but this is not strictly essential, given good natural drainage. It is sufficient to bastard trench, and amend the soil according to its nature. Heavy and clay soils should be made more friable by applying gypsum, and heavily manuring with rotted organic matter throughout, adding lime if more than slightly acid. It is doubtful that the time-honoured practice of digging deep trenches and placing organic matter in layers at the bottom is really rewarding; the trenches often become sumps for drainage water. Light sandy soils, chalk and gravel need stiffening with clay, and moisture holding improved by adding organic matter liberally. A suitable base fertilizer is 2 parts by weight dried blood, 3 parts superphosphate, 1 part sulphate of potash, ½ part sulphate of magnesium, at 3–4 oz. per sq yd, prior to sowing or planting.

Sowing. Sweet Peas are best grown from seeds each year, although propagation by cuttings is possible. To ensure even germination, the hard-coated black seeds are best 'chipped' by removing a tiny piece of the seed coat, away from the hilum or eye, with a sharp knife or file. With brown or mottled seeds this is less necessary. Soaking overnight is often advocated to separate the hard-coated seeds from the others, but should not be prolonged before seeds are sown, or they may rot.

Autumn Sowing. For a long season of bloom, seeds may be sown 1 in. deep, 2–3 in. apart, on well-prepared, porous soil, and sheltered sites, in mid September in the north, to early October in favoured southern counties. Alternatively, seeds are sown under glass, in deep boxes, or preferably in special 'Long-Tom' peat-wood fibre pots, standard compost, and wintered in a cold greenhouse or frame, for planting out in early spring. Alternatively, sowings may be made out of doors in spring; from late February to April out of doors; and if to be hedge-grown, supported by netting or pea-sticks, they may be sown like garden peas in a shallow trench, 2–3 in. apart, 1 in. deep. Alternatively, an early start can be made in the cool greenhouse, as for autumn sowing given above.

Planting Out. Whether sown in autumn, or in the early months of the year, young plants reared under glass for planting out should be grown singly in well-crocked 3-in. pots, or better still in peat-wood fibre 'Long-Toms'; and hardened off. They may be planted out in the first mild break in the weather between late February and the end of April; either 4–6 in. apart, if to be

grown as a hedge, or a group, pea-stick-supported; or 6 in. apart for growing on the cordon system.

The Cordon System. In this method of cultivation each plant is allotted an 8–10 ft cane, tied to a firm framework of two or three horizontal wires, strung between posts, and one selected shoot only is allowed to grow, being fastened to its cane as growth is made with raffia or plastic tape, or rings. Side-shoots at the base are cut out, and lateral shoots removed in their early stages, as with tomatoes, to maintain the single flowering stem. Alternatively, two main shoots (double cordons) may be allowed to develop from the best shoots at the base. It is important that the plants should not go short of moisture, assured by adequate humus material in the soil, and mulching after rain during growth. Regular attention is necessary to maintain the cordon to its single stem. Flowers should be cut close to the base of their stems, and seed formation prevented. A suitable feed is a seaweed derivative in solution to maintain flower production. For exhibition purposes, plants are grown 9–12 in. apart. Flowers should be cut the night before a show, with two or three open per bloom, placed in water up to their lowest bud, and kept cool in the shade until wanted; and then wrapped after drying the stems in soft tissue paper in bunches of twelve, and placed in a stout 6-in.-deep flower box, lined with polythene or wax paper for transport to the show.

Under Glass. A greenhouse with glass to the ground is to be preferred, the Dutch-light type being excellent. The greenhouse must be prepared by a thorough cleansing, and if necessary washing down with a disinfectant (cresylic acid). The soil beds are prepared on the same lines as for out of doors. Plants are sown in late August–late September, to be planted in the beds about mid to late December. They may be grown with peastick supports, but it is more satisfactory to grow on the cordon system, with plants 5 in. apart, and 3½ ft between rows. Regular pinching out of side-shoots and watering are necessary, with minimum temperatures of 5–7° C. (40–45° F.), and ample ventilation to maintain a buoyant atmosphere in the day; and shading is helpful from direct hot sun.

Layering. This is a practice often followed in low greenhouses to accommodate plants to relatively short canes (6–8 ft), and may also be done out of doors. When the plants are growing to the top of their supports, they are taken down, trained along near the base of the canes and refastened, with the end foot or so then tied to grow upright on a cane some feet away. The method is to take 6–9 cordons down, fasten carefully together temporarily to a tall stake; then lower and train the next 6–9 cordons across to train up the empty canes; the first batch of cordons can then be trained in place of those now in position. The time to layer is before the first flush of bloom; roughly towards the latter part of April under glass.

Pot-grown Sweet Peas. The dwarf and semi-dwarf varieties make excellent pot plants for the cold greenhouse, sown four seeds to a 5-in. pot, well-crocked, standard compost. They are also useful for vases and tubs out of doors in sheltered quarters.

Bud-dropping. This is a functional trouble, traceable to the plant's inability to adjust quickly enough to sudden temperature changes, which causes a critical water deficiency in the plant. It is most apt to occur when night temperatures fall drastically after a warm day, as often happens in May–June, when buds are forming. Under glass, a careful watch on and regulation of temperature by daytime shading, and early restriction of ventilation can prevent this trouble. Out of doors, it is important to see there is ample moisture available to the plant, though the trouble is less prevalent after June.

Diseases. The worst infections are caused by viruses; Mosaic, revealed in a mottling, yellow-veining and flecking of leaves; or a speckly mottling of light and dark areas on leaves and colour changes in the flowers; or Streak, showing in a clearing of the veins and mottling of the leaves, with brown or purple streaks on the stems. As there is no remedy, infected plants should be taken up and burnt. Mildew (*Erysiphe polygoni*) may flare up in dry weather,

calling for spraying with a karathane or thiram fungicide. Foot and root rots in slow-germinating seeds are prevented by dressing seeds with a thiram dust before sowing.

Pests. Aphids (*Myzus persicae*) may be troublesome, best controlled with a gamma-BHC or derris insecticide, or prevented by using a systemic insecticide. The Red Spider Mite (*Tetranychus urticae*) may attack under glass, and is best prevented by the use of a systemic insecticide. Mice often take seeds, but a covering of chopped gauze or shredded plastic over seeds will check this, where the mice cannot be controlled by using Warfarin bait.

Sweet Sultan. See *Centaurea moschata*.

Sweet Violet. See *Viola*.

Sweet William (*Dianthus barbatus*, Fam. Caryophyllaceae). A native of southern Europe, Sweet William has been grown in English gardens since 1575. Its colourful, multiple heads of small dianthus-like flowers make a brilliant display. Primarily perennial, they are usually grown as biennials or annuals with relative ease.

Selection. Selected strains are offered, such as 'Sutton's Superb', 'Unwin's Hybrids', to give plants of 1½–2 ft, in white, pinks to reds; 'Giant Auricula-eyed', 1½ ft, distinctive for their bright flowers with a central clear 'eye', and named forms 'Giant White', 'Pink Beauty', 'Harlequin', 'Scarlet' and crimson 'Pheasant Eye'. 'Wee Willie', 6 in., pink and red shades; 'Red Monarch', 9 in., scarlet, are typical hybrid strains to be grown as annuals.

Cultivation. Sow the biennials in June–July, outdoor seed-bed, of porous loam; transplant to flowering quarters, in well-drained soil, pH 6·5, dressed with bone meal, late August–September. Annuals are grown as hardy annuals; sown under glass in February–March, to plant out in April, or where they are to flower in March–April.

Sweet Wivelsfield (*Dianthus barbatus* × *Dianthus* × *allwoodii*). A race of hybrid pinks, with foliage and habit of Sweet William but having a looser inflorescence of larger flowers. Perennial, but usually raised from seeds each year; sown, March, in cool greenhouse, temps. 10–13° C. (50–55° F.), to plant out in

May; or outdoors in April, where they are to flower. There are single and double varieties in a range of colours, white, pink, crimson, etc.

Sword Lily. See *Gladiolus*.

Sycamore. See *Acer pseudoplatanus*.

Sycopsis (si-kop'sis. Fam. Hamamelidaceae). The species chiefly grown, *S. sinensis*, China, is an evergreen shrub, to 10 ft, ornamental for its elliptical, leathery leaves, and early flowers with yellow and red stamens in February–March, of decorative interest.

Cultivation. Plant October–November, or March–April, well-drained loam soil, with leaf-mould or peat, pH 6, sheltered from chill winter winds. Propagation by cuttings under mist, summer; or by layering.

Sylva, Sylvaticus (-a, -um), Sylvestris (-e). Wood or trees of a region, of woods or forests. Ex. *Fagus sylvatica*; *Pinus sylvestris*.

Symbiosis. The living together or association of two dissimilar organisms to their mutual benefit; as of algae and fungi in lichens; of nodule bacteria with leguminous plants; of mycorrhiza between Conifers, Heaths, Orchids, etc., and fungi; though in some cases only one organism may derive advantage, as with Mistletoe and host trees.

Symphoricarpos, St Peter's Wort, Snowberry (sim-por-i-kar'pos. Fam. Caprifoliaceae). Small, hardy, deciduous shrubs, akin to Lonicera, with small white or pink flowers in the axils of opposite paired oval leaves, followed by white berry-like ornamental fruits in autumn.

Selection. S. *albus* (*racemosus*), N. America, to 2½ ft, *orbiculatus*, U.S.A., to 6 ft, red to pink fruits, and v. *variegatus*, green and yellow leaves; *rivularis* (*alba laevigatus*), N. America, to 8 ft, white fruits, naturalized; and hybrids 'Magic Berry' and 'White Hedge'.

Cultivation. Plant November–March, any ordinary soil, sun or shade; good bee plant, and fruits welcomed by game birds.

Propagation. By rooted suckers, detached in winter.

Symphyandra (sim-pi-an'dra. Fam. Campanulaceae). Pretty perennials with heart-shaped leaves, and nodding bell-flowers in summer, for rock gardens or the alpine house.

Selection. S. *cretica*, Crete, 18 in., lilac-blue, August; *hoffmanii*, Bosnia, 1–2 ft, white, summer; *pendula*, Caucasus, 2 ft, cream, summer; and *wanneri*, eastern European Alps, 6 in., blue, summer, often monocarpic.

Cultivation. Plant in well-drained, porous soil, with humus, April; sheltered sunny corners, protect from hard frosts in winter.

Propagation. By seeds in cold frame, April. By cuttings of young shoots, April–May.

Symphytum (sim-pi'tum. Fam. Boragineaceae). Rather rough, hairy perennials of which *S. officinale*, to 4 ft, is the native Comfrey, with white, cream, crimson and purple forms, useful in the wild garden.

Selection. For the waterside or woodland, S. *asperum*, Prickly Comfrey, Caucasus, 4–6 ft, rose to blue, summer, and v. *aureo-variegatum*, with yellow-margined leaves; *peregrinum*, Blue Comfrey, Caucasus, to 6 ft, rose, then blue, heads of flowers, summer, are useful; the v. known as Russian Comfrey is sometimes grown for its large leaves, as animal fodder, and also for providing material for the compost heap; but it should be grown in waste ground, as the thick, tuberous, fusiform roots become difficult to eradicate.

Cultivation. Plant October–March, any ordinary soil, in rougher parts of the garden. Apt to become weed-invasive if not watched.

Symplocos (sim-plo'kos. Fam. Symplocaceae). A large genus of evergreen shrubs of which only S. *paniculata* (*crataegoides*), of China and Japan, growing to 6 ft, with lanceolate, finely toothed leaves, small white, fragrant flowers in panicles, May–June, occasionally followed by brilliant blue berries, when two or more specimens are planted to ensure good pollination.

Cultivation. Plant October–November or March–April, well-drained, peat-enriched soil, warm sunny position, sheltered from cold winds.

Propagation. By cuttings of young firm shoots, July–August, under a handlight, sandy loam.

Syn-. A prefix of compound words,

meaning union. Ex. *syncarpus*—with united carpels.

Synonym (**Syn.** for short). The name of a plant which has been superseded; usually under the rule of priority. *See* Nomenclature.

Synthyris (sin-thi′ris. Fam. Scrophulariaceae). Low-growing hardy perennials of tufted growth, akin to Veronica, from NW. America, for the rock garden or alpine house.

Selection. S. *reniformis*, Oregon, California, 6 in., kidney-shaped, leathery, dark green leaves, clear blue-violet racemes of flowers, April, and v. *cordata*, heart-shaped bronzy leaves, deep blue flowers; and *stellata*, Oregon, 6 in., cordate to rounded leaves, small violet-blue flowers in a dense raceme, April.

Cultivation. Plant April–May, well-drained soil with ample leaf-mould, in cool, partial shade.

Propagation. By careful division, May. By seeds, sown April–May, or when ripe, cold frame.

Syringa, Lilac (si-ring′a. Fam. Oleaceae). Deciduous tall shrubs or small trees, notable for their beautiful panicles of small bell-shaped flowers, often deliciously scented, in May–June.

Selection. There are two sections of Syringa:

1. Privet Lilacs (*Ligustrina*); represented by S. *amurensis*, Manchuria, N. China, to 12 ft, loose panicles of creamy-white scentless flowers, June; its v. *japonica*, Japan, to 30 ft, terminal panicles of white scentless flowers in pairs, June–July; and *pekinensis*, China, to 10 ft, creamy white, privet-like and smelling clustered panicles, June.

2. True Lilacs, of which one group (*Villosae*) produces its flower panicles at the end of young leafy shoots in June, such as S. *emodi*, Himalaya, 12 ft, white to purple; × *henryi*, to 9 ft, pale violet-purple, and vs. 'Lamartine', mauve-pink; *josikaea*, Hungary, to 12 ft, deep lilac; *julianae*, China, to 6 ft, deep lilac, very fragrant; *komarowii*, China, to 12 ft, rose-pink, scentless; *meyeri*, China, 3–6 ft, purple-violet; *microphylla*, China, to 5 ft, lilac, fragrant; × *prestoniae*, Canadian hybrids to 10 ft, in forms 'Audrey', pinkish-mauve; 'Desdemona', pale mauve; 'Hiawatha', pale pink; 'Isabella', pale purple;

reflexa, China, to 10 ft, rich pink; *sweginzowii*, China, to 12 ft, rose-lilac, fragrant; *tomentella*, to 12 ft, China, pale pink-lilac, fragrant; *villosa*, N. China, to 10 ft, lilac-rose; *velutina*, Korea, N. China, to 10 ft, purple and white, fragrant; and *yunnanensis*, China, to 10 ft, pink, fragrant, and v. *rosea*, deeper pink. A second group (*Vulgares*) produces its panicles at the ends of shoots of the previous year, in May, usually in pairs, and includes S. × *chinensis*, Rouen Lilac, to 10 ft, lilac, very fragrant, and vs. *alba*, white; *metensis*, rosy-lilac; and *saugeana*, lilac-red; *persica*, Persian Lilac, Persia to China, 6 ft, lilac, fragrant, and v. *alba*, white; *pinnatifolia*, China, to 8 ft, pinnate leaves, white, pink-tinted; and *vulgaris*, E. Europe, 10–20 ft, lilac, fragrant, and its varieties and hybrids such as 'Ambassadeur', deep blue; 'Charles X', purple red; 'Clarke's Giant', light blue; 'Etna', claret; 'Glory of Horstentein', purple-red; 'Jan Van Thol', white; 'Massena', purple; 'Primrose', pale yellow; 'Souvenir de Louis Spath', reddish purple; and 'Vestale', pure white, which have single flowers; and 'Charles Joly', reddish purple; 'Ellen Willmott', white; 'Katherine Havemeyer', light blue-violet; 'Madame Lemoine', white; 'Michel Buchner', rosy-lilac; 'Mrs Edward Harding', purplish red; 'Paul Thirion', rosy red; 'President Grevy', pinkish mauve; and 'Princess Clementine', cream to white, which have double flowers. S. *microphylla* v. *superba*, China, 2–5 ft, bright lilac, fragrant, May, and *palibiniana*, Korea, to 10 ft, slowly, deep lilac, and white, fragrant, May, are dwarf shrubs, often planted in rock gardens, as growth is so slow.

Cultivation. Plant November–March, well-drained soil, with ample organic content, pH 6·0–6·5, sunny positions. It is best not to allow flowering in the first year. No severe pruning, but when necessary old plants may be thinned in March.

Propagation. Species by seeds, April, outdoor seed-bed. Otherwise by layering in spring. Varieties and hybrids are grafted on S. *vulgaris* rootstocks in spring. By cuttings of half-firm shoots, July–August, under handlights.

No very serious diseases or pests trouble Lilacs. The leaves may be mined by the caterpillars of *Gracilaria syringella*, a tiny Tineid Moth, calling for a gamma-BHC to malathion insecticide in May, or nicotine for summer. Suckers should be suppressed by being torn up, or painted with a 2,4,5-T brushwood herbicide.

Syringe. A good syringe is very useful in greenhouse gardening, to maintain humidity in hot weather by syringing glass, walls and paths. May also be used for applying fungicides and insecticides, but needs thoroughly cleansing afterwards. Pressure sprayers are good alternative appliances. *See* Sprayers.

Systematics. Taxonomy (q.v.), particularly the identification, classification and nomenclature of the groups of plants themselves.

Systemic Insecticides. Insecticides designed to be applied as spray or granules to the soil and/or plants to be absorbed into the sap stream, which is thus made toxic to sap-sucking insects, such as aphids, red spider mites, etc., without harming predator insects. Since they are based on organo-phosphorus compounds, dangerous to man, great care is needed in their use, though formulations for garden use are now available. They should not be used within four weeks of harvest.

T

Tacsonia. A genus now included in *Passiflora* (q.v.). *T. van volxemii*, chiefly grown, is now *P. antioquiensis*.

Tagetes (ta-ge'tes. Fam. Compositae). Pretty, colourful annuals largely with heads in shades of yellow, gold to mahogany, all summer.

Selection. T. erecta, African Marigold, comes from Mexico, is grown in tall strains of $2\frac{1}{2}$–3 ft, such as 'Crackerjack', 'Hawaii', and lemon and orange 'All-double'; F_1 hybrids such as the 'Climax' strain, 3 ft, in yellow, gold and orange; and 'Jubilee' strain, 2 ft, with carnation-like flowers; Carnation-flowered types, $2\frac{1}{2}$ ft, as 'Alaska', pale primrose; 'Apricot Queen' and 'Guinea Gold'; and in dwarf strains, 1–$1\frac{1}{2}$ ft, such as 'Golden Age', 'Spun Gold', 'Spun Yellow' and F_1 hybrid 'Yellow Nugget'. *T. patula*, the parent of French Marigolds, also comes from Mexico, and is grown in dwarf single-flowering vs., such as 'Lemon King', 'Naughty Marietta' and 'Eliza', 6–12 in.; in double-flowering vs., such as the 'Petite' strain of 6 in.; 'Marionette', 6 in.; 'Tangerine', 'Mahogany Red' and 'Spanish Brocade' to 1 ft, and Tall Double French to 2 ft. *T. tenuifolia* (*signata*), Mexican Striped Marigold, has been developed chiefly in v. *pumila*, a dwarf of 6 in., and forms 'Golden Gem' and 'Monarch Lemon Gem', for their cushions of flowers; while 'Irish Lace' is a foliage plant in which the ferny, pinnatisect leaves form green mounds, excellent for edging or contrast. *T. minuta*, S. America, tall to 4 or 6 ft, has been put forward as a weed suppressor on account of its root excretions, but hardly ornamental.

Cultivation. Seeds are sown under glass, March–April, standard compost, bottom heat of 18° C. (65° F.); to be pricked out and hardened off, before planting out of doors 4–9 in. apart, in May. Or seeds may be sown where plants are to grow in late April–May, and thinned subsequently.

Taiwania (ta-i-wa'ni-a. Fam. Pinaceae). The species grown, *T. cryptomerioides*, Formosa, to 120 ft, is a conifer of graceful habit with drooping branchlets, resembling *Cryptomeria*; worth trying in mild localities, planted in March–April, well-drained, lightish loam, peat-enriched, and in warm sun, sheltered from cold drying winds. Propagation by seeds.

Talinum (ta-li'num. Fam. Portulaceae). Pretty succulent-leaved perennials of which two species may be grown in the sheltered rock garden or alpine house.

Selection. T. okanoganense, NW. America, 1–2 in., white, June; and *spinescens*, NW. America, violet flowers, July.

Cultivation. Plant April, well-drained, humus-rich soil; protect from damp cold in winter. Propagated by seeds when available, autumn.

Tamarix, Tamarisk (tam'a-riks. Fam. Tamaricaceae). Maritime or salt-tolerant shrubs esteemed for their graceful stems, dainty foliage and plumose flowers.

Selection. T. anglica, native to SW. England and France, 3–10 ft, white, tinted pink, flowers, July–September; *gallica*, French Tamarisk, France, to 10 ft, pink, June–August; *hispida*, S. Russia, 3–4 ft, bright pink, August–September; *parviflora* (*tetrandra purpurea*), SE. Europe, 15 ft, pink on purple shoots, May; *pentandra*, SE. Europe, to 12 ft, rose-pink, August–September; and *tetrandra*, SE. Europe, 10 ft, bright pink, May.

Cultivation. Plant October–March, porous ordinary, or sandy soil, mild localities, especially valuable for seaside gardens. Prune February–March.

Propagation. By cuttings of firm young shoots, July–August, in cold frame or under handlights, sandy soil, in sheltered shade.

Tanacetum, Tansy (tan-a-ke'tum.

Fam. Compositae). Mostly perennial herbs with smallish composite flower-heads in summer, showy when planted *en masse*.

Selection. T. camphoratum, N. America, 1½ ft, camphor-scented, velvety-silver foliage, golden-yellow, summer, is possible for borders; *herderi*, Turkistan, 3 in., silvery rosettes of leaves, bright yellow, summer, for the rock garden; while *vulgare* is the native Buttons or Tansy, 2–3 ft, camphor-smelling leaves, flat heads of yellow flowers, August, one time grown as a herb for flavouring, and v. *crispum*, curled leaves, may be used for garnishing.

Cultivation. Plant in October–March, any ordinary well-drained soil, in sun.

Propagation. By division, autumn or early spring.

Tanakaea (ta-na-ke'a. Fam. Saxifragaceae). A genus represented by *T. radicans*, Japan, 4 in., a pleasing evergreen perennial with long-stalked, fleshy deep green leaves and plume-like cymes of white flowers in spring; suitable for cool shade, in well-drained, humus-rich soil in the rock garden, or a pan in the alpine house. Propagated by division of rhizomatous root in April.

Tansy. See *Tanacetum*.

Tap-root. The first and main root from a dicotyledonous seed, growing downwards vertically.

Tar, Coal. Most useful for the preservation of timber sunk in the soil, as for stakes and posts.

Tar, Stockholm. A distillate of the wood of *Pinus sylvestris*, which may be used to dress wounds or cuts on trees.

Tar Oil. Derived from the distillation of coal, tar-oil emulsions are chiefly used as winter sprays for fruit trees, to destroy over-wintering aphids' eggs, and cleanse the bark of algae, moss and lichen growth; sometimes used to kill the dog lichen on lawns.

Tares. Seeds of *Vicia* spp., sometimes used for green manure crops.

Tarragon (*Artemisia dracunculus*). A perennial herb of S. Europe, 2 ft, grown for its aromatic, long lanceolate leaves for use in salads, for flavouring sauces and for making tarragon vinegar.

Cultivation. Plant in March, in well-drained light or sandy soil, mild locali-

ties; sunny position. Give winter protection to crowns in the north. Propagated by pulling runners apart in March–April, to plant separately.

Taxodium, Swamp Cypress (taks-o'di-um. Fam. Pinaceae). Deciduous cypresses with pale green yew-like foliage turning bright brown in autumn, natives of Mexico and SE. U.S.A.

Selection. T. ascendens, to 50 ft, and v. *nutans*, with drooping branches; *distichum*, to 100 ft, distinctive for woody protuberances from the roots, known as Cypress Knees, in swampy places; and v. *pendulum*, a drooping form.

Cultivation. Plant October–November or March, in moist or even boggy ground, or will succeed in any ordinary soil, in mid and southern England and Ireland.

Propagation. By seeds, sown March, moist loam. By cuttings of young shoots, July–August, under handlights.

Taxon. A term used for a taxonomic group or unit of classification.

Taxonomy. The study and science of Classification of living organisms, sometimes termed Systematics.

Taxus, Yew (taks'us. Fam. Taxaceae). Hardy, unisexual, evergreen, somewhat slow-growing shrubs or trees, with linear, two-ranked small leaves, long-lived.

Selection. T. baccata, Common Yew, Europe and Britain, 40–50 ft, highly adaptable to fine hedging and topiary work; and vs. *adpressa*, shrub of 8 ft; *dovastonii*, drooping branchlets, good as a specimen; *fastigiata*, upright Irish Yew, and forms *aurea*, golden-leaved; *standishii*, golden leaved; *elegantissima*, long, drooping branches; *neidpathensis*, free-growing; *nana, pygmaea, repandens* are dwarf, and low-growing; and *stricta* an erect bush. *T. canadensis*, eastern N. America, 4–6 ft, bush, and v. *washingtonii*, with drooping branches; *chinensis*, Chinese Yew, to 40 ft, less dense foliage; *cuspidata*, Japanese Yew, to 40 ft, but often shrubby; and various hybrids of which × *hatfieldii*, erect and conical; × *hicksii*, columnar; and × *sargentii*, erect conical growth are useful.

Cultivation. Plant October, or March–April; almost any well-drained soil, including chalk; but with due regard to the fact that shoots and foliage are toxic to stock. Prune in April–May; or clip in June and again in August, for fine hedges.

Propagation. Species by seeds in spring. By cuttings, in sandy soils, in cold frame or under handlights, July–August. By grafting on stocks of common Yew.

Tea Berry. Common name of *Gaultheria procumbens.*

Teasel. See *Dipsacus.*

Tecoma (te-ko'ma. Fam. Bignoniaceae). A genus of erect-growing shrubs with pinnate leaves, and bell-shaped flowers in racemes, of S. America, for the warm greenhouse.

Selection. T. garrocha, Peru, to 12 ft, reddish-brown and yellow flowers, summer; *mollis,* Mexico to Chile, 5 ft, yellow; × *smithii,* 2–3 ft, yellow, tinged orange, autumn (good for pots); and *stans,* Mexico to Peru, to 10 ft, yellow, autumn.

Cultivation. Plant autumn or spring, well-drained loam soil, or in large pots, in the warm greenhouse; watering freely in growth, very moderately in winter, with temp. 13° C. (55° F.) minimum.

Propagation. By seeds, March, standard compost, bottom heat of 21° C. (70° F.). By cuttings, July, in propagating case. For Tecoma Climbers, see *Campsis.*

Tecophilaea (te-ko-pi-le'a. Fam. Amaryllidaceae). The species usually grown is the cormous *T. cyanocrocus,* Chilean Crocus, with blue, white throated flowers in spring, on 6-in. stems; v. *elegans* being more slender, and *leichtlinii,* more white in the throat.

Cultivation. Plant in September–October, 2 in. deep, well-drained, humus-rich soil, in rock garden or alpine house in deep pans.

Propagation. By offsets in September; by seeds, sown in March–April.

Tegumen. The inner layer of a seed-coat.

Tellima (tel'li-ma. Fam. Saxifragaceae). Hardy herbaceous perennials of which *T. grandiflora,* a native of western N. America, 2 ft, with hairy rounded leaves, and greenish, red-tinted flowers in racemes in summer, may be easily grown in woodland or wild garden, being planted October–March, porous lightish soil, with peat; and propagated

by division in March, or by seeds, sown April, out of doors.

Temperature. The temperature in which a plant grows is vital since it virtually regulates the rate at which it can carry out its functions and complex chemistry. There are limits of tolerance for low and high temperature, and an optimum between the limits at which the plant functions most actively. Briefly, low temperatures slow or halt growth; high temperatures prevent it. The temperature range of a plant's native habitat is a reasonable guide to its needs. The Centigrade Scale is universally used in science, and is replacing the Fahrenheit. 5° C. = 3° F. To convert ° C. to ° F., multiply by 9, divide by 5, and add 32 to the result. To convert ° F. to ° C., subtract 32, multiply by 5 and divide by 9.

Tendril. A twining thin extension of a stem (e.g. Vine), leaf (e.g. Pea), used by a plant to attach itself to a support and climb.

FIG. 216   Tendrils (Sweet Pea).

Tenui-. Prefix in compound words, meaning slender or thin.

Tepal. A term used for individual parts of a perianth, where flowers do not have distinct petals and sepals, or the perianth is not differentiated into corolla and calyx, as in flowers of the Amaryllis and Lily families, and Orchids.

Teratology. The study of abnormal growth in plants.

Teres, Terete. Cylindrical, round-stemmed. Ex. *Vanda teres*.

Terminal. At the end of a shoot, not lateral or axillary.

Ternatus (-a, -um). In threes. Ex. *Choisya ternata* (of leaves).

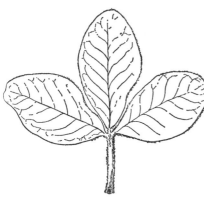

FIG. 217   Ternate leaf (*Cytisus battandieri*).

Ternstroemia (tern-stro'mi-a. Fam. Theaceae). The chief species grown is *T. japonica*, Japan, a somewhat tender evergreen shrub, to 12 ft, with white, fragrant, many-stamened flowers, summer. May be tried in well-drained, humus-rich soil in sheltered, very mild localities outdoors; but elsewhere needs the shelter of a cool greenhouse in winter. Propagation by young shoots, taken in July–August, in propagating frame, with bottom heat of 18° C. (65° F.).

Terrace. A raised levelled area around a house on sloping ground, which may be paved and ornamented with plants in vases or pots, or tubs. With a long slope, a series of terraces can be planned to be planted as separate gardens, with access by steps, and walls adorned with climbers, etc.

Testa. The seed-coat, or protective outer covering of the embryo of a seed plant.

Tetra-. Prefix in compound words, meaning four. Ex. Tetragonous, four-angled.

Tetracentron (te-tra-ken'tron. Fam. Tetracentraceae). The only species, *T. sinense*, of China, makes a tall, elegant tree to 60 ft, with long, slender-pointed, palmate-veined leaves, and small yellowish flowers on thin spikes, June–July; hardy for mild gardens, in warm, sunny, sheltered positions, and well-drained loam soil, planted October–March. Propagation is by seeds, in pots, in cold frame; or by layering in spring.

Tetragonia (te-tra-go'ni-a. Fam. Aizoceae). The only species much grown is *T. expansa* (*tetragonioides*), New Zealand Spinach (q.v.).

Teucrium (tu'kri-um. Fam. Labiatae). A fairly large genus of small shrubs and perennials, but only a few of garden merit.

Selection. *T. chamaedrys*, Wall Germander, Europe and Britain, 9 in., sub-shrub, hairy evergreen leaves, whorled reddish-rose flowers, in spikes, July–August; *fruticans*, S. Europe, 2 ft, blue, summer; *polium*, Europe, 6 in., creamy flowers, July–August; and *subpinosum*, S. Europe, 1 ft, pale lilac, July–August.

Cultivation. Plant October–November or March–April, well-drained soil, with leaf-mould or peat, in warm, sheltered positions, rock garden or alpine house.

Propagation. By cuttings of young shoots, July.

Thalamus. The receptacle of a flower.

Thalictrum, Meadow Rue (thalik'trum. Fam. Ranunculaceae). A genus of herbaceous perennials, containing several of ornamental value for their elegant foliage and attractive flowers.

Selection. *T. aquilegiifolium*, Europe, 2–3 ft, panicles of white, summer, and v. 'Purple Cloud'; *diffusiflorum*, SE. Tibet, 3–10 ft, very large mauve flowers, summer; *dipterocarpum*, W. China, 2–5 ft, mauve, summer; and vs. *album*, white, 'Hewitt's Double', double mauve; and *minus*, Europe, Britain, 1–2 ft, bronzy flowers, summer, and vs., are good border plants; while *T. alpinum*, northern hemisphere, 4 in., greenish-yellow, June; *kiusianum*, Japan, rose-purple, June, and v. *album*, white; and *orientale*, Asia Minor, Greece, 4 in., white,

July, are good for rock gardens or the alpine house.

Cultivation. Plant October or March–April, in good loam soil, well-drained, partial shade, pH 6·0–6·5.

Propagation. By division of roots in late March. Species by seeds, April, cold frame or outdoor seed-bed.

Thallophyta. The lower plants—algae, bacteria, fungi, and lichens—form this division of the Plant Kingdom.

Thallus. The simple vegetative body of a plant, showing no differentiation into organs such as roots, stems and leaves.

Thelesperma (the-les-per'ma. Fam. Compositae). Only one species is much grown, *T. burridgeanum,* an annual from Texas, 1–2 ft, with bi-pinnate leaves, and deep orange, blotched reddish brown, rayed flowers, summer; from seeds sown under glass in March, or out of doors in lightish soil, and sun, in March–April, where to flower.

Thermometer. An instrument for the measuring of temperature (q.v.). The ordinary thermometer, registering the rise and fall of temperature, is useful in the greenhouse, but a Maximum and Minimum Thermometer which records the lowest and highest temperature reached in a chosen period is more informative and useful. It should be placed centrally in a greenhouse, shaded from the sun, out of draughts, to give a reading of the atmosphere. A 'plunging thermometer', with perforated tube, is very useful for testing the heat of mushroom beds and of soil.

Thermopsis (therm-op'sis. Fam. Leguminosae). Hardy perennials with tri-foliolate leaves, and racemes of papilionaceous flowers.

Selection. T. caroliniana, E. U.S.A., 2 ft, yellow erect racemes, July; and *montana,* western N. America, 1½ ft, yellow, June–July.

Propagation. By seeds, March, standard compost, in cool greenhouse, to plant out April–May, well-drained ordinary soil, warm sun.

Thinning. A term used for (*a*) the spacing of seedlings by removing surplus early in growth; (*b*) the thinning of young fruitlets on fruit trees, usually in June; (*c*) the thinning out of shoots and branches of shrubs to improve air circulation and invigorate growth.

Thistle, Blessed. See *Silybum marianum.*

Thistle, Globe. See *Echinops.*

Thistle, Scots. See *Onopordon acanthium.*

Thlaspi (thlas'pi. Fam. Cruciferae). Low growing perennials for the rock garden.

Selection. T. alpinum, European Alps, 4 in., white, yellow-anthered flowers, summer; and *rotundifolium,* European Alps, 2 in., fragrant rose-lilac, summer. *T. arvense* is the annual weed, commonly Pennycress.

Cultivation. Plant October–November or March–April, well-drained scree soil, sun.

Propagation. By shoot cuttings, May–June. By seeds, in cool greenhouse, spring.

Thorn. See *Acacia, Crataegus, Pyracantha.*

Thorn. A sharp-pointed woody spine on a stem.

Thorn Apple. See *Datura stramonium.*

Thrift. See *Armeria.*

Thrips, Thunder Flies. An Order (Thysanoptera) of small, sap-sucking insects, yellow, brownish or black, about $\frac{1}{10}$ in. long, often found on plants, infesting leaves, shoots and flowers, in the open and under glass; one species, *Thrips tabaci,* at least being a vector of virus infection. Controlled by BHC, gamma-BHC, malathion or nicotine insecticides, or in greenhouses by aerosol or smoke forms.

Throat. The top part of a tubular flower.

Throatwort. See *Trachelium caeruleum.*

FIG. 218   Thrips (*Thrips tabaci*).

Thrum-eyed Flower. A flower in which the anthers are borne on long stamens at the top of the corolla tube, above the style and stigma placed half way down; as in some Primulas; opposed to Pin-eyed (q.v.).

Thuja, Thuya (thu'ya. Fam. Pinaceae). Evergreen conifers of pyramidal form, slender flattened branchlets, and male and female flowers on the same tree.

Selection. T. koraiensis, Korea, spreading shrub or small tree to 25 ft, bright green, tansy-scented foliage; *occidentalis,* American Arbor-vitae, 50–60 ft, and many vs., *aurea-spicata,* golden-tipped leaves; *ericoides,* bronzy in winter; *fastigiata,* narrowly erect; *lutescens,* golden; and dwarf forms such as *globosa,* 2–3 ft; *robusta nana* ('Little Gem'; and 'Rheingold', golden yellow; *orientalis,* Chinese Arbor-vitae, 30–40 ft, branches growing vertically; and vs. *argentea,* leaves blotched white; *decussata,* 12 ft, bushy; *elegantissima,* slow-growing, dwarfish; *hillieri,* compact; *minima,* very dwarf; *rosedalis,* dwarf bush; and *semperaurescens,* golden bush; *plicata,* Western Arbor-vitae, Western Red Cedar, western N. America, to 150 ft, provides the timber for greenhouses, etc., pyramidal, branching to ground, reddish trunk, good for hedges and screens; and vs. *atrovirens,* deep green foliage; *fastigiata,* stiffly upright; *hillieri,* charming dwarf; *semperaurescens,* golden-tinged foliage; and *zebrina,* leaves green and gold banded; and *standishii,* Japan, 30 ft, yellowish green foliage.

Cultivation. Plant October or April–May, in well-drained, but moisture-retentive soil, pH 5–6; disliking lime; well sheltered from strong winds, gales or draughts. Best planted young, pot-grown, especially for hedging.

Propagation. Species by seeds, sown April, outdoor seed-bed, sandy loam or in pots. By cuttings, August, in cold frame or under handlight.

Thujopsis (thu-yop'sis. Fam. Pinaceae). The one species, *T. dolabrata* (*Thuja dolobrata*), 40–60 ft, larger leaved, white beneath, than Thuja, and less hardy; but handsome, in vs. *australis,* to 40 ft; *hondai,* taller to 100 ft; and *nana,* low-growing and spreading.

Cultivation. Plant October or March–

May, well-drained, moisture-retentive, lime-free soil, in mild localities of south and south-west; well sheltered from high winds. Propagation as for *Thuja.*

Thunbergia (thun-ber-gi'a. Fam. Acanthaceae). Beautiful evergreen tropical twining climbers, with tubular flowers, summer, for the warm greenhouse.

Selection. T. alata, Black-eyed Susan, S. Africa, to 6 ft, yellow, deep purple throated, flowers, summer, and vs. *alba,* white; and *aurantiaca,* orange; are annual, and grown as half-hardy annuals from seeds. *T. coccinea,* India, 10–25 ft, red flowers, spring; *fragrans,* India, 10 ft, fragrant white, summer; *grandiflora,* N. India, to 30 ft, blue flowers, summer; and *gregorii* (*gibsonii*), E. Africa, orange, summer, are naturally perennial, though often grown as annuals. *T. anatalensis,* S. Africa, a subshrub of 2 ft, blue and yellow, July, can be grown in the cool greenhouse.

Cultivation. Sow seeds in March, standard compost, bottom heat of 18° C. (65° F.), to grow on in pots, or border of well-drained, humus-rich soil, watering freely. If grown perennially, cut back in autumn, training new growth each year. May be propagated by division in spring. Minimum winter temp. 13° C. (55° F.), with very moderate watering.

Thuya. See *Thuja.*

Thyme. Two species are grown as herbs for culinary purposes; *Thymus vulgaris,* Black or Common Thyme, S. Europe, 6–8 in., for general seasoning; and *T.* × *citriodorus,* Lemon Thyme, 6–12 in., for its lemony flavour.

Cultivation. Sow seeds, April, lightish loam soil, warm sunny border; thin to 4–6 in. May also be increased by division in April. Gather shoots for drying when coming into flower, hanging in a cool airy place, in small bunches.

Thymus, Thyme (t(h)i'mus. Fam. Labiatae). A rather large genus of aromatic dwarf shrubs, which may be grouped into the herbal thymes (*see* Thyme), and the ornamental, grown for their flowers, and/or carpeting ground cover, as follows.

Selection. T. carnosus, Portugal, 8 in., fastigiate small bush, pink flowers,

June; *herba-barona*, Corsica, 5 in., deep pink, caraway fragrance, June; *longiflorus*, Spain, 9 in., purple, July; *membranaceus*, Spain, 8 in., white and pink, June; *nitidus*, Marettimo, Sicily, 6 in., lilac-pink, June–July; and *villosus*, Portugal, 4 in., deep rose, July, all need mild, sheltered quarters out of doors, or to be grown in the alpine house. The carpeting thymes are chiefly *T. serpyllum*, Europe, Britain, purple, summer, and v. *alba*, and *carneus*, and *drucei*, Europe and Britain, with pink and white-flowering forms; adaptable to alpine lawns (q.v.).

Cultivation. The shrubby flowering kinds need planting in October–November, or March–April, in well-drained soil in rock gardens or paving, warm sun, mild localities; or to be grown in the alpine house in pans. Carpeting forms are tolerant of most soils, except the waterlogged, planted March–April, and welcome some lime to pH 6·5–7.

Propagation. By green cuttings or rooted runners, early June. By seeds, April, in outdoor bed, sandy soil.

Thyrse. A panicle or cluster of flowers, widest in the middle.

Thyrsiflorus (-a, -um). With flowers in a thyrse, Ex. *Dendrobium thyrsiflorum.*

Tiarella (ti-ar-el'la. Fam. Saxifragaceae). Low-growing herbaceous perennials, pretty flowers freely produced in spring.

Selection. T. cordifolia, Foam-flower, eastern N. America, 1 ft, starry white flowers, April–June; and *wherryi*, Tennessee, etc., 1 ft, starry, rose-tinged white racemes, May–June.

Cultivation. Plant October–March, porous, leaf-mould-enriched soil, cool shade.

Propagation. By division, March–April. By seeds, April, sandy loam seedbed, outdoors.

Tibouchina (Lasiandra) (ti-boo-ki'na. Fam. Melastomataceae). The species chiefly offered and grown is *T. semidecandra*, Brazil, to 10 ft, evergreen shrub with ovate, strongly veined leaves, and large, open, bell-shaped, rich purple flowers in panicles, summer–autumn, and v. *floribunda*, even finer-flowering.

Cultivation. Pot in large pots, or plant

FIG. 219   A Thyrse (*Staphylea colchica*).

in cool greenhouse border, in autumn, sandy loam enriched with peat; keeping just moist in winter, temp. 10° C. (50° F.); water freely in active growth. May be grown as bushes in pots, but repot to avoid being pot-bound; otherwise worth training up a light trellis. Prune flowered shoots back after flowering.

Propagation. By cuttings of young shoots, inserted in propagating case, May–June, bottom heat of 15·5° C. (60° F.).

Tiger Flower. See *Tigrida.*

Tiger Lily. See *Lilium tigrinum.*

Tigridia, Tiger Flower (ti-grid'i-a. Fam. Iridaceae). The species chiefly grown, *T. pavonia*, Flower of Tigris, Peacock Tiger Flower, Mexico, is a bulbous plant, 1–2 ft, bearing bowl-shaped, richly marked red flowers, in summer, opening in the morning, and fading at night; with several vs., such as *alba*, white; *conchiflora*, yellow; and named

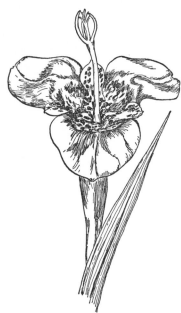

FIG. 220 *Tigridia pavonia,* Peacock Tiger Flower.

forms. Other species, *T. lutea,* Peru, and *pringlei,* S. Mexico, are desirable but seldom offered. Only really suited to sunny districts.

Cultivation. Plant the bulbs 6 in. deep, in April, porous, well-drained soil, peat-enriched, sunny, warm border or terrace. Lift in autumn, to store in frost-proof place as with Gladioli. Propagation is by offsets in spring; or by seeds, in cool greenhouse, to grow on for three years.

Tigrinus (-a, -um). Tiger-like stripes or spots. Ex. *Lilium tigrinum.*

Tilia, Lime, Linden (ti′li-a. Fam. Tiliaceae). A genus of deciduous trees, with handsome foliage and cymes of white or yellowish flowers in June–August, highly attractive to bees.

Selection. T. × *euchlora,* to 50 ft, glossy, bright green, cordate leaves, fragrant flowers, July, and *petiolaris,* Weeping Silver Lime, Europe, 60 ft, dark green leaves, white-felted beneath,

very fragrant flowers, July–August, are good bee trees though sometimes stupefying, and best for gardens; *platyphyllos,* Europe, to 120 ft, is tall-growing, but v. *asplenifolia (laciniata)* is a smaller version, with much lobed leaves, and *fastigiata,* erect-growing; *maximowicziana,* Japan, 70 ft, many-flowered cymes, July, much liked by bees; and *tomentosa,* Silver Lime, SE. Europe, 60 ft, may flower July–August.

FIG. 221 Leaf of the Lime, *Tilia cordata.*

Cultivation. Plant November–March, in good loam, moisture-retentive though draining well; and sun. Limes stand up well to pollarding and pleaching.

Propagation. By layering. By seeds, in spring, but the species hybridize freely and seedlings may vary.

Tillandsia (til-land′si-a. Fam. Bromeliaceae). A large topical genus of epiphytic stemless plants, with richly coloured leaves, and scapes with bracts and flowers; grown as hothouse plants or house plants.

Selection. T. cyanea, Guatemala, 2 ft, blue flowers from a pink-bracted scape, and rosette of strap-shaped leaves, autumn; and *lindeniana,* Peru, 2½ ft, violet-blue flowers from coral-pink bracted scapes, and rosette of arching, narrow, green, empurpled leaves, and vs., make handsome plants.

Cultivation. Pot in spring, in mixture of 3 parts by bulk fibrous peat, 1 part sphagnum moss, 1 part lump charcoal, over crocks or drainage material filling half the pot; in heated greenhouse or well-lighted, airy indoor rooms; temp. 15·5° C. (60° F.); watering and syringing in warm weather months; keeping barely moist in winter.

Propagation. By suckers, rooted as above in pots just big enough to hold them.

Tilth. A term meaning the depth of soil broken up and affected by tillage or cultivation or digging.

Tinctorius (-a, -um). Of Dyers. Ex. *Genista tinctoria.*

Tithonia (ti-tho'ni-a. Fam. Compositae). Annuals of Mexico, central America, and Cuba, known as Mexican Sunflowers, and grown as half-hardy annuals.

Selection. T. diversifolia, to 10 ft, with yellow, rayed flower-heads, summer, and *rotundifolia,* 4–6 ft, rich orange-red flowers, summer.

Cultivation. Sow under glass, March, standard compost, bottom heat of 18° C. (65° F.), to prick off, and plant out in May, in well-drained light soil and sun.

Toad *(Bufo bufo).* Helpful to gardeners, since the toad feeds on woodlice, insects, slugs, etc. Useful to have in the greenhouse.

Toadflax. See *Linaria.*

Toadstool. A common name for umbrella-like fungi of the Class Basidiomycetes, including Mushrooms.

Tobacco *(Nicotiana tabacum).* Although the species from which the varieties of smoking tobacco are derived is an annual or biennially grown plant, native to tropical America, good crops can be grown in most parts of England, given reasonably good soil, and sun; it is quite legal to do so for personal consumption, though not for sale.

Varieties. 'Burley' and its crosses are very suitable and easy to grow, especially on heavy soils; 'Virginian' varieties are popular for cigarettes; 'Havana' is a cigar type; and oriental 'Turkish' provides aromatic leaf.

Culture. Plants are raised from seeds, sown thinly in boxes, JI seed compost, simply pressed into the surface, in cool greenhouse, with bottom heat of 18–21° C. (65–70° F.), and pricked off into small pots or boxes 2 in. apart, when large enough to handle, and grown steadily on with regular watering and

adequate light, until late May. Plant out on an open, sunny site, sheltered from cold winds, in soil reasonably rich in humus and given a base fertilizer, high in potash (1 part by weight ammonium sulphate, 2 parts superphosphate, 1 part sulphate of potash, and 1 part sulphate of magnesium) at 2–3 oz. per square yd, 1½–2 ft apart, in rows 3 ft apart. Weeds must be suppressed. Remove any suckers or side shoots that form, and the terminal flower head before it opens. In late July–early August, remove bottom leaves.

Harvesting. From September onwards, leaves should be removed in dry weather when they mature, shown in slight changes of colour, yellowing or mottling, and curling. The leaves are laid on a clean surface out of doors to wilt for a few hours, as gathered, and then may be stacked in small heaps under cover for 4–5 days to yellow. They must then be dried quickly, hung in a warm, airy, well-ventilated place, threaded on sticks or canes, slightly apart, until the midribs are dry. The mid-ribs may be slit to facilitate drying. When dry, the leaf can be sent to a curing centre. In England, Tilty Tobacco Centre, Tilty, Dunmow, Essex; in Scotland, Scottish Amateur Tobacco Growing and Curing Association, 39 Milton Road, Kirkcaldy, Fife.

Todea (to'de-a. Fam. Osmundaceae). The only species, *T. barbara,* is the Crape Fern of Australia and New Zealand, with fine fronds to 4 ft long, for the cool greenhouse or indoor room; v. *bipinnatifida,* very graceful, and *vromii,* with longer fronds of pale green.

Cultivation. Pot in March–April, mixture of peat and coarse sand, with a little sphagnum moss; small pots, watering moderately; minimum winter temp. 10° C. (50° F.). Tolerates shade. Easily propagated from spores, when ready.

Tolmiea (tol'mi-a. Fam. Saxifragaceae). Represented by a single species, *T. menziesii,* NW. America, a slender, tufted perennial, of 18 in., virtually hardy, but usually grown as a pot plant in cool rooms and shade, distinctive for its habit of producing young plants from buds on the old leaves, giving rise to its common names of Pig-a-Back plant, or Youth-on-Age. Pot in March, standard compost, summer out of doors in cool shady spot; minimum winter temp. 7° C. (45° F.). Propagate by detaching plantlets, after layering and rooting in small pots, during summer.

Tomato (*Lycospersicon esculentum*, Fam. Solonaceae). Introduced in 1595 from Peru, the Tomato was first grown as an ornamental plant and its fruits were called 'Love Apples'. Today it has become indispensable to our diet as a health-giving, vitamin-rich food. The tomato, however, is primarily a tropical plant and non-hardy under temperate conditions; a fact that determines the methods of its culture, for temperature plays a vital part in growing the crop.

Varieties. These are numerous, with most seedsmen offering their own specialities. Of the older varieties 'Early Market', 'Harbinger', 'Money-maker', 'Ailsa Craig' and 'Potentate' (for the north), are good; 'Alicante', 'Histon Ideal', 'Blom's Perfection' are newer introductions; but the F_1 hybrids are becoming more preferable for greater resistance to trouble, such as 'Euro-cross', 'Hertford Cross', 'Kelvedon Cross' and 'Ware Cross'. Although the above varieties will also do well out of doors in good conditions, varieties particularly raised for outdoor-growing include 'Outdoor Girl', 'First in the Field', 'Amateur' and 'Primabel', which are bush types, requiring little staking. Most seedsmen also offer yellow fruiting varieties such as 'Golden Queen' and 'Sunrise'; and ornamental types such as 'Pear', 'Red Cherry' and 'Currant', and so-called 'White' varieties.

Seed-sowing. Whether for indoor or outdoor cropping, plants should be raised from seeds under warm conditions, with bottom heat of 18° C. (65° F.). Sow ¼ in. deep, ½ in. apart, standard compost in seed-boxes or pans, preferably in the greenhouse, though a cold frame can be used for summer sowings. Prick off seedlings as soon as they can be handled by their seed leaves into 3-in. pots, preferably peat-wood fibre, or soil blocks, to grow on at 15·5–18° C. (60–65° F.), until planted out. Sowing times depend upon cropping sequence.

Cold Greenhouse Culture. Plants may be raised from seeds sown in February–March in a propagator, or be bought in to plant when first truss of flower buds are showing, last week of April–mid May. They may be grown in 12–14 in. pots, or 12 by 12 by 18 in. long boxes, two plants per box, filled with rich

FIG. 222 Tomato Flower, fully open and ready to be set: k. knee or elbow.

potting compost, on stages; in well-prepared, organically manured, base-fertilized and watered soil borders; in rings (*see* Ring Culture); or in straw bales (*see* Straw Bale Culture). In a cool greenhouse, when minimum night temperature can be held above 13° C. (55° F.), planting up can be advanced

FIG. 223 Tomato Flower, after fertilization, with embryo fruitlet formed.

by 3–4 weeks. Plants are set 12–18 in. apart, to be trained, single-stemmed, by twining with soft fillis, hung from wires at the top of the house, or, if preferred, by tying to cane supports. For the first 2–3 weeks watering is confined to the soil ball until the plants start growing vigorously. Side-shoots from leaf axils are nipped out as they form. Ventilation should be regulated to maintain an even, fairly high, temp. (15·5-21° C. [60-70° F.]). Flower trusses are tapped when fully open, and mist-sprayed, to ensure setting. First and last trusses, sometimes difficult to set, can be sprayed once with a fruit-setting hormone solution. Increased watering is needed as temperatures rise, and should not be neglected. Capillary watering gives good results when plants cannot be tended during the day. Feeding may begin when the first truss of fruit begins to swell, with a balanced liquid fertilizer or seaweed derivative solution, at fortnightly intervals. Ventilation snould be regulated to maintain a buoyant atmosphere without draughts. Plants should be syringed on hot sunny days, but be dry by nightfall. Too high temperatures (above 27° C. [80° F.]) are not beneficial, and shade should be given on very hot days. Roots may be mulched with moist peat or compost or straw to conserve moisture. There is no need to stop plants, except to confine them to the greenhouse room available, and up to twelve trusses may be set. Lower leaves and yellowing leaves may be removed as fruit develop, but drastic defoliation of plants is not advantageous. Those gardeners who want the utmost yield can use the technique of enriching the carbon dioxide content of the greenhouse atmosphere, during daylight, at temperatures about 18° C. (65° F.), by means of simple cylinder equipment now available.

Heated Greenhouse Culture. With heat, tomatoes can be cropped the year round. Seeds may be sown in late June–mid July in a cold frame to crop at Christmas into the New Year; in August and early September to crop in February–March; in October, in propagating unit or greenhouse, to crop April and May; in mid November to the end of December to crop in May and June; in February, to crop in July.

The limiting factor in winter-cropping is the lack of sunlight, both duration and intensity, and it is only really worth while in the sunnier parts of the country. Winter cropping plants are usually grown to four trusses, in 6-in. pots or rings; spring-cropping in 9-in. pots or rings, to six trusses. Temperatures of 15·5-18° C. (60-65° F.) in the day, and a minimum of 10-13° C. (50-55° F.) at night, should be maintained. Ventilation is simplified by use of an extractor fan. Care should be given to setting fruit by tapping sharply, or using a fruit-setting hormone spray, and watering regulated to give a dryish but buoyant atmosphere. CO_2 atmospheric enrichment can be given on sunny days. F_1 hybrid varieties do well under heated conditions.

Outdoor Culture. Inevitably, outdoor cropping is risky in the British climate, except in warm, sunny and sheltered districts. In the midlands, west and north plants should be grown by a south wall or hedge. Plants are raised from April-sown seeds, to plant out in early June, 18 in. apart, in soil liberally organically manured and base-fertilized, pH 6, or to grow by the Ring Culture or Straw Bale method; or in large pots, half-sunk in the ground, and kept well watered. Climbing varieties are best staked with 4–5 ft canes, and grown single-stemmed as in the greenhouse. Bush varieties welcome short stakes, and may be 'strawed' or mulched with peat or sheet polythene to keep the fruit clean. Cropping is best limited to four trusses. Feeding with liquid dilute manure is helpful after the setting of the first truss, at 7–14-day intervals. Protection against Potato Blight is usually necessary in July–August; and the crop should be grown well away from its relatives, potatoes, if possible.

Cloche Culture. Under the greater warmth and weather protection of cloches, plants may be set out in mid to late April, and the cloches removed in late May–June when the danger of spring frosts is past, to stake and grow on in the open air. Bush varieties, planted 2–3 ft, apart, may be cloche-grown, in barn cloches throughout, though watering needs careful attention. Alternatively, special tall cloches or PVC plastic-covered frames may be used, with a side removable in the hottest weather, for tall plants.

Frame Culture. Tomatoes may also be grown in frames of the tall, span-roofed type or lean-to, in sunny sheltered places. The frame is either placed over well-prepared soil, or filled with a soil compost to give 12 in. headroom at least. Planting may take place from mid April, 18 in. apart, and top lights removed entirely in June, to grow plants on as in normal outdoor culture. Alternatively single-stemmed plants can be grown on as diagonal cordons, on canes, just below the glass surface, and given protection throughout, though the method needs much attention. It is easier to grow bush varieties, allowing them to grow through plastic mesh netting, fixed 6 in. above the soil surface, to harvest clean fruit, and remove top lights in good weather.

Tomato-grafting. Primarily developed as a way of avoiding soil-borne diseases in commercial growing, the grafting of a desirable varietal scion on a rootstock is also found to increase yields and prolong cropping. The best rootstocks are vigorous disease-resistance F_1 hybrids. Seeds of rootstock and scion varieties are sown to produce plants of about 4 in. high, and with stems about $\frac{1}{8}$ in. thick, at the same time. The stem of the rootstock is cut, leaving a pair of leaves, slit downwards for about $\frac{1}{2}$ in., through a little more than half the stem thickness, with a razor blade. A similar cut is made *upwards* at the same angle in the stem of the scion; the cut surfaces are immediately brought together, and bound with grafting tape or a strip of lead foil, and the two plants potted together. When the graft has taken in ten to fourteen days, the root of the scion can be severed, and the grafted plant subsequently planted out.

Diseases. Damping-off and Foot-rot (*Phytophthora* spp., *Corticium solani*) are fungus diseases of seedlings, avoidable by using sterilized composts. Grey Mould (*Botrytis cinerea*) is apt to infect and grow its grey whiskers on wounds, damp fruits, and from dropped flowers and debris left lying, especially under high humidity. Cleanliness, adequate ventilation and painting of trimming cuts with lime-sulphur solution check the fungus. Leaf Mould or Rust (*Cladosporium fulvum*) causes pale yellow patches on leaves, with pale grey to brownish violet mould underneath, particularly with high temperatures and humidity. Seriously infected leaflets should be carefully removed and burnt,

plants sprayed or dusted with a sulphur or zineb fungicide, humidity controlled by ventilation. Wilt, when plants wilt by day and recover by night, may be caused by *Verticillium albo-atrum*, or *V. dahliae*, especially under low temperature conditions; by *Fusarium oxysporum*, or *F. lycopersici*, when temperatures are high; all striking through the soil. Prevention lies in properly sterilized soil. Infected plants may be nursed by mounding soil compost to the stems to encourage fresh roots to form, and regulating temperatures. Blight (*Phytophthora infestans*) may spread from potatoes out of doors, and preventive action by spraying as for potatoes should be taken at similar times.

Virus Infections. Tomatoes are subject to several viruses causing such symptoms as Mosaic or Leaf-mottling, Streak, Bushy Stunt, Distorting Mosaic, Spotted Wilt, etc.; and infected plants are best destroyed. Prevention lies in perfect hygiene; control of insect vectors (Aphids, White-fly); and handling plants with clean hands, especially smokers with nicotine-stained fingers, which can transmit tobacco Mosaic from infected cigarette tobacco.

Functional Disorders. Premature flower-dropping, Dry Set and failure of fruits to swell, Blossom End Rot, when the fruits develop sunken blackish areas opposite to the stalk end, point to a water shortage at a critical period of growth, meriting an overhaul of watering technique. Green Back and Blotchy Ripening may be caused by nutritional deficiency, generally potash and/or phosphorus; though some newer varieties (F_1 hybrids) resist this trouble. Cracking and splitting are usually due to erratic watering or feeding or sudden temperature changes affecting the rate of growth.

Pests. Aphids, chiefly the potato Aphid (*Aulacorthum solani*), should be promptly controlled by nicotine or malathion insecticide (no picking for four days), or derris. White-fly (*Trialeurodes vaporariorum*) is controlled by a gamma-BHC, pyrethrum or malathion insecticide, or more simply repelled by growing a few African Marigolds in the house. Thrips (*Thrips tabaci*) are to be feared chiefly as vectors of the Spotted Wilt virus but are susceptible to the insecticides used for White-fly. Tomato Moth green or brown caterpillars (*Diataraxia oleracea*) may skeletonize leaves but derris usually is effective. Potato root eelworms (*Heterodera rostochiensis*) and Root knot eelworms (*Meloidogyne* spp.) can greatly retard plants, and plants are best destroyed, soil sterilized, or Ring Culture methods adopted. Soil frequenting pests such as Symphylids (*Scutigerella immaculata*), Woodlice and Springtails (*Collembola* spp.) can be controlled by gamma-BHC/DDT dusts, but are better avoided by adopting Ring or Straw Bale Culture, with a new rooting medium each year.

Tomentosus (-a, -um). Tomentose, woolly or thickly hairy. Ex. *Antennaria tomentosa*.

Tools. A gardener's tools and equipment must be adequate according to the size of the garden and the nature of work attempted. It is wise to buy the best tools that can be afforded, seeing to it that they are efficient and pleasant to handle and use, and well cared for, chiefly by inspecting, cleaning and, if necessary, oiling after use. The basic tools are the spade, fork, rake, hoe, trowel and hand-fork. A cultivator, garden line and wheelbarrow are valuable to vegetable gardening. For a lawn, a mowing machine, aerating tool, edging iron, top-dressing distributor, besom and appliance for applying herbicides will be needed. For greenhouse gardening, a thermometer, watering-can, syringe and/or sprayer and hose will be basic. If shrubs, trees and fruit bushes are to be grown, secateurs and a pruning saw will find good use; and for hedging, trimming shears. Where there is much work to be done, powered machines are labour-saving. Before buying ancillary tools, however, it is worth while assessing how often they will be used, their durability and necessity. *See* tools under their separate entries.

Top-dressing. The addition of fresh soil compost or manurial material over the rooting area of plants without disturbing the roots. With pot plants, some of the old surface soil is usually removed first.

Topiary. The art of pruning and trimming shrubs and trees into ornamental, formal or fanciful shapes, most highly popular in the sixteenth and seventeenth centuries. Box, Holly, Thorn and Yew lend themselves to this; the framework of the desired shape being established by careful training of the branches, and the shape itself by regular clipping of twiggy growth in the growing season each year.

Torch Lily. See *Kniphofia*.

Torenia (to-re'ni-a. Fam. Scrophulariaceae). Tender tropical annuals with pretty tubular flowers in short racemes for the warm greenhouse.

Selection. T. atropurpurea, Malaya, decumbent, red-purple flowers, summer; *baillonii*, Indo-China, yellow, purple-throated; and *fournieri*, Indo-China, 1 ft, violet, blue and yellow, and vs. *grandiflora* and *g. alba*, white.

Cultivation. Sow seeds, March–April, standard compost, bottom heat of 18° C. (65° F.), pricking off into pots or baskets, in which they are to flower; in warm greenhouse conditions, watering and syringing freely. May be increased by cuttings of young shoots readily in propagating case or under handlight.

Torreya (tor-reu'a. Fam. Taxaceae. Evergreen trees with linear, spine-pointed leaves in two ranks on shoots, emitting a pungent odour when crushed, and known as the Stinking Yews, though handsome.

Selection. T. californica, California Nutmeg, California, to 60 ft, unisexual, and *nucifera*, Kaya, Japan, bush to 12 ft, horizontal branches.

Cultivation. Plant October–November, or March–April, sheltered warm position, in south or south-west counties; well-drained soil, otherwise ordinary.

Propagation. By cuttings of young shoots, July–August, in cold frame or under handlights. By acorn-like seeds, April, when available.

Torus. The receptacle of a flower.

Trachelium (tra-ke'li-um. Fam. Campanulaceae). Pretty perennial herbs of the Mediterranean region, of doubtful hardiness.

Selection. T. asperuloides, Greece, 1 in., cushiony, lilac-blue flowers, July; *lanceolatum*, Sicily, 6 in., violet-blue panicles of bloom, July–September; and *rumelianum*, Bulgaria, Greece, 8 in., lilac-blue, July, are best grown in pans in the alpine house. *T. caeruleum*, Throatwort, Mediterannean region, 2 ft, large corymbs of small blue flowers, June–August, is usually grown as a biennial in the cool greenhouse, sown in June–July; or as a half-hardy annual, sown in March, and planted out in warm, sunny borders, and well-drained soil.

Cultivation. Pot, and repot, alpine house species in March, standard compost, well-drained pans, trimming after flowering; propagating by young shoot cuttings in June under handlights.

Trachelospermum (tra-kel-o-sper'mum. Fam. Apocynaceae). Evergreen climbing twining shrubs with strongly veined, leathery leaves and clusters of fragrant tubular, lobed flowers, summer.

Selection. *T. asiaticum* (*divaricatum*), Korea, Japan, to 15 ft, creamy white flowers; *jasminoides*, China, to 20 ft, very scented white flowers, and v. *variegatum*, leaves silvered; and *majus*, Japan, to 40 ft, pure white flowers.

Cultivation. Worth attempting on sheltered walls in mild localities, well-drained humus-rich soil; or in a cold greenhouse, somewhat dwarfed in large pots or tubs, watered freely in active growth, shaded from hot direct sun; kept barely moist in winter.

Propagation. By cuttings of firm shoots, July–August, under handlights, cold greenhouse.

Trachycarpus (tra-ki-kar'pus. Fam. Palmaceae). The species chiefly grown is *T. fortunei* (*excelsus, Chamaerops excelsa*), China, the Chusan Fan Palm, 12–40 ft, hardy for very mild localities in warm, well-sheltered spots, ordinary soil; or may be pot-grown in standard compost in a cold greenhouse with liberal watering in summer, very moderate in winter. May be raised from fresh seeds, sown with bottom heat (18° C. [65° F.]), spring.

Trachymene. See *Didiscus*.

Tradescantia (tra-des-kant'i-a. Fam. Commelinaceae). A genus of American perennial herbs of variable habit and attractive foliage.

Selection. *T.* × *andersoniana* (*virginiana*), N. America, the Spiderwort of borders, growing 18 in., is hardy, and well represented by named forms, such

as *alba*, white; *coerulea*, blue; 'Iris Prichard', white, shaded violet; 'J. C. Weguelin', azure blue; 'Osprey', snow white; 'Purple Dome', violet-purple; *rosea*, pink; and *rubra*, rose-red, summer. *T. albiflora*, S. America, small, dark green leaves, white flowers, summer; *blossfeldiana*, Argentine, finely hairy leaves, umbels of pinkish flowers, spring; *fluminensis*, Wandering Jew, S. America, fine foliage, yellow and white striped in v. *aurea*, silvery in *variegata*, are creeping or trailing plants; and *reginae*, Peru, large, light and dark green leaves, and purplish underneath, grows erectly, making fine pot plants for the cool greenhouse or home.

Cultivation. Plant hardy Spiderworts in November–March, ordinary, humus-enriched soil, sun or partial shade. Pot non-hardy S. American plants in March–May, give good light to variegated forms, watering freely in growth; moderately in winger, minimum temp. 7° C. (45° F.).

Propagation. Hardy Spiderworts by division, March. Greenhouse foliage plants by stem cuttings, in spring and summer, standard compost.

Tragopogon (tra-go-po'gon. Fam. Compositae). *T. porrifolius*, N. Europe, 3 ft, is the biennial grown as a vegetable for its roots as Salsify (q.v.). *T. pratensis*, Europe, Goat's Beard, Shepherd's Clock, 2 ft, with large yellow flowerheads, closing in the afternoon, summer, is a biennial, for sowing where it is to flower in June–July, ordinary soil, sun or partial shade.

Translocation. The movement and transport of materials (nutrients, enzymes, foodstuffs, etc.) within a plant in xylem tissues to aerial parts, in phloem from leaves downwards to actively growing cells and storage organs.

Transpiration. The expulsion and loss of moisture, as water vapour, by plants from their leaves, chiefly through stomata (q.v.), also through the cuticle. When excessive it leads to wilting and possibly death but it is vital to the healthy plant. It apparently induces the flow of water solution (transpiration stream) through the plant, carrying nutrient salts, and by reactions stimulates absorption of water and salts from the soil by the roots.

Trapa (tra'pa. Fam. Onagraceae). A

genus of annual floating aquatic plants, of which *T. natans*, Persia, Upper Nile, is interesting in bearing horned or spiny edible fruits known as Jesuit's Nuts or Water Chestnuts in autumn. Not quite hardy, seeds are simply thrown into the water of pools or tubs in a cool greenhouse, early spring.

Traveller's Joy. Common name for the native wilding, *Clematis vitalba*.

Tree. A tall, woody perennial plant with a single stem or trunk from the ground upwards. Sometimes divided into (1) broad-leaved, or hardwood, trees; and (2) conifers, or softwood. The chief genera are covered in separate entries in this book.

Tree Mallow. See *Lavatera arborea*.

Tree of Heaven. See *Ailanthus*.

Tree Peony. See *Paeonia*.

Trees, Dwarfing of. Originating in China, and much further developed in Japan, the art of dwarfing trees, known as Bonzai, is increasingly popular. It implies the cultivation of what are normally large trees to produce themselves in miniature. One method is to discover specimens naturally stunted by adverse conditions in a wild environment, usually in very poor soils and wild exposures in mountainous regions, and carefully make ready for transplantation to a container, by patient rootpruning and trimming, sometimes over a long period. More often today seedling trees are raised or cuttings rooted and grown in small pots, pans or containers, in a soil on the lean side, under cool conditions. The aerial growth of the seedling is regulated to a chosen shape, either by tying or weighing down shoots or branches, or training with the use of annealed wire spirally arranged round a stem, and bent to the desired shape. During growth, all buds and shoots surplus to the conceived shape of the plant are suppressed or trimmed away. Annually, usually in spring before growth begins anew, the roots in their soil ball are turned out of the container, and pruned, coarse roots being cut away, and a little new top soil given on returning the roots to the container. Dwarfed trees usually require cool, airy conditions, shade against hot direct sun, mist-spraying and gentle watering in growth, very moderate watering at other

times, and should be placed outdoors, in shady shelter, during summer months. Repotting is done in early spring; a useful compost being 2 parts by bulk fibrous granular loam, 1 part leaf-mould, 2 parts coarse sand, and feeding confined to weak dilute liquid manure or seaweed derivative. See *A Dwarfed Tree Manual*, S. Newsom (Tokyo News Service, 1963); *Bonzai*, C. Chidamian (D. Van Nostrand, 1955); *The Art of Growing Miniature Trees*, Tatsuo Ishimoto (Crown Publishers Inc., U.S.A., 1956).

Trefoil. See *Trifolium*.

Trellis. A framework of crossing narrow wooden slats, wires or plastic mesh, on which plants may be trained, on walls or in the open, forming screens or open shelters. Trellis on walls should be fixed 3–4 in. out from the wall surface to allow air circulation; in the open, to strong uprights. Wooden trellis is best preserved by painting with an organic solvent preservative, and not creosote, which is toxic to plants.

Tremulus (-a, -um). In constant movement, trembling. Ex. *Populus tremula*.

Trenching. *See* Digging.

Triandrus (-a, -um). Having three stamens. Ex. *Narcissus triandrus*.

Trichinium (tri-kin'i-um. Fam. Amaranthaceae). Half-hardy perennials of which *T. manglesii*, Australia, 9 in., decumbent stems, with fluffy pink flowers, June, makes a charming pot plant for the cool greenhouse; potted in March, standard compost, given ample sunlight, air and water in the growing season, very little after flowering. Propagated by root division, March–April.

Tricho-. Prefix in compound words meaning hairy, or hair-like. Ex. *Trichomanes*, the Bristle Ferns.

Trichomanes (trik-kom'a-nes. Fam. Hymenophyllaceae). A large genus of Bristle Ferns, with delicate fronds, requiring very humid conditions.

Selection. T. radicans, Cup Goldilocks or Killarney Fern, nothern hemisphere, tri-pinnatifid fronds to 12 in., and vs. *andrewsii*, narrower fronds; and *dilatatum*, very dark green, are hardy for shady, humid and mild damp conditions, or for growing in close glass cases or under handlights, rooting in a mixture of soft broken sandstone and fibrous peat, in shade. *T. alatum*, W. Indies; *javanicum*, Java, India, etc., and other tropical species require to be grown by hard pieces of stone, in similar compost, in glass case or under handlights, in the warm greenhouse.

Tricuspidaria. See *Crinodendron*.

Trientalis (tri-en-ta'lis. Fam. Primulaceae). Hardy, rhizomatous perennials, interesting for their flat whorl of elliptical leaves carried at the top of erect stems, and small starry flowers.

Selection. T. borealis, Star Flower, NW. America, 9 in., white flowers, May; and *europaea*, Wintergreen, Britain, N. Europe, white, June–July.

Cultivation. Plant March, well-drained, humus-rich soil, and shade, on rock garden.

Propagation. By seeds, April, under handlight. By division, March.

Trifoliate. With three leaves.

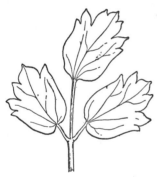

FIG. 224 Trifoliate leaf.

Trifoliolate. With three leaflets from the same point; as in *Trifolium* (Clovers).

Trifolium, Trefoil (tri-fo'li-um. Fam. Leguminosae). A vast genus of annual, biennial or perennial plants, including the Clovers, of agricultural significance.

Selection. T. alpinum, European Alps, 4 in., purple flowers, July; and v. *album*, white; and *uniflorum*, Asia Minor, 2 in., blue-purple and crimson, June–September, and v. *sternbergianum*, white and crimson, are charming for rock gardens. *T. repens*, the native White Clover, is sometimes used for

FIG. 225 Trifoliolate leaf (*Laburnum* sp.)

clover lawns, resistant to drought, and included in orchard grass mixtures; it is also the Shamrock, but variable and four- to six-leaved forms are reputed lucky and not unknown. *T. incarnatum*, S. Europe, is the annual crimson clover of 1 ft, valuable for green manuring.

Cultivation. Plant alpine species in March–April, well-drained soil, sun; or in pans in alpine house.

Propagation. By seeds, when ripe, late summer, in cold frame, or seed-bed out of doors.

Trillium, Wood Lily, Trinity Flower (tril'li-um. Fam. Liliaceae). Rhizomatous-rooted perennials, distinctive for their leaves whorled in threes at the top of stems, and topped by three-parted greenish or white flowers, in May.

Selection. T. erectum, Birth-root, Lamb's Quarters, eastern N. America, 1 ft, claret-purple flowers; v. *album*, greenish white, and *ochroleucum*, yellowish white; *grandiflorum*, Wake Robin, E. U.S.A., 1 ft, white; and *undulatum*, Painted Wood Lily, E. U.S.A., 1 ft, white, striped reddish purple.

Cultivation. Plant September–November, in well-drained deep loam or peat-enriched soil, in shady somewhat moist positions, woodland or border, 3 in. deep.

Propagation. By seeds, when ripe, but take five to six years to flower. By careful division of roots, August–September, every fourth to sixth year.

Trimestris (-e). Of three months' duration. Ex. *Lavatera trimestris.*

Tripetaleia (tri-pet-a-le'i-a. Fam. Ericaceae). The chief species, *T. paniculata*, Japan, 2–4 ft, is an erect-growing deciduous shrub, with panicles of white, tinged pink, cup-shaped flowers, late summer; formerly under *Elliottia.*

Cultivation. Plant November–March, well-drained, lime-free soil, partial shade. Mulch with peat.

Propagation. By cuttings of young shoots, July–August, under handlight.

Triploid. An organism having three times the haploid number of chromosomes in a nucleus. *See* Chromosomes.

Tristis (-e). Sad, dull-coloured. Ex. *Gladiolus tristis.*

Triteleia. See *Brodiaea.*

Tritoma. See *Kniphofia.*

Tritonia, Montbretia (tri-to'ni-a. Fam. Iridaceae). Cormous flowering plants, native to S. Africa, and related to *Crocosmia*, with linear, ensiform leaves, and loose heads of gay, tubular, flared flowers on slender stems.

Selection. T. crocata, 2 ft, orange flowers, May–June, and vs. with orange-red, scarlet, bright red and purple flowers; *hyalina*, 1 ft, pale orange; and *rosea*, 1½ ft, pink, July; and named hybrids in growers' lists.

Cultivation. May be tried in warm, sunny positions, sandy, leaf-mould-enriched soil, in mildest localities, planted 2 in. deep, October–November, winter-protected with litter. Otherwise best grown in cold frames or as pot plants in a cool greenhouse; potted in March–April, five corms to a 7-in. pot, standard compost, 2 in. deep; plunged in a frostproof frame until growth shows; then water increasingly, transfer to greenhouse, and airy position near the glass; reduce watering when leaves yellow, and keep dry until spring and new growth begins. Repot about every fourth year, and propagate by division of the corms.

Trivial Name. The qualifying specific epithet of the botanical name of a plant; or its common name.

Trochodendron (trok-o-den'dron. Fam. Trochodendraceae). Representative of its family and genus, *T. aralioides*, Japan, Formosa, to 15 ft, makes a handsome evergreen small tree, with long-stalked, leathery, glossy green, ovate leaves, and erect racemes of green flowers, June, for mild localities.

Cultivation. Plant March–April, well-drained, peat-enriched soil, warm, sunny shelter.

Propagation. By seeds, April, under glass, bottom heat of 15·5° C. (60° F.). By air layering.

Trollius, Globe Flower (trol'li-us. Fam. Ranunculaceae). Hardy herbaceous perennials with palmately lobed leaves, and showy globular flowers in late spring and summer.

Selection. T. asiaticus, Siberia, Turkistan, 1–1½ ft, dark yellow open flowers, May–June, and v. *aurantiacus*, orange; *chinensis*, N. China, 1½ ft, golden-yellow, June; *europaeus*, Britain, Europe, 1–2 ft, lemon-yellow, summer, and v. *superbus*, soft yellow; *ledebourii*, Siberia, 2 ft, in v. 'Golden Queen', orange-yellow; *pumilus*, N. India, 1 ft, buttercup-yellow; and v. *yunnanensis*, 1½ ft, golden-yellow. Hybrids of distinction include 'Earliest of All', 'Fire Globe', 'Goldquelle' and 'Pritchard's Giant'.

Cultivation. Plant October–March, in rather moist, heavy soil, or by water, sun or partial shade.

Propagation. By division in September–October.

Tropaeolum, Indian Cress, Garden Nasturtium (tro-pe-o'lum. Fam. Tropaeolaceae). A genus of rapid-growing annual and perennial climbers, characterized by flared, funnel-like flowers with a long tubular spur.

Selection. T. majus, strong-growing annual of Peru, its double-flowering v. *flore pleno* and non-climbing *nanum*; non-climbing *minus*, and climbing *peltophorum*, Colombia, Ecuador, are the parental origins of the annual Garden Nasturtiums offered by every seedsman in a galaxy of bright flaming reds, yellow, orange to deep pinks, in climbing and non-climbing races such as 'Gleam Hybrids', 'Jewel', Tom Thumb, Double and Semi-double strains. Seeds may be sown in March–April, porous, light soil, and sun. *T. peltophorum*, red flowers, and vs. 'Lucifer' and 'Spitfire', and *peregrinum*, Canary Creeper, Peru, yellow, may be grown as half-hardy annuals for greenhouse or to plant out in early May. *T. speciosum*, the Flame Nasturtium or Scotch Creeper, Chile, is the hardy herbaceous climber, with orange-red flowers, but requires partial shade, a cool, turfy loam, with peat or leaf-mould, and dislikes lime, if it is to grow to 15 ft, or more, as in West Scotland and the Lake District. Other perennials are less hardy and require the protection of the cold greenhouse, or to have their roots lifted and wintered under cover; including *T. azureum*, Chile, blue flowers, autumn; *pentaphyllum*, S. America, scarlet, summer; *polyphyllum*, Chile, Argentine, yellow, summer; *tricolorum*, Bolivia, Chile, vari-coloured flowers, summer; and *tuberosum*, Peru, orange-scarlet, September.

Cultivation. All the perennials dislike lime, and need turfy loam, enriched with leaf-mould and peat; being planted March–April, in borders or pots in cold greenhouse.

Propagation. Perennials by division of root rhizomes or tubers, March. By seeds, March–April. Tuberous species can be increased by cuttings of wiry stems taken in July.

Trough Gardens. *See* Sink Gardens.

Trowel. The scoop-bladed hand trowel is invaluable for the lifting and transplanting of small plants, preparing planting stations of bedding plants, bulbs, etc. The fern trowel has a narrow blade, useful for working in crevices and in rock gardens.

Truffles. The edible fruit-bodies of the *Tuber* spp., of fungi. *T. aestivum*, found beneath beeches, is the best British species. On the Continent, they are more appreciated, and 'hunted' by poodles and pigs. Attempts at commercial cultivation have not proved very successful.

Trumpet Creeper. See *Campsis*.

Trumpet Flower. A name often used for *Bignonia*, *Campsis*, etc.

Truncatus (-a, -um). Ending abruptly. Ex. *Schlumbergera truncatus*.

Trunk. The single stem of a tree.

Truss. A gardening term for a cluster of terminal flowers from a common

base; increasingly used of the flowers and fruits of tomatoes.

Tsuga, Hemlock Spruce (tsu'ga. Fam. Pinaceae). Hardy, evergreen coniferous trees, branching horizontally, with fine sprays of linear leaves spirally arranged, and solitary cones.

Selection. *T. canadensis*, Eastern Hemlock, eastern N. America, to 90 ft, v. *pendula*, small tree with weeping branches, and several dwarf forms: 'Bennet's *minima*', 'Rugg's Dwarf' and 'Warner's *globosa*'; *caroliniana*, Virginia, Georgia, slow-growing, graceful, 20–40 ft; *chinensis*, Chinese Hemlock, pyramidal, to 30 ft; *diversifolia*, Japanese Hemlock, to 30 ft; *dumosa*, Himalayan Hemlock, to 80 ft, not suitable for cold areas; *heterophylla*, Western Hemlock, western N. America, to 120 ft, very hardy; × *jeffreyi*, to 25 ft; *mertensiana*, Mountain Hemlock, western N. America, to 60 ft, hardy and handsome; *sieboldii*, Japanese Hemlock, Japan, to 60 ft, yew-like; and *yunnanensis*, W. China, to 70 ft, frost-susceptible.

Cultivation. Plant October, or March–April, reasonably well-drained soils, about pH 6.

Propagation. By seeds, outdoor seed-bed of sandy loam, March–April. By cuttings of young shoots, July–August, in cold frame or under handlight.

Tuber. A swollen underground stem, bearing buds or eyes from which new plants may grow. Ex. Jerusalem Artichoke, Potato, Dahlia, etc.

Tubercle. A small tuber-like excrescence or nodule.

Tuberose. See *Polianthes tuberosa*.

Tubs. Wooden tubs are often used for plants of doubtful hardiness, such as Citrus, Bay trees, Palms, Agapanthus and similar summer-flowering plants; enabling them to be moved to shelter for the winter. Oak or teak are the best woods, and should have drainage holes and be well-crocked. It adds to the life of a tub to paint the interior with a bitumen paint or organic solvent preservative.

Tulipa, Tulip (tu'li-pa. Fam. Liliaceae). This genus of bulbous plants is one of the most valuable for its contribution of bloom in a tremendous range of floral shape and colour, for the first half of each year. The species number between seventy and eighty, and originate largely in central and western Asia, particularly the mountains of Asia Minor, Persia, Turkistan and the Caucasus, but also Europe and N. Africa. Interest, however, centres chiefly in the cultivated tulips, which have a somewhat complicated history beginning with their introduction to Europe in 1572, their subsequent development in Holland from 1634 to the present day, with the result that there are over 4,000 varieties of horticultural tulips named and described officially by the Dutch Bulb-growers' Association. Holland remains the principal world supplier of tulip bulbs, though important crops are raised in parts of England, principally Lincolnshire, and parts of western N. America.

Varieties. Current classification groups Tulips into no less than twenty-three sections; the first sixteen of which comprise the Florists' Tulips, the others species groups; brief descriptions are given here, and a selection of renowned varieties, but growers' lists should be consulted for the fuller range and novelties.

1. Very Early, 6 in., 'Duc Van Tol'; March.

2. Single Early, 8–16 in., good for forcing: 'Bellona', golden; 'Brilliant Star', scarlet; 'General de Wet', golden orange, scented; 'Flamingo', deep rose and white; 'Keizerskroon', crimson, edged yellow; 'Mon Tresor', deep golden yellow; 'Pink Beauty', vivid pink, white centre to petals; 'Prince of Austria', orange-scarlet, scented; 'Sunburst', yellow, flushed orange; 'Van der Neer', violet-purple; 'Winter-gold', lemon-yellow; mid April.

3. Double Early, 8–14 in., mid to late April: 'Aga Khan', gold, copper-orange; 'Bonanza', carmine, edged yellow; 'Dante', blood red; 'Electra', cherry-red; 'Goya', salmon-scarlet, streaked apricot; 'Maréchal Niel', yellow, flushed orange; 'Murillo', white, rose; 'Orange Nassau', Indian red; 'Peach Blossom', deep rose; 'Scarlet Cardinal', scarlet; 'Schoonoord', pure white; 'Vuurbaak', scarlet; 'Wilhelm Kordes', orange, flushed red.

4. Mendel, 14–22 in. 'Duc van Thol'

× 'Darwin' hybrids; late April: 'Apricot Beauty', salmon-rose, tinged apricot; 'Athleet', white; 'Golden Triumph', buttercup-yellow; 'Her Grace', white, edged pink; 'John Gay', orange-red; 'Krelage's Triumph', crimson-red; 'Orange Wonder', red, edged orange; 'Van der Eerden', crimson-red; 'Weber', white, edged lilac-rose; 'White Sail', tall, creamy white; 'White Virgin', pure white.

5. Triumph, 20–24 in., late April–early May: 'Alberio', cherry-red, edged yellow; 'Bandoeng', mahogany, orange, flushed yellow; 'Blizzard', creamy white; 'Bruno Walter', orange, flushed purple; 'Crater', crimson; 'Elmus', cherry-red, edged white; 'K and M's Triumph', deep red; 'Korneforos', light red; 'Orient Express', vermilion; 'Pink Glow', satin pink; 'Princess Beatrix', scarlet, edged orange; 'Reforma', sulphur-yellow; 'Telescopium', reddish-violet; 'Virtuoso', lilac-rose.

6. Darwin, 20–28 in., strong stemmed, globular flowers, angular at base; May: 'All Bright'. carmine-red, edged lighter red; 'Aristocrat', violet-rose, edged white; 'Bartigon', cochineal red; 'Bleu Aimable', lilac; 'Clara Butt', salmon-pink; 'Demeter', reddish purple; 'Dorrie Overall', petunia violet, edged mauve; 'Farncombe Sanders', cochineal red; 'Golden Age', buttercup yellow; 'Niphetos', sulphur yellow; 'Philip Snowden', light carmine-rose; 'Pride of Haarlem', cerise-red; 'Princess Elizabeth', rose-pink; 'Queen of Bartigons', salmon-pink; 'Queen of Night', deep maroon; 'Red Pitt', bright red; 'Rose Copeland', lilac-rose; 'Scotch Lassie', deep lavender; 'Sundew', cardinal red; 'Sunkist', golden yellow; 'Sweet Harmony', lemon yellow; 'The Bishop', deep violet; 'William Pitt', red; 'Zwanenburg', pure white.

7. Darwin Hybrids, obtained from Darwin × *T. fosteriana* vs., very tall, 24–30 in.; early May: 'Apeldoorn', orange-scarlet; 'Dover', poppy red; 'General Eisenhower', orange-red; 'Holland's Glory', orange-scarlet; 'Jewel of Spring', sulphur yellow, spotted red; 'Lefeber's Favourite', deep carmine, edged scarlet; 'Red Matador', carmine, edged vermilion; 'Spring Song', scarlet, with salmon glow.

8. Breeder, tall, 26–30 in., very large blooms, for bedding; mid May: 'Admiral Tromp', orange-red and copper, edged yellow; 'Dillenburg', orange, edged apricot; 'Dom Pedro', coffee-brown, shaded maroon; 'Georges Grappe', lavender-mauve; 'Orange Beauty', orange, bronze, edged yellow.

9. Lily-flowered, from *T. retroflexa* × Cottage tulips hybrids; graceful, with reflexing, tapered petals, 20–24 in.; May: 'Aladdin', scarlet, edged yellow; 'Capt. Fryatt', ruby red; 'China Pink', satin pink; 'Dyanito', bright red, yellow base; 'Gisela', rose-pink, salmon tinged; 'Inimitable', yellow; 'Mariette', satin-rose; 'Maytime', purple violet, edged white; 'Queen of Sheba', dark red, edged orange; 'Red Shine', ruby red; 'White Triumphator', white.

10. Cottage, or Single Late, tall, of English origin, 24–30 in., includes Green-flowered forms of *T. viridiflora*; mid to late May flowering mainly: 'Advance', light scarlet, tinted cerise; 'Artist', green to rose and apricot; 'Carrara', pure white; 'Chappaqua', violet-rose; 'Golden Harvest', lemon-yellow; 'Greenland', greenish-yellow, edged pink; 'Magier', white, edged violet-blue; 'Marjorie Bowen', buff and salmon, edged light apricot; 'Marshal Haig', scarlet; 'Mother's Day', lemon yellow; 'Mrs John T. Scheepers', canary yellow; 'Mrs Moon', golden; 'Ossi Oswalda', creamy white, flushed rose; 'Princess Margaret Rose', yellow, edged orange-red; 'Rosy Wings', pink, white base; 'Smiling Queen', rose, edged silvery pink; 'White City', white; *viridiflora praecox*, green outside, yellow-green within.

11. Rembrandt, streaked, flushed, striped or broken Darwins, 24–28 in.; about mid May: 'American Flag', deep red and white; 'Cordell Hull', blood red on off-white background; 'Gondola', salmon-pink, flushed cream; 'Mont-gomery', white, flecked red; 'Union Jack', raspberry red on ivory white.

12. Bizarre, streaked, flushed or broken Breeder and Cottage Tulips, 24–26 in.; May: 'Absalon', yellow, flamed mahogany; 'Insulinde', yellow, bronze, purple on primrose; 'Pierette', lilac, lavender on silvery white ground.

13. Bijbloemen or Bybloem, Breeder

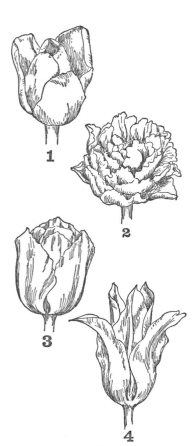

FIG. 226 Types of Tulips: 1. Single Early; 2. Double; 3. Triumph; 4. Lily-flowering.

and Cottage varieties, streaked or veined with red, pink or violet on a white ground, 18–28 in.; May: 'Bright Interval', cherry pink and creamy white; 'Clara', deep pink, scarlet streaking, white ground; 'May Blossom', lilac-purple on creamy white ground; 'Paljas', crimson feathering on white ground.

14. Parrot, large blooms, with fringed, scalloped or wavy petals, somewhat weak stems, 20–24 in.; May: 'Black Parrot', purple-black; 'Blue Parrot', violet-blue; 'Doorman', cherry red, edged yellow; 'Fantasy', salmon-pink, green markings; 'Fire Bird', vermilion; 'Orange Favourite', orange and green; 'Red Champion', cochineal red, flushed scarlet; 'Red Parrot', raspberry red; 'Texas Gold', yellow, red edged.

15. Double Late, or Paeony-flowered, 16–24 in., large blooms, not for pots or windy places; late April–May: 'Brilliant Fire', cherry red to yellow, scented; 'Eros', old rose, scented,; 'Livingstone', cardinal red; 'May Wonder', rose-pink; 'Mount Tacoma', white; 'Nizza', yellow, marked red; 'Orange Triumph', orange-red, edged golden; 'Symphonia', cherry red; 'Uncle Tom', maroon red. Mid May.

16. *T. batalalinii*, a section that includes the species, 6 in., buff-yellow, April, and v. 'Bronze Charm', buff with deep markings.

17. *T. eichleri*, includes the species, 8 in., scarlet, black base with golden band, and v. *excelsa*, with larger, brighter red flowers; April.

18. *T. fosteriana*, includes the species, 8 in., large, bright scarlet, with black basal blotch, March–April, and vs. 'Candela', yellow, 15 in.; 'Cantata', vermilion scarlet, 12 in.; 'Czardas', orange-scarlet, 14 in.; 'Easter Parade', yellow, flushed red, 14 in.; 'Galata', orange-scarlet, 16 in.; 'Madame Lefeber' ('Red Emperor'), vermilion red, 15 in.; 'Princeps', orange-scarlet, 12 in.; 'Purissima', milk-white, 15 in.; 'Rondo', golden, red base, 16 in.; and 'Zombie', carmine, edged yellow, black base, 14 in.

19. *T. greigii*, includes the species, from Turkistan, 10 in., scarlet with dark blotched yellow base, April, and leaves, greyish green, mottled or speckled brown, a feature of the vs. and hybrids:

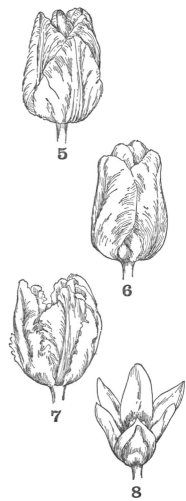

FIG. 227   Types of Tulips: 5. Darwin; 6. Cottage; 7. Parrot; 8. Kaufmanniana hybrid.

'Ali Baba', vermilion; 'Fairy-tale', vermilion, bronzy green, tangerine red outside; 'Margaret Herbst', orange-red, beautifully mottled leaves; 'Oriental Splendour', carmine-red, edged lemon; 'Pandour', pale yellow, flamed carmine; 'Plaisir', carmine, yellow edged; 'Red Riding Hood', pillar-box red, attractive leaves; 'Zampa', primrose yellow, carmine red blotch.

20. *T. kaufmanniana*, includes the species, the Waterlily Tulip of Turkistan, 8 in., flowers with narrow pointed segments, opening wide, waterlily-like, red-streaked, white, yellow, yellow base; March, with increasing number of vs. such as 'Alfred Cortot', scarlet, black base; 'Daylight', scarlet, striped yellow inside; 'Fair Lady', crimson with ivory; 'Fritz Kreisler', salmon-pink, ivory inside; 'Gaiety', cerise-pink, ivory and gold inside; 'Gluck', red, pale yellow, flecked chocolate; 'Johann Strauss', ivory white, marked red, sulphur edge; 'Shakespeare', salmon, apricot and orange, yellow inside; 'Stresa', golden-yellow, marked orange-red; and 'The First', carmine to gold, ivory inside; and 'Rainbow' hybrids, in various colours.

21. *T. marjoletti*, the basis of a group not much developed; the species from Savoy, bearing yellow to white flowers, flushed purple, on 1 ft stems, April.

22. *T. tubergeniana*, the basis of a new group, being a tulip from central Asia, 1 ft, vermilion, with olive blotch, flower, April; being crossed with Darwins, of which 'Candidate', bright red, black centred, is newly introduced.

23. *Other Species* or Botanical Tulips. The more useful include: *T. aucheriana*, Persia, 3 in., pink, bronze blotch, greenish yellow striping outside, on three flowers per stem, April; *clusiana*, Lady Tulip, central Asia, 10 in., cherry-red and white, violet base, April; *hageri*, Greece, Asia Minor, 6 in., coppery-red, olive blotch, green banded, to four flowers per stem, April; *hoogiana*, central Asia, 1 ft, scarlet, edged yellow, May; *linifolia*, Bokhara, 6 in., scarlet, May; *ostrowskiana*, Turkistan, 8 in., bright scarlet, olive blotched, April; *praestans*, central Asia, 10 in., red, to four flowers per stem, and v. 'Fusilier', orange-scarlet; *sprengeri*, Asia Minor, 10 in., scarlet,

May, very late; *stellata*, Himalaya, 6 in., white, pale yellow blotch; and v. *chrysantha*, bright yellow, red reverse, April; *tarda*, Turkistan, 4 in., bright yellow, white edged, to four flowers per stem, May; *urumiensis*, Asia Minor, 2 in., bright yellow, late April; and *violacea*, Persia, 4 in., purple-blue, April.

Cultivation. Species, their varieties and hybrids, are best planted in September–October, 4 in. deep, in well-drained, porous soil, to receive ample spring and summer sun, in the rock garden; and left undisturbed for three to four years, though withered foliage should be removed each year. They may also be potted, about four to a 5-in. pot, standard compost, and kept plunged in a cold frame until showing growth, to flower in the alpine house or cold greenhouse.

Cultivated Tulips grown out of doors are planted 4–6 in. deep, October–November, in soil that is well-drained, enriched with rotted organic matter, and bone meal, pH 6·0–6·5; and may be left until foliage withers before being lifted, dried and stored cool and dry; or if used for bedding, lifted with roots in a soil ball as soon as flowers are spent, and temporarily replanted on a reserve piece of ground to finish growth, and then lifted to store. If bulbs are left in the ground, the withered foliage should be gathered and burnt as a preventive precaution against disease, and the planting top-dressed with organic matter or peat.

Indoor Culture. Pot the bulbs in September–October, using standard compost, or a mixture of 3 parts by bulk fresh fibrous loam, 1 part leaf-mould or moist peat, 1 part sharp sand, 1½–2 in. deep, three to five bulbs per 5- or 6-in. pot, and plunge in cool, shaded spot, under north wall, or in cold frame, covered with 5 in. ashes, coconut fibre, chopped straw or clean soil; or place in cool dark cellar, for 6–9 weeks, or until shoot growth of 3–4 in. shows; then bring to light and warmth gradually; first a week in dark shade at 13° C. (55° F.) to lengthen stems; then to more light and temperature of not more than 15·5° C. (60° F.), until buds are advanced, when temperature should not exceed 20° C. (68° F.).

For earliest flowering, specially pre-pared bulbs of Single Early, Mendel, Triumph, Darwin and Cottage Tulips are available, and should be planted and treated as above immediately received.

Tulips in Bulb Fibre. Bulbs are planted in moist fibre, neck deep, in bowls or containers, September–November, and placed in a dark, cool place for 6–10 weeks, until shoots are 2–3 in. long; and then brought gradually to the light, and increasing warmth; the fibre will need to be kept moist, without over-saturating. When finished, plant on reserve border, under cloches to complete growth.

Diseases. The most common and serious is Fire, caused by the fungus *Botrytis tulipae*; characterized by leaves becoming flecked with pink, yellow and brown markings, which should be detached and burnt. It is best prevented by dusting bulbs before planting with a PCNB fungicidal dust (Botrilex); and growing plants may be sprayed with captan, where the infection is not too advanced. Infected bulbs are best burnt. Grey Bulb Rot (*Sclerotium tuliparum*) affects the growing points of bulbs, preventing shoot development. Infected bulbs are best burnt. Future plantings should be dusted with PCNB dust. Bulbs are often superficially affected by Green Moulds (*Penicillium* spp.) or similar fungi when bought. The brown skin or tunic should be rubbed off, and the bulbs dusted with the PCNB fungicidal dust prior to planting.

Pests. Aphids (*Myzus persicae*, *Macrosiphum euphorbiae*) may attack foliage and need control by a gamma-BHC or malathion insecticide; while *Sappaphis tulipae* sometimes infests bulbs in store under the outer scales; immersion in a gamma-BHC solution for a quarter of an hour will stop this; drying bulbs afterwards. Mice must be defeated by Warfarin-baiting, or use of a repellent, or putting a layer of chopped gorse, short lengths of briar or brambles over the bulbs when planting.

Propagation. By seeds, sown February–March, in cold frame or under handlights, but seedlings take 4–6 years to come to flower. By offset bulbs detached and planted separately in good

soil, to build up to full flowering in three years.

Tulip Tree. See *Liriodendron*.

Tunica (tu′ni-ka. Fam. Caryophyl-laceae). The chief species grown, *T. saxifraga*, S. Europe, 4 in., is a tufted perennial with narrow linear leaves, and white, rose-tinted, flowers, in corymbs, summer, for the rock garden or wall. Plant in March, porous light soil, and sun. Propagate by seeds, sown April, out of doors.

Tunicated. Having a coat or coats, as with bulbs.

Tupelo Tree. See *Nyssa*.

Turbinatus (-a, -um). Turbinate, top-shaped. Ex. *Campanula turbinata*.

Turf. *See* Lawns.

Turfing-iron. A long-handled tool, with a bent shaft attached, with a flat, heart-shaped cutting blade, used to undercut and lift turf for lawn-making, instead of a spade.

Turkey Oak. See *Quercus cerris*.

Turk's Cap Lily. See *Lilium martagon*.

Turnip (*Brassica rapa*, Fam. Cruci-ferae). A hardy biennial of Europe, grown for its edible roots in Britain since the mid seventeenth century.

Varieties. These are divided into two groups: (1) Early, quick growing: 'Early Snowball', 'Early White Stone', 'Early Milan' and 'Model White', which are white-fleshed; and 'Golden Ball', which is yellow-fleshed—for sowing outdoors from early spring to late summer to crop from early summer to autumn. (2) Maincrop: 'Green Top Stone', 'Model Winter' and 'Red Globe'; and 'Purple Top Swede' and 'Bronze Top Swede'; the Swede being a very hardy turnip hybrid—for summer sowing, to crop in autumn. For turnip-top greens, 'Chirk Castle' may be grown.

Cultivation. The art of turnip-growing is to grow them quickly, in cool moist conditions. The soil should be well drained, liberally provided with organic humus-forming material previously, and dressed with 1 part by weight dried blood, 3 parts superphosphate, 1 part sulphate of potash, at 2 oz. per sq. yd, before sowing, and of pH 6·5; partial shade is suitable in sunny districts and the south.

Sowing. Sow seeds in drills ½ in. deep,

12 in. apart, thinning to 6–9 in. apart. Sow early varieties mid March to mid April, and again in May. May be sown as a catch-crop between peas, with celery. Sow maincrops July to end of August. Water freely in dry periods. Dress seeds with gamma-BHC seed dressing to prevent Flea Beetle destruction.

Swedes are hardier than turnips, but take longer to mature, and should be sown in early May in the north, end of May in the south, in drills 15 in. apart, and thinned 1 ft apart. Turnips are subject to the same diseases as other Brassica crops. *See* Cabbage.

Tutsan. See *Hypericum androsaemum*.

Type. In botanical nomenclature, a type or type species is the species chosen as representative of a genus.

Typha (ti'pa. Fam. Typhaceae). Hardy aquatic perennials for pool margins or marshy ground.

Selection. T. angustifolia, Small Reed Mace, Britain, to 4 ft, and *latifolia*, Tall Reed Mace or Cat-tail, mistakenly called Bulrush, Britain, to 8 ft, both with dark brown, velvety flower spikes, are best planted in lakes. For small pools. *T. laxmannii*, SE. Europe, Asia Minor, 2½–4 ft, slender, with brown spikes; and *minima*, Europe, 1–1½ ft, rusty-brown spikes, are less root-invasive, but need planting in containers for safety, in May–June. Propagation is by simple division, at these times.

U

Ulex (u'leks. Fam. Leguminosae). Hardy, spiny evergreen shrubs, with bright golden-yellow flowers.

Selection. U. europaeus, Gorse, Furze, Whin, Europe and Britain, 2–4 ft, golden-yellow, spring; v. *plenus* is more striking with double flowers, and *strictus* is the upright growing, but shy-flowering Irish Gorse; *minor* (*nanus*), dwarf Gorse or Cat-whin, 1–2 ft, golden yellow, July–September, is a useful garden shrub; *gallii*, W. Europe, W. England, to 2 ft, blooms in autumn.

Cultivation. Plant October–November, or March–April, preferably in very poor or sandy heath soil, and sun. Rich soils encourage lanky growth. Prune in February–March, especially if winter-damaged.

Propagation. By seeds, sown outdoors, March–April. By cuttings of young shoots, July–August.

Uliginosus (-a, -um). Growing in marshes. Ex. *Chrysanthemum uliginosum.*

Ulmus, Elm (ul'mus. Fam. Ulmaceae). Hardy deciduous trees of the northern hemisphere, easily grown, with rather harsh textured, toothed leaves, and disk-like, notched fruits (Samara).

Selection. U. carpinifolia, Smooth-leaved Elm, Europe, Britain, W. Asia, to 100 ft. is best in its vs. *cornubiensis* (*U. stricta*), Cornish Elm, to 60 ft, *pendula*, with slender drooping branches, *sarniensis* (*U. wheatleyi*), the Jersey Elm, and *sarniensis aurea*, a rich yellow-leafed form; despite suckering tendencies; *fulva*, Slippery Elm, N. America, to 60 ft, narrow long leaves, uncommon; *glabra*, Wych or Scotch Elm, Britain, N. Europe, to 120 ft, wide-spreading, and vs. *exoniensis*, upright Exeter Elm; *lutescens*, golden-leafed; *pendula*, weeping, for lawns; × *hollandica*, Dutch Elm, to 120 ft, and v. *major*, Europe, Britain, suckers; *parvifolia*, Chinese Elm, to 40 ft, slender-branched, attractive persistent foliage; *procera* (*campestris*), English Elm, to 150 ft, the hedgerow Elm of England, has fine vs. *vanhouttei*, yellow-leafed; *variegata*, marked creamy white; and *viminalis* (*U. viminalis*), to 40 ft; *pumila*, Dwarf Elm, China, Siberia, 12–25 ft, small-leafed; and × *vegata*, Huntingdon Elm, to 100 ft.

Cultivation. Plant November–March, any well-drained soil of loam quality, pH 6–7, open sites.

Propagation. By ripe seeds, March, outdoor seed-bed. By layering, spring or autumn. Varieties of suckering species are usually grafted on rootstocks of *U. glabra.*

Disease. Dutch Elm Disease is caused by a fungus (*Ceratostomella ulmi*), causing leaves to dry up and shrivel, twigs to twist and curl, and sapwood to brown and die. It is spread by bark beetles (*Scolytus* spp.), attracted to dead or dying branches. Control lies in promptly cutting away sick, dead growth and burning. Old infected trees are best cut down and burnt.

Umbel. An inflorescence, umbrella-like, of stalked flowers growing from the

FIG. 228 Umbel (*Allium* sp.).

555

same single point; compound when stalked umbels arise from similarly arranged stems or peduncles.

Umbellatus (-a, -um). Umbellate, arranged in umbels.

Umbellularia (um-bel-lu-la'ri-a. Fam. Lauraceae). The one species, *U. californica*, Californian Laurel, or Spice Bush, is an evergreen tall shrub, to 15 ft, with narrow, oval leathery leaves, and close umbels of yellowish-green flowers, April, for warm, sheltered gardens, planted in March–April, in well-drained, humus-rich loam, pH 5·5–6. Propagation is by layers in spring; by seeds, April.

Umbrella Pine. See *Sciadopitys verticillata*.

Umbrosus (-a, -um). Growing in shade. Ex. *Saxifraga umbrosa*.

Uncinatus (-a, -um). Hooked. Ex. *Echinocactus uncinatus*.

Undulatus (-a, -um). Wavy. Ex. *Stranvaesia undulata*.

Unedo. Means I eat one. Ex. *Arbutus unedo*.

Uni-. Prefix in compound words, meaning one. Ex. Unicellular, one-celled; *uniflorus*, one-flowered; unilateral, one-sided.

Urceolate. Urn-shaped or pitcher-shaped.

FIG. 229 Urceolate flowers (*Pieris* sp.).

Urceolina (ur-ke-o-li'na. Fam. Amaryllidaceae). S. American bulbous plants, with oblong or lanceolate leaves, and heads of long-stalked tubular flowers.

Selection. U. peruviana, Bolivia, Peru, 1 ft, bright red flowers, early summer; and *urceolata*, Peru, 1 ft, bright yellow, green tipped, summer.

Cultivation. Plant October–November or March–April, standard compost, 5-in. pots, and grow as Hippeastrum (q.v.), in cool greenhouse, or indoors, minimum temp. 7° C. (45° F.). Water freely in active growth, very moderately in winter; though more or less evergreen.

Propagation. By offsets, when repotting, March.

Urea, carbamide ($CO(NH_2)_2$). An organic compound that occurs naturally in animal urine, but manufactured synthetically for use as a highly concentrated nitrogenous fertilizer (46 per cent N); often blended in high concentrate fertilizers and liquid manures.

Urens. Stinging.

Urginea (ur-gin'e-a. Fam. Liliaceae). The chief species of interest in these bulbous plants is *U. maritima*, Sea Onion or Squills, of the Mediterranean region, with its spike of starry, white, stained lilac, flowers on 1–3 ft stems, summer.

Cultivation. Plant the large bulbs, one to a 5-in. pot, October, standard compost, to grow in the cold greenhouse; watering freely in growth, drying off when leaves yellow; propagation by offsets, October.

Urine. The liquid excreta of animals contains nitrogen (as urea), potash and a wide range of mineral salts, to render it a valuable manure. It may be diluted with four times its volume of water as a liquid feed; or used to help the decomposition of waste plant matter, straw, etc., and should be conserved in manure or compost heaps. Nevertheless, the urine of carnivorous animals, such as dogs, is often caustic when fresh and damaging to plants, especially lawns.

Ursinia (ur-sin'i-a. Fam. Compositae). Ray-petalled flowering plants of S. Africa, of which the annuals are largely grown.

Selection. U. anthemoides, 1 ft, orange, purple-based flowers, summer, and hybrid strains in shades of orange; *cakeilifolia*, 1 ft, deep orange; and *versicolor*, 1 ft, bright orange, and vs. of other shades.

Cultivation. Sow under glass, March–April, bottom heat of 15·5° C. (60° F.), to prick off, and plant out in May; or sow outdoors, late April–May, where to flower, thinning to 4 in.

Utilis (-e). Useful. Ex. *Betula utilis.*

Utricularia, Bladderwort (u-tri-ku-la'ri-a. Fam. Lentibulariaceae). A large genus of tropical epiphytic and terrestrial plants, and aquatic plants of temperate zones, curious for bladder-like pitchers by which insects are trapped and absorbed.

Selection. U. minor, Lesser Bladderwort, northern hemisphere, pale yellow flowers, summer, and *vulgaris*, Greater Bladderwort, northern hemisphere, yellow, summer, are native aquatic plants which may be grown in the larger garden pool, planted April–May. *U. alpina*, W. Indies, S. America, 6 in., white, yellow-lipped flowers, July; *endresii*, Costa Rica, pale green, lilac to yellow flowers, summer; and *reniformis*, Brazil, 18 in., violet, with darker markings, summer, are epiphytes for the warm greenhouse.

Cultivation. Hardy aquatic species: plant April–May; propagate by division. Tropical epiphytes: plant in spring, in baskets of equal parts fibrous peat and sphagnum moss, with some charcoal; watering liberally in active growth; very moderately in winter, minimum temp. 15·5° C. (60° F.). Propagate by division of rhizomatous roots, April.

Utriculatus (-a, -um). Utriculate, bladder-like. Ex. *Utricularia.*

Uvularia (u-vu-la'ri-a. Fam. Liliaceae). Hardy, herbaceous rhizomatous-rooted perennials of N. America, with sessile or perfoliate, lanceolate leaves, and drooping yellow flowers with long pointed segments in May.

Selection. U. grandiflora, 1 ft, and v. *pallida*, sulphur-yellow flowers; *perfoliata*, 1 ft, and v. *flava*, deeper yellow.

Cultivation. Plant October–November, well-drained, peat-enriched soil, cool partial shade.

Propagation. By division, when leaves die down.

V

Vaccinium (vak-ki'ni-um. Fam. Ericaceae). Deciduous and evergreen shrubs of the northern hemisphere, ornamental for their foliage, autumn colour and edible berries, for lime-free soils.

Selection. Deciduous species are *V. arctostaphylos*, Caucasus, to 10 ft, whitish, purple-tinged flowers, June, dark purple berries, autumn; *corymbosum*, Swamp Blueberry, E. U.S.A., 4–10 ft, white, pink-tinged flowers, May–June, blue-black berries, autumn, with named varieties selected for fruiting; *lamarckii*, eastern N. America, 6–16 in., white flowers, June, bright blue berries; and *parvifolium*, Red Bilberry, western N. America, to 6 ft, green flowers, May–June, coral-red berries, autumn. Evergreen forms include *V. delavayi*, Yunnan, 1–2 ft, white, rose-tinted flowers, June; *glaucoalbum*, Himalaya, 2–4 ft, white flowers, May–June, black berries; *myrsinites*, Evergreen Blueberry, SE. U.S.A., to 2 ft, white or pinkish flower, April, blue-black berries; *ovatum*, western N. America, to 8 ft, white flowers often very late; and *retusum*, E. Himalaya, 1 ft, white, striped red, flowers, May, but shy bearing; and are for sheltered positions in mild localities. *V. macrocarpon* (*Oxycoccus macrocarpus*) American Cranberry, eastern N. America, 1–1½ ft, is grown in selected forms for its acid, scarlet berries commercially; *oxycoccus* (*Oxycoccus oxycoccus*), Small Cranberry, northern hemisphere, creeping, pink-flowering, small red acid berries; and *vitisidaea*, Mountain Cranberry or Cowberry, northern hemisphere, 6 in., red acid berries, may be grown for ground cover on acid soils. *V. myrtillus*, Europe, N. Asia, 1–1½ ft, is the deciduous Bilberry, Whortleberry or Wineberry, pink flowers, May, and sweet blue-black berries, autumn, and available in cultivated forms.

Cultivation. Plant deciduous kinds in November–March; evergreens October–November or March–April, lime-free, moist soils, pH 4·5–5·5.

Propagation. By seeds, April, sandy acid loam. By layering, spring–summer. By cuttings of young shoots, July; by hardwood cuttings, with flower-buds removed, November–December.

Vacuole. A cavity or space in a plant cell, containing cell sap and air.

Vagans. Wandering. Ex. *Erica vagans*.

Valerian. See *Valeriana*.

Valerian, Red. See *Kentranthus*.

Valeriana (va-ler-i-a'na. Fam. Valerianaceae). Perennial herbs, grown for their corymbs of flowers, related to Kentranthus, commonly Valerian.

Selection. *V. officinalis*, All-heal, Cat's Valerian, Europe, Britain, 3 ft, pink flowers, June; *phu*, Caucasus, Europe, 3 ft, white flowers, August, and v. *aurea*, golden in spring; and *pyrenaica*, Pyrenees, 3–4 ft, pale rose, July, are somewhat coarse plants for borders or wild garden. *V. saliunica*, S. Europe, 4 in., pink June flowers; and *supina*, central Europe, 4 in., white, tinged pink, flowers, June–July, may be grown in the rock garden.

Cultivation. Plant October–March, well-drained ordinary soils, sun or partial shade. Remove spent flower heads to prevent self-seeding.

Propagation. By seeds, April, outdoor seed-bed. By division while dormant.

Valerianella (va-ler-i-an-el'la. Fam. Valerianaceae). The species chiefly cultivated is *V. locusta* (*olitoria*), Lamb's Lettuce or Corn Salad (q.v.).

Vallisneria (val-lis-ne'ri-a. Fam. Hydrocharitaceae). Underwater aquatic oxygenating plants for the aquarium or indoor pool.

Selection. *V. spiralis*, Eelgrass, Tapegrass, temperate Europe, has long ribbon-like, grassy leaves, and unisexual flowers, the male breaking off to rise to the surface and release its pollen to fertilize the female greenish flower raised on a slender stalk at the surface; *gigantea*, S. America, has longer, broader leaves, coloured purple in v. *rubrifolia*.

Cultivation. Plant in indoor waters of aquarium or tub or pool, March–June, minimum temp. 10° C. (50° F.).

Propagation. By rooted runners.

Vallota (val-lo′ta. Fam. Amaryllidaceae). The only species, *V. speciosa*, despite its name of Scarborough Lily, S. Africa, is only half-hardy, and a bulbous plant with a head of up to ten glowing scarlet, funnel-shaped flowers on stems of 1–2 ft, summer or autumn; with vs. *alba*, white; *delicata*, salmon-pink; *eximia*, white, crimson markings; and *major*, reddish-scarlet.

FIG. 230   *Vallota speciosa*, Scarborough Lily.

Cultivation. Plant two to three bulbs in an 8-in. pot, standard compost, to their shoulders, June, water thoroughly, stand in cool greenhouse, or indoor window; water liberally during active growth, until the broad linear leaves wither; rest dry from February to May; repot every third year or so, when offsets can be detached for increase.

Vancouveria (van-ku-ve′ri-a. Fam.

Berberidaceae). Pretty, creeping perennials with ferny foliage and spring flowers of western N. America.

Selection. V. hexandra, 6 in., white flowers with reflexed petals, May; and *planipetala*, Redwood Ivy, 9 in., white, lavender tinted, flowers, May.

Cultivation. Plant October–March, peat-enriched soil, partial shade, rock garden or woodland, and increase by division in autumn or March.

Vanda (van′da. Fam. Orchidaceae). A genus of epiphytic orchids, with erect stems, thick recurving leaves and beautiful flowers in racemes, needing hothouse culture, summer temps. 15·5–24° C. (60–75° F.); winter, 13–21° C. (55–70° F.).

Selection. V. caerulescens, Burma, 2½ ft, blue flowering, spring; *caerulea*, Burma, Thai, 2–3 ft, pale to deep blue, autumn, and vs.; *kimballiana*, Shan States, 1–2 ft, white, marked purple, autumn; *sanderiana*, Philippines, 2–3 ft, pink, buff and crimson, autumn; and several vs.; *teres*, Burma, Thai, climber to 4 ft, white, tinged rose to crimson, June–August; *tricolor*, Java, 2½ ft, cream, white, brownish-red, very scented, summer, and several vs.

Cultivation. Pot in March, well-crocked pots, compost of equal parts Osmunda fibre and live sphagnum moss; watering and syringing freely, near glass while growing, shade from hot sun; keeping moderately dry when dormant, December–March. Propagate by offsets, March.

Vanilla (van-ill′a. Fam. Orchidaceae). A genus of tall, climbing orchids of which *V. fragrans*, W. Indies, may be grown in the heated greenhouse for its greenish sweet-scented flowers, summer; which, if hand-pollinated, may form the bean-like pods from which the flavouring, vanilla, is produced.

Cultivation. Pot in March, in small, well-crocked pot, compost of 3 parts by bulk Osmunda fibre and 2 parts sphagnum moss, and train shoots on supports; water and syringe freely in growth, summer temps. 15·5–24° C. (60–75° F.); shading from hot sun; keep moderately dry in winter; temps. 13–21° C. (55–70° F.).

Propagation. By stem cuttings of 3–4 in., in April, with bottom heat of

24° C. (75° F.), in Osmunda fibre, sphagnum moss compost.

Variegation. The irregular variation in the colour of plant leaves, usually in the form of yellow or white patches or marginal markings, may be due to genetical inheritance, chlorosis (q.v.), or an infection, such as mosaic virus disease.

Variegatus (-a, -um). Variegated. Ex. *Cornus alba* v. *variegata*.

Variety. A distinct variation or form of a sub-species or species.

Vascular. Concerned with the vessels or ducts formed in the higher plants which conduct the sap stream.

Vascular Bundle. A longitudinal strand of sap-conducting tissue, largely made up of xylem and phloem (qq.v.).

Vascular Plant. A plant possessing a vascular system (q.v.), with roots, stems and leaves, as in the case with the seed plants (Gymnospermae, Angiospermae) and the cryptogams (Pteridophyta).

Vascular System. The plant tissue or vessels made up chiefly of xylem and phloem which make a continuous sap-conducting system throughout all parts of a vascular plant, conducting water, dissolved salts and synthesized food-stuffs, and lending mechanical support.

Vegetable. Botanically, of the Plant Kingdom. Horticulturally, a plant grown for culinary use, as food, as a whole or in part.

Vegetable Marrow (*Cucurbita pepo ovifera*). The parent species is held to be a native of S. America, though little is known of its introduction to Europe and Britain.

Varieties. These fall into two groups: (1) Trailing, which send out long trailing stems, needing much room, such as 'Long Green Striped', 'Long White' and 'Long Green', yielding large oblongish fruits, and 'Moore's Cream', 'Pen-y-Byd' and 'Rotherside Orange', yielding small, oval or round fruits; and (2) Bush or Clustered, which grow more compactly, such as 'Green Bush', 'White Bush', 'Custard Bush White', 'Tender and True', and continental vs., 'Cocozelle', 'Courgette' and 'Zucchini', which are cut when small, and are considered epicurean delicacies.

Cultivation. Seeds are best sown in April, singly in 2-in. peat-wood fibre pots, standard compost, bottom heat 18° C. (65° F.), to plant out in late May or early June, into prepared soil, well-dug, and liberally manured with organic matter. A layer of lawn mowings, dusted with dried blood, may be placed and firmed under the top spit to advantage, but special raised beds are not essential. Plant trailers about 12 ft apart, bush 4–6 ft. There is no reason why trailers should not be trained up trellis or supports. In warm gardens, seeds can be sown in the soil in May, two to a station, removing the weaker seedling. Throughout growth the plants must have good water supplies, though care must be taken in watering not to let water lodge around the base of stems. Marrows bear male and female flowers separately; the male are produced first with stamens only; the female have an embryo marrow behind them, and the first female flowers can be set by pressing the staminous core of the male into the centre of a female. Excess male flowers can be removed. The main vines can be stopped at 6 ft, to induce laterals to form, which tend to bear flowers that set more readily.

Vegetable Oyster. *See* Salsify.

Vegetables. As food plants garden-grown vegetables provide us with essential health-protective vitamins and minerals, body-regulating roughage and nutriment, and may be harvested at their peak in flavour, succulence and nutriment.

Although personal preference will play a part in choosing which vegetables to grow, consideration must also be given to the influence of such factors as the soil, the climate, space and situation. Carrots and root crops, for instance, require fairly porous, light soils, celery needs ample humus, and potatoes do not do well on chalk. In the north and colder exposures, it is necessary to give priority to the hardier kinds of vegetable. Space and situation will influence the variety of vegetables and the quantity that can be grown.

Site. The vegetable garden should be laid out in the open. Few vegetables do well in shade. The warmest, sunniest and most easily drained part is best reserved for the earliest crops, and half-hardy crops, such as tomatoes. Access paths must be simple and kept to the minimum, and the beds planned for ease in cultivation on a square or rectangular pattern. Perennial crops, such as Asparagus, Globe Artichokes and Rhubarb, must be given well-prepared, weed-free ground at the outset. A herb patch will be invaluable, but for this the soil need not be rich, but well-drained and easy of access.

Drainage. Good subsoil drainage is essential, and should receive first attention (*see* Drainage).

Cultivation. The cropping year begins in autumn, when vacant ground can be taken in hand; though basic cultivations can be carried out, weather permitting, throughout the winter, to late February or early March. Broadly, the heavier the soil, the more desirable it is to cultivate it well ahead of sowing or planting in order to give time for amending treatment to work and for the soil to settle and reintegrate. Under necessity, the soil preparation for potatoes, marrows or tomatoes may be left to the last. When a soil is being brought into cultivation initially it is best to cultivate it as deeply as practical, breaking up any dense hard subsoil or pan. On light and naturally well-drained soils, top spit cultivation may suffice, with liberal organic manuring to the subsoil. Subsequently, it will be beneficial to cultivate the subsoil once in four to six years, and so gain fertility in depth. *See* Digging.

Organic Manuring. Intensive cultivation will mean a more rapid breakdown and loss of organic matter in the soil. This must be made good by regular organic manuring with humus-forming material—animal manures, compost, peat, hop manure, spent hops, shoddy, leaf-mould, etc. Fresh unrotted material must be added well ahead of the sowing or planting time to ensure it decomposes sufficiently to be of value to the crops. After the turn of the year, it is best to use fairly well-rotted matter. Not all crops need organic manuring each year, but with crop rotation, every part of the vegetable garden should be organically manured at least one year in three. It is usually preferable to mix organic manure with the soil throughout, forking or culti-

vating it in, than to place it in buried layers. In the growing season, organic matter can be added in the form of mulches to be forked in after harvest.

Liming. Vegetables grow best in soils of moderate acidity, between pH 6·0 and 6·5. The tendency of most soils in cultivation is to become more acid as rains wash lime salts from the soil. It is sensible, therefore, to periodically test the soil for acidity and, if necessary, amend it by liming. Lime, when needed, is best applied after organic manuring, and the winter months are opportune. Usually, ground for such crops as brassicas, peas and beets benefit most from liming. Where light applications only are needed, it is often most helpful to apply basic slag. *See* pH Scale and Lime.

Fertilizing. Fertilizers are intended to provide nutrients for growing crops, and as such are best applied shortly before sowing or planting. Normal practice is to apply a compound base fertilizer, balanced to meet the nutrient need of the individual crop, in early spring, raked lightly into the soil; and supplement if desired by quick-acting fertilizers or liquid feeding during growth. *See* individual vegetables for recommendations.

Crop Rotation. To avoid one-sided exhaustion of soil fertility, the possible build-up of diseases or pests in a crop, and diminishing yields, it is necessary to practise crop rotation. The guiding principle is that vegetables of the same family should not follow one another on the same piece of ground. The families are:

Chenopodiaceae—Beetroot, Spinach.

Compositae—Globe Artichoke, Jerusalem Artichoke, Chicory, Endive, Lettuce, Salsify.

Cruciferae—Broccoli, Brussels Sprouts, Cabbage, Cauliflower, Kale, Kohl Rabi, Mustard, Savoy, Swede, Turnip, Watercress.

Cucurbitaceae—Cucumber, Marrow, Melon.

Leguminosae—Broad Bean, French Bean, Runner Bean, Peas.

Liliaceae—Asparagus, Garlic, Leek, Onion, Shallot.

Solonaceae—Aubergine, Capsicum, Potato, Tomato.

Umbelliferae—Carrot, Celery, Parsley, Parsnip.

An exception is sometimes made in the case of Onions, but even so, it is wiser to rotate the crop.

In practice a cropping area is divided into three or four equal areas, according to whether it is to be cultivated on a 3-year or a 4-year rotation. A 3-year rotation may be planned as follows:

Plot 1. Early Potatoes (followed by Spring Cabbage, Leeks, Turnips later).
Maincrop Potatoes.
Organic manure in autumn/winter. No lime.

Plot 2. Brassica crops; intercropped with saladings.
Beans, Peas.
Organic manure in autumn. Lime in winter.

Plot 3. Carrots, Parsnips, Beetroot, Spinach.
No organic manure. No lime.

Under this rotation onions are grown on a permanent bed, or included in Plot 2.

In the second year, Plot 1 is cropped as Plot 2; Plot 2 as Plot 3; and Plot 3 as Plot 1.

In the third year, Plot 1 is cropped as Plot 3; Plot 2 as Plot 1; and Plot 3 as Plot 2.

In the fourth year the cycle starts anew.

In a 4-year rotation the ground may be planted as follows:

Plot 1. Early Potatoes (followed by Spring Cabbage).
Maincrop Potatoes.
Organic manure in autumn/winter. No lime.

Plot 2. Broad Beans, French Beans, Peas, Runner Beans, Onions, Leeks, Shallots, Celery.
Organically manure in autumn. Lime in winter.

Plot 3. Carrots, Parsnips, Beetroot and Roots.
No organic manure. No lime.

Plot 4. Brassicas, intercropped with salads.
Organic manure in autumn. Lime in winter.

In the second year, Plot 1 is cropped as Plot 2; Plot 2 as Plot 3; Plot 3 as Plot 4; and Plot 4 as Plot 1.

In the third year Plot 1 is cropped as Plot 3; Plot 2 as Plot 4; Plot 3 as Plot 1; and Plot 4 as Plot 2.

In the fourth year Plot 1 is cropped as Plot 4; Plot 2 as Plot 1; Plot 3 as Plot 2; and Plot 4 as Plot 3.

In the fifth year the cycle begins again as in the first year.

For the cultivation of the individual crops *see* the vegetables under their separate entries.

Vein. The vascular bundle (q.v.) of a leaf; sometimes termed a nerve, or if thick and projecting, a rib. *See* Venation.

Veitchberry. A hybrid Blackberry × Raspberry, cultivated like a Blackberry (q.v.).

Veltheimia (vel-them'i-a. Fam. Liliaceae). Bulbous plants from S. Africa, with strap-like, wavy edged leaves, and handsome tubular, drooping flowers on an erect spike.

Selection. V. capensis, 1 ft, light pink, long-lasting flowers, March–April; vars. *deasii,* 10 in., pink, green-tipped flowers, and *glauca,* 1 ft, whitish flowers, spotted reddish pink, February–March and *viridifolia,* 1½ ft, pinkish purple, March–April.

Cultivation. Pot the large bulbs singly in large pots, standard compost, September; water regularly in growth, cool greenhouse conditions, minimum temp. 10° C. (50° F.); withhold water when leaves yellow and keep dry to September.

Propagation. By offsets when repotting at three- to four-year intervals.

Velutinus (-a, -um). Velvety. Ex. *Quercus velutina.*

Venation. The arrangement of veins in a leaf. In Monocotyledons, the veins usually run parallel with the midrib; in

FIG. 231 Venation: reticulated veined leaf.

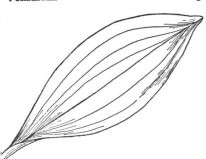

FIG. 232   Venation: parallel-veined leaf (*Hosta* sp.).

Dicotyledons they usually form a network and are reticulated.

Venidium (ve-ni'di-um. Fam. Compositae). Annual S. African flowering plants, of which *V. fatuosum*, 2–3 ft, with grey-green pinnatifid leaves, and golden-yellow ray-petalled flowers, purple at the base, summer, and hybrids in white, ivory, cream and yellows, with maroon base and black disks, are chiefly grown; sown under glass, March, in cool greenhouse, to plant out in May; or in late April, out of doors, where the plants are to flower.

Venidium × Arctotis. A unique F_1 hybrid strain of flowers, raised by Sutton & Sons Ltd, Reading, growing $1\frac{1}{2}$–2 ft, with ray-petalled flowers, summer and autumn, in a wide range of colours from chestnut, through crimson, pink, rose, buff, orange, terra-cotta to white; from plants planted out in May, sunny positions, well-drained ordinary soils, or in cold greenhouse.

Venosus (-a, -um). Strongly veined. Ex. *Verbena venosa*.

Ventilation. See Greenhouses.

Venus's Fly Trap. See *Dionaea muscipula*.

Venus's Looking Glass. See *Specularia speculum*.

Venus's Navelwort. See *Omphalodes linifolia*.

Venustus (-a, -um). Lovely, graceful. Ex. *Calochortus venustus*.

Veratrum, False Hellebore (ver-at'rum. Fam. Liliaceae). Hardy herbaceous perennials with thick poisonous rhizomatous roots, for wild gardens.

Selection. V. album, White Hellebore, Europe, Siberia, 3–4 ft, stemmed raceme of greenish-white flowers, July; *nigrum,* Europe, Siberia, 2–4 ft, dark purple, June; and *viride,* N. America, 3–5 ft, yellowish-green, July.

Cultivation. Plant October–March, rich loam soil, in the wild garden, partial shade.

Propagation. By seeds, April, outdoor seed-bed. By division of roots, February–March.

Veratrum Root. The powdered root of *Veratrum album,* Hellebore Powder, at one time used as an insecticide to control caterpillars.

Verbascum, Mullein (ver-bas'kum. Fam. Scrophulariaceae). A large genus of many biennials and some perennials, with more or less woolly leaves, and spikes or racemes of showy flowers.

Selection. V. blattaria, Moth Mullein, Britain, Europe, 3 ft, bright yellow, summer, and v. *alba,* white; *bombyciferum* ('Broussa'), Asia Minor, 4–6 ft, sulphur-yellow, summer, and v. 'Silver Spire'; *chaixii,* S. Europe, 3 ft, bright yellow, summer; *ovalifolium,* Caucasus, $2\frac{1}{2}$ ft, orange-yellow, July; and *thapsus,* Aaron's Rod, Hag Taper, Britain, Europe, 2–3 ft, yellow, June–July; with × 'Harkness Hybrid', to 10 ft, yellow; and × 'Miss Willmott', 6 ft, white, are biennials. *V. longifolium,* S. Europe, 3–4 ft, golden-yellow, and v. *pannosum,* great rosettes of felted leaves; *nigrum,* Dark Mullein, Europe, Asia, 2–3 ft, deep yellow, and v. *album,* white; *olympicum,* Bithynia, 5–6 ft, golden yellow, summer; *phoeniceum,* Purple Mullein, S. Europe, N. Asia, 2–3 ft, white, pink and violet, summer; *thapsiforme,* Europe, Siberia, 2–5 ft, yellow, summer; *wiedemannianum,* Asia Minor, 3 ft, deep blue to purple, June–September; and hybrids such as × 'C. L. Adams', 6 ft, golden yellow; × 'Gainsborough', 4 ft, pale yellow; × 'Pink Domino', $3\frac{1}{2}$ ft, rose-pink, are border perennials. *V. dumulosum,* Anatolia, 1 ft, small racemes, yellow, crimson blotched flowers, June; *pestalozzae,* Asia Minor, 8 in., clear yellow; and *spinosum,* Crete, 12 in., yellow, August, are sub-shrubby perennials for the rock garden or alpine house.

Cultivation. Plant November or March,

in well-drained soil; excellent on chalk, in warm sun.

Propagation. Biennials and perennials may be raised from seeds, sown April–June, cold frame or outdoor seed-bed; transplanted to flowering stations in September–November. Border perennials by division, March–April. Dwarf kinds by root cuttings in April; by shoot cuttings taken with a heel in May–June.

Verbena, Vervain (ver'be-na. Fam. Verbenaceae).

A large genus of annual, biennial and perennial flowering plants, largely from the warmer regions of the Americas, and not indisputably hardy.

Selection. V. bonariensis, S. America, 3–6 ft, square stems, long, narrow sessile leaves, and short spikes of purple-violet flowers, July–October; *corymbosa,* Chile, 3 ft, panicles of reddish-purple flowers, July–September; may be tried as border perennials in warm sunny gardens, mild localities. Others are half-hardy perennials, grown as half-hardy annuals, and include *V. bipinnatifida,* Mexico, to 1½ ft, ferny foliage, lavender blue clusters, summer; *canadensis,* central and S. U.S.A., 2 ft, magenta, summer, and v. *compacta,* 9 in., violet, for bedding; *hastata,* Canada, U.S.A., to 3 ft, violet, summer; × *hybrida,* Florists' or Garden Verbena, in forms 'Amethyst', blue; 'Compliment', coral-pink; 'Firefly', scarlet; 'Miss Susie Double', salmon-pink; 'Snow Queen', white; and 'Olympia' strain of various colours; *peruviana,* Chile, Patagonia, 3 in. procumbent, scarlet, summer, for the rock garden; *rigida (venosa),* S. America, to 2 ft, purple, and v. *alba,* white; with tuberous roots which may be taken up and wintered in frostproof quarters like those of dahlia, while *officinalis* is the native Vervain, perennial, lavender flowers, summer, but chiefly of herbal interest.

Cultivation. Perennials are best planted in March–April, well-drained, humus-rich soil, warm sun and shelter. Others are raised from seeds, sown March–April, standard compost, bottom heat of 18° C. (65° F.), under glass, pricked off for planting out in late May; or hybrids make good pot plants for the cool greenhouse, when stopped to produce bushy plants.

Propagation. By seeds as above. By cuttings of young shoots, rooted in a frame, summer, to over-winter in a cool greenhouse, kept fairly dry.

Verbena, Lemon-scented. See *Lippia citriodora.*

Verbena, Sand. See *Abronia.*

Veris. Of spring. Ex. *Primula veris.*

Vermiculite. A micaceous mineral expanded by heat treatment to a flaky, granular, sterile material, holding moisture well, and obtainable in horticultural grades, of neutral pH, for the propagation of plants by seeds and cuttings; as an aggregate for soilless culture; as a lightening amendment for heavy soils; and, in dry form, as a storage material for bulbs, tubers, etc., in winter.

Vernalization. The application of cold temperature treatment to plants to effect quicker growth and flowering. Developed largely in Russia, where it is used by first germinating winter varieties of cereals, allowing them to grow to the point when the radicles are just emerging, and then arresting development by subjecting to a temperature just about 0° C. for a few weeks. The seed, when sown later, resumes growth to produce a crop the same year, as a spring variety would. The period from sowing to harvest is thus shortened, and the technique most useful in climates where the summer growing period is short. It is related with day-length, or photoperiodism (q.v.). The concept is applied to other seeds; but horticulturally chiefly to bulbs, in which by careful regulation of temperatures in their later stages of growth, and during storage, flower formation and actual blooming can be accelerated. *See* prepared bulbs, under Hyacinth, Narcissus, and Tulip.

Vernation. The arrangement of leaves in buds.

Vernonia (ver-non'i-a. Fam. Compositae). Although a genus of over 600 species, only a few are worth considering, and then for the mild garden.

Selection. V. altissima, N. America, 5–8 ft, cymes of purple-violet flower-heads, autumn; *crinata,* N. America, 8 ft, purple flower-heads, autumn, and *noveboracensis,* E. U.S.A., 5 ft, purple, August; may be planted in the wild garden, November or March; well-drained ordinary soil, sun.

Propagation. By division, March. By seeds, sown April, outdoor seed-bed.

Vernus (-a, -um). Of spring. Ex. *Gentiana verna.*

Veronica, Speedwell (ver-o'ni-ka. Fam. Scrophulariaceae). A genus of annual and perennial herbs, shrubs and sub-shrubs, often taxonomically confused, with the shrubby kinds often being placed in a separate genus, *Hebe*, by New Zealand and American authorities, though not in Britain.

Selection. Garden-worthy hardy herbaceous perennials are: *V. bonarota*, S. Europe, 4 in., spikes of blue flowers, May–June; *gentianoides*, Caucasus, ½–1 ft, pale blue, June; and v. *pallida*, white; *variegata*, yellow marked leaves; *incana*, Russia, 1–2 ft, blue, July; and vs. *candidissima*, larger in leaf and flower; and *glauca*, deep blue flowers; *longifolia*, central Europe, Asia, 2–3 ft, lilac-blue, summer, and v. *subsessilis*, Japan, purple-blue, compact; *michauxii*, Persia, to 1 ft, pale blue; *spicata*, Britain, Europe, ½–1½ ft, bright blue, summer, and vs. *alba*, white; 'Crater Lake Blue', a deep blue, and *rosea*, purplish-pink; *telephiifolia*, Armenia, 3 in., blue, summer; *teucrium*, S. Europe, ½–2 ft, blue, July; and vs. 'Royal Blue', fine blue; 'Trehane', 6 in., golden leaves; and *vestita*, grey leaves; and *virginica*, eastern N. America, 2–4 ft, white or pale blue, autumn; and v. *alba*, white; *japonica*, Japan, white or blue.

Shrubby species, often listed under *Hebe* or *Parahebe*, are: *V.* × *andersonii*, 4–6 ft, violet to white, August; *anomala*, New Zealand, 3–5 ft, white to pale pink, June–July; *armena*, Armenia, 2 in., bright blue, June–July; *armstrongii*, New Zealand, 1–3 ft, white, July; × 'Autumn Glory', 1½–2 ft, violet, July–August; × 'Bowles Hybrid', 6 in., mauve, summer; *bidwillii*, New Zealand, 6 in., white, pink, June; *brachysiphon* (*traversii*),* New Zealand, to 6 ft, white, July; and v. 'White Gem';* *cinerea*, Asia Minor, 6 in., blue, June–July; *colensoi* v. *glauca*, New Zealand, 1–2 ft, white, July–August; × *edinensis*, 2 ft, white, June–July; *elliptica* (× *franciscana*)*, Chile, New Zealand, to 12 ft, large white, purple-lined flowers, and vs. *latifolia*, mauve; 'Blue Gem'; and *variegata*, yellow marked leaves; ×

'Ettrick Shepherd', 2–4 ft, violet, summer; *fruticans*, Europe, Scotland, 3 in., bright blue, summer; × 'Hielan Lassie', 2 ft, violet-blue, summer; *hulkeana*, New Zealand, to 4 ft, lavender, May–June; *lyallii*, New Zealand, 1–1½ ft, white and rose, July–September; × 'Marjorie',* 3 ft, light violet; × 'Midsummer Beauty',* 3 ft, lavender, summer; *matthewsii*, New Zealand, 3–4 ft, white, July; *pimeleoides*, New Zealand, 1½ ft, purple-blue, July–August, and v. *glauco-caerulea*, dark purple; *pinguifolia*, New Zealand, 1–3 ft, white, June–August, and v. *pagei* (*V. pageana*), 2 ft, white; and *salicifolia*, New Zealand, to 10 ft, lilac, tinged white, June–August, and v. *kirkii*, white. Most hardy kinds marked *. *V. speciosa*, New Zealand, to 5 ft, reddish- or blue-purple flowers, July–September, and vs. 'Evelyn', carmine; *gloriosa*, bright pink; *headfortii*, purplish blue; 'La Seduisante', crimson; 'Purple Queen', purple; and 'Simon Delaux', rich crimson, are tender, but make fine cool greenhouse shrubs outside the warmest, frost-free countries and the Scilly Isles.

Cultivation. Herbaceous perennials are best planted October–November or March, in well-drained soil, and sunny positions; dwarf species do well on rock terraces. The shrubby Hebe section are often of doubtful hardiness, and need sunny sheltered positions, mild localities and soils well-drained but humus-rich; with dwarf forms doing well on rock gardens; preferably plants in March–April.

Propagation. Herbaceous species by division in March; by seeds, March–April, in cold frame. Shrubs, by cuttings of young non-flowered shoots, taken with a heel, July–August, in a frame or under handlights.

Verrucosus (-a, -um). Warted. Ex. *Betula verrucosa.*

Verschaffeltia (vers-kaf-felt'i-a. Fam. Palmaceae). The only species, *V. splendida*, Seychelles, may be grown in large pots, peat-enriched compost, for its large, obovate, bright green, bladed leaves, divided at the edges, to 12–20 ft, under hothouse conditions; potted in March, watered and syringed liberally in growth, shaded from direct sun; and kept just moist in winter, temp. 15·5° C. (60° F.) minimum.

Versicolor. Variously coloured; changing in colours. Ex. *Crodus versicolor.*

Verticillaster. A false whorl or an inflorescence in which the flowers are produced in the leaf axils on opposite sides of a stem, as in the Labiatae.

Verticillatus (-a, -um). Whorled, flowers arranged in a circle around a stem. Ex. *Primula verticillata.*

Vervain. See *Verbena.*

Vesicaria (ve-si-ka′ri-a. Fam. Cruciferae). The chief species grown, *V. graeca*, Greece, is a reasonably hardy perennial, to 18 in., with racemes of yellow flowers, spring, followed by inflated seed pods; for the border or rock garden.

Cultivation. Plant March–April, in well-drained soil, sunny sheltered position, mild localities.

Propagation. By division, March–April. By seeds, April, outdoor seed-bed under handlight.

Vessels, Trachea. Non-living parts of xylem, consisting of tube-like cells, arranged end to end, and forming part of the wood of most flowering plants.

Vetch. See *Vicia.*

Vetch, Bitter. See *Lathyrus vernus* and *Vicia orobus.*

Vetch, Kidney. See *Anthyllis.*

Vetch, Milk. See *Astragalus.*

Vexillum. The standard or large rear petal of a papilionaceous flower. Hence *vexillaris*, with a standard.

Viability. The ability to live, applied to seeds and spores able to germinate.

Viburnum (vi-burn′um. Fam. Caprifoliaceae). A large genus of choice, decorative and attractive flowering shrubs, deciduous and evergreen, easily cultivated.

Selection. V. betulifolium, D., China, to 12 ft, white flowers in clusters, June, red fruits, autumn, on established plants; *bitchiuense*, D., Japan, to 10 ft, fragrant pink to white flower clusters, May; × *bodnantense*, D., to 10 ft, fragrant roseflushed flowers, November–March, and form 'Dawn'; × *burkwoodii*, E., 4–6 ft, fragrant, white clusters, March–April; and 'Park Farm' form; × *carlcephalum*, D., 4–6 ft, fragrant green to white clustered flowers, April; *carlesii*, D., Korea, 4–6 ft, fragrant white, April–

May; *dilatatum*, D., Japan, to 10 ft, pure white clusters, June, handsome red fruits and leaf colour, autumn; *fragrans*, D., N. China, 12 ft, white, tinged pink, fragrant small clusters, November–March; *henryi*, E., China, to 10 ft, pyramidal panicles white flowers, June; *hupehense*, D., China, 6 ft, white clusters, May–June, red fruits, autumn; × *juddii*, D., 4–7 ft, fragrant, pink to white flowers, April–May; *lantana*, D., native

FIG. 233 Flower cluster of *Viburnum carlcephalum.*

Wayfaring Tree, to 15 ft, white, May–June, followed by red to black fruits, autumn leaf colour; *macrocephalum*, Chinese Snowball tree, semi-E., to 12 ft, white globes of sterile flowers, May, for sheltered walls; *opulus*, Guelder Rose, D., Britain, Europe, N. Africa, to 12 ft, flat clusters white flowers, June, followed by bright red berries, good autumn foliage colour, and vs. *compactum*, good dwarf form; 'Notcutt's', large fruits; *sterile*, Snowball Tree, white sterile flowers, v. *roseum*, rose; *rhytidophyllum*, E., China, to 20 ft, large, wrinkled felted leaves, yellowish white flowers, May; *setigerum*, D., China, to 12 ft, white, May–June; *tinus*, E., Laurustinus, SE. Europe, to 12 ft, pink to white terminal flower clusters, December–April, and vs. 'Eve Price', larger clusters; 'French White'; *lucidum*, large-leaved; *variegatum*, yellow variegated leaves; and *tomentosum (plicatum)*, D., China, Japan, to 10 ft, flat clustered flowers, June, good autumn colour; and vs. 'Lanarth', larger leafed; *mariesii*, larger flower

FIG. 234   The winter flower cluster of *Viburnum fragrans*.

clusters; and *plicatum* (sterile), globular pure white flower clusters, June, and *wrightii*, D., Japan, 6–10 ft, white, May, followed by handsome red fruits and brilliant autumn leaf colour.

Cultivation. Deciduous (D., above) kinds may be planted in November–March; evergreen (E., above) in October–November or March–April; well-drained, humus-enriched soil, about pH 6, warm sun. Little pruning is necessary, but when it is, after flowering.

Propagation. Species by seeds, from berries stratified over winter, sown in April, cold frame or outdoor seed-bed. By cuttings of young shoots, July–August, under handlights or in cold frame.

Vicia, Vetch (vi'ki-a. Fam. Leguminosae). Of about 150 species, the most important horticulturally is *V. faba*, the Broad Bean (q.v.).

V. hirsuta, tenuissima and *tetrasperma* are native annuals, known as Tares, sometimes used in green manuring. *V. cracca*, Cow Vetch, climber, 6 ft, bright blue flowers, summer; *orobus*, Bitter Vetch, to 2 ft, white, tinged purple, flowers, summer; and *sylvatica*, Wood Vetch, to 4 ft, white with blue veining, are natives for the wild garden. *V. unijuga (Orobus lathyroides)*, NE. Asia, 1 ft, violet-purple, summer, is sometimes grown. Seeds of vetches may also be used for green manuring. Plants succeed in almost any soil from seeds sown March–September.

Victoria (vik-to'ri-a. Fam. Nymphaeaceae). The chief species, *V. amazonica (regia)*, Queen Victoria's Water-lily, is a rhizomatous rooting aquatic plant of S. America, for 4–6 ft of water, producing enormous rimmed leaves, 4–6 ft across, and white to rose flowers, over 1 ft across, when grown in pools, with water at 27–29° C. (80–85° F.), under glass. Although perennial, it is grown as an annual, from seeds sown in January in pots submerged in water at 29° C. (85° F.); and subsequently planted out in a large tank, in a mixture of rich loam and rotted cow manure, in May.

Villosus (-a, -um). Villous, with long, soft hairs. Ex. *Androsace villosa*.

Vinca, Periwinkle (vin'ka. Fam. Apocynaceae). Trailing evergreens or sub-shrubs, of which the hardy species make pleasing carpeters.

Selection. V. difformis, W. Mediterranean, prostrate-growing, pale blue flowers, autumn, for sheltered corners; *major*, Band Plant, Cut Finger, Britain, Europe, rampant, 2 ft, blue-purple flowers, May–September, and vs. *alba*, white; *pubescens*, hairy, red-purple; and *variegata*, cream-yellow-variegated leaves; *minor*, Britain, Europe, smaller leafed and more prostrate than *V. major*, blue-purple flowers, April–May; and vs. *alba*, white; *atropurpurea*, deep purple; *aureo-variegata*, yellow variegated leaves, blue flowers; 'Bowles Variety', azure blue; 'La Grave', lavender; and *multiplex*, double purple.

Cultivation. Plant November or March,

ordinary soil, to cover banks, under shrubs or trees, and waste ground. Easily propagated by division in March, or by cuttings of running stems, summer.

V. rosea, Madagascar Periwinkle, is a pleasing, tropical evergreen shrub of 1–2 ft, with rose-pink flowers, summer and autumn, and a white v. *alba*. Sow seeds, March–April, standard compost, bottom heat of 18° C. (65° F.), to prick off into small pots, and grow on in the cool greenhouse or on an indoor sill.

Vine. *See* Grape Vine.

Viola (vi′o-la. Fam. Violaceae). A very large genus of small plants, mostly perennial, botanically divided into fourteen sections and several sub-sections, and embracing over 400 species, with many sub-species and varieties. Horticulturally, it is more practical to group them according to their culture into Viola species and varieties, Sweet Violets, Violettas, Violets and Pansies.

Selection. Species and varieties best adapted to the rock garden or alpine house include: *V. biflora*, European Alps, 2–4 in., yellow, veined black, flowers, May; *blanda*, N. America, 3 in., white, veined purple, April; *cornuta*, Pyrenees, 6 in., violet, summer; *elegantula* (*bosniaca*), Yugoslavia, 4–12 in., rosy-mauve, May–June, and vs. *alba*, white; and *lutea*, yellow; *eizanensis*, Japan, 4 in., rose-pink, April; *gracilis*, Asia Minor, to 6 in., deep violet, May–June, and hybrid forms; *pedata*, Bird's Foot Violet, N. America, 4 in., dark and light violet, May–June; and *hispida* (*rothomagensis*), Rouen Violet or Pansy, N. France, 6 in., violet, May–August; all being herbaceous. *V. cazorlensis*, S. Spain, 6 in., rose-lilac, June, and *delphinantha*, Greece, Bulgaria, 4 in., reddish-violet, June–July, are compact shrubby herbaceous plants for the alpine house. *V. calcarata*, European Alps, violet blue or yellow, June; *hederacea*, Australian Violet, violet, flushed white, April; and *yakusimana*, S. Japan, 1 in., tiny white flowers, May–June, are interesting species for the alpine house or sheltered rock garden.

Cultivation. Plant October or March–April; porous, well-drained soil, with leaf-mould, partial shade.

Propagation. By seeds, spring or late summer. By division in April or August; or green cuttings in July. Repot in alpine house after flowering.

Sweet Violets. Derived from *V. odorata*, of Britain, Europe, N. Africa and Asia, sweetly scented, and cultivated in named forms such as 'Cœur d'Alsace', pink; 'Czar', blue; 'Governor Herrick', deep blue; 'Princess of Wales', violet; 'Red Queen', red; 'Rosina Hybrids', various colours; *sulphurea*, creamy yellow; and 'White Czar', white.

FIG. 235 *Viola odorata* v., Sweet Violet.

Cultivation. May be raised from seeds, sown March–April to August in cold frame or outdoor seed-bed. Out of doors, plant May–June or September, in well-drained, humus-rich soil, easterly aspect; pinch off runners for large flowers, next spring. For winter bloom in cool greenhouse or frame, pot plants in September, standard compost, one to a 6-in. pot, and plunge in tan fibre or peat; water carefully, not to wet the leaves, ventilate freely, minimum temp. 7–10° C. (45–50° F.); or may be planted out in 6 in. of good soil compost, over a layer of leaves and rotting manure, or heated sand (at about 13° C. (55° F.)); water regularly, ventilate, but care is needed in foggy, muggy weather. Propagation is by division after flowering, May–June,

Bedding Violas. Sometimes called

Tufted Pansies, and of hybrid origins. Named forms are 'Archie Grant', indigo blue; 'Bridal Morn', light blue; 'Arkwright Ruby', ruby crimson, black blotched; 'Blue Heaven', sky blue; 'Clear Crystals' in yellow, red, blue and white self-colours; 'Chantryland', apricot; 'Goldfinch', yellow, edged violet; 'Maggie Mott', lavender-blue, scented; 'Councillor Waters', bluish-purple; 'Miss Brooks', cerise; 'Moseley Perfection', yellow; 'Primrose Dame', pale yellow; 'Muriel Fearnley', reddish crimson; 'Pickering Blue', bright blue; 'White Swan', white; 6–8 in. high.

Cultivation. By seeds, sown July–August, in boxes, standard compost, cold frame, or outdoor seed-bed; transplanting when large enough in autumn to where plants are to flower the following year. Alternatively, sow under glass, February–March, bottom heat of 15·5° C. (60° F.), to plant out April–May. Plant in well-drained soil, humus-enriched, pH 6·0–6·5, sunny positions or light shade; pinch off spent flower-heads to keep flowering.

Propagation. By basal tufts or cuttings, in pans or boxes, early autumn, housed in a frame.

Violettas. These are plants of compact habit, 4 in., derived from *V. cornuta*, requiring similar culture to Bedding Violas. Named forms include 'Blue Carpet', purple-violet; 'Buttercup', deep yellow; 'Duchess', cream; 'Hansa', violet-blue; 'Jersey Gem', purplish blue; 'Lorna', lavender-purple; 'Northfield Gem', violet; 'Violetta', white.

Pansies. Garden Pansies (from French *Pensée*, reputedly) are hybrids and strains developed from *V. tricolor*, the native Heartsease, and other species, technically grouped under × *wittrockiana*. They differ from Violas chiefly by forming somewhat looser-growing plants, with larger flowers, and are often divided into Fancy varieties, vari-coloured and tinted, with blotched, flamed or edged petals; and Show varieties, more formal and rounded, with self colours; White Ground; and Yellow Ground.

Selection. Bedding Pansies: Bushy habit, about 6 in. tall: 'Apricot Queen', apricot; 'Coronation Gold', golden yellow; 'Beaconsfield', royal purple;

FIG. 236   The face of the Pansy, *Viola* × *wittrockiana*.

'King of the Blacks', purple-black; 'Pacific Toyland F₂ Hybrids', various colours; 'Paperwhite', pure white; and strains such as 'Empress', 'Excelsior' and 'Felix'. Giant Large-Flowering Varieties: 'Alpine Glow', crimson, black blotch; 'Engelmann's Giant' strain; 'Swiss Giant' strain; 'Ullswater', rich blue; 'Westland Giant' strain; and 'Swiss Velvet'. Winter-flowering Varieties: to flower very early in the year; 'Celestial Queen', sky-blue; 'Helios', yellow; 'Ice King', white, dark spotted; 'Jupiter', sky blue; 'Moonlight', primrose; 'Orion', golden yellow; and 'Winter Sun', golden, dark spotted. Fancy and Show varieties in named forms are best sought in specialists' lists.

Cultivation. By seeds at almost any time in the growing season, but usually in late August–September, in pans or boxes, standard compost, in cold frame, to plant out in spring; in June for winter varieties and autumn planting; on outdoor seed-beds, under cloches, if preferred. Plant in humus-rich, moist, but well-drained soil, cool conditions, out of hot midday sun, but not under trees. Keep well picked of spent flowers; water in dry weather.

Propagation. Although perennials, Pansies are usually grown as annuals or biennials, but good kinds can be increased by cuttings of green shoots in the growing season, especially in late summer, rooted in a cold frame, in cool, shady north aspect, or under handlights.

Diseases. Leaf Spot may be caused by various fungi, and seriously affected leaves are best removed and plants treated with a copper fungicide. Black Root Rot (*Thielaviopsis basicola*), Damping Off Rot (*Aphanomyces euteiches*), and Foot and Collar Rots (*Phytophthora*, sp., *Rhizoctonia* sp.) suggest overwet soil, damp conditions and overcrowding; plants should be destroyed and new plantings made under better conditions. Smut (*Urocystis violae*) shows in blackish, bladder-like swellings on leaves and stems, bursting with spores. Affected plants are best destroyed, others sprayed with a copper fungicide, and soil sterilized before planting anew.

Pests. A Gall Midge, *Dasyneura affinis*, sometimes causes distortion and dwarfing of plants in frames, with thickening leaves and rolled margins. Affected leaves must be promptly destroyed, and plants treated with a nicotine insecticide. Red Spider Mites may be troublesome under too dry conditions and need treatment with malathion.

Violaceus (-a, -um). Violet-coloured. Ex. *Calceolaria violacea.*

Violet, African. See *Saintpaulia.*

Violet, Bog. See *Pinguicula.*

Violet, Dame's. See *Hesperis matronalis.*

Violet, Dog's Tooth. See *Erythronium dens-canis.*

Violet, Water. See *Hottonia palustris.*

Viper's Bugloss. See *Echium vulgare.*

Virens. Green. Ex. *sempervirens,* always green.

Virgatus (-a, -um). Virgate, twiggy, wand-like. Ex. *Panicum virgatum.*

Virginia Creeper. See *Parthenocissus quinquefolia.*

Virginian Cowslip. See *Mertensia virginica.*

Virginian Stock. See *Malcolmia maritima.*

Virgin's Bower. Common name used for the climbing forms of *Clematis* (q.v.).

Viridus (-a, -um). Green, **Viridi-** in compound words. Ex. *viridiflorus*, green-flowered, or *Tulipa viridiflora.*

Virus Diseases. Diseases attributed to sub-microscopic organisms, now held to consist of nucleic acid (RNA) within a protein when mature; termed a virion. The viruses multiply within the host plant tissues, and spread to all parts, distorting and crippling growth. Symptoms and effects vary considerably according to the nature of the virus and the type of plant attacked, varying from a chlorotic mosaic of leaves, with curling and rolling, and streaking of shoots, to abnormal distortions and stunting of growth. Beetroot, Brassicas, Cucumber, Dwarf Beans, Lettuce, Peas, Potatoes, Spinach, Tomatoes and Turnips are subject to virus infection; also Apples, Currants (Reversion), Raspberry and Strawberry. Flowering plants may also be affected; virus infection is held to be a cause of Tulip Breaking, though in this case non-fatal. A virus may not kill a plant outright, but weaken it, and carry the risk of being a centre of infection to others. Normally it is wise to destroy infected plants as soon as seen. Viruses are transmitted from plant to plant chiefly by sap-sucking insects, such as aphids, but also by eelworms in some instances and by hand or appliances in others. They may also be spread by the vegetative propagation of infected plants; but are seldom seed-borne.

Viscaria, Rock Lychnis (vis-ka'ri-a. Fam. Caryophyllaceae). Allied to and sometimes included with *Lychnis*, *Viscaria* is a genus of small perennials.

Selection. V. alpina, Britain, Europe, Siberia, to 4 in., pink flowers, summer, and v. *alba*, white; *atropurpurea*, Balkans, 1½ ft, red-purple, May; and *vulgaris*, native Catchfly, 1 ft, rose, summer, and vs. *albiflora*, white; and *splendens flore pleno*, large double rose-pink, summer.

Cultivation. Plant November–March, cool, moist soil, sun or partial shade, on rock garden or border.

Propagation. By seeds, April, in cold frame or out of doors. By division in March.

Viscosus (-a, -um). Viscous, clammy. Ex. *Primula viscosa.*

Viscum, Mistletoe (vis'kum. Fam. Loranthaceae). Although there are many species of this genus of shrubs parasitic on trees, only one is commonly grown in this country, *V. album*, an evergreen unisexual shrub, with soft, tawny-green branches and shoots, opposite, narrowly oblong, round-ended leaves, and inconspicuous sessile flowers in the axils of shoots, which become translucent white berries on a female plant. Propagation is by simply pressing a ripe, one-seeded berry into a crevice or cut notch on the underside of a young host tree branch, near its base, in April–May. The sticky pulp hardens and holds the seed to the branch which then germinates and the radicle grows along the under bark of its host. It takes 5–7 years to come to flowering size and reveal its sex. Obviously, more than one plant must be propagated near enough for cross-pollination to take place. Mistletoe will grow on a wide range of host trees, particularly Apple, Hawthorn and Poplars, but also on Maple, Lime and Ash, but not on Oaks or evergreens. Although native, it is doubtfully hardy north of the Mersey-Humber line, rare in Scotland.

Vitex (vi'teks. Fam. Verbenaceae). Deciduous shrubs of which the chief species grown is *V. agnus-castus*, Chaste Tree of S. Europe, actually a shrub of up to 10 ft, with foliolate leaves of narrow, aromatic greyish leaflets, and racemes of clustered, pale violet, tubular fragrant flowers, September–October; and v. *alba*, white, but only hardy enough for a sheltered wall, in frost-free

FIG. 237 Leaf of *Vitex agnus-castus*, the Chaste Tree.

gardens; planted November–March, well-drained, humus-rich soil, pH 6·0–6·5; or may be tub-grown, and winter-sheltered in a cold greenhouse. Propagated by cuttings of young shoots, July–August, in cold frame, or under handlight.

Vitis (vi'tis, Fam. Vitaceae). A genus of tendril-climbing deciduous shrubs or vines, esteemed for their autumn foliage colours and/or fruits.

Selection. V. amurensis, Manchuria, to 25 ft, broadly ovate, lobed leaves, crimson and purple in autumn; *coignetiae*, Japan, to 60 ft, very large, lobed leaves, most beautiful in crimson, scarlet and gold in autumn; *flexuosa* v. *parvifolia*, Korea, China, to 12 ft, small-leaved, shining bronze-green, purple beneath, leaves, very elegant; *labrusca*, Fox Grape, N. America, to 30 ft, leaves rusty-brown underneath, bunches of musk-flavoured, black grapes; × *pulchra*, to 25 ft, intense autumn leaf colour; *vinifera*, Grape Vine, to 50 ft, has fine ornamental vs. in *apiifolia*, with leaves finely cut; and *purpurea*, claret-red foliage, turning purple.

Cultivation. Plant November–March, well-drained, humus-rich soil, to train up walls on trellis, posts or pergolas or over arbours. May be pruned, if necessary, shortening the previous year's shoots in January.

Propagation. By layering, autumn; by 'eyes' as with grape vines (q.v.).

See *Ampelopsis* and *Parthenocissus* for other species previously listed in this genus.

Vittatus (-a, -um). Stripes lengthways. Ex. *Primula vittata*.

Viviparous. Of plants which have seeds which germinate while still attached to the parent plant; or produce young plants, bulbils or shoots in the inflorescence instead of flowers. Of insects which bring forth living young, as with some aphids.

Vriesia (wres'i-a. Fam. Bromeliaceae). Perennial tropical plants of central and S. America, with rosettes of stiff, beautifully marbled or banded leaves, and a flower stem bearing spikes of showy flowers, colourfully bracted, allied to Tillandsia, for the warm greenhouse or as indoor house plants.

Selection. V. carinata, Brazil, 10 in., yellow flowers, scarlet and yellowish green bracts, October–November; *fenestralis,* Brazil, 3 ft, greenish-yellow flowers, green, spotted brown, bracts, from apple green, beautifully marked leaves, autumn; *hieroglyphica,* Brazil, 3 ft, dull yellow flowers, bluntly keeled bracts, and broad green leaves, handsomely marked dark green, blackish-purple beneath, autumn; *psittacina,* Brazil, 1½ ft, yellow, spotted green, flowers, yellowish green leaves, July; *saundersii,* Brazil, 18 in., sulphur-yellow flowers, broad glaucous green leaves, white spotted, marked purple brown below; *splendens,* Guiana, 3 ft, yellow flowers, bright red bracts, linear green leaves, lighter beneath, summer; and *tessellata,* Brazil, to 6 ft, yellow, green flowers, tessellated green and yellow leaves, late summer, with leaves variegated in v. *sanderae.*

Cultivation. Pot in March–April, well-crocked pots, compost of equal parts by bulk Osmunda fibre, leaf-mould, and half a part each of sphagnum moss and sand, plus a little JI base fertilizer. Keep well watered in active growth; moderately in winter, temp. 15·5° C. (60° F.) minimum.

Propagation. By offsets, in spring.

Vulgaris (-e). Common. Ex. *Primula vulgaris.*

W

Wahlenbergia (wa-len-berg'i-a. Fam. Campanulaceae). A large genus, related to Campanula, and Edraianthus, to which many plants listed as Wahlenbergia belong.

Selection. W. albomarginata, New Zealand, 6 in., bell-shaped, white or blue flowers, June; *matthewsii,* New Zealand, 4 in., tufted linear leaves, erect, bell-shaped, pale lilac, white striped, flowers, July–August; and *saxicola,* Tasmania, 4 in., open, bell-like, pale blue flowers, May. *W. hederacea* is a delightful little native, tiny blue bell flowers, July–August.

Cultivation. Plant in March–April, well-drained but humus-rich soil, in sheltered rock gardens, mild localities, or in pans in the alpine house; keeping fairly dry in winter.

Propagation. By seeds in late summer, in propagating frame.

Wake Robin. See *Trillium grandiflorum.*

Waldsteinia (wald-sten'i-a. Fam. Rosaceae). Dwarf perennial herbs with trifoliolate leaves, and the creeping character of the Strawberry.

Selection. W. fragarioides, E. U.S.A., 2 in., corymbs of yellow flowers, May–June; *geoides,* E. Europe, 8 in., palmately lobed leaves, yellow, April–May; and *ternata,* E. Europe, 3 in., flowers in yellow racemes, April–May.

Cultivation. Plant in October or March–April, well-drained ordinary soil, rock garden or border, sun or light shade.

Propagation. By seeds, April, in cold frame. By division, April.

Walks. *See* Paths.

Wall, Dry. A 'dry' wall is simply a wall built without wet mortar, and may consist of stones or bricks, to mark the division between two garden features, to face terraced ground on a slope, or may be constructed double, with two faces, to enclose a space, or act as a low barrier. Such a wall should be built on a firm footing of well-packed broken stone. The stones are laid in courses, bonded like brickwork with vertical joints overlapping; the face inclined by at least 5 degrees backwards, and stretcher or header stones inserted lengthwise for stability at every 6 ft of wall length and 18 in. of height. A 'mortar' of weed-free, porous soil compost is used, and well firmed behind the wall as it is built. Such a wall is ideal for growing many alpine plants (q.v.), and if made in early spring, these can be planted as the wall grows.

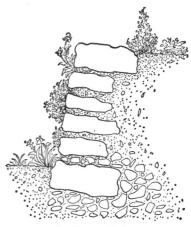

FIG. 238   Dry wall, in section.

Wall Fern. See *Polypodium vulgare.*
Wall Pepper. See *Sedum acre.*
Wall Plants. A short list of suitable plants for dry walls is: *Achillea × lewisii, Aethionema × 'Warley Rose', Androsace saromentosa, Campanula poscharskyana, Cordydalis lutea,* * *Dianthus caesius, D. deltoides, Draba aizoon, Erinus alpinus,* * *Erodium corsicum, Gypsophila repens, Helichrysum belloides,* * *Linaria origanifolia,*

573

Name of Plant	Deci- duous or Evergreen	Aspect of Wall	Flowers in	Remarks
Self-clinging Climbers				
Campsis radicans	D.	S., W.	Aug.–Sept.	For mild localities
Hedera helix	E.	Any	Autumn	Many varieties
Hydrangea petiolaris	D.	N., E., W.	June	
Parthenocissus sp.	D.	Any	—	Autumn colour
Twining Climbers				
Akebia quinata	E.	S., E., W.	May	Not cold exposures
Abutilon megapotamicum	D.	S., W.	Summer	For mild localities
Aristolochia macrophylla	D.	Any	June	Very vigorous
Celastrus orbiculatus	D.	Any	May	Colourful fruits
Lonicera henryi	E.	S., W.	June	Not for cold walls
Lonicera japonica	E.	S., W., E.	Summer	Not entirely frostproof
Lonicera periclymenum	D.	E., W., N.	Summer	
Lonicera tragophylla	D.	E., S., W.	Summer	Likes shelter
Muehlenbeckia complexa	D.	S., W.		For mild localities
Passiflora caerulea	D.	S., W.	July–Aug.	Needs warm shelter
Polygonum baldschuanicum	D.	Any	Summer	Very vigorous
Wisteria sp.	D.	S., W.	May–June	
Clematis spp.	*See Clematis*			
Roses, Climbing	*See Roses*			

Omphalodes verna,* Ramonda myconi,* Saponaria ocymoides,* Saxifraga apiculata,* S. caespitosa, S. moschata,* Sedum spp., *Sempervivum* spp., *Silene alpestris, Thymus serpyllum* and vs., *Cytisus* spp. Strong-growing plants such as *Alyssum saxatile* and vs., *Aubrieta* in variety, *Hypericum reptans,* and *Iberis sempervirens* are best planted to the foot of a dry wall, lest they swamp more delicate plants.

*Indicates tolerance for shade.

Wallflower (*Cheiranthus cheiri*, q.v.) is naturally perennial but is grown as a biennial, and is a favourite flower for a spring display.

Selection. There are now many strains, which may be grouped as: (1) Tall, Giant-flowered, Sweet-scented, such as 'Blood Red'; 'Cloth of Gold', golden yellow; 'Eastern Queen', apricot to bright red; 'Ellen Willmott', ruby red;

'Fire King', orange-red; 'Giant Ruby', ruby red; 'Golden Monarch', golden-yellow; 'Primrose Monarch', deep primrose yellow; 'Rose Queen', apricot, tinted pink; 'Scarlet Emperor', scarlet; and 'Vulcan', velvety crimson; 15–18 in. high. (2) Dwarf, Sweet-scented, Bedding, such as 'Orange Bedder', orange to apricot; 'Scarlet Bedder', scarlet; 'Monarch, Fair Lady', various colours; 'Persian Carpet', various colours; 12 in. (3) Early-flowering, chiefly for cutting, such as 'Phoenix', blood red; 'Yellow Phoenix'; yellow; and early-flowering strains of 'Primrose', 'Fire King', 'Rose Pink' and 'Vulcan'; 2 ft tall. (4) Double flowering; such as 'Christmas Gold'; and Double Mixtures.

Cultivation. Seeds are sown in May, preferably, or not later than June, on outdoor seed-beds, in rows, 12 in. apart, plants thinned to 6 in. apart, or planted out on a reserve bed, prior to planting

Name of Plant	Deciduous or Evergreen	Aspect of Wall	Flowers in	Remarks
Acacia dealbata	D.	S., W.	April	For mild localities
Berberis stenophylla	E.	Any	May–June	To 10 ft
Caryopteris × *clandonensis*	D.	S., W.	Sept.–Oct.	To 5 ft
Ceanothus spp. (q.v.)	E.	S., W.	May–June	To 8–10 ft
Ceratostigma willmottianum	D.	S., W.	Aug.–Sept.	3 ft, low walls
Chaenomeles spp. (q.v.)	D.	Any	March	4–8 ft
Chimonanthus praecox	D.	S., W.	Dec.–Jan.	To 10 ft
Choisya ternata	E.	N., S., W.	May	To 9 ft
Cotoneaster horizontalis	D.	Any	May	To 6 ft, berries
Cotoneaster lactea	E.	Any	July	To 15 ft, berries
Cotoneaster microphylla	E.	Any	June	To 3 ft, berries
Escallonia, various	E.	S., W.	June	5–12 ft
Forsythia spp. (q.v.)	D.	Any	April	8–12 ft
Garrya elliptica	E.	N., S., W.	Feb.	To 12 ft
Hibiscus syriacus	D.	S., W.	Sept.	To 10 ft
Indigofera gerardiana	D.	S., E., W.	Summer	To 10 ft
Jasminum nudiflorum	D.	Any	Winter	To 12 ft
Jasminum officinale	D.	S., W., E.	Summer	To 12 ft
Lippia citriodora	D.	S., W.	Summer	6 ft, tender
Magnolia spp. (q.v.)	D. (E.)	S., W.	Spring	6–15 ft
Osmanthus delavayi	E.	S., W.	April	To 10 ft
Prunus triloba plena	D.	S., W., E.	April	To 9 ft
Pyracantha spp. (q.v.)	E.	Any	May	To 10 ft, berries
Rubus spp.	E.	Any	Summer	To 12 ft
Viburnum × *juddii*	D.	S., W., N.	April–May	To 7 ft
Viburnum opulus vs.	D.	Any	May–June	To 10 ft

in flowering positions in September–October; on well-prepared soil, pH 6·5, enriched with humus from previous organic manuring, and fertilized with bone meal at 3–4 oz. per sq. yd, and ½ oz. sulphate of potash per sq. yd, about 12 in. apart for tall varieties, 6–9 in. for others. In March may be given a light application of a nitrogenous fertilizer, say nitro-chalk at ½ oz. per sq. yd, or dried blood.

Walls. Permanent walls, built of stone, brick, concrete or breeze blocks, may often be used successfully to harbour and shelter plants within their lee, where slightly higher temperatures and more favourable growing conditions than in the open usually obtain. In kitchen gardens, walls of 6 ft or more may be used for the growing of fruit. Apricots, nectarines, peaches, figs and fine dessert plums and gages on warm, sunny, south or westerly facing walls; cordon or espalier apples, plums and cherries, and pears, on south-east, south or west facing walls; and morello cherries on north walls. The trees must be planted 8 in. or so out from the base of the wall in the soil border, and trained to wire supports, which allow air to circulate between wall and plant branches.

High walls, house and structural walls may be made less bleak by the use of ornamental climbing plants, and/or tall-growing shrubs. Climbers may be divided into those which are self-clinging (*see* table, page 574) and those which climb by twining or tendrils and therefore need the support of a trellis or wires.

Many tall-growing shrubs are adaptable to walls and the warm shelter of a wall border is often suitable for species which are not quite robust enough for the open. A selection may be made from those given in the table above.

Walnut. See *Juglans*. The Walnuts grown for their nuts as well as their undoubted timber and ornamental value are chiefly selected varieties of *Juglans regia*, such as: For pickling green nuts in July—'Leeds Castle' and 'Patching'. French varieties for ripe nuts are 'Freyne', 'Mayette', 'Melyannaise' and 'Parisienne', preferably for warm sunny localities, with freedom from late spring frosts. Varieties recommended by the East Malling Research Station, bred to flower late to miss spring frosts, are E.M. 95, 162, 202, 589 and 719. On their own roots, trees may take fifteen to twenty years to come to a flowering and fruiting rhythm. Grafted trees tend to crop earlier, from seven years or so.

Cultivation. Walnuts do well in any well-drained soil of good depth, sited more or less out of reach of spring frosts, and cold north or east air-streams. They do need sun and warmth to yield sound keeping nuts. Planting is best done in October–December.

Harvesting. Nuts for pickling are gathered green in early to late July. Ripe nuts are harvested in early autumn. Beating is only necessary with a long bamboo to get the nuts to fall. The outer husk must be removed with a stiff brush, or churning the nuts up in a tub with an equal amount of sand, covered with water. They are then laid on netting to dry, before storing in layers, covered with sand and a sprinkling of salt, in boxes, under cool conditions, temp. 7–10° C. (45–50° F.).

Wardian Case. A glazed case in which plants may be transported, especially used for plants imported or exported on long sea voyages; and consisting of a wooden framework, with removable top frames, almost airtight, in which potted plants, packed in coconut fibre, were placed. Ornamental adaptations of it were features of Victorian drawing-rooms, etc., planted with ferns and foliage plants. The modern equivalent is the Bottle Garden. By giving a closed atmosphere, moisture is conserved and equable growing conditions for ferns, many succulents and allied plants maintained.

Washingtonia (wash-ing-ton′i-a. Fam. Palmaceae). The species grown, *W. filifera*, California, to 40 ft, is an orna-mental palm, with roundish, fan-like leaves, with deeply cleft blades, which may be grown in pots in the warm greenhouse.

Cultivation. Pot in February–March, compost of loam, moist peat and sharp sand in equal amounts; water freely in active growth, shade from direct sun, water very moderately in winter, minimum temp. 13° C. (55° F.). Propagated from imported seeds, April, standard compost, bottom heat of 29° C. (85° F.), under glass.

Wasps (*Vespoidea*). The black-and-yellow banded swift-flying insects chiefly feared by gardeners are the Common Wasps (*Vespula vulgaris, V. germanica*), which can play havoc with ripening fruit. The Tree Wasp (*V. sylvestris*) is less common, and the large yellow and red Hornet (*Vespa crabo*) even more rare and more docile than the others. Briefly, queen wasps over-winter in hibernation, to found new colonies in spring, making nests of wood-pulp fibre in holes in the ground, in banks, in trees, in attics or outbuildings. The queen may be seen flying in spring, visiting flowers such as those of Cotoneaster for nectar, dead wood and posts for wood pulp, and capturing flies or insects to feed her brood. By June worker wasps emerge to take over the foraging, and in this early phase do much good in reducing insect populations, and are beneficial to gardening. In summer, when they start visiting fruit, it is best to watch their line of flight and trace them to the location of the nest, mark it, and at dusk gently insert a teaspoonful of a DDT or gamma-BHC insecticidal dust in the entrance and withdraw. Inevitably, the insecticide is carried into the colony to its destruction. Wasps do not deliberately sting when foraging unless trapped in clothing, but may sting if disturbed at the nest. The pain of a sting can be reduced by promptly painting with strong ammonia, a paste of sodium bicarbonate and water, or iodine.

Water Garden. The water garden may consist of a single pool or pond, planted with aquatic plants; or a series of pools connected by stream or waterfall to adorn a sloping piece of ground; or the adaptation of a low-lying site to pond with marginal planting and bog garden.

Pool Construction. Within reason and the space available, the larger the pool, the more equable the conditions for plants and fish, and the more easily managed. A minimum maximum depth of 15 in. is desirable, though this need not exceed 30 in. no matter how big the pool; and the depth may be 3–4 in. for marginal planting. Various methods of construction are possible. Concrete is the traditional permanent material used. The pool site is excavated to the required depth and shape, allowing for a 4-in. thickness of concrete at the base and sides. In loose soil a firm base for concreting should be assured by packing with hard core or well-packed broken stone. A suitable concrete mix is 4–5 parts by volume crushed clean stone, gravel or aggregate (¾-in. size), 2 parts clean builder's sand, 1 part cement, plus a waterproofing compound (Pudlo, for instance), thoroughly mixed dry on a clean surface or in a mixing drum, with water added to render plastic without being sloppy. Lay evenly about 2 in. thick over the floor of the pool, then place reinforcement of large mesh wire netting, chain-link netting or reinforcing steel mesh in position, and then the remaining concrete to 4 in., finally smoothing to drain to one end or corner where provision for emptying through a plugged metal or plastic pipe is well worth while. The edges of the base should be criss-crossed or scoured for 4 in. wide to give a key for the walls; the base can then be left covered with damp sacks to harden. It is better to let the walls slant outwards 12–15 degrees, rather than be vertical. They are raised with the help of shuttering—strong board forms firmly placed, 4 in. from the sides of the excavation. The walls can be carried up to form the kerb to a marginal shelf of shallower water. When the concrete has set, and shuttering removed, the surface may be given a smooth rendering coat of a mix of 3 parts by volume sand, 1 part cement, plus waterproofing compound and water, finished with a steel trowel. If desired, cement colourant can be added to this rendering coat. When dry, the concrete must be sealed to prevent harmful alkaline salts dissolving from it into the the water, by painting with a solution

of sodium silicate or water-glass, 1 part by volume to 4 parts water, three or four times, or a proprietary sealant.

Pools may be made more quickly and simply with pliable plastic sheet linings. The pool is first excavated to the size and depth required, and surfaces made smooth and firm by adding sand or sifted soil. The liner is then laid to cover the pool with a good overlap, and secured with bricks or stones laid on at the sides. It is then filled with water, letting the weight of the water take the lining down and fit the excavation. Surplus material beyond 6–12 in. of the

FIG. 239 Water garden pool, constructed of plastic sheeting, laid on sand; with marginal shallows, and soiled for planting.

pool edges may be cut away, and the outer flap then fastened by a flat stone or concrete slab edging to the pool. A lining of heavy-gauge polythene will have a life 5–6 years; for more permanent results either a PVC liner or terylene, plastic coated, liner should be used. The latter are offered in coloured and simulated pebbly finishes. Alternatively, prefabricated pools in resin-bonded glass-fibre can be bought in a variety of sizes and shapes, which only require a suitable excavation to be made to receive them though care should be taken to see that the pool rests firmly supported by the soil or added sand. Plastic pools need no further treatment before filling, and ideally this should be in step with planting.

Planting Pools. Aquatic plant nurseries send out stock between March and September, but the best planting period is April–June. There are two ways. The pool floor may be covered with a 4-in. layer of soil, or the plants may be placed in soil-containing planting baskets, open-weave willow baskets or teak baskets, or better still, plastic open-mesh crates. The soil used should be a rather heavy fibrous loam or clay, to which may be added one-eighth thoroughly rotted cow manure, or a very little dried blood; but no fertilizers. Crates may be lined with an inverted turf before adding soil. A soil bottom to a pool should be well firmed, and topped with half to one inch of coarse sand or fine gravel.

The plants are then placed in the pool in their rooting medium, and water added gradually, a few inches daily, or

FIG. 240 The modern way of planting a water garden pool, with plants in open-work plastic crates.

keeping pace with new growth, so that the water has a chance to warm to an even temperature. It is a good plan to stand a bowl or bucket on a plastic sheet, running the water first into the bowl or bucket slowly, and so not disturb the rooting medium. The water should be soft rain-water if possible, or spring water, but the mains tap water may be used in most districts without much harm.

Choice of Plants. Subsequent clarity of the water will depend upon balanced stocking. The basic need is for (*a*) surface-leafing plants to give shade; supplemented by (*b*) floating plants, which help to defeat algae-formation of greening; and (*c*) submerged oxygenating plants. The most important surface-leafing plants are Water-lilies (*Nymphaea* spp.), which should be chosen according to the depth of water and size of the pool (see *Nymphaea*). Floating plants are *Azolla caroliniana*, Fairy Moss; *Hydrocharis morsus-ranae*, Frog-bit; *Lemna gibba*, Thick Duckweed; *L. minor*, Lesser Duckweed; *L. trisulca*, Ivy-leaved Duckweed; *Stratiotes aloides*, Water Soldier; and *Trianea bogotensis*, American Frog-bit. A plant to every 6–10 sq. ft, of water surface is about

right at first. Later, as the plants multiply, they must be thinned from time to time. Submerged oxygenating plants may be chosen from *Callitriche autumnalis*, *C. verna*, the Starworts; *Ceratophyllum demersum*, Hornwort; *Chara aspara*; *Eleocharis acicularis*, Hair Grass; *Elodea canadensis*, *E. crispa*; *Fontinalis antipyretica*, Willow Moss; *Hottonia palustris*, Water Violet; *Isoetes lacustris*, Quillwort; *Lobelia dortmanna*, Water Lobelia; *Myriophyllum spicatum*, and *M. verticillatum*, Water Milfoils; *Oenanthe fluviatilis*; *Pilularia globulifera*, Pillwort; *Potamogeton crispus*, *P. densus*, *P. pectinatus*, Pondweeds; *Ranunculus aquatilis*, Water Crowfoot; and *Tillaea recurva*, of which ten to fifteen plants per 20 sq. ft of surface area should be planted. *Aponogeton disatchyum*, the Water Hawthorn, may be planted as a surface-leafing companion to Water Lilies in most pools.

Marginal plants for shallows of 3–4 in. of water may be chosen from *Acorus calamus* and v. *variegatus*, Sweet-scented Rush; *Alisma plantago*, Water Plantain; *Butomus umbellatus*, Flowering Rush; *Carex pendula*, Drooping Rush; *Cyperus atrovirens* v. *georgianus*; *Iris laevigata* and vs.; *Juncus glaucus*; *Menyanthes trifoliata*, Bog Bean; *Peltandra virginica*, Arrow Arum; *Pontederia cordata*, Pickerel; *Preslia cervina*; *Ranunculus lingua*, Great Spearwort; *Rumex hydrolapathum*, Water Dock; *Sagittaria graminea*, *S. japonica*, *S. lancifolia*, *S. macrophylla*, *S. sagittifolia*, Arrowheads; *Scirpus albescens*; *S. lacustris*, *S. zebrinus*; *Sparganium ramosum*, Bur Reed; *Typha angustifolia*, *T. gracilis*, *T. latifolia*, Reed Maces; and *Veronica beccabunga*, Brooklime.

Marginal plants for very shallow water or wet soils are *Acorus gramineus* and v. *variegatus*; *Caltha palustris* and v. *plena*; *Cotula coronopifolia*; *Cyperus longus*; *Eriophorum angustifolium*, Cotton Grass; *Iris kaempferi* and vs.; *I. siberica*; *Lysichitum americanum*, *L. camtschatcense*; *Marsilea quadrifolia*; *Mentha aquatica*; *Mimulus luteus*, *M. ringens*; *Myosotis palustris*; *Myriophyllum prosperinacoides*; and *Zantedeschia aethiopeca*, and 'Crowborough variety'.

Fish. It is usually wise to allow a newly planted pool to begin growth and settle down for a few weeks before introducing ornamental fish, which may be chosen from Goldfish (*Carassius auratus* and vs.), Carp (*Cyprinus carpio* and vs.), Orfe (*Idus idus* and vs.) and Golden Tench (*Tinca tinca* v.) as hardy kinds. Approximately five to ten small fish are sufficient for small to medium-sized pools at the beginning. A few fresh-water Snails (*Limnaea stagnalis*), and Ramshorn Snails (*Planorbis corneus*), at one to every 2 sq. ft of surface area may be also introduced to work as scavengers; and a few fresh-water Mussels (*Anodonta cygnea*, *A. anatina*), about half the number of snails.

The Bog Garden. Where the ground is naturally moist, and along the edge of ponds, lakes and streams, moisture-loving perennials which can be grown in addition to those already given for marginal shallow-water planting include *Aconitum napellus*, 4 ft; *Aruncus sulvester*, 5–9 ft; *Arundo donax*, 6–10 ft; *Astilbe arendsii*, and vs., 2–4 ft; *Astrantia major*, 2–3 ft; *Camassia quamash*, 2 ft; *Cyprepedium calceolus*, 15 in.; *Filipendula hexapetala*, 3 ft; *Geum rivale*, 1 ft; *Gunnera manicata*, to 10 ft; *Hemerocallis* sp. and vs., 2–3 ft; *Hosta* spp.; *Inula royleana*, 2 ft; *Iris delavayi*, 5 ft; *I. forrestii*, 1½ ft; *Kirengeshoma palmata*, 5 ft; *Lobelia cardinalis*, 3 ft; *Lysimachia clethroides*, 2–3 ft; *Meconopsis betonicifolia*; *Mimulus guttatus*, and hybrids; *Miscanthus japonicus*, 4 ft; *Primula beesiana*, *P. bulleyana*, *P. denticulata*, *P. japonica*, *P. pulverulenta*, *P. rosea*; *Rheum palmatum*, 8 ft, and vs.; *Rodgersia pinnata* and vs.; *Trollius europeus* and vs.

Maintenance. Probably the greatest immediate problem is achieving clear water in the pool. Discoloration frequently follows planting and stocking, but should clear naturally after a few months. Where the water turns green and blanket weed or flannel weed algae growth appears, as much as possible should be removed by netting and scooping out, and the water may be treated with a suitable algaecide, harmless to other plants and fish. It is also useful to float shade-casting boards in the open water in winter and spring. A cork board, rubber ball or sponge should be floated in winter to absorb the pressure when a pool freezes over. If it is necessary to break the ice to allow the water to 'breathe', it should be done gently, not with a sharp blow, to avoid concussing fish. Periodically underwater plants will need thinning in early spring, and overgrown Water-lilies may be divided and thinned.

Water Hawthorn. See *Apongeton distachyus*.

Water Lily. See *Nymphaea*.

Water Lily, Yellow. See *Nuphar lutea*.

Water Soldier. See *Stratiotes aloides*.

Water Violet. See *Hottonia palustris*.

Watercress. A native of Britain and the northern hemisphere, fresh watercress is a valued health-protecting salading. There are two species grown, *Nasturtium officinale* (*Rorippa nasturtium-aquaticum*), the green-leaved type for summer and autumn cutting, and *N. microphyllum* (*Rorippa macrophyllum*), the bronze or brown-leaved type for winter and spring cutting. Selected strains may be grown commercially. Commercial culture calls for large, specially prepared beds, and a regulated control of clean water. In the garden, watercress may be grown in moisture-retentive beds of soil, in a damp shady spot, well enriched with humus-forming matter, and watered freely in dry weather, with lime to bring to about pH 6·5. Propagation by seeds is possible, but it is easier and quicker to plant cuttings of shoots in March–April; or of the winter type in July–August, where the plants are to grow.

Watering. Water is a constant need of living plants. It is a solvent and is used to carry mineral nutrients to leaf and stem, to distribute foodstuffs to all parts, to provide hydrogen and oxygen, and to facilitate chemical reactions within the plants, and to maintain turgidity and what might be termed the pressure of growth forces. Excess water is constantly being lost in transpiration. Nevertheless, the amount of water available to plants must be in balance with the soil air supply.

Insufficient water leads to a loss of turgidity or wilting, a drooping of growing points, bud, flower and leaf dropping, and, if uncorrected, a yellowing of tissue, and cessation of growth prior to death. Out of doors this is most lkkely to occur in periods of drought, especially in areas of light rainfall, and on porous light or sandy soils. A basic insurance against water shortage lies in adequate stocking of a soil with moisture-retentive humus and organic matter, and of clay colloids. It is important, however, to anticipate a water shortage in outdoor plants, and water before wilting point is reached. Watering, once begun, must be thorough, aimed to soak the soil in some depth; bearing in mind that a dry soil absorbs water slowly and allows it to percolate only gradually. A thorough soaking of lawns, flower-beds, rock gardens, crops, etc., at weekly intervals is better than daily sprinklings. The laying of plastic water-piping below ground, with strategic outlets or stand-pipes, does away with long hoses. Water may be given by means of perforated hose to seep into the soil at soil level; or by overhead watering through sprinkler or oscillating automatic sprayer. The overhead watering has advantages since the water falls more like rain and is oxygenated. Mulching after watering helps to conserve the soil moisture. When watering has to be curtailed because of water shortages, the addition of dilute liquid fertilizer to the water used makes it of more immediate benefit to the struggling plant, and less water goes further.

Plants grown under glass or in the house need meticulous attention to their watering needs. Only general principles can be indicated here. Primarily, plants should be grown under conditions of excellent drainage, in balanced composts, retentive of essential moisture. Watering should be regulated by such factors as temperature—increasing with a rise, decreasing with a fall—ventilation and atmospheric humidity, with its effect on transpiration, and the type, size, and growth activity of the plant. Usually, it is better to saturate at a watering, and then pause until the surface layer begins to dry out, then to water little and often. Syringing plants reduces transpiration losses and reduces soil water requirements, but is most helpful on bright sunny days. It is usually healthiest to water early in the day, and have plants surface dry at night when ventilation is restricted. The use of a system of capillary watering, whereby water can be made available constantly and automatically to plants, is a boon to those who cannot give attention to their greenhouses throughout the day, or when away from home.

The rule of thumb with pot plants is to rap them sharply with a knuckle or small billet of wood; a dull thud indicates no water needed, a ringing noise suggests dryness, but it only works with clay pots. More accurately, a test can be made with a small tensiometer. Pots which have dried out severely should be watered by immersing to the rim in water; the same technique should be followed with seed pans or boxes, drying out.

Soft rain-water is undoubtedly best for plants. When stored in butts or tanks it should be in darkness to avoid algae growth. In doubt, a pinch of potassium permanganate may be added to water as it is drawn off. Where the water has to percolate through much soil, and so warm to the soil's temperature, its initial temperature is not important, but for watering small pots it is useful to have the water at tepidity or approximately greenhouse ground temperature. Mains water is normally acceptable, except when it is a hard water, containing lime salts, and is intended for use with lime-intolerant plants.

Watering-cans are made in various types and sizes, with a tendency for plastic materials to supersede the japanned or galvanized steel. The important points, however, are the balance of the can when full and in use; the provision of good roses, which will give a coarse spray for rapid watering, a fine for delicate plants, seeds and seedlings, without drip, and ease in keeping clean.

Watsonia (wat-son'i-a. Fam. Iridaceae). Herbaceous cormous plants, allied to Gladiolus, of S. Africa, with sword-like leaves and sessile, handsome curving tubular flowers in spikes.

Selection. Culturally the genus falls into two groups: (1) *W. aletroides*, Cape, 1–2 ft, scarlet, June; *alpina*, Transvaal, 2½ ft, pink, June; *coccinea*,

Cape, 1 ft, crimson, June; and *meriana*, Cape, 2–3 ft, rose-red or pink, May–June. (2) *W. ardernei*, Cape, 3–4 ft, white, September; *beatricis*, Cape, 3 ft, orange-red, September; and *galpinii*, Cape, 2½ ft, orange-red, August.

Cultivation. Group 1 may be cultivated like Gladioli in the mildest localities, being planted in February–March, warm, sunny borders, light, porous humus-enriched soil; to be lifted in autumn for storing. Otherwise plant in large pots, October–March, standard compost, to grow in cool greenhouse or deep frame, resting from October or after flowering.

Group 2 are evergreen and require cool greenhouse culture; planted October or March, 3 in. deep in large pots, standard compost, kept more or less only just moist during winter, temp. 10° C. (50° F.); watering very freely with active growth; giving plenty of light and air; moderating after flowering.

Propagation. By offsets when re-repotting. By seeds, when available, April, bottom heat of 18° C. (65° F.), taking three years to flower.

Wattle. See *Acacia*.

Wax Flower. See *Hoya*.

Wayfaring Tree. See *Viburnum lanata*.

Weather. By determining the atmospheric environmental conditions surrounding plants, weather has profound influence on growth, out of doors and under glass. As yet man's attempts to 'make' weather are feeble, and the gardener's chief preoccupations are to take advantage of favourable weather, and offset the affects of adverse. In these days of daily weather forecasts it is often possible to be forewarned and forearmed. *Frost* can be most damaging in spring, when clear nights follow bright sunny days, particularly to fruit tree blossom, young crops, and early growth. It can be offset by interposing some form of cover or canopy between plant and sky, to check radiation losses of warmth and temperature. *Dry weather* in spring threatens newly planted stock, especially evergreens, and should be offset by overhead syringing or watering. *Drought* calls for soaking waterings, and top mulches. *Fog* and similar humidity is hazardous, and usually means that watering should be suspended, and efforts made to get air circulation and temperatures raised, especially under glass. *Dull cloudy* weather and rain mean slower photosynthesis and growth, and watering and feeding may need reduction. *Wind* is important not only for its mechanical force but for its propensity in accentuating whatever weather conditions are prevailing. Good windbreaks and effective tree and shrub planting within a garden can do much to mitigate adverse weather effects. In the greenhouse, weather as far as the plant is concerned is more artificially controlled. Nevertheless, outside weather conditions cannot be ignored. Ventilation has to be regulated according to the direction and force of the wind; watering according to the light available; and heating adjusted according to the temperature. And overriding most weather conditions is the influence of light, its intensity and duration, on daily and seasonal plant life and growth. Hard winter weather when plant life is more or less dormant is probably beneficial on the whole, though hindering to gardening operations. Frost helps to break up the clay in soils. It need not stop planting unless the ground is frozen in depth; it is sufficient to place a frozen surface layer aside, and replace on top after planting. Snow apparently benefits fertility of the soil. But it is wise to dislodge heavy falls from branches of shrubs and trees, particularly evergreens and conifers, which might be broken. Every advantage should be taken of favourable weather for sowing and planting in spring; the old tag 'Sow dry, transplant wet' being basically sound, as the soil must be readily workable for sowing, and moist for ready recovery from transplanting. To sum up, the weather is more friendly than inimical to gardening, if the gardener reads the signs aright as a guide to operations.

Weed. Commonly defined as a plant growing in the wrong place. While most weeds are unwanted native plants, some are introduced exotics, such as soleirolia *soleirolii*, *Oxalis rubra*, *Polygonum cuspidatum*, which become established too freely.

Weed-killers. *See* Herbicides.

Weevils. A large family of small beetles (*Cucurlionidae*), recognizable by their beak-like rostrums or snouts and elbowed antennae, often feeding on plants and fruit trees.

Weigela (Diervilla) (wi-gel'-a. Fam. Caprifoliaceae). Decorative, deciduous shrubs, free-flowering in May–June, with foxglove-like flowers, easily grown.

Selection. W. coraeensis, Japan, to 8 ft, pale rose to carmine; *florida*, China, 6 ft, rose-pink, and vs. *foliis purpureis*, purple-leaved, and *variegata*, leaves margined cream; *japonica*, Japan, 6 ft, white to carmine; *middendorffiana*, N. China, Japan, to 4 ft, fresh green leaves, sulphur-yellow flowers; *praecox*, Korea, to 5 ft, rose-pink, yellow-throated, late April–May, and *venusta*, Korea, 4 ft, rosy pink; while crossing has produced notable hybrids such as 'Abel Carrière', reddish pink; 'Bristol Ruby', ruby-red; Conquête, pale pink; 'Eva Rathke', crimson; 'La Perle', creamy white,

FIG. 242 *Weigela* × 'Eva Rathke'

flushed pink; 'Newport Red', red-crimson; and 'Vanhouttei', bright pink.

Cultivation. Plant October–March, any reasonably well-drained ordinary soil, sun or partial shade, sheltered from spring winds. Prune after flowering.

Propagation. By cuttings of firm young shoots, July–August, under handlights.

Weldenia (wel-den'i-a. Fam. Commelinaceae). The only species, *W. candida*, Mexico, Guatemala, is a rather delightful tuberous-rooted, herbaceous herb, with rosetted, wide strap-like leaves, bearing solitary, sessile, cup-shaped, snow-white flowers in succession, May–June; easily grown in the alpine house, potted in standard compost over good drainage, March–September; little water in winter, increasing with growth. Propagated by seeds, March; or root-cuttings, April.

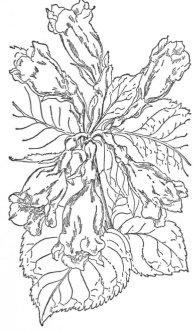

FIG. 241 *Weigela middendorffiana* in flower.

Wellingtonia. Now *Sequoiadendron giganteum* (q.v.).

Welsh Poppy. See *Meconopsis cambrica.*

West Wind, Flower of the. See *Zephyranthes.*

Western Red Cedar. See *Thuja plicata.*

Westringia (west-ring'i-a. Fam. Labiatae). The chief species grown is *W. rosmariniformis*, Victorian Rosemary, an Australian evergreen shrub, to 4 ft, with whorled linear leaves, and pale blue axillary flowers, July; for outdoor sheltered borders in very mild, frost-free localities, and well-drained soil and sun; or for a large pot in a cool greenhouse elsewhere, spending the summer out of doors.

Wetting Agents. *See* Spreaders.

Weymouth Pine. Common name for *Pinus strobus.*

Whin. *See Ulex europaeus.*

White Beam. See *Sorbus aria.*

White-fly. A family of bugs (Aleurodidae), with wings and bodies coated with a white powder. *Aleurodes brassicae* is a pest of Brassicas (q.v.); *Trialeurodes vaporariorum* of greenhouse crops. *See* Tomatoes.

Whitlavia. Included in *Phacelia.*

Whitloof. A form of Chicory (q.v.).

Whitlow Grass. See *Draba.*

Whorl. A ring of organs, usually leaves or flowers, in one plane around a stem.

Whortleberry. See *Vaccinium myrtillus.*

Widdringtonia, Cypress Pine (widdring-ton'i-a. Fam. Pinaceae). Evergreen coniferous shrubs and trees of S. Africa, with soft, small linear leaves, spirally arranged, and dioecious, unfortunately tender.

Selection. W. cupressoides, Saprae, 6–12 ft, bushy with erect branches; *schwarzii*, to 15 ft, small tree; and *whytei*, Milanji Cedar, large timber tree with fragrant wood of Nyasaland (Zambia), may be grown.

Cultivation. Out of doors in the more sheltered, frost-free localities, planted in March–April, well-drained soil. Otherwise in large pots, in the cool greenhouse, to grow as foliage plants while young, watered liberally in active growth, moderately in winter, minimum temp. 10° C. (50° F.).

Propagation. By imported seeds, April, in a pan, bottom heat 21° C. (70° F.). By heeled cuttings in July–August, in propagating frame.

Widow, Mournful. See *Scabiosa atropurpurea.*

Wigandia (wi-gand'i-a. Fam. Hydrophyllaceae). Handsome-leaved tropical perennials from the mountains of Mexico to Colombia, chiefly grown as half-hardy annuals for use in summer bedding.

Selection. W. caracassana, to 8 ft, very large ovate, golden leaves, spikes of lilac and white flowers, summer; *kunthii*, 6–9 ft, sharply toothed leaves, violet-blue flowers, September; and *vigieri*, 6 ft, long-stalked elliptic leaves, blue flowers, summer; unfortunately leaves have stinging hairs.

Cultivation. Sow under glass, standard compost, bottom heat of 21° C. (70° F.); to prick off, harden and plant out in June; or may be grown in pots in cool greenhouse.

Propagation. Roots may be lifted and over-wintered in a cool greenhouse. By cuttings of firm shoots of stems, July–August, in propagating frame or under handlights.

Wild; Wilding. Native; an uncultivated plant.

Willow. See *Salix.*

Willow Herb. See *Epilobium angustifolium.*

Willow, Kilmarnock. See *Salix caprea* v. *pendula.*

Wilt. A description applied to plants when leaves and stems droop and die through a fungus infecting the sap stream through the roots, often by *Verticillium* spp. *See* Asters, Dahlias. Cherries, and Tomatoes.

Wilting. A physiological reaction shown in loss of turgidity and rigidity in cell tissues resulting from a failure of sap pressure due to an insufficient supply of water from the roots. This may be due to the drying out of the soil, or be caused by some injury or infection of the roots disrupting their intake of moisture.

Wind. A forceful movement of a current of air, which by its strength, direction and accompanying weather conditions can have profound effects on plant growth. Winds tend to accelerate transpiration. Dry cold winds of spring are often responsible for the destruction by marginal scorch and browning of leaves, especially of conifers and evergreens. Dry hot winds cause wilting by making water losses in transpiration greater than root absorption can make good. Strong prevailing winds tend to 'prune' growth to make plants lop-sided, leaning to the lee; off-sea winds may carry leaf-blackening salt; and winds from city, town, factory or cement works may be laden with deleterious dust or chemicals. On the other hand, some gentle turbulence and air movement is desirable among plants, both outdoors and in. The force of prevailing winds can be broken by suitable windbreaks or shelter belts, while within the garden, good planting with tough, taller plants affording shelter to the less robust or less hardy, can do much in modifying the garden climate for the better.

Wind Flower. See *Anemone.*

Windbreaks. The purpose of a wind-break, as its name implies, is to break the force of the wind into smaller, less damaging turbulences, filtering it through a physical barrier, screen, shelter belt or hedge of trees or shrubs. A permeable windbreak is better than a solid one, for while the latter gives a lee of quiet air, the wind descends with renewed force beyond this. The best windbreaks are living ones of trees and/ or shrubs. No plant is completely wind-proof, though some are better able to withstand wind than others. The choice of plants is also influenced by the locality, the climatic conditions and the nature of the soil. A well-designed wind-break would reduce the wind-force by 75–80 per cent immediately within its lee, and with lessening effect up to a distance of ten to twelve times its height. To give protection to large areas, a shelter-belt of four or more rows of trees, infilled with shrubs, would be necessary. The most hardy trees are Sycamore, Maples (*Acer* sp.), Ash, Beech, Poplar, Hawthorns and Myrobalan Plum. Austrian Pine, Corsican Pine and Scots Pine are also good, and near the sea, the Monterey Cypress. Trees in a shelter belt are planted 4–6 ft apart, in staggered rows. For smaller areas reliance must be placed on screens and

Hedges (q.v.). As it takes a little time for the plants to establish themselves, temporary windbreaks of trellis, chest-nut paling, chain-link mesh, coir netting or peastick hedging should be placed to the windward. Where it is possible, windbreaks should be planted in crescent, angled or diagonal line to deflect as well as break the force, of the prevailing wind.

Window-box Gardening. Apart from their decorative effects, window-boxes give an outlet to the gardening aspirations of those who lack a garden, or wish to relieve the drabness of town dwellings or buildings.

A window-box may be made of wood, preferably teak, oak or red cedar for durability, though other woods may be used if treated with a suitable preservative (Cuprinol, Presotim, etc.); of sheet metal, preferably aluminium or galvanized steel; of plastic (polystyrene) or of fibreglass. The size should be not less than 6 in. wide, 8 in. deep, and of a length suitable for the window-sill on which it is to rest. It should have feet or wedge-shaped runners, to permit it to stand level on a sloping sill, and to give a space underneath for a tray to catch drainage water. The box should have provision for drainage, in $\frac{1}{2}$–1-in. holes in the base, spaced 6–8 in. apart; and be fixed securely with the help of brackets, or a wire across the front anchored to the window frame.

Each drainage hole should be covered by an inverted crock, and a filling of smaller broken crocks or small stones, gravel or washed clinker, to a depth of 2 in.; on which an inch of sphagnum moss or peat fibre is laid to absorb moisture. The box can then be filled with a standard compost, or mixture of 3 parts good loam, 1 part moist peat, 1 part leaf-mould, and $\frac{1}{2}$ part sharp sand, adding 1 oz. of a balanced organic-based fertilizer to each two-gallon measure of the mixture, to within an inch or so of the top. The box is then ready for planting, after giving a thorough watering, and allowing to drain overnight. The choice of plants will depend partly on personal preferences, partly on the season, and partly on the aspect and exposure.

It is usually best to set out young

plants in a window-box, rather than attempt to raise them from direct sowings. These can be grown separately or bought from a local nurseryman.

For Summer Display. The time to plant is May, and suggestions are: For the front edge *Ageratum* 'Blue Mink', 'White Cushion', etc.; *Alyssum* 'Little Dorrit', 'Royal Carpet', etc.; *Lobelia* 'Cambridge Blue', and dwarf vs.; Dwarf French Marigolds; *Mesambryanthemum crinifolium*; Pansy, 'Clear Crystals', Majestic F_1 Giants; *Petunia multiflora* F_1 single hybrids and *Silene* sp. For the centre *Antirrhinum nanum* vs., and Floral Carpet F_1 hybrids; Aster in Pompone or dwarf vs.; *Dianthus* 'Sweet Wivelsfield'; *Begonia semperflorens*; 'Calceolaria' dwarf hybrids; Celosia; Godetia sp.; Marigold, Dwarf African; *Nemesia* hybrids; *Phlox drummondii*; *Salvia splendens* and vs.; Trysomic seven-week Stocks; *Verbena* 'Sparkle mixed'. For the rear *Antirrhinum* Sprite F_1 hybrids or 'Hyacinth-flowered'; *Aster* 'Lilliput' vs.; *Dahlia* 'Coltness Gem'; *Calendula officinalis*; *Heliotrope* 'Regale hybrids'; *Nicotiana* 'Crimson Bedder', 'Dwarf White'; *Petunia grandiflora*; *Pelargonium zonale* in variety. For foliage, *Coleus*, *Salvia hormimum* (Clary) and *Chlorophytum* sp., may be used; and to trail over the edge of boxes *Tradescantia fluminensis*, *Zebrina pendula* or Pelargoniums 'Pink Galilee' and 'Red Krause' may be planted. For a large box, planting up with young pot-grown *Hydrangea macrophylla* in flower gives a fairly long display; or some of the compact hybrid Fuchsia can be so used.

If it is desired to replace a failing summer planting for an autumn display this can be readily done by having dwarf forms of the early autumn-flowering Pompone Chrysanthemums on hand, such as 'Bronze Fairie', 'Cameo'; 'Denise', 'Glow', 'Imp', 'Orange Bouquet' or 'Trudie'; or the dwarfer forms of Korean Chrysanthemums, or Dwarf Hybrid Michaelmas Daisies such as 'Audrey', 'Hebe', 'Lady in Blue', 'Margaret Rose' and 'Pink Lace'.

For Winter Display. After summer plants have been removed, boxes can be planted with hardy dwarf foliage shrubs in pots sunk in the soil, such as *Aucuba crotonifolia*, *Chamaecyparis lawsoniana* v. *ellwoodii*, *C. l. aurea*; *Juniperus communis* and vs., *Erica carnea* and vs., *Euonymus japonicus*, *E. radicans*, *Picea mariana nana*, *Taxus baccata nana*, and perhaps a few hardy succulents such as *Sedum spathulifolium*, *Sempervivum arachnoideum* and Engleria Saxifrages. Small hardy bulbs can be planted, such as *Crocus*, *Eranthis*, *Iris reticulata*, dwarf *Narcissi*, *Puschkinia scilloides*, *Scilla sibirica* and small Tulips, such as *Tulipa fosteriana* and vs., *T. kaufmanniana* and vs., *T. praestans* and *T. tarda*, for late winter and early spring colour. Alternatively, the box may be planted up in autumn with biennials such as *Bellis perennis* F_1 hybrids; *Cheiranthus allionii*, the Siberian Wallflower; Polyanthus; or Wallflowers. Every second year it will be necessary to replace the soil compost, otherwise the management of a window-box is chiefly one of watering regularly during the warmer weather months, and keeping just moist otherwise. A little weeding may be necessary, and it is good practice to give a feed of liquid manure (such as a seaweed derivative), every two to three weeks in midsummer. Most summer flowers keep blooming if the spent flowers are removed promptly.

Windows, Plants for. The inside sill of windows is a favourite place for decoration with pot plants. Although plants welcome ample light, they should not be subjected to hot direct sun, but have light shade on bright sunny days. The need for some humidity and watering without excess can usually be met by standing the pots on saucers or trays partly filled with small pebbles or gravel, not more than half full of water. Watering should be regulated by growth activity and temperature, and on cold or frosty nights it is wise to withdraw plants from near to the glass. Good flowering plants for windows are *Begonia haageana*, *B. maculata*, *B. metallica*, *Beloperone guttata*, *Bilbergia nutans*, *Calceolaria* hybrids; *Campanula isophylla*, *Echeveria retusa* and vs., *Euphorbia milii*, *Fuchsia* hybrids, *Hoya carnosa*, *Pelargonium zonale*, *Pelargonium* spp., *Schlumbergera gaertneri*, *Solanum pseudocapsicum*, *Sparrmannia africana*, *Primula malacoides*, *P. obconica*, *P.*

stellata, and spring-flowering bulbs, such as Hyacinths, Daffodils and Tulips, and bulbous plants such as Hippeastrums, *Vallota speciosa*, and others, such as Cyclamen. A number of what are now known as House Plants (q.v.) also succeed; and for shaded or north windows a short list is *Agave albicans*, *Aloe variegata*, *Aspidistra lurida*. *Chlorophytum elatum*, × *Fatshedera liazei*, *Hedera helix* and sp., *Pteris cretica*, *Sansevieria* spp., and *Spathiphyllum wallsii*. Many Cacti and succulents make satisfactory window plants.

Wineberry. See *Vaccinium myrtillus*.

Wineberry, Japanese. See *Rubus phoenicolasius*.

Wings. The side petals of the Pea flowers of the Leguminosae.

Winter Aconite. See *Eranthis*.

Winter Cherry. See *Physalis alkekengii*.

Wireworms. The soil-frequenting larvae of Click Beetles (*Agriotes lineatus*, *A. obscurus*, *A. sputator* and *Athous haemorrhoidalis*), yellow or yellow-brown elongated grubs of 22–26 mm. long, not unlike pieces of rusty wire. The adult beetles emerge in spring. After mating the females lay eggs in the soil, which hatch into 'wireworms', which may spend from four to five years in the soil, feeding on organic matter and plant roots. Few plants or crops are immune. Attacks are generally worst on grassland or fallow ground brought newly into cultivation. The incorporation of a gamma-BHC insecticidal dust into the top 4 in. of soil before sowing or planting gives good control; but should not be used prior to cropping with potatoes or root vegetables. Many wireworms can be trapped by baits of cut potato or turnip, impaled on sticks, half-buried in the soil, and inspected periodically to remove the pests caught.

Wisteria (wis-ter'i-a. Fam. Leguminosae). Hardy deciduous twining climbers, with pinnate leaves and drooping racemes of pea-like flowers in May–June.

Selection. W. floribunda, Japan, to 30 ft, fragrant, purplish-blue flowers, June; and vs. *alba*, white; *macrobotrys*, very long flower racemes to 3 ft; and *rosea*, rose-pink; *sinensis*, China, to 60 ft or more, fragrant, mauve, May–June; and vs. *alba*, white; and *flore*

pleno, double flowers; and *venusta*, Japan, to 30 ft, downy shoots and leaves, and white fragrant flowers, May–June.

Cultivation. Plant in October–March, in well-drained, humus-rich soil, pH 6·0–6·5, to grow on walls, up pergolas or old trees; training to the space available. Shorten lateral shoots to half their length in July, and to an inch or so in winter, to encourage flowering spurs. *W. sinensis* and *venusta* may also be trained as standard trees in the open, pruning fairly hard in February to restrict growth, and dealing with laterals as suggested above.

Propagation. By layering of young strong shoots in summer.

Witch Hazel. See *Hamamelis*.

Witches' Brooms, Witch Knots. Clustered bundles of twig-like growths seen on Beech, Birch, Cherry, Fir and other trees; usually caused by fungi, sometimes by Mites; and should be cut out and burnt.

Woad, Dyer's. See *Isatis tinctoria*.

Wolf's Bane. See *Aconitum*.

Wood. When it is necessary to prune or fell timber trees, their burning quality as fuel is well summed up in:

> *Oak* logs will warm you well
>   If they're old and dry.
> *Larch* logs of pinewood smell,
>   But the spark will fly.
> *Beech* logs for Christmas time;
>   *Yew* logs heat well;
> *Scotch Fir* it is a crime
>   For anyone to sell.
> *Birch* logs will burn too fast,
>   *Chestnut* scarce at all;
> *Hawthorn* logs are good to last
>   If cut in the fall.
> *Holly* logs will burn like wax;
>   You should burn them green.
> *Elm* logs like smouldering flax
>   No flame to be seen.
> *Pear* logs and *Apple* logs,
>   They will scent your room.
> *Cherry* logs across the dogs
>   Smell like flowers in bloom.
> But *Ash* logs, all smooth and gray,
>   Burn them green or old;
> Buy all that comes your way:
>   They're worth their weight in gold.

Lime may be rated with Sycamore; coniferous softwood with Larch; but Laburnum, Laurel, Lilac and Hazel all burn well.

Wood Anemone. See *Anemone nemorosa*.

Wood Ashes. *See* Ashes.

Wood Lily. See *Trillium grandiflorum*.

Wood Sorrel. See *Oxalis acetosella.*

Woodbine. See *Lonicera periclymenum.*

Woodlice, Hardbacks, Monkey Peas, Pillbugs, Slaters, Sowbugs. A sub-order of terrestrial crustaceans (Oniscoidea) of which there are thirty-six British species; characterized by two pairs of antennae, seven pairs of legs, and a segmented flattish body, brown to grey, tending to curl up, or roll into a ball in the case of the Pillbug, *Armadillidium vulgare.* Dependent on moisture, they are found in damp places, where rubbish accretes, and feed chiefly on decaying organic matter, but also on tender plants and their roots, and can do much damage in the greenhouse. Dusting the places where they lurk, under pots, containers, bases of walls, etc., with a DDT or gamma-BHC powder is effective. Toads in the greenhouse help considerably, together with good hygiene.

Woodruff. See *Asperula odorata.*

Woodrush. See *Luzula.*

Woodsia (woods'i-a. Fam. Polypodiaceae). A genus of tufted deciduous ferns well adapted to growing in little soil in rock garden crevices or the cool greenhouse.

Selection. W. alpina, 3–6-in. fronds, and *ilvensis,* 4-in. fronds, are native and hardy. *W. mollis,* Mexico, Peru, 6–8-in. fronds; *obtusa,* S. U.S.A. to Peru, 6–9 in. fronds; and *polystichoides,* Japan, 9-in. fronds, are for pot growth in a cool to warm greenhouse.

Cultivation. Plant hardy ferns in October–March, thin soil of sand and leaf-mould, damp parts of the rock garden. Greenhouse kinds in porous mixture of equal parts by volume light loam and peat, with a little charcoal, March; watering liberally in growth moderately in winter; minimum temp. 10° C. (50° F.).

Propagation. By division, October–March.

Woodwardia, Chain Fern (woodward'i-a. Fam. Polypodiaceae). Ever-green ferns with large bi-pinnatifid fronds for the cool greenhouse.

Selection. W. areolata, U.S.A., 1-ft fronds; *japonica,* China and Japan, 6–12-in. fronds; *radicans,* S. Europe to Java, 3–6-ft, fronds, is magnificent, v. *brownii* being a crested form.

Cultivation. Pot in March, equal parts by volume loam and leaf-mould, with a little charcoal; water liberally and syringe often in growth; minimum temp. winter, minimum temp. 7° C. (45° F.).

Propagation. By division of roots, March; by bulbils from the apex of fronds; less often by spores.

Woolly Aphis, American Blight (*Eriosoma lanigerum*). A species of Aphids which infest stems and branches and produce masses of cotton-wool like patches, especially on apple trees (q.v.), but sometimes on pears, and ornamental Pyrus spp. Painting colonies with a neat solution of a tar-oil wash is effective; or malathion may be used in summer.

Woolly Bear. Hairy or furry caterpillars, chiefly of Ermine, or Garden Tiger Moths, often seen feeding on weeds, grasses and plants; seldom doing much damage to garden plants.

Worms. See Earthworms, Eelworms and Hair Worms.

Wulfenia (wul-fe'ni-a. Fam. Scrophulariaceae). The species chiefly grown, *W. carinthiaca,* Balkans, 1–2 ft, is a tufted perennial for the rock garden, with crenate leaves and cylindrical head of blue-violet flowers, summer. *W. baldaccii,* Albania, to 6 in., lilac-blue spikes, May; and *orientalis,* Asia Minor, to 1 ft, heliotrope flowers, May, are more rarely offered.

Cultivation. Plant in well-drained, moisture-retentive soil, in rock garden, in mild localities; giving winter protection from damp; or in pans, in the alpine house.

Propagation. By division in March; by seeds when available.

Wych Elm. See *Ulmus glabra.*

X

Xantho-. A prefix of compound words, meaning yellow.

Xanthoceras (zan-tho'ke-ras. Fam. Sapindaceae). The only species, *X. sorbifolium*, China, is an interesting deciduous tree, to 20 ft, with toothed pinnate leaves, and axillary racemes of white May flowers, with a carmine base, and pear-like small fruits, for mild localities, or sunny, warm, sheltered positions; planted October–March, in well-drained, organically rich soil. May be grown from seeds, sown April; or propagated by root cuttings, March.

Xanthophyll. A yellow-colouring plant pigment contained in chloroplasts and in plastids, and usually the source of yellow colouring in flowers and yellowing leaves in autumn.

Xanthorrhiza (zan-tho-ri'za. Fam. Ranunculaceae). The only species, *X. simplicissima*, Yellowroot of eastern N. America, is a hardy deciduous shrub, 2–3 ft, with small toothed or lobed pinnate leaves, and loose terminal panicles of small purple flowers in March–April before the leaves. May be planted October–March, moisture-retentive loam soil, with shelter from spring frosts. Propagated by layering in summer, autumn.

Xanthosoma (zan-tho-so'ma. Fam. Araceae). Perennial herbs of tropical America, distinctive for their arrow- or spear-shaped leaves, often beautifully veined and variegated; the monoecious flowers on short spadix being less decorative.

Selection. X. atrovirens, Venezuela, dark green, lighter-veined leaves; *lindenii*, Colombia, deep green, white-veined leaves; and *violaceum*, W. Indies, purple-violet veined leaves.

Cultivation. Pot tuberous roots in February–March, compost of equal parts by volume loam, leaf-mould or peat, and sharp sand, a little charcoal; water freely with growth, syringe in hot weather; more or less dry November–February; minimum temp. 10° C. (50° F.); in greenhouse or indoor room.

Propagation. By division of the roots, February–March, planted in small pots, given gentle heat.

Xeranthemum, Everlasting Flower, Immortelle (zer-an'the-mum. Fam. Compositae). Annual flowers, grown for their composite, bracted flower-heads of white, purple and pink, which are cut when freshly open and dried for winter decoration.

Selection. X. annum, S. Europe, purple, and vs. *alba*, white; *roseum*, pink; *purpureum*, purple; and semi-double and double forms—*ligulosum* and *perligulosum*; 2 ft tall.

Cultivation. Sow March, under glass, standard compost, bottom heat of 18° C. (65° F.); to prick off and plant out in sunny border of porous, humus-enriched soil in late May–June; or may be sown outdoors, late April, in warmer counties.

FIG. 243 *Xeranthemum annum* v., Everlasting Flower.

Xerophilous. A plant loving dry conditions.

Xerophyllum (zer-o-pil'lum. Fam. Liliaceae). The species chiefly grown, *X. asphodeloides*, eastern N. America, 3–4 ft, is a rhizomatous-rooted perennial, with linear leaves, and long-stalked fragrant yellowish-white flowers in an upright raceme, summer, sometimes known as Turkey's Beard. Plant March, in moist peaty or boggy soil, or near water; and propagate by division, March–April.

Xerophyte. A plant of a dry habitat, able to grow or thrive through periods of water shortage, such as in deserts; by virtue of a shedding of leaves, rolled leaves, leaves reduced to shoots, spines or thorns, thick cuticle, waxy bloom, hairiness or sunken or protected stomata.

Xiphion, Xiphium. An old generic name for Spanish Iris. See *Iris xiphium.*

Xylem. Wood; inner vascular tissue of plants which conduct the solution of water and mineral salts absorbed by the roots through the plant; and give it physical support; found near the pith.

Xylosoma (zil-os'ma. Fam. Flacourtiaceae). The chief species offered, *X. racemosa*, W. China, to 40 ft, is an evergreen tree, with spiny shoots, ovate leaves, and small fragrant yellow flowers in small racemes, August, hardy for mild localities. Plant March–April, well-drained, humus-rich soil, and sun. Propagation by young firm shoots, July–August, under handlights or in frame.

Y

Yarrow. See *Achillea*.

Yellow Flag. See *Iris pseudocorus*.

Yellow Loosestrife. See *Lysimachia vulgaris*.

Yellow Water Lily. See *Nuphar lutea*.

Yew. See *Taxus*.

Yew, Prince Albert's. See *Saxegothea conspicua*.

Yucca (uk'ka. Fam. Liliaceae). Handsome evergreen shrubs with long, narrow, often spine-tipped leaves in dense clusters, and magnificent spike-like panicles of waxy white flowers; native to southern U.S.A. and central America.

Selection. *Y. filamentosa*, SE. U.S.A., stemless with stiffish leaves, to 2 ft long, and erect, 3 ft, panicle of drooping yellowish-white lily-like flowers, July–August, flowering young; *flaccida*, SE. U.S.A., stemless, similar, but somewhat smaller, yellowish-white flowers, July–August; *glauca*, central U.S.A., stemless, very narrow leaves, greenish-white, drooping flowers on an erect raceme of 3–4 ft, July–August; *gloriosa*, Adam's Needle, SE. U.S.A., short-stemmed, to tree form, stiff, flat leaves, creamy-white flowers, tinged reddish, in 3–6-ft panicles, July–September, and v. *nobilis*, recurving leaves; *recurvifolia*, SE. U.S.A., stems of small tree growth to 6 ft, long recurving leaves, 3–5 ft panicle, creamy-white flowers, July–August; and *whipplei*, SE. U.S.A., stemless, narrow leaves, flowers greenish-white, tipped purple, on erect panicles of 6 ft and more, May–June, are the hardiest species for outdoor cultivation. *Y. aloifolia*, W. Indies, slender-stemmed to 10 ft, creamy-white flowers on panicles of 2–3 ft, May–June; and its vs., *draconis*, branching; *tricolor*, leaves striped yellow and white; and *variegata*, leaves white striped, are only suitable for greenhouse culture.

Cultivation. Plant hardier species in March–May, well-drained, humus-rich soil, sunny warm positions, reasonably mild localities; or in large pots, tubs or vases, moved to winter shelter in exposed cold gardens. *Y. aloifolia* and vs. do well under cool greenhouse conditions, liberal watering in active growth, moderate in winter.

Propagation. By root cuttings of 2–3 in. in standard compost, with bottom heat, 15·5° C. (60° F.), in spring; or by suckers produced at the base of plants in some species.

Yulan. See *Magnolia denudata* (*conspicua*).

Z

Zaluzianskya (zal-u-zi-ansk'i-a. Fam. Scrophulariaceae). Annual or perennial plants from S. Africa, grown as half-hardy annuals, with clammy or hairy foliage and flowers which open at night in summer.

Selection. Z. capensis, ½–1 ft, white or lilac flowers in spikes; and *villosa,* ½–1 ft, white, fragrant, June–August.

Cultivation. Sow seeds in March, standard compost, bottom heat of 18° C. (65° F.), to grow on in pots, in the greenhouse, or plant out in June, warm sunny borders, well-drained lightish soil.

Zantedeschia (Richardia), Arum Lily (zan-te-desk'i-a. Fam. Araceae). Aquatic, rhizomatous-rooting flowering perennials of S. Africa, handsome arrow-shaped leaves, and elegant flowering spathes.

Selection. Z. aethiopica (Richardia africana), Trumpet Lily, Lily of the Nile, Calla Lily, 2–2½ ft, dark green leaves, white spathe to 9 in. long; and vs. *childsiana,* more dwarf but freer flowering; and *gigantea,* very large; may be grown in pools in mild localities, planted April–May, up to 3–6 in. deep. More often they are pot-grown; being potted in October, standard compost, or rich loam, rotted cow manure and sand in equal parts; one plant to a 6-in. pot; watered regularly, in greenhouse, temp. 10° C. (50° F.) minimum; to flower March–May; and after flowering stood out of doors in shade, kept moist, until repotting time, late September–October.

Z. elliottiana, Transvaal, to 3 ft, golden yellow spathe, summer; *melanoleuca,* Natal, 1½ ft, pale yellow spathe, dark purple at base; and *rehmannii,* Natal, bright rose spathe, 1½–2 ft, require warm greenhouse treatment, free watering, with a rest period after flowering.

Propagation. By suckers removed from the base of plants in spring or summer, potted and rooted with bottom heat of 18° C. (65° F.) in frame or greenhouse.

Zanthoxylum (zan-tho-zi'lum. Fam. Rutaceae). A large genus of deciduous or evergreen shrubs or trees, of which a few species deserve attention.

Selection. X. americanum, Prickly Ash, eastern N. America, 6–8 ft, handsome pinnate foliage, small, yellowish-green clusters of flowers, spring; *piperitum,* Japanese Pepper, Korea, Japan, compact shrub to 8 ft, pinnate leaves, greenish flowers, reddish fruits, with black seeds used as a condiment; and *planispinum,* Japan, China, 6–12 ft, spiny, winged leaf-stalks, yellowish flowers, spring.

Cultivation. Plant October–March, well-drained, organically enriched soil, sunny warm shelter, mild localities.

Propagation. By seeds, April, outdoor seed-bed, or frame. By firm young cuttings, July–August, under hand-lights.

Zauschneria, Californian Fuchsia, Humming Bird's Trumpet (zaus-kne'ri-a. Fam. Oenotheraceae). The species chiefly grown, *Z. californica* of California and Mexico, is a half-hardy sub-shrub, of 12 in., with linear leaves, and fuchsia-like bright scarlet flowers in loose spikes, autumn. May be grown from seeds, sown March, under glass, standard compost, bottom heat of 18° C. (65° F.), and potted on; and subsequently increased by cuttings of young shoots, taken July–August.

Zea, Maize, Indian Corn, Guinea Corn, Mealies, Sweet Corn (ze'a. Fam. Gramineae). The sole species, *Z. mays,* of unknown subtropical origin, is very variable. In addition to food-crop varieties, ornamental forms are offered under v. *japonica quadricolor,* 4 ft, leaves striped white, brown, and red on green; and hybrids with vari-coloured seeds on the cobs. For culture *see* Sweet Corn.

Zebrina (ze-brin'na. Fam. Commelinaceae). Akin to Tradescantia, a genus of Mexican trailing or pendulous herbs with colourful foliage, easily grown in the cool greenhouse or as indoor pot plants.

Selection. Z. *pendula*, ovate, pointed leaves, coloured beautifully in longitudinal green, silvery, purple to mauve stripes, small clustered flowers, summer, and v. *quadricolor*, white, red, green, and grey striping; *purpusii*, somewhat more delicate, with greenish-purple leaves, reddish-purple beneath, purplish-rose flowers, October.

FIG. 244 Stems and foliage of *Zebrina pendula*.

Cultivation. Pot in March, standard compost, water freely in active growth, moderately in winter, minimum temp. 7° C. (45° F.), give good light; pinching back shoots in spring and early summer for bushiness.

Propagation. By tip of stem cuttings, spring or summer, with a little gentle heat, 15·5° C. (60° F.).

Zebrinus (-a, -um). Zebra-like striped. Ex. *Scirpus zebrinus.*

Zelkova (zel-ko′va. Fam. Ulmaceae).

Deciduous shrubs or trees, related to the Elms, with somewhat coarsely toothed leaves, rough above, downy beneath, and small green slightly scented flowers in spring.

Selection. Z. *carpinifolia*, Caucasus, to 80 ft, smooth, grey, beech-like trunk; *serrata*, Japan, to 100 ft, elegant and wide spreading; *sinica*, China, to 50 ft, hairy leaves; and *verschaffeltii*, a bushy small tree, Caucasus, deep indented leaves.

Cultivation. Plant October–March, well-drained ordinary soils, open positions.

Propagation. By seeds, sown March–April, outdoor seed-bed, though taking time to make stature.

Zenobia (zen-o′bi-a. Fam. Ericaceae). Now regarded as a genus of one species, Z. *pulverulenta*, deciduous or semi-evergreen, SE. U.S.A., growing to 3–4 ft, with clusters of white, drooping, large lily-of-the-valley-like flowers, June–July; and v. *nuda* (*speciosa*), paler green foliage.

Cultivation. Plant October–November, or March–April, in peat-enriched, acid, lime-free soil, sheltered sunny warm positions, mild localities on the south and west. Prune hard occasionally.

Propagation. By cuttings of firm young shoots, July–August, in cold frame or under handlights; by layering, summer. By seeds when available, in cold frame.

Zephyranthes, Zephyr Lily, Fairy Lily, Flower of the West Wind (ze-pur-an′thes, Fam. Amaryllidaceae). Charming bulbous plants, related to Hippeastrum, from the warmer regions of N. and S. America, and therefore not trustworthily hardy.

Selection. Z. *atamasco*, Atamasco Lily, S. U.S.A., 15 in., white, flushed pink, tubular flared flowers, March–May; and *candida*, Argentina, Uruguay, 1 ft, white, flushed pink flowers, evergreen leaves, September–October, may be attempted out of doors in porous, humus-rich soil, warm, sheltered borders, planted 3–4 in. deep in autumn. Or may be pot-grown in the greenhouse along with Z. *citrina*, British Guiana, Trinidad, 1 ft, golden-yellow flowers, summer; *grandiflora*, Guatemala, W. Indies, 1½ ft, rose-pink, summer; and *rosea*, Guatemala, 8 in., rose-pink, late summer;

FIG. 245   *Zephyranthes grandiflora.*

potting the bulbs, four to a 5-in. pot, standard compost, 3 in. deep, in autumn; in cool greenhouse, winter temp. 10° C. (50° F.), watering increasingly with growth, moderately after flowering, and resting briefly; repot only every third or fourth year.

Propagation. By offsets when re-potting.

Zigadenus (zi-ga-de′nus. Fam. Liliaceae). A little known genus of hardy bulbous plants of which *Z. elegans*, N. America, 9–12 in., with long, thin, linear leaves, and racemes of greenish and white flowers, summer, is worth attempting in a moist, peaty soil, planting in October; or growing from seeds, sown April, in cold frame.

Zinnia (zin′ni-a. Fam. Compositae). A Mexican genus of colourful annuals, of which *Z. elegans*, Youth and Age, a very variable species, has been largely developed, selected and hybridized by American plantsmen to give the various classes now offered under: Double-flowering, 2 ft, in shades of gold, scarlet,

sulphur, violet, rose: 'Envy', greenish flowering; 'Ice Cream', pure white, being outstanding; *robusta grandiflora*, 2½ ft, very large double flowers. Giant Chrysanthemum-flowered, 2½–3 ft, such as 'Glamour Girls', 'Cherry Time', Burpee Hybrids; Giant Dahlia-flowered, 2½ ft, such as 'Canary Bird', yellow; 'Exquisite', cherry red; 'Oriole', orange and gold; 'Scarlet Flame' and others; Giant Mammoth, 2½ ft, such as 'Brightness', rose; 'Daffodil', canary yellow; 'Purity', white, and many others; Gaillardia-flowered, 2 ft, many colours; and dwarf strains, such as Double Lilliput, 1½ ft; 'Tom Thumb', 9 in.; 'Mexicana', 12–15 in., in 'Persian Carpet'; 'Thumbelina', 6 in., and 'Button-flowered', 1 ft, in a wide variety of colours.

Cultivation. Sow seeds under glass, standard compost, late February–April, bottom heat of 18° C. (65° F.), to prick off, and plant out in June. It must be admitted that Zinnias are less successful in the wetter and more clouded west and north. Tall varieties need canes or supports; and all kinds need warm sun, well-drained soil, and shelter from strong prevailing winds.

Zizania (ziz-a′ni-a. Fam. Gramineae). The chief species grown, *Z. aquatica*, Canada Rice, Indian Rice, Water Oats, N. America, is a handsome annual, of to 8 ft, with broad flat leaves, and reedy stems and large terminal panicles of flowers giving way to large grain, beloved by waterfowl, and may be sown broadcast in the marginal waters of lakes or large ponds to attract duck, in spring. *Z. caducifolia*, Manchurian Wild Rice, E. Asia, is perennial, 4–5 ft tall, but does not flower in Britain.

Zygo-. A prefix of compound words, meaning yoked or union. Ex. *Zygopetalum.*

Zygocactus. See *Schlumbergera truncata*.

Zygomorphic. Of a flower, divisible into two equal halves in one plane. Ex. Pea.

Zygopetalum (zi-go-pet′a-lum. Fam. Orchidaceae). A genus of orchids, epiphytic or semi-epiphytic, of S. America, with large and showy flowers, often in winter.

Selection. Z. burkei, Guiana, 1 ft, green, banded and spotted brown, white lipped, flower; *crinitum*, Brazil, 1–1½ ft, large, green, barred brown, white-lipped and fragrant; *intermedium*, Brazil, 1–2½ ft, greenish-yellow, tinged brownish red; *mackaii*, Brazil, 1½–2½ ft, yellow-green, blotched chestnut, and 'Charlesworth variety', pale green with white lip; and *maxillare*, Brazil, to 1½ ft, green, barred chocolate, with bluish-purple lip; all flowering November–December. There are also many beautiful hybrids.

Cultivation. Pot, and repot, in March, compost of equal parts by volume peat, sphagnum moss, loam and charcoal; water liberally in growth, shade from hot sun, in cool, moist house; summer temp. 15·5–24° C. (60–75° F.); moderate watering in winter, with temp. 13–21° C. (55–70° F.).

Propagation. By division, March–April.

Zygophyllum (zig-o-pil'lum. Fam. Zygophyllaceae). Unusual perennial herbs of which *Z. fabago*, Syrian Bean Caper, Syria to Afghanistan, 1–3 ft, with oblongish oval leaves, and terminal, yellow flowers, coppery red at the base of petals, July–August, is worth growing in well-drained, light soil, warm sunny position, from seeds, and increasing by cuttings in July, under glass.

Zygote. A fertilized ovum or ovule.